W9-ALB-986

studysync®

Teacher's Edition

Grade 8 | Volume 1

studysync.com

Send all inquiries to:
BookheadEd Learning, LLC
610 Daniel Young Drive
Sonoma, CA 95476

ISBN 978-1-94-973925-1

2 3 4 5 6 LKV 24 23 22 21 20 19

A

Grade 8

Volume 1 Contents

Authors and Advisors

DR. DOUGLAS FISHER

Dr. Douglas Fisher is Professor of Educational Leadership at San Diego State University and a teacher leader at Health Sciences High & Middle College having been an early intervention teacher and elementary school educator. He is the recipient of a Christa McAuliffe award for excellence in teacher education and is a member of the California Reading Hall of Fame. He is a renowned speaker and author of numerous articles and books and is President of the International Literacy Association (ILA) Board.

DR. TIMOTHY SHANAHAN

Dr. Timothy Shanahan is Distinguished Professor Emeritus at the University of Illinois at Chicago where he is Founding Director of the UIC Center for Literacy. He was Director of Reading for Chicago Public Schools, and, among other awards, received the William S. Gray Citation for Lifetime Achievement and the Albert J. Harris Award for outstanding research on reading disability from the International Literacy Association (ILA). He is the author/editor of more than 200 publications and books, and his research emphasizes the connections between learning to read and learning to write, literacy in the disciplines, and improvement of reading achievement.

DR. MICHELLE H. MARTIN

Dr. Michelle H. Martin is the Beverly Cleary Endowed Professor for Children and Youth Services in the Information School at the University of Washington and from 2011-2016 was the inaugural Augusta Baker Endowed Chair in Childhood Literacy at the University of South Carolina. She published Brown Gold: Milestones of African-American Children's Picture Books, 1845-2002 (Routledge, 2004), and is the founder of Read-a-Rama, a non-profit that uses children's books as the springboard for year-round and summer camp programming.

CATLIN TUCKER

Catlin Tucker is a Google Certified Innovator, bestselling author, international trainer, and frequent Edtech speaker, who teaches in Sonoma County where she was named Teacher of the Year in 2010. Her books Blended Learning in Grades 4-12 and Blended Learning In Action are both bestsellers. She is currently in the doctoral program at Pepperdine University, and writes the Techy Teacher column for ASCD's Educational Leadership.

JEFF ANDERSON

Jeff has inspired writers and teachers with the power and joy of the writing process. His particular area of interest is in making editing and grammar in context a meaning-making experience for students and teachers. He has written five books on writing and teaching writing. More recently, he has taken up writing middle grade novels, including Zack Delacruz: Me and My Big Mouth, which was selected for the Keystone State Reading List in Pennsylvania.

DR. PATRICIA MORALES

Dr. Patricia Morales is founder of ellservices©, consultant, and a professional development provider in English as a Second Language (ESL), Bilingual Education, and Dual Language Education. She is also an independent educational consultant at the Teaching and Learning Division of the Harris County Department of Education in Houston, Texas. She has taught university courses focusing on language acquisition and pedagogy, and continues to prepare thousands of teachers pursuing certifications in bilingual education and English as a Second Language in Texas.

JESSICA ROGERS

Jessica Rogers is a Lecturer at Baylor University and founder of Rogers Education Consulting, which specializes in Balanced Literacy professional development. She has over fifteen years experience in education, including teaching ESL, inclusion, gifted and talented, self-contained classrooms, mentoring teachers, and designing and implementing professional development. Her passion is making abstract educational theory and cutting-edge techniques practical for the classroom teacher.

GERRIT JONES-ROOY

Gerrit Jones-Rooy is Director of Literacy at Collegiate Academies in New Orleans as well as a 9th grade teacher. Previously he worked as a Staff Developer for the Reading and Writing Project, leading work across the country as well as in Saudi Arabia, Colombia, Poland and Thailand. He is the author or co-author of several Teachers College units including "Turning Every Kid into a Reader, Really" and "All About Books: Writing in Non-fiction."

DR. MARCELA FUENTES

Dr. Marcela Fuentes is an Assistant Professor of Creative Writing and Latinx Literature at Texas A&M University. She is a graduate of the Iowa Writers' Workshop, and was the 2016-2017 James C. McCreight Fellow in Fiction at the Wisconsin Institute for Creative Writing. She co-founded The Iowa Youth Writing Project, a nonprofit dedicated to promoting writing programs and events for K-12 students in the Iowa City area.

J. SCOTT BROWNLEE

J. Scott Brownlee is a Career & Talent Development Consultant at UT-Austin's McCombs School of Business, and a core faculty member for Brooklyn Poets, a NYC-based literary nonprofit. The author of four books of poetry, he received the Texas Institute of Letters 2015 Bob Bush Award for Best First Book of Poetry, as well as the 2014 Robert Phillips Prize from Texas Review Press.

DR. LYNNE KNOWLES

Dr. Lynn Knowles spent the majority of her 28-year teaching career at Flower Mound High School in Texas, where she served as English department chair and taught English II pre-AP and Humanities, as well as AP Capstone. She holds a bachelor's degree in Journalism from The University of Texas, a master's in Humanities from the University of Texas at Dallas, and a Ph.D. in Rhetoric from Texas Woman's University.

RICHARD ORLOPP

Richard Orlopp moved to Texas after graduating from Rutgers University with degrees in English and Journalism. He never left. He has taught English for the past 17 years and currently teaches AP Literature and Composition and International Baccalaureate seniors at Coppell High School.

WENDY MASSEY

Wendy Massey has taught high school for 20 years now. She has experience teaching grades 9-12 but primarily has taught English II Pre-AP and PSAT/SAT Prep. She has served several years now as the English department co-chair; in addition, she has served on the curriculum writing team for her district and has been the Academic Decathlon language coach.

MUHAMMAD SHIMAL

Mr. Shimal has been teaching for eleven years now. His teaching experience spans high school to college classes domestically and internationally. He current ly teaches English Language AP/Dual Credit for Juniors and College Prep classes for Seniors. He holds a Bachelor's degree in English Language and Literature, a Masters degree in Linguistics, and is currently finishing his PhD in English at the University of Texas at San Antonio.

VALENTINA GONZALES

Valentina Gonzalez is a Professional Development Specialist for English Language Learners in Texas, coaching teachers in ELL strategies and leading professional development at the state and national level. She has a natural love of language stemming from her experience as an immigrant from Serbia, Yugoslavia. Her years in education include roles as a classroom teacher, ESL Specialty Support Teacher, and ESL Facilitator. She holds a bachelor's degree in Interdisciplinary Studies from The University of Houston, and a master's in Educational Administration from Lamar University.

UNIT 1

Everyone Loves a Mystery

What attracts us to the mysterious?

SyncStart introduces students and teachers to the routines and skills they will need throughout the year.

Integrated Reading and Writing

Genre Focus: FICTION

The Extended Writing Project prompts students to consider a unit's theme and essential question as they develop extended responses in a variety of writing forms.

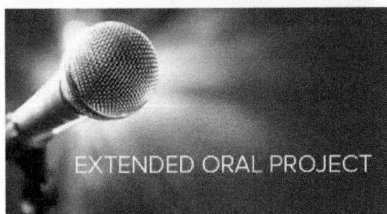

English Language Learner Resources offer instruction using texts written at four distinct levels that serve as structural and thematic models of authentic texts in the unit.

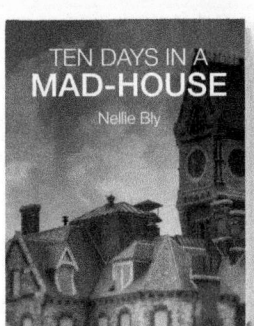

End-of Unit Assessments gauge students' understanding of key instuctional content and mastery of standards covered in the unit.

UNIT 1

Author Biographies

NELLIE BLY

Reporter Nellie Bly (1864–1922) feigned insanity to gain admittance to the Blackwell's Island Insane Asylum in New York City, the subject of her 1886 exposé, which began as a series of newspaper articles and was eventually published as a book, *Ten Days in a Mad-House* (1887). Her report on the inhuman conditions she encountered there—from mandatory ice baths to confinement in small, damp, vermin-infested rooms—resulted in increased government oversight and improved overall conditions. Bly's pioneering tactic developed into modern investigative journalism.

PAUL LAURENCE DUNBAR

In his lifetime, Paul Laurence Dunbar (1872–1906) achieved national recognition for his writing reflecting black life in turn-of-the-century America. Known for his innovative use of dialect in his poems, his first collection of poems, *Oak and Ivy* (1893), was written in dialect and in standard English. It includes "Sympathy," one of his most popular poems addressing the plight of black people in American society, which contains the famous line "I know why the caged bird sings," the inspiration for the title of Maya Angelou's autobiography.

RUDOLPH FISHER

Considered one of the central literary figures of the Harlem Renaissance, Rudolph Fisher (1897–1934) was also a practicing physician and esteemed orator. Much of his work dealt with the adjustment of Southern black migrants to the urban enclave of Harlem. His second novel, *The Conjure-Man Dies* (1932), is regarded as the first detective novel by an African American author. Fisher published at least two novels and two short stories before his untimely death at the age of thirty-seven.

NEIL GAIMAN

A self-described "feral child who was raised in libraries," Neil Gaiman (b. 1960) devoured fantasy and science-fiction books from a young age. Best known for his novella *Coraline* (2002), he is credited with being one of the first creators of modern comics and an author of genre works that refuse to stay true to their genres. Gaiman's *The Graveyard Book* (2008), conceived of as a take on Kipling's Mowgli stories, involves an orphaned toddler finding a safe haven in the local graveyard.

ALFRED HITCHCOCK

British film director Alfred Hitchcock (1899–1980) earned the nickname "The Master of Suspense" over the course of his long and prolific career. His distinct directorial style in films like *Rear Window* (1954), *Psycho* (1960), and *The Birds* (1963) had a lasting impact on cinema. Film critic Peter Conrad wrote that in his work, "Hitchcock diagnosed the discontents that chafe and rankle beneath the decorum of civilization."

W.W. JACOBS

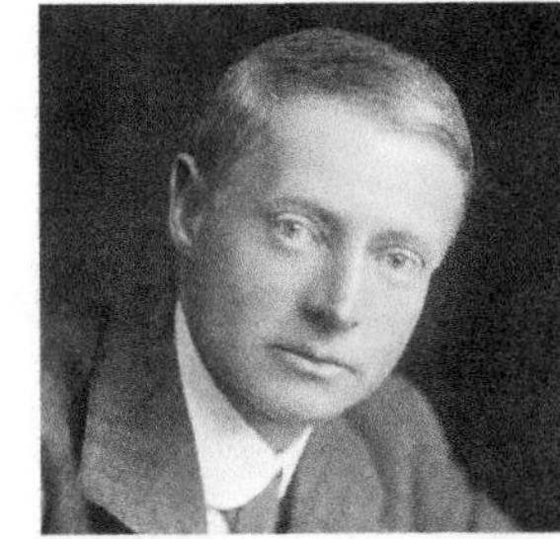

English short-story writer and novelist W. W. Jacobs (1863–1943) grew up in a house on a River Thames wharf. His is best known for his horror story, "The Monkey's Paw," published in his 1902 collection, *The Lady of the Barge*. In the story, a couple is presented with a magical monkey's paw from India. Set in Victorian England, the ensuing tale of superstition and terror unfolds in a domestic setting. Jacobs's first collection had immediate success and he published more than a dozen volumes in his lifetime.

SHIRLEY JACKSON

Called the master of the creepy story, Shirley Jackson (1916–1965) was interested in witchcraft, she writes, as "a way of embracing and channeling female power at a time when women in America often had little control over their lives." Her stories and novels of the supernatural included the well-known short story "The Lottery" and the best-selling novel *The Haunting of Hill House* (1959). When the former was first published in The New Yorker in 1948, it generated the largest volume of mail ever received by the magazine, most of it hateful.

WALTER DEAN MYERS

American children's book author Walter Dean Myers (1937–2014) wrote books that reflected the lives of young people he met visiting schools and prisons around the country, whose life experiences often resonated with his own. Although he wrote over a hundred books in his lifetime, he is best known for *Monster*, his 1999 drama about a teenager who writes a movie script while incarcerated. This stylistically innovative work alternates between suspenseful courtroom scenes and introspective journal entries.

EDGAR ALLEN POE

Widely regarded as one of the foremost progenitors of modern Gothic literature, Edgar Allan Poe (1809–1849) was born the son of two actors in Boston, but grew up in foster care in Richmond, Virginia. Much of his work, especially his best-known horror tales, achieve a psychological intensity through the use of a first-person narrator. Poe had written numerous short stories, poems, and works of criticism by the time he died at the age of forty from suspected alcohol poisoning.

JOHN FLEISCHMAN

John Fleischman (b. 1948) began writing non-fiction for young adults when he noticed how engrossed a group of adolescents was looking at a scientific display of the skull of Phineas Gage. The subject of Fleischman's first book, Gage was a construction foreman who became an important case study in the field of neurology when he miraculously survived a freak accident. Fleischman has also published three non-fiction books about the history of his adopted city, Cincinnati, Ohio, and has written articles for numerous science magazines.

UNIT 2

Past and Present

What makes you, you?

Every lesson in the unit features integrated scaffolding and differentiation for all levels of English Language Learners, Approaching grade-level readers, and Beyond grade-level readers.

Integrated Reading and Writing

Genre Focus: POETRY

Grammar instruction is embedded in the Extended Writing Project. Additional grammar lessons are available in the Skills library.

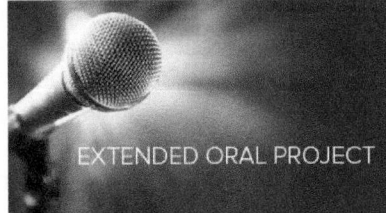

Each Core ELA Unit contains two options for Novel Study with lessons supporting the close reading of the complete text.

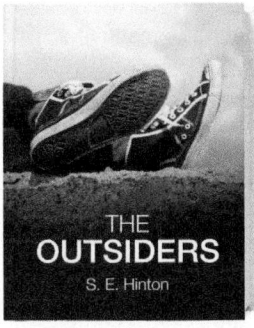

Author Biographies

SWIN CASH

Swin Cash (b. 1979) played fourteen seasons in the WNBA, winning three championships, appearing on four all-star teams, and winning two Olympic gold medals. In addition to her stellar playing record, she has worked to establish the WNBA players' union and to increase community involvement where she's lived. In a 2016 essay announcing her retirement, she paid tribute to the women who paved the way for her and made clear her commitment to ensuring that subsequent generations of women could play basketball professionally.

SANDRA CISNEROS

Regarded as a prominent figure in the Chicana literary movement, Sandra Cisneros (b. 1954) is a dual citizen of the United States and Mexico. In works like her classic coming-of-age novel, *The House on Mango Street* (2009), about a Latina girl growing up in a Chicago barrio, Cisneros explores themes related to Latina identity and working-class culture. In an *Electric Literature* interview, she said "the more you reach into the different things that make you who you are, the more you hold up a mirror to what makes you different from others."

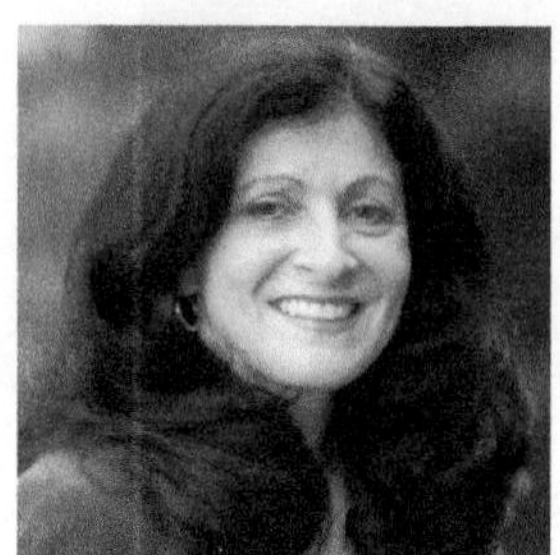

JUDITH ORTIZ COFER

Born in Hormigueros, a small town in Puerto Rico, Judith Ortiz Cofer (1952–2016) moved with her family to Augusta, Georgia, at the age of fifteen. With characteristic vitality, Cofer's writing addresses the experience of living in the breach between these disparate cultures. Best known for her works of creative nonfiction, Cofer also published at least four collections of poetry, several novels, and a memoir.

EMILY DICKINSON

As early as 1850, just a few years after dropping out of Mount Holyoke and moving back into her family's estate in Amherst, Massachusetts, Emily Dickinson (1830–1886) started thinking of writing her life's work. She recognized that her aims in life were different from those of her peers and began to retreat from polite society. As a result, the speakers in Dickinson's poetry are often sharply critical of society and express a desire to be liberated from its constraints.

ROBERT FROST

Though he was born in San Francisco, Robert Frost (1874–1963) wrote mostly about New England, where he moved in 1884 following his father's death. He became known for his innovative use of New England vernacular in his writing. Objects, people, or events sparked meditations on large concepts in his poems. In "The Road Not Taken," one of Frost's most iconic poems, a fork in a woodland path becomes a metaphor.

S.E. HINTON

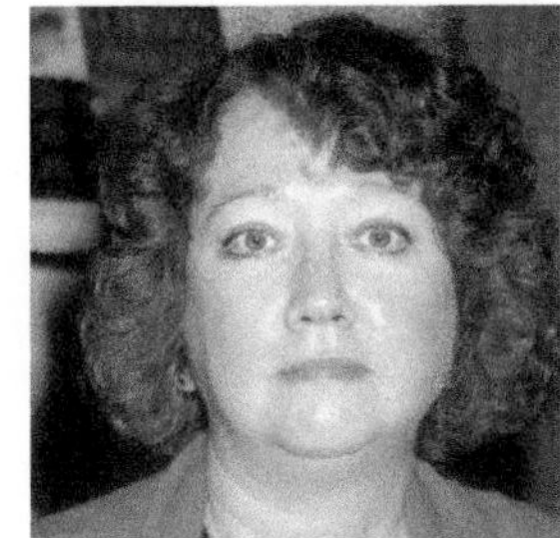

With her influential coming-of-age novel *The Outsiders* (1967) S. E. Hinton (b. 1948), who was seventeen at the time of writing, in large part inaugurated the young adult fiction genre. Set in Tulsa, Oklahoma, where she was born and has lived for the majority of her life, Hinton's novel about violence, prejudice, and class conflict in 1960s America stood out for its nuanced portrayals of teenage life. Four of Hinton's novels have been adapted into film, including *The Outsiders*, which has also been translated into thirty languages.

YUSEF KOMUNYAKAA

Born in Bogalusa, Louisiana, Yusef Komunyakaa (b. 1947) considers his first exposure to poetry to be the Old Testament–inflected cadence of his grandparents' voices. Komunyakaa would assert his distinctive style combining personal narrative, jazz rhythms, and vernacular language in two poetry collections in particular: *Magic Bus* (1992), about growing up in the South in the 1950s, and *Neon Vernacular: New and Selected Poems* (1994), which also dealt with the culture of the South as well as war in Southeast Asia, urban life, and music.

MICHELLE OBAMA

Lawyer, writer, public servant, and former First Lady, Michelle Obama (b. 1964) grew up on the South Side of Chicago, studied sociology and African American studies at Princeton University, and graduated from Harvard Law School. She has led initiatives to empower youth through higher education and to aid underserved communities throughout the United States, among many others. In her 2016 commencement address delivered at the Santa Fe Indian School, she reflects on how her family background shaped her character and contributed to her lifetime achievements.

NATASHA TRETHEWEY

Being born black and biracial in Gulfport, Mississippi, is one of the two "existential wounds" poet Natasha Trethewey (b. 1966) says she's been writing with her whole adult life. The other was losing her mother at the age of nineteen. In poetry collections like *Native Guard* (2006), *Bellocq's Ophelia* (2002), and *Domestic Work* (2000), she explores how her personal history is tied to larger historical narratives and the way private recollection often diverges from collective memory.

NAOMI SEPISO

Naomi Sepiso (b. 1998) is a writer of Kenyan and Zambian descent living in Australia. Her work often deals with the immigrant experience and the experience of being a young person of color. Her 2016 essay "So where are you from?" considers the sometimes damaging implications of this seemingly innocuous question.

THANHHÀ LAI

Children's book author Thanhhà Lai (b. 1965) was born in Saigon, Vietnam, and immigrated to Montgomery, Alabama, in 1975. Like the main character, Hà, of her first novel, Inside Out and Back Again (2011), Lai witnessed the harsh realities of the Vietnam War, had a father who was missing in action, and fled with her family to the United States. The emotions Lai conveys through her character Hà powerfully resonate with immigrant experiences everywhere. Lai's second novel, Listen, Slowly (2015) also explores themes related to heritage and identity.

UNIT 3

No Risk, No Reward

Why do we take chances?

Independent Reads provide opportunities to focus on reading comprehension and skills application.

Students self-select a text that corresponds to the unit's theme and essential question and then write a response.

Integrated Reading and Writing

Genre Focus: INFORMATIONAL TEXT

814 | Extended Writing Project and Grammar

In the Extended Oral Project, students apply the structure and approach of the Extended Writing Project to an oral presentation.

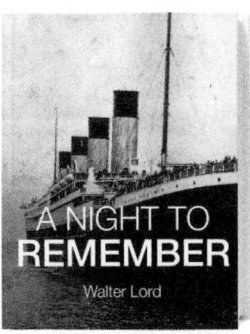

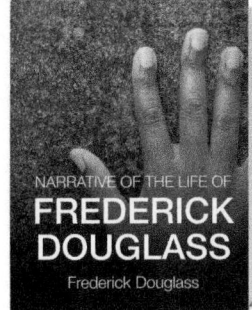

UNIT 3

Author Biographies

FREDERICK DOUGLASS

Born into slavery in Baltimore, Maryland, Frederick Douglass (1818–1895) was twenty years old when he escaped to freedom and became an active abolitionist. He taught himself to read despite laws prohibiting enslaved people from doing so, and only seven years after attaining his freedom, published the first of his three memoirs, *Narrative of the Life of Frederick Douglass, An American Slave* (1845). An account of his journey from slavery to freedom, it played a key role in fueling the abolitionist movement prior to the Civil War.

ANYA GRONER

A resident of New Orleans, Louisiana, Anya Groner has written essays, stories, and poems covering a wide range of subjects, from her childhood growing up in Virginia to the politics of drinking water. In "The Vanishing Island" (2017), Groner discusses the plight of the Native American inhabitants of the Isle de Jean Charles off the coast of Louisiana, as rising water levels threaten their ancestral homeland.

FRANCES ELLEN WATKINS HARPER

Writer, abolitionist, and civil rights activist Frances Ellen Watkins Harper (1825–1911) is credited with establishing the tradition of African American protest poetry. Born a free woman in Baltimore, Maryland, Harper traveled extensively throughout the eastern United States, often under hazardous circumstances, to voice her opposition to slavery and to advocate for the burgeoning feminist movement. As a result of her constant effort to raise awareness around these issues, she was elected vice president of the National Association of Colored Women in 1897.

LANGSTON HUGHES

Now regarded as a leading figure of the 1920's cultural and intellectual movement known as the Harlem Renaissance, Langston Hughes (1902–1967) initially faced widespread criticism from African American intellectuals for his unvarnished portrayals of African American life in his poetry. Despite the criticism he received, he maintained his commitment to writing for and about regular people throughout his life, earning him the moniker "poet of the people."

JACK LONDON

Turn-of-the-century American novelist and short-story writer Jack London (1876–1916) is best known for his novels *The Call of the Wild* (1903) and *White Fang* (1906) about wild wolf dogs in the Yukon Territory and the Northwest Territories of Canada during the Klondike Gold Rush of the 1890s. Writing between the Civil War and World War I, London's work reflected the nation's transformation into a modern, industrial society, and appealed to readers desiring a sense of adventure and vitality.

THOMAS PONCE

An animal rights activist and citizen lobbyist from Casselberry, Florida, Thomas Ponce (b. 2000) became a vegetarian at age four, attended his first protest at age five, and founded the animal rights organization Lobby For Animals at age twelve. He now works as a coordinator for Fin Free Florida, working to limit the sale, distribution, and trade of shark fins and shark fin products in the state of Florida. For his dedication to animal rights, he has received awards from major organizations like PETA and the Farm Animal Rights Movement.

RONALD REAGAN

Though he had an average, midwestern upbringing, Ronald Reagan (1911–2004) became the fortieth president of the United States and is the only Hollywood actor ever to become president. He is remembered for his conservative political beliefs and his policies toward the dissolution of Soviet communism. A major event of his presidency was the explosion of the Space Shuttle *Challenger* resulting in the deaths of its seven passengers. His address to the nation on January 28, 1986, lauded the bravery of the fallen crew.

NINA GREGORY

Throughout her career, news editor and journalist Nina Gregory has covered topics ranging from the financial crisis to elections, and has interviewed many influential figures including director Ava DuVernay and Facebook COO Sheryl Sandberg. One of her most intriguing stories profiles Richard Turere, a young boy living among the Maasai people near Nairobi National Park, a refuge for endangered lions in Kenya. As a thirteen-year-old, Turere came up with an inventive solution for protecting both the locals' livestock and the encroaching lions.

WALTER LORD

Walter Lord (1917–2002) had been obsessed with the story of the RMS Titanic since he came across a small book written by a survivor of the shipwreck in his aunt's home in 1927. Lord studied American and modern European history at Princeton University, but it wasn't until an editor friend suggested he turn his obsession with the Titanic into a book that he undertook the endeavor. With A Night to Remember (1955), Lord popularized the story and developed an innovative technique of telling history through the eyes of those who lived it.

MAHVASH SABET

Teacher, principal, and Bahá'í community leader Mahvash Sabet (b. 1953) was fired from her job and blocked from working in public education following the Islamic Revolution of 1979. She and the rest of the seven leaders that comprised an informal council working to support Iran's 300,000-member Bahá'í community were arrested in 2008. While serving her twenty-year prison sentence, she began writing poetry, and in 2013 published her first collection in English translation.

Bring Literature to Life

- Instructional choice from thematic units, novel studies, and teacher-created units.
- Interchangeable print and digital use.
- A continuously growing library of over 1,600 classic & contemporary texts.

Student Print Edition

Novel Options

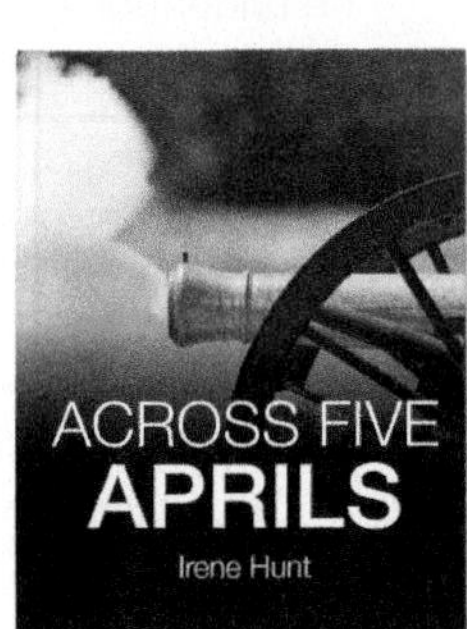

- Extensive writing and research practice.
- Automatically embedded scaffolds so ALL students reach their potential.
- Data-driven assessment to track progress and inform instruction.

Teacher Print Edition

Data Driven Assesment

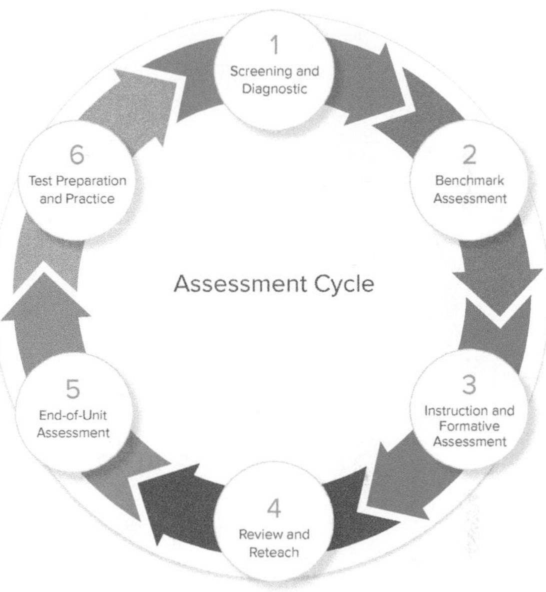

Comprehensive Student and Teacher Digital Experience

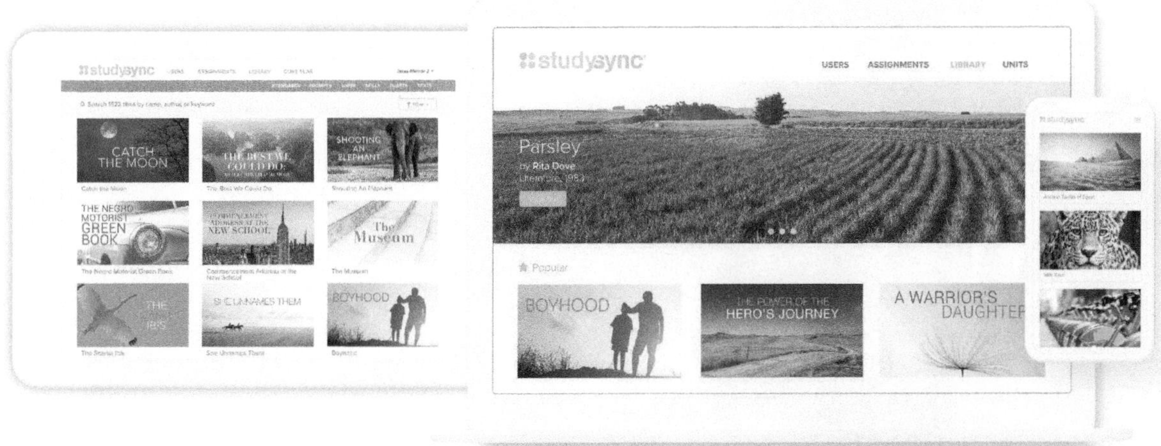

Lead to Achievement

StudySync's integrated reading and writing routines hone foundational language, reading comprehension, and analytical reading and writing skills as students respond to multiple genres of increasingly complex texts.

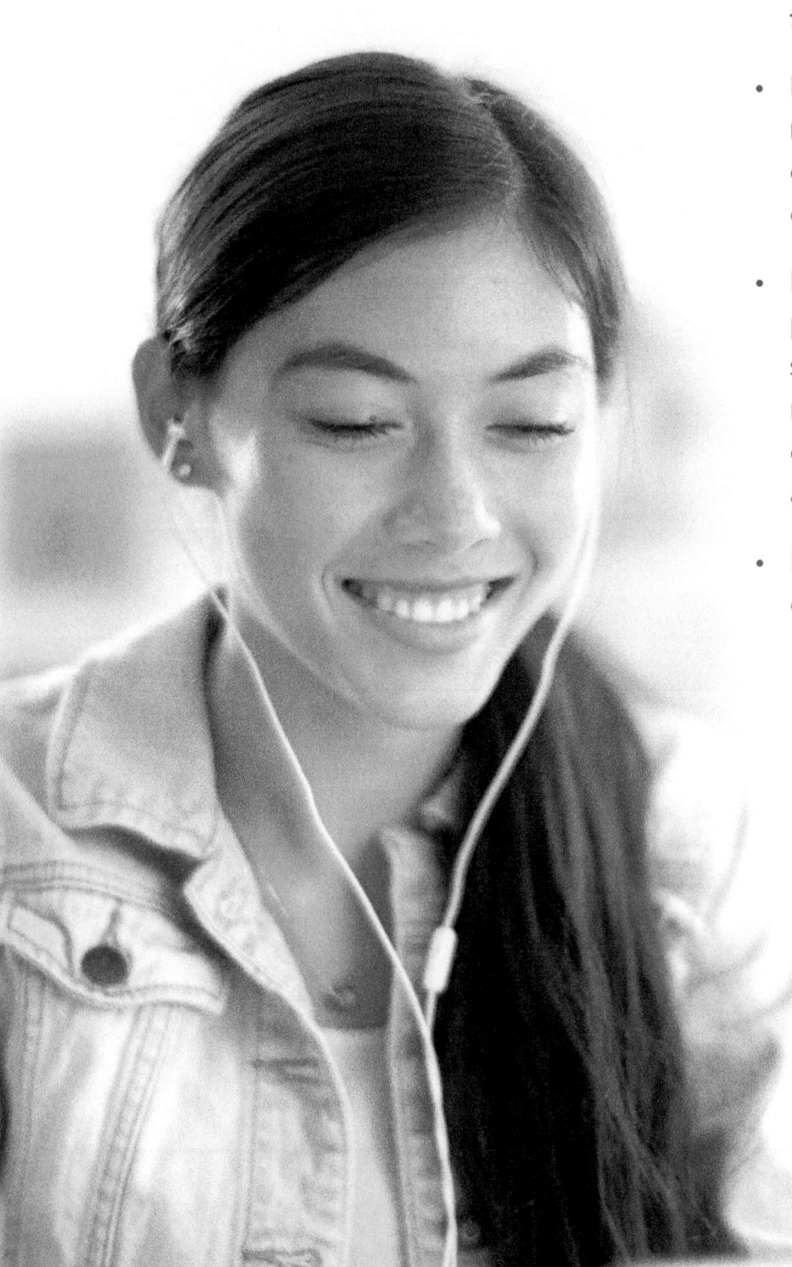

- StudySync's close reading routines ensure progress toward standards mastery.
- Novel Studies provide teachers with key vocabulary, reading quizzes, comparative texts, and other curriculum supports to teach from any of the 12 complete works suggested in each grade.
- Independent and self-selected reading lessons provide students opportunities to practice and apply skills while exercising more choice over their readings and responsesTwo comparative text sets in every unit challenge students to make connections and compare texts within and across genres.
- Extended Writing Projects teach writing with embedded grammar instruction.

Support Every Student

With StudySync, every student has the same opportunity and access regardless of native language, learning level, or physical, social and emotional ability.

Supports for English Language Learners

- Targeted scaffolds for 4 different levels of English Language Learners automatically appear with every digital assignment.
- Two leveled texts per unit introduce English Language Learners to the text types they'll encounter in the core curriculum.
- Additional ELL skills lessons emphasize/ vocabulary development, language acquisition, spelling and grammar, and reading comprehension.
- Extended Oral Projects build language proficiency and offer students opportunities to collaborate and build academic language skills.

Supports for Approaching and Beyond Grade-level Learners

- Intentional scaffolds such as annotation guides, and sentence frames help Approaching-level students interact meaningfully with on grade-level curriculum.
- A digital Library of 1000s of additional skill mini-lessons and texts is searchable by standard and Lexile, allowing teachers to quickly and easily differentiate, remediate, or extend lessons.
- Lesson-specific suggestions such as Beyond the Book and Prepare for Advanced Courses drive Beyond grade-level learners to further engage with texts and extend their learning.

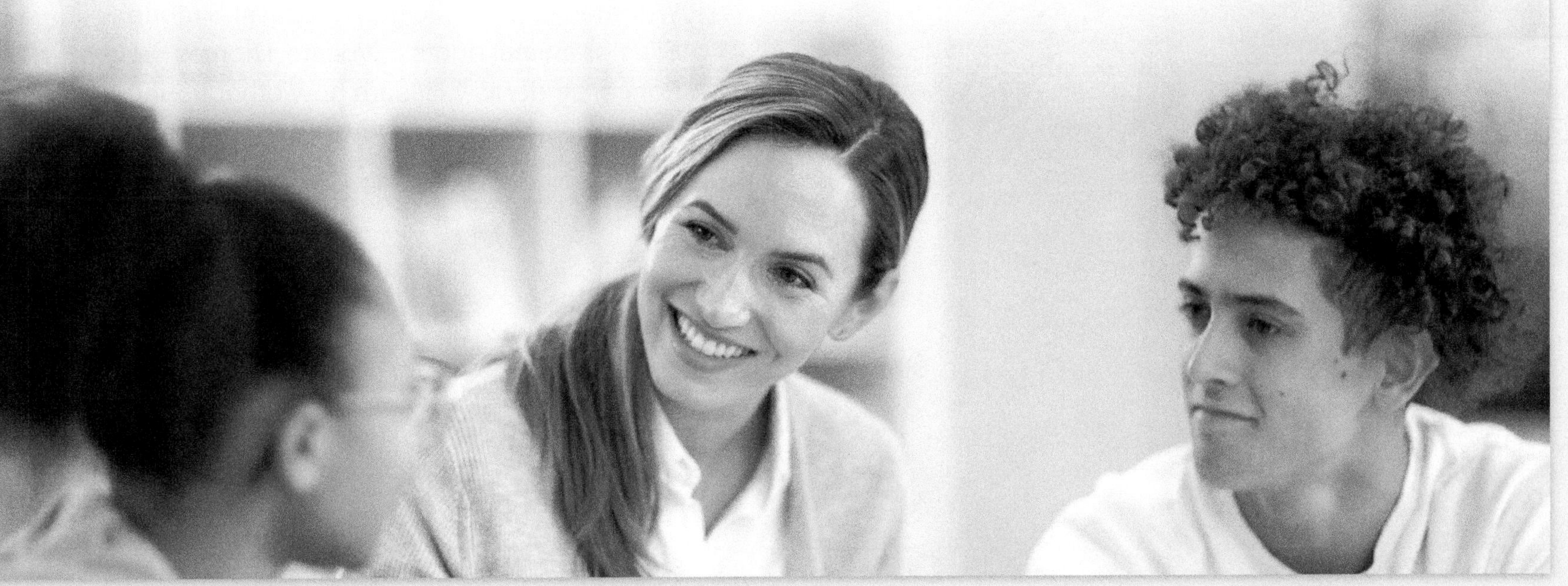

Amplify Student Voices

StudySync helps students think critically and thoughtfully. All StudySync students see themselves in their curriculum. StudySync encourages students to develop their own unique voices while they grow as readers, writers, and future leaders in college and career settings.

- StudySync's curriculum is centered around students. Lesson activities and the digital platform enable teachers to easily facilitate peer review and other on and offline collaborative approaches that transform classrooms into workshops of great reading and writing.
- The Table of Contents for every grade features at least 50% of texts written by female authors and at least 50% of texts written by authors from diverse backgrounds.
- Each grade's Table of Contents includes stories about extraordinary young people. Whether it's Olympic gold medalist Simone Biles or animal rights advocate Thomas Ponce, students will learn how other young people like them are changing the world today.

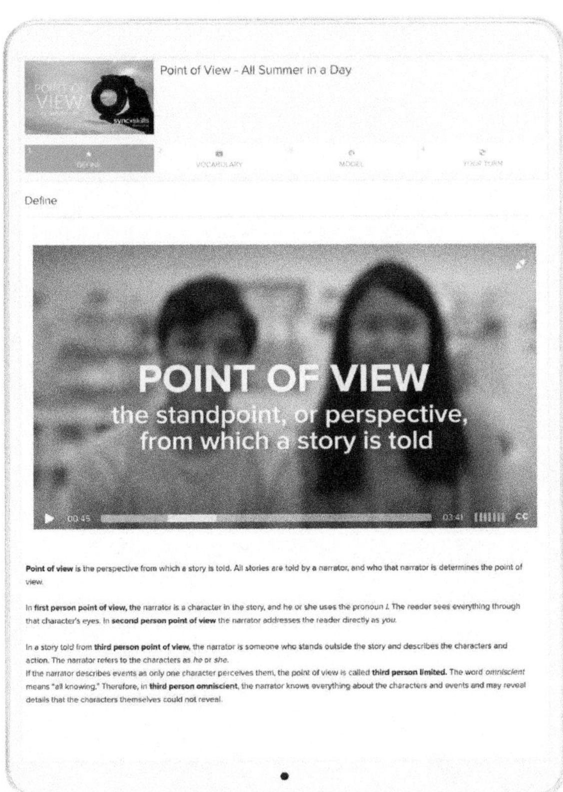

- Integrated media such as StudySyncTV and SkillsTV models collaborative and academic conversations, providing students the roadmap they need to develop their own voices.
- Unique media like the "School of Thought" podcast series helps teachers meet multimedia and digital literacy standards with high-quality resources that are relevant to the lives of today's students.

- Blast lessons help students understand the most important issues in today's world. Teachers have access to a brand new Blast article - leveled for 3 different Lexiles - every single school day, helping them deliver a fresh, relevant learning experience every year.

Everyone Loves a Mystery

What attracts us to the mysterious?

UNIT 1

Everyone Loves a Mystery

ESSENTIAL QUESTION

What attracts us to the mysterious?

Hairs rising on the back of your neck? Lips curling up into a wince? Palms a little sweaty? These are tell-tale signs that you are in the grips of suspense.

But what attracts us to mystery and suspense? We may have wondered what keeps us from closing the book or changing the channel when confronted with something scary, or what compels us to experience in stories the very things we spend our lives trying to avoid. Why do we do it?

Those are the questions your students will explore in this Grade 8 unit.

Edgar Allan Poe. Shirley Jackson. W. W. Jacobs. Masters of suspense stories are at work in this unit, with its focus on fiction. And there's more: Alfred Hitchcock, the "master of suspense" at the movies, shares tricks of the trade in a personal essay. Students will also read a suspenseful excerpt of a novel presented as a screenplay by award-winning YA fiction writer Walter Dean Myers. After reading classic thrillers and surprising mysteries within and across genres, your students will try their own hands at crafting fiction, applying what they have learned about suspense to their own narrative writing projects. Students will begin this unit as readers, brought to the edge of their seats by hair-raising tales, and they will finish as writers, leading you and their peers through hair-raising stories of their own.

Integrated Reading and Writing

Genre Focus:
FICTION

Extended Writing Project and Grammar

English Language Learner Resources

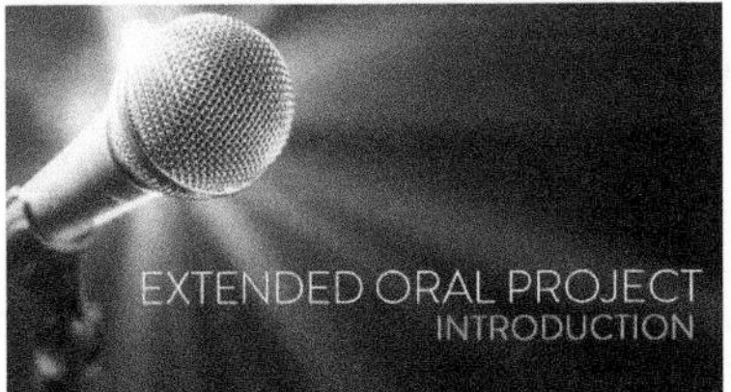

326 | Novel Study Choices

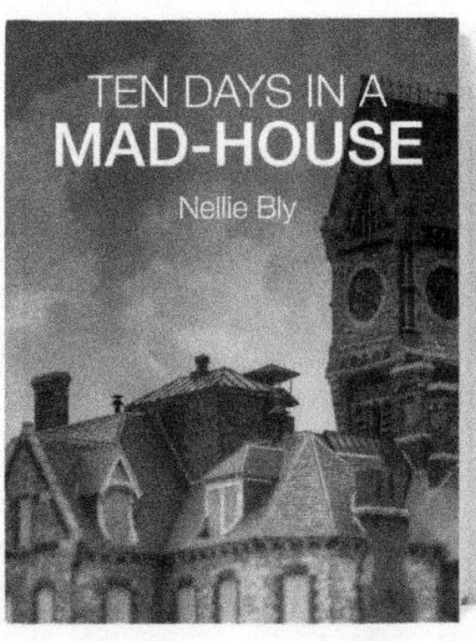

329 | End-of-Unit Assessment

Everyone Loves a Mystery

(tv) StudySyncTV or SkillsTV Episode

Pacing Guide

Days	Readings	Skill and Standard Instruction	Skill Practice and Spiraling
1-5	**SyncStart: The Tell-Tale Heart** (tv) p. 12	• Annotation • Context Clues • Reading Comprehension • Text Dependent Responses • Textual Evidence • Language, Style, and Audience • Collaborative Conversations • Short Constructed Responses • Peer Review	• Literary Analysis Writing • Collaborative Conversations
6-7	Essential Question **The Big Idea: What attracts us to the mysterious?** p. 48	• Recognizing Genre: Fiction • Academic Vocabulary	• Write: Analyzing Genre
8-10	**Monster** (tv) p. 52	• Character	• Textual Evidence • Narrative Writing • Collaborative Conversations
11-13	**Let 'Em Play God** p. 72	• Generating Questions • Author's Purpose and Point of View (tv)	• Textual Evidence • Literary Analysis Writing
14-17	PAIRED READINGS **Sympathy** p. 90 **Ten Days in a Mad-House (Chapter IV)** (tv) p. 100	• Personal Response • Author's Purpose and Point of View • Compare and Contrast (tv)	• Textual Evidence • Comparative Writing • Collaborative Conversations

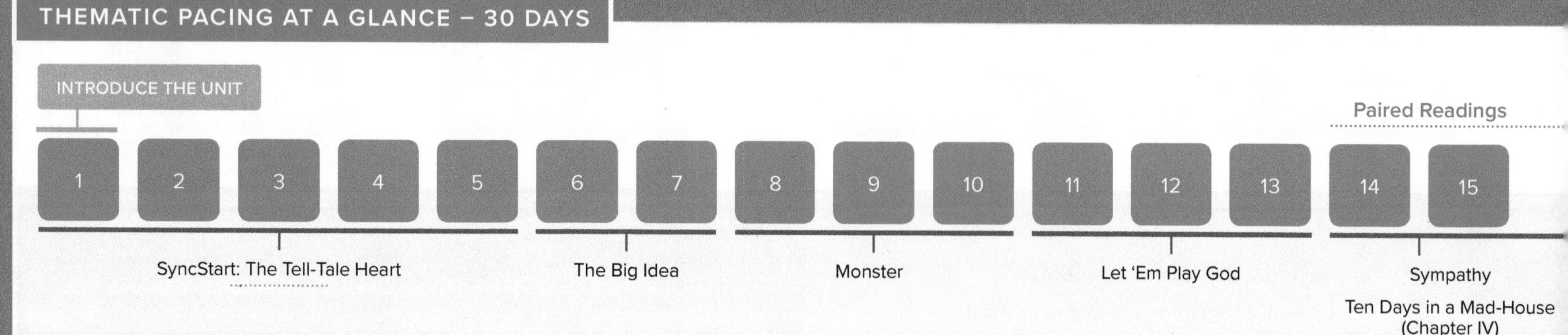

Days	Readings	Skill and Standard Instruction	Skill Practice and Spiraling
18-20	**The Lottery** tv p. 122	• Making and Confirming Predictions • Theme • Allusion	• Textual Evidence • Literary Analysis Writing • Collaborative Conversations
21-24	PAIRED READINGS **The Graveyard Book** p. 148 **The Conjure-Man Dies: A Mystery Tale of Dark Harlem** p. 178 **The Monkey's Paw** tv p. 192	• Plot • Story Structure	• Textual Evidence • Character • Comparative Writing • Collaborative Conversations
25-27	**Phineas Gage: A Gruesome but True Story About Brain Science** p. 220	• Central or Main Idea • Textual Evidence • Write: Analyzing Genre	• Author's Purpose and Point of View • Informative Writing
28	**Self-Selected Reading and Response** p. 240	• Independent Reading	• Personal Response Writing

Review and Assessment See page 328.

Days	Review and Assessment	Skill Practice and Assessment
29	**Skills Review** p. 328	Students will have the opportunity to complete one or more Spotlight skill lessons in order to improve understanding and further practice skills from the unit that they found most challenging.
30	**End-of-Unit Assessment** p. 329	For more detail, please see the End-of-Unit Assessment information for Grade 8 Unit 1 on page 329.

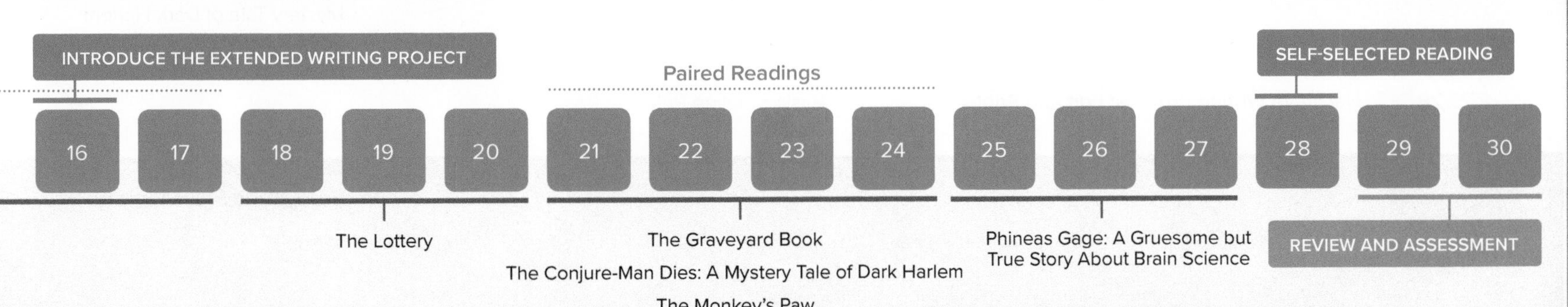

Extended Writing Project and Grammar

Pacing Guide

In the second half of the unit, students continue exploring texts that address the unit's Essential Question and begin crafting a longer composition to share their own ideas about the Essential Question in the Extended Writing Project. The writing project will take your students through the writing process to produce a narrative essay.

Extended Writing Project Prompt

What happens when fear comes from an unlikely source?

Use the techniques you've learned in this unit to write your own suspenseful narrative. Your characters may experience suspense in a familiar place or while they're with people they know and trust. Perhaps the fear comes from an everyday object or situation.

Days	Extended Writing Project and Grammar	Skill and Standard Instruction	Connect to Mentor Texts
16	**Narrative Writing Process: Plan** p. 250		
17-18	**Narrative Writing Process: Draft** p. 261	• Organizing Narrative Writing	• The Tell-Tale Heart
19-24	**Narrative Writing Process: Revise** p. 282	• Story Beginnings • Narrative Techniques • Descriptive Details • Transitions • Conclusions	• Monster • Ten Days in a Mad-House (Chapter IV) • The Lottery • The Graveyard Book • The Conjure-Man Dies: A Mystery Tale of Dark Harlem • The Monkey's Paw
25-28	**Narrative Writing Process: Edit and Publish** p. 291	• Basic Spelling Rules I • Dashes • Commas After Transitions	Additional grammar lessons can be found in the StudySync Skills Library.

Research

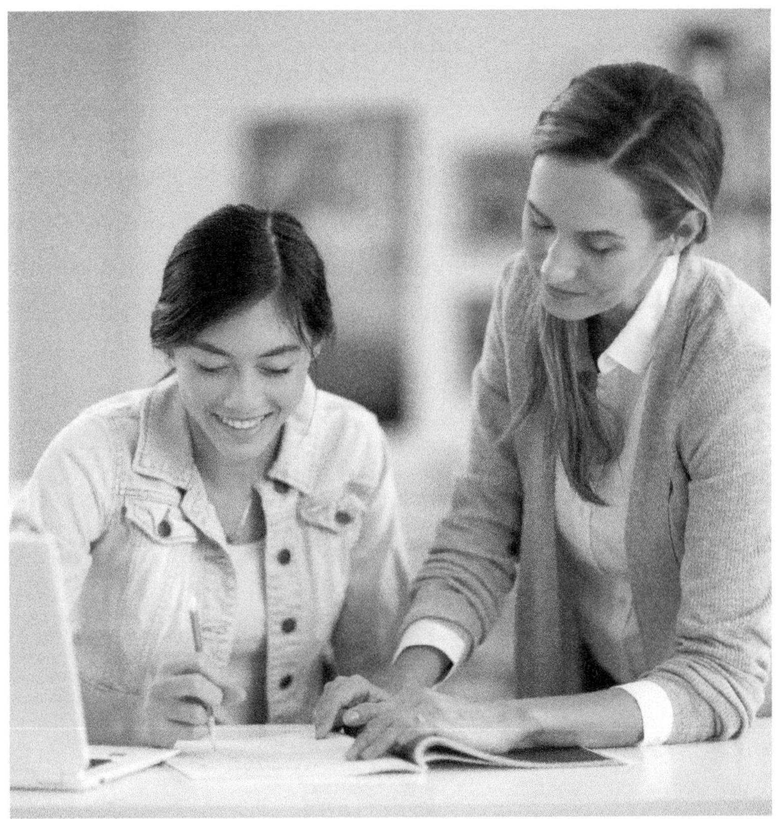

The following lessons include opportunities for research:

Blast **Blast Away!** Research Links*

First Read **The Tell-Tale Heart** Activate Prior Knowledge and Experiences

Blast **Everyone Loves a Mystery** Research Links*

First Read **Monster** Activate Prior Knowledge and Experiences

Blast **Teen Talk** Research Links*

First Read **Let 'Em Play God** Activate Prior Knowledge and Experiences

Independent Read **Sympathy** Activate Prior Knowledge and Experiences

Close Read **The Lottery** Beyond the Book

Independent Read **The Graveyard Book** Activate Prior Knowledge and Experiences

Independent Read **The Conjure-Man Dies** Beyond the Book

First Read **The Monkey's Paw** Activate Prior Knowledge and Experiences

Blast **Life's Great Mysteries** Research Links*

*See the teacher lesson plan online

Self-Selected Reading Prompt

After reading a self-selected text, students will respond to the following narrative prompt:

Famous novelist Leo Tolstoy once said, "Music is the shorthand of emotion." In other words, music has the power to communicate emotions that might be difficult to explain using words alone.

What is the music of a great mystery?

Imagine that you have the opportunity to create the soundtrack for a film adaptation of the selection you've just read. What songs would you include? Why? How do these songs capture the feelings you experienced while reading this text? Write a response in which you describe your reactions to moments or events from the text and identify songs that best capture your feelings.

Integrated Scaffolding

ELL and Approaching grade-level students receive scaffolds for every lesson, whether in the Thematic, Novel Study or ELL Resources sections of the unit. Specific scaffolds are intentionally designed to support the needs of English Language Learners and Approaching grade-level students in the ELA classroom. Other scaffolds exist as part of the many standard features in the StudySync digital platform and can be strategically utilized to support students' comprehension and engagement.

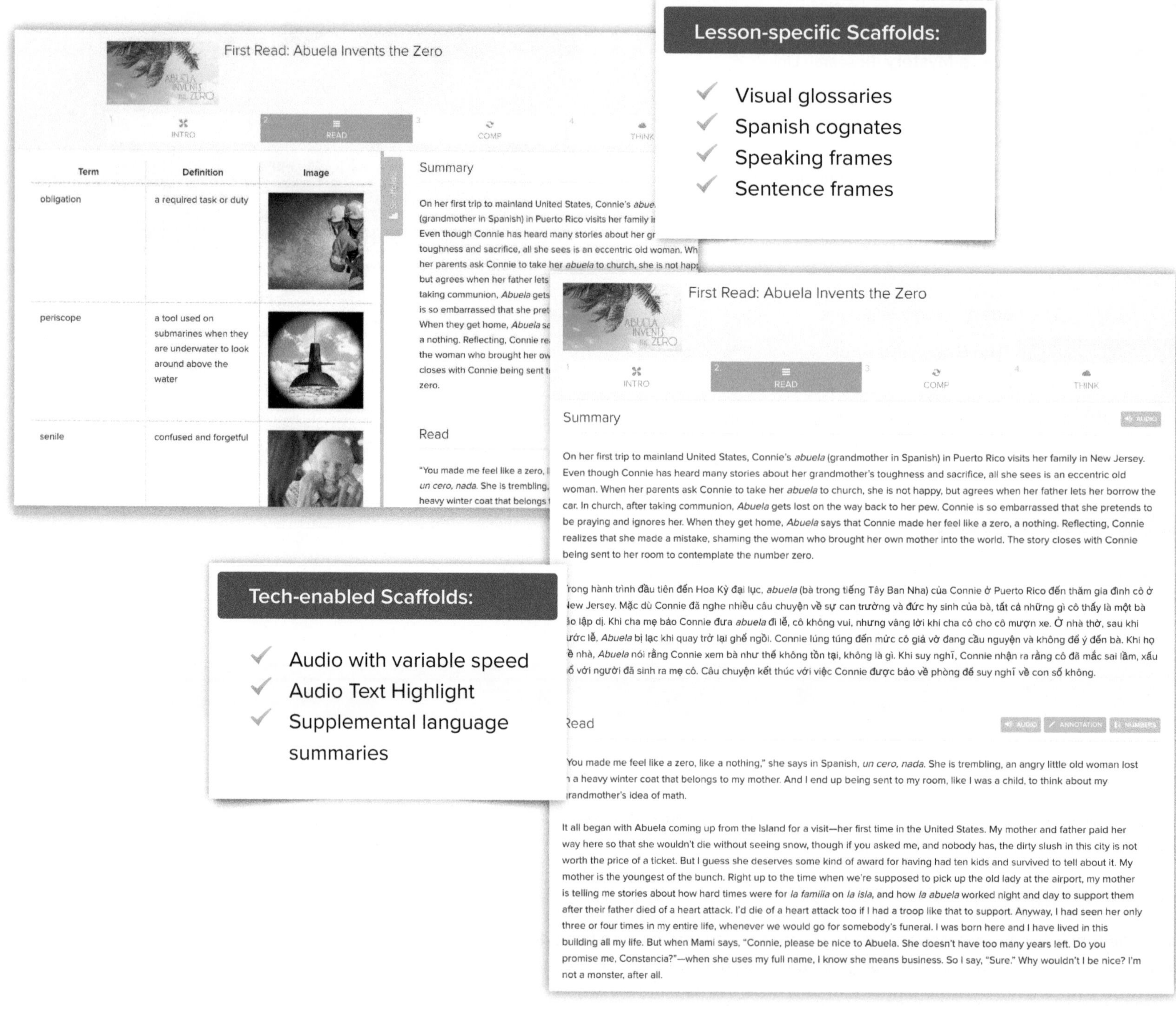

English Language Learner Resources

Both Thematic and Novel Study units include English Language Learner resources designed to match the thematic focus, text structures, and writing form of the unit. ELL resources include two leveled texts and an extended oral project.

ELL Texts	Differentiated Text Levels	Skill and Standard Instruction
 	BEGINNING N/A I 327 words INTERMEDIATE N/A I 398 words ADVANCED N/A I 456 words ADVANCED HIGH N/A I 533 words Use this text in place of or as an extension to *Monster*.	• Sight Vocabulary and High-Frequency Words • Analyzing Expressions • Conveying Ideas • Spelling Patterns and Rules
 	BEGINNING 380L I 377 words INTERMEDIATE 420L I 416 words ADVANCED 570L I 467 words ADVANCED HIGH 690L I 569 words Use this text in place of or as an extension to "The Monkey's Paw."	• Classroom Vocabulary • Taking Notes • Language Structures • Retelling and Summarizing • Subject-Verb Agreement
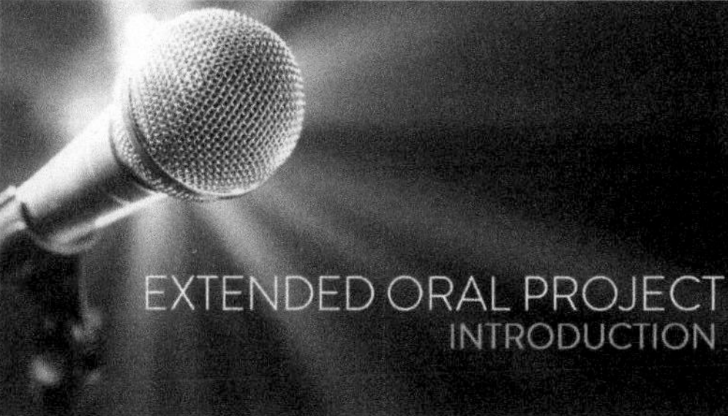 	In this Extended Oral Project, students will write and perform a dramatic scene. This may be assigned in place of this unit's EWP.	• Acquiring Vocabulary • Sentence Lengths

Focus on English Language Proficiency Levels

ADVANCED HIGH
ADVANCED
INTERMEDIATE
BEGINNING

ELL Resources provide targeted support for four levels of proficiency: Beginning, Intermediate, Advanced, and Advanced High. Instruction and scaffolds, as well as the texts themselves, are differentiated based on these levels.

Additional differentiated scaffolds include visual glossaries, speaking and writing frames, and suggested grouping for peer and teacher support. Lessons also include suggested extension activities to challenge Advanced and Advanced High students as they progress through the year.

Assessment

DAYS 29-30

Assessment in StudySync is built upon a recursive cycle that includes assessment, instruction, and review. Screening, placement, and benchmark assessments help teachers establish baselines and determine scaffold needs. Throughout the course of instruction, teachers regularly assess student progress using formative and summative measures, and use the individualized data from those assessments to guide choices about instruction, review, remediation, and enrichment to bring all students to standards mastery and College and Career Readiness.

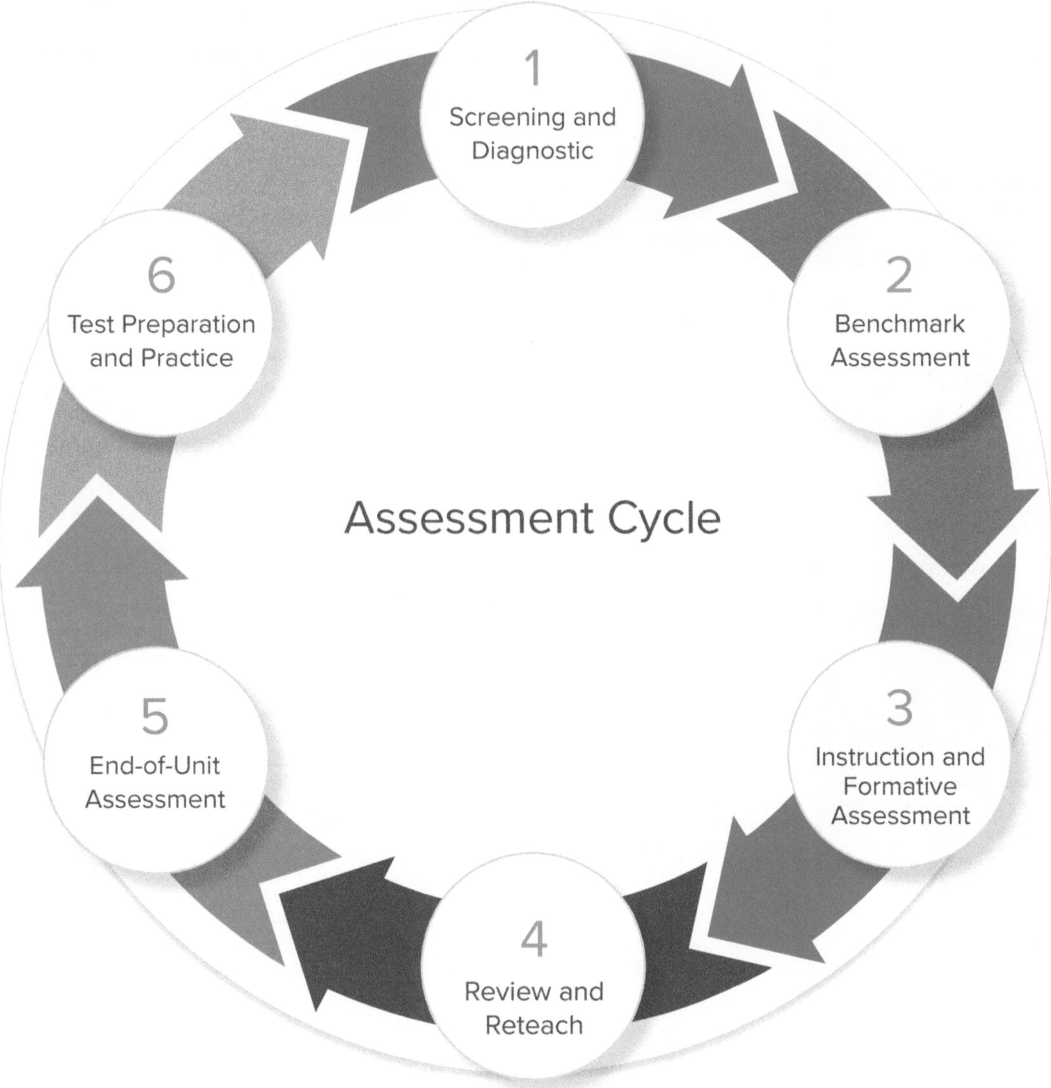

What's Next?

Assessment results can be viewed by item, standard, and skill to monitor mastery and make decisions for upcoming instruction.

- ✓ Reteach skills that students have not yet mastered, using Spotlight Skills or the Test Preparation and Practice book.
- ✓ Revise your teaching plan to provide more or less explicit instruction into a skill or text, using Beyond the Book activities for enrichment.
- ✓ Regroup students and levels of scaffolding based on standards progress.

Review

Spotlight Skills Review

A review day before the end-of-unit assessment gives you an opportunity to review difficult concepts with students using Spotlight Skills lessons. Spotlight Skills are targeted lessons that provide you resources to reteach or remediate without assigning additional readings. Every Core ELA Skill lesson has a corresponding Spotlight Skill lesson. Spotlight Skills can be assigned at any point in the year, but the end of each unit provides a natural moment to pause, review data collected throughout the unit, and reteach skills students have not yet mastered.

Progress Monitoring

The Progress Monitoring charts that appear before every text in this unit identify standards and associated Spotlight Skills. On review day, you may want to give preference to reteaching skills that are not revisited in later units. You can see where Skills are covered again in the Opportunities to Reteach column.

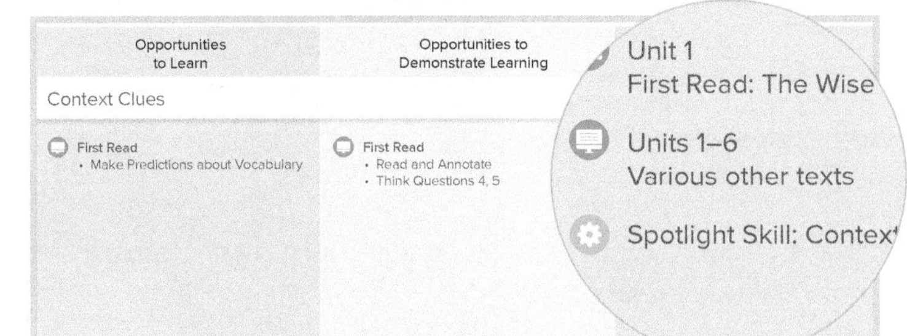

StudySync Gradebook

As students submit assignments on StudySync, their mastery of skills and standards is tracked via the gradebook. The gradebook can be sorted and viewed in a variety of ways. Sorting by assignment shows overall student performance, while sorting by standards or by Skill lessons displays student progress toward mastery goals.

	First Rea	Skill: Text	Close Re	
MAX SCORE	10	2	12	
STUDENT				
Tate O'Brien	10	2	9	
Olivia Adams	8	1	11	

Skills Library

Spotlight Skills are located in the Skills section of the StudySync Library. You can assign Spotlight Skills to individual students or groups of students. Search tools allow you to search by Skill type or name.

End-of-Unit Assessment

Assessed Reading Skills

- ✓ Allusion
- ✓ Author's Purpose and Point of View
- ✓ Central or Main Idea
- ✓ Character
- ✓ Compare and Contrast
- ✓ Context Clues
- ✓ Language, Style, and Audience
- ✓ Plot
- ✓ Story Structure
- ✓ Textual Evidence
- ✓ Theme

Assessed Revising and Editing Skills

- ✓ Basic Spelling Rules I
- ✓ Commas After Transitions
- ✓ Conclusions
- ✓ Dashes
- ✓ Descriptive Details
- ✓ Narrative Techniques
- ✓ Organizing Narrative Writing
- ✓ Story Beginnings
- ✓ Transitions

Introduction

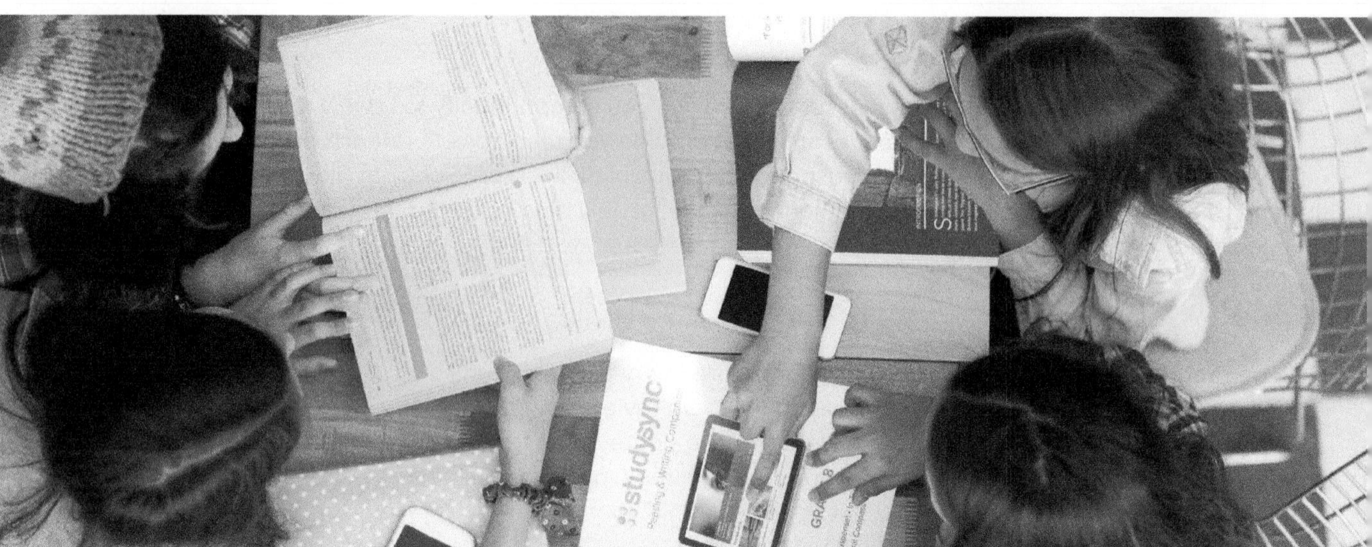

How do I use StudySync? More importantly, how does StudySync design learning today to help my students in the future? SyncStart introduces students and teachers to the instructional routines that figure prominently in StudySync. Built around an existing, grade-level text, each SyncStart Unit instructs and assesses the habits and skills needed to tap students' maximum potential for learning. With SyncStart, teachers have detailed plans for their first two weeks of StudySync instruction. Students and teachers alike reap the benefits of a strong start to a new program—a SyncStart.

What does it take to be a strong reader and writer? Is it enough to just recognize the words on a page or know how to spell or use punctuation? Are some people born good at it, while others struggle? Attitudes toward learning, particularly learning how to read and write, have changed dramatically over time. What we've now found is that there are a number of specific, individual skills and strategies that can improve the way we access and write about the texts we read.

In this SyncStart unit, students develop these skills in the context of a StudySync reading routine. The unit begins by instructing to foundational best practices for reading—using annotation to record notes and ideas, drawing on context clues to predict the meanings of unknown words, and applying reading comprehension strategies to break down complex texts. From there, students will slowly go through the routine of a First Read, Reading Skills, and a Close Read, pausing intermittently to dive deeply into additional skills and strategies. For example, before participating in their first StudySyncTV-style Discussion, students will complete a lesson on Collaborative Conversations that explicitly instructs to the behaviors that lead to a successful peer discussion. Similarly, before and after students submit their first Close Read Response, they will analyze and practice the skills of writing Short Constructed Responses and Peer Reviews. Throughout this unit, students are introduced to the skills that will help them grow as readers and writers as they continue to practice throughout the year.

What's different about SyncStart?

In the SyncStart unit, teachers and students become familiar with the lessons, routines, and skills in the StudySync curriculum. StudySync provides this preparation within the curriculum to prepare students for the year ahead in four ways:

1 Routines

The SyncStart unit starts with a Blast and then follows the Integrated Reading and Writing routine of First Read, Skill Lesson, and Close Read. Targeted skill lessons like Short Constructed Response and Peer Review introduce specific skills and give students the instructional tools they'll need for the year ahead.

2 Habits of Learning

In addition to establishing the routines students will use in StudySync, other skill lessons allow students to develop the skills they will need every day in class, like Annotation, Text-Dependent Responses, and Collaborative Conversation. These skills create a foundation of best practices for students so that they can more effectively interact with texts, respond to questions, and collaborate with their peers.

3 PREP

PREP sections in each SyncStart lesson plan explain the purpose behind StudySync's instructional routines. Over the course of the SyncStart lessons, teachers will come to understand and master best practices for the instructional moments in each StudySync lesson.

4 Teaching Lab Videos

These videos show teachers what the routine looks like in action and appear in the Instructional Path alongside the lesson plan for the lesson they illustrate.

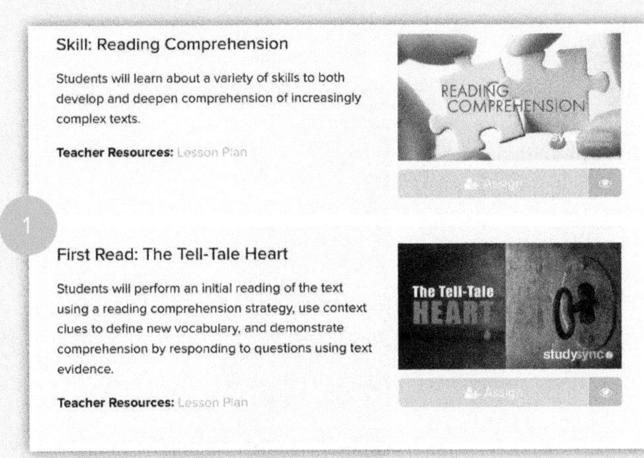

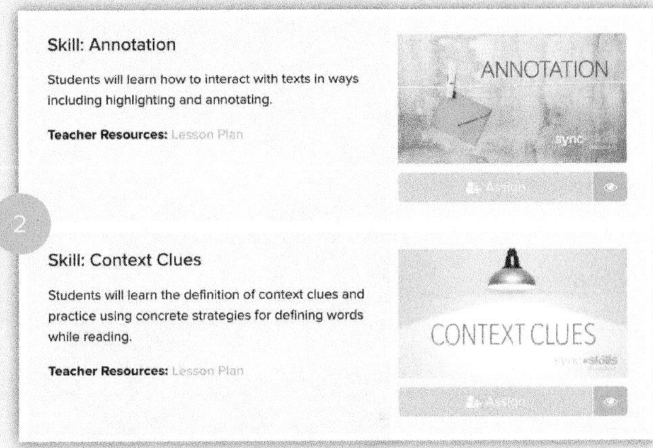

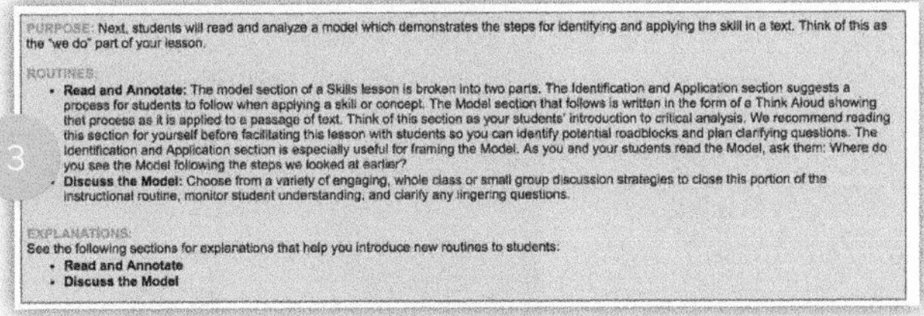
PURPOSE: Next, students will read and analyze a model which demonstrates the steps for identifying and applying the skill in a text. Think of this as the "we do" part of your lesson.

ROUTINES:

- **Read and Annotate:** The model section of a Skills lesson is broken into two parts. The Identification and Application section suggests a process for students to follow when applying a skill or concept. The Model section that follows is written in the form of a Think Aloud showing that process as it is applied to a passage of text. Think of this section as your students' introduction to critical analysis. We recommend reading this section for yourself before facilitating this lesson with students so you can identify potential roadblocks and plan clarifying questions. The Identification and Application section is especially useful for framing the Model. As you and your students read the Model, ask them: Where do you see the Model following the steps we looked at earlier?
- **Discuss the Model:** Choose from a variety of engaging, whole class or small group discussion strategies to close this portion of the instructional routine, monitor student understanding, and clarify any lingering questions.

EXPLANATIONS:

See the following sections for explanations that help you introduce new routines to students:

- **Read and Annotate**
- **Discuss the Model**

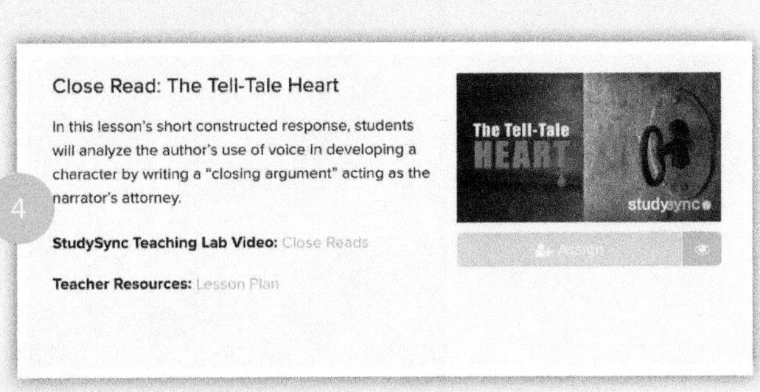

The Tell-Tale Heart

FICTION
Edgar Allan Poe
1843

Introduction

studysync tv

The works of Edgar Allan Poe (1809–1849) set the standard for Gothic fiction. "The Tell-Tale Heart" is one of his most famous and widely read stories. Convinced that officers at his house can hear the dead man's heart beating through the floorboard, Poe's narrator confesses to killing an old man in his care, despite the fact he bore the man no grudge. In a dramatic monologue of increasing volume and intensity—as well as mental disintegration—the "perfectly sane" murderer painstakingly describes how the "vulture eye" of his victim drove him to commit the horrible act.

Driven mad by the sight of an old man's vulture-like eye, the narrator recounts how he set out to murder him. Throughout the story, he presents one unhinged rationalization after another, but the narrator maintains that he is perfectly sane. For seven days, he visits the old man's room at midnight but always finds the eye closed. On the eighth night, when the narrator's lantern light shines on the old man's face, that narrator sees that the eye is open, which spurs him to kill the old man. He dismembers the body and hides it beneath the floorboards. The police arrive the next morning, stating that a scream had been reported. The narrator confidently shows them around, convincing them of his innocence. All seems well until he hears the old man's heart beating through the floor. As the sound gets louder, the narrator becomes convinced that the police can also hear it, so he confesses.

ELL Proficiency-leveled summaries and summaries in multiple languages are available digitally.

 Audio and audio text highlighting are available with this text.

CONNECT TO ESSENTIAL QUESTION

What attracts us to the mysterious?

How do we know when a narrator is reliable? In Edgar Allan Poe's classic short story "The Tell-Tale Heart", the central mystery about the main character concerns his sanity in the midst of a terrible murder confession. Will he give himself away, or get away with murder?

Access Complex Text

LEXILE: 950L **WORD COUNT:** 2,163

The following areas may be challenging for students, particularly ELL English Language Learners and A Approaching grade-level learners.

Genre	Sentence Structure	Specific Vocabulary
• This classic short story, told in first-person point of view, may challenge some students as the narrator alternates between external description and internal thought. • Readers will need to distinguish between fact and perception.	• Long sentences are broken by dashes and capital letters to indicate the narrator's anxious, fragmented thinking. • Poe uses nonstandard font, punctuation, and other devices as visual cues to the narrator's emotional state.	• Difficult vocabulary, such as *unperceived* and *over-acuteness*, may present a challenge to readers. Remind readers to use context clues, as well as knowledge of Greek and Latin roots and affixes, to help them define unknown words.

SCAFFOLDS  **ENGLISH LANGUAGE LEARNERS**  **APPROACHING GRADE LEVEL**  **BEYOND GRADE LEVEL**

These icons identify differentiation strategies and scaffolded support for a variety of students. See the digital lesson plan for additional differentiation strategies and scaffolds.

Instructional Path

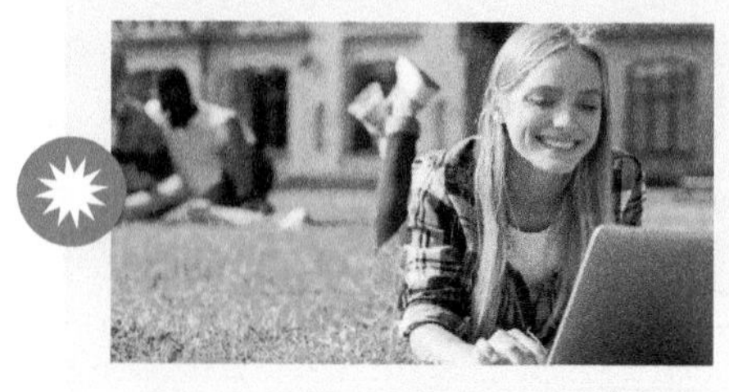

Blast: Blast Away!

Objectives: Students will explore background information and research links in order to answer a question with a 140-character response.

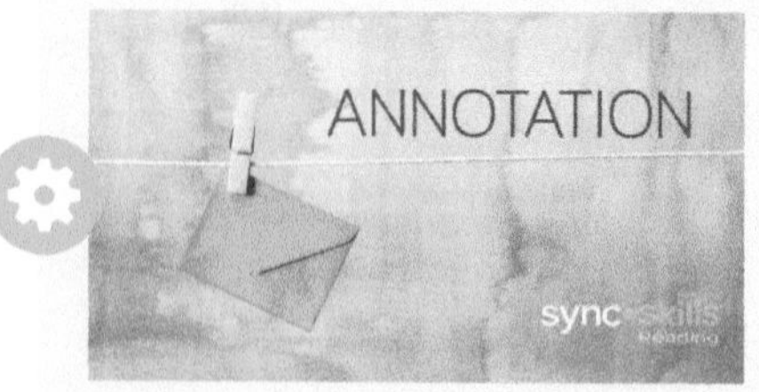

Skill: Annotation

Objectives: After reading and discussing a model, students will be able to write annotations to ask questions, track the development of an idea, and respond to the text.

DIGITAL ONLY

Skill: Context Clues

Objectives: After rereading and discussing a model of close reading, students will be able to use context clues, such as definition, comparison, contrast, and examples, to clarify the meanings of words.

DIGITAL ONLY

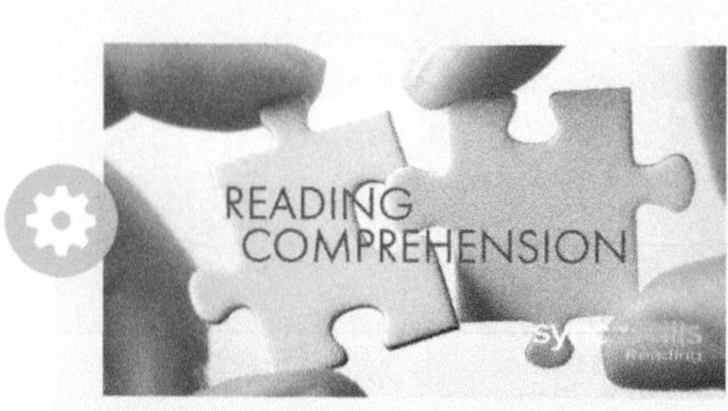

Skill: Reading Comprehension

Objectives: After rereading and discussing a model of close reading, students will be able to use reading comprehension strategies to develop and deepen comprehension of increasingly complex texts.

DIGITAL ONLY

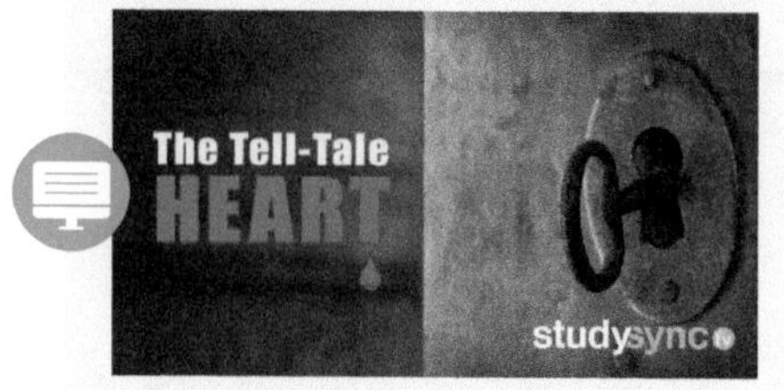

First Read: The Tell-Tale Heart

Objectives: After an initial reading and discussion of the short story, students will be able to implement a reading comprehension strategy, use context clues to define new vocabulary, and demonstrate comprehension by responding to questions using textual evidence.

Skill: Text-Dependent Responses

Objectives: Students will be able to cite textual evidence that most strongly supports analysis of the text.

The print teacher's edition includes essential point-of-use instruction and planning tools. Complete lesson plans and program documents appear in your digital teacher account.

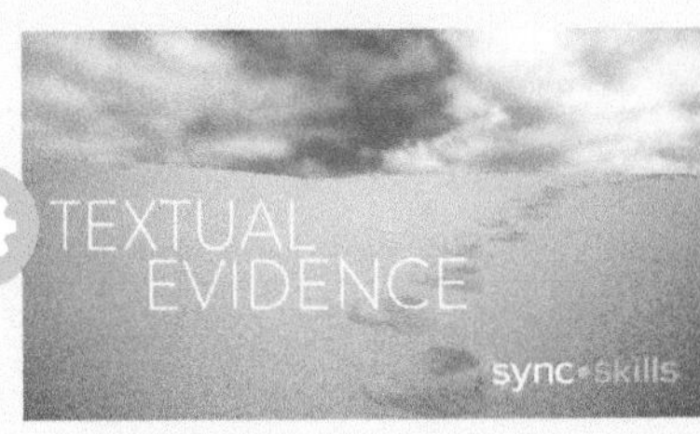

Skill: Textual Evidence

Objectives: Students will be able to cite textual evidence to support analysis of what the text says explicitly, as well as inferences drawn from the text.

Skill: Language, Style, and Audience

Objectives: Students will be able to analyze how an author's use of words and phrases impact the meaning and tone in a work of fiction.

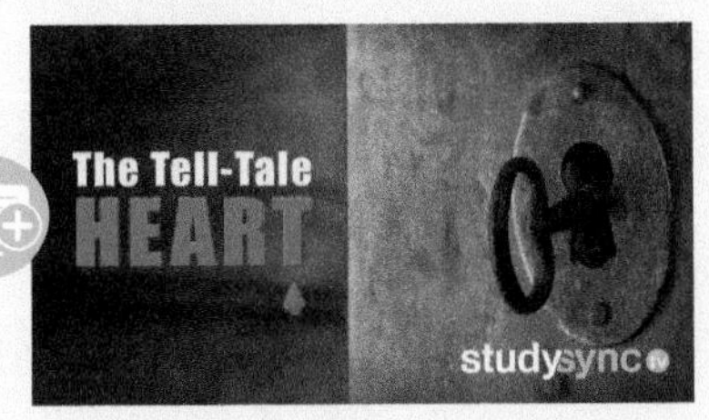

Close Read: The Tell-Tale Heart

Objectives: Students will be able to analyze the author's word choice and tone and use textual evidence to support that analysis in order to participate in a collaborative conversation and write a short constructed response.

Skill: Collaborative Conversations

Objectives: Students will be able to analyze what elements contribute to successful collaborative conversations.

Skill: Short Constructed Responses

Objectives: Students will be able to analyze how to plan and write a brief, organized response to a prompt.

Skill: Peer Review

Objectives: Students will be able to understand and apply the elements of effective and constructive peer review.

Progress Monitoring

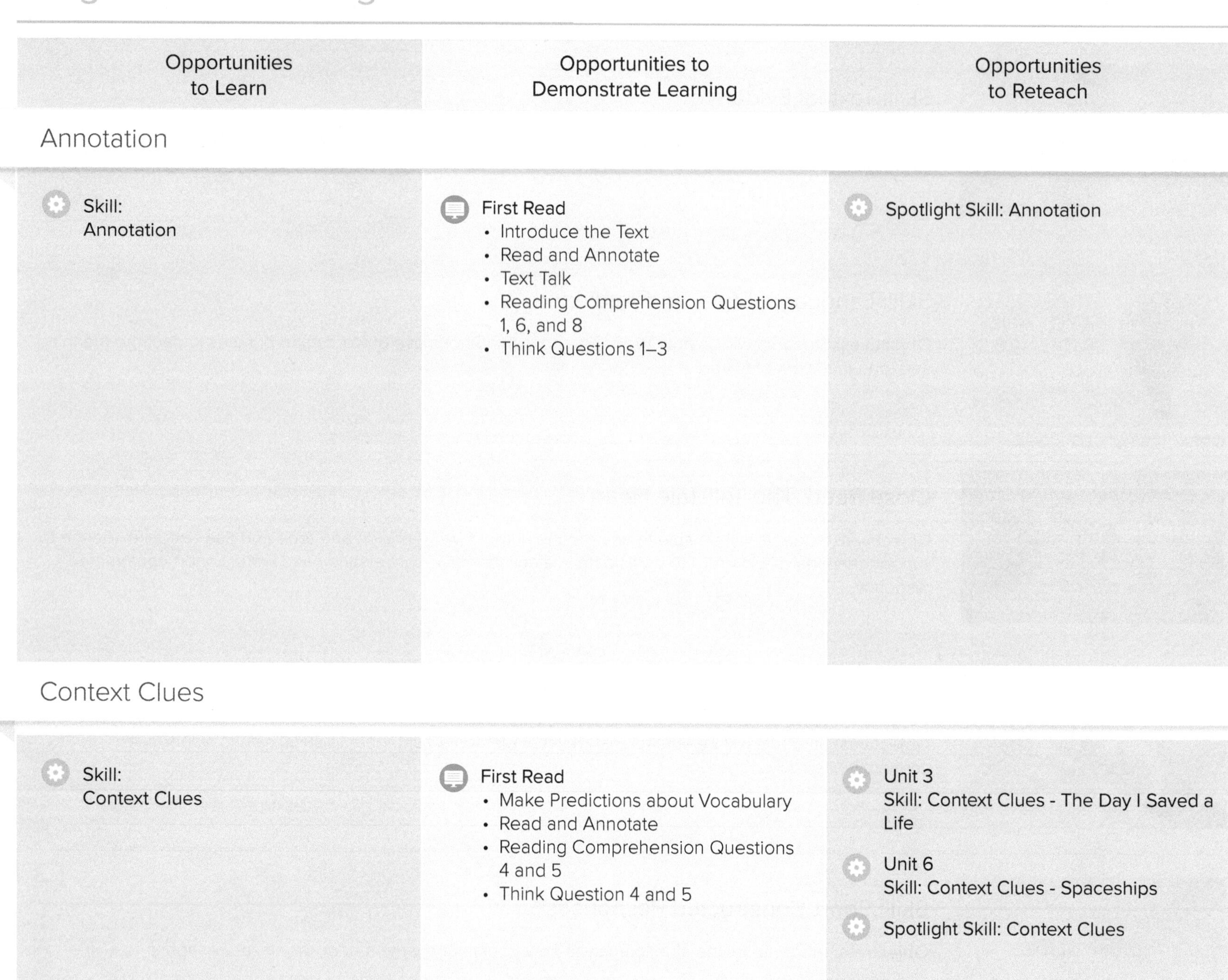

Opportunities to Learn	Opportunities to Demonstrate Learning	Opportunities to Reteach
Annotation		
Skill: Annotation	First Read • Introduce the Text • Read and Annotate • Text Talk • Reading Comprehension Questions 1, 6, and 8 • Think Questions 1–3	Spotlight Skill: Annotation
Context Clues		
Skill: Context Clues	First Read • Make Predictions about Vocabulary • Read and Annotate • Reading Comprehension Questions 4 and 5 • Think Question 4 and 5	Unit 3 Skill: Context Clues - The Day I Saved a Life Unit 6 Skill: Context Clues - Spaceships Spotlight Skill: Context Clues

Reading Comprehension

Skill:
Reading Comprehension

First Read
- Read and Annotate

Spotlight Skill: Reading Comprehension

Text-Dependent Responses

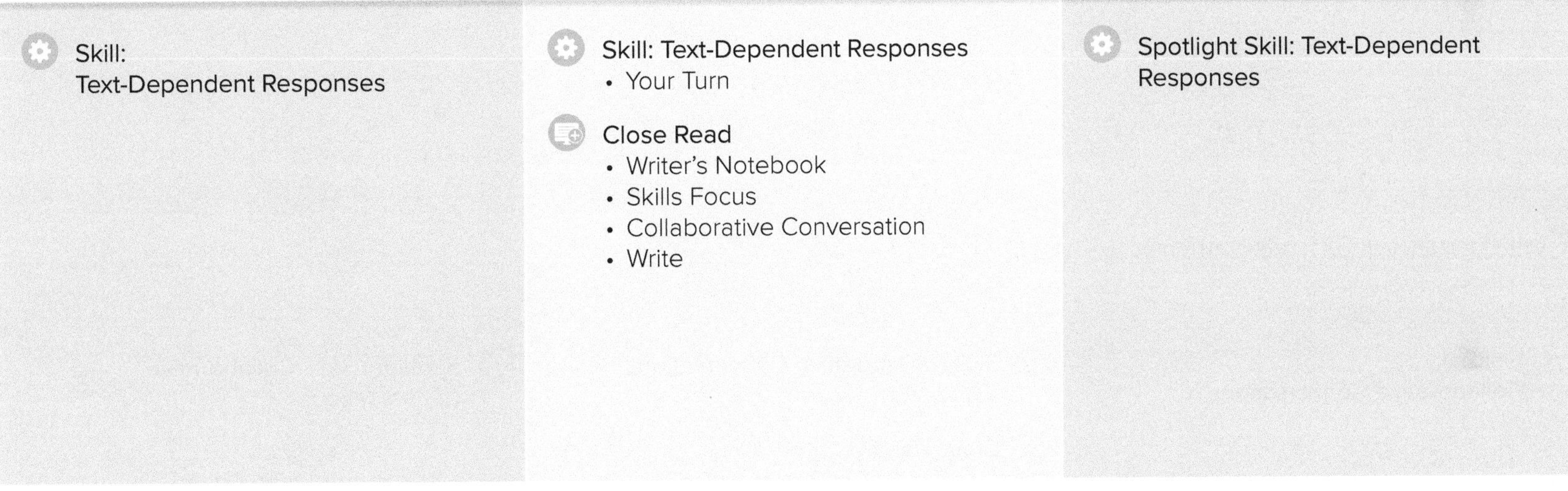

Skill:
Text-Dependent Responses

Skill: Text-Dependent Responses
- Your Turn

Close Read
- Writer's Notebook
- Skills Focus
- Collaborative Conversation
- Write

Spotlight Skill: Text-Dependent Responses

Textual Evidence

Skill:
Textual Evidence

Skill: Textual Evidence
- Your Turn

Close Read
- Writer's Notebook
- Skills Focus
- Collaborative Conversation
- Write

Unit 1
Skill: Textual Evidence - Phineas Gage: A Gruesome but True Story About Brain Science

Unit 2
Skill: Textual Evidence - The Outsiders

Spotlight Skill: Textual Evidence

Progress Monitoring

Language, Style, and Audience

Skill: Language, Style, and Audience	Skill: Language, Style, and Audience • Your Turn Close Read • Complete Vocabulary Chart • Skills Focus • Write	Unit 3 Skill: Language, Style, and Audience - The Call of the Wild Unit 4 Skill: Language, Style, and Audience - Speech to the Ohio Women's Conference: Ain't I a Woman? Spotlight Skill: Language, Style, and Audience

Collaborative Conversations

Skill: Collaborative Conversations	Skill: Collaborative Conversations • Your Turn Close Read • Collaborative Conversation	Spotlight Skill: Collaborative Conversations

Progress Monitoring

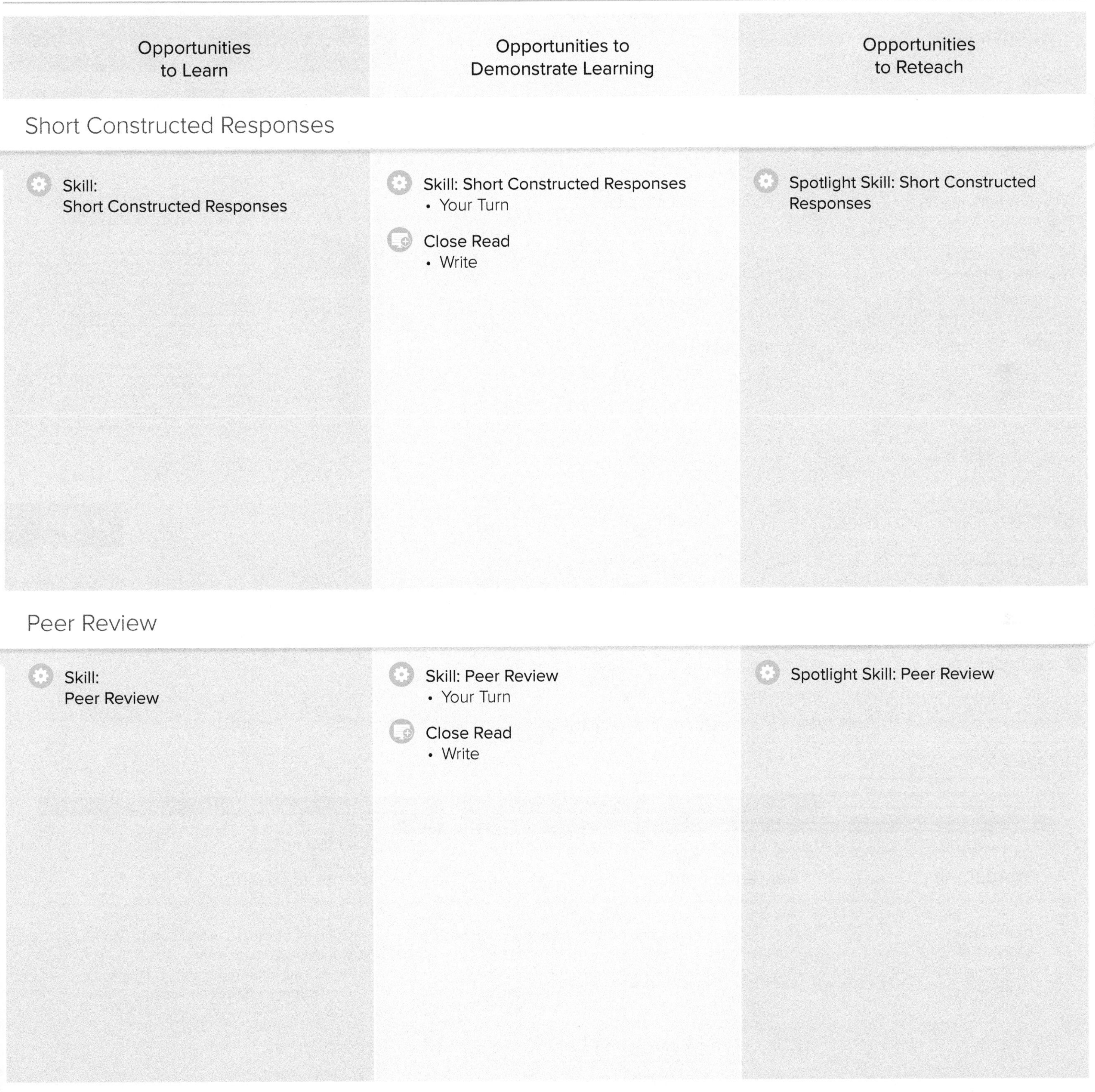

Opportunities to Learn	Opportunities to Demonstrate Learning	Opportunities to Reteach
Short Constructed Responses		
Skill: Short Constructed Responses	Skill: Short Constructed Responses • Your Turn Close Read • Write	Spotlight Skill: Short Constructed Responses
Peer Review		
Skill: Peer Review	Skill: Peer Review • Your Turn Close Read • Write	Spotlight Skill: Peer Review

Blast: Blast Away!

How do contemporary issues and culture shape your worldview?

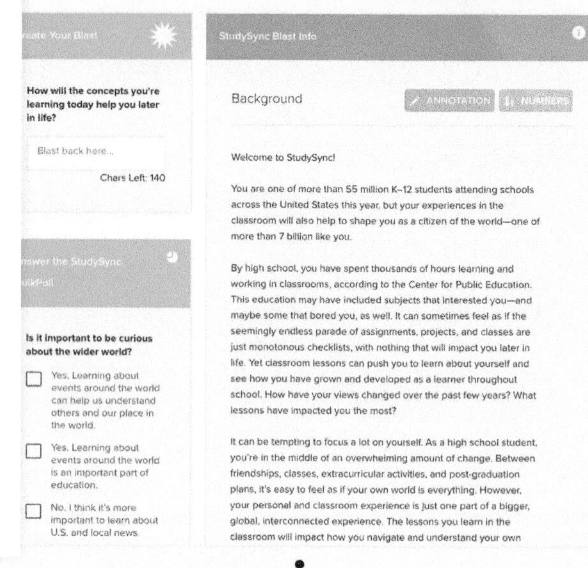

TEXT TALK

Where might you already be thinking critically and voicing your opinion about events?

Paragraph 3: Some places include Facebook, Twitter, and Snapchat.

What is a trending topic? What are some current trending topics?

Paragraph 3: A trending topic is one that shows up again and again. Examples might include global, environmental, political, or cultural issues.

What are some activities included in a StudySync Blast?

Paragraphs 4 and 5: Weigh in on issues, read an article, research sources, respond to a question, complete a Number Crunch and QuikPoll, and write a Blast.

What are some opinions about our access to information?

Paragraph 6: Some people think that the world is getting worse, but Ray Kurzweil disagrees.

Create Your Own Blast

SCAFFOLDS

Ask students to write a 140-character Blast after they complete the QuikPoll.

Use the scaffolds below to differentiate instruction for your ELL English Language Learners.

BEGINNING Write a response using the word bank to complete the sentence frame.

INTERMEDIATE Write a response using the sentence frame.

ADVANCED, ADVANCED HIGH Write a response using the sentence starter.

BEGINNING	BEGINNING / INTERMEDIATE	ADVANCED, ADVANCED HIGH
Word Bank	**Sentence Frame**	**Sentence Starter**
perspective knowledge understanding ideas thinking	Contemporary issues and culture shape my worldview by expanding my ____ and ____.	• Contemporary issues and culture shape my worldview by expanding . . . • When I am informed about . . . I think . . . • Contemporary issues and culture shape how I . . .

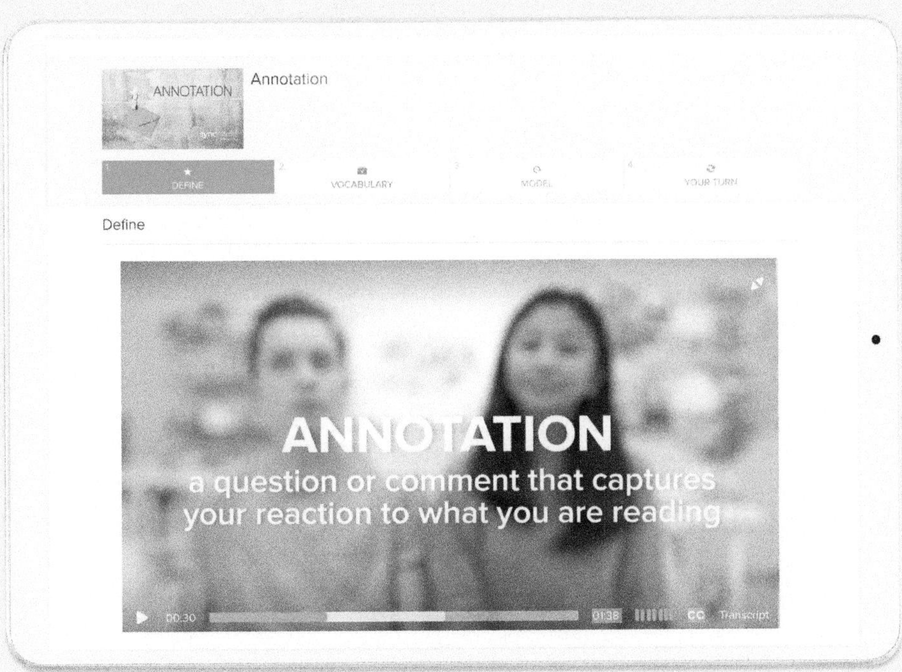

Skill: Annotation

Introduce the Skill

Watch the Concept Definition video and read the following definition with your students.

An **annotation** is a question or comment that you write directly on a text to capture your reaction to what you are reading. When annotating a text, a writer may ask a **question**, **track** the development of an idea, or **respond** with a personal experience.

Annotations may also include a reader's inferences and evaluations about the text. An **inference** is an idea that a reader forms about a text by combining textual evidence and his or her own reasoning and prior knowledge. An **evaluation** is a judgment about a text's content or the effectiveness of the writer's craft.

To record an annotation, a reader may use the StudySync annotation tool to highlight a selection of text and leave a comment or underline a passage of printed text and write a note in the margin.

Your Turn

Ask students to complete the Your Turn activity.

Highlighted Text	Annotation	Category
"dissimulation"	What does this word mean? Maybe it means "well-planned" because the narrator is using it to describe how he enters the old man's bedroom.	Ask Questions
"Oh, you would have laughed to see how cunningly I thrust it in! I moved it slowly—very, very slowly, so that I might not disturb the old man's sleep."	I can't believe he's laughing about this! This thought reveals that he is a disturbed person.	Track
"And this I did for seven long nights—every night just at midnight—but I found the eye always closed . . . "	He planned to kill the old man from the beginning, but he can't do it unless he can see the eye open.	Track
"And every morning, when the day broke, I went boldly into the chamber, and spoke courageously to him, calling him by name in a hearty tone, and inquiring how he had passed the night.	This is so twisted! My neighbors and I chat all the time. I would never suspect that one might want to secretly harm me.	Respond

TURN AND TALK

1. What are annotations?
2. What are three purposes of annotations?

ELL SPEAKING FRAMES

- Annotations are ____.
- One purpose of annotations is to ____.

Skill: Context Clues

Introduce the Skill

Watch the Concept Definition video  and read the following definition with your students.

When readers come across words they don't know, they often use context to determine the meanings of the unfamiliar words. **Context clues** are hints in the surrounding text that a reader can use to **infer** the meaning of an unfamiliar word. Some common types of context clues include the following:

- **Definition**: an explanation of the word's meaning before or after the word appears, usually set off by a comma
- **Example**: one or more examples in a text that may demonstrate the meaning of a word
- **Comparison**: determining a word's meaning based on how it is like something else in the text
- **Contrast**: determining a word's meaning based on how it is unlike something else in the text

In addition, the genre of a text and what it is about also provide context clues for a word's meaning. Readers can verify their preliminary definitions of words or phrases by using a print or digital resource.

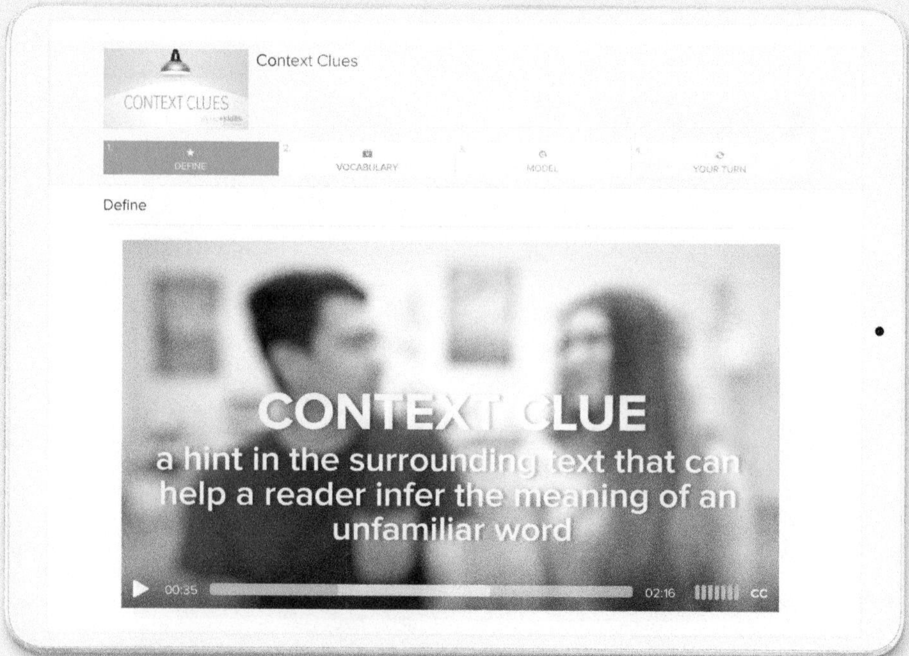

TURN AND TALK

1. What are context clues?

2. What are four different types of context clues?

SPEAKING FRAMES

- Context clues are ____.
- One type of context clue is ____.
- It provides a clue to the meaning of a word through ____.

Your Turn

Ask students to complete the Your Turn activity.

QUESTION 1

Part A

A. Incorrect. The speaker "talked more quickly," but the text doesn't say anything about his volume.

B. Correct. The speaker "gasped" and "talked more quickly," suggesting that he is becoming more emotional and passionate.

C. Incorrect. The speaker "talked more fluently . . . with a heightened voice," which means that he did not sound flat or monotone.

D. Incorrect. The noise was "such a sound as a watch makes when enveloped in cotton," not the speaker's voice.

Part B

A. Incorrect. This describes the noise that the speaker heard, not the speaker's voice.

B. Correct. The description of "a high key and with violent gesticulations" suggests emotion and passion.

C. Incorrect. This describes the noise that the speaker heard, not the speaker's voice.

D. Incorrect. This describes the speaker's appearance, not the speaker's voice.

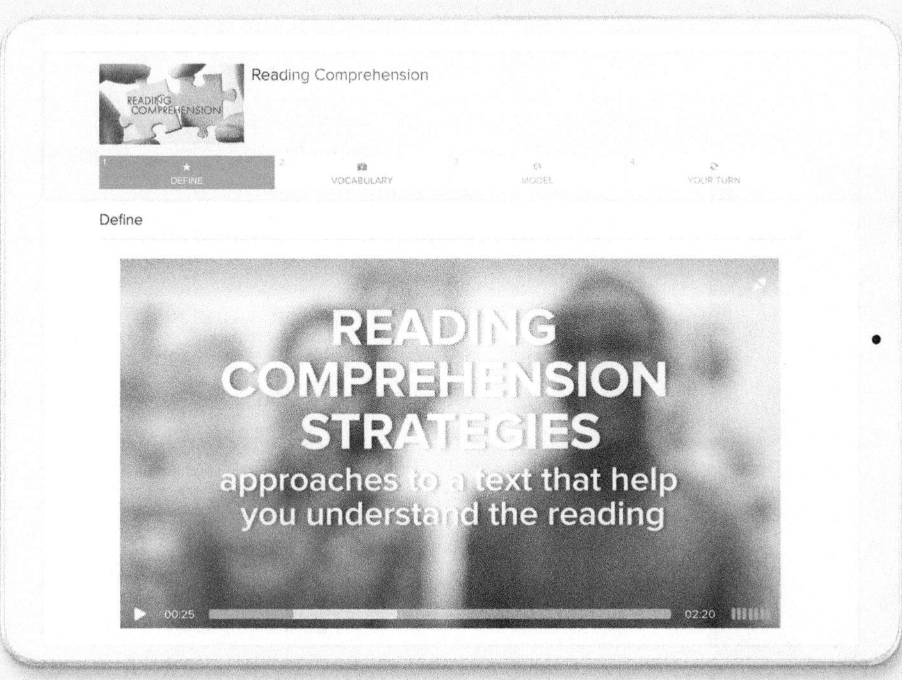

Skill: Reading Comprehension

Introduce the Skill

Watch the Concept Definition video and read the following definition with your students.

Do you ever reach a point in your reading where you no longer understand what is happening? Have you ever felt overwhelmed by the information in a text? Many readers sometimes share this feeling, but there are many **reading comprehension strategies** that can help you. Reading comprehension strategies are conscious, deliberate plans — a set of steps that readers can use to make sense of a text and help them become active readers in control of their own reading comprehension.

Occasionally you will employ a reading comprehension strategy before you begin reading a text, such as **setting a purpose for reading** or **generating questions**. To set a purpose for reading means to identify the reason for reading a text.

Generating questions means to ask and answer questions before, during, and after reading a text. During reading, you might apply one or a combination of strategies that will help you feel confident as you read challenging texts.

Your Turn

Ask students to complete the Your Turn activity.

Text	Annotation	Strategy
His room was as black as pitch with the thick darkness (for the shutters were close fastened through fear of robbers), and so I knew that he could not see the opening of the door . . .	I can picture his dark room, and the narrator ever-so-slowly opening the door. Creepy!	visualizing
I had my head in, and was about to open the lantern, when my thumb slipped upon the tin fastening . . .	The old man woke up! I bet that the narrator will get caught.	making and confirming predictions
I kept quite still and said nothing. For a whole hour I did not move a muscle, and in the meantime I did not hear him lie down.	Is the old man really still listening? Did he maybe fall back asleep?	generating questions
He was still sitting up in the bed, listening;—just as I have done, night after night, hearkening to the death watches in the wall.	I think the narrator might mean that the old man knows his life is coming to an end.	making inferences

TURN AND TALK

1. Have you ever used a reading comprehension strategy before? If so, which ones have worked for you?

SPEAKING FRAMES

- When I compare, I look at how ____.
- When I contrast, I look at how ____.
- Comparing and contrasting texts helps me to demonstrate and ____ my understanding of the texts.

First Read

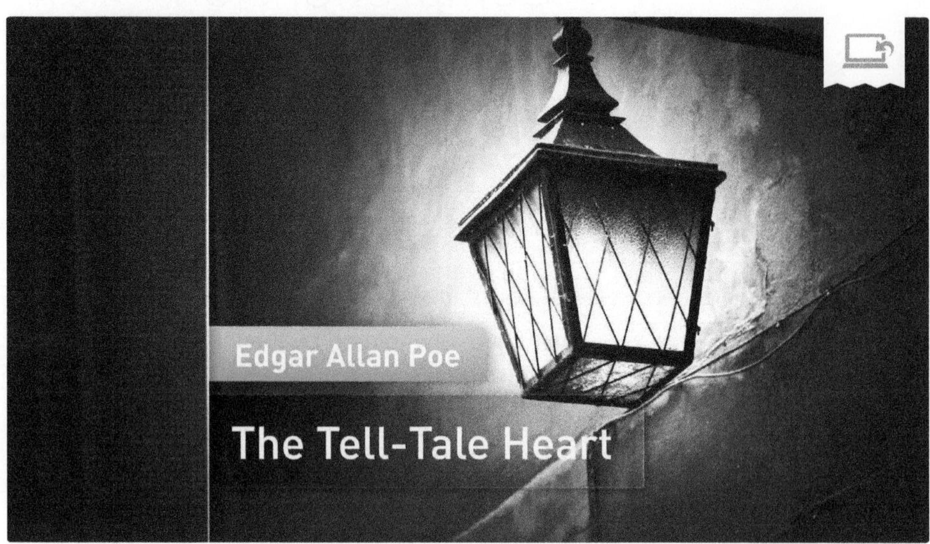

Introduce the Text

As a class, watch the video preview and have students read the introduction in pairs to make connections to the video preview.

To activate prior knowledge and experiences, ask students:

- How do the images, words, and music in this video make you feel?
- What kind of story are you going to read? How do you know?

ELL SENTENCE FRAMES

- The ____ in the video makes me think ____.
- The video shows ____. This makes me wonder ____.
- I think the text will ____. I think this because ____.
- I predict that there will be ____. I believe this because ____.

Entry Point

As students prepare to read "The Tell-Tale Heart," share the following information with them to provide context.

✓ Although Edgar Allan Poe is best known for his tales of horror, he considered himself primarily a poet. "The Raven" established his national reputation, while the haunting "Annabel Lee" was devoted to his deceased young wife. Poe was also respected for his literary criticism and reviews and has been called the "father of the modern detective story."

✓ Poe did not invent the horror story, or gothic fiction. In the early 1800s, inexpensive books called "Penny Dreadfuls" told sensational stories of horror, torture, and supernatural events. Poe, however, did lend to the genre the craft of a superior writer.

✓ "All things in heaven and on earth" is a common phrase, used in the Bible and elsewhere. Poe's narrator expands the reference: "I heard all things in the heaven and in the earth. I heard many things in hell." Students might discuss the impact of this opening line on the reader.

"You fancy me mad. Madmen know nothing. But you should have seen me."

NOTES

1 True!—nervous—very, very dreadfully nervous I had been and am; but why will you say that I am mad? The disease had sharpened my senses—not destroyed—not dulled them. Above all was the sense of hearing **acute.** I heard all things in the heaven and in the earth. I heard many things in hell. How, then, am I mad? Hearken! and observe how healthily—how calmly I can tell you the whole story.

2 It is impossible to say how first the idea entered my brain; but once conceived, it haunted me day and night. Object there was none. Passion there was none. I loved the old man. He had never wronged me. He had never given me insult. For his gold I had no desire. I think it was his eye! yes, it was this! He had the eye of a vulture—a pale blue eye, with a film over it. Whenever it fell upon me, my blood ran cold; and so by degrees—very gradually—I made up my mind to take the life of the old man, and thus rid myself of the eye forever.

Hooded vulture

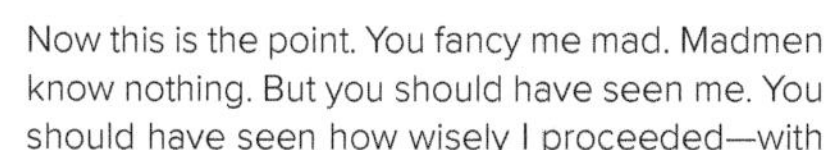

3 Now this is the point. You fancy me mad. Madmen know nothing. But you should have seen me. You should have seen how wisely I proceeded—with what caution—with what foresight—with what dissimulation I went to work! I was never kinder to the old man than during the whole week before I killed him. And every night, about midnight, I turned the latch of his door and opened it—oh so gently! And then, when I had made an opening **sufficient** for my head, I put in a dark lantern, all closed, closed, that no light shone out, and then I thrust in my head. Oh, you would have laughed to see how cunningly I thrust it in! I moved it slowly—very, very slowly, so that I might not disturb the old man's sleep. It took me an hour to place my whole head within the opening so far that I could see him as he lay upon his bed. Ha! would a madman have been so wise as this, And then, when my head was well in the room, I undid the lantern cautiously-oh, so cautiously—cautiously (for the hinges creaked)—I undid it just so much that a single thin ray fell upon the vulture eye. And this I did for seven long nights—every night just at

Skill: Text-Dependent Responses

The narrator claims to love the old man. So why does he want to kill him because of his eye? That's crazy. The narrator is obsessed!

Skill: Textual Evidence

The last line does not make sense, since he says in the previous paragraph that he liked the old man. How can the narrator be a sane, kind person like he claims to be? If someone kills a person that they like, it usually means they are neither kind nor sane.

Analyze Vocabulary Using Context Clues

In paragraph 1, focus on the sentence that uses the word *acute*. Point out these context clues:

1. First, I notice that in the previous sentence, the speaker explains that his disease has sharpened, not dulled, his senses.
2. This means that his senses, such as his hearing, have become sharper, or more perceptive.
3. So, *acute* must mean "sharp" or "perceptive."

Skills Focus

QUESTION 5: Connect to Essential Question

Few people would describe someone's eye as looking like a vulture's eye. It's also strange that a person would kill someone just because of their eye. This makes the reader wonder whether the old man actually has a strange eye, or if it is all in the narrator's imagination.

Text-Dependent Responses

What was the first step the reader took to respond to the first Think Question?

The reader recalled details from the text and reviewed his annotations to confirm his thinking.

Textual Evidence

What explicit meaning does the reader examine? Why does this confuse the reader?

The reader notes that the narrator claims he is not "mad" or insane. This doesn't make sense because he is doing something a madman would do: killing a person he likes.

SELECTION VOCABULARY

acute / agudo/a ***adjective*** wise, perceptive

sufficient / suficiente ***adjective*** describing a quantity that can fulfill a need without being abundant; being enough COGNATE

- What event(s) are taking place in this part of the story?
- What is the narrator's feeling in this part of the story? Is it positive or negative?

TEXT TALK

Why does the narrator decide to kill the old man?

See paragraph 2: The old man has an eye that reminds the narrator of a vulture's eye.

Skills Focus

QUESTION 2: Textual Evidence

The narrator explicitly refers to the eye—"it" —separately from the old man to whom "it" belongs. This word choice from the author implies the narrator sees the eye as its own force of power acting against him, which supports the idea of him being insane, since someone's eyes don't actually have this much power in real life.

midnight—but I found the eye always closed; and so it was impossible to do the work; for it was not the old man who vexed me, but his Evil Eye. And every morning, when the day broke, I went boldly into the chamber, and spoke courageously to him, calling him by name in a hearty tone, and inquiring how he has passed the night. So you see he would have been a very **profound** old man, indeed, to suspect that every night, just at twelve, I looked in upon him while he slept.

4 Upon the eighth night I was more than usually cautious in opening the door. A watch's minute hand moves more quickly than did mine. Never before that night had I felt the extent of my own powers—of my **sagacity.** I could scarcely contain my feelings of triumph. To think that there I was, opening the door, little by little, and he not even to dream of my secret deeds or thoughts. I fairly chuckled at the idea; and perhaps he heard me; for he moved on the bed suddenly, as if startled. Now you may think that I drew back—but no. His room was as black as pitch with the thick darkness, (for the shutters were close fastened, through fear of robbers,) and so I knew that he could not see the opening of the door, and I kept pushing it on steadily, steadily. I had my head in, and was about to open the lantern, when my thumb slipped upon the tin fastening, and the old man sprang up in bed, crying out—"Who's there?" I kept quite still and said nothing. For a whole hour I did not move a muscle, and in the meantime I did not hear him lie down. He was still sitting up in the bed listening;—just as I have done, night after night, hearkening to the death watches in the wall.

5 Presently I heard a slight groan, and I knew it was the groan of mortal terror. It was not a groan of pain or of grief—oh, no!—it was the low stifled sound that arises from the bottom of the soul when overcharged with awe. I knew the sound well. Many a night, just at midnight, when all the world slept, it has welled up from my own bosom, deepening, with its dreadful echo, the terrors that distracted me. I say I knew it well. I knew what the old man felt, and pitied him, although I chuckled at heart. I knew that he had been lying awake ever since the first slight noise, when he had turned in the bed. His fears had been ever since growing upon him. He had been trying to fancy them causeless, but could not. He had been saying to himself—"It is nothing but the wind in the chimney—it is only a mouse crossing the floor," or "It is merely a cricket which has made a single chirp." Yes, he had been trying to comfort himself with these suppositions: but he had found all in vain. All in vain; because Death, in approaching him had stalked with his black shadow before him, and enveloped the victim. And it was the mournful influence of the unperceived shadow that caused him to feel—although he neither saw nor heard—to feel the presence of my head within the room.

6 When I had waited a long time, very patiently, without hearing him lie down, I resolved to open a little—a very, very little crevice in the lantern. So I opened

TEXT TALK

What makes the old man spring up in his bed and cry out on the eighth night?

See paragraph 4: The narrator's thumb slips on the lantern he is holding, making a loud noise.

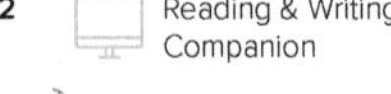

SELECTION VOCABULARY

profound / profundo/a *adjective* very great or intense COGNATE

- Who is the narrator talking about?
- What is important about this person?

sagacity / la sagacidad *noun* an exceptionally keen ability to see things or discern ideas COGNATE

- What event(s) are taking place in this part of the story?
- What nearby words describe *sagacity*? Are they positive or negative?

NOTES

it—you cannot imagine how stealthily, stealthily—until, at length a simple dim ray, like the thread of the spider, shot from out the crevice and fell full upon the vulture eye. It was open—wide, wide open—and I grew furious as I gazed upon it. I saw it with perfect distinctness—all a dull blue, with a hideous veil over it that chilled the very marrow in my bones; but I could see nothing else of the old man's face or person: for I had directed the ray as if by instinct, precisely upon the damned spot. And have I not told you that what you mistake for madness is but over-acuteness of the sense?—now, I say, there came to my ears a low, dull, quick sound, such as a watch makes when enveloped in cotton. I knew that sound well, too. It was the beating of the old man's heart. It increased my fury, as the beating of a drum stimulates the soldier into courage.

7 But even yet I refrained and kept still. I scarcely breathed. I held the lantern motionless. I tried how steadily I could maintain the ray upon the eve. Meantime the hellish tattoo of the heart increased. It grew quicker and quicker, and louder and louder every instant. The old man's terror must have been extreme! It grew louder, I say, louder every moment!—do you mark me well I have told you that I am nervous: so I am. And now at the dead hour of the night, amid the dreadful silence of that old house, so strange a noise as this excited me to uncontrollable terror. Yet, for some minutes longer I refrained and stood still. But the beating grew louder, louder! I thought the heart must burst. And now a new anxiety seized me—the sound would be heard by a neighbour! The old man's hour had come! With a loud yell, I threw open the lantern and leaped into the room. He shrieked once—once only. In an instant I dragged him to the floor, and pulled the heavy bed over him. I then smiled gaily, to find the deed so far done. But, for many minutes, the heart beat on with a muffled sound. This, however, did not vex me; it would not be heard through the wall. At length it ceased. The old man was dead. I removed the bed and examined the corpse. Yes, he was stone, stone dead. I placed my hand upon the heart and held it there many minutes. There was no pulsation. He was stone dead. His eye would trouble me no more.

8 If still you think me mad, you will think so no longer when I describe the wise precautions I took for the concealment of the body. The night waned, and I worked hastily, but in silence. First of all I dismembered the corpse. I cut off the head and the arms and the legs. I then took up three planks from the flooring of the chamber, and deposited all between the scantlings. I then replaced the boards so cleverly, so cunningly, that no human eye—not even his—could have detected any thing wrong. There was nothing to wash out—no stain of any kind—no blood-spot whatever. I had been too wary for that. A tub had caught all—ha! ha! When I had made an end of these labors, it was four o'clock—still dark as midnight. As the bell sounded the hour, there came a knocking at the street door. I went down to open it with a light heart,—for what had I now to fear? There entered three men, who introduced themselves,

Skill: Language, Style, and Audience

The narrator is still trying to convince us he's sane. The author uses words like "wise," "cleverly," and "cunningly" to describe the narrator's actions. But he's talking about hiding the body of a person he just murdered! We can't trust him. When he laughs at his own cleverness in hiding the body, he seems mad, like a killer in a scary movie.

Skills Focus

QUESTION 3: Language, Style, & Audience

When the author has the narrator laughing and chuckling at himself for doing such a thorough job of cutting up and disposing of the old man's dead body, he is suggesting that the narrator might be losing his mind. It's not normal for someone to feel excitement and pride after cutting up a dead body; most sane people would feel disgust just by looking at a dead body, let alone cutting it up.

Skills Focus

QUESTION 4: Language, Style, & Audience

When the author has the narrator directly address the reader, it seems like he knows the reader will think he is insane. The author has the narrator keep trying to convince the reader he is not "mad," which makes me think he knows he might be mad because his mental state is clearly on his mind. Someone who tries this hard to convince people comes across as untrustworthy because of their insecurity and overeagerness.

Skills Focus

QUESTION 5: Language, Style, & Audience

The author's use of the word "audacity" makes it clear that the narrator is risky and bold. How can someone like this be trusted? For example, here he knowingly puts his chair on top of the old man's dead body despite the fact that that makes it more likely the police officers could realize his guilt. This must mean he loves danger and toying with people, which makes him impossible to trust. What if he is toying with the reader in the same way he toys with the cops?

Language, Style, and Audience

How does the use of language in paragraph 8 increase the reader's understanding of the author's meaning and tone?

The narrator's continued insistence that he isn't crazy along with his weird laughter convince the reader that he is unreliable, or not to be trusted.

TEXT TALK

What does the narrator do to the old man when he hears his heart beating louder and louder?

See paragraph 7: The narrator kills the old man.

How does the narrator hide the old man's body?

See paragraph 8: The narrator cuts up the old man's body and puts the body parts under the floorboards.

Skills Focus

QUESTION 3: Language, Style, & Audience

The narrator's insistence that he hears the old man's beating heart only increases throughout this paragraph. The old man is dead, which means it would be impossible to hear his heartbeat. The author repeats the word *louder* four times to establish the narrator's loss of sanity; he is hearing things that simply aren't there.

Skills Focus

QUESTION 5: Connect to Essential Question

The narrator is convinced he hears the old man's heartbeat, but this is mysterious to readers, because how could you hear a dead man's heartbeat? The narrator's insistence on this unbelievable fact creates a mystery for readers. Readers are left wondering what is real; does the narrator actually hear a heartbeat or is this his crazed imagination?

with perfect suavity, as officers of the police. A shriek had been heard by a neighbour during the night; suspicion of foul play had been aroused; information had been lodged at the police office, and they (the officers) had been deputed to search the premises. I smiled,—for what had I to fear? I bade the gentlemen welcome. The shriek, I said, was my own in a dream. The old man, I mentioned, was absent in the country. I took my visitors all over the house. I bade them search—search well. I led them, at length, to his chamber. I showed them his treasures, secure, undisturbed. In the enthusiasm of my confidence, I brought chairs into the room, and desired them here to rest from their fatigues, while I myself, in the wild **audacity** of my perfect triumph, placed my own seat upon the very spot beneath which reposed the corpse of the victim.

9 The officers were satisfied. My manner had convinced them. I was singularly at ease. They sat, and while I answered cheerily, they chatted of familiar things. But, ere long, I felt myself getting pale and wished them gone. My head ached, and I fancied a ringing in my ears: but still they sat and still chatted. The ringing became more distinct:—It continued and became more distinct: I talked more freely to get rid of the feeling: but it continued and gained definiteness—until, at length, I found that the noise was not within my ears. No doubt I now grew very pale;—but I talked more fluently, and with a heightened voice. Yet the sound increased—and what could I do? It was a low, dull, quick sound—much such a sound as a watch makes when enveloped in cotton. I gasped for breath—and yet the officers heard it not. I talked more quickly—more **vehemently;** but the noise steadily increased. I arose and argued about trifles, in a high key and with violent gesticulations; but the noise steadily increased. Why would they not be gone? I paced the floor to and fro with heavy strides, as if excited to fury by the observations of the men—but the noise steadily increased. Oh God! what could I do? I foamed—I raved—I swore! I swung the chair upon which I had been sitting, and grated it upon the boards, but the noise arose over all and continually increased. It grew louder—louder—louder! And still the men chatted pleasantly, and smiled. Was it possible they heard not? Almighty God!—no, no! They heard!—they suspected!—they knew!—they were making a mockery of my horror!-this I thought, and this I think. But anything was better than this agony! Anything was more tolerable than this derision! I could bear those hypocritical smiles no longer! I felt that I must scream or die! and now—again!—hark! louder! louder! louder! louder!

10 "Villains!" I shrieked, "dissemble no more! I admit the deed!—tear up the planks! here, here!—It is the beating of his hideous heart!"

TEXT TALK

Even though the officers don't suspect anything, the narrator is convinced they know of the old man's death. What makes him certain of this?

See paragraphs 9 and 10: The narrator hears the old man's heart beating louder and louder.

What other questions can you ask and answer?

Answers will vary.

Ask each Beyond grade-level student to write one additional discussion question. Then have one or two students facilitate a discussion, using their questions to guide the conversation.

SELECTION VOCABULARY

audacity / la audacia ***noun*** the act of taking risks COGNATE

- What event(s) are taking place in this part of the story?
- What nearby words describe *audacity*? Are they positive or negative?

vehemently / vehementemente ***adverb*** with energy and passion COGNATE

- What event(s) are taking place in this part of the story?
- What is the narrator's feeling in this part of the story? Is it positive or negative?

Reading Comprehension OPTIONAL

Have students complete the digital reading comprehension questions ✓ when they finish reading.

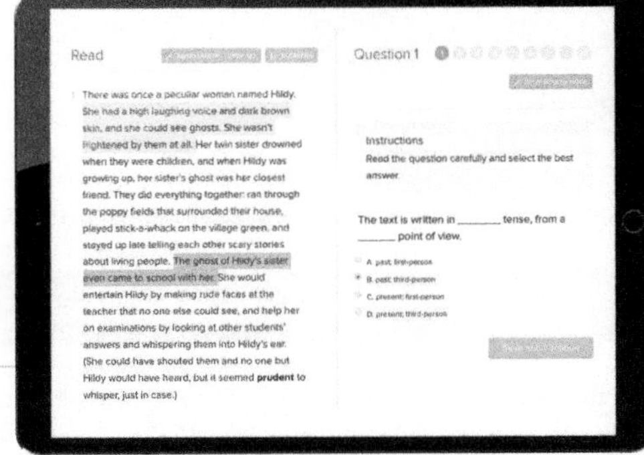

ANSWER KEY

QUESTION 1: A
QUESTION 2: C
QUESTION 3: A
QUESTION 4: D
QUESTION 5: B
QUESTION 6: D
QUESTION 7: D
QUESTION 8: B
QUESTION 9:
See first chart.
QUESTION 10:
See second chart.

Synonym	Word
enough	sufficient
wisdom	sagacity
boldness	audacity
sharp	acute
intelligent	profound

First	Second	Third	Fourth
The narrator spies on the old man in his sleep.	The narrator murders the old man in the night.	The narrator hears the pounding of the old man's heart beneath the floor.	The narrator confesses to the police what he has done.

Connect and Extend OPTIONAL

CONNECT TO EXTENDED WRITING PROJECT

Students can use "The Tell-Tale Heart" as a mentor text for their Extended Writing Project. They may adopt some of Edgar Allan Poe's methods for creating suspense as they craft their own suspenseful narratives.

BEYOND THE BOOK

Mock Trial: The Insanity Defense

Turn your class into a courtroom to try the story's narrator for the murder of the old man. Have students role play the judge, jury, defense team, prosecution, and key witnesses. The narrator and his defense team should plead not guilty by reason of insanity. During the trial:

1. Allow the prosecution to call witnesses and present its case using evidence from the text and other reasonable inferences they can make based on the story.
2. Have the defense take its turn.
3. Allow both sides to present a brief closing argument to the jury.
4. Ask the jury to take a few minutes to deliberate and then share its verdict with the class. Be sure to have the jury explain which parts of the case they believed the prosecution and defense made most compellingly.

Think Questions

Circulate as students answer Think Questions independently. Scaffolds for these questions are shown on the opposite page.

QUESTION 1: Textual Evidence

The narrator claims that he "loved the old man." The narrator says he decided to kill the old man because he could not stand the old man's "eye of a vulture" looking at him anymore.

QUESTION 2: Textual Evidence

The narrator is probably not trustworthy. The narrator says he is "very, very dreadfully nervous," which would seem to show he understands himself. However, he goes on to ask, 'why will you say that I am mad?" which suggests he might be crazed.

QUESTION 3: Textual Evidence

The narrator confesses to the murder because he says he hears the beating of the old man's heart getting louder. Referring to the supposed sound of the old man's heart, he says, "It grew louder—louder—louder!" before he confesses in the final lines of the story.

QUESTION 4: Context Clues

The word *sufficient* means "enough." According to the story, the narrator is trying to open the door to the old man's room just enough for his head and a lantern to fit in so that he does not "disturb the old man's sleep."

QUESTION 5: Context Clues

In the story, the narrator is proud of his ability to remain unseen by the old man when he opens the door. It is not until the eighth night of practice that he feels aware of his own "powers" or "sagacity." The fact that the word *sagacity* is used as a synonym for *powers* gives me a clue about what it must mean. I can infer that *sagacity* means "smart" or "clever" because the narrator has to be smart and clever to avoid being seen or heard by the old man.

First Read

Read "The Tell-Tale Heart." After you read, complete the Think Questions below.

THINK QUESTIONS

1. Write two or three sentences explaining how the narrator feels about the old man and why he decides to murder him.
2. Does the narrator seem trustworthy as he gives his account of the events in the story? Cite evidence from the text to explain your opinions.
3. What sound does the narrator hear at the end of the story that causes him to confess to the murder? Provide evidence to support your inference.
4. Find the word **sufficient** in paragraph 3 of "The Tell-Tale Heart." Use context clues in the surrounding sentences, as well as the sentence in which the word appears, to determine the word's meaning. Write your definition here and identify clues that helped you figure out its meaning.
5. Use context clues to determine the meaning of **sagacity** as it is used in paragraph 4 of "The Tell-Tale Heart." Write your definition here and identify clues that helped you figure out its meaning. Then check the meaning in a dictionary.

Think Questions

SCAFFOLDS

Use the scaffolds below to differentiate instruction for your ELL English Language Learners and A Approaching grade-level learners.

ELL **BEGINNING** Write a response using the word bank and sentence frames.

INTERMEDIATE Write a response using the sentence frames.

ADVANCED, ADVANCED HIGH Write a response using the Text-Dependent Question Guide.

A **APPROACHING** Write a response using the Text-Dependent Question Guide.

BEGINNING | INTERMEDIATE | APPROACHING / ADVANCED, ADVANCED HIGH

Word Bank	Sentence Frames	Text-Dependent Question Guide
disease wide loves beating heart less successful guilty head officers enough calm wrong crazy vulture's eye power	The narrator ____ the old man. I know this because the old man has never done anything ____ to the narrator. The narrator decides to murder the old man because he can not stand his ____.	1. • How does the narrator feel about the old man? • How do I know the narrator feels this way? • Why does the narrator decide to murder the old man?
	The narrator has a ____ that might affect his thinking. The narrator accuses the reader of thinking the narrator is ____. The narrator feels both nervous and ____. This makes him seem ____ trustworthy because these feelings don't go together.	2. • What is wrong with the narrator's health? • What does the narrator accuse the reader of thinking about the narrator? • What different feelings does the narrator have? Does this make him seem more or less trustworthy?
	The narrator hears the old man's ____. The ____ cannot hear this sound. The narrator confesses to the murder because he thinks the officers suspect that he is ____ of killing the old man.	3. • What sound does the narrator hear at the end of the story? • Can the officers hear the sound? • Why does this cause the narrator to confess to the murder?
	No light shines through the opening in the door after the narrator puts in a lantern and his ____. This means that he only opens the door ____ enough to fit these things in. This gives me a clue that *sufficient* means "____."	4. • Read: "And then, when I had made an opening **sufficient** for my head, I put in a dark lantern, all closed, closed, that no light shone out, and then I thrust in my head." • What does the narrator put inside the opening in the door? • What does the fact that the lantern can fit into the door tell me about the meaning of *sufficient*?
	The narrator feels ____. This gives me a clue that *sagacity* means "____."	5. • Read: "Never before that night had I felt the extent of my own powers—of my **sagacity**." • What new feeling does the narrator have in this paragraph? • What does that tell me about the meaning of the word *sagacity*?

Skill: Text-Dependent Responses

Introduce the Skill

Watch the Concept Definitions video and read the following definition with your students.

Whether you are reading fiction or poetry, a play or nonfiction, **text-dependent responses** are short, concise answers to questions about a selection that include supporting evidence from the text. In StudySync, every First Read lesson includes a set of Think Questions that require a text-dependent response. To answer a Think Question, you need to use details from the text to make an inference or draw a conclusion, and cite these details to support your response. The strength of your response depends on your ability to use **textual evidence**, or details that a reader can use to support his or her ideas and opinions about a text. Answering such questions allows you to demonstrate your **comprehension**, or understanding of the text before moving on to a deeper analysis in future lessons.

Skill: Text-Dependent Responses

Use the Checklist to analyze Text-Dependent Responses in "The Tell-Tale Heart." Refer to the sample student annotations about Text-Dependent Responses in the text.

••• CHECKLIST FOR TEXT-DEPENDENT RESPONSES

In order to cite textual evidence that most strongly supports an analysis, consider the following:

- ✓ details from the text to make a strong inference or draw a strong conclusion
- ✓ read carefully and consider why an author gives particular details and information
  - think about what you already know, and use your own knowledge and experiences to help you figure out what the author does not state directly
  - cite textual evidence, or the specific words, phrases, sentences, or paragraphs that led you to make an inference
- ✓ details to support your ideas and opinions about a text
- ✓ explicit evidence of a character's feelings or motivations, or the reasons behind an historical event in a nonfiction text
  - explicit evidence is stated directly in the text and must be cited accurately to strongly support a text-dependent answer or analysis

To cite the textual evidence that most strongly supports an analysis, consider the following questions:

- ✓ What types of textual evidence can I use to support an analysis of a text?
- ✓ What explicit evidence can I use to support my analysis?
- ✓ If I infer things in the text that the author does not state directly, what evidence from the text, along with my own knowledge, can I use to support my analysis?
- ✓ How do I know that I've used textual evidence that offers the strongest support for my analysis?

TURN AND TALK

1. What are some things that you do when writing text-dependent responses?
2. How do you think finding textual evidence to support a response might improve your comprehension of the text?

SPEAKING FRAMES

- Text-dependent responses are ____ that include ____.
- The strength of your response depends on your ability to use ____.
- Answering text-dependent responses allows you to demonstrate your ____ of the text before moving on to deeper analysis.

SKILL VOCABULARY

text dependent response / la respuesta que depende del texto *noun* short and concise answer to questions about a text that include supporting evidence from the text

textual evidence / la evidencia del texto *noun* details from the text that a reader can use to support his or her ideas and opinions about a text

comprehension / la comprensión *noun* the ability to understand what the text says COGNATE

Skill: Text-Dependent Responses

Read the second Think question from the First Read lesson for "The Tell-Tale Heart" and answer the follow-up question below. Then, complete the chart by deciding which evidence from the text reveals when the narrator is trustworthy or untrustworthy.

YOUR TURN

Follow-Up Question
Does the narrator seem trustworthy as he gives his account of the events in the story? Cite textual evidence to explain your opinions.

	Textual Evidence Options
A	"Yet, for some minutes longer I refrained and stood still."
B	"You should have seen how wisely I proceeded—with what caution—with what foresight—with what dissimulation I went to work!"
C	"Never before that night had I felt the extent of my own powers—of my sagacity."
D	"I moved it slowly—very, very slowly, so that I might not disturb the old man's sleep."
E	". . . because Death, in approaching him, had stalked with his black shadow before him and enveloped the victim."
F	"Above all was the sense of hearing acute. I heard all things in the heaven and in the earth."

Trustworthy	Untrustworthy

Your Turn

Ask students to complete the Your Turn activity.

Trustworthy	Untrustworthy
"You should have seen how wisely I proceeded—with what caution—with what foresight—with what dissimulation I went to work!"	"Above all was the sense of hearing acute. I heard all things in the heaven and in the earth."
"I moved it slowly—very, very slowly, so that I might not disturb the old man's sleep."	"Never before that night had I felt the extent of my own powers—of my sagacity."
"Yet, for some minutes longer I refrained and stood still."	". . . because Death, in approaching him, had stalked with his black shadow before him and enveloped the victim."

Skill: Textual Evidence

Introduce the Skill

Watch the Concept Definition video and read the following definition with your students.

Any time you're discussing a text, you need to **cite**, or point out, **textual evidence**, the details that readers use to support their ideas and opinions. Readers may cite evidence that is directly stated, or **explicit**, in the text. Other times, textual evidence may be **implicit**, which means it is suggested but not directly stated. One way to interpret implicit meanings is to **make inferences**, using clues from the text and your own experiences to make logical decisions about characters and events that are not stated directly.

Readers must also refer to textual evidence when they **analyze** and examine the different parts of a text. Analyzing specific parts of the text, such as the actions of a character or the cause-and-effect relationships between events in nonfiction, helps a reader **interpret** and explain the meaning, theme, or central idea of the text as a whole. When you cite textual evidence, someone else can look back at a particular part of a text you read and understand your analysis.

TURN AND TALK

1. When have you had to cite textual evidence in conversations with others?
2. What is the purpose of citing textual evidence? What kinds of textual evidence might we cite?

SPEAKING FRAMES

- One conversation where I had to cite textual evidence was ____.
- Textual evidence is what readers use to support their ____ and ____.
- Readers might cite textual evidence that is ____, or directly stated in the text, or textual evidence might be ____, or suggested but not stated.

The Tell-Tale Heart

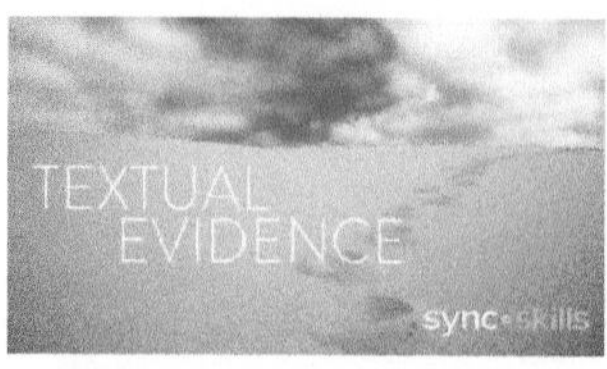

Skill: Textual Evidence

Use the Checklist to analyze Textual Evidence in "The Tell-Tale Heart." Refer to the sample student annotations about Textual Evidence in the text.

••• CHECKLIST FOR TEXTUAL EVIDENCE

In order to support an analysis by citing textual evidence that is explicitly stated in the text, do the following:

- ✓ read the text closely and critically
- ✓ identify what the text says explicitly
- ✓ find the most relevant textual evidence that supports your analysis
- ✓ consider why an author explicitly states specific details and information
- ✓ cite the specific words, phrases, sentences, or paragraphs from the text that support your analysis
- ✓ cite evidence from the text that most strongly supports your analysis

In order to interpret implicit meanings in a text by making inferences, do the following:

- ✓ combine information directly stated in the text with your own knowledge, experiences, and observations
- ✓ cite the specific words, phrases, sentences, or paragraphs from the text that support this inference

In order to cite textual evidence to support an analysis of what the text says explicitly, as well as inferences drawn from the text, consider the following questions:

- ✓ Have I read the text closely and critically?
- ✓ What inferences am I making about the text? What textual evidence am I using to support these inferences?
- ✓ Am I quoting the evidence from the text correctly?
- ✓ Does my textual evidence logically relate to my analysis?
- ✓ What textual evidence most strongly supports your analysis?

V SKILL VOCABULARY

cite / citar *verb* to quote as evidence to support a response COGNATE

textual evidence / la evidencia del texto *noun* details from the text that a reader can use to support his or her ideas and opinions about the text

explicit / explícito/a *adjective* precisely and clearly expressed COGNATE

implicit / implícito/a *adjective* implied but not stated directly COGNATE

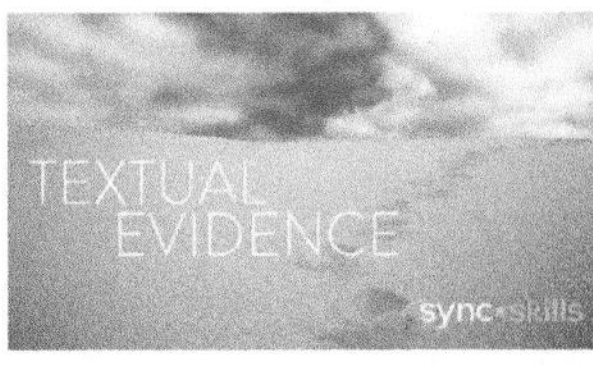

Skill: Textual Evidence

Reread paragraphs 3, 8, and 9 of "The Tell-Tale Heart." Then, using the Checklist instructions on the previous page, complete the chart below by writing the explicit and implicit meaning of each paragraph. The first one is done for you.

YOUR TURN

Text	Explicit Meaning	Implicit Meaning
And every morning, when the day broke, I went boldly into the chamber, and spoke courageously to him, calling him by name in a hearty tone, and inquiring how he has passed the night.	The narrator speaks to the old man every morning, asking him how he slept the previous night.	The narrator is trying to figure out whether or not the old man heard the narrator spying on him the previous night.
There was nothing to wash out—no stain of any kind—no blood-spot whatever. I had been too wary for that. A tub had caught all—ha! ha!		
The officers were satisfied. My manner had convinced them. I was singularly at ease. They sat, and while I answered cheerily, they chatted of familiar things. But, ere long, I felt myself getting pale and wished them gone.		

SKILL VOCABULARY

make inferences / hacer inferencias *verb* to use your understanding of a text and your own experiences to draw conclusions

analyze / analizar *verb* to consider in detail and discover essential features or meaning COGNATE

interpret / interpretar *verb* to explain the meaning of (information, words, or actions) COGNATE

Your Turn

Ask students to complete the Your Turn activity.

Text	Evidence found explicitly in the text	Inference drawn from the text
And every morning, when the day broke, I went boldly into the chamber, and spoke courageously to him, calling him by name in a hearty tone, and inquiring how he has passed the night.	The narrator speaks to the old man every morning, asking him how he slept the previous night.	The narrator is trying to figure out whether or not the old man heard the narrator spying on him the previous night.
There was nothing to wash out—no stain of any kind—no blood-spot whatever. I had been too wary for that. A tub had caught all—ha! ha!	After the narrator kills the old man, there are no blood stains to clean up. The stains ended up in a tub. The narrator laughs.	The narrator feels proud of himself for covering up the crime so well. His laughs are a sign of success and happiness.
The officers were satisfied. My manner had convinced them. I was singularly at ease. They sat, and while I answered cheerily, they chatted of familiar things. But, ere long, I felt myself getting pale and wished them gone.	The police officers do not find any evidence of a crime during their search. The narrator feels safe. The policemen sit and talk. After a while, the narrator's face turns pale and he hopes the police officers will leave.	The narrator is calm at first because he feels confident the police do not suspect a crime happened. However, then he gets nervous that they will realize he murdered the old man if they keep sitting in his house. His pale face shows his anxiety.

Skill: Language, Style, and Audience

Introduce the Skill

Watch the Concept Definition video and read the following definition with your students.

Authors use language to convey meaning or to affect the way their audience thinks and perceives. An **audience** is the intended reader or listener. Readers can analyze an author's style to better understand the tone and meaning of a text.

Style refers to the way an author uses language (words, sentences, paragraphs) to achieve a purpose. One element of style is word choice. **Word choice** is a technique in which writers choose specific words for precise meaning or to convey a certain tone. **Meaning** is a reader's interpretation of the text's deeper messages, themes, or ideas. **Tone** expresses a writer's **attitude** (or thoughts and feelings) toward his or her subject. Tone can be described, for example, as formal, casual, conversational, ironic, sad, bitter, humorous, or serious.

The Tell-Tale Heart

Skill: Language, Style, and Audience

Use the Checklist to analyze Language, Style, and Audience in "The Tell-Tale Heart." Refer to the sample student annotations about Language, Style, and Audience in the text.

••• CHECKLIST FOR LANGUAGE, STYLE, AND AUDIENCE

In order to determine an author's style, do the following:

- ✓ identify and define any unfamiliar words or phrases
- ✓ use context, including the meanings of surrounding words and phrases
- ✓ note possible reactions to the author's word choice
- ✓ examine your reaction to the author's word choice
- ✓ identify any analogies, or comparisons in which one part of the comparison helps explain the other

To analyze the impact of specific word choice on meaning and tone, ask the following questions:

- ✓ How did your understanding of the language change during your analysis?
- ✓ How do the writer's word choices impact or create meaning in the text?
- ✓ How do the writer's word choices impact or create a specific tone in the text?
- ✓ How could various audiences interpret this language? What different possible emotional responses can you list?
- ✓ What analogies do you see? Where might an analogy have clarified meaning or created a specific tone?

10  Reading & Writing Companion

TURN AND TALK

1. Can you think of a book, movie, or TV show that used specific word choices or style of writing to help you understand the characters or story better?
2. How did the word choice or style of writing help you understand more about the story or characters?

ELL SPEAKING FRAMES

- One movie, TV show, or book where the word choice helped me understand the characters better was ____. The word choice helped me understand more because ____.

V SKILL VOCABULARY

style / el estilo *noun* a way of expressing something that is characteristic of the person or time period COGNATE

word choice / la elección de palabras *noun* specific words chosen for precise meaning or to generate an emotional response

tone / el tono *noun* the writer's or speaker's attitude toward his or her subject matter COGNATE

Skill: Language, Style, and Audience

Reread paragraphs 9 and 10 of "The Tell-Tale Heart." Then, using the Checklist on the previous page, answer the multiple-choice questions below.

YOUR TURN

1. What effect do the punctuation choices in paragraphs 9 and 10 have on the tone?
   - A. The dashes and exclamation marks reveal that the narrator is losing control.
   - B. The italics make it clear that the narrator's words aren't to be trusted.
   - C. The semicolons introduce a formal tone into an informal speech.
   - D. The frequent questions reveal the narrator's attempt to engage the reader.

2. Which phrase from the passage most clearly suggests the narrator's disturbed mental state at the end of the story?
   - A. "but I talked more fluently"
   - B. "Why would they not be gone?"
   - C. "It grew louder—louder—louder!"
   - D. "And still the men chatted pleasantly"

SKILL VOCABULARY

attitude / la actitud *noun* a state involving beliefs and feelings that causes a person to think or act in a certain way COGNATE

audience / la audiencia *noun* the people who read a written text, listen to an oral response or presentation, or watch a performance COGNATE

meaning / el significado *noun* what is meant by a word; the general message of a text or idea

Your Turn

Ask students to complete the Your Turn activity.

QUESTION 1

A. Correct. The dashes and exclamation marks make the narrator's voice seem fast-paced and agitated, showing that he is growing increasingly upset.

B. Incorrect. The italics emphasize certain words; they do not have an impact on how trustworthy the narrator seems.

C. Incorrect. The semicolons do not affect the tone of the passage, which remains informal.

D. Incorrect. The frequent questions show that the narrator is losing control; they are not an attempt to engage the reader.

QUESTION 2

A. Incorrect. This phrase hints that the narrator is becoming slightly agitated, but it is not the best choice to reveal his disturbed mental state.

B. Incorrect. This excerpt suggests that the narrator wishes the police would leave, but it is not the best choice to reveal his disturbed mental state.

C. Correct. This excerpt reveals that the sound of the beating heart, which does not really exist, is growing louder and louder in the narrator's mind as he loses control.

D. Incorrect. This phrase tells us about the mental state of the police officers, not the narrator.

Close Read

Skills Focus

QUESTION 1: Textual Evidence

Paragraph 1: The author's explicit word choice stating that the narrator can tell the story in a calm manner contradicts the earlier description about the narrator being nervous, which might mean that the author is implying his troubled nature and tendency to lie about his mental health

QUESTION 2: Textual Evidence

See paragraph 3.

QUESTION 3: Language, Style, & Audience

See paragraphs 8 and 9.

QUESTION 4: Language, Style, & Audience

See paragraph 8.

QUESTION 5: Connect to Essential Question

See paragraph 2.

Close Read

Reread "The Tell-Tale Heart." As you reread, complete the Skills Focus questions below. Then use your answers and annotations from the questions to help you complete the Write activity.

SKILLS FOCUS

1. What inferences can you draw about the narrator's mental state based on the author's word choices?
2. What does the author imply about the narrator's mental state through the descriptions of the narrator's feelings about how the old man looks at him with the "eye of a vulture"?
3. Identify word choices the author uses to indicate that the narrator might be losing his mind. How do the word choices and tone indicate the narrator's troubled mental state?
4. What language does the author use to make the narrator seem untrustworthy? How does this language reveal the narrator's dishonest nature?
5. Explain how the author uses the narrator's personality to create a feeling of mystery for the reader.

WRITE

LITERARY ANALYSIS: Can the narrator of "The Tell-Tale Heart" be trusted? Consider the author's word choice, tone, and description of events as you draw conclusions about the narrator's state of mind. Be sure to support your ideas with evidence from the text.

Writer's Notebook

Give students time to reflect on "The Tell-Tale Heart" by freewriting in their Writer's Notebooks. For students who prefer to write to a prompt, consider using a modified version of this lesson's writing prompt: Can the narrator of "The Tell-Tale Heart" be trusted?

Beginning & Intermediate

Read aloud the prompt. Encourage students to draw their reflections or allow students to write in their native language. Circulate the room, prompting students for their thoughts as they respond orally or through pantomime.

Advanced & Advanced High

Allow students to share their reflections orally in pairs or small groups before freewriting.

StudySyncTV

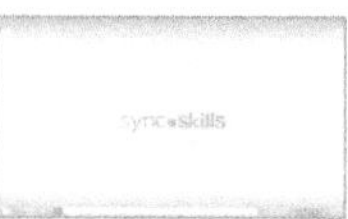

Project the StudySyncTV episode and pause at the following times to prompt discussion:

1:55 How do Katie and Olivia arrive at different interpretations of the narrator's personality?

5:48 What evidence do the students use to support their conclusion that the narrator has a guilty conscience?

7:30 How do the students gain new insights about the meaning of the story by comparing it to a typical horror movie?

TURN AND TALK

1. How can you make sure a collaborative conversation stays on topic?
2. How can you respectfully disagree with someone during a collaborative conversation?

ELL **SPEAKING FRAMES**

- I can keep a conversation on track by ____.
- I can be respectful by ____.

Skill: Collaborative Conversations

Introduce the Skill

Watch the Concept Definition video and read the following definition with your students.

A **collaborative conversation** is a discussion among individuals in which the participants engage in collaboration. **Collaboration** is the process of working together to achieve a shared goal.

Collaborative conversation involves offering insights and ideas, listening carefully to the ideas of others, and responding thoughtfully to each other. Participants in a collaborative conversation choose language that is respectful and encouraging and are careful not to dismiss or ignore others' opinions. Participants must **reflect** on the ideas of others and **adjust** their own responses when **valid evidence** indicates an adjustment is warranted. When defending or challenging an author's **claim**, a speaker must use relevant **text evidence**. The outcome of the collaboration is, ideally, the fulfillment of a stated plan or goal.

Learning to listen to and respond appropriately and thoughtfully to the ideas of others and working to express your own relevant ideas and opinions are essential life skills.

Your Turn

Ask students to complete the Your Turn activity.

Helps the Collaborative Conversation	Distracts from the Collaborative Conversation
"Whoa, whoa! Can someone read the prompt first?"	"She should think of it as an unexpected present."
"Oh yeah! She explains it at the beginning of the story."	"An ugly sweater that smells like cottage cheese?"

StudySyncTV

Project the StudySyncTV episode and pause at the following times to prompt discussion:

1:55 How do Katie and Olivia arrive at different interpretations of the narrator's personality?

5:48 What evidence do the students use to support their conclusion that the narrator has a guilty conscience?

7:30 How do the students gain new insights about the meaning of the story by comparing it to a typical horror movie?

Collaborative Conversation

Break students into collaborative conversation groups to discuss the Close Read prompt. Ask students to use the StudySyncTV episode as a model for their discussion. Remind them to reference their Skills Focus annotations in their discussion.

Can the narrator of "The Tell-Tale Heart" be trusted? Consider the author's word choice, tone, and description of events as you draw conclusions about the narrator's state of mind. Be sure to support your ideas with evidence from the text.

Use the scaffolds below to differentiate instruction for your ELL English Language Learners and A Approaching grade-level learners.

BEGINNING, INTERMEDIATE Use the discussion guide and speaking frames to facilitate the discussion with support from the teacher.

ADVANCED, ADVANCED HIGH Use the discussion guide and speaking frames to facilitate the discussion in mixed-level groups.

APPROACHING Use the discussion guide to facilitate the discussion in mixed-level groups.

APPROACHING
ADVANCED, ADVANCED HIGH
BEGINNING, INTERMEDIATE

Discussion Guide	Speaking Frames
1. What lies does the author have the narrator tell in the story? On the other hand, what does he seem to be telling the truth about?	• One lie the narrator tells in the story is ____. • On the other hand, he seems to be telling the truth when ____.
2. Does the narrator ever contradict himself? If so, where in the story does this happen?	• The narrator contradicts himself when ____.
3. Based on the author's words and tone, does the narrator seem like he can be trusted? Why or why not?	• The narrator seems like he (can / cannot) be trusted because ____.

Review Prompt and Rubric

Before students begin writing, review the writing prompt and rubric with the class.

LITERARY ANALYSIS: Can the narrator of "The Tell-Tale Heart" be trusted? Consider the author's word choice, tone, and description of events as you draw conclusions about the narrator's state of mind. Be sure to support your ideas with evidence from the text.

ELL PROMPT GUIDE

A
- What is a trustworthy narrator?
- What words would you use to describe the author's tone and description of the narrator?
- How does the author describe the events in the story?
- Based on the author's tone and description of events, do you think the narrator can be trusted?

Score	Textual Evidence	Language, Style, and Audience	Language and Conventions
4	The writer clearly analyzes and explains the narrator's trustworthiness. The writer provides exemplary analysis, using relevant evidence from the text.	The writer clearly analyzes and explains the author's word choice and tone. The writer provides exemplary analysis, using relevant evidence from the text.	The writer demonstrates a consistent command of grammar, punctuation, and usage conventions. Although minor errors may be evident, they do not detract from the fluency or the clarity of the writing.
3	The writer analyzes and explains the narrator's trustworthiness. The writer provides sufficient analysis, using relevant evidence from the text most of the time.	The writer analyzes and explains the author's word choice and tone. The writer provides sufficient analysis, using relevant evidence from the text most of the time.	The writer demonstrates an adequate command of grammar, punctuation, and usage conventions. Although some errors may be evident, they create few (if any) disruptions in the fluency or the clarity of the writing.
2	The writer begins to analyze or explain the narrator's trustworthiness, but the analysis is incomplete. The writer uses relevant evidence from the text only some of the time.	The writer begins to analyze or explain the author's word choice and tone, but the analysis is incomplete. The writer uses relevant evidence from the text only some of the time.	The writer demonstrates a partial command of grammar, punctuation, and usage conventions. Some distracting errors may be evident, at times creating minor disruptions in the fluency or clarity of the writing.
1	The writer attempts to analyze or explain the narrator's trustworthiness, but the analysis is not successful. The writer uses little or no relevant evidence from the text.	The writer attempts to analyze or explain the author's word choice and tone, but the analysis is not successful. The writer uses little or no relevant evidence from the text.	The writer demonstrates little or no command of grammar, punctuation, and usage conventions. Serious and persistent errors create disruptions in the fluency of the writing and sometimes interfere with meaning.
0	The writer does not provide a relevant response to the prompt or does not provide a response at all.	The writer does not provide a relevant response to the prompt or does not provide a response at all.	Serious and persistent errors overwhelm the writing and interfere with the meaning of the response as a whole, making the writer's meaning impossible to understand.

Skill: Short Constructed Responses

Introduce the Skill

Watch the Concept Definition video and read the following definition with your students.

A **short constructed response** is a brief, organized written composition that answers a prompt. A **prompt** asks you to define, explain, analyze, interpret, or respond to a topic, idea, or issue. The prompt may include statements and questions to guide or inspire a reader's response.

Types of responses vary for different texts and lessons. For instance, you may analyze an extended metaphor in a poem, argue your point of view after reading an article, or even imagine yourself as a character in a short story.

To write your response, you first paraphrase the prompt to guide your thinking. To **paraphrase** means to restate the directions of the prompt in your own words. Next, you plan your analysis and write your response using text evidence collected in annotations. **Text evidence** refers to the details from the text that you can use to support your ideas.

Writing short constructed responses helps you to develop a routine to support your thinking with evidence, as well as giving you practice using newly acquired content and academic vocabulary.

TURN AND TALK

1. What was the last prompt you had to respond to in a class?
2. What did you do to plan your analysis and support your ideas?

SPEAKING FRAMES

- As you plan and write your analysis, include ____ to support your ideas.

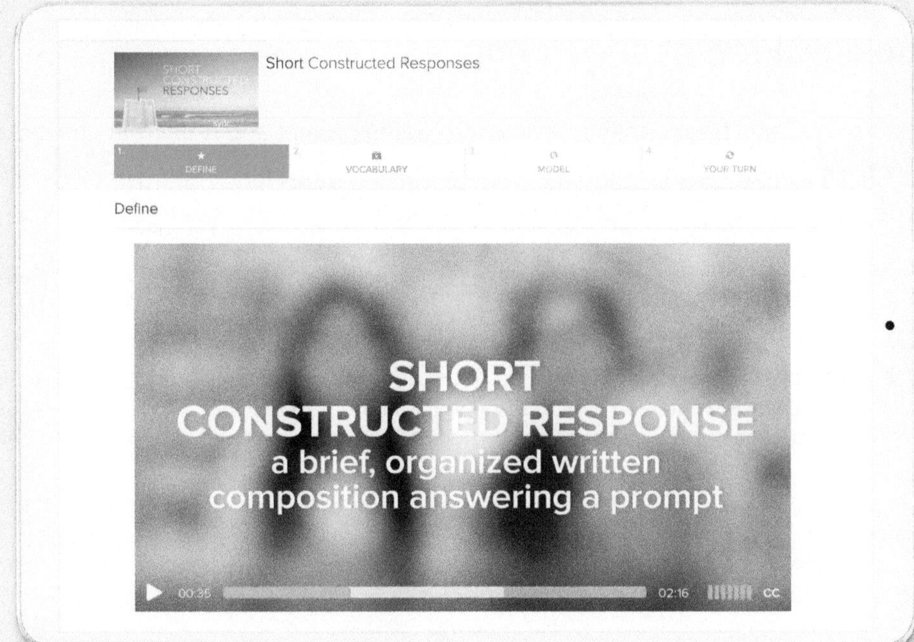

Your Turn

Ask students to complete the Your Turn activity.

QUESTION 1

A. Correct. The sentence paraphrases the prompt correctly.

B. Incorrect. This sentence does not clearly paraphrase the prompt because it includes "figurative language" and "plot," neither of which are mentioned in the prompt.

C. Incorrect. This sentence leaves out the part of the prompt that says to consider the author's word choice and description of events.

D. Incorrect. This sentence leaves out the part of the prompt that says to consider the author's word choice and description of events.

QUESTION 2

A. Incorrect. This evidence supports the claim because the narrator refers to himself as "Death" as if he is watching what he is doing from another vantage point.

B. Correct. This evidence does not support the claim because there is no language that reveals the narrator has the power to see and know everything.

C. Incorrect. This evidence supports the claim because the narrator claims to know what the officers are thinking ("my manner had convinced them") when it is impossible for him to know.

D. Incorrect. This evidence supports the claim because the narrator claims to know that the officers "heard," "suspected," "knew," and "were making a mockery" of the narrator, even though he cannot possibly know this.

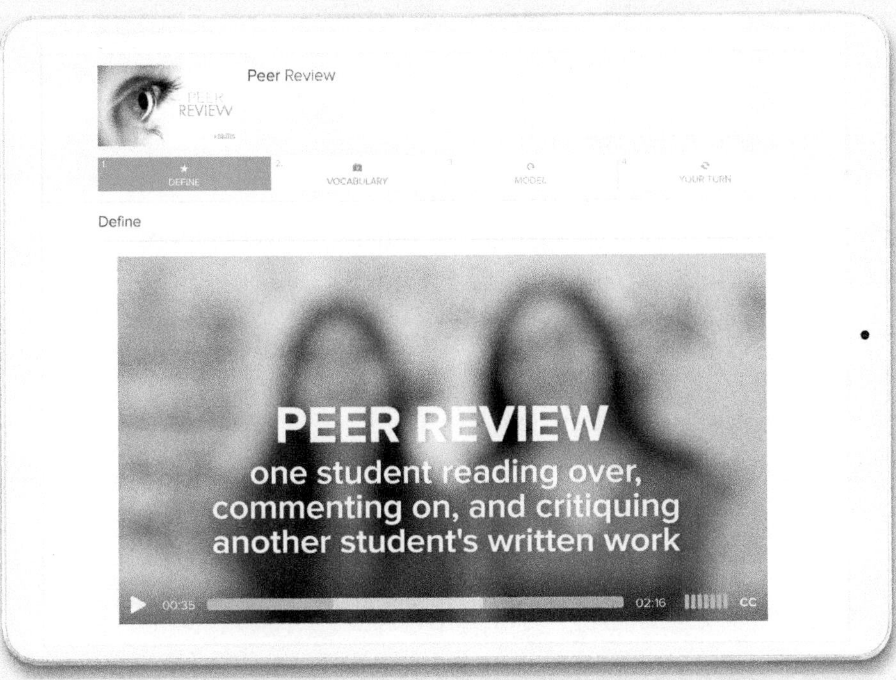

Skill: Peer Review

Introduce the Skill

Watch the Concept Definition video and read the following definition with your students.

Peer review is the act of one student reading over, commenting on, and **critiquing** another student's written work. This collaborative process allows for input from a variety of perspectives, providing a writer with more complete feedback on his or her writing. What one reviewer notices, another might miss.

Peer reviewers should strive to give **constructive** feedback that will help the writer improve his or her work. To provide constructive feedback, include **specific comments** that identify strengths or areas for improvement, and offer clear suggestions on how to improve the writing. Peer reviewers should always maintain a **respectful tone**. That means expressing their thoughts and opinions in a way that shows consideration for the writer's feelings, keeping in mind that it can be difficult for a writer to receive criticism.

Your Turn

Ask students to complete the Your Turn activity.

Descriptions	Peer Reviews
Specific	The textual evidence in your second paragraph is very strong.
Vague	I like how you used textual evidence.
Positive	You did a really great job of selecting details from the story!
Negative	I don't like the quotes that you chose.
Constructive	You may want to add an explanation after your first paragraph; the evidence is good but I'm not sure how it supports your claim.

TURN AND TALK

1. What are the most important things to keep in mind when writing a peer review?
2. What are some ways you can phrase negative feedback so that it is respectful and not discouraging to the writer?

SPEAKING FRAMES

- A peer review is ____. It is helpful because it gives a writer input from ____.
- Peer reviewers should provide feedback that is ____ and ____.
- A specific comment identifies a strength or an area for improvement and offers a suggestion for ____.
- Peer reviewers should maintain a ____ tone in order to show consideration for the writer's feelings.

Write

SCAFFOLDS

Ask students to complete the writing assignment using textual evidence to support their answers.

Use the scaffolds below to differentiate instruction for your ELL English Language Learners and A Approaching grade-level learners.

ELL **BEGINNING** With the help of the word bank, write a response using paragraph frame 1.

INTERMEDIATE With the help of the word bank, write a response using paragraph frames 1 and 2.

ADVANCED, ADVANCED HIGH Write a response of differentiated length using the sentence starters.

A **APPROACHING** Write a response of differentiated length using the sentence starters.

BEGINNING / INTERMEDIATE	INTERMEDIATE		ADVANCED, ADVANCED HIGH / APPROACHING
Word Bank	**Paragraph Frame 1**	**Paragraph Frame 2**	**Sentence Starters**
possible tone describes trusted laughs	The narrator of the story cannot be ____. The author ____ him as hearing a dead man's heartbeat. This is not ____. He also feels proud of himself for the murder and ____ about killing the old man. I can see how the author's description of events and the author's word choice and ____ make the narrator untrustworthy.	At the beginning of the story, the author describes the narrator as ____. He then says the opposite when he describes himself as ____. This helps me understand that he cannot be trusted because he is the type of person who ____.	• The narrator (can / cannot) be trusted because . . . • An example of this is when the narrator . . . • The way the author describes events in the story makes the narrator seem . . . • For example, when . . . • This shows that the narrator . . .

Peer Review

Students should submit substantive feedback to two peers using the instructions below.

- How well does this response answer the prompt?
- How well does the writer support his or her ideas with details and examples from the text?
- Which sentence in the writer's response made you think differently about the text?
- What did the writer do well in this response? What does the writer need to work on?

Rate

Respond to the following with a point rating that reflects your opinion.

	1	2	3	4
Ideas	■	■	■	□
Evidence	■	■	■	■
Language and Conventions	■	■	□	□

Submit

ELL A

SENTENCE FRAMES

- You were able to (completely / partly / almost) answer the prompt.
- You could answer the prompt more completely by ____.
- You supported the idea of ____ with the detail of ____.
- One idea that needs more support is ____.
- I thought differently about the texts after reading ____.
- My favorite part of your response is ____.

Unit Preview

Introduce the Unit

As a class, watch the unit preview and discuss the questions below.

- What two words would you use to describe this video?
- What key words or images from the video do you think will be most important to this unit?

Instructional Path

Big Idea Blast

Objectives: After exploring background information and research links about a topic, students will respond to a question with a 140-character response.

Skill: Recognize Genre

Objectives: After learning about the genre of fiction, students will be able to identify and describe characteristics of mystery, fantasy, and realistic fiction.

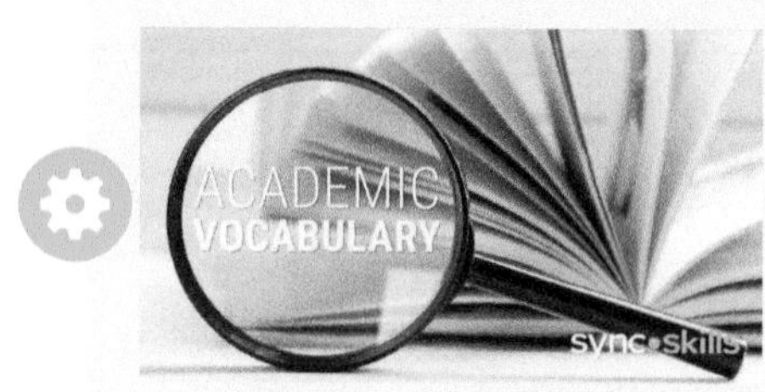

Skill: Academic Vocabulary

Objectives: After learning the meanings of ten academic vocabulary words, students will be able to recognize and use them in a variety of contexts.

DIGITAL ONLY

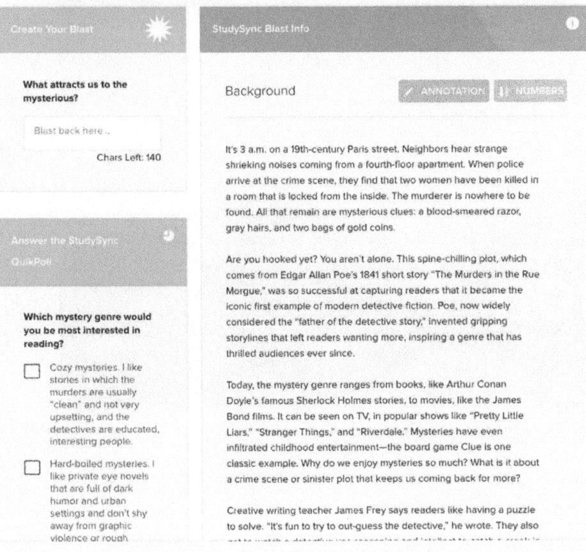

Blast: Everyone Loves a Mystery

What attracts us to the mysterious?

TEXT TALK

How did Edgar Allan Poe contribute to the mystery genre?

Poe created the first detective story.

In what media do we see mysteries?

Mysteries appear in books, movies, television shows, and games.

Where else have you experienced mystery stories?

Possible responses include theater, radio, and around a campfire, for example.

How do different writers view the appeal of mysteries?

One says that people like to "out-guess" the detective, and another says that, through fiction, people can feel what it's like both to solve a mystery and commit a crime.

Create Your Own Blast

SCAFFOLDS

Ask students to write a 140-character Blast after they complete the QuikPoll.

Use the scaffolds below to differentiate instruction for your ELL English Language Learners.

ELL **BEGINNING** Write a response using the word bank to complete the sentence frame.

INTERMEDIATE Write a response using the sentence frame.

ADVANCED, ADVANCED HIGH Write a response using the sentence starter.

BEGINNING	INTERMEDIATE	ADVANCED, ADVANCED HIGH
Word Bank	**Sentence Frame**	**Sentence Starter**
fun exciting interesting scared surprised uncertain	People love mysteries because it can be ____ to feel ____.	• I like how you ____. • I would change ____. • Your response (is / is not) clear because ____.

Skill: Recognize Genre

Introduce the Genre: Fiction

Watch the Concept Definition video  and read the following definition with your students.

Fiction is writing about invented people, places, and events. It includes both long and short written works. **Novels** are long works of fiction. **Short stories**, myths, and folktales are examples of short works of fiction. Short fiction focuses on a small number of events or on just one event. You can usually read a short work of fiction in a single sitting. Short works contain the same elements as do longer works of fiction. These elements include character, plot, setting, point of view, and theme.

In addition, there are many different **literary genres**, or specific categories, of fiction writing. Examples of literary genres include realistic fiction, adventure stories, historical fiction, mysteries, humor, myths, fantasy, and science fiction. Each literary genre has certain characteristics that define the content of the writing.

TURN AND TALK

1. How do literary genres differ from one another?
2. How can you use your knowledge of the features of fiction to tell literary genres apart?

SPEAKING FRAMES

- Literary genres are different because ____.
- One thing I know about features of fiction is ____. I can use this to tell literary genres apart by ____.

Your Turn

Ask students to complete the Your Turn activity.

Literary Genre	Feature of Fiction
Fantasy	The main character is guided by a magic compass.
Realistic Fiction	The story is set in a middle school in Chicago.
Folktale	The evil prince and the good prince battle over the princess's hand in marriage.
Mysteries	The plot centers on a stolen ancient artifact.
Historical Fiction	The main character is Susan B. Anthony.
Science Fiction	The plot tells about a space mission gone wrong.

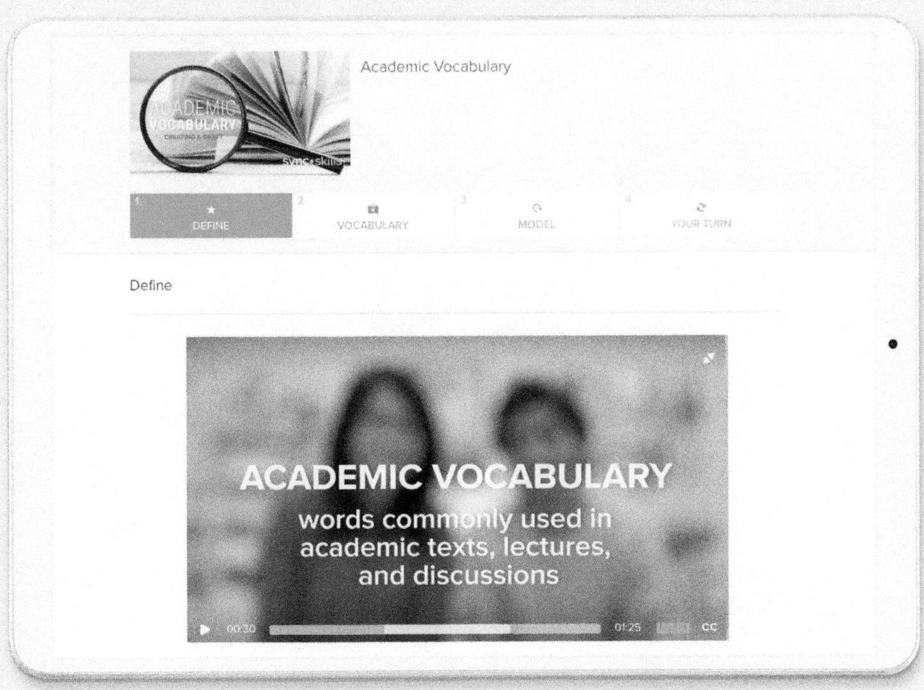

Your Turn

Ask students to complete the Your Turn activities.

Your Turn 1

QUESTION 1: A **QUESTION 2:** B **QUESTION 3:** A **QUESTION 4:** A **QUESTION 5:** B

Your Turn 2

QUESTION 1: B **QUESTION 2:** D **QUESTION 3:** A **QUESTION 4:** C **QUESTION 5:** C

Your Turn 3

See digital teacher's edition for sample answers.

Skill: Academic Vocabulary

Introduce the Terms

access / acceder ***verb*** to reach or gain access to COGNATE

amend / mejorar ***verb*** to correct or make better

consult / consultar ***verb*** to seek information from COGNATE

emerge / emerger ***verb*** to become known or apparent COGNATE

expose / exponer ***verb*** to show or make visible or apparent COGNATE

modify / modificar ***verb*** to make minor changes in order to make something better COGNATE

monitor / monitorear ***verb*** to check, track, and observe COGNATE

objective / objetivo/a ***adjective*** undistorted by emotion or personal bias COGNATE

occupy / ocupar ***verb*** to be on the mind of COGNATE

target / el objetivo ***noun*** an objective or result toward which efforts are directed

Practice Using Vocabulary

Divide the vocabulary words into two lists. Pair students and give each student one half of the list. Challenge students to have a casual conversation with each other that uses every word on their list. Students should aim to insert their vocabulary words in a way that sounds natural. You may wish to turn this activity into a game, allowing partners to award each other points if they effectively use each word on their list.

Monste

FICTION
Walter Dean Myer
1999

Introduction

Monster is one of the most unique and unforgettable wo author Walter Dean Myers (1937–2014). Myers's prolific features more than one hundred books for young readers young adult literature and nonfiction. Monster is about a teenage Harmon, age 16, who decides to write a movie script about his curre He's in jail and on trial, accused of acting as lookout in a drugstore r a man was shot and killed. This excerpt introduces Steve's screen introducing Steve to the reader.

Sixteen-year-old Steve Harmon wakes up every day in jail as if in a nightmare, surrounded by strangers who want to harm him. In order to cope with this difficult new reality, Steve decides to write a film script depicting his struggle. The camera fades in on Steve's cell as he gets dressed for court. Someone asks Steve if he is going to eat his breakfast, but he isn't hungry. At the courthouse, Steve meets his lawyer, Kathy O'Brien, who informs him that he is on trial for felony murder and the prosecutor is excellent. O'Brien instructs him how to act inside the courtroom—no smiling or waving to his friends. The jury needs to see that he takes the situation seriously. Steve asks O'Brien if she thinks they will win. Her response doesn't give him much hope.

 Proficiency-leveled summaries and summaries in multiple languages are available digitally.

 Audio and audio text highlighting are available with this text.

CONNECT TO ESSENTIAL QUESTION

What attracts us to the mysterious?

Suspense is created not only by the supernatural or eerie. With the harsh realism of *Monster*, Walter Dean Myers draws readers into the tense story of a teenage boy on trial for murder. Did he commit the crime? What will the verdict be? And is the question of his guilt or innocence even relevant in a criminal justice system that is not always just?

Access Complex Text

LEXILE: 590L **WORD COUNT:** 1,391

The following areas may be challenging for students, particularly ELL English Language Learners and A Approaching grade-level learners.

Organization	Sentence Structure	Specific Vocabulary
• Students may find it confusing that this novel excerpt consists mainly of a screenplay as imagined by the main character. The opening text is a prologue in the form of a journal entry by the character.	• Students may not be used to the high proportion of short sentences, which mirror the brusque nature of the criminal justice system.	• The text includes some vocabulary specific to prisons and courtrooms, including *cell block, stenographer,* and *U-bolt*. • Students should use a dictionary and context clues to find the meanings of unfamiliar words.

SCAFFOLDS ELL ENGLISH LANGUAGE LEARNERS A APPROACHING GRADE LEVEL B BEYOND GRADE LEVEL

These icons identify differentiation strategies and scaffolded support for a variety of students. See the digital lesson plan for additional differentiation strategies and scaffolds.

Instructional Path

The print teacher's edition includes essential point-of-use instruction and planning tools. Complete lesson plans and program documents appear in your digital teacher account.

First Read: Monster

Objectives: After an initial reading and discussion of the novel excerpt, students will be able to generate their own questions about the text to gain information and deepen their understanding, use context clues to define new vocabulary, and demonstrate comprehension by responding to questions using textual evidence.

Skill: Character

Objectives: After rereading and discussing a model of close reading, students will be able to analyze dialogue and incidents to determine what is revealed about characters.

Close Read: Monster

Objectives: After engaging in a close reading and discussion of the text, students will be able to demonstrate how incidents and dialogue reveal aspects of character in a short, written response.

Blast: Teen Talk

Objectives: After exploring background information and research links about a topic, students will respond to a question with a 140-character response.

Progress Monitoring

Opportunities to Learn	Opportunities to Demonstrate Learning	Opportunities to Reteach
Character		
Skill: Character	Skill: Character • Your Turn Close Read • Skills Focus • Write	Unit 2 Skill: Character - The Outsiders Unit 4 Skill: Character - /HUG Spotlight Skill: Character

First Read

Introduce the Text

As a class, watch the video preview  and have students read the introduction in pairs to make connections to the video preview.

To activate prior knowledge and experiences, ask students:

- What two words would you use to describe this video?
- How do the images, words, and music in the video connect to the information in the introduction?
- What is one prediction you can make about the novel excerpt you're going to read?

ELL **SENTENCE FRAMES**

- The ____ in the video makes me think ____.
- The video shows ____. This makes me wonder ____.
- I think the text will ____. I think this because ____.
- I predict that there will be ____. I believe this because ____.

Entry Point

As students prepare to read *Monster*, share the following information with them to provide context.

- ✓ According to his website, Walter Dean Myers devoured books as a young boy ("I found solace in books") but felt he had to hide his love of reading by carrying books home from the library in a brown paper bag. A high school teacher encouraged his writing, but it was not until he read James Baldwin's short story "Sonny's Blues" as an adult that he realized he could write about his own African American experience.
- ✓ Like much of his work, *Monster* involves the real-world problems and harsh reality faced by many inner city young people, an experience that Myers felt was not represented in literature, especially literature for young adults.
- ✓ The excerpt of *Monster* that students will read focuses mainly on the screenplay the main character, Steve, is writing, but throughout the novel the screenplay is interspersed with Steve's journal entries that directly reveal the character's thoughts, feelings, and fears.

"I'll call it what the lady who is the prosecutor called me."

NOTES

1 They say you get used to being in jail, but I don't see how. Every morning I wake up and I am surprised to be here. If your life outside was real, then everything in here is just the opposite. We sleep with strangers, wake up with strangers, and go to the bathroom in front of strangers. They're strangers but they still find reasons to hurt each other.

2 Sometimes I feel like I have walked into the middle of a movie. It is a strange movie with no plot and no beginning. The movie is in black and white, and grainy. Sometimes the camera moves in so close that you can't tell what is going on and you just listen to the sounds and guess. I have seen movies of prisons but never one like this. This is not a movie about bars and locked doors. It is about being alone when you are not really alone and about being scared all the time.

Skill: Character

teve is the rotagonist. He's been rrested and thrown in il, and now he feels lone and scared. His ecision to write a creenplay about what's appening to him shows e Steve is someone ho tries to deal with a ad situation by emoving himself from it motionally.

3 I think to get used to this I will have to give up what I think is real and take up something else. I wish I could make sense of it.

4 Maybe I could make my own movie. I could write it out and play it in my head. I could block out the scenes like we did in school. The film will be the story of my life. No, not my life, but of this experience. I'll write it down in the notebook they let me keep. I'll call it what the lady who is the **prosecutor** called me.

MONSTER **Monday, July 6th**

Monster!

5 **FADE IN: INTERIOR: Early morning in CELL BLOCK D, MANHATTAN DETENTION CENTER. Camera goes slowly down grim, gray corridor. There are sounds of inmates yelling from cell to cell; much of it is obscene. Most of the voices are clearly Black or Hispanic. Camera stops and slowly turns toward a cell.**

6 **INTERIOR: CELL. Sixteen-year-old STEVE HARMON is sitting on the edge of a metal cot, head in hands. He is thin, brown skinned. On the cot next to him are the suit and tie he is to wear to court for the start of his trial.**

7 **CUT TO: ERNIE, another prisoner, sitting on john, pants down.**

Analyze Vocabulary Using Context Clues

In paragraph 4, focus on the sentence that uses the word *prosecutor*. Point out these context clues:

1. The text tells me that Steve is in a jail cell, and the lady who is a prosecutor called him a monster.
2. I know lawyers are involved in court cases. Some lawyers work for the person on trial, and some work against him. They try to prove he is guilty.
3. I think the prosecutor may be the lawyer who is trying to prove that Steve is guilty. I can keep reading to see if that conclusion is correct.

Character

What does the reader note about Steve's character in the journal entry?

The reader notes how the incident of being put in jail has made Steve feel alone and scared, but he's dealing with these feelings by deciding to write a screenplay to remove himself emotionally.

SELECTION VOCABULARY

prosecutor / el/la fiscal *noun* a lawyer who works for the government

TEXT TALK

Where is the narrator of this novel?

See paragraph 1: He is in jail.

What does the narrator decide to do with his experience?

See paragraph 4: He decides to make it into a movie.

Skills Focus

QUESTION 1: Character

Steve responds to other characters by pulling a blanket over his head. His way to deal with his bad situation is to block it out. He doesn't like to face reality.

Prepare for Advanced Courses

Use the activity below to differentiate instruction for your B Beyond grade-level learners.

Direct students to reread paragraphs 1–4, paying attention to the sentence structure.

Have students analyze how sentence structure relates to the purpose and content of the text. Ask students: What sentence structure is typical in the first three paragraphs? Why do you think the author chose this structure?

Then ask: What sentence structure is typical in the fourth paragraph? Why do you think the author chose this structure for this paragraph?

NOTES

8 **CUT TO: SUNSET, another prisoner, pulling on T-shirt.**

9 **CUT TO: STEVE pulling blanket over his head as screen goes dark.**

VOICE-OVER (VO)

10 Ain't no use putting the blanket over your head, man. You can't cut this out; this is reality. This is the real deal.

11 **VO continues with anonymous PRISONER explaining how the Detention Center is the real thing. As he does, words appear on the screen, just like the opening credits of the movie *Star Wars,* rolling from the bottom of the screen and shrinking until they are a blur on the top of the screen before rolling off into space.**

12 **Monster!**
The Story of
My
Miserable
Life

13 **Starring**
Steve Harmon

14 **Produced by**
Steve Harmon

15 **Directed by**
Steve Harmon

16 (Credits continue to roll.)
The incredible story
of how one guy's life
was turned around
by a few events
and how he might
spend the rest of his life
behind bars.
Told as it
actually
happened!

17 **Written and directed by Steve Harmon**
Featuring. . .

18 **Sandra Petrocelli**
as the Dedicated Prosecutor

19 **Kathy O'Brien**
as the Defense Attorney with Doubts

SELECTION VOCABULARY

anonymous / anónimo/a *adjective* having no name; not identified COGNATE

- Who is the Voice-Over, or VO, speaking to?
- What does the reader not know about this person?

NOTES

20 James King
as the Thug

21 Richard “Bobo” Evans
as the Rat

22 Osvaldo Cruz, member of the Diablos,
as the Tough Guy Wannabe

23 Lorelle Henry
as the Witness
Jose Delgado. . .
he found the body

24 *And Starring*
16-year-old Steve Harmon
As the Boy on Trial for Murder!

25 Filmed at the Manhattan Detention Center

26 Set design, handcuffs, and prison outfits by
The State of New York

VO

27 Yo, Harmon, you gonna eat something? Come on and get your breakfast, man. I'll take your eggs if you don't want them. You want them?

STEVE (subdued)

28 I'm not hungry.

SUNSET

29 His trial starts today. He up for the big one. I know how that feels.

30 **CUT TO: INTERIOR: CORRECTIONS DEPT. VAN. Through the bars at the rear of the van, we see people going about the business of their lives in downtown New York. There are men collecting garbage, a female traffic officer motioning for a taxi to make a turn, students on the way to school. Few people notice the van as it makes its way from the DETENTION CENTER to the COURTHOUSE.**

31 **CUT TO: PRISONERS, handcuffed, coming from back of van. STEVE is carrying a notebook. He is dressed in the suit and tie we saw on the cot. He is seen only briefly as he is herded through the heavy doors of the courthouse.**

32 **FADE OUT as last prisoner from the van enters rear of courthouse.**

33 **FADE IN: INTERIOR COURTHOUSE. We are in a small room used for prisoner-lawyer interviews. A guard sits at a desk behind STEVE.**

SELECTION VOCABULARY

subdued / rendido/a ***adjective*** showing little energy or enthusiasm; glum

- Who is subdued?
- Why might a person not be hungry at mealtime?

TEXT TALK

Who stars in the movie? Why is he on trial?

See paragraph 24: The movie stars Steve Harmon, who is on trial for murder.

Character

What does the reader note about the character of O'Brien?

The reader notes that their dialogue reveals that O'Brien is direct, businesslike, and knows what she is doing.

Skills Focus

QUESTION 3: Connect to Essential Question

The dialogue here creates suspense because it leaves what will happen to Steve up in the air. His lawyer might think that winning means he doesn't get the death penalty, which means Steve could still go to prison. More suspense is created when James King, the man on trial with Steve for murder, glares at him. This incident is menacing.

Skills Focus

QUESTION 2: Character

This dialogue reveals how unconcerned the stenographer and guard are about Steve and his situation. The stenographer cares only about getting paid, and the guard is very cynical. He thinks Steve will just get locked up. He even makes fun of Steve by calling him a name. They don't support him at all.

NOTES

34 **KATHY O'BRIEN, STEVE's lawyer, is petite, red-haired, and freckled. She is all business as she talks to STEVE.**

O'BRIEN

35 Let me make sure you understand what's going on. Both you and this King character are on trial for felony murder. Felony murder is as serious as it gets. Sandra Petrocelli is the prosecutor, and she's good. They're pushing for the death penalty, which is really bad. The jury might think they're doing you a big favor by giving you life in prison. So you'd better take this trial very, very seriously.

36 When you're in court, you sit there and you pay attention. You let the jury know that you think the case is as serious as they do. You don't turn and wave to any of your friends. It's all right to **acknowledge** your mother.

37 I have to go and talk to the judge. The trial will begin in a few minutes. Is there anything you want to ask me before it starts?

STEVE

38 You think we're going to win?

O'BRIEN (seriously)

39 It probably depends on what you mean by "win."

40 **CUT TO: INTERIOR: HOLDING ROOM. We see STEVE sitting at one end of bench. Against the opposite wall, dressed in a sloppy-looking suit, is 23-year-old JAMES KING, the other man on trial. King looks older than 23. He looks over at STEVE with a hard look and we see STEVE look away. Two GUARDS sit at a table away from the prisoners who are handcuffed. The camera finds the GUARDS in a MEDIUM SHOT (MS). They have their breakfast in aluminum take-out trays that contain eggs, sausages, and potatoes. A Black female STENOGRAPHER[1] pours coffee for herself and the GUARDS.**

STENOGRAPHER

41 I hope this case lasts two weeks. I can sure use the money.

GUARD 1

42 Six days—maybe seven. It's a motion[2] case. They go through the motions; then they lock them up.

43 **(Turns and looks off camera toward STEVE.)**

44 Ain't that right, bright eyes?

Skill: Character

O'Brien talks to Steve very directly and doesn't mince words. This tells me she's very businesslike and probably knows what she's doing. And she's maybe a little sarcastic with "what you mean by win," but she's trying to show Steve how serious his situation is.

1. **stenographer** a person whose job is to transcribe spoken or recorded speech
2. **motion** in legal terms, a request for a ruling

TEXT TALK

Who is O'Brien?

See paragraph 34: Kathy O'Brien is Steve Harmon's lawyer.

SELECTION VOCABULARY

acknowledge / reconocer *verb* to show that one recognizes or notices someone or something

- What does Steve's lawyer tell Steve not to do?
- Whom does she allow Steve to acknowledge?

NOTES

45 **CUT TO: STEVE, who is seated on a low bench. He is handcuffed to a U-bolt put in the bench for that purpose. STEVE looks away from the GUARD.**

46 **CUT TO: DOOR. It opens, and COURT CLERK looks in.**

COURT CLERK

47 Two minutes!

48 **CUT TO: GUARDS, who hurriedly finish breakfast. STENOGRAPHER takes machine into COURTROOM. They unshackle STEVE and take him toward door.**

49 **CUT TO: STEVE is made to sit down at one table. At another table we see KING and two attorneys. STEVE sits alone. A guard stands behind him. There are one or two spectators in the court. Then four more enter.**

50 **CLOSE-UP (CU) OF STEVE HARMON. The fear is evident on his face.**

51 **MS: People are getting ready for the trial to begin. KATHY O'BRIEN sits next to STEVE.**

O'BRIEN

52 How are you doing?

STEVE

53 I'm scared.

O'BRIEN

54 Good; you should be. Anyway, just remember what we've been talking about. The judge is going to rule on a motion that King's lawyer made to suppress Cruz's **testimony**, and a few other things. Steve, let me tell you what my job is here. My job is to make sure the law works for you as well as against you, and to make you a human being in the eyes of the jury. Your job is to help me. Any questions you have, write them down and I'll try to answer them. What are you doing there?

STEVE

55 I'm writing this whole thing down as a movie.

O'BRIEN

56 Whatever. Make sure you pay attention. Close attention.

Excerpted from *Monster* by Walter Dean Myers, published by HarperCollins Publishers.

TEXT TALK

How do you know that the last paragraphs are set in a courtroom?

See paragraphs 46–51: Answers will vary but should include characters such as "Court Clerk" and other details.

B Ask each Beyond grade-level student to write one additional discussion question. Then have one or two students facilitate a discussion, using their questions to guide the conversation.

SELECTION VOCABULARY

unshackle / desencadenar ***verb*** to take off handcuffs

ELL
- Where is Steve before he is unshackled?
- Who unshackles Steve?

testimony / el testimonio ***noun*** statements that a person makes as a witness in court COGNATE

- Who is Cruz?
- Why might James King's lawyer be concerned about Cruz?

Think Questions

Circulate as students answer Think Questions independently. Scaffolds for these questions are shown on the opposite page.

QUESTION 1: Textual Evidence

Steve credits himself as the star actor, producer, director, and writer of the movie. He also credits himself as "The Boy on Trial for Murder."

QUESTION 2: Textual Evidence

Kathy tells Steve to pay attention and let the jury know that he thinks the case is as serious as they do. She also tells him not to wave to his friends in court, but that it's okay to acknowledge his mother.

QUESTION 3: Textual Evidence

The stenographer hopes the trial lasts two weeks so that she can make more money, but the guard says that it will be over sooner than that and Steve will go to prison. He thinks that the whole trial is just going "through the motions."

QUESTION 4: Context Clues

Anonymous means "not named or identified." In paragraphs 9 and 10, I know that Steve is pulling his blanket over his head and the Voice-Over character is speaking to him. But in paragraph 11, the VO is speaking with an "anonymous prisoner." It could be Steve with the blanket over his head, or it could be any prisoner. In this context, I think anonymous must mean "unidentifiable" or "faceless," because the reader can't be sure of the prisoner's identity.

QUESTION 5: Context Clues

Subdued means "quiet; with little energy." The opening text says that Steve is in a jail cell, feeling alone and scared. In the stage direction, he has his head in his hands. He says he's not hungry when asked if he wants his breakfast. These clues tell me that Steve is feeling bad or low on energy because he's up for trial soon. These context clues help me to understand that *subdued* must mean "not talkative" or maybe even "depressed."

First Read

Read *Monster*. After you read, complete the Think Questions below.

THINK QUESTIONS

1. How does Steve Harmon introduce himself in the opening credits of the screenplay?
2. What advice does Kathy O'Brien, Steve's lawyer, have for Steve?
3. What do the stenographer and the guard say about Steve's case?
4. Find the word **anonymous** in paragraph 11 of *Monster*. Use context clues in the surrounding sentences, as well as the sentence in which the word appears, to determine the word's meaning. Write your definition here and identify clues that helped you figure out its meaning.
5. Use context clues to determine the meaning of **subdued** as it is used to describe Steve's dialogue for paragraph 28. Write your definition of *subdued* here and and identify clues that helped you figure out its meaning. Then check the meaning in a dictionary.

SCAFFOLDS

Think Questions

Use the scaffolds below to differentiate instruction for your ELL English Language Learners and A Approaching grade-level learners.

ELL **BEGINNING** Write a response using the word bank and sentence frames.

INTERMEDIATE Write a response using the sentence frames.

ADVANCED, ADVANCED HIGH Write a response using the Text-Dependent Question Guide.

A **APPROACHING** Write a response using the Text-Dependent Question Guide.

BEGINNING	INTERMEDIATE	APPROACHING / ADVANCED, ADVANCED HIGH
Word Bank	**Sentence Frames**	**Text-Dependent Question Guide**
wave prison serious	Steve lists himself as the star ____. He lists himself as ____. Finally, Steve lists himself as the writer and ____.	1. • How does Steve list himself first? • How does Steve list himself next? • How does Steve list himself last?
actor hands weeks	Kathy O'Brien tells Steve to sit and pay ____ to what is going on. She tells him to let the jury know he is ____. O'Brien tells him not to turn and ____ to friends.	2. • What does Kathy O'Brien tell Steve to do when he is in court? • What does O'Brien tell him to do about the jury? • What does O'Brien tell him *not* to do?
nameless producer director	The stenographer hopes that the trial lasts two ____. The guard says the trial will end with Steve in ____. The trial is just going "through the ____."	3. • How long does the stenographer want the trial to last? • What does the guard think will happen to Steve?
name hungry attention	*Anonymous* means "to be ____." This is a clue that anonymous means "without a known ____."	4. • Who is the Voice-Over speaking to in paragraph 10? • Who is the Voice-Over speaking to in paragraph 11? • What does the reader not know about this person?
motions quiet depressed	The text says that Steve has his head in his ____. He is not ____ and speaks little. These clues suggest that "subdued" means he is ____. He may be ____.	5. • How does Steve feel? • How is Steve sitting? • What does Steve say when a prisoner asks if he wants his food? • What do these clues suggest about someone who is *subdued*?

Reading Comprehension OPTIONAL

Have students complete the digital reading comprehension questions when they finish reading.

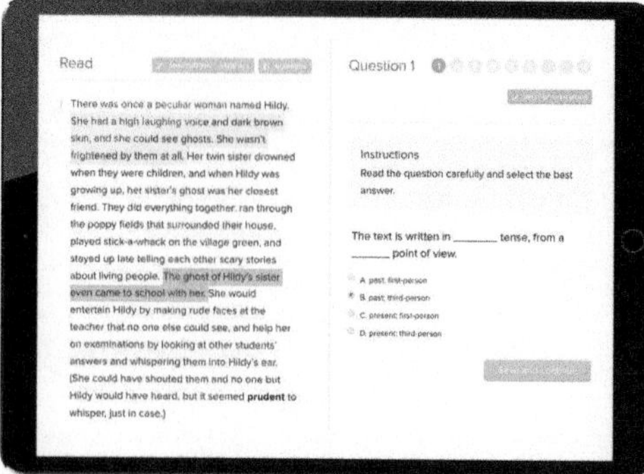

ANSWER KEY

QUESTION 1: C
QUESTION 2: B
QUESTION 3: A
QUESTION 4: B
QUESTION 5: A
QUESTION 6: B
QUESTION 7: B
QUESTION 8: D
QUESTION 9: *See first chart.*
QUESTION 10: *See second chart.*

Definition	Word
without a name or face	anonymous
a person who carries out legal matters	prosecutor
quiet and possibly depressed	subdued
to remove from restraints	unshackle
to admit	acknowledge

Attribute	Character
Shell-shocked	Steve
No-nonsense	Kathy
Spine-chilling	James King
Matter-of-fact	Stenographer

Connect and Extend OPTIONAL

CONNECT TO EXTENDED WRITING PROJECT

While writing their literary analyses, students can find inspiration from Walter Dean Myers's *Monster* for their Extended Writing Project. They may consider how Myers uses his characters and the events in the story, as well as structural elements of drama, to create suspense.

BEYOND THE BOOK

Graphic Story: Monster

Students will take the screenplay in Monster and use it to design a graphic story of Steve's experience in jail and court.

Ask students to:

- Read through the screenplay, focusing on the bold screen directions and noting all the places where the scenes change.
- Create a storyboard with rough sketches to organize the story, portraying each scene as an image.
- Use details from the screen directions and dialogue to create a visual depiction of each scene. Students can use pen and paper or an online comic creator to create their graphic stories.
- Publish stories for feedback from the class.

To reflect, ask students:

- What was the most challenging part of turning this screenplay into a graphic story?
- Which scene was toughest to portray visually?
- How did you use color and other details to reflect Steve's emotional state in each scene?

Skill: Character

Use the Checklist to analyze Character in *Monster*. Refer to the sample student annotations about Character in the text.

••• CHECKLIST FOR CHARACTER

In order to determine how dialogue or incidents in a story propel the action, reveal aspects of a character, or provoke a decision, note the following:

- ✓ the characters in the story, including the protagonist and antagonist
- ✓ key dialogue and how it reveals character traits and moves the action, or the events of the plot, forward
- ✓ characters' responses and reactions to other characters or events, and what this reveals about them
- ✓ when an event or another character's actions or dialogue provokes a character to make a decision
- ✓ the resolution and how it affects the characters

To analyze how particular lines of dialogue or incidents in a story or drama propel the action, reveal aspects of a character, or provoke a decision, consider the following questions:

- ✓ How does the dialogue propel, or move forward, the action in the story?
- ✓ How does the dialogue reveal different aspects or traits of each character?
- ✓ Did an event or a character provoke another character to make a decision? What was it, and how did it affect the events of the plot?
- ✓ How does the resolution affect the characters?

Skill: Character

Introduce the Skill

Watch the Concept Definition video ▶ and read the following definition with your students.

A **character** is a person, animal, or other being portrayed in a story. Every kind of fiction and drama needs characters. Characters' thoughts, feelings, actions, and reactions drive the **plot**, or the events that take place in the story. The **resolution** is the final outcome of the story's conflict. Writers use several techniques to develop characters and reveal aspects of their personality including **dialogue**, or conversation, description, and plot events. Character **traits** are the defining qualities of personality or behavior, good or bad, that make that character unique.

The main character—the one the story revolves around and who usually has a problem to solve—is called the **protagonist**. The character who opposes the protagonist is called the **antagonist**. Minor characters provide support for the protagonist or antagonist, helping to reveal aspects of their personalities.

TURN AND TALK

1. What is your favorite play or movie, and who were the characters?
2. How did understanding the dialogue and action help you understand the characters and the meaning of the story?

ELL SPEAKING FRAMES

- My favorite play or movie is ____.
- The characters are ____.
- The dialogue helped me see that ____.
- The action helped me see that ____.

SKILL VOCABULARY

character / el personaje ***noun*** an individual in a literary work whose thoughts, feelings, actions, and reactions move the action of the plot forward

plot / la trama ***noun*** the sequence of events that form a story

resolution / la resolución ***noun*** the final outcome of the story's conflict COGNATE

dialogue / el diálogo ***noun*** the conversation between characters COGNATE

Your Turn

Ask students to complete the Your Turn activity.

QUESTION 1

Part A

A. Correct. The dialogue and descriptions in this passage most strongly support this response because O'Brien clearly explains her role, what is about to happen, and what Steve can do.

B. Incorrect. Steve says that he is scared, but O'Brien does not.

C. Incorrect. O'Brien does not say or imply that the trial will turn out well for Steve.

D. Incorrect. O'Brien does not say or imply that the trial will not turn out well for Steve.

Part B

A. Incorrect. This question does not reveal that O'Brien is honest.

B. Incorrect. This statement does not reveal that O'Brien is honest.

C. Correct. This statement shows that O'Brien is clearly explaining her role in this scene.

D. Incorrect. This statement does not reveal that O'Brien is honest.

QUESTION 2

A. Incorrect. This comment does not show lack of concern with Steve's feelings. O'Brien wants to explain to Steve what she does during the trial.

B. Incorrect. This comment does not show lack of concern with Steve's feelings.

C. Incorrect. This comment does not show lack of concern with Steve's feelings.

D. Correct. In this line of dialogue, O'Brien is not concerned with how Steve feels, but that he understands the importance of his trial.

Skill: Character

Reread paragraphs 52–56 from *Monster*. Then, using the Checklist on the previous page, answer the multiple-choice questions below.

YOUR TURN

1. This question has two parts. First, answer Part A. Then, answer Part B.

Part A: Which of the following is one character trait that O'Brien shows in this passage?

- A. honesty
- B. fearfulness
- C. optimism
- D. pessimism

Part B: Which of the following lines of dialogue BEST reveals the character trait selected in Part A?

- A. "How are you doing?"
- B. "Anyway, just remember what we've been talking about."
- C. "My job is to make sure the law works for you as well as against you, and to make you a human being in the eyes of the jury."
- D. "Any questions you have, write them down and I'll try to answer them."

2. Which line shows that O'Brien is not overly concerned with Steve's feelings?

- A. "Steve, let me tell you what my job is here."
- B. "Your job is to help me."
- C. "What are you doing there?"
- D. "Whatever."

SKILL VOCABULARY

trait / el rasgo ***noun*** an aspect of a character's behavior and attitude that make up that character's personality

protagonist / el/la protagonista ***noun*** the main character—the one the story revolves around and who usually has a problem to solve COGNATE

antagonist / el/la antagonista ***noun*** the character whose goals work against the protagonist COGNATE

Close Read

eread *Monster*. As you reread, complete the Skills Focus questions below. Then use your answers and nnotations from the questions to help you complete the Write activity.

SKILLS FOCUS

What do Steve's responses to other characters or events in the story reveal about him?

. Minor characters in a story may support the protagonist or antagonist. How does the dialogue reveal character traits of some of the minor characters in *Monster*? Do they support Steve?

3. Identify ways in which suspense is created through events, characters, and dialogue. How does the use of suspense help to attract the reader to the novel's mysteriousness?

WRITE

NARRATIVE: Choose a section from the screenplay in *Monster*, and rewrite it as as story rather than a screenplay. Include lines of dialogue, but also add descriptions about the characters' feelings and responses to one another.

Close Read

Skills Focus

QUESTION 1: Character

See paragraphs 7–10.

QUESTION 2: Character

See paragraphs 41–44.

QUESTION 3: Connect to Essential Question

See paragraphs 37–40.

CHECK FOR SUCCESS

If students struggle to respond to Skills Focus question 1, ask them the following questions:

- Which parts of the text tell what Steve says or how he acts?
- What do you learn about Steve in each of these parts?

Have students transition to read and annotate independently once they have successfully completed the first Skills Focus prompt.

Writer's Notebook

Connect to Essential Question: Give students time to reflect on how *Monster* connects to the unit's essential question "What attracts us to the mysterious?" by freewriting in their Writer's Notebooks.

Beginning & Intermediate

Read aloud the unit's essential question: "What attracts us to the mysterious?" Encourage students to draw their connections or allow students to write in their native language. Circulate the room, prompting students for their thoughts as they respond orally or through pantomime.

Advanced & Advanced High

Allow students to share their connections orally in pairs or small groups before freewriting.

StudySyncTV

Project the StudySyncTV episode and pause at the following times to prompt discussion:

1:34 Dakota thinks that Steve is not guilty of murder. What example does she cite to support her belief?

2:18 How does Colin explain Steve's reasons for writing the screenplay? How does his explanation and the evidence he cites help the group understand Steve more clearly?

4:13 How does the group characterize Steve? Do you agree? What evidence supports their characterization?

Collaborative Conversation

Break students into collaborative conversation groups to discuss the Close Read prompt. Ask students to use the StudySyncTV episode as a model for their discussion. Remind them to reference their Skills Focus annotations in their discussion.

Choose a section from the screenplay in *Monster* and rewrite it as as story rather than a screenplay. Include lines of dialogue, but also add descriptions about the characters' feelings and responses to one another.

Use the scaffolds below to differentiate instruction for your ELL English Language Learners and A Approaching grade-level learners.

ELL **BEGINNING, INTERMEDIATE** Use the discussion guide and speaking frames to facilitate the discussion with support from the teacher.

ADVANCED, ADVANCED HIGH Use the discussion guide and speaking frames to facilitate the discussion in mixed-level groups.

A APPROACHING Use the discussion guide to facilitate the discussion in mixed-level groups.

APPROACHING
ADVANCED, ADVANCED HIGH
BEGINNING, INTERMEDIATE

Discussion Guide	Speaking Frames
1. Who are the characters in *Monster*?	• The main character is ____. • The minor characters are ____.
2. What do you learn about the characters from their dialogue and reactions?	• I learn that ____ is ____ when (he / she) says ____. • I learn that ____ is ____ when (he / she) ____.

Review Prompt and Rubric

Before students begin writing, review the writing prompt and rubric with the class.

NARRATIVE: Choose a section from the screenplay in *Monster* and rewrite it as as story rather than a screenplay. Include lines of dialogue, but also add descriptions about the characters' feelings and responses to one another.

PROMPT GUIDE

- Who are the characters in *Monster*?
- What do you learn about the characters from their dialogue and reactions?

Score	Character	Language and Conventions
4	The writer effectively rewrites part of the screenplay as a story, adding clear and accurate descriptions of the characters' feelings and responses to one another.	The writer demonstrates a consistent command of grammar, punctuation, and usage conventions. Although minor errors may be evident, they do not detract from the fluency or the clarity of the writing.
3	The writer rewrites part of the screenplay as a story, adding accurate descriptions of the characters' feelings and responses to one another.	The writer demonstrates an adequate command of grammar, punctuation, and usage conventions. Although some errors may be evident, they create few (if any) disruptions in the fluency or the clarity of the writing.
2	The writer rewrites the screenplay as a story, adding some descriptions of the characters' feelings and responses to one another.	The writer demonstrates a partial command of grammar, punctuation, and usage conventions. Some distracting errors may be evident, at times creating minor disruptions in the fluency or clarity of the writing.
1	The writer attempts to rewrite the screenplay as a story but includes few or unclear descriptions of the characters' feelings and responses to one another.	The writer demonstrates little or no command of grammar, punctuation, and usage conventions. Serious and persistent errors create disruptions in the fluency of the writing and sometimes interfere with meaning.
0	The writer does not provide a relevant response to the prompt or does not provide a response at all.	Serious and persistent errors overwhelm the writing and interfere with the meaning of the response as a whole, making the writer's meaning impossible to understand.

Write

SCAFFOLDS

Ask students to complete the writing assignment using textual evidence to support their answers.

Use the scaffolds below to differentiate instruction for your ELL English Language Learners and A Approaching grade-level learners.

ELL **BEGINNING** With the help of the word bank, write a response using paragraph frame 1.

INTERMEDIATE With the help of the word bank, write a response using paragraph frames 1 and 2.

ADVANCED, ADVANCED HIGH Write a response of differentiated length using the sentence starters.

A **APPROACHING** Write a response of differentiated length using the sentence starters.

BEGINNING | INTERMEDIATE | ADVANCED, ADVANCED HIGH | APPROACHING

Word Bank	Paragraph Frame 1	Paragraph Frame 2	Sentence Starters
alone jail quietly mean frightened	The scene takes place in ____. "Yo, Harmon, you gonna eat something? Come on and get your breakfast, man. I'll take your eggs if you don't want them. You want them?" VO asked. He was not being ____, just hungry. "I'm not hungry," Steve mumbled ____. Steve felt too ____ and ____ to think about food.	"His trial starts today. He up for the big one. I know how that feels," Sunset said ____. Sunset was ____. He understood ____.	• The scene is . . . • . . . , Steve said. He is . . . • . . . , O'Brien said. She is . . .

Peer Review

Rate

Respond to the following with a point rating that reflects your opinion.

	1	2	3	4
Ideas	■	■	■	□
Evidence	■	■	■	■
Language and Conventions	■	■	□	□

Submit

Students should submit substantive feedback to two peers using the review instructions below.

- How well does this response answer the prompt?
- How effectively and accurately does the writer portray the characters through descriptions and responses?
- What did the writer do well in this response? What does the writer need to work on?

ELL A

SENTENCE FRAMES

- You were able to (completely / partly / almost) answer the prompt because ____ .
- You could answer the prompt better by ____ .
- The characters were portrayed ____ .
- My favorite part of your response is ____.

Let 'Em Play God

INFORMATIONAL TEXT
Alfred Hitchcock
1948

Introduction

With films that consistently put viewers on the edge of their seats, British film director Alfred Hitchcock earned the nickname "The Master of Suspense." In the following excerpt from a 1948 essay, Hitchcock describes how he creates suspense by letting the audience "play God"—by providing them with certain information not known to characters in a movie—and illustrates how he used the technique to create dramatic tension in his 1948 thriller, *Rope*.

British film director Alfred Hitchcock explains that the secret for suspense is letting the audience play God. When the audience has information that the characters aren't aware of, the audience becomes emotionally involved in the characters' actions. As an example, Hitchcock cites his film *Rope,* in which the audience knows from the beginning that a young man was killed and his body was hidden in a chest. Soon thereafter, the dead man's family arrives for a party, and the suspense grows as the audience wonders whether the dead body will be discovered. Hitchcock shares two final secrets for creating suspense. One, the characters and situations must be believable, and two, Hitchcock explains how contrast can make a dark situation seem more sinister, such as by using a charming or serene background.

 Proficiency-leveled summaries and summaries in multiple languages are available digitally.

 Audio and audio text highlighting are available with this text.

CONNECT TO ESSENTIAL QUESTION

What attracts us to the mysterious?

Anyone who creates thrillers or mysteries knows that it's crucial to keep the reader or the audience guessing. How does a filmmaker keep an audience's interest in movie after movie? In this essay, the "master of suspense," Alfred Hitchcock, shares his secret for creating unforgettable suspense films.

Access Complex Text

LEXILE: 1070L **WORD COUNT:** 752

The following areas may be challenging for students, particularly ELL English Language Learners and A Approaching grade-level learners.

Prior Knowledge	Specific Vocabulary	Connection of Ideas
• Many Hitchcock films, such as *Shadow of a Doubt* (1943), *Rope* (1948), and *North by Northwest* (1959), generate suspense through fugitives on the run. • Students may benefit from watching excerpts or trailers from the films to build context.	• Idiomatic expressions, such as "cry for joy" and "work like the devil," may need to be explained. • It may be helpful for the teacher to provide sample sentences applying these idioms in context.	• Abstract ideas, such as suspense and the idea of an audience "playing God," are developed with concrete examples. • Students may benefit by viewing an excerpt from the film *Rope* to better understand Hitchcock's points about it.

SCAFFOLDS  ENGLISH LANGUAGE LEARNERS  APPROACHING GRADE LEVEL  BEYOND GRADE LEVEL

These icons identify differentiation strategies and scaffolded support for a variety of students. See the digital lesson plan for additional differentiation strategies and scaffolds.

Instructional Path

The print teacher's edition includes essential point-of-use instruction and planning tools. Complete lesson plans and program documents appear in your digital teacher account.

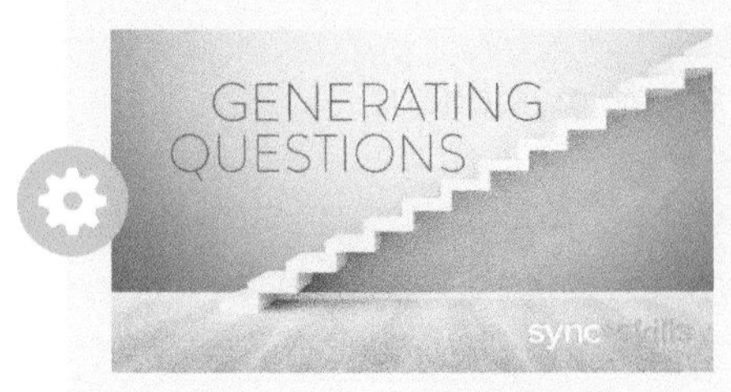

DIGITAL ONLY

Skill: Generating Questions

Objectives: After reading and discussing a model, students will be able to generate questions before, during, and after reading to ensure understanding and gain information.

First Read: Let 'Em Play God

Objectives: After an initial reading and discussion of the essay, students will be able to generate their own questions about the text to gain information and deepen their understanding, use context clues to define new vocabulary, and demonstrate comprehension by responding to questions using textual evidence.

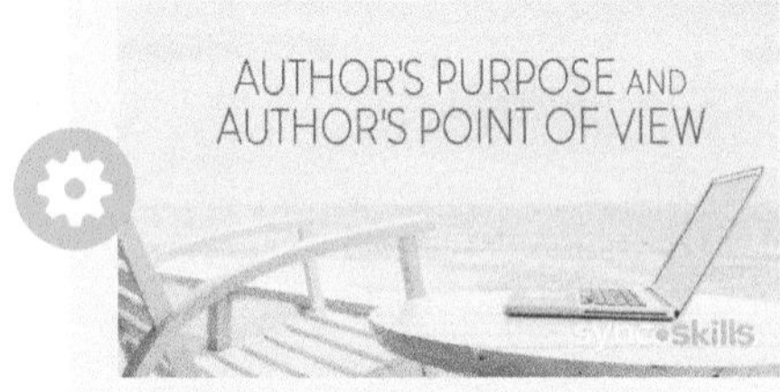

Skill: Author's Purpose and Point of View

Objectives: After rereading and discussing a model of close reading, students will be able to explain the author's purpose and point of view within a text.

Close Read: Let 'Em Play God

Objectives: After engaging in a close reading and discussion of the text, students will be able to analyze the author's purpose and point of view in a short, written response.

Progress Monitoring

Opportunities to Learn	Opportunities to Demonstrate Learning	Opportunities to Reteach
Generating Questions		
Skill: Generating Questions	First Read • Read And Annotate	Unit 6 First Read: Everybody Out (from 'What If?') Spotlight Skill: Generating Questions
Author's Purpose and Point of View		
Skill: Author's Purpose and Point of View	Skill: Author's Purpose and Point of View • Your Turn Close Read • Skills Focus • Write	Unit 1 Skill: Author's Purpose and Point of View - Ten Days in a Mad-House Unit 5 Skill: Author's Purpose and Point of View - Long Walk to Freedom Spotlight Skill: Author's Purpose and Point of View

First Read

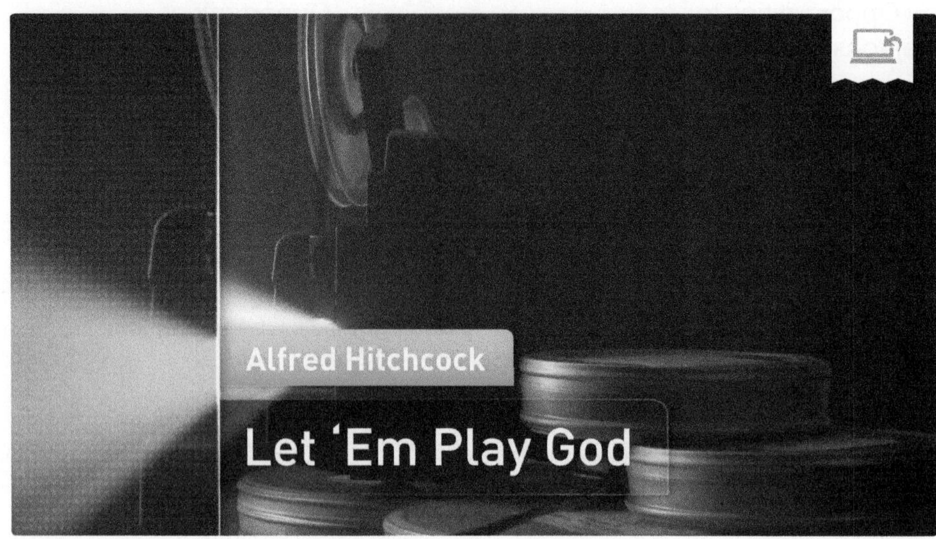

Introduce the Text

As a class, watch the video preview  and have students read the introduction in pairs to make connections to the video preview.

To activate prior knowledge and experiences, ask students:

- What part of the video stood out to you the most?
- What is one question you have about what you are going to read?

ELL SPEAKING FRAMES

- The ____ in the video makes me think ____.
- The video shows ____. This makes me wonder ____.
- I think the text will ____. I think this because ____.
- I predict that there will be ____. I believe this because ____.

Entry Point

As students prepare to read "Let 'Em Play God," share the following information with them to provide context.

- ✓ British film director Alfred Hitchcock (1899–1980) entered the film industry in 1920 as an artist who drew sets and was first given a chance to direct in 1923. He made films in a variety of genres, but he focused on suspense as he developed. Many of Hitchcock's films were popular, and critics often praised them for their craft.
- ✓ In 1948, Hitchcock published "Let 'Em Play God" in *The Hollywood Reporter*. In this essay, he explains how he gets audiences "on the edge of their seats." He cites scenes from one of his films, *Rope*, as evidence to support his claims.
- ✓ Since suspense is a popular genre of books, films, and TV shows, students can share their own definitions of that term and then compare them to Hitchcock's definition after they read this essay.

"As far as I'm concerned, you have suspense when you let the audience play God."

NOTES

Skill: Author's Purpose and Point of View

Hitchcock is answering a question, but is he writing to inform or explain?

He starts to answer the question by describing how suspense is created, so he must be writing to explain. I'm just not sure what he means yet.

From "Let 'Em Play God"

1 Every maker of mystery movies aims at getting the audience on the edge of their seats. The **ingredient** to keep them there is called "suspense." Producers[1] cry for it, writers cry in agony to get it, and actors cry for joy when they do get it. I've often been asked what it is.

2 As far as I'm concerned, you have suspense when you let the audience play God.

3 Suppose, for instance, you have six characters involved in a mystery. A man has been murdered and all six are possible **suspects** but no one is sure including the audience.

4 One of the characters, a young man, is standing in a shadowy room with his back to the door when an unidentified character in a cloak and black hat sneaks in and slugs him into **insensibility.** It's a brutal act, but if the audience does not know whether the young man is a killer or a hero they will not know whether to cheer or weep.

5 If the audience does know, if they have been told all the secrets that the characters do not know, they'll work like the devil for you because they know what fate is facing the poor actors. That is what is known as "playing God." That is suspense.

6 For 17 years I have been making pictures described alternately as thriller, dark mysteries, and chillers, yet I have never actually directed a whodunit[2] or a puzzler. Offhand this may sound like **debunking,** but I do not believe that puzzling the audience is the essence of suspense.

7 Take, for instance, the drama I recently filmed at Warner Bros. called *Rope*. It stars James Stewart with Joan Chandler, our new discovery, in the feminine lead.

1. **Producers** the people who oversee the production of a film
2. **whodunit** a story about a murder in which the murderer's identity is concealed until the conclusion of the narrative

Analyze Vocabulary Using Context Clues

In paragraph 1, focus on the sentence that uses the word *ingredient*. Point out these context clues:

1. First, I notice that the author uses the pronoun *it* to refer to *suspense*. That tells me that *ingredient* is a noun.
2. When I read the sentences again, I notice producers, writers, and actors want to use suspense as an ingredient in order to make audiences feel a certain way.
3. I know that movies have a lot of parts, and suspense is just one of them. Based on this, I can figure out that *ingredient* means "one part of a mixture."

Author's Purpose and Point of View

How did the reader use details to draw conclusions about Hitchcock's purpose?

She noted that Hitchcock is answering a question.

TEXT TALK

What does it mean to let the audience "play God"?

See paragraphs 2–5: Giving the audience information that the characters do not know is what Hitchcock means by this phrase.

SELECTION VOCABULARY

ingredient / el ingrediente ***noun*** one of the things in a mixture COGNATE

suspects / el/la sospechoso/a ***noun*** a person who might be guilty of a crime COGNATE

- What is the relationship between the six characters and the crime?

insensibility / la inconsciencia ***noun*** not conscious, especially after being hit

- Would a person most likely remain awake and aware after such a "brutal act"?

debunk / desacreditar ***verb*** to expose something as being untrue

- What difference does Hitchcock point out between how people describe his movies and how he sees his own films?

Skills Focus

QUESTION 2: Author's Purpose and Point of View

Hitchcock shows the difference between a whodunit and the films he makes. He advises that revealing the killers helps make the movie more suspenseful. Future filmmakers may follow this model in creating their own films.

Skills Focus

QUESTION 3: Connect to Essential Question

Hitchcock imagines that audiences will constantly ask questions about what will happen next. The audience already knows who the killers are, so they are driven by the mystery of whether or not the criminals will get caught.

TEXT TALK

What does Hitchcock mean by "whodunit"? Make an inference.

See paragraph 9: *Whodunit*, or "who done, or did, it," refers to figuring out who committed the crime in a mystery.

Why isn't *Rope* a "whodunit" film?

See paragraph 9: The audience already knows who the killer is.

What kinds of characters and situations are needed to create suspense?

See paragraph 11: Plausible, or realistic, characters and situations are needed to create suspense.

Why doesn't Hitchcock create spooky settings through bad weather, shadows, or creaky doors?

See paragraphs 13–15: He wishes to create contrast between the suspenseful plot and the characters' situations.

Ask each Beyond grade-level student to write one additional discussion question. Then have one or two students facilitate a discussion, using their questions to guide the conversation.

NOTES

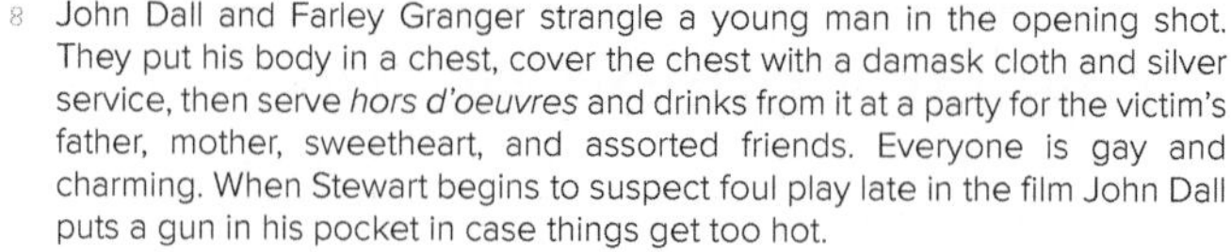

8 John Dall and Farley Granger strangle a young man in the opening shot. They put his body in a chest, cover the chest with a damask cloth and silver service, then serve *hors d'oeuvres* and drinks from it at a party for the victim's father, mother, sweetheart, and assorted friends. Everyone is gay and charming. When Stewart begins to suspect foul play late in the film John Dall puts a gun in his pocket in case things get too hot.

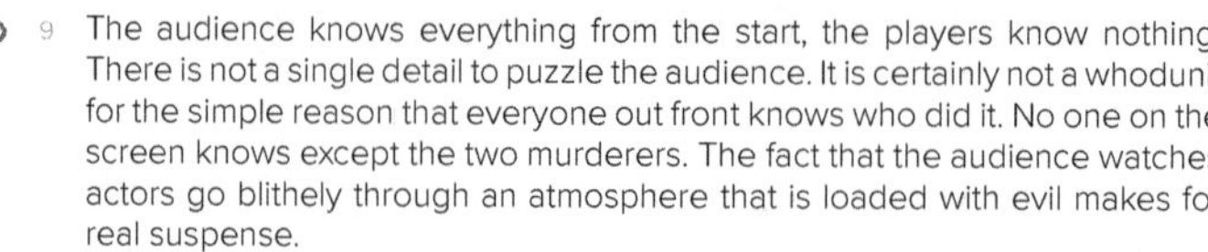

9 The audience knows everything from the start, the players know nothing. There is not a single detail to puzzle the audience. It is certainly not a whodunit for the simple reason that everyone out front knows who did it. No one on the screen knows except the two murderers. The fact that the audience watches actors go blithely through an atmosphere that is loaded with evil makes for real suspense.

10 These are the questions, now, that constantly pop up. Will the murderers break and give themselves away? When the victim does not show up for the party will his father suspect? Will Jimmy get killed before he discovers the actual crime? How long will that body lie in its wooden grave at a champagne party without being discovered? If we are successful we'll have the audience at such a pitch that they want to shout every time one of the players goes near that chest.

11 In order to achieve this, one of the necessary ingredients of the formula is a series of **plausible** situations with people that are real. When characters are unbelievable you never get suspense, only surprise.

12 Just because there is a touch of murder and an air of mystery about a story it is not necessary to see transoms opening, clutching fingers, hooded creatures, and asps on the Chinese rug.

13 *Spellbound* was based on complete psychiatric truth. *Foreign Correspondent* was simply the story of a man hammering away at events with a woman who was not much help. *Notorious* concerned a woman caught in a web of world events from which she could not extricate herself and *The Paradine Case* was a love story embedded in the emotional quicksand of a murder trial.

14 In none of these was the house filled with shadows, the weather dull and stormy throughout, the moor windswept, and the doors creaky. In fact, it is important in a story with sinister implications to use counterpoint, great contrast between situation and background, as we did in *Rope*.

15 John Dall is guilty of a bestial crime which the audience sees him perform with young Granger. But throughout the film he is grace and charm itself and his apartment is gay and beautifully appointed. And when Granger plays the piano he picks a light and childish piece, a minuet. Suspense involves contrast.

SELECTION VOCABULARY

plausible / factible *adjective* believable, reasonable

- What kinds of people does Hitchcock include as characters in his films?
- What kinds of things does Hitchcock say are not necessary to create suspense?

Reading Comprehension OPTIONAL

Have students complete the digital reading comprehension questions ✔ when they finish reading.

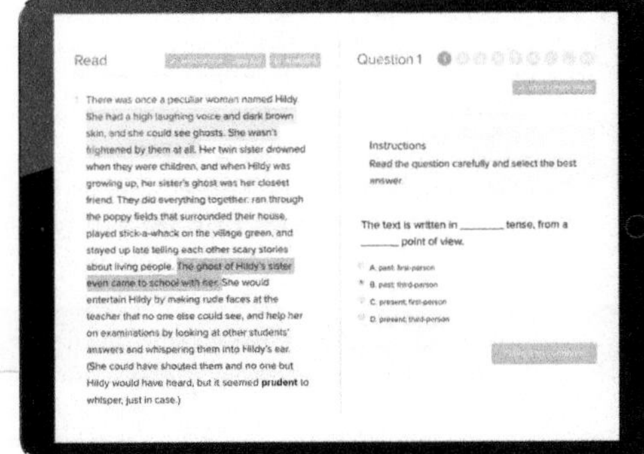

ANSWER KEY

QUESTION 1: C
QUESTION 2: A
QUESTION 3: A
QUESTION 4: C
QUESTION 5: *See chart.*

Suspenseful	Not Suspenseful
Allow the audience to know who has committed the crime.	Include characters with exaggerated personalities.
Make characters unknowingly interact with the criminal.	Keep the audience from knowing who the suspect is in the film.
Allow the audience to ponder when and how a crime will be resolved.	Puzzle the audience with details that cause confusion.

Connect and Extend OPTIONAL

CONNECT TO EXTENDED WRITING PROJECT

Students can use “Let 'Em Play God” as a mentor text for their Extended Writing Project. They may adopt some of Alfred Hitchcock's methods for creating suspense as they craft their own suspenseful narratives.

BEYOND THE BOOK

Performance: The Suspense Is Killing Me

Place students in small groups. Challenge them to construct a short, suspenseful scene that allows the audience to “play God,” or see everything. Students must collaboratively create the scenario and decide how they will tell the audience the secrets of the scene while keeping characters in the dark.

To reflect, follow each performance with a class conversation about the following questions:

- What secrets were clear to the audience but not the characters?
- How did you feel as you watched?
- What could the group have done to make the scene even more suspenseful?

Think Questions

Circulate as students answer Think Questions independently. Scaffolds for these questions are shown on the opposite page.

QUESTION 1: Textual Evidence

Hitchcock makes suspenseful movies. For example, he talks about "six characters involved in a mystery" and a man "who has been murdered" as part of the plot of this imaginary movie. He then shows the need to let audiences know information that characters do not know instead of confusing them. This creates a feeling of suspense.

QUESTION 2: Textual Evidence

Hitchcock summarizes the plot of his movie *Rope*. He then explains that "There is not a single detail to puzzle the audience. It is certainly not a whodunit for the simple reason that everyone out front knows who did it." He says that suspense is created when the audience knows secrets that the characters do not.

QUESTION 3: Textual Evidence

Hitchcock includes some questions he thinks the audience will ask, such as "Will the murderers break and give themselves away? When the victim does not show up for the party, will his father suspect? Will Jimmy get killed before he discovers the actual crime?" Such questions build suspense because they show that the audience does not know what will happen next.

QUESTION 4: Context Clues

I think *suspects* must mean "people who may be guilty of a crime." The word is used to describe characters in a movie in which a person has been killed. One of the characters must be the murderer, but the audience does not know which one it is.

QUESTION 5: Context Clues

I think *plausible* must mean "believable." The word is used to describe situations with "people that are real." I know that Hitchcock is talking about people in a movie, so I think he must mean people and situations that seem realistic or believable.

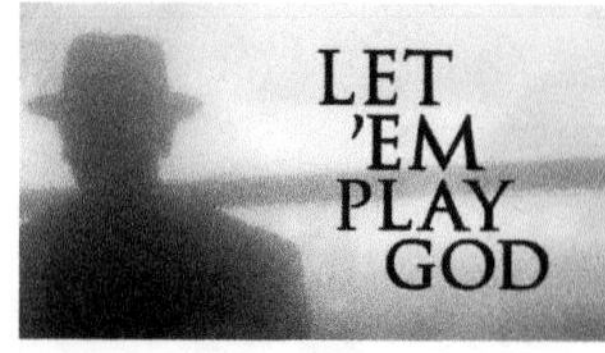

First Read

Read "Let 'Em Play God." After you read, complete the Think Questions below.

THINK QUESTIONS

1. What does the imaginary movie that Hitchcock describes in paragraphs 3 and 5 tell you about the kinds of movies he makes? Use evidence from the text to explain your answer.

2. Hitchcock says, "I do not believe that puzzling the audience is the essence of suspense." What kinds of examples does he use to help him support that statement?

3. What kinds of questions does Hitchcock hope his audience will ask while they watch the movie *Rope*? How do they build suspense? Refer to one or more details from the text to support your answer.

4. Find the word **suspects** in paragraph 3 of "Let 'Em Play God." Use context clues in the surrounding sentences, as well as the sentence in which the word appears, to determine the word's meaning. Write your definition here and identify clues that helped you figure out its meaning.

5. Use context clues to determine the meaning of **plausible** as it is used in paragraph 11 of "Let 'Em Play God." Write your definition here and identify clues that helped you figure out its meaning. Then check the meaning in a dictionary.

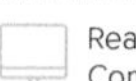

Think Questions

SCAFFOLDS

Use the scaffolds below to differentiate instruction for your ELL English Language Learners and A Approaching grade-level learners.

ELL **BEGINNING** Write a response using the word bank and sentence frames.

INTERMEDIATE Write a response using the sentence frames.

ADVANCED, ADVANCED HIGH Write a response using the Text-Dependent Question Guide.

A **APPROACHING** Write a response using the Text-Dependent Question Guide.

BEGINNING	INTERMEDIATE	APPROACHING / ADVANCED, ADVANCED HIGH
Word Bank	**Sentence Frames**	**Text-Dependent Question Guide**
party body real crime killers suspense unbelievable suspects happen mistake murdered characters believable	Hitchcock makes ____ films. He describes characters who are ____ in a crime.	1. • What details does Hitchcock give about the plot? • How does he want audiences to react? • What kinds of movies make audiences react like that?
	Rope is not a puzzler or whodunit film because the audience already knows who the ____ are. The suspense comes from the audience knowing information that the ____ do not know.	2. • What happens at the beginning of *Rope*? • Why isn't *Rope* a puzzler or whodunit film? • How does Hitchcock build suspense?
	In *Rope*, the killers murder someone and then have a ____. Audiences might wonder if the killers will make a ____. They might wonder if the guests will find the ____. These questions build suspense because the audience does not know what will ____.	3. • What happens in the plot of *Rope*? • What might the audience wonder about the killers? • What might the audience wonder about the guests?
	The mystery is who ____ the man. This gives me a clue that *suspects* means "people who may be guilty of a ____."	4. • Read: "Suppose, for instance, you have six characters involved in a mystery. A man has been murdered and all six are possible **suspects** but no one is sure including the audience." • What is the mystery described in the paragraph? • What does that tell me about the meaning of the word *suspects*?
	Hitchcock describes people who are ____. He wants to avoid characters who are ____. This gives me a clue that *plausible* means "____."	5. • Read: "In order to achieve this, one of the necessary ingredients of the formula is a series of **plausible** situations with people that are real. When characters are unbelievable you never get suspense, only surprise." • What kinds of people are described? • What kinds of characters does Hitchcock want to avoid? • What does that tell me about the meaning of the word *plausible*?

Skill: Author's Purpose and Point of View

Introduce the Skill

Watch the Concept Definition video and read the following definition with your students.

Author's purpose is the author's reason for writing. Authors typically write for one or more of the following purposes: to entertain, to inform, to persuade, or to explain something to readers. The **author's point of view** refers to the way the author looks at a topic or a subject, and his or her attitude toward it. In order to fully understand an author's purpose for writing, it is often necessary to identify the author's point of view on the subject he or she has chosen to write about, including how it is conveyed or expressed in the text. Sometimes an author's point of view is directly stated. When it is implied, the reader will need to look at textual evidence to infer the author's point of view.

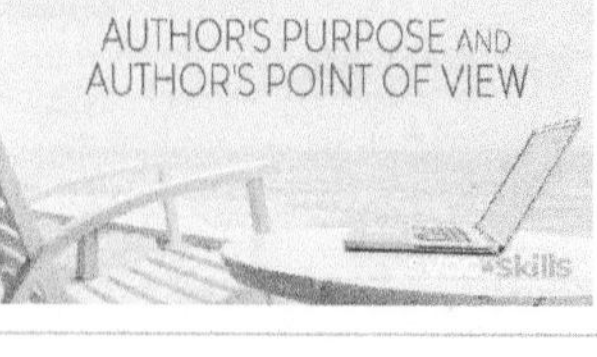

Skill: Author's Purpose and Point of View

Use the Checklist to analyze Author's Purpose and Point of View in "Let 'Em Play God." Refer to the sample student annotations about Author's Purpose and Point of View in the text.

••• CHECKLIST FOR AUTHOR'S PURPOSE AND POINT OF VIEW

In order to identify author's purpose and point of view, note the following:

- ✓ descriptions that present a complicated process in plain language, which may indicate that an author is writing to explain
- ✓ facts, statistics, and graphic aids, as these indicate that an author is writing to inform
- ✓ the author's use of emotional or figurative language, which may indicate the author is trying to persuade readers or stress an opinion
- ✓ the language the author uses, as figurative and emotional language can be clues to the author's point of view on a subject or topic
- ✓ whether the author acknowledges and responds to conflicting evidence or points of view that contradict his or her own

To determine the author's purpose and point of view in a text, consider the following questions:

- ✓ How does the author convey, or communicate, information in the text?
- ✓ Does the author use figurative or emotional language? What does this indicate?
- ✓ Are charts, graphs, maps, and other graphic aids included in the text? For what purpose?
- ✓ Does the author acknowledge contradictory or conflicting evidence or other points of view? How does the author respond to or address them?

TURN AND TALK

1. Think about the last text you wrote. Why did you write it? Was it to to entertain, inform, persuade, explain, or a combination of these?
2. What was the overall point of view that you wanted to share? How did you use details to communicate that message?

ELL SPEAKING FRAMES

- The last text I wrote was ____. I wrote it to (entertain / inform / persuade / explain).
- My point of view was ____.
- A detail I used to show that point of view was ____.

SKILL VOCABULARY

author's purpose / el propósito del autor ***noun*** an author's reason for writing, such as to entertain, to inform, or to persuade

author's point of view / punto de vista del autor ***noun*** an author looks at a topic or subject, and his or her attitude toward it

Let 'Em Play God

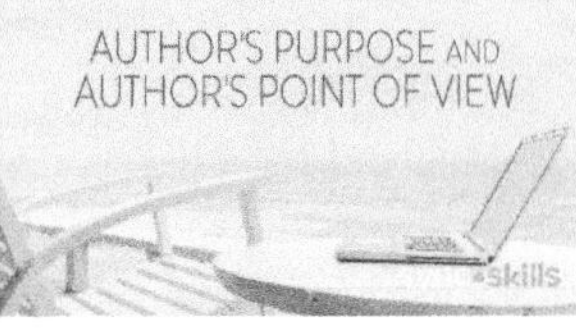

Skill: Author's Purpose and Point of View

Reread paragraphs 9 and 10 of "Let 'Em Play God." Then, using the Checklist on the previous page, answer the multiple-choice questions below.

YOUR TURN

1. Based on Hitchcock's explanation of suspense in paragraph 9, the reader can conclude that—
   - A. The author thinks that suspense is stronger when the characters know everything.
   - B. The author believes that whodunit films are not as suspenseful as thrillers.
   - C. The author prefers to keep suspenseful details from his audiences.
   - D. The author likes building suspense by telling the audience when characters are in danger.

2. The questions Hitchcock includes in paragraph 10 reveal his point of view. He believes that suspense builds when the audience—
   - A. knows how the film will end.
   - B. tries to guess what will happen.
   - C. is confused about the movie.
   - D. makes noise during the movie.

3. Based on the details Hitchcock gives in paragraphs 9 and 10, the reader can conclude that his purpose in writing these paragraphs is—
   - A. to explain.
   - B. to entertain and persuade.
   - C. to persuade only.
   - D. to entertain and inform.

SkillsTV

Project the SkillsTV episode and pause at the following times to prompt discussion:

0:52 What are some reasons why authors write?

1:11 How can you find clues to an author's purpose?

2:10 Why is it important to recognize the author's purpose?

Your Turn

Ask students to complete the Your Turn activity.

QUESTION 1

A. Incorrect. Hitchcock thinks that suspense is stronger when the audience knows everything.

B. Incorrect. Hitchcock says that his film is not a whodunit, but he does not suggest that whodunits are not as suspenseful as thrillers.

C. Incorrect. Hitchcock prefers to share suspenseful details with his audiences.

D. Correct. Hitchcock says that suspense comes from the audience knowing details that the characters do not.

QUESTION 2

A. Incorrect. Nothing in the paragraph indicates that the audience knows how the film will end.

B. Correct. Hitchcock includes the questions to show guesses the audience might make about what will happen next in the film.

C. Incorrect. Hitchcock is not suggesting that the audience is confused about the film.

D. Incorrect. Shouting does not cause suspense. Hitchcock wants the audience to shout because they are excited by the suspense.

QUESTION 3

A. Correct. In paragraphs 9 and 10, Hitchcock writes to explain how to create suspense.

B. Incorrect. In paragraphs 9 and 10, Hitchcock is not mainly writing to entertain and persuade. He is writing to explain how to create suspense.

C. Incorrect. In paragraphs 9 and 10, Hitchcock is not mainly writing to persuade. He is writing to explain how to create suspense.

D. Incorrect. In paragraphs 9 and 10, Hitchcock is not mainly writing to entertain and inform. He is writing to explain how to create suspense.

Your Turn

QUESTION 4

A. Incorrect. In this excerpt, Hitchcock explains how an audience reacts to a scene after they have already learned key information about it.

B. Correct. In this excerpt, Hitchcock explains how an audience can become held in suspense.

C. Incorrect. In this excerpt, Hitchcock shares an example of a scene that does not puzzle audiences.

D. Incorrect. In this excerpt, Hitchcock shares an example of a scene in which audiences know what has happened in the past, but they do not know what will happen next.

QUESTION 5

A. Incorrect. Paragraphs 9 and 10 include facts, but they do not include statistics and graphic aids.

B. Incorrect. Paragraphs 9 and 10 include possible questions from audiences, but they do not share their reviews of the film.

C. Correct. Paragraphs 9 and 10 provide details about how and why an audience develops suspense.

D. Incorrect. Paragraphs 9 and 10 do not include examples of evidence that conflicts with the author's point of view.

4. How does the author achieve his purpose in paragraphs 9 and 10?

   - ○ A. The author achieves his purpose by explaining how he shares information with the audience instead of the players.
   - ○ B. The author achieves his purpose by explaining how he has built suspense in a film that he is making.
   - ○ C. The author achieves his purpose by sharing an example of a film that interested audiences by puzzling them.
   - ○ D. The author achieves his purpose by sharing an example of a film in which audiences always know what will happen next.

5. Which of the following best describes the supporting details that the author includes in paragraphs 9 and 10?

   - ○ A. facts, statistics, and graphic aids
   - ○ B. questions from audience members with conflicting reviews of his film
   - ○ C. clear details about how and why an audience experiences suspense
   - ○ D. conflicting evidence and the author's response to it

Close Read

Reread "Let 'Em Play God." As you reread, complete the Skills Focus questions below. Then use your answers and annotations from the questions to help you complete the Write activity.

SKILLS FOCUS

1. Identify textual evidence that reveals Hitchcock's purpose for writing "Let 'Em Play God." Explain why you think Hitchcock is willing to expose his personal style for making films.
2. Identify textual evidence that reveals Hitchcock's point of view on creating suspense in a movie. Explain the effect his advice may have on future filmmakers.
3. Hitchcock gives clear recommendations for how to craft a successful mystery or suspense film. Identify examples of audiences' viewpoints that he acknowledges in his argument. Explain what these examples suggest about how Hitchcock attracts audiences to the mysterious.

WRITE

LITERARY ANALYSIS: What is Hitchcock's purpose and point of view in "Let 'Em Play God"? How does his point of view emerge throughout the essay? Write a response of at least 300 words. Support your writing with evidence from the text.

Close Read

Skills Focus

QUESTION 1: Author's Purpose and Point of View

See paragraph 5: Hitchcock is writing to explain what suspense is. He uses plain language to describe how he builds suspense so that readers can better understand the concept of suspense and follow his personal style.

QUESTION 2: Author's Purpose and Point of View

See paragraph 9.

QUESTION 3: Connect to Essential Question

See paragraph 10.

CHECK FOR SUCCESS

If students struggle to respond to Skills Focus question 1, ask them the following questions:

- What scene does Hitchcock describe in paragraph 4?
- How does he describe the effect of the scene in paragraph 5?
- Why does Hitchcock describe two different ways that audiences can react to a scene?
- What does that tell you about Hitchcock's purpose for writing?

Have students transition to read and annotate independently once they have successfully completed the first Skills Focus prompt.

Writer's Notebook

Connect to Essential Question: Give students time to reflect on how "Let 'Em Play God" connects to the unit's essential question "What attracts us to the mysterious?" by freewriting in their Writer's Notebooks.

Beginning & Intermediate

Read aloud the unit's essential question: "What attracts us to the mysterious?" Encourage students to draw their connections or allow students to write in their native language. Circulate the room, prompting students for their thoughts as they respond orally or through pantomime.

Advanced & Advanced High

Allow students to share their connections orally in pairs or small groups before freewriting.

Collaborative Conversation

SCAFFOLDS

Break students into collaborative conversation groups to discuss the Close Read prompt. Ask students to use the StudySyncTV episode as a model for their discussion. Remind them to reference their Skills Focus annotations in their discussion.

What is Hitchcock's purpose and point of view in "Let 'Em Play God"? How does his point of view emerge throughout the essay? Write a response of at least 300 words. Support your writing with evidence from the text.

Use the scaffolds below to differentiate instruction for your ELL English Language Learners and A Approaching grade-level learners.

ELL **BEGINNING, INTERMEDIATE** Use the discussion guide and speaking frames to facilitate the discussion with support from the teacher.

ADVANCED, ADVANCED HIGH Use the discussion guide and speaking frames to facilitate the discussion in mixed-level groups.

A **APPROACHING** Use the discussion guide to facilitate the discussion in mixed-level groups.

APPROACHING
ADVANCED, ADVANCED HIGH
BEGINNING, INTERMEDIATE

Discussion Guide	Speaking Frames
1. What does the audience need to be given in order to "play God"?	• The audience needs ____. • This is important because ____.
2. According to Hitchcock, what does not build suspense?	• ____ does not help build suspense. • This is important to Hitchcock's point of view because ____.
3. What does the audience learn at the beginning of the film *Rope*? What doesn't the audience know as they watch the film *Rope*?	• The audience learns ____. The audience does not know ____. • This helps build suspense because ____.

Review Prompt and Rubric

Before students begin writing, review the writing prompt and rubric with the class.

LITERARY ANALYSIS: What is Hitchcock's purpose and point of view in "Let 'Em Play God"? How does his point of view emerge throughout the essay? Write a response of at least 300 words. Support your writing with evidence from the text.

PROMPT GUIDE

- What is an author's purpose?
- What is an author's point of view?
- What is Hitchcock's purpose in writing this essay?
- What does Hitchcock say is necessary to develop suspense?
- How does Hitchcock's point of view emerge from the details he includes in a text?

Score	Author's Purpose and Point of View	Language and Conventions
4	The writer clearly analyzes and explains the author's purpose and development of his point of view. The writer provides exemplary analysis, using relevant evidence from the text.	The writer demonstrates a consistent command of grammar, punctuation, and usage conventions. Although minor errors may be evident, they do not detract from the fluency or the clarity of the writing.
3	The writer analyzes and explains the author's purpose and development of his point of view. The writer provides sufficient analysis, using relevant evidence from the text most of the time.	The writer demonstrates an adequate command of grammar, punctuation, and usage conventions. Although some errors may be evident, they create few (if any) disruptions in the fluency or the clarity of the writing.
2	The writer begins to analyze or explain the author's purpose and development of his point of view, but the analysis is incomplete. The writer uses relevant evidence from the text only some of the time.	The writer demonstrates a partial command of grammar, punctuation, and usage conventions. Some distracting errors may be evident, at times creating minor disruptions in the fluency or clarity of the writing.
1	The writer attempts to analyze or explain the author's purpose and development of his point of view, but the analysis is unsuccessful. The writer uses little or no relevant evidence from the text.	The writer demonstrates little or no command of grammar, punctuation, and usage conventions. Serious and persistent errors create disruptions in the fluency of the writing and sometimes interfere with meaning.
0	The writer does not provide a relevant response to the prompt or does not provide a response at all.	Serious and persistent errors overwhelm the writing and interfere with the meaning of the response as a whole, making the writer's meaning impossible to understand.

Write

Ask students to complete the writing assignment using textual evidence to support their answers.

Use the scaffolds below to differentiate instruction for your ELL English Language Learners and A Approaching grade-level learners.

ELL **BEGINNING** With the help of the word bank, write a response using paragraph frame 1.

INTERMEDIATE With the help of the word bank, write a response using paragraph frames 1 and 2.

ADVANCED, ADVANCED HIGH Write a response of differentiated length using the sentence starters.

A **APPROACHING** Write a response of differentiated length using the sentence starters.

BEGINNING: Word Bank, Paragraph Frame 1
INTERMEDIATE: Word Bank, Paragraph Frame 1, Paragraph Frame 2
ADVANCED, ADVANCED HIGH / APPROACHING: Sentence Starters

Word Bank	Paragraph Frame 1	Paragraph Frame 2	Sentence Starters
suspense guess killers point of view audiences	Hitchcock's ____ is that ____ is created when ____ know information that the characters do not know. In *Rope*, the ____ are revealed at the beginning of the film. Suspense comes when audiences try to ____ what will happen next. This example helps me to understand the author's point of view.	Hitchcock imagines that audiences ____ while watching suspense films like *Rope*. They feel ____ to find out ____. This suggests that suspense comes from ____, not from confusing the audience.	• Hitchcock's point of view is that suspense is created when . . . • The film *Rope* shows an example of this because . . . • At the beginning of the film, . . . • Then audiences try to guess . . . • This shows how suspense is developed because . . . • This helps me understand the author's point of view because . . .

Peer Review

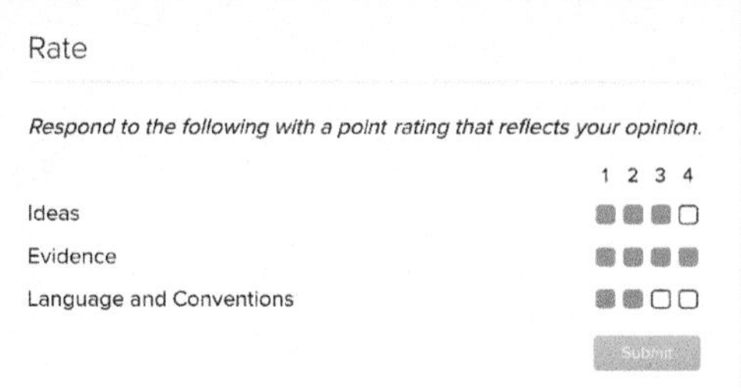

Students should submit substantive feedback to two peers using the review instructions below.

- How well does this response answer the prompt?
- How well does the writer support his or her claim with details and examples from the text?
- Which sentence in the writer's response most clearly explained his or her ideas about the author's point of view? Why?
- What did the writer do well in this response? What does the writer need to work on?

SENTENCE FRAMES

- Your response (completely / partly) answers the prompt because ____.
- You could answer the prompt more completely by ____.
- You (always / sometimes / rarely) support your claim by ____.
- The sentence that most clearly explains your idea is ____.
- One idea that needs more support is ____.
- My favorite part of your response is ____.

Sympathy

POETRY
Paul Laurence Dunbar
1899

Introduction

Paul Laurence Dunbar was one of the first nationally acclaimed African American poets. The son of people who were formerly enslaved, Dunbar was born after the Civil War and the abolition of slavery but at a time when African Americans continued to face the horrors of racism and discrimination. Dunbar was a gifted writer from a young age and published his first poems when he was only sixteen years old. His poem "Sympathy" includes the famous line "I know why the caged bird sings," the inspiration for the title of Maya Angelou's autobiography.

Paul Dunbar was the child of formerly enslaved people and was born after the abolition of slavery, but during a time when African Americans faced harsh racism and discrimination. In this poem, Dunbar uses the metaphor of a caged bird to portray the thoughts and feelings of African Americans. In the first stanza, he writes about what a caged bird feels when it sees the sun and the wind playing upon the grass. When the first bud opens and its scent steals into the cage, the bird is still stuck inside, longing to be free. In the second stanza, the bird beats itself bloody against the bars, because he would much rather be on a tree branch than clinging listlessly to the perch in his cage. In the third stanza, the bird sings even though he's bruised and sore. It is not a happy song, but rather a prayer from deep inside his heart, longing for freedom.

 Proficiency-leveled summaries and summaries in multiple languages are available digitally.

 Audio and audio text highlighting are available with this text.

COMPARING WITHIN AND ACROSS GENRES

 Creating suspense is a tactic that writers use to engage and thrill readers. The authors of "Sympathy" and *Ten Days in a Mad-House* achieve this effect through their works.

Access Complex Text

LEXILE: N/A **WORD COUNT:** 186

The following areas may be challenging for students, particularly ELL English Language Learners and A Approaching grade-level learners.

Prior Knowledge	Organization	Specific Vocabulary
• The poem was written during the post-Reconstruction era in the United States, when African Americans faced Jim Crow laws, segregation, discrimination, and harsh economic realities. • Explain that although African Americans had been liberated from slavery and given basic rights as citizens, they still faced discrimination and oppression.	• The poem is made up of three stanzas. There is a repeating phrase at the beginning and end of each stanza, the first stating, "I know what the caged bird feels," the second affirming, "I know why the caged bird beats his wing," and the third stanza asserting, "I know why the caged bird sings." • Explain to students that line repetition in poems is often used to emphasize meaning(s).	• Poetic and archaic vocabulary, such as *opes* ("open") and *fain* ("with pleasure; gladly"), may need defining. • Remind students to use context clues while reading, and also to use a dictionary to define unfamiliar words.

  ENGLISH LANGUAGE LEARNERS  APPROACHING GRADE LEVEL  BEYOND GRADE LEVEL

These icons identify differentiation strategies and scaffolded support for a variety of students. See the digital lesson plan for additional differentiation strategies and scaffolds.

Instructional Path

The print teacher's edition includes essential point-of-use instruction and planning tools. Complete lesson plans and program documents appear in your digital teacher account.

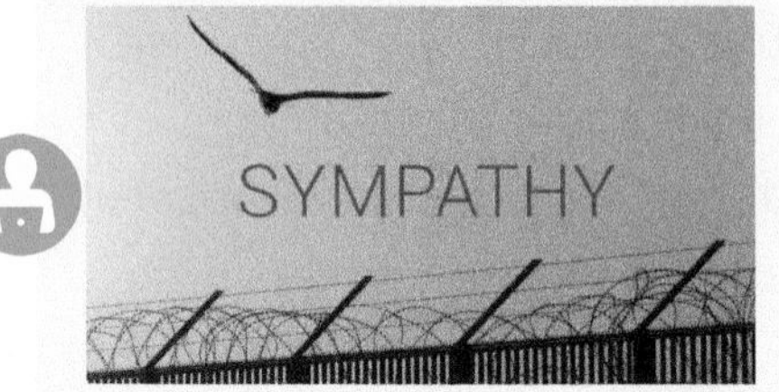

Independent Read: Sympathy

Objectives: After reading the text, students will write a short response that demonstrates their understanding of the poem through a personal connection.

Independent Read

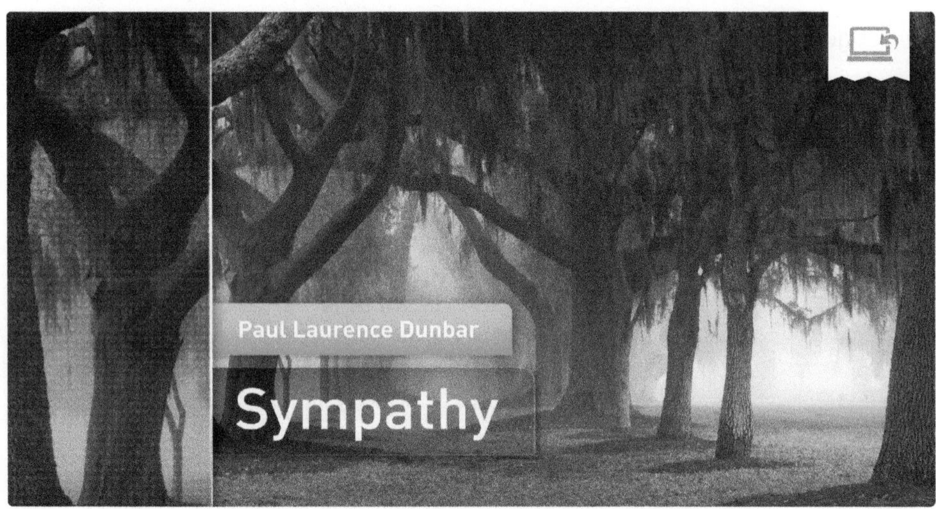

Introduce the Text

As a class, watch the video preview and have students read the introduction in pairs to make connections to the video preview.

- How do the images complement the narration? How does each make you feel?
- What kind of text are you about to read? How can you tell?

ELL **SPEAKING FRAMES**
- The video shows ____. This makes me wonder ____.
- I think the text will ____. I think this because ____.
- I predict that there will be ____ because ____.

Entry Point

As students prepare to read "Sympathy," share the following information with them to provide context.

- ✓ Paul Laurence Dunbar (1872–1906) was the son of two formerly enslaved people. His mother was emancipated at the end of the Civil War, and his father escaped during the war. They had both been enslaved in Kentucky but met and married in Ohio, where Dunbar was born and raised.
- ✓ Always an avid learner, Dunbar began writing poetry and stories at a young age. He was educated by his mother until he started high school as the only African American student. Dunbar was embraced by his all-white school and became the leader of several clubs and publications.
- ✓ The connections Dunbar forged through his literary fame helped him become involved in the civil rights movement of the late-19th century.

"I know what the caged bird feels!"

NOTES

I know what the caged bird feels, **alas**!
When the sun is bright on the upland slopes;
When the wind stirs soft through the springing grass,
And the river flows like a stream of glass;
When the first bird sings and the first bud opes[1],
And the faint perfume from its **chalice** steals—
I know what the caged bird feels!

I know why the caged bird beats his wing
Till its blood is red on the cruel bars;
For he must fly back to his perch and cling
When he fain[2] would be on the **bough** a-swing;
And a pain still throbs in the old, old scars
And they pulse again with a **keener** sting—
I know why he beats his wing!

I know why the caged bird sings, ah me,
When his wing is bruised and his bosom sore,—
When he beats his bars and he would be free;
It is not a carol of joy or glee,
But a prayer that he sends from his heart's deep core,
But a plea, that upward to Heaven he flings—
I know why the caged bird sings!

1. **opes** an archaic way of saying "opens"
2. **fain** gladly

Analyze Vocabulary Using Context Clues

As students read the text, ask them to make predictions about each bold vocabulary word based on the context clues in the sentence.

TEXT TALK

What does the speaker describe in the first stanza, in contrast to the caged bird?

See lines 2–5: The speaker contrasts the caged bird with the freedom and openness of nature: the sun, wind, river, "first bird," and "first bud."

What does the caged bird do to himself in the second stanza?

See lines 8 and 9: The bird beats his wings against the bars of the cage until they bleed.

What type of song does the caged bird sing in the third stanza?

See lines 19 and 20: The bird sings a "prayer" and a "plea" that it could be free.

B Ask each Beyond grade-level student to write one additional discussion question. Then have one or two students facilitate a discussion, using their questions to guide the conversation.

V SELECTION VOCABULARY

alas / ay *interjection* an expression of sadness, disappointment, or regret

ELL
- What is the speaker describing when he uses the word *alas*?
- What emotion might this word express?

chalice / el cáliz *noun* the bowl-shaped interior of a flower

ELL
- What is the chalice a part of?
- What sense does the chalice appeal to?

WRITE

PERSONAL RESPONSE: Paul Laurence Dunbar uses the imagery of a caged bird to communicate feelings of oppression and a lack of freedom. What images from the poem were effective in communicating these feelings? How does it make you feel? Can you sympathize with someone who feels trapped like this? Choose several moments in the poem that you felt were effective and explain your reaction. Make sure to include details from the poem and your own thoughts and feelings in your response.

SELECTION VOCABULARY

bough / la rama ***noun*** a tree branch

- Where is the bird forced to fly back to?
- Where might the bird rather be sitting?

keen / cortante ***adjective*** sharper; more intense

- How would the sting of a scar feel?
- How would the sting of many scars feel?

Reading Comprehension OPTIONAL

Have students complete the digital reading comprehension questions ✓ when they finish reading.

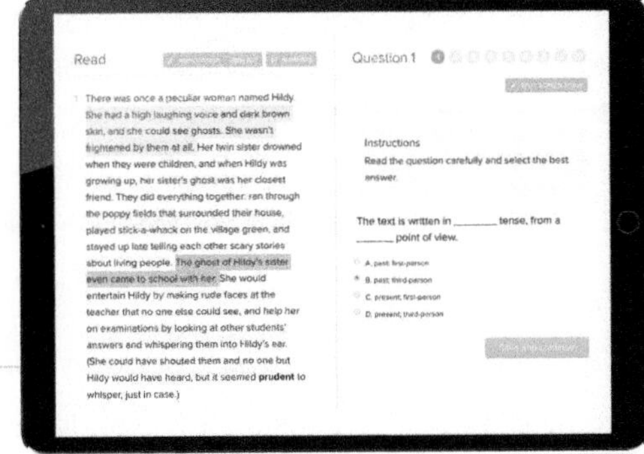

ANSWER KEY

QUESTION 1: A
QUESTION 2: D
QUESTION 3: C
QUESTION 4: B
QUESTION 5: *See chart.*

Unused Phrases	Condition of Bird
the wind stirs soft	pain still throbs
the faint perfume	his wing is bruised
sun is bright	his bosom sore

Connect and Extend OPTIONAL

CONNECT TO EXTENDED WRITING PROJECT

Students can find inspiration from "Sympathy" for their suspenseful narratives. Have them work to create images that elicit strong emotions in readers and help them sympathize and perhaps even identify with characters.

BEYOND THE BOOK

Photography: Where do you see the word *sympathy*?

Take students outside your classroom and work in pairs or groups of three. Give students 10 minutes to take a series of three photographs that are inspired by the emotions or descriptions in the poem. After all groups have finished, return to the classroom to have them share their images as their group rereads the poem aloud for the class.

To reflect, ask groups:

- How do your images reflect the feeling or emotion of the poem?
- What words might you use to describe your images?

Collaborative Conversation

Post the writing prompt to generate a discussion in small groups. Ask students to first break down the prompt before they discuss relevant ideas and textual evidence.

Paul Laurence Dunbar uses the imagery of a caged bird to communicate feelings of oppression and a lack of freedom. What images from the poem were effective in communicating these feelings? How does it make you feel? Can you sympathize with someone who feels trapped like this? Choose several moments in the poem that you felt were effective and explain your reaction. Make sure to include details from the poem and your own thoughts and feelings in your response.

Use the scaffolds below to differentiate instruction for your ELL English Language Learners and A Approaching grade-level learners.

ELL **BEGINNING, INTERMEDIATE** Use the discussion guide and speaking frames to facilitate the discussion with support from the teacher.

ADVANCED, ADVANCED HIGH Use the discussion guide and speaking frames to facilitate the discussion in mixed-level groups.

A **APPROACHING** Use the discussion guide to facilitate the discussion in mixed-level groups.

APPROACHING
ADVANCED, ADVANCED HIGH
BEGINNING, INTERMEDIATE

Discussion Guide	Speaking Frames
1. What image helped to show show a lack of freedom?	• One image that showed lack of freedom is ____.
2. How did this image make you feel?	• This image made me feel ____.
3. Can you sympathize with someone who feels trapped like this?	• I can sympathize because ____.

Review Prompt and Rubric

Before students begin working, review with the class the writing prompt and rubric.

PERSONAL RESPONSE: Paul Laurence Dunbar uses the imagery of a caged bird to communicate feelings of oppression and a lack of freedom. What images from the poem were effective in communicating these feelings? How does it make you feel? Can you sympathize with someone who feels trapped like this? Choose several moments in the poem that you felt were effective and explain your reaction. Make sure to include details from the poem and your own thoughts and feelings in your response.

PROMPT GUIDE

- What image helped to show a lack of freedom?
- How did this image make you feel?
- Can you sympathize with someone who feels trapped like this?

Score	Personal Response	Language and Conventions
4	The writer clearly explains his or her personal connection to the text, using relevant evidence from the text as needed.	The writer demonstrates a consistent command of grammar, punctuation, and usage conventions. Although minor errors may be evident, they do not detract from the fluency or the clarity of the writing.
3	The writer sufficiently explains his or her personal connection to the text, using relevant evidence from the text most of the time.	The writer demonstrates an adequate command of grammar, punctuation, and usage conventions. Although some errors may be evident, they create few (if any) disruptions in the fluency or the clarity of the writing.
2	The writer begins to explain his or her personal connection to the text, but the explanation is incomplete. The writer uses relevant evidence from the text only some of the time.	The writer demonstrates a partial command of grammar, punctuation, and usage conventions. Some distracting errors may be evident, at times creating minor disruptions in the fluency or clarity of the writing.
1	The writer attempts to explain his or her personal connection to the text, but the explanation is not successful. The writer uses little or no relevant evidence from the text.	The writer demonstrates little or no command of grammar, punctuation, and usage conventions. Serious and persistent errors create disruptions in the fluency of the writing and sometimes interfere with meaning.
0	The writer does not provide a relevant response to the prompt or does not provide a response at all.	Serious and persistent errors overwhelm the writing and interfere with the meaning of the response as a whole, making the writer's meaning impossible to understand.

Write

SCAFFOLDS

Ask students to complete the writing assignment using textual evidence to support their answers.

Use the scaffolds below to differentiate instruction for your ELL English Language Learners and A Approaching grade-level learners.

ELL **BEGINNING** With the help of the word bank, write a response using paragraph frame 1.

INTERMEDIATE With the help of the word bank, write a response using paragraph frames 1 and 2.

ADVANCED, ADVANCED HIGH Write a response of differentiated length using the sentence starters.

A **APPROACHING** Write a response of differentiated length using the sentence starters.

BEGINNING / INTERMEDIATE / ADVANCED, ADVANCED HIGH / APPROACHING

Word Bank	Paragraph Frame 1	Paragraph Frame 2	Sentence Starters
sympathize sorry blood trapped free	An effective image from "Sympathy" is the red ____ from the bird beating its wings. The bird wants to be ____, and the speaker does too. The image made me feel ____ for the bird and the speaker. I can ____ with them. It is hard to feel ____.	Another effective image in the poem is ____. This image tells me ____. This image makes me ____. When I think about the speaker, I ____.	• One image that is effective is . . . • It really conveys . . . • This image made me feel . . . • This image made me realize . . . • I can sympathize with the speaker because . . .

Peer Review

Students should submit substantive feedback to two peers using the review instructions below.

- How well does this response answer the prompt?
- Which of the author's comments inspired you to think differently or more deeply about the text?
- What did the writer do well in this response? What does the writer need to work on?

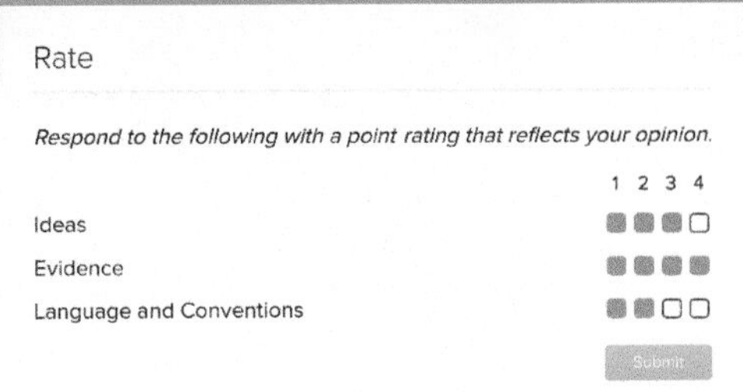

SENTENCE FRAMES

- You were able to (completely / partly / almost) answer the prompt.
- You could answer the prompt more completely by ____.
- I thought differently or more deeply about the poem after reading ____.
- My favorite part of your response is ____.

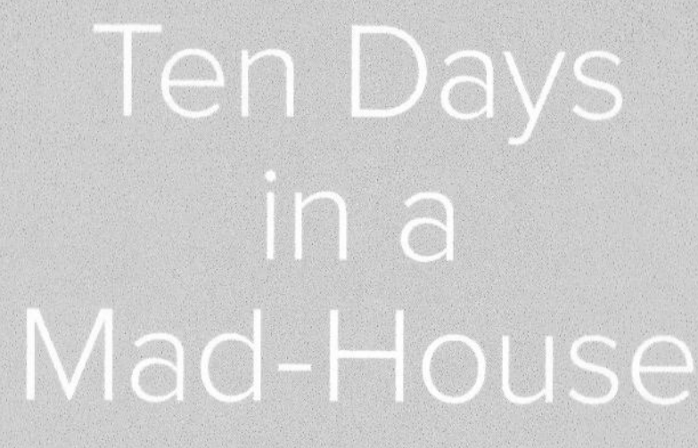

Ten Days in a Mad-House

INFORMATIONAL TEXT
Nellie Bly
1887

Introduction

In 1887, reporter Nellie Bly (1864–1922) went on an undercover assignment for a New York newspaper, the *World*, for which she feigned insanity in order to get committed to the Blackwell's Island Insane Asylum. Her exposé of the conditions inside the Women's Lunatic Asylum launched a criminal investigation that later led to an $850,000 budget increase from the Department of Public Charities and Corrections. *Ten Days in a Mad-House* began as a series of newspaper articles and was eventually published as a book.

In this article from 1887, journalist Nellie Bly fakes insanity in order to report on the conditions at Wards Island, a New York hospital for the mentally ill. After causing a disturbance at her lodging house—owned by Mrs. Stanard—Bly is picked up by the police and taken to court in order to obtain a judgment of her sanity. The judge has sympathy for Bly because she is well-dressed, speaks perfect English, and is clearly not lower class. Bly hopes to be sent to Wards Island, but she is worried that her appearance will prevent the judge from sending her there. Ultimately, the judge follows the suggestion of one of the court officers and sentences her to the island. Mrs. Stanard wails in grief over Nellie's fate, but Bly secretly rejoices.

 Proficiency-leveled summaries and summaries in multiple languages are available digitally.

 Audio and audio text highlighting are available with this text.

COMPARING WITHIN AND ACROSS GENRES

 Journalist Nellie Bly, on assignment for her paper in 1887, goes undercover to get inside an insane asylum, or mad-house, to report on what she finds there. The result is the book *Ten Days in a Mad-House*. What draws her to this mysterious other world? What will she find?

Access Complex Text

LEXILE: 1170L **WORD COUNT:** 2,002

The following areas may be challenging for students, particularly ELL English Language Learners and A Approaching grade-level learners.

Organization	Specific Vocabulary	Prior Knowledge
• The first-person narrative switches back and forth between the account of Bly's feigned insanity and her thoughts regarding the success of her scheme. Readers may benefit by highlighting Bly's thoughts to separate them from the insanity scheme.	• Some idiomatic expressions, such as a description of a judge "dealing out the milk of human kindness by wholesale," may present challenges for some readers. In this case, it refers to a judge who is exceedingly kind.	• Students may be unfamiliar with investigative journalism. • Students may be unfamiliar with the practice of court-ordered assignment to an insane asylum without the commission of a crime.

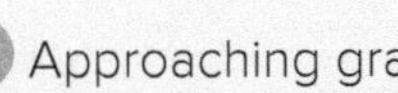

SCAFFOLDS  ENGLISH LANGUAGE LEARNERS  APPROACHING GRADE LEVEL  BEYOND GRADE LEVEL

These icons identify differentiation strategies and scaffolded support for a variety of students. See the digital lesson plan for additional differentiation strategies and scaffolds.

Instructional Path

The print teacher's edition includes essential point-of-use instruction and planning tools. Complete lesson plans and program documents appear in your digital teacher account.

First Read: Ten Days in a Mad-House

Objectives: After an initial reading and discussion of the text, students will be able to use the reading comprehension strategy of making and confirming predictions, use context clues to define new vocabulary, and demonstrate comprehension by responding to questions using textual evidence.

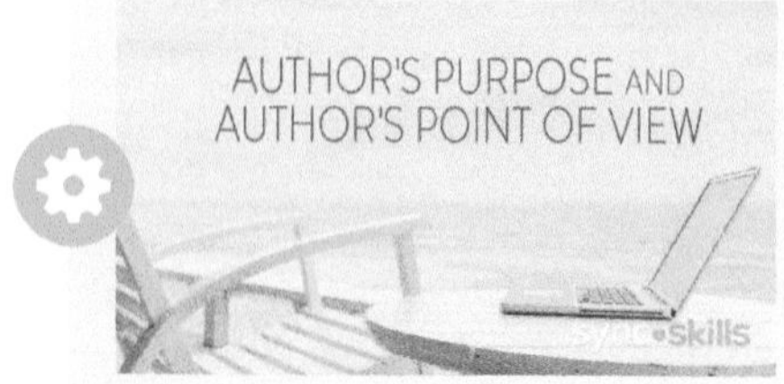

Skill: Author's Purpose and Point of View

Objectives: After rereading and discussing a model of close reading, students will be able to analyze an author's purpose and point of view within a text.

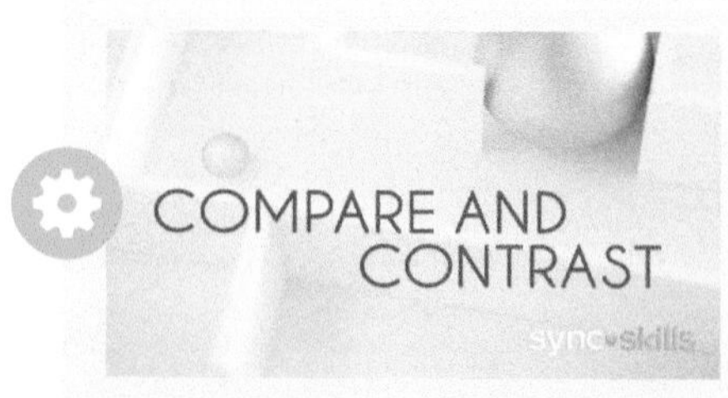

Skill: Compare and Contrast

Objectives: After rereading and discussing a model of close reading, students will be able to demonstrate an understanding of texts by comparing and contrasting sources within and across genres.

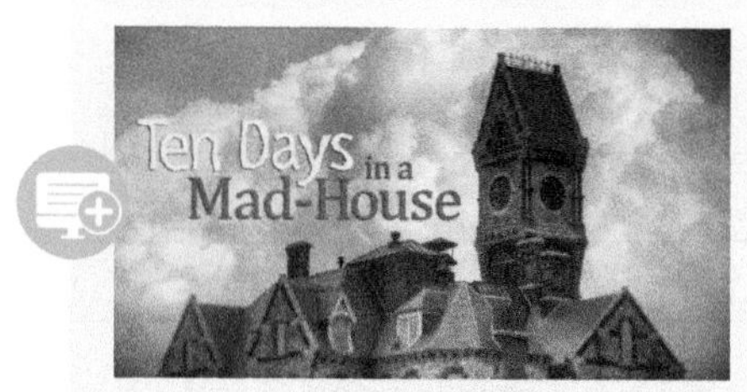

Close Read: Ten Days in a Mad-House

Objectives: After engaging in a close reading and discussion of the text, students will be able to analyze author's purpose and point of view and to compare and contrast texts in a short, written response.

Progress Monitoring

Opportunities to Learn	Opportunities to Demonstrate Learning	Opportunities to Reteach
Author's Purpose and Point of View		
Skill: Author's Purpose and Point of View	Skill: Author's Purpose and Point of View • Your Turn Close Read • Skills Focus • Write	Unit 5 Skill: Author's Purpose and Point of View - Long Walk to Freedom Spotlight Skill: Author's Purpose and Point of View
Compare and Contrast		
Skill: Compare and Contrast	Skill: Compare and Contrast • Your Turn Close Read • Skills Focus • Write	Unit 4 Skill: Compare and Contrast - Gaming Communities Spotlight Skill: Compare and Contrast

First Read

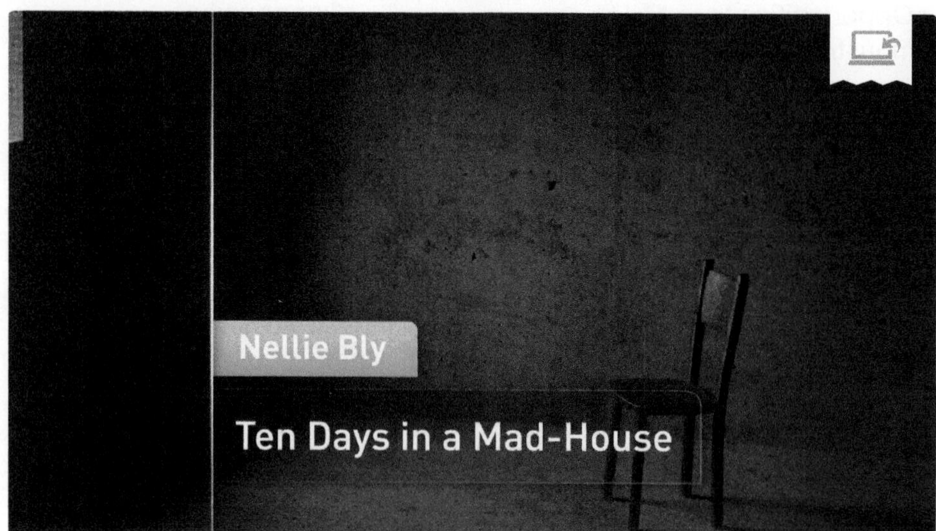

Introduce the Text

As a class, watch the video preview and have students read the introduction in pairs to make connections to the video preview.

To activate prior knowledge and experiences, ask students:

- How do you think the images and music from the video are preparing you for the selection you are about to read? What makes you think that?
- What is one prediction you can make about the selection you're going to read?

SPEAKING FRAMES

- The ____ in the video makes me think ____.
- The video shows ____. This makes me think about ____.
- I think the text will ____. I think this because ____.
- I predict that there will be ____. I believe this because ____.

Entry Point

As students prepare to read an excerpt from *Ten Days in a Mad-House*, share the following information with them to provide context.

- ✓ Nellie Bly (1864–1922) was an investigative journalist who started her career in Pittsburgh. She went on to document her undercover investigation of the Women's Lunatic Asylum in New York City, later published as the book *Ten Days in a Mad-House*. She followed up this assignment by traveling around the world in 72 days—a world record. Her journey was documented and published in the *New York World* newspaper. In later life, she became a profitable inventor and continued her journalism career by covering the Women's Suffrage movement.
- ✓ The Women's Lunatic Asylum on Blackwell's Island (now Roosevelt Island) in New York City was well known for the cruel mistreatment of the women committed there.
- ✓ Following the excerpt presented here, Bly is successfully admitted to the asylum and recounts the horrors she experiences there, including interviews with many women who had been forcibly admitted but appear completely sane.

"At last the question of my sanity or insanity was to be decided."

NOTES

Chapter IV: Judge Duffy and the Police

1 "Are you Nellie Brown?" asked the officer. I said I supposed I was. "Where do you come from?" he asked. I told him I did not know, and then Mrs. Stanard gave him a lot of information about me—told him how strangely I had acted at her home; how I had not slept a wink all night, and that in her opinion I was a poor unfortunate who had been driven crazy by inhuman treatment. There was some discussion between Mrs. Stanard and the two officers, and Tom Bockert was told to take us down to the court in a car.

2 "Come along," Bockert said, "I will find your trunk[1] for you." We all went together, Mrs. Stanard, Tom Bockert, and myself. I said it was very kind of them to go with me, and I should not soon forget them. As we walked along I kept up my refrain about my trunks, injecting occasionally some remark about the dirty condition of the streets and the curious character of the people we met on the way. "I don't think I have ever seen such people before," I said. "Who are they?" I asked, and my companions looked upon me with expressions of pity, evidently believing I was a foreigner, an emigrant or something of the sort. They told me that the people around me were working people. I remarked once more that I thought there were too many working people in the world for the amount of work to be done, at which remark Policeman P. T. Bockert eyed me closely, evidently thinking that my mind was gone for good. We passed several other policemen, who generally asked my sturdy guardians what was the matter with me. By this time quite a number of ragged children were following us too, and they passed remarks about me that were to me original as well as amusing.

3 "What's she up for?" "Say, kop, where did ye get her?" "Where did yer pull 'er?" "She's a daisy!"

4 Poor Mrs. Stanard was more frightened than I was. The whole situation grew interesting, but I still had fears for my fate before the judge.

1. **trunk** (archaic) a large piece of luggage

Analyze Vocabulary Using Context Clues

In paragraph 15, focus on the sentences that use and relate to the word *incredulous*. Point out these context clues:

1. First, I notice the word *incredulous* is an adjective and describes how Bly is trying to look.
2. When I read the sentences again, I see that she is arguing with an officer. He is trying to tell her that she is in New York, and she is pretending to not know where she is.
3. Since Bly is trying to act like she doesn't believe the officer, and *incredulous* is describing how she is trying to appear, I think *incredulous* must mean "not willing to believe something."

Skills Focus

QUESTION 1: Author's Purpose and Point of View

The police officers want to know what is wrong with Bly. The children want to know what she did. Their reactions show that people taken into custody are treated like they are already guilty.

TEXT TALK

Why does Mrs. Stanard ask the officers for help?

See paragraph 1: Mrs. Stanard believes that Bly is mentally ill and needs help.

What reason does Tom Bockert give to Bly for bringing her to the courthouse?

See paragraph 2: He says he will help her find her missing trunks.

5 At last we came to a low building, and Tom Bockert kindly volunteered the information: "Here's the express office. We shall soon find those trunks of yours."

6 The entrance to the building was surrounded by a curious crowd and I did not think my case was bad enough to permit me passing them without some remark, so I asked if all those people had lost their trunks.

7 "Yes," he said, "nearly all these people are looking for trunks."

8 I said, "They all seem to be foreigners, too." "Yes," said Tom, "they are all foreigners just landed. They have all lost their trunks, and it takes most of our time to help find them for them."

9 We entered the courtroom. It was the Essex Market Police Courtroom. At last the question of my sanity or insanity was to be decided. Judge Duffy sat behind the high desk, wearing a look which seemed to indicate that he was dealing out the milk of human kindness by wholesale. I rather feared I would not get the fate I sought, because of the kindness I saw on every line of his face, and it was with rather a sinking heart that I followed Mrs. Stanard as she answered the summons to go up to the desk, where Tom Bockert had just given an account of the affair.

The Essex Market Police Court, Essex Street, Lower East Side, New York City, circa 1857

10 "Come here," said an officer. "What is your name?"

11 "Nellie Brown," I replied, with a little accent. "I have lost my trunks, and would like if you could find them."

12 "When did you come to New York?" he asked.

13 "I did not come to New York," I replied (while I added, mentally, "because I have been here for some time.").

14 "But you are in New York now," said the man.

15 "No," I said, looking as **incredulous** as I thought a crazy person could, "I did not come to New York."

TEXT TALK

What is Bly's first impression of the judge?

See paragraph 9: He looks kind.

SELECTION VOCABULARY

incredulous / incrédulo/a ***adjective*** not willing to admit or accept something as true COGNATE

16 "That girl is from the west," he said, in a tone that made me tremble. "She has a western accent."

17 Someone else who had been listening to the brief dialogue here asserted that he had lived south and that my accent was southern, while another officer was positive it was eastern. I felt much relieved when the first spokesman turned to the judge and said:

18 "Judge, here is a peculiar case of a young woman who doesn't know who she is or where she came from. You had better attend to it at once."

19 I **commenced** to shake with more than the cold, and I looked around at the strange crowd about me, composed of poorly dressed men and women with stories printed on their faces of hard lives, abuse and poverty. Some were consulting eagerly with friends, while others sat still with a look of utter hopelessness. Everywhere was a sprinkling of well-dressed, well-fed officers watching the scene passively and almost **indifferently.** It was only an old story with them. One more unfortunate added to a long list which had long since ceased to be of any interest or concern to them.

20 "Come here, girl, and lift your veil," called out Judge Duffy, in tones which surprised me by a harshness which I did not think from the kindly face he possessed.

21 "Who are you speaking to?" I inquired, in my stateliest manner.

22 "Come here, my dear, and lift your veil. You know the Queen of England, if she were here, would have to lift her veil," he said, very kindly.

23 "That is much better," I replied. "I am not the Queen of England, but I'll lift my veil."

24 As I did so the little judge looked at me, and then, in a very kind and gentle tone, he said: "My dear child, what is wrong?"

25 "Nothing is wrong except that I have lost my trunks, and this man," indicating Policeman Bockert, "promised to bring me where they could be found."

26 "What do you know about this child?" asked the judge, sternly, of Mrs. Stanard, who stood, pale and trembling, by my side.

27 "I know nothing of her except that she came to the home yesterday and asked to remain overnight."

28 "The home! What do you mean by the home?" asked Judge Duffy, quickly.

NOTES

Skill: Author's Purpose and Point of View

The hopeless people are at the courthouse because they need help, but it looks like the officers are not willing to help them. I think the author's point of view here is that not enough is being done to help people in need.

Skills Focus

QUESTION 2: Author's Purpose and Point of View

The officer uses a forceful tone. This shows that he does not treat mentally ill people very well.

Author's Purpose and Point of View

How did the reader determine the author's point of view?

The reader noted that the author's descriptions of two groups of people suggest that the officers are not willing to help people in need.

TEXT TALK

How does the judge respond to Bly at first?

See paragraphs 20–24: At first the judge is harsh with Bly. Then he is nicer to her after she pretends she doesn't know to whom he's talking.

SELECTION VOCABULARY

commence / comenzar ***verb*** to take the first step or steps in carrying out an action; to start or begin COGNATE

- What did she "commence" to do?
- Was she always doing that? Or did she just start?

indifferent / indiferente ***adjective*** not at all interested in something COGNATE

ELL

- Who is behaving indifferently?
- How do they feel about what is happening?

Text to World

Use the activity below to differentiate instruction for your B Beyond grade-level learners.

To write *Ten Days in a Mad-House*, Nellie Bly went undercover to investigate the treatment of the mentally ill in 1887. Her reports led to a criminal investigation and budget increase of $850,000 from the Department of Public Charities and Corrections. Ask students to conduct informal research to answer the following questions: How else did Nellie Bly's reporting change the way the people with mental illnesses were treated? How can you see the impact of her work in the way people with mental illnesses are treated today?

29 "It is a temporary home kept for working women at No. 84 Second Avenue."

30 "What is your position there?"

31 "I am assistant matron[2]."

32 "Well, tell us all you know of the case."

33 "When I was going into the home yesterday I noticed her coming down the avenue. She was all alone. I had just got into the house when the bell rang and she came in. When I talked with her she wanted to know if she could stay all night, and I said she could. After awhile she said all the people in the house looked crazy, and she was afraid of them. Then she would not go to bed, but sat up all the night."

34 "Had she any money?"

35 "Yes," I replied, answering for her, "I paid her for everything, and the eating was the worst I ever tried."

36 There was a general smile at this, and some murmurs of "She's not so crazy on the food question."

37 "Poor child," said Judge Duffy, "she is well dressed, and a lady. Her English is perfect, and I would stake everything on her being a good girl. I am positive she is somebody's darling."

38 At this announcement everybody laughed, and I put my handkerchief over my face and endeavored to choke the laughter that threatened to spoil my plans, in despite of my **resolutions.**

39 "I mean she is some woman's darling," hastily amended the judge. "I am sure someone is searching for her. Poor girl, I will be good to her, for she looks like my sister, who is dead."

40 There was a hush for a moment after this announcement, and the officers glanced at me more kindly, while I silently blessed the kind-hearted judge, and hoped that any poor creatures who might be afflicted as I pretended to be should have as kindly a man to deal with as Judge Duffy.

41 "I wish the reporters were here," he said at last. "They would be able to find out something about her."

2. **matron** a woman in charge of managing students at a school or residents of a boarding house

TEXT TALK

Why does the judge wish reporters were there?

See paragraphs 39–41: He believes that someone must be searching for Bly, and he thinks reporters could help figure out who she is.

B Ask each Beyond grade-level student to write one additional discussion question. Then have one or two students facilitate a discussion, using their questions to guide the conversation.

SELECTION VOCABULARY

resolution / la resolución *noun* determination COGNATE

- What are Bly and the crowd doing?
- Did Bly mean to do this?

42 I got very much frightened at this, for if there is anyone who can ferret out a mystery it is a reporter. I felt that I would rather face a mass of expert doctors, policemen, and detectives than two bright specimens of my craft, so I said:

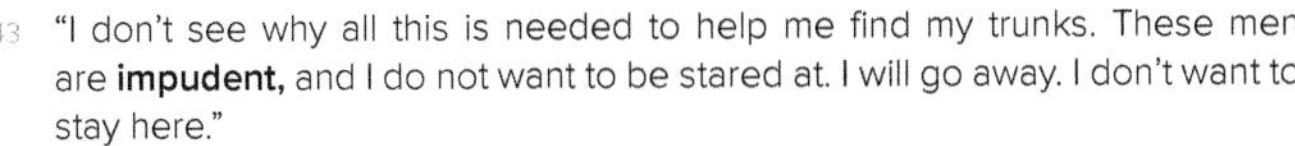

43 "I don't see why all this is needed to help me find my trunks. These men are **impudent,** and I do not want to be stared at. I will go away. I don't want to stay here."

44 So saying, I pulled down my veil and secretly hoped the reporters would be detained elsewhere until I was sent to the asylum.

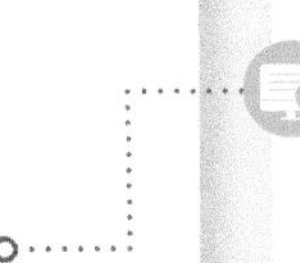

45 "I don't know what to do with the poor child," said the worried judge. "She must be taken care of."

46 "Send her to the Island," suggested one of the officers.

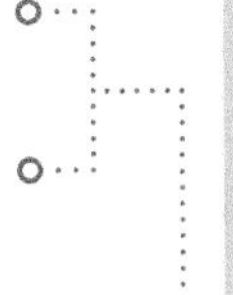

47 "Oh, don't!" said Mrs. Stanard, in evident alarm. "Don't! She is a lady and it would kill her to be put on the Island."

48 For once I felt like shaking the good woman. To think the Island was just the place I wanted to reach and here she was trying to keep me from going there! It was very kind of her, but rather provoking under the circumstances.

Skills Focus

QUESTION 3: Author's Purpose and Point of View

Bly is worried that reporters will figure out the truth about who she is. That shows that there is a purpose to her disguise.

Skills Focus

QUESTION 5: Connect to Essential Question

The Island seems to be the place where women are sent when officers don't know what else to do with them. Mrs. Stanard's strong reaction to the mention of the Island hints that it is not good place, but the officer wants to send Bly there without a second thought. Bly is curious to figure out what is happening at the asylum and the women who get sent there. This shows that people are attracted to the mysterious because they want to try to figure it out.

Skills Focus

QUESTION 4: Compare and Contrast

Mrs. Stanard panics at the idea of sending Bly to the Island. This suggests that the asylum is not a good place. This is similar to the "Sympathy" speaker's feelings, because it shows that being locked up or imprisoned is a bad thing. However, Bly wants to go to the Island. This is a strong contrast to the speaker's feelings in the poem because he wants to escape his own kind of imprisonment.

SELECTION VOCABULARY

impudent / insolente ***adjective*** bold and disrespectful

ELL
- Who is described as "impudent"?
- What is he or she doing? Does Bly view this person's actions as positive or negative?

Think Questions

Circulate as students answer Think Questions independently. Scaffolds for these questions are shown on the opposite page.

QUESTION 1: Textual Evidence

Bly pretends to be a mentally ill woman named Nellie Brown. She writes that she has convinced Mrs. Stanard that she is "a poor unfortunate who has been driven crazy by inhumane treatment." She hopes that she will be sent to "the Island," which is an asylum—a place for mentally ill people.

QUESTION 2: Textual Evidence

Answers will vary, but may include the following textual evidence that describes behaviors Bly adopts when she is pretending to be mentally ill:

- ". . . how strangely I had acted at her home; how I had not slept a wink all night;"
- "'No,' I said, looking as incredulous as I thought a crazy person could, 'I did not come to New York.'"

QUESTION 3: Textual Evidence

Bly purposefully answers the judges' questions rudely in the hopes that he will send her to the asylum. She fears that she has made a mistake when the judge seems charmed by her. The judge says he wishes a reporter could help find her family, which makes Bly worry that he will not send her to the Island as planned.

QUESTION 4: Context Clues

I think *indifferently* must mean "to not care or be interested." The word is used to describe the actions of the officers, who are watching "passively." The text also says that the events "ceased to be of any interest or concern to them."

QUESTION 5: Context Clues

I think *impudent* must mean "disrespectful." Bly calls the men "impudent" because they are staring at her, even though she does not want to be stared at. That is disrespectful behavior.

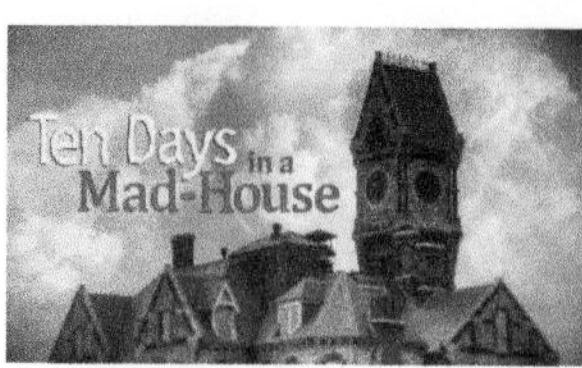

First Read

Read *Ten Days in a Mad-House*. After you read, complete the Think Questions below.

THINK QUESTIONS

1. Nellie Bly is a reporter. Who does she pretend to be, and why? Cite textual evidence from the selection to support your answer.
2. How does Bly alter her behavior to convince Mrs. Stanard, Tom Bockert, and the officers that she is mentally ill? Cite textual evidence from the selection to support your answer.
3. Write two to three sentences describing how Bly reacts to the judge's questions and comments.
4. Use context clues to determine the meaning of **indifferently** as it is used in paragraph 19 of the excerpt from *Ten Days in a Mad-House*. Write your definition here, and identify clues that help you figure out its meaning.
5. Use context clues to determine the meaning of **impudent** as it is used in paragraph 43 of the excerpt from *Ten Days in a Mad-House*. Write your definition here, and identify clues that helped you figure out the word's meaning.

SCAFFOLDS

Think Questions

Use the scaffolds below to differentiate instruction for your ELL English Language Learners and A Approaching grade-level learners.

ELL **BEGINNING** Write a response using the word bank and sentence frames.

INTERMEDIATE Write a response using the sentence frames.

ADVANCED, ADVANCED HIGH Write a response using the Text-Dependent Question Guide.

A **APPROACHING** Write a response using the Text-Dependent Question Guide.

Word Bank (BEGINNING)	Sentence Frames (BEGINNING, INTERMEDIATE)	Text-Dependent Question Guide (APPROACHING; ADVANCED, ADVANCED HIGH)
slept like not courthouse trunks rudely staring refuses darling asylum interest mentally ill disrespectful Nellie Brown	Nellie Bly pretends to be a woman named ____. She wants to convince people that she is ____. She wants to be sent to an ____.	1. • What does Nellie Bly say her name is? • What does Bly want people to believe about her? • Where does Bly want to be sent?
	Mrs. Stanard says that Bly had not ____ all night. Bly asks Tom Bockert if all the people at the courthouse lost their ____. Bly ____ to admit that she is in New York.	2. • What does Mrs. Stanard say about Bly's behavior? • What does Bly ask Tom Bockert about the people at the courthouse? • How does Bly respond to the officer in the courtroom?
	At the ____, Bly meets a judge. Bly reacts ____ to the judge's questions. The judge believes that Bly must be somebody's "____."	3. • How does Bly respond to the judge's questions? • What does the judge assume about Bly's family? • What does Bly fear?
	The officers have stopped having "any ____ or concern." This gives me a clue that *indifferently* means "____ having any interest."	4. • Read: "Everywhere was a sprinkling of well-dressed, well-fed officers watching the scene passively and almost **indifferently**. It was only an old story with them. One more unfortunate added to a long list which had long since ceased to be of any interest or concern to them." • Who is behaving *indifferently*? • How do they feel about what is happening around them?
	The men are ____ at Bly. She does not ____ their actions. This gives me a clue that *impudent* means "____."	5. • Read: "These men are **impudent**, and I do not want to be stared at. I will go away. I don't want to stay here." • What are the men doing? How does Bly respond to their actions? • What does that tell me about the meaning of the word *impudent*?

Reading Comprehension OPTIONAL

Have students complete the digital reading comprehension questions ✓ when they finish reading.

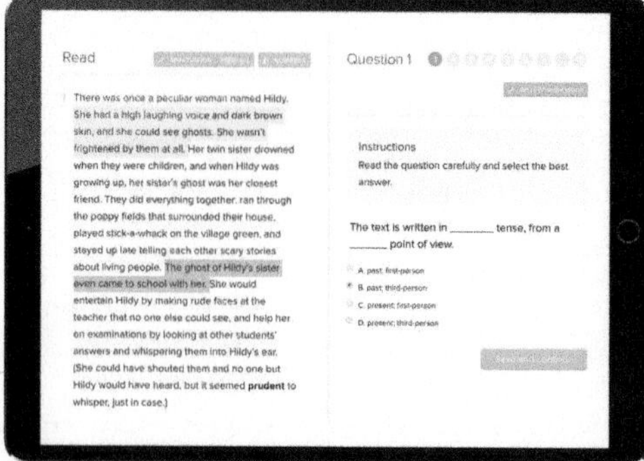

ANSWER KEY

QUESTION 1: D
QUESTION 2: A
QUESTION 3: B
QUESTION 4: C
QUESTION 5: B
QUESTION 6: C
QUESTION 7: D
QUESTION 8: B
QUESTION 9: *See first chart.*
QUESTION 10: *See second chart.*

Dialogue	Individual
"I know nothing of her except that she came to the home yesterday and asked to remain overnight."	Mrs. Stanard
I would stake everything on her being a good girl. I am positive she is somebody's darling."	Judge Duffy
"She's a daisy!"	a ragged child
Here's the express office. We shall soon find those trunks of yours."	Officer Bockert

True	False
stays up all night and says her housemates are crazy	barks like a dog and flashes her teeth in court
fixates on finding her trunks	resembles Judge Duffy's dead sister
accuses the people around her of being foreigners	tells the judge about the home for working women she helps to run
pretends to not know where she is from	dresses well and speaks in perfect English

Connect and Extend OPTIONAL

CONNECT TO EXTENDED WRITING PROJECT

Students can use Nellie's Bly's reportage in *Ten Days in a Mad-House* as inspiration for their Extended Writing Project. They may gather ideas to create situations, settings, and characters for fiction.

BEYOND THE BOOK

Debate: Ethical Journalism

Divide the class into two groups to debate this proposition: It's okay for journalists to pretend to be someone they are not to gain access to people and places they could not otherwise observe.

- Assign one group to argue in favor of the proposition and one group to argue against it.
- Have students prepare for the formal debate by compiling examples and evidence from *Ten Days in a Mad-House* and other contemporary examples of undercover journalism.
- When it's time to conduct the debate, consider bringing in an outside panel (e.g., a principal) to judge the winner and explain which examples and evidence swayed their decision.

To reflect, ask students to consider:

- What evidence most effectively proved your group's point? Why?

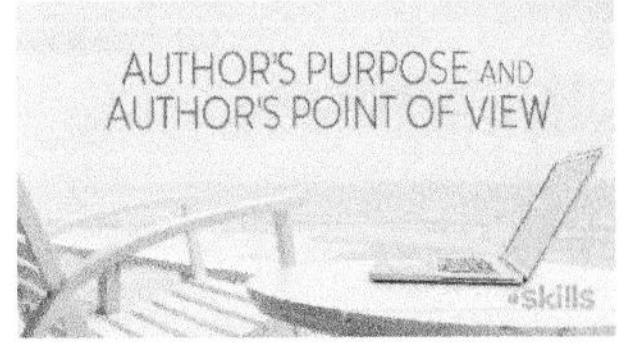

Skill: Author's Purpose and Point of View

Use the Checklist to analyze Author's Purpose and Point of View in *Ten Days in a Mad-House*. Refer to the sample student annotations about Author's Purpose and Point of View in the text.

••• CHECKLIST FOR AUTHOR'S PURPOSE AND POINT OF VIEW

In order to identify author's purpose and point of view, note the following:

- ✓ facts, statistics, and graphic aids, as these indicate that an author is writing to inform
- ✓ the author's use of emotional or figurative language, which may indicate the author is trying to persuade readers or stress an opinion
- ✓ descriptions that present a complicated process in plain language, which may indicate that an author is writing to explain
- ✓ the language the author uses, such as figurative and emotional language, can be clues to the author's point of view on a subject or topic
- ✓ whether the author acknowledges and responds to conflicting evidence or points of view that contradict his or her own

To determine the author's purpose and point of view in a text, consider the following questions:

- ✓ How does the author convey, or communicate, information in the text?
- ✓ Does the author use figurative or emotional language? What does this indicate?
- ✓ Are charts, graphs, maps, and other graphic aids included in the text? For what purpose?
- ✓ Does the author acknowledge contradictory or conflicting evidence or other points of view? How does the author respond to or address them?

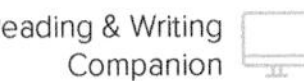

SKILL VOCABULARY

author's purpose / el propósito del autor ***noun*** the author's reason for writing, such as to entertain, to inform, or to persuade

author's point of view / punto de vista del autor ***noun*** the way authors look at a topic or subject, and their attitude toward it

Skill: Author's Purpose and Point of View

Introduce the Skill

Watch the Concept Definition video ▶ and read the following definition with your students.

Author's purpose is the author's reason for writing. Authors typically write for one or more of the following purposes: to entertain, to inform, to persuade, or to explain something to readers. The **author's point of view** refers to the way the author looks at a topic or a subject, and his or her attitude toward it. In order to fully understand an author's purpose for writing, it is often necessary to identify the author's point of view on the subject he or she has chosen to write about, including how it is conveyed or expressed in the text. Sometimes an author's point of view is directly stated. When it is implied, the reader will need to look at textual evidence to infer the author's point of view.

TURN AND TALK

1. Think about the last text you read. What was the author's purpose for writing it?
2. Think of a text you have read that was both entertaining and informative. Explain how the author used details and examples to achieve both purposes.

SPEAKING FRAMES

- The last text I read was ____. The author's purpose was to (inform / entertain / persuade).
- A detail the author used to entertain was ____.
- A detail the author used to inform was ____.

Your Turn

Ask students to complete the Your Turn activity.

QUESTION 1

A. Incorrect.

B. Incorrect.

C. Correct. Mrs. Stanard's panicked reaction suggests that the women who are sent to the Island are not treated well.

D. Incorrect.

QUESTION 2

A. Incorrect. Although Bly does fool people, this is not her main purpose for writing.

B. Incorrect. Bly is not writing to entertain.

C. Incorrect. Although Bly does tell how Mrs. Stanard is kind, this is not the author's main purpose for writing.

D. Correct. The author is trying to get sent to the asylum so she can inform readers about the treatment that mentally ill people receive there.

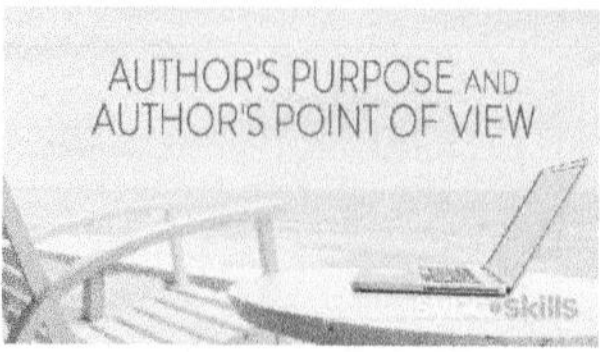

Skill: Author's Purpose and Point of View

Reread paragraphs 43–48 of *Ten Days in a Mad-House*. Then, using the Checklist on the previous page, answer the multiple-choice questions below.

YOUR TURN

1. Which paragraph best shows Bly's point of view to be that mentally ill people receive poor treatment?

   - A. 43
   - B. 44
   - C. 47
   - D. 48

2. Based on details in paragraph 48, the reader can infer that Bly's purpose in writing is—

   - A. to describe how to fool people to get what you want.
   - B. to entertain readers with a funny story from her real life.
   - C. to persuade readers that Mrs. Stanard is a very kind lady.
   - D. to inform readers about the treatment of mentally ill people.

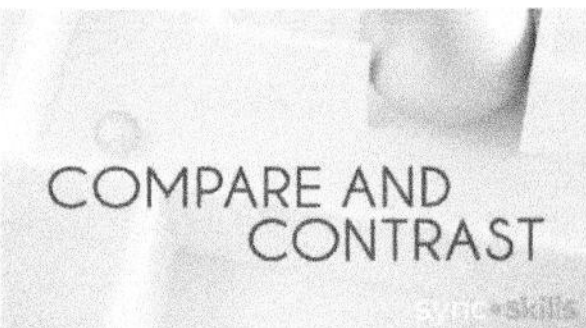

Skill: Compare and Contrast

Use the Checklist to analyze Compare and Contrast in *Ten Days in a Mad-House*. Refer to the sample student annotations about Compare and Contrast in the text.

••• CHECKLIST FOR COMPARE AND CONTRAST

In order to determine how to compare and contrast information in two or more texts that provide conflicting information on the same topic, use the following steps:

- ✓ first, choose two or more texts that present information on the same topic or subject
- ✓ next, identify the information each text offers
- ✓ after, identify the main ideas in each text, as well as the details that support these ideas
- ✓ then, identify the conflicting information each text offers on the same topic
- ✓ finally, explain where the texts disagree, both in their presentation of facts or their interpretation of events

To analyze a case in which two or more texts provide conflicting information on the same topic, consider the following questions:

- ✓ What kind of information does each text offer?
- ✓ How do the main ideas and supporting details differ? How are they the same? How does it result in conflicting information?
- ✓ In what ways do the authors of each text disagree? How does this contribute to the conflicting information that they provide?

Skill: Compare and Contrast

Introduce the Skill

Watch the Concept Definition video and read the following definition with your students.

To **compare** two or more texts means to explain how they are similar. To **contrast** texts means to explain how they are different. A reader may compare and contrast texts within and across genres. **Genre** refers to a specific category of literary text, such as science fiction, satire, historical drama, epic poetry, and the essay. Genre may also refer to a specific category of creative expression in other **media**, such as film, fine art, and music—examples include the Western, Impressionism, and jazz.

Readers may write or deliver **comparative responses** in which they use evidence to analyze the similarities and differences between two or more texts or other media. **Textual evidence** refers to details from the texts that support ideas and opinions about similarities and differences between them. Evidence may be **quoted** directly by including the author's exact words and placing them within quotation marks. Readers may also **paraphrase**, or restate the evidence in their own words.

TURN AND TALK

1. Think about your two favorite books, movies, or TV shows. How are they similar? How are they different?

2. Think about the last two texts we read in class. How were they similar? What made them different from one another?

SPEAKING FRAMES

- My favorite (books / movies / TV shows) are ____. They are similar because ____.
- The last two texts we read were the same because ____.
- The last two texts we read were different because ____.

Your Turn

Ask students to complete the Your Turn activity.

QUESTION 1

Ten Days in a Mad-House	Both	"Sympathy"
The narrator has to adjust what she says and does, such as putting on a veil, because people react in ways she can't predict.	Both the narrators are hoping for their situations to change.	The narrator understands the feelings of frustration that one would experience if they were trapped.
When people try to prevent the narrator from being sent away, she feels upset thinking her plans will be ruined.	Both narrators are affected emotionally because other people are in control of their circumstances	The narrator understands that desperation can lead people to act wildly.

Ten Days in a Mad-House (Chapter IV)

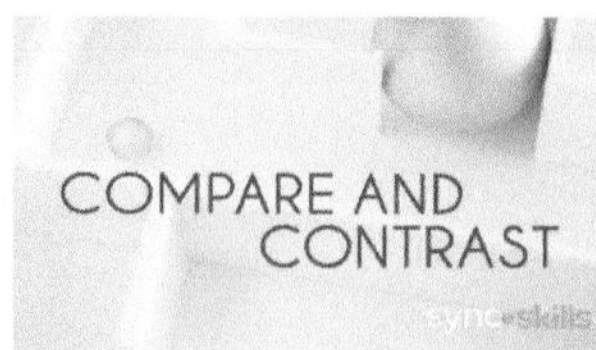

Skill: Compare and Contrast

Reread paragraphs 41–48 from *Ten Days in a Mad-House* and lines 15–21 from "Sympathy." Then, using the Checklist on the previous page, complete the chart below to compare and contrast the passages.

YOUR TURN

	Observation Options
A	When people try to prevent the narrator from being sent away, she feels upset, thinking her plans will be ruined.
B	The narrator has to adjust what she says and does, such as putting on a veil, because people react in ways she can't predict.
C	The narrator understands the feelings of frustration that one would experience if they were trapped.
D	Both the narrators are affected emotionally because other people are in control of their circumstances
E	The narrator understands that desperation can lead people to act wildly.
F	Both the narrators are hoping for their situations to change.

Ten Days in a Mad-House	Both	"Sympathy"

44 Reading & Writing Companion

SKILL VOCABULARY

compare / comparar ***verb*** to explain how two or more things are similar COGNATE

contrast / contrastar ***verb*** to explain how two or more things are different COGNATE

genre / el género ***noun*** the different categories or types of literature, in which the main categories are fiction, nonfiction, poetry, and drama

media / los medios ***noun*** the plural form of the word *medium*; a means of sending a communication to an intended audience

comparative response / la respuesta comparativa ***noun*** an oral or written response in which a reader explains the similarities and differences between two or more things

textual evidence / la evidencia del texto ***noun*** details from the text that a reader can use to support his or her ideas and opinions about the text

quote / citar ***verb*** to use an author's exact words and place them within quotation marks

paraphrase / parafrasear ***verb*** to restate the author's words in your own words COGNATE

Close Read

Reread *Ten Days in a Mad-House*. As you reread, complete the Skills Focus questions below. Then use your answers and annotations from the questions to help you complete the Write activity.

SKILLS FOCUS

1. Reread the first eight paragraphs of *Ten Days in a Mad-House*. Identify details in the text that show people's reactions to Nellie Bly being brought into the courthouse. Explain how these details reveal the author's point of view about how people taken into custody by the police are treated.
2. Identify details in the excerpt from *Ten Days in a Mad-House* that describe the officials in the courthouse. Explain how these details reveal the author's point of view about the treatment mentally ill people receive from these officials.
3. Identify evidence in the text that shows what Bly is trying to accomplish in her conversation with the judge. Explain what her actions reveal about her purpose for writing *Ten Days in a Mad-House*.
4. Identify examples of emotional responses to imprisonment in the excerpt from *Ten Days in a Mad-House*. Then compare and contrast these examples with those in in the poem "Sympathy."
5. Identify evidence in the text that shows what motivates Bly to occupy herself with the mystery of the conditions inside the asylum. Explain what Bly's curiosity suggests about why people are attracted to the mysterious.

WRITE

COMPARATIVE: Nellie Bly wants to access a "mad-house" from which other people would want to escape. Imagine that the speaker of "Sympathy" is an inmate being wrongly held there and that Bly conducts an interview with the inmate. Write a brief account of the interview, similar to what Bly might write for her newspaper. Be sure to show the contrasts between the two situations, relying on evidence from both texts.

Close Read

Skills Focus

QUESTION 1: Author's Purpose and Point of View

See paragraphs 2 and 3.

QUESTION 2: Author's Purpose and Point of View

See paragraph 16.

QUESTION 3: Author's Purpose and Point of View

See paragraph 42.

QUESTION 4: Compare and Contrast

See paragraphs 47 and 48.

QUESTION 5: Connect to Essential Question

See paragraphs 45–47.

CHECK FOR SUCCESS

If students struggle to respond to Skills Focus question 1, ask them the following questions:

- What do the other police officers ask about Bly in paragraph 2?
- What do the children say about Bly in paragraph 3?
- How does Mrs. Stanard react to being brought into the courthouse in paragraph 4?

Have students transition to read and annotate independently once they have successfully completed the first Skills Focus prompt.

Writer's Notebook

Connect to Essential Question: Give students time to reflect on how *Ten Days in a Mad-House* connects to the unit's essential question "What attracts us to the mysterious?" by freewriting in their Writer's Notebooks.

Beginning & Intermediate

Read aloud the unit's essential question: "What attracts us to the mysterious?" Encourage students to draw their connections or allow students to write in their native language. Circulate the room, prompting students for their thoughts as they respond orally or through pantomime.

Advanced & Advanced High

Allow students to share their reflections orally in pairs or small groups before freewriting.

StudySyncTV

Project the StudySyncTV episode and pause at the following times to prompt discussion:

1:17 Why does the group struggle to identify the real Nellie Bly in the beginning of the discussion? What inferences are they able to make once they read more closely?

2:17 Samrah states that Nellie Bly feels for the people in the Women's Lunatic Asylum. What textual evidence supports her inference? How does Samrah's point help the group better understand Bly?

4:23 Samrah describes Bly as clever. What textual evidence supports this idea?

Collaborative Conversation

Break students into collaborative conversation groups to discuss the Close Read prompt. Ask students to use the StudySyncTV episode as a model for their discussion. Remind them to reference their Skills Focus annotations in their discussion.

Nellie Bly wants to access a "mad-house" from which other people would want to escape. Imagine that the speaker of "Sympathy" is an inmate being wrongly held there and that Bly conducts an interview with the inmate. Write a brief account as Bly might for her newspaper. Be sure to show the contrasts between the two situations, relying on evidence from both texts.

Use the scaffolds below to differentiate instruction for your ELL English Language Learners and A Approaching grade-level learners.

ELL **BEGINNING, INTERMEDIATE** Use the discussion guide and speaking frames to facilitate the discussion with support from the teacher.

ADVANCED, ADVANCED HIGH Use the discussion guide and speaking frames to facilitate the discussion in mixed-level groups.

A **APPROACHING** Use the discussion guide to facilitate the discussion in mixed-level groups.

APPROACHING
ADVANCED, ADVANCED HIGH
BEGINNING, INTERMEDIATE

Discussion Guide	Speaking Frames
1. What might Bly ask the speaker of the poem about imprisonment?	• Why do you feel like imprisonment is ____? • How would you feel if ____?
2. How would the speaker answer the question?	• The word *caged* makes me feel ____. • I think of ____ when I think about imprisonment.
3. How might the speaker's answers reveal the differences in their situations?	• The speaker of the poem thinks that ____. However, Bly wants to ____. • Their actions show that their feelings about ____ are different. Their attitudes are different because ____.

Review Prompt and Rubric

Before students begin writing, review the writing prompt and rubric with the class.

COMPARATIVE: Nellie Bly wants to access a "mad-house" from which other people would want to escape. Imagine that the speaker of "Sympathy" is an inmate being wrongly held there and that Bly conducts an interview with the inmate. Write a brief account as Bly might for her newspaper. Be sure to show the contrasts between the two situations, relying on evidence from both texts.

PROMPT GUIDE

A

- Why does Bly want to access a place that most people would want to escape from?
- How would the speaker in the poem feel about being inside the insane ward on the Island?
- How are Bly's feelings about imprisonment and escape different from the speaker's?

Score	Compare and Contrast	Language and Conventions
4	The writer clearly shows contrasts between both texts to develop ideas. The writer is clear and coherent and provides exemplary development of ideas, using relevant evidence from the texts.	The writer demonstrates a consistent command of grammar, punctuation, and usage conventions. Although minor errors may be evident, they do not detract from the fluency or the clarity of the writing.
3	The writer shows contrasts between both texts to develop ideas. The writer is mostly clear and provides sufficient development of ideas, using relevant evidence from the texts most of the time.	The writer demonstrates an adequate command of grammar, punctuation, and usage conventions. Although some errors may be evident, they create few (if any) disruptions in the fluency or the clarity of the writing.
2	The writer begins to show contrasts between both texts to develop ideas, but the piece is incomplete or lacks enough development of ideas. The writer uses relevant evidence from the texts only some of the time.	The writer demonstrates a partial command of grammar, punctuation, and usage conventions. Some distracting errors may be evident, at times creating minor disruptions in the fluency or clarity of the writing.
1	The writer attempts to show contrasts between both texts to develop ideas, but the piece is unclear and incoherent. The writer uses little or no relevant evidence from the text.	The writer demonstrates little or no command of grammar, punctuation, and usage conventions. Serious and persistent errors create disruptions in the fluency of the writing and sometimes interfere with meaning.
0	The writer does not provide a relevant response to the prompt or does not provide a response at all.	Serious and persistent errors overwhelm the writing and interfere with the meaning of the response as a whole, making the writer's meaning impossible to understand.

Write

Ask students to complete the writing assignment using textual evidence to support their answers.

Use the scaffolds below to differentiate instruction for your ELL English Language Learners and A Approaching grade-level learners.

ELL **BEGINNING** With the help of the word bank, write a response using paragraph frame 1.

INTERMEDIATE With the help of the word bank, write a response using paragraph frames 1 and 2.

ADVANCED, ADVANCED HIGH Write a response of differentiated length using the sentence starters.

A **APPROACHING** Write a response of differentiated length using the sentence starters.

BEGINNING: Word Bank, Paragraph Frame 1
INTERMEDIATE: Word Bank, Paragraph Frame 1, Paragraph Frame 2
ADVANCED, ADVANCED HIGH / APPROACHING: Sentence Starters

Word Bank	Paragraph Frame 1	Paragraph Frame 2	Sentence Starters
imprisonment trapped sacrifice escape access	I met an inmate who wanted to ____ from the Island. I asked the woman how she felt about her wrongful ____. She told me that she felt ____ because she did not belong in the asylum. She did not understand why I wanted to ____ my freedom. I explained that I wanted to ____ the asylum to write about what it is like there.	I think our situations are very ____. Going into the asylum was my ____. The inmate says that she prays to escape, but ____. Maybe I would also feel trapped if ____.	• I met an inmate who wants to . . . • I asked her how she felt about . . . • She told me that she felt . . . • My situation is (similar to / different from) hers. • One way that our situations are different is . . . • It was my choice to . . . • This is important because . . .

Peer Review

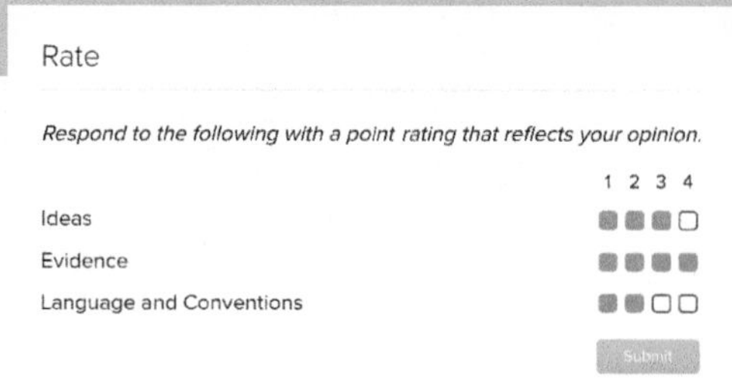

Students should submit substantive feedback to two peers using the review instructions below.

- Does this response answer the prompt? What additional details and explanations would complete the response or make it better?
- Does the writer support his or her ideas with details and examples from each text? Is there additional textual evidence the writer could have cited?
- Which sentence in the writer's response made you think differently about each text?
- What did the writer do well in this response? What does the writer still need to work on?

SENTENCE FRAMES

A

- You were able to (completely / partly / almost) answer the prompt because ____.
- Another detail you could include is ____.
- You supported the idea of ____ with the detail of ____.
- One idea that needs more support is ____.
- I thought differently about the texts after reading ____.
- One thing you do well in your response is ____.
- One thing that you could improve is ____.

The Lottery

FICTION
Shirley Jackson
1948

Introduction

studysync

When this story appeared in *The New Yorker* in 1948, the response was loud, but divided: many distressed readers wrote in to cancel their subscriptions. Others asked which town it was modeled after so they could be spectators of such an event. Called "an icon in the history of the American short story," Shirley Jackson's piece may be controversial, but once read, it engraves itself in readers' psyches forever.

On a quaint summer day, the inhabitants of a village gather for its annual lottery, a tradition that helps ensure a good harvest. With their pockets filled with stones, the children gather first, followed by the adults. Mr. Summers arrives with a shabby black wooden box that has always been used in the lottery. The mood of the crowd is jovial. The ceremony begins with one man from each family drawing a slip of paper. When everyone has a slip, they open them at the same time to discover who has the slip with the black mark. This year, Bill Hutchinson pulled the marked slip, but his wife Tessie complains that the draw was not conducted fairly. The next round of the lottery requires each member of the Hutchinson family to draw one slip. This time, Tessie picks the slip with the black mark. Quickly, she is surrounded by the villagers, and as she raises her arms, they begin to stone her.

 Proficiency-leveled summaries and summaries in multiple languages are available digitally.

 Audio and audio text highlighting are available with this text.

CONNECT TO ESSENTIAL QUESTION

What attracts us to the mysterious?

Shirley Jackson's short story caused a sensation when it was first published. How could a tale about a tradition in an ordinary American town create such powerful interest?

Access Complex Text

LEXILE: 1090L **WORD COUNT:** 3,379

The following areas may be challenging for students, particularly ELL English Language Learners and A Approaching grade-level learners.

Genre	Prior Knowledge	Sentence Structure
• "The Lottery" reads like a detailed report on an event, and the slow development of the plot may challenge some readers. • Teachers might preview that writers of horror and suspense often create plot twists in ordinary settings.	• The strict adherence to tradition is critical to understanding the story's theme and may be difficult to grasp. • Discussion of traditions in their own families or cultures may help prepare students for the narrative.	• Jackson's use of compound, complex, and compound-complex sentences may be a challenge for some readers. • Annotating and highlighting sections of longer sentences may help unlock meaning.

SCAFFOLDS  **ENGLISH LANGUAGE LEARNERS**  **APPROACHING GRADE LEVEL**  **BEYOND GRADE LEVEL**

These icons identify differentiation strategies and scaffolded support for a variety of students. See the digital lesson plan for additional differentiation strategies and scaffolds.

Instructional Path

The print teacher's edition includes essential point-of-use instruction and planning tools. Complete lesson plans and program documents appear in your digital teacher account.

DIGITAL ONLY

Skill: Making and Confirming Predictions

Objectives: After reading and discussing a model, students will be able make and confirm predictions in order to improve reading comprehension.

First Read: The Lottery

Objectives: After an initial reading and discussion of the short story, students will be able to identify and describe characters and setting details as well as articulate events that are central to the story's plot.

Skill: Theme

Objectives: After rereading and discussing a model of close reading, students will be able to determine a theme or central idea of a text and analyze its development over the course of the text, including its relationship to the setting.

Skill: Allusion

Objectives: After rereading and discussing a model of close reading, students will be able to analyze how a modern work of fiction draws on themes, patterns of events, or character types from myths, traditional stories, or religious works such as the Bible, including describing how the material is rendered new.

Close Read: The Lottery

Objectives: After engaging in a close reading and discussion of the text, students will be able to write a short response analyzing how an author can use the setting of a story and allusions to develop theme.

Progress Monitoring

Opportunities to Learn	Opportunities to Demonstrate Learning	Opportunities to Reteach
Making and Confirming Predictions		
Skill: Making and Confirming Predictions	First Read • Read And Annotate	Spotlight Skill: Making and Confirming Predictions
Theme		
Skill: Theme	Skill: Theme • Your Turn Close Read • Skills Focus • Write	Unit 2 Skill: Theme - Abuela Invents the Zero Unit 4 Skill: Theme - /HUG Spotlight Skill: Theme
Allusion		
Skill: Allusion	Skill: Allusion • Your Turn Close Read • Skills Focus • Write	Unit 2 Skill: Allusion - Slam, Dunk, & Hook Unit 4 Skill: Allusion - The Adventures of Tom Sawyer (Chapter 2) Spotlight Skill: Allusion

First Read

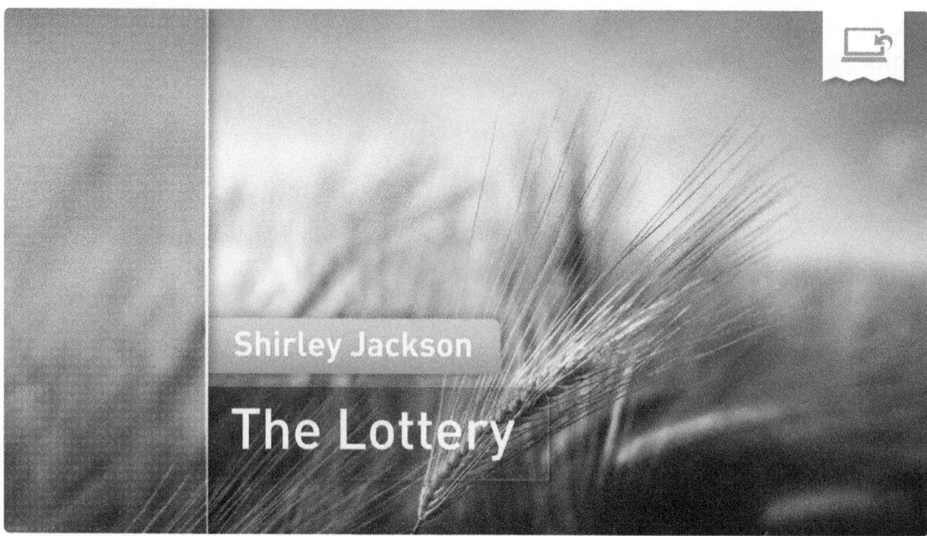

Introduce the Text

As a class, watch the video preview  and have students read the introduction in pairs to make connections to the video preview.

To activate prior knowledge and experiences, ask students:

- How do the images contrast with the narration? Why do you think that is? How does it make you feel?
- What is one prediction you can make about the story you're going to read?

ELL **SPEAKING FRAMES**

- The ____ in the video makes me think ____.
- The video shows ____. This makes me wonder ____.
- I think the text will ____. I think this because ____.
- I predict that there will be ____. I believe this because ____.

Entry Point

As students prepare to read "The Lottery," share the following information with them to provide context.

- ✓ Shirley Jackson (1916–1965) began writing when she was young and continued developing as a writer, even though her family did not understand her interest in it. Jackson published her first short story at Syracuse University and went on to publish novels, short stories, and essays after graduating. Her work often mixed humor with horror and psychological drama. It also provided readers with a sense of the struggles that women faced in society during the mid-20th century.
- ✓ "The Lottery" was published in 1948, almost four years after the end of World War II. During that time, a widespread fear of Communism in the United States was developing.
- ✓ "The Lottery" prompted a record number of readers to write to *The New Yorker* with divided reviews. Some readers were outraged by the story, and others admired it.

“I tell you it wasn’t fair. You didn’t give him time enough to choose.”

1 The morning of June 27th was clear and sunny, with the fresh warmth of a full-summer day; the flowers were blossoming profusely and the grass was richly green. The people of the village began to gather in the square, between the post office and the bank, around ten o’clock; in some towns there were so many people that the lottery took two days and had to be started on June 26th, but in this village, where there were only about three hundred people, the whole **lottery** took less than two hours, so it could begin at ten o’clock in the morning and still be through in time to allow the villagers to get home for noon dinner.

2 The children assembled first, of course. School was recently over for the summer, and the feeling of liberty sat uneasily on most of them; they tended to gather together quietly for a while before they broke into boisterous play, and their talk was still of the classroom and the teacher, of books and reprimands. Bobby Martin had already stuffed his pockets full of stones, and the other boys soon followed his example, selecting the smoothest and roundest stones; Bobby and Harry Jones and Dickie Delacroix—the villagers pronounced this name “Dellacroy”—eventually made a great pile of stones in one corner of the square and guarded it against the raids of the other boys. The girls stood aside, talking among themselves, looking over their shoulders at the boys, and the very small children rolled in the dust or clung to the hands of their older brothers or sisters.

3 Soon the men began to gather, surveying their own children, speaking of planting and rain, tractors and taxes. They stood together, away from the pile of stones in the corner, and their jokes were quiet and they smiled rather than laughed. The women, wearing faded house dresses and sweaters, came shortly after their menfolk. They greeted one another and exchanged bits of gossip as they went to join their husbands. Soon the women, standing by their husbands, began to call to their children, and the children came reluctantly, having to be called four or five times. Bobby Martin ducked under his mother’s grasping hand and ran, laughing, back to the pile of stones. His father spoke up sharply, and Bobby came quickly and took his place between his father and his oldest brother.

NOTES

Skill: Allusion

Why are the boys playing with stones in this scene? Since they’re saving ones that are smooth and round, it seems like they’re searching for stones that are good for throwing. I wonder what they’ll use them for?

Skill: Theme

The fact that villagers are talking about simple things like the weather or gossip shows that the setting of the village is at first presented as a very ordinary place, but later events in the story are anything but!

SELECTION VOCABULARY

lottery / la lotería *noun* an event in which the result is determined by chance COGNATE

Analyze Vocabulary Using Context Clues

In paragraph 1, focus on the sentence that uses the word *lottery*. Point out these context clues:

1. First, I notice that the word *lottery* refers to events in different towns.
2. I see that the lottery is different depending on how many people reside in a town. The number of people involved will affect the outcome.
3. Based on this, I can infer that *lottery* is “an event with an unpredictable outcome.”

Allusion

How does the reader identify an allusion?

First, the reader notices that the boys are collecting stones in paragraph 2 and wonders how they’ll be used. Next the reader notes how the stones will be used in paragraph 74 and considers that this is an allusion to punishment that happens in stories from the Bible.

Theme

How did the reader use setting details to draw conclusions about the villagers?

The reader noted that the villagers treat the occasion of this horrific tradition as a fairly ordinary day.

TEXT TALK

Who gathers in the town square, and how do they arrange themselves?

See paragraphs 1–3: Children, men, and women gather, grouped by family.

Skills Focus

QUESTION 5: Connect to Essential Question

The author includes details that help readers visualize what the lottery looks like and what it means to the villagers. These details create a sense of mystery because we don't know what the lottery is for. Readers become interested to find out more about it.

NOTES

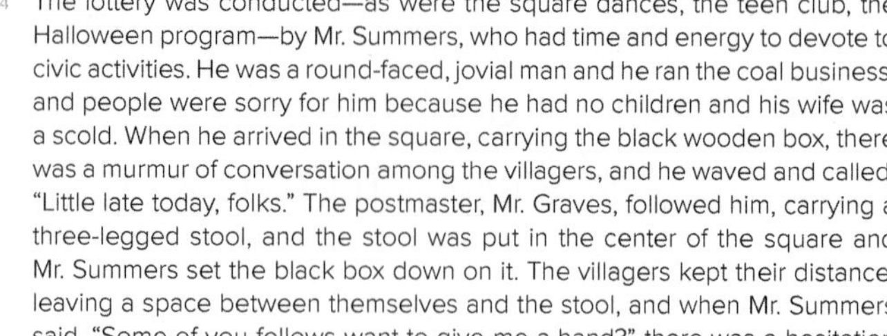

4 The lottery was conducted—as were the square dances, the teen club, the Halloween program—by Mr. Summers, who had time and energy to devote to civic activities. He was a round-faced, jovial man and he ran the coal business, and people were sorry for him because he had no children and his wife was a scold. When he arrived in the square, carrying the black wooden box, there was a murmur of conversation among the villagers, and he waved and called, "Little late today, folks." The postmaster, Mr. Graves, followed him, carrying a three-legged stool, and the stool was put in the center of the square and Mr. Summers set the black box down on it. The villagers kept their distance, leaving a space between themselves and the stool, and when Mr. Summers said, "Some of you fellows want to give me a hand?" there was a hesitation before two men, Mr. Martin and his oldest son, Baxter, came forward to hold the box steady on the stool while Mr. Summers stirred up the papers inside it.

5 The original **paraphernalia** for the lottery had been lost long ago, and the black box now resting on the stool had been put into use even before Old Man Warner, the oldest man in town, was born. Mr. Summers spoke frequently to the villagers about making a new box, but no one liked to upset even as much **tradition** as was represented by the black box. There was a story that the present box had been made with some pieces of the box that had preceded it, the one that had been constructed when the first people settled down to make a village here. Every year, after the lottery, Mr. Summers began talking again about a new box, but every year the subject was allowed to fade off without anything's being done. The black box grew shabbier each year: by now it was no longer completely black but splintered badly along one side to show the original wood color, and in some places faded or stained.

6 Mr. Martin and his oldest son, Baxter, held the black box securely on the stool until Mr. Summers had stirred the papers thoroughly with his hand. Because so much of the ritual had been forgotten or discarded, Mr. Summers had been successful in having slips of paper substituted for the chips of wood that had been used for generations. Chips of wood, Mr. Summers had argued, had been all very well when the village was tiny, but now that the population was more than three hundred and likely to keep on growing, it was necessary to use something that would fit more easily into the black box. The night before the lottery, Mr. Summers and Mr. Graves made up the slips of paper and put them in the box, and it was then taken to the safe of Mr. Summers' coal company and locked up until Mr. Summers was ready to take it to the square next morning. The rest of the year, the box was put way, sometimes one place, sometimes another; it had spent one year in Mr. Graves's barn and another year underfoot in the post office; and sometimes it was set on a shelf in the Martin grocery and left there.

TEXT TALK

What is inside the black box?

See paragraph 6: Pieces of paper with the names of all the villagers are inside the box.

SELECTION VOCABULARY

paraphernalia / la parafernalia ***noun*** objects used for a particular purpose or activity COGNATE

- What objects are mentioned in these paragraphs?
- Why are these objects important?

tradition / la tradición ***noun*** an inherited pattern of thought or action COGNATE

- Why is Old Man Warner mentioned in the paragraph?
- Why don't the villagers make a new box for the lottery?

NOTES

7 There was a great deal of fussing to be done before Mr. Summers declared the lottery open. There were the lists to make up—of heads of families, heads of households in each family, members of each household in each family. There was the proper swearing-in of Mr. Summers by the postmaster, as the official of the lottery; at one time, some people remembered, there had been a recital of some sort, performed by the official of the lottery, a **perfunctory,** tuneless chant that had been rattled off duly each year; some people believed that the official of the lottery used to stand just so when he said or sang it, others believed that he was supposed to walk among the people, but years and years ago this part of the ritual had been allowed to **lapse.** There had been, also, a ritual salute, which the official of the lottery had had to use in addressing each person who came up to draw from the box, but this also had changed with time, until now it was felt necessary only for the official to speak to each person approaching. Mr. Summers was very good at all this; in his clean white shirt and blue jeans, with one hand resting carelessly on the black box, he seemed very proper and important as he talked interminably to Mr. Graves and the Martins.

8 Just as Mr. Summers finally left off talking and turned to the **assembled** villagers, Mrs. Hutchinson came hurriedly along the path to the square, her sweater thrown over her shoulders, and slid into place in the back of the crowd. "Clean forgot what day it was," she said to Mrs. Delacroix, who stood next to her, and they both laughed softly. "Thought my old man was out back stacking wood," Mrs. Hutchinson went on, "and then I looked out the window and the kids was gone, and then I remembered it was the twenty-seventh and came a-running." She dried her hands on her apron, and Mrs. Delacroix said, "You're in time, though. They're still talking away up there."

9 Mrs. Hutchinson craned her neck to see through the crowd and found her husband and children standing near the front. She tapped Mrs. Delacroix on the arm as a farewell and began to make her way through the crowd. The people separated good-humoredly to let her through; two or three people said, in voices just loud enough to be heard across the crowd, "Here comes your Missus, Hutchinson," and "Bill, she made it after all." Mrs. Hutchinson reached her husband, and Mr. Summers, who had been waiting, said cheerfully, "Thought we were going to have to get on without you, Tessie." Mrs. Hutchinson said, grinning, "Wouldn't have me leave m'dishes in the sink, now, would you, Joe?" and soft laughter ran through the crowd as the people stirred back into position after Mrs. Hutchinson's arrival.

10 "Well, now," Mr. Summers said soberly, "guess we better get started, get this over with, so's we can go back to work. Anybody ain't here?"

11 "Dunbar," several people said. "Dunbar, Dunbar."

TEXT TALK

Who is late for the lottery?

See paragraph 8: Mrs. Tessie Hutchinson is late for the lottery.

SELECTION VOCABULARY

perfunctory / indiferente ***adjective*** done in a hurry and as a matter of routine

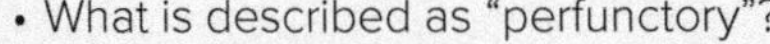

- What is described as "perfunctory"?
- How else is that thing described?

lapse / caducar ***verb*** to run out, to end

- What was allowed to "lapse"?
- What other traditions are mentioned? What happened to them?

12 Mr. Summers consulted his list. "Clyde Dunbar," he said. "That's right. He's broke his leg, hasn't he? Who's drawing for him?"

13 "Me, I guess," a woman said, and Mr. Summers turned to look at her. "Wife draws for her husband," Mr. Summers said. "Don't you have a grown boy to do it for you, Janey?" Although Mr. Summers and everyone else in the village knew the answer perfectly well, it was the business of the official of the lottery to ask such questions formally. Mr. Summers waited with an expression of polite interest while Mrs. Dunbar answered.

14 "Horace's not but sixteen yet," Mrs. Dunbar said regretfully. "Guess I gotta fill in for the old man this year."

15 "Right," Mr. Summers said. He made a note on the list he was holding. Then he asked, "Watson boy drawing this year?"

16 A tall boy in the crowd raised his hand. "Here," he said. "I'm drawing for m'mother and me." He blinked his eyes nervously and ducked his head as several voices in the crowd said things like "Good fellow, Jack," and "Glad to see your mother's got a man to do it."

17 "Well," Mr. Summers said, "guess that's everyone. Old Man Warner make it?"

18 "Here," a voice said, and Mr. Summers nodded.

19 A sudden hush fell on the crowd as Mr. Summers cleared his throat and looked at the list. "All ready?" he called. "Now, I'll read the names—heads of families first—and the men come up and take a paper out of the box. Keep the paper folded in your hand without looking at it until everyone has had a turn. Everything clear?"

20 The people had done it so many times that they only half listened to the directions; most of them were quiet, wetting their lips, not looking around. Then Mr. Summers raised one hand high and said, "Adams." A man disengaged himself from the crowd and came forward. "Hi, Steve," Mr. Summers said, and Mr. Adams said, "Hi, Joe." They grinned at one another humorlessly and nervously. Then Mr. Adams reached into the black box and took out a folded paper. He held it firmly by one corner as he turned and went hastily back to his place in the crowd, where he stood a little apart from his family, not looking down at his hand.

21 "Allen," Mr. Summers said. "Anderson. . . . Bentham."

TEXT TALK

What do the heads of families do?

See paragraphs 19 and 20: They draw slips of paper from the box.

SELECTION VOCABULARY

assembled / reunido/a ***adjective*** the state of being gathered together

- What is described as "assembled"?
- What are they doing? How are they grouped?

NOTES

22 "Seems like there's no time at all between lotteries any more," Mrs. Delacroix said to Mrs. Graves in the back row. "Seems like we got through with the last one only last week."

23 "Time sure goes fast," Mrs. Graves said.

24 "Clark. . . . Delacroix."

25 "There goes my old man," Mrs. Delacroix said. She held her breath while her husband went forward.

26 "Dunbar," Mr. Summers said, and Mrs. Dunbar went steadily to the box while one of the women said, "Go on, Janey," and another said, "There she goes."

27 "We're next," Mrs. Graves said. She watched while Mr. Graves came around from the side of the box, greeted Mr. Summers gravely and selected a slip of paper from the box. By now, all through the crowd there were men holding the small folded papers in their large hands, turning them over and over nervously. Mrs. Dunbar and her two sons stood together, Mrs. Dunbar holding the slip of paper.

28 "Harburt. . . . Hutchinson."

29 "Get up there, Bill," Mrs. Hutchinson said, and the people near her laughed.

30 "Jones."

31 "They do say," Mr. Adams said to Old Man Warner, who stood next to him, "that over in the north village they're talking of giving up the lottery."

32 Old Man Warner snorted, "Pack of crazy fools," he said. "Listening to the young folks, nothing's good enough for them. Next thing you know, they'll be wanting to go back to living in caves, nobody work any more, live that way for a while. Used to be a saying about 'Lottery in June, corn be heavy soon.' First thing you know, we'd all be eating stewed chickweed and acorns. There's always been a lottery," he added petulantly. "Bad enough to see young Joe Summers up there joking with everybody."

33 "Some places have already quit lotteries," Mrs. Adams said.

34 "Nothing but trouble in that," Old Man Warner said stoutly. "Pack of young fools."

35 "Martin." And Bobby Martin watched his father go forward. "Overdyke. . . . Percy."

Skills Focus

QUESTION 2: Theme

Old Man Warner remembers that the lottery used to be done to ensure there was a good harvest. The fact that some people want to change things suggests that the history behind the tradition has been forgotten.

NOTES

36 "I wish they'd hurry," Mrs. Dunbar said to her older son. "I wish they'd hurry."

37 "They're almost through," her son said.

38 "You get ready to run tell Dad," Mrs. Dunbar said.

39 Mr. Summers called his own name and then stepped forward precisely and selected a slip from the box. Then he called, "Warner."

40 "Seventy-seventh year I been in the lottery," Old Man Warner said as he went through the crowd. "Seventy-seventh time."

41 "Watson." The tall boy came awkwardly through the crowd. Someone said, "Don't be nervous, Jack," and Mr. Summers said, "Take your time, son."

42 "Zanini."

43 After that, there was a long pause, a breathless pause, until Mr. Summers, holding his slip of paper in the air, said, "All right, fellows." For a minute, no one moved, and then all the slips of paper were opened. Suddenly, all the women began to speak at once, saying, "Who is it?" "Who's got it?" "Is it the Dunbars?" "Is it the Watsons?" Then the voices began to say, "It's Hutchinson. It's Bill," "Bill Hutchinson's got it."

44 "Go tell your father," Mrs. Dunbar said to her older son.

45 People began to look around to see the Hutchinsons. Bill Hutchinson was standing quiet, staring down at the paper in his hand. Suddenly, Tessie Hutchinson shouted to Mr. Summers, "You didn't give him time enough to take any paper he wanted. I saw you. It wasn't fair!"

46 "Be a good sport, Tessie, " Mrs. Delacroix called, and Mrs. Graves said, "All of us took the same chance."

47 "Shut up, Tessie," Bill Hutchinson said.

48 "Well, everyone," Mr. Summers said, "that was done pretty fast, and now we've got to be hurrying a little more to get done in time." He consulted his next list. "Bill," he said, "you draw for the Hutchinson family. You got any other households in the Hutchinsons?"

49 "There's Don and Eva," Mrs. Hutchinson yelled. "Make them take their chance!"

50 "Daughters draw with their husbands' families, Tessie," Mr. Summers said gently. "You know that as well as anyone else."

TEXT TALK

What do the Hutchinsons have to do, and why?

See paragraphs 43–63: They have to draw among their family because Bill's slip had the black spot in the first drawing.

NOTES

51 "It wasn't fair," Tessie said.

52 "I guess not, Joe," Bill Hutchinson said regretfully. "My daughter draws with her husband's family, that's only fair. And I've got no other family except the kids."

53 "Then, as far as drawing for families is concerned, it's you," Mr. Summers said in explanation, "and as far as drawing for households is concerned, that's you, too. Right?"

54 "Right," Bill Hutchinson said.

55 "How many kids, Bill?" Mr. Summers asked formally.

56 "Three," Bill Hutchinson said. "There's Bill, Jr., and Nancy, and little Dave. And Tessie and me."

57 "All right, then," Mr. Summers said. "Harry, you got their tickets back?"

58 Mr. Graves nodded and held up the slips of paper. "Put them in the box, then," Mr. Summers directed. "Take Bill's and put it in."

59 "I think we ought to start over," Mrs. Hutchinson said, as quietly as she could. "I tell you it wasn't fair. You didn't give him time enough to choose. Everybody saw that."

60 Mr. Graves had selected the five slips and put them in the box, and he dropped all the papers but those onto the ground, where the breeze caught them and lifted them off.

61 "Listen, everybody," Mrs. Hutchinson was saying to the people around her.

62 "Ready, Bill?" Mr. Summers asked, and Bill Hutchinson, with one quick glance around at his wife and children, nodded.

63 "Remember," Mr. Summers said, "take the slips and keep them folded until each person has taken one. Harry, you help little Dave." Mr. Graves took the hand of the little boy, who came willingly with him up to the box. "Take a paper out of the box, Davy," Mr. Summers said. Davy put his hand into the box and laughed. "Take just one paper," Mr. Summers said. "Harry, you hold it for him." Mr. Graves took the child's hand and removed the folded paper from the tight fist and held it while little Dave stood next to him and looked up at him wonderingly.

64 "Nancy next," Mr. Summers said. Nancy was twelve, and her school friends breathed heavily as she went forward, switching her skirt, and took a slip

Skills Focus

QUESTION 3: Allusion

A gravestone can be used to mark the life and death of a person. I think that relates to Mr. Graves in this story. He is in charge of placing the lottery tickets back in the box. Whoever chooses a marked ticket will be killed by the other villagers. The name Mr. Graves is an allusion to graves and death because he is in charge of organizing and delivering death to someone.

Prepare for Advanced Courses

Use the activity below to differentiate instruction for your B Beyond grade-level learners.

Shirley Jackson purposefully created names for her characters, and each name represents or describes the character a little further. In the story, Mrs. Hutchinson is the only character who seems to be speaking out against the lottery.

Look at paragraph 59:

"I think we ought to start over," Mrs. Hutchinson said, as quietly as she could. "I tell you it wasn't fair. You didn't give him time enough to choose. Everybody saw that."

Some believe that the author wrote this character after Anne Hutchinson from history. Have your students conduct informal research to answer the following questions: What connections can you make between Anne Hutchinson and Tessie Hutchinson in "The Lottery"?

Skills Focus

QUESTION 4: Setting and Theme

At the beginning of the story, the stones seemed like a small setting detail. But now I know that they will be used as weapons, which is a surprising twist. It is also surprising how eager the women are to use the stones, since earlier in the story they seemed friendly.

Allusion

How is the act of throwing stones rendered new in "The Lottery"?

Answers will vary but should indicate that the community still practices this lethal tradition because they value tradition over an individual's well-being.

daintily from the box. "Bill, Jr.," Mr. Summers said, and Billy, his face red and his feet overlarge, nearly knocked the box over as he got a paper out. "Tessie," Mr. Summers said. She hesitated for a minute, looking around defiantly, and then set her lips and went up to the box. She snatched a paper out and held it behind her.

65 "Bill," Mr. Summers said, and Bill Hutchinson reached into the box and felt around, bringing his hand out at last with the slip of paper in it.

66 The crowd was quiet. A girl whispered, "I hope it's not Nancy," and the sound of the whisper reached the edges of the crowd.

67 "It's not the way it used to be," Old Man Warner said clearly. "People ain't the way they used to be."

68 "All right," Mr. Summers said. "Open the papers. Harry, you open little Dave's."

69 Mr. Graves opened the slip of paper and there was a general sigh through the crowd as he held it up and everyone could see that it was blank. Nancy and Bill. Jr., opened theirs at the same time, and both beamed and laughed, turning around to the crowd and holding their slips of paper above their heads.

70 "Tessie," Mr. Summers said. There was a pause, and then Mr. Summers looked at Bill Hutchinson, and Bill unfolded his paper and showed it. It was blank.

71 "It's Tessie," Mr. Summers said, and his voice was hushed. "Show us her paper, Bill."

72 Bill Hutchinson went over to his wife and forced the slip of paper out of her hand. It had a black spot on it, the black spot Mr. Summers had made the night before with the heavy pencil in the coal company office. Bill Hutchinson held it up, and there was a stir in the crowd.

73 "All right, folks," Mr. Summers said. "Let's finish quickly."

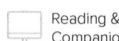

Skill: Allusion

The villagers will use the stones to throw at Mrs. Hutchinson, and this changes the tone of the story from a civil to horrific one. They might use stones because they're following an old tradition. In the Bible, people threw stones at a person as punishment, but Mrs. Hutchinson didn't commit a crime.

74 Although the villagers had forgotten the ritual and lost the original black box, they still remembered to use stones. The pile of stones the boys had made earlier was ready; there were stones on the ground with the blowing scraps of paper that had come out of the box. Mrs. Delacroix selected a stone so large she had to pick it up with both hands and turned to Mrs. Dunbar. "Come on," she said. "Hurry up."

75 Mrs. Dunbar had small stones in both hands, and she said, gasping for breath, "I can't run at all. You'll have to go ahead and I'll catch up with you."

NOTES

76 The children had stones already, and someone gave little Davy Hutchinson a few pebbles.

77 Tessie Hutchinson was in the center of a cleared space by now, and she held her hands out desperately as the villagers moved in on her. "It isn't fair," she said. A stone hit her on the side of the head.

78 Old Man Warner was saying, "Come on, come on, everyone." Steve Adams was in the front of the crowd of villagers, with Mrs. Graves beside him.

79 "It isn't fair, it isn't right," Mrs. Hutchinson screamed and then they were upon her.

TEXT TALK

What happens to Mrs. Hutchinson as a result of the lottery?

See paragraphs 77–79: All the villagers throw stones at her and kill her.

B Have one or two students facilitate a discussion to answer the following question: Why do you think the townspeople continue with the tradition of the lottery?

Think Questions

Circulate as students answer Think Questions independently. Scaffolds for these questions are shown on the opposite page.

QUESTION 1: Textual Evidence

In the first paragraph, we learn the date (June 27), the time (about 10:00 AM), the temperature (warm, clear, and sunny), and the place (the village square of a small town) where the lottery takes place. The pleasant setting contrasts with the events that lead to a woman being stoned to death.

QUESTION 2: Textual Evidence

Old Man Warner cites the saying "Lottery in June, corn be heavy soon." This saying indicates that the original purpose of the lottery was to ensure a good harvest. Warner's comment that "First thing you know, we'd all be eating stewed chickweed and acorns" indicates that he still believes harvests might fail without the lottery and that the townspeople would suffer as a result.

QUESTION 3: Textual Evidence

In paragraph 72, when Bill discovers that Tessie has drawn the slip of paper with the black spot, he holds up the paper so the whole town can see. This action shows that Bill is willing to go along with the tradition of the lottery, even if it means sacrificing a member of his family.

QUESTION 4: Context Clues

The text links the black box with tradition when it says, "no one liked to upset even as much tradition as was represented by the black box." Based on these clues, I think that *tradition* means "a custom or belief that has been passed down from one generation to another."

QUESTION 5: Context Clues

The text refers to "a recital of some sort" and "a perfunctory, tuneless chant that has been dones so many times that it is no longer special." Based on these clues, I think *perfunctory* means "done as a matter of routine."

First Read

Read "The Lottery." After you read, complete the Think Questions below.

THINK QUESTIONS

1. Describe the day on which the lottery takes place. How does the description of this day contrast with the events that take place later on? Cite textual evidence from the selection to support your answer.

2. What saying does Old Man Warner recite about the lottery in paragraph 32? What does this tell you about the original reason for holding the lottery? Cite specific textual evidence to support your statements.

3. How does the lottery affect Tessie and Bill Hutchinson at the end of the story? Cite specific textual evidence to support your statements.

4. Find the word **tradition** in paragraph 5 of "The Lottery." Use context clues in the surrounding sentences, as well as the sentence in which the word appears, to determine the word's meaning. Write your definition here and identify clues that helped you figure out its meaning.

5. Use context clues to determine the meaning of **perfunctory** as it is used in paragraph 7 of "The Lottery." Write your definition here and identify clues that helped you figure out its meaning. Then check the meaning in a dictionary.

Think Questions

SCAFFOLDS

Use the scaffolds below to differentiate instruction for your ELL English Language Learners and A Approaching grade-level learners.

ELL **BEGINNING** Write a response using the word bank and sentence frames.

INTERMEDIATE Write a response using the sentence frames.

ADVANCED, ADVANCED HIGH Write a response using the Text-Dependent Question Guide.

A **APPROACHING** Write a response using the Text-Dependent Question Guide.

BEGINNING	INTERMEDIATE	APPROACHING / ADVANCED, ADVANCED HIGH
Word Bank	**Sentence Frames**	**Text-Dependent Question Guide**
mark year crops sunny blossoming heavy sacrifice generation green save fools oldest killed routine tuneless	The story takes place in the town square on a ____ summer day. Flowers are ____, and the grass is ____. These positive images contrast with the events because Mrs. Hutchinson is hit with stones and ____ at the end of the lottery.	1. • Where and when does the story take place? • What are the flowers doing? What does the grass look like? • How do the positive images contrast with the events that take place at the end of the lottery?
	Old Man Warner recalls the saying "Lottery in June, corn be ____ soon." The saying suggests that the purpose of the lottery is to make a sacrifice so that ____ will grow. Old Man Warner calls people who want to give up the lottery " ____."	2. • What does Old Man Warner say comes after a "Lottery in June"? • Based on that saying, what can we infer is the purpose of the lottery? • What does Old Man Warner call people who want to end the lottery?
	Readers might expect a husband to ____ his wife. Bill holds up Tessie's piece of paper so everyone can see the ____. This action shows that Bill was affected by the lottery because he is willing to ____ her.	3. • How might you expect a husband to react to his wife being chosen? • What does Bill Hutchinson do at the end of the second drawing? • What does Bill's behavior suggest about how he may be affected by the tradition of the lottery?
	The black box has been used since before the ____ man in town was born. This gives me a clue that *tradition* means something that is passed down from one ____ to another.	4. • Reread paragraph 5. • How long has the black box been used? • What does that tell me about the meaning of the word *tradition*?
	The chant is also described as ____. It is done the same way every ____. This gives me a clue that *perfunctory* means "something that is done as a matter of ____."	5. • Reread paragraph 7. • What other word is used to describe the chant? • What does that tell me about the meaning of the word *perfunctory*?

Reading Comprehension OPTIONAL

Have students complete the digital reading comprehension questions ✓ when they finish reading.

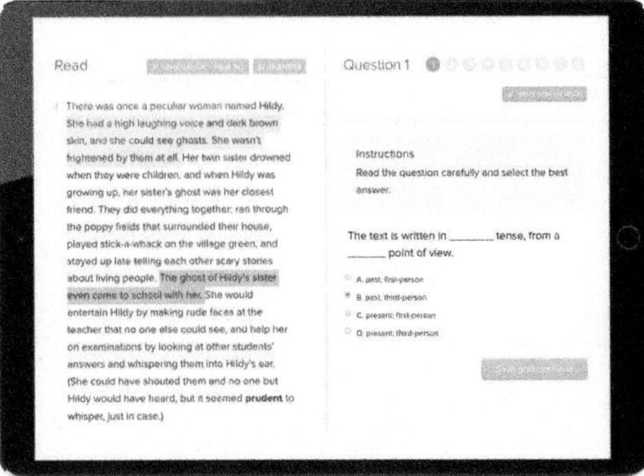

ANSWER KEY

QUESTION 1: D
QUESTION 2: A
QUESTION 3: A
QUESTION 4: B
QUESTION 5: C
QUESTION 6: C
QUESTION 7: A
QUESTION 8: C
QUESTION 9: C
QUESTION 10: *See chart.*

Description	Character
The oldest living participant in the annual tradition	Old Man Warner
The person conducting the ceremony	Mr. Summers
Not in attendance at this year's lottery because of a broken leg	Clyde Dunbar
Father of three and husband to Tessie	Bill Hutchinson

Connect and Extend OPTIONAL

CONNECT TO EXTENDED WRITING PROJECT

Students can use "The Lottery" as a mentor text for their Extended Writing Project. They may take inspiration from Shirley Jackson's setting or theme for suspenseful action to occur.

BEYOND THE BOOK

Research Project: Unusual Traditions

Divide students into small groups to identify and learn more about traditions in a part of the world that fascinates them. The tradition they focus on does not need to be as dark or foreboding as the one Shirley Jackson creates in "The Lottery." Examples for your students might include things like the Palio di Siena in Italy or La Tomatina in Spain. Ask students to consider:

- What are the origins of the tradition?
- How has it changed over time?
- What objects symbolize the meaning of the tradition?
- What meaning does the tradition hold for members of the culture?

Have groups answer these questions as they share their findings with the class.

Skill: Theme

Use the Checklist to analyze Theme in "The Lottery." Refer to the sample student annotations about Theme in the text.

••• CHECKLIST FOR THEME

In order to identify a theme, or central idea, of a text, note the following:

- ✓ the subject of the text and a theme that might be stated directly in the text
- ✓ details in the text that help to reveal theme
  - the title and chapter headings
  - details about the setting
  - a narrator's or speaker's tone
  - characters' thoughts, actions, and dialogue
  - the central conflict in a story's plot
  - the climax, or turning point, in the story
  - the resolution of the conflict
  - shifts in characters, setting, or plot events
- ✓ analyze the development of the theme and its relationship to the characters, setting, and plot
  - a setting, such as a rugged wilderness or a boat lost at sea, can prevent characters from accomplishing something and affect them in some way
  - the time and place, such as a narrative set in the past or future, can affect how a character responds to events

To determine a theme, or central idea, of a text and analyze its development over the course of the text, including its relationship to the characters, setting, and plot, use the following questions as a guide:

- ✓ What is a theme, or central idea, of the text? When did you become aware of that theme?
- ✓ How does the theme relate to the characters, setting, and plot?
- ✓ How does the theme develop over the course of the text?

SKILL VOCABULARY

topic / el tema ***noun*** the subject of a literary work, usually expressed as a single word or phrase in the form of a noun

theme / el tema ***noun*** the central idea or message of a work of literature, often expressed as a general statement about life

infer / inferir ***verb*** to determine something by using reasoning and evidence from the text COGNATE

Skill: Theme

Introduce The Skill

Watch the Concept Definition video ▶ and read the following definition with your students.

The **topic** of a literary work is the subject of the work. It is usually expressed as a noun. The **theme** is the central idea or message of a work of literature. It is often expressed as a general statement about life. For example, the topic of a literary work might be love. The theme would be what the writer suggests about love: that it is wonderful or painful or maybe both at once. A literary work may have more than one theme.

Sometimes a writer states a theme directly. More often, though, theme is revealed gradually. In short stories, novels, and dramas, theme is revealed through elements such as character, setting, and plot, what the characters do and say, and how these elements affect the events that take place. When a theme is not stated directly, a reader will have to infer the theme. To **infer** means to determine something by using reasoning and textual evidence.

TURN AND TALK

1. What are some examples of memorable themes from books, TV shows, or movies?
2. How did the setting connect to the theme of the book, episode, or movie?

ELL SPEAKING FRAMES

- One memorable theme is ____. I remember the theme well because ____.
- The setting was connected to the theme ____.
- Some setting details that connected to the theme were ____.

Your Turn

Ask students to complete the Your Turn activity.

QUESTION 1

Part A

A. Incorrect. The villagers have changed routines over time. For example, they replaced the chips of wood that they used to add to the black box with slips of paper.

B. Correct. The villagers know that parts of the tradition have been changed and lost, but they do not question their current practices.

C. Incorrect. The villagers do not question rituals that do not have a clear meaning.

D. Incorrect. The villagers debate about different ways rituals used to be practiced, but most villagers do not argue that the lottery should be stopped.

Part B

A. Correct. This detail shows that the villagers debate about past practices and are not sure why they have been changed, but they still accept the current practices.

B. Incorrect. This detail describes one ritual, but it does not show the villagers' view of it.

C. Incorrect. This detail describes how two villagers prepare for the ritual, but it does not show the villagers' view of it.

D. Incorrect. This detail describes one scene during "The Lottery," but it does not show the villagers' view of current practices.

Skill: Theme

Reread paragraphs 6 and 7 of "The Lottery." Then, using the Checklist on the previous page, answer the multiple-choice questions below.

YOUR TURN

1. This question has two parts. First, answer Part A. Then, answer Part B.

Part A: Which of the following describes most villagers' view of the lottery?

- A. One should not follow or change any routines that have not been done in the past.
- B. The current version of the tradition should be practiced even though parts of it have been let go or lost.
- C. A routine should be changed when the villagers no longer understand the meaning behind it.
- D. Most villagers think that the lottery should be stopped, but they do not have the power to stop it.

Part B: Which of the following details BEST supports the conclusion drawn in Part A?

- A. ". . . some people believed that the official of the lottery used to stand just so when he said or sang it, others believed that he was supposed to walk among the people, but years and years ago this part of the ritual had been allowed to lapse."
- B. "There was a great deal of fussing to be done before Mr. Summers declared the lottery open. There were the lists to make up—of heads of families, heads of households in each family, members of each household in each family."
- C. "The night before the lottery, Mr. Summers and Mr. Graves made up the slips of paper and put them in the box, and it was then taken to the safe of Mr. Summers' coal company and locked up until Mr. Summers was ready to take it to the square next morning."
- D. "Mr. Summers was very good at all this; in his clean white shirt and blue jeans, with one hand resting carelessly on the black box, he seemed very proper and important as he talked interminably to Mr. Graves and the Martins."

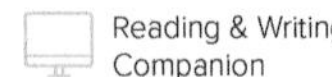

2. Paragraph 6 describes where the villagers keep the black box during the lottery and where they have kept it throughout the rest of the year. What does that description imply about this tradition?

   - A. Historic objects are an essential part of practicing traditions, so they need to be carefully preserved.
   - B. As part of the tradition, the box needs to be stored in a different place each year so that everyone shares the responsibility for taking care of it.
   - C. No one wants to be in charge of the black box during the year because it is used to determine who will be sacrificed in the lottery.
   - D. The object associated with the lottery is an accepted part of village life, as much as the post office or grocery store is.

3. Based on the interactions between characters and the setting details in paragraphs 6 and 7, the reader can conclude that a possible theme is—

   - A. Small changes can make old traditions seem new and exciting.
   - B. Traditions can become less meaningful over time.
   - C. Failing to pass down a tradition can be hurtful to a community.
   - D. It can be dangerous to blindly stick to traditions.

QUESTION 2

A. Incorrect. There is no evidence that this box is carefully preserved during the year. Sometimes it is even "set on a shelf in the Martin grocery and left there."

B. Incorrect. There is no evidence that this box is shared by villagers in an organized way or that everyone shares the responsibility for taking care of it.

C. Incorrect. The text does not say that people want to avoid storing the black box during the year.

D. Correct. The box and what it represents have become so expected, that it is stored without careful consideration. For example, it is sometimes even "set on a shelf in the Martin grocery and left there."

QUESTION 3

A. Incorrect. Although changes have been made to the tradition, they do not make the lottery seem new and exciting.

B. Incorrect. There is no evidence to support the idea that the lottery has grown less meaningful over time.

C. Incorrect. There are no details in the passage about failing to pass down a tradition.

D. Correct. The villagers go through the motions of the lottery without questioning its senseless violence.

Skill: Allusion

Introduce The Skill

Watch the Concept Definition video and read the following definition with your students.

An **allusion** is a reference to something, usually made in an indirect way. The reference may be to a literary work, a work of art, a historical event, a famous person, or something else that a reader or listener is expected to understand without an explanation. For example, referring to someone as "a Scrooge" alludes to the stingy character of that name in Charles Dickens's *A Christmas Carol*. Through the allusion, the many qualities of Ebenezer Scrooge may be transferred quickly to another character or person.

Works of literature often draw on themes, patterns of events, or characters from other works, and these allusions have an impact on the meaning and tone of a work. Readers may not know the **source material** authors borrow from or allude to, but a familiarity with a variety of works such as Greek myths, the Bible, and the plays of William Shakespeare may deepen a reader's experience of the newer material.

Skill: Allusion

Use the Checklist to analyze Allusion in "The Lottery." Refer to the sample student annotations about Allusion in the text.

••• CHECKLIST FOR ALLUSION

In order to identify an allusion, note the following:

- ✓ references or clues that suggest a reference to a myth, religious works such as The Bible, a story, person, historical event, object, idea, or other work of art with which readers may be familiar
- ✓ the theme, event, character, or situation in a text to which the references or clues add information
- ✓ patterns of events or character types that are used in other familiar texts

To better understand the allusion in a work of literature, do the following:

- ✓ use a print or digital resource to look up what you think might be an allusion
- ✓ list details about the allusion that relate to themes, events, or character types

To analyze how a modern work of fiction draws on themes, events, patterns of events, or character types from myths, traditional stories, or religious works, consider the following questions:

- ✓ What theme/event/character is referenced in the fiction I am reading? How do I know?
- ✓ How does that theme/event/character relate to what is happening in this new text?

To describe how the material is rendered new, consider the following questions:

- ✓ What does the modern version of the story add to the previous story?
- ✓ How does the inclusion of allusions impact the meaning or tone of the story?
- ✓ How does the theme/event/character change from its origin or source text?

TURN AND TALK

1. Have you ever read a book or seen a movie or show that makes an allusion to another story that you already know?
2. What did this allusion add to the book/movie/show?

SPEAKING FRAMES

- One (book / movie / show) that makes an allusion is ____.
- It makes an allusion to ____.
- I know that this is an allusion because ____.
- I think this allusion adds ____ to the (book / movie / show).

SKILL VOCABULARY

allusion / la alusión *noun* a reference to a person, place, thing, or idea COGNATE

source material / el material de referencia *noun* the work of literature or other source to which an allusion, or reference, is made, or from which themes and characters are borrowed

Skill: Allusion

Reread paragraphs 4 and 5 of "The Lottery." Then, using the Checklist on the previous page, answer the multiple-choice questions below.

YOUR TURN

1. In paragraph 4, which of the following could be a theme or event that the black box is referencing?

   - A. The black box is most likely an allusion to one year when crops did not grow.
   - B. The black box is most likely an allusion to a theme about fear because all of the villagers want to stay away from it.
   - C. The black box is most likely an allusion to a ceremonial object, so it could be a reference to a theme about tradition.
   - D. The black box is most likely an allusion to a theme about preserving natural resources because Mr. Summers also runs a coal business, and the box is made out of wood.

2. The condition of the black box is described in paragraph 5. What does its condition reveal to readers about the state of this village tradition?

   - A. The black box has lost many of its original qualities, and this village tradition has also lost many of the original practices.
   - B. The black box has been carefully preserved since it was first used, and this village tradition has also been carefully preserved over time.
   - C. In this village, each generation adds new material to this black box, and each generation adds a new practice to this village tradition.
   - D. The black box is fading, and it is evident that the yearly observance of this tradition will fade over time as well.

Your Turn

Ask students to complete the Your Turn activity.

QUESTION 1

A. Incorrect. Although this tradition is based on the need for an abundant crop yield, there is no evidence that the box is a reference to one year when crops did not grow.

B. Incorrect. While many of the villagers do keep their distance from the black box, there is no evidence that Mr. Summers fears the black box.

C. Correct. A local leader carries the box to the lottery and places it at the center of the village square. This is an allusion to ceremonial objects, which are important parts of some traditions.

D. Incorrect. While wood and coal are mentioned throughout the story, there is no evidence that the black box is making a reference to a theme about preserving natural resources.

QUESTION 2

A. Correct. The black box is not the original box, and it is losing important qualities like its color and shape. Similarly, the tradition that the villagers practice is not the original one, and it may have also lost important qualities over time.

B. Incorrect. The black box has not been carefully preserved since it is losing its paint color and shape. Similarly, the tradition has not been carefully preserved over time since village residents have different stories about what used to be practiced.

C. Incorrect. Although the box may include some material from the original box, the village residents resist changing their version of the black box and their version of the tradition.

D. Incorrect. There is no evidence that this village tradition will fade or stop being practiced in the near future.

Close Read

Skills Focus

QUESTION 1: Setting and Theme

See paragraph 1: The village seems warm and welcoming. The weather is pleasant. Jackson uses simple descriptions that could be used to describe any village. It makes the exact setting seem ambiguous.

QUESTION 2: Theme

See paragraph 32.

QUESTION 3: Allusion

See paragraph 57–60.

QUESTION 4: Setting and Theme

See paragraph 74.

QUESTION 5: Connect to Essential Question

See paragraph 5.

CHECK FOR SUCCESS

If students struggle to respond to Skills Focus question 1, ask them the following questions:

- What details describe the village in paragraph 1?
- What details describe the villagers in paragraph 3?
- Does the village seem special or ordinary? Why?

Have students transition to read and annotate independently once they have successfully completed the first Skills Focus prompt.

Close Read

Reread "The Lottery." As you reread, complete the Skills Focus questions below. Then use your answers and annotations from the questions to help you complete the Write activity.

SKILLS FOCUS

1. Identify clues about the village where "The Lottery" is set. Consider why the author may have decided to leave the village's exact location ambiguous, or unclear. Explain why an ambiguous setting connects to the story's theme about traditions.
2. Identify evidence of Old Man Warner's feelings about the lottery and what he thinks about stopping the tradition. Explain how his character's dialogue helps develop the story's theme.
3. Some of the last names in "The Lottery" make allusions to important characters, events, and themes, and "Mr. Graves" is an example of one of those names. What connections can you make to this character's name? How might the name be an allusion? Use evidence from the text to explain your answer.
4. Identify setting details and examples of surprising behavior in the story's conclusion. Explain how living in the village has influenced the characters' beliefs and values.
5. Identify mysterious elements in "The Lottery" related to the story's setting, events, characters, and theme. Explain how these examples work together to create reader interest in the story.

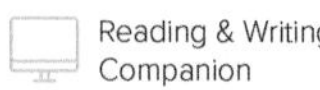

WRITE

LITERARY ANALYSIS: Sometimes terrible things happen in places that seem safe and pleasant on the surface. How did your knowledge about the setting of "The Lottery" expand or change as you read the story? What is one theme that the setting helped to develop as a result? Write a response of at least 300 words. Monitor details from the story to show how Shirley Jackson uses the setting not only to surprise readers, but also to develop the theme.

Writer's Notebook

Connect to Essential Question: Give students time to reflect on how "The Lottery" connects to the unit's essential question "What attracts us to the mysterious?" by freewriting in their Writer's Notebooks.

Beginning & Intermediate

Read aloud the unit's essential question: "What attracts us to the mysterious?" Encourage students to draw their connections or allow students to write in their native language. Circulate the room, prompting students for their thoughts as they respond orally or through pantomime.

Advanced & Advanced High

Allow students to share their connections orally in pairs or small groups before freewriting.

StudySyncTV

Project the StudySyncTV episode and pause at the following times to prompt discussion:

1:43 How do the students use textual evidence to determine the setting of "The Lottery"?

4:05 Miles, Paige, and Rebecca debate the purpose of the lottery. What textual evidence do they use to support their claims? How does this bring the group closer to identifying the theme?

5:52 How does the group use historical context to determine a possible theme of the story?

Collaborative Conversation

Break students into collaborative conversation groups to discuss the Close Read prompt. Ask students to use the StudySyncTV episode as a model for their discussion. Remind them to reference their Skills Focus annotations in their discussion.

Sometimes terrible things happen in places that seem safe and pleasant on the surface. How did your knowledge about the setting of "The Lottery" expand or change as you read the story? What is one theme that the setting helped to develop as a result? Write a response of at least 300 words. Monitor details from the story to show how Shirley Jackson uses the setting not only to surprise readers, but also to develop the theme.

Use the scaffolds below to differentiate instruction for your ELL English Language Learners and A Approaching grade-level learners.

ELL **BEGINNING, INTERMEDIATE** Use the discussion guide and speaking frames to facilitate the discussion with support from the teacher.

ADVANCED, ADVANCED HIGH Use the discussion guide and speaking frames to facilitate the discussion in mixed-level groups.

A **APPROACHING** Use the discussion guide to facilitate the discussion in mixed-level groups.

APPROACHING

ADVANCED, ADVANCED HIGH

BEGINNING, INTERMEDIATE

Discussion Guide	Speaking Frames
1. How does the setting relate to theme in this story?	• At first, the village square seems ____ because ____. • In the end, the village square seems ____ because ____. • This surprising change could help develop a theme about ____.
2. How does an allusion deepen your understanding of the text and its themes?	• In this story, ____ is an allusion to ____. • This allusion helps me see ____ in a new way because ____. • This allusion could help develop a theme about ____.
3. Think about the setting and allusion that you have analyzed. What is one theme that they both help develop in this story?	• This setting and allusion both relate to a theme about ____. • The author uses setting and allusion to develop this theme: ____.

Review Prompt and Rubric

Before students begin writing, review the writing prompt and rubric with the class.

LITERARY ANALYSIS: Sometimes terrible things happen in places that seem safe and pleasant on the surface. How did your knowledge about the setting of "The Lottery" expand or change as you read the story? What is one theme that the setting helped to develop as a result? Write a response of at least 300 words. Monitor details from the story to show how Shirley Jackson uses the setting not only to surprise readers, but also to develop the theme.

ELL **PROMPT GUIDE**

- Did the setting details that you monitored change your impression of the village as you read this story?
- How does this change relate to themes in this story?
- Are any details allusions to themes, characters, or events from older stories?
- How does this allusion deepen your understanding of the text and its themes?
- Think about the setting and allusion that you have analyzed. What is one theme that they both help develop in this story?

Score	Theme	Allusion	Language and Conventions
4	The writer clearly analyzes and explains how the setting develops a theme. The writer provides exemplary analysis, using relevant evidence from the text.	The writer clearly analyzes and explains how one or more allusions from "The Lottery" are rendered new in the story and help develop a theme. The writer provides exemplary analysis, using relevant evidence from the text.	The writer demonstrates a consistent command of grammar, punctuation, and usage conventions. Although minor errors may be evident, they do not detract from the fluency or the clarity of the writing.
3	The writer analyzes and explains how the setting develops a theme. The writer provides sufficient analysis, using relevant evidence from the text most of the time.	The writer analyzes and explains how one or more allusions from "The Lottery" are rendered new in the story and help develop a theme. The writer provides sufficient analysis, using relevant evidence from the text most of the time.	The writer demonstrates an adequate command of grammar, punctuation, and usage conventions. Although some errors may be evident, they create few (if any) disruptions in the fluency or the clarity of the writing.
2	The writer begins to analyze or explain how the setting develops a theme. However, the analysis is incomplete because the writer uses relevant evidence from the text only some of the time.	The writer begins to analyze or explain how one or more allusions from "The Lottery" are rendered new in the story and help develop a theme. However, the analysis is incomplete because the writer uses relevant evidence from the text only some of the time.	The writer demonstrates a partial command of grammar, punctuation, and usage conventions. Some distracting errors may be evident, at times creating minor disruptions in the fluency or clarity of the writing.
1	The writer attempts to analyze or explain how the setting develops a theme, but the analysis is not successful. The writer uses little or no relevant evidence from the text.	The writer attempts to analyze or explain how one or more allusions from "The Lottery" are rendered new in the story and help develop a theme, but the analysis is not successful. The writer uses little or no relevant evidence from the text.	The writer demonstrates little or no command of grammar, punctuation, and usage conventions. Serious and persistent errors create disruptions in the fluency of the writing and sometimes interfere with meaning.
0	The writer does not provide a relevant response to the prompt or does not provide a response at all.	The writer does not provide a relevant response to the prompt or does not provide a response at all.	Serious and persistent errors overwhelm the writing and interfere with the meaning of the response as a whole, making the writer's meaning impossible to understand.

SCAFFOLDS

Write

Ask students to complete the writing assignment using textual evidence to support their answers.

Use the scaffolds below to differentiate instruction for your ELL English Language Learners and A Approaching grade-level learners.

ELL **BEGINNING** With the help of the word bank, write a response using paragraph frame 1.

INTERMEDIATE With the help of the word bank, write a response using paragraph frames 1 and 2.

ADVANCED, ADVANCED HIGH Write a response of differentiated length using the sentence starters.

A **APPROACHING** Write a response of differentiated length using the sentence starters.

BEGINNING / INTERMEDIATE | ADVANCED, ADVANCED HIGH / APPROACHING

Word Bank	Paragraph Frame 1	Paragraph Frame 2	Sentence Starters
orderly allusion ancient theme tradition	Shirley Jackson's "The Lottery" develops a theme about ____ by using the setting of a village square and an ____ to stone-throwing. The setting changes from ____ to violent as villagers follow each part of the lottery. The villagers throw stones at a person who loses the lottery. This is an allusion to an ____ form of punishment that happens in The Bible. The setting and allusion reveal a ____ that it is dangerous to follow old traditions and not question them.	The tradition is ____ because the villagers use ____ to kill the person who ____ the lottery. This scene ____ shows that people can easily participate in ____ actions because those actions have been done for many years.	• This story develops a theme about . . . • The setting of this story is . . . • It changes from . . . to . . . because . . . • At the end of this tradition, the villagers . . . • This is an allusion to . . . • The setting and allusion help to reveal . . .

Peer Review

Students should submit substantive feedback to two peers using the review instructions below.

- How clearly does the writer express a theme from the story?
- Does the writer clearly analyze and explain how the setting helps develop a theme?
- Does the writer clearly identify an allusion and explain how it helps develop a theme?
- What did the writer do well in this response? What does the writer need to work on?

Rate

Respond to the following with a point rating that reflects your opinion.

	1	2	3	4
Ideas	■	■	■	□
Evidence	■	■	■	■
Language and Conventions	■	■	□	□

Submit

ELL A **SENTENCE FRAMES**

- One of the story's themes was (clearly / not clearly) stated. It was ____.
- You could express the theme more clearly by ____.
- You (do / do not) explain how a setting helps develop a theme because ____.
- You (do / do not) explain how an allusion helps develop a theme because ____.
- One of the strongest parts of this response is ____.
- You can improve this response by ____.

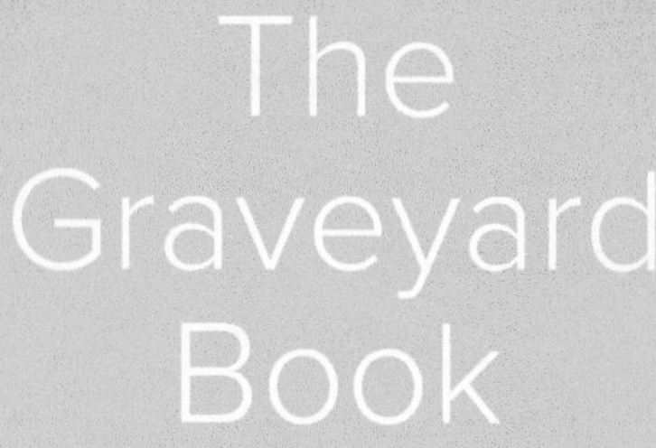

The Graveyard Book

FICTION
Neil Gaiman and
P. Craig Russell
2014

Introduction

Children's author Neil Gaiman is best known for his novella *Coraline*, which won international praise and was adapted into a graphic novel as well as a high-budget film. Like *Coraline*, the British author's graphic novel version of *The Graveyard Book* was both a bestseller and critically acclaimed. Through Gaiman's text and P. Craig Russell's award-winning illustrations, this Newbery Medal-winning story tells of a boy who, after his family is murdered by the man Jack, is raised in a cemetery by ghosts.

Awoken in his crib by the sound of his parents' murder, a toddler escapes to a nearby cemetery, where a ghost couple named Owens find him. As Mr. and Mrs. Owens wonder what to do, the ghost of the toddler's mother appears and asks Mrs. Owens to protect the baby from Jack, her murderer. Jack has followed the baby to the cemetery, but just as he is getting close, the Owen couple disappears with the baby boy. Silas, the graveyard's caretaker, confronts Jack and escorts him out the front gate. Then Silas flies to the middle of the graveyard, where the rest of the ghosts discuss how to take care of the baby. Silas volunteers to be the boy's guardian because he is the only one who can leave the cemetery to find food. The ghosts propose names for the boy, eventually settling on Nobody Owens. Silas thinks the name will help keep the boy safe.

 Proficiency-leveled summaries and summaries in multiple languages are available digitally.

 Audio and audio text highlighting are available with this text.

COMPARING WITHIN AND ACROSS GENRES

 What do a wandering baby in a graveyard, a New York City murder, and a monkey's paw talisman have in common? Each tells a tale of mystery but with different story structures. Reading them together will help students analyze how structure contributes to the meaning and style of a text.

Access Complex Text

LEXILE: 1070L **WORD COUNT:** 829

The following areas may be challenging for students, particularly ELL English Language Learners and A Approaching grade-level learners.

Genre	Organization	Connection of Ideas
• The original novel by Neil Gaiman was turned into a graphic novel, which includes illustrated panels, text boxes, and speech bubbles unique to that form.	• The arrangement of the illustrations on each page, containing story details essential for following the narrative, may not be clear for some students.	• Readers must link the details from the illustrations, the content of the speech bubbles, and the narration in the panels to follow the complete story. • Students may need to restate the narrative in their own words in annotations.

 SCAFFOLDS

 ENGLISH LANGUAGE LEARNERS  APPROACHING GRADE LEVEL  BEYOND GRADE LEVEL

These icons identify differentiation strategies and scaffolded support for a variety of students. See the digital lesson plan for additional differentiation strategies and scaffolds.

Instructional Path

The print teacher's edition includes essential point-of-use instruction and planning tools. Complete lesson plans and program documents appear in your digital teacher account.

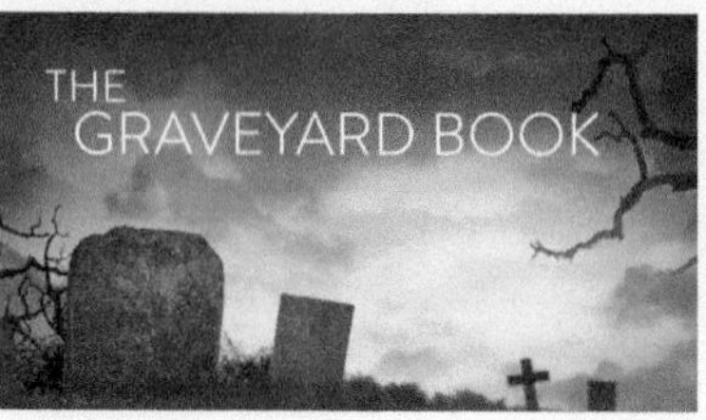

Independent Read: The Graveyard Book

Objectives: After reading the text, students will demonstrate understanding by responding to comprehension questions, participating in a collaborative conversation, and writing a personal response.

Independent Read

Introduce the Text

As a class, watch the video preview and have students read the introduction in pairs to make connections to the video preview.

- What feeling or mood is created by the images and narration in the video?
- What questions do you have about the text?
- How does the information provided in the introduction relate to the mood created by the video preview?

ELL **SPEAKING FRAMES**

- The ____ in the video makes me think ____.
- The video shows ____. This makes me wonder ____.
- I think the text will ____. I think this because ____.
- I predict that there will be ____ because ____.

Entry Point

As students prepare to read *The Graveyard Book*, share the following information with them to provide context.

- ✓ Neil Gaiman writes novels, short stories, and essays, and this book won the Newbery Medal for the most outstanding contribution to children's literature in 2009.
- ✓ Artist P. Craig Russell worked with a team of other comic book artists to adapt the novel into a graphic novel. Gaiman reported that a different artist worked on each chapter.
- ✓ There's a saying in this story that "It takes a graveyard to raise a child," and it is based on the proverb "It takes a village to raise a child." Students can discuss why the author might have used this saying after they have read the story.

"Are you . . . is that . . . a ghost?!"

NOTES

Analyze Vocabulary Using Context Clues

As students read the text, ask them to make predictions about each vocabulary word based on the context clues in the sentence.

TEXT TALK

What happens when the baby boy hears a crash?

See page 64: He climbs out of his crib and walks toward an open door.

NOTES

NOTES

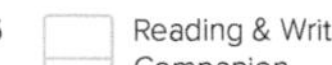

TEXT TALK

Where does the boy go?

See pages 65 and 66: He wanders into a graveyard, where there appear to be ghosts of a man and a woman.

NOTES

I DARESAY THAT IS A QUESTION, AND YET, IT IS NOT OUR QUESTION. FOR THIS HERE BABY IS UNQUESTIONABLY ALIVE, AND AS SUCH IS NOTHING TO DO WITH US AND IS NO PART OF OUR WORLD.
LOOK AT HIM SMILE!
THERE NOW. IT'S THE BABE'S FAMILY, COME TO BRING HIM BACK TO ITS LOVING BOSOM. LEAVE THE LITTLE MAN BE.
HE DUN'T LOOK LIKE NOBODY'S FAMILY, THAT ONE.

The Graveyard Book

NOTES

TEXT TALK

What event takes the ghosts by surprise?

See pages 68 and 69: A spirit of a woman screams, "He is trying to harm my baby!"

How do you know that a man is after the baby? What questions does this raise for you?

See page 69: Answers will vary but should include that a man is pictured jumping into the graveyard, and the same man is shown holding a knife in a panel that sits side-by-side next to a panel showing the little boy.

Analyze for Enrichment

Use the activity below to differentiate instruction for your B Beyond grade-level learners.

Look at the illustrations on page 70:

In graphic novels, color and shading show feelings, moods, and emotions. What mood is the author trying to evoke? How are the colors helping the reader understand the story? Is the author's use of color effective?

TEXT TALK

What happens to the boy in the graveyard?

See page 70: The ghosts of the old couple, the Owenses, take him and the three of them disappear in a mist so the man with the knife—the man Jack—can't see him.

NOTES

CAN I HELP YOU?
THE MAN JACK WAS TALL. THIS MAN WAS TALLER. THE MAN JACK WORE DARK CLOTHES. THIS MAN'S CLOTHES WERE DARKER. PEOPLE WHO NOTICED THE MAN JACK WHEN HE WAS ABOUT HIS BUSINESS FOUND THEMSELVES TROUBLED.
THE MAN JACK LOOKED UP AT THE STRANGER, AND IT WAS THE MAN JACK WHO WAS TROUBLED.
I WAS LOOKING FOR SOME-ONE.
IN A LOCKED GRAVEYARD, AT NIGHT?
I WAS JUST PASSING WHEN I HEARD A BABY CRY. WELL, WHAT WOULD ANYONE DO?
I APPLAUD YOUR PUBLIC-SPIRITEDNESS. YET HOW WERE YOU PLANNING TO GET OUT OF HERE WITH IT? YOU CAN'T CLIMB BACK OVER THE WALL HOLDING A BABY.
I WOULD HAVE CALLED UNTIL SOMEONE LET ME OUT.
WELL, THAT WOULD HAVE BEEN ME, THEN.
I WOULD HAVE HAD TO LET YOU OUT.
FOLLOW ME.
ARE YOU THE CARE-TAKER, THEN?
AM I?
CERTAINLY, IN A MANNER OF SPEAKING.

NOTES

IF THERE WAS A BABY, IT WOULDN'T HAVE BEEN HERE IN THE GRAVEYARD.
MUCH MORE LIKELY THAT YOU HEARD A NIGHTBIRD, AND SAW A CAT, PERHAPS, OR A FOX. THEY DECLARED THIS PLACE A NATURE RESERVE THIRTY YEARS AGO, AROUND THE TIME OF THE LAST FUNERAL.
PERHAPS YOU WERE MISTAKEN.
NOW THINK CAREFULLY, AND TELL ME YOU ARE CERTAIN THAT IT WAS A CHILD THAT YOU SAW.
A FOX. THEY MAKE THE MOST UNCOMMON NOISES, NOT UNLIKE A PERSON CRYING.
NO, YOUR VISIT TO THE GRAVEYARD WAS A MIS-STEP. SOMEWHERE THE CHILD YOU SEEK AWAITS YOU...
...BUT HE IS NOT HERE.

NOTES

TEXT TALK

What makes the man Jack leave the graveyard?

See page 73: A very tall man dressed like a vampire lets him out with a key, and for some reason, the man Jack decides to go.

SELECTION VOCABULARY

acquaintance / el/la conocido/a *noun* someone known casually, not a close friend

- What are The Stranger and Jack doing by the cemetery gate?
- How well do The Stranger and Jack know each other?

SELECTION VOCABULARY

perpetuity / la perpetuidad ***noun*** the state of continuing forever COGNATE

- How much time has passed since the cemetery was bought?
- How does that time frame give a clue about the meaning of *perpetuity*?

obdurate / obstinado/a ***adjective*** stubborn and hard-hearted

- What character does the word *obduracy* refer to?
- How do that character's actions give a clue about the meaning of *obduracy*?

NOTES

MY *DEAR* WOMAN...

I AM *NOT* YOUR DEAR WOMAN.

TEXT TALK

What does the tall man witness in the graveyard?

See pages 74 and 75: The tall man sees the ghosts talking about the baby as the old woman ghost holds him.

NOTES

SELECTION VOCABULARY

draw / atraer *verb* to attract; to pull someone's attention

- Does The Stranger want to discuss the baby?
- What makes The Stranger join the conversation?

TEXT TALK

How does the tall man, Silas, settle the argument among the ghosts?

See page 76: He decides that the whole graveyard will look after the baby boy.

Academic Vocabulary in Context

Use the activity below to differentiate instruction for your B Beyond grade-level learners.

Look at the word *expression* in the last panel on page 77:

Explain to students that *expression* is an academic vocabulary word with four meanings:

1. the communication (in speech or writing) of one's beliefs or opinions
2. the feelings expressed on a person's face
3. a word or phrase that particular people use in particular situations
4. communication without words

Ask students: Which definition of *expression* best matches the word as it's being used in the text? Using that knowledge, explain what Silas means when he says "pardon the expression."

NOTES

V SELECTION VOCABULARY

flattery / la adulación ***noun*** praise that is insincere

- How does the phrase "push the minds" give a clue about the meaning of flattery?
- What other word is used to describe The Stranger's abilities?
- What "tools" does Silas like to use on humans?
- Do these tools work on the dead?

immune / immune ***adjective*** unable to be affected by something

- What does Mrs. Owens's expression show us about what it means to be "not immune" to something?
- If she is "not immune," what does it mean to be immune to something?

NOTES

TEXT TALK

What name does Silas give the baby?

See page 78: He names the baby Nobody.

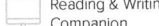

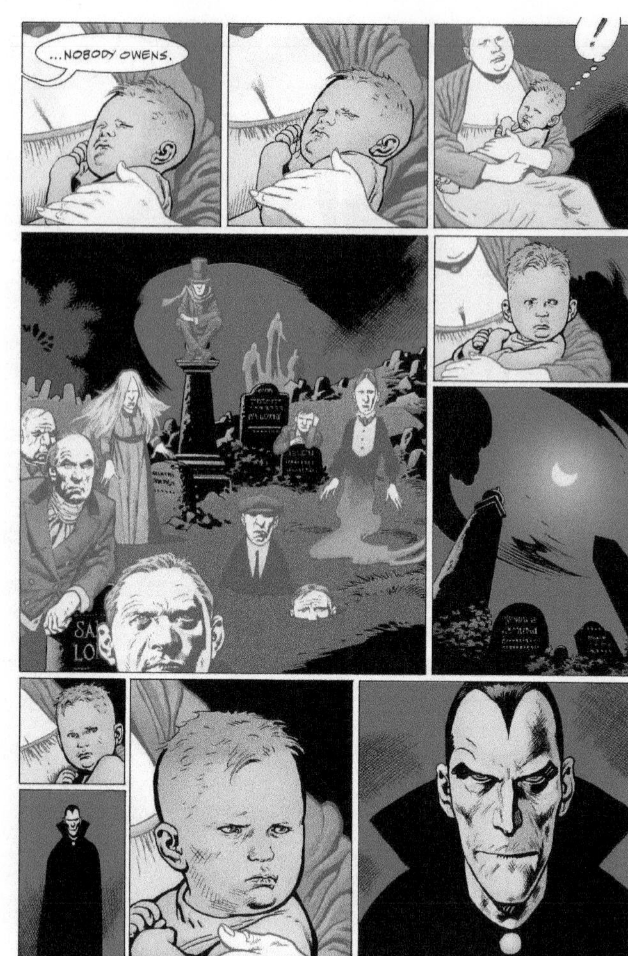
...NOBODY OWENS.

NOTES

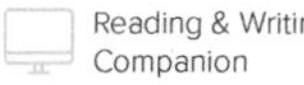

TEXT TALK

What is the response to the boy's new name? Why does Silas like the name?

See page 80: Everyone looks upset by the name, but the tall man says it will keep the baby safe.

NOTES

MRS. OWENS WAITED OUTSIDE THE FUNERAL CHAPEL, A LITTLE CHAPEL IN AN OVERGROWN GRAVEYARD THAT HAD BECOME UNFASHIONABLE. THE TOWN COUNCIL HAD PADLOCKED IT AND WERE WAITING FOR IT TO FALL DOWN.
SLEEP MY LITTLE BABY-- OH SLEEP UNTIL YOU WAKEN WHEN YOU'RE GROWN YOU'LL SEE THE WORLD ----
SOMETHING SOMETHING DUM - DE - DUM
AAAND SOME HAIRY BACON.
HERE WE GO, MISTRESS OWENS. LOTS OF GOOD THINGS FOR A GROWING BOY.
TINK
WE CAN KEEP IT IN THE CRYPT, EH?

NOTES

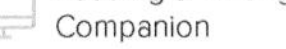

TEXT TALK

What is the challenge for the ghosts in taking care of the baby?

See pages 81 and 82: They have to figure out where to keep him and how to feed him.

NOTES

I CAN'T GIVE HIM UP. NOT AFTER WHAT I PROMISED HIS MAMA.
DO YOU THINK WE WILL HAVE LONG TO WAIT?
NOT LONG.
BUT HE WAS WRONG ABOUT THAT.
A GRAVEYARD IS NOT NORMALLY A DEMOCRACY, AND YET DEATH IS THE GREAT DEMOCRACY, AND EACH OF THE DEAD HAD AN OPINION AS TO WHETHER THE LIVING CHILD SHOULD BE ALLOWED TO STAY.
WE HAVE TO CONSIDER IT WAS THE OWENSES THAT GOT US INTO THIS NONSENSE.
THEY ARE RESPECTABLE.
TRUE.
AND THEY'RE NOT SOME FLIBBERTIGIBBET JOHNNY-COME-LATELIES.
TRUE.
NEVER BEFORE.
SLIPPERY SLOPE.
WELL WHY NOT?
ALWAYS A FIRST TIME.
SILAS *HAS* VOLUNTEERED TO BE HIS GUARDIAN.
STILL, SILAS IS NOT ONE OF US.
WE MUST GIVE WEIGHT TO THAT.
REGRET IT.
JUST NOT DONE.
BUT STILL... BUT STILL...
NEHEMIAH TROT, THE POET, HAD BEGUN TO DECLAIM HIS THOUGHT ON THE MATTER...
AHEM.
...WHEN SOMETHING HAPPENED.
SOMETHING TO SILENCE EACH OPINIONATED MOUTH.
SOMETHING UNPRECEDENTED IN THE HISTORY OF THE GRAVEYARD.

THEY KNEW HER, THE GRAVEYARD FOLK, FOR EACH OF US ENCOUNTERS THE LADY ON THE GREY AT THE END OF OUR DAYS, AND THERE IS NO FORGETTING HER.
THE DEAD ARE NOT SUPERSTITIOUS, NOT AS A RULE, BUT THEY WATCHED HER AS A ROMAN AUGER MIGHT HAVE WATCHED THE SACRED CROWS CIRCLE, SEEKING WISDOM, SEEKING A CLUE.

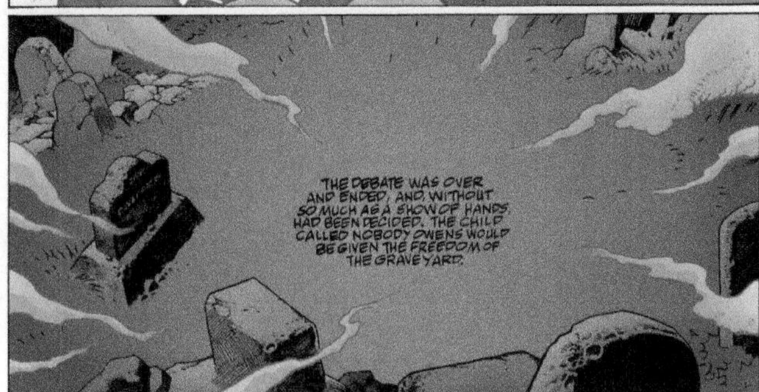

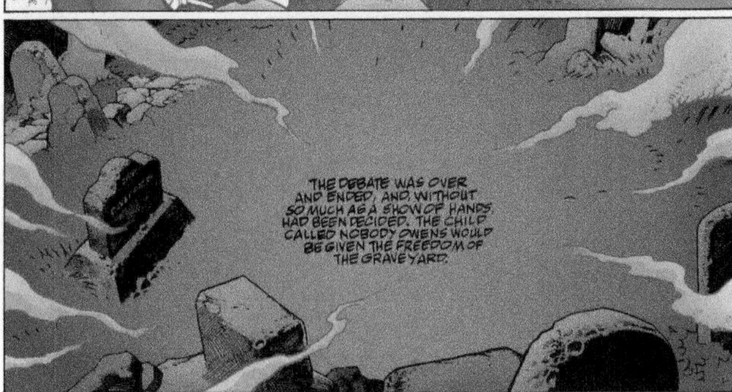

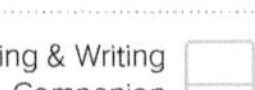

TEXT TALK

What are the ghosts debating in the last pages? How is the debate settled?

See pages 83–85: The ghosts do not agree about keeping and raising the baby. A lady on a grey horse shows up, tells them to have charity, and then rides away. Through her power, it's decided that the child will live in the graveyard.

B Ask each Beyond grade-level student to write one additional discussion question. Then have one or two students facilitate a discussion, using their questions to guide the conversation.

WRITE

PERSONAL RESPONSE: Think about the title of this book and the excerpt that follows. What kind of story did you expect to read based on the title? Why? Did your expectations change after you read the excerpt? Use quotations and descriptions from the excerpt to explain whether or not the book matched what you expected from the title.

Reading Comprehension OPTIONAL

Have students complete the digital reading comprehension questions ✓ when they finish reading.

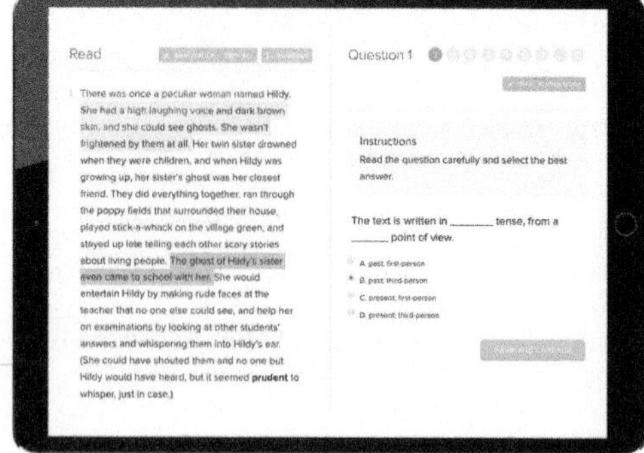

ANSWER KEY

QUESTION 1: D
QUESTION 2: D
QUESTION 3: A
QUESTION 4: B
QUESTION 5: C
QUESTION 6: B
QUESTION 7: D
QUESTION 8: C
QUESTION 9: *See first chart.*
QUESTION 10: *See second chart.*

First	Second	Third	Fourth
Something crashes on the floor in the baby's house.	Jack lifts a knife behind The Stranger's back.	The graveyard citizens argue over adopting the baby.	The baby is named "Nobody."

Dialogue	Character
"The Stranger reached them as silently as the fog itself, and he watched the proceedings unfold from the shadows."	The Narrator
"If there was a baby, it wouldn't have been here in the graveyard."	The Stranger
"I was just passing when I heard a baby cry. Well, what would anyone do?"	Jack
"I can look after him. I'm holding him, aren't I?"	Mistress Owens

Connect and Extend OPTIONAL

CONNECT TO EXTENDED WRITING PROJECT

Students can use *The Graveyard Book* as a mentor text for their Extended Writing Project. They may take inspiration from Neil Gaiman's supernatural elements to create their own narratives.

BEYOND THE BOOK

Art: Graphic Transformation

The Graveyard Book is a graphic novel version of the original novel. Challenge students to transform another story (or a portion of another story) from this unit into a graphic story using pictures and dialogue. When they've finished creating their graphic stories, place students in small groups to share their works with their classmates.

To reflect, ask students:

- What aspects of the story were easiest to transform into graphic panels? What was most difficult?
- Did the graphic story medium alter the meaning or the content of the story? Why or why not?

SCAFFOLDS

Collaborative Conversation

Post the writing prompt to generate a discussion in small groups. Ask students to first break down the prompt before they discuss relevant ideas and textual evidence.

Think about the title of this book and the excerpt that follows. What did you expect from the title? Did your expectations change after you read the excerpt? Use quotations and descriptions from the excerpt to explain whether or not the book matched what you expected from the title.

Use the scaffolds below to differentiate instruction for your ELL English Language Learners and A Approaching grade-level learners.

ELL **BEGINNING, INTERMEDIATE** Use the discussion guide and speaking frames to facilitate the discussion with support from the teacher.

ADVANCED, ADVANCED HIGH Use the discussion guide and speaking frames to facilitate the discussion in mixed-level groups.

A **APPROACHING** Use the discussion guide to facilitate the discussion in mixed-level groups.

APPROACHING
ADVANCED, ADVANCED HIGH
BEGINNING, INTERMEDIATE

Discussion Guide	Speaking Frames
1. What did you expect about the graphic novel based on the title, *The Graveyard Book*?	• I expected the graphic novel to be ____.
2. Did your expectations change after you read the excerpt? How?	• After reading, I thought ____. • The (plot / characters / theme) surprised me because ____.
3. Which quotations and images from the excerpt matched or differed from your expectations?	• One (quotation / image) that matched my expectations was ____. • One (quotation / image) that differed from my expectations was ____.

Review Prompt And Rubric

Before students begin working, review the writing prompt and rubric with the class.

PERSONAL RESPONSE: Think about the title of this book and the excerpt that follows. What kind of story did you expect to read based on the title? Why? Did your expectations change after you read the excerpt? Use quotations and descriptions from the excerpt to explain whether or not the book matched what you expected from the title.

PROMPT GUIDES

- What did you expect about the graphic novel based on the title, *The Graveyard Book?*
- Did your expectations change after you read the excerpt? How?
- What quotations and images from the excerpt matched or differed from your expectations?

Score	Personal Response	Language and Conventions
4	The writer clearly explains how his or her expectations about the book were affected by reading the excerpt, using relevant evidence from the text as needed.	The writer demonstrates a consistent command of grammar, punctuation, and usage conventions. Although minor errors may be evident, they do not detract from the fluency or the clarity of the writing.
3	The writer sufficiently explains how his or her expectations about the book were affected by reading the excerpt, using relevant evidence from the text most of the time.	The writer demonstrates an adequate command of grammar, punctuation, and usage conventions. Although some errors may be evident, they create few (if any) disruptions in the fluency or the clarity of the writing.
2	The writer begins to explain how his or her expectations about the book were affected by reading the excerpt, but the explanation is incomplete. The writer uses relevant evidence from the text only some of the time.	The writer demonstrates a partial command of grammar, punctuation, and usage conventions. Some distracting errors may be evident, at times creating minor disruptions in the fluency or clarity of the writing.
1	The writer attempts to explain how his or her expectations about the book were affected by reading the excerpt, but the explanation is not successful. The writer uses little or no relevant evidence from the text.	The writer demonstrates little or no command of grammar, punctuation, and usage conventions. Serious and persistent errors create disruptions in the fluency of the writing and sometimes interfere with meaning.
0	The writer does not provide a relevant response to the prompt or does not provide a response at all.	Serious and persistent errors overwhelm the writing and interfere with the meaning of the response as a whole, making the writer's meaning impossible to understand.

SCAFFOLDS

Write

Ask students to complete the writing assignment using textual evidence to support their answers.

Use the scaffolds below to differentiate instruction for your ELL English Language Learners and A Approaching grade-level learners.

ELL **BEGINNING** With the help of the word bank, write a response using paragraph frame 1.

INTERMEDIATE With the help of the word bank, write a response using paragraph frames 1 and 2.

ADVANCED, ADVANCED HIGH Write a response of differentiated length using the sentence starters.

A **APPROACHING** Write a response of differentiated length using the sentence starters.

BEGINNING / INTERMEDIATE	BEGINNING / INTERMEDIATE	INTERMEDIATE	ADVANCED, ADVANCED HIGH / APPROACHING
Word Bank	**Paragraph Frame 1**	**Paragraph Frame 2**	**Sentence Starters**
different scare ghosts protect cemetery	I expected *The Graveyard Book* to be a story about ____. The setting matched my expectations because the story takes place in a ____. However, the characters were ____ from my expectations. Usually ghosts try to ____ people. The ghosts in the story decide to ____ the child.	One part of the plot that matched expectations for a scary story is ____. A scary (image / quotation) is ____. The theme of the story is surprising because ____. The way the ghosts take care of the child is ____.	• I expected the story to be . . . because . . . • Most ghost stories are . . . • The ghosts in this story . . . • An image or quotation that matched my expectations is . . . • An image or quotation that differed from my expectations is . . . • Before I read the excerpt, I thought . . . , but now I think . . .

Peer Review

Students should submit substantive feedback to two peers using the review instructions below.

- How well does the writer support his or her ideas about the text?
- Which of the writer's ideas was most surprising or interesting to you?
- What did the writer do well in this response? What does the writer need to work on?

Rate

Respond to the following with a point rating that reflects your opinion.

	1	2	3	4
Ideas				
Evidence				
Language and Conventions				

Submit

ELL A **SENTENCE FRAMES**

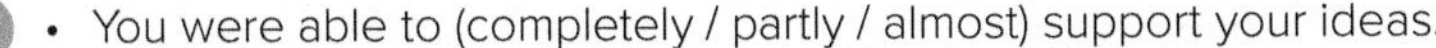

- You were able to (completely / partly / almost) support your ideas.
- Another (image / quotation) that could support your ideas is ____.
- I thought your idea about ____ was interesting because ____.
- The most surprising part of your response is ____.

The Conjure-Man Dies

FICTION
Rudolph Fisher
1932

Introduction

Originally published in 1932, *The Conjure-Man Dies: A Mystery Tale of Dark Harlem* is widely considered the first detective novel by an African-American author. Though writer Rudolph Fisher (1897–1934) published only two short stories and two novels before his untimely death at 37 years of age, he is still considered one of the central literary figures of the Harlem Renaissance. In this passage from the novel, Harlem physician Dr. Archer casts his keen analytical eye and medical expertise on the mysterious circumstances surrounding the sudden death of a local conjure-man, or fortune teller.

On a cold winter night in 1930s Harlem, Dr. Archer is summoned to tend to Frimbo, a fortune teller who was found unresponsive by Jinx and Bubber. Dr. Archer inspects the body and announces that Frimbo is dead. Looking closer, the doctor finds blood in Frimbo's hair and suspects foul play. Trying to determine what happened, he questions the two men, who explain that they were visiting Frimbo to seek advice about a business project. Jinx states that he had been with Frimbo while Bubber waited outside. Jinx claims that Frimbo was talking normally until he mumbled something about his vision and then suddenly lost consciousness.

ELL Proficiency-leveled summaries and summaries in multiple languages are available digitally.

Audio and audio text highlighting are available with this text..

COMPARING WITHIN AND ACROSS GENRES

In an excerpt from a novel, *The Conjure-Man Dies: A Mystery Tale of Dark Harlem*, Dr. Archer is called upon to examine the mysterious circumstances surrounding the death of a local conjure-man, or fortune teller.

Access Complex Text

LEXILE: 1010L **WORD COUNT:** 1,710

The following areas may be challenging for students, particularly ELL English Language Learners and A Approaching grade-level learners.

Specific Vocabulary	Genre	Sentence Structure
• Vocabulary specific to the setting, such as *Harlem, Battery Park,* and *Seventh Avenue*, set the novel in New York City. • Professions noted, such as *undertaker* and *psychist*, as well as other vocabulary, may need to be defined.	• The novel is divided into chapters, noted with numerals. • The narration establishes the time period, locations, characters, and mystery to be solved, but students may need to use highlighting to follow key events.	• The compound, complex, and compound-complex sentences, as well as descriptive phrases in the narration, may require simplifying.

SCAFFOLDS

 ENGLISH LANGUAGE LEARNERS  APPROACHING GRADE LEVEL  BEYOND GRADE LEVEL

These icons identify differentiation strategies and scaffolded support for a variety of students. See the digital lesson plan for additional differentiation strategies and scaffolds.

Instructional Path

The print teacher's edition includes essential point-of-use instruction and planning tools. Complete lesson plans and program documents appear in your digital teacher account.

Independent Read: The Conjure-Man Dies

Objectives: After reading an excerpt from the novel, students will write a short response to demonstrate their understanding of how setting details and description create a sense of mystery.

Independent Read

Introduce the Text

As a class, watch the video preview and have students read the introduction in pairs to make connections to the video preview.

- How do the images contrast with the narration? Why do you think that is? How does it make you feel?
- What kind of story are you about to read? How can you tell?

ELL SPEAKING FRAMES

- The ____ in the video makes me think ____.
- The video shows ____. This makes me wonder ____.
- I think the text will ____. I think this because ____.
- I predict that there will be ____ because ____.

Entry Point

As students prepare to read *The Conjure-Man Dies: A Mystery Tale of Dark Harlem*, share the following information with them to provide context.

- ✓ The Harlem Renaissance was a ground-shaking creative movement among African American intellectuals, artists, musicians, and writers in Harlem in the 1920s. Writers such as Langston Hughes, Zora Neale Hurston, and Rudolph Fisher celebrated the richness of African American life.
- ✓ Fisher was a physician and medical professor, but he also became the first Harlem Renaissance writer to be published in the mainstream press when his short story "City of Refuge" appeared in the *Atlantic Monthly* in 1925.
- ✓ Fisher intended for *The Conjure-Man Dies* to become a play but died before he could finish the project. Fellow Renaissance writer Countee Cullen aided in turning the novel into a drama, and it was presented on the stage of a Harlem theater in 1936.

"But all of black Harlem was not thus gay and bright."

NOTES

1.

1 Encountering the bright-lighted gaiety of Harlem's Seventh Avenue, the frigid midwinter night seemed to relent a little. She had given Battery Park a chill stare and she would undoubtedly freeze the Bronx. But here in this midrealm of rhythm and laughter she seemed to grow warmer and friendlier, observing, perhaps, that those who dwelt here were mysteriously dark like herself.

2 Of this favor the Avenue promptly took advantage. Sidewalks barren throughout the cold white day now sprouted life like fields in spring. Along swung boys in camels' hair beside girls in bunny and muskrat; broad, flat heels clacked, high narrow ones clicked, reluctantly leaving the disgorging theaters or eagerly seeking the **voracious** dance halls. There was loud jest and louder laughter and the frequent uplifting of merry voices in the moment's most popular song:

3 *"I'll be glad when you're dead, you rascal you,*
I'll be glad when you're dead, you rascal you.
What is it that you've got
Makes my wife think you so hot?
Oh you dog—I'll be glad when you're gone!"

4 But all of black Harlem was not thus gay and bright. Any number of dark, chill, silent side streets declined the relenting night's favor. 130th Street, for example, east of Lenox Avenue, was at this moment cold, still, and narrowly forbidding; one glanced down this block and was glad one's destination lay elsewhere. Its **concentrated** gloom was only intensified by an occasional spangle of electric light, splashed ineffectually against the blackness, or by the unearthly pallor of the sky, into which a wall of dwellings rose to hide the moon.

5 Among the houses in this looming row, one reared a little taller and gaunter than its fellows, so that the others appeared to shrink from it and huddle together in the shadow on either side. The basement of this house was quite black; its first floor, high above the sidewalk and approached by a long

Analyze Vocabulary Using Context Clues

As students read the text, ask them to make predictions about each vocabulary word based on the context clues in the sentence.

TEXT TALK

How does the house of Samuel Crouch and N. Frimbo differ from other houses on the street?

See paragraph 5: The house is taller and gloomier.

SELECTION VOCABULARY

voracious / voraz *adjective* an intense craving for food COGNATE

ELL
- Who is seeking the "voracious" dance halls? How do they feel?
- What can be heard inside the hall?

concentrated / la concentración *adjective* gathered together; condensed into one area or location COGNATE

- How is black Harlem described in the first sentence?
- What words are used to describe the side streets?

NOTES

graystone stoop, was only dimly lighted; its second floor was lighted more dimly still, while the third, which was the top, was vacantly dark again like the basement. About the place hovered an oppressive silence, as if those who entered here were warned beforehand not to speak above a whisper. There was, like a footnote, in one of the two first-floor windows to the left of the entrance a black-on-white sign reading:

6 "Samuel Crouch, Undertaker."

7 On the narrow panel to the right of the doorway the silver letters of another sign obscurely glittered on an onyx background:

8 "N. Frimbo, Psychist."

9 Between the two signs receded the high, narrow vestibule, terminating in a pair of tall glass-paneled doors. Glass curtains, tightly stretched in vertical folds, dimmed the already too subdued illumination beyond.

2.

10 It was about an hour before midnight that one of the doors rattled and flew open, revealing the bare headed, short, round figure of a young man who manifestly was **profoundly** agitated and in a great hurry. Without closing the door behind him, he rushed down the stairs, sped straight across the street, and in a moment was frantically pushing the bell of the dwelling directly opposite. A tall, slender, light-skinned man of obviously habitual composure answered the excited summons.

11 "Is—is you him?" stammered the agitated one, pointing to a shingle labeled "John Archer, M.D."

12 "Yes—I'm Dr. Archer."

13 "Well, arch on over here, will you, doc?" urged the caller. "Sump'm done happened to Frimbo."

14 "Frimbo? The fortune teller?"

15 "Step on it, will you, doc?"

16 Shortly, the physician, bag in hand, was hurrying up the graystone stoop behind his guide. They passed through the still open door into a hallway and mounted a flight of thickly carpeted stairs.

17 At the head of the staircase a tall, lank, angular figure awaited them. To this person the short, round, black, and by now quite breathless guide panted, "I

TEXT TALK

How does Bubber know where to find a doctor?

See paragraphs 10–12: A shingle says "John Archer, M.D."

SELECTION VOCABULARY

profoundly / profundo/a ***adjective*** very great or intense; heartfelt

COGNATE

ELL

- What word does *profoundly* describe?
- What other adjective follows *profoundly* and is connected by *and* in the sentence?
- How does the young man act?

got one, boy! This here's the doc from 'cross the street. Come on, doc. Right in here."

18 Dr. Archer, in passing, had an impression of a young man as long and lean as himself, of a similarly light complexion except for a **profusion** of dark brown freckles, and of a curiously scowling countenance that glowered from either ill humor or apprehension. The doctor rounded the banister head and strode behind his pilot toward the front of the house along the upper hallway, midway of which, still following the excited short one, he turned and swung into a room that opened into the hall at that point. The tall fellow brought up the rear.

19 Within the room the physician stopped, looking about in surprise. The chamber was almost entirely in darkness. The walls appeared to be hung from ceiling to floor with black velvet drapes. Even the ceiling was covered, the heavy folds of cloth converging from the four corners to gather at a central point above, from which dropped a chain suspending the single strange source of light, a device which hung low over a chair behind a large desk-like table, yet left these things and indeed most of the room unlighted. This was because, instead of shedding its radiance downward and outward as would an ordinary shaded droplight, this mechanism focused a horizontal beam upon a second chair on the opposite side of the table. Clearly the person who used the chair beneath the odd spotlight could remain in relative darkness while the occupant of the other chair was brightly illuminated.

20 "There he is—jes' like Jinx found him."

21 And now in the dark chair beneath the odd lamp the doctor made out a huddled, shadowy form. Quickly he stepped forward.

22 "Is this the only light?"

23 "Only one I've seen."

24 Dr. Archer procured a flashlight from his bag and swept its faint beam over the walls and ceiling. Finding no sign of another lighting fixture, he directed the instrument in his hand toward the figure in the chair and saw a bare black head **inclined** limply sidewise, a flaccid countenance with open mouth and fixed eyes staring from under drooping lids.

25 "Can't do much in here. Anybody up front?"

26 "Yes, suh. Two ladies."

27 "Have to get him outside. Let's see. I know. Downstairs. Down in Crouch's. There's a sofa. You men take hold and get him down there. This way."

SELECTION VOCABULARY

profusion / la profusión *noun* an abundance of something COGNATE

- What does the phrase "except for" indicate?
- What contrasts with "profusion of dark brown freckles"?

inclined / inclinar *adjective* angled COGNATE

- What does the doctor see when he shines the flashlight on the chair?
- How is the head inclined?

TEXT TALK

What is strange about the single light in the room Dr. Archer enters?

See paragraphs 19–21: The light shines over one chair at the opposite side of the table. The other person seated would be in complete darkness.

NOTES

28 There was some hesitancy. "Mean us, doc?"

29 "Of course. Hurry. He doesn't look so hot now."

30 "I ain't none too warm, myself," murmured the short one. But he and his friend obeyed, carrying out their task with a dispatch born of distaste. Down the stairs they followed Dr. Archer, and into the undertaker's dimly lighted front room.

31 "Oh, Crouch!" called the doctor. "Mr. Crouch!"

32 "That 'mister' ought to get him."

33 But there was no answer. "Guess he's out. That's right—put him on the sofa. Push that other switch by the door. Good."

34 Dr. Archer inspected the supine figure as he reached into his bag. "Not so good," he commented. Beneath his black satin robe the patient wore ordinary clothing—trousers, vest, shirt, collar and tie. Deftly the physician bared the chest; with one hand he palpated the heart area while with the other he adjusted the ear-pieces of his stethoscope. He bent over, placed the bell of his instrument on the motionless dark chest, and listened a long time. He removed the instrument, disconnected first one, then the other, rubber tube at their junction with the bell, blew **vigorously** through them in turn, replaced them, and repeated the operation of listening. At last he stood erect.

35 "Not a twitch," he said.

36 "Long gone, huh?"

37 "Not so long. Still warm. But gone."

38 The short young man looked at his scowling freckled companion. "What'd I tell you?" he whispered.

39 "Was I right or wasn't I?"

40 The tall one did not answer but watched the doctor. The doctor put aside his stethoscope and inspected the patient's head more closely, the parted lips and half-open eyes. He extended a hand and with his extremely long fingers gently palpated the scalp. "Hello," he said. He turned the far side of the head toward him and looked first at that side, then at his fingers.

41 "Wh-what?"

42 "Blood in his hair," announced the physician. He procured a gauze dressing from his bag, wiped his moist fingers, thoroughly sponged and reinspected the wound. Abruptly he turned to the two men, whom until now he had treated

SELECTION VOCABULARY

vigorously / vigorosamente ***adverb*** energetically or forcefully COGNATE

- Why does the doctor decide to check his stethoscope?
- What does the doctor do to check his stethoscope?
- Why does the doctor blow his stethoscope this way?

quite impersonally. Still imperturbably, but incisively, in the manner of lancing an abscess, he asked, "Who are you two gentlemen?"

43 "Why—uh—this here's Jinx Jenkins, doc. He's my buddy, see? Him and me—"

44 "And you—if I don't presume?"

45 "Me? I'm Bubber Brown—"

46 "Well, how did this happen, Mr. Brown?"

47 "'Deed I don' know, doc. What you mean—is somebody killed him?"

48 "You don't know?" Dr. Archer regarded the pair curiously a moment, then turned back to examine further. From an instrument case he took a probe and proceeded to explore the wound in the dead man's scalp. "Well—what do you know about it, then?" he asked, still probing. "Who found him?" "Jinx," answered the one who called himself Bubber. "We jes' come here to get this Frimbo's advice 'bout a little business project we thought up."

49 "Jinx went in to see him. I waited in the waitin' room. Presently Jinx come bustin' out pop-eyed and beckoned to me. I went back with him—and there was Frimbo, jes' like you found him. We didn't even know he was over the river."

50 "Did he fall against anything and strike his head?"

51 "No, suh, doc." Jinx became **articulate.** "He didn't do nothin' the whole time I was in there. Nothin' but talk. He tol' me who I was and what I wanted befo' I could open my mouth. Well, I said that I knowed that much already and that I come to find out sump'm I didn't know. Then he went on talkin', tellin' me plenty. He knowed his stuff all right. But all of a sudden he stopped talkin' and mumbled sump'm 'bout not bein' able to see. Seem like he got scared, and he say, 'Frimbo, why don't you see?' Then he didn't say no more. He sound' so funny I got scared myself and jumped up and grabbed that light and turned it on him—and there he was."

TEXT TALK

Why does Dr. Archer ask, "Who are you two gentlemen?"

See paragraphs 42–48: Dr. Archer knows Frimbo is dead, and he wants to know what happened.

Why does Jinx get scared?

See paragraph 49–51: Frimbo sounded funny and stopped talking.

B Ask each Beyond grade-level student to write one additional discussion question. Then have one or two students facilitate a discussion, using their questions to guide the conversation.

SELECTION VOCABULARY

articulate / elocuente *adjective* a characteristic of expressing yourself clearly

- Did Jinx talk at all before this time?
- How much does he talk at this point?

WRITE

PERSONAL RESPONSE: In the first section of *The Conjure-Man Dies*, the author describes Harlem in great detail. Reread this section and note your reaction. What can you see or hear? What phrases are particularly effective, and why? How does the author use this description to gradually create a sense of mystery? Be sure to cite textual evidence.

Reading Comprehension OPTIONAL

Have students complete the digital reading comprehension questions ✓ when they finish reading.

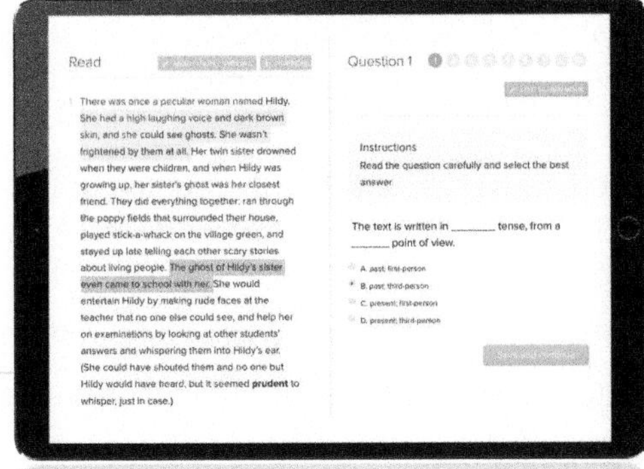

ANSWER KEY

QUESTION 1: B
QUESTION 2: B
QUESTION 3: A
QUESTION 4: C
QUESTION 5: D
QUESTION 6: C
QUESTION 7: A
QUESTION 8: B
QUESTION 9: *See first chart.*
QUESTION 10: *See second chart.*

Dialogue	Character
"Did he fall against anything and strike his head?"	Dr. Archer
"Frimbo, why don't you see?"	Frimbo
"We jes' come here to get this Frimbo's advice 'bout a little business project we thought up."	Bubber
"He sound' so funny I got scared myself and jumped up and grabbed that light and turned it on—and there he was."	Jinx

First	Second	Third	Fourth
Bubber runs across the street to Dr. Archer's office.	Jinx and Bubber carry Frimbo downstairs to Crouch's office.	Dr. Archer examines Frimbo and finds a bloody wound on his skull.	Bubber explains to Dr. Archer why he and Jinx came to see Frimbo.

Connect and Extend OPTIONAL

CONNECT TO EXTENDED WRITING PROJECT

Students can use *The Conjure-Man Dies: A Mystery Tale of Dark Harlem* as a mentor text for their Extended Writing Project. They may adopt Rudolph Fisher's style of description for their own narratives.

BEYOND THE BOOK

Research Project: The Harlem Renaissance

Rudolph Fisher was a central literary figure of the Harlem Renaissance. Place students into small groups to research the following aspects of the literary and cultural movement:

- Harlem, New York City
- the time period of the Harlem Renaissance
- key themes and ideas of the movement
- prominent Harlem Renaissance authors
- culture, music, and fashion

Allow groups time to present their key findings to the class.

To reflect, ask students:

- What authors, artists, and musicians were most interesting to you? Why?
- What other historical figures might you continue to learn about on your own?

Collaborative Conversation

SCAFFOLDS

Post the writing prompt to generate a discussion in small groups. Ask students to first break down the prompt before they discuss relevant ideas and textual evidence.

In the first section of *The Conjure-Man Dies*, the author describes Harlem in great detail. Reread this section and note your reaction. What can you see or hear? What phrases are particularly effective, and why? How does the author use this description to gradually create a sense of mystery? Be sure to cite textual evidence.

Use the scaffolds below to differentiate instruction for your ELL English Language Learners and A Approaching grade-level learners.

ELL **BEGINNING, INTERMEDIATE** Use the discussion guide and speaking frames to facilitate the discussion with support from the teacher.

ADVANCED, ADVANCED HIGH Use the discussion guide and speaking frames to facilitate the discussion in mixed-level groups.

A **APPROACHING** Use the discussion guide to facilitate the discussion in mixed-level groups.

APPROACHING
ADVANCED, ADVANCED HIGH
BEGINNING, INTERMEDIATE

Discussion Guide	Speaking Frames
1. What is a phrase that helps you see or hear Harlem?	• A phrase that helps me see Harlem is ____. • A phrase that helps me hear Harlem is ____.
2. What makes a phrase descriptive?	• A descriptive phrase ____.
3. What kinds of things are mysterious to you? Why?	• An example of something mysterious is ____. • It is mysterious because ____. Now I think ____.

Review Prompt and Rubric

Before students begin writing, review the writing prompt and rubric with the class.

PERSONAL RESPONSE: In the first section of *The Conjure-Man Dies*, the author describes Harlem in great detail. Reread this section and note your reaction. What can you see or hear? What phrases are particularly effective, and why? How does the author use this description to gradually create a sense of mystery? Be sure to cite textual evidence.

PROMPT GUIDE

A

- What is a phrase that helps you see or hear Harlem?
- What makes a phrase descriptive?
- What kinds of things are mysterious to you? Why?

Score	Personal Response	Language and Conventions
4	The writer clearly explains his or her response to the descriptions in the text, using relevant evidence from the text as needed.	The writer demonstrates a consistent command of grammar, punctuation, and usage conventions. Although minor errors may be evident, they do not detract from the fluency or the clarity of the writing.
3	The writer sufficiently explains his or her response to the descriptions in the text, using relevant evidence from the text most of the time.	The writer demonstrates an adequate command of grammar, punctuation, and usage conventions. Although some errors may be evident, they create few (if any) disruptions in the fluency or the clarity of the writing.
2	The writer begins to explain his or her response to the descriptions in the text, but the explanation is incomplete. The writer uses relevant evidence from the text only some of the time.	The writer demonstrates a partial command of grammar, punctuation, and usage conventions. Some distracting errors may be evident, at times creating minor disruptions in the fluency or clarity of the writing.
1	The writer attempts to explain his or her response to the descriptions in the text, but the explanation is not successful. The writer uses little or no relevant evidence from the text.	The writer demonstrates little or no command of grammar, punctuation, and usage conventions. Serious and persistent errors create disruptions in the fluency of the writing and sometimes interfere with meaning.
0	The writer does not provide a relevant response to the prompt or does not provide a response at all.	Serious and persistent errors overwhelm the writing and interfere with the meaning of the response as a whole, making the writer's meaning impossible to understand.

Write

SCAFFOLDS

Ask students to complete the writing assignment using textual evidence to support their answers.

Use the scaffolds below to differentiate instruction for your ELL English Language Learners and A Approaching grade-level learners.

ELL **BEGINNING** With the help of the word bank, write a response using paragraph frame 1.

INTERMEDIATE With the help of the word bank, write a response using paragraph frames 1 and 2.

ADVANCED, ADVANCED HIGH Write a response of differentiated length using the sentence starters.

A **APPROACHING** Write a response of differentiated length using the sentence starters.

BEGINNING / INTERMEDIATE	BEGINNING / INTERMEDIATE	INTERMEDIATE	ADVANCED, ADVANCED HIGH / APPROACHING
Word Bank	**Paragraph Frame 1**	**Paragraph Frame 2**	**Sentence Starters**
see scary mysterious happy hear	The phrase "loud jest and louder laughter" helps me ____ the scene. I think the phrase sounds ____. The phrase "dark, chill, silent side streets" helps me ____ another scene. The phrase makes the story ____. The details about the setting are ____.	Another phrase that is descriptive is ____ because it helps me ____. The phrase ____ creates mystery because it ____.	• A phrase that helps me see an image is . . . • A phrase that helps me hear a sound is . . . • A phrase that is descriptive is . . . • This phrase is descriptive because . . . • A phrase that creates mystery is . . .

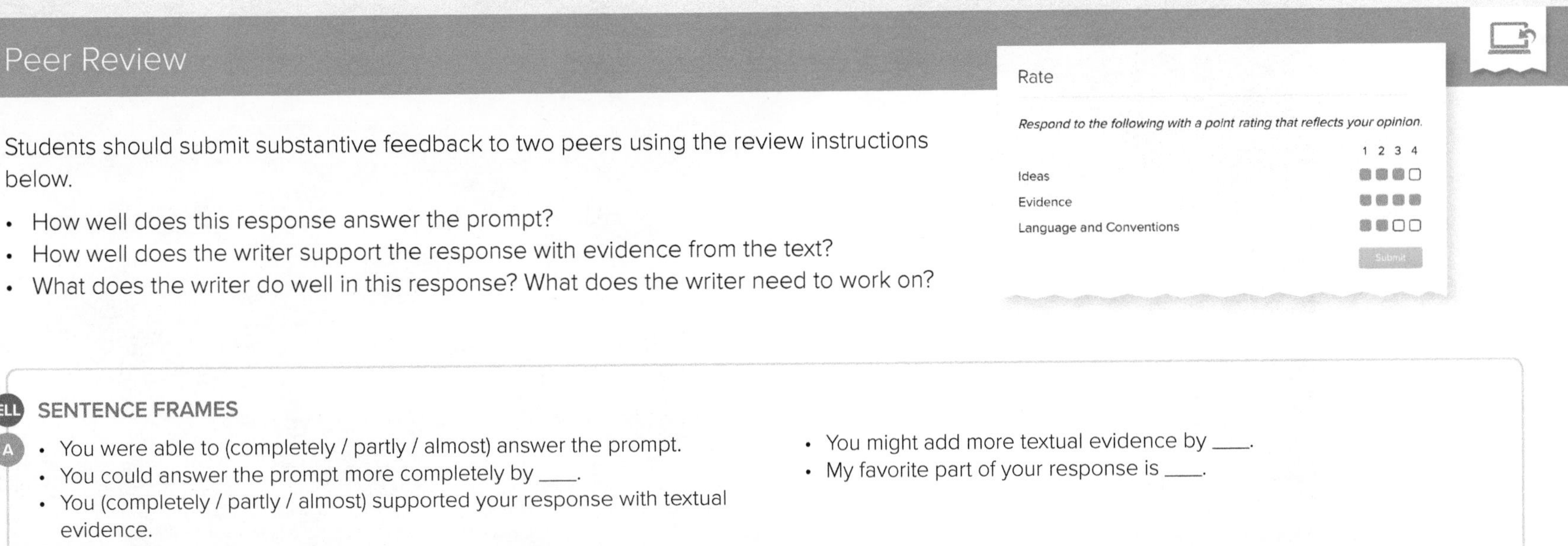

Peer Review

Students should submit substantive feedback to two peers using the review instructions below.

- How well does this response answer the prompt?
- How well does the writer support the response with evidence from the text?
- What does the writer do well in this response? What does the writer need to work on?

ELL A

SENTENCE FRAMES

- You were able to (completely / partly / almost) answer the prompt.
- You could answer the prompt more completely by ____.
- You (completely / partly / almost) supported your response with textual evidence.
- You might add more textual evidence by ____.
- My favorite part of your response is ____.

The Monkey's Paw

FICTION
W. W. Jacobs
1902

Introduction

studysync

W. W. Jacobs (1863–1943) wrote numerous humorous short stories, but it is for his works of horror that he is mainly remembered. In "The Monkey's Paw," his cautionary tale from 1902, a well-to-do family in Victorian England is presented with a dubious opportunity to increase their fortunes. A magical monkey's paw from India has the power to make three wishes come true—but what will be the price?

In Victorian England, a soldier pays a visit to the White family. He shows Mr. White a magical monkey's paw that will grant three wishes but warns him to throw the cursed thing away. Mr. White ignores the warning and wishes for £200 to pay off his mortgage. The next day, an agent from their son's workplace arrives to inform Mr. and Mrs. White that their son was killed in an on-the-job accident. As compensation, he offers Mr. and Mrs. White £200. After their son's funeral, Mrs. White convinces her husband to use the paw to bring their son back. Mr. White wishes for their son to be alive again. Soon thereafter, they hear a knock at the door. Mrs. White rushes to the door, but Mr. White is afraid of what she will find. The story ends with Mr. White making an unknown final wish as Mrs. White opens the door to a deserted road.

 Proficiency-leveled summaries and summaries in multiple languages are available digitally.

 Audio and audio text highlighting are available with this text.

COMPARING WITHIN AND ACROSS GENRES

 In the classic story of suspense "The Monkey's Paw" by W. W. Jacobs, we see the White family drawn to the mystery of the monkey's paw. Readers have the chance to consider what they would do in a similar situation. Would they be able to resist the mystery of the monkey's paw, or would they be drawn to it like the family was?

Access Complex Text

LEXILE: 940L **WORD COUNT:** 3,940

The following areas may be challenging for students, particularly  English Language Learners and  Approaching grade-level learners.

Genre	Prior Knowledge	Specific Vocabulary
• The author creates suspense and develops a major theme in this classic short story as readers begin to suspect, through foreshadowing and dialogue, that the consequences of wishes may be terrible. • Highlighting examples of literary elements may help students uncover the theme.	• The story is set in Victorian England, when the British Empire extended to India, and students may be unfamiliar with Indian cultural references. • Explain that the phrase "old temples and fakirs" refers to religious locations and the Muslims or Hindus who lived on alms, or charity.	• Difficult vocabulary, such as *presumptuous* (behavior that does not observe limits as to what is proper) and *doggedly* (in a manner of persistence), may need defining. • Remind students to use context clues while reading, and also to use a dictionary to define unfamiliar words.

SCAFFOLDS  **ENGLISH LANGUAGE LEARNERS**  **APPROACHING GRADE LEVEL**  **BEYOND GRADE LEVEL**

These icons identify differentiation strategies and scaffolded support for a variety of students. See the digital lesson plan for additional differentiation strategies and scaffolds.

Instructional Path

The print teacher's edition includes essential point-of-use instruction and planning tools. Complete lesson plans and program documents appear in your digital teacher account.

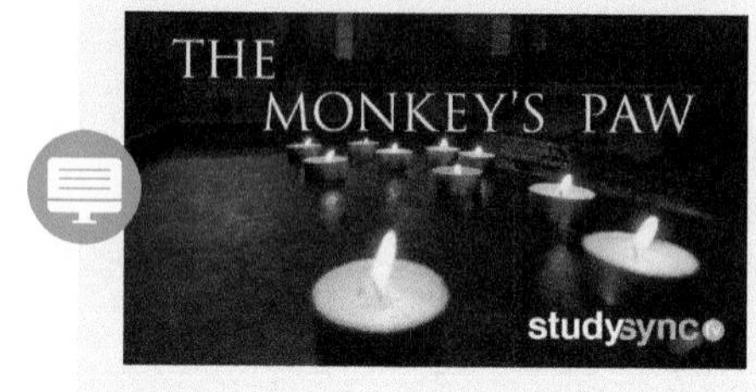

First Read: The Monkey's Paw

Objectives: Before, during, and after an initial reading and discussion of the short story, students will be able to identify and describe characters and setting details, as well as articulate events that are central to the story's plot.

Skill: Plot

Objectives: After rereading and discussing a model of close reading, students will be able to explain how dialogue propels the plot forward in the text.

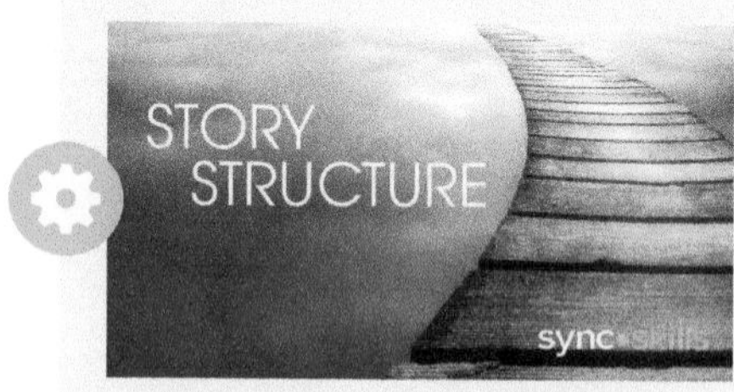

Skill: Story Structure

Objectives: After rereading and discussing a model of close reading, students will be able to compare and contrast the structure of two texts and analyze how the differing structures affect meaning and style.

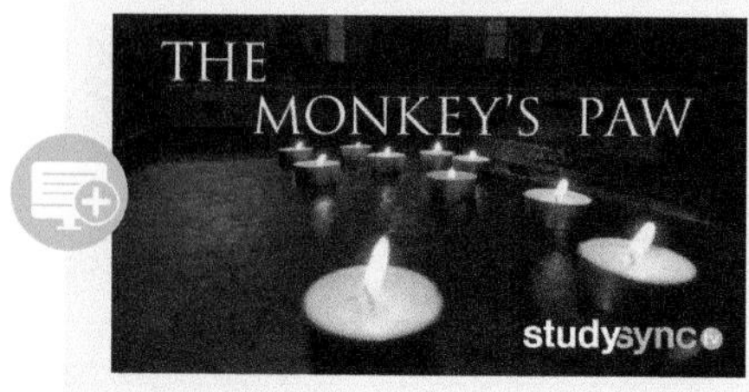

Close Read: The Monkey's Paw

Objectives: After engaging in a close reading and discussion, students will be able to analyze and compare how story structure contributes to the meaning of two texts in a short, written response.

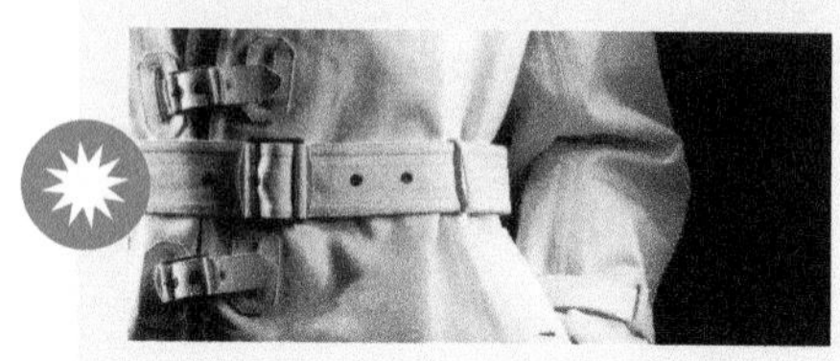

Blast: Life's Great Mysteries

Objectives: After exploring background information and research links about a topic, students will respond to a question by writing a 140-character response.

Progress Monitoring

Opportunities to Learn	Opportunities to Demonstrate Learning	Opportunities to Reteach
Plot		
Skill: Plot	Skill: Plot • Your Turn Close Read • Skills Focus • Write	Unit 2 Skill: Plot - Abuela Invents the Zero Unit 5 Skill: Plot - Teen Mogul Spotlight Skill: Plot
Story Structure		
Skill: Story Structure	Skill: Story Structure • Your Turn Close Read • Skills Focus • Write	Unit 6 Skill: Story Structure - There Will Come Soft Rains Unit 6 Skill: Story Structure - Children of Blood and Bone Spotlight Skill: Story Structure

First Read

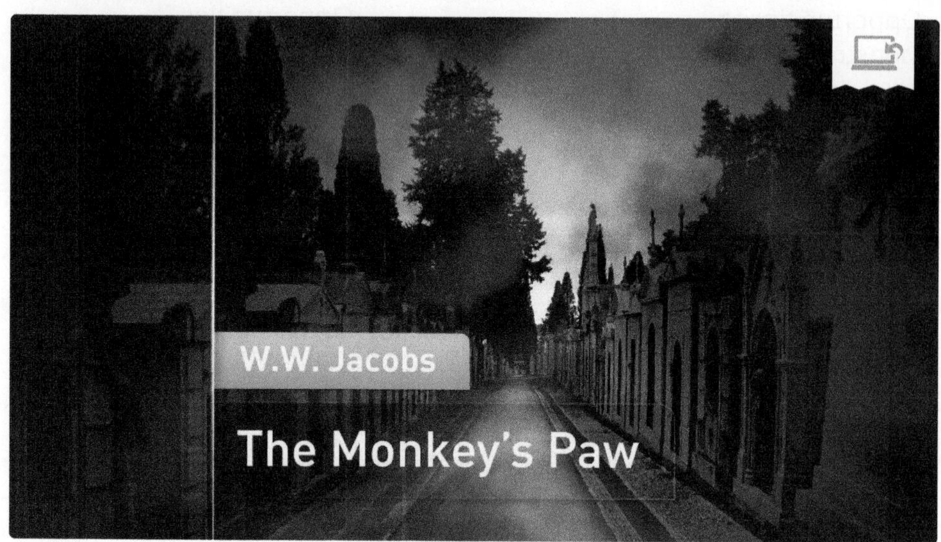

Introduce the Text

As a class, watch the video preview and have students read the introduction in pairs to make connections to the video preview.

To activate prior knowledge and experiences, ask students:

- How do the images, words, and music in this video make you feel?
- What kind of story are you about to read? How can you tell?

ELL **SENTENCE FRAMES**

- The ____ in the video makes me think ____.
- The video shows ____. This makes me wonder ____.
- I think the text will ____. I think this because ____.
- I predict that there will be ____. I believe this because ____.

Entry Point

As students prepare to read "The Monkey's Paw," share the following information with them to provide context.

- ✓ "The Monkey's Paw" by W. W. Jacobs is what is known as a classic short story. Short fiction in a classic sense has a clear beginning, middle, and end, and includes the recognized structure of exposition, rising action, climax, falling action, and resolution. "The Monkey's Paw" is often ranked as one of the best short stories of all time, but that ranking may also be a matter of taste, for this is a horror story.
- ✓ A classic short story generally is centered around one of the four major conflicts: man versus man, man versus self, man versus society, or man versus nature. In the case of "The Monkey's Paw," the conflict centers on man versus self, but also on man versus the supernatural.
- ✓ There's an old saying: "Be careful what you wish for, for you will surely get it." Students can return to that question after they complete the reading.

"Hold it up in your right hand and wish aloud," said the sergeant-major, "but I warn you of the consequences."

I.

1 Without, the night was cold and wet, but in the small parlour of Laburnam Villa the blinds were drawn and the fire burned brightly. Father and son were at chess, the former, who possessed ideas about the game involving **radical** changes, putting his king into such sharp and unnecessary perils that it even provoked comment from the white-haired old lady knitting placidly by the fire.

2 "Hark at the wind," said Mr. White, who, having seen a fatal mistake after it was too late, was amiably desirous of preventing his son from seeing it.

3 "I'm listening," said the latter, grimly surveying the board as he stretched out his hand. "Check."

4 "I should hardly think that he'd come to-night," said his father, with his hand poised over the board.

5 "Mate," replied the son.

6 "That's the worst of living so far out," bawled Mr. White, with sudden and unlooked-for violence; "of all the beastly, slushy, out-of-the-way places to live in, this is the worst. Pathway's a bog, and the road's a torrent. I don't know what people are thinking about. I suppose because only two houses in the road are let, they think it doesn't matter."

7 "Never mind, dear," said his wife, soothingly; "perhaps you'll win the next one."

8 Mr. White looked up sharply, just in time to intercept a knowing glance between mother and son. The words died away on his lips, and he hid a guilty grin in his thin grey beard.

9 "There he is," said Herbert White, as the gate banged to loudly and heavy footsteps came toward the door.

SELECTION VOCABULARY

radical / radical *adjective* major; extreme and far beyond the norm COGNATE

Analyze Vocabulary Using Context Clues

In paragraph 1, focus on the sentence that uses the word *radical*. Point out the following context clues:

1. First, I notice that the word *radical* is describing the word *changes*, which means that it is an adjective.
2. When I read the sentence again, I notice that *radical* is related to Father's attitude toward the chess game. In this game, he is "putting his king into such sharp and unnecessary perils."
3. It sounds like Father is making extreme and risky decisions with his king, which makes me think that *radical* is another way of saying *extreme*.

Skills Focus

QUESTION 5: Connect to Essential Question

Is the monkey's paw magic? Here the White family learns about the mysterious "magic" of the monkey's paw. But what if the whole thing was just a series of coincidences?

10 The old man rose with hospitable haste, and opening the door, was heard condoling with the new arrival. The new arrival also condoled with himself, so that Mrs. White said, "Tut, tut!" and coughed gently as her husband entered the room, followed by a tall, burly man, beady of eye and rubicund of visage.

11 "Sergeant-Major Morris," he said, introducing him.

12 The sergeant-major shook hands, and taking the proffered seat by the fire, watched contentedly while his host got out whiskey and tumblers and stood a small copper kettle on the fire.

13 At the third glass his eyes got brighter, and he began to talk, the little family circle regarding with eager interest this visitor from distant parts, as he squared his broad shoulders in the chair and spoke of wild scenes and doughty deeds; of wars and plagues and strange peoples.

14 "Twenty-one years of it," said Mr. White, nodding at his wife and son. "When he went away he was a slip of a youth in the warehouse. Now look at him."

15 "He don't look to have taken much harm," said Mrs. White, politely.

16 "I'd like to go to India myself," said the old man, "just to look round a bit, you know."

17 "Better where you are," said the sergeant-major, shaking his head. He put down the empty glass, and sighing softly, shook it again.

18 "I should like to see those old temples and fakirs and jugglers," said the old man. "What was that you started telling me the other day about a monkey's paw or something, Morris?"

A fakir rests on a bed of nails in a display of public penance in Calcutta, India, circa 1930.

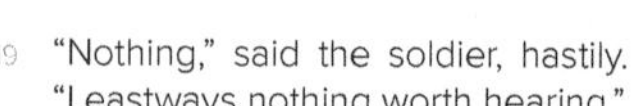

19 "Nothing," said the soldier, hastily. "Leastways nothing worth hearing."

20 "Monkey's paw?" said Mrs. White, curiously.

21 "Well, it's just a bit of what you might call magic, perhaps," said the sergeant-major, offhandedly.

22 His three listeners leaned forward eagerly. The visitor absent-mindedly put his empty glass to his lips and then set it down again. His host filled it for him.

TEXT TALK

Where does the monkey's paw come from?

See paragraphs 18 and 26: The monkey's paw comes from a "fakir" in India.

23 "To look at," said the sergeant-major, fumbling in his pocket, "it's just an ordinary little paw, dried to a mummy."

24 He took something out of his pocket and proffered it. Mrs. White drew back with a grimace, but her son, taking it, examined it curiously.

25 "And what is there special about it?" inquired Mr. White as he took it from his son, and having examined it, placed it upon the table.

26 "It had a spell put on it by an old fakir," said the sergeant-major, "a very holy man. He wanted to show that fate ruled people's lives, and that those who interfered with it did so to their sorrow. He put a spell on it so that three separate men could each have three wishes from it."

27 His manner was so impressive that his hearers were conscious that their light laughter jarred somewhat.

28 "Well, why don't you have three, sir?" said Herbert White, cleverly.

29 The soldier regarded him in the way that middle age is wont to regard **presumptuous** youth. "I have," he said, quietly, and his blotchy face whitened.

30 "And did you really have the three wishes granted?" asked Mrs. White.

31 "I did," said the sergeant-major, and his glass tapped against his strong teeth.

32 "And has anybody else wished?" persisted the old lady.

33 "The first man had his three wishes. Yes," was the reply; "I don't know what the first two were, but the third was for death. That's how I got the paw."

34 His tones were so grave that a hush fell upon the group.

35 "If you've had your three wishes, it's no good to you now, then, Morris," said the old man at last. "What do you keep it for?"

36 The soldier shook his head. "Fancy, I suppose," he said, slowly. "I did have some idea of selling it, but I don't think I will. It has caused enough mischief already. Besides, people won't buy. They think it's a fairy tale; some of them, and those who do think anything of it want to try it first and pay me afterward."

37 "If you could have another three wishes," said the old man, eyeing him keenly, "would you have them?"

38 "I don't know," said the other. "I don't know."

Skill:
Plot

When the sergeant-major says that the first man's final wish was for death, Mr. and Mrs. White never question why. These lines of dialogue build tension. I want to find out what happens when a wish is made with the monkey's paw.

Plot

How does the reader analyze dialogue at the beginning of the text?

The reader notes how lines of dialogue and characters' responses help to build tension and propel the plot forward.

SELECTION VOCABULARY

presumptuous / impertinente *adjective* overconfident, inappropriate

- What is described as "presumptuous"?
- What is the sergeant-major's feeling in this part of the story? Is it positive or negative?

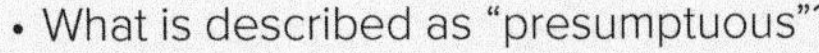

TEXT TALK

What information does the sergeant-major have about the monkey's paw that he does not completely share with Mr. White?

See paragraphs 28–31: The sergeant-major does not tell the Whites what his wishes were and what the outcome of the wishes was.

Skills Focus

QUESTION 4: Plot

After hearing about the powers of the cursed monkey's paw, Mr. White decides to save the paw from the fire. This decision moves the plot forward because the monkey's paw is the source of the story's conflict. Every time a wish is granted, something bad happens.

Skills Focus

QUESTION 1: Character

Herbert is lighthearted and jokes frequently with his father. His behavior shows that he doesn't think through the consequences of wishing on the monkey's paw. Likely, he doesn't believe it has power.

Story Structure

How does the reader determine similarities in the texts?

The reader notes that inciting incidents in both texts occur near the beginning of the story and drive the characters' actions.

Skill: Story Structure

The inciting incident creates a feeling that something bad will happen.

39 He took the paw, and dangling it between his forefinger and thumb, suddenly threw it upon the fire. White, with a slight cry, stooped down and snatched it off.

40 "Better let it burn," said the soldier, solemnly.

41 "If you don't want it, Morris," said the other, "give it to me."

42 "I won't," said his friend, doggedly. "I threw it on the fire. If you keep it, don't blame me for what happens. Pitch it on the fire again like a sensible man."

43 The other shook his head and examined his new possession closely. "How do you do it?" he inquired.

44 "Hold it up in your right hand and wish aloud," said the sergeant-major, "but I warn you of the **consequences**."

45 "Sounds like the Arabian Nights[1]," said Mrs. White, as she rose and began to set the supper. "Don't you think you might wish for four pairs of hands for me?"

46 Her husband drew the talisman from pocket, and then all three burst into laughter as the sergeant-major, with a look of alarm on his face, caught him by the arm.

47 "If you must wish," he said, gruffly, "wish for something sensible."

48 Mr. White dropped it back in his pocket, and placing chairs, motioned his friend to the table. In the business of supper the talisman was partly forgotten, and afterward the three sat listening in an enthralled fashion to a second installment of the soldier's adventures in India.

49 "If the tale about the monkey's paw is not more truthful than those he has been telling us," said Herbert, as the door closed behind their guest, just in time for him to catch the last train, "we sha'nt make much out of it."

50 "Did you give him anything for it, father?" inquired Mrs. White, regarding her husband closely.

51 "A trifle," said he, colouring slightly. "He didn't want it, but I made him take it. And he pressed me again to throw it away."

52 "Likely," said Herbert, with pretended horror. "Why, we're going to be rich, and famous and happy. Wish to be an emperor, father, to begin with; then you can't be henpecked."

1. **Arabian Nights** a collection of Middle Eastern folktales told by the legendary Scheherazade, also frequently called *One Thousand and One Nights*

SELECTION VOCABULARY

consequence / la consecuencia *noun* outcome, result COGNATE

- What are the sergeant-major and Mr. White talking about when they mention "consequences"?
- What consequences do they mention?

NOTES

53 He darted round the table, pursued by the maligned Mrs. White armed with an antimacassar[2].

54 Mr. White took the paw from his pocket and eyed it dubiously. "I don't know what to wish for, and that's a fact," he said, slowly. "It seems to me I've got all I want."

55 "If you only cleared the house, you'd be quite happy, wouldn't you?" said Herbert, with his hand on his shoulder. "Well, wish for two hundred pounds[3], then; that 'll just do it."

56 His father, smiling shamefacedly at his own **credulity,** held up the talisman, as his son, with a solemn face, somewhat marred by a wink at his mother, sat down at the piano and struck a few impressive chords.

57 "I wish for two hundred pounds," said the old man distinctly.

58 A fine crash from the piano greeted the words, interrupted by a shuddering cry from the old man. His wife and son ran toward him.

59 "It moved," he cried, with a glance of disgust at the object as it lay on the floor.

60 "As I wished, it twisted in my hand like a snake."

61 "Well, I don't see the money," said his son as he picked it up and placed it on the table, "and I bet I never shall."

62 "It must have been your fancy, father," said his wife, regarding him anxiously.

63 He shook his head. "Never mind, though; there's no harm done, but it gave me a shock all the same."

64 They sat down by the fire again while the two men finished their pipes. Outside, the wind was higher than ever, and the old man started nervously at the sound of a door banging upstairs. A silence unusual and depressing settled upon all three, which lasted until the old couple rose to retire for the night.

65 "I expect you'll find the cash tied up in a big bag in the middle of your bed," said Herbert, as he bade them good-night, "and something horrible squatting up on top of the wardrobe watching you as you pocket your ill-gotten gains."

2. **antimacassar** an ornamental cloth placed over the back of a chair to protect it
3. **pounds** British units of currency

Skills Focus

QUESTION 2: Character

Mr. White doesn't really seem like he wants or needs to make a wish. Still, Herbert persuades him to wish for 200 pounds, a sum of money that could pay off the mortgage on his home. This wish sets the tragic events of the story in motion.

Skills Focus

QUESTION 3: Plot

Herbert suggests that his father wish for 200 pounds. Even though Mr. White is ashamed to believe in the monkey's paw, he wishes for the money. That wish drives the action of the plot because soon after, Herbert dies.

SELECTION VOCABULARY

credulity / la credulidad *noun* the habit of believing anything COGNATE

ELL

- Who is described as having "credulity?"
- What is this character doing?

TEXT TALK

What is Mr. White's first wish?

See paragraph 57: Mr. White wishes for 200 pounds.

NOTES

66 He sat alone in the darkness, gazing at the dying fire, and seeing faces in it. The last face was so horrible and so simian that he gazed at it in amazement. It got so vivid that, with a little uneasy laugh, he felt on the table for a glass containing a little water to throw over it. His hand grasped the monkey's paw, and with a little shiver he wiped his hand on his coat and went up to bed.

II.

67 In the brightness of the wintry sun next morning as it streamed over the breakfast table he laughed at his fears. There was an air of prosaic wholesomeness about the room which it had lacked on the previous night, and the dirty, shrivelled little paw was pitched on the sideboard with a carelessness which betokened no great belief in its virtues.

68 "I suppose all old soldiers are the same," said Mrs. White. "The idea of our listening to such nonsense! How could wishes be granted in these days? And if they could, how could two hundred pounds hurt you, father?"

69 "Might drop on his head from the sky," said the frivolous Herbert.

70 "Morris said the things happened so naturally," said his father, "that you might if you so wished attribute it to coincidence."

71 "Well, don't break into the money before I come back," said Herbert as he rose from the table. "I'm afraid it'll turn you into a mean, avaricious man, and we shall have to disown you."

72 His mother laughed, and following him to the door, watched him down the road; and returning to the breakfast table, was very happy at the expense of her husband's credulity. All of which did not prevent her from scurrying to the door at the postman's knock, nor prevent her from referring somewhat shortly to retired sergeant-majors of bibulous habits when she found that the post brought a tailor's bill.

73 "Herbert will have some more of his funny remarks, I expect, when he comes home," she said, as they sat at dinner.

74 "I dare say," said Mr. White, pouring himself out some beer; "but for all that, the thing moved in my hand; that I'll swear to."

75 "You thought it did," said the old lady soothingly.

76 "I say it did," replied the other. "There was no thought about it; I had just—What's the matter?"

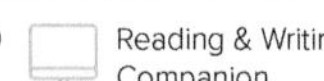

77 His wife made no reply. She was watching the mysterious movements of a man outside, who, peering in an undecided fashion at the house, appeared to be trying to make up his mind to enter. In mental connection with the two hundred pounds, she noticed that the stranger was well dressed, and wore a silk hat of glossy newness. Three times he paused at the gate, and then walked on again. The fourth time he stood with his hand upon it, and then with sudden resolution flung it open and walked up the path. Mrs. White at the same moment placed her hands behind her, and hurriedly unfastening the strings of her apron, put that useful article of apparel beneath the cushion of her chair.

78 She brought the stranger, who seemed ill at ease, into the room. He gazed at her furtively, and listened in a preoccupied fashion as the old lady apologized for the appearance of the room, and her husband's coat, a garment which he usually reserved for the garden. She then waited as patiently as her sex would permit, for him to broach his business, but he was at first strangely silent.

79 "I—was asked to call," he said at last, and stooped and picked a piece of cotton from his trousers. "I come from 'Maw and Meggins.'"

80 The old lady started. "Is anything the matter?" she asked, breathlessly. "Has anything happened to Herbert? What is it? What is it?"

81 Her husband interposed. "There, there, mother," he said, hastily. "Sit down, and don't jump to conclusions. You've not brought bad news, I'm sure, sir;" and he eyed the other wistfully.

82 "I'm sorry—" began the visitor.

83 "Is he hurt?" demanded the mother, wildly.

84 The visitor bowed in assent. "Badly hurt," he said, quietly, "but he is not in any pain."

85 "Oh, thank God!" said the old woman, clasping her hands. "Thank God for that! Thank—"

86 She broke off suddenly as the sinister meaning of the assurance dawned upon her and she saw the awful confirmation of her fears in the other's averted face. She caught her breath, and turning to her slower-witted husband, laid her trembling old hand upon his. There was a long silence.

87 "He was caught in the machinery," said the visitor at length in a low voice.

88 "Caught in the machinery," repeated Mr. White, in a dazed fashion, "yes."

89 He sat staring blankly out at the window, and taking his wife's hand between his own, pressed it as he had been wont to do in their old courting-days nearly forty years before.

90 "He was the only one left to us," he said, turning gently to the visitor. "It is hard."

91 The other coughed, and rising, walked slowly to the window. "The firm wished me to convey their sincere sympathy with you in your great loss," he said, without looking round. "I beg that you will understand I am only their servant and merely obeying orders."

92 There was no reply; the old woman's face was white, her eyes staring, and her breath inaudible; on the husband's face was a look such as his friend the sergeant might have carried into his first action.

93 "I was to say that 'Maw and Meggins' disclaim all responsibility," continued the other. "They admit no liability at all, but in consideration of your son's services, they wish to present you with a certain sum as **compensation."**

94 Mr. White dropped his wife's hand, and rising to his feet, gazed with a look of horror at his visitor. His dry lips shaped the words, "How much?"

95 "Two hundred pounds," was the answer.

96 Unconscious of his wife's shriek, the old man smiled faintly, put out his hands like a sightless man, and dropped, a senseless heap, to the floor.

III.

97 In the huge new cemetery, some two miles distant, the old people buried their dead, and came back to a house steeped in shadow and silence. It was all over so quickly that at first they could hardly realize it, and remained in a state of expectation as though of something else to happen —something else which was to lighten this load, too heavy for old hearts to bear.

98 But the days passed, and expectation gave place to resignation—the hopeless resignation of the old, sometimes miscalled, **apathy.** Sometimes they hardly exchanged a word, for now they had nothing to talk about, and their days were long to weariness.

99 It was about a week after that the old man, waking suddenly in the night, stretched out his hand and found himself alone. The room was in darkness, and the sound of subdued weeping came from the window. He raised himself in bed and listened.

100 "Come back," he said, tenderly. "You will be cold."

TEXT TALK

How is his wish fulfilled?

See paragraphs 80–95: Herbert dies in an accident at work, and the family is compensated with 200 pounds.

SELECTION VOCABULARY

compensation / la compensación *noun* pay or other benefits given for service or loss; repayment COGNATE

- Who is giving the compensation?
- What are they offering?

NOTES

101 "It is colder for my son," said the old woman, and wept afresh.

102 The sound of her sobs died away on his ears. The bed was warm, and his eyes heavy with sleep. He dozed fitfully, and then slept until a sudden wild cry from his wife awoke him with a start.

103 "The paw!" she cried wildly. "The monkey's paw!"

104 He started up in alarm. "Where? Where is it? What's the matter?"

105 She came stumbling across the room toward him. "I want it," she said, quietly. "You've not destroyed it?"

106 "It's in the parlour, on the bracket," he replied, marvelling. "Why?"

107 She cried and laughed together, and bending over, kissed his cheek.

108 "I only just thought of it," she said, hysterically. "Why didn't I think of it before? Why didn't you think of it?"

109 "Think of what?" he questioned.

110 "The other two wishes," she replied, rapidly. "We've only had one."

111 "Was not that enough?" he demanded, fiercely.

112 "No," she cried, triumphantly; "we'll have one more. Go down and get it quickly, and wish our boy alive again."

113 The man sat up in bed and flung the bedclothes from his quaking limbs. "Good God, you are mad!" he cried, aghast.

114 "Get it," she panted; "get it quickly, and wish—Oh, my boy, my boy!"

115 Her husband struck a match and lit the candle. "Get back to bed," he said, unsteadily. "You don't know what you are saying."

116 "We had the first wish granted," said the old woman, feverishly; "why not the second?"

117 "A coincidence," stammered the old man.

118 "Go and get it and wish," cried his wife, quivering with excitement.

119 The old man turned and regarded her, and his voice shook. "He has been dead ten days, and besides he—I would not tell you else, but—I could only recognize him by his clothing. If he was too terrible for you to see then, how now?"

SELECTION VOCABULARY

apathy / la apatía ***noun*** not caring, lacking interest COGNATE

- What is "apathy" sometimes confused with?
- Who is showing apathy? How are they behaving?

Plot

How does the reader identify the turning point in the story?

The reader identified a character's decision in the dialogue that propelled the action toward a resolution.

120 "Bring him back," cried the old woman, and dragged him toward the door. "Do you think I fear the child I have nursed?"

121 He went down in the darkness, and felt his way to the parlour, and then to the mantelpiece. The talisman was in its place, and a horrible fear that the unspoken wish might bring his mutilated son before him ere he could escape from the room seized upon him, and he caught his breath as he found that he had lost the direction of the door. His brow cold with sweat, he felt his way round the table, and groped along the wall until he found himself in the small passage with the unwholesome thing in his hand.

Skill: Plot

Mr. White gives in to his wife and wishes again. This decision in the lines of dialogue is a turning point that moves the plot forward because the wish will bring their son back.

122 Even his wife's face seemed changed as he entered the room. It was white and expectant, and to his fears seemed to have an unnatural look upon it. He was afraid of her.

123 "Wish!" she cried, in a strong voice.

124 "It is foolish and wicked," he faltered.

125 "Wish!" repeated his wife.

126 He raised his hand. "I wish my son alive again."

127 The talisman fell to the floor, and he regarded it fearfully. Then he sank trembling into a chair as the old woman, with burning eyes, walked to the window and raised the blind.

128 He sat until he was chilled with the cold, glancing occasionally at the figure of the old woman peering through the window. The candle-end, which had burned below the rim of the china candlestick, was throwing pulsating shadows on the ceiling and walls, until, with a flicker larger than the rest, it expired. The old man, with an unspeakable sense of relief at the failure of the talisman, crept back to his bed, and a minute or two afterward the old woman came silently and apathetically beside him.

129 Neither spoke, but lay silently listening to the ticking of the clock. A stair creaked, and a squeaky mouse scurried noisily through the wall. The darkness was oppressive, and after lying for some time screwing up his courage, he took the box of matches, and striking one, went downstairs for a candle.

130 At the foot of the stairs the match went out, and he paused to strike another; and at the same moment a knock, so quiet and stealthy as to be scarcely audible, sounded on the front door.

TEXT TALK

What is Mr. White's second wish? Why does he make this wish?

See paragraphs 123–126: He wishes his son were alive again. His wife urges him to make this wish.

Ask each Beyond grade-level student to write one additional discussion question. Then have one or two students facilitate a discussion, using their questions to guide the conversation.

131 The matches fell from his hand and spilled in the passage. He stood motionless, his breath suspended until the knock was repeated. Then he turned and fled swiftly back to his room, and closed the door behind him. A third knock sounded through the house.

132 "What's that?" cried the old woman, starting up.

133 "A rat," said the old man in shaking tones—"a rat. It passed me on the stairs."

134 His wife sat up in bed listening. A loud knock resounded through the house.

135 "It's Herbert!" she screamed. "It's Herbert!"

136 She ran to the door, but her husband was before her, and catching her by the arm, held her tightly.

137 "What are you going to do?" he whispered hoarsely.

138 "It's my boy; it's Herbert!" she cried, struggling mechanically. "I forgot it was two miles away. What are you holding me for? Let go. I must open the door."

139 "For God's sake don't let it in," cried the old man, trembling.

140 "You're afraid of your own son," she cried, struggling. "Let me go. I'm coming, Herbert; I'm coming."

141 There was another knock, and another. The old woman with a sudden wrench broke free and ran from the room. Her husband followed to the landing, and called after her appealingly as she hurried downstairs. He heard the chain rattle back and the bottom bolt drawn slowly and stiffly from the socket. Then the old woman's voice, strained and panting.

142 "The bolt," she cried, loudly. "Come down. I can't reach it."

143 But her husband was on his hands and knees groping wildly on the floor in search of the paw. If he could only find it before the thing outside got in. A perfect fusillade of knocks reverberated through the house, and he heard the scraping of a chair as his wife put it down in the passage against the door. He heard the creaking of the bolt as it came slowly back, and at the same moment he found the monkey's paw, and frantically breathed his third and last wish.

144 The knocking ceased suddenly, although the echoes of it were still in the house. He heard the chair drawn back, and the door opened. A cold wind rushed up the staircase, and a long loud wail of disappointment and misery from his wife gave him courage to run down to her side, and then to the gate beyond. The street lamp flickering opposite shone on a quiet and deserted road.

Prepare for Advanced Courses

Use the activity below to differentiate instruction for your B Beyond grade-level learners.

Direct students to reread paragraphs 78 and 79.

Ask students: What is the purpose of the narrator in these two paragraphs? What does the narrator describe, and how do those descriptions have an impact on the narrative?

TEXT TALK

What other questions can you ask and answer?

Answers will vary.

Think Questions

Circulate as students answer Think Questions independently. Scaffolds for these questions are shown on the opposite page.

QUESTION 1: Textual Evidence

It's a cursed, mummified monkey's paw that grants wishes. Herbert is curious about the paw but doubtful of its power. He says, "We sha'nt make much out of it" after the sergeant-major leaves.

QUESTION 2: Textual Evidence

After Mr. White makes his first wish, he feels shocked and disgusted by the paw because he thinks the paw moved when he made his wish. After Mr. White makes his second wish to bring Herbert back to life, he feels fearful about the power of the paw.

QUESTION 3: Textual Evidence

Answers will vary but may include the following examples:

- "I don't know what the first two were, but the third was for death."
- "He sat alone in the darkness, gazing at the dying fire, and seeing faces in it. The last face was so horrible and so simian that he gazed at it in amazement."

Student descriptions should explain why the selection hints at later events such as Herbert's death, his "resurrection," Mr. White wishing him back into the grave, or the family's overall misery.

QUESTION 4: Context Clues

When Mr. White retrieves the monkey's paw from the fire, the sergeant-major warns Mr. White of the "consequences." Based on these clues, I think *consequence* must mean "an outcome, an effect, or a result."

QUESTION 5: Context Clues

I think *compensation* must mean "repayment." The word is used to describe what the visitor from Herbert's work is giving to the parents. He brings them 200 pounds after Herbert dies in an accident. This makes me think that *compensation* means "a type of payment in exchange for something."

First Read

Read "The Monkey's Paw." After you read, complete the Think Questions below.

THINK QUESTIONS

1. What is "the monkey's paw"? What is Herbert's attitude toward the monkey's paw? Cite textual evidence from the selection to support your answer.
2. Write two to three sentences describing how Mr. White's feelings change about the monkey's paw after he makes his first wish and second wish.
3. Foreshadowing is a literary device in which a writer gives a subtle hint of what is to come later in the story. Can you identify an example of foreshadowing from the beginning of "The Monkey's Paw" that suggests making wishes on the paw will lead to tragedy? Cite textual evidence from the selection to support your answer.
4. Find the word **consequence** in paragraph 44 of "The Monkey's Paw." Use context clues in the surrounding sentences, as well as the sentence in which the word appears, to determine the word's meaning. Write your definition here and identify clues that helped you figure out its meaning.
5. Use context clues to determine the meaning of **compensation** as it is used in paragraph 93 of "The Monkey's Paw." Write your definition here and identify clues that helped you figure out its meaning. Then check the meaning in a dictionary.

SCAFFOLDS

Think Questions

Use the scaffolds below to differentiate instruction for your ELL English Language Learners and A Approaching grade-level learners.

ELL **BEGINNING** Write a response using the word bank and sentence frames.

INTERMEDIATE Write a response using the sentence frames.

ADVANCED, ADVANCED HIGH Write a response using the Text-Dependent Question Guide.

A **APPROACHING** Write a response using the Text-Dependent Question Guide.

BEGINNING	INTERMEDIATE	APPROACHING / ADVANCED, ADVANCED HIGH
Word Bank	**Sentence Frames**	**Text-Dependent Question Guide**
throw away grant wishes doubts warns fearful repayment jokes result shock and disgust dangerous accident	The monkey's paw is magical. The monkey's paw has the power to ____. Herbert ____ that the monkey's paw works. I know this because Herbert makes ____ about the monkey's paw.	1. • What is "the monkey's paw"? • How does Herbert feel about the monkey's paw? • How do I know how Herbert feels?
	Mr. White feels ____ after his first wish. He feels ____ after his second wish.	2. • How does Mr. White feel after his first wish? • How does Mr. White feel after his second wish? • How does Mr. White feel after his third wish?
	The sergeant-major wants to ____ the monkey's paw. He thinks the paw is ____.	3. • The monkey's paw grants wishes, but the Whites are sad in the end. • Are there clues in the story that this will happen? • What are the clues?
	The sergeant-major ____ Mr. White about the "consequences" of making a wish. This gives me a clue that a *consequence* is a ____.	4. • Read: "Hold it up in your right hand and wish aloud," said the sergeant-major, "but I warn you of the **consequences**." • What is the result of the wish?
	Compensation is another way of saying "____." The visitor is giving the parents money after Herbert dies in an ____.	5. • "Read: "I was to say that 'Maw and Meggins' disclaim all responsibility," continued the other. "They admit no liability at all, but in consideration of your son's services, they wish to present you with a certain sum as **compensation**." • What is the visitor offering the parents? • Why is he giving this to the parents?

Reading Comprehension OPTIONAL

Have students complete the digital reading comprehension questions ✓ when they finish reading.

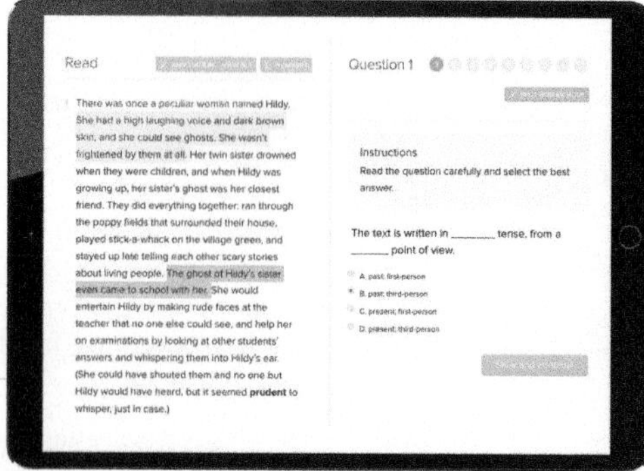

ANSWER KEY

QUESTION 1: C
QUESTION 2: C
QUESTION 3: D
QUESTION 4: D
QUESTION 5: B
QUESTION 6: A
QUESTION 7: A
QUESTION 8: B
QUESTION 9: B
QUESTION 10: *See chart.*

Dialogue	Character
"Better let it burn."	Sergeant-Major Morris
"It's my boy! It's Herbert!"	Mrs. White
"Well don't break into the money before I come back."	Herbert White
"I dare say. But for all that, the thing moved in my hand; that I'll swear to."	Mr. White

Connect and Extend OPTIONAL

CONNECT TO EXTENDED WRITING PROJECT

Students can use "The Monkey's Paw" as a mentor text for their Extended Writing Projects. They may adopt some of W. W. Jacobs's methods for creating suspense as they craft their own narratives.

BEYOND THE BOOK

Writing: Six Random Objects

Provide all students in the class the same random list of objects. Come up with your own list or use this one:

- toothbrush, rubber band, washing machine, tennis racket, bird seed, wedding ring

Ask students to write a short mystery story that somehow incorporates all six objects. At least one of the objects should play a significant role in the plot of the story. When they've finished, place students in small groups to share their writing with their classmates.

To reflect, ask students:

- Did the constraint of using the six objects make writing this story easier or more difficult? Why?

Skill:
Plot

Use the Checklist to analyze Plot in "The Monkey's Paw." Refer to the sample student annotations about Plot in the text.

••• CHECKLIST FOR PLOT

In order to identify plot elements in a story or drama, note the following:

- ✓ dialogue or conversations between two or more characters
- ✓ incidents or notable events throughout the story's plot
- ✓ central conflict
- ✓ characters' responses or decisions to incidents
- ✓ the ways in which the characters affect the resolution of the conflict

To analyze how particular lines of dialogue or incidents in a story or drama propel the action or provoke a decision, consider the following questions:

- ✓ What happens as a result of a dialogue between two characters?
- ✓ How does the plot unfold in the story?
- ✓ Do characters respond or change as the plot advances? How?
- ✓ What causes a character to act or make a decision? What events occur as a result of their actions or decisions?

Skill: Plot

Introduce the Skill

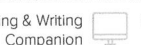

Watch the Concept Definition video ▶ and read the following definition with your students.

The events that take place in a story or **narrative** are called the **plot**. These events give the story a beginning, a middle, and an end, and they are influenced by literary elements such as character and setting. Events in a story begin with the **inciting incident**, or the moment in which the **conflict**, or main problem, is introduced. As characters attempt to solve the problem, it may become more complicated, and the characters may undergo changes as they respond to rising tension. For example, the main character may learn the value of patience as he or she works toward finding a solution, or may begin to understand or sympathize with another character's difficulties. The **turning point** in a plot occurs when a key event or decision leads to a **resolution**, or a way to solve the problem.

TURN AND TALK

1. What are some of your favorite books, TV shows, or movies with a lot of suspense or tension?
2. What's the most intense incident or moment from your favorite book, TV show, or movie? What happens after that incident?

SPEAKING FRAMES

- One of my favorite (books / TV shows / movies) is ____. I like this (book / TV show / movie) because ____.
- A tense incident or moment is ____. The moment builds suspense because ____.
- The next thing that happens is ____.

SKILL VOCABULARY

narrative / la narración ***noun*** a story, real or imagined, consisting of connected events

plot / la trama ***noun*** the sequence of events that form a story

inciting incident / el incidente generador ***noun*** the first event in which the conflict becomes apparent

conflict / el conflicto ***noun*** the main problem or struggle that characters face in a story COGNATE

Your Turn

Ask students to complete the Your Turn activity.

QUESTION 1

A. Incorrect. The dialogue shows that the sergeant-major's warning about the monkey's paw was correct.

B. Incorrect. No mention is made of a plan for Herbert to ask for a raise at work.

C. Correct. Mr. White speculates about how the wish could be granted, while Mrs. White and Herbert make jokes about how it could happen.

D. Incorrect. Even though the monkey's paw is "pitched on a sideboard," the family does not stop talking about it.

QUESTION 2

A. Incorrect. This sentence is descriptive and does not directly propel the plot.

B. Incorrect. This shows how Mrs. White feels, but it does not reveal an event to come.

C. Incorrect. This shows an ordinary part of the day for the Whites.

D. Correct. Mrs. White is distracted and focused on a mysterious man pacing outside the White's home, which builds suspense by hinting at events to come.

QUESTION 3

A. Incorrect. There is no evidence that suggests the Whites will receive money.

B. Incorrect. Mrs. White's response indicates that she is aware of bad news.

C. Correct. Mrs. White's responses, such as watching the man outside and immediately asking about Herbert, show that she knows something has happened to her son.

D. Incorrect. Mrs. White talks to the men freely.

Skill: Plot

Reread paragraphs 67–80 of "The Monkey's Paw." Then, using the Checklist on the previous page, answer the multiple-choice questions below.

YOUR TURN

1. The author uses the dialogue between Mr. White, Mrs. White, and Herbert in paragraphs 68–70 to—

   - A. reveal that the sergeant-major is not credible.
   - B. provoke Herbert to ask for a raise at work.
   - C. build suspense about how the wish will be granted.
   - D. reveal that Mr. White, Mrs. White, and Herbert no longer care about the monkey's paw.

2. Which of the following is an example of an inciting incident?

   - A. In the brightness of the wintry sun next morning as it streamed over the breakfast table he laughed at his fears.
   - B. "Herbert will have some more of his funny remarks, I expect, when he comes home," she said, as they sat at dinner.
   - C. His mother laughed, and following him to the door, watched him down the road; and returning to the breakfast table, was very happy at the expense of her husband's credulity.
   - D. His wife made no reply. She was watching the mysterious movements of a man outside, who, peering in an undecided fashion at the house, appeared to be trying to make up his mind to enter.

3. The author builds tension at the end of the excerpt by—

   - A. hinting that the Whites will soon receive the 200 pounds.
   - B. indicating Mrs. White is unaware of what is happening.
   - C. suggesting that Mrs. White suspects there is something wrong.
   - D. implying that Mrs. White is uncomfortable talking to the man.

SKILL VOCABULARY

turning point / el clímax ***noun*** a moment when the series of events in a plot suddenly changes

resolution / la resolución ***noun*** the final outcome of the story's conflict COGNATE

Skill: Story Structure

Use the Checklist to analyze Story Structure in "The Monkey's Paw." Refer to the sample student annotations about Story Structure in the text.

••• CHECKLIST FOR STORY STRUCTURE

In order to determine how to compare and contrast the structure of two or more texts, note the following:

- ✓ the order of events, including the exposition, inciting incident, rising action, climax, falling action, and resolution in each text
- ✓ when the conflict is introduced in each text
- ✓ the use of flashback or foreshadowing in each text
- ✓ how the structure of each text contributes to its meaning and style
- ✓ the similarities and differences between the structures in each text

To compare and contrast the structure of two or more texts and analyze how the structure of each text contributes to its meaning and style, ask the following questions:

- ✓ How is each text structured?
- ✓ How are the structures of each text the same? How are they different?
- ✓ How does the structure of each text contribute to its meaning and style?

SKILL VOCABULARY

story structure / la estructura de la historia *noun* the outline a writer uses to organize and tell a story

plot / la trama *noun* the sequence of events that form a story

flashback / la escena retrospectiva *noun* a scene in a story, play, movie, or TV show that is set in a time earlier than the events in the main story

Skill: Story Structure

Introduce the Skill

Watch the Concept Definition video ▶ and read the following definition with your students.

Story structure is the framework writers use to develop the events of the **plot**. Any plot has a central problem or conflict which the story introduces, builds to a climax, and finally solves. The story may be character-driven, exploring one person's emotions, or it could be driven by suspense, with a complicated sequence of events that takes many twists and turns. The events may or may not be presented in chronological order. For example, an author who wishes to build tension may begin with a dramatic **flashback** before introducing the present situation in a story. A character-driven novel might describe events from the point of view of one character, and how the events change him or her. Whatever story structure an author chooses to use, **analyzing** how the events of a chapter or scene fit into the overall structure can help readers identify how it also contributes to the development of the **theme** and **setting**.

TURN AND TALK

1. Think about the last movie or TV show you saw that was based on a book. How did the movie or TV version compare with the original story? What was similar between the two versions? What made them different?

SPEAKING FRAMES

- The [movie / TV show] had the same ____ as the original story.
- The [movie / TV show] changed ____ from the original story.

Your Turn

Ask students to complete the Your Turn activity.

The Conjure-Man Dies	Both	"The Monkey's Paw"
A character is in an unfamiliar room with two strangers and a dead body.	The scene shows rising action in the plot.	A character makes a decision, and a supernatural event occurs.
The scene suggests the style of a mystery novel.	The scene helps the reader understand the meaning and style of the story.	The scene suggests the style of a spooky, horror story.

Skill: Story Structure

Reread paragraphs 54–59 of "The Monkey's Paw" and paragraphs 40–42 of *The Conjure-Man Dies*. Then, using the Checklist on the previous page, complete the chart below to compare and contrast the passages.

YOUR TURN

	Observation Options
A	The scene helps the reader understand the meaning and style of the story.
B	A character is in an unfamiliar room with two strangers and a dead body.
C	The scene shows rising action in the plot.
D	The scene suggests the style of a mystery novel.
E	A character makes a decision, and a supernatural event occurs.
F	The scene suggests the style of a spooky, horror story.

The Conjure-Man Dies	Both	"The Monkey's Paw"

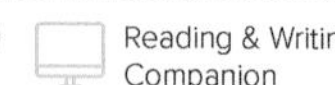

SKILL VOCABULARY

analyze / analizar *verb* to consider in detail and discover essential features or meaning COGNATE

theme / el tema *noun* the central idea or message of a work of literature, often expressed as a general statement about life

setting / el escenario *noun* the time and place of the story

Close Read

Reread "The Monkey's Paw." As you reread, complete the Skills Focus questions below. Then use your answers and annotations from the questions to help you complete the Write activity.

SKILLS FOCUS

1. Identify evidence of Herbert's behavior in the story and explain how it influences events. Be sure to cite textual evidence to support your claims.
2. To wish or not to wish on the monkey's paw: this is the central conflict of W. W. Jacobs's story. Identify evidence of Mr. and Mrs. White's motivations in the story, and explain how their actions influence the resolution of the conflict. Be sure to cite evidence from the text to support your claims.
3. How do specific incidents or lines of dialogue in "The Monkey's Paw" propel the action of the plot? Be sure to use examples from the text to explain how the incident or dialogue drives action in the plot forward.
4. In *The Conjure-Man Dies*, something mysterious happens to Frimbo the conjure-man, leading Bubber Brown to hurriedly run to get help from Dr. Archer. Identify incidents in "The Monkey's Paw" that similarly provoke characters' decisions. How do these incidents drive the plot forward? How does the story structure contribute to the meaning of the texts?
5. Ghosts from the distant past and a figure cloaked in black help to create the mystery of the graveyard in *The Graveyard Book*. In "The Monkey's Paw," the mystery lies in the reader's interpretation of events. Identify one event from "The Monkey's Paw" and explain what makes it mysterious.

WRITE

COMPARE AND CONTRAST: "The Monkey's Paw" (a short story), *The Conjure-Man Dies* (an excerpt from a novel), and *The Graveyard Book* (a graphic novel excerpt) have different story structures. How do these different structures contribute to the meanings of the texts? How do they impact the development of each plot? Compare and contrast how structure helps reveal the meaning of "The Monkey's Paw" against the *The Conjure-Man Dies* or *The Graveyard Book*. Remember to support your ideas with evidence from the texts.

Close Read

Skills Focus

QUESTION 1: Character

See paragraph 52.

QUESTION 2: Character

See paragraphs 54 and 55.

QUESTION 3: Plot

See paragraphs 55–57.

QUESTION 4: Plot

See paragraph 39.

QUESTION 5: Connect to Essential Question

See paragraph 21.

CHECK FOR SUCCESS

If students struggle to respond to Skills Focus question 1, ask them the following questions:

- What is Herbert doing in paragraph 55?
- How does Mr. White respond in paragraph 57?
- What does that tell you about Mr. White?

Have students transition to read and annotate independently once they have successfully completed the first Skills Focus prompt.

Writer's Notebook

Connect to Essential Question: Give students time to reflect on how "The Monkey's Paw" connects to the unit's essential question "What attracts us to the mysterious?" by freewriting in their Writer's Notebooks.

Beginning & Intermediate

Read aloud the unit's essential question: "What attracts us to the mysterious? Encourage students to draw their connections or allow students to write in their native language. Circulate the room, prompting students for their thoughts as they respond orally or through pantomime.

Advanced & Advanced High

Allow students to share their connections orally in pairs or small groups before freewriting.

StudySyncTV

Project the StudySyncTV episode and pause at the following times to prompt discussion:

1:38 How do the students use textual evidence to determine the setting of "The Monkey's Paw"?

2:50 Amanda and Andrew agree that Mr. White is being "greedy." What textual evidence supports this characterization? How does this bring the group closer to identifying the theme?

3:45 How does the group build on Amanda's first idea of the theme "be careful what you wish for"? What evidence do they use to narrow the focus of their theme?

Collaborative Conversation

Break students into collaborative conversation groups to discuss the Close Read prompt. Ask students to use the StudySyncTV episode as a model for their discussion. Remind them to reference their Skills Focus annotations in their discussion.

"The Monkey's Paw" (a short story), *The Conjure-Man Dies* (an excerpt from a novel), and *The Graveyard Book* (a graphic novel excerpt) have different story structures. How do these different structures contribute to the meanings of the texts? How do they impact the development of each plot? Compare and contrast how structure helps reveal the meaning of "The Monkey's Paw" against *The Conjure-Man Dies* or *The Graveyard Book*. Remember to support your ideas with evidence from the texts.

Use the scaffolds below to differentiate instruction for your ELL English Language Learners and A Approaching grade-level learners.

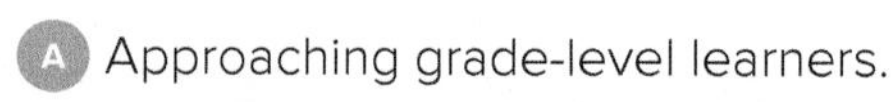

ELL **BEGINNING, INTERMEDIATE** Use the discussion guide and speaking frames to facilitate the discussion with support from the teacher.

ADVANCED, ADVANCED HIGH Use the discussion guide and speaking frames to facilitate the discussion in mixed-level groups.

A **APPROACHING** Use the discussion guide to facilitate the discussion in mixed-level groups.

APPROACHING
ADVANCED, ADVANCED HIGH
BEGINNING, INTERMEDIATE

Discussion Guide	Speaking Frames
1. What is the inciting incident in "The Monkey's Paw"? What events does it lead to, or cause to happen?	• The inciting incident is when ____. • It leads to ____.
2. What is the inciting incident in the other text you chose? What events does it lead to, or cause to happen?	• The inciting incident is when ____. • It leads to ____.
3. How are the stories alike? How are the story structures different?	• The stories are alike in that ____. • The stories are different in that ____.

Review Prompt and Rubric

Before students begin writing, review the writing prompt and rubric with the class.

COMPARE AND CONTRAST: "The Monkey's Paw" (a short story), *The Conjure-Man Dies* (an excerpt from a novel), and *The Graveyard Book* (a graphic novel excerpt) have different story structures. How do these different structures contribute to the meanings of the texts? How do they impact the development of each plot? Compare and contrast how structure helps reveal the meaning of "The Monkey's Paw" against *The Conjure-Man Dies* or *The Graveyard Book*. Remember to support your ideas with evidence from the texts.

PROMPT GUIDE

A

- What is the inciting incident in each story?
- What kinds of events does the inciting incident lead to?
- How does this structure help you understand the story?
- How are the stories similar?
- How are the story structures different?

An additional rubric item for Language and Conventions appears in your digital teacher and student accounts.

Score	Plot	Story Structure
4	The writer effectively analyzes how the plot of each story is affected by its structure. The writer includes sufficient details about the plots that support this analysis.	The writer clearly analyzes and explains how the structure of each text helps reveal its meaning and compares and contrasts the two structures.. The writer provides exemplary analysis, using relevant evidence from the texts.
3	The writer analyzes how the plot of each story is affected by its structure. The writer includes some details about the plots that support this analysis.	The writer analyzes and explains how the structure of each text helps reveal its meaning and compares and contrasts the two structures. The writer provides sufficient analysis, using relevant evidence from the texts most of the time.
2	The writer attempts to analyze how the plot of each story is affected by its structure, but is not entirely successful. The writer includes a few details about the plots that attempt to support this analysis.	The writer begins to analyze or explain how the structure of each text helps reveal its meaning and to compare and contrast the two structures, but the analysis is incomplete. The writer uses relevant evidence from the texts only some of the time.
1	The writer does not analyze how the plot of each story is affected by its structure. The writer includes few or no details about the plots.	The writer attempts to analyze or explain how the structure of each text helps reveal its meaning and to compare and contrast the two structures, but the analysis is not successful. The writer uses little or no relevant evidence from the texts.
0	The writer does not provide a relevant response to the prompt or does not provide a response at all.	The writer does not provide a relevant response to the prompt or does not provide a response at all.

Write

SCAFFOLDS

Ask students to complete the writing assignment using textual evidence to support their answers.

Use the scaffolds below to differentiate instruction for your ELL English Language Learners and A Approaching grade-level learners.

ELL **BEGINNING** With the help of the word bank, write a response using paragraph frame 1.

INTERMEDIATE With the help of the word bank, write a response using paragraph frames 1 and 2.

ADVANCED, ADVANCED HIGH Write a response of differentiated length using the sentence starters.

A **APPROACHING** Write a response of differentiated length using the sentence starters.

Word Bank	Paragraph Frame 1	Paragraph Frame 2	Sentence Starters
BEGINNING, INTERMEDIATE	BEGINNING, INTERMEDIATE	INTERMEDIATE	ADVANCED, ADVANCED HIGH, APPROACHING
mystery monkey's paw horror story suspense doctor	In "The Monkey's Paw," conflict is introduced when Mr. White snatches the ____. In *The Conjure-Man Dies*, the inciting incident is when the man runs to get the ____. Both incidents or events create ____. The conflict in "The Monkey's Paw" fits with the structure of a ____ because the paw is supernatural and scary. The conflict in *The Conjure-Man Dies* fits with the structure of a ____ because readers don't know how Frimbo died.	In "The Monkey's Paw," readers wonder ____. In *The Conjure-Man Dies*, you wonder ____. For each story, the structure helps ____.	• In "The Monkey's Paw," the story structure . . . • Similarly, in *The Conjure-Man Dies*, . . . • The two stories are alike because . . . • One way that the story structures are different is . . . • Another way that they are different is . . .

Peer Review

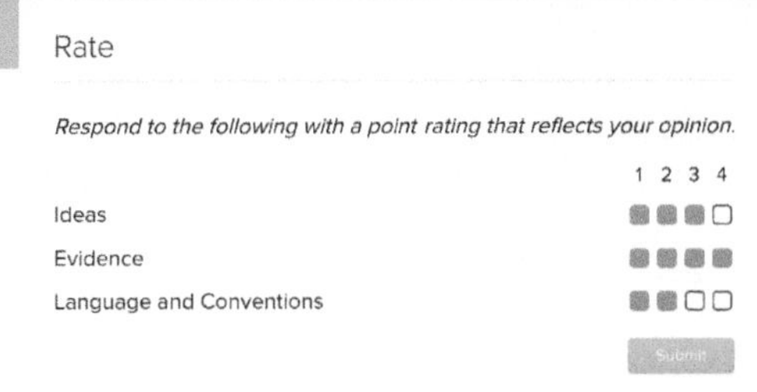

Students should submit substantive feedback to two peers using the review instructions below.

- How well does this response answer the prompt?
- How well does the writer explain each structure and how it helps reveal the meaning of the story?
- Did the writer include enough textual evidence to support his or her ideas?
- What did the writer do well in this response? What does the writer need to work on?

SENTENCE FRAMES

A

- You were able to (completely / partly / almost) answer the prompt because ____.
- You could answer the prompt more completely by ____.
- You supported the idea that the texts were alike with the detail of ____.
- You supported the idea that the texts were different with the detail of ____.
- One idea that needs more support is ____.
- I thought differently about the texts after reading ____. My favorite part of your response is ____.

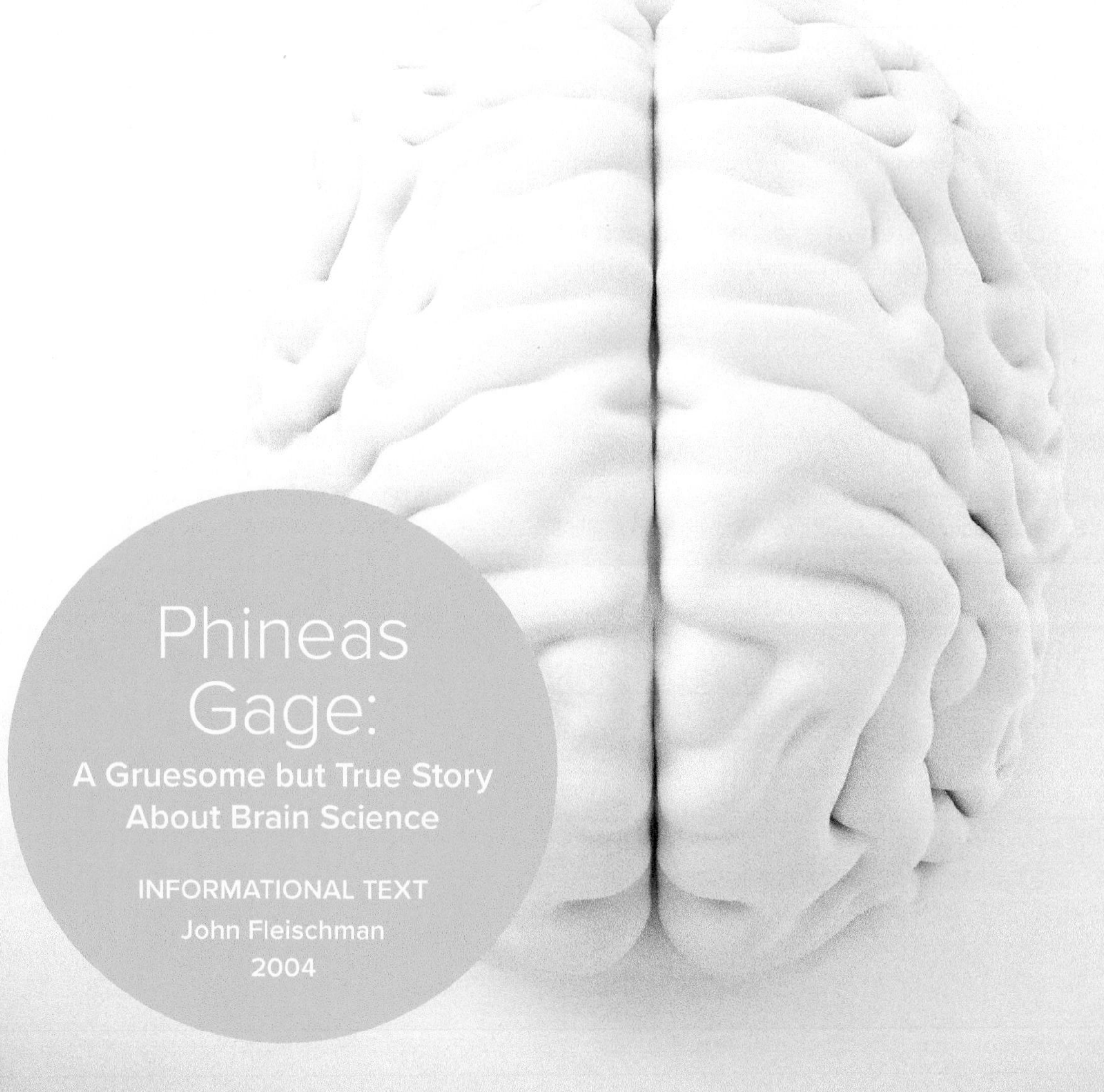

Phineas Gage:

A Gruesome but True Story About Brain Science

INFORMATIONAL TEXT
John Fleischman
2004

Introduction

After surviving a horrific accident that should have killed him instantly, Phineas Gage went on to live for eleven more years. What became of him after this accident—and why—would forever impact what scientists know about the human brain and how it functions. In the first chapter of *Phineas Gage: A Gruesome but True Story About Brain Science*, author John Fleischman draws readers into Phineas's shocking and fascinating story with a lively and engrossing account of the freak accident.

Phineas Gage: A Gruesome but True Story About Brain Science

In 1848, while working on the construction of a railroad in Vermont, 26-year-old Phineas Gage had a horrific accident. One day while he was setting a charge, it exploded and sent a rod through his skull, leaving him with open wounds on his cheek and at the top of his head. It was the kind of injury that should have killed him, yet Gage remained lucid and calm. When the doctor arrived, he found Gage sitting on the porch of his hotel. When Gage told the doctor what happened, the doctor did not believe him. Gage physically recovered, but people close to him claimed that his personality changed. The injuries from the accident ultimately killed Gage eleven years later. To this day, doctors still study Gage's case and how he survived for so many years.

ELL Proficiency-leveled summaries and summaries in multiple languages are available digitally.

Audio and audio text highlighting are available with this text.

CONNECT TO ESSENTIAL QUESTION

What attracts us to the mysterious?

When a man amazingly survives a freak accident, he and his brain become a world-famous mystery, especially to psychologists, medical researchers, and doctors.

Access Complex Text

LEXILE: 970L **WORD COUNT:** 1,396

The following areas may be challenging for students, particularly ELL English Language Learners and A Approaching grade-level learners.

Prior Knowledge	Purpose	Organization
• Phineas Gage is the foreman of a railroad crew. References to railroad construction may need explanation. • Gage's accident injured the frontal lobe of his brain. This area is the "control panel" of personality and the ability to communicate.	• The selection is an informational text that is told as a narrative. Because of the narrative elements, the author's purpose may need to be clarified for students.	• The text does not follow a chronological structure or use past tense, which may challenge some students. • Events that appear out of chronological order include the introduction of the accident and Gage's death in the introductory paragraphs.

SCAFFOLDS

 ENGLISH LANGUAGE LEARNERS  APPROACHING GRADE LEVEL  BEYOND GRADE LEVEL

These icons identify differentiation strategies and scaffolded support for a variety of students. See the digital lesson plan for additional differentiation strategies and scaffolds.

Instructional Path

The print teacher's edition includes essential point-of-use instruction and planning tools. Complete lesson plans and program documents appear in your digital teacher account.

First Read: Phineas Gage: A Gruesome but True Story About Brain Science

Objectives: After an initial reading and discussion of a nonfiction text, students will be able to identify and restate the text's key ideas and details.

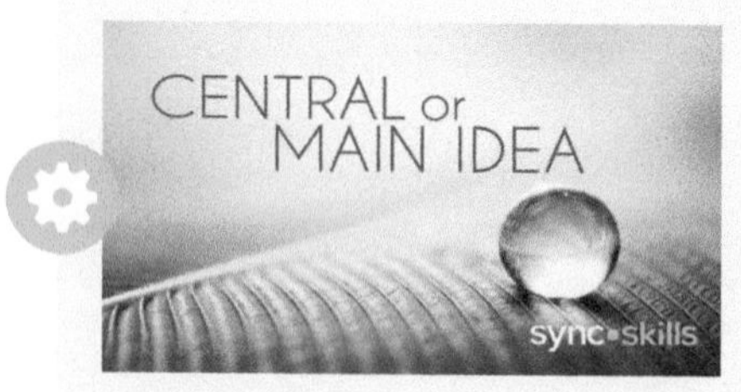

Skill: Central or Main Idea

Objectives: After rereading and discussing a model of close reading, students will be able to analyze the development of central or main ideas throughout a text.

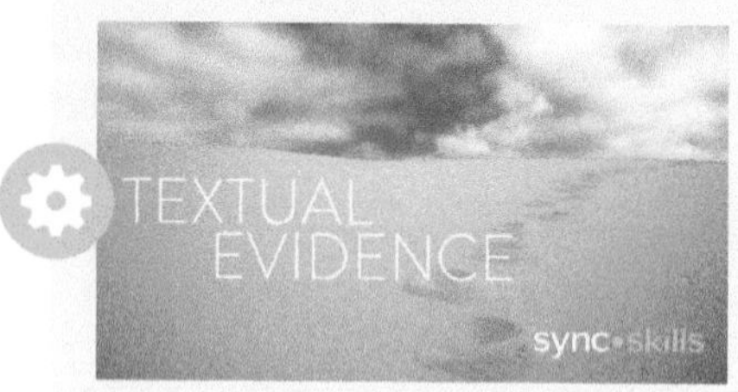

Skill: Textual Evidence

Objectives: After rereading and discussing a model of close reading, students will be able to cite textual evidence that strongly supports analysis of what the text says explicitly as well as inferences drawn from the text.

Close Read: Phineas Gage: A Gruesome but True Story About Brain Science

Objectives: After engaging in a close reading and discussion, students will be able to to identify and analyze the central or main idea and cite textual evidence to write a short response.

Progress Monitoring

Opportunities to Learn	Opportunities to Demonstrate Learning	Opportunities to Reteach
Central or Main Idea		
Skill: Central or Main Idea	Skill: Central or Main Idea • Your Turn Close Read • Skills Focus • Write	Unit 2 Skill: Central or Main Idea - So where are you from? Unit 6 Skill: Central or Main Idea - Universal Declaration of Human Rights Spotlight Skill: Central or Main Idea
Textual Evidence		
Skill: Textual Evidence	Skill: Textual Evidence • Your Turn Close Read • Writer's Notebook • Skills Focus • Collaborative Conversation • Write	Unit 2 Skill: Textual Evidence - The Outsiders Unit 5 Skill: Textual Evidence - Farewell to Manzanar Spotlight Skill: Textual Evidence

First Read

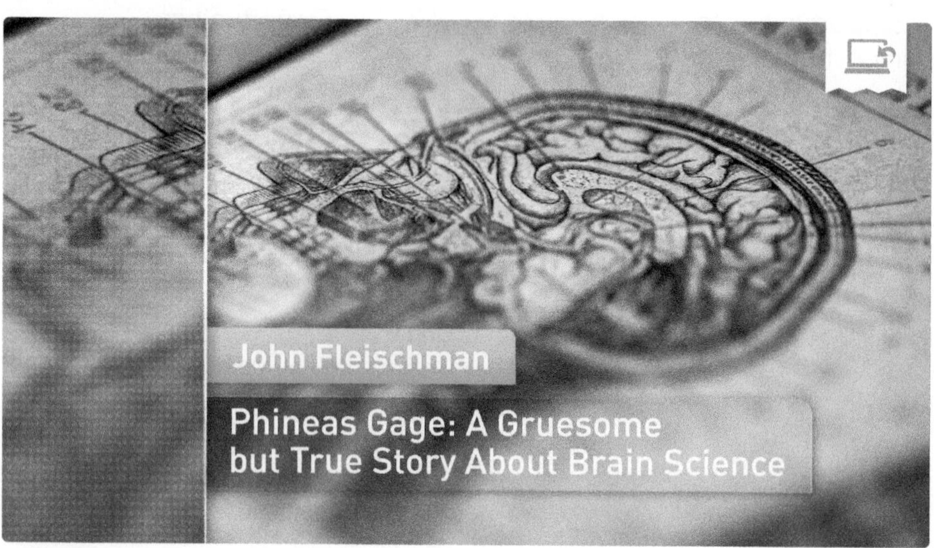

Introduce the Text

As a class, watch the video preview  and have students read the introduction in pairs to make connections to the video preview.

To activate prior knowledge and experiences, ask students:

- What part of the video stood out to you the most?
- What is one question you have about what you are going to read?

ELL SPEAKING FRAMES

- The ____ in the video makes me think ____.
- The video shows ____. This makes me wonder ____.
- I think the text will ____. I think this because ____.
- I predict that there will be ____. I believe this because ____.

Entry Point

As students prepare to read *Phineas Gage: A Gruesome but True Story About Brain Science*, share the following information with them to provide context.

- ✓ In 1848, Phineas Gage was the respected foreman of a crew that was building a railroad. That work involved igniting explosives to blast through rock as the crew worked to clear a path for a railway.
- ✓ While doing this work, Gage was hurt in an accident. He suffered severe damage in the frontal lobe of his brain, and his personality changed as a result. This case spurred neuroscientists to study the relationship between personality and the frontal lobe of the brain.
- ✓ The text will ask an important question: "Was Gage lucky or unlucky?" Students can return to this question after they complete their reading.

"Phineas will never be his old self again."

"Horrible Accident in Vermont"

NOTES

. . .

1 Phineas is the foreman of a track construction gang that is in the process of blasting a railroad right-of-way through granite bedrock near the small town of Cavendish, Vermont. Phineas is twenty-six years old, unmarried, and five feet, six inches tall, short for our time but about average for his. He is good with his hands and good with his men, "possessing an iron **will** as well as an iron frame," according to his doctor. In a moment, Phineas will have a horrible accident.

2 It will kill him, but it will take another eleven years, six months, and nineteen days to do so. In the short run, Phineas will make a full recovery, or so it will seem to those who didn't know him before. Old friends and family will know the truth. Phineas will never be his old self again. His "character" will change. The ways in which he deals with others, **conducts** himself, and makes plans will all change. Long after the accident, his doctor will sum up his case for a medical journal. "Gage," his doctor will write, "was no longer Gage." Phineas Gage's accident will make him world famous, but fame will do him little good. Yet for many others—psychologists, medical researchers, doctors, and especially those who suffer brain injuries—Phineas Gage will become someone worth knowing.

Skill: Central or Main Idea

The author notes that Gage's accident changed his behavior. Gage also became the subject of medical research. These supporting ideas and details tell me that the author's central or main idea relates to how the accident affected Gage's brain.

3 That's why we know so much about Phineas. It's been 150 years since his accident, yet we are still learning more about him. There's also a lot about Phineas we don't know and probably never will. The biggest question is the simplest one and the hardest to answer: Was Phineas lucky or unlucky? Once you hear his story, you can decide for yourself. But right now, Phineas is working on the railroad and his time has nearly come.

4 Building a railroad in 1848 is muscle work. There are no bulldozers or power shovels to open a way through Vermont's Green Mountains for the Rutland & Burlington Railroad. Phineas's men work with picks, shovels, and rock drills. Phineas's special skill is blasting. With well-placed charges of black

SELECTION VOCABULARY

will / la voluntad ***noun*** state of mind to persevere

conduct / la conducta ***verb*** to behave or act in a certain way COGNATE

- Who "conducts" and what does the person "conduct"?
- Which words and phrases are context clues for *conducts*?

Analyze Vocabulary Using Context Clues

In paragraph 1, focus on the sentence that uses the word *will*. Point out these context clues:

1. A *will* is something that a person possesses, or has. Based on that clue, I think *will* is a noun.
2. I read the sentence again. I notice that the sentence is describing Gage, and that *iron frame* refers to Gage's strong body.
3. I think that the author is saying that Gage has a strong body and mind. So, *will* must refer to the mind.

Central or Main Idea

How did the reader move closer to identifying the author's central or main idea?

The reader paid attention to how the supporting ideas and facts in the text build on each other.

TEXT TALK

What is Phineas Gage's job?

See paragraphs 1 and 5: He is the foreman of a construction gang that is blasting bedrock to clear the way for a railroad right-of-way.

How did Phineas Gage become "famous"?

See paragraph 2: He survived a horrible accident that should have killed him, and he became a well-known case study for brain injuries.

What does Gage's tool look like?

See paragraph 4: Gage's tamping iron is long, heavy, and thin. It has a fat, round end and a pointy end.

Skills Focus

QUESTION 2: Author's Purpose and Point of View

The author continues to list the very detailed work the people working on the railroad have to do. I think the author makes a point to write all of these details because he thinks their job is difficult.

Skills Focus

QUESTION 3: Textual Evidence

Working with gunpowder is risky because it can explode without warning if it is not handled properly.

Skills Focus

QUESTION 4: Central or Main Idea

The author describes how Gage or someone on his team made a big mistake. This is an important detail because it leads to the accident.

Textual Evidence

How did the reader use textual evidence to support her inference about Gage?

The reader noticed details about Gage's daily responsibilities, such as "All day, Phineas must keep an eye on his drillers to make sure they stay ahead."

NOTES

gunpowder, he shatters rock. To set those charges, he carries the special tool of the blasting trade, his "tamping iron." Some people confuse a tamping iron with a crowbar, but they are different tools for different jobs. A crowbar is for lifting up or prying apart something heavy. A tamping iron is for the delicate job of setting explosives. Phineas had his tamping iron made to order by a neighborhood blacksmith. It's a tapering iron rod that is three feet, seven inches long and weighs thirteen and a half pounds. It looks like an iron spear. At the base, it's fat and round, an inch and three quarters in diameter. The fat end is for tamping—packing down—loose powder. The other end comes to a sharp, narrow point and is for poking holes through the gunpowder to set the **fuse.** Phineas's tamping iron is very smooth to the touch, smooth from the blacksmith's **forge** as well as from constant use.

5 His task is to blast the solid rock into pieces small enough for his crew to dig loose with hand tools and haul away in ox carts. The first step is to drill a hole in the bedrock at exactly the right angle and depth, or the explosion will be wasted. All day, Phineas must keep an eye on his drillers to make sure they stay ahead. All day, Phineas must keep an eye on his diggers to make sure they keep up. All the time between, Phineas and his assistant are working with touchy explosives.

Skill: Textual Evidence

Gage has a dangerous job working with explosives. He also manages a crew. It must have been hard to keep track of so many things. These details show that Gage must have been a very hard worker to do such a difficult job.

6 They follow a strict **routine.** His assistant "charges" each new hole by filling the bottom with coarse-grained gunpowder. Phineas uses the narrow end of his iron to carefully press the ropelike fuse down into the powder. The assistant then fills up the rest of the hole with loose sand to act as a plug. Phineas will tamp the sand tight to bottle up the explosion, channeling the blast downward into the rock to shatter it. While his assistant is pouring the sand, Phineas flips his tamping iron around from the pointy end to the round end for tamping. Black powder is ticklish stuff. When it's damp, nothing will set it off. When it's too dry or mixed in the wrong formula, almost anything can set it off, without warning. But Phineas and his assistant have done this a thousand times—pour the powder, set the fuse, pour the sand, tamp the sand plug, shout a warning, light the fuse, and run like mad.

7 But something goes wrong this time. The sand is never poured down the hole; the black powder and fuse sit exposed at the bottom. Does his assistant forget, or does Phineas forget to look? Witnesses disagree. A few yards behind Phineas, a group of his men are using a hand-cranked derrick crane to hoist a large piece of rock. Some of the men remember seeing Phineas standing over the blast hole, leaning lightly on the tamping iron. Others say Phineas was sitting on a rock ledge above the hole, holding the iron loosely between his knees.

TEXT TALK

Why is working with gunpowder dangerous?

See paragraph 6: When it's damp, it doesn't explode, and when it's too dry it can go off without warning.

SELECTION VOCABULARY

fuse / el detonador *noun* a long string used to light explosives so they will explode

ELL

- What action is *fuse* associated with?
- How does the description of Gage's actions give a clue to the meaning of *fuse*?

8 There is no argument about what happens next. Something or someone distracts Phineas. Does he hear his name called? Does he spot someone goofing off? Whatever the reason, Phineas turns his head to glance over his right shoulder. The fat end of his tamping iron slips down into the hole and strikes the granite. A spark flies onto the exposed blasting powder. Blam! The drill hole acts as a gun barrel. Instead of a bullet, it fires Phineas's rod straight upward. The iron shrieks through the air and comes down with a loud clang about thirty feet away.

9 This is what happens. Imagine you are inside Phineas's head, watching in extreme slow motion: See the pointy end of the rod enter under his left cheekbone, pass behind his left eye, through the front of his brain, and out the middle of his forehead just above the hairline. It takes a fraction of a fraction of a second for the iron rod to pass from cheekbone to forehead, through and through.

10 Amazingly, Phineas is still alive. The iron throws him flat on his back, but as his men come running through the gunpowder smoke, he sits up. A minute later, he speaks. Blood is pouring down his face from his forehead, but Phineas is talking about the explosion. His men insist on carrying him to an ox cart for the short ride into town. They gently lift him into the back of the cart so he can sit up with his legs out before him on the floor. An Irish workman grabs a horse and races ahead for the doctor while the ox cart ambulance rumbles slowly down the half-mile to Cavendish. Phineas's excited men crowd alongside, walking next to their injured boss. Still acting as a foreman, Phineas calls out for his time book and makes an entry as he rolls toward town.

Skill: Textual Evidence

After the accident, Gage is talking and working. I'd expect him to be in pain. It seems he has no pain and doesn't know how badly he's hurt. This shows that the brain can trick a person into thinking that he's fine when he is not.

11 Something terrible has happened, yet Phineas gets down from the cart without help. He climbs the steps of the Cavendish hotel, where he has been living, and takes a seat on the porch beside his landlord, Joseph Adams. A few minutes earlier, Adams had seen the Irishman ride past shouting for Dr. Harlow, the town physician. Dr. Harlow was not to be found, so the rider was sent on to the next village to fetch Dr. Williams. Now Phineas takes a neighborly seat on the porch and tells his landlord what happened to him.

12 That's how Dr. Edward Williams finds Phineas nearly thirty minutes after the accident. Dr. Williams pulls up in his buggy at the hotel porch, and there is Phineas, talking away. Friends, workmates, and the curious crowd around as Dr. Williams climbs down from his carriage. "Well, here's work enough for you, Doctor," Phineas says to him quite cheerfully.

Textual Evidence

How did the reader identify textual evidence that she can use as support in a written response about the brain?

She notices Gage's actions following the accident and combines them with background knowledge about accidents.

TEXT TALK

How did Gage behave immediately after the accident?

See paragraphs 10 and 11: He behaved the same as always, despite the blood pouring down his face.

SELECTION VOCABULARY

forge / la fragua ***noun*** a furnace or oven where metal is heated and shaped

ELL
- Who has a "forge"?
- How is this person a clue to the word's meaning?

routine / la rutina ***noun*** a repeating pattern of actions COGNATE

ELL
- What actions make up the "routine"?
- How often are those actions performed?

13 Dr. Williams examines Phineas's head. He can't believe that this man is still alive. His skull is cracked open, as if something has popped out from the inside. Accident victims are often too shaken to know what happened, so Dr. Williams turns to Phineas's workmen for the story, but Phineas insists on speaking for himself. He tells Dr. Williams that the iron went right through his head.

14 Dr. Williams does not believe him.

Excerpted from *Phineas Gage: A Gruesome but True Story About Brain Science* by John Fleischman, published by HMH Books for Young Readers.

TEXT TALK

What does the doctor think when he examines Phineas's head after the accident? What questions does it raise for you?

See paragraphs 13 and 14: He doesn't believe what Phineas tells him about the accident. Additional questions will vary.

B Ask each Beyond grade-level student to write one additional discussion question. Then have one or two students facilitate a discussion, using their questions to guide the conversation.

Reading Comprehension OPTIONAL

Have students complete the digital reading comprehension questions ✓ when they finish reading.

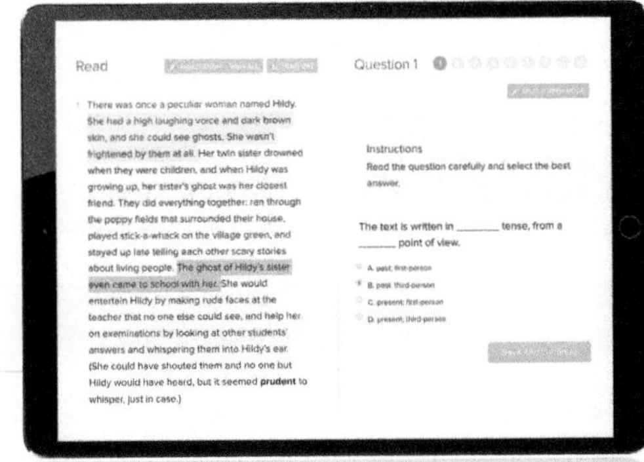

ANSWER KEY

QUESTION 1: C
QUESTION 2: B
QUESTION 3: D
QUESTION 4: A
QUESTION 5: D
QUESTION 6: C
QUESTION 7: A
QUESTION 8: B
QUESTION 9: *See first chart.*
QUESTION 10: *See second chart.*

FIRST	SECOND	THIRD	FOURTH
Phineas and his assistant work on blasting rock.	A blast throws Phineas's own tamping iron into his head.	Dr. Williams does not believe that an iron went through Phineas's head.	Phineas Gage "was no longer Gage."

Definition	Word
a blacksmith's workshop or factory	forge
behave	conduct
determination or resolve	will
a sequence or pattern	routine
a wire used to detonate an explosive device	fuse

Connect and Extend OPTIONAL

CONNECT TO EXTENDED WRITING PROJECT

Students can use *Phineas Gage: A Gruesome but True Story About Brain Science* as a resource when writing their suspenseful narratives. John Fleischman's style may suggest ideas for students' writing.

BEYOND THE BOOK

Comic Strip: Tell the Whole Story of Phineas Gage

The story of Phineas Gage is told in horrible detail, but there are pieces of information missing. The sand is never poured down the hole. What happened? Something or someone distracts Phineas. What was it?

Ask students to create comic strip panels depicting this tragic scene. They should use the details from the first chapter to show what is known and use their imaginations to fill in the missing information to tell the whole story of what happened that day.

Think Questions

Circulate as students answer Think Questions independently. Scaffolds for these questions are shown on the opposite page.

QUESTION 1: Textual Evidence

The author says Gage is "good with his hands and good with his men" before the accident. His doctor says he has an "iron will as well as an iron frame." The author also says that "The ways in which he deals with others, conducts himself, and makes plans will all change" after the accident. His doctor says he "was no longer Gage." Based on this textual evidence, I can infer that Gage might not be able to do his job or relate to people in the same positive way as he could before.

QUESTION 2: Textual Evidence

An explosion shoots an iron rod through Gage's head. Instead of killing him, the accident seems to have little effect. Doctors studied him and learned a lot about brain injuries that is still helpful more than 150 years after his accident.

QUESTION 3: Textual Evidence

Answers will vary but may include the following examples:

- "Amazingly, Phineas is still alive."
- "Dr. Williams pulls up in his buggy at the hotel porch, and there is Phineas, talking away."
- "Accident victims are often too shaken to know what happened, so Dr. Williams turns to Phineas's workmen for the story, but Phineas insists on speaking for himself."

Student descriptions should explain that Dr. Williams thinks anyone who had this kind of accident would be dead or at least unable to speak.

QUESTION 4: Word Meaning

Definition 3 most closely matches the meaning of the word *conduct* in paragraph 2. The verb is used to tell something about what Gage does himself, not to other people, and when I replace *conducts* with "behaves" the sentence still makes sense.

First Read

Read *Phineas Gage: A Gruesome but True Story About Brain Science.* After you read, complete the Think Questions below.

THINK QUESTIONS

1. How is Phineas Gage described by the author in the beginning of the excerpt? How might the accident affect or change his behavior? Explain, citing specific textual evidence.
2. Using textual evidence, summarize in three sentences what happens to Phineas Gage on this fateful day and why it is remembered centuries later.
3. Why doesn't Dr. Edward Williams believe Phineas's account of what happened? Explain, citing specific textual evidence.
4. Read the following dictionary entry:

   conduct
   con•duct \kən ˈdəkt\ *verb*

   1. organize or direct something
   2. transmit energy
   3. behave in a specified way or manner

   Which definition most closely matches the meaning of **conduct** as it is used in paragraph 2? Write the correct definition of *conduct* here and explain how you figured out the correct meaning.
5. Find the word **routine** in paragraph 6 of *Phineas Gage: A Gruesome but True Story About Brain Science.* Use context clues in the surrounding sentences, as well as the sentence in which the word appears, to determine the word's meaning. Write your definition here and identify clues that helped you figure out its meaning.

QUESTION 5: Context Clues

I think *routine* refers to "the usual way of doing something." In the text, *routine* refers to the series of actions Gage and his workers complete every time they set off an explosion. This is something they've done the same way many times.

SCAFFOLDS

Think Questions

Use the scaffolds below to differentiate instruction for your ELL English Language Learners and A Approaching grade-level learners.

ELL **BEGINNING** Write a response using the word bank and sentence frames.

INTERMEDIATE Write a response using the sentence frames.

ADVANCED, ADVANCED HIGH Write a response using the Text-Dependent Question Guide.

A **APPROACHING** Write a response using the Text-Dependent Question Guide.

BEGINNING	INTERMEDIATE	APPROACHING / ADVANCED, ADVANCED HIGH
Word Bank	**Sentence Frames**	**Text-Dependent Question Guide**
job Gage usual daily brain interacts men talk explain cracked explosion	Before the accident, Gage works well with his hands and with his ____. After the accident, the way he ____ with others changes. Based on these details, I can infer that Gage might not be able to do his ____ as well as he did before.	1. • What does the author say about Phineas before the accident? • What does the author say will change about Phineas after the accident? • What can you infer from this textual evidence?
	Gage is injured when an ____ causes an iron rod to pass through his head. Afterward, Gage still was able to ____ and move. Doctors have learned a lot about ____ injuries based on Gage's story.	2. • What happened during the accident? • How did Gage act after the accident? • Why is Gage's story important to people today?
	Dr. Williams discovers that Gage's head is ____ open. Usually, people who have such injuries cannot ____ what happened to them. However, ____ has no trouble telling the doctor what happened.	3. • What does Dr. Williams discover when he examines Gage? • How do accident victims usually act? • How is Gage's behavior different?
	Conduct as used in the text matches definition #____.	4. • "The ways in which he deals with others, **conducts** himself, and makes plans will all change." • Is Gage organizing or directing himself? (#1) • Is Gage transmitting energy? (#2) • Is Gage behaving a certain way? (#3)
	The word *routine* refers to the way Gage and his team do their job ____. This gives me a clue that *routine* means "something that is the ____ way of doing something."	5. • Read: "They follow a strict **routine**." • What actions are described after this sentence? • What do the sentences after this one tell me about the meaning of the word *routine*?

Skill: Central or Main Idea

Introduce the Skill

Watch the Concept Definition video and read the following definition with your students.

The **central idea** of a nonfiction text is the most important point that an author makes about a **topic**. The statement of a central idea answers the question *What's it all about?* In order to find the answer, look for **supporting ideas** that help develop the central idea. Authors also include **details** as textual evidence to support the central idea about the topic. Readers **analyze** these supporting ideas or details to see what they have in common. What do they support, explain, or describe? Answering this question will help identify the central or main idea.

Skill: Central or Main Idea

Use the Checklist to analyze Central or Main Idea in *Phineas Gage: A Gruesome but True Story About Brain Science*. Refer to the sample student annotations about Central or Main Idea in the text.

••• CHECKLIST FOR CENTRAL OR MAIN IDEA

In order to identify a central idea of a text, note the following:

- ✓ the central or main idea, if it is explicitly stated
- ✓ when the central idea emerges
- ✓ ways in which supporting ideas relate to the central idea
- ✓ key details and supporting ideas that connect to the author's point or message

To determine a central idea of a text and analyze its development over the course of the text, including its relationship to supporting ideas, consider the following questions:

- ✓ What main idea(s) do the details in each paragraph explain or describe?
- ✓ What bigger idea do all the paragraphs support?
- ✓ What is the best way to state the central idea?
- ✓ How do the supporting ideas and details help develop the central idea over the course of the text?
- ✓ How might you objectively summarize the text and message? What details would you include?

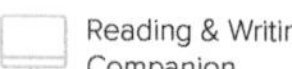

TURN AND TALK

1. What was the topic of an informational text you read and really liked?
2. What was the central or main idea of that text? How do you know?

SPEAKING FRAMES

- I liked an informational text about ____.
- I think the central or main idea of that text is ____.
- I think that is the central idea because the author mainly talked about ____.

SKILL VOCABULARY

central or main idea / la idea central o principal ***noun*** the most important point an author makes about a topic or in a section of text

topic / el tema ***noun*** the subject of a literary work, usually expressed as a single word or phrase in the form of a noun

supporting idea / la idea secundaria ***noun*** a focused explanation or argument that helps develop the central idea

Skill: Central or Main Idea

Reread paragraphs 11–14 of *Phineas Gage: A Gruesome but True Story About Brain Science*. Then, using the Checklist on the previous page, answer the multiple-choice questions below.

YOUR TURN

1. Based on how Gage behaves in paragraph 11, the reader can conclude that a central or main idea is —

   ○ A. The landlord and Gage know each other very well.
   ○ B. Gage is behaving very strangely for an accident victim.
   ○ C. The author is exaggerating how bad the accident really was.
   ○ D. Doctors in the 1800s were not as skillful as they are today.

2. The description of the "curious crowd" in paragraph 12 supports the central or main idea that—

   ○ A. Gage is well-liked.
   ○ B. Life in the town is dull.
   ○ C. What is happening is very unusual.
   ○ D. People in Vermont tend to be curious.

3. Details in paragraphs 13 and 14 build the central or main idea that—

   ○ A. Gage needed to receive medical attention sooner.
   ○ B. The town would benefit from more experienced doctors.
   ○ C. This is likely the first time someone survived such an accident.
   ○ D. Dr. Williams thinks Gage is not telling the truth about what happened.

SKILL VOCABULARY

detail / el detalle *noun* a fact, a description, an example, or a reason that further explains a key idea COGNATE

analyze / analizar *verb* to consider in detail and discover essential features or meaning COGNATE

Your Turn

Ask students to complete the Your Turn activity.

QUESTION 1

A. Incorrect. Although they most likely did know each other well, this is not an important idea.

B. Correct. Gage is chatting with his landlord as if nothing is wrong just after an iron rod went completely through his head.

C. Incorrect. The author is not exaggerating. It was a very bad accident.

D. Incorrect. Details in the passage do not support this opinion.

QUESTION 2

A. Incorrect. Although the author suggests that Gage is well liked, it is not a central idea.

B. Incorrect. Details in the passage do not support this idea.

C. Correct. A "curious crowd" gathers because Gage's accident is unbelievable.

D. Incorrect. Details in the passage do not support this idea.

QUESTION 3

A. Incorrect. Although Gage does have to wait for the doctor, the details do not suggest that his outcome would have changed if he were treated sooner.

B. Incorrect. The text does not support this idea.

C. Correct. The doctor's shocked reaction suggests that he has never seen such a case before.

D. Incorrect. Although paragraph 14 reveals the doctor's doubts, this is not the central idea.

Skill: Textual Evidence

Introduce the Skill

Watch the Concept Definition video and read the following definition with your students.

Any time you're discussing a text, you need to **cite**, or point out, **textual evidence**, the details that readers use to support their ideas and opinions. Readers may cite evidence that is directly stated, or **explicit**, in the text. Other times, textual evidence may be **implicit**, which means it is suggested but not directly stated. One way to interpret implicit meanings is to **make inferences**, using clues from the text and your own experiences to make logical decisions about characters and events that are not stated directly.

Readers must also refer to textual evidence when they **analyze** and examine the different parts of a text. Analyzing specific parts of the text, such as the actions of a character or the cause-and-effect relationships between events in nonfiction, helps a reader **interpret** and explain the meaning, theme, or central idea of the text as a whole. When you cite textual evidence, someone else can look back at a particular part of a text you read and understand your analysis.

Skill:
Textual Evidence

Use the Checklist to analyze Textual Evidence in *Phineas Gage: A Gruesome but True Story About Brain Science*. Refer to the sample student annotations about Textual Evidence in the text.

••• CHECKLIST FOR TEXTUAL EVIDENCE

In order to support an analysis by citing textual evidence that is explicitly stated in the text, do the following:

- ✓ read the text closely and critically
- ✓ identify what the text says explicitly
- ✓ find the most relevant textual evidence that supports your analysis
- ✓ consider why an author explicitly states specific details and information
- ✓ cite the specific words, phrases, sentences, or paragraphs from the text that support your analysis
- ✓ cite evidence from the text that most strongly supports your analysis

In order to interpret implicit meanings in a text by making inferences, do the following:

- ✓ combine information directly stated in the text with your own knowledge, experiences, and observations
- ✓ cite the specific words, phrases, sentences, or paragraphs from the text that support this inference

In order to cite textual evidence to support an analysis of what the text says explicitly, as well as to support inferences drawn from the text, consider the following questions:

- ✓ Have I read the text closely and critically?
- ✓ What inferences am I making about the text? What textual evidence am I using to support these inferences?
- ✓ Am I quoting the evidence from the text correctly?
- ✓ Does my textual evidence logically relate to my analysis?
- ✓ What textual evidence from the text most strongly supports your analysis?

TURN AND TALK

1. Think of an informational text you've read. What was the author's central or main idea?
2. How did the author use textual evidence to support the central or main idea?

SPEAKING FRAMES

- An informational text I've read is ____. The author's central or main idea was ____.
- The author supported (his / her) central idea by using textual evidence like ____.

SKILL VOCABULARY

cite / citar ***verb*** to quote as evidence to support a response COGNATE

textual evidence / la evidencia del texto ***noun*** details from the text that a reader can use to support his or her ideas and opinions about the text

explicit / explícito/a ***adjective*** precisely and clearly expressed COGNATE

implicit / implícito/a ***adjective*** implied but not stated directly COGNATE

Phineas Gage: A Gruesome but True Story About Brain Science

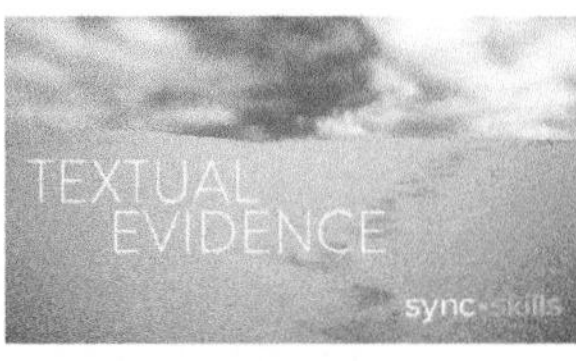

Skill: Textual Evidence

Reread paragraphs 6–9 of *Phineas Gage: A Gruesome but True Story About Brain Science*. Then, using the Checklist on the previous page, answer the multiple-choice questions below.

YOUR TURN

1. Which response best shows an understanding of the text that is supported by textual evidence?

   - A. The accident shows that gunpowder was too dangerous to be used safely.
   - B. The incident proves that accidents can happen to even the most experienced experts.
   - C. The confusion after the accident suggests that witnesses are unreliable.
   - D. Gage deserved what happened because it was his fault.

2. Which paragraph best supports the inference that the cause of the accident is unknown?

   - A. 6
   - B. 7
   - C. 8
   - D. 9

3. Which textual evidence best supports the inference that the accident happens too quickly to be fully observed?

   - A. "When it's too dry or mixed in the wrong formula, almost anything can set it off, without warning."
   - B. "A few yards behind Phineas, a group of his men are using a hand-cranked derrick crane to hoist a large piece of rock."
   - C. "A spark flies onto the exposed blasting powder. Blam!"
   - D. "It takes a fraction of a fraction of a second for the iron rod to pass from cheekbone to forehead, through and through."

SKILL VOCABULARY

make inferences / hacer inferencias *verb* to use your understanding of a text and your own experiences, to draw conclusions

analyze / analizar *verb* to consider in detail and discover essential features or meaning COGNATE

interpret / interpretar *verb* to explain the meaning of (information, words, or actions) COGNATE

Your Turn

Ask students to complete the Your Turn activity.

QUESTION 1

A. Incorrect. Textual evidence in paragraph 6 shows that Gage and his team have used gunpowder safely many times.

B. Correct. Textual evidence shows that Gage and his team have a lot of experience, but the accident happens anyway.

C. Incorrect. Although textual evidence in paragraph 7 does support the inference that witnesses do not agree on what happened, this is not the most reasonable conclusion to draw from the passage.

D. Incorrect. There is no evidence to support the idea that Gage deserved what happened.

QUESTION 2

A. Incorrect. There is no textual evidence in the paragraph to suggest that the cause of the accident is unknown.

B. Correct. Textual evidence in paragraph 7 shows that witnesses' accounts of what happened varied.

C. Incorrect. There is no textual evidence in the paragraph to suggest that the cause of the accident is unknown.

D. Incorrect. There is no textual evidence in the paragraph to suggest that the cause of the accident is unknown.

QUESTION 3

A. Incorrect. This textual evidence shows that gunpowder is likely to explode, not that the accident itself happened quickly.

B. Incorrect. This textual evidence suggests that the men didn't fully observe the accident because they were busy, not because it happened too quickly.

C. Incorrect. This textual evidence helps readers imagine the blast, but it does not sufficiently support the inference that the accident was quick.

D. Correct. This textual evidence shows that the rod passed through Gage's skull in less than a second, suggesting that the whole incident happened too quickly to be fully observed.

Close Read

Skills Focus

QUESTION 1: Central or Main Idea

See paragraph 3: The author's central or main idea is that Phineas Gage's story is important because of what it taught scientists about brain injuries.

QUESTION 2: Author's Purpose and Point of View

See paragraph 6.

QUESTION 3: Textual Evidence

See paragraph 6.

QUESTION 4: Central or Main Idea

See paragraph 7.

QUESTION 5: Connect to Essential Question

See paragraph 2: Gage's accident didn't kill him right away, but it caused his personality to change. No one knows why that happened, which makes it a very intriguing mystery.

CHECK FOR SUCCESS

If students struggle to respond to Skills Focus question 1, ask them the following questions:

- What happened to Phineas Gage?
- What details in paragraph 3 stand out to you?
- What do we learn from the first three paragraphs?

Have students transition to read and annotate independently once they have successfully completed the first Skills Focus prompt.

Phineas Gage: A Gruesome but True Story About Brain Science

Close Read

Reread *Phineas Gage: A Gruesome but True Story About Brain Science*. As you reread, complete the Skills Focus questions below. Then use your answers and annotations from the questions to help you complete the Write activity.

SKILLS FOCUS

1. Reread the first three paragraphs of *Phineas Gage: A Gruesome but True Story About Brain Science*. Identify a key detail in paragraph 3, and explain the central or main idea that is revealed by the beginning of the excerpt.
2. Reread paragraphs 4–6. Does the author think people who work on the railroad have a difficult job or an easy job? Describe the author's point of view about railroad workers, citing textual evidence.
3. An important idea in paragraph 6 is that working with gunpowder is risky. Identify textual evidence that supports this idea, and explain what makes working with gunpowder so risky.
4. Reread paragraphs 7–9. Identify a detail that reveals a central or main idea in this section of *Phineas Gage: A Gruesome but True Story About Brain Science*. Explain the central or main idea and how the textual evidence supports it.
5. In paragraph 3, the author states that 150 years after Phineas Gage's accident there is still a lot we don't know. Why are people still interested in Gage's story? Identify a detail that makes Gage's story still intriguing 150 years later.

WRITE

INFORMATIVE: Explain how Gage's reaction to his serious injury impacts Dr. Williams. How do the details about the interaction between Phineas Gage and Dr. Williams connect to the central or main idea of the overall text? Be sure to cite specific textual evidence to support your claim.

122 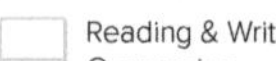 Reading & Writing Companion

Writer's Notebook

Connect to Essential Question: Give students time to reflect on how *Phineas Gage: A Gruesome but True Story About Brain Science* connects to the unit's essential question "What attracts us to the mysterious?" by freewriting in their Writer's Notebooks.

Beginning & Intermediate

Read aloud the unit's essential question: "What attracts us to the mysterious?" Encourage students to draw their connections or allow students to write in their native language. Circulate the room, prompting students for their thoughts as they respond orally or through pantomime.

Advanced & Advanced High

Allow students to share their reflections orally in pairs or small groups before freewriting

SCAFFOLDS

Collaborative Conversation

Break students into collaborative conversation groups to discuss the Close Read prompt. Ask students to use the StudySyncTV episode as a model for their discussion. Remind them to reference their Skills Focus annotations in their discussion.

Explain how Gage's reaction to his serious injury impacts Dr. Williams. How do the details about the interaction between Phineas Gage and Dr. Williams connect to the central or main idea of the overall text? Be sure to cite specific textual evidence to support your claim.

Use the scaffolds below to differentiate instruction for your ELL English Language Learners and A Approaching grade-level learners.

ELL **BEGINNING, INTERMEDIATE** Use the discussion guide and speaking frames to facilitate the discussion with support from the teacher.

ADVANCED, ADVANCED HIGH Use the discussion guide and speaking frames to facilitate the discussion in mixed-level groups.

A **APPROACHING** Use the discussion guide to facilitate the discussion in mixed-level groups.

APPROACHING
ADVANCED, ADVANCED HIGH
BEGINNING, INTERMEDIATE

Discussion Guide	Speaking Frames
1. Describe Phineas's behavior in the time period right after his accident.	• Phineas was able to ____. • Phineas felt and acted in a ____ way.
2. What is the central or main idea of *Phineas Gage: A Gruesome but True Story About Brain Science*?	• The central or main idea of *Phineas Gage: A Gruesome but True Story About Brain Science* is ____. • A detail that reveals this message is ____.
3. How does the doctor's reaction to Phineas Gage connect to the central idea of the text?	• The doctor reacts to Phineas by ____. • The doctor's reaction to Phineas Gage connects to the central idea because ____.

Review Prompt and Rubric

Before students begin writing, review the writing prompt and rubric with the class.

INFORMATIVE: Explain how Gage's reaction to his serious injury impacts Dr. Williams. How do the details about the interaction between Phineas Gage and Dr. Williams connect to the central or main idea of the overall text? Be sure to cite specific textual evidence to support your claim.

PROMPT GUIDE

- What is the central or main idea in *Phineas Gage: A Gruesome but True Story About Brain Science*? What textual evidence supports this main idea?
- How would you expect someone to act after an accident like Phineas's? How does Phineas react?
- What was shocking to the doctor about how Phineas was acting?

Score	Central or Main Idea	Textual Evidence	Language and Conventions
4	The writer clearly identifies and analyzes the central or main idea in the text. The writer provides exemplary analysis, using relevant evidence from the text.	The writer cites the strongest textual evidence to support exemplary analysis.	The writer demonstrates a consistent command of grammar, punctuation, and usage conventions. Although minor errors may be evident, they do not detract from the fluency or the clarity of the writing.
3	The writer identifies and analyzes the central or main idea in the text. The writer provides sufficient analysis, using relevant evidence from the text most of the time.	The writer cites textual evidence to support sufficient analysis.	The writer demonstrates an adequate command of grammar, punctuation, and usage conventions. Although some errors may be evident, they create few (if any) disruptions in the fluency or the clarity of the writing.
2	The writer begins to identify and analyze the central or main idea in the text, but the analysis is incomplete. The writer uses relevant evidence from the text only some of the time.	The writer begins to cite textual evidence to support an appropriate response, but analysis is incomplete.	The writer demonstrates a partial command of grammar, punctuation, and usage conventions. Some distracting errors may be evident, at times creating minor disruptions in the fluency or clarity of the writing.
1	The writer attempts to identify and analyze the central or main idea in the text, but the analysis is not successful. The writer uses little or no relevant evidence from the text.	The writer attempts to cite textual evidence to support an appropriate response, but the analysis is not successful.	The writer demonstrates little or no command of grammar, punctuation, and usage conventions. Serious and persistent errors create disruptions in the fluency of the writing and sometimes interfere with meaning.
0	The writer does not provide a relevant response to the prompt or does not provide a response at all.	The writer does not provide a relevant response to the prompt or does not provide a response at all.	Serious and persistent errors overwhelm the writing and interfere with the meaning of the response as a whole, making the writer's meaning impossible to understand.

SCAFFOLDS

Write

Ask students to complete the writing assignment using textual evidence to support their answers.

Use the scaffolds below to differentiate instruction for your ELL English Language Learners and A Approaching grade-level learners.

ELL **BEGINNING** With the help of the word bank, write a response using paragraph frame 1.

INTERMEDIATE With the help of the word bank, write a response using paragraph frames 1 and 2.

ADVANCED, ADVANCED HIGH Write a response of differentiated length using the sentence starters.

A **APPROACHING** Write a response of differentiated length using the sentence starters.

BEGINNING | INTERMEDIATE | ADVANCED, ADVANCED HIGH | APPROACHING

Word Bank	Paragraph Frame 1	Paragraph Frame 2	Sentence Starters
cheerfully shocks unusual explain expect	When Dr. Williams finds Phineas he is ____ talking with friends. Phineas's head is hurt and he is bleeding so the doctor doesn't ____ Phineas to be able to explain what happened, but he does. Phineas's reaction to his injury ____ the doctor. Phineas's ability to talk with other people and ____ what happened support the central idea of this text. The central idea of this text is that the accident and how it affected Phineas were extremely ____.	Phineas's tamping iron went ____, but he could ____. His interaction with the doctor connects to the central or main idea of this story because it shows that the accident and its effects on Phineas were ____.	• When someone has a serious injury, I would expect them to . . . • After Phineas's accident he . . . • By the time Dr. Williams finds Phineas, he is . . . • This interaction with the doctor connects to the central or main idea of this story by showing . . .

Peer Review

Students should submit substantive feedback to two peers using the instructions below.

- How well does this response answer the prompt?
- Did the writer clearly identify the central or main idea in the text?
- How well does the writer support his or her ideas with details and examples from the text?
- What did the writer do well in this response? What does the writer need to work on?

Rate

Respond to the following with a point rating that reflects your opinion.

ELL

SENTENCE FRAMES

- You were able to (completely / partly / almost) answer the prompt.
- You could answer the prompt more completely by ____.
- You supported the idea of ____ with the detail of ____.
- One idea that needs more support is ____.

Blast: Judge a Book by Its Cover

How do you judge a book by its cover?

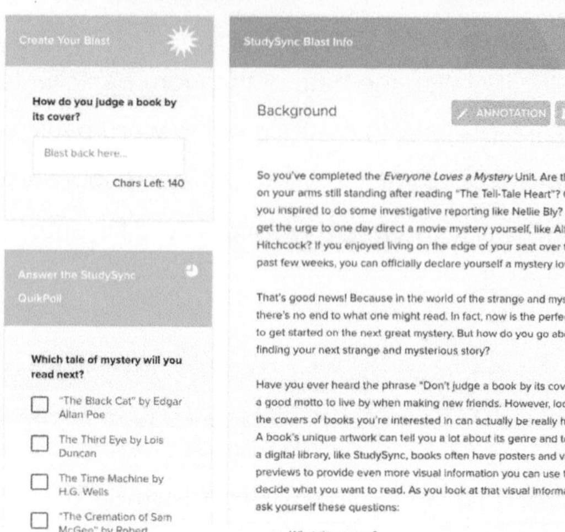

TEXT TALK

What is one strategy you can use for self-selecting a new text? How does it work?

Answers may vary.

What should you do once you choose a text that interests you?

Start reading the text to confirm my interest. If I like it, I should keep reading.

Create Your Own Blast

Ask students to write a 140-character Blast after they complete the QuikPoll.

Use the scaffolds below to differentiate instruction for your ELL English Language Learners.

ELL **BEGINNING** Write a response using the word bank to complete the sentence frame.

INTERMEDIATE Write a response using the sentence frame.

ADVANCED, ADVANCED HIGH Write a response using the sentence starter.

BEGINNING		ADVANCED, ADVANCED HIGH
	INTERMEDIATE	
Word Bank	**Sentence Frame**	**Sentence Starter**
interested decide video preview visual information poster	I can judge a text's ____ in order to ____ what to read. ____ and ____ can help me become ____ in a story.	• I can judge a text's . . . • I can judge a book by its cover using . . .

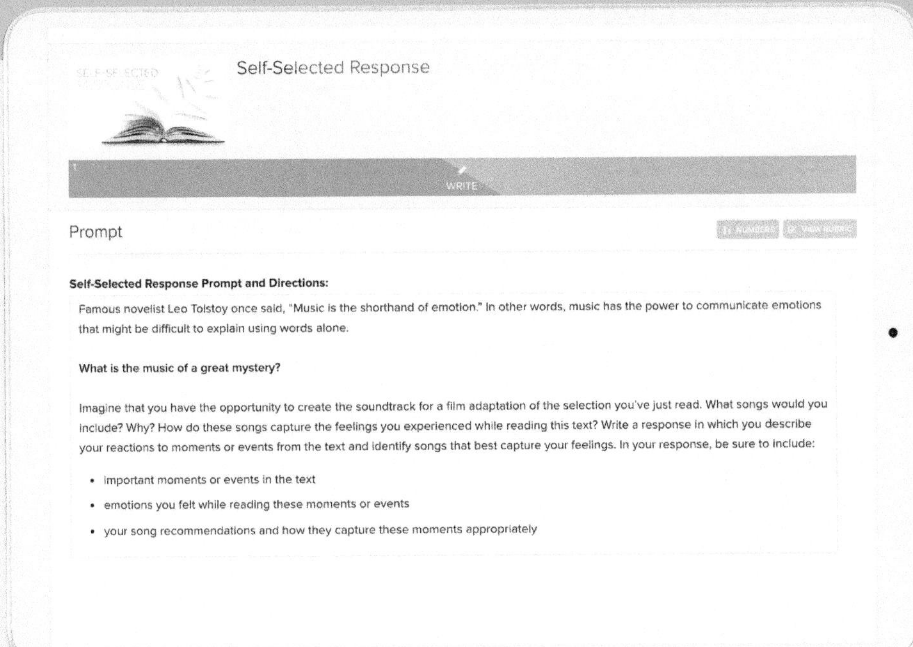
Self-Selected Response

Prompt

Self-Selected Response Prompt and Directions:

Famous novelist Leo Tolstoy once said, "Music is the shorthand of emotion." In other words, music has the power to communicate emotions that might be difficult to explain using words alone.

What is the music of a great mystery?

Imagine that you have the opportunity to create the soundtrack for a film adaptation of the selection you've just read. What songs would you include? Why? How do these songs capture the feelings you experienced while reading this text? Write a response in which you describe your reactions to moments or events from the text and identify songs that best capture your feelings. In your response, be sure to include:

- important moments or events in the text
- emotions you felt while reading these moments or events
- your song recommendations and how they capture these moments appropriately

Self-Selected Response

Introduce the Prompt

Read aloud the prompt. Ask students to discuss:

- What is the prompt asking you to do?
- Why might it be a good idea to think about our own reactions to a text before choosing a song?

Write

SCAFFOLDS

Ask students to complete the writing assignment using text evidence to support their answers.

Use the scaffolds below to differentiate instruction for your ELL English Language Learners and A Approaching grade level readers.

ELL **BEGINNING** With the help of the word bank, write a response using paragraph frame 1.

INTERMEDIATE With the help of the word bank, write a response using paragraph frames 1 and 2.

ADVANCED, ADVANCED HIGH Write a response of differentiated length using the sentence starters.

A **APPROACHING** Write a response of differentiated length using the sentence starters.

BEGINNING, INTERMEDIATE	BEGINNING	INTERMEDIATE	ADVANCED, ADVANCED HIGH, APPROACHING
Word Bank	**Paragraph Frame 1**	**Paragraph Frame 2**	**Sentence Starters**
happy sad angry surprised excited nervous tense anxious frustrated relieved	I read the text (title) ____ by (author) ____. One important event is ____. I felt ____ when I read this event. A song that captures my feelings is (song) ____ by (artist) ____. Another important event is ____. I felt ____ when I read this event. A song that captures my feelings is (song)____ by (artist) ____.	I chose the first song because ____. I chose the second song because ____.	• I read the text . . . by . . . • One important event from the story is . . . • I felt . . . while reading this event . . . • A song that I would choose to capture my feelings in reaction to this event is . . . • This song is appropriate because . . . • Another key moment from the story is . . .

Extended Writing Project

The Extended Writing Project (EWP) in Grade 8, Unit 1 focuses on narrative writing. Students probe the unit's essential question—What attracts us to the mysterious?—as they write a narrative about a suspenseful experience that comes in a familiar place or an everyday situation. The multiple pieces of suspenseful fiction in the unit, as well as an account of time in a madhouse and an essay by the "master of suspense," serve as mentor texts for students to analyze and emulate. Specific skill lessons teach developing ideas, organization, and conventions, while other skill lessons focus on story beginnings, descriptive details, and dialogue and help students develop their unique voices. Directed revision leads students through the process of revising for clarity, development, organization, word choice, and sentence variety. Throughout the EWP, students have the opportunity to practice using created student writing, authentic texts, and their own work.

 Audio and audio text highlighting are available in select lessons in the Extended Writing Project.

CONNECT TO ESSENTIAL QUESTION

What attracts us to the mysterious?

In analyzing the texts in this unit, students learned how authors manipulate plot, characters, setting, dialogue, and other story elements to build suspense for their readers. Now students will apply those strategies to their own suspenseful narrative.

Extended Writing Project Prompt

What happens when fear comes from an unlikely source?

Use the techniques you've learned in this unit to write your own suspenseful narrative. Your characters may experience suspense in a familiar place or while they're with people they know and trust. Perhaps the fear comes from an everyday object or situation.

These icons identify differentiation strategies and scaffolded support for a variety of students. See the digital lesson plan for additional differentiation strategies and scaffolds.

Instructional Path

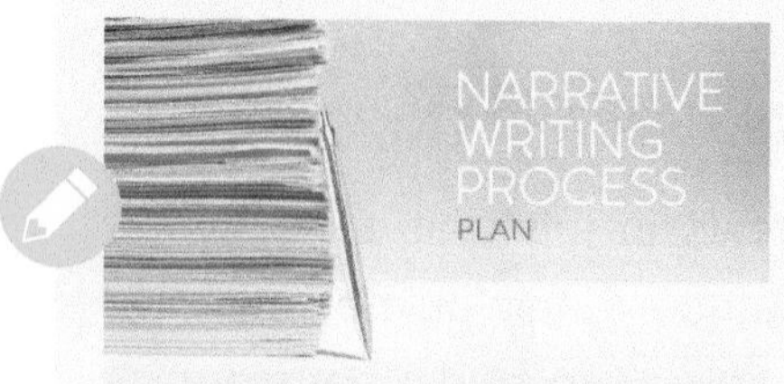

Narrative Writing Process: Plan

Objectives: After learning about genre characteristics and craft, students will analyze a sample Student Model and plan a meaningful narrative in response to a prompt.

Skill: Organizing Narrative Writing

Objectives: After reading and discussing a model of student writing, students will develop their drafts by organizing their narrative effectively.

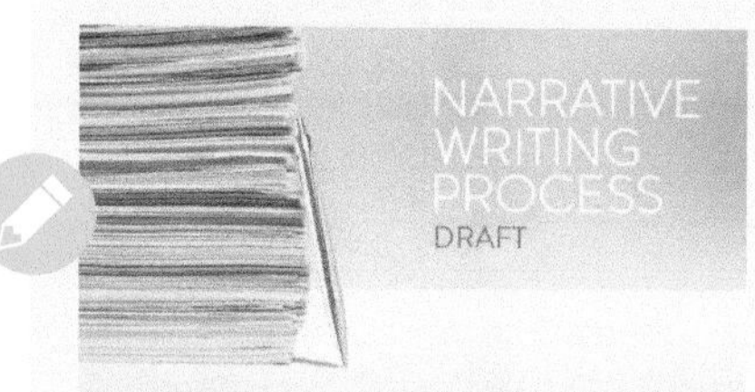

Narrative Writing Process: Draft

Objectives: After reading a Student Model draft and reviewing a writing checklist, students will draft a meaningful narrative in response to a prompt.

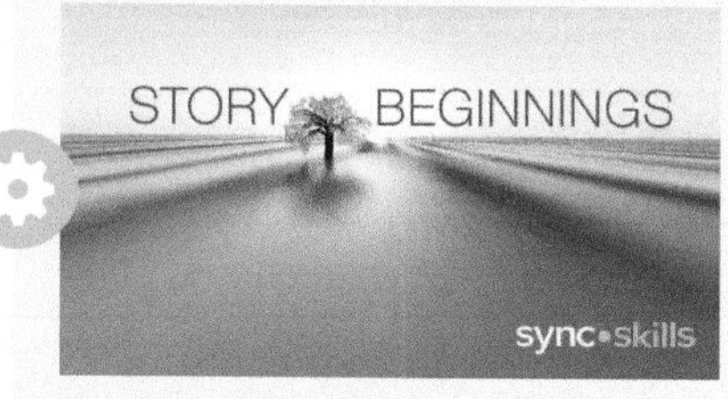

Skill: Story Beginnings

Objectives: After reading and discussing a model of student writing, students will develop their drafts by improving their story beginning.

Skill: Narrative Techniques

Objectives: After reading and discussing a model of student writing, students will develop their drafts by using narrative techniques, such as dialogue, pacing, description, and reflection, to develop experiences, events, and/or characters.

Skill: Descriptive Details

Objectives: After reading and discussing a model of student writing, students will develop their drafts by using relevant descriptive details to capture the action and convey experiences and events.

The print teacher's edition includes essential point-of-use instruction and planning tools. Complete lesson plans and program documents appear in your digital teacher account.

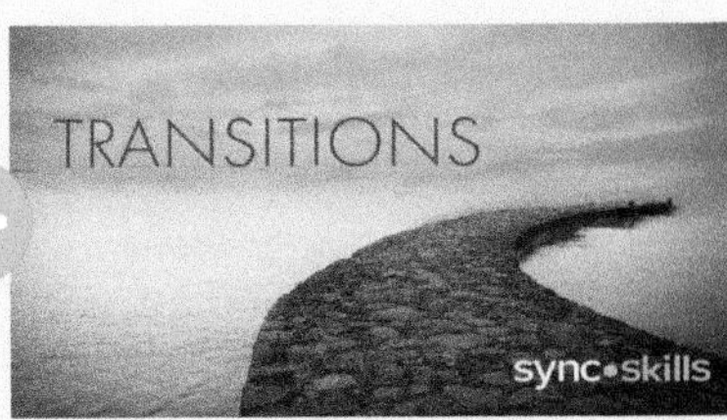

Skill: Transitions

Objectives: After reading and discussing a model of student writing, students will use a variety of transition words, phrases, and clauses to convey sequence, signal shifts from one time frame or setting to another, and show the relationships among experiences and events.

Skill: Conclusions

Objectives: After reading and discussing a model of student writing, students will provide a conclusion that follows from and reflects on the narrated experiences or events.

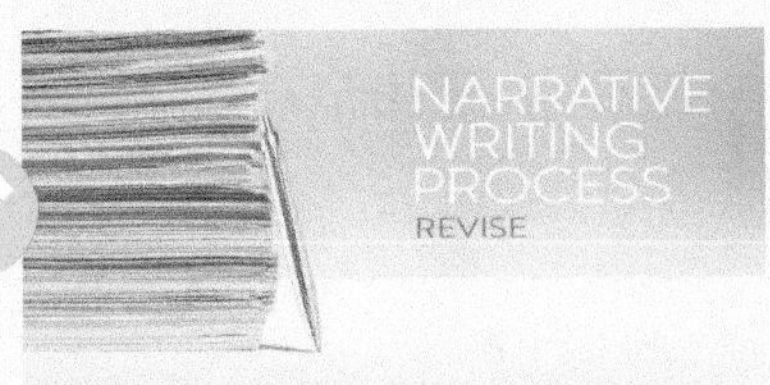

Narrative Writing Process: Revise

Objectives: Students will use a revision guide to revise the draft of their narrative for clarity, development, organization, style, diction, and sentence variety.

Grammar: Basic Spelling Rules I

Objectives: After learning about a set of basic spelling rules and seeing how they are used in text examples, students will practice using these basic spelling rules correctly.

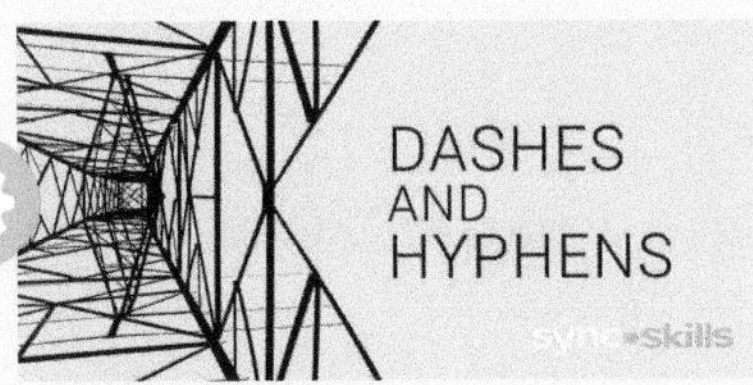

Grammar: Dashes and Hyphens—Dashes

Objectives: After learning about dashes and seeing how they are used in text examples, students will practice using dashes correctly.

Grammar: Commas After Transitions

Objectives: After learning about commas after transitions and seeing how they are used in text examples, students will practice using commas after transitions correctly.

Narrative Writing Process: Edit and Publish

Objectives: After seeing an example of editing in the Student Model and reviewing an editing checklist, students will edit and publish the final draft of their narrative.

Progress Monitoring

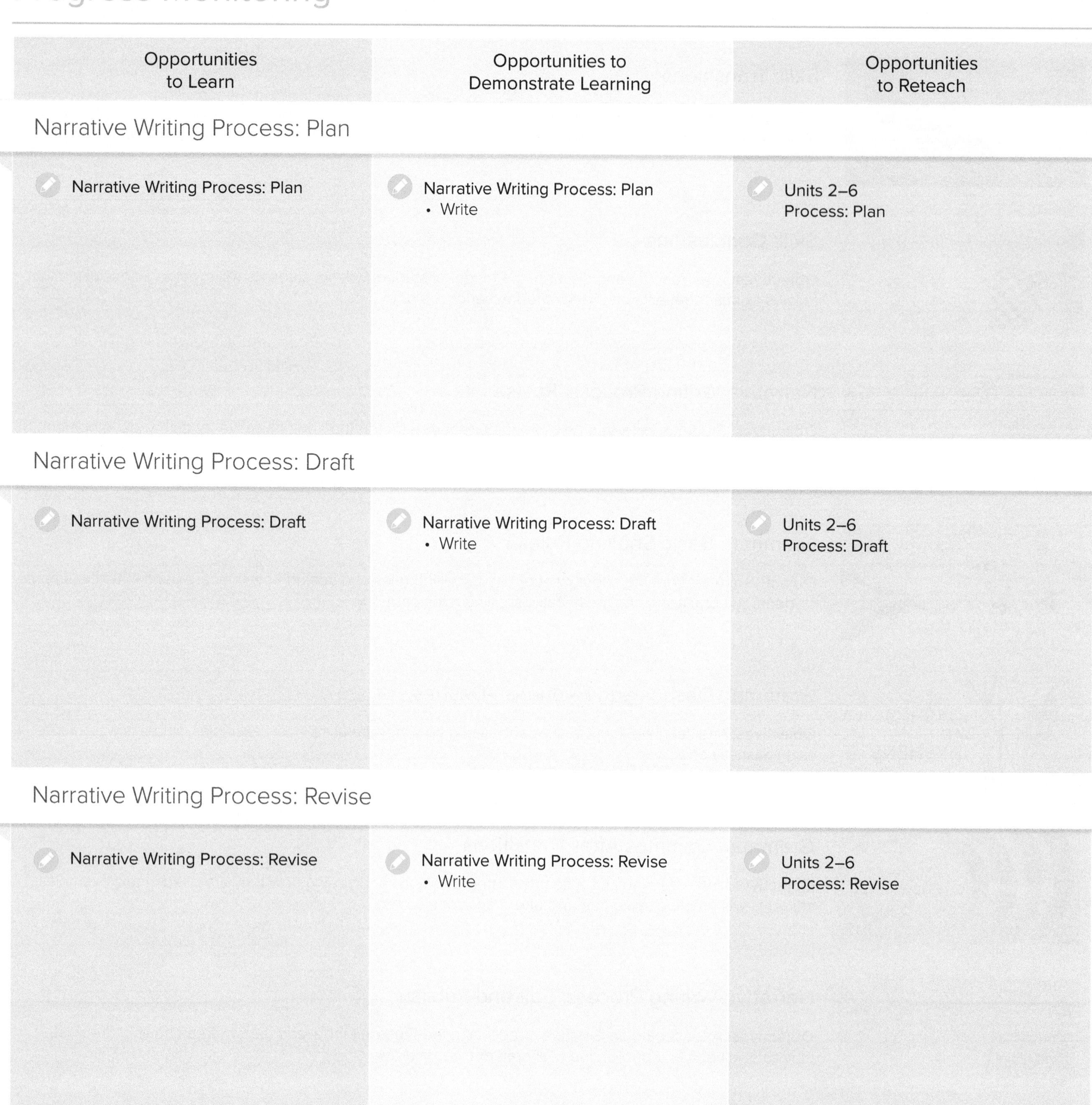

Opportunities to Learn	Opportunities to Demonstrate Learning	Opportunities to Reteach
Narrative Writing Process: Plan		
Narrative Writing Process: Plan	Narrative Writing Process: Plan • Write	Units 2–6 Process: Plan
Narrative Writing Process: Draft		
Narrative Writing Process: Draft	Narrative Writing Process: Draft • Write	Units 2–6 Process: Draft
Narrative Writing Process: Revise		
Narrative Writing Process: Revise	Narrative Writing Process: Revise • Write	Units 2–6 Process: Revise

Narrative Writing Process: Edit and Publish

Narrative Writing Process: Edit and Publish	Narrative Writing Process: Edit and Publish • Write	Units 2–4, 6 Process: Edit and Publish Unit 5 Process: Edit and Present

Organizing Narrative Writing

Skill: Organizing Narrative Writing	Skill: Organizing Narrative Writing • Your Turn Narrative Writing Process: Draft	Spotlight Skill: Organizing Narrative Writing

Story Beginnings

Skill: Story Beginnings	Skill: Story Beginnings • Your Turn Narrative Writing Process: Revise	Spotlight Skill: Story Beginnings

Narrative Techniques

Skill: Narrative Techniques	Skill: Narrative Techniques • Your Turn Narrative Writing Process: Revise	Spotlight Skill: Narrative Techniques

Descriptive Details

Skill: Descriptive Details	Skill: Descriptive Details • Your Turn Narrative Writing Process: Revise	Spotlight Skill: Descriptive Details

Transitions

Skill: Transitions	Skill: Transitions • Your Turn Narrative Writing Process: Revise	Units 2–6 Skill: Transitions Spotlight Skill: Transitions

Conclusions

Skill: Conclusions	Skill: Conclusions • Your Turn Narrative Writing Process: Revise	Units 2–6 Skill: Conclusions Spotlight Skill: Conclusions

Basic Spelling Rules I

Grammar: Basic Spelling Rules I	Grammar: Basic Spelling Rules I • Your Turn Narrative Writing Process: Edit and Publish	Grammar: Spelling—Prefixes

Dashes and Hyphens—Dashes

Grammar: Dashes and Hyphens—Dashes	Grammar: Dashes and Hyphens—Dashes • Your Turn Narrative Writing Process: Edit and Publish	Grammar: Colons and Semicolons—Colons

Commas After Transitions

Grammar: Commas After Transitions	Grammar: Commas After Transitions • Your Turn Narrative Writing Process: Edit and Publish	Grammar: Commas—Misuse of Commas Grammar: Commas—With Introductory Phrases

Narrative Writing Process: Plan

Introduce the Extended Writing Project

- What is the prompt asking you to do?
- Which characteristics of narrative writing will you need to learn more about in order to respond to the prompt?
- What are the five characteristics of narrative writing?
- What elements of craft do narrative writers use?

DIFFERENTIATED QUESTIONS

- What does **unlikely** mean?
- What are some situations that would probably not be scary?
- What might make one of those situations scary?

Review the Rubric

Have students examine the "Narrative Writing Rubric—Grade 8" grading rubric. Inform students that this is the same rubric that will be used to evaluate their completed Narrative Extended Writing Project.

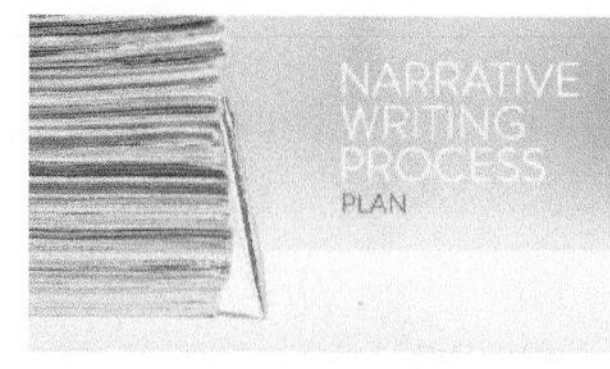

Narrative Writing Process: Plan

PLAN | DRAFT | REVISE | EDIT AND PUBLISH

Authors often create suspense from unlikely sources. The old man in "The Tell-Tale Heart" had no reason to fear the man who lived in a room in his home . . . until he was murdered. In "The Lottery," a town's annual summer gathering takes a horrifying turn of events.

WRITING PROMPT

What happens when fear comes from an unlikely source?

Use the techniques you've learned in this unit to write your own suspenseful narrative. Your characters may experience suspense in a familiar place or while they're with people they know and trust. Perhaps the fear comes from an everyday object or situation. Regardless of which unlikely source you choose, be sure your narrative includes the following:

- a plot with a beginning, middle, and end
- a clear setting
- characters and dialogue
- a feeling of suspense
- a clear theme

Introduction to Narrative Writing

Narrative writing tells a story of experiences or events that have been imagined by a writer or that have happened in real life. Good narrative writing effectively uses genre characteristics and craft such as relevant descriptive details and a purposeful structure with a series of events that contain a beginning, middle, and end. The characteristics of fiction writing include:

- setting
- characters
- plot
- theme/reflection
- point of view

In addition to these characteristics, narrative writers also carefully craft their work through their use of dialogue, details, word choice, and figurative language. These choices help to shape the tone, mood, and overall style of the text. Effective narratives combine these genre characteristics and craft to engage the reader.

As you continue with this Extended Writing Project, you'll receive more instruction and practice at crafting each of the characteristics of fiction writing to create your own suspenseful narrative.

Before you get started on your suspenseful narrative, read a narrative that one student, Lucia, wrote in response to the writing prompt. As you read the Model, highlight and annotate the features of narrative writing that Lucia included in her narrative.

STUDENT MODEL

NOTES

1 The microwave timer chimes and I push the button to release the door. A wave of butter-scented popcorn hits my face, and my taste buds long to try it. I pour it eagerly into a big wooden bowl and shake on some salt, humming to myself. My cell phone rings. It's Mom.

2 "Just checking in!" Mom chirps.

3 "I'm fine. I promise," I say, rolling my eyes, which of course she can't see.

4 "Okay, okay. I'll let you go. But Ella—" Mom trails off. I can tell she wants to say something.

5 "Yes?" I ask.

6 "Not too much ZeldaZee, okay?"

7 "Sure, Mom. I promise." She also couldn't see my fingers, which are crossed.

8 While carrying the bowl of popcorn under one arm and a tall glass of fizzy water in one hand, I shuffle in my slippered feet down the hallway to my bedroom in record-breaking time. The house hums contentedly around me. It is Friday night, and I have the whole place to myself. Mom is at a work dinner, and my younger brother, Tom the Slob, is at a sleepover. The quiet feels like a rare treat, but most exciting of all is the promise of uninterrupted time with my favorite YouTube star, ZeldaZee.

Read and Annotate

As students read, have them use the Annotation Tool to identify and label the characteristics of narrative writing:

- setting
- characters
- plot
- theme/reflection
- point of view

When students finish reading, ask them to share their annotations in small groups.

ANNOTATION GUIDE

Find the following quotes in the Student Model. Then, use the Annotation Tool to label each quote as an example of setting, character, plot, or point of view.

- My cell phone rings. It's Mom.
- I shuffle in my slippered feet down the hallway to my bedroom in record-breaking time.
- Here's what I can tell you about ZeldaZee: She's sixteen.
- Suddenly, ZeldaZee whirls around to face the screen.
- I'm just swinging my legs over the side of the bed when I hear it: the creak of floorboards just outside my door.
- To my horror, the doorknob begins to twist.

READ AND ANNOTATE

Pair students with on-grade-level peers to complete the annotation activity.

TEXT TALK

Structure and Organization

Where does Lucia introduce the conflict in her story?

See paragraphs 6–7: Ella crosses her fingers when she promises to obey her mom. This shows that she is not being honest.

Organization and Focus

How does Lucia focus on the setting in her opening paragraphs to create a calm tone at the beginning of her narrative?

See paragraph 8: Ella's description of her quiet evening at home includes specific details about her slippers and how the house "hums" around her. It allows readers to focus on the way the house feels.

9 Once I make it to my bedroom without spilling a thing, I climb up onto my neatly made bed—Mom's a stickler for asking me to make it. My open laptop has already fallen asleep there, but I awaken the screen with one click. ZeldaZee's channel is queued up and ready to go. So I toss a kernel of popcorn into my mouth and hit play.

10 Here's what I can tell you about ZeldaZee: She's sixteen. She has a little brother (just like me!) whom she calls Stinker, but I'm pretty sure that's not his real name. She has two Siamese cats, who often show up in her videos, dressed in different outfits or draped in some of her jewelry. She lives in the suburbs but I'm not sure where—she keeps it vague. ZeldaZee covers a lot of different topics—school life, fashion, family, beauty—but the thing I love about her is her personality; I swear it feels like she's talking right to me. When she looks into the camera and tells a story about her day, I laugh as though one of my friends were talking to me. Sometimes, I find myself responding to her out loud. I have to remind myself she can't hear me.

11 The title of this video is "How Not to Get Lost in Your Own Neighborhood." It shows ZeldaZee walking through her neighborhood on a sunny afternoon, pointing at familiar landmarks. "Look for street names!" she instructs, and the camera swings up to hold on the names of the cross streets: Magnolia and Pine. *Hey, wait a second*, I think. *We have an intersection of Magnolia and Pine not too far from here!* I take a sip of fizzy water, thinking a wonderful thought: What if ZeldaZee lives in my neighborhood? I've wondered it before. I swear she drove by a nearby mini mall in her episode "How To Shop Like a Boss." However, ZeldaZee has over twelve million followers. She's a star! If she lived in my neighborhood, wouldn't I have heard about it?

12 On screen, meanwhile, ZeldaZee continues down the list. "Ask a friendly-looking neighbor!" ZeldaZee instructs. She waves to an old woman in gardening gloves, repotting some tulips. "Hey!" calls ZeldaZee. "Do I look familiar to you?"

13 I squint at the screen. I'm almost positive I've seen that old lady before. Didn't she used to give me piano lessons? Miss Gomez, wasn't it? A feeling of unease creeps down my spine and it takes me

TEXT TALK

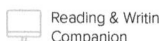

Development of Ideas and Details

How does Lucia use specific details to contribute to her narrative?

Answers will vary. Sample answer: In paragraph 10, Lucia provides details about ZeldaZee to make her seem more realistic.

Conventions

Can you find an example of a comma after a transition word or phrase? What ideas is this word or phrase connecting?

Answers will vary. Sample answer: Yes, in paragraph 12, the author says, "On screen, meanwhile, ZeldaZee continues down the list." The author uses "meanwhile" to transition from her thoughts about the show to what is currently happening on screen.

Organization and Coherence

Where does Lucia use a transition to begin building suspense?

Answers will vary. Sample answer: In paragraph 13, Ella says, "A feeling of unease creeps down my spine" when she realizes that Miss Gomez died.

a second to realize why: Last week, Mom had told me that Miss Gomez died.

14 Suddenly, ZeldaZee whirls around to face the screen. In a low voice she says, "Ella, I have something to tell you."

15 The popcorn kernel in my fingers is frozen halfway to my open mouth. Ella. That's me.

16 "Don't freak out," says ZeldaZee, still in that same low voice. "But there's someone in your house."

17 My blood turns to ice in my veins. Then I shake it off. She can't possibly be talking to me. I look to the door of my room, force myself to laugh. "Whatever," I say aloud.

18 "You still have time," ZeldaZee continues. I search her face for the usual glint of mischief, but her eyes are oddly blank. "Ella, you need to act fast. Pick up your phone."

19 I scan the room, searching for my cell phone, but I am filled with a sense of dread once I realize that I left it in the kitchen.

20 "He's coming down the hallway," ZeldaZee tells me, her voice almost a whisper. "Now's your chance."

21 This can't be right. I snap the laptop shut. "Weird," I say. But the word sounds more casual than I feel. I'm just swinging my legs over the side of the bed when I hear it: the creak of floorboards just outside my door.

22 "Hello?" My voice makes a tiny scratchy sound as it leaves my throat.

23 To my horror, the doorknob begins to twist.

24 I run for the window. I'm on the second floor, but that hardly matters. As I scramble onto the roof, I see the door to my room swing open. "Ella! Ella!"

25 It's ZeldaZee. She's calling to me. But where is she? I peer over the ledge of the roof. My familiar front lawn looms in front of me, a map of shadows. *I'll climb down the trellis*, I tell myself. Once on the ground, I can run to a neighbor's house for help.

TEXT TALK

Word Choice

Where do you find Lucia's word choice especially strong or expressive?

Answers will vary. Sample answer: In paragraph 14, Lucia writes that ZeldaZee "whirls" around to face the screen. I think that's a really good verb and a good choice to use instead of something more common, like "turns."

Sentence Fluency

Choose one sentence that you think is really effective. Why do you think it's so strong?

Answers will vary. Sample answer: I think the sentence "I snap the laptop shut" in paragraph 21 is really strong. I can visualize how quickly she closes her computer.

NOTES

26 As I twist my body to try and catch hold of the trellis with my feet, I see through my bedroom window. Inside, someone rushes through the room. "Ella!"

27 My foot slips. I start to fall. I open my mouth to scream, but no sound comes out.

28 "Ella! Wake up!"

29 I jolt upright. I'm sitting in my room, blinking up into . . . Mom's face.

30 She looks concerned. "You were having a nightmare."

31 "Was I?" I look around. The bowl of popcorn has capsized on the bed, kernels dusting over the open laptop's keyboard as a result. "I must've fallen asleep."

32 "Watching ZeldaZee, I presume," says Mom. She doesn't try to conceal the disapproval in her voice.

33 Was it really all a dream? I click the keyboard and watch as my computer lurches to life. According to the screen, I've watched eleven episodes of ZeldaZee. That's funny, I can only remember the first.

34 "I had the weirdest dream," I say.

35 Mom is shaking her head. "And what have I told you about food in your room?"

36 "I'm sorry," I say.

37 "Just don't do it again."

38 "Oh, believe me," I say, meaning it this time. "I won't!" One look at ZeldaZee's face on my screen and my stomach clenches up. Now that the feelings of fear and confusion are wearing off, there's one consolation, though: I think I'm finally cured of my obsession with ZeldaZee!

TEXT TALK

Development of Ideas

Was there a theme in this story?

Answers will vary. Sample answer: This story shows that dreams can sometimes help us improve our habits because Ella's suspenseful dream helped her stop obsessing over a YouTube series.

WRITE

Writers often take notes about story ideas before they sit down to write. Think about what you've learned so far about narrative writing to help you begin prewriting.

- **Purpose:** What issue do you want to write about, and why is it a problem?
- **Audience:** Who is your audience and what message do you want to express to your audience?
- **Setting:** Where and when will your story be set? What kinds of problems might these characters face? How might the setting of your story affect the characters and problem?
- **Characters:** What types of characters would you like to write about in your narrative?
- **Plot:** What events will lead to the resolution of the conflict while keeping a reader engaged?
- **Theme/Reflection:** If you are writing an imagined narrative, what general message about life do you want to express? If you are writing a real narrative, what careful thoughts about the significance of your experience will you include?
- **Point of View:** From which point of view should your story be told, and why?

Response Instructions

Use the questions in the bulleted list to write a one-paragraph summary. Your summary should describe what will happen in your narrative.

Don't worry about including all of the details now; focus only on the most essential and important elements. You will refer to this short summary as you continue through the steps of the writing process.

Write

Circulate as students use the questions in the bulleted list to plan their writing. See the instructions for scaffolding and differentiating that follow.

CHECK FOR SUCCESS

If students struggle to come up with answers for the questions in the lesson, work with students to provide an answer to one question and then help them build from there.

For example, start by asking students, "Where is your story happening?" or "What is the least suspenseful situation you can think of?" Once students have answered one question, help them to work through a second question until they've begun to build some momentum. It may be helpful to start with a different question than the one that's listed first in the lesson.

Review Prompt and Rubric

Before students begin writing, review the writing prompt and rubric with the class.

Response Instructions

Use the questions in the bulleted list to write a one-paragraph summary. Your summary should describe what will happen in your narrative.

Don't worry about including all of the details now; focus only on the most essential and important elements. You will refer to this short summary as you continue through the steps of the writing process.

Score	Plan	Language and Conventions
4	The writer responds to the questions, and the writing is clear and focused.	The writer demonstrates a consistent command of grammar, punctuation, and usage conventions. Although minor errors may be evident, they do not detract from the fluency or clarity of the writing.
3	The writer responds to the questions, but the writing is not always clear or focused.	The writer demonstrates an adequate command of grammar, punctuation, and usage conventions. Although some errors may be evident, they create few (if any) disruptions in the fluency or clarity of the writing.
2	The writer responds to the questions, but the writing is somewhat unclear and unfocused.	The writer demonstrates a partial command of grammar, punctuation, and usage conventions. Some distracting errors may be evident, at times creating minor disruptions in the fluency or clarity of the writing.
1	The writer responds to the questions, but the writing is very unclear and unfocused.	The writer demonstrates little or no command of grammar, punctuation, and usage conventions. Serious and persistent errors create disruptions in the fluency of the writing and sometimes interfere with meaning.
0	The writer does not provide a relevant response to the questions or does not provide a response at all.	Serious and persistent errors overwhelm the writing and interfere with the meaning of the response as a whole, making the writer's meaning impossible to understand.

Write

SCAFFOLDS

Use the scaffolds below to differentiate instruction for your ELL English Language Learners and A Approaching grade-level learners.

ELL **BEGINNING, INTERMEDIATE** With the help of the word bank, write a response using the paragraph frame.

ADVANCED, ADVANCED HIGH Write a response using the sentence starters.

A **APPROACHING** Write a response using the sentence starters.

BEGINNING / INTERMEDIATE		ADVANCED, ADVANCED HIGH / APPROACHING
Word Bank	**Paragraph Frame**	**Sentence Starters**
problem home boy surprised school girl succeed	My story will be about ____. The main character is ____. The setting of my story is ____. In the beginning of the story, ____. In the middle of the story, ____. At the end of the story, ____.	• My story will be about . . . • It will take place . . . • First, . . . • Then, . . . • It will end . . .

Peer Review

Students should submit substantive feedback to two peers using the review instructions below.

- How well does this response answer the prompt?
- What part of the suspenseful narrative are you most excited to read about?
- Are there any ideas that could be improved on? How so?

Rate

Respond to the following with a point rating that reflects your opinion.

	1	2	3	4
Ideas	■	■	■	□
Evidence	■	■	■	■
Language and Conventions	■	■	□	□

Submit

ELL A **SENTENCE FRAMES**

- The response does a good job of addressing ____ from the prompt.
- The response would improve by addressing ____ from the prompt.
- I am most excited to read about ____.
- I think you could improve ____ by (adding / clarifying / describing) ____.

Skill: Organizing Narrative Writing

Introduce the Skill

Watch the Concept Definition video and read the following definition with your students.

In **narrative writing**, a writer creates a story out of real or imagined events. A narrative is usually organized by the **plot**, or the series of events that take place. The plot is driven by a **conflict**, or a problem that the characters face.

Many narratives arrange the story with a clear beginning, middle, and end, moving through five stages:

Exposition—provides background information
Rising action—develops the conflict
Climax—the point of highest interest or suspense
Falling action—what happens after the climax
Resolution—how the conflict is solved

When organizing a narrative, orient the reader with information about the characters and setting. Create an **inciting incident** that pushes a character into the main action of the story and the problem the character must solve. The events that lead to a solution should unfold naturally and logically, as in a series of cause-and-effect relationships.

Skill: Organizing Narrative Writing

CHECKLIST FOR ORGANIZING NARRATIVE WRITING

As you consider how to organize your narrative, use the following questions as a guide:

- Who is the narrator and who are the characters in the story?
- From what point of view will the story be told?
- Where will the story take place?
- What conflict or problem will the characters have to resolve?
- Does my plot flow logically and naturally from one event to the next?

Here are some strategies to help you organize your narrative:

- Introduce a narrator and/or characters.
  > Characters can be introduced all at once or throughout the narrative.
  > Choose the role each character will play.
  > Choose a point of view.
    - A first-person narrator can be a participant or character in the story.
    - A third-person narrator tells the story as an outside observer.
- Establish a context.
  > Begin with your exposition—decide what background information your readers need to know about the characters, setting, and conflict.
  > List the events of the rising action—be sure that these events build toward the climax.
  > Describe what will happen during the climax of the story—make sure that this is the point of highest interest, conflict, or suspense in your story.
  > List the events of the falling action—make sure that these events show what happens to the characters as a result of the climax.
  > Explain the resolution of the main conflict in your story.

TURN AND TALK

Turn to your partner and explain how your favorite movie follows (or doesn't follow) the basic structure of narrative writing provided in the Concept Definition video.

SPEAKING FRAMES

- My favorite movie is ____.
- It follows the basic structure of narrative writing because ____.

SKILL VOCABULARY

narrative writing / la escritura narrativa *noun* a story made out of real or imagined events

plot / la trama *noun* the sequence of events that form a story

conflict / el conflicto *noun* the main problem or struggle that characters face in a story COGNATE

exposition / la exposición *noun* the background information provided in the beginning of a story about the characters, the setting, and the conflict COGNATE

YOUR TURN

Complete the chart below by matching each event to its correct place in the narrative sequence.

	Options
A	He doesn't see anything familiar, but he decides to walk around and figure out where he is.
B	The main character wakes up in a world he doesn't recognize.
C	He figures out he has to stay in the new world.
D	He tries to find a way home but is unable to.
E	He realizes the new world is similar to his old one, and he can be happy there.

Narrative Sequence	Event
Exposition	
Rising Action	
Climax	
Falling Action	
Resolution	

Your Turn

Ask students to complete the Your Turn activity.

Exposition	B
Rising Action	A
Climax	D
Falling Action	C
Resolution	E

SKILL VOCABULARY

rising action / la tensión dramática creciente *noun* a series of events that work to create tension, interest, or suspense and result in the story's climax

climax / el clímax *noun* the point in the plot with the highest interest, conflict, or suspense COGNATE

falling action / la acción decreciente *noun* a series of events that occur after the climax and lead to the resolution of the story's conflict

resolution / la resolución *noun* the final outcome of the story's conflict COGNATE

inciting incident / el incidente generador *noun* the first event in which the conflict becomes apparent

Your Turn

Ask students to complete the Your Turn activity. Answers will vary.

Exposition	My story will be set in a small town on a sunny day, but it will be deserted except for a 65-year-old woman named Ana. She is on her way to a park to lead a nature walk for the 50th year in a row. As she walks, she thinks about what that route used to be like when she was a kid.
Rising Action	She walks through the town center and does not see anyone around. To try to find people, she goes into several places, like the bank, the grocery store, and the post office, but she finds that they are all empty and closed.
Climax	She calls the police station to ask what has happened. The chief of police reminds her that it is a bank holiday, but no one is sleeping in: Everyone is waiting at the park to go on her nature walk and thank her for her years of community service.
Falling Action	When Ana gets to the park, a large crowd breaks into applause.
Resolution	The mayor, wearing hiking boots, presents Ana with a plaque to honor her for her 50 years of community service. The plaque says that the town would not be a community without her.

Extended Writing Project

YOUR TURN

Complete the chart below by writing a short summary of what will happen in each section of your narrative.

Narrative Sequence	Summary
Exposition	
Rising Action	
Climax	
Falling Action	
Resolution	

132 Reading & Writing Companion

Writer's Notebook

Choose five items from your classroom (for example, a pencil, a marker, a spoon, a calendar, and a remote control). Place these items somewhere in the room where students can see all of them. Ask students to create a story using those items for the five parts of their plot diagram. Students should label each part of their story and write a one- or two-sentence summary of events for each image, like Lucia did in the Student Model.

TURN AND TALK

Allow students to share their summaries orally in pairs or small groups before freewriting.

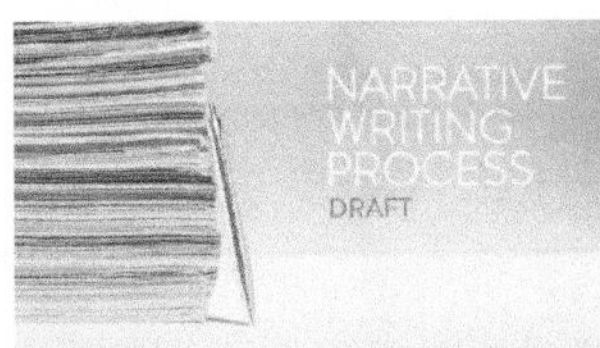

Narrative Writing Process: Draft

PLAN | DRAFT | REVISE | EDIT AND PUBLISH

You have already made progress toward writing your suspenseful short story. Now it is time to draft your suspenseful short story.

WRITE

Use your plan and other responses in your Binder to draft your narrative. You may also have new ideas as you begin drafting. Feel free to explore those new ideas as you have them. You can also ask yourself these questions:

- Have I included specifics about my setting, characters, plot, theme, and point of view?
- Have I made my conflict clear to the reader?
- Does the sequence of events in my story make sense?

Before you submit your draft, read it over carefully. You want to be sure that you've responded to all aspects of the prompt.

Narrative Writing Process: Draft

Write

Ask students to complete the writing assignment.

CHECK FOR SUCCESS

If students struggle to begin drafting their suspenseful narratives, ask them the following questions:

- Who is your story about?
- What is happening to that character?
- Where is the story happening?
- When is the story happening?
- Why is the character fearful of something unexpected?

DRAFT CHECKLIST

- ☐ Does my exposition explain the setting, characters, and conflict?
- ☐ Did I provide information about my characters with descriptions? With dialogue?
- ☐ Is the order of my story easy for readers to follow?
- ☐ Does my resolution solve the conflict?

Peer Review

Students should submit substantive feedback to two peers using the instructions below.

- Do any elements of narrative writing need to be added or further developed?
- How well has the writer developed suspense in this narrative?
- What suggestions can you make to help the writer improve the organization of the story?
- Are there any ideas that could be improved on? How so?

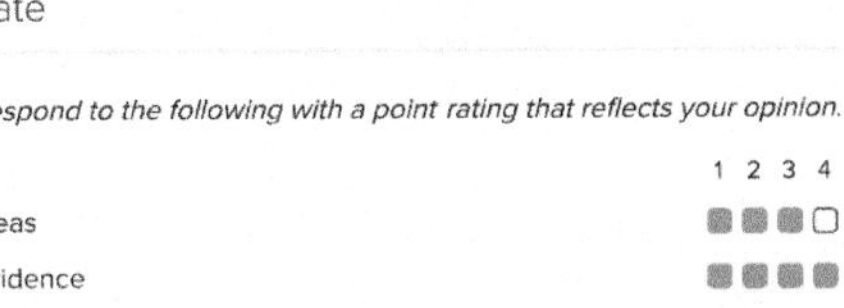

SENTENCE FRAMES

- The ____ could be further developed by ____.
- The suspense is (always / sometimes / rarely) effective because ____.
- The organization of the story can be improved by ____ .
- I like the ____ because ____. You could improve it by ____.

Analyze Student Model

Have students discuss the questions in the lesson as well as the Student Model draft. Ask:

- What important background information does Lucia present to her readers in the exposition?
- Which narrative techniques does Lucia use to begin her story?
- How does Lucia's use of dialogue and description reveal information about her characters?

Encourage students to share ideas for their own narratives based on the questions in the lesson.

SPEAKING FRAMES

- In the exposition, the writer presents important details such as ____.
- The writer grabs readers' attention with narrative techniques like ____.
- The writer uses dialogue to reveal ____.
- The writer uses description to reveal ____.
- An idea that I have for my narrative involves ____.

Story Beginnings

Discuss the Model

1. The model shows how Lucia changed the beginning of her story. How did she change it? Lucia added descriptive details and action to share information about the characters, setting, and conflict in an engaging way.
2. How do those changes improve her story? Answers will vary, but they may include adding more details to help readers better imagine the scene and reveal more information about Ella.
3. How could Lucia use a different story beginning technique to grab her readers' attention? Answers will vary.

SPEAKING FRAMES

- Lucia changed the beginning of her story by ____.
- These changes improved her story because ____.
- Lucia could use a different story beginning, like ____.

Extended Writing Project

Here is Lucia's short story draft. As you read, identify details that Lucia includes in her exposition. As she continues to revise and edit her narrative, she will find and improve weak spots in her writing, as well as correct any language or punctuation mistakes.

STUDENT MODEL: FIRST DRAFT

A Quiet Friday Night

~~I am standing in my kitchen when my cell phone rings. The screen tells me that it's my Mom.~~

~~"Just checking in!"~~

~~"I'm fine. I promise," I say.~~

~~"Okay, okay. I'll let you go. But . . ." Mom trails off.~~

~~"Yes?"~~

~~"Not too much ZeldaZee, okay?"~~

~~"Sure, Mom. I promise."~~

The microwave timer chimes and I push the button to release the door. A wave of butter-scented popcorn hits my face, and my taste buds long to try it. I pour it eagerly into a big wooden bowl and shake on some salt, humming to myself. My cell phone rings. It's Mom.

"Just checking in!" Mom chirps.

"I'm fine. I promise," I say, rolling my eyes, which of course she can't see.

"Okay, okay. I'll let you go. But Ella—" Mom trails off. I can tell she wants to say something.

"Yes?" I ask.

"Not too much ZeldaZee, okay?"

"Sure, Mom. I promise." She also couldn't see my fingers, which are crossed.

Skill: Story Beginnings

Lucia adds action and description to help readers better imagine the opening scene. She describes what her character is doing as she talks to her mom, and these actions reveal parts of the main character's personality.

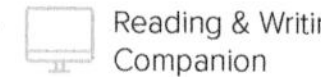

EMULATE A MENTOR TEXT

Have students choose a sentence or passage from one of the mentor texts in the unit that they find particularly effective. Allow students time to discuss their selections in a small group, exploring why the passage stood out to them. Was it the structure? Writing style? Something else? Then, encourage students to emulate their mentor text in a section of their own writing.

While carrying the bowl of popcorn under one arm and a tall glass of fizzy water in one hand I shuffle in my slippered feet down the hallway to my bedroom in record-breaking time. The house was queit around me. It is Friday night, and I have the whole place to myself. Mom is at a work dinner, and my younger brother, Tom the Slob, is at a sleepover. I'm excited, but most exciteing of all is the promise of unterrupted time with my favorite YouTube star, ZeldaZee.

I climb up onto my neatly made bed, and my open laptop has fallen asleep there. With one click, I awaken the screen. ZeldaZee's channel is queued up and ready to go. I toss a kernel of popcorn into my mouth and hit play.

Here's what I can tell you about ZeldaZee: She's sixteen. She has a little brother and two Siamese cats.They lives in a suburb. I don't know which one. ZeldaZee covers a lot of different topics-- school life, fashion, family, beauty-- but the thing I love about her is her personality; I swear it feels like she's talking right to me. When she looks into the camera and tells a story from her day, I laugh as though one of my friends is talking to me. Sometimes, I find myself responding to her out loud. I have to remind myself she can't hear me.

I watched "How Not to Get Lost in Your Own Neighborhood." It shows ZeldaZee walking through her nieghborhood on a sunny afternoon, pointing at familiar landmarks. "Look for street names!" she instructs, and the camera shows the name of the cross-street: Magnolia and Pine. *Hey wait a second*, I think. *We have an intersection of Magnolia and Pine not too far from here!* I think: ~~What if ZeldaZee lives in my neighborhood? I've wondered it before. I swear she drove by a nearby mini mall in one episode—. ZeldaZee has over twelve million followers. She's a star! If she lived in my nieghborhood, I think I would know?~~

~~On screen ZeldaZee continues down the list. "Ask a friendely-looking neighbor!" ZeldaZee instructs. She waves to an old woman. "Hey!" calls ZeldaZee. "Do I look familiar to you?"~~

~~I squint at the screen because I'm almost positive that I've seen that old lady before. A feeling of unease creeps down my spine.~~

SPEAKING FRAMES

- This scene starts when ____. That is followed by ____.
- Lucia added these transition words and phrases to this section of her story: ____.
- These transitions improve her story because ____.
- Another transition (word / phrase / clause) that Lucia could use is ____.
- This transition would improve her story because ____.

Story Beginnings

Connect to Mentor Text

Project the following examples of story beginnings and discuss with your students:

- The morning of June 27th was clear and sunny, with the fresh warmth of a full-summer day; the flowers were blossoming profusely and the grass was richly green. ("The Lottery")
- Encountering the bright-lighted gaiety of Harlem's Seventh Avenue, the frigid midwinter night seemed to relent a little. ("The Conjure-Man Dies")

Ask students:

- What do you notice about these beginnings?
- What about the beginnings appeals to you as a reader?
- Does the language make you interested, nervous, curious, or something else?

Transitions

Discuss the Model

1. What is the order of events in this scene?
   1. Ella wonders if ZeldaZee could live in her neighborhood. 2. Ella recognizes a neighbor whom ZeldaZee greets in the show. 3. Ella remembers that this neighbor passed away recently and becomes upset.
2. Which transition words, phrases, or clauses did Lucia add to this section of her story?
   Lucia added the transition words "However" and "meanwhile." She also added the phrase "Last week."
3. How do those changes improve her story?
   Answers will vary, but students should point out that the transition words show shifts in sequence, time, and settings. They also show the relationships among experiences and events.

Transitions

Connect to Mentor Text

Project the following excerpt from *The Graveyard Book* and discuss with your students:

That night, he had been woken by the sound of something on the floor beneath him falling with a crash. Awake, he soon became bored, and had begun looking for a way out of his crib. It had high sides, like the walls of his playpen downstairs, but he was convinced that he could scale it. All he needed was a step . . .

He pulled his large, golden teddy bear into the corner of the crib, then, holding the railing in his tiny hands, he put his foot onto the bear's lap, the other foot up on the bear's head, and he pulled himself up into a standing position, and then he half-climbed, half-toppled over the railing and out of the crib.

Ask students:

- What is the order of events in this scene? Is it clear and logical?
- How does the author show shifts in time, setting, and action?

NOTES

Skill: Transitions

Lucia adds transition words to signal important shifts in the plot of her story and show a relationship between events that are happening at the same time. She uses the word "however" to show how Ella's thoughts shift from supporting her idea about where ZeldaZee could live to doubting it.

What if ZeldaZee lives in my neighborhood? I've wondered it before. I swear she drove by a nearby mini mall in her episode "How To Shop Like a Boss." However, ZeldaZee has over twelve million followers. She's a star! If she lived in my neighborhood, wouldn't I have heard about it?

On screen, meanwhile, ZeldaZee continues down the list. "Ask a friendly-looking neighbor!" ZeldaZee instructs. She waves to an old woman in gardening gloves, repotting some tulips. "Hey!" calls ZeldaZee. "Do I look familiar to you?"

I squint at the screen. I'm almost positive I've seen that old lady before. Didn't she used to give me piano lessons? Miss Gomez, wasn't it? A feeling of unease creeps down my spine and it takes me a second to realize why: Last week, Mom had told me that Miss Gomez died.

Suddenly, ZeldaZee whirls around to face the screen. In a low voice she says "Ella."

The popcorn kernel in my fingers are frozen, halfway to my open mouth. Ella. That's me.

~~"Don't freak out, said ZeldaZee, still in that same low voice. "But there's someone in your house."~~

~~I'm scared. Then I shake it off. She can't possibly be talking to me. I look to the door of my room. "Whatever," I say aloud.~~

~~"You still have time." I search her face for the usual glint of mischief, but her eyes are oddly blank.~~

~~I scan the room, searching for my cellphone, but I realize that I left it in the kitchen. It must be near the microwave!~~

~~He's coming down the hallway," ZeldaZee tells me, her voice almost a whisper.~~

"Don't freak out," says ZeldaZee, still in that same low voice. "But there's someone in your house."

Narrative Techniques

Discuss the Model

1. Which narrative techniques did Lucia use to revise her story? She improved the dialogue, changed the pacing, added description, and added a brief reflection.
2. How did Lucia build more suspense in her story? Lucia built suspense by speeding up the pace of this scene. She did that by shortening sentences and removing unnecessary details.
3. How can Lucia use these narrative techniques to further develop her story? Answers will vary. Sample answer: Lucia can add description after some of her dialogue to show the difference between what a character says out loud and what the character actually thinks or feels.

SPEAKING FRAMES

- Lucia used ____, a narrative technique, to revise her story.
- Lucia built more suspense in her story by ____.
- Another narrative technique that Lucia could use in her story is ____.
- This change would improve her story because ____.

My blood turns to ice in my veins. Then I shake it off. She can't possibly be talking to me. I look to the door of my room, force myself to laugh. "Whatever," I say aloud.

"You still have time," ZeldaZee continues. I search her face for the usual glint of mischief, but her eyes are oddly blank. "Ella, you need to act fast. Pick up your phone."

I scan the room, searching for my cell phone, but I am filled with a sense of dread once I realize that I left it in the kitchen.

"He's coming down the hallway," ZeldaZee tells me, her voice almost a whisper. "Now's your chance."

This can't be right. There's no way she's right as she's talking to me through my computer. I decide to ignore her words as I fold the screen on my laptop shut. "Weird," I say. But the word sounds more casual than I feel. I'm just swinging my legs over the side of the bed when I hear it: the creak of floorboards just outside my door.

"Hello?" My voice makes a tiny scratchy sound as it leaves my throat.

To my horror, the doorknob begins to twist.

~~I run for the window. I'm on the second floor, but that hardly matters. I climb onto the roof. The door to my room opens. "Ella! Ella!"~~

~~ZeldaZee is calling to me. But where is she? I peer over the ledge of the roof. *I'll climb down the trellis*, I tell myself. Once on the ground, I can run to a neighbor's house for help.~~

~~As I try and catch hold of the trellis with my feet, I see through my bedroom window. Inside, someone is moving around. "Ella!"~~

~~My foot slips. I start to fall. I open my mouth to scream, but I can't.~~

I run for the window. I'm on the second floor, but that hardly matters. As I scramble onto the roof, I see the door to my room swing open. "Ella! Ella!"

It's ZeldaZee. She's calling to me. But where is she? I peer over the ledge of the roof. My familiar front lawn looms in front of me, a map

Skill: Narrative Techniques

Lucia improves her use of dialogue, including more description, and building more suspense in this part of her story. She adds an identifying name to a line of dialogue to make sure that readers know who is saying it. She also builds suspense by speeding up the pacing, removing unnecessary details, and breaking long sentences into short, simple ones.

Skill: Descriptive Details

Lucia adds more descriptive details to her draft so readers can better imagine what is happening during the climax of the story. She wants to show readers what Ella is experiencing at this tense moment, so she adds sensory language.

Narrative Techniques

Connect to Mentor Text

Project the following example of the use of narrative techniques from *Ten Days in a Mad-House* and discuss with your students:

"Poor child," said Judge Duffy, "she is well dressed, and a lady. Her English is perfect, and I would stake everything on her being a good girl. I am positive she is somebody's darling."

At this announcement everybody laughed, and I put my handkerchief over my face and endeavored to choke the laughter that threatened to spoil my plans, in despite of my resolutions.

Ask students:

- What is happening in this scene?
- Can you find examples of narrative techniques that the writer has used in this scene?
- How does each technique contribute to the scene?

Descriptive Details

Discuss the Model

1. How do descriptive details help readers connect with a story? Answers will vary, but students will likely mention that such details help readers imagine what a character sees, hears, feels, smells, or tastes.
2. What kinds of descriptive details does Lucia add to her draft? She adds details that help readers imagine how things look, feel, and sound.
3. How do those changes improve her story? Answers will vary.

ELL SPEAKING FRAMES

- Descriptive details help readers imagine ____.
- Lucia adds details that appeal to readers' senses of ____, ____, and ____.
- These changes improve her story because ____.
- Lucia could have added a sight / touch detail such as ____.

Descriptive Details

Connect to Mentor Text

Project the following excerpt from *Monster* as an example of using descriptive details and discuss with your students:

Sometimes I feel like I have walked into the middle of a movie. It is a strange movie with no plot and no beginning. The movie is in black and white, and grainy. Sometimes the camera moves in so close that you can't tell what is going on and you just listen to the sounds and guess. I have seen movies of prisons but never one like this. This is not a movie about bars and locked doors. It is about being alone when you are not really alone and about being scared all the time.

Ask students:

- What do you notice about the author's use of descriptive details?
- What do these descriptive details allow you to imagine?

Conclusions

Discuss the Model

1. The model shows how Lucia changed the conclusion of her story. How did she change it? She added several sentences in which Ella shared her thoughts and feelings about the experience.
2. How do those changes improve her story? Answers will vary. Sample answer: Lucia's changes clarified what happened in the story, showed how two characters felt about it, and reflected on why these events are important.
3. What are some other ways that Lucia could have concluded this story? Answers will vary.

SPEAKING FRAMES

- Lucia changed her conclusion by ____.
- These changes improved her story because ____.
- Lucia could also write a conclusion in which ____.

Extended Writing Project

NOTES

of shadows. *I'll climb down the trellis*, I tell myself. Once on the ground, I can run to a neighbor's house for help.

As I twist my body to try and catch hold of the trellis with my feet, I see through my bedroom window. Inside, someone rushes through the room. "Ella!"

My foot slips. I start to fall. I open my mouth to scream, but no sound comes out.

"Ella! Wake up!"

I jolt upright. I'm sitting in my room, blinking up into . . . Mom's face.

She looks concerned. "You were having a nightmare."

"Was I?" I look around. "Watching ZeldaZee, I presume." says Mom.

She knows me too well. The bowl of popcorn is spilled all over my bed and laptop. "I must've fallen asleep."

~~Was it realy all a dream? I click the keyboard and watch as my computer lurched to life. According to the screen, I've watched eleven episodes of ZeldaZee. That's funny. I can only remember the first.~~

~~Mom is shakeing her head. "And what have I told you about food in your room."~~

~~"I'm sorry," I say.~~

~~"Just don't do it again."~~

~~"Oh beleive me, I won't!"~~

Was it really all a dream? I click the keyboard and watch as my computer lurches to life. According to the screen, I've watched eleven episodes of ZeldaZee. That's funny, I can only remember the first.

"I had the weirdest dream," I say.

Mom is shaking her head. "And what have I told you about food in your room?"

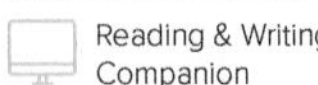

Skill: Conclusions

To improve her conclusion, Lucia adds important details that briefly summarize what has happened to Ella and show both characters' thoughts and feelings about the events.

NOTES

"I'm sorry," I say.

"Just don't do it again."

"Oh, believe me," I say, meaning it this time. "I won't!" One look at ZeldaZee's face on my screen and my stomach clenches up. Now that the feelings of fear and confusion are wearing off, there's one consolation, though: I think I'm finally cured of my obsession with ZeldaZee!

Conclusions

Connect to Mentor Text

Project the following examples of conclusions and discuss with your students:

- A cold wind rushed up the staircase, and a long loud wail of disappointment and misery from his wife gave him courage to run down to her side, and then to the gate beyond. The street lamp flickering opposite shone on a quiet and deserted road. ("The Monkey's Paw")
- "It isn't fair, it isn't right," Mrs. Hutchinson screamed and then they were upon her. ("The Lottery")

Ask students:

- What do you notice about these conclusions?
- What narrative techniques does each author use?
- What thoughts or feelings are the characters expressing in each conclusion?

Skill: Story Beginnings

Introduce the Skill

Watch the Concept Definition video and read the following definition with your students.

A **story beginning** is the opening section of a story in which the writer orients the reader by providing essential information, or **context:**

- **characters**—people or animals in the story
- **setting**—the time and place in which the action of a story occurs
- **conflict**—the problem that one or more of the characters must face

This essential background information for the story is called the **exposition**.

The best story beginnings also engage readers by grabbing their attention and tempting them to keep reading. Writers use a variety of techniques to start their stories and introduce the elements of the exposition in an engaging way. This includes establishing the **narrator,** or the one telling the story. The narrator can be a character in the story or someone outside the story who is never described. The narrator's relationship to the story is called the narrative **point of view**.

Skill: Story Beginnings

CHECKLIST FOR STORY BEGINNINGS

Before you write the beginning of your narrative, ask yourself the following questions:

- What information does my reader need to know at the beginning of the story about the narrator, main character, setting, and the character's conflict?
- What will happen to my character in the story?
- Who is the narrator of my story?

There are many ways you can engage and orient your reader. Here are some strategies to help you establish a context, show a point of view, and introduce the narrator and/or characters:

- Action
  - > Instead of beginning with a description of a character, have the character doing something that will reveal his or her personality.
  - > Opening a story with an immediate conflict, either between characters or due to an event in the plot, can help grab a reader's attention.
- Description
  - > Use description to quickly establish the setting and establish a context for the story.
  - > If the story is science or historical fiction, provide specific details about where and when the story takes place.
- Dialogue
  - > Dialogue can immediately establish the point of view in a story.
    - first person: narrator is a character in the story
    - third person: narrator is outside the story
    - third-person omniscient: narrator knows the thoughts and actions of all the characters
    - third-person limited: narrator knows the thoughts and actions of only one character
  - > A character's internal thoughts can provide information that only the reader knows.

TURN AND TALK

Turn to your partner and brainstorm a list of movies, TV shows, or books that have exciting beginnings.

ELL SPEAKING FRAMES

- The movie / TV show / book ____ begins with ____.
- An example of an exciting beginning is ____.

V SKILL VOCABULARY

story beginning / el comienzo de la historia ***noun*** the opening to a story

context / el contexto ***noun*** the set of facts or circumstances that surround a situation or event COGNATE

character / el personaje ***noun*** an individual in a literary work whose thoughts, feelings, actions, and reactions move the action of the plot forward

setting / el escenario ***noun*** the time and place of the story

 YOUR TURN

Choose the best answer for each question.

1. Below is a section from a previous draft of Lucia's story. The meaning of the underlined sentence is unclear. What changes should Lucia make to improve the clarity of the sentence?

> It is Friday night, and I have the whole house to myself. Mom is at a work dinner, and my younger brother, Tom the Slob, is at a sleepover. <u>The quiet feels cool.</u> However, the most exciting of all is the promise of uninterrupted time with my favorite YouTube star, ZeldaZee.

- ○ A. Change "cool" to "awesome."
- ○ B. Change "cool" to "soothing."
- ○ C. Change "quiet" to "absolute silence."
- ○ D. Change "quiet" to "quietly."

2. Lucia wants to improve the beginning of a previous draft of her story. How can she rewrite the underlined sentence to provide more detail and imagery?

> I haven't been home alone for months. Thankfully, tonight, my brother is at a sleepover and Mom is at a work dinner, so I have the place to myself for the next three hours. <u>The house feels so great right now.</u>

- ○ A. It feels exciting to have the house all to myself.
- ○ B. The house has not felt this empty since Halloween, when the rest of the family was out in their costumes trick-or-treating and I got to stay home all alone—my first time without our normal babysitter.
- ○ C. I love the house when it is this quiet and empty.
- ○ D. For once, I can actually hear the calming buzz of the air-conditioning and the quiet purr of my cat, without the nagging reminders of my mom and the loud laughter of my brother to drown them out.

 WRITE

Use the questions and techniques in the checklist to revise the beginning of your suspenseful narrative.

 SKILL VOCABULARY

conflict / el conflicto ***noun*** the main problem or struggle that characters face in a story COGNATE

exposition / la exposición ***noun*** the background information provided in the beginning of a story about the characters, the setting, and the conflict COGNATE

narrator / el narrador ***noun*** someone who tells a story COGNATE

point of view / el punto de vista ***noun*** the standpoint, or perspective, from which a story is told

Your Turn

Ask students to complete the Your Turn activity.

QUESTION 1

A. Incorrect. "Awesome" is often used as a general positive statement, and its meaning in this context is not more clear than "cool."

B. Correct. "Feels soothing" provides a more formal and specific description of how the quiet feels.

C. Incorrect. "Absolute silence" does not clarify what "cool" means in this context.

D. Incorrect. A noun is needed here, not an adverb.

QUESTION 2

A. Incorrect. This sentence does not provide more detail and imagery.

B. Incorrect. This sentence adds more detail, but not more imagery.

C. Incorrect. This sentence does not provide more detail and imagery.

D. Correct. This sentence adds more detail about how the house feels and also adds more imagery, engaging the reader's sense of sound.

Write

Ask students to complete the writing assignment.

ELL **REWRITE CHECKLIST**

A **Action**

- ☐ What action could help reveal information about my character or conflict?
- ☐ How might an exciting moment grab my readers' attention?

Description

- ☐ What specific details should I include to introduce the characters, setting, and conflict?

Dialogue

- ☐ How can I use dialogue to establish the point of view in my story?
- ☐ How can a character's internal thoughts provide information that is only for the reader?

Skill: Narrative Techniques

Introduce the Skill

Watch the Concept Definition video and read the following definition with your students.

When writing a narrative, authors use a variety of tools to develop the plot and characters or to explore their own personal experiences. **Narrative techniques** include dialogue, description, pacing, reflection, and multiple plot lines.

Narratives often have **dialogue**, or a conversation between characters. Dialogue can be used to develop characters or to move the plot forward. In addition, authors use **description** outside of dialogue to develop the setting, characters, and plot events. While narratives often have one plot, some have multiple **plot lines**.

Authors use pacing to control the flow of the narrative. **Pacing** is the speed at which a story is told. For example, a writer might speed up the pace as the story nears a climax, or slow it down to reflect a character's indecision. The author or narrator might also want to comment on the events or theme. This technique is called **reflection**, and it is particularly effective in a personal narrative.

Extended Writing Project

Skill:
Narrative Techniques

••• CHECKLIST FOR NARRATIVE TECHNIQUES

As you begin to develop the techniques you will use in your narrative, ask yourself the following questions:

- Is it clear which character is talking in a dialogue?
- How quickly or slowly do I want the plot to move?
- Which literary devices can I add to strengthen my characters or plot? How can I better engage my reader?
- What insight or personal reflection could I add to the overall message of my narrative?

Here are some methods that can help you write dialogue, pacing, description, and reflection to develop experiences, events, and/or characters in your narrative:

- Use dialogue to explain events or move the action forward.
  - > Use quotation marks correctly.
  - > Include identifying names as needed before or after quotation marks.
- Include description to help the reader visualize the characters, setting, and other elements.
  - > Include only those descriptions relevant to the reader's understanding of the element being described.
- Use pacing effectively to convey a sense of urgency or calm.
  - > To speed up the pace, try using limited description, short paragraphs, brief dialogue, and simpler sentences.
  - > To slow down the pace, try using detailed description, longer paragraphs, and more complex sentence structures.
- Add reflection, if appropriate, to comment on the overall message.
  - > Include characters' inner thoughts or your own insight.
- Use any combination of the above techniques.

 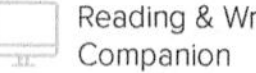

TURN AND TALK

Turn and talk to your partner about a suspenseful scene from a book, movie, or TV show. Did the writer or writers use any of the narrative techniques provided in the Concept Definition video? If so, how did that technique contribute to the scene?

SPEAKING FRAMES

- A movie / TV show / book with a memorable scene is ____.
- An example of a narrative technique in that scene is ____.

SKILL VOCABULARY

narrative techniques / las técnicas narrativas ***noun*** the tools authors use to develop a story COGNATE

dialogue / el diálogo ***noun*** the conversation between characters COGNATE

description / la descripción ***noun*** the use of literary devices to enhance readers' engagement with the story COGNATE

YOUR TURN

Read each quote below. Then, complete the chart by matching each quote with the narrative technique that it best illustrates.

Quote Options	
A	Now that the feelings of fear and confusion are wearing off, there's one consolation, though: I think I'm finally cured of my obsession with ZeldaZee!
B	"I had the weirdest dream," I say.
C	It's ZeldaZee. She's calling to me. But where is she?
D	My blood turns to ice in my veins.

Narrative Technique	Quote
Dialogue	
Pacing	
Description	
Reflection	

SKILL VOCABULARY

plot line / la línea argumental ***noun*** a series of events in a narrative focused on a particular action, setting, and set of characters; a narrative may have more than one plot line

pacing / el ritmo ***noun*** the rate at which the plot of the narrative unfolds

reflection / la reflexión ***noun*** an author's thoughts about events in the narrative COGNATE

Your Turn

Ask students to complete the Your Turn activity.

Dialogue	B
Pacing	C
Description	D
Reflection	A

Your Turn

Ask students to complete the Your Turn activity. Answers will vary.

Dialogue	"Hi, Sally! Do you need to finish up today's lab experiment too?" "No, I finished it, but—" "But what?" "There were strange results."
Pacing	The clock ticked behind us. The period would end any second, but nothing had changed. The reaction did not happen.
Description	Ms. Cubas's lab was pristine. The lab tables were so clean that it looked like each experiment was being done upside down in them, and we used our bristled test tube cleaners as often as we used pens.
Reflection	I wanted my hypothesis to be right. I wanted to make a breakthrough this year, but my experiment failed, and now I need to start again. This time, I'm going to try to remember that wanting something to be a fact doesn't make it one.

Extended Writing Project

YOUR TURN

Complete the chart below by rewriting part of your narrative using each narrative technique.

Narrative Technique	Rewrite
Dialogue	
Pacing	
Description	
Reflection	

144 Reading & Writing Companion

Writer's Notebook

Ask students to review the plot diagram of the story based on five items from the classroom. How can students use narrative techniques to develop one scene from this story? Ask students to write one scene in which they apply more than one narrative technique.

TURN AND TALK

Allow students to share their ideas orally in pairs or small groups before freewriting.

Skill: Descriptive Details

••• CHECKLIST FOR DESCRIPTIVE DETAILS

First, reread the draft of your narrative and identify the following:

- where descriptive details are needed to convey experiences and events
- vague, general, or overused words and phrases
- places where you want to tell how something looks, sounds, feels, smells, or tastes, such as:
  - > experiences
  - > events
  - > action

Use precise words and phrases, relevant descriptive details, and sensory language to capture the action and convey experiences and events, using the following questions as a guide:

- What experiences and events do I want to convey in my writing?
- Have I included relevant and descriptive details?
- Where can I add descriptive details to describe the characters and the events of the plot?
- How can I use sensory language, or words that describe sights, sounds, feelings, smells, or tastes, to help my reader create a picture of the action, experiences, and events?
- What can I refine or revise in my word choice to make sure that the reader can picture what is taking place?

V SKILL VOCABULARY

descriptive detail / el detalle descriptivo *noun* a detail that helps readers imagine the world in which the story takes place and the characters who live in it

context / el contexto *noun* the set of facts or circumstances that surround a situation or event COGNATE

precise language / el lenguaje preciso *noun* exact language that includes specific nouns and action verbs COGNATE

Skill: Descriptive Details

Introduce the Skill

Watch the Concept Definition video ▶ and read the following definition with your students.

Descriptive details are details that writers include to help readers imagine the world in which the story takes place and the characters who live in it. These details are important because they help to orient the reader by establishing a **context** or the circumstances that form the setting of events or a situation in a story.

Descriptive details often use **precise language**—specific nouns and action verbs—to convey experiences or events. Many descriptive details use sensory language to appeal to one or more of the reader's five senses. **Sensory details** tell how something looks, sounds, feels, smells, or tastes.

In a story, it is easy to include many interesting details, but not every detail is **relevant**, that is, important, appropriate, and purposeful. Think about what the reader really needs to know in order to understand or picture what is happening. This will help you select and include only the most relevant details for your story.

TURN AND TALK

Turn to your partner and brainstorm five descriptive adjectives that appeal to each of your senses: sight, sound, smell, touch, and taste.

SPEAKING FRAMES

- A word or phrase that appeals to my sense of sight / smell / touch / sound / taste is ____.

Your Turn

Ask students to complete the Your Turn activity.

QUESTION 1

A. Incorrect. This sentence does not use sensory language.

B. Correct. This sentence uses sensory language to help readers imagine how comfortable Ella felt at this time.

C. Incorrect. This sentence uses sensory language, but it focuses on how something tastes, not how it feels.

D. Incorrect. This sentence uses sensory language, but it focuses on how something sounds, not how it feels.

QUESTION 2

A. Incorrect. Ella does not fall, because in the next sentence, she considers climbing down.

B. Incorrect. Ella does not get smaller.

C. Correct. Ella looks or gazes over the ledge of the roof to see the ground below.

D. Incorrect. Ella looks at, rather than hears, the ground below.

YOUR TURN

Choose the best answer to each question.

1. Below is a sentence from one of Lucia's previous drafts. Lucia wants to use sensory language to show readers how comfortable she felt just before she watched ZeldaZee. Which revision BEST helps readers imagine how she felt?

> Before I started to watch ZeldaZee, I sat on my bed with my popcorn, and my back was against some pillows.

- A. I now had everything I needed to start the show—popcorn, water, pillows, and my laptop.
- B. I kept my bowl of puffy popcorn beside me and sat with my back against a mound of fluffed pillows. I was now ready to click play.
- C. After enjoying a handful of salty, buttery popcorn and a sip of the refreshing fizzy water, I clicked play on the latest ZeldaZee video.
- D. I sat on my bed with my back against a pillow, allowing the silence of my house to be filled with the sound of ZeldaZee's voice and perfectly timed background music.

2. Below is a section of one of Lucia's previous drafts. In the underlined sentence, Lucia did not use the most appropriate word to describe the main character, Ella's, actions. Which of the following is the best replacement for the word *see*?

> I hear her. ZeldaZee is calling to me. But I can't hear her. Where is she? I see over the ledge of the roof. *I'll climb down the trellis*, I tell myself. Once I am on the ground, I can run to a neighbor's house for help.

- A. fall
- B. shrink
- C. gaze
- D. hear

SKILL VOCABULARY

sensory detail / el detalle sensorial ***noun*** a detail that appeals to the sense of sight, sound, smell, touch, or taste

relevant / relevante ***adjective*** appropriate and logically related to the topic COGNATE

YOUR TURN

Complete the chart by writing a descriptive detail that appeals to each sense for your narrative.

Sense	Descriptive Detail
Sight	
Smell	
Touch	
Taste	
Sound	

Your Turn

Ask students to complete the Your Turn activity. Answers will vary.

Sight	I could see nothing but shadows after the sun went down.
Smell	The telltale scent of a campfire told me I wasn't alone.
Touch	I was drenched with sweat.
Taste	I looked at the barren trees and longed for the sweet crunch of breakfast cereal.
Sound	A twig snapped in the distance.

Writer's Notebook

Project these five sentences and senses on the board. Ask students to rewrite each sentence, adding sensory details that appeal to each sense.

- I opened the window. (sight)
- I walked into the kitchen. (smell)
- I took off my shoes. (touch)
- I turned on the radio. (sound)
- I went to the grocery store. (taste)

TURN AND TALK

Allow students to share their ideas orally in pairs or small groups before freewriting.

Skill: Transitions

Introduce the Skill

Watch the Concept Definition video and read the following definition with your students.

Transitions are connecting words, phrases, and clauses that writers use to **clarify** the relationships among ideas and details in a text. Transitions have different functions depending on whether the text is argumentative, informative, or narrative.

In an argumentative essay, writers state claims and provide reasons and evidence for their claims. To clarify a relationship between a claim and a reason or supporting evidence, transitions such as *although* and *on the other hand* help make connections clear.

For informative essays, transitions such as *however*, *in addition*, and *for example* may help create **cohesion** among ideas and concepts.

In narrative writing, authors use a variety of words, phrases, and clauses to signal shifts in time, setting, and action. Transitions such as *until now*, *meanwhile*, and *once it was over* may make narrative events more **coherent**.

Transitions also help to connect ideas both within and across paragraphs and between major sections of text.

Extended Writing Project

Skill: Transitions

••• CHECKLIST FOR TRANSITIONS

Before you revise your current draft to include transitions, think about:

- the order of events, including the rising action, climax, falling action, and resolution
- moments where the time or setting changes
- relationships between characters and plot events

Next, reread your current draft and note areas in your narrative where:

- the order of events is unclear or illogical
- changes in time or setting are confusing or unclear. Look for:
  - > sudden jumps
  - > missing or illogical plot events or character experiences
  - > places where you could add more context or exposition, such as important background information about the narrator, setting, characters, and conflict

Revise your draft to use a variety of transition words, phrases, and clauses to convey sequence, signal shifts from one time frame or setting to another, and show the relationships among experiences and events, using the following questions as a guide:

- Do the events of the rising action, climax, falling action, and resolution flow naturally and logically?
- Are there better transition words I can use to show shifts in time, setting, and relationships between experiences and events?
  - > Transitions such as "moreover," "likewise," and "by the same token" show relationships between experiences and events.
  - > Transitions such as "simultaneously" or "afterward" signal shifts in time and settings.
- Do the characters' experiences logically and naturally relate to the plot events?

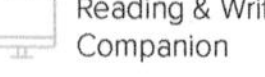

TURN AND TALK

Turn to your partner and tell him or her about one scene from your favorite book, movie, or TV show. Which part of the plot could this scene be from? What transitions do readers need to follow in order to understand what is happening?

SPEAKING FRAMES

- One of my favorite books / movies / TV shows is ____.
- I remember one scene in which ____.
- This scene takes place in ____, one part of the plot.
- One transition that happens in this scene is ____.

SKILL VOCABULARY

transition / la transición *noun* a connecting word or phrase that a writer may use to clarify the relationship between ideas in a text; set off with a comma COGNATE

clarify / aclarar *verb* to make clear and more comprehensible

cohesion / la cohesión *noun* the quality of parts working together as a whole COGNATE

coherent / coherente *adjective* marked by being orderly and logical; easy to understand COGNATE

YOUR TURN

Choose the best answer to each question.

1. Below is a section from a previous draft of Lucia's story. The connection between the first sentence and the underlined sentence is unclear. What transition word, phrase, or clause can be added to the underlined sentence to make the connection clear?

> I start to open up the bag of popcorn. <u>ZeldaZee made the perfect bowl of popcorn.</u> There were no unpopped kernels in it! Could mine be as good? Steam fogs up my glasses while I open the bag and begin to pour out the popcorn. It is hard to see, but I hear the jangle of unpopped kernels hit the bowl. They needed more time.

- ○ A. As a result,
- ○ B. In the last episode of the show,
- ○ C. With masterful microwaving skills,
- ○ D. Similarly,

2. Below is a section of one of Lucia's previous drafts. The transition from the second sentence to the underlined sentence is not clear. Which transition word, phrase, or clause can Lucia use to connect the two ideas?

> What if ZeldaZee lives in my neighborhood? I've wondered it before, and I swear that she drove by a nearby mini mall in one episode. <u>She is a celebrity with twelve million followers.</u> If she lived down the street, I would have to know about it!

- ○ A. Although
- ○ B. On the other hand,
- ○ C. In fact,
- ○ D. In contrast,

Your Turn

Ask students to complete the Your Turn activity.

QUESTION 1

A. Incorrect. The transition phrase "as a result" does not connect the events in a logical or clear way.

B. Correct. This transition phrase helps readers see the connection between a current event and a past episode of ZeldaZee.

C. Incorrect. This transition phrase "with masterful microwaving skills" does not connect the events in a logical or clear way.

D. Incorrect. This transition word does not connect the events in a logical or clear way since Ella points out that she did not make popcorn without unpopped kernels this time.

QUESTION 2

A. Incorrect. "Although" shows a surprising connection between two different ideas, but it would make the underlined sentence incomplete.

B. Correct. "On the other hand" connects two different ideas about the same topic, and the sentence stays complete.

C. Incorrect. Writers can use "in fact" to add a supporting detail to an idea, but Ella is sharing a reason why her idea might not be true in this case.

D. Incorrect. "In contrast" is used to compare opposites, but a sentence about ZeldaZee's fame is not the opposite of the sentence before it.

Your Turn

Ask students to complete the Your Turn activity. Answers will vary.

Convey sequence	Ivan ran up to the stage to take a selfie in front of the set while an actor was reviewing his lines behind a cardboard tree.
Signal shifts from one time frame or setting to another	When the house lights dimmed, the audience's chatter quieted down, and a spotlight fell on the actor whom Ivan had seen in his selfie.
Show a relationship among experiences and events	Just like Ivan, the character of Narcissus was obsessed with his appearance.

YOUR TURN

Complete the chart below by writing a sentence for each listed purpose using transition words, phrases, and clauses.

Purpose	Sentence
Convey sequence	
Signal shifts from one time frame or setting to another	
Show a relationship among experiences and events	

Writer's Notebook

Use transition words, phrases, and clauses to describe one exciting day on a dream vacation. Which shifts in sequence, time, or setting need to be clear? How can you show relationships between events or experiences?

TURN AND TALK

Allow students to share their ideas orally in pairs or small groups before freewriting.

Skill: Conclusions

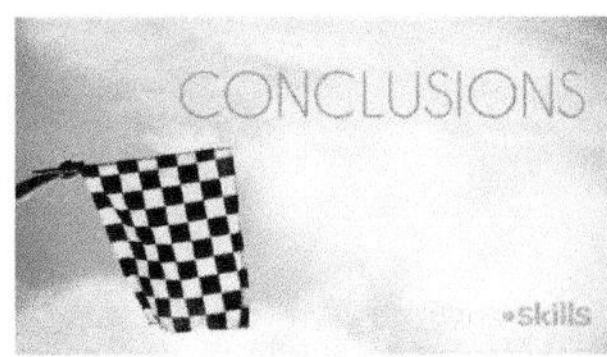

Skill: Conclusions

CHECKLIST FOR CONCLUSIONS

Before you write your conclusion, ask yourself the following questions:

- What important details should I include in my conclusion?
- What other thoughts and feelings could characters share with readers in the conclusion?
- Should I use dialogue or characters' actions to show readers the importance of the events in my narrative?

Below are two strategies to help you provide a conclusion that follows from and reflects on the narrated experiences or events:

- Peer discussion
  > After you have written your introduction and body paragraphs, talk with a partner about possible endings for your narrative, writing notes about your discussion.
  > Review your notes and think about how you want to end your story.
  > Briefly summarize the events in the narrative through the narrator or one of the characters.
  > Describe how the narrator feels about the events he or she experienced.
  > Reveal to readers why the experiences in the narrative matter through a character's reflections or dialogue.
  > Write your conclusion.
- Freewriting
  > Freewrite for ten minutes about what you might include in your conclusion. Don't worry about grammar, punctuation, or writing down fully formed ideas.
  > Review your notes and think about how you want to end your story.
  > Briefly summarize the events in the narrative through the narrator or one of the characters.
  > Describe how the narrator feels about the events he or she experienced.
  > Reveal to readers why the experiences in the narrative matter through a character's reflections or dialogue.
  > Write your conclusion.

Introduce the Skill

Watch the Concept Definition video and read the following definition with your students.

A **conclusion** is the closing paragraph or section of an essay, argument, or narrative. It is where the writer brings an essay to a close by restating the main idea or **thesis statement** or the **claim** in an argument. It also summarizes the evidence and research that support the claim or thesis. The conclusion should follow logically from the information, explanations, or claim that has been presented. A conclusion is a good way to suggest to your readers that you have accomplished what you set out to do. In addition, try to leave readers with an interesting final impression. This might be accomplished by closing with a quote, an anecdote, or a call to action.

In a **narrative**, a conclusion should follow logically from the events of the plot and what the characters have experienced. It might include characters reflecting on events, why they matter, and how they feel about them.

SKILL VOCABULARY

conclusion / la conclusión *noun* the closing paragraph or section of an essay; a closing argument in an argumentative text COGNATE

thesis statement / la presentación de la tesis *noun* a statement that shares the main idea of an argumentative or informational essay

claim / la afirmación *noun* the writer's or speaker's position on a debatable issue or problem

narrative / la narración *noun* a story, real or imagined, consisting of connected events

TURN AND TALK

Turn to your partner and brainstorm a list of movies, TV shows, or books that have memorable conclusions. Discuss what makes each example memorable.

ELL SPEAKING FRAMES

- One (book / movie / TV show) that I added to our list is ____.
- At the end of this (book / movie / TV show), this is what happens: ____.
- I think this is memorable because ____.
- ____ is one narrative technique that this ending includes.

Your Turn

Ask students to complete the Your Turn activity.

QUESTION 1

A. Incorrect. This revision does not show how Ella's feelings changed when she heard that her mother was home.

B. Incorrect. This revision shares a question that Ella had after she heard that her mother was home, but it does not show how her feelings changed.

C. Correct. This description shows how Ella's feelings changed when she heard that her mother was home.

D. Incorrect. This revision does not show how Ella's feelings changed when she heard that her mother was home.

QUESTION 2

A. Correct. This sentence adds an important detail that explains why Ella had such a strange and frightening experience in this story and how she feels about it.

B. Incorrect. This line makes an unclear comment about the events, but it does not add an important detail to the conclusion.

C. Incorrect. This line does not add an important detail about the story to the conclusion.

D. Incorrect. This line does not add an important detail about the story to the conclusion.

YOUR TURN

Choose the best answer to each question.

1. Lucia wants to revise the dialogue in her conclusion from a previous draft to reveal how Ella felt during the dialogue. How can she use descriptive language to show how Ella's feelings changed when she heard the underlined line?

> I call out the window to my neighbor, "Ms. Barton! Can you hear me? Can you help?!" Her dog barks repeatedly as she runs onto the front yard beneath my window.
>
> "Ella! How can I help? Would you like me to get your mom?" Ms. Barton asks and points toward the front door.
>
> "There's no time for that now!" I shouted. "Can you help me climb—"
>
> "Oh! But she just got home a minute ago," Ms. Barton said.

- A. "What?!" I asked and shouted at the same time.
- B. "Wow. How did it get that late?" I wondered.
- C. My look of terror dissolved, and I breathed a sigh of relief.
- D. I was speechless.

2. In a previous draft, Lucia had left out an important detail. She wants to add that detail after the underlined line below. Which sentence uses dialogue to add an important detail to the conclusion?

> "Ella! Ella! I'm home. Are you okay?" My mom rushes over and hugs me.
>
> I look around the room. The bowl of popcorn has spilled all over my bed and laptop.
>
> "Oh, no! Mom, I'm sorry." I run to my laptop to clear off the kernels, and it wakes up again. According to the screen, I've watched eleven episodes of ZeldaZee, but I can only remember the first.
>
> "Watching ZeldaZee, I presume." She shakes her head and begins to help me pick up the popcorn.

- A. "I must have had a nightmare," I tell her as I stare at the floor.
- B. "What a Friday night," I say as I gather up the kernels.
- C. "Do you want to watch a different show after we pick all this up?" I ask her.
- D. "How was your work dinner?" I ask her to try to change the subject.

 WRITE

Use the questions in the checklist section to revise the conclusion of your suspenseful narrative.

Write

Ask students to complete the writing assignment.

ELL **REWRITE CHECKLIST**

A **Important details**

- ☐ What questions about the plot still need to be answered?
- ☐ What details can I use to briefly address them?

Characters' feelings about the events

- ☐ What feelings do the characters share about the events?
- ☐ How do they share them?

Characters' thoughts about the events

- ☐ What thoughts do the characters share about the events?
- ☐ How do they share them?

Reflection

- ☐ Why did these events matter?
- ☐ How can I show that through the characters' dialogue or actions?

Writer's Notebook

Ask students to reread the conclusions from two or three novels or stories that they read during this unit. In their Writer's Notebook, students can then mimic how an author concluded each narrative by writing two or three different conclusions for their own suspenseful narrative.

 **TURN AND TALK**

Allow students to share their conclusions orally in pairs or small groups before writing.

Narrative Writing Process: Revise

Review Revision Guide

Break the class into five groups, and assign each group a category of the revision guide. Ask:

- What is the purpose of this section of the guide?
- How did it improve Lucia's writing?
- How will it help to improve your writing?

Allow groups to share their ideas with the class.

ELL SPEAKING FRAMES

- I think (clarity / sentence variety / word choice / organization / development) improved Lucia's writing by ____.
- I think (clarity / sentence variety / word choice / organization / development) will improve my writing because ____.

Extended Writing Project

Narrative Writing Process: Revise

PLAN | DRAFT | REVISE | EDIT AND PUBLISH

You have written a draft of your suspenseful narrative. You have also received input from your peers about how to improve it. Now you are going to revise your draft.

REVISION GUIDE

Examine your draft to find areas for revision. Keep in mind your purpose and audience as you revise for clarity, development, organization, and style. Use the guide below to help you review:

Review	Revise	Example
	Clarity	
Annotate any places where important information about an experience, event, or character seems unclear.	Use narrative techniques like dialogue, pacing, description, and reflection to develop those parts of your story.	"Just checking in!" Mom chirps. "I'm fine. I promise," I say, rolling my eyes, which of course she can't see. "Okay, okay. I'll let you go. But Ella—" Mom trails off. I can tell she wants to say something. "Yes?" I ask.

154 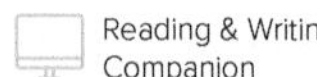 Reading & Writing Companion

Review	Revise	Example
	Development	
Identify suspenseful moments leading up to the climax. Annotate places where you don't feel anxious about what's going to happen next.	Focus on a single event and add descriptive details such as sounds, sights, smells, touch, taste, or characters' thoughts and feelings to build suspense.	I squint at the screen. I'm almost positive I've seen that old lady before. Didn't she used to give me piano lessons? Miss Gomez, wasn't it? A feeling of unease creeps down my spine and it takes me a second to realize why: Last week, Mom had told me that Miss Gomez died.
	Organization	
Identify shifts between times, settings, experiences, and events in your draft. Annotate places where those changes seem illogical or need transitions to make them clear.	Revise any events that seem illogical and use transitions to show readers clear relationships between different times, settings, experiences, and events in your story.	"You still have time," ZeldaZee continues. I search her face for the usual glint of mischief, but her eyes are oddly blank. "Ella, you need to act fast. Pick up your phone." I scan the room, searching for my cell phone, but I am filled with a sense of dread once I realize that I left it in the kitchen.
	Style: Word Choice	
Identify every form of the verb *to be* (*am, is, are, was, were, be, being, been*).	Select sentences to rewrite using action verbs.	Inside, someone ~~is moving around~~ rushes through the room.

Revise

Students should start this activity with a copy of their drafts either printed on paper or open in a word-processing program, such as Google Docs. Allow students time to revise their drafts using the instructions in the revision guide. Once students have finished revising their narrative, have them submit their work.

CHECK FOR SUCCESS

Circulate around the room to spend time with individual students. Ask:

- What category are you working on?
- Why are you revising this specific section?
- How are you revising it?
- How does this change support your purpose?
- Does this change make your writing appropriate for your audience?

If students struggle while revising their drafts, choose an exemplary revision to share with the class while the student talks through the process. You could also invite a student to share a dilemma in the revision process and allow the class to offer feedback or suggestions.

WORD CHOICE

Revise your draft, focusing on word choice. Select words from your draft that could be replaced with a stronger synonym.

Write

Ask students to complete their writing assignment.

ELL A REVISION CHECKLIST

- ☐ Find a word that you feel is weak.
- ☐ Use a thesaurus or your notes to find a stronger synonym.
- ☐ Replace the weak word with the stronger word choice.

Review	Revise	Example
Style: Sentence Variety		
Think about a key event where you want your reader to feel a specific emotion. Long sentences can draw out a moment and make a reader think; short sentences can show urgent actions or danger.	Rewrite a key event making your sentences longer or shorter to achieve the emotion you want your reader to feel.	This can't be right. ~~There's no way she's right as she's talking to me through my computer. I decide to ignore her words as~~ I ~~fold the screen on~~ snap the laptop shut.

WRITE

Use the guide above, as well as your peer reviews, to help you evaluate your suspenseful narrative to determine areas that should be revised.

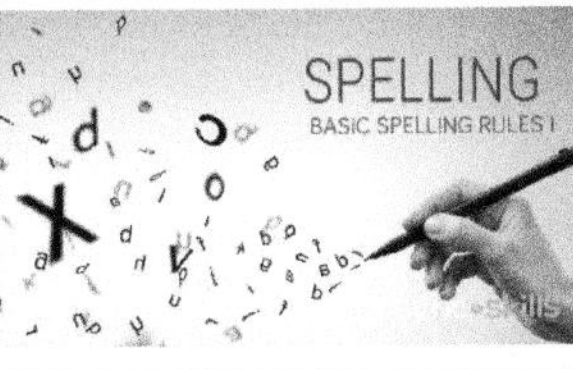

Grammar:
Basic Spelling Rules I

uffixes and the Silent *e*

Spelling Patterns	Base Words	Correct Spelling	Incorrect Spelling
When adding a suffix that begins with a consonant to a word that ends with a silent ***e***, keep the ***e***.	atone displace	atonement displacement	atonment displacment
When adding a suffix that begins with a vowel to a word that ends with a silent ***e***, usually drop the ***e***.	console admire adore	consolation admirable adoring	consoleation admireable adoreing
When adding ***-ly*** to a word that ends in ***l*** plus the silent ***e***, drop the ***le***.	forcible prickle	forcibly prickly	forciblely pricklely

Suffixes and the Final *y*

Spelling Conventions	Base Words	Correct Spelling	Incorrect Spelling
When a word ends in a consonant + ***y***, change the ***y*** to ***i*** before adding a suffix.	clarify witty	clarification witticism	clarifycation wittycism
When a word ends in a vowel + ***y***, keep the ***y***.	deploy relay	deployment relaying	deploiment relaing

Grammar: Basic Spelling Rules I

Introduce the Skill

Review the image and definition for basic spelling rules as a class.

- suffix - an affix attached to the end of a word; may change the spelling of the base word depending on the suffix
- unstressed vowel - a sound that is not emphasized when the word is spoken; using related words can help with choosing unstressed vowels

Discuss the Model

1. How does recognizing spelling patterns help writers know how to spell words? Answers will vary, but students may mention knowing when to keep or drop a silent *e*, when to change a *y* to an *i* while adding a suffix, etc.
2. Why is it helpful to understand that there are exceptions to common spelling patterns? Answers will vary, but students may say that it is still important to check the spelling of a word since that word may not follow common spelling rules.

Your Turn

Ask students to complete the Your Turn activity.

QUESTION 1

A. Incorrect.

B. Incorrect.

C. Correct. The *y* at the end of *mystery* changes to an *i* before addition of the suffix *-ous*.

D. Incorrect.

QUESTION 2

A. Correct. The base word *notice* ends in a silent *e*, which stays in plays when the suffix *-able* is added.

B. Incorrect.

C. Incorrect.

D. Incorrect.

QUESTION 3

A. Incorrect.

B. Incorrect.

C. Incorrect.

D. Correct. The sentence contains no spelling errors.

QUESTION 4

A. Incorrect.

B. Correct. The first e in *literate* is unstressed, so it easy to misspell. Similar words, such as *considerate*, might have helped you conclude that *literate* was the correct spelling.

C. Incorrect.

D. Incorrect.

YOUR TURN

1. How should the spelling error in this sentence be corrected?

> Alfred Hitchcock wrote about how he achieved a suspenseful atmosphere without mysteryous special effects.

- A. Change **achieved** to **acheived**.
- B. Change **suspenseful** to **suspensful**.
- C. Change **mysteryous** to **mysterious**.
- D. No change needs to be made to this sentence.

2. How should the spelling error in this sentence be corrected?

> As Hitler rose to power there was a noticable surge in the mistreatment of Jews, with the perpetrators seemingly immunized from punishment.

- A. Change **noticable** to **noticeable**.
- B. Change **perpetrators** to **perpetraters**.
- C. Change **immunized** to **immuneized**.
- D. No change needs to be made to this sentence.

3. How should the spelling error in this sentence be corrected?

> In the story *Home*, a father who tries to discipline his young son wonders about the complexity and responsibility of being both self-indulgent and a parent.

- A. Change **complexity** to **complexty**.
- B. Change **responsibility** to **responsability**.
- C. Change **self-indulgent** to **self-indulgeant**.
- D. No change needs to be made to this sentence.

4. How should the spelling error in this sentence be corrected?

> Living under slavery, young Frederick was illitarate, but he was so desirous of learning that he traded food for instruction.

- A. Change **slavery** to **slavry**.
- B. Change **illitarate** to **illiterate**.
- C. Change **desirous** to **desireous**.
- D. No change needs to be made to this sentence.

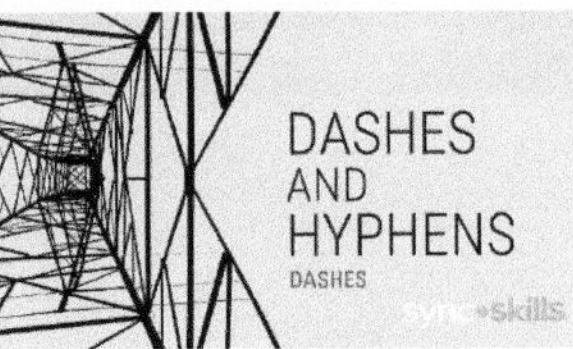

Grammar: Dashes and Hyphens—Dashes

A dash (—) looks like a long hyphen. When you are writing a sentence, use a dash or dashes to show a sudden break or a change of thought or speech. Using a dash or dashes is also an effective way of emphasizing a thought or giving new information.

Rule	Text
Use a pair of dashes if the new thought or emphasized information is in the middle of a sentence.	The creek he knew was frozen clear to the bottom—**no creek could contain water in that arctic winter**—but he knew also that there were springs that bubbled out from the hillsides and ran along under the snow and on top the ice of the creek. To Build a Fire
Use one dash if the new thought or emphasized information is at the end of a sentence.	But when Mami says, "Connie, please be nice to Abuela. She doesn't have too many years left. Do you promise me, Constancia?"—**when she uses my full name, I know she means business.** Abuela Invents the Zero
Do not use dashes if the additional or emphasized information is not a sudden break in the text.	Due to a shortage of wood, barracks were built with green pine that shrank and left cracks between the boards, **allowing sand and insects to seep and creep inside**. Dear Miss Breed

Grammar: Dashes and Hyphens—Dashes

Introduce the Skill

Review the image and definition for dashes as a class.

- dash (indicates break in text) - indicates an abrupt break or change in thought within a sentence; typed using two hyphens
- dash (sets off or emphasizes text) - sets off and emphasizes supplemental information or parenthetical statements; typed using two hyphens

Discuss the Model

1. Why might a writer add a break in text to a sentence instead of starting a new one? Answers will vary. Sample answer: A writer may want to emphasize information, show an interruption, or share a new thought within a sentence.
2. How can you use dashes to show a break in text in the middle of a sentence? Use a pair of dashes around a break in text that happens in the middle of a sentence. One dash is placed before the break in text, and the other dash is placed after it.
3. How can you use a dash to show a break in text at the end of a sentence? Use one dash before a break in text at the end of the sentence.
4. When should you avoid using dashes in a sentence? Do not use dashes if the additional or emphasized information is not a sudden break in the text; instead, it is part of a continued and developing thought.

Your Turn

Ask students to complete the Your Turn activity.

QUESTION 1

A. Incorrect.

B. Correct. The change in thought *it's only been open two months* needs to be set off by dashes on both sides.

C. Incorrect.

D. Incorrect.

QUESTION 2

A. Incorrect.

B. Incorrect.

C. Incorrect.

D. Correct. The sentence that interrupts the main sentence, *it's been advertised as "You could be a millionaire!,"* is correctly punctuated and is set off by dashes.

QUESTION 3

A. Correct. The phrase *the star's breakout hit* is interrupting the main sentence and is set off by dashes.

B. Incorrect.

C. Incorrect.

D. Incorrect.

QUESTION 4

A. Incorrect.

B. Correct. *"Push button to start"* is additional information and should be set off by dashes on both sides.

C. Incorrect.

D. Incorrect.

YOUR TURN

1. How should this sentence be changed?

> That new restaurant—it's only been open two months is always swamped with eager diners.

- A. Remove the dash after **restaurant**.
- B. Put a dash after **months**.
- C. Put a dash after **swamped**.
- D. No change needs to be made to this sentence.

2. How should this sentence be changed?

> The contest—it's been advertised as "You could be a millionaire!"—starts next week.

- A. Remove the dash after **millionaire!"**
- B. Remove the dash after **contest**.
- C. Insert a dash after **starts**.
- D. No change needs to be made to this sentence.

3. How should this sentence be changed?

> The movie the star's breakout hit was a huge success at the box office.

- A. Put dashes after **movie** and **hit**.
- B. Put a dash after **movie**.
- C. Put a dash after **success**.
- D. No change needs to be made to this sentence.

4. How should this sentence be changed?

> The instructions for the machine—"Push button to start" were printed in large red letters.

- A. Remove the dash after **machine**.
- B. Insert a dash after **start"**.
- C. Insert a dash after **printed**.
- D. No change needs to be made to this sentence.

Grammar: Commas After Transitions

Transition words and phrases help connect ideas in a text. Transitions can improve the flow in a piece of writing, and they can help readers better understand the ideas presented in the text. Examples of transition words and phrases include *for instance*, *however*, *as a result*, *therefore*, *first*, *on the other hand*, and *in addition*. Use a comma after transition words or phrases at the beginning of a sentence.

Correct	Incorrect
Therefore, Grace decided to change her study habits last semester.	**Therefore** Grace decided to change her study habits last semester.
In fact, Miguel surprised his mom by baking her favorite cake.	**In fact** Miguel surprised his mom by baking her favorite cake.

Follow this additional rule when using commas with transitions:

Rule	Text
Use a pair of commas to set off a transition that interrupts the flow of thought in the middle of a sentence.	He thought he was lazy and, **worse**, spoiled by the trappings of being middle class. Born Worker

Grammar: Commas After Transitions

Introduce the Skill

Review the image and definition for commas after transitions as a class.

- comma - punctuation to indicate a pause in a sentence or to separate items in a list
- transition - links details such as comparisons for coherence; set off with a comma

Discuss the Model

1. Why do writers use transitions? Answers will vary. Sample answer: Writers use transitions to connect ideas in a text. They can improve the flow in a piece of writing, and they can help readers understand the ideas that they're expressing.
2. How are transitions punctuated when they are used at the beginning of a sentence? Writers should use a comma after transition words or phrases at the beginning of a sentence.
3. How are transitions punctuated when they interrupt the flow of thought in the middle of a sentence? Writers should use a pair of commas to set off transitions that interrupt the flow of thought in the middle of a sentence.

Your Turn

Ask students to complete the Your Turn activity.

QUESTION 1

A. Correct. A comma belongs after the transition phrase *for example* at the beginning of the sentence.

B. Incorrect.

C. Incorrect.

D. Incorrect.

QUESTION 2

A. Incorrect.

B. Correct. Adding a comma after the word *all* sets the transition phrase *after all* apart from the rest of the sentence.

C. Incorrect.

D. Incorrect.

QUESTION 3

A. Incorrect.

B. Incorrect.

C. Incorrect.

D. Correct. This sentence correctly includes a comma after the transition phrase.

QUESTION 4

A. Correct. Inserting a comma here sets off the transition phrase *in fact* from the rest of the sentence.

B. Incorrect.

C. Incorrect.

D. Incorrect.

YOUR TURN

1. How should this sentence be changed?

   For example Daniel plans to play a Mozart piece at his next piano recital.

   - A. Insert a comma after **example**.
   - B. Insert a comma after **Daniel**.
   - C. Insert a comma after **next**.
   - D. No change needs to be made to this sentence.

2. How should this sentence be changed?

   Mozart, after all is his favorite classical composer.

   - A. Delete the comma after **Mozart**.
   - B. Insert a comma after **all**.
   - C. Insert a comma after **favorite**.
   - D. No change needs to be made to this sentence.

3. How should this sentence be changed?

   In addition, Daniel loves the music of Beethoven, Chopin, and Debussy.

   - A. Insert a comma after **In**.
   - B. Delete the comma after **addition**.
   - C. Delete the comma after **Beethoven**.
   - D. No change needs to be made to this sentence.

4. How should this sentence be changed?

   Daniel in fact, wants to continue studying music in high school and beyond.

   - A. Insert a comma after **Daniel**.
   - B. Delete the comma after **fact**.
   - C. Insert a comma after **music**.
   - D. No change needs to be made to this sentence.

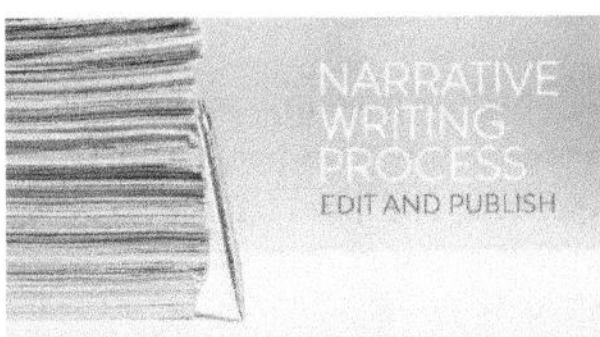

Narrative Writing Process: Edit and Publish

PLAN | DRAFT | REVISE | EDIT AND PUBLISH

You have revised your suspenseful narrative based on your peer feedback and your own examination.

Now, it is time to edit your narrative. When you revised, you focused on the content of your narrative. You probably looked at your story's beginning, descriptive details, and transitions. When you edit, you focus on the mechanics of your story, paying close attention to things like grammar and punctuation.

Use the checklist below to guide you as you edit:

- ☐ Have I followed spelling rules?
- ☐ Have I followed the guidelines for using dashes?
- ☐ Have I used commas to set off transitions when needed?
- ☐ Do I have any sentence fragments or run-on sentences?
- ☐ Have I punctuated everything correctly?

Notice some edits Lucia has made:

- followed spelling rules for words that contain *ie* and *ei*
- followed spelling rules for adding a suffix to a word that ends in a silent *e*
- followed spelling rules for adding prefixes to words
- followed the guidelines for using dashes
- followed the rules for using commas after transitions

Narrative Writing Process: Edit and Publish

Practice with Student Model (Optional)

Provide groups with a different section of Lucia's draft. Each group should practice editing Lucia's model using the checklist in the lesson. Has she:

- ☐ followed spelling rules?
- ☐ followed the guidelines for using dashes?
- ☐ used commas to set off transitions when needed?
- ☐ used any sentence fragments or run-on sentences?
- ☐ punctuated everything correctly?

After the groups have finished, call volunteers from each group to make edits until all the mistakes have been found and edited, pausing to discuss points of disagreement.

SPEAKING FRAMES

- ____ is spelled incorrectly. The correct spelling is ____.
- Lucia did / did not use dashes correctly when she wrote ____.
- Lucia did / did not use commas with transitions correctly when she wrote ____.
- ____ is an example of a run-on sentence / sentence fragment that Lucia has / has not corrected.
- ____ is punctuated incorrectly. The correct punctuation is ____.

Write

After students finish editing, suggest, if there's time, that they set their essays aside for a few minutes, and that they then proofread them one more time. Once students have completed their writing, have them submit their work.

CHECK FOR SUCCESS

If students struggle to edit successfully, help them determine where edits are needed and what changes need to be made.

Direct students to the grammar lessons in this unit if they are uncertain about the rules for specific concepts.

READ ALOUD

Encourage students to read their stories aloud to themselves or to a partner in order to catch any remaining mistakes.

READ ALOUD

Encourage students to read their stories aloud to themselves or to an on-grade-level peer in order to catch any remaining mistakes.

WRITE A BLURB

Have students review their story and determine where their writing was most effective. Allow students to write a blurb like they might find on the back of a book that highlights and praises the best qualities of their work. Alternatively, have students write blurbs for the students in the class and post them around the room.

While carrying the bowl of popcorn under one arm and a tall glass of fizzy water in one hand, I shuffle in my slippered feet down the hallway to my bedroom in ~~record breaking time~~ record-breaking time. The house hums contentedly around me. It is Friday night, and I have the whole place to myself. Mom is at a work dinner, and my younger brother, Tom the Slob, is at a sleepover. The ~~queit~~ quiet feels like a rare treat, but most ~~exciteing~~ exciting of all is the promise of ~~unterrupted~~ uninterrupted time with my favorite YouTube star, ZeldaZee.

Once I make it to my bedroom without spilling a thing, I climb up onto my neatly made bed~~and my open laptop has fallen asleep there.~~—Mom's a stickler for asking me to make it. My open laptop has already fallen asleep there, but I awaken the screen with one click. ~~With one click, I awaken the screen.~~ ZeldaZee's channel is queued up and ready to go. So I toss a kernel of popcorn into my mouth and hit play.

WRITE

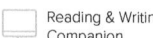

Use the questions on the previous page, as well as your peer reviews, to help you evaluate your suspenseful narrative to determine areas that need editing. Then edit your narrative to correct those errors.

Once you have made all your corrections, you are ready to publish your work. You can distribute your writing to family and friends, hang it on a bulletin board, or post it on your blog. If you publish online, share the link with your family, friends, and classmates.

English Language Learner Resources

studysync USERS ASSIGNMENTS

GRADE 8 › UNIT

Everyone Loves a Mystery
Core ELA
Grade 8
30 Days

Unit Overview
Integrated Reading and Writing
Extended Writing Project
ELL Resources
Novel Study
End-of-Unit Assessment

Instructional Path

Inside the House

The Lucky Coin

Skill: Classroom Vocabulary

Students will learn and recognize classroom vocabulary words and practice using them in a variety of contexts.

Teacher Resources: Lesson Plan

Assign

Skill: Taking Notes

Students will learn and practice the skill of taking notes when they listen to or read a text.

Teacher Resources: Lesson Plan

Assign

Add to

Lessons in the English Language Learner Resources section offer explicit ELL instruction. These lessons share a thematic and genre focus with all other lessons in the Core ELA unit.

The twenty ELL Resources are developed around two texts, "Inside the House" and "Lucky Coin," and an Extended Oral Project. Each text is written at four distinct levels. For ELLs, these texts serve as structural and thematic models of authentic texts in the Integrated Reading and Writing section of the unit. Thus, teachers may use the ELL texts in place of or as extensions for "Monster" and "The Monkey's Paw."

ELL lessons modify the routines used with texts in the Integrated Reading and Writing section. Explicit vocabulary instruction is emphasized, and reading and writing Skills lessons focus strongly on language acquisition and reading comprehension.

After reading texts about the scary and mysterious, students will complete an Extended Oral Project that can be used in place of or as an extension to the Extended Writing Project. In this unit, students will plan and present a suspenseful scene in the form of a group presentation.

Focus on English Language Proficiency Levels

- ADVANCED HIGH
- ADVANCED
- INTERMEDIATE
- BEGINNING

ELL Resources provide targeted support for four levels of proficiency: Beginning, Intermediate, Advanced, and Advanced High. Instruction and scaffolds, as well as the texts themselves, are differentiated based on these levels.

Additional differentiated scaffolds include visual glossaries, speaking and writing frames, and suggested grouping for peer and teacher support. Lessons also include suggested extension activities to challenge Advanced and Advanced High students as they progress through the year.

ELL Resources

ELL TEXTS

Inside the House

- Skill: Sight Vocabulary and High-Frequency Words
- Skill: Seeking Clarification
- First Read
- Skill: Analyzing Expressions
- Skill: Conveying Ideas
- Skill: Spelling Patterns and Rules
- Close Read

The Lucky Coin

- Skill: Classroom Vocabulary
- Skill: Taking Notes
- First Read
- Skill: Language Structures
- Skill: Retelling and Summarizing
- Skill: Subject-Verb Agreement
- Close Read

EXTENDED ORAL PROJECT

- Introduction
- Skill: Acquiring Vocabulary
- Plan
- Skill: Sentence Lengths
- Practice
- Present

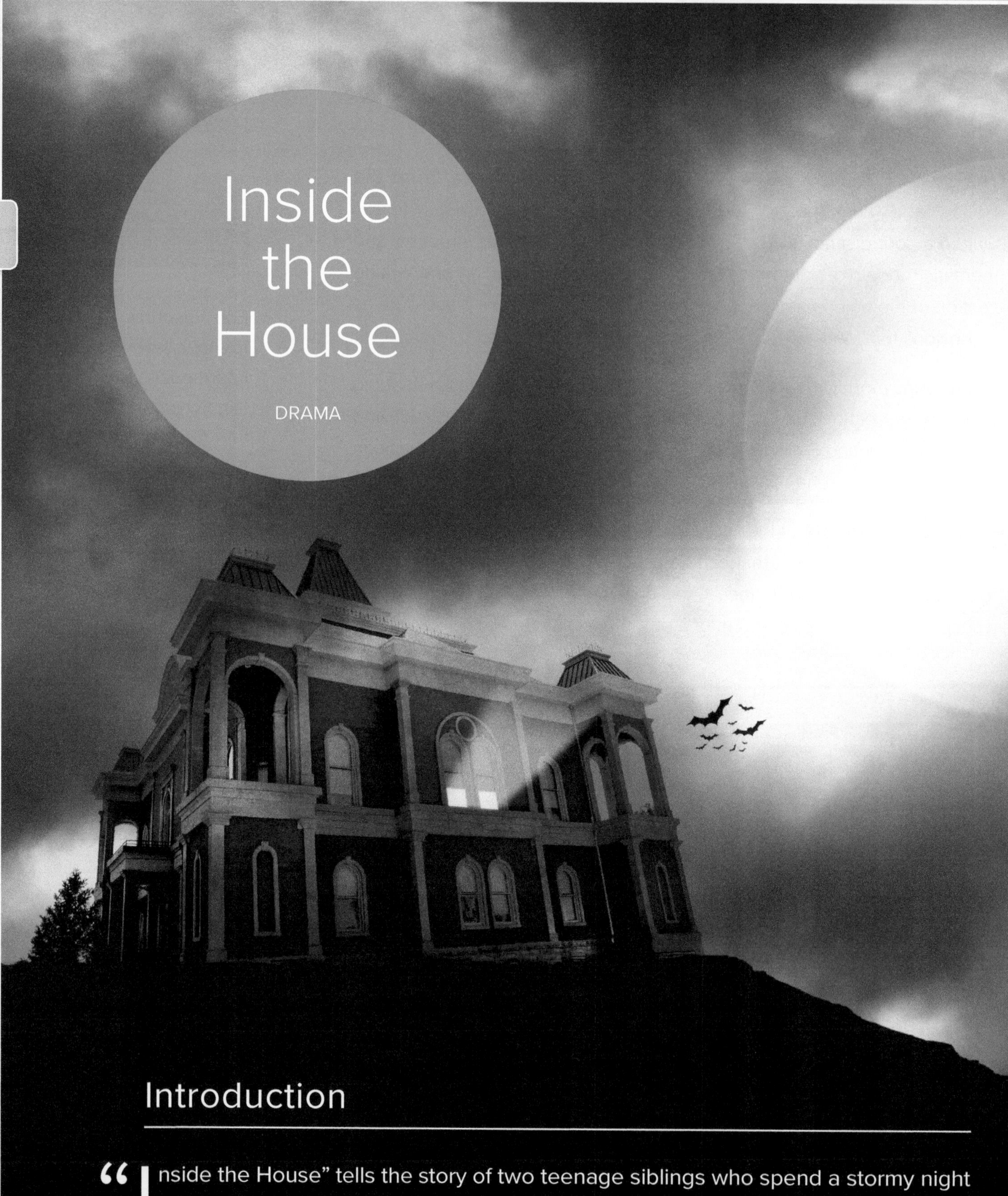

Inside the House

DRAMA

Introduction

"Inside the House" tells the story of two teenage siblings who spend a stormy night alone telling scary stories. In this scene from the play, Cristina and Fernando learn just how scary a story can be when their real life starts to match a tale they've told. The author uses dialogue, sound effects, and foreshadowing to build suspense

Fifteen-year-old twins Fernando and Cristina are home alone while a thunderstorm rages outside. The power is out, so to pass the time, they tell each other scary stories. The scene opens as Cristina finishes her story, explaining that the killer is already inside the house. Fernando makes fun of her predictable ending and boasts that he could tell a scarier story. However, before he gets the chance, Cristina announces that it's bedtime and heads to her room. Left alone, Fernando hears knocking outside his window. Frightened, he calls Cristina. She doesn't believe him and tells Fernando that he's imagining things. He pleads for her to close the door and stay with him. As soon as she complies, they hear knocking outside the bedroom door, and the doorknob slowly turns.

 Summaries in multiple languages are available digitally.

 Audio and audio text highlighting are available with this text.

CONNECT TO ESSENTIAL QUESTION

What attracts us to the mysterious?

In this short play, two siblings swap scary stories before finding themselves in a scary situation of their own. Will Cristina believe her brother's concerns before it's too late?

Core ELA Connections

Texts	Theme	Genre
Monster	On a stormy night, siblings Cristina and Fernando are telling each other scary stories, when they hear strange sounds. The play builds on the ideas of fear and uncertainty.	A short drama, "Inside the House" uses dialogue, sound effects, and foreshadowing to build suspense.

Differentiated Text Levels

ELL LEVEL	BEGINNING	INTERMEDIATE	ADVANCED	ADVANCED HIGH
WORD COUNT	327	398	456	533
LEXILE	N/A	N/A	N/A	N/A

Instructional Path

The print teacher's edition includes essential point-of-use instruction and planning tools. Complete lesson plans and program documents appear in your digital teacher account.

Skill: Sight Vocabulary and High-Frequency Words

DIGITAL ONLY

Objectives: Students will be able to learn and recognize sight vocabulary and high-frequency words in English.

Objectives: Students will be able to recognize sight vocabulary and high-frequency words when listening and reading, and produce sight vocabulary and high-frequency words when speaking and writing.

Skill: Seeking Clarification

DIGITAL ONLY

Objectives: Students will be able to learn and practice the skill of seeking clarification when they do not understand spoken language.

Objectives: Students will be able to seek clarification when they do not understand spoken language.

First Read: Inside the House

Objectives: Students will be able to perform an initial reading of a text using the strategy of seeking confirmation.

Objectives: Students will be able to demonstrate comprehension of a text by responding to questions orally and in writing using textual evidence.

Skill: Analyzing Expressions

Objectives: Students will be able to analyze expressions to improve comprehension.

Objectives: Students will be able to analyze expressions when reading text.

Skill: Conveying Ideas

Objectives: Students will be able to use different strategies to convey ideas.

Objectives: Students will be able to use different strategies to convey ideas when speaking.

Skill: Spelling Patterns and Rules

Objectives: Students will be able to recognize and apply spelling patterns and rules.

Objectives: Students will be able to recognize spelling patterns and rules when reading and apply spelling patterns and rules when writing.

Close Read: Inside the House

Objectives: Students will be able to perform a close reading of a text in order to analyze expressions.

Objectives: Students will be able to demonstrate analysis of expressions by participating in a collaborative conversation and writing a short constructed response.

Progress Monitoring

Opportunities to Learn	Opportunities to Demonstrate Learning	Opportunities to Reteach
Sight Vocabulary and High-Frequency Words		
Skill: Sight Vocabulary and High-Frequency Words	Skill: Sight Vocabulary and High-Frequency Words • Your Turn First Read • Sight Vocabulary and High-Frequency Words	Spotlight Skill: Sight Vocabulary and High-Frequency Words
Seeking Clarification		
Skill: Seeking Clarification	Skill: Seeking Clarification • Your Turn First Read • Skills Focus	Spotlight Skill: Seeking Clarification
Analyzing Expressions		
Skill: Analyzing Expressions	Skill: Analyzing Expressions • Your Turn	Spotlight Skill: Analyzing Expressions
Conveying Ideas		
Skill: Conveying Ideas	Skill: Conveying Ideas • Your Turn Close Read • Complete Skills Focus • Write	Spotlight Skill: Conveying Ideas
Spelling Patterns and Rules		
Skill: Spelling Patterns and Rules	Skill: Spelling Patterns and Rules • Your Turn Close Read • Write	Spotlight Skill: Spelling Patterns and Rules

First Read

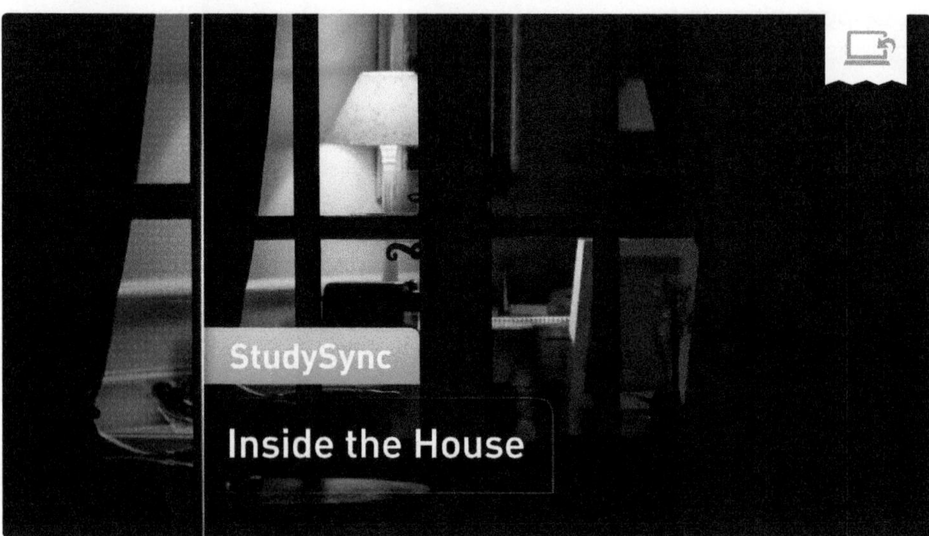

Introduce the Text

As a class, watch the video preview and have students read the introduction in pairs to make connections to the video preview. Ask students various "wh" questions such as:

- What did you see in the video? How does it make you feel?
- What do you think the text will be about?
- Is there something in the video or introduction that surprised you?

Beginning & Intermediate

SPEAKING FRAMES

- I see ____. I feel ____.
- I think the text will be about ____.
- I was surprised by ____.

Practice Prereading Skill

Remind students that Seeking Clarification:

helps you better understand the text you read and the conversations you have with others. When you discover that you do not understand a word in a text or a conversation, you can use different questions to seek clarification. To help you understand, someone may speak slower or use gestures.

Have students work in small, on-level groups to choral read or listen to the audio of the summary. Remind students to seek clarification from you or their peers as needed.

- *What does this word mean?*
- *Would you repeat that?*

Activate Prior Knowledge and Experiences OPTIONAL

Have students make connections while practicing their oral language by discussing what they know about scary stories.

Generate a list (on the board or on paper) of any information or ideas your students have about scary stories.

Ask students to share where their background knowledge came from. For example, did their ideas come from a movie, friend, television show, book, or family member?

VOCABULARY

predictable
easily guessed or expected

anxious
nervous or afraid

sarcastic
meaning the opposite of what is said to express humor, irritation, or meanness

embarrassed
feeling foolish or ashamed

scratching
rubbing against something with a rough or sharp object

NOTES

READ

1 [SCENE: *A teenager's bedroom on a stormy night. Thunder rumbles. Lightning flashes outside the window. Fifteen-year-old twins* CRISTINA *and* FERNANDO *sit together on the floor. Their only light is a flashlight. They are home alone. The power is out. They are telling scary stories.* CRISTINA *finishes her story as the scene begins.*]

2 CRISTINA [*speaking quickly*]: Suddenly, the knocking stopped. The bedroom door flew open. They reached for the phone, but it was too late. The killer was already inside the house! [*She smiles proudly.*]

3 FERNANDO [*coldly*]: That was not scary. Of course the killer was already inside the house. The killer is always already inside the house! Nice try, Tina. But that ending was so **predictable**.

4 CRISTINA: Can you do better?

5 FERNANDO: Yes! [*Eager to tell a scarier tale.*] This guy was camping alone in the woods. . .

AUDIO TEXT HIGHLIGHTING

Allow students to use the audio text highlight feature to follow along as they read. Alternately, you may wish to work directly with students or group them in twos or threes for partner reading or choral reading.

Preteach Vocabulary

Model the first word and example for the class.

1. The first word is *predictable,* and its meaning is "easily guessed or expected."
2. When I hear the word *predictable*, I think of events or outcomes that I can guess will happen.
3. For example, if I stay up very late before going to bed, it is *predictable* that I will be tired the next morning.
4. This is an example of something that is *predictable* because it is not surprising.

Continue this exercise with each word in the glossary, calling on individuals or groups of students to share out.

Beginning

PRETEACH VOCABULARY

Use the gestures to clarify meanings.

- **predictable** (Make a guess.)
- **sarcastic** (Roll your eyes and make a sarcastic comment.)
- **scratching** (Scratch your nails against the board or desk to make a noise.)
- **anxious** (Pantomime nervousness by rubbing your hands together slowly and looking around.)
- **embarrassed** (Pantomime looking down, covering your face.)

Sight Vocabulary and High-Frequency Words Focus

Remind students of the sight vocabulary and high-frequency words that they studied at the beginning of the unit. Point out that some of the words may be useful as they think about and discuss the text. For example:

- both (**Both** Cristina and Fernando . . .)
- don't (They **don't** know what the sound is . . .)
- right (I don't believe Fernando is **right** . . .)
- tell (Fernando should **tell** Cristina . . .)
- which (I'm not sure **which** character to trust . . .)

TEXT TALK

Have students discuss the questions in small groups. Circulate and check for understanding.

1. What is the story about?
2. Who are the story's characters?
3. Where does the story take place?
4. How does the story make you feel?

All Levels

SPEAKING FRAMES

Giving Information:

- This story is about ____.
- The story's characters are ____.
- This story takes place in ____.
- This story makes me feel ____.

Asking for Information:

- Can you explain ____?
- What do you think about ____?
- Why do you think ____?

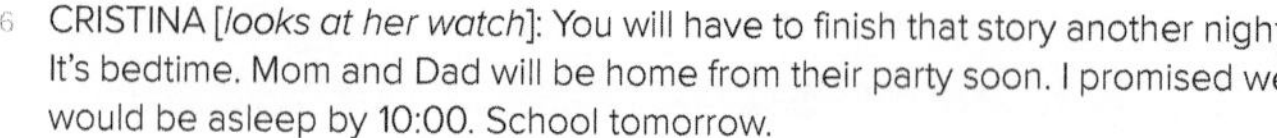

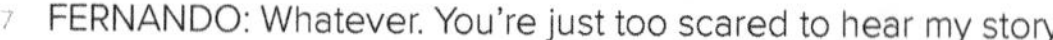

NOTES

6 CRISTINA [*looks at her watch*]: You will have to finish that story another night. It's bedtime. Mom and Dad will be home from their party soon. I promised we would be asleep by 10:00. School tomorrow.

7 FERNANDO: Whatever. You're just too scared to hear my story.

8 CRISTINA [***sarcastic***]: Yeah, that's it. I am just too scared—and too tired. [*stands*] Go to bed, Fernando.

9 [CRISTINA *leaves the room. She closes the door.* FERNANDO *gets into bed. The rain gets louder. We hear a persistent* ***scratching*** *on the window.*]

10 FERNANDO [*jumping up*]: Cristina!

11 CRISTINA [*rushing in*]: What's wrong?

12 FERNANDO [***anxious*** *and* ***embarrassed***]: I don't know. I heard something. A scratching. By the window.

13 CRISTINA [*doubtful*]: You did not. You are trying to scare me. We're twins. I know how you think. Go to bed. We have a big test in the morning.

14 [CRISTINA *leaves again. She slams the door. There are three loud knocks against the window.*]

15 FERNANDO: Tina!

16 CRISTINA [*opening the door, annoyed*]: What?

17 FERNANDO [*terrified*]: Tell me you heard that.

18 CRISTINA: Heard what?

19 FERNANDO: That knocking! On the window!

20 CRISTINA: There is nobody knocking on the window. You are not going to scare me. [*turns to go*]

21 FERNANDO: Wait. I heard it when you closed my door. Close the door again.

22 CRISTINA: Fine. But this isn't funny.

23 FERNANDO: You're right. It's not. There is somebody out there.

24 [CRISTINA *closes the door. She turns toward her brother.* FERNANDO *waits to hear another noise.* CRISTINA *stays quiet. Someone knocks three times against the bedroom door. The doorknob begins to turn.*]

First Read

Read the story. After you read, answer the Think Questions below.

THINK QUESTIONS

1. Who are the main characters in the story? What is their relationship?

   The main characters are ____________ and ____________.

   They are ____________.

2. Where does the story take place? What kind of night is it?

   The story takes place ____________.

   It is a ____________.

3. At the end of the story, why do the characters get scared?

   The characters get scared because ____________
   ____________.

4. Use context to confirm the meaning of the word *annoy* as it is used in "Inside the House." Write your definition of *annoy* here.

   Annoy means ____________.

   A context clue is ____________.

5. What is another way to say that someone is *anxious*?

   Someone is ____________.

Think Questions

Circulate as students answer Think Questions independently. Answers will vary.

QUESTION 1: Comprehension

Cristina and Fernando. They are twins/siblings.

QUESTION 2: Comprehension

The characters are at home. It is a stormy night. The power is out.

QUESTION 3: Comprehension

Answers will vary, but may include the following examples:

- "There are three loud knocks against the window."
- "Someone knocks three times. . . . The doorknob begins to turn."

Student responses should provide an example from the text and an explanation that describes how the example causes the characters to get scared.

QUESTION 4: Language

Cristina feels bothered and frustrated by Fernando calling her back in the room. *Annoy* means "to bother."

QUESTION 5: Language

That person is nervous.

Skill: Analyzing Expressions

Introduce the Skill

Watch the Concept Definition video and read the definition for Analyzing Expressions.

Skill: Analyzing Expressions

DEFINE

When you read, you may find English expressions that you do not know. An **expression** is a group of word that communicates an idea. Three types of expressions are idioms, sayings, and figurative language. They ca be difficult to understand because the meanings of the words are different from their **literal**, or usual, meanings

An **idiom** is an expression that is commonly known among a group of people. For example: "It's raining cat and dogs" means it is raining heavily. **Sayings** are short expressions that contain advice or wisdom. Fo instance: "Don't count your chickens before they hatch" means do not plan on something good happenin before it happens. **Figurative** language is when you describe something by comparing it with somethin else, either directly (using the words *like* or *as*) or indirectly. For example, "I'm as hungry as a horse" mean I'm very hungry. None of the expressions are about actual animals.

CHECKLIST FOR ANALYZING EXPRESSIONS

To determine the meaning of an expression, remember the following:

- ✓ If you find a confusing group of words, it may be an expression. The meaning of words in expression may not be their literal meaning.
  - Ask yourself: Is this confusing because the words are new? Or because the words do not make sense together?
- ✓ Determining the overall meaning may require that you use one or more of the following:
  - context clues
  - a dictionary or other resource
  - teacher or peer support
- ✓ Highlight important information before and after the expression to look for clues.

TURN AND TALK

1. What does it mean to analyze expressions?
2. Why might it be difficult to analyze expressions?
3. What can you do if you are struggling to analyze expressions?

Beginning & Intermediate

SPEAKING FRAMES

- When I don't understand an expression, I ____.
- To determine the meaning of an expression, ____.

Advanced & Advanced High

SPEAKING FRAMES

- When I don't understand an expression, I ____. For example, ____.
- To determine the meaning of an expression, ____. For example, ____.

SKILL VOCABULARY

expression / la expresión *noun* a phrase used to express an idea COGNATE

idiom / el modismo *noun* a common expression that cannot be taken literally

saying / el dicho *noun* an expression that contains advice or wisdom

literal / literal *adjective* describing the usual meaning of a word COGNATE

YOUR TURN

Read the following excerpt from "Inside the House". Then, complete the multiple-choice questions below.

from **"Inside the House"**

FERNANDO [*jumping up*]: Cristina!

CRISTINA [*rushing in*]: What's wrong?

FERNANDO [*anxious and embarrassed*]: I don't know. I heard something. A scratching. By the window.

CRISTINA [*doubtful*]: You did not. You are trying to scare me. We're twins. I know how you think. Go to bed. We have a big test in the morning.

1. What does Cristina mean when she says "I know how you think?"
   - A. She can read Fernando's mind.
   - B. Fernando told Cristina he wanted to scare her.
   - C. Cristina and Fernando think alike.
   - D. Cristina tells Fernando what to think.

2. Which context clue helped you determine the meaning of the expression?
   - A. "What's wrong?"
   - B. "I don't know. I heard something."
   - C. "You are trying to scare me. We're twins."
   - D. "Go to bed. We have a big test in the morning."

Your Turn

Ask students to complete the Your Turn Activity.

QUESTION 1: C) Cristina and Fernando think and act like each other.

QUESTION 2: C) This clue reveals that Cristina and Fernando are twins, which means they are very close.

Discuss the Skill Model

1. What does the student not understand?

   She doesn't understand the meaning of the expression, "The door flew open."

2. How does the student analyze the expression?

   She searches for context clues.

3. What context clue does the student highlight? What does he conclude in her annotation?

   "Suddenly the knocking stopped" and "but it was too late." She concludes that something is happening quickly and that this is the meaning of the expression.

4. What does the student do to confirm her analysis of the expression?

   The student asks her teacher or peers what the expression means.

5. How does knowing the meaning of the expression help the student?

   The student better understands the text.

ELL **Beginning & Intermediate**

Have students use the speaking frames and helpful terms to participate in the group discussion. If beginning students are hesitant to participate in a discussion, encourage them by prompting with *yes* or *no* questions.

Advanced & Advanced High

Have students use the speaking frames to participate in the group discussion.

SPEAKING FRAMES

- The student does not understand the expression ____.
- The student analyzes the expression by searching for ____ in the text.
- The student highlights ____.
- The student believes the expression means ____.
- The student ____ to confirm her understanding.
- The student improves her understanding of the text by ____.

HELPFUL TERMS FOR DISCUSSION

• context clues	• able	• expression
• analyze	• confirm	• understanding
• highlight	• improve	• text

Skill: Conveying Ideas

Introduce the Skill

Watch the Concept Definition video ▶ and read the definition for Conveying Ideas.

Skill:
Conveying Ideas

 DEFINE

Conveying ideas means communicating a **message** to another person. When speaking, you might not kno what word to use to convey your ideas. When you do not know the exact English word, you can try differen strategies. For example, you can ask for help from classmates or your teacher. You may use gestures an physical movements to act out the word. You can also try using **synonyms** or **defining** and describing th meaning you are trying to express.

••• CHECKLIST FOR CONVEYING IDEAS

To convey ideas for words you do not know when speaking, use the following learning strategies:

- ✓ Request help.
- ✓ Use gestures or physical movements.
- ✓ Use a synonym for the word.
- ✓ Describe what the word means using other words.
- ✓ Give an example of the word you want to use.

TURN AND TALK

1. What does it mean to convey ideas?
2. Why might it be difficult to convey your ideas?
3. What can you do if you are struggling to convey your ideas?

Beginning & Intermediate

SPEAKING FRAMES
- To convey an idea means to relay a ____.
- You may not be able to ____.
- You could use physical movements or ____.
- You could also say ____.

Advanced & Advanced High

SPEAKING FRAMES
- To convey an idea means ____.
- You may not be able to ____ because ____.
- You could use physical movements or ____.
- You could also try using strategies like ____ or ____.

 SKILL VOCABULARY

convey / verbalizar ***verb*** to express

message / el mensaje ***noun*** a piece of information COGNATE

synonym / el sinónimo ***noun*** a word or phrase that means the same as another word or phrase COGNATE

define / definar ***verb*** to give the meaning of a word COGNATE

YOUR TURN

nagine that someone is trying to convey the meaning of the word *knocking*. Find the correct example for ach strategy to complete the chart below.

	Examples
A	The person says, "It is like when you go to someone's house and you want them to let you inside."
B	The person uses the similar word *tapping*.
C	The person mimes hitting the door with her first.
D	The person explains that the word means making a noise on a door or wall to get someone's attention.

Strategies	Examples
Use gestures or physical movements.	
Use a synonym for the word.	
Describe what the word means using other words.	
Give examples of the word you want to use.	

Your Turn

Ask students to complete the Your Turn activity.

Examples
The person mimes hitting the door with her fist.
The person uses the similar word *tapping*.
The person explains that the word means "making a noise on a door or wall to get someone's attention."
The person says it is like when you go to someone's house and you want them to let you inside.

Discuss the Skill Model

1. What is the student trying to do?

   The student is trying to share their annotation.

2. Why is the student struggling?

   The student can't remember a word.

3. What strategies does the student use?

   Answers will vary, but should include: The student describes the word. The students says a synonym. The student asks for help.

ELL Beginning & Intermediate

Have students use the speaking frames and helpful terms to participate in the group discussion. If beginning students are hesitant to participate in a discussion, encourage them by prompting with *yes* or *no* questions.

Advanced & Advanced High

Have students use the speaking frames to participate in the group discussion.

SPEAKING FRAMES

- The student is trying to expand on his ____.
- The student is struggling because he can't ____ a word.
- First, the student ____.
- The student also ____.

HELPFUL TERMS FOR DISCUSSION

- convey
- synonym
- asks
- explain
- ideas
- help

Close Read

Model Skills Focus

Remind students of the Reading Skill Analyzing Expressions. Tell students that one way you can analyze expressions you do not know in a story is to look for context clues about those expressions while you are reading. Direct students to the Skills Focus and remind them to track as you read aloud.

Find context clues that help you analyze expressions in the play.

Model this activity for students:

- I am going to focus on expressions that I do not understand well.
- I reread the story and look at my annotations. I notice that I highlighted the part when Cristina leaves the room.
- I didn't understand the phrase, "*She slams the door.*"
- I look for context clues. In the previous sentence, I know that Cristina leaves the room. I also know that Cristina is not happy in this moment because Fernando did not like her story. These are all important clues. Now I understand that the expression means that Cristina shut the door when she left the room, but not in a quiet way. She shut the door loudly.

Complete Skills Focus

Divide students into pairs. Have each pair identify expressions in the story to analyze.

- Have both partners look for context clues to help determine the meaning of each expression.
- Have the partners ask each other what they believe each expression means based on the context clues.
- Have partners explain how the context clues helped them analyze and understand each expression.

Circulate and monitor groups as they work.

Close Read

WRITE

PERSONAL NARRATIVE: In "Inside the House," Cristina and Fernando are home alone when something scary happens. Tell about a time something scary happened to you, using specific details. How did you feel? How did you react? Pay attention to spelling patterns as you write.

Use the checklist below to guide you as you write:

- [ ] What is a scary experience that you've had?
- [ ] How did you feel while it was happening?
- [ ] How did you react? What did you do?

Use the sentence frames to organize and write your personal narrative.

A scary experience that I had is ______________________.

It happened when ______________________.

I felt very ______________________.

I thought ______________________.

I reacted by ______________________.

It helped me ______________________.

Collaborative Conversation

Group students so they have a representative from each of the original pairs. Prompt partners to make a list of all the expressions they analyzed and what they mean.

- How did context clues help you to analyze these expressions?
- How did asking other students help confirm your understanding?
- How did analyzing the expressions help your understanding of the story?

Collaborative Conversation

SCAFFOLDS

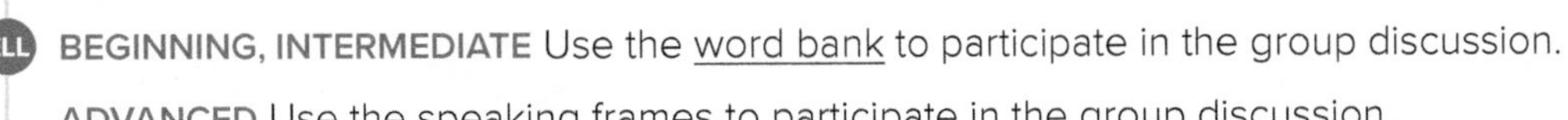

ELL **BEGINNING, INTERMEDIATE** Use the word bank to participate in the group discussion.

ADVANCED Use the speaking frames to participate in the group discussion.

BEGINNING, INTERMEDIATE	ADVANCED
Word Bank	**Speaking Frames**
• helped me understand • now I understand • character • plot • action • description	• Context clues helped me because ____. • Asking other students helped me because ____. • Analyzing the expressions helped me better understand ____ about the story.

Write

Ask students to complete the writing assignment. Remind students to pay attention to spelling patterns in words.

ELL **BEGINNING** Write a response using the paragraph frames and word bank.

INTERMEDIATE Write a response using the paragraph frames.

INTERMEDIATE / BEGINNING	BEGINNING
Paragraph Frames	**Word Bank**
• A scary experience that I had is ____. It happened when ____. • I felt very ____. I thought ____. • I reacted by ____. It helped me ____.	• terrified • dangerous • trouble • calm • behave

The Lucky Coin

FICTION

Introduction

Maggie is a hard-working teen who doesn't believe in magic. At least, she doesn't until her grandfather gives her a lucky coin that makes her every wish come true. But when she accidentally loses the coin, Maggie also loses her confidence in herself. "The Lucky Coin" tells the story of Maggie's journey from skeptic to believer and back again.

Maggie has always worked hard, practicing to make the basketball team and studying for school. One day, her grandpa gives her a lucky coin and tells her that it will make her wishes come true. Maggie doesn't believe in magic, but she puts the coin in her pocket anyway. The next day, her teacher surprises the class with a test. Maggie hasn't done the reading, so out of panic, she clutches the lucky coin. The test turns out to be on last week's assignment. Getting used to the power of the coin, Maggie wishes to become the captain of the basketball team and for her team to win every game. Soon thereafter, she becomes her team's captain, and her team makes it to the championship. However, Maggie loses the coin, and with it, her ability to shoot the ball. Her coach calls a timeout and asks Maggie to bring her usual magic. Back in the game, Maggie takes a deep breath and throws the ball.

 Summaries in multiple languages are available digitally.

 Audio and audio text highlighting are available with this text.

CONNECT TO ESSENTIAL QUESTION

What attracts us to the mysterious?

A young girl receives a "lucky coin" from her grandfather. She is skeptical of its magical powers, but is tempted to give it a try. Will this coin give her everything she wishes for?

Core ELA Connections

Texts	Theme	Genre
The Monkey's Paw	Maggie receives a lucky coin as a gift from her grandfather. The text builds on the ideas of superstition, luck, and rewards.	"The Lucky Coin" is a mystery that leaves readers wondering the cause of Maggie's success.

Differentiated Text Levels

ELL LEVEL	BEGINNING	INTERMEDIATE	ADVANCED	ADVANCED HIGH
WORD COUNT	377	416	467	569
LEXILE	380L	420L	570L	690L

Instructional Path

The print teacher's edition includes essential point-of-use instruction and planning tools. Complete lesson plans and program documents appear in your digital teacher account.

Skill: Classroom Vocabulary

DIGITAL ONLY

Objectives: Students will be able to learn and recognize classroom vocabulary words in English.

Objectives: Students will be able to recognize classroom vocabulary words when listening and reading, and produce and practice classroom vocabulary words when speaking and writing.

Skill: Taking Notes

DIGITAL ONLY

Objectives: Students will be able to learn and practice the skill of taking notes when listening to or reading a text.

Objectives: Students will be able to take notes when listening to or reading a text.

First Read: The Lucky Coin

Objectives: Students will be able to perform an initial reading of a text using the strategy of taking notes.

Objectives: Students will be able to demonstrate comprehension of a text by responding to questions orally and in writing using textual evidence.

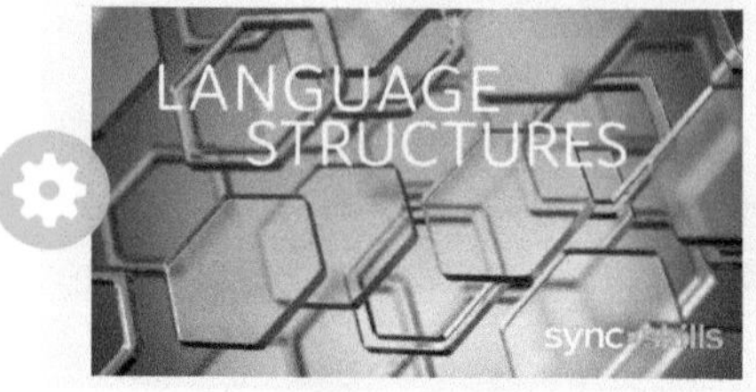

Skill: Language Structures

Objectives: Students will be able to understand the basic subject-verb-object language structure.

Objectives: Students will be able to understand the basic subject-verb-object language structure when they read.

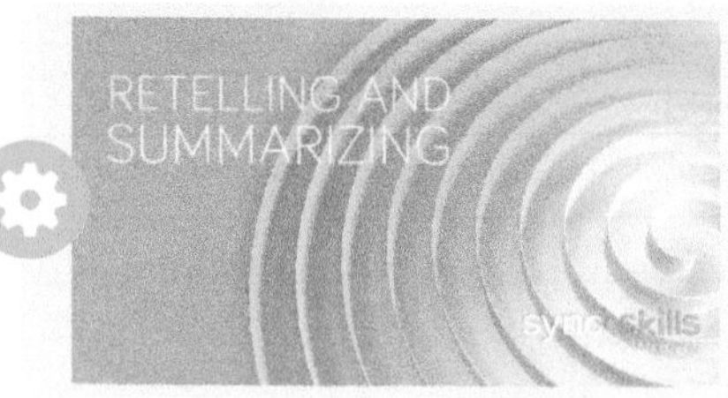

Skill: Retelling and Summarizing

Objectives: Students will be able to retell and summarize to demonstrate comprehension.

Objectives: Students will be able to retell and summarize a text they read.

Skill: Subject-Verb Agreement

Objectives: Students will be able to recognize and apply rules for subject-verb agreement.

Objectives: Students will be able to apply rules for subject-verb agreement when writing.

Close Read: The Lucky Coin

Objectives: Students will be able to perform a close reading of a text in order to retell and summarize.

Objectives: Students will be able to demonstrate retelling and summarizing by participating in a collaborative conversation and writing a short constructed response.

Progress Monitoring

Opportunities to Learn	Opportunities to Demonstrate Learning	Opportunities to Reteach
Classroom Vocabulary		
Skill: Classroom Vocabulary	Skill: Classroom Vocabulary • Your Turn First Read • Classroom Vocabulary	Spotlight Skill: Classroom Vocabulary
Taking Notes		
Skill: Taking Notes	Skill: Taking Notes • Your Turn First Read • Skills Focus	Spotlight Skill: Taking Notes
Language Structures		
Skill: Language Structures	Skill: Language Structures • Your Turn	Spotlight Skill: Language Structures
Retelling and Summarizing		
Skill: Retelling and Summarizing	Skill: Retelling and Summarizing • Your Turn Close Read • Complete Skills Focus • Write	Spotlight Skill: Retelling and Summarizing
Subject-Verb Agreement		
Skill: Subject-Verb Agreement	Skill: Subject-Verb Agreement • Your Turn Close Read • Write	Spotlight Skill: Subject-Verb Agreement

First Read

Introduce the Text

As a class, watch the video preview and have students read the introduction in pairs to make connections to the video preview. Ask students various "wh" questions such as:

- What did you see in the video? How does it make you feel?
- What do you think the text will be about?
- Is there something in the video or introduction that surprised you?

Beginning & Intermediate

SPEAKING FRAMES

- I see ____. I feel ____.
- I think the text will be about ____.
- I was surprised by ____.

Practice Prereading Skill

Remind students that Taking Notes:

helps you to stay focused on the information you are reading or hearing. When you begin to read or listen to information, write the main ideas and important details in an outline or chart. Taking notes like this lets you organize the information. This helps you understand it more easily, talk about the main ideas more clearly, and study better.

Have students work in small, on-level groups to create an outline of the summary using the main ideas and details chart.

As students are working in small groups, circulate to listen for sample questions like:

- *What are the main ideas?*
- *What are the important details?*

Activate Prior Knowledge and Experiences OPTIONAL

Have students make connections while practicing their oral language by discussing what they know about luck.

Generate a list (on the board or on paper) of any information or ideas your students have about luck.

Ask students to share where their background knowledge came from. For example, did their ideas come from a movie, friend, television show, book, or family member?

VOCABULARY

ridiculous
absurd; very silly

undefeated
having no losses; never beaten

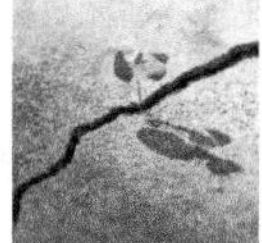

miracle
an extremely amazing or unlikely event, thing, or accomplishment

confidence
a feeling of certainty in one's own abilities

captain
a person who leads a team or group

READ

NOTES

1 Maggie did not believe in magic. She worked hard to make her dreams come true. When she wanted to make the basketball team, she practiced for a month. So when her grandpa gave her a lucky coin, Maggie thought it was a joke.

2 "Your future will be bright," Grandpa said. "But if you need some luck, hold this coin and make a wish. The coin will do the rest."

3 Maggie laughed, "I don't believe in magic."

4 Grandpa winked. "The coin is very powerful. Promise me you will use it responsibly."

5 Maggie put the coin in her pocket. She thought, *A lucky coin. How* ***ridiculous!***

AUDIO TEXT HIGHLIGHTING

Allow students to use the audio text highlight feature to follow along as they read. Alternately, you may wish to work directly with students or group them in twos or threes for partner reading or choral reading.

Preteach Vocabulary

Model the first word and example for the class.

1. The first word is *ridiculous,* and its meaning is "absurd; very silly."
2. When I hear the word *ridiculous,* I think of something unusual, such as clothing with lots of patterns and colors.
3. For example, the clown was easy to spot because of his *ridiculous* clothing covered with multicolored stripes and polka dots.
4. This is an example of something that is *ridiculous* because it is very silly.

Continue this exercise with each word in the glossary, calling on individuals or groups of students to share.

Beginning

PRETEACH VOCABULARY

Use the gestures to clarify meanings.

- **ridiculous** (Make a funny face.)
- **miracle** (Pantomime winning the lottery.)
- **captain** (Pantomime giving orders like you're the captain of a basketball team.)
- **undefeated** (Clasp your hands together and hold them up like you're the champion of something.)
- **confidence** (Smile broadly.)

Classroom Language Focus

Remind students of the sight vocabulary and high-frequency words that they studied at the beginning of the unit. Point out that some of the words may be useful as they think about and discuss the text. For example:

- computer (The **computers** at school are . . .)
- use (Maggie liked to **use** . . .)
- search (Maggie did not **search** for . . .)
- type (I like to **type**, but Maggie's grandpa probably prefers to . . .)
- Internet (The **Internet** is where I . . .)

6 The next day Maggie's teacher surprised the class with a quiz. Maggie was nervous. She forgot to do the reading assignment. *What am I going to do?* Maggie realized that the coin was in her pocket. *This is silly, but what have I got to lose? I wish for a* ***miracle***.

7 Maggie took a deep breath and looked down at the quiz. It was about a story she read last week! *It's a miracle! The coin worked!*

8 The bell rang for lunch. Maggie's stomach grumbled. *I know exactly what to wish for next: pizza.* She made her wish. Maggie cheered when she saw the menu in the cafeteria. As she bit into her second slice of pizza she thought, *I could get used to this.*

9 Maggie wished to be chosen as **captain** of the basketball team. Then she wished that the team would win all their games. Soon she was leading the **undefeated** team into the championship.

10 Then one day, Maggie led the team on an outdoor run. The coin bounced out of her pocket somewhere along the trail. It was gone.

11 On the morning of the championship game, Maggie couldn't do anything right. She didn't sink a basket during the first half of the game. Her teammates struggled without Maggie's **confidence** to guide them. It looked like the team would lose. The referee blew his whistle, announcing a time-out. Maggie ignored her coach's pep talk. *I didn't used to believe in magic. Now I can't do anything without it. I wish I'd never heard of that lucky coin!*

12 "Hey, Maggie! Are you listening?"

13 Maggie snapped to attention.

14 Her coach said, "We need some of your usual magic, or we don't have a chance. Can we count on you?"

15 A second whistle called the team back. Within seconds, the ball was in Maggie's hands. She took a deep breath and took a shot.

TEXT TALK

Have students discuss the questions in small groups. Circulate and check for understanding.

1. What is the story about?
2. Who are the story's characters?
3. Where does the story take place?
4. How does the story make you feel?

All Levels

SPEAKING FRAMES

Giving Information:

- This story is about ____.
- The story's characters are ____.
- This story takes place in ____.
- This story makes me feel ____.

Asking for Information:

- Can you explain ____?
- What do you think about ____?
- Why do you think ____?

First Read

Read the story. After you read, answer the Think Questions below.

THINK QUESTIONS

1. **Who are the main characters in the story? What is their relationship?**

   The main characters are ____________________.

   They are ____________________.

2. **What happens at the beginning of the story?**

   At the beginning of the story ____________________.

3. **At the end of the story, why is Maggie upset?**

   Maggie is upset because ____________________.

4. **Use context to confirm the meaning of the word *miracle* as it is used in "The Lucky Coin." Write your definition of *miracle* here.**

   Miracle means ____________________.

   A context clue is ____________________.

5. **What is another way to say that a lucky coin is *ridiculous*?**

   A lucky coin is ____________________.

Think Questions

Circulate as students answer Think Questions independently. Answers will vary.

QUESTION 1: Comprehension

Maggie and Grandpa. Grandpa is Maggie's grandfather.

QUESTION 2: Comprehension

Grandpa gives Maggie a lucky coin. She doesn't believe in it at first.

QUESTION 3: Comprehension

Maggie lost her lucky coin. She is worried that she will have bad luck.

QUESTION 4: Language

Maggie forgot to read her assignment. The teacher gives the class a surprise test. Maggie hopes for a *miracle*. The test is on a text she read last week. I think *miracle* means "something incredible that happens."

QUESTION 5: Language

A lucky coin is very silly.

Skill: Language Structures

Introduce the Skill

Watch the Concept Definition video and read the definition for Language Structures.

TURN AND TALK

1. Have you ever read a sentence that confused you?
2. Why was it confusing?

Beginning & Intermediate

SPEAKING FRAMES

- A sentence that confused me is ____.
- It was confusing because ____.

Advanced & Advanced High

SPEAKING FRAMES

- Once I was confused by ____.
- It was confusing because ____ so I ____.

The Lucky Coin

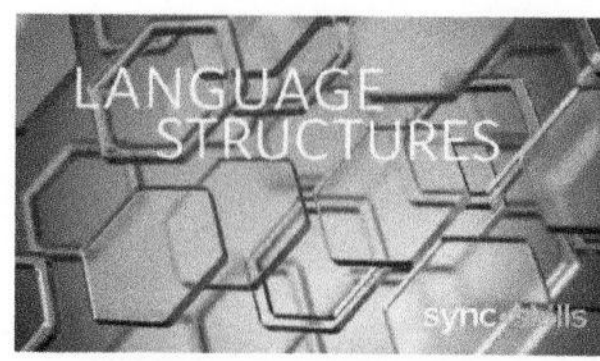

Skill: Language Structures

DEFINE

In every language, there are rules that tell how to **structure** sentences. These rules define the correct order of words. In the English language, for example, a **basic** structure for sentences is subject, verb, and object. Some sentences have more **complicated** structures.

You will encounter both basic and complicated **language structures** in the classroom materials you read. Being familiar with language structures will help you better understand the text.

••• CHECKLIST FOR LANGUAGE STRUCTURES

To improve your comprehension of language structures, do the following:

✓ Monitor your understanding.

- Ask yourself: Why do I not understand this sentence? Is it because I do not understand some of the words? Or is it because I do not understand the way the words are ordered in the sentence?

✓ Break down the sentence into its parts.

- In English, most sentences share the same pattern: subject + verb + object.
  - > The **subject** names who or what is doing the action.
  - > The **verb** names the action or state of being.
  - > The **object** answers questions such as Who?, What?, Where?, and When?
- Ask yourself: What is the action? Who or what is doing the action? What details do the other words provide?

✓ Confirm your understanding with a peer or teacher.

SKILL VOCABULARY

structure / la estructura ***noun*** the order of parts COGNATE

basic / básico ***adjective*** the most important parts without anything extra COGNATE

complicated / complicado ***adjective*** having many parts COGNATE

language structure / la estructura de lenguaje ***noun*** the order of words in a sentence COGNATE

YOUR TURN

Read the following excerpt from "The Lucky Coin." Then, complete the chart by writing the words and phrases into the "Subject," "Verb," and "Object" columns. The first row has been done as an example.

from **"The Lucky Coin"**

Maggie wished to be chosen as captain of the basketball team. Then she wished that the team would win all their games. Soon she was leading the undefeated team into the championship.

Then one day, Maggie led the team on an outdoor run. The coin bounced out of her pocket somewhere along the trail. It was gone.

Sentence	Subject	Verb	Object
Maggie wished to be chosen as captain of the basketball team.	Maggie	wished	to be chosen
Then she wished that the team would win all their games.			
Soon she was leading the undefeated team into the championship.			
Then one day, Maggie led the team on an outdoor run.			
The coin bounced out of her pocket somewhere along the trail.			

Your Turn

Ask students to complete the Your Turn activity.

Subject	Verb	Object
she	wished	that the team would win
she	was leading	the undefeated team
Maggie	led	the team
The coin	bounced	out of her pocket

Discuss the Skill Model

1. Why does the reader highlight the sentence in yellow?

   He highlights it in yellow because he does not understand it.

2. Why does the reader highlight the sentence in different colors?

   He uses different colors to identify the parts of the sentence.

3. How does this help the reader?

   He gets an idea of the meaning of the sentence. And he identifies the part of the sentence that is confusing.

4. What does the reader do to confirm his understanding?

   He asks his teacher if his understanding is right.

ELL

Beginning & Intermediate

Have students use the speaking frames and helpful terms to participate in the group discussion.
If beginning students are hesitant to participate in a discussion, encourage them by prompting with *yes* or *no* questions.

Advanced & Advanced High

Have students use the speaking frames to participate in the group discussion.

SPEAKING FRAMES

- The reader highlights in yellow to show that he does not ____.
- The reader highlights in different colors to identify ____.
- This helps the reader to get an idea of ____. He is able to identify ____.
- Finally the reader asks his teacher to ____.

HELPFUL TERMS FOR DISCUSSION

- determine
- identify
- understanding
- analyze
- teacher
- confusing
- discover
- confirm
- highlight

Skill: Retelling and Summarizing

Introduce the Skill

Watch the Concept Definition video ▶ and read the definition for Retelling and Summarizing.

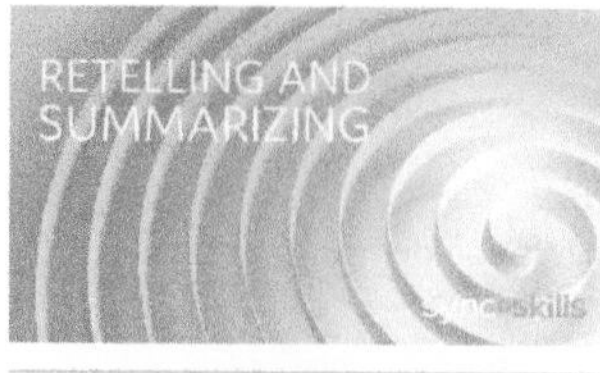

Skill: Retelling and Summarizing

★ DEFINE

You can retell and summarize a text after reading to show your understanding. **Retelling** is telling a story again in your own words. **Summarizing** is giving a short explanation of the most important ideas in a text.

Keep your retelling or summary **concise**. Only include important information and keywords from the text. By summarizing and retelling a text, you can improve your comprehension of the text's ideas.

••• CHECKLIST FOR RETELLING AND SUMMARIZING

In order to retell a story or summarize text, note the following:

✓ Identify the main events of the story.

- Ask yourself: What happens in this text? What are the main events that happen at the beginning, the middle, and the end of the text?

✓ Identify the main ideas in a text.

- Ask yourself: What are the most important ideas in the text?

✓ Determine the answers to the six WH questions.

- Ask yourself: After reading this text, can I answer Who?, What?, Where?, When?, Why?, and How? questions.

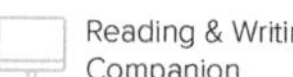

TURN AND TALK

1. Have you ever told a friend about a movie you watched or a news article you read?
2. Why have you told a friend about the movie or news article?
3. What are some of the things that you have told your friend about the movie or news article?

Beginning & Intermediate

SPEAKING FRAMES

- I have told my friend about ____. I wanted my friend to ____.
- I told my friend about the main ____.

Advanced & Advanced High

SPEAKING FRAMES

- I told my friend about a movie or news article because ____.
- I told my friend about ____. For example, ____.

SKILL VOCABULARY

retell / volver a contar ***verb*** to tell a story again in your own words

summarize / resumir ***verb*** to give a short explanation of the most important ideas in a text

concise / conciso/a ***adjective*** short COGNATE

YOUR TURN

Read the following excerpt from "The Lucky Coin." Then, write each event in the beginning, middle, or end of the chart to retell what happened in the story.

from "**The Lucky Coin**"

On the morning of the championship game, Maggie couldn't do anything right. She didn't sink a basket during the first half of the game. Her teammates struggled without Maggie's confidence to guide them. It looked like the team would lose. The referee blew his whistle, announcing a time-out. Maggie ignored her coach's pep talk. *I didn't used to believe in magic. Now I can't do anything without it. I wish I'd never heard of that lucky coin!*

Event Options		
Maggie thinks it is because of the coin	The team was probably going to lose.	Maggie didn't sink a basket in the first half.

Beginning	
Middle	
End	

Your Turn

Ask students to complete the Your Turn activity.

Beginning	Maggie didn't sink a basket in the first half.
Middle	The team was probably going to lose.
End	Maggie thinks it is because of the coin.

Discuss the Skill Model

1. Why does the reader want to retell the excerpt?

   to show her understanding of it

2. What does the reader highlight in the paragraph?

   Answers will vary.

3. Why does she highlight these details?

   These details show the beginning, the middle, and the end events of the paragraph.

4. Why does the reader answer the six WH questions?

   The answers help the reader retell the details of the paragraph.

ELL

Beginning & Intermediate

Have students use the speaking frames and helpful terms to participate in the group discussion.
If beginning students are hesitant to participate in a discussion, encourage them by prompting with *yes* or *no* questions.

Advanced & Advanced High

Have students use the speaking frames to participate in the group discussion.

SPEAKING FRAMES

- The reader wants to retell the paragraph to show her ____.
- The reader highlights the ____ in the paragraph.
- These details show the ____, the ____, and the ____.
- The reader answers the six WH questions because ____.

HELPFUL TERMS FOR DISCUSSION

- details
- middle
- highlight
- main event
- end
- retell
- beginning
- understanding
- explain

Close Read

Model Skills Focus

Remind students of the Reading Skill Retelling and Summarizing. Tell students that one way to improve your understanding of a story or text is to retell the main events of a story or the main ideas of a text. Direct students to the Skills Focus and remind them to track as you read aloud.

Form an opinion about how well the descriptions and events help readers understand why Maggie starts believing in magic.

Model this activity for students:

- I know from the story that Maggie does not believe in magic at the beginning, but does at the end.
- I am going to focus on the things that happen to Maggie that make her believe in luck or magic.
- I will reread the story and look at my annotations.
- I notice that after Maggie gets the pizza she wished for, she plans to wish for more things. She also did well on her quiz even though she didn't do her assignment.
- These events show me that Maggie was getting lucky. She started believing in magic because of the good things that happened to her.
- Identifying these events shows my understanding of the story and tells me how well the descriptions and events in the story help me understand why Maggie starts to believe in magic.

Complete Skills Focus

Divide students into three equal groups. Assign each group with one of the following focus areas:

- Identify one detail that helps readers understand why Maggie starts believing in magic.
- Identify one event that helps readers understand why Maggie starts believing in magic.
- Identify one question you have about Maggie's belief in magic.

Circulate and monitor groups as they work.

The Lucky Coin

Close Read

WRITE

ARGUMENTATIVE--LITERARY ANALYSIS: How do the descriptions and events help readers understand why Maggie makes the choices she does? Write a response to this question. Support your writing with evidence from the text. Pay attention to subject-verb agreement as you write.

Use the checklist below to guide you as you write.

- ☐ Which details tell how Maggie feels about magic?
- ☐ Which event first leads Maggie to believe that magic is real?
- ☐ What does Maggie start doing after this event?
- ☐ What is one negative decision Maggie makes because of her belief in magic?

Use the sentence frames to organize and write your literary analysis.

At first, Maggie does not believe in ______________________.

She thinks the lucky coin is silly.

Then, Maggie forgets to read her homework. The teacher gives her a ______________________
______________________.

Maggie is nervous. She makes a wish with the lucky coin. The quiz is about something she already read.

Other events like this start happening.

For example, ______________________.

Then, ______________________.

These examples show why Maggie starts to ______________________.

176 Reading & Writing Companion

Collaborative Conversation

Group students so they have a representative from each of the original three groups. Prompt groups to combine their examples and form an opinion about how well the examples help them understand why Maggie starts believing in magic.

- How did you choose examples?
- How did the examples help students understand why Maggie starts believing in magic?
- What questions do they still have about Maggie's new belief in magic?

SCAFFOLDS

Collaborative Conversation

BEGINNING, INTERMEDIATE Use the word bank to participate in the group discussion.

ADVANCED Use the speaking frames to participate in the group discussion.

BEGINNING, INTERMEDIATE

Word Bank

- support my opinion
- why she believes
- character
- describe
- action
- belief

ADVANCED

Speaking Frames

- I chose examples that ____.
- The examples helped because ____.
- One question that I still have about Maggie's new belief is ____.

Write

Ask students to complete the writing assignment. Remind students to pay attention to correct subject-verb agreement.

BEGINNING Write a response using the paragraph frames and word bank.

INTERMEDIATE Write a response using the paragraph frames.

INTERMEDIATE

BEGINNING

Paragraph Frames

- At first, Maggie does not believe in ____. She thinks the lucky coin is silly.
- Then, Maggie forgets to read her homework. The teacher gives her a ____. Maggie is nervous. She makes a wish with the lucky coin. The quiz is about something she already read.
- Other events like this start happening. For example, ____. Then, ____. These examples show why Maggie starts to ____.

Word Bank

- lunch
- basketball
- believe
- magic
- confidence

In the Extended Oral Project, students plan, draft, practice, and deliver an oral presentation that ties into the theme of the unit and spans informative, argumentative, and narrative genres. Lessons provide explicit instruction to prepare students for the unique challenges of an oral presentation, and to help break down the genre characteristics of each prompt. At each step in the process, students focus in-depth on specific writing and speaking skills as they brainstorm, organize, and refine their presentation. Students also receive discussion prompts and frames to guide them in providing effective peer feedback as they practice and discuss in small groups before presenting to the class on the final day.

CONNECT TO ESSENTIAL QUESTION

What attracts us to the mysterious?

In this unit, students practiced effective collaborative communication skills, as well as note-taking and retelling skills, while reading and analyzing two texts about mysteries. Now students will apply those skills to work together in writing and performing a dramatic scene.

Developing Effective Presentations

Form	Language and Conventions	Oral Language Production
Students may struggle with the creative demands of developing the dramatic scene, such as characters and plot.	Students should be encouraged to experiment with new sentence patterns and lengths to make their dialogue sound natural and realistic.	Students may make mistakes when they transfer grammatical forms from their native languages into English. Remind students to monitor their use of the letter *s* when indicating countable plural nouns and possessive nouns.

SCAFFOLDS

ENGLISH LANGUAGE LEARNERS

Vocabulary, discussion, and peer and teacher support in the Extended Oral Project is differentiated for Beginning, Intermediate, Advanced, and Advanced High English Language Learners. See individual lesson plans for additional scaffolding and support.

Instructional Path

All Extended Oral Project lessons lesson plans appear in your digital teacher account.

DIGITAL ONLY

Introduction

Objectives: Students will be able to identify the components of a suspenseful scene in order to brainstorm and plan their own scene.

Objectives: Students will be able to record ideas for a suspenseful scene in writing.

DIGITAL ONLY

Skill: Acquiring Vocabulary

Objectives: Students will be able to use a graphic organizer to make connections between words and acquire new vocabulary for their suspenseful scene.

Objectives: Students will be able to brainstorm new words to use in writing their scene.

DIGITAL ONLY

Plan

Objectives: Students will be able to plan and write a first draft of their scene.

Objectives: Students will be able to organize their first draft using an outline.

DIGITAL ONLY

Skill: Sentence Lengths

Objectives: Students will be able to apply knowledge of sentence lengths to revise the dialogue in their suspenseful scene.

Objectives: Students will be able to vary sentence lengths orally and in writing.

DIGITAL ONLY

Practice

Objectives: Students will be able to practice and revise their suspenseful scene based on peer feedback.

Objectives: Students will be able to practice a suspenseful scene orally and make revisions in writing.

DIGITAL ONLY

Present

Objectives: Students will be able to observe and perform a suspenseful scene in order to give and receive peer feedback.

Objectives: Students will be able to use varied sentence lengths in an oral presentation and give peer feedback orally and in writing.

Novel Study

Each Core ELAR Unit contains two texts designated for Novel Study. The Novel Study supports the close reading of the complete text through its associated Reading Guide and a series of comparative reading and writing lessons. Novel Studies are not a part of each grade-level's 180 days of instruction; however, teachers may choose to draw from them if they wish to incorporate materials from other disciplines or develop an alternative, novel-based approach to instruction.

Each novel comes with a **Reading Guide** that provides both teacher and student support. Each lesson provides key vocabulary words and close reading questions, as well as a key passage that will help teachers guide students through an exploration of the essential ideas, events, and character development in the novel. This passage will also serve as the point from which students will engage in their own StudySyncTV-style group discussion. Each novel study's **Comparative Reading and Writing** lessons contain resources to support comparative analyses. Students read passages of other texts drawn from across the disciplines and compare those passages to specific sections of the novel in written responses.

Suggested Novel Studies

Title	Genre	Summary	Themes and Topics
Ten Days in a Mad-House (1887)	Journalism	In the late 19th century, New York's mental health system was rife with institutional cruelty, theft, and murder. To expose this, journalist Nellie Bly went undercover, getting herself committed to the women's asylum on Blackwell's Island.	• Journalism • Activism • Mental Illness
Great Tales and Poems (various)	Fiction/Poetry	Edgar Allan Poe invented the mystery genre, wrote a handful of poetry's most quoted lines, and penned finely tuned horror tales that haunt readers to this day.	• Horror • Mystery • Gothic Literature

OPTION 1

Ten Days in a Mad-House

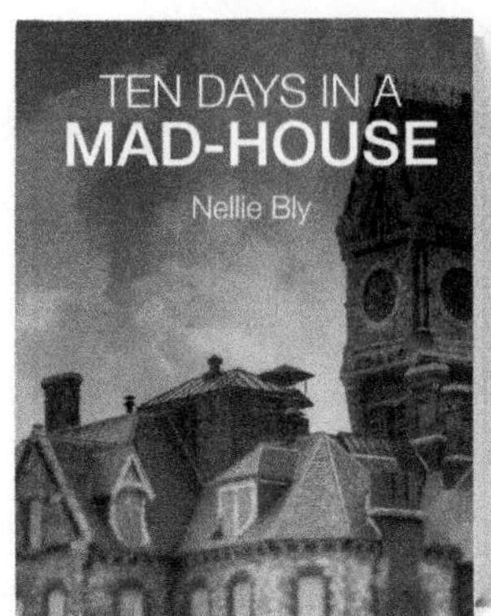

Ten Days in a Mad-House is an example of muckraking, in which a writer examines a societal issue or exposes a wrongdoing in hopes of creating public pressure for change. To shine a light on deplorable conditions in mental hospitals, author Nellie Bly convinced a judge she was "insane." She was committed to the New York City women's asylum on Blackwell's Island, where she witnessed everything from starvation and extreme cold to physical abuse and torture.

Nellie Bly, or Elizabeth Seaman Cochrane (1864–1922), wrote the series of articles collected in this book for the newspaper *New York World* in 1887. The response to Bly's reports was immediate; after a grand jury investigation, the state granted a million-dollar increase in funding for the Department of Public Charities and Corrections.

OPTION 2

Great Tales and Poems

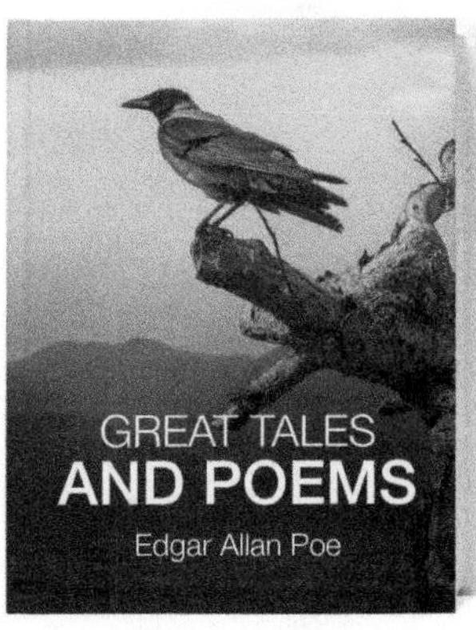

A talking raven visits a distraught man at midnight... A razor-sharp pendulum swings back and forth over a bound prisoner... A masked ball has one uninvited guest... Edgar Allan Poe's timeless stories and poems are filled with indelible images of the macabre that laid the foundations of literary mystery and horror. Here are many of the author's most famous works including "The Raven," "The Bells," "The Pit and the Pendulum," "The Masque of the Red Death," "The Cask of Amontillado," and more.

Edgar Allan Poe (1809–1849) was the first American to earn a living as a writer, though he struggled in poverty much of his life. Known mostly as a literary critic in his day, his stories and poems have shaped his legacy since. His house in Baltimore is a National Historic Landmark.

Spotlight Skills Review

A review day before the end-of-unit assessment gives you an opportunity to review difficult concepts with students using Spotlight Skills lessons. Spotlight Skills are targeted lessons that provide you with resources to reteach or remediate without assigning additional readings. Every Core ELA Skill lesson has a corresponding Spotlight Skill lesson. Spotlight Skills can be assigned at any point in the year, but the end of each unit provides a natural moment to pause, review data collected throughout the unit, and reteach skills students have not yet mastered.

Progress Monitoring

The Progress Monitoring charts that appear before every text in this unit identify standards and associated Spotlight Skills. On review day, you may want to give preference to reteaching skills that are not revisited in later units. You can see where skills are covered again in the Opportunities to Reteach column.

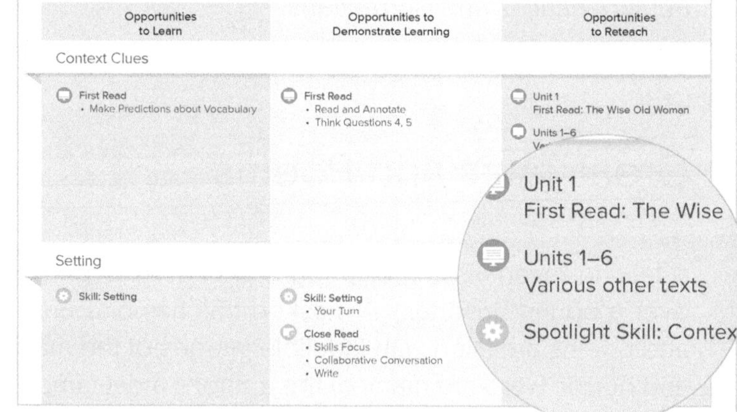

Opportunities to Learn
Opportunities to Demonstrate Learning
Opportunities to Reteach
Context Clues
First Read
• Make Predictions about Vocabulary
First Read
• Read and Annotate
• Think Questions 4, 5
Unit 1
First Read: The Wise Old Woman
Units 1–6
Unit 1
First Read: The Wise
Units 1–6
Various other texts
Spotlight Skill: Contex
Setting
Skill: Setting
Skill: Setting
• Your Turn
Close Read
• Skills Focus
• Collaborative Conversation
• Write

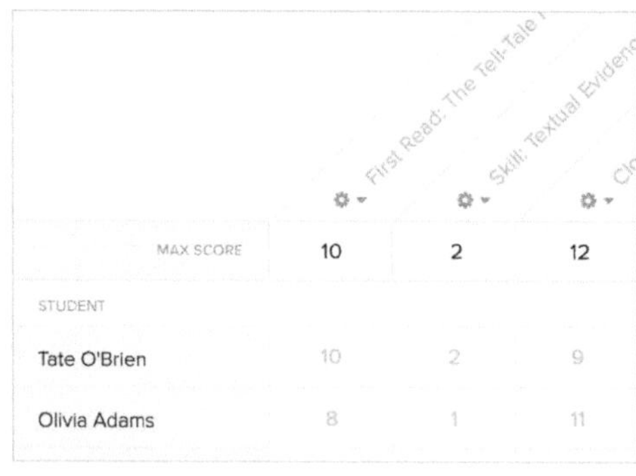

	First Read: The Tell-Tale	Skill: Textual Evidence	Cl
MAX SCORE	10	2	12
STUDENT			
Tate O'Brien	10	2	9
Olivia Adams	8	1	11

StudySync Gradebook

As students submit assignments on StudySync, their mastery of skills and standards is tracked via the gradebook. The gradebook can be sorted and viewed in a variety of ways. Sorting by assignment shows overall student performance, while sorting by standards or by Skill lessons displays student progress toward mastery goals.

Skills Library 

Spotlight Skills are located in the Skills section of the StudySync Library. You can assign Spotlight Skills to individual students or groups of students. Search tools allow you to search by skill type or name.

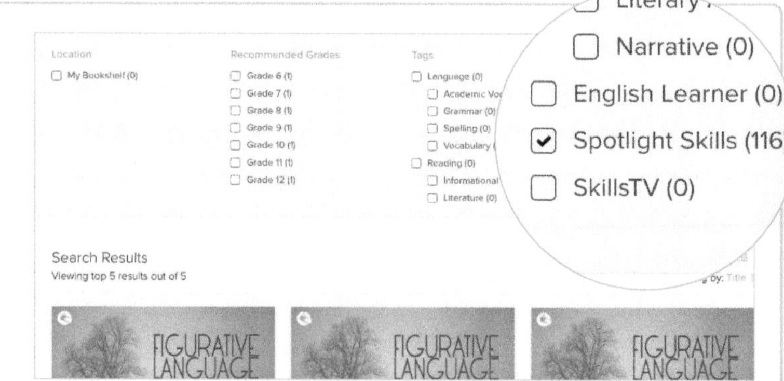

End-of-Unit Assessment

The end-of-unit assessment can be found in two places. The digital version of the assessment can be assigned from the Online Assessment tab inside your ConnectED account. The paper-based version of the assessment can be printed from the End-of-Unit Assessment tab inside this unit in your StudySync account.

Assessment Section	Content	Assessed Skills	
READING	The Mystery and Wonder of Science Genre: Nonfiction Word Count: 479 Lexile: 1060L	• Central or Main Idea • Author's Purpose and Point of View	• Textual Evidence • Context Clues
	The Cave of Eternal Night Genre: Fiction Word Count: 517 Lexile: 1020L	• Context Clues • Plot	• Theme • Language, Style, and Audience
	The Pencil Bandit Genre: Fiction Word Count: 532 Lexile: 1050L	• Context Clues • Language, Style, and Audience • Theme	• Plot • Story Structure • Text-Dependent Responses • Textual Evidence
	In the Dark Genre: Fiction Word Count: 938 Lexile: 1040L	• Language, Style, and Audience • Plot • Textual Evidence	• Theme • Context Clues
REVISING and **EDITING**	Student Passage #1	• Commonly Misspelled Words • Dashes	• Commas After Transitions
	Student Passage #2	• Organizing Writing • Beginnings • Narrative Techniques	• Transition Words • Descriptive Details • Conclusions
WRITING	Prompt: Narrative Writing	• Narrative Writing	

What's Next?

Assessment results can be viewed by item, standard, and skill to monitor mastery and make decisions for upcoming instruction.

RETEACH skills that students have not yet mastered, using Spotlight Skills or the Test Preparation and Practice book.

REVISE your teaching plan to provide more or less explicit instruction into a skill or text, using Beyond the Book activities for enrichment.

REGROUP students and levels of scaffolding based on standards progress.

Past and Present

What makes you, you?

UNIT 2

Past and Present

ESSENTIAL QUESTION

What makes you, you?

What makes us who we are? As we form bonds with other people and our communities over time, we realize that experiences from our past shape who we are in the present. With a genre focus on poetry, this Grade 8 unit prepares students to explore questions about how we see ourselves in the world.

Poets Yusef Komunyakaa, Robert Frost, and Natasha Trethewey use description and figurative language to examine ideas related to identity and community. Author Thanhhà Lai approaches questions of belonging in a novel written in verse. WNBA star Swin Cash's essay and former First Lady Michelle Obama's speech discuss the people and events who helped make them who they are. Judith Ortiz Cofer and Sandra Cisneros use fiction to inspire students to think about how characters' identities are affected by the world around them. After reading about these ideas within and across genres, your students will write a literary analysis, applying what they have learned from the unit's literature, speeches, and essays to an argumentative writing project.

Students in this unit will discover what it means to be yourself, to make tough decisions, and even to feel on top of the world, using the lens of figurative language to understand how authors express varied ideas about identity and belonging, past and present.

Integrated Reading and Writing

Genre Focus: POETRY

Extended Writing Project and Grammar

English Language Learner Resources

614 | Novel Study Choices

The Outsiders
Fiction
S.E. Hinton

Inside Out and Back Again
Fiction
Thanhhà Lai

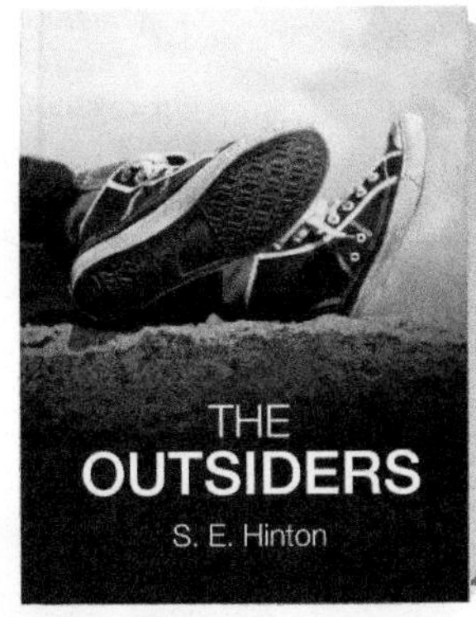

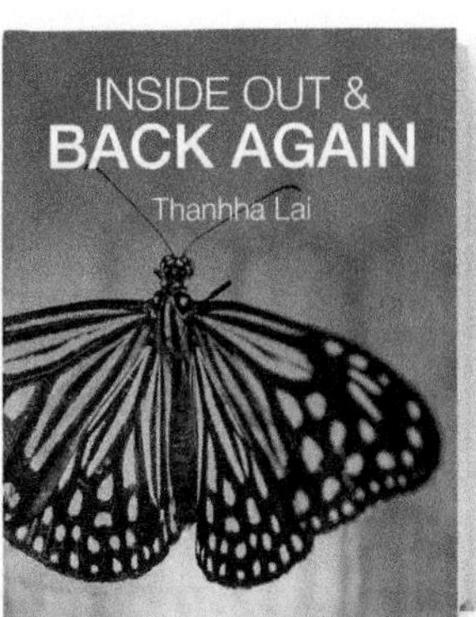

617 | End-of-Unit Assessment

THEMATIC PACING GUIDE

Past and Present

(tv) StudySyncTV or SkillsTV Episode

Pacing Guide

Days	Readings	Skill and Standard Instruction	Skill Practice and Spiraling
1–2	Essential Question **The Big Idea: What makes you, you?** p. 342	• Recognizing Genre: Poetry • Academic Vocabulary	• Write: Analyzing Genre
3–4	**I'm Nobody! Who are you?** p. 346	• Poetic Elements and Structure (tv)	• Textual Evidence • Theme • Character • Poetry Writing
5–8	**Commencement Address to the Santa Fe Indian School** p. 362	• Making Inferences • Arguments and Claims	• Textual Evidence • Author's Purpose and Point of View • Argumentative Writing
9–11	PAIRED READINGS **Curtain Call** p. 384 **So where are you from?** p. 394	• Visualizing • Central or Main Idea (tv)	• Textual Evidence • Comparative Writing
12–14	**The Outsiders** (tv) p. 410	• Character • Textual Evidence (tv)	• Literary Analysis Writing • Collaborative Conversations

THEMATIC PACING AT A GLANCE – 30 DAYS

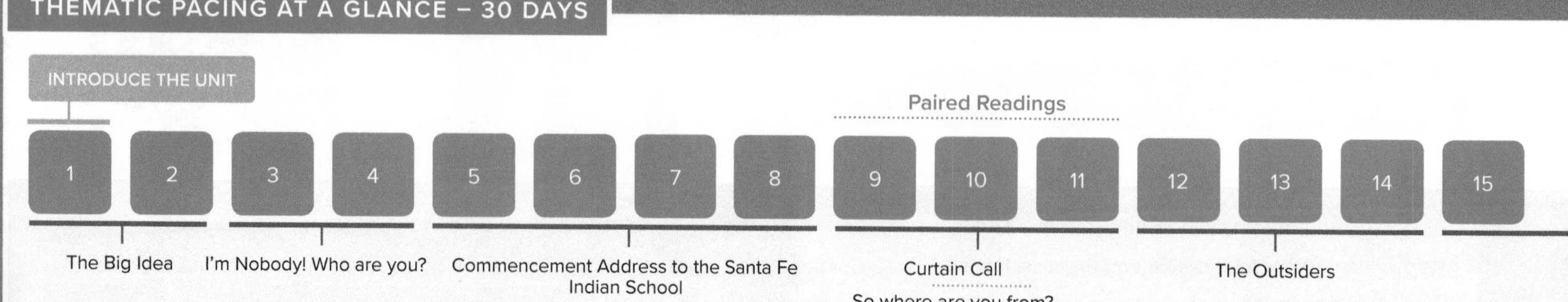

Days	Readings	Skill and Standard Instruction	Skill Practice and Spiraling
15–17	**Slam, Dunk, & Hook** p. 430	• Poetic Elements and Structure • Allusion	• Textual Evidence • Discussion
18–20	**Abuela Invents the Zero** p. 448	• Plot • Theme	• Textual Evidence • Narrative Writing
21–24	PAIRED READINGS **Inside Out and Back Again** tv p. 468 **Theories of Time and Space** p. 482 **The Road Not Taken** tv p. 492	• Poetic Elements and Structure tv • Figurative Language	• Textual Evidence • Theme • Comparative Writing • Collaborative Conversations
25–27	**The House on Mango Street** tv p. 510	• Figurative Language • Summarizing • Write: Analyzing Genre	• Textual Evidence • Argumentative Writing • Collaborative Conversations
28	**Self-Selected Reading and Response** p. 530	• Independent Reading	• Personal Response Writing

Review and Assessment See page 616.

Days	Review and Assessment	Skill Practice and Assessment
29	**Skills Review** p. 616	Students will have the opportunity to complete one or more Spotlight skill lessons in order to improve understanding and further practice skills from the unit that they found most challenging.
30	**End-of-Unit Assessment** p. 617	For more detail, please see the End-of-Unit Assessment information for Grade 8 Unit 2 on page 617.

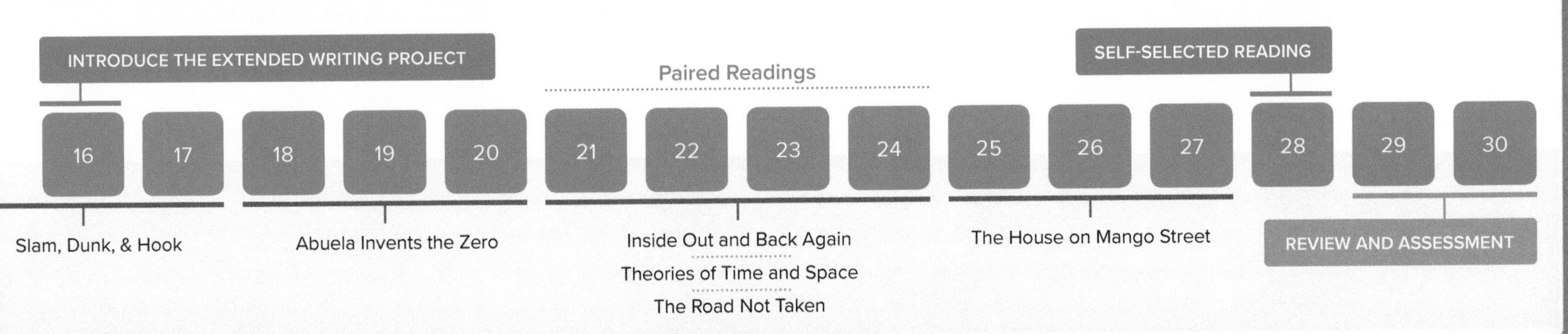

Extended Writing Project and Grammar

Pacing Guide

In the second half of the unit, students continue exploring texts that address the unit's Essential Question and begin crafting a longer composition to share their own ideas about the Essential Question in the Extended Writing Project. The writing project will take your students through the writing process to produce a literary analysis essay.

Extended Writing Project Prompt

What is the power of a metaphor?

Examine the texts from this unit and select three powerful metaphors that deepen our understanding of identity and belonging. Your analysis should explain each metaphor and make an argument about how the metaphor reveals something about each speaker, character, or author.

Days	Extended Writing Project and Grammar	Skill and Standard Instruction	Connect to Mentor Texts
16	**Literary Analysis Writing Process: Plan** p. 540		
17-20	**Literary Analysis Writing Process: Draft** p. 556	• Organizing Argumentative Writing • Thesis Statement • Reasons and Relevant Evidence	• Commencement Address to the Santa Fe Indian School • Curtain Call
21-25	**Literary Analysis Writing Process: Revise** p. 572	• Introductions • Transitions • Style • Conclusions	• I'm Nobody! Who are you? • Commencement Address to the Santa Fe Indian School • So where are you from?
26-28	**Literary Analysis Writing Process: Edit and Publish** p. 580	• Active and Passive Voice • Verb Moods • Consistent Verb Voice and Mood	Additional grammar lessons can be found in the StudySync Skills Library.

Research

The following lessons include opportunities for research:

Blast **Past and Present** Research Links*

First Read **Commencement Address to the Santa Fe Indian School** Independent Research (Beyond)

Close Read **Commencement Address to the Santa Fe Indian School** Text to World (Beyond)

Independent Read **Curtain Call** Independent Research (Beyond)

Blast **Your Six Words** Research Links*

Blast **Poetry in Action** Research Links*

Independent Read **Inside Out and Back Again** Beyond the Book

*See the teacher lesson plan online

Self-Selected Reading Prompt

After reading a self-selected text, students will respond to the following literary analysis prompt:

A great text can make us laugh, cry, or hide underneath our beds. A great text can also illuminate the things in our past that make us who we are today. Sometimes what makes a text memorable is the impact it has on our thoughts and perspectives.

How can a text change the way you think?

Using your self-selected text, write a journal entry in response to this question. In your entry, be sure to explain how a word, phrase, line, or passage changed the way you think about an idea, individual, or event.

Integrated Scaffolding

ELL and Approaching grade-level students receive scaffolds for every lesson, whether in the Thematic, Novel Study or ELL Resources sections of the unit. Specific scaffolds are intentionally designed to support the needs of English Language Learners and Approaching grade-level students in the ELA classroom. Other scaffolds exist as part of the many standard features in the StudySync digital platform and can be strategically utilized to support students' comprehension and engagement.

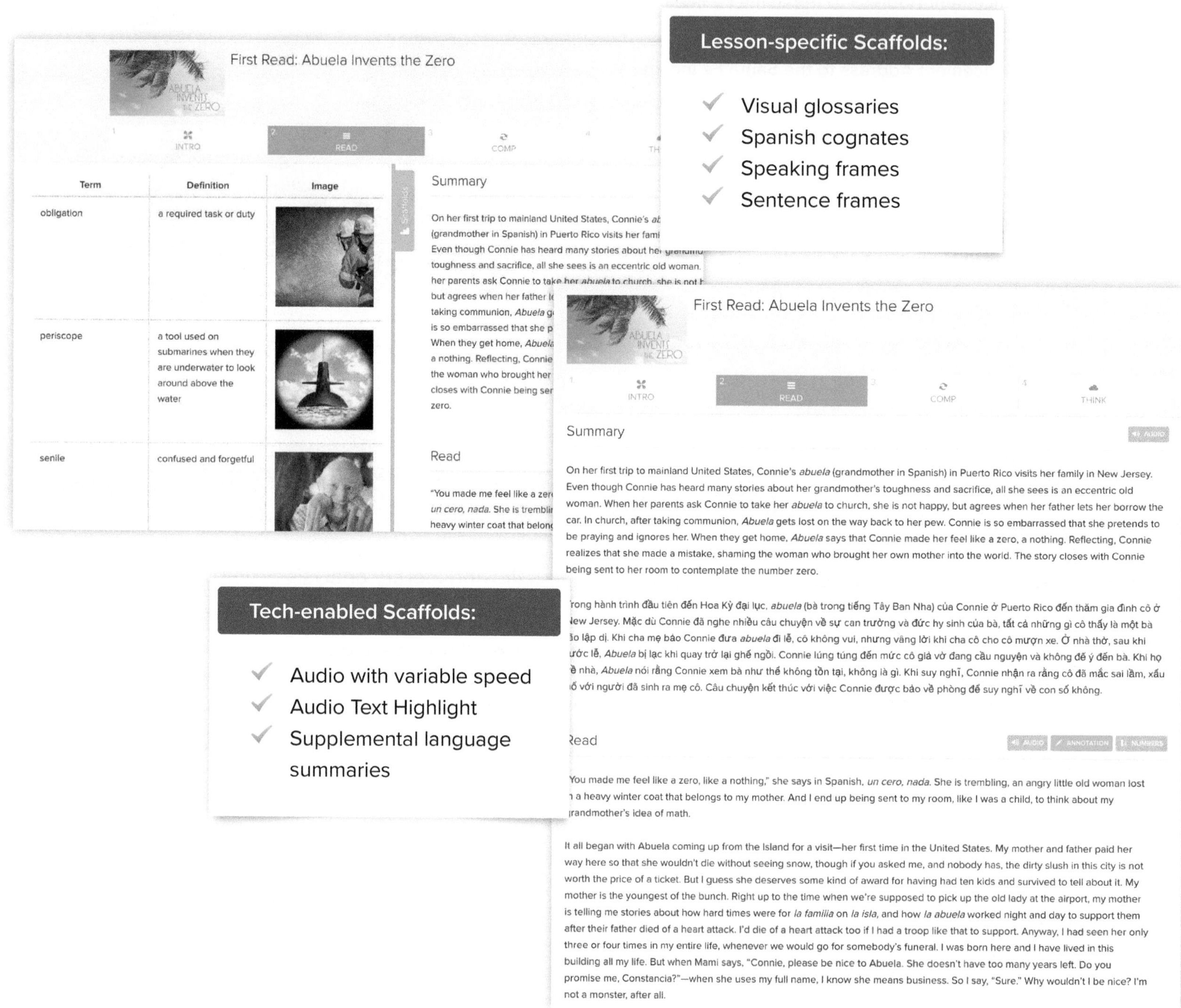

English Language Learner Resources

Both Thematic and Novel Study units include English Language Learner resources designed to match the thematic focus, text structures, and writing form of the unit. ELL resources include two leveled texts and an extended oral project.

ELL Texts	Differentiated Text Levels	Skill and Standard Instruction
	BEGINNING 270L | 259 words INTERMEDIATE 510L | 357 words ADVANCED 590L | 443 words ADVANCED HIGH 710L | 543 words Use this text in place of or as an extension to *The Outsiders*.	• Sight Vocabulary and High-Frequency Words • Demonstrating Listening Comprehension • Analyzing Expressions • Sharing Information • Spelling Patterns and Rules
	BEGINNING 400L | 349 words INTERMEDIATE 590L | 406 words ADVANCED 780L | 504 words ADVANCED HIGH 760L | 578 words Use this text in place of or as an extension to "Abuela Invents the Zero."	• Classroom Vocabulary • Generating Questions • Language Structures • Drawing Inferences and Conclusions • Verb Tenses
	In this Extended Oral Project, students will write debate points and participate in a debate. This may be assigned in place of this unit's EWP.	• Acquiring Vocabulary • Connecting Words

Focus on English Language Proficiency Levels

ADVANCED HIGH
ADVANCED
INTERMEDIATE
BEGINNING

ELL Resources provide targeted support for four levels of proficiency: Beginning, Intermediate, Advanced, and Advanced High. Instruction and scaffolds, as well as the texts themselves, are differentiated based on these levels.

Additional differentiated scaffolds include visual glossaries, speaking and writing frames, and suggested grouping for peer and teacher support. Lessons also include suggested extension activities to challenge Advanced and Advanced High students as they progress through the year.

Assessment

DAYS 29-30

Assessment in StudySync is built upon a recursive cycle that includes assessment, instruction, and review. Screening, placement, and benchmark assessments help teachers establish baselines and determine scaffold needs. Throughout the course of instruction, teachers regularly assess student progress using formative and summative measures, and use the individualized data from those assessments to guide choices about instruction, review, remediation, and enrichment to bring all students to standards mastery and College and Career Readiness.

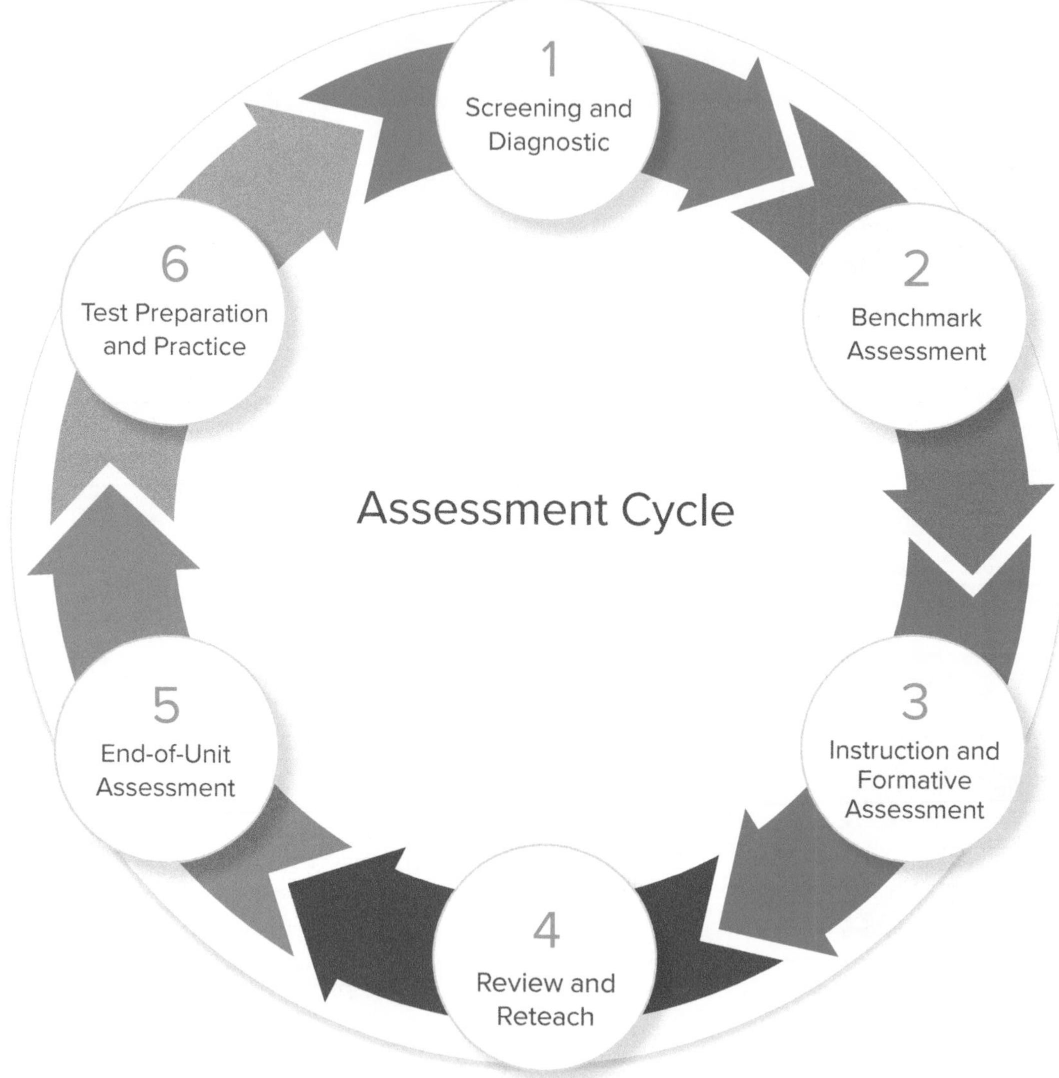

What's Next?

Assessment results can be viewed by item, standard, and skill to monitor mastery and make decisions for upcoming instruction.

- ✓ Reteach skills that students have not yet mastered, using Spotlight Skills or the Test Preparation and Practice book.
- ✓ Revise your teaching plan to provide more or less explicit instruction into a skill or text, using Beyond the Book activities for enrichment.
- ✓ Regroup students and levels of scaffolding based on standards progress.

Review

Spotlight Skills Review

A review day before the end-of-unit assessment gives you an opportunity to review difficult concepts with students using Spotlight Skills lessons. Spotlight Skills are targeted lessons that provide you resources to reteach or remediate without assigning additional readings. Every Core ELA Skill lesson has a corresponding Spotlight Skill lesson. Spotlight Skills can be assigned at any point in the year, but the end of each unit provides a natural moment to pause, review data collected throughout the unit, and reteach skills students have not yet mastered.

Progress Monitoring

The Progress Monitoring charts that appear before every text in this unit identify standards and associated Spotlight Skills. On review day, you may want to give preference to reteaching skills that are not revisited in later units. You can see where Skills are covered again in the Opportunities to Reteach column.

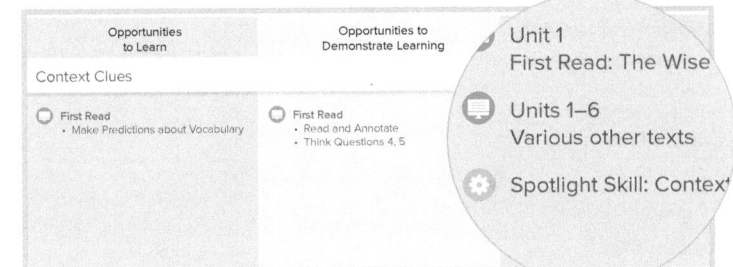

StudySync Gradebook

As students submit assignments on StudySync, their mastery of skills and standards is tracked via the gradebook. The gradebook can be sorted and viewed in a variety of ways. Sorting by assignment shows overall student performance, while sorting by standards or by Skill lessons displays student progress toward mastery goals.

Skills Library

Spotlight Skills are located in the Skills section of the StudySync Library. You can assign Spotlight Skills to individual students or groups of students. Search tools allow you to search by Skill type or name.

End-of-Unit Assessment

Assessed Reading Skills

- Allusion
- Arguments and Claims
- Central or Main Idea
- Character
- Figurative Language
- Plot
- Poetic Elements and Structure
- Summarizing
- Textual Evidence
- Theme

Assessed Revising, Editing, and Writing Skills

- Active and Passive Voice
- Conclusions
- Consistent Verb Voice and Mood
- Introductions
- Organizing Argumentative Writing
- Reasons and Relevant Evidence
- Style
- Thesis Statement
- Transitions
- Verb Moods

Unit Preview

Introduce the Unit

As a class, watch the unit preview and discuss the questions below.

- What two words would you use to describe this video?
- What key words or images from the video do you think will be most important to this unit?

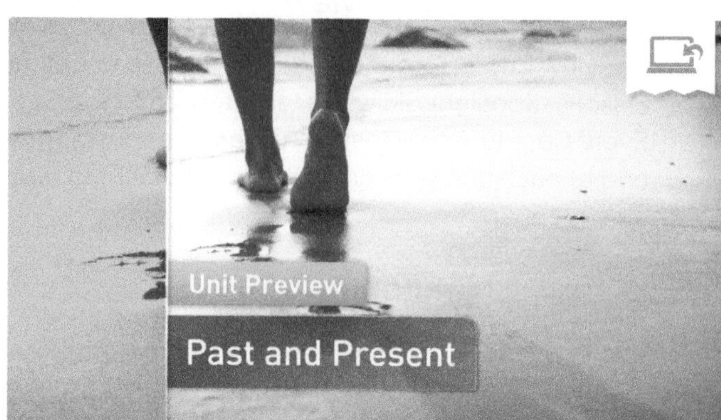

Instructional Path

Big Idea Blast

Objectives: After exploring background information and research links about a topic, students will respond to a question with a 140-character response.

DIGITAL ONLY

Skill: Recognize Genre

Objectives: After learning about the genre of poetry, students will be able to identify and describe characteristics of poetry.

DIGITAL ONLY

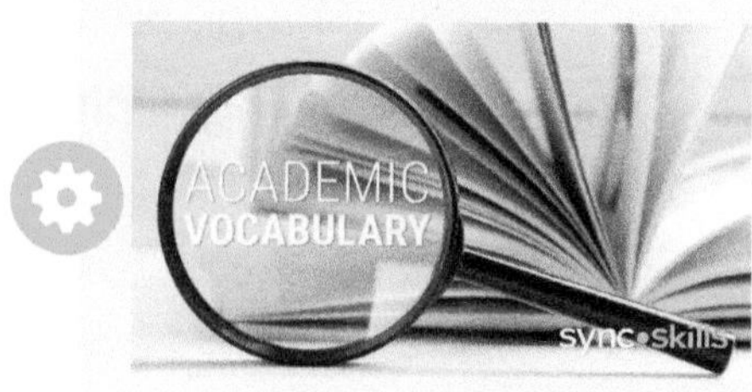

Skill: Academic Vocabulary

Objectives: After learning the meanings of ten academic vocabulary words, students will be able to recognize and use them in a variety of contexts.

DIGITAL ONLY

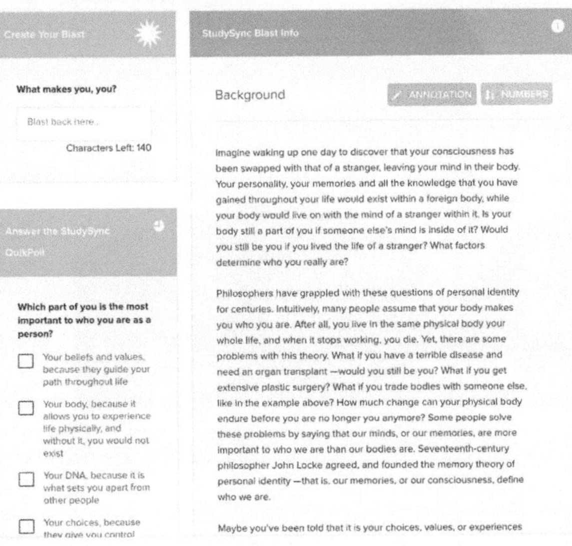

Blast: Past and Present

What makes you, you?

TEXT TALK

What defines a person according to John Locke's theory?

Memories or consciousness define a person.

What defines a person according to Valerie Jarrett?

Jarrett says a person's experiences make them who they are.

How do people change over the course of their life?

Cells die and are replaced; people develop different values and beliefs; people like different foods, etc.

Create Your Own Blast

SCAFFOLDS

Ask students to write a 140-character Blast after they complete the QuikPoll.

Use the scaffolds below to differentiate instruction for your ELL English Language Learners.

ELL **BEGINNING** Write a response using the word bank to complete the sentence frame.

INTERMEDIATE Write a response using the sentence frame.

ADVANCED, ADVANCED HIGH Write a response using the sentence starter.

BEGINNING	BEGINNING / INTERMEDIATE	ADVANCED, ADVANCED HIGH
Word Bank	**Sentence Frame**	**Sentence Starter**
experiences, memories, personality, body, beliefs, values	What makes you, you is your ____ and ____.	• What makes you, you is . . .

Skill: Recognize Genre

Introduce the Genre: Fiction

Watch the Concept Definitions video  and read the following definition with your students.

Fiction is writing about invented people, places, and events. It includes both long and short written works. **Novels** are long works of fiction. **Short stories,** myths, and folktales are examples of short works of fiction. Short fiction focuses on a small number of events or on just one event. You can usually read a short work of fiction in a single sitting. Short works contain the same elements as do longer works of fiction. These elements include character, plot, setting, point of view, and theme.

In addition, there are many different **literary genres,** or specific categories, of fiction writing. Examples of literary genres include realistic fiction, adventure stories, historical fiction, mysteries, humor, myths, fantasy, and science fiction. Each literary genre has certain characteristics that define the content of the writing.

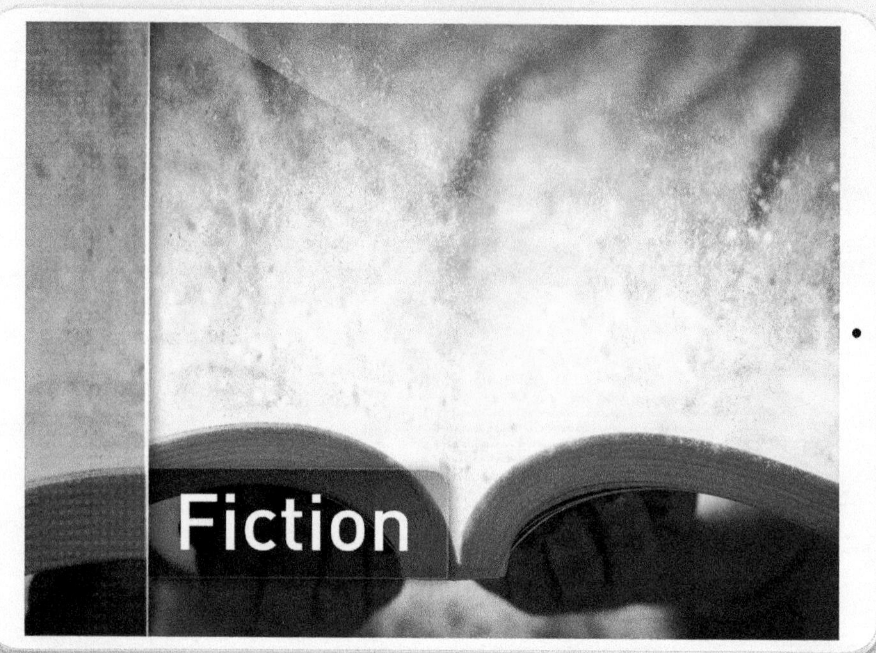

TURN AND TALK

1. How can an author create an emotion in a poem?
2. What are some poems you've read with a specific emotion?

SPEAKING FRAMES

- A poet can use a ____ to create emotion.
- One poem I have read is "____." It had the emotion of ____.

Your Turn

Ask students to complete the Your Turn activity.

Examples from Poems	Poetic Device
She sells sea shells by the sea shore.	sound device
The fall leaves were like broken glass beneath his feet	imagery
What if you had to go to the school dance alone?	line break
Once upon a dreary day a boat left port to sail the bay	rhyme scheme

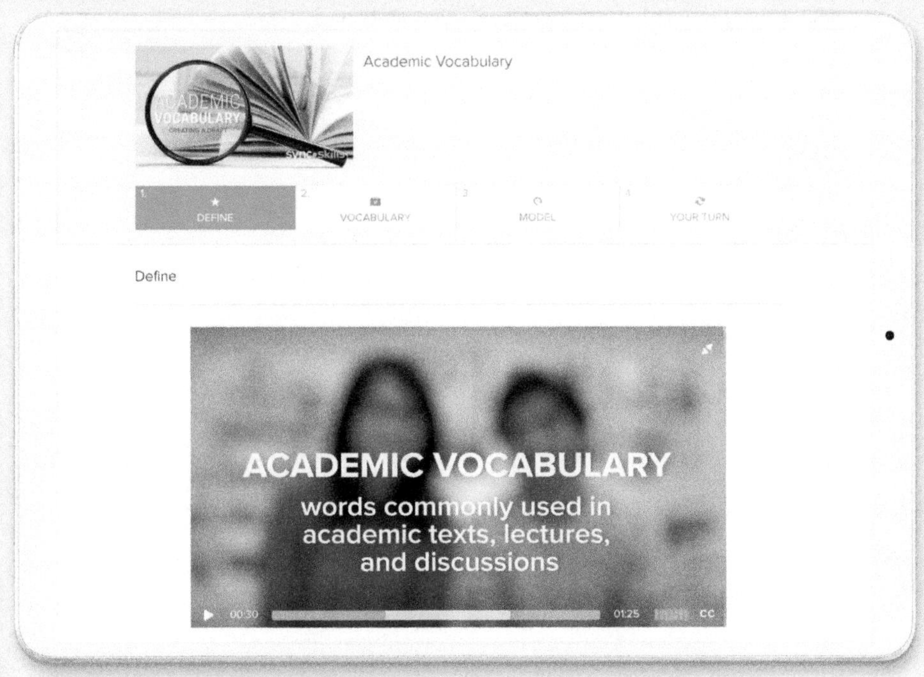

Your Turn

Ask students to complete the Your Turn activities.

Your Turn 1

Original Word	Change	Affix	Related Word
communicate	Change the word into a noun.	-ion	communication
contrast	Change the word into an adjective.	-ing	contrasting
debate	Change the word into an adjective.	-able	debatable
obvious	Change the word into an adverb.	-ly	obviously
option	Change the word into an adjective.	-al	optional

Your Turn 2

QUESTION 1: B **QUESTION 2:** C **QUESTION 3:** A **QUESTION 4:** C **QUESTION 5:** C

Your Turn 3

See digital teacher's edition for complete sample activity.

Skill: Academic Vocabulary

Introduce the Terms

attitude / la actitud ***noun*** a state involving beliefs and feelings that causes a person to think or act in a certain way COGNATE

circumstance / la circunstancia ***noun*** a condition that influences some event or activity

communicate / comunicar ***verb*** to express thoughts or feelings COGNATE

constrain / restringir ***verb*** to hold back

contrast / contrastar ***verb*** to explain how two or more things are different COGNATE

debate / el debate ***noun*** a discussion in which reasons are advanced for and against some proposal COGNATE

obvious / obvio/a ***adjective*** easily perceived by the senses or grasped by the mind COGNATE

option / la opción ***noun*** one of a number of things from which only one can be chosen COGNATE

overall / total ***adjective*** general and including everything

professional / profesional ***adjective*** having or showing the skill and attitude appropriate to a professional person COGNATE

Practice Using Vocabulary

Divide students into pairs or small groups. Assign each group a word from the list and prompt them to act out a short scene that demonstrates the meaning of their word. Then, have groups take turns performing their scene for the class.

I'm Nobody! Who are you?

POETRY

Emily Dickinson

1891

Introduction

Emily Dickinson (1830–1886), who barely left her family's house and never married, published only a handful of poems during her lifetime. After her death, hundreds more were found stacked under her bed. Today they are considered to be among the best and most influential poems ever written. In this poem, "I'm Nobody! Who are you?" Dickinson explains in a few short phrases the difference between an identity lived privately and one lived true to oneself—and the circus of life in the public eye.

In this poem, the speaker celebrates living a private life. She asks if the reader is a nobody like she is. If so, she warns the reader not to tell anyone. In the second stanza, the speaker muses about how dull life would be to be known, to be a somebody. The speaker thinks that having to say her name all the time would be exhausting.

 Proficiency-leveled summaries and summaries in multiple languages are available digitally.

 Audio and audio text highlighting are available with this text.

CONNECT TO ESSENTIAL QUESTION

What makes you, you?

In "I'm Nobody! Who are you?" by Emily Dickinson, privacy and personal identity are examined through lyric poetry. Although it's a short poem, it leaves a lasting effect on the reader, who is left questioning, "What makes you, you?"

Access Complex Text

LEXILE: N/A WORD COUNT: 52

The following areas may be challenging for students, particularly ELL English Language Learners and A Approaching grade-level learners.

Genre	Specific Vocabulary	Connection of Ideas
• Dickinson often ignored rules of poetry, rhyme, grammar, and punctuation. • Point out that while the second stanza of this poem uses a conventional *abcb* rhyme scheme, the first stanza uses half-rhyme (*too*, *know*).	• The definitions of *Nobody* (someone who is not important) and *Somebody* (someone who is important) as used in the poem may need to be explained.	• The images in Dickinson's poems are often very ordinary. They reflect the simplicity of the everyday objects in her private world. However, she connects them via metaphor to unconventional or intense ideas. • The poem uses mostly simple one- and two-syllable words. This simplicity makes every word important. It also draws attention to longer words, such as *advertise*.

SCAFFOLDS ELL ENGLISH LANGUAGE LEARNERS  APPROACHING GRADE LEVEL  BEYOND GRADE LEVEL

These icons identify differentiation strategies and scaffolded support for a variety of students. See the digital lesson plan for additional differentiation strategies and scaffolds.

Instructional Path

The print teacher's edition includes essential point-of-use instruction and planning tools. Complete lesson plans and program documents appear in your digital teacher account.

First Read: I'm Nobody! Who are you?

Objectives: After an initial reading and discussion of the poem, students will be able to generate questions to analyze and understand the ideas presented in the poem.

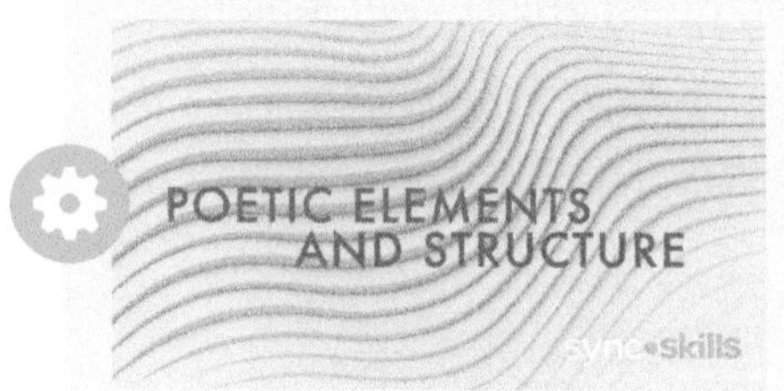

Skill: Poetic Elements and Structure

Objectives: After rereading and discussing a model of close reading, students will be able to analyze the ways in which the structure of a text contributes to its meaning.

Close Read: I'm Nobody! Who are you?

Objectives: After engaging in a close reading and discussion of the text, students will be able to write a short response analyzing how the poetic elements and structure contribute to the poem's meaning.

Progress Monitoring

Opportunities to Learn	Opportunities to Demonstrate Learning	Opportunities to Reteach
Poetic Elements and Structure		
Skill: Poetic Elements and Structure	Skill: Poetic Elements and Structure • Your Turn Close Read • Skills Focus • Write	Unit 2 Skill: Poetic Elements and Structure - Slam, Dunk, & Hook Unit 2 Skill: Poetic Elements and Structure - The Road Not Taken Spotlight Skill: Poetic Elements and Structure

First Read

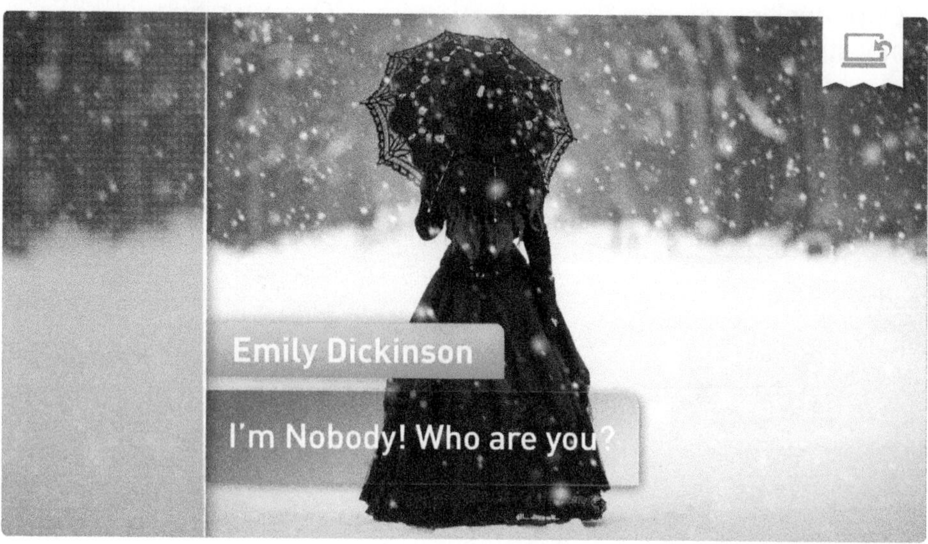

Introduce the Text

As a class, watch the video preview and have students read the introduction in pairs to make connections to the video preview.

To activate prior knowledge and experiences, ask students:

- What other images could you imagine using in this video?
- What kind of poem are you about to read? How can you tell?

SPEAKING FRAMES

- The ____ in the video makes me think ____.
- The video shows ____. This makes me wonder ____.
- I think the text will ____. I think this because ____.
- I predict that there will be ____. I believe this because ____.

Entry Point

As students prepare to read "I'm Nobody! Who are you?" share the following information with them to provide context.

- ✓ Emily Dickinson (1830–1886) was not a famous poet during her lifetime, and she chose to spend most of her time at home in Amherst, Massachusetts. However, she was an avid reader and frequently wrote to acquaintances.
- ✓ During Dickinson's lifetime, only about a dozen of her poems were published. After her death in 1886, however, Dickinson's younger sister found her full collection of nearly 1,800 poems.
- ✓ The first volume of Dickinson's work was published in 1899, and the final volume of her work was published in 1955.

"I'm Nobody! Who are you? Are you – Nobody – too?"

I'm Nobody! Who are you?
Are you – Nobody – too?
Then there's a pair of us!
Don't tell! they'd **advertise** – you know!

How **dreary** – to be – Somebody!
How **public** – like a Frog –
To tell one's name – the **livelong** June –
To an admiring **Bog!**

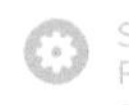

Skill: Poetic Elements and Structure

Lines one and two rhyme, and the fourth line almost rhymes with them. For meter, the first line has 7 syllables, the next two lines have 6, the last one 8.

This stanza has irregular rhyme and meter. It begins with a rhyme scheme and then breaks out of it.

SELECTION VOCABULARY

advertise / promocionar ***verb*** to promote or draw attention to something

dreary / deprimente ***adjective*** depressing, literally or figuratively dark

- What does the word *dreary* describe?
- In this poem, how does the word *dreary* relate to be "Somebody"?

Analyze Vocabulary Using Context Clues

In line 4, focus on the use of the word *advertise*. Point out these context clues:

1. First, I notice that the speaker says "Don't tell!" earlier in the line. It's like she wants to keep a secret.
2. Based on this, I can guess that *advertise* might mean the opposite of keeping a secret. I think *advertise* means "telling a lot of people about something."
3. I read the line again with this meaning in mind. The speaker asks the reader not to "tell" others, because she wants to prevent someone else from telling a lot of people about her.

CHECK FOR SUCCESS

If students are unable to make predictions, revisit the checklist section of the Grade 8 Context Clues lesson with the class. After revisiting, guide students as they make predictions about the next bold word in the text in line 5 using the following routine:

- Is the word a noun, a verb, an adjective, or an adverb?
- What does the word *dreary* describe?
- In this poem, how does the word *dreary* relate to being "Somebody"?

Poetic Elements and Structure

What does the reader notice about Dickinson's rhyme scheme and meter?

Neither one is regular, and the reader notes that this must be deliberate.

TEXT TALK

How does the speaker identify herself?

See line 1: She says "I'm Nobody."

What relationship between the speaker and reader is suggested by the word *pair*?

See lines 3 and 4: They're alike and are apart from the rest of the world.

What image do you create in your mind when you read the word *Somebody*?

Answers will vary.

How does the speaker describe being Somebody?

See lines 5 and 6: She thinks it is "dreary" and "public."

What image do you create in your mind when you read the word *bog*?

Answers will vary.

According to the speaker, how is the frog "public," and is this viewed as a positive trait? Explain.

Answers will vary.

Skills Focus

QUESTION 1: Poetic Elements and Structure

Lines 1–8: Only two of the four lines rhyme in each stanza. In lines 1–4, the first and second lines rhyme, and they are both questions that open conversation with the reader.

In lines 5–8, the second and fourth lines rhyme because they end with *Frog* and *Bog*. Those words end with consonants that cut the lines short, and the words sound humorous together. It makes it hard to take "Somebody" seriously.

QUESTION 2: Theme

Line 5: In this poem, the speaker conveys the theme that a private life is better than a public life. This line helps develop that theme because the word *dreary* means "gloomy and unpleasant." So the speaker is saying that it must be unpleasant to be someone who is widely known.

QUESTION 3: Character

Lines 1–8: This poem includes four characters: the speaker, the reader, "Somebody," and a frog. The speaker declares that she is "Nobody," which means that she isn't widely known. She also assumes that the reader is a "Nobody."

In her mind, "Somebody" is a famous person, and she compares his or her life to the life of a frog that wastes a summer month repeating its name to a bog.

QUESTION 4: Connect to Essential Question

Lines 1–8: The first stanza includes the word "you" and the speaker asks the reader a question. It feels conversational and interesting because the speaker and reader can connect.

In contrast, the second stanza does not include the word "you" or any questions. Instead, the speaker compares "Somebody" with the "Frog."

SELECTION VOCABULARY

public / público/a ***adjective*** openly known or accessible to the general population COGNATE

- What nearby words or phrases are context clues for *public*?
- Does the speaker think *public* is positive or negative?

livelong / todo el día ***adjective*** complete, whole, entire

- What word parts do you see in *livelong*?
- How do the word parts help you understand the meaning of *livelong*?

bog / el pantano ***noun*** marsh; muddy, spongy ground

- What nearby words or phrases are context clues for *bog*?
- Does *bog* have a positive or negative connotation?

Reading Comprehension OPTIONAL

Have students complete the digital reading comprehension questions ✓ when they finish reading.

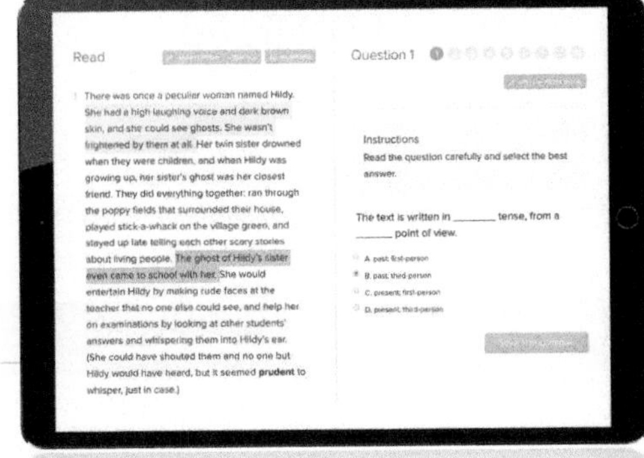

ANSWER KEY

QUESTION 1: A
QUESTION 2: D
QUESTION 3: B
QUESTION 4: D

QUESTION 5:
See chart below.

Definition	Word
dark or gloomy	dreary
muddy or swampy ground	bog
to do something to get other people's attention	advertise
exposed to open view	public
entire or whole	livelong

Connect and Extend OPTIONAL

CONNECT TO EXTENDED WRITING PROJECT

Students can use Emily Dickinson's poem "I'm Nobody! Who are you?" as a resource when writing their literary analyses. Have them analyze and reflect on the poet's use of figurative language.

BEYOND THE BOOK

Writing: Real Identity vs. Social Media Identity

In this poem, Emily Dickinson celebrates a private identity. Today, many people share a public identity on social media that may or may not match their private identity.

Ask students to reflect on the following questions in writing:

- How would you describe your "true" identity?
- What do you value?
- Who do you enjoy spending time with?
- What is your day-to-day life like? Are you generally happy/sad/lonely/energized?

Next, have students compare their written reflections with what they've posted on social media. (Have students without social media accounts compare their reflections to what they generally share with others each day.)

Then give them time to discuss the following questions with a small group of peers.

- Do the images and updates posted to your social media accounts (or shared with others) accurately reflect you?
- Why might people create social media profiles that are strikingly different from their "real" lives and identities?
- How do you feel after scrolling through other people's social media accounts? Why do you think you feel this way?

Think Questions

Circulate as students answer Think Questions independently. Scaffolds for these questions are shown on the opposite page.

QUESTION 1: Textual Evidence

The speaker is using the second-person pronoun *you* to talk directly to the reader. She uses the pronoun *they* to refer to people who are different from you and her. I know this because she says that you and she are "a pair."

QUESTION 2: Textual Evidence

The speaker says, "How dreary – to be – Somebody!" This description has negative connotations and shows that the speaker thinks that being "Somebody" is overrated. She also thinks being "Somebody" is too "public."

QUESTION 3: Textual Evidence

The speaker compares living in "public" to being a frog that repeats its own name over and over to the empty "admiring bog" around it. Based on this comparison, I can infer that the speaker thinks there is no value in being well known.

QUESTION 4: Context Clues

The speaker contrasts "Don't tell!" with *advertise*, so *advertise* means "to tell a lot of people about something."

QUESTION 5: Context Clues

The frog is saying its own name aloud to the land that surrounds it. Based on this context, I can guess that *bog* refers to "wet, swampy land" where the frog lives. When I check a dictionary, I see that I am right.

I'm Nobody!
Who are you?

First Read

Read "I'm Nobody! Who are you?" After you read, complete the Think Questions below.

THINK QUESTIONS

1. To whom is the speaker speaking in the first stanza? In other words, who is "you" and who are "they"? Cite textual evidence from the selection to support your answer.
2. The speaker doesn't want to be a "Somebody." Explain why she believes that being a "Somebody" is overrated. Cite specific lines in your answer.
3. In line 6, Dickinson uses a rather unusual figure of speech, or comparison, to describe what being "public" is like. Explain this comparison in line 6 in your own words. What do you think the speaker means in this line?
4. Which context clues helped you figure out the meaning of the word **advertise** in line 4? Write your own definition of *advertise* and explain how you figured out the meaning of the word.
5. Based on context clues, can you guess the definition of the word **bog** in line 8? Write your own definition of *bog* here, identifying any clues that helped you define it. Once you have written your own definition, check a print or online dictionary to verify its meaning.

SCAFFOLDS

Think Questions

Use the scaffolds below to differentiate instruction for your ELL English Language Learners and A Approaching grade-level learners.

ELL **BEGINNING** Write a response using the word bank and sentence frames.

INTERMEDIATE Write a response using the sentence frames.

ADVANCED, ADVANCED HIGH Write a response using the Text-Dependent Question Guide.

A **APPROACHING** Write a response using the Text-Dependent Question Guide.

BEGINNING	INTERMEDIATE	APPROACHING / ADVANCED, ADVANCED HIGH
Word Bank	**Sentence Frames**	**Text-Dependent Question Guide**
name wet tell value frog unlike pair dreary dictionary public people negative surrounds reader	The speaker uses *you* to refer directly to the ____. The speaker uses *they* to refer to people who are ____ herself. I know this because the speaker says that she and *you* are a ____, so "they" must mean people who are different.	1. • What does the speaker mean by "you"? • What does the speaker mean by "they"? • How do you know?
	In line 5, the speaker says it is ____ to be "Somebody." She thinks being "Somebody" is overrated because it is too ____. I know that the speaker does not want to be "Somebody" because she describes it in a ____ way.	2. • Why doesn't the speaker want to be "Somebody"? • Why does the speaker think that being "Somebody" is overrated, or not so great? • What details show the speaker's opinions?
	Dickinson compares living a public life to being a ____. The frog repeats its own ____ over and over again to the land around it. I think the speaker means that being well known has no ____.	3. • What two things are being compared using the word *like*? • What does the frog tell over and over again? To whom is it speaking? • What does this tell you about the speaker's opinion of being well known to the public?
	The speaker tells the reader, "Don't ____!" This gives me a clue that *advertise* means to tell a lot of ____ about something.	4. • Read line 4: "Don't tell! they'd **advertise** – you know!" • What doesn't the speaker want the reader to do? • What does that tell me about the meaning of the word *advertise*?
	The frog is saying its own name aloud to the area that ____ it. This gives me a clue that *bog* refers to the ____ land where the frog lives. I can look in a ____ to check the word's meaning.	5. • Read line 7: "To an admiring **Bog!**" • What is the frog doing in this stanza? • What does that tell me about the meaning of the word *bog*?

Skill: Poetic Elements and Structure

Introduce the Skill

Watch the Concept Definition video and read the following definition with your students.

Poetic structure describes the organization of words and lines in a poem as well as its rhyme scheme and meter. Poems consist of words that are divided into **lines**. A group of lines is called a **stanza**.

Other elements of poetry that contribute to structure include rhyme and rhythm. **Rhyme** is the repetition of the same or similar vowel sounds. The **rhyme scheme** of a poem is the pattern formed by the rhyming words at the end of lines. **Rhythm** is the pattern of unstressed and stressed syllables in a line of poetry. A regular pattern is called **meter,** and it gives a line of poetry a predictable rhythm.

The poet's choice of **poetic form**, or arrangement and style of a poem, will help determine the structure. Common forms include haiku, limerick, and sonnet, each with its own rules. Poetry without a consistent meter, rhyme, or stanza length is called **open form**.

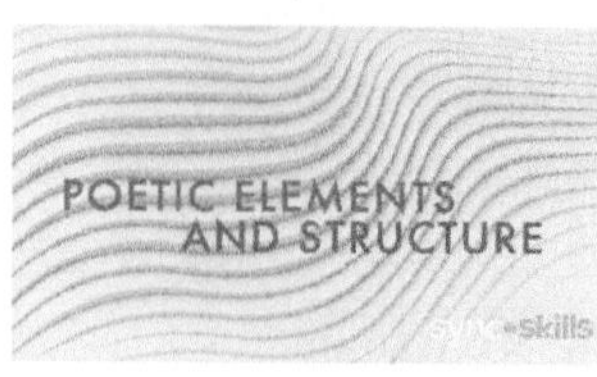

Skill: Poetic Elements and Structure

Use the Checklist to analyze Poetic Elements and Structure in "I'm Nobody! Who are you?" Refer to the sample student annotations about Poetic Elements and Structure in the text.

••• CHECKLIST FOR POETIC ELEMENTS AND STRUCTURE

In order to determine how to analyze the ways in which the structure of a text contributes to its meaning, look for the following:

- ✓ the organization of words and lines
- ✓ the relationships between words, lines, or stanzas
- ✓ the rhyme, rhythm, and meter, if present
- ✓ ways the poet uses punctuation or capitalization and how it affects the rhythm or meaning of the poem
- ✓ ways that the poem's structure connects to the poem's meaning

To analyze how poetic elements and structure contribute to a poem's meaning and style, consider the following questions:

- ✓ Do any of the words, lines, or stanzas have important similarities?
- ✓ Do any of the words, lines, or stanzas have important differences?
- ✓ Does this poem's structure relate to any of its themes?
- ✓ Does this poem's structure affect the overall meaning of the poem?

TURN AND TALK

- How do you identify poetry when you see it?
- Do you like poems with or without a clear structure, rhyme scheme, and meter? Why?

SPEAKING FRAMES

- I can identify a poem by ____.
- I like poems that (do / do not) have a (clear structure / rhyme scheme / meter).
- I like these kinds of poems because ____.

SKILL VOCABULARY

poetic structure / la estructura poética *noun* the organization of words and lines as well as the rhyme and meter of a poem COGNATE

line / el verso *noun* a string of words in a poem, not necessarily a full sentence or phrase

stanza / la estrofa *noun* the basic unit of a poem, made up of a series of lines

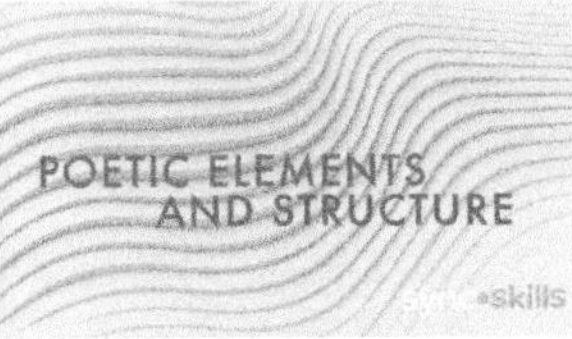

Skill: Poetic Elements and Structure

Reread lines 5–8 of "I'm Nobody! Who are you?" Then, using the Checklist on the previous page, answer the multiple-choice questions below.

YOUR TURN

1. The word *Somebody* is capitalized in the poem because—
   - A. it is a proper pronoun.
   - B. it is the proper name of a character in the poem.
   - C. it conveys an idea of being well known.
   - D. the poet does not know how to capitalize properly.

2. The dashes mainly affect the poem by—
   - A. acting like periods to indicate the end of a thought.
   - B. breaking the flow of language so the poem is easier to read.
   - C. dividing the lines into sections that have the same meter.
   - D. emphasizing the humorous connections Dickinson makes.

SKILL VOCABULARY

meter / la métrica ***noun*** a regular pattern of unstressed and stressed syllables in a line of poetry

rhyme / la rima ***noun*** the repetition of the same or similar sounds in a poem

open form / la forma abierta ***noun*** poetic form without consistent meter, rhyme, or stanza length

Your Turn

Ask students to complete the Your Turn activity.

QUESTION 1

A. Incorrect. *Somebody* is not a proper pronoun.

B. Incorrect. There is nothing to suggest that *Somebody* is an actual person.

C. Correct. The capitalized *Somebody* suggests an idea or concept of being known out in public.

D. Incorrect. Any choice made by the poet would be deliberate.

QUESTION 2

A. Incorrect. The dashes interrupt, but they do not indicate the end of a thought.

B. Incorrect. The dashes do not make the poem easier or more difficult to read.

C. Incorrect. The words and phrases on either side of the dashes do not have the same meter.

D. Correct. The dashes draw the reader's attention to Dickinson's humorous comparison that being "Somebody" is like being a frog.

SkillsTV

Project the SkillsTV episode and pause at the following times to prompt discussion:

0:30 What can readers look for to begin understanding how a poem is structured?

2:00 What do the students notice about Dickinson's use of capitalization? How does this surprise them?

2:48 What do the students notice about Dickinson's punctuation? What does this discussion of structure reveal for them?

Close Read

Skills Focus

QUESTION 1: Poetic Elements and Structure

See lines 1–8.

QUESTION 2: Theme

See line 5.

QUESTION 3: Character

See lines 1–8.

QUESTION 4: Connect to Essential Question

See lines 1–8.

CHECK FOR SUCCESS

If students struggle to respond to Skills Focus question 1, ask them the following questions:

- How is the structure of the lines in the first stanza similar and different to the structure of the lines in the second stanza?
- How is the rhyme scheme in the first stanza similar and different to the rhyme scheme in the second stanza?

Have students transition to read and annotate independently once they have successfully completed the first Skills Focus prompt.

Close Read

Reread "I'm Nobody! Who are you?" As you reread, complete the Skills Focus questions below. Then us your answers and annotations from the questions to help you complete the Write activity.

SKILLS FOCUS

1. Compare the line structure and rhyme scheme in the first stanza (lines 1–4) to the second stanza (lines 5–8).
2. Choose a line from the poem that shows the theme. Explain how or why this line is the best choice for the theme you are discussing.
3. Choose specific words from the poem that mention characters. Also be sure to state what these characters do and how they are referenced in the poem.
4. What is something unique about this poem Identify specific words and phrases that make th poem stand out. Also discuss what the speake does to make her perspective different fro others'.

WRITE

POEM: Write a poem in which the speaker declares who he or she is: "I'm ____." Structure your poem to include rhyme, rhythm, meter, and at least two stanzas. The poetic elements and structure should help show the speaker's attitude toward the topic and convey a theme that is important to you.

Writer's Notebook

Connect to Essential Question: Give students time to reflect on how "I'm Nobody! Who are you?" connects to the unit's essential question "What makes you, you?" by freewriting in their Writer's Notebooks.

Beginning & Intermediate

Read aloud the unit's essential question: "What makes you, you?" Encourage students to draw their connections or allow students to write in their native language. Circulate the room, prompting students for their thoughts as they respond orally or through pantomime.

Advanced & Advanced High

Allow students to share their connections orally in pairs or small groups before freewriting.

SCAFFOLDS

Collaborative Conversation

Break students into collaborative conversation groups to discuss the Close Read prompt. Ask students to use the StudySyncTV episode as a model for their discussion. Remind them to reference their Skills Focus annotations in their discussion.

Write a poem in which the speaker declares who he or she is: "I'm _____." Structure your poem to include rhyme, rhythm, meter, and at least two stanzas. The poetic elements and structure should help show the speaker's attitude toward the topic and convey a theme that is important to you.

Use the scaffolds below to differentiate instruction for your ELL English Language Learners and A Approaching grade-level learners.

ELL **BEGINNING, INTERMEDIATE** Use the discussion guide and speaking frames to facilitate the discussion with support from the teacher.

ADVANCED, ADVANCED HIGH Use the discussion guide and speaking frames to facilitate the discussion in mixed-level groups.

A APPROACHING Use the discussion guide to facilitate the discussion in mixed-level groups.

APPROACHING

ADVANCED, ADVANCED HIGH

BEGINNING, INTERMEDIATE

Discussion Guide	Speaking Frames
1. What is the structure of "I'm Nobody! Who are you?"	• The poem has ____ stanzas of ____ lines. • The poem's structure calls attention to ideas such as ____.
2. How does (rhyme / rhythm / meter) help show the author's attitude toward the topic?	• One example of (rhyme / rhythm / meter) in this poem is ____. • This helps show the author's attitude toward the topic because ____.
3. How does (rhyme / rhythm / meter) help convey a theme in this poem?	• The (rhyme / rhythm / meter) calls attention to key words and phrases such as ____. • This helps develops the theme that ____.

Review Prompt and Rubric

Before students begin writing, review the writing prompt and rubric with the class.

POEM: Write a poem in which the speaker declares who he or she is: "I'm _____." Structure your poem to include rhyme, rhythm, meter, and at least two stanzas. The poetic elements and structure should help show the speaker's attitude toward the topic and convey a theme that is important to you.

PROMPT GUIDE

- What is the speaker's attitude in "I'm Nobody! Who are you?"
- What attitude do you want the speaker in your poem to have?
- What is one theme in "I'm Nobody! Who are you?"
- What theme would you like your poem to convey?
- Which rhyming words can you use in your poem?
- How many beats, or syllables, will your lines have?

Score	Poetic Elements and Structure	Language and Conventions
4	The writer effectively uses poetic elements and structure to compose a poem that is at least two stanzas long. The rhyme, rhythm, and meter clearly help reveal the speaker's attitude toward the topic and contribute to a theme.	The writer demonstrates a consistent command of grammar, punctuation, and usage conventions. Although minor errors may be evident, they do not detract from the fluency or the clarity of the writing.
3	The writer uses poetic elements and structure to compose a poem that is at least two stanzas long. The rhyme, rhythm, and meter help reveal the speaker's attitude toward the topic and contribute to a theme.	The writer demonstrates an adequate command of grammar, punctuation, and usage conventions. Although some errors may be evident, they create few (if any) disruptions in the fluency or clarity of the writing.
2	The writer attempts to use poetic elements and structure to compose a poem that is at least two stanzas long. The writer attempts to use some rhyme, rhythm, and meter to reveal the speaker's attitude and contribute to a theme, but both are difficult to identify.	The writer demonstrates a partial command of grammar, punctuation, and usage conventions. Some distracting errors may be evident, at times creating minor disruptions in the fluency or clarity of the writing.
1	The writer does not successfully use poetic elements and structure to compose a poem that is at least two stanzas long. The poem does not use rhyme, rhythm, or meter to reveal the speaker's attitude or contribute to a theme.	The writer demonstrates little or no command of grammar, punctuation, and usage conventions. Serious and persistent errors create disruptions in the fluency of the writing and sometimes interfere with meaning.
0	The writer does not provide a relevant response to the prompt or does not provide a response at all.	Serious and persistent errors overwhelm the writing and interfere with the meaning of the response as a whole, making the writer's meaning impossible to understand.

Write

SCAFFOLDS

Ask students to complete the writing assignment using textual evidence to support their answers.

Use the scaffolds below to differentiate instruction for your ELL English Language Learners and A Approaching grade-level learners.

ELL **BEGINNING** With the help of the word bank, write a response using paragraph frame 1.

INTERMEDIATE With the help of the word bank, write a response using paragraph frames 1 and 2.

ADVANCED, ADVANCED HIGH Write a response of differentiated length using the sentence starters.

A **APPROACHING** Write a response of differentiated length using the sentence starters.

BEGINNING / INTERMEDIATE	BEGINNING / INTERMEDIATE	INTERMEDIATE	ADVANCED, ADVANCED HIGH / APPROACHING
Word Bank	**Paragraph Frame 1**	**Paragraph Frame 2**	**Sentence Starters**
rhyme scheme theme meter attitude rhythm	In my poem, I will develop a ____, or a message that I want to convey to readers. I will use descriptive words and phrases. They will show the speaker's ____ about a topic. I can also use words that ____ at the end of lines. They will follow a pattern, so my poem will have a clear ____. I also want to surprise readers by changing the ____, or pace of the poem, at the end.	The word I will use to describe my speaker's identity is ____. A descriptive word or phrase that will show this quality is ____. A detail I can include to develop in my poem is ____.	• The speaker in my poem will declare "I'm ____!" • The speaker's attitude toward the topic will be . . . • The theme I want to convey is . . . • I will use rhyme to . . . • I will use rhythm to . . .

Peer Review

Students should submit substantive feedback to two peers using the review instructions below.

- How well does the writer convey the speaker's attitude in the poem?
- Does the poem include rhyme, rhythm, and meter?
- Did the poetic elements and structure contribute to the meaning of the poem?

Rate

Respond to the following with a point rating that reflects your opinion.

	1	2	3	4
Ideas	■	■	■	□
Evidence	■	■	■	■
Language and Conventions	■	■	□	□

Submit

ELL A **SENTENCE FRAMES**

- I think that one theme in this poem is ____ because ____.
- I think that speaker's attitude toward the topic is ____ because ____.
- You (did / did not) include (rhyme / rhythm / meter) because ____.
- The poetic elements and structure (did / did not) contribute to the meaning of the poem because ____.

Commencement Address to the Santa Fe Indian School

INFORMATIONAL TEXT
Michelle Obama
2016

Introduction

The Santa Fe Indian School is a small high school in New Mexico with a graduating class of about a hundred students. So it was much to their surprise when former First Lady Michelle Obama (b. 1964) accepted an invitation to be the school's commencement speaker. In her speech, Mrs. Obama did not shy away from acknowledging the American government's troublesome relationship with the school. The school had been founded in 1890 as an institution of enforced assimilation, during a period when the U.S. government believed the only options in dealing with Native Americans were "to civilize or exterminate them." However, the school would undergo a major transformation in the century that followed, becoming dedicated to preserving the history of its students. Today, the student body represents a multinational demographic incorporating the twenty-two tribal nations of New Mexico. Mrs. Obama spoke to the students about the power of education for her family and celebrated the achievements of the school's seniors, who were nearly all heading to college and had earned over $5 million in scholarships.

Speaking to the graduating class of Santa Fe Indian School, former First Lady Michelle Obama shares how her family faced discrimination during the times of slavery and segregation. She states that their experiences strengthened their commitment to their children's futures. Although her parents never went to college, they did all they could to ensure that she would, which is why she views her college degrees as the fulfillment of her and her family's dreams. She also praises the school's values—respect, integrity, and perseverance—because she learned the same at home. The school is an expression of Native American culture, and Obama encourages students to continue giving back to their communities. To be successful, she advises them to seek help when they are struggling, persevere in the face of obstacles, draw strength from their difficulties, and remember that their culture is a source of pride.

ELL Proficiency-leveled summaries and summaries in multiple languages are available digitally.

Audio and audio text highlighting are available with this text.

CONNECT TO ESSENTIAL QUESTION

What makes you, you?

In a commencement address given at a small Native American high school in New Mexico, former First Lady Michelle Obama explores how her own family and experiences have helped turn her into the woman she is today. Likewise, she encourages the students to remain true to themselves and their values as they move forward.

Access Complex Text

LEXILE: 1280L **WORD COUNT:** 2,826

The following areas may be challenging for students, particularly ELL English Language Learners and A Approaching grade-level learners.

Prior Knowledge	Purpose	Connection of Ideas
• Santa Fe is in New Mexico, a state that contains a significant Native American population and is defined by Native American history, which includes confinement to reservations and an attempt in earlier decades to wipe out Native American culture.	• Commencement addresses traditionally offer a personal take on how to be effective in life. • As First Lady, Michelle Obama speaks in an official capacity. Her support for Native Americans and for their culture carries a special import.	• Obama repeatedly emphasizes the importance of education. Her family endured many setbacks but never gave up on the goal of educating their children. The emphasis on education is appropriate to a commencement speech.

SCAFFOLDS ELL ENGLISH LANGUAGE LEARNERS  A APPROACHING GRADE LEVEL  B BEYOND GRADE LEVEL

These icons identify differentiation strategies and scaffolded support for a variety of students. See the digital lesson plan for additional differentiation strategies and scaffolds.

Instructional Path

The print teacher's edition includes essential point-of-use instruction and planning tools. Complete lesson plans and program documents appear in your digital teacher account.

Skill: Making Inferences

Objectives: After reading and discussing a model, students will be able to make inferences in order to improve reading comprehension.

First Read: Commencement Address to the Santa Fe Indian School

Objectives: After an initial reading and discussion of the speech, students will be able to identify and restate key ideas and details.

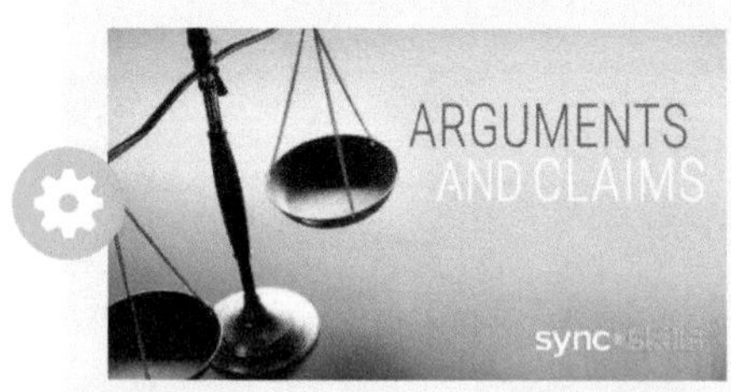

Skill: Arguments and Claims

Objectives: After rereading and discussing a model of close reading, students will be able to delineate and evaluate the argument and specific claims in a text.

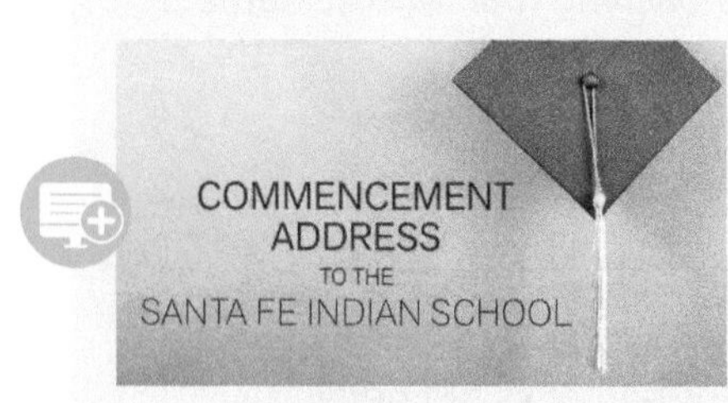

Close Read: Commencement Address to the Santa Fe Indian School

Objectives: After engaging in a close reading and discussion of the text, students will be able to delineate and evaluate the argument and specific claims in a text in a short written response.

Progress Monitoring

Opportunities to Learn	Opportunities to Demonstrate Learning	Opportunities to Reteach
Making Inferences		
Skill: Making Inferences	First Read • Read and Annotate	Spotlight Skill: Making Inferences
Arguments and Claims		
Skill: Arguments and Claims	Skill: Arguments and Claims • Your Turn Close Read • Skills Focus • Collaborative Conversation • Write	Unit 4 Skill: Arguments and Claims - Gaming Communities Unit 4 Skill: Arguments and Claims - Gettysburg Address Spotlight Skill: Arguments and Claims

First Read

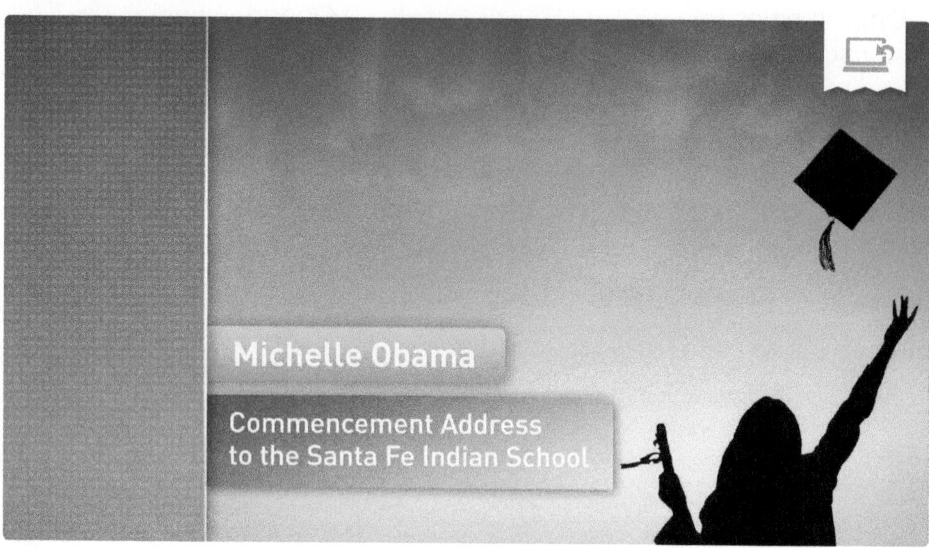

Introduce the Text

As a class, watch the video preview  and have students read the introduction in pairs to make connections to the video preview.

To activate prior knowledge and experiences, ask students:

- What part of the video stood out to you the most?
- What information does the video provide that the introduction does not?

ELL **SENTENCE FRAMES**

- The ____ in the video makes me think ____.
- The video shows ____. This makes me wonder ____.
- I think the text will ____. I think this because ____.
- I predict that there will be ____. I believe this because ____.

Entry Point

As students prepare to read "Commencement Address to the Santa Fe Indian School," share the following information with them to provide context.

- ✓ Michelle Obama was first lady from 2009 to 2017, when her husband, Barack Obama, was president. She was the first African American first lady, and he was the first African American president. Michelle Obama is a graduate of Princeton University and Harvard Law School, and she has worked for causes ranging from support for military families to promoting better school nutrition and physical activity. She has been voted the Most Admired Woman according to a Gallup poll.
- ✓ While commencement addresses are given at both high school and college graduation ceremonies, a celebrity speaker is invited usually only at the college level. The students at the Santa Fe Indian School had asked the White House if either the first lady or the president would be their commencement speaker, and they were surprised when told that Michelle Obama had accepted their invitation.

Commencement Address to the Santa Fe Indian School

"I want to tell you about the people who came before me and how they made me who I am today."

NOTES

1 Please, please, be seated. Good afternoon, everyone. It is beyond an honor and a pleasure to be with you all today.

2 Of course, I want to start by thanking Hanna and Michael for their wonderful introduction. And I want to recognize all of the other outstanding student leaders who have graced us with their words today. I'm so proud of you all.

3 I also want to thank the governors, the tribal leaders, elders, the board of trustees, along with the superintendent and your amazing principal, your teachers and staff. I wish I could meet you all, I wish I could spend a whole week with you. I also want to thank the Tewa dancers who performed for us today—absolutely.

4 And of course, last but not least, to the class of 2016: You all did it! Woo! You're here! You did it! You made it! After so many long afternoons and late nights studying for exams, writing papers; after countless hours preparing to present your senior honors projects to your communities; after all those jalapeño nachos you ate at the EAC—yes, I heard about that—you did it. You're here. You made it. And we are all so very, very proud of you. I love you all so much.

5 And today, I want just to take a moment once again to look around this beautiful auditorium at the people who helped you on your journey—your families and friends, everyone in your school and your communities—all the people who pushed you and poured their love into you and believed in you even when you didn't believe in yourselves sometimes. Today is their day, too, right? So let's, graduates, give them a big, old, loud shout-out and love to our families. Thank you all. Yes!

6 And that's actually where I want to start today—with family, in particular with my own family. I want to tell you about the people who came before me and how they made me who I am today.

7 I am the great-great-granddaughter of Jim Robinson, who was born in South Carolina, lived as a slave, and is likely buried in an unmarked grave on the

Skill: Arguments and Claims

Michelle mentions students' families and friends and the support they offered. Then she makes a statement about how her own family supported her. This claim is part of her argument: how families and friends help us on our journey.

Analyze Vocabulary Using Context Clues

In paragraph 7, focus on the sentence that uses the word *entrepreneur*. Point out these context clues:

1. First, I notice that the word *entrepreneur* is used as a noun in the sentence because the word *an* comes before it.
2. I also see that the phrase "selling newspapers and shoes" is a context clue to the word's meaning.
3. Based on syntax and context clues, I think an entrepreneur is someone who starts their own business and does well.

CHECK FOR SUCCESS

If students are unable to make predictions, revisit the Checklist section of the Grade 8 Context Clues lesson with the class. After revisiting, guide students as they make predictions about the next bold word in the text in paragraph 12 using the following routine:

- Is the word a noun, a verb, an adjective, or an adverb?
- What word part is a clue to the meaning of *infuse*?
- How does the phrase "handed down to me" help you understand the meaning of *infuse*?

Arguments and Claims

How does the reader use the structure of the text to identify a claim?

The reader notices that two statements about family come before the example Obama presents from her own family.

Arguments and Claims

How does the reader delineate Obama's argument?

She notes the sequence of statements that back a claim and then expresses the argument in her own words.

Skills Focus

QUESTION 3: Textual Evidence

Her father was really hard-working, even when he was sick. He sacrificed so his daughter could go to college. I think she wants the students to understand that.

plantation where he worked. I am the great-granddaughter of Fraser Robinson, an illiterate houseboy who taught himself to read and became an **entrepreneur,** selling newspapers and shoes. I am the granddaughter of Fraser Robinson Jr., who left the only life he'd ever known to move his family north, seeking a place where his children's dreams wouldn't be so limited by the color of their skin.

8 And I am the daughter of Fraser Robinson III and Marian Robinson, who raised me and my brother in a tiny apartment on the South Side of Chicago, just upstairs from my elderly great aunt and uncle, who my parents cared for, and just blocks away from our extended family—a host of grandparents and aunts and uncles and cousins who were always in and out of each other's homes and lives, sharing stories and food and talking and laughing for hours.

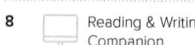

Skill: Arguments and Claims

Michelle gives factual information from her own life to support her argument: how families and friends help us on our journey. She talks about her mother volunteering at school and her father saving money for her college tuition.

9 And while my parents were products of segregated schools, and neither of them had an education past high school, they knew with every bone in their bodies that they wanted their kids to go to college. That was their mission from the day we were born. So my mother volunteered at our school so that she could make sure we were taking our studies seriously. And my father worked as a pump operator at the city water plant, saving every penny for our college tuition. And when my father was diagnosed with Multiple Sclerosis—a disease that affected his muscles and made it hard for him to walk and even dress himself in the morning—I remember he hardly ever missed a day of work, no matter how sick he was, no matter how much pain he was in.

10 And let me tell you, I will never forget the look of pride on his face and on my mom's face as I walked across the stage at Princeton University, and three years later at Harvard Law School to accept my diplomas—degrees that have given me opportunities that my parents never could have dreamed of for themselves.

11 So, graduates, this is my story. And I'm sharing this with you because when I heard that—when you were first brainstorming about who to invite to your commencement and someone suggested me or my husband, some of you thought that that was an impossible dream, that it just wasn't realistic to think that people like us would ever visit a school like yours. Well, today, I want you to know that there is nowhere I would rather be than right here with all of you.

12 Because while I might have grown up across the country, and while my journey may be a bit different than yours, when I learned about all of you, it was clear to me that our stories are connected, and that your values—the values that **infuse** this school—are the very same values that my parents handed down to me.

TEXT TALK

What was Michelle Obama's parents' "mission"?

See paragraph 9: They wanted their children to go to college, which was something they had been unable to do.

Why does Obama believe she and the students at the school are connected?

See paragraph 12: They have similar values, including what her parents handed down to her.

SELECTION VOCABULARY

entrepreneur / emprendedor/a ***noun*** successful business person who organizes business practices

infuse / llenar ***verb*** to introduce, add, or fill

- What word part is a clue to the meaning of *infuse*?
- How does the phrase "handed down to me" help you understand the meaning of *infuse*?

NOTES

13 See, I learned respect from how my parents cared for my great aunt and uncle—how my mother would wake up in the middle of the night to check on my great aunt, how my father would prop himself up against the bathroom sink each morning, leaning hard on his crutches, to give my great uncle a shave. I learned **integrity** from my parents—that living a good life is not about being wealthy or powerful, it's about being honest and doing what you say you're going to do. It's about how you act when no one is watching, and whether you're the same person on the outside as you are on the inside.

14 My parents—yes. My parents also taught me about giving back—that when someone is sick, you show up, maybe with a home-cooked meal; when someone's down on their luck, you quietly slip them whatever's in your wallet, even if you're not doing so well yourself.

15 And finally, my parents—especially my dad—taught me about **perseverance.** See, my dad had been an athlete his whole life, a swimmer and a boxer. But if he was frustrated or disappointed by his illness, he never let on. He just woke up extra early each day, slowly fastened each button on his uniform, and eased himself down the steps one leg at a time, to get to his job and provide for our family.

16 So, graduates, I wanted to be here with you at your commencement because your values are my values—the values that carried me all the way from the South Side of Chicago to where I am today, standing before you as the First Lady of the United States. I also wanted to be here because your stories—your achievements, your contributions and the story of this school—inspire me.

17 As we all know, this school was founded as part of a **deliberate,** systematic effort to extinguish your culture; to literally annihilate who you were and what you believed in. But look at you today. The Native languages that were once strictly forbidden here now echo through hallways and in your dorm room conversations at night. The traditions that this school was designed to destroy are now expressed in every square foot of this building—in the art on your walls, in the statue in your MSC building, in the Po Pay Day song and dance performances in your plaza, in the prayers and blessings that you offer in your heart room.

Buffalo Round Up mural at the Santa Fe Indian School

18 And the endless military drills and manual labor that those early students endured have been replaced by one of the best academic curriculums in the

Skills Focus

QUESTION 4: Connect to Essential Question

Obama tells about lessons she learned from her parents. For example, she learned about integrity by watching how her parents lived their lives. These values helped make Obama who she is today.

Skills Focus

QUESTION 1: Compare and Contrast

The school used to forbid students to speak their native languages! Now they can and do use them. It also apparently forbid cultural traditions like art, dances, and prayers, but these are now allowed.

SELECTION VOCABULARY

integrity / la integridad *noun* the quality of being honest or having strong moral principles COGNATE

- What is an example of an action by Obama's parents that shows integrity?
- What nearby words describe *integrity*? Are they positive or negative?

perseverance / la perseverancia *noun* the act of continuing to do something even though it is difficult COGNATE

- How does Obama's father show "perseverance"?
- What is special about perseverance? Is it positive or negative?

deliberate / deliberado/a *adjective* done in a way that shows careful thought COGNATE

- What action was "deliberate"?
- What other words describe the deliberate action?

Skills Focus

QUESTION 2: Author's Purpose and Point of View

Obama's purpose is to persuade the students to keep their Native American traditions and values and to serve their communities and the world. She reveals this purpose when she explains why the community needs the students.

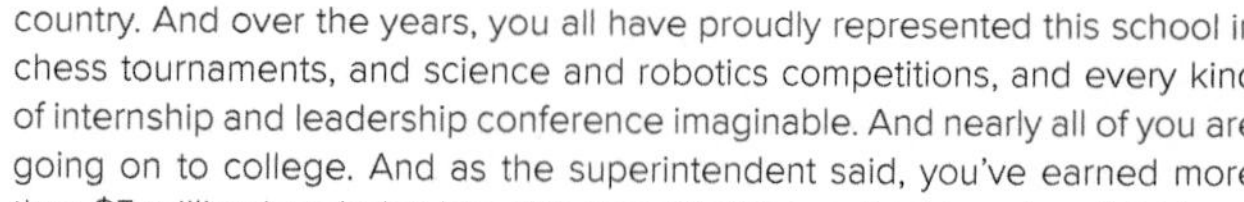

NOTES

country. And over the years, you all have proudly represented this school in chess tournaments, and science and robotics competitions, and every kind of internship and leadership conference imaginable. And nearly all of you are going on to college. And as the superintendent said, you've earned more than $5 million in scholarships this year. That is breathtaking—breathtaking.

19 And whether you're saying an ancient blessing over your hydroponically-grown crops, or using cutting-edge computer technology to understand the biology and hydrology of your ancestral lands, every day at this school, you've been weaving together thousands of years of your heritage with the realities of your modern lives. And all of that preparation and hard work, graduates, is so critically important, because make no mistake about it, you all are the next generation of leaders in your communities, and not years from now or decades from now, but right now.

20 Through your senior honors projects, you've already become experts on urgent issues like addiction and poverty, education and economic development. And so many of you have already stepped up to **implement** your projects in your communities, hosting a fun run to raise awareness about domestic violence and diabetes, leading a traditional foods cooking demonstration, supporting seniors and teen parents, and doing so much more.

21 And as you begin the next phase of your journey, please remember that your communities need even more of your energy and expertise. They need you to bring home additional knowledge and skills to more effectively address the challenges your communities face. That's why it is so important for all of you to hold fast to your goals, and to push through any obstacles that may come your way.

22 And here's the thing: I guarantee you that there will be obstacles—plenty of them. For example, when you get to college or wherever else you're going next, it's going to be an adjustment. College was certainly a huge adjustment for me. I had never lived away from home, away from my family for any length of time. So there were times when I felt lonely and overwhelmed during my freshman year.

23 And what I want you to remember is if that happens to you, I want you to keep pushing forward. Just keep pushing forward. And I want you to reach out and ask for help. I know your teachers tell you that all the time, but please understand that no one gets through college—or life, for that matter—alone. No one. I certainly didn't.

24 So the minute you feel like you're struggling—*the minute*—I want you to ask for help. Don't wait. Seek out a professor you trust. Go to the writing center or

TEXT TALK

What future does Obama see for the graduating students?

See paragraph 19: They are the next generation of leaders in their communities.

How did Obama feel when she first went to college?

See paragraph 22: She felt lonely and overwhelmed because she had never lived away from home.

SELECTION VOCABULARY

implement / implementar *verb* to begin or put a plan into action COGNATE

- How does the phrase "stepped up" reveal the meaning of *implement*?
- What do students do to implement their projects?

NOTES

the counseling center. Talk to older students who know the ropes and can give you some advice. And if the first person you ask isn't friendly or helpful, then ask a second person, and then a third and a fourth. My point is, keep asking until you get the answers you need to get you back on track. Do you understand me?

25 I am so passionate about this because your communities need you. They need you to develop your potential and become who you're meant to be. And that goes for every student in here who is thinking about dropping out, who is feeling discouraged. Your community needs you. And more than ever before, our world needs you, too.

26 And you don't need your First Lady to tell you that. All you have to do is tune in to the news and you'll see that right now, some of the loudest voices in our national conversation are saying things that go against every single one of the values that you've been living at this school. They're telling us that we should disrespect others because of who they are or where they come from or how they worship. They're telling us that we should be selfish—that folks who are struggling don't deserve our help, that we should just take what we can from life and not worry about anyone else. And they're saying that it's okay to keep harming our planet and using our land, our air, our water however we wish.

27 But, graduates, you all know that those are not the values that shape good citizens. Those are not the values that build strong families and communities and nations. You know this. So we desperately need your voices and your values in this conversation reminding us that we're all connected, we're all obligated to treat one another with respect, to act with integrity, to give back to those in need.

28 Now, I know that perhaps I'm asking a lot of all of you. And I know that sometimes all those obligations might feel like a heavy burden. I also know that many of you have already faced and overcome challenges in your lives that most young people can't even begin to imagine—challenges that have tested your courage, your confidence, your faith, and your trust.

29 But, graduates, those struggles should never be a source of shame—never—and they are certainly not a sign of weakness. Just the opposite. Those struggles are the source of your greatest strengths. Because by facing adversity head on and getting through it, you have gained wisdom and maturity beyond your years. I've seen it in you. You've developed resilience that will sustain you throughout your lives. You've deepened a well of compassion within yourselves that will help you connect with and give back to others who struggle.

Prepare for Advanced Courses

Use the activity below to differentiate instruction for your B Beyond grade-level learners.

Look at paragraph 29.

"Those struggles are the source of your greatest strengths."

Have students conduct informal research on famous singers, authors, athletes, etc. who took a struggle in their life and turned it into a strength or used it to motivate themselves to work harder. Have students compare and contrast the people they learned about and the students at Sante Fe Indian School.

TEXT TALK

Why does Obama ask the graduates to stay true to their values?

See paragraph 26: Many people in the world are selfish and have negative attitudes.

Skills Focus

QUESTION 5: Connect to Essential Question

Obama says that much of what I am comes from family, but I also have my own dreams, and they are not impossible to achieve. My dreams make me an individual.

30 And most of all, you have taken your place in the long line of those before you whose continued survival in the face of overwhelming threats should inspire you every day of your lives—every day. I'm talking about many of your ancestors who came together to lead a revolt, risking their lives to preserve their traditions. I'm talking about your predecessors at this school who defied the rules by speaking their languages and running away to attend ceremonial dances back home. And I'm talking about the leaders who reclaimed and reopened this school for you, rebuilding it in your image and the image of your communities.

31 Graduates, all of these people, and so many more, have worked so hard and sacrificed so much so that you could be sitting in these seats on this glorious day celebrating your graduation. And as we honor their legacy today, I'm reminded of how some of your communities have seeds that your ancestors have been planting and harvesting for thousands of years, long before America was even an idea.

32 And just as they have been blessing those crops and lovingly preserving those seeds through storms and droughts, struggles and upheavals so that they could keep handing them down, generation after generation, so, too, have they handed down their wisdom, and their values and their dreams, fighting to save them in the face of unthinkable odds, spurred on by their devotion to those who came before them and those who would come after.

33 And, graduates, today, all of that—all of that—lives inside of you. All of that history, all of that sacrifice, all of that love lives within you. And you all should feel so proud and so blessed to have the privilege of continuing that story. Because with the education you've gotten from this amazing school and with the values that you've learned from your families and your communities, your big, impossible dreams are actually just the right size—big. And you have everything you need to achieve them.

34 Now, of course, it won't be easy. But standing here today with all of you, I am filled with hope. It's the same hope I feel when I think about my own story — how my great-great grandfather was another man's property, my great-grandfather was another man's servant, my grandparents and parents felt the sting of segregation and discrimination. But because they refused to be defined by anyone else's idea of who they were and what they could be, because they held fast to their impossible dreams for themselves and their children, today, my two daughters wake up each morning in the White House.

35 And every day, I try my best to pass down to my girls that same love and that same dreaming spirit that Marian and Fraser Robinson passed down to me, that same love and spirit that your ancestors passed down to all of you and that you will soon pass on to your children and grandchildren.

TEXT TALK

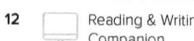

What does Obama say fills her with hope?

See paragraph 34: People who are discriminated against can still succeed and help make the world better.

B Ask each Beyond grade-level student to write one additional discussion question. Then have one or two students facilitate a discussion, using their questions to guide the conversation.

36 Because in the end, I believe that that is the true path of history in this country. It is long—it is. It is long. It is winding. And at times it can be very painful. But ultimately, it flows in the direction of hope, dignity and justice, because people like you stand up for your values—people like you who stay true to who you are and where you've come from, and who work every day to share the blessings you've had with others.

37 So, graduates, in closing, I hope that you will always remember your story, and that you will carry your story with you as proudly as I carry mine. I am so proud of you. I am so excited for you to continue this extraordinary journey. And I can't wait to see everything you'll achieve and bring back to your communities.

38 Thank you all. Love you.

Think Questions

Circulate as students answer Think Questions independently. Scaffolds for these questions are shown on the opposite page.

QUESTION 1: Textual Evidence

Answers will vary but may include the following examples:

- It was founded to end Native American culture, but now the school helps preserve Native American languages and traditions.
- The military training and manual labor have been replaced by one of the best academic curriculums in the country.

QUESTION 2: Textual Evidence

Obama remembers her time in college and advises students that "no one gets through college—or life, for that matter—alone." She tells students to "keep pushing forward" and to "reach out and ask for help" if they need it.

QUESTION 3: Textual Evidence

She thinks the students can gain lessons about integrity and perseverance from her father. She recalls how her father took care of her great uncle, and how "he hardly ever missed a day of work" to support his family despite a painful illness. Obama thinks the lessons will be important to the students "because your values are my values."

QUESTION 4: Context Clues

I think *perseverance* must mean "continuing to do something." The word is used to describe Michelle Obama's father when he keeps working at a demanding job even when he is sick. Context clues from the text include that if he "was frustrated or disappointed by his illness, he never let on."

QUESTION 5: Word Meaning

Definition 1 most closely matches the meaning of the word *integrity* in paragraph 13. The context clues in the sentence support this meaning because Obama talks about acts of kindness her parents performed and "doing what you say you're going to do."

First Read

Read "Commencement Address to the Santa Fe Indian School." After you read, complete the Think Questions below.

THINK QUESTIONS

1. What was the Santa Fe Indian School like in its early years? What is it like when Michelle Obama speaks there in 2016? Use details from Obama's speech as evidence.
2. What advice does Michelle Obama give to students who may face difficulties in college? Cite specific evidence from the text to support your response.
3. What lessons does Michelle Obama think that the students in her audience can gain from her father's life experience? Explain, citing details from the text.
4. Use context clues to determine the meaning of **perseverance** as it is used in paragraph 15. Write your definition here and identify clues that helped you figure out its meaning.
5. Read the following dictionary entry:

   integrity
   in•teg•ri•ty \ in ˈte grə dē \ *noun*

   1. the quality of having strong values or morals
   2. the state of being whole or unified
   3. the condition of being solid or sturdy in construction

   Which definition most closely matches the meaning of **integrity** as it is used in paragraph 13? Write the correct definition of *integrity* here and explain how you figured out the correct meaning.

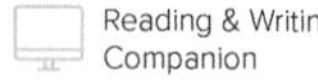

SCAFFOLDS

Think Questions

Use the scaffolds below to differentiate instruction for your ELL English Language Learners and A Approaching grade-level learners.

ELL **BEGINNING** Write a response using the word bank and sentence frames.

INTERMEDIATE Write a response using the sentence frames.

ADVANCED, ADVANCED HIGH Write a response using the Text-Dependent Question Guide.

A **APPROACHING** Write a response using the Text-Dependent Question Guide.

BEGINNING	INTERMEDIATE	APPROACHING / ADVANCED, ADVANCED HIGH
Word Bank	**Sentence Frames**	**Text-Dependent Question Guide**
push end help labor always academic sick share honesty tradition continuing overwhelmed	The school was founded to ____ Native American culture. Now the school honors Native American ____. Students at the school used to spend their days doing manual ____. Now they have an excellent ____ curriculum.	1. • Why was the school founded? • What is the school like now? • How have the students' activities changed?
	Obama says that she felt ____ when she started college. She tells the students to ____ forward. She tells them to ask for ____ until they get the answers they need.	2. • How did Michelle Obama feel when she first got to college? • What does she tell students to do when they start to have a problem?
	Obama learned lessons about ____ and hard work from her father. She tells students that her father kept working even though he was ____. These lessons are important to the students because she believes they ____ the same values.	3. • What values did Obama learn from her father? • How did Obama's father's actions show those values? • Why are those lessons important to the students?
	Obama describes the way her father ____ worked hard to provide for the family. This gives me a clue that *perseverance* means "____ to work hard even if something is difficult."	4. • Read: "And finally, my parents—especially my dad—taught me about **perseverance**." • What actions are being described in this paragraph? • What does that tell me about the meaning of *perseverance*?
	Integrity as used in the text matches definition #____.	5. • "I learned **integrity** from my parents—that living a good life is not about being wealthy or powerful, it's about being honest and doing what you say you're going to do." • Does *integrity* relate to strong values or morals? (#1) • Does *integrity* relate to being whole or unified? (#2) • Does *integrity* relate to being strong or sturdy? (#3)

Reading Comprehension OPTIONAL

Have students complete the digital reading comprehension questions ✓ when they finish reading.

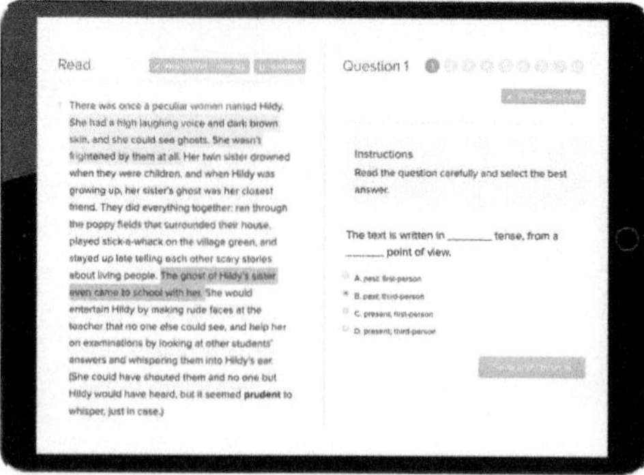

ANSWER KEY

QUESTION 1: B
QUESTION 2: B
QUESTION 3: B
QUESTION 4: D
QUESTION 5: A
QUESTION 6: D
QUESTION 7: A
QUESTION 8: A
QUESTION 9: *See first chart.*
QUESTION 10: *See second chart.*

Synonym	Word
fill	infuse
on purpose	deliberate
carry out	implement
determination	perseverance
morality	integrity
businessperson	entrepreneur

First Lady	Students
Parents who grew up during segregation and did not graduate high school	Participating in projects in education and economic development
Ancestors who were enslaved people and servants	Schools where ancestors' languages were once forbidden
Feeling lonely and overwhelmed upon arriving at college	Jalapeño nachos at the EAC
Grandparents who moved north to avoid discrimination	A community whose history predates the existence of the nation

Connect and Extend OPTIONAL

CONNECT TO EXTENDED WRITING PROJECT

Students can use Michelle Obama's "Commencement Address to the Santa Fe Indian School" as a resource when writing their literary analyses. Have them analyze Obama's use of language as they craft their own writing.

BEYOND THE BOOK

Writing: Digital Storytelling

Ask students to create a digital story detailing their academic journey from kindergarten to their 8th-grade commencement. Digital stories can combine text, images, videos, narration, and/or music.

Digital stories should:

- Identify important people (family, friends, teachers) and their impact.
- Include important moments or events.
- Highlight challenges faced and lessons learned.
- State specific goals they have for the future.

Students can use an online video creator to design and publish their digital stories. Encourage students to share these digital stories with friends, family, and teachers.

To reflect, ask students:

- What has had the biggest impact on you as a student?
- What is the biggest lesson you have learned in school?

Skill: Arguments and Claims

Use the Checklist to analyze Arguments and Claims in "Commencement Address to the Santa Fe Indian School." Refer to the sample student annotations about Arguments and Claims in the text.

••• CHECKLIST FOR ARGUMENTS AND CLAIMS

In order to identify the speaker's argument and claims, note the following:

- ✓ clues that reveal the author's opinion in the title, opening remarks, or concluding statement
- ✓ declarative statements that come before or follow a speaker's anecdote or story

To delineate a speaker's argument and specific claims, do the following:

- ✓ note the information that the speaker introduces in sequential order
- ✓ describe the speaker's argument in your own words

To evaluate the argument and specific claims, consider the following questions:

- ✓ Does the writer support each claim with reasoning and evidence?
- ✓ Do the writer's claims work together to support the writer's overall argument?
- ✓ Which claims are not supported, if any?

Skill: Arguments and Claims

Introduce the Skill

Watch the Concept Definition video and read the following definition with your students.

In an **argument,** a writer or speaker expresses an opinion about a topic and defends that opinion. A writer or speaker defends his or her argument using claims, evidence, and reasoning. **Claims** are statements that convey the writer's or speaker's position on an issue or problem. **Evidence** consists of facts, examples, and expert opinions that uphold the claim. **Reasoning** is a combination of statements, questions, and rhetorical appeals that attempt to explain or emphasize why a reader or audience should consider the evidence that is presented and accept the claim.

Arguments are **debatable**, meaning they can be proven or disproven. Effective arguments use claims that are supported by the writer's reasons and evidence. Furthermore, the writer's reasoning is sufficient and logical, and the evidence is grounded in factual information. To determine whether an argument is effective, you **delineate** (trace or outline) the writer's argument, analyze his or her reasoning, and research the relevance of the evidence.

TURN AND TALK

1 When have you felt someone was trying to inspire or otherwise persuade you?

2 What kinds of facts and evidence did the person present to support his or her argument?

ELL SPEAKING FRAMES

- A person who tried to [inspire / persuade] me was ____.
- [He / she] tried to [inspire / persuade] me to ____.
- [He / she] tried to [inspire / persuade] me by ____.

V SKILL VOCABULARY

argument / el argumento ***noun*** a set of claims, evidence, and reasons designed to persuade others to adopt a certain point of view or to take a certain action COGNATE

claim / la afirmación ***noun*** the writer's or speaker's position on a debatable issue or problem

evidence / la evidencia ***noun*** facts, examples, and expert opinions that support a claim COGNATE

Your Turn

Ask students to complete the Your Turn activity.

QUESTION 1

Part A

A. Incorrect. This is evidence that the speaker presents to support the counterclaim that the obligation to give back to one's community can be too much of a burden.

B. Incorrect. This is evidence that the speaker uses to support the claim that many widely heard leaders are making statements that oppose the values that students have learned.

C. Incorrect. The speaker asks students to develop themselves to their full potential and contribute to their communities.

D. Correct. The speaker addresses the challenges that students have overcome by saying "Those struggles are the source of your greatest strengths."

Part B

A. Incorrect. This is a claim from paragraph 25.

B. Correct. This is evidence that supports the claim in paragraph 29.

C. Incorrect. This is a reason from paragraph 27. It explains how evidence from paragraph 27 supports the claim that the students' communities need them.

D. Incorrect. This is a claim from paragraph 28.

Skill: Arguments and Claims

Reread paragraphs 25–29 of "Commencement Address to the Santa Fe Indian School." Then, using the Checklist on the previous page, answer the multiple-choice questions below.

 YOUR TURN

1. This question has two parts. First, answer Part A. Then, answer Part B.

Part A: Which of the following statements is one claim that the speaker makes in this passage?

- ○ A. The students have already faced more difficult challenges than many other young people.
- ○ B. Many leaders are saying that it is not a problem if one causes damage to the environment.
- ○ C. The students need to use their education to contribute to their community instead of focusing on developing themselves.
- ○ D. Students can find significant strengths in the struggles that they have already overcome.

Part B: Which of the following statements supports the claim selected in Part A?

- ○ A. "Your community needs you. And more than ever before, our world needs you, too."
- ○ B. "Because by facing adversity head on and getting through it, you have gained wisdom and maturity beyond your years. I've seen it in you."
- ○ C. "So we desperately need your voices and your values in this conversation reminding us that we're all connected, we're all obligated to treat one another with respect, to act with integrity, to give back to those in need."
- ○ D. "Now, I know that perhaps I'm asking a lot of all of you."

SKILL VOCABULARY

reasoning / el razonamiento ***noun*** statements, questions, and appeals that explain why a reader should consider the evidence that is presented and accept the claim

debatable / debatible ***adjective*** open for discussion or argument COGNATE

delineate / describir ***verb*** to describe precisely

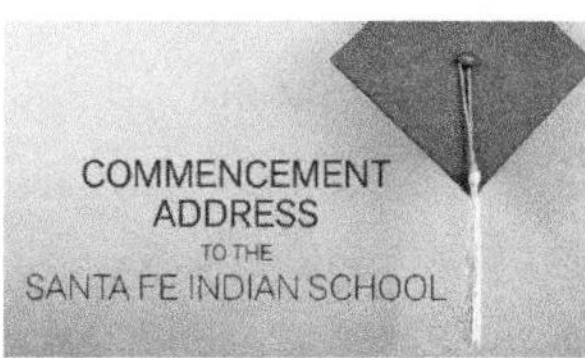

Close Read

Reread "Commencement Address to the Santa Fe Indian School." As you reread, complete the Skills Focus questions below. Then use your answers and annotations from the questions to help you complete the Write activity.

SKILLS FOCUS

1. What was the Santa Fe Indian School like in its early years? Compare and contrast it to what it was like when Michelle Obama gave her commencement speech there in 2016. Use details from Obama's speech as textual evidence.
2. Identify evidence that reveals Obama's purpose for writing this speech. Explain what her purpose is and how you know.
3. What lessons does Michelle Obama think that the students in her audience can gain from her father's life? Explain, citing details from the text to support your analysis.
4. Michelle Obama makes an analogy between her personal history and the history of the students at the school. Identify examples in the text where Obama describes her family's history. Using those details, explain how she might answer the question, *What makes you, you?*
5. How can Obama's speech help students at the school to further establish their individuality? Cite specific evidence from the text in your response.

WRITE

ARGUMENTATIVE: Write a speech of 300 words or more to be given to students at your grade level at the end of the year. Use the First Lady's speech as a template to help you focus on a major part of your life and its history thus far: your education, your family life, your greatest achievements, or a particular struggle you've faced. Use details from that experience to write a speech that attempts to inspire graduates who are about to embark on new journeys and overcome obstacles that may have proven problematic without such advice.

Close Read

Skills Focus

QUESTION 1: Compare and Contrast

See paragraph 17.

QUESTION 2: Author's Purpose and Point of View

See paragraph 21.

QUESTION 3: Textual Evidence

See paragraph 9.

QUESTION 4: Connect to Essential Question

See paragraph 13.

QUESTION 5: Connect to Essential Question

See paragraph 33.

CHECK FOR SUCCESS

If students struggle to respond to Skills Focus question 1, ask them the following questions:

- How does Obama describe the school in its early years in paragraphs 17 and 18?
- What happens in the school today?
- In what ways does the school seem different?

Have students transition to read and annotate independently once they have successfully completed the first Skills Focus prompt.

Writer's Notebook

Connect to Essential Question: Give students time to reflect on how "Commencement Address to the Santa Fe Indian School" connects to the unit's essential question "What makes you, you?" by freewriting in their Writer's Notebooks.

Beginning & Intermediate

Read aloud the unit's essential question: "What makes you, you?" Encourage students to draw their reflections or allow students to write in their native language. Circulate, prompting students for their thoughts as they respond orally or through pantomime.

Advanced & Advanced High

Allow students to share their reflections orally in pairs or small groups before freewriting.

Collaborative Conversation

Break students into collaborative conversation groups to discuss the Close Read prompt. Ask students to use the StudySyncTV episode as a model for their discussion. Remind them to reference their Skills Focus annotations in their discussion.

Write a speech of 300 words or more to be given to students at your grade level at the end of the school year. Use the First Lady's speech as a template to help you focus on a major part of your life and its history thus far: your education, your family life, your greatest achievements, or a particular struggle you've faced. Use details from that experience to write a speech that attempts to inspire graduates who are about to embark on new journeys and overcome obstacles that may have proven problematic without such advice.

Use the scaffolds below to differentiate instruction for your ELL English Language Learners and A Approaching grade-level learners.

ELL **BEGINNING, INTERMEDIATE** Use the discussion guide and speaking frames to facilitate the discussion with support from the teacher.

ADVANCED, ADVANCED HIGH Use the discussion guide and speaking frames to facilitate the discussion in mixed-level groups.

A **APPROACHING** Use the discussion guide to facilitate the discussion in mixed-level groups.

APPROACHING
ADVANCED, ADVANCED HIGH
BEGINNING, INTERMEDIATE

Discussion Guide	Speaking Frames
1. What people or experiences from her own life does Michelle Obama use to inspire the students?	• Obama uses ____.
2. What people or experiences from your lives might inspire students?	• Inspiring people include ____. • Inspiring experiences include ____.
3. What could you tell other students about these people and experiences to inspire them?	• I would tell about ____.

Review Prompt and Rubric

Before students begin writing, review the writing prompt and rubric with the class.

ARGUMENTATIVE: Write a speech of 300 words or more to be given to students at your grade level at the end of the year. Use the First Lady's speech as a template to help you focus on a major part of your life and its history thus far: your education, your family life, your greatest achievements, or a particular struggle you've faced. Use details from that experience to write a speech that attempts to inspire graduates who are about to embark on new journeys and overcome obstacles that may have proven problematic without such advice.

ELL A **PROMPT GUIDE**

- What people or experiences from her own life does Obama use to inspire the students?
- What people or experiences from your lives might inspire students?
- What could you tell other students about these people and experiences to inspire them?

Score	Arguments and Claims	Language and Conventions
4	The writer clearly writes an inspirational speech about embarking on a new journey and overcoming obstacles. The writer uses details from personal experience.	The writer demonstrates a consistent command of grammar, punctuation, and usage conventions. Although minor errors may be evident, they do not detract from the fluency or the clarity of the writing.
3	The writer writes a fairly inspirational speech about embarking on a new journey and overcoming obstacles. The writer uses some details from personal experience.	The writer demonstrates an adequate command of grammar, punctuation, and usage conventions. Although some errors may be evident, they create few (if any) disruptions in the fluency or clarity of the writing.
2	The writer attempts to write an inspirational speech about embarking on a new journey and overcoming obstacles. The writer uses few details from personal experience.	The writer demonstrates a partial command of grammar, punctuation, and usage conventions. Some distracting errors may be evident, at times creating minor disruptions in the fluency or clarity of the writing.
1	The writer does not produce an inspirational speech about embarking on a new journey and overcoming obstacles. The writer uses few or no details from personal experience.	The writer demonstrates little or no command of grammar, punctuation, and usage conventions. Serious and persistent errors create disruptions in the fluency of the writing and sometimes interfere with meaning.
0	The writer does not provide a relevant response to the prompt or does not provide a response at all	Serious and persistent errors overwhelm the writing and interfere with the meaning of the response as a whole, making the writer's meaning impossible to understand.

Write

SCAFFOLDS

Ask students to complete the writing assignment using textual evidence to support their answers.

Use the scaffolds below to differentiate instruction for your ELL English Language Learners and A Approaching grade-level learners.

ELL **BEGINNING** With the help of the word bank, write a response using paragraph frame 1.

INTERMEDIATE With the help of the word bank, write a response using paragraph frames 1 and 2.

ADVANCED, ADVANCED HIGH Write a response of differentiated length using the sentence starters.

A **APPROACHING** Write a response of differentiated length using the sentence starters.

BEGINNING / INTERMEDIATE	BEGINNING / INTERMEDIATE	INTERMEDIATE	ADVANCED, ADVANCED HIGH / APPROACHING
Word Bank	**Paragraph Frame 1**	**Paragraph Frame 2**	**Sentence Starters**
obstacles achieve family values struggle	My ____ inspired and helped me. They taught me good ____ like not giving up. Sometimes I ____ with English. But I am learning more and more each day. You too can overcome ____ by not giving up. You can ____ your dreams by always trying hard.	I also learned ____ from ____. [He / she] had a hard time when ____. But [he / she] ____. Remember that it is important to ____.	• ____ inspired me because . . . • I was inspired when . . . • I struggled when . . . Yet I . . . • You should . . . • Always remember to . . .

Peer Review

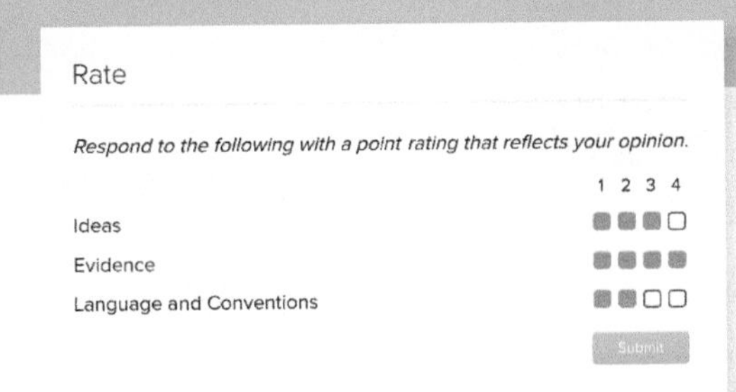

Students should submit substantive feedback to two peers using the review instructions below.

- How well does this response answer the prompt?
- How well does the writer inspire readers?
- How well does the writer use interesting and relevant examples from his or her own personal experience?
- What did the writer do well in this response? What does the writer need to work on?

SENTENCE FRAMES

- You were able to (completely / partly / almost) answer the prompt because ____.
- You could answer the prompt more completely by ____.
- You could inspire even more by ____.
- Another example of personal experience might help because ____.
- My favorite part of your response is ____.

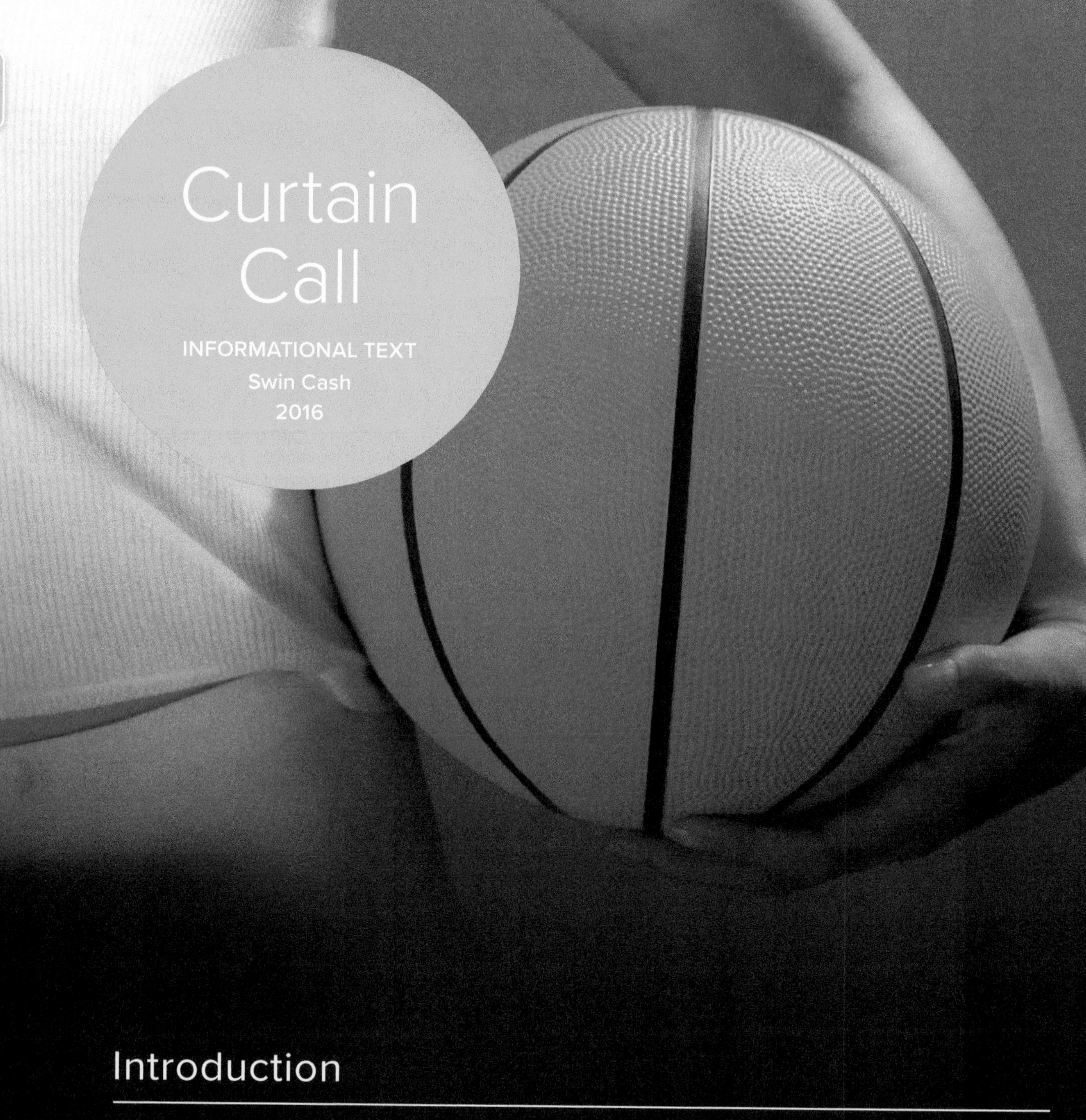

Curtain Call

INFORMATIONAL TEXT
Swin Cash
2016

Introduction

Swin Cash (b. 1979) played 14 seasons in the WNBA, winning three championships, appearing on four all-star teams, and winning two Olympic gold medals along the way. Despite all of those accomplishments, Cash was equally known for her work establishing the WNBA players union and her involvement in the community within the various cities she played in. In 2016, she announced her upcoming retirement in this essay for The Players' Tribune, looking back on her proudest accomplishments and wondering what would come next.

In this essay, Swin Cash, a former Olympian and Women's National Basketball Association (WNBA) star, announces her retirement from basketball. Reflecting on the struggles of female players, she is proud that she helped create a players' union, ensuring the rights of future women in the sport. Cash says that she fought hard because the women who came before her made sacrifices so that she would have the chance to play. Likewise, she wants to make sure that the next generation is also afforded similar opportunities. Cash reflects on the importance of the people she met through basketball, including her teammates and all the fans in the different cities in which she played. Ultimately, Cash acknowledges that her larger purpose is to empower others. With twenty-seven games left, Cash looks forward to continuing to serve as a role model after her retirement.

 Proficiency-leveled summaries and summaries in multiple languages are available digitally.

Audio and audio text highlighting are available with the text.

COMPARING WITHIN AND ACROSS GENRES

 In her short personal essay "Curtain Call," WNBA star Swin Cash discusses how her view of herself and others changes as she approaches the end of her career. How did the people and events of her past make her the successful woman she became? This selection pairs nicely with Naomi Sepiso's essay "So where are you from?" in which the author reflects on how people's questions affect her identity and view of herself.

Access Complex Text

LEXILE: 740L **WORD COUNT:** 608

The following areas may be challenging for students, particularly ELL English Language Learners and A Approaching grade-level learners.

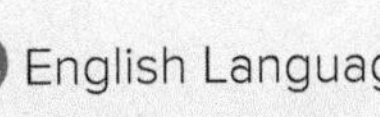

Prior Knowledge	Connection of Ideas	Sentence Structure
• Swin Cash played for the Women's National Basketball Association. Students may need to research this organization. • The term "curtain call" is a theater term, meaning to take a bow after a performance. Cash uses it as a term for retirement.	• Cash alludes to unions, discrimination, pay, and other aspects of playing professional basketball as a woman. • Cash connects struggles to the importance of giving back to those who helped her succeed. Highlighting may help readers make connections.	• Cash includes several one-sentence paragraphs. These are used for effect, or to draw attention to the emotions behind the statements, and readers may need to annotate to explain them.

 SCAFFOLDS  ENGLISH LANGUAGE LEARNERS  APPROACHING GRADE LEVEL  BEYOND GRADE LEVEL

These icons identify differentiation strategies and scaffolded support for a variety of students. See the digital lesson plan for additional differentiation strategies and scaffolds.

Instructional Path

The print teacher's edition includes essential point-of-use instruction and planning tools. Complete lesson plans and program documents appear in your digital teacher account.

Independent Read: Curtain Call

Objectives: Read a text and demonstrate understanding by responding to comprehension questions, participating in a collaborative conversation, and writing a personal response.

Independent Read

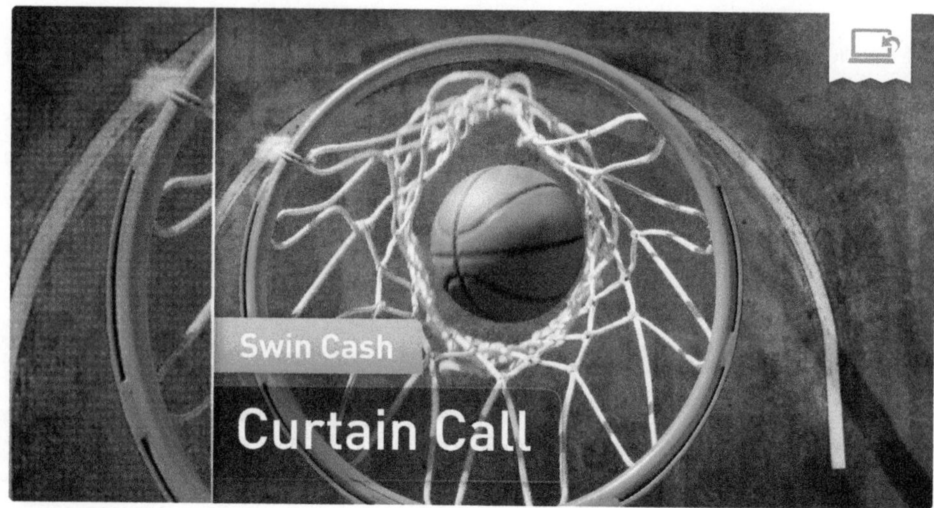

Introduce the Text

As a class, watch the video preview and have students read the introduction in pairs to make connections to the video preview.

- What key words or images from the video do you think will be most important to the essay you are about to read?
- What do you think you'll learn about in this text?
- Why do you think it's important to learn about this person's experiences?

ELL SPEAKING FRAMES

- The ____ in the video makes me think ____.
- The video shows ____. This makes me wonder ____.
- I think the text will ____. I think this because ____.
- I predict that there will be ____. I believe this because ____.

Entry Point

As students prepare to read "Curtain Call," share the following information with them to provide context.

✓ Swin Cash's retirement announcement, "Curtain Call," was published in The Players' Tribune, a media outlet started by former New York Yankees baseball player Derek Jeter. The Tribune publishes stories and articles written by athletes themselves, and includes videos and podcasts in addition to written texts.

✓ The Women's National Basketball Association is a professional basketball league and is the women's counterpart to the men's National Basketball Association. It began in 1997 and currently has teams in twelve cities and states: Atlanta, Chicago, Connecticut, Dallas, Indiana, Las Vegas, Los Angeles, Minnesota, New York, Phoenix, Seattle, and Washington.

"I've always been training for something. What happens when that's gone?"

NOTES

1 While my playing career will soon be coming to an end, I will never be able to completely walk away. I care so much about whether the league will be around for another 20 years—and more. We had to fight to get where we are. We had to fight **apathy.**

2 We still fight apathy, but with trust that change will come.

3 We—the players—had to fight for the **union,** and fight to make it better. This is **critical** to our success. Many don't understand but *those are things we don't get paid for.*

4 I've done all of this because many women before me sacrificed so that I could get my shot. And I did. So why wouldn't I make sure that the **generation** behind me got theirs?

5 I remember coming into the league and seeing some of the players who helped launch the WNBA—players like Lisa Leslie, Sheryl Swoopes, Teresa Weatherspoon. They were playing not just for the love of the game, but because it was so important for the future. Futures that weren't even theirs.

6 *My* future.

7 I was part of the generation of players right after that **inaugural** wave, and we never forgot their legacy. I'm so proud now when I see my nieces dribble a basketball. That's something the women before me inspired. That's something I inspired. I would live this particular life all over again to ensure young women recognize and embrace the queens they are within.

8 This wasn't an easy decision.

9 It never is, no matter how well you've prepared.

10 Most people don't get to wake up every day and do something they're passionate about. You always feel you can give more, but at some point you have to do what's right for yourself. Maybe every athlete goes through that when they retire. It's hard to open up your hands and let go of what you know.

Analyze Vocabulary Using Context Clues

As students read the text, ask them to make predictions about each bold vocabulary word based on the context clues in the sentence.

TEXT TALK

What is Swin Cash's concern about the WNBA?

See paragraph 1: Cash is retiring and wants to make sure that after as she leaves the sport, women's basketball is around for future generations.

What is Cash's point about the WNBA union?

See paragraphs 2–5: The union is important to Cash because she and other players had to fight for it, so she doesn't want future players to stop caring about it.

What does Cash see as her legacy? What image does she use to express it?

See paragraph 7: She and players like her inspired young girls to play basketball. She describes her nieces dribbling a ball.

SELECTION VOCABULARY

apathy / la apatía ***noun*** not caring, lacking interest COGNATE

ELL
- How does Cash feel about the league?
- Why did she and other basketball players have to fight to get where they are?

union / el sindicato ***noun*** group of workers that protects those workers' rights

- Who had to fight for the union?
- What does the word tell you about the players?

critical / crítico/a ***adjective*** urgently needed; absolutely necessary COGNATE

- What does the word *this* refer to?
- Is success important or not?

NOTES

You hold on because it's so much a part of your routine—and your life. I've always been training for something. What happens when that's gone? I've told that kind of story about other athletes in my broadcast work, but now I'm on the other side.

11 *This is real.*

12 At the end of your career, you do a lot of **reflecting.** I've played for multiple teams in the WNBA, and they've all felt like home: Detroit and Seattle, where I won championships, and Chicago, Atlanta and New York, my last stops. And the fans in each of those cities became something like family to me. They're the reason I'm announcing my decision now. I want to spend this season showing my gratitude to everyone who's been a part of this journey. It's been rich not just because of the accomplishments and wins, but also because of the people in my life: family, teammates, mentors and fans.

13 I came into this game unapologetically fearless, as the woman I felt I was called to be. From the way I carried myself on and off the court, to using my voice for the union, to speaking out against discrimination, to fighting for all the kids in my Cash for Kids charity—all of this is bigger than me. It's bigger than my career.

14 There's no greater legacy than a legacy of lasting impact.

15 Basketball gave me the vehicle to inspire and empower. That was my purpose.

16 I have 27 regular season games left. I'll be taking in every moment as I look to the future, whatever it may hold. I understand there's a new life waiting for me after that last whistle.

17 May God allow it to be as blessed as this one has been—and a blessing to others, as well.

WRITE

PERSONAL RESPONSE: Swin Cash says, "Basketball gave me the vehicle to inspire and empower." Who do you want to inspire and empower? Like Swin Cash, do you have a passion that allows you to inspire others or empower those who feel powerless? What is it? Reflect on your own thoughts, feelings, or dreams for the future as you respond to each of these questions.

TEXT TALK

Why is Cash announcing her retirement before the season ends?

See paragraph 12: She wants to spend the last season showing her gratitude to the fans.

What does Cash see as her purpose for playing basketball?

See paragraph 15: She sees that inspiring others and making them feel they have the power to do things is her purpose in life.

B Ask each Beyond grade-level student to write one additional discussion question. Then have one or two students facilitate a discussion, using their questions to guide the conversation.

SELECTION VOCABULARY

generation / la generación ***noun*** all the people living at the same time or of approximately the same age COGNATE

ELL • Who does Cash talk about in this sentence and in the first sentence?

inaugural / inaugural ***adjective*** first; first to happen COGNATE

ELL • Which generation of players were Leslie, Swoopes, and Weatherspoon part of?

reflect / refleccionar ***verb*** to think deeply or carefully, sometimes about the past

ELL
- When is Cash "reflecting"?
- What does someone often do near the end of their career?

Reading Comprehension OPTIONAL

Have students complete the digital reading comprehension questions ✓ when they finish reading.

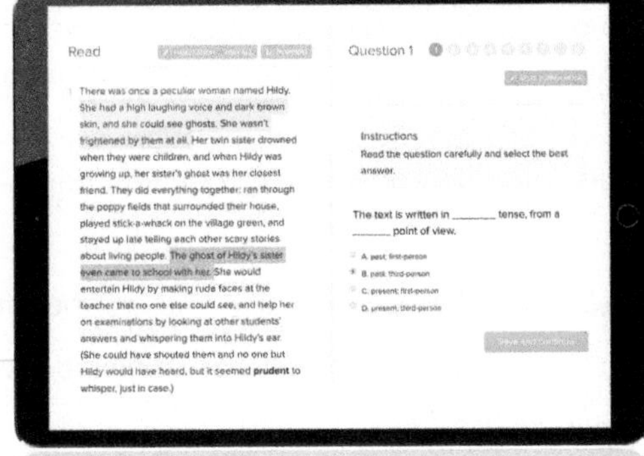

ANSWER KEY

QUESTION 1: D
QUESTION 2: D
QUESTION 3: A
QUESTION 4: B
QUESTION 5: A
QUESTION 6: D
QUESTION 7: B
QUESTION 8: A
QUESTION 9: *See first chart.*
QUESTION 10: *See second chart.*

Synonym	Word
indifference	apathy
crucial	critical
first	inaugural
contemplate	reflect
enable	empower

True	False
Voluntarily established a players union	Part of the first wave of WNBA players
Created a charity with her name on it	Won championships in Atlanta and New York
Played on five different teams	Experienced nothing but enthusiasm toward the WNBA
Embraced every city she played in	Announced retirement after the final game she ever played

Connect and Extend OPTIONAL

CONNECT TO EXTENDED WRITING PROJECT

Students can find inspiration from “Curtain Call” when writing their literary analyses. Have them analyze and reflect on how Swin Cash uses basketball to explain ideas of belonging.

BEYOND THE BOOK

Speech: Your Legacy in 60 Seconds

In her personal essay, Swin Cash reflects on her legacy. Challenge students to write and deliver an elevator speech—a brief speech that outlines or pitches an idea in the time it takes to travel in an elevator—about the legacy they want to create.

Ask students to:

- Think about the legacy they would like to leave behind.
- Prepare a 60-second elevator speech that clearly and concisely articulates their purpose in life and describes the legacy they want to leave behind.
- Practice their elevator speeches with a partner.
- Present for the class.

To reflect, ask students:

- Was it challenging to identify your purpose in life?
- Why do so many people hope to leave a legacy after they retire?
- How might setting goals help you eventually create a legacy?

Collaborative Conversation

SCAFFOLDS

Post the writing prompt to generate a discussion in small groups. Ask students to first break down the prompt before they discuss relevant ideas and textual evidence.

Swin Cash says, "Basketball gave me the vehicle to inspire and empower." Who do you want to inspire and empower? Like Swin Cash, do you have a passion that allows you to inspire others or empower those who feel powerless? What is it? Reflect on your own thoughts, feelings, or dreams for the future as you respond to each of these questions.

Use the scaffolds below to differentiate instruction for your ELL English Language Learners and A Approaching grade-level learners.

ELL **BEGINNING, INTERMEDIATE** Use the discussion guide and speaking frames to facilitate the discussion with support from the teacher.

ADVANCED, ADVANCED HIGH Use the discussion guide and speaking frames to facilitate the discussion in mixed-level groups.

A **APPROACHING** Use the discussion guide to facilitate the discussion in mixed-level groups.

APPROACHING
ADVANCED, ADVANCED HIGH
BEGINNING, INTERMEDIATE

Discussion Guide	Speaking Frames
1. Who do you want to inspire and empower? Why do you want to inspire and empower them?	• I want to inspire and empower ____ because ____.
2. What is your passion? How can it inspire and empower others?	• My passion is ____. • It can inspire and empower others by ____.
3. What are your thoughts, feelings, or dreams for the future? How can your passion help make them a reality?	• I want to make the future better by ____. • My passion can make my dreams come true because ____.

Review Prompt and Rubric

Before students begin writing, review the writing prompt and rubric with the class.

PERSONAL RESPONSE: Swin Cash says, "Basketball gave me the vehicle to inspire and empower." Who do you want to inspire and empower? Like Swin Cash, do you have a passion that allows you to inspire others or empower those who feel powerless? What is it? Reflect on your own thoughts, feelings, or dreams for the future as you respond to each of these questions.

ELL **PROMPT GUIDE**

A

- Who do you want to inspire and empower? Why do you want to inspire and empower them?
- What is your passion? How can it help inspire and empower others?
- What are your thoughts, feelings, or dreams about the future? How can your passion help make them a reality?

Score	Personal Response	Language and Conventions
4	The writer clearly explains his or her personal connection to the text, using relevant evidence from the text as needed.	The writer demonstrates a consistent command of grammar, punctuation, and usage conventions. Although minor errors may be evident, they do not detract from the fluency or the clarity of the writing.
3	The writer sufficiently explains his or her personal connection to the text, using relevant evidence from the text most of the time.	The writer demonstrates an adequate command of grammar, punctuation, and usage conventions. Although some errors may be evident, they create few (if any) disruptions in the fluency or clarity of the writing.
2	The writer begins to explain his or her personal connection to the text, but the explanation is incomplete. The writer uses relevant evidence from the text only some of the time	The writer demonstrates a partial command of grammar, punctuation, and usage conventions. Some distracting errors may be evident, at times creating minor disruptions in the fluency or clarity of the writing.
1	The writer attempts to explain his or her personal connection to the text, but the explanation is not successful. The writer uses little or no relevant evidence from the text.	The writer demonstrates little or no command of grammar, punctuation, and usage conventions. Serious and persistent errors create disruptions in the fluency of the writing and sometimes interfere with meaning.
0	The writer does not provide a relevant response to the prompt or does not provide a response at all	Serious and persistent errors overwhelm the writing and interfere with the meaning of the response as a whole, making the writer's meaning impossible to understand.

Write

Ask students to complete the writing assignment using textual evidence to support their answers.

Use the scaffolds below to differentiate instruction for your ELL English Language Learners and A Approaching grade-level learners.

ELL **BEGINNING** With the help of the word bank, write a response using paragraph frame 1.

INTERMEDIATE With the help of the word bank, write a response using paragraph frames 1 and 2.

ADVANCED, ADVANCED HIGH Write a response of differentiated length using the sentence starters.

A **APPROACHING** Write a response of differentiated length using the sentence starters.

BEGINNING / INTERMEDIATE		INTERMEDIATE	ADVANCED, ADVANCED HIGH / APPROACHING
Word Bank	**Paragraph Frame 1**	**Paragraph Frame 2**	**Sentence Starters**
sister influence strength younger help	I want to inspire and empower ____. I want to inspire and empower ____ because ____. My passion is ____. My passion can inspire and empower people to ____. Inspiring and empowering people will change the future because ____.	In the future, I hope people will ____. One way I can inspire and empower people to do this is ____. Like Swin Cash, I hope to ____.	• I want to inspire and empower . . . • I want to inspire and empower . . . because . . . • My passion is . . . • My passion can inspire and empower people to . . . • My dream for the future is . . . • The future can be changed to . . .

Peer Review

Rate

Respond to the following with a point rating that reflects your opinion.

	1	2	3	4
Ideas	■	■	■	□
Evidence	■	■	■	■
Language and Conventions	■	■	□	□

Submit

Students should submit substantive feedback to two peers using the review instructions below.

- How well does this response answer the prompt?
- Which of the author's comments inspired you to think differently about the text?
- What did the writer do well in this response? What does the writer need to work on?

SENTENCE FRAMES

A

- You were able to (completely / partly / almost) answer the prompt.
- You could answer the prompt more completely by ____.
- I thought differently about the text after reading ____.
- My favorite part of your response is ____.

So where are you from?

INFORMATIONAL TEXT
Naomi Sepiso
2016

Introduction

Most people might chalk up the question "Where are you from?" as innocent small-talk. But seventeen-year-old Naomi Sepiso senses that for people whose appearance causes them to feel like an outsider, the question's meaning can cut much deeper. In this essay, Sepiso explains why being asked about her origin is a line in the sand between her and the asker. The question, in Sepiso's eyes, immediately ostracizes her as "the other"—someone who is from somewhere else. She describes having a "pre-rehearsed answer" she often uses, keeping her truer feelings buried beneath the many layers and complexities of her own identity.

In this essay, 17-year-old Naomi Sepiso explains why being asked where she's from causes painful emotions. As a Kenyan immigrant living in Australia, she is used to the question. However, the answer is not simple. Although her roots trace back to one country, she grew up in another. Furthermore, she feels like a foreigner everywhere because she doesn't understand her parents' native language. In the end, she rebels against the ethnic identity others ascribe to her. She learns how to see herself as her own country, believing that one day people will see her as an individual and stop trying to classify her.

COMPARING WITHIN AND ACROSS GENRES

How would you feel if someone asked you where you're from? How does that question create distance between the person asking and the person asked? In the essay "So where are you from?" 17-year-old Naomi Sepiso discusses how a seemingly simple question makes her feel like she doesn't belong. Readers will make similar connections to "Curtain Call" as they begin to question whether who we are is a product of our history, or rather a product of our choices.

ELL Proficiency-leveled summaries and summaries in multiple languages are available digitally.

 Audio and audio text highlighting are available with this text.

Access Complex Text

LEXILE: 800L **WORD COUNT:** 484

The following areas may be challenging for students, particularly ELL English Language Learners and A Approaching grade-level learners.

Purpose	Genre	Connection of Ideas
• Students may need assistance understanding that the author wishes that others could more fully understand her experiences. Immigrants have rich backgrounds and histories that deserve to be approached thoughtfully.	• The text is an informational essay, but it uses the third-person point of view. The author's use of the third-person point of view is a device that may help her express a feeling of alienation. However, the essay is rooted in her real-life experiences.	• While the author focuses on her specific experiences as an immigrant in Australia, the text has universal implications. The author's personal experiences help illuminate what many immigrants to other countries around the world experience.

SCAFFOLDS

ELL ENGLISH LANGUAGE LEARNERS

A APPROACHING GRADE LEVEL

B BEYOND GRADE LEVEL

These icons identify differentiation strategies and scaffolded support for a variety of students. See the digital lesson plan for additional differentiation strategies and scaffolds.

Instructional Path

The print teacher's edition includes essential point-of-use instruction and planning tools. Complete lesson plans and program documents appear in your digital teacher account.

DIGITAL ONLY

Skill: Visualizing

Objectives: After reading and discussing a model, students will be able create mental images in order to improve reading comprehension.

First Read: So where are you from?

Objectives: After an initial reading and discussion of the essay, students will be able to use the reading comprehension strategy of visualizing, use context clues to define new vocabulary, and demonstrate comprehension by responding to questions using textual evidence.

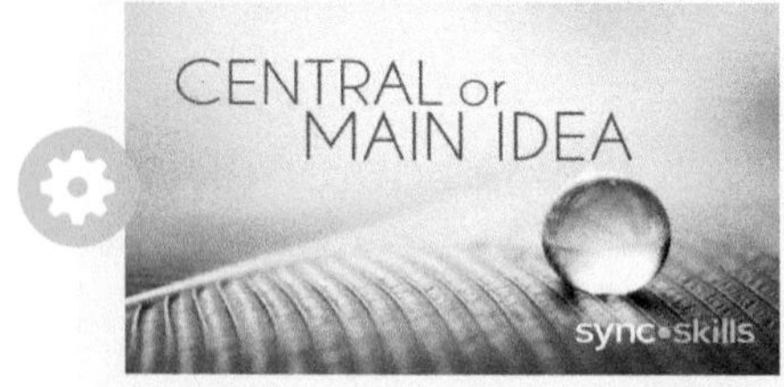

Skill: Central or Main Idea

Objectives: After rereading and discussing a model of close reading, students will be able to analyze the central or main idea with supporting evidence in an informational text.

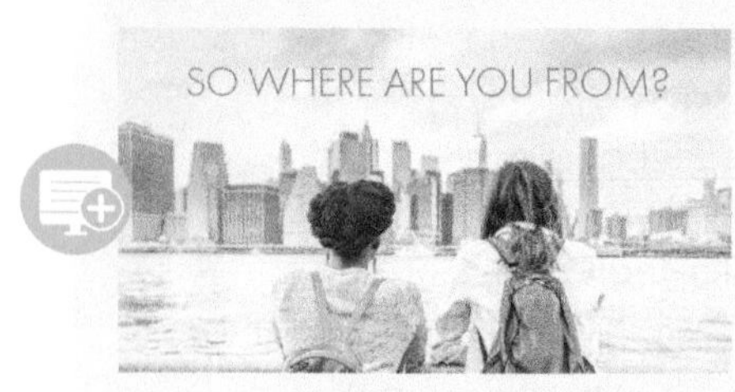

Close Read: So where are you from?

Objectives: After engaging in a close reading and discussion of the text, students will be able to analyze the central or main idea and supporting evidence in order to participate in a collaborative conversation and write a short, constructed response.

Blast: Your Six Words

Objectives: After exploring background information and research links about a topic, students will respond to a question with a 140-character response.

Progress Monitoring

Opportunities to Learn	Opportunities to Demonstrate Learning	Opportunities to Reteach
Visualizing		
Skill: Visualizing	First Read • Read and Annotate	Spotlight Skill: Visualizing
Central or Main Idea		
Skill: Central or Main Idea	Skill: Central or Main Idea • Your Turn Close Read • Skills Focus • Write	Unit 6 Skill: Central or Main Idea - Universal Declaration of Human Rights Spotlight Skill: Central or Main Idea

First Read

Introduce the Text

As a class, watch the video preview and have students read the introduction in pairs to make connections to the video preview.

To activate prior knowledge and experiences, ask students:

- What other images could you imagine using in this video?
- Why do you think it's important to learn about this person?

ELL SPEAKING FRAMES

- The ____ in the video makes me think ____.
- The video shows ____. This makes me wonder ____.
- I think the text will ____. I think this because ____.
- I predict that there will be ____. I believe this because ____.

Entry Point

As students prepare to read "So where are you from?" share the following information with them to provide context.

- ✓ The author of this selection is an immigrant who lives in Australia, and she wrote this personal narrative when she was 17 years old.
- ✓ In a personal narrative, a writer often shares one specific and meaningful event from his or her life. These pieces usually include descriptive details and dialogue that help convey a theme.
- ✓ Henri Tajfel and John Turner, two social psychologists, developed social identity theory in 1979. They argue that part of a person's sense of self can be based on groups in which they belong. As a result, a question like "So where are you from?" can make a person feel as if they do not belong to an "in-group," or a group in which they thought they belonged.

"She was not someone from a place. She made a home of kind words and warm feelings."

NOTES

Skill:
Central or Main Idea

I think the main idea is about belonging. "Always" shows she gets this question a lot. "Originally" sounds like someone's not Australian if they were born elsewhere. The author uses third-person like she's distancing herself from others.

1 'So where are you from?' They always asked that question; a **subtle** reminder that she was not one of them.

2 'What do you mean?' she asked. They only asked that question when they were afraid of placing her into a box. As though they were giving her the option of which box she wanted to climb into.

3 'Well... you're obviously not from here... I mean... you live here, but where are you *from*... like, originally?'

4 There it was. *Originally*. The word suggesting that she cannot **validate** her sense of belonging to this place. The **implication** being that her 'exotic' genetic makeup excludes her from her right to belong to this land.

5 She gave the long pre-rehearsed answer they often dug for. They love a good story. She told them where her mother came from, where her father came from. She told them how her parents met in a land far from their own where she was born. She told them of how they moved around from town to town and across the ocean to a place that sometimes felt like 'home'. They smiled. Happy endings always leave a crowd feeling good.

6 What she doesn't tell them is how she feels her pre-rehearsed response drag up her throat, as though she didn't pick the right words from those that whirl at the bottom of her stomach in response. She doesn't tell them that being born out of her mother's country makes her a foreigner to a land she could have called home. Or that her official documents are marked with the Coat of Arms of a land she never felt safe in. That she cannot have conversations with the grandparents she has not seen in years because her tongue will always stumble over the **nuances** of languages that never fit quite right.

7 Sometimes she felt tired of being watered down to belonging to a foreign location on a map. To being a friend that made someone else a little more 'cultured' by simple association. As though everything else she had to offer became lacking in value every time someone asked her the question.

SELECTION VOCABULARY

subtle / sutil *adjective* barely noticeable

validate / validar *verb* to prove, or confirm COGNATE

- Why does the question make the author want to validate where she belongs?
- What word suggests she cannot validate where she is living?

Analyze Vocabulary Using Context Clues

In paragraph 1, focus on the sentence that uses the word *subtle*. Point out these context clues:

1. First, I notice that the word *subtle* is an adjective. It describes the noun *reminder*, which means "a message that prompts you to remember."
2. In the next paragraph, the author writes, "they only asked that question when they were afraid of placing her in a box." If the people asking her the question are afraid of what the author might think, then they probably aren't asking a direct, confrontational question.
3. Since it's not obvious that the question asks whether the author belongs, and the people asking it are afraid of what she might think, *subtle* must mean "indirect"or "not obvious".

Central or Main Idea

How does the reader begin to infer the author's main idea? What details help him?

The reader notices that the pronoun *they* and the author's use of third-person point of view show a separation between the author and others. The word *originally* helps the reader make the connection to a main idea about identity.

TEXT TALK

What question do people ask the author?

See paragraphs 1 and 3: They ask her, "So where are you from?"

What doesn't the author tell about how she feels?

See paragraph 6: She doesn't tell them that she feels like a foreigner to her mother's homeland and to her grandparents, or that she felt unsafe in the land of her birth.

Skills Focus

QUESTION 1: Central or Main Idea

The question "So where are you from?" makes the author feel she doesn't belong. It reminds her that people see her as different and as belonging to a country other than the one she lives in.

Skills Focus

QUESTION 3: Connect to Essential Question

The author hopes that eventually people will stop putting her in a group or category because of where she came from.

NOTES

8 She was not someone from a place. She made a home of kind words and warm feelings. Her soul became a safe nest deep inside the **confines** of her body.

"Her soul became a safe nest deep inside the confines of her body."

9 'What is the value of a land I come from. We are all of this land. We came the same way and we leave the same way.' By the time the words fought their way out of her mouth everyone else had moved on.

10 One day they would come to understand, she thought. She was not the land of her mother and father. She was her own country, with her own history of civil wars, revolutions, healing and growth. One day they would learn to keep their boxes away from her. One day they would see that she will never, *ever*, fit.

"So where are you from?" published by Sula Collective at sulacollective.com. Used by permission of Sula Collective.

TEXT TALK

What does she want others to understand?

See paragraphs 8–10: She wants others to understand that she is an individual, and she doesn't want to be put in a box or thought of as different because of her family background.

Is the author's self-esteem and sense of identity affected by people questioning where she's from? Explain.

Answers will vary.

SELECTION VOCABULARY

implication / la implicación *noun* an indirect suggestion COGNATE

What does the author feel is the "implication" of her family background?

confines / los confines *noun* limits or boundaries COGNATE

- What is compared to a "safe nest" in paragraph 8?
- How does not fitting in a box connect to the word *confines*?

nuance / el matiz *noun* slight variation or difference

- Why does the author have difficulty talking with her grandparents?
- What nearby words help explain "the nuances of languages"?

Reading Comprehension OPTIONAL

Have students complete the digital reading comprehension questions when they finish reading.

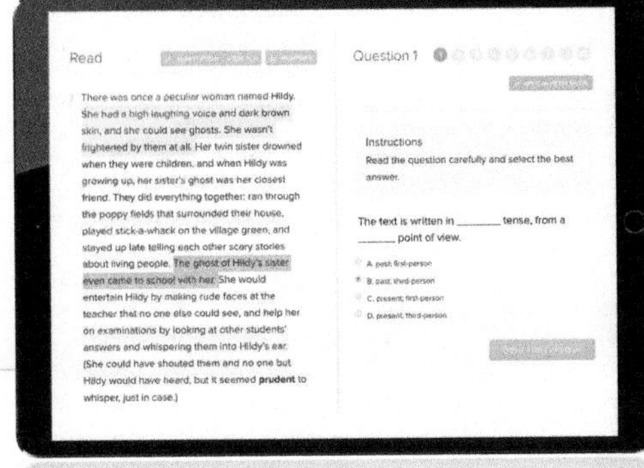

ANSWER KEY

QUESTION 1: D
QUESTION 2: C
QUESTION 3: A
QUESTION 4: D
QUESTION 5: *See chart.*

Synonym	Word
prove	validate
nonnative	exotic
suggestion	implication
cultivated	cultured
subtlety	nuance

Connect and Extend OPTIONAL

CONNECT TO EXTENDED WRITING PROJECT

Students can find inspiration from "So where are you from?" when writing their literary analyses. Have them analyze and reflect on Naomi Sepiso's use of figurative language to explore identity.

BEYOND THE BOOK

Art: A Cinematic Self-Portrait

In Naomi Sepiso's essay, she writes, "She was her own country, with her own history of civil wars, revolutions, healing and growth." Ask students to create a cinematic self-portrait designed to explore their complex identities. Encourage them to think about and include images that reveal how their identities have been impacted by the following:

- Trauma and challenges
- Social status
- Gender
- Family dynamics
- Belief systems

Students can use an online video creator tool to combine original photography and/or artwork with music to design a dynamic film exploring their individual identity.

Once students have completed their films, they can share them with the class or post them online.

Think Questions

Circulate as students answer Think Questions independently. Scaffolds for these questions are shown on the opposite page.

QUESTION 1: Textual Evidence

People always ask the author where she comes from. When she asks what they mean, they use the word *originally* because they want to know where she and her parents were born. The word bothers her because it suggests she doesn't belong in the country she lives in.

QUESTION 2: Textual Evidence

The author believes she is from where she now lives. Her idea differs from what others believe. Their idea seems to be that people come from where they or their parents were born.

QUESTION 3: Textual Evidence

A box is a container that holds things. The author feels people want to put her in a box because she is different, but they don't know which box to put her in. The author says that she won't ever fit in a box.

QUESTION 4: Context Clues

The author explains that for other people, her "sense of belonging" to this country can't be justified. In the sentence before the one with *implication,* she uses the word *suggesting.* The word *suggesting* is a clue that *implication* means "suggestion."

QUESTION 5: Context Clues

The author says her soul is safe "deep inside" her body. This gives me a clue that *confines* means something like "a limited area."

First Read

Read "So where are you from?" After you read, complete the Think Questions below.

THINK QUESTIONS

1. What question is the author frequently asked? Why do people use the word *originally* when they ask this question? Explain, citing evidence from the text.
2. Write two or three sentences explaining how the author's idea of where she's from differs from what other people think.
3. The author mentions a "box" in paragraph 2 and "boxes" in paragraph 10. How would you explain what she means? Cite textual evidence from the selection to support your answer.
4. Use context clues to determine the meaning of **implication** as it is used in paragraph 4 of "So where are you from?" Write your definition here and identify clues that helped you figure out its meaning.
5. Use context clues to determine the meaning of **confines** as it is used in paragraph 8. Write your definition here and identify clues that helped you figure out its meaning.

SCAFFOLDS

Think Questions

Use the scaffolds below to differentiate instruction for your ELL English Language Learners and A Approaching grade-level learners.

ELL **BEGINNING** Write a response using the word bank and sentence frames.

INTERMEDIATE Write a response using the sentence frames.

ADVANCED, ADVANCED HIGH Write a response using the Text-Dependent Question Guide.

A **APPROACHING** Write a response using the Text-Dependent Question Guide.

BEGINNING	INTERMEDIATE	APPROACHING / ADVANCED, ADVANCED HIGH
Word Bank	**Sentence Frames**	**Text-Dependent Question Guide**
living different belong where suggestion background born inside limits or boundaries holds	People ask the author ____ she comes from. They want to know her ____. The question suggests she doesn't ____.	1. • What question is the author always asked? • What do the people mean? • Why does the question upset her?
	The author believes she is from where she is ____. The others believe that a person comes from where he or she is ____.	2. • Where does the author believe she is from? • What do others believe it means to come from a place? • How do the ideas differ?
	A box is a container. It ____ things. People put the author in a box because they think she is ____. The author says that she won't ever fit in a box.	3. • What are boxes used for? • Why do people put the author in a box? • Why doesn't the author like boxes?
	The word *originally* suggests that she doesn't belong. The implication is also that she doesn't belong. I think the word *suggesting* is a clue that *implication* must mean "a ____."	4. • Read: "*Originally*. The word suggesting that she cannot validate her sense of belonging to this place. The **implication** being that her 'exotic' genetic makeup excludes her from her right to belong to this land." • What does the word *originally* suggest? • How does the suggestion of not belonging give a clue to the meaning of *implication*?
	The author's soul is ____ her body. This gives me a clue that *confines* means something like "____."	5. • Read: "Her soul became a safe nest deep inside the **confines** of her body." • Where is her soul? • What does that tell me about the meaning of the word *confines*?

Skill: Central or Main Idea

Introduce the Skill

Watch the Concept Definition video and read the following definition with your students.

The **central idea** of a nonfiction text is the most important point that an author makes about a **topic.** The statement of a central idea answers the question *What's it all about?* In order to find the answer, look for **supporting ideas** that help develop the central idea. Authors also include **details** as textual evidence to support the central idea about the topic. Readers **analyze** these supporting ideas or details to see what they have in common. What do they support, explain, or describe? Answering this question will help identify the central or main idea.

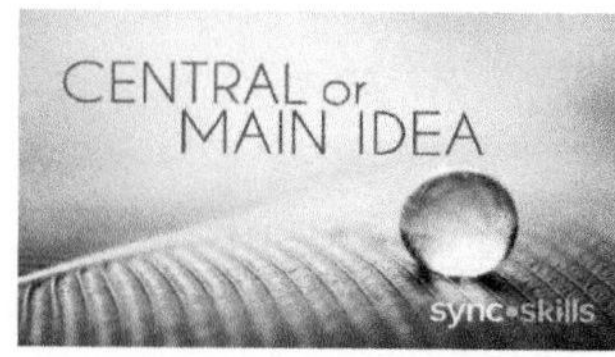

Skill: Central or Main Idea

Use the Checklist to analyze Central or Main Idea in "So where are you from?" Refer to the sample student annotations about Central or Main Idea in the text.

••• CHECKLIST FOR CENTRAL OR MAIN IDEA

In order to identify a central or main idea of a text, note the following:

- ✓ the central or main idea, if it is explicitly stated
- ✓ when the central idea emerges
- ✓ ways in which supporting ideas relate to the central idea
- ✓ key details and supporting ideas that connect to the author's point or message

To determine a central or main idea of a text and analyze its development over the course of the text, including its relationship to supporting ideas, consider the following questions:

- ✓ What main idea(s) do the details in each paragraph explain or describe?
- ✓ What bigger idea do all the paragraphs support?
- ✓ What is the best way to state the central idea?
- ✓ How do the supporting ideas and details help develop the central idea over the course of the text?
- ✓ How might you objectively summarize the text and message? What details would you include?

TURN AND TALK

1. Think of a recent magazine or newspaper article you read about current events. What was the main idea in the article?
2. What evidence, such as examples or expert opinions, did you use to determine the main idea?

SPEAKING FRAMES

- One recent article I read was about ____.
- The most important idea in the article was ____.
- The author supported the idea with ____.

SKILL VOCABULARY

central or main idea / la idea central o principal ***noun*** the most important point an author makes about a topic or in a section of text

topic / el tema ***noun*** the subject of a literary work, usually expressed as a single word or phrase in the form of a noun

supporting idea / la idea secundaria ***noun*** a focused explanation or argument that helps develop the central idea

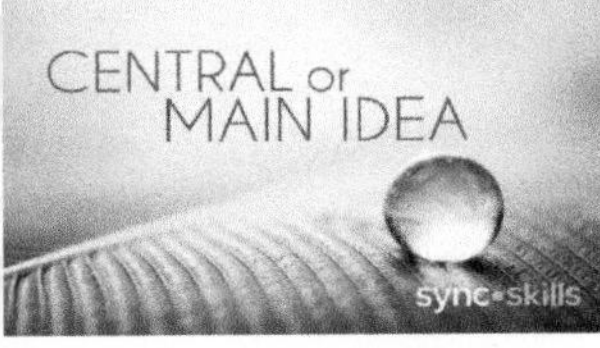

Skill: Central or Main Idea

Reread paragraphs 7–10 of "So where are you from?" Then, using the Checklist on the previous page, answer the multiple-choice questions below.

YOUR TURN

1. This question has two parts. First, answer Part A. Then, answer Part B.

   Part A: What idea is supported by the evidence the author gives in paragraph 7?

   - A. The author doesn't like being valued only because she comes from a foreign place.
   - B. The author is flattered that others assume she is from a different country.
   - C. The author feels she has less value to others because she looks different.
   - D. The author likes people to ask where she is from so that she can tell her story.

   Part B: How does the author further develop the idea from Part A in paragraph 8?

   - A. She shares the story of her background with those who ask where she is from.
   - B. She tells readers that they should treat wherever they are living as their home.
   - C. She defines her version of a home as a collection of positive words and feelings that she keeps with her, not a geographic location.
   - D. She guesses that others must find value in positive words and feelings, and she wishes people would share those with her as well.

2. Which paragraph provides support for the author's belief that she and the others all belong to the same land?

   - A. 7
   - B. 8
   - C. 9
   - D. 10

3. What main idea is expressed in the last paragraph?

   - A. The author wishes to return to the land where she fits in.
   - B. The author wants to be seen as her own person.
   - C. The author is tired of civil wars and revolutions in the world.
   - D. The author hopes one day that everyone will accept her.

SKILL VOCABULARY

detail / el detalle *noun* a fact, a description, an example, or a reason that further explains a key idea COGNATE

analyze / analizar *verb* to consider in detail and discover essential features or meaning COGNATE

Your Turn

Ask students to complete the Your Turn activity.

QUESTION 1

Part A

A. Correct. The author says she doesn't want to be valued for making others feel more "cultured."

B. Incorrect. The author never says she feels flattered to be asked about her origins.

C. Incorrect. The author feels she has more to offer than just being from another place.

D. Incorrect. Being asked where she comes from makes the author feel others don't see the total person she is.

Part B

A. Incorrect. The author does not say that she shares this information with people who ask her where she is from.

B. Incorrect. The author is defining what home means to the subject of this essay, and she is not directly addressing readers.

C. Correct. The author says, "She was not someone from a place. She made a home of kind words and warm feelings."

D. Incorrect. The author says that her version of a home is made of "kind words and warm feelings" that she has already experienced.

QUESTION 2

A. Incorrect.

B. Incorrect.

C. Correct. The author says where she came from doesn't matter. "We are all of this land."

D. Incorrect.

QUESTION 3

A. Incorrect. The author questions the value of a land she comes from.

B. Correct. The author says she hopes that people will understand she can't fit in a "box."

C. Incorrect. The author's references to wars are personal.

D. Incorrect. The author says that someday people will "see that she will never, *ever*, fit."

Close Read

Skills Focus

QUESTION 1: Central or Main Idea

See paragraph 10.

QUESTION 2: Language, Style, and Audience

See paragraph 5: The author uses the pronouns *she* and *her* to refer to herself. Writing in the third-person suggests that the author's experience and feelings are shared by others who live in countries where they were not born.

QUESTION 3: Connect to Essential Question

See paragraph 10.

CHECK FOR SUCCESS

If students struggle to respond to Skills Focus question 1, ask them the following questions:

- In paragraph 1, what does the question remind the author of?
- In the last paragraph, what does the author say will never happen?
- What do the details tell you about the important idea?

Have students transition to read and annotate independently once they have successfully completed the first Skills Focus prompt.

So where are you fror

Close Read

Reread "So where are you from?" As you reread, complete the Skills Focus questions below. Then use yo answers and annotations from the questions to help you complete the Write activity.

SKILLS FOCUS

1. Read the first and last paragraphs of "So where are you from?" and pay particular attention to the last sentence in both paragraphs. What overall idea do they share? Cite evidence from paragraphs 3–8 in support of the main or central idea.
2. How does the author's choice to use the third-person pronouns *she* and *her* support the central or main idea? Cite textual evidence.
3. It is important to the author to be accepted for th qualities that make her the individual she i Identify examples in "So where are you from? that show her feelings, and explain how they ar connected to the text's main idea.

WRITE

LITERARY ANALYSIS: *Where are you from?* seems like a question with an obvious answer, but the answer is clearly more complicated according to the essay's author, Naomi Sepiso. How does Sepiso respond to this question? What supporting evidence does she include to develop her central or main idea? Be sure to use ideas and evidence from her essay to support your analysis.

Writer's Notebook

Connect to Essential Question: Give students time to reflect on how "So where are you from?" connects to the unit's essential question "What makes you, you?" by freewriting in their Writer's Notebooks.

Beginning & Intermediate

Read aloud the unit's essential question: "What makes you, you?" Encourage students to draw their connections or allow students to write in their native language. Circulate, prompting students for their thoughts as they respond orally or through pantomime.

Advanced & Advanced High

Allow students to share their reflections orally in pairs or small groups before freewriting.

SCAFFOLDS

Collaborative Conversation

Break students into collaborative conversation groups to discuss the Close Read prompt. Ask students to use the StudySyncTV episode as a model for their discussion. Remind them to reference their Skills Focus annotations in their discussion.

"Where are you from?" seems like a question with an obvious answer, but the answer is clearly more complicated according to the essay's author, Naomi Sepiso. How does Sepiso respond to this question? What supporting evidence does she include to develop her central or main idea? Be sure to use ideas and evidence from her essay to support your analysis.

Use the scaffolds below to differentiate instruction for your ELL English Language Learners and A Approaching grade-level learners.

ELL **BEGINNING, INTERMEDIATE** Use the discussion guide and speaking frames to discuss with support from the teacher.

ADVANCED, ADVANCED HIGH Use the discussion guide and speaking frames to discuss in mixed-level groups.

A APPROACHING Use the discussion guide to discuss in mixed-level groups.

APPROACHING
ADVANCED, ADVANCED HIGH
BEGINNING, INTERMEDIATE

Discussion Guide	Speaking Frames
1. What question comes up at the beginning of the essay? What do those who ask the question mean?	• Others ask the author ____. • They use the word *originally* to suggest ____.
2. What example shows how the author responds to the question?	• The author tells where ____. • This is evidence because ____.
3. What does she hope that people will come to understand?	• The author hopes people will understand that she is ____. • She hopes they will stop putting her in a box because ____.

Review Prompt and Rubric

Before students begin writing, review the writing prompt and rubric with the class.

LITERARY ANALYSIS: "Where are you from?" seems like a question with an obvious answer, but the answer is clearly more complicated according to the essay's author, Naomi Sepiso. How does Sepiso respond to this question? What supporting evidence does she include to develop her main idea? Be sure to use ideas and evidence from her essay to support your analysis.

PROMPT GUIDE

- What question comes up at the beginning of the essay?
- What do those who ask the question mean?
- How does the author feel about this question?
- What example shows how the author responds to the question?

Score	Central or Main Idea	Language and Conventions
4	The writer clearly analyzes and explains the central or main idea with supporting evidence. The writer provides exemplary analysis, using relevant evidence from the text.	The writer demonstrates a consistent command of grammar, punctuation, and usage conventions. Although minor errors may be evident, they do not detract from the fluency or the clarity of the writing.
3	The writer analyzes and explains the central or main idea with supporting evidence. The writer provides sufficient analysis, using relevant evidence from the text most of the time.	The writer demonstrates an adequate command of grammar, punctuation, and usage conventions. Although some errors may be evident, they create few (if any) disruptions in the fluency or clarity of the writing.
2	The writer begins to analyze or explain the central or main idea with supporting evidence, but the analysis is incomplete. The writer uses relevant evidence from the text only some of the time.	The writer demonstrates a partial command of grammar, punctuation, and usage conventions. Some distracting errors may be evident, at times creating minor disruptions in the fluency or clarity of the writing.
1	The writer attempts to analyze or explain the central or main idea with supporting evidence, but the analysis is not successful. The writer uses little or no relevant evidence from the text.	The writer demonstrates little or no command of grammar, punctuation, and usage conventions. Serious and persistent errors create disruptions in the fluency of the writing and sometimes interfere with meaning.
0	The writer does not provide a relevant response to the prompt or does not provide a response at all.	Serious and persistent errors overwhelm the writing and interfere with the meaning of the response as a whole, making the writer's meaning impossible to understand.

Write

SCAFFOLDS

Ask students to complete the writing assignment using textual evidence to support their answers.

Use the scaffolds below to differentiate instruction for your ELL English Language Learners and A Approaching grade-level learners.

ELL **BEGINNING** With the help of the word bank, write a response using paragraph frame 1.

INTERMEDIATE With the help of the word bank, write a response using paragraph frames 1 and 2.

ADVANCED, ADVANCED HIGH Write a response of differentiated length using the sentence starters.

A **APPROACHING** Write a response of differentiated length using the sentence starters.

BEGINNING / INTERMEDIATE — ADVANCED, ADVANCED HIGH / APPROACHING

Word Bank	Paragraph Frame 1	Paragraph Frame 2	Sentence Starters
where feel belongs evidence family	The author begins with the question about ____ she is from. It shows that she doesn't feel like she ____. One example that she gives is the story about her ____ background. This supporting ____ helps me understand the main idea. It helps me understand how the question makes the author ____.	Another example of supporting evidence is ____. This shows ____. This helps me to better understand the main idea because ____.	• The author begins by stating the question . . . • The question suggests that the author's main idea is about . . . • One example of supporting evidence is . . . • Another example of evidence is . . . • In the end, the author hopes that one day . . . • This helps me understand the main idea because . . .

Peer Review

Rate

Respond to the following with a point rating that reflects your opinion.

	1	2	3	4
Ideas				
Evidence				
Language and Conventions				

Submit

Students should submit substantive feedback to two peers using the instructions below.

- How well does this response answer the prompt?
- How well does the writer support the analysis of the central or main idea?
- Which sentence in the writer's response made you think differently about the text?
- What did the writer do well in this response? What does the writer need to work on?

ELL A **SENTENCE FRAMES**

- You were able to (completely / partly / almost) answer the prompt because ____.
- You could support the main idea more completely by ____.
- You supported the idea of ____ with the evidence of ____.
- One idea that needs more support is ____.
- I thought differently about the text after reading ____.
- My favorite part of your response is ____.

The Outsiders

FICTION

S. E. Hinton

1967

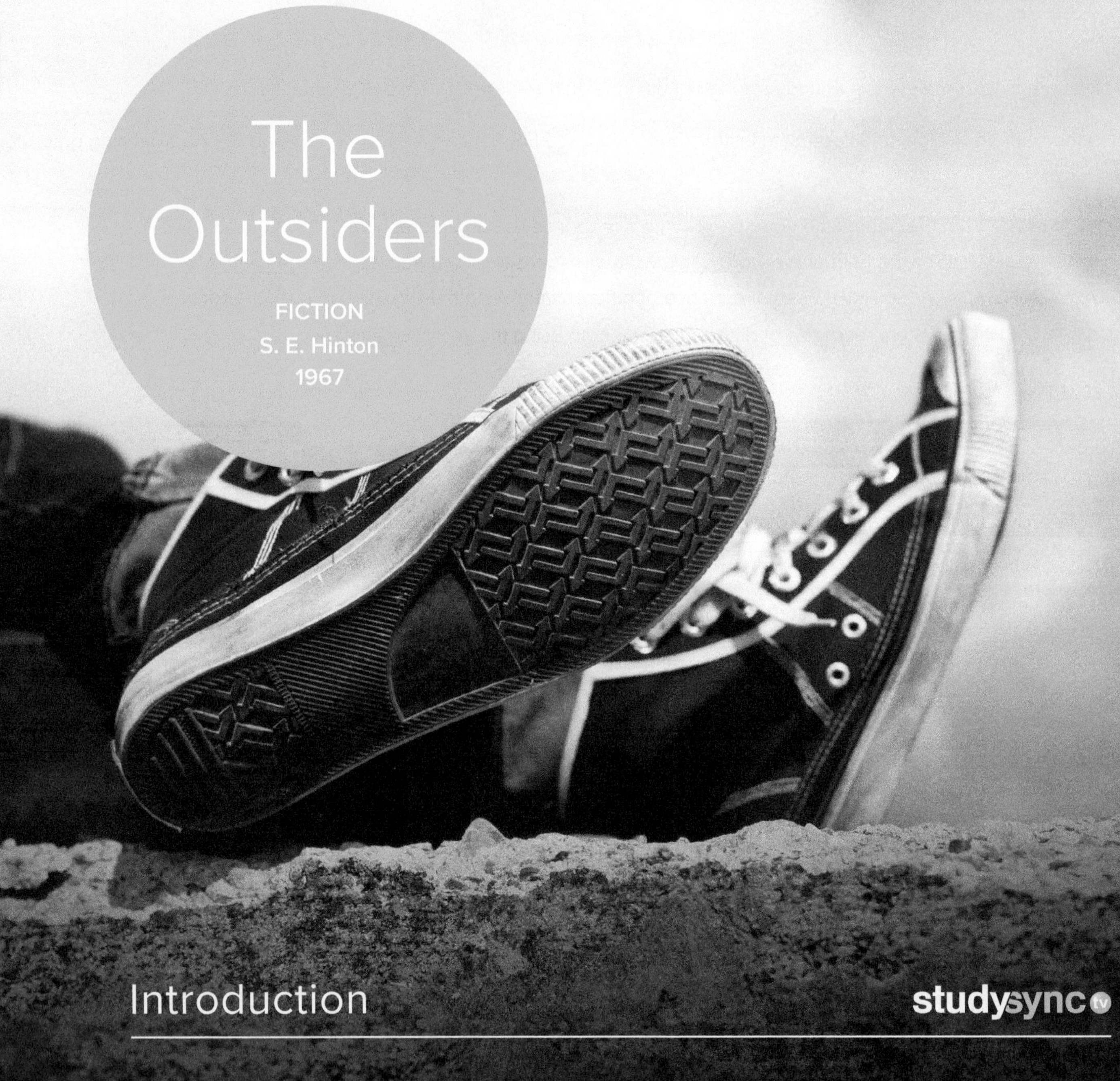

Introduction

studysync tv

Susan Eloise Hinton (b. 1948) was only seventeen years old when her groundbreaking novel *The Outsiders* was first published. Her publisher believed the novel would sell better if the author's gender remained unknown, so it was published under Hinton's initials. The novel explores the hearts and minds of a gang with no voice, telling the story of class conflict between the lower-class "Greasers" and the upper-class "Socs" (short for "Socials" and pronounced "Soshes") in 1960's middle America. In this excerpt from early in the novel, the Greasers learn that the rival Socs have viciously attacked a fellow Greaser named Johnny.

In 1960s Middle America, members of a gang called the Greasers find Johnny, one of its members, badly beaten. In this excerpt, Ponyboy relates to Cherry how Johnny was accosted by four members of the Socs, an upper-class gang. Having grown up in a violent home, Johnny was used to aggression, but this beating changes him and he begins to carry a knife for protection. Cherry, a member of the Socs, explains that not all Socs would do such a thing. She also says that rich kids have problems just like everyone else. Ponyboy considers how much the Socs and the Greasers actually have in common and decides it's money that separates them. Cherry disagrees because she thinks the two groups hold different values. The Socs are sophisticated and cold while the Greasers are emotional, which Cherry admires.

 Proficiency-leveled summaries and summaries in multiple languages are available digitally.

 Audio and audio text highlighting are available with this text.

CONNECT TO ESSENTIAL QUESTION

What makes you, you?

What happens when being part of a group defines who you are? In this excerpt from the classic novel *The Outsiders,* members of rival gangs begin to question how they see themselves and how they see each other.

Access Complex Text

LEXILE: 660L **WORD COUNT:** 1,060

The following areas may be challenging for students, particularly ELL English Language Learners and A Approaching grade-level learners.

Prior Knowledge	Connection of Ideas	Genre
• The text is infused with the class conflict and cultural divides of the United States in the 1950s and 1960s. The characters label themselves based on their affiliations, and their differences are expressed in their lifestyles.	• The text connects the violence happening in a small Midwestern city to the violence happening at the same time in New York City. • 1950s car culture and the gang conflicts described in the musical *West Side Story* provide further context.	• Students may benefit from considering the text as an excerpt. Since *The Outsiders* is a novel, it takes more time with moments over a longer narrative. The conversation between Ponyboy and Cherry is one example.

SCAFFOLDS  ENGLISH LANGUAGE LEARNERS  APPROACHING GRADE LEVEL  BEYOND GRADE LEVEL

These icons identify differentiation strategies and scaffolded support for a variety of students. See the digital lesson plan for additional differentiation strategies and scaffolds.

Instructional Path

The print teacher's edition includes essential point-of-use instruction and planning tools. Complete lesson plans and program documents appear in your digital teacher account.

First Read: The Outsiders

Objectives: After an initial reading and discussion of the excerpt, students will be able to use the reading comprehension strategy of making inferences, using context clues to define new vocabulary, and demonstrating comprehension by responding to questions using textual evidence.

Skill: Character

Objectives: After rereading and discussing a model of close reading, students will be able to analyze how dialogue and incidents in a story can reveal aspects of a character.

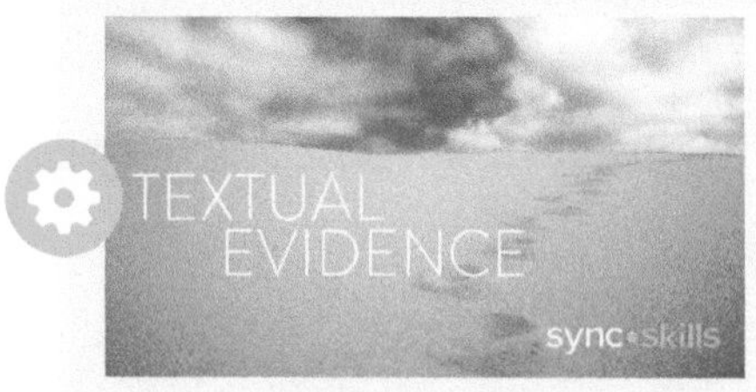

Skill: Textual Evidence

Objectives: After rereading and discussing a model of close reading, students will be able to cite the textual evidence that most strongly supports an analysis of what the text says explicitly as well as inferences drawn from the text.

Close Read: The Outsiders

Objectives: After engaging in a close reading and discussion of an excerpt from the text, students will be able to analyze how an author uses dialogue and incidents in a story to develop characters in order to participate in a collaborative conversation and write a short literary analysis.

Progress Monitoring

Opportunities to Learn	Opportunities to Demonstrate Learning	Opportunities to Reteach
Character		
Skill: Character	Skill: Character • Your Turn Close Read • Skills Focus • Write	Unit 4 Skill: Character - /HUG Spotlight Skill: Character
Textual Evidence		
Skill: Textual Evidence	Skill: Textual Evidence • Your Turn Close Read • Writer's Notebook • Skills Focus • Collaborative Conversation • Write	Unit 5 Skill: Textual Evidence - Farewell to Manzanar Spotlight Skill: Textual Evidence

First Read

Introduce the Text

As a class, watch the video preview  and have students read the introduction in pairs to make connections to the video preview.

To activate prior knowledge and experiences, ask students:

- What two words would you use to describe this video?
- What questions do you have after reading the introduction?

ELL SPEAKING FRAMES

- The ____ in the video makes me think ____.
- The video shows ____. This makes me wonder ____.
- I think the text will ____. I think this because ____.
- I predict that there will be ____. I believe this because ____.

Entry Point

As students prepare to read *The Outsiders*, share the following information with them to provide context.

✓ Susan Eloise Hinton (S. E. Hinton) was born in Tulsa, Oklahoma, in 1948. She developed an interest in reading and writing early in life, and she wrote *The Outsiders* while she was in high school.

✓ Hinton explains that she did not think teenagers were accurately portrayed in fiction at that time, so she wrote a novel with a plot that reflected her experience. She also cites several authors and movies as influences. The authors include Shirley Jackson, Ray Bradbury, and Margaret Mitchell; the movies include *West Side Story* and *Rebel Without a Cause.*

✓ S. E. Hinton's novel *The Outsiders* was published in 1967, and it was marketed to adults. At first the novel did not sell well, but the publisher saw that teachers were buying the book to share with students. This discovery contributed to the development of YA literature as a genre.

"We have troubles you've never heard of. . . . Things are rough all over."

Skill: Character

Ponyboy describes how Johnny often got beaten by his father, but this beating from the Socs was even worse. This helps us understand that Johnny is a character who struggles to stand up for himself. But Ponyboy and Steve both seem concerned, so we know that Johnny is also a character who has people who care about him.

1 We were used to seeing Johnny banged up—his father clobbered him around a lot, and although it made us madder than heck, we couldn't do anything about it. But those beatings had been nothing like this. Johnny's face was cut up and bruised and swollen, and there was a wide gash from his temple to his cheekbone. He would carry that scar all his life. His white T-shirt was splattered with blood. I just stood there, trembling with sudden cold. I thought he might be dead; surely no one could be beaten like that and live. Steve closed his eyes for a second and muffled a groan as he dropped on his knees beside Soda.

2 Somehow the gang sensed what had happened. Two-Bit was suddenly there beside me, and for once his comical grin was gone and his dancing gray eyes were stormy. Darry had seen us from our porch and ran toward us, suddenly skidding to a halt. Dally was there, too, swearing under his breath, and turning away with a sick expression on his face. I wondered about it vaguely. Dally had seen people killed on the streets of New York's West Side. Why did he look sick now?

3 "Johnny?" Soda lifted him up and held him against his shoulder. He gave the limp body a slight shake. "Hey, Johnnycake."

4 Johnny didn't open his eyes, but there came a soft question. "Soda?"

5 "Yeah, it's me," Sodapop said. "Don't talk. You're gonna be okay."

6 "There was a whole bunch of them," Johnny went on, swallowing, ignoring Soda's **command.** "A blue Mustang full . . . I got so scared . . ." He tried to swear, but suddenly started crying, fighting to control himself, then sobbing all the more because he couldn't. I had seen Johnny take a whipping with a two-by-four from his old man and never let out a whimper. That made it worse to see him break now. Soda just held him and pushed Johnny's hair back out of his eyes. "It's okay, Johnnycake, they're gone now. It's okay."

7 Finally, between sobs, Johnny managed to gasp out his story. He had been hunting our football to practice a few kicks when a blue Mustang had pulled

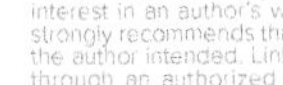

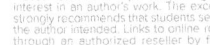

SELECTION VOCABULARY

command / la orden ***noun*** a direction or instruction to do something

Analyze Vocabulary Using Context Clues

In paragraph 6, focus on the sentence that uses the word *command*. Point out these context clues:

1. Johnny is ignoring Soda's command by talking in this sentence.
2. If Johnny's actions show that he is ignoring Soda's command, then it makes sense that Soda was telling Johnny what to do.
3. Based on this context, a *command* is "an order to do something."

Character

How did the reader begin to understand Johnny's character traits?

The reader noticed that Ponyboy mentions that Johnny often gets hit by his father, but his friends obviously care about him. This helps us understand that Johnny is a sympathetic character in the group.

Skills Focus

QUESTION 1: Character

Ponyboy uses the pronoun *we* to show that he is part of a group: the Greasers. He says that all the Greasers are concerned about Johnny, showing that they all care for one another. In this world, the identity of one person is tied to the values of a whole group. This is a theme of the excerpt.

TEXT TALK

What happens to Johnny at home?

See paragraph 1: Johnny's father mistreats him.

Why is Johnny's face so badly cut?

See paragraph 7: One of the Socs who attacked him had been wearing a lot of rings on his hand.

Skills Focus

QUESTION 3: Character

The author includes dialogue to reveal Cherry's character traits. Cherry says that not all Socs are like the ones who attacked Johnny and reminds Ponyboy that one of the Greasers has also attacked people. Ponyboy admits that she is right. This helps us see that Cherry is a character who is capable of seeing from multiple perspectives. She is sympathetic and honest.

Skills Focus

QUESTION 4: Connect to Essential Question

Cherry says that most people probably think the Socs are lucky rich kids. This gives readers a clue about how other people see the Socs, including the Greasers. She also says that the Socs have troubles, too. I think that this difference between how they're seen and how they really feel is a big part of the Socs' identity.

TEXT TALK

What does Cherry tell Ponyboy about the Socs?

See paragraph 13: She tells Ponyboy the Socs have "troubles."

NOTES

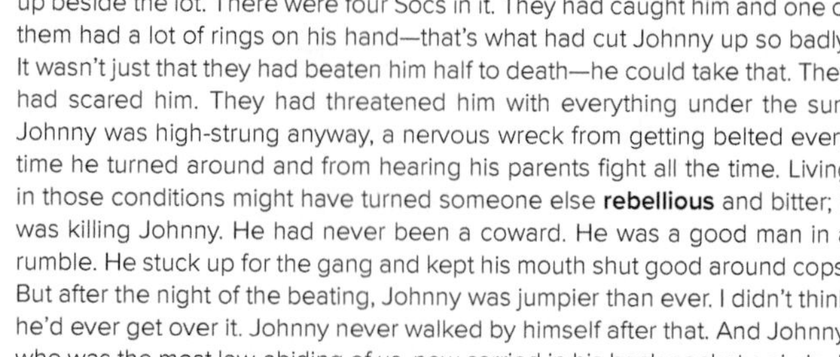
up beside the lot. There were four Socs in it. They had caught him and one of them had a lot of rings on his hand—that's what had cut Johnny up so badly. It wasn't just that they had beaten him half to death—he could take that. They had scared him. They had threatened him with everything under the sun. Johnny was high-strung anyway, a nervous wreck from getting belted every time he turned around and from hearing his parents fight all the time. Living in those conditions might have turned someone else **rebellious** and bitter; it was killing Johnny. He had never been a coward. He was a good man in a rumble. He stuck up for the gang and kept his mouth shut good around cops. But after the night of the beating, Johnny was jumpier than ever. I didn't think he'd ever get over it. Johnny never walked by himself after that. And Johnny, who was the most law-abiding of us, now carried in his back pocket a six-inch switchblade. He'd use it, too, if he ever got jumped again. They had scared him that much. He would kill the next person who jumped him. Nobody was ever going to beat him like that again. Not over his dead body. . . .

8 I had nearly forgotten that Cherry was listening to me. But when I came back to reality and looked at her, I was startled to find her as white as a sheet.

9 "All Socs aren't like that," she said. "You have to believe me, Ponyboy. Not all of us are like that."

10 "Sure," I said.

11 "That's like saying all you greasers are like Dallas Winston. I'll bet he's jumped a few people."

12 I **digested** that. It was true. Dally had jumped people. He had told us stories about muggings in New York that had made the hair on the back of my neck stand up. But not all of us are that bad.

13 Cherry no longer looked sick, only sad. "I'll bet you think the Socs have it made. The rich kids, the West-side Socs. I'll tell you something, Ponyboy, and it may come as a surprise. We have troubles you've never heard of. You want to know something?" She looked me straight in the eye. "Things are rough all over."

14 "I believe you," I said. "We'd better get out there with the popcorn or Two-Bit'll think I ran off with his money."

. . .

15 After the movie was over it suddenly came to us that Cherry and Marcia didn't have a way to get home. Two-Bit **gallantly** offered to walk them home—the west side of town was only about twenty miles away—but they wanted to call

SELECTION VOCABULARY

rebellious / rebelde ***adjective*** refusing to follow rules or accepted ways of behaving COGNATE

- What does Ponyboy say might make someone rebellious?
- What other word does Ponyboy use to describe a person living that way?

digest / asimilar ***verb*** to think about something

- What does Cherry say about the Socs and the Greasers to Ponyboy?
- What does Ponyboy think about after Cherry tells him these things?

gallantly / galantemente ***adverb*** in a manner showing special courtesy or respect, particularly toward women COGNATE

- What is Cherry and Marcia's problem?
- What does Two-Bit offer to do?

NOTES

their parents and have them come and get them. Two-Bit finally talked them into letting us drive them home in his car. I think they were still half-scared of us. They were getting over it, though, as we walked to Two-Bit's house to pick up the car. It seemed funny to me that Socs—if these girls were any example—were just like us. They liked the Beatles and thought Elvis Presley was out, and we thought the Beatles were rank and that Elvis was tuff, but that seemed the only difference to me. Of course greasy girls would have acted a lot tougher, but there was a basic sameness. I thought maybe it was money that separated us.

16 "No," Cherry said slowly when I said this. "It's not just money. Part of it is, but not all. You Greasers have a different set of values. You're more emotional. We're **sophisticated**—cool to the point of not feeling anything. Nothing is real with us. You know, sometimes I'll catch myself talking to a girl-friend, and I realize I don't mean half of what I'm saying. I don't really think a beer blast on the river bottom is super-cool, but I'll rave about one to a girl-friend just to be saying something." She smiled at me. "I never told anyone that. I think you're the first person I've ever really gotten through to."

Excerpted from *The Outsiders* by S. E. Hinton, published by the Penguin Group.

TEXT TALK

How does Cherry feel about Ponyboy?

See paragraph 16: She feels like she connects with Ponyboy.

What can you infer about Cherry based on what she tells Ponyboy at the end of the excerpt?

Answers will vary.

Based on the excerpt, what do you think is at the heart of the rivalry between the Greasers and the Socs? Why do their differences cause so much hostility?

Answers will vary.

Ask each Beyond grade-level student to write one additional discussion question. Then have one or two students facilitate a discussion, using their questions to guide the conversation.

SELECTION VOCABULARY

sophisticated / sofisticado/a ***adjective*** complicated, highly developed, or advanced COGNATE

- How does Cherry describe the Greasers?
- How does Cherry describe being "sophisticated"? How does this compare with her description of the Greasers?

Think Questions

Circulate as students answer Think Questions independently. Scaffolds for these questions are shown on the opposite page.

QUESTION 1: Textual Evidence

The Greasers seem close-knit, and they also seem to care about each other. They all seem upset and concerned about Johnny's attack. Ponyboy is terrified because he thinks Johnny might be dead. He says he was "trembling with sudden cold." Two-Bit's "stormy" eyes show that he is angry. Sodapop tries to reassure Johnny. Dally shows that he is angry, and his expression shows that he is disturbed by his friend's condition.

QUESTION 2: Textual Evidence

The attack makes Johnny more fearful. Following the attack, Ponyboy says that Johnny would not walk alone anymore, and he begins to carry a knife with him. Ponyboy says that "Nobody was ever going to beat him like that again."

QUESTION 3: Textual Evidence

Ponyboy realizes that they are more or less the same and that money was what separated the two groups. He says, "Of course greasy girls would have acted a lot tougher, but there was a basic sameness. I thought maybe it was money that separated us."

QUESTION 4: Context Clues

I think *gallantly* means "in a way that shows special courtesy" because Two-Bit is being kind to Cherry and Marcia by offering to walk them home.

QUESTION 5: Word Meaning

Definition 2 most closely matches the meaning of the word *digested* in paragraph 12. Ponyboy says that he digested something that Cherry says. Then he describes differences between Dally and other members of his gang, which shows that he has thought about what Cherry said about there being differences among the Greasers.

First Read

Read *The Outsiders*. After you read, complete the Think Questions below.

THINK QUESTIONS

1. How would you describe the relationships among the Greasers? Cite textual evidence from the selection to support your answer.
2. What effect does the attack have on Johnny? Cite textual evidence from the selection to support your answer.
3. What observation does Ponyboy make about the Greasers and the Socs? Cite textual evidence from the selection to support your answer.
4. Use context clues to determine the meaning of **gallantly** as it is used in paragraph 15 of the excerpt from *The Outsiders*. Write your definition here and identify clues that helped you figure out its meaning.
5. Read the following dictionary entry:

   digest

   di•gest \dī ˈjest\ *verb*

   1. to break down food into a form that the body can use
   2. to think about something and try to understand it
   3. to arrange in a particular order

   Which definition most closely matches the meaning of **digested** as it is used in paragraph 12? Write the correct definition of *digested* here and explain how you figured out the correct meaning.

SCAFFOLDS

Think Questions

Use the scaffolds below to differentiate instruction for your ELL English Language Learners and A Approaching grade-level learners.

ELL **BEGINNING** Write a response using the word bank and sentence frames.

INTERMEDIATE Write a response using the sentence frames.

ADVANCED, ADVANCED HIGH Write a response using the Text-Dependent Question Guide.

A **APPROACHING** Write a response using the Text-Dependent Question Guide.

BEGINNING	INTERMEDIATE	APPROACHING / ADVANCED, ADVANCED HIGH
Word Bank	**Sentence Frames**	**Text-Dependent Question Guide**
money special courtesy concerned similar help knife angry alone fearful twenty miles close	The Greasers have a ____ relationship. I know this because they feel ____ and ____ when they see that Johnny has been beaten.	1. • How does each member respond to seeing Johnny badly beaten? • What do these reactions reveal about their feelings? • What do their feelings suggest about their relationship?
	After the attack, Johnny becomes ____. He never walks ____ again, and he carries a ____ around with him.	2. • How does Johnny's mood change after his attack? • How do Johnny's actions change after his attack?
	Ponyboy thinks that the Greasers and the Socs are____, but ____ separates the two groups.	3. • What does Ponyboy find funny about the two groups? • What differences does he notice between the groups? • Which differences does he see as significant?
	Two-Bit offers to ____ Cherry and Marcia get home, which is more than ____ away. This gives me a clue that *gallantly* means "to do something in a way that shows ____."	4. • Read: "Two-Bit **gallantly** offered to walk them home—the west side of town was only about twenty miles away—but they wanted to call their parents and have them come and get them." • What action is being described in this paragraph? • What does that tell me about the meaning of the word *gallantly*?
	Digested as used in the text matches definition #____.	5. • "I **digested** that. It was true. Dally had jumped people. He had told us stories about muggings in New York that had made the hair on the back of my neck stand up. But not all of us are that bad." • Does *digest* mean "to break down food into a form that the body can use"? (#1) • Does *digest* mean "to think about something and try to understand it"? (#2) • Does *digest* mean "to arrange in a particular order"? (#3)

Reading Comprehension OPTIONAL

Have students complete the digital reading comprehension questions ✓ when they finish reading.

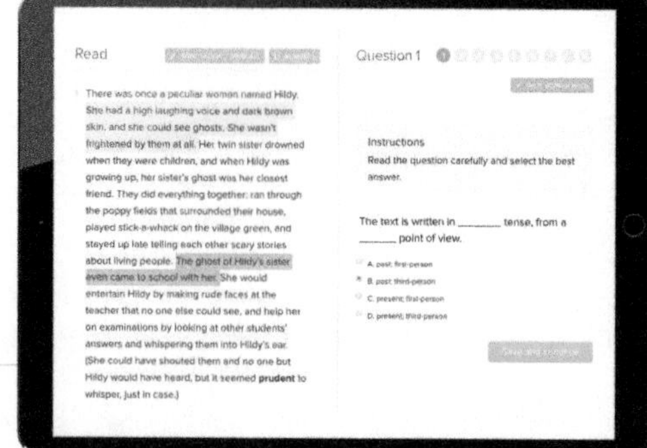

ANSWER KEY

QUESTION 1: A
QUESTION 2: C
QUESTION 3: D
QUESTION 4: C
QUESTION 5: C
QUESTION 6: B
QUESTION 7: A
QUESTION 8: D
QUESTION 9: *See first chart.*
QUESTION 10: *See second chart.*

First	Second	Third	Fourth
Johnny cries.	Johnny carries a switchblade wherever he goes	Cherry says not all Socs are violent.	Cherry feels a connection to the narrator.

Dialogue	Character
"Don't talk. You're gonna be okay."	Soda
"A blue Mustang full... I got so scared..."	Johnny
"You have to believe me, Ponyboy. Not all of us are like that."	Cherry
"We'd better get out there with the popcorn or Two-Bit'll think I ran off with his money."	Ponyboy

Connect and Extend OPTIONAL

CONNECT TO EXTENDED WRITING PROJECT

Students can find inspiration from *The Outsiders* when writing their literary analyses. Have them reflect on S. E. Hinton's characterization of teens as they work to find a sense of belonging.

BEYOND THE BOOK

Writing: Dally's Interior Monologue

When Johnny returns beaten, Dally's response surprises Ponyboy. He says, "Dally had seen people killed on the streets of New York's West Side. Why did he look sick now?"

Ask students to write Dally's interior monologue in this moment to reveal what he is thinking, feeling, and/or remembering that makes him look sick. An interior monologue is a literary device that allows the reader into a character's mind and can be written as a stream of consciousness, or a flow of thoughts.

Once students have written their interior monologues, pair them up to exchange papers with partners. After students have read their partners' interior monologues, ask pairs to discuss the similarities and differences between their pieces.

To reflect, ask students:

- What details from the text helped you write this interior monologue?
- What was most challenging about getting inside Dally's mind?

CHARACTER

Skill: Character

Use the Checklist to analyze Character in *The Outsiders*. Refer to the sample student annotations about Character in the text.

••• CHECKLIST FOR CHARACTER

In order to determine how dialogue or incidents in a story propel the action, reveal aspects of a character, or provoke a decision, note the following:

- ✓ the characters in the story, including the protagonist and antagonist
- ✓ key dialogue and how it reveals character traits and moves the action, or the events of the plot, forward
- ✓ characters' responses and reactions to other characters or events, and what this reveals about them
- ✓ when an event or another character's actions or dialogue provokes a character to make a decision
- ✓ the resolution and ways it affects the characters

To analyze how particular lines of dialogue or incidents in a story or drama propel the action, reveal aspects of a character, or provoke a decision, consider the following questions:

- ✓ How does the dialogue propel, or move forward, the action in the story?
- ✓ How does the dialogue reveal different aspects or traits of each character?
- ✓ How do the events, actions, and reactions reveal different aspects or traits of each character?
- ✓ Did an event or a character provoke another character to make a decision? What was it, and how did it affect the events of the plot?
- ✓ How does the resolution affect the characters?

 SKILL VOCABULARY

character / el personaje ***noun*** an individual in a literary work whose thoughts, feelings, actions, and reactions move the action of the plot forward

plot / la trama ***noun*** the sequence of events that form a story

resolution / la resolución ***noun*** the final outcome of the story's conflict COGNATE

Skill: Character

Introduce the Skill

Watch the Concept Definition video ▶ and read the following definition with your students.

A **character** is a person, animal, or other being portrayed in a story. Every kind of fiction and drama needs characters. Characters' thoughts, feelings, actions, and reactions drive the **plot**, or the events that take place in the story. The resolution is the final outcome of the story's conflict. Writers use several techniques to develop characters and reveal aspects of their personality including **dialogue**, or conversation, description, and plot events. Character **traits** are the defining qualities of personality or behavior, good or bad, that make that character unique.

The main character—the one the story revolves around and who usually has a problem to solve—is called the **protagonist**. The character who opposes the protagonist is called the **antagonist**. Minor characters provide support for the protagonist or antagonist, helping to reveal aspects of their personalities.

TURN AND TALK

1. What are some qualities of your favorite characters from books, TV, or movies? What helps you figure out that the characters have these qualities?

2. How does dialogue help you understand a character? How do events in a story help you understand a character?

 SPEAKING FRAMES

- My favorite character from books, TV, or movies is ____, and that character is ____.
- I know the character has this quality because ____.
- The dialogue and events in a story help you understand a character because ____.

Your Turn

Ask students to complete the Your Turn activity.

QUESTION 1

A. Correct. Two-Bit wants to make sure the girls get home safely, regardless of whether or not they are Socs.

B. Incorrect. Two-Bit does not have bad intentions.

C. Incorrect. Cherry and Marcia "were starting to get over" their fear of the Greasers, though they are not overly eager to get along with them, either.

D. Incorrect. Although Cherry and Marcia seem at first to be suspicious of Two-Bit's offer to drive them home, there is no mention of the Socs owing the Greasers anything in return.

QUESTION 2

A. Incorrect. Details in the paragraph do not indicate that either character is lonely.

B. Incorrect. This exchange does not indicate anything about how tough the characters are.

C. Correct. Ponyboy realizes that both groups have more similarities than they might know about. He says the Socs "were just like us."

D. Incorrect. Cherry and Ponyboy both start to see from one another's point of view.

QUESTION 3

A. Incorrect. This detail does not show that Cherry feels pressure to fit in with the Socs.

B. Incorrect. This detail does not show that Cherry feels pressure to fit in with the Socs.

C. Correct. This detail shows that Cherry sometimes says things just so she will fit in with the Socs.

D. Incorrect. This detail does not show that Cherry feels pressure to fit in with the Socs.

Skill: Character

Reread paragraphs 15 and 16 of *The Outsiders*. Then, using the Checklist on the previous page, answer the multiple-choice questions below.

YOUR TURN

1. Based on Two-Bit's offer to help Cherry and Marcia get home in paragraph 15, the reader can conclude that—

   - A. Two-Bit is a nice guy, despite the reputation that most Greasers have.
   - B. Two-Bit is just as bad as his Greaser reputation implies.
   - C. Cherry and Marcia are afraid of Two-Bit and acting out of fear.
   - D. Cherry and Marcia do not want to owe the Greasers any favors.

2. Based on the dialogue between Ponyboy and Cherry in paragraphs 15 and 16, the reader can conclude that both characters share which of the following character traits?

   - A. Both Cherry and Ponyboy are lonely for company.
   - B. Both Cherry and Ponyboy are tough.
   - C. Both Cherry and Ponyboy are becoming aware of the commonalities they share.
   - D. Both Cherry and Ponyboy are stubborn when it comes to seeing things from another perspective.

3. Which piece of dialogue best shows that Cherry feels pressure to fit in with the Socs?

   - A. "You Greasers have a different set of values."
   - B. "We're sophisticated—cool to the point of not feeling anything."
   - C. "You know, sometimes I'll catch myself talking to a girl-friend, and I realize I don't mean half of what I'm saying."
   - D. "I never told anyone that. I think you're the first person I've ever really gotten through to."

SKILL VOCABULARY

dialogue / el diálogo ***noun*** the conversation between characters COGNATE

trait / el rasgo ***noun*** an aspect of a character's behavior and attitude that make up that character's personality

protagonist / el/la protagonista ***noun*** the main character—the one the story revolves around and who usually has a problem to solve COGNATE

Skill: Textual Evidence

Use the Checklist to analyze Textual Evidence in "The Outsiders." Refer to the sample student annotations about Textual Evidence in the text.

••• CHECKLIST FOR TEXTUAL EVIDENCE

In order to support an analysis by citing textual evidence that is explicitly stated in the text, do the following:

- ✓ read the text closely and critically
- ✓ identify what the text says explicitly
- ✓ find the most relevant textual evidence that supports your analysis
- ✓ consider why an author explicitly states specific details and information
- ✓ cite the specific words, phrases, sentences, or paragraphs from the text that support your analysis
- ✓ cite evidence from the text that most strongly supports your analysis

In order to interpret implicit meanings in a text by making inferences, do the following:

- ✓ combine information directly stated in the text with your own knowledge, experiences, and observations
- ✓ cite the specific words, phrases, sentences, or paragraphs from the text that support this inference

In order to cite textual evidence to support an analysis of what the text says explicitly as well as inferences drawn from the text, consider the following questions:

- ✓ Have I read the text closely and critically?
- ✓ What inferences am I making about the text? What textual evidence am I using to support these inferences?
- ✓ Am I quoting the evidence from the text correctly?
- ✓ Does my textual evidence logically relate to my analysis?
- ✓ What textual evidence from the text most strongly supports your analysis?

SKILL VOCABULARY

cite / citar *verb* to quote as evidence to support a response COGNATE

textual evidence / la evidencia del texto *noun* details from the text that a reader can use to support his or her ideas and opinions about the text COGNATE

make inferences / hacer inferencias *verb* to use your understanding of a text and your own experiences to draw conclusions

Skill: Textual Evidence

Introduce the Skill

Watch the Concept Definition video ▶ and read the following definition with your students.

Any time you're discussing a text, you need to **cite**, or point out, **textual evidence**, the details that readers use to support their ideas and opinions. Readers may cite evidence that is directly stated, or **explicit**, in the text. Other times, textual evidence may be **implicit**, which means it is suggested but not directly stated. One way to interpret implicit meanings is to **make inferences**, using clues from the text and your own experiences to make logical decisions about characters and events that are not stated directly.

Readers must also refer to textual evidence when they **analyze** and examine the different parts of a text. Analyzing specific parts of the text, such as the actions of a character or the cause-and-effect relationships between events in nonfiction, helps a reader **interpret** and explain the meaning, theme, or central idea of the text as a whole. When you cite textual evidence, someone else can look back at a particular part of a text you read and understand your analysis.

TURN AND TALK

1. What are some opinions or ideas you have about a favorite book or movie?
2. How can you use a detail from the book or movie to support your opinions or ideas about it?

ELL SPEAKING FRAMES

- One idea I had about [book or movie title] was ____.
- One detail from [book or movie title] to support my idea is ____.

Your Turn

Ask students to complete the Your Turn activity.

QUESTION 1

A. Incorrect. The narrator makes the point that Johnny had always been somewhat nervous and "high-strung," not calm.

B. Correct. The passage shows how Johnny was made jumpier because of the beating by the Socs, and the narrator fears that Johnny may never get over the beating.

C. Incorrect. It is true that the narrator says that Johnny's home life had made him nervous, but it doesn't show that he was afraid of authority.

D. Incorrect. Nothing in the paragraph suggests that the beating turned him into a coward.

QUESTION 2

A. Incorrect. The paragraph is more concerned with Johnny's state of mind after he was beaten by the Socs, not before.

B. Incorrect. This quotation shows that Johnny was brave and loyal, but the paragraph is more concerned with how the beating affected him.

C. Correct. This quotation supports the inference that Johnny changed as a result of the Socs' beating, perhaps permanently.

D. Incorrect. This quotation supports the inference that Johnny was probably the most sensitive member of the gang, but the paragraph is more concerned with how the beating affected him.

QUESTION 3

A. Incorrect. The quote is incorrect, and this is not why he carried the switchblade.

B. Incorrect. The rest of the quote is "he would kill the next person who jumped him," not necessarily a member of the Socs.

C. Correct. These quotes are correct and demonstrate that he was carrying it to defend himself if needed.

D. Incorrect. This doesn't happen in the text.

The Outsiders

Skill: Textual Evidence

Reread the end of paragraph 7 from "The Outsiders." Then, using the Checklist on the previous page, answer the multiple-choice questions below.

YOUR TURN

1. Which of the following inferences can be supported by specific textual evidence from the passage?
   - A. Johnny had been the calmest one of the Greasers before the beating.
   - B. The beating by the Socs changed Johnny, perhaps permanently.
   - C. Being beaten by his father had made Johnny afraid of authority.
   - D. The beating by the Socs turned Johnny, who had been brave, into a coward.

2. Which sentence from the passage supports your answer to the previous question?
   - A. "Johnny was high-strung anyway, a nervous wreck from getting belted every time he turned around and from hearing his parents fight all the time."
   - B. "He stuck up for the gang and kept his mouth shut good around cops."
   - C. "But after that night of the beating, Johnny was jumpier than ever. I didn't think he'd ever get over it."
   - D. "Living in those conditions might have turned someone else rebellious and bitter; it was killing Johnny."

3. Why does the text say that Johnny "now carried in his back pocket a six-inch switchblade?"
   - A. It says he carried a switchblade because "he had always been a coward."
   - B. It says he decided "he would kill the next" Socs member he found.
   - C. It says that Johnny would "use it" to "kill the next person who jumped him." which shows that he might be afraid but will protect himself at all costs from now on.
   - D. It says his father gave it to him after the beating.

SkillsTV

Project the SkillsTV episode and pause at the following times to prompt discussion:

1:13 What did the students notice about the textual evidence they found?

1:43 What are two ways that textual evidence may be stated in the text?

3:30 How did the textual evidence help make and confirm an inference about the text?

Close Read

Reread *The Outsiders*. As you reread, complete the Skills Focus questions below. Then use your answers and annotations from the questions to help you complete the Write activity.

SKILLS FOCUS

1. Identify clues that reveal the character traits that the Greasers all possess. Explain how the author's choice to include these details about the group helps you better understand a theme of the excerpt.
2. Explain how the incident with the Socs changed Johnny's character.
3. Identify evidence from the text that helps you understand Cherry's unique character traits.
4. How might the Greasers and the Socs answer the question *What makes you, you?* Identify details that show what influences one group's identity, and explain how they see themselves in relation to others.

WRITE

LITERARY ANALYSIS: One theme of the novel *The Outsiders* has to do with the pressure to remain loyal to a group. Explain how interacting with Cherry has changed Ponyboy's understanding of similarities and differences between the Greasers and the Socs. How does his conversation with Cherry begin to change his overall character? Be sure to support your ideas with evidence from the text.

Close Read

Skills Focus

QUESTION 1: Character

See paragraph 1.

QUESTION 2: Character

See paragraph 6: Johnny was a character who experienced violence, but getting beaten up by the Socs was different. He was strong and silent when his dad beat him, but the beating from the Socs actually causes him to break down. We see that he is changed by this event—it makes him weaker.

QUESTION 3: Character

See paragraphs 9–12.

QUESTION 4: Connect to Essential Question

See paragraph 13.

CHECK FOR SUCCESS

If students struggle to respond to Skills Focus question 1, ask them the following questions:

- What traits do the characters seem to have in this excerpt from *The Outsiders?*
- How do the characters help you better understand the theme?

Have students transition to read and annotate independently once they have successfully completed the first Skills Focus prompt.

Writer's Notebook

Connect to Essential Question: Give students time to reflect on how *The Outsiders* connects to the unit's essential question "What makes you, you?" by freewriting in their Writer's Notebooks.

Beginning & Intermediate

Read aloud the unit's essential question, "What makes you, you?" Encourage students to draw their connections or allow students to write in their native language. Circulate the room, prompting students for their thoughts as they respond orally or through pantomime.

Advanced & Advanced High

Allow students to share their connections orally in pairs or small groups before freewriting.

StudySyncTV

Project the StudySyncTV episode and pause at the following times to prompt discussion:

2:05 How do the students use textual evidence to identify the cycle of violence within the novel?

3:15 How do the students use textual evidence to better understand the characters' unique character traits?

6:33 How does the group build on the idea that the Socs and Greasers have more in common than expected? What evidence do they use to support this idea?

Collaborative Conversation

Break students into collaborative conversation groups to discuss the Close Read prompt. Ask students to use the StudySyncTV episode as a model for their discussion. Remind them to reference their Skills Focus annotations in their discussion.

One theme of the novel *The Outsiders* has to do with the pressure to remain loyal to a group. Explain how interacting with Cherry has changed Ponyboy's understanding of similarities and differences between the Greasers and the Socs. How does his conversation with Cherry begin to change his overall character? Be sure to support your ideas with evidence from the text.

Use the scaffolds below to differentiate instruction for your ELL English Language Learners and A Approaching grade-level learners.

ELL **BEGINNING, INTERMEDIATE** Use the discussion guide and speaking frames to facilitate the discussion with support from the teacher.

ADVANCED, ADVANCED HIGH Use the discussion guide and speaking frames to facilitate the discussion in mixed-level groups.

A **APPROACHING** Use the discussion guide to facilitate the discussion in mixed-level groups.

APPROACHING
ADVANCED, ADVANCED HIGH
BEGINNING, INTERMEDIATE

Discussion Guide	Speaking Frames
1. What does Ponyboy think about the Socs before talking to Cherry?	• Ponyboy thinks Socs ____. • This is important because ____.
2. How does talking to Cherry start to change Ponyboy's mind?	• Cherry supports her claim by explaining that ____. • She wants to show Ponyboy that ____.
3. How does this conversation start to change the type of person Ponyboy is and the traits he has? What kind of person is he becoming?	• Talking to Cherry is making Ponyboy a more ____ type of person. • This change might end up making him a person who ____.

Review Prompt and Rubric

Before students begin writing, review the writing prompt and rubric with the class.

LITERARY ANALYSIS: One theme of the novel *The Outsiders* has to do with the pressure to remain loyal to a group. Explain how interacting with Cherry has changed Ponyboy's understanding of similarities and differences between the Greasers and the Socs. How does his conversation with Cherry begin to change his overall character? Be sure to support your ideas with evidence from the text.

PROMPT GUIDE

- What does Ponyboy think about the Socs before talking to Cherry?
- How does talking to Cherry start to change Ponyboy's mind?
- How does this conversation start to change the type of person Ponyboy is and the traits he has? What kind of person is he becoming?

Score	Character	Language and Conventions
4	The writer clearly analyzes and explains the changes in the character. The writer provides exemplary analysis, using relevant evidence from the text.	The writer demonstrates a consistent command of grammar, punctuation, and usage conventions. Although minor errors may be evident, they do not detract from the fluency or the clarity of the writing.
3	The writer analyzes and explains the changes in the character. The writer provides sufficient analysis, using relevant evidence from the text most of the time.	The writer demonstrates an adequate command of grammar, punctuation, and usage conventions. Although some errors may be evident, they create few (if any) disruptions in the fluency or clarity of the writing.
2	The writer begins to analyze or explain the changes in the character, but the analysis is incomplete. The writer uses relevant evidence from the text only some of the time.	The writer demonstrates a partial command of grammar, punctuation, and usage conventions. Some distracting errors may be evident, at times creating minor disruptions in the fluency or clarity of the writing.
1	The writer attempts to analyze or explain the changes in the character, but the analysis is not successful. The writer uses little or no relevant evidence from the text.	The writer demonstrates little or no command of grammar, punctuation, and usage conventions. Serious and persistent errors create disruptions in the fluency of the writing and sometimes interfere with meaning.
0	The writer does not attempt to analyze or explain the changes in the character or does not provide a response at all.	Serious and persistent errors overwhelm the writing and interfere with the meaning of the response as a whole, making the writer's meaning impossible to understand.

Write

Ask students to complete the writing assignment using textual evidence to support their answers.

Use the scaffolds below to differentiate instruction for your ELL English Language Learners and A Approaching grade-level learners.

ELL **BEGINNING** With the help of the word bank, write a response using paragraph frame 1.

INTERMEDIATE With the help of the word bank, write a response using paragraph frames 1 and 2.

ADVANCED, ADVANCED HIGH Write a response of differentiated length using the sentence starters.

A **APPROACHING** Write a response of differentiated length using the sentence starters.

BEGINNING / INTERMEDIATE | ADVANCED, ADVANCED HIGH / APPROACHING

Word Bank	Paragraph Frame 1	Paragraph Frame 2	Sentence Starters
Greasers alike empathetic violent common	At first Ponyboy thinks the Socs are ____ because they attacked Johnny. Ponyboy starts to change his mind when Cherry says not all Socs are ____. Ponyboy also notices that Cherry and Marcia are just like the ____. Ponyboy's character is starting to change because he realizes that the Socs and Greasers have a lot in ____. He is becoming a more ____ character.	One piece of textual evidence that shows how Ponyboy is starting to change is ____. This evidence shows ____. Another piece of evidence that shows that Ponyboy is more empathetic is ____. This evidence shows ____.	• Interacting with Cherry changes Ponyboy because . . . • Before he met Cherry, Ponyboy thought . . . • After talking with her, he realizes . . . • His character is becoming . . .

Peer Review

Rate

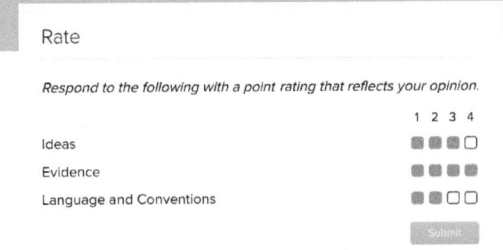

Respond to the following with a point rating that reflects your opinion.

1 2 3 4

Ideas

Evidence

Language and Conventions

Submit

Students should submit substantive feedback to two peers using the review instructions below.

- How well does this response answer the prompt?
- How well does the writer support his or her ideas with details and examples from the text?
- Which sentence in the writer's response made you think differently about the text?
- What did the writer do well in this response? What does the writer need to work on?

SENTENCE FRAMES

A

- You were able to (completely / partly / almost) answer the prompt because ____.
- You could answer the prompt more completely by ____.
- You supported the idea of ____ with the detail of ____.
- One idea that needs more support is ____.
- I thought differently about the texts after reading ____.
- My favorite part of your response is ____.

Slam, Dunk, & Hook

POETRY
Yusef Komunyakaa
1991

Introduction

"Slam, Dunk, & Hook" is a poem by Pulitzer Prize-winning poet Yusef Komunyakaa (b. 1947). It is included in Komunyakaa's *Magic Bus*, his 1992 collection of poems that draw on his experiences growing up as an African American in the 1950s in Bogalusa, a small city in northeastern Louisiana. While "Slam, Dunk, & Hook" primarily describes the feelings of playing basketball as a youth, the racial tensions that defined the 1950s Deep South seem to exist just outside the edges of both the poem and the "roundhouse" where the boys play

Set in the 1950s Deep South, the African American speaker of this poem remembers playing basketball with his friends. He describes their athleticism, confidence, fast-moving Nike sneakers, and the silky swish of the net. He also mentions how the boys played better when girls were cheering for them. However, basketball was also an outlet for grief. When Sonny Boy's mother died, Sonny played so hard that the backboard wore down. Later, using the blackjack as a symbol, the poem hints that they faced trouble in their lives, but the boys still stuck with basketball. At their physical prime, the boys were full of joy, recognizing their beauty and power on the court.

ELL Proficiency-leveled summaries and summaries in multiple languages are available digitally.

Audio and audio text highlighting are available with this text.

CONNECT TO ESSENTIAL QUESTION

What makes you, you?

How can you create a sense of belonging when you don't feel welcome in your community? The poem draws on the experiences of poet Yusef Komunyakaa, who grew up as an African American in the 1950s in a small city in northeastern Louisiana.

Access Complex Text

LEXILE: N/A **WORD COUNT:** 183

The following areas may be challenging for students, particularly ELL English Language Learners and A Approaching grade-level learners.

Genre	Specific Vocabulary	Connection of Ideas
• The poem is free verse. Students may need assistance understanding that a sentence may break over several lines. • Highlighting single sentences that break over two or more lines may help students see the complete thoughts. Modeling may also help students understand how to read the poem.	• Specialized vocabulary, such as *roundhouse* and *blackjack*, may challenge some readers. Remind students to use context clues while reading, and also to use a dictionary to define unfamiliar words.	• The poem is about the speaker's love of basketball, but it also expresses larger ideas about life. Elevated language such as "hope & good intention," "metaphysical," and "beautiful & dangerous" help to convey the reality of the lives of the players.

SCAFFOLDS  ENGLISH LANGUAGE LEARNERS  APPROACHING GRADE LEVEL  BEYOND GRADE LEVEL

These icons identify differentiation strategies and scaffolded support for a variety of students. See the digital lesson plan for additional differentiation strategies and scaffolds.

Instructional Path

The print teacher's edition includes essential point-of-use instruction and planning tools. Complete lesson plans and program documents appear in your digital teacher account.

First Read: Slam, Dunk, & Hook

Objectives: After an initial reading and discussion of the poem, students will be able to visualize imagery in order to have a deeper understanding of the text.

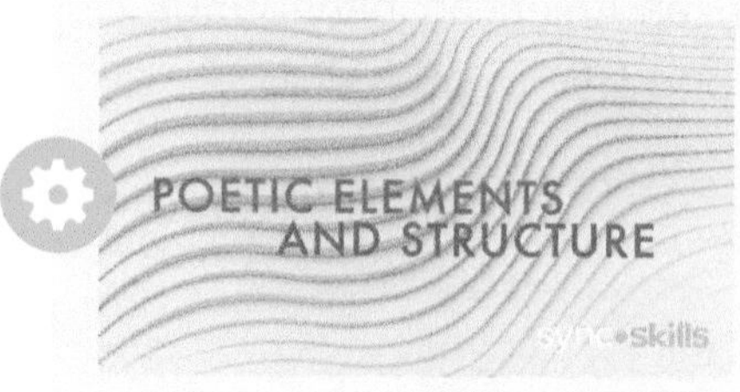

Skill: Poetic Elements and Structure

Objectives: After rereading and discussing a model of close reading, students will be able to analyze the effect of structure and elements, such as punctuation and line length, in poems across a variety of poetic forms.

Skill: Allusion

Objectives: After rereading and discussing a model of close reading, students will be able to identify and understand allusions made in a poem.

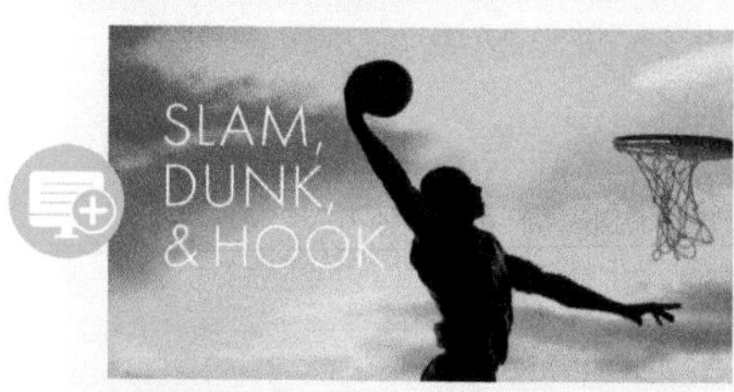

Close Read: Slam, Dunk, & Hook

Objectives: Students will closely read the text to analyze poetic structure and allusion in order to participate in a collaborative conversation and write a short, constructed response.

Blast: Poetry in Action

Objectives: After exploring background information and research links about a topic, students will respond to a question with a 140-character response.

Progress Monitoring

Opportunities to Learn	Opportunities to Demonstrate Learning	Opportunities to Reteach
Poetic Elements and Structure		
Skill: Poetic Elements and Structure	Skill: Poetic Elements and Structure • Your Turn Close Read • Skills Focus • Write	Unit 2 Skill: Poetic Elements and Structure - The Road Not Taken Spotlight Skill: Poetic Elements and Structure
Allusion		
Skill: Allusion	Skill: Allusion • Your Turn Close Read • Complete Vocabulary Chart • Skills Focus • Write	Unit 4 Skill: Allusion - The Adventures of Tom Sawyer (Chapter 2) Spotlight Skill: Allusion

First Read

Introduce the Text

As a class, watch the video preview ▶ and have students read the introduction in pairs to make connections to the video preview.

To activate prior knowledge and experiences, ask students:

- What part of the video stood out to you the most?
- What is one question you have about what you are going to read?

SPEAKING FRAMES

- The ____ in the video makes me think ____.
- The video shows ____. This makes me wonder ____.
- I think the text will ____. I think this because ____.
- I predict that there will be ____. I believe this because ____.

Entry Point

As students prepare to read "Slam, Dunk, & Hook," share the following information with them to provide context.

✓ Yusef Komunyakaa is a Pulitzer Prize-winning poet and teacher whose poems combine personal history, jazz rhythm, and everyday language, including slang, called *vernacular*. He often writes about jazz and blues, the Vietnam War in which he served, and race.

✓ Free verse is poetry that is "free" from the constraints of traditional poetry, such as meter, rhyme, and fixed form. It often follows natural speech patterns but still allows for great expression of feeling. Walt Whitman in the 1800s was among the earliest poets experimenting with this form, but since the early 1900s, most lyric poetry has been free verse.

✓ "Slam, Dunk, & Hook" was first published in 1991 but has appeared in different poetry collections since then. A video of Yusef Komunyakaa reading his poem is available online.

"Lay ups. Fast breaks.

Fast breaks. Lay ups. With Mercury's
Insignia on our sneakers,
We outmaneuvered to footwork
Of bad angels. Nothing but a hot
Swish of strings like silk
Ten feet out. In the roundhouse
Labyrinth our bodies
Created, we could almost
Last forever, **poised** in midair
Like storybook sea monsters.
A high note hung there
A long second. Off
The rim. We'd corkscrew
Up & dunk balls that exploded
The skullcap of hope & good
Intention. Lanky, all hands
& feet . . . sprung **rhythm**.
We were **metaphysical** when girls
Cheered on the sidelines.
Tangled up in a falling,
Muscles were a bright motor
Double-flashing to the metal hoop
Nailed to our oak.
When Sonny Boy's mama died
He played nonstop all day, so hard
Our backboard splintered.
Glistening with sweat,
We rolled the ball off
Our fingertips. Trouble
Was there slapping a blackjack
Against an open palm.
Dribble, drive to the inside,
& glide like a sparrow hawk.
Lay ups. Fast breaks.
We had moves we didn't know

NOTES

Skill: Poetic Elements and Structure

There's no regular meter or rhyme scheme, so this is open form. The line breaks and capitalized words within the lines make me pause and imagine the "sneakers" and "footwork." When I read this aloud, the rhythm sounds like a basketball pounding on the court.

Skill: Allusion

Sea monsters are powerful creatures from folklore. I've seen movies where they rise up out of the sea to attack ships. As with the allusion to Mercury at the beginning of the poem, the speaker is describing the players as having superhuman qualities.

SELECTION VOCABULARY

insignia / la insignia ***noun*** a mark or sign to represent a specific thing COGNATE

labyrinth / el laberinto ***noun*** maze-like or something confusing COGNATE

- What game are the "we" playing?
- Where do the players position their "bodies"?

Analyze Vocabulary Using Context Clues

In lines 1–4, focus on the sentence that uses the word *insignia*. Point out these context clues:

1. First, I notice that the insignia is something on their shoes, and the word *sign*, which means "a symbol or mark," is inside the word *insignia*.
2. When I read the sentence again, using *sign* in place of *insignia*, the sentence makes sense. The symbol for Mercury was on the sneakers, and Mercury was a Roman god known for speed.

Poetic Elements and Structure

What poetic structure does the reader note? How does she explain its effect?

The reader notes that short lines help to emphasize imagery and to create a rhythm that resembles the pounding of a basketball.

Allusion

What does the reader note about the second allusion?

He notes how it describes the players and compares it with the first allusion to identify a theme that the speaker is developing to describe the players.

TEXT TALK

Why are sneakers important to the players of this game?

See lines 1–4: Players have to show "footwork," or move fast on their feet to outplay opponents.

What are some of the players' moves?

See lines 1, 9, 13, 14, 28, 29, and 32–34: They make fast breaks and layups. They stop "midair," twist and turn while jumping, pass a ball off their "fingertips," and "dribble, drive to the inside, / & glide."

Skills Focus

QUESTION 5: Connect to Essential Question

The players learned they could move in ways they didn't know they could. Realizing this makes them feel powerful. It gives them "joy" and lets them know they are not only "beautiful" but also "dangerous" to anyone who plays against them.

We had. Our bodies spun
On swivels of bone & faith,
Through a lyric slipknot
Of joy, & we knew we were
Beautiful & dangerous.

"Slam, Dunk, & Hook" from *Pleasure Dome: New and Collected Poems.*

TEXT TALK

Why is basketball a kind of release for the players?

See lines 29–40: It helps them let out their feelings in action.

Why do you think this experience is expressed as a poem?

Answers will vary.

Ask each Beyond grade-level student to write one additional discussion question. Then have one or two students facilitate a discussion, using their questions to guide the conversation.

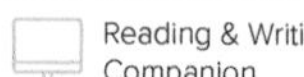

SELECTION VOCABULARY

poised / equilibrado/a ***adjective*** balanced and ready to move COGNATE

- How do the phrases "last forever" and "in midair" help explain *poised*?

rhythm / el ritmo ***noun*** a regular pattern of sounds or movements

- What does "A high note hung there / A long second" have to do with *rhythm*?

metaphysical / metafísico/a ***adjective*** relating to ideas about life and existence; beyond physical COGNATE

- *Meta-* is a prefix meaning "more than." How does putting together the meaning of *meta-* and the meaning of *physical* help you understand *metaphysical*?

Reading Comprehension OPTIONAL

Have students complete the digital reading comprehension questions when they finish reading.

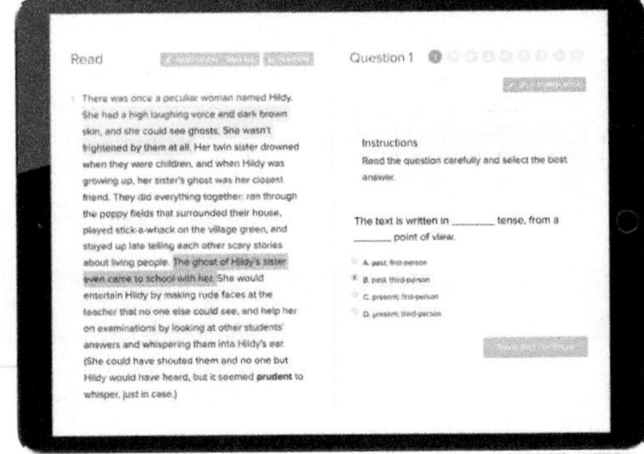

ANSWER KEY

QUESTION 1: A
QUESTION 2: B
QUESTION 3: A
QUESTION 4: D
QUESTION 5: *See chart.*

Synonym	Word
transcendent	metaphysical
logo	insignia
balanced	poised
maze	labyrinth
tempo	rhythm

Connect and Extend OPTIONAL

CONNECT TO EXTENDED WRITING PROJECT

Students can use "Slam, Dunk, & Hook" as a resource when writing their literary analyses. Have them analyze how Yusef Komunyakaa uses the game of basketball to explore identity.

BEYOND THE BOOK

Writing: Larger Than Life

In "Slam, Dunk, & Hook," the speaker describes how playing basketball made him feel larger than life and helped him escape the difficult realities of his life.

Ask students to reflect on the following questions:

- What do you do that makes you feel larger than life?
- Do you feel it's important to have an activity that helps you escape from your day-to-day life? Why or why not?

In three separate diary entries, students should reflect on specific moments in their lives when they engaged in a particular pastime, hobby, sport, or activity to escape from a challenging situation.

Tell students that their diary entries should:

- Include a date for each entry.
- Identify a situation, person, or problem that sometimes requires an escape.
- Describe a pastime, hobby, sport, or activity and how it makes them feel, using rich sensory details.

Think Questions

Circulate as students answer Think Questions independently. Scaffolds for these questions are shown on the opposite page.

QUESTION 1: Textual Evidence

Lines 1–17 describe boys playing basketball. For example, in lines 9 and 10 the poet describes the boys as being "poised in midair / Like storybook sea monsters." In lines 13 and 14 the boys "corkscrew / Up & dunk balls that exploded."

QUESTION 2: Textual Evidence

Sonny Boy's mother dies. He reacts by playing all day without stopping. He plays so hard that pieces of the backboard break off. Sonny Boy works off the sadness and anger of losing his mother by playing basketball.

QUESTION 3: Textual Evidence

"Sprung rhythm," "muscles were a bright motor," "glide like a sparrow hawk," and "Through a lyric slipknot / of joy" have positive connotations. They suggest that the players and the game are beautiful, strong, and powerful.

QUESTION 4: Context Clues

"In the roundhouse" suggests the circle of play around the ball. As players dart around, their movements are hard to follow. The dictionary definition of *labyrinth* is "a complicated network of passages in which it is difficult to find one's way."

QUESTION 5: Word Meaning

Definition 1 most closely matches the meaning of *poised* in line 9. The player is "balanced" in the air. Students may also suggest that the players, who "could almost / Last forever," had a composed or self-assured manner in the way they played.

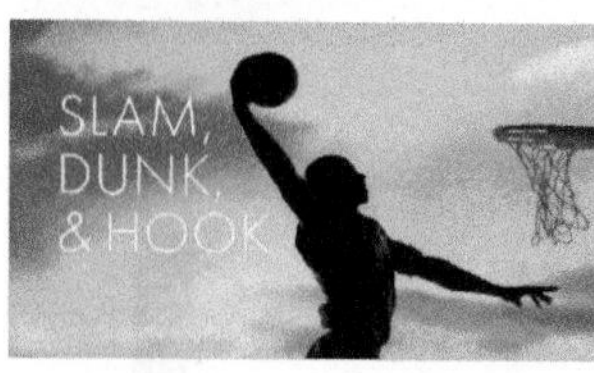

First Read

Read "Slam, Dunk, & Hook." After you read, complete the Think Questions below.

THINK QUESTIONS

1. What do lines 1–17 of the poem describe? Who appears in these lines? Cite textual evidence from the poem to support your answer.
2. What troubling event happens to Sonny Boy? How does he react? Use textual evidence to support your answer.
3. What words and phrases suggest the power and beauty of the basketball game? Explain your answer.
4. Read lines 6–9. Then use context clues to determine the meaning of **labyrinth** as it is used in the poem.
5. Read the following dictionary entry:

   poised
   poised \poizd\ *adjective*

   1. marked by balance or equilibrium
   2. having a composed or self-assured manner

   Explain which definition most closely matches the meaning of **poised** as it is used in line 9. Do yo[u] think either of these meanings could work, or i[s] one more accurate than the other? Explain.

SCAFFOLDS

Think Questions

Use the scaffolds below to differentiate instruction for your ELL English Language Learners and A Approaching grade-level learners.

ELL **BEGINNING** Write a response using the word bank and sentence frames.

INTERMEDIATE Write a response using the sentence frames.

ADVANCED, ADVANCED HIGH Write a response using the Text-Dependent Question Guide.

A **APPROACHING** Write a response using the Text-Dependent Question Guide.

BEGINNING	INTERMEDIATE	APPROACHING / ADVANCED, ADVANCED HIGH
Word Bank	**Sentence Frames**	**Text-Dependent Question Guide**
basketball angry glide hard graceful mother boys fast joyful confusing day	The lines describe teenage ____. They play ____ . The game is ____.	1. • Who is wearing sneakers and dunking balls? • What game has dunking? • What does the game in the poem look like?
	In the poem, Sonny Boy's ____ dies. Then Sonny Boy plays basketball all ____. He plays ____. He feels ____.	2. • Who dies in the poem? • What does Sonny Boy do? • Why are these lines important?
	The players are beautiful because they are ____. The game is beautiful because it is____. A positive word in the poem is ____.	3. • What makes the players "Beautiful & dangerous"? • What words describe movement? • What are some positive words in the poem?
	The word *roundhouse* tells about the word *labyrinth*. It suggests a circle or arena. The players try to get the ball. Their fast movements make the game ____ to follow. This gives me a clue that *labyrinth* means "something that is ____."	4. • Read: "In the roundhouse / **Labyrinth** our bodies / Created, we could almost / Last forever" • What is being described in these lines? • What does that tell me about the meaning of the word *labyrinth*?
	Poised as used in the text best matches definition #____. *Poised* may also suggest the players are sure of their moves, or definition # ____.	5. • Read: "**poised** in midair, / Like storybook sea monsters." • Are the players "balanced" or "composed" in "midair"? • Which definition best describes where the players are? • Sometimes poets use words that have double meanings. Is it possible that the word *poised* suggests more than one meaning in these lines?

Skill: Poetic Elements and Structure

Introduce the Skill

Watch the Concept Definition video ▶ and read the following definition with your students.

Poetic structure describes the organization of words and lines in a poem as well as its rhyme scheme and meter. Poems consist of words that are divided into **lines**. A group of lines is called a **stanza**.

Other elements of poetry that contribute to structure include rhyme and rhythm. **Rhyme** is the repetition of the same or similar vowel sounds. The **rhyme scheme** of a poem is the pattern formed by the rhyming words at the end of lines. **Rhythm** is the pattern of unstressed and stressed syllables in a line of poetry. A regular pattern is called **meter**, and it gives a line of poetry a predictable rhythm.

The poet's choice of **poetic form**, or arrangement and style of a poem, will help determine the structure. Common forms include haiku, limerick, and sonnet, each with its own rules. Poetry without a consistent meter, rhyme, or stanza length is called **open form**.

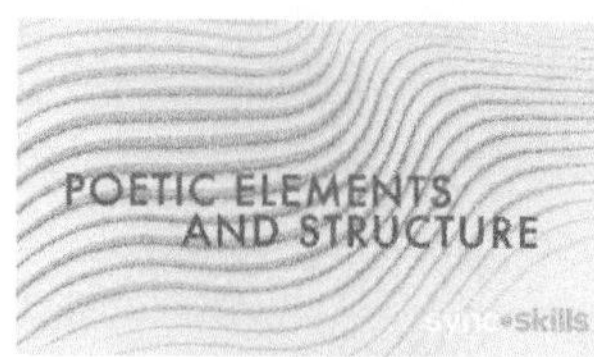

Skill:
Poetic Elements and Structure

Use the Checklist to analyze Poetic Elements and Structure in "Slam, Dunk, & Hook." Refer to the sample student annotations about Poetic Elements and Structure in the text.

••• CHECKLIST FOR POETIC ELEMENTS AND STRUCTURE

In order to determine how to compare and contrast the structures of two or more poems, look for the following:

- ✓ the forms and overall structures of the poems
- ✓ the rhyme, rhythm, and meter, if present
- ✓ lines and stanzas in the poems that suggest the poems' meanings and styles
- ✓ ways that the poems' structures connect to the poems' meanings

To compare and contrast the structures of two or more poems and analyze how the differing structures contribute to each poem's meaning and style, consider the following questions:

- ✓ What forms do the poets use?
- ✓ How do the poems compare to each other in their structures?
- ✓ How does the choice of form or structure affect the overall meaning of each poem? How do they compare?

TURN AND TALK

1. What are some things you like about poems?
2. What are some examples of how poems look on a page? Why do people like to hear a poem read aloud?

SPEAKING FRAMES

- One thing I like about poems is ____.
- Poems do not all look alike. Some poems ____. Other poems ____.
- Poems with ____ are fun to listen to.

SKILL VOCABULARY

poetic structure / la estructura poética ***noun*** the organization of words and lines as well as the rhyme and meter of a poem COGNATE

line / el verso ***noun*** a string of words in a poem, not necessarily a full sentence or phrase

stanza / la estrofa ***noun*** the basic unit of a poem, made up of a series of lines

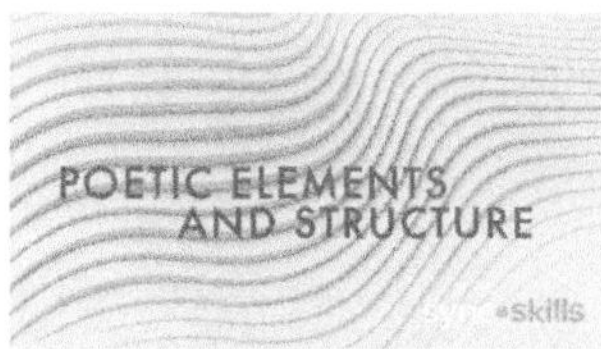

Skill: Poetic Elements and Structure

Reread lines 27–40 of "Slam, Dunk, & Hook." Then, using the Checklist on the previous page, answer the multiple-choice questions below.

YOUR TURN

1. The capital letter *T* in *Trouble* in line 29 shows—
   - ○ A. the beginning of a new thought.
   - ○ B. the beginning of a new line in the poem.
   - ○ C. a proper noun.
   - ○ D. a mistake because it should not be a capital letter.

2. Line 34 in the poem is an example of—
   - ○ A. the use of rhyme in the poem.
   - ○ B. the complete thought contained in each line.
   - ○ C. the short lines in the structure of the poem.
   - ○ D. the use of repetition in the poem.

3. Which lines have one complete thought that best sums up the meaning of the poem?
   - ○ A. lines 27–29
   - ○ B. lines 31–32
   - ○ C. lines 32–33
   - ○ D. lines 36–40

Your Turn

Ask students to complete the Your Turn activity.

QUESTION 1

A. Correct. The thought begins with *Trouble* and ends with *palm*.

B. Incorrect. *Trouble* doesn't begin a new line.

C. Incorrect. *Trouble* is not a proper noun.

D. Incorrect. The capital letter is correct.

QUESTION 2

A. Incorrect. This poem does not have rhyme.

B. Incorrect. Complete thoughts are not always contained in one line in this poem.

C. Correct. The poem has short lines to express the quick pace of the game.

D. Incorrect. The example does not show repetition.

QUESTION 3

A. Incorrect. These lines have one thought, but it describes only one move.

B. Incorrect. These lines are part of two different complete thoughts.

C. Incorrect. The lines have one complete thought, but it is an example and does not best sum up the meaning of the poem.

D. Correct. The complete thought begins with "Our bodies spun" in line 36. Basketball is important to the players because they find "joy" in the game and gain confidence in knowing that they play well and are dangerous opponents.

SKILL VOCABULARY

rhythm / el ritmo ***noun*** the pattern of unstressed and stressed syllables in a line of poetry

meter / la métrica ***noun*** a regular pattern of unstressed and stressed syllables in a line of poetry

rhyme / la rima ***noun*** the repetition of the same or similar sounds in a poem

rhyme scheme / el patrón de rima ***noun*** the pattern formed by the rhyming words at the end of lines in a poem

poetic form / la forma poética ***noun*** the particular set of rules guiding the arrangement of words and lines in a poem COGNATE

open form / la forma abierta ***noun*** poetic form without consistent meter, rhyme, or stanza length

Skill: Allusion

Introduce the Skill

Watch the Concept Definition video and read the following definition with your students.

An **allusion** is a reference to something, usually made in an indirect way. The reference may be to a literary work, a work of art, a historical event, a famous person, or something else that a reader or listener is expected to understand without an explanation. For example, referring to someone as "a Scrooge" alludes to the stingy character of that name in Charles Dickens's *A Christmas Carol*. Through the allusion, the many qualities of Ebenezer Scrooge may be transferred quickly to another character or person.

Works of literature often draw on themes, patterns of events, or characters from other works, and these allusions have an impact on the meaning and tone of a work. Readers may not know the **source material** authors borrow from or allude to, but a familiarity with a variety of works such as Greek myths, the Bible, and the plays of William Shakespeare may deepen a reader's experience of the newer material.

Skill: Allusion

Use the Checklist to analyze Poetic Elements and Structure in "Slam, Dunk, & Hook." Refer to the sample student annotations about Poetic Elements and Structure in the text.

••• CHECKLIST FOR ALLUSION

In order to identify an allusion, note the following:

- ✓ references or clues that suggest a reference to a myth, mythological creature, famous person, historical event, work of art, or work of literature
- ✓ the theme, event, character, or situation in a text to which the references or clues add information
- ✓ patterns of events or character types

To better understand the allusion in a work of literature, do the following:

- ✓ use a print or digital resource to look up what you think might be an allusion
- ✓ list details about the allusion that relate to themes, events, or character types

To analyze how a modern work of fiction or poetry draws on themes, events, patterns of events, or character types from myths, traditional stories, or religious works and describe how the material is rendered new, consider the following questions:

- ✓ What theme/event/character is referenced in the text I am reading? How do I know?
- ✓ How does that theme/event/character relate to what is happening in this new text?
- ✓ What does the modern version add to the previous story?
- ✓ How does the inclusion of allusions impact the meaning or tone of the story or poem?

TURN AND TALK

1. How would you describe the players and the action in your favorite sport?
2. What other people or events—either real or fictional—do the players or the action remind you of?

SPEAKING FRAMES

- My favorite sport is ____.
- The players move like ____.
- The action is ____.
- The players remind me of ____.
- The action reminds me of ____.

V SKILL VOCABULARY

allusion / la alusión ***noun*** a reference to a person, place, thing, or idea COGNATE

source material / el material de referencia ***noun*** the work of literature or other source to which an allusion, or reference, is made, or from which themes and characters are borrowed

Skill: Allusion

Reread lines 3–17 of "Slam, Dunk, & Hook." Then, using the Checklist on the previous page, answer the multiple-choice questions below.

YOUR TURN

1. Which phrase from the poem is a Biblical allusion that describes the opponents of the players as supernatural creatures who have fallen from grace?

   - ○ A. "We outmaneuvered to footwork / Of bad angels."
   - ○ B. "A high note hung there / A long second."
   - ○ C. "We'd corkscrew / Up & dunk balls"
   - ○ D. "Lanky, all hands / & feet . . . sprung rhythm."

2. Which phrase from the poem is an allusion to a Greek myth that involves a complicated system of moving around?

   - ○ A. "Nothing but a hot / Swish of strings like silk"
   - ○ B. "In the roundhouse / Labyrinth our bodies / Created"
   - ○ C. "we could almost / Last forever, poised in midair"
   - ○ D. "The skullcap of hope & good / Intention."

Your Turn

Ask students to complete the Your Turn activity.

QUESTION 1

A. Correct. "Bad angels" is a Biblical reference to fallen angels. It describes the boys the speaker's team is playing against.
B. Incorrect. This description is not a Biblical allusion and does not describe the opponents.
C. Incorrect. This description is not a Biblical allusion and does not describe the opponents.
D. Incorrect. This description is not a Biblical allusion and does not describe the opponents.

QUESTION 2

A. Incorrect. This description is not an allusion to a Greek myth and does not describe a complicated system of moving around.
B. Correct. *Labyrinth* is an allusion to a Greek myth that involves a maze-like structure.
C. Incorrect. This description is not an allusion to a Greek myth and does not describe a complicated system of moving around.
D. Incorrect. This description is not an allusion to a Greek myth and does not describe a complicated system of moving around.

Close Read

Skills Focus

QUESTION 1: Poetic Elements and Structure

See lines 1–4: The speaker uses *our* and *we*. A basketball player is speaking, and he's speaking about playing the game. So the structure of the poem mimics the action of a basketball game.

QUESTION 2: Poetic Elements and Structure

See lines 11–17: All the lines are short and about the same length. One thought may extend to two or more lines. The short line length suggests the action in the game is fast.

QUESTION 3: Allusion

See lines 1–10: In Roman mythology, Mercury was the messenger of the Gods, with wings on his hat and feet. This allusion suggests that the boys are moving so fast, it appears they have wings on their feet. *Labyrinth* is an allusion to a structure in Greek mythology. It was a complicated network of passages or paths in which it was difficult to find one's way.

QUESTION 4: Poetic Elements and Structure

See lines 21–33: *Motor* suggests energy and power. It describes the players. *Died*, *hard*, and *splintered* suggest the sadness and anger Sonny Boy felt at the death of his mother.

QUESTION 5: Connect to Essential Question

See lines 36–40.

Close Read

Reread "Slam, Dunk, & Hook." As you reread, complete the Skills Focus questions below. Then use your answers and annotations from the questions to help you complete the Write activity.

SKILLS FOCUS

1. Look at the first lines of the poem. From whose point of view is the poem being told? How does this information help to establish and contribute to the poetic structure of the poem? Cite specific textual evidence to help support your claims.
2. Identify the connection between line length and meaning in the poem. Cite evidence from lines in the poem.
3. Allusion is a brief reference to a work of art, a character from a myth or story, or an event in history. For example, a mention of Scrooge is an allusion to a character in *A Christmas Carol* by Charles Dickens. Identify examples of allusion in "Slam, Dunk, & Hook." Explain how the allusions add to your understanding.
4. Analyze the line breaks in the poem. What types of words appear at the ends of lines? What effect do they have on the meaning of the poem?
5. Is there a sport or activity that makes you feel as passionate as Komunyakaa feels about basketball? Citing specific evidence from the text, respond to Komunyakaa's attitude towards basketball based on your experience.

WRITE

DISCUSSION: How is the identity of the speaker and other basketball players tied to the game of basketball? Discuss this question with a group of your peers. To prepare for your discussion, use the graphic organizer to identify the poet's use of structure and allusions, and explain how they help communicate the game's importance to the identity of individual players and the team as a whole. After your discussion, you will write a reflection.

Writer's Notebook

Connect to Essential Question: Give students time to reflect on how "Slam, Dunk, & Hook" connects to the unit's essential question "What makes you, you?" by freewriting in their Writer's Notebooks.

Beginning & Intermediate

Read aloud the unit's essential question: "What makes you, you?" Encourage students to draw their connections or allow students to write in their native language. Circulate the room, prompting students for their thoughts as they respond orally or through pantomime.

Advanced & Advanced High

Allow students to share their connections orally in pairs or small groups before freewriting.

Collaborative Conversation

Post the writing prompt to generate a discussion in small groups. Ask students to first break down the prompt before they discuss relevant ideas and textual evidence.

How is the identity of the speaker and other basketball players tied to the game of basketball? Discuss this question with a group of your peers. To prepare for your discussion, use the graphic organizer to identify the poet's use of structure and allusions, and explain how they help communicate the game's importance to the identity of individual players and the team as a whole.

Use the scaffolds below to differentiate instruction for your ELL English Language Learners and A Approaching grade-level learners.

ELL **BEGINNING, INTERMEDIATE** Use the discussion guide and speaking frames to facilitate the discussion with support from the teacher.

ADVANCED, ADVANCED HIGH Use the discussion guide and speaking frames o facilitate the discussion in mixed-level groups.

A APPROACHING Use the discussion guide to facilitate the discussion in mixed-level groups.

APPROACHING
ADVANCED, ADVANCED HIGH
BEGINNING, INTERMEDIATE

Discussion Guide	Speaking Frames
1. How does the speaker describe himself and his team as basketball players?	• The speaker describes the players as ____ and ____. • This description shows that the players see themselves as ____.
2. What situations show how important the game is to the players?	• When Sonny Boy's mother dies, he ____. • When trouble was around, the players ____.
3. How do the structure and allusions communicate the game's importance to the identity of the players?	• The structure communicates the importance of the game by ____. • The allusions communicate the importance of the game by ____.

Review Prompt and Rubric

Before students begin writing, review the writing prompt and rubric with the class.

REFLECTION: As you write, make sure to

- evaluate how well everyone followed the rules when making decisions affecting the group
- evaluate your own participation in the discussion
- reflect on how well you posed questions that connected the ideas of several speakers and responded to others' questions and comments with relevant evidence, observations, and ideas

PROMPT GUIDE

- How does the speaker see himself and his team?
- How important is the game to the players?
- How do the structure and allusions help communicate the game's importance?

Score	Reflection	Language and Conventions
4	The writer clearly reflects on how well he or she posed questions and responded to others' comments as well as his or her own participation. The writer consistently refers to specific examples from the discussion.	The writer demonstrates a consistent command of grammar, punctuation, and usage conventions. Although minor errors may be evident, they do not detract from the fluency or the clarity of the writing.
3	The writer reflects on how well he or she posed questions and responded to others' comments as well as his or her own participation. The writer refers to specific examples from the discussion most of the time.	The writer demonstrates an adequate command of grammar, punctuation, and usage conventions. Although some errors may be evident, they create few (if any) disruptions in the fluency or clarity of the writing.
2	The writer begins to reflect on how well he or she posed questions and responded to others' comments as well as his or her own participation. The writer refers to specific examples from the discussion some of the time.	The writer demonstrates a partial command of grammar, punctuation, and usage conventions. Some distracting errors may be evident, at times creating minor disruptions in the fluency or clarity of the writing.
1	The writer attempts to reflect on how well he or she posed questions and responded to others' comments as well as his or her own participation, but with little success. The writer refers to few, if any, examples from the discussion.	The writer demonstrates little or no command of grammar, punctuation, and usage conventions. Serious and persistent errors create disruptions in the fluency of the writing and sometimes interfere with meaning.
0	The writer does not provide a relevant response to the prompt or does not provide a response at all.	Serious and persistent errors overwhelm the writing and interfere with the meaning of the response as a whole, making the writer's meaning impossible to understand.

SCAFFOLDS

Write

Have students write a reflection that evaluates their own and others' participation in the discussion group.

Use the scaffolds below to differentiate instruction for your ELL English Language Learners and A Approaching grade-level learners.

ELL **BEGINNING** With the help of the word bank, write a response using paragraph frame 1.

INTERMEDIATE With the help of the word bank, write a response using paragraph frames 1 and 2.

ADVANCED, ADVANCED HIGH Write a response of differentiated length using the sentence starters.

A **APPROACHING** Write a response of differentiated length using the sentence starters.

BEGINNING | INTERMEDIATE | ADVANCED, ADVANCED HIGH | APPROACHING

Word Bank	Paragraph Frame 1	Paragraph Frame 2	Sentence Starters
good average identity structure questions comments allusions text	My discussion group talked about ____. We included ____ and ____ as examples. I think my group did a(n) ____ job following the discussion rules. I think this because ____. I added to the discussion by ____.	First, we talked about how basketball ____. One allusion we cited was ____. I participated when I ____.	• My opinion of my group's performance is . . . • I have this opinion because . . . • I contributed to the discussion by . . . • I posed a question about . . . • I responded to a comment with . . . • If I could change one thing about my contributions, it would be . . . • Next time, my discussion goal will be to . . .

Peer Review

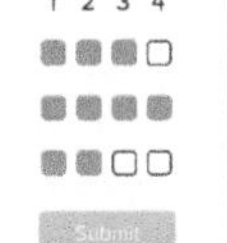

Rate

Respond to the following with a point rating that reflects your opinion.

	1	2	3	4
Ideas	■	■	■	□
Evidence	■	■	■	■
Language and Conventions	■	■	□	□

Submit

Students should submit substantive feedback to two peers using the review instructions below.

- How well does the writer refer to specific examples from the discussion?
- What does the writer do well in this reflection? What does the writer need to work on?

ELL A **SENTENCE FRAMES**

- You included examples (most of the time / some of the time / not often).
- One idea you expressed well is ____.
- You might improve by ____.

Abuela Invents the Zero

FICTION
Judith Ortiz Cofer
1996

Introduction

Judith Ortiz Cofer's (1952–2016) writing reflects the differences between her two childhood homes: one on the island of Puerto Rico and one in a barrio (neighborhood) on the mainland. In this short story, Constancia is a teenager whose abuela (grandmother) comes to visit her in New Jersey. Caught between her American and Puerto Rican identities, Constancia feels embarrassed by the "bizarre" behavior of her abuela at church and hides her face in shame. Later, she is left to contemplate the meaning of "zero."

Connie's *abuela* ("grandmother" in Spanish) from Puerto Rico visits her family in New Jersey. It is Abuela's first trip to the United States mainland. Even though Connie has heard many stories about her grandmother's toughness and sacrifice, all she sees is an eccentric old woman. When her parents ask Connie to take her abuela to church, she is not happy, but she agrees when her father lets her borrow the car. In church, after taking communion, Abuela gets lost on the way back to her pew. Connie is so embarrassed that she pretends to be praying and ignores her. When they get home, Abuela says that Connie made her feel like a zero, a nothing. Reflecting, Connie realizes that she made a mistake, shaming the woman who brought her own mother into the world. The story closes with Connie being sent to her room to contemplate the number zero.

 Proficiency-leveled summaries and summaries in multiple languages are available digitally.

Audio and audio text highlighting are available with this text.

CONNECT TO ESSENTIAL QUESTION

What makes you, you?

How can generational and cultural differences affect a family? In this short story, the main character learns a tough lesson about acceptance after she is rude to her grandmother, who is visiting from Puerto Rico.

Access Complex Text

LEXILE: 970L **WORD COUNT:** 1,583

The following areas may be challenging for students, particularly ELL English Language Learners and A Approaching grade-level learners.

Purpose	Organization	Specific Vocabulary
• Readers need to recognize that on the surface, the story appears to be humorous and entertaining, but actually it is meant to teach a moral or lesson.	• Students need to recognize that the events in the story are not linear. The story starts with the ending, jumps back to the past, and then returns to that same beginning point later in the story.	• The story features Spanish words with which some readers may not be familiar. Point out that the use of Spanish helps identify the culture as well as the cultural friction between the narrator and her grandmother. • Most of the time the author translates for readers, as when she writes, in the fourth paragraph, "*el Polo Norte*, as she calls New Jersey, the North Pole." Sometimes, however, students will have to use context clues to figure out the meaning of certain Spanish words and phrases.

SCAFFOLDS  ENGLISH LANGUAGE LEARNERS  APPROACHING GRADE LEVEL  BEYOND GRADE LEVEL

These icons identify differentiation strategies and scaffolded support for a variety of students. See the digital lesson plan for additional differentiation strategies and scaffolds.

Instructional Path

The print teacher's edition includes essential point-of-use instruction and planning tools. Complete lesson plans and program documents appear in your digital teacher account.

First Read: Abuela Invents the Zero

Objectives: After an initial reading and discussion of the short story, students will be able to use the reading comprehension strategy of making inferences, use context clues to define new vocabulary, and demonstrate comprehension by responding to questions using textual evidence.

Skill: Plot

Objectives: After rereading and discussing a model of close reading, students will be able to analyze how particular lines of dialogue or incidents in a story or drama propel the action or provoke a decision.

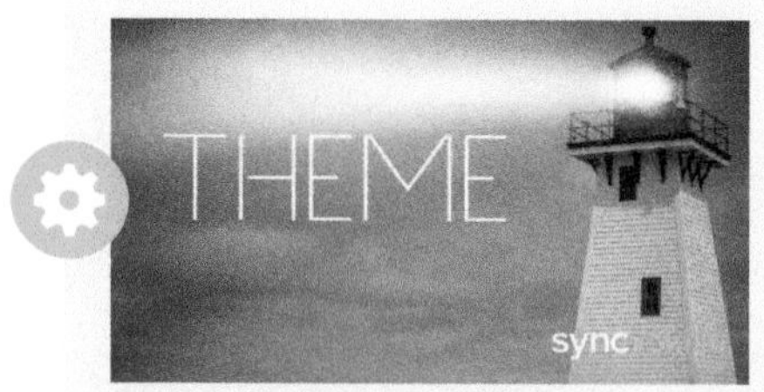

Skill: Theme

Objectives: After rereading and discussing a model of close reading, students will be able to identify details in the text that help reveal the theme.

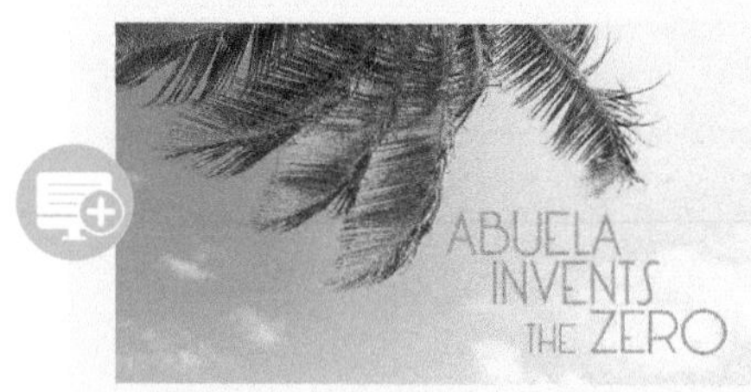

Close Read: Abuela Invents the Zero

Objectives: After engaging in a close reading and discussion of the text, students will be able to analyze how the plot and theme of the story are developed through the character's responses to incidents or decisions in a short, written response.

Progress Monitoring

Opportunities to Learn	Opportunities to Demonstrate Learning	Opportunities to Reteach
Plot		
Skill: Plot	Skill: Plot • Your Turn Close Read • Skills Focus • Write	Unit 5 Skill: Plot - Teen Mogul Spotlight Skill: Plot
Theme		
Skill: Theme	Skill: Theme • Your Turn Close Read • Writer's Notebook • Skills Focus	Unit 4 Skill: Theme - /HUG Unit 6 Skill: Theme - Manuel and the Magic Fox Spotlight Skill: Theme

First Read

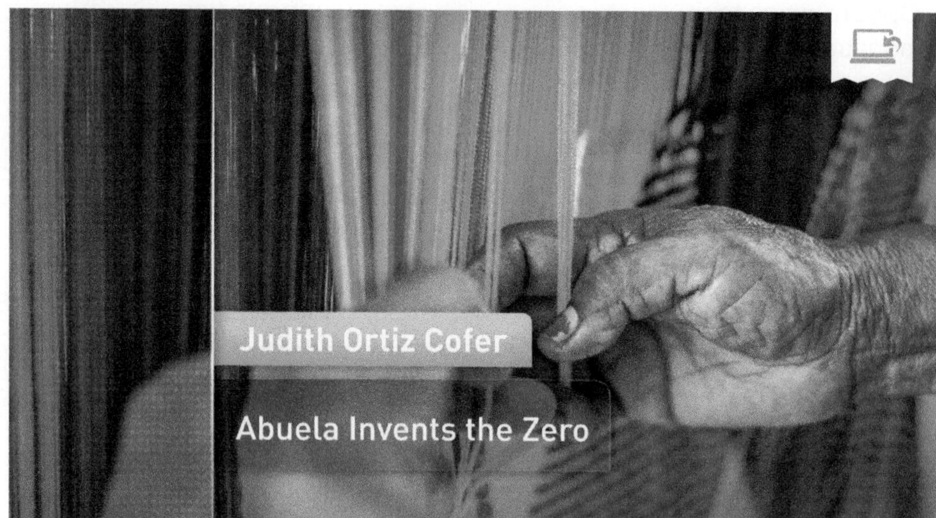

Introduce the Text

As a class, watch the video preview ▶ and have students read the introduction in pairs to make connections to the video preview.

To activate prior knowledge and experiences, ask students:

- What key words or images from the video do you think will be most important to the story you are about to read?
- What behaviors would you consider to be bizarre, and why might they be embarrassing?

SPEAKING FRAMES

- The ____ in the video makes me think ____.
- The video shows ____. This makes me wonder ____.
- I think the text will ____. I think this because ____.
- I predict that there will be ____. I believe this because ____.

Entry Point

As students prepare to read "Abuela Invents the Zero," share the following information with them to provide context.

- ✓ Judith Ortiz Cofer was an award-winning poet, short story writer, essayist, and novelist, mainly of young adult fiction. When Ortiz Cofer was four years old, her military father was transferred from her Puerto Rican homeland to New Jersey, which is the setting of "Abuela Invents the Zero." She spent much of her childhood going back and forth between the two family bases and cultures.
- ✓ Ortiz Cofer said she inherited her talent for storytelling from her abuela: "When my abuela sat us down to tell a story, we learned something from it, even though we always laughed. That was her way of teaching. So early on I instinctively knew storytelling was a form of empowerment."
- ✓ While a young child may unquestionably accept relatives, the teenage years are often marked by self-consciousness, insecurity, and a desire to "fit in." The teenage first-person narrator of "Abuela Invents the Zero" reflects these feelings.

"You made me feel like a zero, like a nothing."

NOTES

1 "You made me feel like a zero, like a nothing," she says in Spanish, *un cero, nada*. She is trembling, an angry little old woman lost in a heavy winter coat that belongs to my mother. And I end up being sent to my room, like I was a child, to think about my grandmother's idea of math.

2 It all began with Abuela coming up from the Island for a visit—her first time in the United States. My mother and father paid her way here so that she wouldn't die without seeing snow, though if you asked me, and nobody has, the dirty slush in this city is not worth the price of a ticket. But I guess she deserves some kind of award for having had ten kids and survived to tell about it. My mother is the youngest of the bunch. Right up to the time when we're supposed to pick up the old lady at the airport, my mother is telling me stories about how hard times were for *la familia* on *la isla*, and how *la abuela* worked night and day to support them after their father died of a heart attack. I'd die of a heart attack too if I had a troop like that to support. Anyway, I had seen her only three or four times in my entire life, whenever we would go for somebody's funeral. I was born here and I have lived in this building all my life. But when Mami says, "Connie, please be nice to Abuela. She doesn't have too many years left. Do you promise me, Constancia?"—when she uses my full name, I know she means business. So I say, "Sure." Why wouldn't I be nice? I'm not a monster, after all.

Skill: Plot

It seems strange that Connie would have to promise to be nice to her own grandmother. I wonder if this dialogue hints at a source of conflict in the story between Connie and her parents.

3 So we go to Kennedy to get *la abuela*, and she is the last to come out of the airplane, on the arm of the cabin attendant, all wrapped up in a black shawl. He hands her over to my parents like she was a package sent airmail. It is January, two feet of snow on the ground, and she's wearing a shawl over a thick black dress. That's just the start.

4 Once home, she refuses to let my mother buy her a coat because it's a waste of money for the two weeks she'll be in *el Polo Norte*, as she calls New Jersey, the North Pole. So since she's only four feet eleven inches tall, she walks around in my mother's big black coat looking ridiculous. I try to walk far behind them in public so that no one will think we're together. I plan to stay very busy the whole time she's with us so that I won't be asked to take her anywhere, but my plan is ruined when my mother comes down with the flu

Analyze Vocabulary Using Context Clues

In paragraph 8, focus on the sentence that uses the word *compromise*. Point out these context clues:

1. I know that the subject of the sentence *we* refers to the narrator and her father, I also know that the narrator wants to borrow the car and her father wants her to take Abuela to church. So I think a compromise is an agreement.
2. When I read the sentence again, using *agreement* in place of *compromise*, the sentence makes sense: "Needless to say, we come to an *agreement* very quickly."
3. It also fits within the context of this part of the story, in which the narrator doesn't want to take Abuela to church, but she wants to borrow the car more.

Plot

What did the reader note when she analyzed the dialogue between Connie and her mother?

The reader noted it was strange that Connie would have to be reminded to be nice to her grandmother. She also noted that this might be a clue about the story's central conflict.

TEXT TALK

What language does Abuela speak?

See paragraph 1: Abuela speaks Spanish.

What is Abuela wearing when she arrives?

See paragraph 3: Abuela is wearing a shawl over a black dress.

Why does Abuela refuse to let the narrator's mother buy her a coat?

See paragraph 4: Abuela thinks it's a waste of money.

Why does Connie have to take Abuela to church?

See paragraph 4: Connie's mother comes down with the flu.

Plot

What does the reader notice about how Connie responded to her decision to take Abuela to church?

The reader noticed that Connie regretted this decision, because she was embarrassed and more concerned about what others think.

Prepare for Advanced Courses

Use the activity below to differentiate instruction for your B Beyond grade-level learners.

Direct students to reread paragraphs 5–12.

Ask students: How does the author convey the narrator's attitude in the story? How does this attitude cause the conflict?

Answers will vary; sample answer: The author uses first-person narration and present tense to show that the narrator, Connie, is impatient. Still, Connie is aware of her world in many ways, as when her father plays a game with the car keys, and as she describes the church. However, she is focused only on her own responses, and this creates the conflict with Abuela.

and Abuela absolutely *has* to attend Sunday mass or her soul will be eternally damned. She's more Catholic than the Pope. My father decides that he should stay home with my mother and that I should escort *la abuela* to church. He tells me this on Saturday night as I'm getting ready to go out to the mall with my friends.

NOTES

5 "No way," I say.

6 I go for the car keys on the kitchen table: he usually leaves them there for me on Friday and Saturday nights. He beats me to them.

7 "No way," he says, pocketing them and grinning at me.

8 Needless to say, we come to a **compromise** very quickly. I do have a responsibility to Sandra and Anita, who don't drive yet. There is a Harley-Davidson fashion show at Brookline Square that we *cannot* miss.

9 "The mass in Spanish is at ten sharp tomorrow morning, *entiendes*?" My father is dangling the car keys in front of my nose and pulling them back when I try to reach for them. He's really enjoying himself.

10 "I understand. Ten o'clock. I'm out of here." I pry his fingers off the key ring. He knows that I'm late, so he makes it just a little difficult. Then he laughs. I run out of our apartment before he changes his mind. I have no idea what I'm getting myself into.

11 Sunday morning I have to walk two blocks on dirty snow to retrieve the car. I warm it up for Abuela as instructed by my parents, and drive it to the front of our building. My father walks her by the hand in baby steps on the slippery snow. The sight of her little head with a bun on top of it sticking out of that huge coat makes me want to run back into my room and get under the covers. I just hope that nobody I know sees us together. I'm dreaming, of course. The mass is packed with people from our block. It's a holy day of **obligation** and everyone I ever met is there.

Skill: Plot

Connie already regrets taking Abuela to mass. She is embarrassed to be seen with her grandmother and more concerned about what others will think. I think Connie's feelings will lead to the central conflict with Abuela.

12 I have to help her climb the steps, and she stops to take a deep breath after each one, then I lead her down the aisle so that everybody can see me with my bizarre grandmother. If I were a good Catholic, I'm sure I'd get some purgatory time taken off for my sacrifice. She is walking as slow as Captain Cousteau exploring the bottom of the sea, looking around, taking her sweet time. Finally she chooses a pew, but she wants to sit in the other end. It's like she had a spot picked out for some unknown reason, and although it's the most inconvenient seat in the house, that's where she has to sit. So we squeeze by all the people already sitting there, saying, "Excuse me, please, *con permiso*, pardon me," getting annoyed looks the whole way. By the time

SELECTION VOCABULARY

compromise / ceder ***noun*** the settlement of an argument or disagreement in which each side agrees to give up some part of its claims or demands

obligation / la obligación ***noun*** something that is required and must be done COGNATE

- Where is the narrator when she uses the word *obligation*?
- How many other people are there? Why are there so many people?

we settle in, I'm drenched in sweat. I keep my head down like I'm praying so as not to see or be seen. She is praying loud, in Spanish, and singing hymns at the top of her creaky voice.

13 I ignore her when she gets up with a hundred other people to go take communion. I'm actually praying hard now—that this will all be over soon. But the next time I look up, I see a black coat dragging around and around the church, stopping here and there so a little gray head can peek out like a **periscope** on a submarine. There are giggles in the church, and even the priest has frozen in the middle of a blessing, his hands above his head like he is about to lead the congregation in a set of jumping jacks.

Skill: Theme

Abuela gets lost in church, forcing Connie, the narrator, to make a choice. This choice is uncomfortable for Connie, so she decides to stay seated. It's clear she doesn't want to be seen in public with her grandmother.

14 I realize to my horror that my grandmother is lost. She can't find her way back to the pew. I am so embarrassed that even though the woman next to me is shooting daggers at me with her eyes, I just can't move to go get her. I put my hands over my face like I'm praying, but it's really to hide my burning cheeks. I would like for her to disappear. I just know that on Monday my friends, and my enemies, in the barrio will have a lot of **senile**-grandmother jokes to tell in front of me. I am frozen to my seat. So the same woman who wants me dead on the spot does it for me. She makes a big deal out of getting up and hurrying to get Abuela.

15 The rest of the mass is a blur. All I know is that my grandmother kneels the whole time with her hands over *her* face. She doesn't speak to me on the way home, and she doesn't let me help her walk, even though she almost falls a couple of times.

16 When we get to the apartment, my parents are at the kitchen table, where my mother is trying to eat some soup. They can see right away that something is wrong. Then Abuela points her finger at me like a judge passing a **sentence** on a criminal. She says in Spanish, "You made me feel like a zero, like a nothing." Then she goes to her room.

17 I try to explain what happened. "I don't understand why she's so upset. She just got lost and wandered around for a while," I tell them. But it sounds lame, even to my own ears. My mother gives me a look that makes me cringe and goes in to Abuela's room to get her version of the story. She comes out with tears in her eyes.

18 "Your grandmother says to tell you that of all the hurtful things you can do to a person, the worst is to make them feel as if they are worth nothing."

19 I can feel myself shrinking right there in front of her. But I can't bring myself to tell my mother that I think I understand how I made Abuela feel. I might be sent into the old lady's room to apologize, and it's not easy to admit you've

TEXT TALK

What is Abuela's problem at church?

See paragraph 14: She gets lost coming back from communion.

What does the narrator's mother do after she hears what happened at church?

See paragraphs 17 and 18: She cries and tells Connie what Abuela said about her.

Theme

What part of the story did the reader annotate to show that Abuela forced Connie to make a choice about her behavior

The reader highlighted the moment that Abuela got lost and needed help.

Skills Focus

QUESTION 3: Plot and Character

Connie does not want to be associated with her grandmother because of the way she is dressed, so she ignores her in church.

Skills Focus

QUESTION 2: Plot

When Connie realizes that her grandmother is lost and cannot find her way back to the pew in church, her first thought is not to go to Abuela's rescue. Instead she wants Abuela to disappear.

Skills Focus

QUESTION 1: Plot

Abuela tells Connie she made her feel like a zero. Until this point, Connie thinks it's fine to ignore Abuela, without consideration for how it might make her grandmother feel. She claims to not understand why Abuela is upset.

Skills Focus

QUESTION 4: Plot and Theme

Even after Connie's mother clearly tells her how bad she made Abuela feel, Connie just sits there. She still refers to her grandmother as "the old lady" and is reluctant to apologize because of the way it would make *her* feel. Connie still does not realize how her behavior has hurt Abuela, and she still thinks only of herself and her own feelings.

Skills Focus

Question 5: Connect to Essential Question

Before Abuela visited, Connie's mother begged her to be nice, and Connie thought that since she's not a monster, her behavior would be good enough. It isn't until Connie's mother points out Abuela's value and their connection to each other that Connie starts to understand. She made Abuela feel like zero, or nothing, and in the last line of the story, Connie finally thinks about how zero must feel in a whole new way.

NOTES

been a jerk—at least, not right away with everybody watching. So I just sit there not saying anything.

20 My mother looks at me for a long time, like she feels sorry for me. Then she says, "You should know, Constancia, that if it wasn't for the old woman whose existence you don't seem to value, you and I would not be here."

21 That's when *I'm* sent to *my* room to consider a number I hadn't thought much about—until today.

TEXT TALK

How can Connie build a relationship and find common ground with Abuela?

Answers will vary.

Ask each Beyond grade-level student to write one additional discussion question. Then have one or two students facilitate a discussion, using their questions to guide the conversation.

SELECTION VOCABULARY

periscope / el periscopio ***noun*** a device used to look around or above an obstacle COGNATE

- What is Abuela doing when she is compared to a "periscope"?
- How is this like a submarine?

senile / senil ***adjective*** relating to or showing characteristics of old age, especially with regard to loss of memory COGNATE

- Who is "senile"? Is it positive or negative?
- What is Abuela doing in this paragraph?

sentence / la sentencia ***noun*** a punishment given for a particular offense COGNATE

- Who passes a "sentence"?
- Who receives a "sentence"?

Reading Comprehension OPTIONAL

Have students complete the digital reading comprehension questions ✓ when they finish reading.

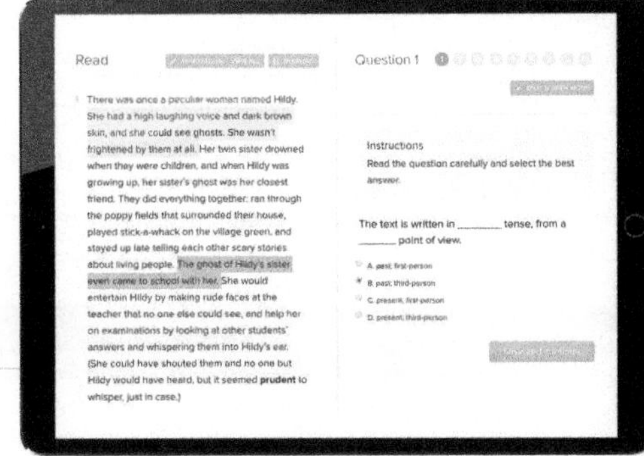

ANSWER KEY

QUESTION 1: B
QUESTION 2: C
QUESTION 3: C
QUESTION 4: D
QUESTION 5: D
QUESTION 6: A
QUESTION 7: A
QUESTION 8: C
QUESTION 9: *See first chart.*
QUESTION 10: *See second chart.*

Definition	Vocabulary Word
a viewing tool	periscope
duty or requirement	obligation
punishment for a particular offense	sentence
suffering from a loss of mental function	senile
an agreement	compromise

First	Second	Third	Fourth
Abuela wears a shawl in the middle of an East Coast winter.	The narrator is bribed into taking Abuela to church.	The narrator does not help her abuela when she is lost.	The narrator learns the meaning of "zero" (as it is used in the title of the story).

Connect and Extend OPTIONAL

CONNECT TO EXTENDED WRITING PROJECT

Students can find inspiration from "Abuela Invents the Zero" when writing their literary analyses. Have them reflect on Judith Ortiz Cofer's characterization of the narrator as she grapples with identity.

BEYOND THE BOOK

Photography: Nothing to Something

Sometimes we may treat others as if they were nothing, or, as Connie treats her abuela, as if they were "zero." To change this, have students do the following:

Find or take a photograph of someone whom others might ignore, dismiss, or not always notice during the course of a busy day.

- The photo may be of either someone you know or a stranger.
- The portrait may be in color or black and white.

Choose one type of brief caption to write to tell the story of the person in the photo.

- A narrative describing the person and circumstances; or
- A monologue in the voice of the person. If you do an actual interview, use quotation marks.

Display the portraits and stories. To reflect, ask students:

- What do the portraits and words make you think about?
- How might you look at strangers differently now?

Think Questions

Circulate as students answer Think Questions independently. Scaffolds for these questions are shown on the opposite page.

QUESTION 1: Textual Evidence

Connie hardly knows her grandmother. She says she only met her grandmother three or four times in Puerto Rico when she was there for family funerals. So, Connie doesn't have the kind of close relationship with Abuela that other young people have with a grandparent who lives nearby or whom they visit often.

QUESTION 2: Textual Evidence

Connie thinks Abuela's clothes are inappropriate for the winter in New Jersey, and the coat she borrows is way too big for her and makes her look silly. Connie thinks Abuela looks odd when she goes to church with her head sticking out of the oversized coat.

QUESTION 3: Textual Evidence

Answers will vary but may include the following examples:

- "I am so embarrassed"
- "I put my hands over my face"

Student descriptions should explain that Connie's reaction is dramatic and does not include trying to help her grandmother.

QUESTION 4: Context Clues

The word *obligation* describes a "holy day." I know that Connie is in church, and the church is "packed with people." It must be a special day and the people are there because they feel they have to be. This helps me figure out that an *obligation* is something that is required to be done.

QUESTION 5: Word Meaning

Noun definition 2 most closely matches the meaning of the word *sentence* in paragraph 16. The *sentence* is something that Abuela is "passing," so it must be one of the noun options. The word *judge* as well as the word *criminal* are clues in the sentence that helped me figure out that *sentence* must mean "a punishment given for a particular offense."

First Read

Read "Abuela Invents the Zero." After you read, complete the Think Questions below.

THINK QUESTIONS

1. Describe Constancia's relationship with Abuela prior to her grandmother's visit to New Jersey. Cite details from the text to support your response.
2. Refer to details from the text to explain why Constancia considers her grandmother to be, in her eyes, "ridiculous" and "bizarre."
3. How does Constancia respond when Abuela becomes lost in the church? Describe her reaction, and support your answer with evidence from the text.
4. Use context to determine the meaning of the word **obligation** as it is used in "Abuela Invents the Zero" in paragraph 11. Write your definition of *obligation* here and explain how you found it.
5. Read the following dictionary entry:

   sentence
   sen•tence \ˈsen(t)əns\

   noun

   1. a complete statement, command, question, etc., containing one or more words
   2. a punishment given for a particular offense

   verb

   1. to punish or pass judgment (on someone), typically in a court of law

   Which definition most closely matches the meaning of **sentence** as it is used in paragraph 16? Write the appropriate definition of *sentence* here and explain how you figured out the correct meaning.

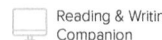

SCAFFOLDS

Think Questions

Use the scaffolds below to differentiate instruction for your ELL English Language Learners and A Approaching grade-level learners.

ELL **BEGINNING** Write a response using the word bank and sentence frames.

INTERMEDIATE Write a response using the sentence frames.

ADVANCED, ADVANCED HIGH Write a response using the Text-Dependent Question Guide.

A **APPROACHING** Write a response using the Text-Dependent Question Guide.

BEGINNING	INTERMEDIATE	APPROACHING / ADVANCED, ADVANCED HIGH
Word Bank	**Sentence Frames**	**Text-Dependent Question Guide**
know help clothes embarrassed big required times pray packed close coat ridiculous	Connie does not ____ Abuela very well. Connie only met her grandmother a few ____. Connie is not ____ to Abuela.	1. • How well does Connie know Abuela? • How much time have they spent together in the past? • How does Connie feel about Abuela? • How do I know this?
	Connie thinks Abuela's ____ are wrong for winter. The ____ Abuela borrows is too ____ for her. Connie thinks Abuela looks ____.	2. • Why does Connie think Abuela looks weird? • Why does Connie think Abuela acts differently? • Why doesn't Connie want people to see her with Abuela?
	Connie feels ____. Connie pretends to ____. She does not get up to ____ Abuela.	3. • Which words in the text tell Connie's reaction? • What does Connie do when Abuela looks for her? • How would you describe Connie's reaction in your own words?
	There are more people at church than usual, and Connie says that the mass is ____. This is a clue that *obligation* means they have to, or are ____ to, go.	4. • Read: "The mass is packed with people from our block. It's a holy day of **obligation** and everyone I ever met is there." • What does *obligation* describe? • What does Connie notice about how many people are at church?
	Sentence as used in the text matches definition #____.	5. • Read: "Then Abuela points her finger at me like a judge passing a **sentence** on a criminal." • Is a *sentence* a complete statement or command? (#1) • Is a *sentence* a punishment? (#2) • Does *sentence* mean "to punish"? (#3)

Skill: Plot

Introduce the Skill

Watch the Concept Definition video and read the following definition with your students.

The events that take place in a story or **narrative** are called the **plot**. These events give the story a beginning, a middle, and an end, and they are influenced by literary elements such as character and setting. Events in a story begin with the **inciting incident**, or the moment in which the **conflict**, or main problem, is introduced. As characters attempt to solve the problem, it may become more complicated, and the characters may undergo changes as they respond to rising tension. For example, the main character may learn the value of patience as he or she works toward finding a solution, or may begin to understand or sympathize with another character's difficulties. The **turning point** in a plot occurs when a key event or decision leads to a **resolution**, or a way to solve the problem.

Skill:
Plot

Use the Checklist to analyze Plot in "Abuela Invents the Zero." Refer to the sample student annotations abo Plot in the text.

••• CHECKLIST FOR PLOT

In order to identify plot elements in a story or drama, note the following:

- ✓ dialogue or conversations between two or more characters
- ✓ incidents or notable events throughout the story's plot
- ✓ central conflict
- ✓ characters' responses to or decisions about incidents
- ✓ the ways in which the characters affect the resolution of the conflict

To analyze how particular lines of dialogue or incidents in a story or drama propel the action or provoke decision, consider the following questions:

- ✓ What happens as a result of a dialogue between two characters?
- ✓ How does the plot unfold in the story?
- ✓ Do characters respond or change as the plot advances? How?
- ✓ What causes a character to act or make a decision? What events occur as a result of these actior or decisions?

TURN AND TALK

1. What is the conflict, or problem, in your favorite book or movie?
2. How is the conflict resolved by the end of the story?

SPEAKING FRAMES

- One problem in [book title / movie title] was ____.
- Another problem was ____.
- I think the main conflict is ____.
- The conflict was resolved when ____.

SKILL VOCABULARY

narrative / la narración ***noun*** a story, real or imagined, consisting of connected events

plot / la trama ***noun*** the sequence of events that form a story

inciting incident / el incidente generador ***noun*** the first event in which the conflict becomes apparent

conflict / el conflicto ***noun*** the main problem or struggle that characters face in a story COGNATE

Skill: Plot

Reread paragraphs 4–10 of "Abuela Invents the Zero." Then, using the Checklist on the previous page, answer the multiple-choice questions below.

YOUR TURN

1. How does the decision that Connie's father makes in paragraph 4 affect the events that follow?

   - A. Connie's father decides that Connie should take Abuela to church.
   - B. Connie's mother comes down with the flu.
   - C. Connie's father tells her that she should take Abuela to church and Connie refuses.
   - D. Abuela decides she doesn't need to go to church.

2. How does the dialogue in paragraphs 5–7 influence the decision Connie makes about taking Abuela to church?

   - A. The dialogue in paragraphs 5–7 influences Connie to take Abuela to the Brookline Square Mall.
   - B. Connie decides to take Abuela to church because her father says "No way" when she asks for the car keys to head to a fashion show.
   - C. Connie decides to take Abuela to church because her father says she has to.
   - D. Connie tells her father "No way" when he tells her to take Abuela to church because she wants to go to the fashion show.

SKILL VOCABULARY

turning point / el clímax ***noun*** a moment when the series of events in a plot suddenly changes

resolution / la resolución ***noun*** the final outcome of the story's conflict COGNATE

Your Turn

Ask students to complete the Your Turn activity.

QUESTION 1

A. Incorrect, even though this is the decision her father makes, this does not answer how it affects the events that follow.

B. Incorrect. Connie's mother gets sick before her father decides that Connie should take Abuela to church.

C. Correct. Connie says "No way," when her father tells her to take Abuela to church.

D. Incorrect. This doesn't happen in the story.

QUESTION 2

A. Incorrect. The dialogue between Connie and her father in paragraphs 5–7 influences Connie to take Abuela to church, because otherwise, her father won't let her take the car to the the fashion show.

B. Correct. Connie's father says "No Way" when she asks for the car keys. He responds by saying the same thing when she tries to take the keys to drive, which influences her decision to take Abuela to church.

C. Incorrect. Connie tells her dad "No way" when he tells her to take Abuela to church. He responds by saying the same thing when she tries to take the car keys, which influences her decision to take Abuela to church.

D. Incorrect. Connie tells her father "No way" because she doesn't want to take Abuela to church at all. He responds by saying the same thing when she tries to take the keys to drive to the fashion show, which influences her decision to take Abuela to church.

Skill: Theme

Introduce the Skill

Watch the Concept Definition video and read the following definition with your students.

The **topic** of a literary work is the subject of the work. It is usually expressed as a noun. The **theme** is the central idea or message of a work of literature. It is often expressed as a general statement about life. For example, the topic of a literary work might be love. The theme would be what the writer suggests about love: that it is wonderful or painful or maybe both at once. A literary work may have more than one theme.

Sometimes a writer states a theme directly. More often, though, theme is revealed gradually. In short stories, novels, and dramas, theme is revealed through elements such as character, setting, and plot, what the characters do and say, and how these elements affect the events that take place. When a theme is not stated directly, a reader will have to infer the theme. To **infer** means to determine something by using reasoning and textual evidence.

Skill: Theme

Use the Checklist to analyze Theme in "Abuela Invents the Zero." Refer to the sample student annotations about Theme in the text.

••• YOUR TURN

In order to identify a theme or central idea of a text, note the following:

- ✓ the subject of the text and a theme that might be stated directly in the text
- ✓ details in the text that help to reveal theme
  - the title and chapter headings
  - details about the setting
  - a narrator's or speaker's tone
  - characters' thoughts, actions, and dialogue
  - the central conflict in a story's plot
  - the climax, or turning point, in the story
  - the resolution of the conflict
  - shifts in characters, setting, or plot events
- ✓ analyze the development of the theme and its relationship to the characters, setting, and plot
  - the time and place, such as a narrative set in the past or future, can affect how a character responds to events
  - characters' responses and reactions to events in a text can reveal themes in a story
  - the story's conflict or resolution may help to determine the theme

To determine a theme or central idea of a text and analyze its development over the course of the text, including its relationship to the characters, setting, and plot, use the following questions as a guide:

- ✓ What is a theme or central idea of the text? When did you become aware of that theme?
- ✓ How does the theme relate to the characters, setting, and plot?
- ✓ How does the theme develop over the course of the text?

TURN AND TALK

1. In your favorite book or movie, what message do you take away from the story?
2. How does that message get revealed throughout the story?

SPEAKING FRAMES

- My favorite book or movie was about ____.
- In my favorite book or movie, the message I took away from the story was ____.
- I learned that message when ____ happened in the story.

SKILL VOCABULARY

topic / el tema *noun* the subject of a literary work, usually expressed as a single word or phrase in the form of a noun

theme / el tema *noun* the central idea or message of a work of literature, often expressed as a general statement about life

infer / inferir *verb* to determine something by using reasoning and evidence from the text COGNATE

Abuela Invents the Zero

Skill: Theme

Reread paragraphs 15–17 of "Abuela Invents the Zero." Then, using the Checklist on the previous page, answer the multiple-choice questions below.

YOUR TURN

1. Referring to paragraph 15, how does Abuela react to Connie?

  - ○ A. She seeks help from her granddaughter and uses her for support.
  - ○ B. She apologizes to her granddaughter for embarrassing her in church.
  - ○ C. She ignores her granddaughter and refuses Connie's help.
  - ○ D. She is angry with her granddaughter and yells at her on the way home.

2. Which quote from the story demonstrates how Abuela feels about Connie's behavior in church?

  - ○ A. She says in Spanish, "You made me feel like a zero, like a nothing."
  - ○ B. I try to explain what happened. "I don't understand why she's so upset. She just got lost and wandered around for a while," I tell them.
  - ○ C. They can see right away that something is wrong.
  - ○ D. But I can't bring myself to tell my mother that I think I understand how I made Abuela feel.

3. Referring to paragraph 17, whose reaction changes the narrator's opinion of her grandmother?

  - ○ A. Her parents' reaction when they can see right away that something is wrong.
  - ○ B. Abuela's reaction when she says in Spanish, "You made me feel like a zero, like a nothing."
  - ○ C. Abuela's reaction when she doesn't speak on the way home.
  - ○ D. Her mother's reaction when she has tears in her eyes and tells her what Abuela said.

Your Turn

Ask students to complete the Your Turn activity.

QUESTION 1

A. Incorrect. This does not accurately reflect what happened in the text.

B. Incorrect. This does not accurately reflect what happened in the text.

C. Correct. Abuela puts her hands over her face in church and walks by herself on the way home.

D. Incorrect. This does not accurately reflect what happened in the text.

QUESTION 2

A. Correct. These are Abuela's words, and they are the first time she has spoken to her granddaughter about the mistreatment she received in church.

B. Incorrect. This is the narrator explaining things to her parents, it does not refer to Abuela's feelings.

C. Incorrect. This refers to what her parents know, not to Abuela's feelings.

D. Incorrect. This refers to the narrator's feelings, it does not refer to Abuela's feelings.

QUESTION 3

A. Incorrect. The narrator still tries to defend herself and explain what happened after seeing her parents' reaction.

B. Incorrect. The narrator still tries to defend herself and explain what happened after seeing Abuela's reaction.

C. Incorrect. The narrator still tries to defend herself and explain what happened after hearing Abuela's reaction.

D. Correct. It is finally after seeing her mom's tears and hearing what Abuela told her that the narrator begins to understand how she made Abuela feel.

Close Read

Skills Focus

QUESTION 1: Plot

See paragraphs 16 and 17.

QUESTION 2: Plot

See paragraph 14.

QUESTION 3: Plot and Character

See paragraph 13.

QUESTION 4: Plot and Theme

See paragraphs 18 and 19.

QUESTION 5: Connect to Essential Question

See paragraphs 20 and 21.

CHECK FOR SUCCESS

If students struggle to respond to Skills Focus question 1, ask them the following questions:

- What does Connie's mother ask her to do in paragraph 2? Why?
- How does Connie respond?
- What does Connie tell her father in paragraph 5? Why?

Have students transition to read and annotate independently once they have successfully completed the first Skills Focus prompt.

Close Read

Reread "Abuela Invents the Zero." As you reread, complete the Skills Focus questions below. Then use your answers and annotations from the questions to help you complete the Write activity.

SKILLS FOCUS

1. Which lines of dialogue in the story reveal that Connie is unaware of the consequences her actions can have? Cite evidence in the text to support your answer.
2. Analyzing specific incidents and events in a story or drama can help readers determine the theme as it develops over the course of the text. Reread paragraphs 13–15. Cite specific evidence that suggests the incident at the church is a turning point in the relationship between Connie and Abuela, and what it reveals or communicates about the theme.
3. How does the author reveal the importance Connie places on clothes and appearance throughout the story, and how does this character trait serve to create a distance between grandmother and granddaughter? Cite evidence in the text that supports your answer.
4. Reread paragraphs 17–21 of the story. Which paragraphs suggest that Connie still doesn't fully realize how much her behavior has hurt her grandmother? Cite textual evidence that supports your answer.
5. Explain how Connie considers herself to be before Abuela comes to visit, and how this opinion changes by the end of the story. Cite textual evidence to support your response.

WRITE

NARRATIVE: Write a letter that continues the story in which Constancia apologizes to Abuela and resolves the conflict between them. In your letter, include an example of Connie's responses to a decision or incident. In connection to the story's central idea or theme, explain what Connie has learned and how she has changed.

Writer's Notebook

Connect to Essential Question: Give students time to reflect on how "Abuela Invents the Zero" connects to the unit's essential question "What makes you, you?" by freewriting in their Writer's Notebooks.

Beginning & Intermediate

Read aloud the unit's essential question: "What makes you, you?" Encourage students to draw their connections or allow students to write in their native language. Circulate the room, prompting students for their thoughts as they respond orally or through pantomime.

Advanced & Advanced High

Allow students to share their connections orally in pairs or small groups before freewriting.

Collaborative Conversation

SCAFFOLDS

Break students into collaborative conversation groups to discuss the Close Read prompt. Ask students to use the StudySyncTV episode as a model for their discussion. Remind them to reference their Skills Focus annotations in their discussion.

Write a letter that continues the story in which Constancia apologizes to Abuela and resolves the conflict between them. In your letter, include an example of Connie's responses to a decision or incident. In connection to the story's central idea or theme, explain what Connie has learned and how she has changed.

Use the scaffolds below to differentiate instruction for your ELL English Language Learners and A Approaching grade-level learners.

ELL **BEGINNING, INTERMEDIATE** Use the discussion guide and speaking frames to discuss with support from the teacher.

ADVANCED, ADVANCED HIGH Use the discussion guide and speaking frames to discuss in mixed-level groups.

A **APPROACHING** Use the discussion guide to discuss in mixed-level groups.

APPROACHING
ADVANCED, ADVANCED HIGH
BEGINNING, INTERMEDIATE

Discussion Guide	Speaking Frames
1. What is an example of how Connie responds to a decision or incident?	• Connie responds ____ when ____. • Another example is when Connie ____.
2. What do you think Connie has learned from this?	• Connie has learned ____ because ____. • Connie will change by ____.
3. How does the lesson Connie learns connect to the central idea or theme of the story?	• The central idea or theme is ____. • This connects to Connie's lesson because ____.

Review Prompt and Rubric

Before students begin writing, review the writing prompt and rubric with the class.

NARRATIVE: Write a letter that continues the story in which Constancia apologizes to Abuela and resolves the conflict between them. In your letter, include an example of Connie's responses to a decision or incident. In connection to the story's central idea or theme, explain what Connie has learned and how she has changed.

PROMPT GUIDE

- What did Connie do that requires an apology to Abuela?
- What has Connie learned?
- How has Connie changed?
- How does the lesson Connie learns connect to the central idea or theme of the story?

An additional rubric for Language and Conventions appears in your digital teacher and student accounts.

Score	Plot	Theme
4	The writer effectively extends the plot of the story, providing a strong resolution that clearly shows how the character has changed. The writer includes details about the plot that follow clearly and effectively from the events in the story.	The writer effectively explains what Connie has learned, providing a strong connection to the central idea or theme of the story.
3	The writer extends the plot of the story, providing a reasonable resolution that attempts to show how the character has changed. The writer includes details about the plot that mostly follow from the events of the story.	The writer explains what Connie has learned, providing a reasonable attempt to connect to the central idea or theme of the story.
2	The writer attempts to extend the plot of the story, but the resolution mostly restates details from the story or does not show how the character has changed. The writer attempts to include details about the plot, but it does not follow clearly from the events of the story.	The writer attempts to explain what Connie has learned, but does not make a reasonable attempt to connect to the central idea or theme of the story.
1	The writer does not extend the plot of the story or provide a resolution to the conflict. The writer does not attempt to include details about the plot or show how the character has changed.	The writer does not explain what Connie has learned or make a reasonable attempt to connect to the central idea or theme of the story.
0	The writer does not provide a relevant response to the prompt or does not provide a response at all.	The writer does not provide a relevant response to the prompt or does not provide a response at all.

Write

SCAFFOLDS

Ask students to complete the writing assignment using textual evidence to support their answers.

Use the scaffolds below to differentiate instruction for your ELL English Language Learners and A Approaching grade-level learners.

ELL **BEGINNING** With the help of the word bank, write a response using paragraph frame 1.

INTERMEDIATE With the help of the word bank, write a response using paragraph frames 1 and 2.

ADVANCED, ADVANCED HIGH Write a response of differentiated length using the sentence starters.

A **APPROACHING** Write a response of differentiated length using the sentence starters.

BEGINNING | INTERMEDIATE | ADVANCED, ADVANCED HIGH | APPROACHING

Word Bank	Paragraph Frame 1	Paragraph Frame 2	Sentence Starters
hurt nice Abuela ignored Love	Dear ____, I'm sorry I ____ you at church. It was not ____, and I will never do that again. Now I know that my bad actions ____ your feelings. ____, Connie	Dear ____, I'm sorry I ____you at church. It was not ____, and I will never do that again. Now I know that my bad actions ____ your feelings. When you arrived I ____. Now I ____. I hope ____. ____, Connie	• I'm sorry I . . . • When you arrived I . . . • Now I . . . • I hope . . .

Peer Review

Students should submit substantive feedback to two peers using the instructions below.

- How well does this response answer the prompt?
- How well does the writer include relevant references to Connie's responses to a decision or incident?
- Did the letter connect to the story's central idea or theme?
- What did the writer do well in this response? What does the writer need to work on?

Rate

Respond to the following with a point rating that reflects your opinion.

	1	2	3	4
Ideas	■	■	■	□
Evidence	■	■	■	■
Language and Conventions	■	■	□	□

Submit

ELL A **SENTENCE FRAMES**

- You were able to (completely / partly / almost) answer the prompt.
- You could answer the prompt better by ____.

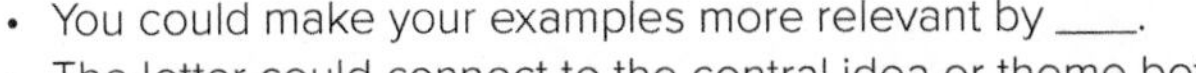

- You could make your examples more relevant by ____.
- The letter could connect to the central idea or theme better by ____.
- My favorite part of your letter is ____.

Inside Out and Back Again

FICTION
Thanhhà Lai
2011

Introduction

In many ways, the first novel by Thanhhà Lai (b. 1965) mirrors her own childhood experience. Like the main character, Hà, in *Inside Out and Back Again*, Thanhhà Lai witnessed the harsh reality of the Vietnam War, had a father who was missing in action, and fled with her family to America. Through Hà's character, Lai captures many of the universal feelings refugees experience in an unfamiliar place. In the four excerpts here, written in verse as first-person journal entries, Hà feels a rush of emotions as she repeats the fourth grade in her new home: Alabama.

In these four journal entries, a Vietnamese refugee named Hà describes her experience when she has to repeat the fourth grade after immigrating to Alabama. In the morning, Hà's mother ignores her request for a bicycle and tells her to make some friends at school. Hà worries that she won't be able to make any friends because she will be the oldest student in her grade. Nervous, she arrives to class, where she doesn't understand the language. When Hà says her name, the teacher mistakes it for laughter. Looking around the room, Hà realizes that she is the only person with black hair and olive skin. Later, in the cafeteria, she observes how the students eat separately: those with light skin sit on one side of the room and the dark-skinned students congregate on the other. With her medium-tone skin, Hà wonders where to sit.

 Proficiency-leveled summaries and summaries in multiple languages are available digitally.

 Audio and audio text highlighting are available with this text.

COMPARING WITHIN AND ACROSS GENRES

 How can moving to a new place change the way you see yourself? In the excerpt from *Inside Out and Back Again*, a novel written in verse by Thanhhà Lai, the main character adjusts to life in Alabama after moving to the United States from Vietnam. The selection, which is paired with "Theories of Time and Space" and "The Road Not Taken," allows readers to reflect on how sense of self relates to new beginnings.

Access Complex Text

LEXILE: N/A **WORD COUNT:** 521

The following areas may be challenging for students, particularly ELL English Language Learners and A Approaching grade-level learners.

Genre	Connection of Ideas	Sentence Structure
• Thanhhà Lai wrote this novel in the form of verse. Traditionally, poetry focuses on images and emotion, which may be why the author chose this form.	• The story of a child's assimilation to American culture is told in bursts of images, centered around going to a new school • Readers will need to connect the moments to follow the plot. Annotating may help readers make connections.	• Lai uses a variety of structures, including dates as in a journal, stanzas, and one-sentence paragraphs in italics to indicate dialogue. • Reading sections aloud, alone or in pairs, may help readers follow the events of the plot.

SCAFFOLDS  ENGLISH LANGUAGE LEARNERS  APPROACHING GRADE LEVEL  BEYOND GRADE LEVEL

These icons identify differentiation strategies and scaffolded support for a variety of students. See the digital lesson plan for additional differentiation strategies and scaffolds.

Instructional Path

The print teacher's edition includes essential point-of-use instruction and planning tools Complete lesson plans and program documents appear in your digital teacher account.

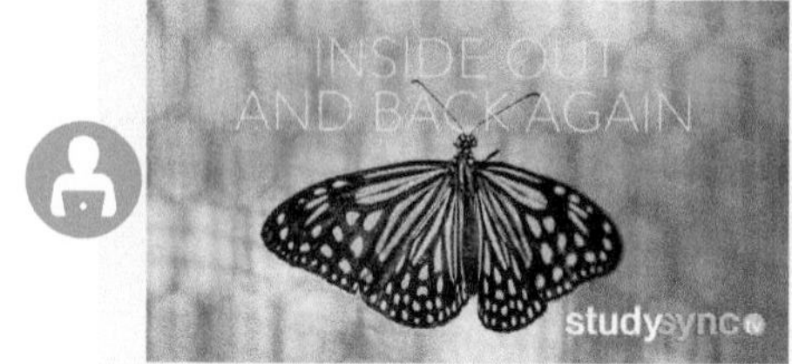

Independent Read: Inside Out and Back Again

Objectives: After reading an excerpt from the text, students will demonstrate understanding by responding to comprehension questions, participating in a collaborative conversation, and writing a personal response.

Independent Read

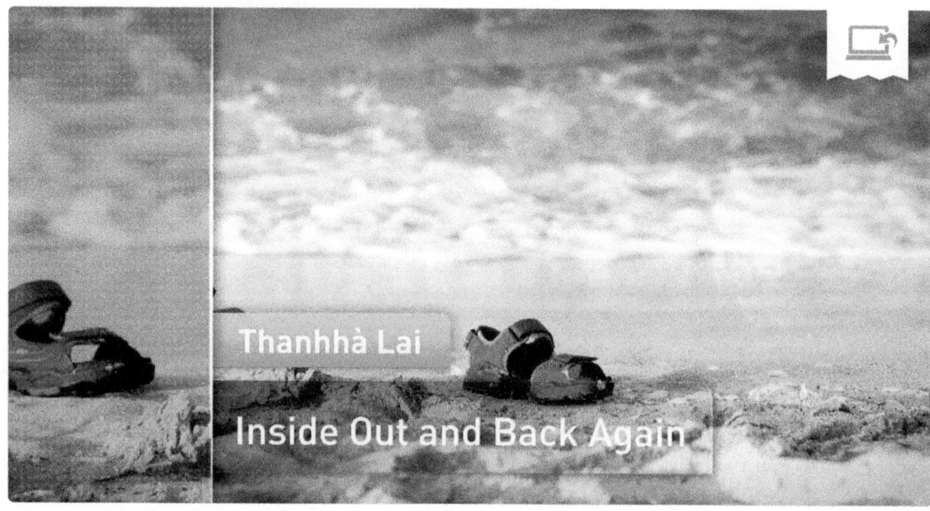

Introduce the Text

As a class, watch the video preview and have students read the introduction in pairs to make connections to the video preview.

- What key words or images from the video do you think will be most important to the selection you are about to read?
- What kind of story are you about to read? What is unusual about the genre or form?
- How does this information connect to something you already know?

ELL **SPEAKING FRAMES**

- The ____ in the video makes me think ____.
- The video shows ____. This makes me wonder ____.
- I think the text will ____. I think this because ____.
- I predict that there will be ____. I believe this because ____.

Entry Point

As students prepare to read *Inside Out and Back Again*, share the following information with them to provide context.

✓ Thanhhà Lai won the National Book Award for Young People's Literature, as well as a Newbery Honor, for *Inside Out and Back Again*, her first novel. She has written a second novel, *Listen, Slowly.*

✓ The Vietnam War was a civil war fought between South Vietnam and North Vietnam; the South was aided by the United States. The narrator and main character, Hà, lives in Saigon, the capital of South Vietnam, and flees with her family to the United States when Saigon falls to the North Vietnamese toward the end of the war. Hà's family lives in a tent city for refugees before relocating to the setting of the excerpt.

✓ Though considered a novel, *Inside Out and Back Again* is not written in prose; it is written in free verse and belongs to a literary form called a verse novel.

“Deep breaths.
I’m the first student in class.”

NOTES

The Outside

Starting tomorrow
everyone must
leave the house.

Mother starts sewing
at a factory;
Brother Quang begins
repairing cars.

The rest of us
must go to school,
repeating the last grade,
left unfinished.

Brother Vũ wants
to be a cook
or teach martial arts,
not waste a year
as the oldest senior.

Mother says
one word:
College.

Brother Khôi
gets an old bicycle to ride,
but Mother says
I’m too young for one
even though I’m
a ten-year-old
in the fourth grade,
when everyone else
is nine.

Analyze Vocabulary Using Context Clues

As students read the text, ask them to make predictions about each bold vocabulary word based on the context clues in the sentence.

CHECK FOR SUCCESS

If students are unable to determine the meaning of one or more bolded vocabulary words, project the Checklist from the Grade 8 Context Clues lesson with the class. After revisiting, guide students as they make predictions about the bold word in line 77 using the following routine:

- Is the word a noun, a verb, an adjective, or an adverb?
- Who is not impressed in this sentence?
- Is *impress* a positive or negative word?

TURN AND TALK

Have students discuss their original vocabulary predictions with a neighbor. Come to a consensus as a class before confirming their definitions.

TEXT TALK

In the section “Outside,” what is happening with the family?

See lines 1–19: The family is heading out into the world, either to work or go to school.

Mother says,
Worry instead
about getting sleep
because from now on
no more naps.
You will eat lunch
at school
with friends.

What friends?

You'll make some.

What if I can't?

You will.

What will I eat?

What your friends eat.

But what will I eat?

Be surprised.

I hate surprises.

Be agreeable.

Not without knowing
what I'm agreeing to.

Mother sighs,
walking away.

September 1

Sadder Laugh

School!

I wake up with
dragonflies
zipping through
my gut.

TEXT TALK

What does the text in italics represent? What is the narrator told by her mother in the first text with italics?

See lines 29–48: The italics sections contain dialogue. The narrator learns from her mother that she will no longer be at home on her own schedule. She will go to school and have to make friends.

What images does the narrator use to describe going to school?

See lines 53 and 54: She explains her nervousness as "dragonflies / zipping through / my gut."

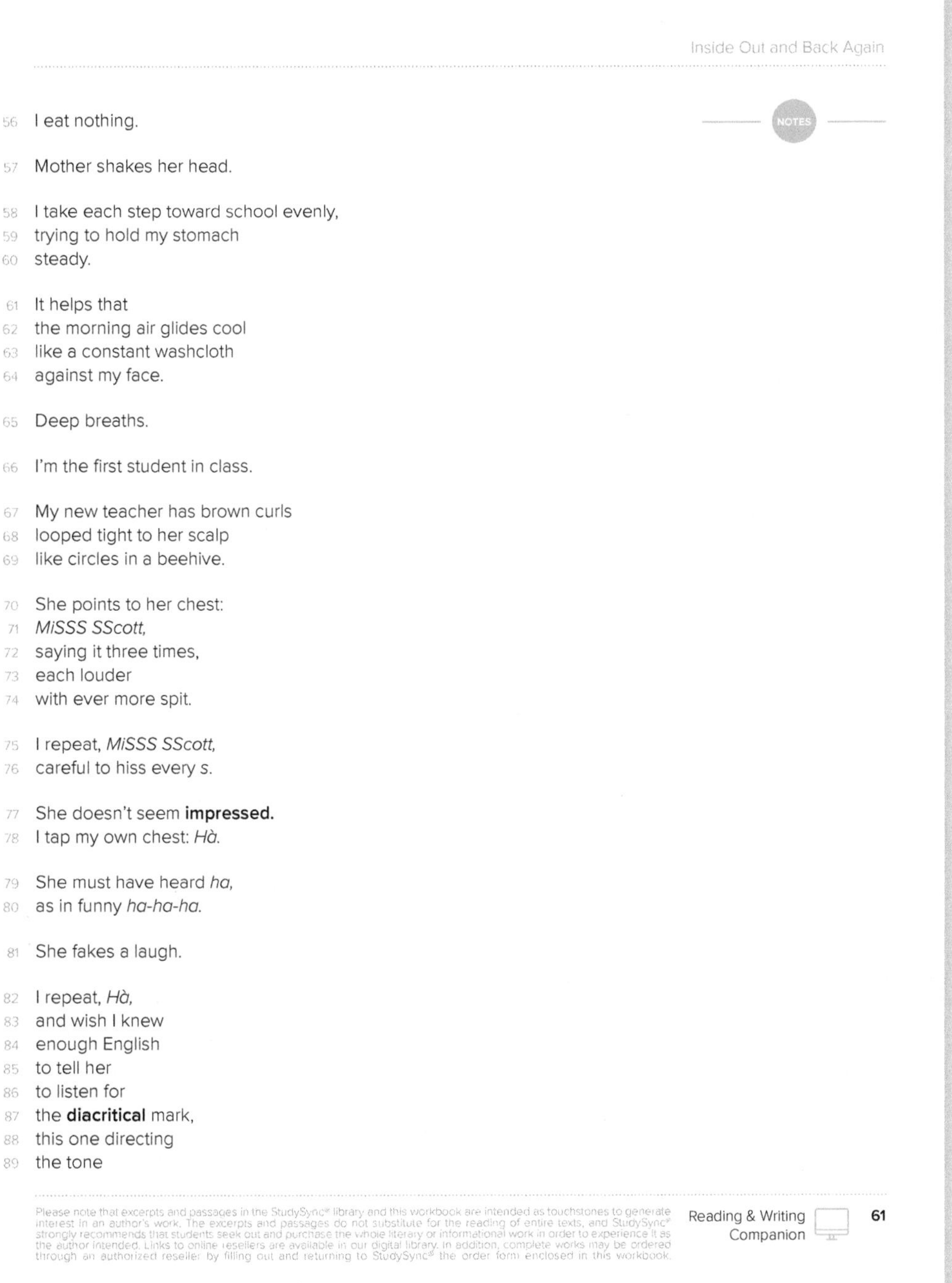

NOTES

I eat nothing.

Mother shakes her head.

I take each step toward school evenly,
trying to hold my stomach
steady.

It helps that
the morning air glides cool
like a constant washcloth
against my face.

Deep breaths.

I'm the first student in class.

My new teacher has brown curls
looped tight to her scalp
like circles in a beehive.

She points to her chest:
MiSSS SScott,
saying it three times,
each louder
with ever more spit.

I repeat, *MiSSS SScott,*
careful to hiss every *s.*

She doesn't seem **impressed.**
I tap my own chest: *Hà.*

She must have heard *ha,*
as in funny *ha-ha-ha.*

She fakes a laugh.

I repeat, *Hà,*
and wish I knew
enough English
to tell her
to listen for
the **diacritical** mark,
this one directing
the tone

V SELECTION VOCABULARY

impress / impresionar *verb* to create a strong effect; to have a forceful impact COGNATE

diacritical / diacrítico/a ***adjective*** showing how a word should be said COGNATE

ELL

- What noun does *diacritical* describe in this sentence?
- How does Miss Scott say Hà's name incorrectly?

downward.

My new teacher
tilts her head back,
fakes
an even sadder laugh.

September 2
Morning

Rainbow

I face the class.
MiSSS SScott speaks.
Each classmate says something.

I don't understand,
but I see.

Fire hair on skin dotted with spots.
Fuzzy dark hair on skin shiny as **lacquer.**
Hair the color of root on milky skin.
Lots of braids on milk chocolate.
White hair on a pink boy.
Honey hair with orange ribbons on see-through skin.
Hair with barrettes in all colors on bronze bread.

I'm the only
straight black hair
on olive skin.

September 2
Midmorning

Black and White and Yellow and Red

The bell rings.
Everyone stands.
I stand.

They line up;
so do I.

Down a hall.
Turn left.
Take a tray.

TEXT TALK

What images does the narrator use to describe her teacher and classmates?

See lines 67–109: She describes the teacher's hair and her emphasis on the letter *s* for pronunciation. She describes her classmates by hair and skin type.

Ask each Beyond grade-level student to write one additional discussion question. Then have one or two students facilitate a discussion, using their questions to guide the conversation.

SELECTION VOCABULARY

lacquer / la laca *noun* a liquid used to make wood shiny

- What adjective in this sentence describes *lacquer*?
- What word is compared to *laquer* in this sentence?

NOTES

Receive food.
Sit.

On one side
of the bright, noisy room,
light skin.
Other side,
dark skin.

Both laughing, chewing,
as if it never occurred
to them
someone **medium**
would show up.

I don't know where to sit
any more than
I know how to eat
the pink sausage
snuggled inside bread
shaped like a corncob,
smeared with sauces
yellow and red.

I think
they are making fun
of the Vietnamese flag[1]
until I remember
no one here likely knows
that flag's colors.

I put down the tray
and wait
in the hallway.

September 2
11:30 am

1. **Vietnamese flag** until 1975, the South Vietnamese flag consisted of a yellow background with three horizontal red stripes

Analyze for Enrichment

Use the activity below to differentiate instruction for your B Beyond grade-level learners.

Look at lines 125–143.

The author uses all the senses here to paint a picture for the reader. Explain to students that when poets use language that is appealing to the senses, they are evoking emotions in the reader.

Ask students: As you read this section, what emotions do you feel? How is this use of language contributing to the tone and mood of the text? How did the specific description evoke these emotions?

V SELECTION VOCABULARY

medium / medio/a ***adjective*** halfway between two extremes COGNATE

ELL
- What is described as medium in this sentence?
- How is Hà different than the two groups of students in the lunchroom?

smear / untar ***verb*** to spread

ELL
- What is being smeared in this sentence?
- What is it smeared on to?

WRITE

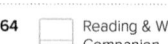

PERSONAL NARRATIVE: Hà doesn't know much English, so she describes her surroundings based on how she sees them. For example, she doesn't know what a hot dog is and describes it as "the pink sausage / snuggled inside bread / shaped like a corncob, / smeared with sauces / yellow and red." Choose a place from your own life—your classroom, the hallways, the library, your school's lunchroom—and describe it avoiding terms usually associated with the thing you describe. As you write your description, use the excerpt from *Inside Out and Back Again* as inspiration.

TEXT TALK

What happens at lunchtime?

See lines 125–137: The narrator has trouble finding a place to sit and does not feel that she belongs. The food is unusual to her.

If you could give advice to the narrator on her first day at a new school, what would you tell her and why?

Answers will vary.

Reading Comprehension OPTIONAL

Have students complete the digital reading comprehension questions ✓ when they finish reading.

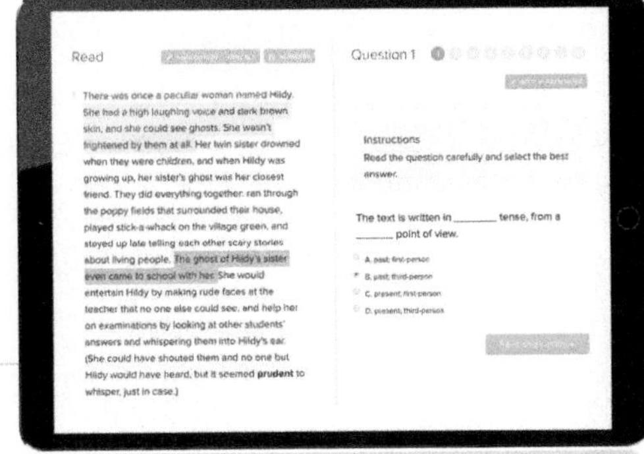

ANSWER KEY

QUESTION 1: C
QUESTION 2: B
QUESTION 3: C
QUESTION 4: B
QUESTION 5: A
QUESTION 6: C
QUESTION 7: A
QUESTION 8: B
QUESTION 9: *See first chart.*
QUESTION 10: *See second chart.*

First	Second	Third	Fourth
Hà complains to her mother about having to repeat the fourth grade.	Miss Scott teaches her class how to pronounce her name.	Hà notices the different physical features of her classmates.	Hà realizes that a hot dog probably has nothing to do with the Vietnamese flag.

Description	Character
Confused by Ha's unfamiliar name	Miss Scott
About to begin working at a sewing factory	Mother
Doesn't want to repeat his senior year of high school	Brother Vũ
Doesn't know where to sit in the cafeteria	Hà

Connect and Extend OPTIONAL

CONNECT TO EXTENDED WRITING PROJECT

Students can use *Inside Out and Back Again* as a resource when writing their literary analyses. Have them reflect on Thanhhà Lai's use of figurative language as the narrator seeks to belong in her new surroundings.

BEYOND THE BOOK

Research Project: A Refugee's Perspective

Ask students to:

- Select a specific group of refugees to research.
- Research news articles, podcasts, and/or interviews to learn about their refugee experience.
- Find a refugee with an interesting story or perspective.
- Learn everything you can about that person and his/her experience.
- Write a series of first-person journal entries in verse that explore his/her experience as a refugee.
- Use your imagination to fill in missing details.

To reflect, ask students:

- What did you learn about the refugee experience that you did not know before writing these journals?
- What aspects of your journal entries were based on facts and which details did you have to invent?

StudySyncTV

Project the StudySyncTV episode and pause at the following times to prompt discussion:

2:43 Why does the group focus on dialogue between Hà and her mom? What does it reveal about her worries?

4:01 How does Breanna help enrich the group's understanding of Hà's first day of school?

4:56 What details from the text illustrate how Hà's first day was different from that of her classmates? What evidence leads the students to conclude that Hà also shares some regular first school day experiences with her classmates?

Collaborative Conversation

Post the writing prompt to generate a discussion in small groups. Ask students to first break down the prompt before they discuss relevant ideas and textual evidence. Ask students to use the StudySyncTV episode as a model for their discussion.

Hà doesn't know much English, so she describes her surroundings based on how she sees them. For example, she doesn't know what a hot dog is and describes it as "the pink sausage / snuggled inside bread / shaped like a corncob, / smeared with sauces / yellow and red." Choose a place from your own life—your classroom, the hallways, the library, your school's lunchroom—and describe it avoiding terms usually associated with the thing you describe. As you write your description, use the excerpt from *Inside Out and Back Again* as inspiration.

Use the scaffolds below to differentiate instruction for your ELL English Language Learners and A Approaching grade-level learners.

ELL **BEGINNING, INTERMEDIATE** Use the discussion guide and speaking frames to facilitate the discussion with support from the teacher.

ADVANCED, ADVANCED HIGH Use the discussion guide and speaking frames to facilitate the discussion in mixed-level groups.

A APPROACHING Use the discussion guide to facilitate the discussion in mixed-level groups.

APPROACHING
ADVANCED, ADVANCED HIGH
BEGINNING, INTERMEDIATE

Discussion Guide	Speaking Frames
1. What words are usually used to describe a place from your life?	• When people describe ____ they usually say ____.
2. Hà makes sense of the hot dog by comparing it to a corncob. What comparisons could someone make up about your place?	• My place reminds me of a ____. • Someone who had never seen my place might think ____.

Review Prompt and Rubric

Before students begin writing, review the writing prompt and rubric with the class.

PERSONAL NARRATIVE: Hà doesn't know much English, so she describes her surroundings based on how she sees them. For example, she doesn't know what a hot dog is and describes it as "the pink sausage / snuggled inside bread / shaped like a corncob, / smeared with sauces / yellow and red." Choose a place from your own life—your classroom, the hallways, the library, your school's lunchroom—and describe it avoiding terms usually associated with the thing you describe. As you write your description, use the excerpt from *Inside Out and Back Again* as inspiration.

ELL **PROMPT GUIDE**

- What words are usually used to describe a place in your life?
- How would someone describe a place in your life if they were not familiar with it?

Score	Personal Narrative	Language and Conventions
4	The writer is able to skillfully convey the location and describe aspects of it in innovative ways.	The writer demonstrates a consistent command of grammar, punctuation, and usage conventions. Although minor errors may be evident, they do not detract from the fluency or the clarity of the writing.
3	The writer is able to clearly convey the location and describe aspects in a clear way.	The writer demonstrates an adequate command of grammar, punctuation, and usage conventions. Although some errors may be evident, they create few (if any) disruptions in the fluency or clarity of the writing.
2	The writer is able to convey some sense of the location but may not be able to describe it in a creative way.	The writer demonstrates a partial command of grammar, punctuation, and usage conventions. Some distracting errors may be evident, at times creating minor disruptions in the fluency or clarity of the writing.
1	Because the description is presented in a random or illogical way, the writer is not able to convey a sense of the location.	The writer demonstrates little or no command of grammar, punctuation, and usage conventions. Serious and persistent errors create disruptions in the fluency of the writing and sometimes interfere with meaning.
0	The writer does not provide a relevant response to the prompt or does not provide a response at all.	Serious and persistent errors overwhelm the writing and interfere with the meaning of the response as a whole, making the writer's meaning impossible to understand.

Write

SCAFFOLDS

Ask students to complete the writing assignment using textual evidence to support their answers.

Use the scaffolds below to differentiate instruction for your ELL English Language Learners and A Approaching grade-level learners.

ELL **BEGINNING** With the help of the word bank, write a response using paragraph frame 1.

INTERMEDIATE With the help of the word bank, write a response using paragraph frames 1 and 2.

ADVANCED, ADVANCED HIGH Write a response of differentiated length using the sentence starters.

A **APPROACHING** Write a response of differentiated length using the sentence starters.

BEGINNING | INTERMEDIATE | ADVANCED, ADVANCED HIGH | APPROACHING

Word Bank	Paragraph Frame 1	Paragraph Frame 2	Sentence Starters
flowers cafeteria students tables fields	When I first go into the ____, I see ____ and chairs. They remind me of ____ of grass. The room is filled with ____. They remind me of ____ because they grow and learn here.	Then I notice ____. I see ____. It reminds me of ____. It makes me feel ____.	• When I go into this place, . . . • The people here are . . . • This place makes me feel . . .

Peer Review

Students should submit substantive feedback to two peers using the review instructions below.

- How well does this response answer the prompt?
- Which of the writer's descriptions was most surprising to you?
- What did the writer do well in this response? What does the writer need to work on?

Rate

Respond to the following with a point rating that reflects your opinion.

	1	2	3	4
Ideas	■	■	■	□
Evidence	■	■	■	■
Language and Conventions	■	■	□	□

Submit

SENTENCE FRAMES

A

- You were able to (completely / partly / almost) answer the prompt.
- I was surprised by your description of ____.
- I thought differently about the text after reading ____.
- My favorite part of your response is ____.

Theories of Time and Space

POETRY

Natasha Trethewey

2006

Introduction

Natasha Trethewey (b. 1966) has been a State Poet Laureate of Mississippi and a United States Poet Laureate, and she has won a Pulitzer Prize. Her poems combine reflections about the history of African Americans in Mississippi with her own experience growing up biracial in the South. Trethewey wrote "Theories of Time and Space" as the introduction to her book of poems *Native Guard*. That title refers to the Louisiana Native Guards, a group of black Union soldiers who watched over imprisoned Confederate soldiers on Ship Island, off the coast of Mississippi. Like other poems in the collection, "Theories of Time and Space" takes readers on a tour of the American South, while pondering how the passage of time makes everything different than what came before.

In this poem, the speaker alludes to the idea that the passing of time makes each moment in life unique. To exemplify this, she gives driving directions. The speaker instructs the reader to take a road until it reaches a dead end, where there is a port. From there, the reader should board a boat bound for an island, taking only his or her memory as luggage. Before boarding the boat, the reader's picture will be taken. Upon returning, the photograph will be presented to the reader to illustrate how the trip changed them.

COMPARING WITHIN AND ACROSS GENRES

How do our experiences change our identity? Drawing on the experience of growing up biracial in Mississippi, poet Natasha Trethewey takes readers on a tour of her area of the American South in "Theories of Time and Space." The speaker reflects on how the passage of time makes everything different from what came before. The poem complements *Inside Out and Back Again* and "The Road Not Taken" by allowing readers to explore the human process of making decisions and finding one's self in the world.

ELL Proficiency-leveled summaries and summaries in multiple languages are available digitally.

Audio and audio text highlighting are available with this text.

Access Complex Text

LEXILE: N/A **WORD COUNT:** 121

The following areas may be challenging for students, particularly ELL English Language Learners and A Approaching grade-level learners.

Genre	Specific Vocabulary	Purpose
• This is a free verse poem, meaning there is no rhyme scheme or regular meter. • The speaker directly addresses the reader in second person, so the reader must assume a role while reading.	• Specialized vocabulary, such as *mangrove swamp* and *riggings of shrimp boats*, indicates geographical features of the Deep South around the Gulf of Mexico. • The term *mile markers* relates to travel, which is key to the poem's themes.	• The poem is one in which the speaker gives advice to a reader. Highlighting and annotating may help readers follow the poet's purpose.

SCAFFOLDS

ENGLISH LANGUAGE LEARNERS

APPROACHING GRADE LEVEL

BEYOND GRADE LEVEL

These icons identify differentiation strategies and scaffolded support for a variety of students. See the digital lesson plan for additional differentiation strategies and scaffolds.

Instructional Path

The print teacher's edition includes essential point-of-use instruction and planning tools. Complete lesson plans and program documents appear in your digital teacher account.

Independent Read: Theories of Time and Space

Objectives: After reading the text, students will write a short poem that demonstrates their understanding of poetic elements through a personal connection.

Independent Read

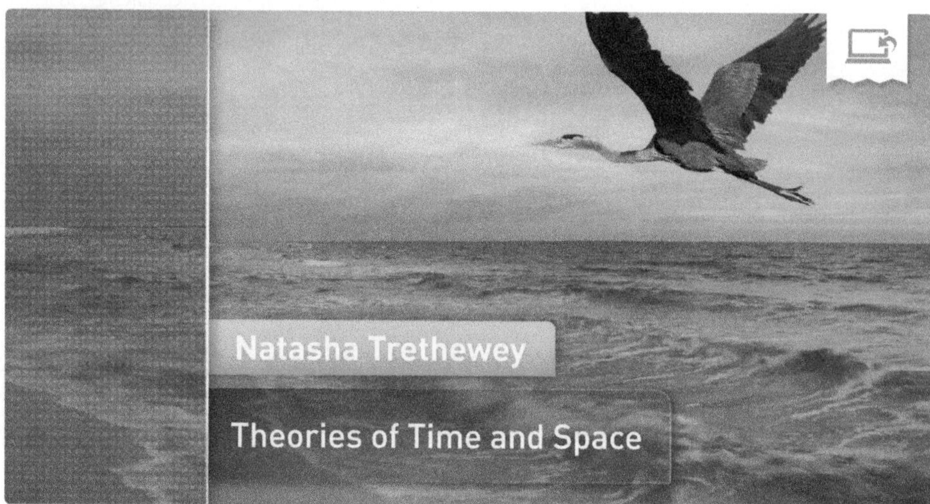

Introduce the Text

As a class, watch the video preview  and have students read the introduction in pairs to make connections to the video preview.

- How do the images contrast with the narration? Why do you think that is? How does it make you feel?
- What kind of poem are you about to read? How can you tell?

ELL **SPEAKING FRAMES**

- The ____ in the video makes me think ____.
- The video shows ____. This makes me wonder ____.
- I predict that there will be ____ because ____.

Entry Point

As students prepare to read "Theories of Time and Space," share the following information with them to provide context.

✓ Natasha Trethewey was born in Gulfport, Mississippi, in 1966. She became an avid reader as a child and later studied English and creative writing. Trethewey has received many awards for her work, including the Pulitzer Prize for the book in which this poem is published, *Native Guard* (2007). She was the U.S. Poet Laureate from 2012–2014.

✓ Einstein's theory of special relativity shows that measures of time and space depend on an observer's point of view. Students who are interested in science may enjoy researching this theory to find connections between Trethewey's poem and physics.

"Everywhere you go will be somewhere you've never been."

You can get there from here, though
there's no going home.

Everywhere you go will be somewhere
you've never been. Try this:

head south on Mississippi 49, one-
by-one mile markers ticking off

another minute of your life. Follow this
to its natural **conclusion**—dead end

at the coast, the pier at Gulfport where
riggings[1] of shrimp boats are loose stitches

in a sky threatening rain. Cross over
the man-made beach, 26 miles of sand

dumped on the mangrove[2] swamp—buried
terrain of the past. Bring only

what you must carry—**tome** of memory,
its random blank pages. On the dock

where you board the boat for Ship Island,
someone will take your picture:

the photograph—who you were—
will be waiting when you return.

1. **riggings** ropes used to operate sails aboard a ship
2. **mangrove** a type of tropical tree and shrub

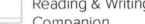

SELECTION VOCABULARY

conclusion / la conclusión *noun* end of something COGNATE

- What is the location of the pier at Gulfport in the speaker's trip?
- What does the speaker do after she reaches the pier?

Analyze Vocabulary Using Context Clues

As students read the text, ask them to make predictions about each bold vocabulary word based on the context clues in the sentence.

TURN AND TALK

Have students discuss their original vocabulary predictions with a neighbor. Come to a consensus as a class before confirming their definitions.

TEXT TALK

What is the speaker of the poem asking the reader to do? How can you tell?

See lines 1–4: The speaker is talking about traveling. The phrases "You can get there from here" and "Everywhere you go" suggest travel, and "Try this:" sounds like an idea for going somewhere.

What is this poem's setting? How do you know?

See lines 5–10: The poem is set in the Deep South of the United States, near the ocean, since it mentions "Mississippi 49" and references "pier at Gulfport" and "shrimp boats."

What images does the speaker use about the places on this journey?

See lines 11–14: Images include "man-made beach" and "mangrove swamp."

Prepare for Advanced Courses

Use the activity below to differentiate instruction for your B Beyond grade-level learners.

Direct students to reread the poem "Theories of Time and Space."

Ask students: What does "Ship Island" symbolize in the poem? Which details in the poem lead you to that conclusion?

Answers will vary; sample answer: The trip out to Ship Island symbolizes the journey everyone must take to become who they are. At the beginning of the poem, the speaker says, "Everywhere you go will be somewhere / you've never been." She tells the reader to "Try this: . . . ," and although "this" involves "boarding the boat for Ship Island," really it could be any destination or goal that will have meaning for a reader.

NOTES

WRITE

POEM: "Theories of Time and Space" seems to be about a journey, more specifically the speaker's personal rules of the road. Imagine that you, like the speaker, go on a journey of your own. What do you see? What do you record in your "tome of memory"? Write a poem in any style to express your journey.

TEXT TALK

What are the final images in this poem?

See lines 17–20: The final images include "a boat for Ship Island" and a "photograph" of the traveler, maybe the reader, just before leaving.

Make an inference: What might be the significance of the line "the photograph—who you were—will be waiting when you return"?

Answers will vary.

SELECTION VOCABULARY

terrain / el terreno ***noun*** land and its features COGNATE

- How are the sand and mangrove swamp layered?
- What is buried?

tome / el tomo ***noun*** a large, heavy book filled with knowledge COGNATE

- What does the speaker say to carry?
- What does the speaker suggest to record on the trip?

Reading Comprehension OPTIONAL

Have students complete the digital reading comprehension questions ✓ when they finish reading.

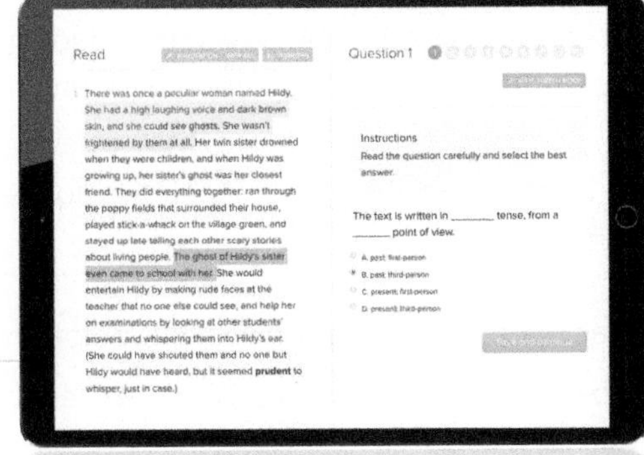

ANSWER KEY

QUESTION 1: B
QUESTION 2: B
QUESTION 3: C
QUESTION 4: D
QUESTION 5: *See chart.*

First	Second	Third	Fourth
Drive south on Mississippi 49.	Cross the man-made beach.	Get on the boat for Ship Island.	Be changed by your visit to the island.

Connect and Extend OPTIONAL

CONNECT TO EXTENDED WRITING PROJECT

Students can use the poem "Theories of Time and Space" as a resource when writing their literary analyses. Have them analyze how Natasha Trethewey explores travel through metaphor.

BEYOND THE BOOK

Writing: The Streets and Your Story

Students will use a geographic location to inspire a poem about a specific moment in their lives.

Ask students to:

- Select a geographic location where you have a strong memory.
- Use an online map to zoom into this geographic location.
- Explore the details in the map and use them to inspire a poem that tells a story anchored in this geographic location.
- Incorporate street names and physical landmarks in your poem.
- Publish poems by sharing them in class or posting them online.

To reflect, ask students:

- How did using the online map help you remember details from this moment that you may not have remembered otherwise?
- How did including details from the physical location impact your poem?

Collaborative Conversation

SCAFFOLDS

Post the writing prompt to generate a discussion in small groups. Ask students to first break down the prompt before they discuss relevant ideas and textual evidence.

"Theories of Time and Space" seems to be about a journey, more specifically the speaker's personal rules of the road. Imagine that you, like the speaker, go on a journey of your own. What do you see? What do you record in your "tome of memory"? Write a poem in any style to express your journey.

Use the scaffolds below to differentiate instruction for your ELL English Language Learners and A Approaching grade-level learners.

ELL **BEGINNING, INTERMEDIATE** Use the discussion guide and speaking frames to facilitate the discussion with support from the teacher.

ADVANCED, ADVANCED HIGH Use the discussion guide and speaking frames to facilitate the discussion in mixed-level groups.

A **APPROACHING** Use the discussion guide to facilitate the discussion in mixed-level groups.

APPROACHING
ADVANCED, ADVANCED HIGH
BEGINNING, INTERMEDIATE

Discussion Guide	Speaking Frames
1. What do you think is meaningful about a journey to Ship Island?	• I think visiting Ship Island is meaningful because ____.
2. What connections can you make between the poem and your knowledge and experiences?	• This poem reminds me of ____. • This poem connects to ____.
3. How has the poem changed the way you think about journeys?	• The poem has made me realize that ____. • I used to think ____. Now I think ____.

Review Prompt and Rubric

Before students begin writing, review the writing prompt and rubric with the class.

POEM: "Theories of Time and Space" seems to be about a journey, more specifically the speaker's personal rules of the road. Imagine that you, like the speaker, go on a journey of your own. What do you see? What do you record in your "tome of memory"? Write a poem in any style to express your journey.

PROMPT GUIDE

A
- What do you think is meaningful about a journey to Ship Island?
- What connections can you make between the poem and your knowledge and experiences?
- How has the poem changed the way you think about journeys?

Score	Poem	Language and Conventions
4	The writer clearly writes a poem about a personal journey, using inspiration or relevant evidence from the text as needed.	The writer demonstrates a consistent command of grammar, punctuation, and usage conventions. Although minor errors may be evident, they do not detract from the fluency or the clarity of the writing.
3	The writer sufficiently writes a poem about a personal journey, using inspiration or relevant evidence from the text most of the time.	The writer demonstrates an adequate command of grammar, punctuation, and usage conventions. Although some errors may be evident, they create few (if any) disruptions in the fluency or clarity of the writing.
2	The writer begins to write a poem about a personal journey, but the poem is incomplete. The writer uses inspiration or relevant evidence from the text only some of the time.	The writer demonstrates a partial command of grammar, punctuation, and usage conventions. Some distracting errors may be evident, at times creating minor disruptions in the fluency or clarity of the writing.
1	The writer attempts to write a poem about a personal journey, but the attempt is not successful. The writer uses little or no inspiration or relevant evidence from the text.	The writer demonstrates little or no command of grammar, punctuation, and usage conventions. Serious and persistent errors create disruptions in the fluency of the writing and sometimes interfere with meaning.
0	The writer does not provide a relevant response to the prompt or does not provide a response at all.	Serious and persistent errors overwhelm the writing and interfere with the meaning of the response as a whole, making the writer's meaning impossible to understand.

Write

Ask students to complete the writing assignment using textual evidence to support their answers.

Use the scaffolds below to differentiate instruction for your ELL English Language Learners and A Approaching grade-level learners.

ELL **BEGINNING** With the help of the word bank, write a response using paragraph frame 1.

INTERMEDIATE With the help of the word bank, write a response using paragraph frames 1 and 2.

ADVANCED, ADVANCED HIGH Write a response of differentiated length using the sentence starters.

A **APPROACHING** Write a response of differentiated length using the sentence starters.

BEGINNING / INTERMEDIATE | ADVANCED, ADVANCED HIGH / APPROACHING

Word Bank	Paragraph Frame 1	Paragraph Frame 2	Sentence Starters
beach	I am going on a journey to ____.	I will remember ____.	• I took a journey to . . .
park	I see ____.	I think ____.	• The place is meaningful because . . .
trees	I hear ____.	I am changed because ____.	• I changed . . .
water	I feel ____.		• I feel . . .
leaves	I will remember ____.		• I used to think . . .
waves	I think ____.		• Now I think . . .
feelings			
happy			
thoughtful			
good			

Peer Review

Rate

Respond to the following with a point rating that reflects your opinion.

	1	2	3	4
Ideas	■	■	■	□
Evidence	■	■	■	■
Language and Conventions	■	■	□	□

Submit

Students should submit substantive feedback to two peers using the review instructions below.

- How well does this response answer the prompt?
- Which of the author's comments inspired you to think differently about the text?
- What did the writer do well in this response? What does the writer need to work on?

ELL

SENTENCE FRAMES

- You were able to (completely / partly / almost) answer the prompt.
- You could answer the prompt more completely by ____.
- I thought differently about the text after reading ____.
- My favorite part of your response is ____.

The Road Not Taken

POETRY
Robert Frost
1915

Introduction

studysync tv

Robert Frost (1874–1963) was a United States Poet Laureate, and his poetry earned him four Pulitzer Prizes. Frost's classic poem "The Road Not Taken" is often interpreted as a nod to non-conformism, but some see it differently. When asked about the sigh in the last stanza, Frost wrote a friend, "It was my rather private jest at the expense of those who might think I would yet live to be sorry for the way I had taken in life."

In this poem, the speaker is walking in the woods when he reaches a fork in the road. He laments that he cannot take both routes. He spends some time looking down both paths and ultimately chooses the one covered in grass because it had clearly not been used much. That morning, both paths were covered in leaves, and the speaker understands that neither path had been used that day. Although the speaker chooses the grassy route, he hopes to be able to travel down the other road at some point. At the same time, he recognizes that both paths lead to unexpected places and he may never come back. He imagines himself in the future, explaining how he took the path less traveled and how his choice made a major difference in the course of his life.

 Proficiency-leveled summaries and summaries in multiple languages are available digitally.

Audio and audio text highlighting are available with this text.

COMPARING WITHIN AND ACROSS GENRES

 How can your decisions affect how you feel about yourself and your life? In this classic poem, "The Road Not Taken" by Robert Frost, the speaker has to choose between two roads as he takes a walk through the woods. The speaker leads readers through his thought process and reflections on how his choice affects the rest of his life. The poem is paired with two selections that echo this theme of entering new territory: an excerpt from *Inside Out and Back Again* by Thanhhà Lai, and the poem "Theories of Time and Space" by Natasha Trethewey.

Access Complex Text

LEXILE: N/A **WORD COUNT:** 144

The following areas may be challenging for students, particularly 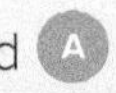 English Language Learners and Ⓐ Approaching grade-level learners.

Connection of Ideas	Prior Knowledge	Specific Vocabulary
• The poem is about a walk in the woods, but it addresses life issues. The way the speaker evaluates the roads and makes his choice relates to how people make choices throughout life.	• Some students may not be familiar with the types of woods and trails described in the poem. Explain that in some areas, people have access to forest preserves, and the preserves often contain many old trails.	• Specialized vocabulary, such as *trodden*, may challenge some readers. Remind students to use context clues while reading, and also to use a dictionary to define unfamiliar words.

SCAFFOLDS  **ENGLISH LANGUAGE LEARNERS**  **APPROACHING GRADE LEVEL**  **BEYOND GRADE LEVEL**

These icons identify differentiation strategies and scaffolded support for a variety of students. See the digital lesson plan for additional differentiation strategies and scaffolds.

Instructional Path

The print teacher's edition includes essential point-of-use instruction and planning tools. Complete lesson plans and program documents appear in your digital teacher account.

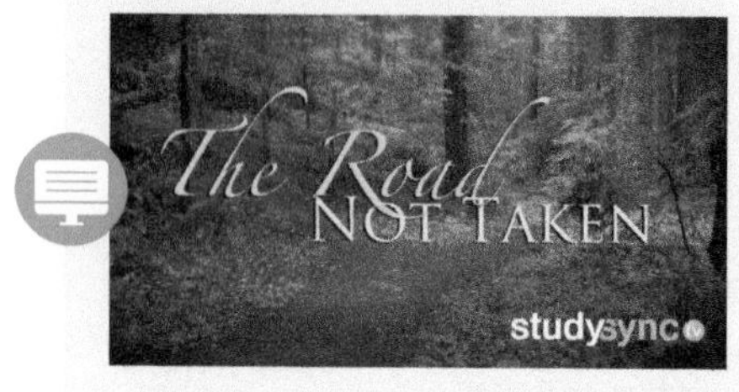

First Read: The Road Not Taken

Objectives: After an initial reading and discussion of the poem, students will be able to identify and describe key details and lines, as well as articulate the overall narrative of the poem.

Skill: Poetic Elements and Structure

Objectives: After rereading and discussing a model of close reading, students will be able to demonstrate an understanding of texts by comparing and contrasting how the poetic structures of two or more poems contribute to meaning and style.

Skill: Figurative Language

Objectives: After rereading and discussing a model of close reading, students will be able to analyze an author's use of figurative language.

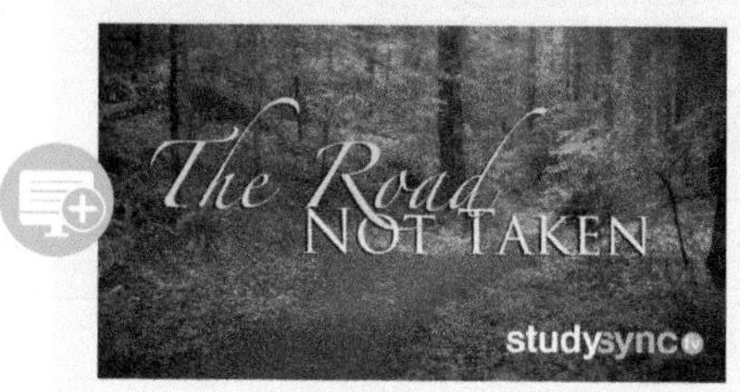

Close Read: The Road Not Taken

Objectives: After engaging in a close reading and discussion of the text, students will be able to analyze how the poetic structure and figurative language helps to develop the theme of the poem and use that analysis as inspiration for a short poem.

Progress Monitoring

Opportunities to Learn	Opportunities to Demonstrate Learning	Opportunities to Reteach
Poetic Elements and Structure		
Skill: Poetic Elements and Structure	Skill: Poetic Elements and Structure • Your Turn Close Read • Skills Focus • Write	Spotlight Skill: Poetic Elements and Structure
Figurative Language		
Skill: Figurative Language	Skill: Figurative Language • Your Turn Close Read • Complete Vocabulary Chart • Skills Focus • Write	Unit 2 Skill: Figurative Language - The House on Mango Street Unit 3 Skill: Figurative Language - Narrative of the Life of Frederick Douglass, An American Slave Spotlight Skill: Figurative Language

First Read

Introduce the Text

As a class, watch the video preview and have students read the introduction in pairs to make connections to the video preview.

To activate prior knowledge and experiences, ask students:

- What is one question you have about what you are going to read?

ELL SENTENCE FRAMES

- The ____ in the video makes me think ____.
- The video shows ____. This makes me wonder ____.
- I think the text will ____. I think this because ____.
- I predict that there will be ____. I believe this because ____.

Entry Point

As students prepare to read "The Road Not Taken," share the following information with them to provide context.

- ✓ Robert Frost's career and reputation as a poet became firmly established in England, where he and his wife moved in 1912. There he was influenced by British poets such as Robert Graves and Rupert Brooke, became friends with Ezra Pound, and had two poetry collections published. Upon his return to the United States in 1915, he became the most celebrated poet in the country.
- ✓ Frost's poetry generally reflects New England life and follows traditional poetic forms, but his themes are largely universal, and he uses contemporary language. His poetry is modern and accessible.
- ✓ Frost wrote "The Road Not Taken" as a joke about a friend he would often walk with. When faced with a choice of paths, the friend would always regret the choice he made and moan about the one not taken.

"Two roads diverged in a wood, and I— I took the one less traveled by"

Two roads **diverged** in a yellow wood,
And sorry I could not travel both
And be one traveler, long I stood
And looked down one as far as I could
To where it bent in the **undergrowth;**

Then took the other, as just as fair[1],
And having perhaps the better **claim,**
Because it was grassy and wanted wear;
Though as for that the passing there
Had worn them really about the same,

And both that morning equally lay
In leaves no step had **trodden** black.
Oh, I kept the first for another day!
Yet knowing how way leads on to way,
I doubted if I should ever come back.

I shall be telling this with a sigh
Somewhere ages and ages **hence:**
Two roads diverged in a wood, and I—
I took the one less traveled by,
And that has made all the difference.

NOTES

Skill: Figurative Language

The speaker comes across two roads. He wants to take them both, but that's impossible. He has to make a choice. Along with the title, I think the purpose of these lines might be to introduce an extended metaphor about making choices.

Skill: Poetic Elements and Structure

Like the speaker in "Theories of Time and Space," the speaker here is also concerned with time and space.

Fork in the road

1. **fair** sufficient

SELECTION VOCABULARY

diverge / divergir *verb* to move in different directions COGNATE

undergrowth / el matorral *noun* low plant growing on a forest floor

- What word parts do you recognize in *undergrowth*?
- What does the speaker's location in the forest suggest about the meaning of *undergrowth*?

Analyze Vocabulary Using Context Clues

In stanza 1, focus on the line that uses the word *diverged*. Point out these context clues:

1. First, I notice that the word *diverged* refers to two roads.
2. I keep reading and notice the speaker regrets not being able to travel both roads at the same time.
3. The speaker's ideas show that the roads must be traveling in two different directions. I think *diverge* must mean "to move in different directions."

Figurative Language

How did the reader use descriptive details to identify the extended metaphor in the poem?

The reader noticed that the speaker wants to take both roads, but he has to make a choice, which also connects to the poem's title. This implies an extended metaphor about making choices.

Poetic Elements and Structure

How does the reader use his understanding of poetic structure to help him make meaning of the poems?

The reader notes that the poems are both concerned with the passage of time and that the structure helps to indicate each speaker's understanding of how time and choices affect us.

Skills Focus

QUESTION 2: Figurative Language

The speaker realizes that he probably cannot ever return and choose the first road. This develops the extended metaphor about choices because it shows that you cannot undo a choice once you've made it.

TEXT TALK

Where is the speaker?

See line 1: The speaker is walking in the forest.

What does the speaker notice about the second road?

See line 8: The second road is covered in more grass than the first one is.

What do the roads look like that morning?

See lines 11 and 12: Both roads have leaves on them.

What does the speaker doubt?

See lines 13–15: The speaker doubts that he will be able to return to the first road.

Which road does the speaker choose and why?

See line 19: The speaker chooses the second road because fewer people have taken that road.

What other inferences can you make about the speaker?

Answers will vary.

Make an inference: Why does the speaker doubt that he will be able to return to the first road?

Answers will vary.

QUESTION 1: Poetic Structure

See lines 1–4: These lines have the same number of stressed syllables. This choice reflects how life moves along at a steady pace. The poet rhymes the words *wood, stood,* and *could* to call attention to the speaker's choice and actions, showing that the speaker's choice is a tough one that requires a lot of thought. This structural choice mirrors the way people make decisions throughout their lives.

QUESTION 3: Theme

See lines 16 and 17: The speaker thinks that he will have an emotional reaction when he talks about his choice many years after he's made it. This detail helps develop the message that the choices we make now will affect us for the rest of our lives. This is both similar to and different from Hà in *Inside Out and Back Again* because Hà also has an emotional reaction to her experiences, but she seems much more negative while the speaker of the poem has a brighter outlook.

QUESTION 4: Connect to Essential Question

See lines 6–10: The speaker notices that the second road looks similar to the first, but since fewer people had recently traveled down that way, he chooses the second path. This is significant because it shows that we all make similar choices in life. I would also choose the second path because I would feel a little more adventurous taking that road.

SELECTION VOCABULARY

claim / el reclamo ***noun*** a statement that you have a right to something; a statement that something belongs to you

- What is the speaker describing in these line
- What nearby words describe the "claim"? Are they positive or negative?

trodden / pisar ***verb*** stepped on, trampled

- What observation does the speaker make about the roads?
- How does the word *step* relate to *trodden*?

hence / a partir de aquí ***adverb*** from this time or place

- When does the speaker imagine telling the story?
- Where does the speaker imagine telling the story?

Reading Comprehension OPTIONAL

Have students complete the digital reading comprehension questions ✓ when they finish reading.

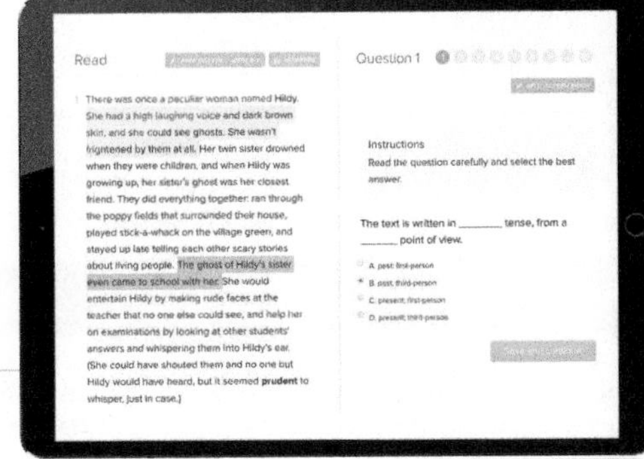

ANSWER KEY

QUESTION 1: B
QUESTION 2: C
QUESTION 3: B
QUESTION 4: D

QUESTION 5:
See chart.

First	Second	Third	Fourth
The narrator stands at a crossroads and tries to decide which path to take.	He chooses the second road, the one that looks like fewer people have taken it.	He thinks about the first road but realizes it's not very likely he'll get another chance to take it.	He says that one day he'll look back on his decision and realize how it shaped his future.

Connect and Extend

CONNECT TO EXTENDED WRITING PROJECT

Students can find inspiration in the poem "The Road Not Taken" when writing their literary analyses. Have students reflect on Robert Frost's themes related to choices and their consequences in shaping who we are.

BEYOND THE BOOK

Reflection: Life Choices

Ask students to write a journal entry about a moment in their lives when they were given a choice between two different roads, or life choices. Have them reflect on the possible outcome if they had made a different choice in that moment.

In their journal entries, have students respond to the following:

- Explain the situation.
  - > What choice were you presented with?
  - > Which choice felt more like the "road less traveled"?
  - > Which choice felt more comfortable or familiar?
- How did you decide which road to take?
- Thinking back, did you make the right choice?
- What might have happened if you had selected the other road?

Think Questions

Circulate as students answer Think Questions independently. Scaffolds for these questions are shown on the opposite page.

QUESTION 1: Textual Evidence

The speaker regrets not being able to take both roads. In lines 2 and 3, he says, "And sorry I could not travel both / And be one traveler . . . ." He also examines the roads carefully before he makes his choice. In lines 3 and 4, he says, "long I stood / And looked down one as far as I could . . . ."

QUESTION 2: Textual Evidence

The speaker believes that his life will be affected by his decision. He imagines telling the story about his choices "somewhere ages and ages hence" and concludes that choosing "the one less traveled by" will have "made all the difference." In other words, he imagines that his choice will determine the path his life takes.

QUESTION 3: Textual Evidence

The speaker is tempted by the other road and hopes to return to it another time. In line 13 he says, "Oh, I kept the first for another day!" However, he doubts that he will be able to follow through with that plan because the road he has chosen will take him somewhere else. In lines 14 and 15, he admits, "Yet knowing how way leads on to way, / I doubted if I should ever come back."

QUESTION 4: Word Meaning

Definition 2 most closely matches the meaning of the word *claim* in line 7. The speaker decides that one road is better suited to travel. So *claim* must mean "a statement that you have a right to something." In this context, the road the speaker chooses has the better "right" to be traveled.

QUESTION 5: Context Clues

I think *hence* must mean "away from this time and place." The word is used to describe the future, when the speaker is somewhere far away many years from now.

First Read

Read "The Road Not Taken." After you read, complete the Think Questions below.

THINK QUESTIONS

1. What evidence in the text of the poem shows you that the speaker is uncertain about which road to choose? Cite evidence from the text to support your answer.
2. What do lines 16–20 tell you about how the speaker imagines his future? Use evidence from the text to support your answer.
3. How does the speaker feel about the road he didn't take? Cite evidence from the text to support your answer.
4. Read the following dictionary entry:

   claim
   claim \klām\ *noun*

   1. a demand or request for something that is owed
   2. a statement that you have a right to something
   3. a piece of land that is owned by someone

   Which definition most closely matches the meaning of **claim** as it is used in line 7 of "The Road Not Taken"? Write the correct definition of *claim* here, and explain how you figured out the correct meaning
5. Find the word **hence** in line 17 of "The Road Not Taken." Use context clues in the surrounding lines, as well as the line in which the word appears, to determine the word's meaning. Write your definition here and identify clues that helped you figure out its meaning.

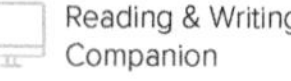

SCAFFOLDS

Think Questions

Use the scaffolds below to differentiate instruction for your ELL English Language Learners and A Approaching grade-level learners.

ELL **BEGINNING** Write a response using the word bank and sentence frames.

INTERMEDIATE Write a response using the sentence frames.

ADVANCED, ADVANCED HIGH Write a response using the Text-Dependent Question Guide.

A **APPROACHING** Write a response using the Text-Dependent Question Guide.

BEGINNING	INTERMEDIATE	APPROACHING / ADVANCED, ADVANCED HIGH
Word Bank	**Sentence Frames**	**Text-Dependent Question Guide**
road place looks affect return somewhere lead time doubts years regrets difference	The speaker ____ that he cannot travel down both roads. In order to make his decision, the speaker ____ at the roads carefully.	1. • How does the speaker react when he sees the roads? • What does the speaker do to make his decision? • How do the speaker's actions show uncertainty?
	The speaker has to choose which ____ to take. The speaker believes that his choice will ____ the way his life turns out. I know this because he says that choosing "the one less traveled by" will make a ____.	2. • What choice does the speaker make? • What will happen in the speaker's life? • How can I tell the speaker feels this way?
	The speaker hopes to ____ to the first road someday. However, he ____ that he will be able to follow his plan because the second road will ____ him somewhere else.	3. • What does the speaker plan to do about the first road? • Does the speaker believe that he will be able to follow his plan? • Why or why not?
	Claim as used in the text matches definition #____.	4. • Read: "Then took the other, as just as fair, / And having perhaps the better **claim,** / Because it was grassy and wanted wear" • Is *claim* in the poem a demand or request? (#1) • Is *claim* in the poem a statement? (#2) • Is *claim* in the poem a piece of land that someone owns? (#3)
	The speaker imagines telling the story ____ else many ____ from now. This gives me a clue that *hence* means "away from this ____ and ____."	5. • Read: "I shall be telling this with a sigh / Somewhere ages and ages **hence**" • When and where does the speaker imagine telling the story? • What does that tell me about the meaning of the word *hence*?

Skill: Poetic Elements and Structure

Introduce the Skill

Watch the Concept Definition video and read the following definition with your students.

Poetic structure describes the organization of words and lines in a poem as well as its rhyme scheme and meter. Poems consist of words that are divided into **lines.** A group of lines is called a **stanza.**

Other elements of poetry that contribute to structure include rhyme and rhythm. **Rhyme** is the repetition of the same or similar vowel sounds. The **rhyme scheme** of a poem is the pattern formed by the rhyming words at the end of lines. **Rhythm** is the pattern of unstressed and stressed syllables in a line of poetry. A regular pattern is called **meter,** and it gives a line of poetry a predictable rhythm.

The poet's choice of **poetic form**, or arrangement and style of a poem, will help determine the structure. Common forms include haiku, limerick, and sonnet, each with its own rules. Poetry without a consistent meter, rhyme, or stanza length is called **open form**.

POETIC ELEMENTS AND STRUCTURE

Skill: Poetic Elements and Structure

Use the Checklist to analyze Poetic Elements and Structure in "The Road Not Taken." Refer to the sampl student annotations about Poetic Elements and Structure in the text.

••• CHECKLIST FOR POETIC ELEMENTS AND STRUCTURE

In order to determine how to compare and contrast the structures of two or more poems, look fo the following:

- ✓ the forms and overall structures of the poems
- ✓ the rhyme, rhythm, and meter, if present
- ✓ lines and stanzas in the poems that suggest the poems' meanings and styles
- ✓ ways that the poems' structures connect to the poems' meanings

To compare and contrast the structures of two or more poems and analyze how the differing structure o each text contributes to its meaning and style, consider the following questions:

- ✓ What forms do the poets use?
- ✓ How do the poems compare to each other in their structures?
- ✓ How does the choice of form or structure affect the overall meaning of each poem?
- ✓ How do the meanings of each poem compare?

TURN AND TALK

1. How is the structure of a poem different from stories or other texts you've read?
2. What is one poem that you love? How does the structure of that poem help you understand its meaning?

ELL SPEAKING FRAMES

- The structure of a poem is different from other texts because ____.
- My favorite poem is ____. The structure helps me understand it because ____.

SKILL VOCABULARY

poetic structure / la estructura poética ***noun*** the organization of words and lines as well as the rhyme and meter of a poem COGNATE

line / el verso ***noun*** a string of words in a poem, not necessarily a full sentence or phrase

stanza / la estrofa ***noun*** the basic unit of a poem, made up of a series of lines

POETIC ELEMENTS AND STRUCTURE

sync•skills

Skill: Poetic Elements and Structure

Reread lines 9–14 of "Theories of Time and Space" and lines 11–15 of "The Road Not Taken." Then, using the Checklist on the previous page, complete the chart below to compare and contrast the passages.

YOUR TURN

	Observation Options
A	Poem has a structured rhyme scheme and meter.
B	Poem has no rhyme scheme or meter.
C	The structure helps communicate the way that man has negatively affected the natural world.
D	Both the narrators are influenced by the world as they encounter it.
E	Both poems have consistent line length.
F	The structure helps to communicate the beauty of nature.

"Theories of Time and Space"	Both	"The Road Not Taken"

Your Turn

Ask students to complete the Your Turn activity.

"Theories of Time and Space"	Both	"The Road Not Taken"
Poem has no rhyme scheme or meter.	Both poems have consistent line length.	Poem has a structured rhyme scheme and meter.
The structure helps communicate the way that man has negatively affected the natural world.	Both the narrators are influenced by the world as they encounter it.	The structure helps communicate the beauty of nature.

SKILL VOCABULARY

rhythm / el ritmo *noun* the pattern of unstressed and stressed syllables in a line of poetry COGNATE

meter / la métrica *noun* a regular pattern of unstressed and stressed syllables in a line of poetry COGNATE

rhyme / la rima *noun* the repetition of the same or similar sounds in a poem COGNATE

rhyme scheme / el patrón de rima *noun* the pattern formed by the rhyming words at the end of lines in a poem

poetic form / la forma poética *noun* the particular set of rules guiding the arrangement of words and lines in a poem COGNATE

open form / la forma abierta *noun* poetic form without consistent meter, rhyme, or stanza length

Skill: Figurative Language

Introduce the Skill

Watch the Concept Definition video and read the following definition with your students.

Figurative language is language used for descriptive effect, often to illustrate or imply ideas indirectly. Types of figurative language include simile, metaphor, and personification. A **simile** uses the words *like* or *as* to compare two seemingly unlike things. A **metaphor** directly compares two seemingly unlike things without using *like* or *as*. **Personification** is a **figure of speech** in which an animal, object, force of nature, or an idea is given human qualities.

When reading prose, and especially poetry, readers use **context**—including when and where a text was written, for example—to analyze the impact of word choice and to help determine or interpret the meaning of figurative words and phrases.

Skill: Figurative Language

Use the Checklist to analyze Figurative Language in "The Road Not Taken." Refer to the sample student annotations about Figurative Language in the text.

••• CHECKLIST FOR FIGURATIVE LANGUAGE

To determine the meaning of figures of speech in a text, note the following:

- ✓ words that mean one thing literally but suggest something else
- ✓ similes, such as "strong as an ox"
- ✓ metaphors, such as "her eyes were stars"
- ✓ analogies, or comparisons of two unlike things based on a specific similarity, used for clarification
    - remarking, "Life is like a ball game; anybody can have a losing day."
    - in Shakespeare's Sonnet 18, "Shall I compare thee to a summer's day? / Thou art more lovely and more temperate."
- ✓ extended metaphors, which make an implied comparison through the entirety of a text

In order to interpret the meaning of a figure of speech in context, ask the following questions:

- ✓ Does any of the descriptive language in the text compare two seemingly unlike things?
- ✓ Do any descriptions include *like* or *as*, indicating a simile?
- ✓ Is there a direct comparison that suggests a metaphor?

TURN AND TALK

1. How can figurative language help you better express your ideas?
2. When was the last time you used figurative language to make a point? What kind of figurative language did you use?

ELL SPEAKING FRAMES

- Using figurative language lets me ____. This helps me express my ideas because ____.
- One example of figurative language I used recently is ____. It helped me make a point because ____.
- This figurative language was an example of a/an ____.

V SKILL VOCABULARY

figurative language / el lenguaje figurativo *noun* expressions used for descriptive or rhetorical effect that are not literally true but express some truth beyond the literal level COGNATE

simile / el símil *noun* a figure of speech that uses the words *like* or *as* to compare two seemingly unlike things COGNATE

metaphor / la metáfora *noun* a figure of speech that compares two seemingly unlike things but implies a comparison instead of stating it directly with the words *like* or *as* COGNATE

Skill: Figurative Language

Reread lines 6–10 of "The Road Not Taken." Then, using the Checklist on the previous page, answer the multiple-choice questions below.

YOUR TURN

1. Based on the descriptive details in lines 6–8, the reader can conclude that—
   - A. Both roads are equally worthy of being chosen.
   - B. The second road is longer than the first road.
   - C. Fewer people choose to travel down the second road.
   - D. The first road is paved, but the second road is not.

2. Lines 6–10 best contribute to the extended metaphor in the poem by—
   - A. suggesting that there are no "right" choices in life.
   - B. showing that people make choices with the information they have.
   - C. introducing the idea that decisions are not important.
   - D. hinting that everyone ends up in the same place no matter what road they take.

SKILL VOCABULARY

personification / la personificación *noun* a figure of speech in which an animal, object, force of nature, or idea is given human form or qualities COGNATE

figure of speech / la figura literaria *noun* a word or phrase not meant to be taken literally, but rather used for effect

context / el contexto *noun* the set of facts or circumstances that surround a situation or event COGNATE

Your Turn

Ask students to complete the Your Turn activity.

QUESTION 1

A. Incorrect. The speaker says the second road was the better "claim."

B. Incorrect. There is no evidence in lines 6–8 to support this conclusion.

C. Correct. The descriptive details, such as "grassy" and "wanted wear," suggest that fewer people choose the second road.

D. Incorrect. Although the second road is described as "grassy," there is no evidence to suggest that the first road is paved.

QUESTION 2

A. Incorrect. The stanza does not develop ideas about "right" or "wrong" choices.

B Correct. The speaker notices that the paths are equally worn, but that one seems to have been walked upon less than the other. The speaker is making a decision based on this observation, or the best way he knows how.

C. Incorrect. The stanza does not suggest that decisions are unimportant.

D. Incorrect. The details in the poem suggest that people have taken both paths at one time or another, but there is nothing to suggest the paths end in the same place.

Close Read

Skills Focus

QUESTION 1: Poetic Structure

See lines 1–4.

QUESTION 2: Figurative Language

See lines 14 and 15.

QUESTION 3: Theme

See lines 16 and 17.

QUESTION 4: Connect to Essential Question

See lines 6–10.

CHECK FOR SUCCESS

If students struggle to respond to Skills Focus question 1, ask them the following questions:

- What words rhyme in lines 1–5?
- What punctuation mark appears at the end of line 5?
- What do those elements tell you about the theme?

Have students transition to read and annotate independently once they have successfully completed the first Skills Focus prompt.

Close Read

Reread "The Road Not Taken." As you reread, complete the Skills Focus questions below. Then use your answers and annotations from the questions to help you complete the Write activity.

SKILLS FOCUS

1. Reread the first stanza of "The Road Not Taken," and look for clues that reveal the poem's structure. Identify a line or lines that contain elements that build that structure, such as rhyme, meter, or other elements. Then explain how the poet's choice to use such a structure helps him develop the theme that life is a journey.
2. Reread the third stanza of "The Road Not Taken." Identify a detail that develops the extended metaphor in the poem, and explain the idea it communicates about making choices. Cite evidence from the poem to support your answer.
3. "The Road Not Taken," *Inside Out and Back Again*, and "Theories of Time and Space" each deal with the idea of turning points in our lives. Identify details in "The Road Not Taken" that reveal the speaker's thoughts on the turning point he faces. Explain how his thoughts are similar to or different from Hà's in *Inside Out and Back Again* and the speaker's in "Theories of Time and Space." Use specific evidence from the text(s) to support your claims.
4. The speaker of the poem implies that both roads are actually very similar. If that is true, then what is the significance of choosing one over the other? Which road would you choose and why? Use specific evidence from the text to support your claims.

WRITE

POETRY: Think about a time you had to make an important choice. Write a poem to show the journey and the risk involved in that experience, as well as how it changed you. Your poem may use regular rhyme and meter or be in free verse, may be humorous or serious, and should include figurative language to develop ideas. Include a final line that states the poem's theme as it relates to your speaker and the events.

Writer's Notebook

Connect to Essential Question: Give students time to reflect on how "The Road Not Taken" connects to the unit's essential question "What makes you, you?" by freewriting in their Writer's Notebooks.

Beginning & Intermediate

Read aloud the unit's essential question: "What makes you, you?" Encourage students to draw their connections or allow students to write in their native language. Circulate the room, prompting students for their thoughts as they respond orally or through pantomime.

Advanced & Advanced High

Allow students to share their connections orally in pairs or small groups before freewriting.

StudySyncTV

Project the StudySyncTV episode and pause at the following times to prompt discussion:

1:32 How do the students determine some possible tones of "The Road Not Taken"?

3:21 What strategy do the students use to determine how the speaker feels about his choice?

4:46 What do the students do when they become confused by the concepts in the poem? How do they work through their confusion?

Collaborative Conversation

Break students into collaborative conversation groups to discuss the Close Read prompt. Ask students to use the StudySyncTV episode as a model for their discussion. Remind them to reference their Skills Focus annotations in their discussion.

Think about a time when you had to make an important choice. Write a poem to show the journey and the risk involved in that experience, as well as how it changed you. Your poem may use regular rhyme and meter or be in free verse, may be humorous or serious, and should include figurative language to express different ideas. Include a final line that states the poem's theme as it relates to your speaker and the events.

Use the scaffolds below to differentiate instruction for your ELL English Language Learners and A Approaching grade-level learners.

ELL **BEGINNING, INTERMEDIATE** Use the discussion guide and speaking frames to facilitate the discussion with support from the teacher.

ADVANCED, ADVANCED HIGH Use the discussion guide and speaking frames to facilitate the discussion in mixed-level groups.

A **APPROACHING** Use the discussion guide to facilitate the discussion in mixed-level groups.

APPROACHING
ADVANCED, ADVANCED HIGH
BEGINNING, INTERMEDIATE

Discussion Guide	Speaking Frames
1. How does the poet use an extended metaphor to show the process of making an important choice?	• A detail that develops the extended metaphor is ____. • This shows the process of making a choice because ____.
2. How do these details help develop the theme of the poem?	• One theme of the poem is ____. • A detail that develops this theme is ____ because ____.
3. What experience and theme do I want to develop in my own poem?	• An experience I can write about is ____. • A theme I can develop is ____.

Review Prompt and Rubric

Before students begin writing, review the writing prompt and rubric with the class.

POETRY: Think about a time when you had to make an important choice. Write a poem to show the journey and the risk involved in that experience, as well as how it changed you. Your poem may use regular rhyme and meter or be in free verse, may be humorous or serious, and should include figurative language to develop ideas. Include a final line that states the poem's theme as it relates to your speaker and the events.

PROMPT GUIDE

- What is an important choice I've had to make?
- How does Frost use an extended metaphor to show the process of making an important choice?
- How does Frost use details to develop the theme of the poem?
- What theme do I want to develop in my own poem?

Score	Poetic Elements and Structure	Figurative Language	Language and Conventions
4	The writer successfully crafts a clear structure for the poem.	The writer successfully uses figurative language to communicate ideas and develop a theme. The writer includes a clear and effective final line that shows the poem's theme.	The writer demonstrates a consistent command of grammar, punctuation, and usage conventions. Although minor errors may be evident, they do not detract from the fluency or the clarity of the writing.
3	The writer mostly crafts a clear structure for the poem.	The writer mostly uses figurative language to communicate ideas. The writer includes a final line that shows the poem's theme.	The writer demonstrates an adequate command of grammar, punctuation, and usage conventions. Although some errors may be evident, they create few (if any) disruptions in the fluency or clarity of the writing.
2	The writer attempts to craft a clear structure for the poem.	The writer attempts to use figurative language to communicate ideas or develop a theme. The writer includes a final line that gives a clue about the poem's theme.	The writer demonstrates a partial command of grammar, punctuation, and usage conventions. Some distracting errors may be evident, at times creating minor disruptions in the fluency or clarity of the writing.
1	The writer attempts to craft a clear structure for the poem but is not successful.	The writer attempts to use figurative language but is not successful. The writer does not include a final line that points to the poem's theme.	The writer demonstrates little or no command of grammar, punctuation, and usage conventions. Serious and persistent errors create disruptions in the fluency of the writing and sometimes interfere with meaning.
0	The writer does not provide a relevant response to the prompt or does not provide a response at all.	The writer does not provide a relevant response to the prompt or does not provide a response at all.	Serious and persistent errors overwhelm the writing and interfere with the meaning of the response as a whole, making the writer's meaning impossible to understand.

SCAFFOLDS

Write

Ask students to complete the writing assignment using textual evidence to support their answers.

Use the scaffolds below to differentiate instruction for your ELL English Language Learners and A Approaching grade-level learners.

ELL **BEGINNING** With the help of the word bank, write a response using paragraph frame 1.

INTERMEDIATE With the help of the word bank, write a response using paragraph frames 1 and 2.

ADVANCED, ADVANCED HIGH Write a response of differentiated length using the sentence starters.

A **APPROACHING** Write a response of differentiated length using the sentence starters.

BEGINNING | INTERMEDIATE | ADVANCED, ADVANCED HIGH | APPROACHING

Word Bank	Paragraph Frame 1	Paragraph Frame 2	Sentence Starters
choices important roads difference fewer	Robert Frost includes two ____ in his poem. This introduces the extended metaphor of making ____. The speaker decides to take the road traveled by ____ people. At the end of the poem, the speaker feels like his choice made a ____ in his life. This supports the theme that people's choices are ____. The theme of my poem will be ____. I can write my poem about my experience ____.	The theme of my poem will be ____. I can write my poem about my experience ____. I can develop this idea with details such as ____. A detail I can use to show this theme is ____.	• Robert Frost uses an extended metaphor to . . . • A detail that introduces this metaphor is . . . It develops the idea that . . . • The theme of the poem is . . . Details that develop this theme include . . . • In my own poem, I plan to develop the extended metaphor of . . . • A theme that builds from this extended metaphor is . . .

Peer Review

Students should submit substantive feedback to two peers using the review instructions below.

- How well does this response answer the prompt?
- How well does the writer craft the structure of his or her poem?
- How clearly does the writer use figurative language to develop and express a theme?
- What did the writer do well in this response? What does the writer need to work on?

Rate

Respond to the following with a point rating that reflects your opinion.

	1	2	3	4
Ideas				
Evidence				
Language and Conventions				

Submit

SENTENCE FRAMES

- You were able to (completely / partly / almost) answer the prompt.
- You could answer the prompt more completely by ____.
- You introduced the extended metaphor of ____ with the detail of ____.
- You developed the theme of ____ by ____.
- One idea that needs more development is ____.
- My favorite part of your response is ____.

The House on Mango Street

FICTION
Sandra Cisneros
1984

Introduction

studysync tv

Sandra Cisneros (b. 1954) is regarded as a prominent writer in the Chicana literary movement. She has won numerous awards, including the National Medal of Arts and The National Book Award. Her first novel, *The House on Mango Street*, is a series of compressed, lyrical vignettes which center around a Latina girl growing up in a Chicago barrio. From her little red house, the protagonist Esperanza describes her life and the neighborhood around her. In this excerpt, Esperanza gives readers a glimpse into her dissatisfaction with the present and her hopes for the future.

In the first vignette, Esperanza does not like her family's new house on Mango Street. Small and crumbling, it does not have a yard and has only one bathroom. Even though her parents tell her that it's only temporary, she knows that they can't afford anything bigger. In the second vignette, Esperanza reflects on her name, which comes from her great-grandmother, who was a wild woman. Apparently, her great-grandmother was forced into marriage and then spent the rest of her life staring out the window. Esperanza wonders if her great-grandmother made the best of her life or filled her days with self-pity. In the third and final vignette, Esperanza explains how she relates to the four skinny trees in front of her house. She feels as though they are the only things that understand her because they also possess a secret strength despite their appearance.

ELL Proficiency-leveled summaries and summaries in multiple languages are available digitally.

 Audio and audio text highlighting are available with this text.

CONNECT TO ESSENTIAL QUESTION

What makes you, you?

In this excerpt from the novel *The House on Mango Street* by Sandra Cisneros, the young narrator struggles to define herself when she feels challenged by her surroundings and longs for a house that would always belong to her family.

Access Complex Text

LEXILE: 850L **WORD COUNT:** 950

The following areas may be challenging for students, particularly ELL English Language Learners and A Approaching grade-level learners.

Prior Knowledge	Organization	Connection of Ideas
• Sandra Cisneros was born in Chicago. Her father was Mexican and her mother was Mexican American. Her experiences as a Chicana (Mexican American) caught between two cultures influenced her depiction of the main character in this novel.	• The novel is organized as a series of vignettes—short descriptive scenes. • Each vignette has a title and is a self-contained story. Have students identify the three scenes that are included in this excerpt.	• Cisneros uses a poetic style exemplified by imagery and figurative language. Students may need guidance understanding the metaphors and similes, how the figurative language draws the reader into the story, and how it contributes to the theme.

SCAFFOLDS ELL ENGLISH LANGUAGE LEARNERS A APPROACHING GRADE LEVEL B BEYOND GRADE LEVEL

These icons identify differentiation strategies and scaffolded support for a variety of students. See the digital lesson plan for additional differentiation strategies and scaffolds.

Instructional Path

The print teacher's edition includes essential point-of-use instruction and planning tools. Complete lesson plans and program documents appear in your digital teacher account.

First Read: The House on Mango Street

Objectives: After an initial reading and discussion of the novel excerpt, students will be able to identify and describe characters and setting details, as well as articulate events that are central to the story's plot.

Skill: Figurative Language

Objectives: After rereading and discussing a model of close reading, students will be able to describe how the author's use of figurative language achieves specific purposes.

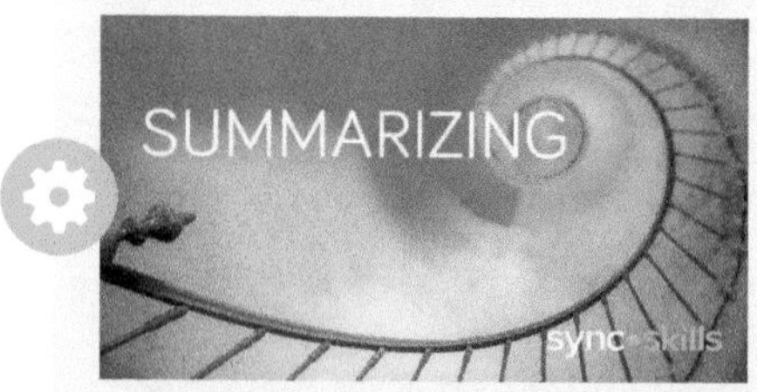

Skill: Summarizing

Objectives: After rereading and discussing a model of close reading, students will be able to determine how to write an objective summary of a text.

Close Read: The House on Mango Street

Objectives: After engaging in a close reading and discussion of the excerpt, students will be able to analyze figurative language in order to participate in a collaborative conversation and write a short, constructed response.

Progress Monitoring

Opportunities to Learn	Opportunities to Demonstrate Learning	Opportunities to Reteach
Figurative Language		
Skill: Figurative Language	Skill: Figurative Language • Your Turn Close Read • Complete Vocabulary Chart • Skills Focus • Write	Unit 3 Skill: Figurative Language - Narrative of the Life of Frederick Douglass, An American Slave Unit 4 Skill: Figurative Language - The Adventures of Tom Sawyer (Chapter 2) Spotlight Skill: Figurative Language
Summarizing		
Skill: Summarizing	Skill: Summarizing • Your Turn Close Read • Skills Focus • Write	Unit 3 Skill: Summarizing - Address to the Nation on the Explosion of the Space Shuttle *Challenger* Unit 6 Skill: Summarizing - Everybody Out (from 'What If?') Spotlight Skill: Summarizing

First Read

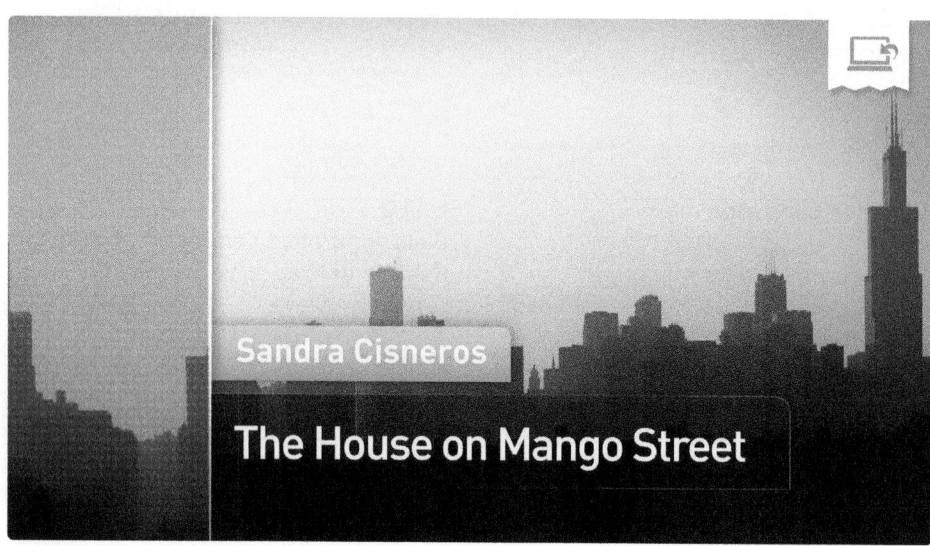

Introduce the Text

As a class, watch the video preview and have students read the introduction in pairs to make connections to the video preview.

To activate prior knowledge and experiences, ask students:

- What part of the video stood out to you the most?
- How do the images, words, and music in the video connect to the information in the introduction?

SPEAKING FRAMES

- The ____ in the video makes me think ____.
- The video shows ____. This makes me wonder ____.
- I think the text will ____. I think this because ____.
- I predict that there will be ____. I believe this because ____.

Entry Point

As students prepare to read *The House on Mango Street,* share the following information with them to provide context.

- ✓ Sandra Cisneros was born in Chicago, Illinois, in 1954. She is a Mexican American author who has received many awards for her work. They include a MacArthur Fellowship and a National Medal of Arts.
- ✓ Cisneros published *The House on Mango Street* in 1984. This novel is a portrait of a young Latina girl and the neighborhood in which she grows up.
- ✓ *The House on Mango Street* is made up of vignettes. A vignette is a short description of a scene or event. It does not follow the traditional structure of a narrative. However, it often includes many descriptive details and helps develop a theme.

"I have inherited her name, but I don't want to inherit her place by the window."

The House on Mango Street

1 They always told us that one day we would move into a house, a real house that would be ours for always so we wouldn't have to move each year. And our house would have running water and pipes that worked. And inside it would have real stairs, not hallway stairs, but stairs inside like the houses on TV. And we'd have a basement and at least three washrooms so when we took a bath we wouldn't have to tell everybody. Our house would be white with trees around it, a great big yard and grass growing without a fence. This was the house Papa talked about when he held a lottery ticket and this was the house Mama dreamed up in the stories she told us before we went to bed.

2 But the house on Mango Street is not the way they told it at all. It's small and red with tight steps in front and windows so small you'd think they were holding their breath. Bricks are crumbling in places, and the front door is so swollen you have to push hard to get in. There is no front yard, only four little elms the city planted by the curb. Out back is a small garage for the car we don't own yet and a small yard that looks smaller between the two buildings on either side. There are stairs in our house, but they're ordinary hallway stairs, and the house has only one washroom. Everybody has to share a bedroom—Mama and Papa, Carlos and Kiki, me and Nenny.

Skill: Figurative Language

The description of windows "so small you'd think they were holding their breath" is an example of personification. I can picture windows sucking in their breath, so small they can't let any air out even when they're open.

3 Once when we were living on Loomis, a nun[1] from my school passed by and saw me playing out front. The **laundromat** downstairs had been boarded up because it had been robbed two days before and the owner had painted on the wood YES WE'RE OPEN so as not to lose business.

4 Where do you live? she asked.

5 There, I said pointing up to the third floor.

6 You live *there?*

1. **nun** a female member of a religious order, often the staff and faculty at Catholic schools

Analyze Vocabulary Using Context Clues

In paragraph 3, focus on the sentence that uses the word *laundromat*. Point out these context clues:

1. First, I notice the letters *l-a-u-n-d-r* at the beginning of the word *laundromat*. These letters are also found at the beginning of the word *laundry*. I know that laundry is what we do when we wash our clothes.
2. The words *owner* and *business* are clues that a *laundromat* is a kind of shop or store.
3. A *laundromat* must be a place where customers pay to wash their clothes.

Figurative Language

How does the reader interpret the use of personification in the second paragraph?

The reader notes Esperanza's use of personification to describe windows "so small you'd think they were holding their breath." This helps her picture windows sucking in their breath, so small they can't let any air out even when they're open.

SELECTION VOCABULARY

laundromat / la lavandería *noun* a business that features coin-operated laundry machines

TEXT TALK

What sort of house do Mama and Papa want for their family?

See paragraph 1: They want a big, white house with trees and a big yard. It will have running water, stairs inside, a basement, and at least three washrooms.

What is the house on Mango Street like?

See paragraph 2: It is small and red. It has "tight steps," small windows, "crumbling bricks," a front door that is "swollen," four little trees, a small yard, and one washroom.

Figurative Language

How does the reader interpret the metaphor "a wild horse of a woman"?

The reader recognizes Esperanza's comparison of her great-grandmother to a "wild horse." She understands that this comparison shows that her great-grandmother was independent.

Summarizing

Why does the reader only highlight the first sentence in paragraphs 13 and 14?

The reader highlights the first sentence in paragraph 13 because it expresses one reason why Esperanza doesn't like her first name. The first sentence in paragraph 14 describes the kind of name she wants.

Skills Focus

QUESTION 2: Figurative Language

Esperanza uses a simile and a metaphor to compare her name to the number nine and a muddy color. There are nine letters in Esperanza's name, and she feels it is too long. She wishes she had a nickname like her sister. Comparing her name to a muddy color implies that Esperanza is not an identifiable color, like green or yellow. She feels she has no identity.

Skills Focus

QUESTION 3: Figurative Language

Esperanza compares the way her classmates say her name to something painful—so painful that it cannot be said aloud without hurting your mouth. This shows that Esperanza feels like she does not belong with her classmates.

NOTES

7 *There.* I had to look to where she pointed—the third floor, the paint peeling, wooden bars Papa had nailed on the windows so we wouldn't fall out. You live *there?* The way she said it made me feel like nothing. *There.* I lived *there.* I nodded.

8 I knew then I had to have a house. A real house. One I could point to. But this isn't it. The house on Mango Street isn't it. For the time being, Mama says. Temporary, says Papa. But I know how those things go.

...

My Name

Skill: Figurative Language

The metaphor "a wild horse of a woman" doesn't use like or as. This communicates that the author's great-grandmother was independent. The simile "as if she were a fancy chandelier" implies how valuable she was to her great-grandfather.

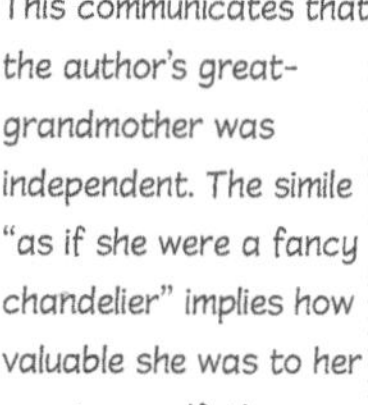

9 In English my name means hope. In Spanish it means too many letters. It means sadness, it means waiting. It is like the number nine. A muddy color. It is the Mexican records my father plays on Sunday mornings when he is shaving, songs like sobbing.

10 It was my great-grandmother's name and now it is mine. She was a horse woman too, born like me in the Chinese year of the horse—which is supposed to be bad luck if you're born female—but I think this is a Chinese lie because the Chinese, like the Mexicans, don't like their women strong.

11 My great-grandmother. I would've liked to have known her, a wild horse of a woman, so wild she wouldn't marry. Until my great-grandfather threw a sack over her head and carried her off. Just like that, as if she were a fancy **chandelier**. That's the way he did it.

Skill: Summarizing

Esperanza wants to be her own person instead of having a name related to her heritage. She wants to separate herself from her parents and sister. Changing her name seems to her an important step in that direction.

12 And the story goes she never forgave him. She looked out the window her whole life, the way so many women sit their sadness on an elbow. I wonder if she made the best with what she got or was she sorry because she couldn't be all the things she wanted to be. Esperanza. I have inherited her name, but I don't want to **inherit** her place by the window.

13 At school they say my name funny as if the syllables were made out of tin and hurt the roof of your mouth. But in Spanish my name is made out of a softer something, like silver, not quite as thick as sister's name—Magdalena—which is uglier than mine. Magdalena who at least can come home and become Nenny. But I am always Esperanza.

14 I would like to **baptize** myself under a new name, a name more like the real me, the one nobody sees. Esperanza as Lisandra or Maritza or Zeze the X. Yes. Something like Zeze the X will do.

...

SELECTION VOCABULARY

chandelier / el candelabro ***noun*** a decorative hanging light

- What word describes *chandelier*?
- Who is compared to a chandelier? What does that tell you about *chandelier*?

Four Skinny Trees

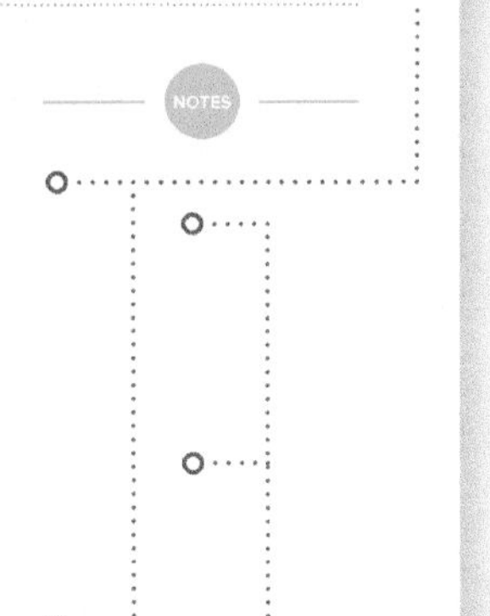

15 They are the only ones who understand me. I am the only one who understands them. Four skinny trees with skinny necks and pointy elbows like mine. Four who do not belong here but are here. Four raggedy excuses planted by the city. From our room we can hear them, but Nenny just sleeps and doesn't appreciate these things.

16 Their strength is secret. They send **ferocious** roots beneath the ground. They grow up and they grow down and grab the earth between their hairy toes and bite the sky with violent teeth and never quit their anger. This is how they keep.

17 Let one forget his reason for being, they'd all droop like tulips in a glass, each with their arms around the other. Keep, keep, keep, trees say when I sleep. They teach.

Excerpted from *The House on Mango Street* by Sandra Cisneros, published by Vintage Books.

Skills Focus

QUESTION 4: Summarizing

Esperanza compares herself to the trees in front of her house. She says they are skinny but strong and persistent. They were part of her disappointment, but now they seem to represent her feelings. Like the trees, she feels out of place but determined to persist.

Skills Focus

QUESTION 5: Connect to Essential Question

Esperanza compares herself to the trees, which are skinny but strong. This shows that Esperanza wants to be strong like the trees and survive in a place where she feels she doesn't belong. Coming to terms with her real self is an important part of understanding herself.

TEXT TALK

What are the four little trees like?

See paragraphs 15 and 16: They are skinny but have strong roots.

What does Esperanza think of the house on Mango Street? Does she consider it "home"?

Answers will vary.

SELECTION VOCABULARY

inherit / heredar *verb* to receive or be left with (something) from a former owner

ELL
- Who does Esperanza "inherit" something from?
- What does she inherit? What does she not want to inherit?

ferocious / feroz *adjective* very violent and fierce COGNATE

- What do the roots do?
- What emotion does Esperanza think the roots feel?

baptize / bautizar *verb* to bless or christen

- How would Esperanza like to "baptize" herself?
- Why does she want to make this change?

Think Questions

Circulate as students answer Think Questions independently. Scaffolds for these questions are shown on the opposite page.

QUESTION 1: Textual Evidence

The dream house would be big, well maintained, and permanent. It would have stairs like "houses on TV," be surrounded by trees, and have "a great big yard." In contrast, the house on Mango Street is small, deteriorating, and temporary. It has only one bedroom and only "a small yard" out back.

QUESTION 2: Textual Evidence

Esperanza is upset and ashamed after the encounter with the the nun. The nun's comment suggests that her home above the laundromat with its peeling paint and bars nailed over the windows is not acceptable. Esperanza "feels like nothing." She wants to live in a "real house" that will make her proud.

QUESTION 3: Textual Evidence

Esperanza identifies with the four trees outside her window because they represent the way she feels about herself and her sense of belonging. The trees are skinny like Esperanza, with "skinny necks" and "pointy elbows." The trees "do not belong here," and she doesn't feel like she belongs.

QUESTION 4: Word Meaning

In paragraph 10, Esperanza says, "It was my great-grandmother's name and now it is mine." Then in paragraph 12, she says, "I have inherited her name, but I don't want to inherit her place by the window." So *inherited* in this selection must mean "to have something, such as a position or attitude, after someone who came before you."

QUESTION 5: Context Clues

The word *ferocious* describes *roots* in the sentence. Other words in the surrounding sentences that describe roots or what they do are *strength*, *grab*, *bite*, *violent*, and *anger*. All of these words suggest that *ferocious* must mean "strong," "determined," and "vicious." I think that *ferocious* means something like "fierce and wild."

First Read

Read *The House on Mango Street*. After you read, complete the Think Questions below.

THINK QUESTIONS

1. How is the family's dream house different from their real house on Mango Street? Cite evidence from the selection to support your answer.

2. How does Esperanza's encounter with the nun affect her? Explain how she feels after this brief encounter. Cite evidence from the text.

3. Why do you think Esperanza identifies with the four skinny trees outside her window? What does this tell you about her? Cite evidence from the text.

4. Read the following dictionary entry:

   inherit
   in•her•it \in ˈher it\ *verb*

   1. to receive money or property from someone who has died
   2. to receive a genetic trait from a parent or ancestor
   3. to have something, such as a job or attitude, after someone who came before you

   Which definition most closely matches the meaning of **inherit** as it is used in paragraph 12? Write the appropriate definition of *inherit* here and explain how you figured out the correct meaning.

5. Find the word **ferocious** in paragraph 16 of *The House on Mango Street*. Use context clues in the surrounding sentences, as well as the sentence in which the word appears, to determine the word's meaning. Write your definition here and identify clues that helped you figure out its meaning.

Think Questions

SCAFFOLDS

Use the scaffolds below to differentiate instruction for your ELL English Language Learners and A Approaching grade-level learners.

ELL **BEGINNING** Write a response using the word bank and sentence frames.

INTERMEDIATE Write a response using the sentence frames.

ADVANCED, ADVANCED HIGH Write a response using the Text-Dependent Question Guide.

A **APPROACHING** Write a response using the Text-Dependent Question Guide.

BEGINNING	INTERMEDIATE	APPROACHING / ADVANCED, ADVANCED HIGH
Word Bank	**Sentence Frames**	**Text-Dependent Question Guide**
lives grab fierce red yard upsets strong big ashamed belong anger white bite small	A "dream house" is the house the parents hope to have one day. It will be ____ and ____, and it will have a large ____. The house on Mango Street is ____ and ____.	1. • What is a "dream house"? • How do Esperanza's parents describe their dream house? • What is the house on Mango Street like?
	The nun asks Esperanza where she ____. Esperanza points out her home. What the nun says ____ Esperanza and makes her feel ____.	2. • What does the nun ask Esperanza? • What does the nun say when Esperanza points to her home? • How does this make Esperanza feel?
	The trees are skinny. They don't seem to ____ where they were planted. The trees' roots are ____. This teaches Esperanza to be tough.	3. • What are the trees like Esperanza? • What does Esperanza see that is good in the trees? • How do the trees help her?
	Inherit as used in the text matches definition # ____.	4. • "I have inherited her name, but I don't want to **inherit** her place by the window." • Does *inherit* mean "to receive money or property"? (#1) • Does *inherit* mean "to receive a genetic trait"? (#2) • Does *inherit* mean "to have something after someone who came before you"? (#3)
	As the roots grow, they ____ the earth and ____ the sky. They also feel ____. These words give me a clue that *ferocious* means "something that is ____."	5. • Read: "They send **ferocious** roots beneath the ground. They grow up and they grow down and grab the earth between their hairy toes and bite the sky with violent teeth and never quit their anger. " • What word does *ferocious* describe? • How do the trees grow? • What other words are clues to the meaning of *ferocious*?

Reading Comprehension OPTIONAL

Have students complete the digital reading comprehension questions when they finish reading.

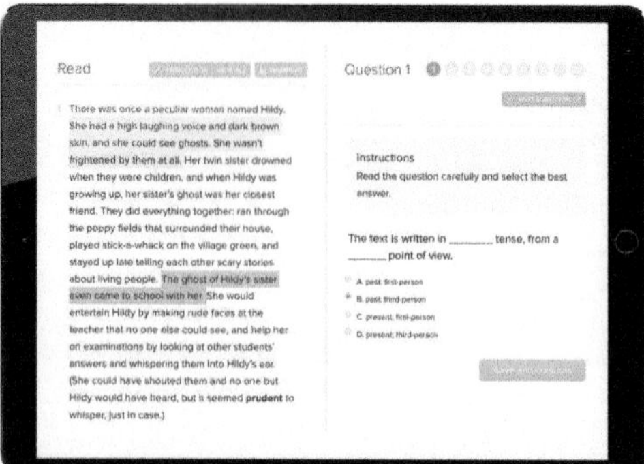

ANSWER KEY

QUESTION 1: B
QUESTION 2: A
QUESTION 3: C
QUESTION 4: D
QUESTION 5: B
QUESTION 6: D
QUESTION 7: A
QUESTION 8: C
QUESTION 9: *See first chart.*
QUESTION 10: *See second chart.*

Synonym	Word
light fixture	chandelier
fierce	ferocious
acquire	inherit
cleaners	laundromat
christen	baptize

What It Represents	Image or Element
How unrealistic their dream house is	lottery ticket
How unsafe Esperanza's home life is	boarded-up laundromat
Bad luck or omen for women	Year of the Horse myth
Escape that Esperanza does not have	Nenny
Hope that Esperanza can power through to a better life	four skinny trees

Connect and Extend OPTIONAL

CONNECT TO EXTENDED WRITING PROJECT

Students can use the novel *The House on Mango Street* as a resource when writing their literary analyses. Have them analyze how Sandra Cisneros uses the metaphor of a house to explore belonging.

BEYOND THE BOOK

Art: Ideal Home or The Story of Your Name

Ask students to select and complete one of the two assignments below.

1. Describe in minute detail your "ideal" home.
   - What would it look like inside and out?
   - What color would it be?
   - How many rooms would it have?
   - How would you feel in this home?

   Draw a picture or cut out images from magazines to create a collage of this ideal home.

2. Tell the story of your name.
   - What does your name mean?
   - What inspired your name?
   - Were you named after anyone?

   Draw an artistic representation of your name in which each letter of your name is an object or image that represents part of your personality or identity.

To reflect, ask students:

- Why did you choose the assignment you completed? What attracted you to it over the other option?
- What does your "ideal" home or the story behind your name reveal about your identity? Is there any connection?

The House on Mango Street

Skill: Figurative Language

Use the Checklist to analyze Figurative Language in *The House on Mango Street*. Refer to the sample student annotations about Figurative Language in the text.

••• CHECKLIST FOR FIGURATIVE LANGUAGE

To determine the meaning of figurative language in a text, note the following:

- ✓ words that mean one thing literally but suggest something else
- ✓ similes, such as "strong as an ox," or metaphors, such as "her eyes were stars"
- ✓ the use of personification, which gives human traits and qualities to something nonhuman, such as "the flowers smiled at us as we walked through the garden"
- ✓ puns, or plays on words, such as saying, "Let's branch out," while walking in the woods with friends

In order to interpret the meaning of a figure of speech in context, ask the following questions:

- ✓ How does descriptive language in the text compare two seemingly unlike things?
- ✓ Are there any similes or metaphors in the text? How do you know?
- ✓ Are there any examples of personification?
- ✓ Do you see any words that have two meanings that are used deliberately for humor or a pun?
- ✓ How does the use of figurative language change your understanding of the thing or person being described?

In order to analyze the impact of figurative language on the meaning of a text, use the following questions as a guide:

- ✓ Where does figurative language appear in the text? What does it mean?
- ✓ What impact do specific word choices have on meaning and tone, or the writer's attitude toward the subject or audience?

SKILL VOCABULARY

figurative language / el lenguaje figurativo *noun* expressions used for descriptive or rhetorical effect that are not literally true but express some truth beyond the literal level COGNATE

simile / el símil *noun* a figure of speech that uses the words *like* or *as* to compare two seemingly unlike things COGNATE

metaphor / la metáfora *noun* a figure of speech that compares two seemingly unlike things but implies a comparison instead of stating it directly with the words *like* or *as* COGNATE

Skill: Figurative Language

Introduce the Skill

Watch the Concept Definition video ▶ and read the following definition with your students.

Figurative language is language used for descriptive effect, often to illustrate or imply ideas indirectly. Types of figurative language include simile, metaphor, and personification. A **simile** uses the words *like* or *as* to compare two seemingly unlike things. A **metaphor** directly compares two seemingly unlike things without using *like* or *as*. **Personification** is a **figure of speech** in which an animal, object, force of nature, or an idea is given human qualities.

When reading prose, and especially poetry, readers use **context**—including when and where a text was written, for example—to analyze the impact of word choice and to help determine or interpret the meaning of figurative words and phrases.

TURN AND TALK

1. Think about a close friend. What qualities does he or she have that you like?
2. What comparisons can you think of to describe those qualities?

SPEAKING FRAMES

- My friend ___ (verb) like ___.
- My friend is as ___ as ___.
- My friend is a/an ___.
- My friend has ___ that is/are like ___.
- My friend has ___ that is/are as ___ as a ___.

Your Turn

Ask students to complete the Your Turn activity.

QUESTION 1

A. Incorrect. There are no details in this excerpt that support that interpretation.

B. Incorrect. There are no details in this excerpt that support that interpretation.

C. Correct. Esperanza describes the trees as though they have body parts and says that they are like her own body parts.

D. Incorrect. There are no details in this excerpt that support that interpretation.

QUESTION 2

A. Incorrect. There are no details in this excerpt that support that interpretation. The personification suggests that the trees are strong, not weak.

B. Incorrect. There are no details in this excerpt that support that interpretation.

C. Correct. Esperanza says that their "strength is secret." The personification of the trees helps show that the trees are firmly rooted in the ground.

D. Incorrect. Esperanza does describe the trees as *ferocious* and *violent*, but there are no details in this excerpt to suggest that the trees might cause anyone harm.

QUESTION 3

A. Correct. The image of drooping tulips helps communicate a loss of purpose.

B. Incorrect. All of the tulips are drooping, so they are not providing support for one another.

C. Incorrect. The image of drooping tulips communicates a lack of strength.

D. Incorrect. The image of drooping tulips communicates giving up, not determination.

Skill: Figurative Language

Reread paragraphs 15–17 of *The House on Mango Street*. Then, using the Checklist on the previous page, answer the multiple-choice questions below.

YOUR TURN

1. The personification in paragraph 15 helps show that—
   - A. Esperanza thinks the trees are dying.
   - B. Esperanza feels annoyed by the trees.
   - C. Esperanza feels a connection to the trees.
   - D. Esperanza is the only person who sees the trees.

2. The personification in paragraph 16 helps communicate that the trees are—
   - A. weak.
   - B. aging.
   - C. strong.
   - D. dangerous.

3. The simile in paragraph 17 helps the reader understand—
   - A. defeat.
   - B. support.
   - C. strength.
   - D. determination.

SKILL VOCABULARY

personification / la personificación ***noun*** a figure of speech in which an animal, object, force of nature, or idea is given human form or qualities COGNATE

figure of speech / la figura literaria ***noun*** a word or phrase not meant to be taken literally, but rather used for effect

context / el contexto ***noun*** the set of facts or circumstances that surround a situation or event COGNATE

Skill: Summarizing

Use the Checklist to analyze Summarizing in *The House on Mango Street*. Refer to the sample student annotations about Summarizing in the text.

••• CHECKLIST FOR SUMMARIZING

In order to determine how to write an objective summary of a text, note the following:

- ✓ in a nonfiction text, examine the details to identify the main idea, making notations in a notebook or graphic organizer
- ✓ in literature, note the setting, characters, and events in the plot and their relationship to the theme
- ✓ answers to the basic questions *who, what, where, when, why,* and *how*
- ✓ stay objective, and do not add your own personal thoughts, judgments, or opinions to the summary

To provide an objective summary of a text, consider the following questions:

- ✓ What are the answers to basic *who, what, where, when, why,* and *how* questions in literature and works of nonfiction?
- ✓ In what order should I put the main ideas and most important details in a work of nonfiction to make my summary logical?
- ✓ In a work of literature, have I included details that reflect the relationship of the setting, characters, and events in the plot to the theme?
- ✓ Is my summary objective, or have I added my own thoughts, judgments, and personal opinions?

Skill: Summarizing

Introduce the Skill

Watch the Concept Definition video ▶ and read the following definition with your students.

When you **summarize** a text, you briefly state the main points and most important details in your own words. Summarizing can help you organize, explain, and remember concepts in an informational text or the events that take place in a story.

To summarize, you must decide what is most important as you read. Ask the basic questions: *who, what, when, where, why,* and *how*. Using your own words, write your answers to these questions from an **objective** point of view, without inserting your own feelings and opinions.

Summarizing is sometimes confused with paraphrasing. When you **paraphrase**, you do not condense a text to its most important details. Instead, you restate the entire text in your own words. A summary is much shorter than the original text, while a paraphrase may be the same length as the original text.

V SKILL VOCABULARY

summarize / resumir ***verb*** to restate briefly the most important points in a text

objective / objetivo/a ***adjective*** undistorted by emotion or personal bias COGNATE

paraphrase / parafrasear ***verb*** to restate the author's words in your own words COGNATE

TURN AND TALK

1. Think about your favorite book or movie. Can you describe who did what, where, when, why, and how without including your thoughts and feelings about it?
2. Why do you think we leave out our own thoughts and feelings when we summarize?

SPEAKING FRAMES

- The [book / movie] took place in ____.
- In [book or movie title], the main character was ____ and in the [book / movie] they ____.
- The reason the main character did what they did was to ____.
- The [movie / book] ended when ____.

Your Turn

Ask students to complete the Your Turn activity.

QUESTION 1

Part A

A. Incorrect. Esperanza thinks about how her name influences her identity, but she does not argue that her entire identity is based on it.

B. Incorrect. Esperanza shares a story about her name, but she does not mention that everyone has a story to tell about their name.

C. Incorrect. While Esperanza is a unique character, she is not the only person who has that name.

D. Correct. Esperanza thinks about how her name has influenced the way she sees herself and the challenges she expects to face.

Part B

A. Correct. Esperanza describes her great-grandmother as a strong woman. Since her great-grandmother also faced difficulties due to her strength, she is concerned about the conflicts that she will most likely face as well.

B. Incorrect. At the end of this passage, Esperanza hopes that she will have a future that differs from the experience that her grandmother had.

C. Incorrect. Esperanza mentions her father's music in this passage, but she does not mention asking her father about his name.

D. Incorrect. Esperanza describes similarities between her great-grandmother and herself.

QUESTION 2

A. Incorrect. Esperanza never calls her great-grandmother weak.

B. Incorrect. This is a minor detail and doesn't explain how she feels about her great-grandmother.

C. Correct. Esperanza says she would have liked to have known her great-grandmother for her "wild streak," but does not want to inherit her "place by the window."

D. Incorrect. At no point does Esperanza say she dislikes her great-grandmother for being sad.

The House on Mango Street

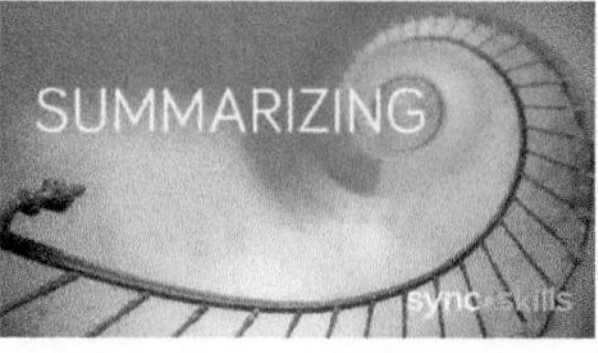

Skill: Summarizing

Reread paragraphs 9–12 of *The House on Mango Street*. Then, using the Checklist on the previous page, answer the multiple-choice questions below.

YOUR TURN

1. This question has two parts. First, answer Part A. Then, answer Part B.

Part A: Which of the following is the theme or central idea of this passage?

- A. A person's identity is defined by the name that he or she was given.
- B. Every person has a story to tell about their names.
- C. Esperanza's name makes her unique.
- D. A name can influence a person's identity.

Part B: How does the character relate to the theme you selected in Part A?

- A. Esperanza's name is both a source of strength and a concern for her.
- B. Esperanza thinks that she has no control over her future because of her name.
- C. Esperanza shares the story behind her name and wants to learn the story behind her father's name.
- D. Esperanza thinks that her name shows that she is different from everyone else.

2. Summarize Esperanza's feelings about her great-grandmother.

- A. She seems to think she was weak.
- B. She seems to like her because, like her great-grandmother, Esperanza was born in the Chinese year of the horse.
- C. She seems to admire her, describing in detail her great-grandmother's independent streak, but at the same time does not want to inherit her sadness.
- D. She seems to dislike her because she was sad all the time.

84 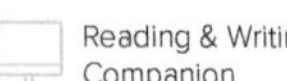 Reading & Writing Companion

The House on Mango Street

3. During this passage, Esperanza mentions some reasons why she doesn't like her name. Summarize her feelings towards her name.

   ○ A. Esperanza dislikes her name for many reasons, including that it means "sadness" and "waiting" and has too many letters.

   ○ B. Esperanza dislikes her name because it means "hope" in English.

   ○ C. Esperanza dislikes her name because it reminds her of the sad records her father plays while he is shaving.

   ○ D. Esperanza likes names that contain fewer syllables.

QUESTION 3

A. Correct. This is a good summary because it lists the three main reasons why Esperanza dislikes her name, and the other reasons only add to these same feelings.

B. Incorrect. Esperanza mentions that her name means "hope" in English, but she does not give this as a reason for why she dislikes it.

C. Incorrect. This is only one reason why Esperanza dislikes her name.

D. Incorrect. Esperanza actually says her name has too many letters, not syllables.

Close Read

Skills Focus

QUESTION 1: Summarizing

See paragraph 2: Esperanza is disappointed that the house is not what she had hoped for. Her disappointment shows that Esperanza does not feel good about the house. She describes the windows as "so small you'd think they were holding their breath," which sounds confining.

QUESTION 2: Figurative Language

See paragraph 9.

QUESTION 3: Figurative Language

See paragraph 13.

QUESTION 4: Summarizing

See paragraphs 15–17.

QUESTION 5: Connect to Essential Question

See paragraphs 15 and 16.

CHECK FOR SUCCESS

If students struggle to respond to Skills Focus question 1, ask them the following questions:

- What does the house on Mango Street look like?
- What did Esperanza want the house to be like?

Have students transition to read and annotate independently once they have successfully completed the first Skills Focus prompt.

Close Read

Reread *The House on Mango Street*. As you reread, complete the Skills Focus questions below. Then use your answers and annotations from the questions to help you complete the Write activity.

SKILLS FOCUS

1. Provide a descriptive summary of Esperanza's feelings toward the house on Mango Street. Include as many relevant details as possible, being sure to cite the text when necessary.
2. Identify the figurative language in paragraph 9 of the excerpt from *The House on Mango Street*. Explain what ideas Esperanza is expressing through her use of figurative language.
3. Identify the figurative language in paragraph 13 of the excerpt from *The House on Mango Street*. Explain how the figurative comparison helps the reader understand how Esperanza feels.
4. Summarize Esperanza's thoughts about the trees. What do they seem to represent to her, and why are they significant enough to be a focal point within her narrative?
5. Like many others, Esperanza struggles with who she is. Identify examples of this struggle and explain what makes the narrator uncomfortable. Be sure to emphasize how coming to terms with one's identity is an important part of determining what makes someone themselves.

WRITE

ARGUMENTATIVE: Esperanza faces several internal and external struggles. Overall, what are Esperanza's biggest challenges? Summarize the challenges Esperanza faces in each section of the text, and explain how figurative language is used to convey those challenges. Be sure to support your ideas with evidence from the text.

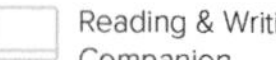

Writer's Notebook

Connect to Essential Question: Give students time to reflect on how *The House on Mango Street* connects to the unit's essential question "What makes you, you?" by freewriting in their Writer's Notebooks.

Beginning & Intermediate

Read aloud the unit's essential question: "What makes you, you?" Encourage students to draw their reflections or allow students to write in their native language. Circulate, prompting students for their thoughts as they respond orally or through pantomime.

Advanced & Advanced High

Allow students to share their reflections orally in pairs or small groups before freewriting.

StudySyncTV

Project the StudySyncTV episode and pause at the following times to prompt discussion:

2:08 Esperanza has conflicting feelings about her name. What does the group say about this?

3:42 What do Renata and Katie say about how hope is discussed in the text? What textual evidence does Chris provide to show Esperanza's definition of a "real house"?

5:32 What takes the group back to discussing Esperanza's conflict about her name? What evidence does Renata read to explain how Esperanza feels about her name?

Collaborative Conversation

SCAFFOLDS

Break students into collaborative conversation groups to discuss the Close Read prompt. Ask students to use the StudySyncTV episode as a model for their discussion. Remind them to reference their Skills Focus annotations in their discussion.

Esperanza faces several internal and external struggles. Overall, what are Esperanza's biggest challenges? Summarize the challenges Esperanza faces in each section of the text, and explain how figurative language is used to convey those challenges. Be sure to support your ideas with evidence from the text.

Use the scaffolds below to differentiate instruction for your ELL English Language Learners and A Approaching grade-level learners.

ELL **BEGINNING, INTERMEDIATE** Use the discussion guide and speaking frames to facilitate the discussion with support from the teacher.

ADVANCED, ADVANCED HIGH Use the discussion guide and speaking frames to facilitate the discussion in mixed-level groups.

A **APPROACHING** Use the discussion guide to facilitate the discussion in mixed-level groups.

APPROACHING
ADVANCED, ADVANCED HIGH
BEGINNING, INTERMEDIATE

Discussion Guide	Speaking Frames
1. Why is Esperanza embarrassed about the house on Loomis?	• Esperanza is embarrassed about the house on Loomis when the nun ____. • Esperanza says she feels like ____.
2. What does Esperanza think about the house on Mango Street?	• Esperanza thinks the house is ____. • Esperanza describes the house as ____.
3. Why does Esperanza compare herself to trees in the excerpt from *The House on Mango Street*?	• Esperanza compares herself to the trees because they are ____. • Esperanza says she can learn from the trees because they are ____.

Review Prompt and Rubric

Before students begin writing, review the writing prompt and rubric with the class.

ARGUMENTATIVE: Esperanza faces several internal and external struggles. Overall, what are Esperanza's biggest challenges? Summarize the challenges Esperanza faces in each section of the text, and explain how figurative language is used to convey those challenges. Be sure to support your ideas with evidence from the text.

PROMPT GUIDE

- What challenges has Esperanza faced in her life?
- What figurative language is used in the text to show these challenges?
- How does the figurative language help us better understand the challenges Esperanza has faced?

An additional rubric item for Language and Conventions appears in your digital teacher and student accounts.

Score	Theme	Figurative Language
4	The writer clearly summarizes the overall challenges that Esperanza faces in her life. The writer provides exemplary summarization in their own words, using relevant evidence from the text.	The writer clearly analyzes and explains how each section uses figurative language to effectively convey the overall challenges that Esperanza faces in her life. The writer provides exemplary analysis, using relevant evidence from the text.
3	The writer summarizes the overall challenges that Esperanza faces in her life. The writer provides sufficient summarization in their own words, using relevant evidence from the text most of the time.	The writer analyzes and explains how each section uses figurative language to effectively convey the overall challenges that Esperanza faces in her life. The writer provides sufficient analysis, using relevant evidence from the text most of the time.
2	The writer summarizes some of the challenges that Esperanza faces in her life, but the summarization is incomplete. The writer uses relevant evidence from the text only some of the time.	The writer begins to analyze or explain how each section uses figurative language to effectively convey the overall challenges that Esperanza faces in her life, but the analysis is incomplete. The writer uses relevant evidence from the text only some of the time.
1	The writer attempts to summarize the challenges that Esperanza faces in her life, but the summarization is not successful. The writer uses little or no relevant evidence from the text.	The writer attempts to analyze or explain how each section uses figurative language to effectively convey the overall challenges that Esperanza faces in her life, but the analysis is not successful. The writer uses little or no relevant evidence from the text.
0	The writer does not provide a relevant response to the prompt or does not provide a response at all.	The writer does not provide a relevant response to the prompt or does not provide a response at all.

SCAFFOLDS

Write

Ask students to complete the writing assignment using textual evidence to support their answers.

Use the scaffolds below to differentiate instruction for your ELL English Language Learners and A Approaching grade-level learners.

ELL **BEGINNING** With the help of the word bank, write a response using paragraph frame 1.

INTERMEDIATE With the help of the word bank, write a response using paragraph frames 1 and 2.

ADVANCED, ADVANCED HIGH Write a response of differentiated length using the sentence starters.

A **APPROACHING** Write a response of differentiated length using the sentence starters.

BEGINNING / INTERMEDIATE		INTERMEDIATE	ADVANCED, ADVANCED HIGH / APPROACHING
Word Bank	**Paragraph Frame 1**	**Paragraph Frame 2**	**Sentence Starters**
metaphor struggles sorry figurative language embarrassed	Esperanza ____ with how she feels about herself. In the first section, Esperanza is ____ about her old home. The author uses ____ when she writes that the windows in the red house are "so small you'd think they were holding their breath." In the second section, Esperanza thinks about her great-grandmother. The author uses a ____ when she writes that Esperanza's grandmother was like women who "sit their sadness on an elbow." This figurative language shows that she doesn't want to end up feeling ____ for herself.	In the final section, the author uses ____. Esperanza compares herself to four trees because the trees ____, just as Esperanza feels ____.	• In *The House on Mango Street*, Esperanza struggles with . . . • Her challenge in the first section is . . . • The figurative language in the first section shows . . . • Her challenge in the second section is . . . • The figurative language in the second section shows . . . • Her challenge in the final section is . . . • The figurative language in the last section shows . . .

Peer Review

Students should submit substantive feedback to two peers using the review instructions below.

- How well does this response answer the prompt?
- How well does the writer summarize the narrator's challenges?
- How well does the writer support the ideas figurative language from the text?
- Which sentence in the writer's response made you think differently about the text?

Rate

Respond to the following with a point rating that reflects your opinion.

	1	2	3	4
Ideas	■	■	■	□
Evidence	■	■	■	■
Language and Conventions	■	■	□	□

Submit

ELL A **SENTENCE FRAMES**

- You were able to (completely / partly / almost) answer the prompt.
- You supported the idea of ____ with the figurative language examples of ____.
- One idea that needs more support is ____.
- I thought differently about the text after reading ____.
- My favorite part of your response is ____.

Blast: Author! Author! Read All About It!

How can researching information about an author help you self-select a text?

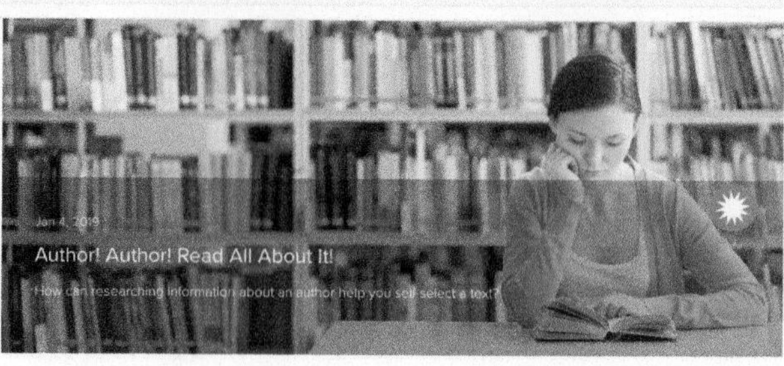

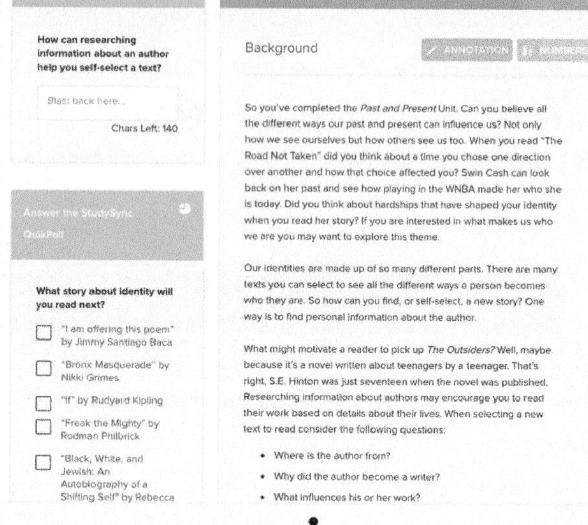

TEXT TALK

What is one strategy you can use for self-selecting a new text? How does it work?

I can research information about an author before reading their work. While I am finding information, I can use the suggested questions as a guide.

What should you do once you choose a text that interests you?

Start reading the text to confirm my interest. If I like it, I should keep reading.

Create Your Own Blast

SCAFFOLDS

Ask students to write a 140-character Blast after they complete the QuikPoll.

Use the scaffolds below to differentiate instruction for your ELL English Language Learners.

ELL **BEGINNING** Write a response using the word bank to complete the sentence frame.

INTERMEDIATE Write a response using the sentence frame.

ADVANCED, ADVANCED HIGH Write a response using the sentence starter.

BEGINNING	BEGINNING / INTERMEDIATE	ADVANCED, ADVANCED HIGH
Word Bank	**Sentence Frames**	**Sentence Starters**
relatable interesting reading connection author	I can research ____ information about an ____ before ____ their work. This can help me find a ____ with the ____.	• I can research information about an author . . . • This information can help me . . .

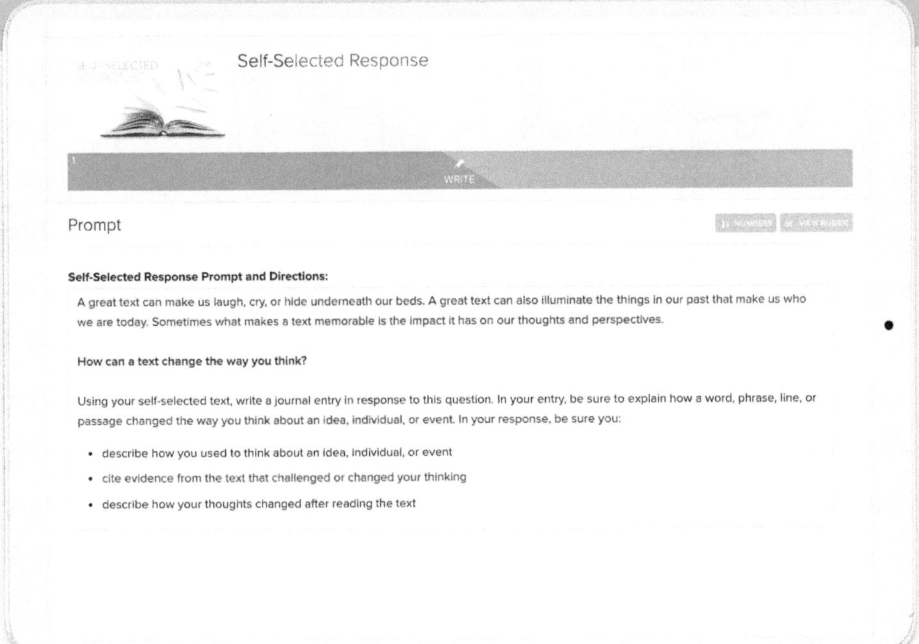

Self-Selected Response

WRITE

Prompt

Self-Selected Response Prompt and Directions:

A great text can make us laugh, cry, or hide underneath our beds. A great text can also illuminate the things in our past that make us who we are today. Sometimes what makes a text memorable is the impact it has on our thoughts and perspectives.

How can a text change the way you think?

Using your self-selected text, write a journal entry in response to this question. In your entry, be sure to explain how a word, phrase, line, or passage changed the way you think about an idea, individual, or event. In your response, be sure you:

- describe how you used to think about an idea, individual, or event
- cite evidence from the text that challenged or changed your thinking
- describe how your thoughts changed after reading the text

Self-Selected Response

Introduce the Prompt

Read aloud the prompt. Ask students to discuss:

- What is the prompt asking you to do?
- Why might it be useful to reflect on how a text can change the way you think?

Write

SCAFFOLDS

Ask students to complete the writing assignment using text evidence to support their answers.

Use the scaffolds below to differentiate instruction for your ELL English Language Learners and A Approaching grade level learners.

ELL **BEGINNING** With the help of the word bank, write a response using paragraph frame 1.

INTERMEDIATE With the help of the word bank, write a response using paragraph frames 1 and 2.

ADVANCED, ADVANCED HIGH Write a response of differentiated length using the sentence starters.

A **APPROACHING** Write a response of differentiated length using the sentence starters.

BEGINNING INTERMEDIATE	BEGINNING	INTERMEDIATE	ADVANCED, ADVANCED HIGH APPROACHING
Word Bank	**Paragraph Frame 1**	**Paragraph Frame 2**	**Sentence Starters**
love family war friendship sports difficult easy hardest enjoyable challenging	I read the text (title) ____ by (author) ____. I used to think ____. I thought this because ____. Now, I think ____. I think this because the text says, "____."	I read the text (title) ____ by (author) ____. I used to think ____. I thought this because ____. Now, I think ____. I think this because the text says, "____." This made me think ____. Therefore, ____ changed the way I think about ____.	• I read the text . . . by . . . • I used to think . . . • I thought this because . . . • Now I think . . . • I think this because in the text it says, " . . . " • This changed my thinking because . . .

Extended Writing Project

The Extended Writing Project (EWP) in Grade 8, Unit 2 focuses on literary analysis, a form of argumentative writing. The students probe the unit's essential question—What makes you, you?—as they write a literary analysis about the power of metaphor in texts. The multiple pieces of poetry in the unit, as well as fiction focused on identity and a commencement address, serve as resources for students in creating an analysis. Specific skill lessons teach thesis statements, organization, and conventions, while other skill lessons focus on supporting details, introductions and conclusions, and body paragraphs to help students craft a strong analysis. Directed revision leads students through the process of revising for clarity, development, organization, word choice, and sentence variety. Throughout the EWP, students have the opportunity to practice using created student writing, authentic texts, and their own work.

 Audio and audio text highlighting are available in select lessons in the Extended Writing Project.

CONNECT TO ESSENTIAL QUESTION

What makes you, you?

The texts in this unit showed the myriad ways characters, speakers, and narrators in texts define their individuality. Students are asked to think about the specific technique of metaphor and what it reveals about the character, speaker, or narrator. Students will structure their discussion of metaphor around an argument supported by coherent body paragraphs.

Extended Writing Project Prompt

What is the power of a metaphor?

Examine the texts from this unit and select three powerful metaphors that deepen our understanding of identity and belonging. Your analysis should explain each metaphor and make an argument about how the metaphor reveals something about each speaker, character, or author.

 ENGLISH LANGUAGE LEARNERS  APPROACHING GRADE LEVEL  BEYOND GRADE LEVEL

These icons identify differentiation strategies and scaffolded support for a variety of students. See the digital lesson plan for additional differentiation strategies and scaffolds.

Instructional Path

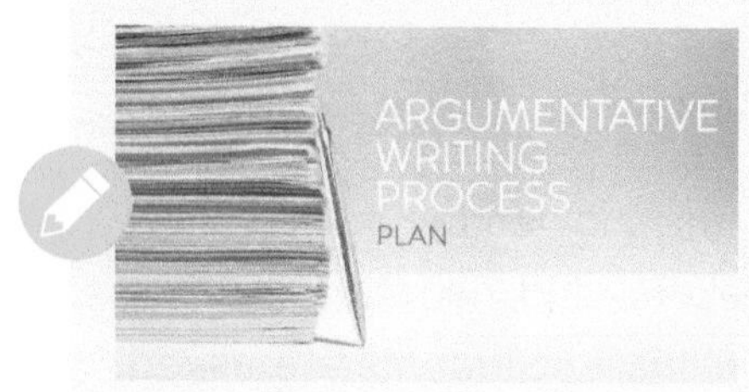

Argumentative Writing Process: Plan

Objectives: After learning about genre characteristics and craft, students will analyze a sample Student Model and plan a meaningful literary analysis in response to a prompt.

Skill: Organizing Argumentative Writing

Objectives: After reading and discussing a model of student writing, students will develop their drafts by organizing their arguments effectively.

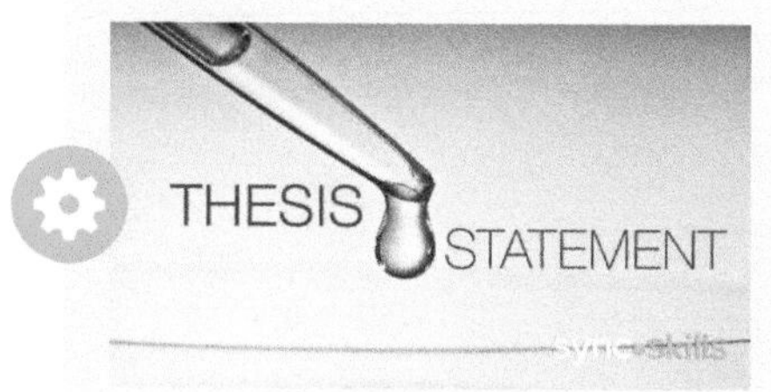

Skill: Thesis Statement

Objectives: After reading and discussing a model of student writing, students will compose a clear thesis statement in response to a prompt.

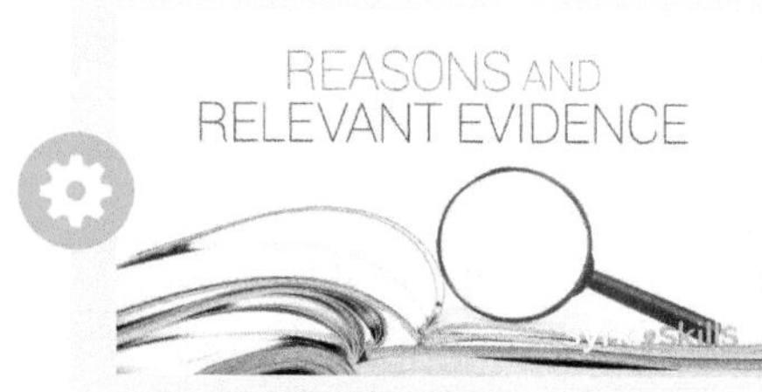

Skill: Reasons and Relevant Evidence

Objectives: After reading and discussing a model of student writing, students will support claim(s) with logical reasoning and relevant evidence, using accurate and credible sources.

Argumentative Writing Process: Draft

Objectives: After reading a Student Model draft and reviewing a writing checklist, students will draft a meaningful literary analysis in response to a prompt.

The print teacher's edition includes essential point-of-use instruction and planning tools. Complete lesson plans and program documents appear in your digital teacher account.

Skill: Introductions

Objectives: After reading and discussing a model of student writing, students will introduce claim(s). They will also acknowledge and distinguish those claim(s) from alternate or opposing claims.

Skill: Transitions

Objectives: After reading and discussing a model of student writing, students will use words, phrases, and clauses to create cohesion and clarify the relationships among claim(s), counterclaims, reasons, and evidence.

Skill: Style

Objectives: After reading and discussing a model of student writing, students will establish and maintain a formal style.

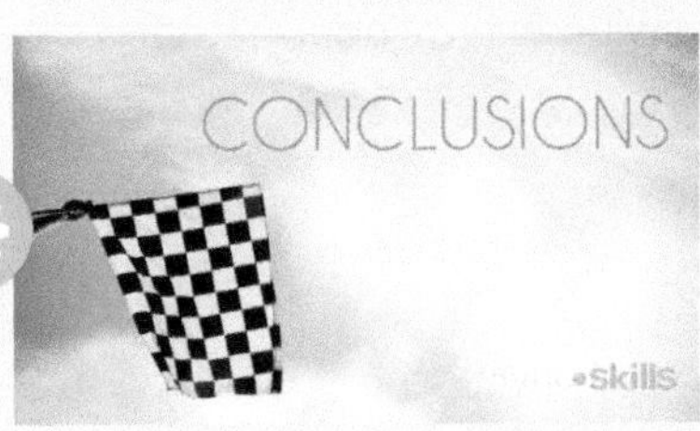

Skill: Conclusions

Objectives: After reading and discussing a model of student writing, students will provide a conclusion that follows from and reflects on the narrated experiences or events.

Argumentative Writing Process: Revise

Objectives: Students will use a revision guide to revise the draft of their literary analysis for clarity, development, organization, style, diction, and sentence effectiveness.

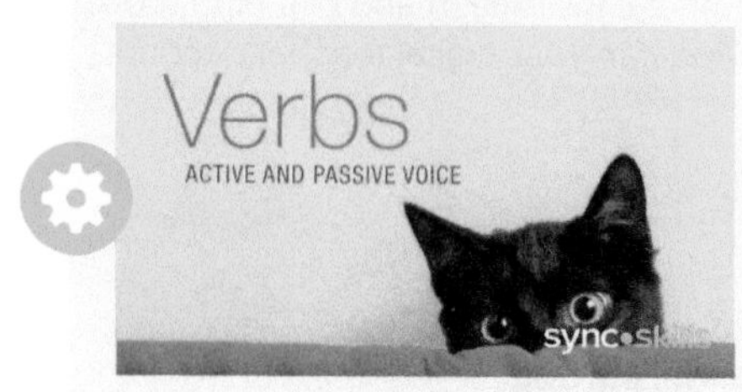

Grammar: Active and Passive Voice

Objectives: After learning about active and passive voice and seeing how they are used in text examples, students will practice using active and passive voice correctly.

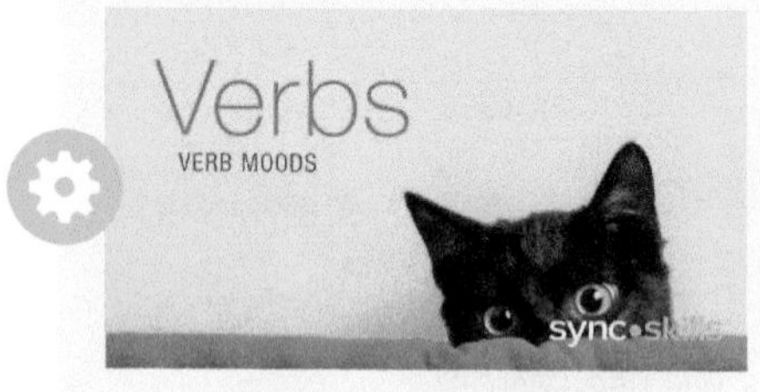

Grammar: Verb Moods

Objectives: After learning about verb moods and seeing how they are used in text examples, students will practice using verb moods correctly.

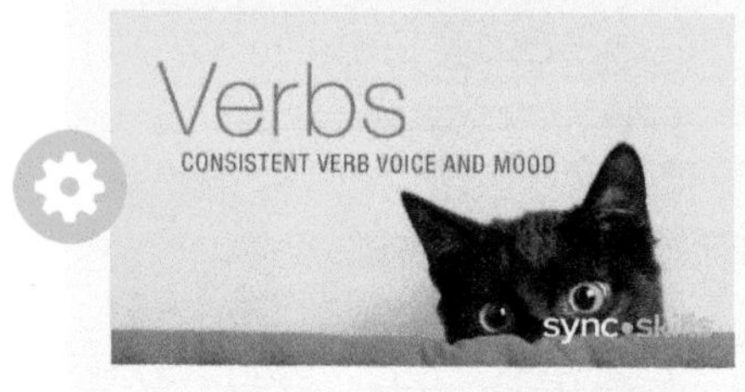

Grammar: Consistent Verb Voice and Mood

Objectives: After learning about consistent verb voice and mood and seeing how they are used in text examples, students will practice using consistent verb voice and mood correctly.

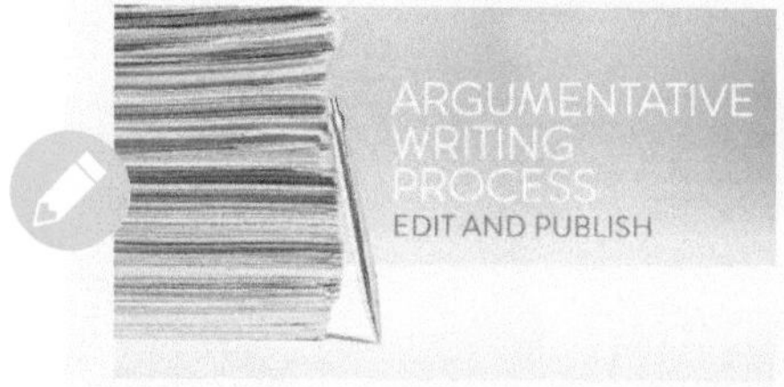

Argumentative Writing Process: Edit and Publish

Objectives: After seeing an example of editing in the Student Model and reviewing an editing checklist, students will edit and publish the final draft of their literary analysis.

Progress Monitoring

Opportunities to Learn	Opportunities to Demonstrate Learning	Opportunities to Reteach
Argumentative Writing Process: Plan		
Argumentative Writing Process: Plan	Argumentative Writing Process: Plan • Write	Units 3–6 Process: Plan
Argumentative Writing Process: Draft		
Argumentative Writing Process: Draft	Argumentative Writing Process: Draft • Write	Units 3–6 Process: Draft
Argumentative Writing Process: Revise		
Argumentative Writing Process: Revise	Argumentative Writing Process: Revise • Write	Units 3–6 Process: Revise

Argumentative Writing Process: Edit and Publish

Argumentative Writing Process: Edit and Publish	Argumentative Writing Process: Edit and Publish • Write	Units 3–4, 6 Process: Edit and Publish Unit 5 Process: Edit and Present

Organizing Argumentative Writing

Skill: Organizing Argumentative Writing	Skill: Organizing Argumentative Writing • Your Turn Argumentative Writing Process: Draft	Unit 4 Skill: Organizing Argumentative Writing Spotlight Skill: Organizing Argumentative Writing

Thesis Statement

Skill: Thesis Statement	Skill: Thesis Statement • Your Turn Argumentative Writing Process: Draft	Units 3–4 Skill: Thesis Statement Spotlight Skill: Thesis Statement

Reasons and Relevant Evidence

Skill: Reasons and Relevant Evidence	Skill: Reasons and Relevant Evidence • Your Turn Argumentative Writing Process: Draft	Units 4–5 Skill: Reasons and Relevant Evidence Spotlight Skill: Reasons and Relevant Evidence

Introductions

Skill: Introductions	Skill: Introductions • Your Turn Argumentative Writing Process: Revise	Units 3–4 Skill: Introductions Spotlight Skill: Introductions

Transitions

Skill: Transitions	Skill: Transitions • Your Turn Argumentative Writing Process: Revise	Units 3–4 Skill: Transitions Spotlight Skill: Transitions

Style

Skill: Style	Skill: Style • Your Turn Argumentative Writing Process: Revise	Units 3–4 Skill: Style Spotlight Skill: Style

Conclusions

Skill: Conclusions	Skill: Conclusions • Your Turn Argumentative Writing Process: Revise	Units 3–4 Skill: Conclusions Spotlight Skill: Conclusions

Active and Passive Voice

Grammar: Active and Passive Voice	Grammar: Active and Passive Voice • Your Turn Argumentative Writing Process: Edit and Publish	Grammar: Verbs—Direct Objects Grammar: Verbs—Main and Helping Verbs

Verb Moods

Grammar: Verb Moods	Grammar: Verb Moods • Your Turn Argumentative Writing Process: Edit and Publish	Grammar: Sentence Structure—Sentence Types Grammar: Writing for Effect

Consistent Verb Voice and Mood

Grammar: Consistent Verb Voice and Mood	Grammar: Consistent Verb Voice and Mood • Your Turn Argumentative Writing Process: Edit and Publish	Grammar: Verbs—Consistent Verb Tenses

Argumentative Writing Process: Plan

Introduce the Extended Writing Project

- What is the prompt asking you to do?
- Which characteristics of literary analysis writing will you need to learn more about in order to respond to the prompt?
- What are the six characteristics of argumentative and literary analysis writing?

DIFFERENTIATED QUESTIONS

- What does it mean to **belong?**
- How does a metaphor help explain how a person belongs or show what a person feels?
- Which texts from the unit best show metaphors?

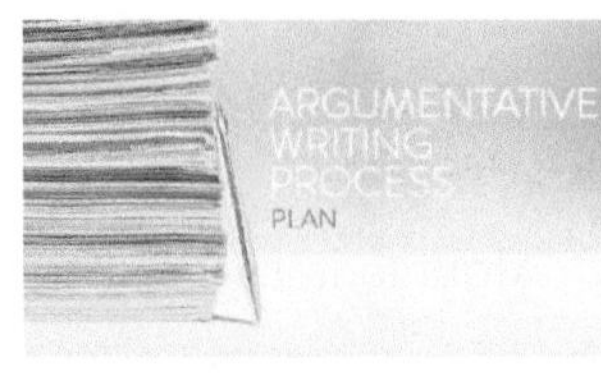

Argumentative Writing Process: Plan

PLAN | DRAFT | REVISE | EDIT AND PUBLISH

It's not always easy to define who we are. However, many of this unit's authors use metaphors to communicate an individual's perspective on his or her identity or sense of belonging. In *The House on Mango Street*, Esperanza describes her name by saying, "It is the Mexican records my father plays on Sunday mornings when he is shaving, songs like sobbing." In the poem "Slam, Dunk, & Hook," the speaker artfully describes how he and his friends play in sync during a basketball game: "Our bodies spun / On swivels of bone & faith." In the story "Abuela Invents the Zero," Abuela also uses a metaphor to express what it feels like to be rejected by a family member: "You made me feel like a zero, like a nothing."

WRITING PROMPT

What is the power of a metaphor?

Examine the texts from this unit and select three powerful metaphors that deepen our understanding of identity and belonging. Your analysis should explain each metaphor and make an argument about how the metaphor reveals something about each speaker, character, or author. Be sure your literary analysis includes the following:

- an introduction
- a claim
- coherent body paragraphs
- reasons and relevant evidence
- a formal style

Introduction to Argumentative Writing

An argumentative essay is a form of persuasive writing where the writer makes a claim about a topic and then provides evidence—facts, details, examples, and quotations—to convince readers to accept and agree with the writer's claim. In order to provide convincing supporting evidence for an argumentative essay, the writer must often do outside research as well as cite the sources of the evidence that is presented in the essay.

A literary analysis is a form of argumentative writing that tries to persuade readers to accept the writer's interpretation of a literary text. Good literary analysis writing builds an argument with a strong claim, convincing reasons, relevant textual evidence, and a clear structure with an introduction, body, and conclusion. The characteristics of argumentative and literary analysis writing include:

- introduction
- claim
- thesis statement
- textual evidence
- transitions
- formal style
- conclusion

As you continue with this Extended Writing Project, you'll receive more instruction and practice at crafting each of the characteristics of argumentative writing to create your own literary analysis.

Review the Rubric

Have students examine the "Argumentative Writing Rubric—Grade 8" grading rubric. Inform students that this is the same rubric that will be used to evaluate their completed Argumentative Extended Writing Project.

Read and Annotate

As students read, have them use the Annotation Tool to identify and label the characteristics of argumentative and literary analysis writing:

- introduction
- claim
- thesis statement
- textual evidence
- transitions
- formal style
- conclusion

When students finish reading, ask them to share their annotations in small groups.

ANNOTATION GUIDE

Find the following quotes in the Student Model. Then, use the Annotation Tool to label each quote as an example of introduction, thesis statement, reason, textual evidence, or conclusion.

- *Who are you?* At first this question seems easy. A person might answer it by saying his or her name. However, a name is just one small part of a person's identity.
- Each one of these metaphors helps readers see how a character's community can influence his or her identity.
- In *The House on Mango Street*, Esperanza uses her name as a metaphor for the way she sees herself and her place in her community.
- He also uses the metaphor of a labyrinth to show how strong every member of the group feels when they play basketball together: "In the roundhouse / Labyrinth our bodies / Created, we could almost / Last forever, poised in midair / Like storybook sea monsters" (lines 7–10).
- In the poem, the speaker and his friends create a strong community based on basketball.
- In each text, figurative language helps readers understand how a community can influence the way people see themselves.

READ AND ANNOTATE

Pair students with on-grade-level peers to complete the annotation activity.

Extended Writing Project

Before you get started on your own literary analysis, read this literary analysis that one student, Donovan, wrote in response to the writing prompt. As you read the Model, highlight and annotate the features of argumentative writing that Donovan included in his narrative.

STUDENT MODEL

What's in a Name? How Metaphor Can Express Identity

1 *Who are you?* At first this question seems easy. A person might answer it by saying his or her name. However, a name is just one small part of a person's identity. Identity includes memories, goals, thoughts, and actions. While one could argue that those aspects of a person can never be captured in writing, authors can use figurative language to reveal complex parts of a character's unique identity. In the excerpts from *The House on Mango Street*, the main character's name is a metaphor for how she feels about the world around her. Likewise, in the poem "Slam, Dunk, & Hook," the game of basketball, a labyrinth, and a sea monster are used to act as metaphors for a strong community. They drastically differ from the metaphor that Abuela uses in "Abuela Invents the Zero." In that story, the number zero is used by Abuela to express how it feels to be excluded by a group. Each one of these metaphors helps readers see how a character's community can influence his or her identity.

2 In *The House on Mango Street*, Esperanza uses her name as a metaphor for the way she sees herself and her place in her community. Esperanza's name is defined in this selection, and she also defines what it means to her: "In English my name means hope. In Spanish it means too many letters. It means sadness, it means waiting. It is like the number nine. A muddy color" (paragraph 9). As a reflection of her name, Esperanza does have some hope that her parents will purchase a house that they have promised her. She thinks that a better home might make her feel more proud about her place in the community. Even if that dream were to come true, however, Esperanza would still see her own name as a barrier to belonging. This is evident when she says, "At school they say my name funny as if the syllables were made out of tin and hurt the roof of your mouth" (paragraph 13). Esperanza's name is a major part of her identity, so she feels out of place when her classmates struggle with it. In this excerpt, she even wants to change her name to solve

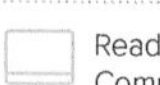

TEXT TALK

Structure and Organization

Where does Donovan identify the structure and purpose of his analysis?

See paragraph 1: Donovan explains that he will compare three selections to discuss the way each text uses figurative language.

Organization and Focus

How does Donovan focus his ideas about the selections?

See paragraphs 2–4: In each body paragraph, Donovan analyzes the use of figurative language in one of the texts.

NOTES

the problem. As a result, her name acts as a metaphor, and it holds more than one meaning in this selection. It shows her desire to belong to a community and the difficulty of doing that.

3 Like Esperanza, the speaker in the poem "Slam, Dunk, & Hook" wants to connect with other people. In the poem, the speaker and his friends create a strong community based on basketball. In fact, the speaker even speaks on behalf of the group by using the pronouns *we* and *our* instead of *I* throughout the poem. These pronouns emphasize that the speaker is describing experiences he has shared with his friends. He also uses the metaphor of a labyrinth to show how strong every member of the group feels when they play basketball together: "In the roundhouse / Labyrinth our bodies / Created, we could almost / Last forever, poised in midair / Like storybook sea monsters" (lines 7–10). The metaphor shows that the speaker and his friends feel invincible when they play. A labyrinth is a huge, complex maze, so the speaker's comparison suggests that their moves are highly developed and impressive. In addition, the comparison to "storybook sea monsters" shows that playing basketball makes the speaker and his friends feel as if they are tough competitors who are ready to destroy their opponents. One could argue that this excerpt includes "mixed metaphors," disconnected comparisons that sound like nonsense when strung together; however, they do have important connections. A labyrinth and a sea monster are both associated with myths and legends, so they imply that these friends have superhuman strength and endurance when they play together. Furthermore, a labyrinth and sea monster are made up of many parts that work together to create entities that can be "beautiful & dangerous," like this group of friends (line 40). Although there are multiple metaphors in this poem, they show readers that a strong community can help each member thrive.

4 As a contrast, the short story "Abuela Invents the Zero" shows how insignificant a person can feel when he or she does not conform to a community's expectations. In this story, Constancia and her family are visited by Abuela, and Constancia notices that her grandmother looks out of place everywhere they go. When they go to church, for example, she compares Abuela to the explorer Captain Cousteau, trying to make sense of a new underwater world. When Abuela has trouble finding her seat, Constancia then ignores her because she is

TEXT TALK

Development of Ideas

Are Donovan's ideas developed and well supported?

Answers will vary. See paragraphs 2–4. Sample answer: Yes, I think Donovan includes clear reasons to support his claim in each body paragraph along with specific textual evidence.

Organization and Coherence

Where does Donovan use a transition to compare and contrast two of the selections?

Answers will vary. Sample answer: To begin paragraph 3, Donovan uses the transition "Like Esperanza" to compare Esperanza's point of view with the speaker's point of view in the poem "Slam, Dunk, & Hook."

Development of Ideas and Evidence

How does Donovan use specific text evidence to contribute to his analysis?

Answers will vary. Sample answer: In paragraph 3, Donovan quotes lines of the poem to support his ideas.

Word Choice

Where do you find Donovan's word choice especially strong?

Answers will vary. Sample answer: In paragraph 3, Donovan uses the phrase "highly developed and impressive" to describe the speaker's moves. The phrase shows how the poet's words affect the writer's understanding of the speaker.

Sentence Fluency

Choose one sentence that you think is really effective. Why do you think it's so strong?

Answers will vary. Sample answer: I think the sentence in paragraph 4 is strong: "As a contrast, the short story 'Abuela Invents the Zero' shows how insignificant a person can feel when he or she does not conform to a community's expectations." Donovan uses a transition phrase that connects the sentence to the previous paragraph along with verbs in the active voice and indicative mood. They make the statement both strong and clear.

overwhelmed with embarrassment. After they return home, Abuela tells Constancia how she felt when Constancia failed to help her: "You made me feel like a zero, like a nothing" (paragraph 16). She uses a simile, a comparison that includes the words *like* or *as*, to express her feelings of worthlessness. The "Zero" in the story's title, "Abuela Invents the Zero," also shows how important this simile is. It suggests that Constancia does not realize how much neglect can hurt another person until her grandmother explains it. As a result, Abuela's simile shows the need to help relatives find ways to be a part of a community, even if that community is unfamiliar to them.

5 *The House on Mango Street*, "Slam, Dunk, & Hook," and "Abuela Invents the Zero" each use metaphor to show readers how community can affect a person's identity. In *The House on Mango Street*, Esperanza's name reveals a longing to feel like she belongs in her community. The speaker in "Slam, Dunk, & Hook" also offers a different perspective by using metaphors to illustrate how a person can find strength in community bonds. Under different circumstances, Constancia abandons her grandmother when she is lost in "Abuela Invents the Zero." Abuela then uses the number zero as a metaphor to explain how that disrespect made her feel. In each text, figurative language helps readers understand how a community can influence the way people see themselves.

TEXT TALK

Conventions

Does Donovan write his essay in active or passive voice? Can you find an example of an active voice verb Donovan uses?

Answers will vary. Sample answer: Donovan uses the active voice. Paragraph 5 shows active verbs in the first sentence: "*The House on Mango Street*, 'Slam, Dunk, & Hook,' and 'Abuela Invents the Zero' each use metaphor to show readers how community can affect a person's identity." In this sentence, "use" and "can affect" are examples of active verbs.

WRITE

Writers often take notes before they sit down to write. Think about what you've learned so far about literary analyses to help you begin prewriting.

- Which texts from the unit would you like to write about?
- How do the characters, narrators, speakers, or authors of those texts express their ideas about identity and belonging?
- What kind of figurative language do the characters, narrators, speakers, or authors use?
- How does that figurative language, including metaphor, help them communicate their ideas in a unique way?
- What kinds of textual evidence might you use to support your ideas?
- What kinds of transition words and phrases could you use to connect your ideas in a logical way?

Response Instructions

Use the questions in the bulleted list to write a one-paragraph summary. Your summary should identify the texts you want to write about and at least one idea about how the characters, speakers, or authors of those texts use metaphor and other figurative language to express themselves.

Don't worry about including all of the details now; focus only on the most essential and important elements. You will refer back to this short paragraph as you continue through the steps of the writing process.

Write

Circulate as students use the questions in the bulleted list to plan their writing. See the instructions for scaffolding and differentiation that follow.

CHECK FOR SUCCESS

If students struggle to come up with answers for the questions in the lesson, work with students to provide an answer to one question and then help them build from there.

For example, start by asking students, "How does the character/narrator/speaker/author express his or her identity?" or "What metaphor does the author include in the selection?" Once students have answered one question, help them to work through a second question until they've begun to build some momentum. It may be helpful to start with a different question than the one that's listed first in the lesson.

Review Prompt and Rubric

Before students begin writing, review the writing prompt and rubric with the class.

Response Instructions

Use the questions in the bulleted list to write a one-paragraph summary. Your summary should identify the texts you want to write about and at least one idea about how the characters, speakers, or authors of those texts use metaphor and other figurative language to express themselves.

Don't worry about including all of the details now; focus only on the most essential and important elements. You will refer back to this short paragraph as you continue through the steps of the writing process.

Score	Plan	Language and Conventions
4	The writer responds to the questions, and the writing is clear and focused.	The writer demonstrates a consistent command of grammar, punctuation, and usage conventions. Although minor errors may be evident, they do not detract from the fluency or clarity of the writing.
3	The writer responds to the questions, but the writing is not always clear or focused.	The writer demonstrates an adequate command of grammar, punctuation, and usage conventions. Although some errors may be evident, they create few (if any) disruptions in the fluency or clarity of the writing.
2	The writer responds to the questions, but the writing is somewhat unclear and unfocused.	The writer demonstrates a partial command of grammar, punctuation, and usage conventions. Some distracting errors may be evident, at times creating minor disruptions in the fluency or clarity of the writing.
1	The writer responds to the questions, but the writing is very unclear and unfocused.	The writer demonstrates little or no command of grammar, punctuation, and usage conventions. Serious and persistent errors create disruptions in the fluency of the writing and sometimes interfere with meaning.
0	The writer does not provide a relevant response to the prompt or does not provide a response at all.	Serious and persistent errors overwhelm the writing and interfere with the meaning of the response as a whole, making the writer's meaning impossible to understand.

Write

SCAFFOLDS

Use the scaffolds below to differentiate instruction for your ELL English Language Learners and A Approaching grade-level learners.

ELL BEGINNING, INTERMEDIATE With the help of the word bank, write a response using the paragraph frame.

ADVANCED, ADVANCED HIGH Write a response using the sentence starters.

A APPROACHING Write a response using the sentence starters.

BEGINNING / INTERMEDIATE		ADVANCED, ADVANCED HIGH / APPROACHING
Word Bank	**Paragraph Frame**	**Sentence Starters**
The House on Mango Street basketball "Abuela Invents the Zero" zero "Slam, Dunk, & Hook" community name	The authors of ____, ____, and ____ use metaphor to show why it is important to be part of a community. In *The House on Mango Street*, Esperanza's ____ is a metaphor for how she looks at the world. In "Slam, Dunk, & Hook," ____ is a metaphor. The speaker and his friends create a ____ when they play together. In "Abuela Invents the Zero," the number ____ is a metaphor for feeling left out.	• The authors of ____, ____, and ____ use metaphor to show . . . • ____ is a metaphor for . . . • The character shows how she feels about herself when . . . • The speaker in the poem feels like he belongs when . . . • The character ____ feels like . . .

Peer Review

Rate

Respond to the following with a point rating that reflects your opinion.

	1 2 3 4
Ideas	
Evidence	
Language and Conventions	

Submit

Students should submit substantive feedback to two peers using the review instructions below.

- Does the writer identify three texts he or she is going to write about?
- Does the writer identify ideas about identity and belonging in each text?
- Does the writer identify how figurative language conveys those ideas in each text?
- Has the writer found strong textual evidence to support each idea?
- Are there any ideas that could be improved upon? How so?

SENTENCE FRAMES

- The writer (does / does not) address each part of the prompt because ____.
- Each idea (is / is not) clearly supported by textual evidence because ____.
- I think you could improve ____ by (adding / clarifying / describing) ____.

Skill: Organizing Argumentative Writing

Introduce the Skill

Watch the Concept Definition video and read the following definition with your students.

Argumentative writing intends to convince readers of an author's position or point of view on a subject. To build an argument, authors introduce **claims**, which are arguments they will support with logical and valid reasoning and relevant evidence from reliable sources. In order to make a convincing argument, authors must distinguish their claim or claims from opposing points of view, or **counterclaims**.

When a writer is planning an argumentative essay, he or she will need to choose an organizational structure to present the argument in a logical and persuasive way. An **organizational structure** is the order or pattern that a writer uses to structure and present ideas or events. A writer of an argumentative text may do one of the following:

- discuss a claim or claims in order of importance
- compare and contrast ideas
- present cause-and-effect relationships
- list advantages and disadvantages
- describe a problem and offer a solution

Skill: Organizing Argumentative Writing

••• CHECKLIST FOR ORGANIZING ARGUMENTATIVE WRITING

As you consider how to organize your writing for your argumentative essay, use the following questions as a guide:

- What is my position on this topic?
- Have I chosen the best organizing structure to present my information logically?
- Have I acknowledged, or recognized, opposing claims and presented evidence to distinguish them from my own?
- Can my claim be supported by logical reasoning and relevant evidence?
- Do I have enough evidence to support my claim?

Follow these steps to plan out the organization of your argumentative essay, including organizing your reasons and evidence logically:

- Identify your claim.
  > Write a statement that will present your claim in the first paragraph.
- Choose an organizing structure that will present your claim logically.
- Recognize claims that oppose or disagree with your claim, and present evidence that distinguishes your claim from others.
- Identify reasons and evidence that support your claim.
- Note that textual evidence can be proven to be true in other sources, and may be in the form of:
  > numbers or statistics
  > quotes from experts
  > names or dates
  > reference sources

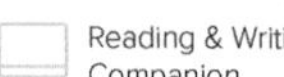

TURN AND TALK

Turn to your partner and explain the kind of structure you used in the last essay you wrote and why you chose that structure. If you aren't sure about the structure, describe your essay to your partner to figure out which one you used.

SPEAKING FRAMES

- I used a ____ structure in the last essay I wrote.
- I chose that structure because ____.
- The structure helped me express my ideas about ____.
- It was an effective way to organize my writing because ____.

YOUR TURN

Read the quotations from a student's argumentative essay called "Mirrors and Windows" below. Then, complete the chart by matching each quotation with its correct place in the outline.

	Quotations
A	To deepen their understanding of shared and diverse experiences, people need to read books that act like mirrors and books that act like windows.
B	Books that act like windows show readers cultural backgrounds, experiences, and challenges that are not familiar to them. They help readers learn about experiences that they have not had and see the world in new ways.
C	How can books act like mirrors and windows?
D	Books that act like mirrors show readers cultural backgrounds, experiences, and challenges that are familiar to them. They can help readers see their experiences in new ways.
E	One can argue that all good literature acts like a mirror and a window since it should include universal themes and unique perspectives. However, it is important to read books with characters from a wide range of backgrounds to learn about different cultures, struggles, and points of view.

Outline	Quotation
Introductory Statement:	
Thesis Statement:	
Main Idea 1:	
Main Idea 2:	
Main Idea 3:	

Your Turn

Ask students to complete the Your Turn activity.

Introductory Statement:	C
Thesis Statement:	A
Main Idea 1:	D
Main Idea 2:	B
Main Idea 3:	E

SKILL VOCABULARY

argumentative writing / la escritura argumentativa *noun* a genre of writing in which a writer presents a central claim and provides reasons and evidence to support that claim COGNATE

claim / la afirmación *noun* the writer's or speaker's position on a debatable issue or problem

counterclaim / el contraargumento *noun* an idea that is contrary to the author's position or point of view; an opposing claim

organizational structure / la estructura organizativa *noun* the order or pattern that a writer uses to organize information, such as cause and effect or compare and contrast COGNATE

Your Turn

Ask students to complete the Your Turn activity. Answers will vary.

Introductory Statement:	How is an identity formed? And can it be changed?
Thesis Statement:	These texts use metaphor to show different ways that people may develop their identities.
Main Idea 1:	In "The Road Not Taken," the speaker uses a divide in a road as a metaphor for a major decision that shapes the kind of life he will lead.
Main Idea 2:	In "Theories of Time and Space," the narrator uses travel as a metaphor to show that our identities are constantly changing as we face unknowns.
Main Idea 3:	In "So Where Are You From," the narrator uses the idea of a country as a metaphor for one person's unique identity.

YOUR TURN

Complete the chart below by writing a short summary of what you will focus on in each section of your essay.

Outline	Summary
Introductory Statement:	
Thesis Statement:	
Main Idea 1:	
Main Idea 2:	
Main Idea 3:	

Writer's Notebook

Project a basic outline on the board. Ask students to fill in their own outlines based on the basic outline, as Donovan did in the Student Model.

TURN AND TALK

Allow students to share their outlines orally in pairs or small groups before freewriting.

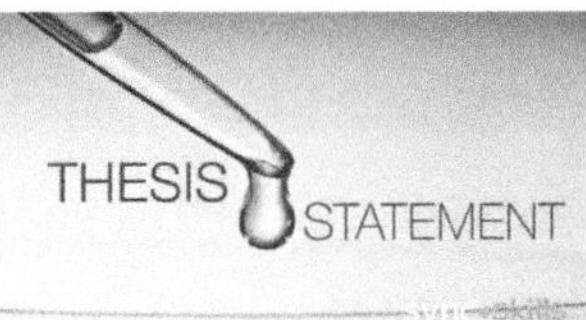

Skill: Thesis Statement

••• CHECKLIST FOR THESIS STATEMENT

Before you begin writing your thesis statement, ask yourself the following questions:

- What is the prompt asking me to write about?
- What is the topic of my essay? How can I state it clearly for the reader?
- What claim do I want to make about the topic of this essay? Is my opinion clear to my reader?
- Does my thesis statement introduce the body of my essay?
- Where should I place my thesis statement?

Here are some methods to introduce and develop your claim and topic clearly:

- Think about the topic and central idea of your essay.
  > The central idea of an argument is stated as a claim, or what will be proven or shown to be true.
  > Identify as many claims as you intend to prove.
- Write a clear statement about the central idea or claim. Your thesis statement should:
  > let the reader anticipate the body of your essay
  > respond completely to the writing prompt
- Consider the best placement for your thesis statement.
  > If your response is short, you may want to get right to the point. Your thesis statement may be presented in the first sentence of the essay.
  > If your response is longer (as in a formal essay), you can build up your thesis statement. In this case, you can place your thesis statement at the end of your introductory paragraph.

V SKILL VOCABULARY

thesis statement / la presentación de la tesis *noun* a statement that shares the main idea of an argumentative or informational essay

introduction / la introducción *noun* the opening paragraph or section of an essay COGNATE

body paragraph / el párrafo del cuerpo *noun* a paragraph that appears between the introduction and the conclusion of an essay

conclusion / la conclusión *noun* the closing paragraph or section of an essay; a closing argument in an argumentative text COGNATE

Skill: Thesis Statement

Introduce the Skill

Watch the Concept Definition video and read the following definition with your students.

In an essay, a **thesis statement** expresses the writer's main idea about a topic. The thesis statement usually appears in the **introduction**, or opening paragraph of your essay, and is often the last sentence of the introduction. The **body paragraphs** of the essay should offer a thorough explanation of the thesis statement as well as supporting details, reasons, and relevant evidence. The thesis is often restated in the **conclusion** of an essay.

TURN AND TALK

Turn to your partner and think of a situation in which the ability to make a clear, strong thesis statement might help you and your audience. As examples, that might be necessary during sports events, interviews, group meetings, when writing to leaders, or when writing for publications.

ELL SPEAKING FRAMES

- A clear, strong thesis statement can help the writer / speaker ____.
- A clear, strong thesis statement can help a reader / an audience ____.

Your Turn

Ask students to complete the Your Turn activity.

B	A
C	D
E	F

Write

Ask students to complete the writing assignment.

ELL REWRITE CHECKLIST

A Topic

- ☐ What question is the writing prompt asking?
- ☐ Does your thesis statement respond to each part of that question?
- ☐ Does your thesis statement let readers know how you will support it?

Clarity

- ☐ Is your claim an opinion that readers can debate?
- ☐ Is your claim clear?

Organization

- ☐ What information do you need to share before presenting your thesis statement?
- ☐ If this is a short response, did you place your thesis statement in the first sentence?
- ☐ If this is a multi-paragraph response, did you place your thesis statement at the end of the introductory paragraph?

YOUR TURN

Read the sentences below. Then, complete the chart by sorting them into those that are effective thesis statements and those that are not.

	Sentences
A	Shirley Jackson's "The Lottery" is set in a small town.
B	In "The Monkey's Paw," W. W. Jacobs warns readers about the perils of mocking superstition.
C	Walter Dean Myers's *Monster* shows that a person's environment can change the way they see themselves.
D	Walter Dean Myers's *Monster* is both a novel and a screenplay.
E	"The Lottery" serves as a warning against blindly following tradition without considering the consequences.
F	"The Monkey's Paw" is a suspenseful story.

Effective Thesis Statement	Ineffective Thesis Statement

WRITE

Follow the steps in the checklist section to draft a thesis statement for your literary analysis.

Writer's Notebook

Project a famous speech, such as Patrick Henry's Speech to the Second Virginia Convention or Abraham Lincoln's Gettysburg Address, on the board. Have students identify the thesis statement in the speech and write why the author's method of communicating his claim or claims is effective.

ELL TURN AND TALK

Allow students to share their thesis statements orally in pairs or small groups before writing.

Skill: Reasons and Relevant Evidence

Introduce the Skill

Watch the Concept Definition video and read the following definition with your students.

An **argument** is a set of reasons designed to persuade others to adopt a certain point of view or take a certain action. The **claim** is the main idea of the argument. The structure of an argument consists of a claim and the support for that claim. Support for the claim includes reasons and evidence. **Reasons** are logical explanations that state why the author believes in his or her claim and why others should accept the claim. **Relevant evidence** consists of facts, statistics, specific examples, and expert opinions and quotations from reliable sources that uphold the claim. To be relevant and reliable, evidence for an argument must come from **credible sources** that contain verifiable information closely connected to the topic and essential to the reader's understanding of the argument.

TURN AND TALK

Turn to your partner and discuss the last time you tried to convince your parents or guardian to let you do something. What kinds of supporting details did you include in your argument? How did they help you make your case?

SPEAKING FRAMES

- I tried to convince my ____ to let me ____.
- A supporting detail I used was ____.
- It helped me make my case because ____.
- My argument was / was not successful because ____.

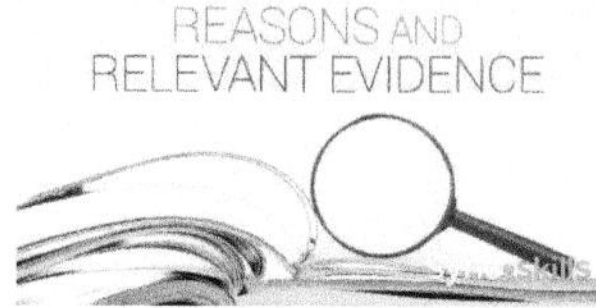

Skill: Reasons and Relevant Evidence

••• CHECKLIST FOR REASONS AND RELEVANT EVIDENCE

As you begin to determine what reasons and relevant evidence will support your claim(s), use the following questions as a guide:

- What is the claim (or claims) that I am making in my argument?
- What textual evidence am I using to support this claim? Is it relevant?
- Am I quoting the source accurately?
- Does my evidence display logical reasoning and relate to the claim I am making?

Use the following steps as a guide to help you determine how you will support your claim(s) with logical reasoning and relevant evidence, using accurate and credible sources:

- Identify the claim(s) you will make in your argument.
- Select evidence from credible sources that will convince others to accept your claim(s).
  - > Look for reliable and relevant sources of information online, such as government or educational websites.
  - > Search print resources such as books written by an expert or authority on a topic.
- Explain the connection between your claim(s) and the evidence selected in which you demonstrate an understanding of the topic or text.
- Think about whether your reasoning is logical and develops naturally from the evidence you have found to support your claim.

SKILL VOCABULARY

argument / el argumento *noun* a set of claims, evidence, and reasons designed to persuade others to adopt a certain point of view or to take a certain action COGNATE

claim / la afirmación *noun* the writer's or speaker's position on a debatable issue or problem

reason / la razón *noun* an explanation that states why others should accept a claim

Your Turn

Ask students to complete the Your Turn activity.

A	B
E	C
F	D

YOUR TURN

Read each piece of text evidence from *The House on Mango Street* below. Then, complete the chart by sorting them into those that support Donovan's thesis statement and those that do not.

	Text Evidence
A	You live *there*? The way she said it made me feel like nothing. *There*. I lived *there*.
B	Once when we were living on Loomis, a nun from my school passed by and saw me playing out front. The laundromat downstairs had been boarded up because it had been robbed two days before and the owner had painted on the wood YES WE'RE OPEN so as not to lose business.
C	This was the house Papa talked about when he held a lottery ticket and this was the house Mama dreamed up in the stories she told us before we went to bed.
D	The house on Mango Street isn't it. For the time being, Mama says. Temporary, says Papa.
E	They are the only ones who understand me. I am the only one who understands them. Four skinny trees with skinny necks and pointy elbows like mine. Four who do not belong here but are here.
F	In English my name means hope. In Spanish it means too many letters. It means sadness, it means waiting. It is like the number nine. A muddy color. It is the Mexican records my father plays on Sunday mornings when he is shaving, songs like sobbing.

Supports Thesis Statement	Does Not Support Thesis Statement

SKILL VOCABULARY

relevant / relevante ***adjective*** appropriate and logically related to the topic COGNATE

evidence / la evidencia ***noun*** facts, examples, and expert opinions that support a claim COGNATE

credible source / la fuente confiable ***noun*** a source that is trustworthy and believable

YOUR TURN

Complete the chart below by identifying textual evidence from each selection you've chosen that you can use to develop your own thesis statement.

Selection	Textual Evidence
Selection #1	
Selection #2	
Selection #3	

Your Turn

Ask students to complete the Your Turn activity. Answers will vary.

Selection #1	In "The Road Not Taken," the speaker uses a divide in the road as a metaphor for a major decision that has helped shape who he is: "Two roads diverged in a wood, and I— / I took the one less traveled by, / And that has made all the difference" (lines 18–20).
Selection #2	In "Theories of Time and Space," the narrator shows that identities are constantly changing as we move through each day, so even one's home is never the same once you have left it: "You can get there / from here, though / there's no going home. / Everywhere you go will be somewhere / you've never been" (lines 1–4).
Selection #3	In "So Where Are You From?," the narrator uses the metaphor of a country to describe the main character as a unique and complex individual: "She was her own country, with her own history of civil wars, revolutions, healing and growth."

Writer's Notebook

Ask students to think of an extracurricular activity or school club they belong to. Ask them to pretend they want a new student to join this group. They should think of a claim along with reasons and relevant evidence that support their claim. Have students use that information to write a short dialogue in which they make their argument and imagine the new student's responses to it.

TURN AND TALK

Allow students to share their dialogues orally in pairs or small groups before writing the short dialogues in their Writer's Notebook.

Argumentative Writing Process: Draft

Write

Ask students to complete the writing assignment.

CHECK FOR SUCCESS

If students struggle to begin drafting their literary analysis, ask them the following questions:

- What is your claim? Is it included in your thesis statement?
- What reasons do you have for supporting your claim?
- What textual evidence best supports your reasons?
- How will the organization of your essay help readers understand your claim?

DRAFT CHECKLIST

- ☐ Did I include a clear and strong thesis statement?
- ☐ Did I include three logical reasons to support that statement?
- ☐ Is the order of my essay easy for readers to follow?
- ☐ Does my conclusion restate my thesis statement?

Extended Writing Project

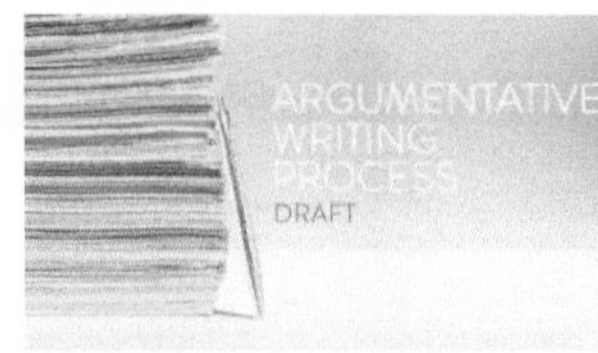

Argumentative Writing Process: Draft

PLAN | DRAFT | REVISE | EDIT AND PUBLISH

You have already made progress toward writing your literary analysis. Now it is time to draft your literary analysis.

 WRITE

Use your plan and other responses in your Binder to draft your literary analysis. You may also have new ideas as you begin drafting. Feel free to explore those new ideas as you have them. You can also ask yourself these questions:

- Have I stated my claim clearly?
- Have I supported my claim with logical reasons and relevant evidence?
- Does my organization make sense?

Before you submit your draft, read it over carefully. You want to be sure that you've responded to all aspects of the prompt.

102 Reading & Writing Companion

Peer Review

Students should submit substantive feedback to two peers using the review instructions below.

- Does the writer's thesis statement include a clear claim and a preview of how he or she will support that claim?
- Has the writer strongly supported the claim with reasons and relevant evidence? Could support be added or improved?
- Are there any ideas that could be improved on? How so?

SENTENCE FRAMES

- The thesis statement is ____.
- One example of strong support for a claim is ____.
- You can (add / improve) the ____ by ____.

Here is Donovan's literary analysis draft. There may be mistakes in the draft, but he can correct those later in the process. As you read, identify reasons and relevant evidence that develop the argument in his thesis statement.

STUDENT MODEL: FIRST DRAFT

NOTES

What's In A Name? How Metaphor Can Express Identity

~~It can be hard to define who you are. In fiction, authors have to define their characters for readers. Characters' unique identities are shown through figurative language, such as metaphors. In *The House on Mango Street*, "Slam, Dunk, & Hook," and "Abuela Invents the Zero," metaphors show not only who the characters are, but why it is important to be part of a community.~~

Who are you? At first this question seems easy. A person might answer it by saying his or her name. However, a name is just one small part of a person's identity. Identity includes memories, goals, thoughts, and actions. While one could argue that those aspects of a person can never be captured in writing, authors can use figurative language to reveal complex parts of a character's unique identity. In the excerpts from *The House on Mango Street,* the main character's name is a metaphor for how she feels about the world around her. Likewise, in the poem "Slam, Dunk, & Hook," the game of basketball, a labyrinth, and a sea monster are used to act as metaphors for a strong community. They drastically differ from the metaphor that Abuela uses in "Abuela Invents the Zero." In that story, the number zero is used by Abuela to express how it feels to be excluded by a group. Each one of these metaphors helps readers see how a character's community can influence his or her identity.

Skill: Introductions

Donovan revises his paragraph to include an interesting hook, a preview of the argument that he will make in his essay, and a claim that clearly relates to the rest of the paragraph.

~~When I read this part of *The House On Mango Street*, I saw that Esperanza uses her name to show her identity. It also shows that her relationship is connected to her community. Esperanza's name and what it means to her is defined in this selection: "In English my name means hope. In Spanish it means too many letters. It means sadness, it means waiting. It is like the number nine. A muddy color" (paragraph 9). You can see that Esperanza has some hope. She hopes that her parents will get a nice house. If they do, she can then have freinds over to hang out. There's no way that'll happen until~~

EMULATE A MENTOR TEXT

Have students choose a sentence or passage from one of the mentor texts in the unit that they find particularly effective. Allow students time to discuss their selections in a small group, exploring why the passage stood out to them. Was it the structure? Writing style? Something else? Then, encourage students to emulate their mentor text in a section of their own writing.

Analyze Student Model

Have students discuss the questions in the lesson as well as the Student Model draft. Ask:

- How does Donovan build toward his thesis statement?
- What is effective about the way Donovan organizes his ideas?
- How does Donovan's use of reasons and evidence help support his thesis statement?

Encourage students to share ideas for their own literary analyses based on the questions in the lesson.

SPEAKING FRAMES

- The writer builds toward his thesis statement with details like ____. This approach (is / is not) effective because ____.
- The writer structured his or her argument by ____. This organization (is / is not) effective because ____.
- The writer's reasons / evidence support his or her thesis statement because ____.
- An idea that I have for my literary analysis is ____.

Introductions

Discuss the Model

1. The Skill Model shows how Donovan changed the introduction of his literary analysis. How did he change it? He made his claim more specific, added a hook, and previewed his argument.
2. How do those changes improve his literary analysis? Answers will vary. Sample answer: Donovan added an engaging hook, considered a counterclaim, and added necessary information.

SPEAKING FRAMES

- Donovan changed the introduction of his literary analysis by ____.
- These changes improved his literary analysis because ____.

Introductions

Connect to Mentor Text

Project the following example of an introduction from the Big Idea Blast: What makes you, you? Discuss with your students:

> What if you woke up one day with your mind in someone else's body? Your personality, your memories, and all of your knowledge would live on in a different body. Meanwhile, your body would continue to live with the mind of a stranger within it. Is your body still a part of you if someone else's mind is inside of it? Would you still be you if you lived the life of a stranger?

Ask students:

- What do you notice about this introduction?
- What about the introduction appeals to you as a reader?

Style

Discuss the Model

1. What nonfiction that you've recently read is written in a formal style? Answers will vary. Sample answers: an informational article, an op-ed, a magazine article, a peer's essay
2. How does Donovan make the language in his draft more formal? Donovan replaced slang with more formal language and found opportunities to add the academic term "metaphor" to his work. He also removed his use of the first-person point of view.
3. How does Donovan change the structure of some sentences in his draft? Donovan varied the length of his sentences by combining two short sentences with conjunctions and transitions and breaking a long sentence into two independent clauses.
4. What are examples of some conventions that Donovan corrects? Donovan placed end quotes outside of periods in his revision, corrected the capitalization in the book title, corrected the spelling of "friends," and replaced a sentence with an inconsistent voice. However, he still needs to work on making sure that each sentence has a consistent voice and mood.

NOTES

~~they get that house though. And even with the house, Esperanza would still never really be cool. She says, "At school they say my name funny as if the syllables were made out of tin and hurt the roof of your mouth" (paragraph 13). Like my name, Esperanza's name is a major part of her identity, so she feels out of place when her classmates can't say it. She even wants to change her name to solve the problem. Her name acts as a metaphor. It holds more than one meaning in this selection. It shows her desire to belong to a community and the difficulty of doing that.~~

Skill: Style

Donovan looks for ways to make the style more formal. He spells out contractions and removes slang terms like "hang out" and "never really be cool." He also replaces the first-person pronoun I and second-person pronoun you with third-person pronouns. Donovan replaces a phrase with the term metaphor, one example of academic language. To vary his sentences and avoid confusing readers, Donovan combines several shorter sentences into longer sentences that are easier to follow.

In *The House on Mango Street*, Esperanza uses her name as a metaphor for the way she sees herself and her place in her community. Esperanza's name is defined in this selection, and she also defines what it means to her: "In English my name means hope. In Spanish it means too many letters. It means sadness, it means waiting. It is like the number nine. A muddy color" (paragraph 9). As a reflection of her name, Esperanza does have some hope that her parents will purchase a house that they have promised her. She thinks that a better home might make her feel more proud about her place in the community. Even if that dream were to come true, however, Esperanza would still see her own name as a barrier to belonging. This is evident when she says, "At school they say my name funny as if the syllables were made out of tin and hurt the roof of your mouth" (paragraph 13). Esperanza's name is a major part of her identity, so she feels out of place when her classmates struggle with it. In this excerpt, she even wants to change her name to solve the problem. As a result, her name acts as a metaphor, and it holds more than one meaning in this selection. It shows her desire to belong to a community and the difficulty of doing that.

Like Esperanza, the speaker in the poem "Slam, Dunk, & Hook" wants to connect with other people. In the poem, the speaker and his friends create a strong community based on basketball. The speaker even uses the pronouns we and *our* instead of *I* throughout the poem. The metaphors of a labyrinth and a sea monster also show how they feel when they play basketball together: "In the roundhouse / Labyrinth our bodies / Created, we could almost / Last forever, poised in midair / Like storybook sea monsters" (lines 7–10). The labyrinth and sea monster are made up of multiple parts that work together to create something that can be "beautiful &

SPEAKING FRAMES

- I recently read ____, which was written in a formal style.
- Donovan makes the language in his draft more formal by ____.
- Donovan changes the structure of some sentences by ____.
- One example of a convention that Donovan corrected is ____.

dangerous," a phrase that is used by the speaker to describe his group of friends (line 40). Although there are multiple metaphors in this poem, they show readers that a strong community can help each member thrive.

~~The short story "Abuela Invents the Zero" shows how insignificant a person can feel when he or she does not try to conform with a community's expectations. When Abuela visits Constancia and her family, she notices that Abuela is out of place everywhere they go. They go to church. She compares Abuela to Captain Cousteau trying to make sense of a new underwater world. Instead of helping her grandmother figure out where to go, Constancia would ignore her, and Abuela ends up getting lost.~~

As a contrast, the short story "Abuela Invents the Zero" shows how insignificant a person can feel when he or she does not conform to a community's expectations. In this story, Constancia and her family are visited by Abuela, and Constancia notices that her grandmother looks out of place everywhere they go. When they go to church, for example, she compares Abuela to the explorer Captain Cousteau, trying to make sense of a new underwater world. When Abuela has trouble finding her seat, Constancia then ignores her because she is overwhelmed with embarrassment.

Skill:
Transitions

Donovan strengthens the cohesion between these paragraphs by starting the topic sentence with the phrase "As a contrast." This transition shows readers that the third body paragraph will include reasons and evidence that significantly differ from the reasons and evidence that Donovan presented in the second body paragraph. However, both of these paragraphs still work together to support his claim.

After they return home, Abuela tells Constancia how she felt when Constancia failed to help her: "You made me feel like a zero, like a nothing" (paragraph 16). Her feelings of worthlessness are shown through this smile, a comparison that would include the words "like" or "as." "Zero" is also used in the story's title "Abuela Invents the Zero." It shows how important this simile is. It suggests that Constancia do not realize how much neglect can hurt another person until this is explained by her grandmother. So see how Abuela's simile shows the need to help relatives find ways to be a part of a community, even if that community is unfamiliar to them.

~~In conclusion, metaphor is used in *The House on Mango Street*, "Slam, Dunk, & Hook," and "Abuela Invents the Zero" to show different ideas about people and their communities. Esperanza shows how difficult it is when you have trouble fitting into a community, while strength in community bonds is found by the~~

ELL SPEAKING FRAMES

- Donovan used the transition ____ to show readers that ____.
- In Donovan's draft, a sudden jump in ideas happens when ____.
- Donovan could also have used the transition ____ to improve his paragraph by ____.

Transitions

Discuss the Model

1. How did Donovan clarify the relationship between this body paragraph and the one that precedes it? Donovan used the phrase "As a contrast" to show that this paragraph presents a reason for supporting the claim that significantly differs from the reason he presented in the paragraph before it.
2. In Donovan's draft, what is an example of a sudden jump in ideas? Answers will vary. One jump is when Donovan says that Constancia and her grandmother go to church, and then Constancia compares her grandmother to an explorer. It is not clear how these ideas are connected.
3. What is a different way that Donovan could use transitions to clarify the relationship between those ideas? Answers will vary.

Transitions

Connect to Mentor Text

Project the following examples of transitions from Michelle Obama's Commencement Address to the Santa Fe Indian School and discuss with your students:

> That's why it is so important for all of you to hold fast to your goals, and to push through any obstacles that may come your way.
>
> And here's the thing: I guarantee you that there will be obstacles—plenty of them. For example, when you get to college or wherever else you're going next, it's going to be an adjustment. College was certainly a huge adjustment for me. I had never lived away from home, away from my family for any length of time. So there were times when I felt lonely and overwhelmed during my freshman year.
>
> And what I want you to remember is if that happens to you, I want you to keep pushing forward.

Ask students:

- How does the speaker use transitions to show how the claim, reason, and evidence relate to one another in this speech?

Conclusions

Discuss the Model

1. The Skill Model shows how Donovan revised the conclusion of his essay. What changes did he make? Donovan restated his thesis statement in a new way and added a sentence to leave a lasting impression on his readers. He reviewed and clarified the reasons he had used to support his claim in the essay.
2. How did those changes improve his essay? Answers will vary. Sample answer: The changes made his conclusion clearer and more meaningful.
3. What are some other ways that Donovan could have concluded his essay? Answers will vary.

SPEAKING FRAMES

- Donovan revised his conclusion by ____.
- Those changes improved his conclusion because ____.
- Donovan could also write a conclusion in which ____.

Conclusions

Connect to Mentor Text

Project the following example of conclusions from Michelle Obama's Commencement Address to the Santa Fe Indian School and discuss with your students:

> So, graduates, in closing, I hope that you will always remember your story, and that you will carry your story with you as proudly as I carry mine. I am so proud of you. I am so excited for you to continue this extraordinary journey. And I can't wait to see everything you'll achieve and bring back to your communities.

Ask students:

- What claim does the speaker rephrase in this conclusion?
- How does she show that it is an important one?

NOTES

Skill: Conclusions

Donovan revises his conclusion to make it clearer and more engaging. Rather than repeating his thesis statement in the same words that he used in the introduction, Donovan decides to rephrase it. The rephrased thesis statement at the beginning of the conclusion shows how Donovan's argument has evolved over the course of the essay.

~~speaker in the poem. Under different circumstances, Constancia abandons her grandmother when she is lost in "Abuela Invents the Zero," and Abuela uses the number zero as a metaphor to explain how that disrespect makes her feel.~~

The *House on Mango Street*, "Slam, Dunk, & Hook," and "Abuela Invents the Zero" each use metaphor to show readers how community can effect a person's identity. In *The House on Mango Street*, Esperanza's name reveals a longing to feel like she belongs in her community. The speaker in "Slam, Dunk, & Hook" also offers a different perspective by using metaphors to illustrate how a person can find strength in community bonds. Under different circumstances, Constancia abandons her grandmother when she is lost in "Abuela Invents the Zero," and Abuela uses the number zero as a metaphor to explain how that disrespect made her feel. In each text, figurative language helps readers understand how a community can influence the way people see themselves.

Skill: Introductions

Introduce the Skill

Watch the Concept Definition video and read the following definition with your students.

The **introduction** is the opening paragraph or section of an essay or other nonfiction text. To begin an argumentative essay, writers identify the **topic**, or what the essay will be about. The most important part of the introduction in an argumentative essay is the **thesis statement**. This statement contains the writer's **claim**, or main argument, and it states something that the writer believes to be true.

In an informative/explanatory text, the introduction should provide readers with necessary information in order to introduce a topic. It should state the thesis, which in an informative/explanatory essay is a short statement that summarizes the main point of the essay and previews the ideas that will follow in the text. In an informative/explanatory essay, many writers also include one or two sentences that are called a "hook." They are intended to engage readers' interest and grab their attention so they keep reading.

Skill: Introductions

••• CHECKLIST FOR INTRODUCTIONS

Before you write your introduction, ask yourself the following questions:

- What is my claim? Have I recognized opposing claims that disagree with mine or use a different perspective? How can I use them to make my own claim more unique and specific?
- How can I introduce my topic clearly?
- How will your "hook" grab your readers' interest? You might:
  - > start with an attention-grabbing statement
  - > begin with an intriguing question
  - > use descriptive words to set a scene

Below are two strategies to help you introduce your claim and topic clearly in an introduction:

- Peer Discussion
  - > Discuss your thesis statement and plan for supporting it with a partner.
  - > Discuss claims that disagree with yours and how your claim is different from other claims on your topic.
  - > Review your thesis statement and consider revising it based on your discussion.
  - > Write ways you can introduce your thesis statement.
  - > Write a possible "hook."
  - > You may also add a counterclaim and address it.
- Freewriting
  - > Freewrite for ten minutes about your topic. Don't worry about grammar, punctuation, or having fully formed ideas. The point of freewriting is to discover ideas.
  - > Review your thesis statement and consider revising it based on ideas you have discovered.
  - > Write ways you can introduce your thesis statement.
  - > Write a possible "hook."
  - > You may also add a counterclaim and address it.

TURN AND TALK

Turn to your partner and discuss radio, television, or print advertisements that catch your attention, and explain what makes them effective and memorable.

ELL SPEAKING FRAMES

- An effective television / radio / print advertisement is ____.
- The advertisement catches my attention because ____.
- I remember the advertisement because ____.

SKILL VOCABULARY

introduction / la introducción ***noun*** the opening paragraph or section of an essay COGNATE

topic / el tema ***noun*** the subject of a literary work, usually expressed as a single word or phrase in the form of a noun

thesis statement / la presentación de la tesis ***noun*** a statement that shares the main idea of an argumentative or informational essay

Your Turn

Ask students to complete the Your Turn activity.

QUESTION 1

A. Correct. This sentence starts with an attention-grabbing description that relates to the essay topic, and it transitions into sentence 1.

B. Incorrect. This sentence provides an obvious definition and does not transition.

C. Incorrect. This sentence provides an obvious definition.

D. Incorrect. This sentence does not relate to sentence 1.

QUESTION 2

A. Incorrect. This sentence mentions only one of the three selections.

B. Incorrect. This sentence makes a general statement about metaphors in fiction and poetry.

C. Correct. This sentence lists the three selections that Donovan will analyze as a way to preview how he will support his claim.

D. Incorrect. The first clause in this sentence states a counterclaim, but it does not preview the argument that Donovan will make.

Write

Ask students to complete the writing assignment.

YOUR TURN

Choose the best answer to each question.

1. Below is Donovan's introduction from a previous draft. Donovan would like to add a sentence to grab his readers' attention. Which sentence could he add before sentence 1 to help achieve this goal?

> (1) It is not easy to capture someone's identity in a limited number of words. (2) However, authors often use figurative language, such as metaphor, to reveal characters' qualities and experiences in unique ways. (3) Authors can use metaphor to show why it is important to be part of a community.

○ A. How can you ever really understand another person?
○ B. Metaphors are comparisons between two seemingly unlike things.
○ C. Identity refers to all of the qualities that make someone who they are.
○ D. Being part of a community is an important aspect of identity.

2. Below is the introduction from a previous draft of Donovan's essay. Donovan would like to preview the main ideas that follow in his essay by revising sentence 3. Which of the following revisions will achieve that goal?

> (1) It is not easy to capture someone's identity in a limited number of words. (2) However, authors often use figurative language, such as metaphor, to reveal characters' qualities and experiences in unique ways. (3) *The House on Mango Street*, "Slam, Dunk, & Hook," and "Abuela Invents the Zero" use metaphor to show why it is important to be part of a community.

○ A. In texts like *The House on Mango Street*, Esperanza uses her name as a way to express her identity, and that kind of metaphor shows why it is important to be a part of the community.
○ B. In fiction and poetry, authors use metaphor to show why it is important to be part of a community.
○ C. *The House on Mango Street*, "Slam, Dunk, & Hook," and "Abuela Invents the Zero" use metaphor to show why it is important to be part of a community.
○ D. While some may argue that metaphors are not useful, authors can use metaphor to show why it is important to be part of a community.

WRITE

Use the steps in the checklist section to revise the introduction of your literary analysis.

 **REWRITE CHECKLIST**

 **Hook**

- ☐ What attention-grabbing statement could you include?
- ☐ How could descriptive details establish a scene that introduces your ideas?

Clarification

- ☐ Have you introduced your topic clearly?
- ☐ Have you given readers a preview of how you will support your claim?

Claim

- ☐ How is your claim different from other views of this topic?
- ☐ How can you use other views to make your claim more unique and specific?

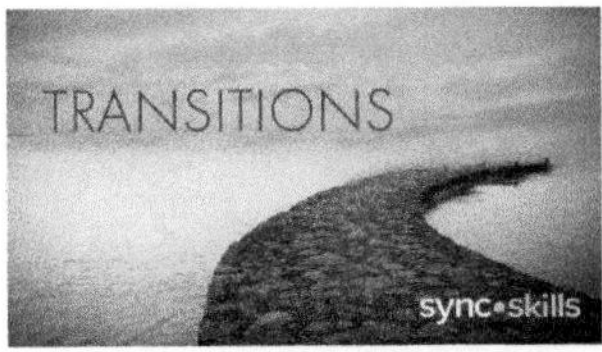

Skill: Transitions

••• CHECKLIST FOR TRANSITIONS

Before you revise your current draft to include transitions, think about:

- the key ideas you discuss in your body paragraphs
- how your paragraphs connect together to support your claim(s)
- the relationships among your claim(s), reasons, and evidence
- the logical progression of your argument

Next, reread your current draft and note areas in your essay where:

- the relationships between your claim(s) and the reasons and evidence are unclear, identifying places where you could add linking words or other transitional devices to make your argument more cohesive. Look for:
  - > sudden jumps in your ideas
  - > breaks between paragraphs where the ideas in the next paragraph are not logically following from the previous one

Revise your draft to use words, phrases, and clauses to create cohesion and clarify the relationships among claim(s) and reasons, using the following questions as a guide:

- Are there unifying relationships between the claims, reasons, and evidence I present in my argument?
- Have I clarified, or made clear, these relationships?
- What linking words (such as conjunctions), phrases, or clauses could I add to my argument to clarify the relationships between the claims, reasons, and evidence I present?

Skill: Transitions

Introduce the Skill

Watch the Concept Definition video and read the following definition with your students.

Transitions are connecting words, phrases, and clauses that writers use to **clarify** the relationships among ideas and details in a text. Transitions have different functions depending on whether the text is argumentative, informative, or narrative.

In an argumentative essay, writers state claims and provide reasons and evidence for their claims. To clarify a relationship between a claim and a reason or supporting evidence, transitions such as *although* and *on the other hand* help make connections clear.

For informational essays, transitions such as *however, in addition,* and *for example* may help create **cohesion** among ideas and concepts.

In narrative writing, authors use a variety of words, phrases, and clauses to signal shifts in time, setting, and action. Transitions such as *until now, meanwhile,* and *once it was over* may make narrative events more **coherent**.

Transitions also help to connect ideas both within and across paragraphs and between major sections of text.

V SKILL VOCABULARY

transition / la transición ***noun*** a connecting word or phrase that a writer may use to clarify the relationship between ideas in a text COGNATE

clarify / aclarar ***verb*** to make clear and more comprehensible

cohesion / la cohesión ***noun*** the quality of parts working together as a whole COGNATE

coherent / coherente ***adjective*** marked by being orderly and logical; easy to understand COGNATE

TURN AND TALK

Turn to your partner and brainstorm a list of one transition word, phrase, and clause. Discuss examples of when you might use each one.

SPEAKING FRAMES

- One example of a transition word / phrase / clause is ____, and I can use it when ____.

Your Turn

Ask students to complete the Your Turn activity.

QUESTION 1

A. Correct. This sentence is the topic sentence of the first body paragraph. It transitions from Donovan's claim in the introduction to the first body paragraph. That body paragraph shows how one of the texts supports his claim.

B. Incorrect. This sentence summarizes the issue that Donovan explores in this paragraph, but it does not show how that issue is logically connected to the claim in the introduction above it.

C. Incorrect. This sentence mentions a metaphor, but it does not clearly show how that metaphor relates to the claim in the introduction above it.

D. Incorrect. This sentence shares an opinion about the main character. However, that statement does not clearly relate to the claim in the introduction above it, and the second part of it is not supported by evidence in the second paragraph.

QUESTION 2

A. Incorrect. "Similarly" is a word used to show how one idea relates to another idea that is like it.

B. Correct. "For example" shows how a reason relates to evidence that supports it.

C. Incorrect. "In addition to that detail" adds evidence to information that has already been presented.

D. Incorrect. "As a result" is a phrase that shows the relationship between a cause and its effect.

 YOUR TURN

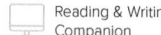

Choose the best answer to each question.

1. Below is a body paragraph from a previous draft of Donovan's literary analysis. Donovan notices a sudden jump in ideas at the beginning of the second paragraph in this excerpt. Which of the following could replace the underlined sentence in this body paragraph and provide the most effective transition to the ideas that follow?

> The metaphors in these texts help readers understand why it is important to be part of a community.
>
> <u>At the beginning of *The House on Mango Street*, Esperanza does not like any of the places where she has lived</u>. She describes the condition of one small apartment that a nun from her school saw: "the third floor, the paint peeling, wooden bars Papa had nailed on the windows so we wouldn't fall out" (paragraph 7). She is ashamed of these conditions, and she wants to show other people a home that makes her proud.

- ○ A. At the beginning of *The House on Mango Street*, Esperanza does not think that she can be a part of her community because she is not proud of where she lives.
- ○ B. At the beginning of *The House on Mango Street*, Esperanza focuses on her home and why she is ashamed of it.
- ○ C. At the beginning of *The House on Mango Street*, Esperanza does not live in a house even though houses become a metaphor in this story.
- ○ D. At the beginning of *The House on Mango Street*, Esperanza needs to find a way to feel proud of herself and her community.

2. Below is a body paragraph from a previous draft of Donovan's literary analysis. Donovan would like to add a transition word or phrase to help readers move from sentence 4 to sentence 5. Which transition will work best?

(1) In "Slam, Dunk, & Hook," a game of basketball is used as a metaphor for a strong and supportive community. (2) Throughout the poem, the narrator uses the first-person plural to describe his friends' perspective as a whole, rather than his own. (3) This point of view emphasizes that they all share the amazing experience that he describes. (4) When these friends play together, they surpass what they can do on their own. (5) The narrator says, "Lay ups. Fast breaks. / We had moves we didn't know / We had. Our bodies spun / On swivels of bone & faith, / Through a lyric slipknot / Of joy" (lines 34–39).

- ○ A. Similarly,
- ○ B. For example,
- ○ C. In addition to that detail,
- ○ D. As a result,

WRITE

Use the questions in the checklist section to revise one of your body paragraphs. Look for a variety of ways to use words, phrases, and clauses to create cohesion and clarify the relationships among ideas in this section. Those ideas may include your claim, counterclaims, reasons, and evidence.

Write

Ask students to complete the writing assignment.

ELL **REWRITE CHECKLIST**

A **Logical progression of the argument**

- ☐ Is there a clear connection between this paragraph and the paragraph before it?
- ☐ Is there a clear flow of information from one idea to another within the paragraph?
- ☐ Do you use a variety of transitions to make those connections clear?

Relationships among claim(s) and reasons

- ☐ What is the claim in this paragraph?
- ☐ What reasons support it?
- ☐ Do you clearly show readers the relationship between each reason and the claim?
- ☐ Do you use a variety of transition words, phrases, or clauses to show those connections?

Relationships among reasons and evidence

- ☐ What evidence have you used to support each claim?
- ☐ Do you clearly show readers how that evidence supports a claim?
- ☐ Do you use a variety of transition words, phrases, or clauses to help show the relationship between your evidence and a claim?

Writer's Notebook

Write a short argument about your identity in one paragraph. State one claim about your identity in a sentence and support that claim with reasons and evidence from your past actions and experiences. Then, look for ways to use a variety of transitions to show how your claim, reasons, and evidence are connected.

TURN AND TALK

Allow students to share their paragraphs orally in pairs or small groups before writing.

Skill: Style

Introduce the Skill

Watch the Concept Definition video and read the following definition with your students.

Style is the way a writer uses language to express ideas and convey information. It is revealed through the writer's choice of words and sentence construction. Style also involves being aware of the rules for writing standard English.

Choosing an appropriate style depends on the audience and the purpose for writing. Different subjects require different styles of writing. For both argumentative and informative writing, writers must use a formal style. With a **formal style**, a writer chooses **academic** language—the type of vocabulary used in school texts, for example—rather than informal or conversational language. The writer might also use special vocabulary unique to a particular topic, sometimes called **domain-specific** language.

Finally, to help maintain a formal style, writers must be sure to follow conventional rules for grammar, spelling, capitalization, and punctuation.

Skill: Style

CHECKLIST FOR STYLE

First, reread the draft of your argumentative essay and identify the following:

- places where you use slang, contractions, abbreviations, and a conversational tone
- areas where you could use subject-specific or academic language in order to help persuade or inform your readers
- moments where you use first person (*I*) or second person (*you*)
- areas where sentence structure lacks variety
- incorrect uses of the conventions of standard English for grammar, spelling, capitalization, and punctuation

Establish and maintain a formal style in your essay, using the following questions as a guide:

- Have I avoided slang in favor of academic language?
- Did I consistently use a third-person point of view, using third-person pronouns (*he*, *she*, *they*)?
- Have I varied my sentence structure and the length of my sentences? Apply these specific questions where appropriate:
  - > Where should I make some sentences longer by using conjunctions to connect independent clauses, dependent clauses, and phrases?
  - > Where should I make some sentences shorter by separating any independent clauses?
- Did I follow the conventions of standard English, including:
  - > grammar?
  - > spelling?
  - > capitalization?
  - > punctuation?

TURN AND TALK

Turn to your partner and discuss examples of situations in which you've needed to use formal language, and think about why there is a need for that style.

SPEAKING FRAMES

- I have needed to use formal language when ____.
- There is a need for a formal style of speaking because ____.
- There is a need for a formal style of writing because ____.

SKILL VOCABULARY

style / el estilo ***noun*** a way of expressing something that is characteristic of the person or time period COGNATE

formal style / el estilo formal ***noun*** a writing style or way of writing for academic essays

academic / académico/a ***adjective*** having to do with school COGNATE

domain-specific / específico/a del campo ***adjective*** having to do with a particular topic

YOUR TURN

Choose the best answer to each question.

1. Below is a section from a previous draft of Donovan's literary analysis. He sees that he needs to make sentence 2 shorter by dividing it into independent clauses that are written in a formal style. Which revision successfully divides the sentence into independent clauses that are written in a formal style?

> (1) The speaker in the poem "Slam, Dunk, & Hook" has found a way to connect with a group of friends who play basketball. (2) The poet emphasizes that he and his friends are interconnected by using first-person plural pronouns like *we* and *us* instead of *I*, and he uses the metaphor of a labyrinth to show how his friends feel when they play basketball together. (3) He says, "In the roundhouse / Labyrinth our bodies / Created, we could almost / Last forever, poised in midair / Like storybook sea monsters."

- ○ A. The poet emphasizes that he and his friends are interconnected. He uses first-person plural pronouns like *we* and *us* instead of *I*. He uses the metaphor of a labyrinth to show how his friends feel when they play basketball together.
- ○ B. By using first-person plural pronouns like *we* and *us* instead of *I*, the poet emphasizes that he and his friends are interconnected. And he uses the metaphor of a labyrinth to show how his friends feel when they play basketball together.
- ○ C. The poet emphasizes that he and his friends are interconnected by using first-person plural pronouns like *we* and *us* instead of *I*. He also uses the metaphor of a labyrinth to show how his friends feel when they play basketball together.
- ○ D. The poet emphasizes that he and his friends are interconnected by using first-person plural pronouns like *we* and *us* instead of *I* and the metaphor of a labyrinth. This shows how his friends feel when they play basketball together.

Your Turn

Ask students to complete the Your Turn activity.

QUESTION 1

A. Incorrect. The independent sentence has been broken into separate sentences, but it is not clear how these ideas are connected.

B. Incorrect. The second sentence is not an independent clause because it starts with the conjunction "And."

C. Correct. This sentence breaks a lengthy sentence into two clearer independent clauses. The second sentence also uses a transition to show how the ideas are connected.

D. Incorrect. The first sentence is confusing because it is not clear how "the metaphor of the labyrinth" relates to the point about the pronouns that the speaker uses.

QUESTION 2

A. Incorrect. The verb "to get" should be replaced with a more formal verb.

B. Incorrect. This sentence includes the second person ("you").

C. Incorrect. This sentence uses a contraction and misspells "their" as "they're."

D. Correct. This is an independent clause that uses academic language, and it is written in the third person.

Write

Ask students to complete the writing assignment.

ELL **REWRITE CHECKLIST**

A **Language**

- ☐ Can you find examples of slang in this paragraph?
- ☐ How can you replace those words or phrases with more formal language?
- ☐ Do you see opportunities to add academic language to this paragraph?

Sentence structure

- ☐ Do all of your sentences follow the same pattern, or do they have different structures?
- ☐ Where can you make some sentences longer and clearer?
- ☐ Where can you make some hard-to-follow sentences shorter?

Conventions

- ☐ Did you follow the conventions of standard English, including:
    - ☐ grammar?
    - ☐ spelling?
    - ☐ capitalization?
    - ☐ punctuation?

2. Below is a section from a previous draft of Donovan's literary analysis. Donovan wants to add a sentence after the quotation in sentence 3 to explain why that textual evidence is important. Based on the checklist, which version of his sentence works best?

> (1) The speaker in the poem "Slam, Dunk, & Hook" has found a way to connect with a group of friends who play basketball. (2) The poet emphasizes that he and his friends are interconnected by using first-person plural pronouns like *we* and *us* instead of *I*, and he uses the metaphor of a labyrinth to show how his friends feel when they play basketball together. (3) He says, "In the roundhouse / Labyrinth our bodies / Created, we could almost / Last forever, poised in midair / Like storybook sea monsters."

- ○ A. Each basketball player in this group gets more power and skills when they play together, so they are an example of a strong community.
- ○ B. This group of friends shows you an example of a strong community because they gain power and skills from their connection to one another.
- ○ C. When they're playing basketball together, they're power and skills increase.
- ○ D. The labyrinth is a metaphor for a strong community that gives every member more power and skills than they could have on their own.

 WRITE

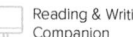

Use the steps in the checklist section to add to or revise the language of one paragraph from your draft by establishing and maintaining a formal style.

Writer's Notebook

Can you switch your writing style? In a short response, write two versions of a recommendation for a movie that should be shown or a game that should be played at a school event. Use an informal style to write the first version for students in your class. Then, rewrite that recommendation for teachers, parents, and administrators by establishing and maintaining a formal style.

 **TURN AND TALK**

Allow students to share their recommendations orally in pairs or small groups before writing.

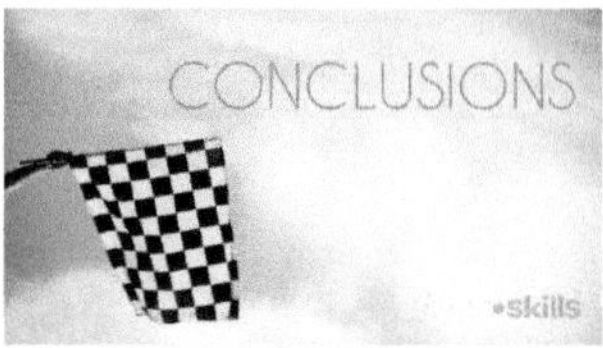

Skill: Conclusions

CHECKLIST FOR CONCLUSIONS

Before you write your conclusion, ask yourself the following questions:

- How can I rephrase the thesis statement in my concluding section or statement? What impression can I make on my reader?
- How can I write my conclusion so that it supports and follows logically from my argument?
- Should I include a call to action?
- How can I conclude with a memorable comment?

Below are two strategies to help you provide a concluding statement or section that follows from and supports the argument presented:

- Peer Discussion
  - > After you have written your introduction and body paragraphs, talk with a partner and tell him or her what you want readers to remember, writing notes about your discussion.
  - > Review your notes and think about what you wish to express in your conclusion.
  - > Do not simply repeat your claim or thesis statement. Rephrase your main idea to show the depth of your knowledge, convey the importance of your idea, and encourage readers to adopt your view.
  - > Write your conclusion.
- Freewriting
  - > Freewrite for ten minutes about what you might include in your conclusion. Don't worry about grammar, punctuation, or having fully formed ideas. The point of freewriting is to discover ideas.
  - > Review your notes and think about what you wish to express in your conclusion.
  - > Do not simply repeat your claim or thesis statement. Rephrase your main idea to show the depth of your knowledge, support for your argument, and the importance of your idea, and to encourage readers to adopt your view.
  - > Write your conclusion.

SKILL VOCABULARY

conclusion / la conclusión *noun* the closing paragraph or section of an essay; a closing argument in an argumentative text COGNATE

thesis statement / la presentación de la tesis *noun* a statement that shares the main idea of an argumentative or informational essay

Skill: Conclusions

Introduce the Skill

Watch the Concept Definition video and read the following definition with your students.

A **conclusion** is the closing paragraph or section of an essay, argument, or narrative. It is where the writer brings an essay to a close by restating the main idea or **thesis statement** or the **claim** in an argument. It also summarizes the evidence and research that support the claim or thesis. The conclusion should follow logically from the information, explanations, or claim that has been presented. A conclusion is a good way to suggest to your readers that you have accomplished what you set out to do. In addition, try to leave readers with an interesting final impression. This might be accomplished by closing with a quote, an anecdote, or a call to action.

In a **narrative**, a conclusion should follow logically from the events of the plot and what the characters have experienced. It might include characters reflecting on events, why they matter, and how they feel about them.

TURN AND TALK

Turn to your partner and talk about the similarities and differences between a strong conclusion to a narrative and a strong conclusion to an argument like a speech or essay.

SPEAKING FRAMES

- A strong conclusion in a narrative includes ____.
- A strong conclusion in an argument includes ____.
- They can be similar because ____.
- One important difference is ____.

Your Turn

Ask students to complete the Your Turn activity.

QUESTION 1

A. Incorrect. While style is important, it will not help Donovan show that his conclusion logically follows from his argument.

B. Correct. Donovan can summarize the textual evidence from his essay and remind readers how it supports the claim that he has rephrased in his conclusion.

C. Incorrect. If the terms need to be defined, Donovan should define them when they first occur, and that happens earlier in the essay.

D. Incorrect. Donovan needs to show how his conclusion is connected to his entire argument rather than focusing on how it is connected to one body paragraph.

QUESTION 2

A. Incorrect. This sentence states a question about rejection, rather than summarizing Donovan's argument about the three stories.

B. Incorrect. This sentence discusses overcoming challenges, rather than the main topic of the essay, which is the effect of the figurative language in all three stories.

C. Correct. This sentence summarizes Donovan's argument about the effect of the figurative language in all three stories.

D. Incorrect. This sentence comments on the story titles, rather than the effect of figurative language in the stories.

Extended Writing Project

 YOUR TURN

Choose the best answer to each question.

1. Below is the conclusion from Donovan's first draft. Donovan's peer said that he needed to show readers that the conclusion supports and follows logically from his argument. What is an effective way to do that?

> The saying "a picture is worth one thousand words" is challenged by the authors of these three texts. That is because they use figurative language to reveal who these characters are and how they relate to their communities. So no selfies are needed to help readers understand these individuals—just similes and metaphors.

- A. Make the style of the language more formal.
- B. Summarize the evidence that supports this claim and show how it is connected to the claim.
- C. Define the terms *figurative language*, *simile*, and *metaphor* for readers.
- D. Add a transition word, phrase, or clause that shows how this paragraph relates to the one that precedes it.

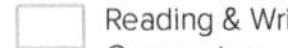

116  Reading & Writing Companion

SKILL VOCABULARY

claim / la afirmación ***noun*** the writer's or speaker's position on a debatable issue or problem

narrative / la narración ***noun*** a story, real or imagined, consisting of connected events

2. Below is the conclusion from a later draft of Donovan's essay. Donovan would like to add a sentence to bring his essay to a more effective close. Which sentence could he add after sentence 4 to help achieve this goal?

(1) Authors of all three stories use metaphor to teach readers how belonging to a community can affect a person's identity. (2) Esperanza's experience in *The House on Mango Street* shows how hard it is when you have trouble fitting into a community. (3) The speaker's experiences in "Slam, Dunk, & Hook" show how a person can find strength in being a part of a community. (4) The conflict between Constancia and her grandmother in "Abuela Invents the Zero" shows how painful it is to be rejected, especially by someone you love.

- ○ A. How would you respond to being rejected by someone you love?
- ○ B. Each of these characters is brave for overcoming challenges and showing leadership despite their fear, which is not an easy thing for most people, including me, to do.
- ○ C. Even though each of these individuals has a unique identity, the figurative language used to tell their stories makes their experiences more relatable to the reader.
- ○ D. The title of each story is important in relaying themes to the reader.

 WRITE

Use the questions in the checklist section to revise the conclusion of your argumentative essay.

Write

Ask students to complete the writing assignment.

ELL **REWRITE CHECKLIST**

A **Restated thesis statement**

- ☐ How has your understanding of the thesis statement deepened while writing this essay?
- ☐ How can you rephrase the thesis statement from the introduction to show this new understanding and keep readers engaged?

Brief summary

- ☐ Have you reviewed the reasons and evidence that you used to support your claim?
- ☐ Is your summary of that argument both brief and clear?

The final impression

- ☐ Why is your argument important for readers to understand?
- ☐ How can you show readers that your argument is important?

Writer's Notebook

Ask students to reread the conclusions from the mentor texts that they studied in this lesson and note how the author made a lasting impression on her audience. In their Writer's Notebook, students can then freewrite to develop at least three ways that they can close their essays with a sentence that makes a lasting impression on their audiences.

 **TURN AND TALK**

Allow students to share their closing sentences orally in pairs or small groups before writing.

Argumentative Writing Process: Revise

Review Revision Guide

Break the class into five groups, and assign each group a category of the revision guide. Ask:

- What is the purpose of this section of the guide?
- How did it improve Donovan's writing?
- How will it help to improve your writing?

Allow groups to share their ideas with the class.

SPEAKING FRAMES

- I think ____ (clarity / development / organization / word choice / sentence variety) improved Donovan's writing by ____.
- I think ____ (clarity / development / organization / word choice / sentence variety) will improve my writing because ____.

Revise

Students should start this activity with a copy of their drafts either printed on paper or open in a word-processing program, such as Google Docs. Allow students time to revise their drafts using the instructions in the revision guide. Once students have finished revising their narrative, have them submit their work.

Extended Writing Project

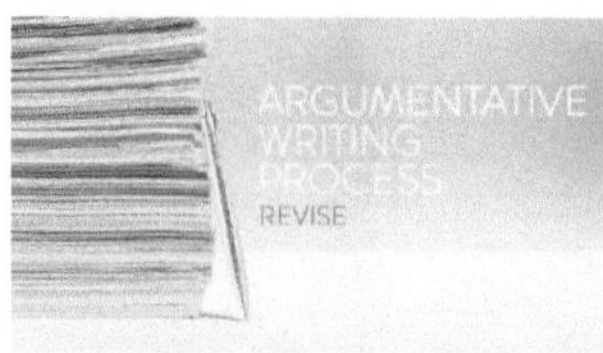

Argumentative Writing Process: Revise

PLAN | DRAFT | REVISE | EDIT AND PUBLISH

You have written a draft of your literary analysis. You have also received input from your peers about how to improve it. Now you are going to revise your draft.

REVISION GUIDE

Examine your draft to find areas for revision. Keep in mind your purpose and audience as you revise for clarity, development, organization, and style. Use the guide below to help you review:

Review	Revise	Example
	Clarity	
Reread your literary analysis and see if each idea flows into the next idea. Annotate places where the connection between ideas is not clear.	Focus on a paragraph that has the most annotations. Then, revise that section by using words, phrases, and clauses to clarify relationships among your claim, counterclaims, reasons, and evidence.	In this excerpt, ~~She~~ she even wants to change her name to solve the problem. As a result, ~~Her~~ her name acts as a metaphor, and ~~It~~ it holds more than one meaning in this selection.
	Development	
Identify each claim in your literary analysis. Annotate any places where a reason does not clearly support a claim or where evidence does not clearly support a reason.	Focus on a single place where a reason or evidence does not clearly support a claim. Then, revise that section by adding a reason or textual evidence that clearly supports the claim.	In the poem, the speaker and his friends create a strong community based on basketball. In fact, ~~The~~ the speaker even ~~uses~~ speaks on behalf of the group by using the pronouns *we* and *our* instead of *I* throughout the poem. These pronouns emphasize that the speaker is describing experiences he has shared with his friends.

CHECK FOR SUCCESS

Circulate around the room to spend time with individual students. Ask:

- What category are you working on?
- Why are you revising this specific section?
- How are you revising it?
- How does this change support your purpose?
- Does this change make your writing appropriate for your audience?

If students struggle while revising their drafts, choose an exemplary revision to share with the class while the student talks through the process. You could also invite a student to share a dilemma in the revision process and allow the class to offer feedback or suggestions.

Review	Revise	Example
	Organization	
Reread your thesis statement, and annotate any parts of the statement that need to be updated to reflect discoveries that you made while you were writing your draft or the revisions that you have made so far.	Use the annotations that you have made to revise your thesis statement. Your revised statement should include any updated claims and let readers anticipate how you have supported them in the body of your literary analysis.	Each one of these metaphors ~~shows not only who the characters are, but why it is important to be part of a community.~~ helps readers see how a character's community can influence his or her identity.
	Style: Word Choice	
Identify sentences that have a conversational style, and replace those with sentences that have a formal style.	Select one to two sentences to rewrite by using a formal style.	. . . ~~Like my name,~~ Esperanza's name is a major part of her identity, so she feels out of place when her classmates ~~can't say~~ struggle with it.
	Style: Sentence Variety	
Read your literary analysis aloud. Annotate places where there are too many long sentences or short sentences in a row. Take note of long sentences and short sentences that are hard to follow as well.	Select one long sentence to revise or a set of shorter sentences to combine.	Under different circumstances, Constancia abandons her grandmother when she is lost in "Abuela Invents the Zero~~,~~." ~~and~~ Abuela then uses the number zero as a metaphor to explain how that disrespect made her feel.

WRITE

Use the guide above, as well as your peer reviews, to help you evaluate your literary analysis to determine areas that should be revised.

ELL DEVELOPMENT

Revise your draft, focusing on development. Identify places in your draft where reasons and textual evidence do not strongly support your claims.

DEVELOPMENT

Tell students to revise their drafts using the revision guide, focusing on development. In addition, have students make revisions that focus on word choice, as practiced in the previous unit.

Write

Ask students to complete their writing assignment.

ELL A REVISION CHECKLIST

- ☐ Look for claims that lack support.
- ☐ Provide strong reasons and relevant textual evidence that support your claim.
- ☐ Revise the sentence or paragraph to include stronger support.

Grammar: Active and Passive Voice

Introduce the Skill

Review the image and definition for active and passive voice as a class.

- active voice - action verb when the subject of the sentence performs the action
- passive voice - action verb when the action is performed on the subject

Discuss the Model

1. In good writing, why do most sentences use the active voice? Sentences that use the active voice often sound stronger and clearer than sentences that use the passive voice.
2. When is the passive voice useful in good writing? Writers can use the passive voice to show that the "doer" of the action in a sentence is unknown. They can also use the passive voice when the "doer" of an action is not as important as the action or direct object in a sentence. The direct object is the noun on which the action is performed in a sentence.

Extended Writing Project

Grammar:
Active and Passive Voice

Active and Passive Voice

Generally speaking, the active voice makes a stronger impression than the passive voice. It helps make writing clearer for readers. In good writing, most sentences will use active voice.

Voice	Text
Active	**The passengers in their cabins felt** the jar too, and tried to connect it with something familiar. *A Night to Remember*
Active	**Her husband drew the talisman** from his pocket, and then all three burst into laughter as the sergeant-major, with a look of alarm on his face, caught him by the arm. "The Monkey's Paw"

However, passive voice is useful when the "doer" of an action is unknown or if it is less important than the action or the object. Passive voice is only possible if there is a direct object in the sentence. To form the passive voice, use a form of the auxiliary verb *be* with the past participle of the verb. The tense of the auxiliary verb determines the tense of the passive verb.

Voice	Sentence
Passive	A war cabinet **has been formed** of five members, representing, with the Labour, Opposition, and Liberals, the unity of the nation. *Blood, Toil, Tears and Sweat*
Passive	At last the question of my sanity or insanity **was to be decided**. *Ten Days in a Mad-House*

Reading & Writing Companion

YOUR TURN

1. Read the sentence below. Then pick the version that correctly changes it to the active voice.

   The heavens were studied by ancient astronomers.

   - ○ A. Ancient astronomers studied the heavens.
   - ○ B. The heavens would have been studied by ancient astronomers.
   - ○ C. The heavens were of interest to ancient astronomers.
   - ○ D. No change needs to be made to this sentence.

2. Read the sentence below. Then pick the version that correctly changes it to the passive voice.

   Hipparchus established an observatory in the third century BC.

   - ○ A. In the third century BC, Hipparchus established an observatory.
   - ○ B. Hipparchus will establish an observatory in the third century BC.
   - ○ C. An observatory was established by Hipparchus in the third century BC.
   - ○ D. No change needs to be made to this sentence.

3. Read the sentence below. Then pick the version that correctly changes it to the active voice.

   A solar eclipse was predicted by Thales of Miletus in 585 BC.

   - ○ A. A solar eclipse has been predicted by Thales of Miletus in 585 BC.
   - ○ B. Thales of Miletus predicted a solar eclipse in 585 BC.
   - ○ C. Miletus was the place where a solar eclipse was predicted by Thales in 585 BC.
   - ○ D. No change needs to be made to this sentence.

4. Read the sentence below. Then pick the version that correctly changes it to the passive voice.

   In 1543, Copernicus, a Polish astronomer, suggested the theory that the earth orbits the sun.

   - ○ A. In 1543, the theory that the earth orbits the sun was suggested by Copernicus, a Polish astronomer.
   - ○ B. Copernicus, a Polish astronomer, suggested the theory that the earth orbits the sun in 1543.
   - ○ C. A Polish astronomer, Copernicus, suggested the theory that the earth orbits the sun in 1543.
   - ○ D. No change needs to be made to this sentence.

Your Turn

Ask students to complete the Your Turn activity.

QUESTION 1

A. Correct. The subject, ancient astronomers, performs the action.

B. Incorrect.

C. Incorrect.

D. Incorrect.

QUESTION 2

A. Incorrect.

B. Incorrect.

C. Correct. The subject receives the action of the verb.

D. Incorrect.

QUESTION 3

A. Incorrect.

B. Correct. The subject, Thales of Miletus, performs the action.

C. Incorrect.

D. Incorrect.

QUESTION 4

A. Correct. The subject, Copernicus, receives that action of the verb.

B. Incorrect.

C. Incorrect.

D. Incorrect.

Grammar: Verb Moods

Introduce the Skill

Review the image and definition for verb moods as a class.

- indicative mood - makes a statement of fact or reality
- imperative mood - expresses a command or makes a request
- interrogative mood - asks a question
- subjunctive mood (recommend or suggest) - expresses indirectly a demand, recommendation, suggestion, or statement of necessity
- subjunctive mood (condition or wish contrary to fact) - states a condition or a wish that is imaginary or contrary to fact

Discuss the Model

1. Why are indicative sentences the most common type of sentence in written work? Indicative sentences state facts or opinions about reality in nonfiction or a character's reality in fiction. Those types of statements are more common than questions, commands, recommendations, and wishes.
2. What is the difference between the imperative and interrogative moods? A person uses the imperative mood when giving a command or making a request, like "Please do not order the special." A person uses the interrogative mood when they ask a question like "Would you like to order the special?"
3. When do writers need to use the subjunctive mood? Writers should use the subjunctive mood when they are making suggestions like "I recommend that you audition for the play." They should also use the subjunctive mood when they are talking about wishes or possibilities that are not currently true: "If I were to audition, I'd need to memorize those lines."

Extended Writing Project

Grammar:
Verb Moods

Mood can be indicative, imperative, interrogative, or subjunctive. Of these four, indicative will make up the majority of a written work. However, because subjunctive is the least used, it is the easiest to get wrong, so familiarize yourself with this mood to avoid problems.

Mood	Text
Indicative	Inside the floating cloak he was tall, thin, and bony; and his hair was red beneath the black cap. *Lord of the Flies*
Imperative	"Go and get it and wish," cried his wife, quivering with excitement. "The Monkey's Paw"
Interrogative	Will the murderers break and give themselves away? When the victim does not show up for the party will his father suspect? *Let 'Em Play God*
Subjunctive	"You know the Queen of England, if she were here, would have to lift her veil," he said, very kindly. *Ten Days in a Mad-House*

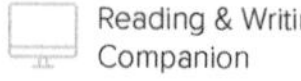
Reading & Writing Companion

YOUR TURN

1. This sentence is indicative. How could this be rewritten to make it interrogative?

   When you get home, I'd appreciate it if you'd let the dog out.

   - A. When you get home, let the dog out.
   - B. When you get home, could you let the dog out?
   - C. When you get home, please let the dog out.
   - D. No change needs to be made to this sentence.

2. This sentence is imperative. How could this be rewritten to make it indicative?

   Mow the lawn this weekend.

   - A. Don't forget to mow the lawn.
   - B. This weekend, mow the lawn.
   - C. You need to mow the lawn this weekend.
   - D. No change needs to be made to this sentence.

3. This sentence is in the subjunctive. How could this be rewritten to make it indicative?

   I wish there were more people signed up for the lecture series.

   - A. I wish there was more people signed up for the lecture series.
   - B. We need to have more people signed up for the lecture series.
   - C. If I were planning a lecture series, I would want more people to sign up.
   - D. No change needs to be made to this sentence.

4. This sentence is indicative. How could this be rewritten to make it subjunctive?

   They will serve roast chicken at the dinner this evening.

   - A. I recommend that roast chicken be served at the dinner this evening.
   - B. Will roast chicken be served at the dinner this evening?
   - C. They are serving dinner this evening, and it might be chicken.
   - D. No change needs to be made to this sentence.

Your Turn

Ask students to complete the Your Turn activity.

QUESTION 1

A. Incorrect.

B. Correct. Questions are interrogative mood.

C. Incorrect.

D. Incorrect.

QUESTION 2

A. Incorrect.

B. Incorrect.

C. Correct. This is indicative.

D. Incorrect.

QUESTION 3

A. Incorrect.

B. Correct. This is a statement, not a wish.

C. Incorrect.

D. Incorrect.

QUESTION 4

A. Correct. "I recommend" used with "be" makes the sentence subjunctive.

B. Incorrect.

C. Incorrect.

D. Incorrect.

Grammar: Consistent Verb Voice and Mood

Introduce the Skill

Review the image and definition for verb voice and mood as a class.

- consistent verb voice - the state of verbs that are consistent in voice within a clause or sentence; maintaining either active voice or passive voice
- inconsistent verb voice - the state of verbs that are not consistent in voice within a clause or sentence; shifting from active to passive, or from passive to active
- consistent verb mood - the state of verbs that are consistent in mood within a clause or sentence; maintaining indicative, imperative, or subjunctive moods
- inconsistent verb mood - the state of verbs that are not consistent in mood within a clause or sentence; shifting among indicative, imperative, or subjunctive moods

Discuss the Model

1. Why should writers avoid using different verb voices in a sentence or clause? Answers will vary. A sentence or clause with different verb voices can be difficult to follow. In contrast, a sentence or clause with a consistent verb voice is more likely to be strong and clear.
2. Look at the incorrect sentences under "Mood" in the model. Based on these sentences, why should writers avoid using different verb moods in a sentence or clause? Answers will vary. Sample answer: A sentence or clause with different verb moods can make it nonsensical or difficult to follow; however, a sentence or clause with a consistent verb mood is more likely to make sense and be clear.

Extended Writing Project

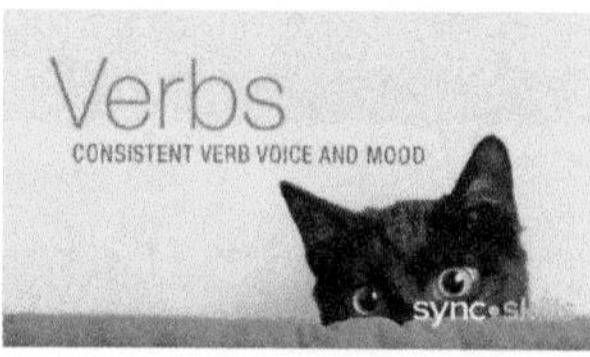

Grammar: Consistent Verb Voice and Mood

Voice

Voice is either active or passive. Consistent voice makes writing better and stronger. Though consistency is possible with the passive voice, and the passive voice is sometimes needed, active voice is more common.

Mood

Mood can be indicative, imperative, interrogative, or subjunctive. Of these four, indicative will make up the majority of a written work.

Correct	Incorrect
We are going to the store, and we are leaving now.	We are going to the store, and leave now. (The indicative shifts to the imperative.)
Get your coat and come with me.	Get your coat and are you coming? (The imperative shifts to the interrogative.)
If I were in charge, then I would make certain things were done correctly.	If I were in charge, then I will make certain things will be done correctly. (The subjunctive shifts to the indicative.)

Rule	Text
Voice should remain consistent within a sentence.	Someone else who had been listening to the brief dialogue here asserted that he had lived south and that my accent was southern, while another officer was positive it was eastern. *Ten Days in a Mad-House*
Mood should remain consistent within a sentence.	In a few minutes it really did seem as if kind spirits had been at work there. *Little Women*

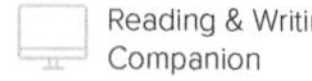
Reading & Writing Companion

YOUR TURN

1. Decide whether the voice is consistent. If not, pick the change that will make the sentence correct.

   Lions are the top predators in Africa, and gazelles are hunted by them.

   - A. Change **Lions are the top predators** to **Africa's top predators are lions**.
   - B. Change **gazelles are hunted by them** to **they hunt gazelles**.
   - C. Change **gazelles are hunted by them** to **gazelles will be hunted by them**.
   - D. No change needs to be made to this sentence.

2. Decide whether the mood is consistent. If not, pick the change that will make the sentence correct.

   Buy tickets for the movie, and will you come with us?

   - A. Change **will you come with us?** to **come with us**.
   - B. Change **will you come with us?** to **have you come with us?**
   - C. Change **Buy tickets for the movie** to **Buy tickets for the show**.
   - D. No change needs to be made to this sentence.

3. Decide whether the verb mood is consistent. If not, pick the change that will make the sentence correct.

   If I were more interested in this subject, I will probably do better in this class.

   - A. Change **If I were more interested** to **I had been more interested**.
   - B. Change **I will probably do better** to **I would probably do better**.
   - C. Change **I will probably do better** to **I have done better**.
   - D. No change needs to be made to this sentence.

4. Decide whether the voice is consistent. If not, pick the change that will make the sentence correct.

   The state legislature will consider the proposed laws, and then the bill will be voted on.

   - A. Change **will consider** to **had considered**.
   - B. Change **bill will be voted on** to **bill will have been voted on**.
   - C. Change **the bill will be voted on** to **they will vote on the bill**.
   - D. No change needs to be made to this sentence.

Your Turn

Ask students to complete the Your Turn activity.

QUESTION 1

A. Incorrect.

B. Correct. This change makes the voice consistently active.

C. Incorrect.

D. Incorrect.

QUESTION 2

A. Correct. This makes the mood consistently imperative.

B. Incorrect.

C. Incorrect.

D. Incorrect.

QUESTION 3

A. Incorrect.

B. Correct. This makes the verb mood consistently subjunctive.

C. Incorrect.

D. Incorrect.

QUESTION 4

A. Incorrect.

B. Incorrect.

C. Correct. This makes the voice of the sentence consistently active.

D. Incorrect.

Argumentative Writing Process: Edit and Publish

Practice with Student Model (Optional)

Provide groups with a different section of Donovan's draft. Each group should practice editing Donovan's model using the checklist in the lesson. Has he:

- ☐ used active and passive voice effectively?
- ☐ used verb mood correctly?
- ☐ used verb voice and mood consistently in each sentence?
- ☐ corrected any sentence fragments or run-on sentences?
- ☐ spelled everything correctly?

After the groups have finished, call on volunteers from each group to make edits until all the mistakes have been found and edited, pausing to discuss points of disagreement.

SPEAKING FRAMES

- Donovan did / did not use passive and active voice effectively when he wrote ____.
- Donovan did / did not use verb mood correctly when he wrote ____.
- Donovan did / did not use verb voice and verb mood consistently when he wrote ____.
- ____ is an example of a run-on sentence / sentence fragment that Donovan has / has not corrected.
- ____ is spelled incorrectly. The correct spelling is ____.

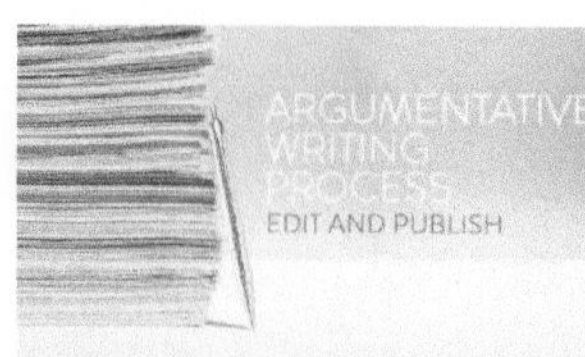

Argumentative Writing Process: Edit and Publish

PLAN | DRAFT | REVISE | EDIT AND PUBLISH

You have revised your literary analysis based on your peer feedback and your own examination.

Now, it is time to edit your literary analysis. When you revised, you focused on the strength of the argument in your literary analysis. You probably looked at the claim in your thesis statement, organization, style, and the cohesion of your ideas. When you edit, you focus on the mechanics of your literary analysis, paying close attention to things like grammar and punctuation.

Use the checklist below to guide you as you edit:

- ☐ Have I used active and passive voice effectively throughout the literary analysis?
- ☐ Does each sentence have a consistent verb voice?
- ☐ Is the mood of each verb correct?
- ☐ Does each sentence have a consistent verb mood?
- ☐ Do I have any sentence fragments or run-on sentences?
- ☐ Have I spelled everything correctly?

Notice some edits Donovan has made:

- Used active voice instead of passive voice to make a statement stronger.
- Corrected a spelling mistake.
- Made verb voice consistent within a sentence.
- Corrected verb mood.
- Made verb mood consistent within a sentence.

After they return home, Abuela tells Constancia how she felt when Constancia failed to help her: "You made me feel like a zero, like a nothing" (paragraph 16). ~~Her feelings of worthlessness are shown through this~~ She uses a ~~smile~~ simile, a comparison that ~~would~~ includes the words "like" or "as," to express her feelings of worthlessness. The "Zero" ~~is also used~~ in the story's title, "Abuela Invents the Zero:," ~~It~~ also shows how important this simile is. It suggests that Constancia ~~do~~ does not realize how much neglect can hurt another person until ~~this is explained by~~ her grandmother explains it. ~~So see how~~ As a result, Abuela's simile shows the need to help relatives find ways to be a part of a community, even if that community is unfamiliar to them.

WRITE

Use the questions on the previous page, as well as your peer reviews, to help you evaluate your literary analysis to determine areas that need editing. Then edit your literary analysis to correct those errors.

Once you have made all your corrections, you are ready to publish your work. You can distribute your writing to family and friends, hang it on a bulletin board, or post it on your blog. If you publish online, share the link with your family, friends, and classmates.

Write

After students finish editing, suggest, if there's time, that they set aside their literary analyses for a few minutes and then proofread them one more time. Once students have completed their writing, have them submit their work.

CHECK FOR SUCCESS

If students struggle to edit successfully, help them determine where edits are needed and what changes need to be made.

Direct students to the grammar lessons in this unit if they are uncertain about the rules for specific concepts.

READ ALOUD

Encourage students to read their stories aloud to themselves or to a partner in order to catch any remaining mistakes.

READ ALOUD

Encourage students to read their stories aloud to themselves or to an on-grade-level peer in order to catch any remaining mistakes.

WRITE A BLURB

Have students review their literary analyses and determine where their writing was most effective. Allow students to write a blurb like they might find on the back of a book that highlights and praises the best qualities of their work. Alternatively, have students write blurbs for the students in the class and post them around the room.

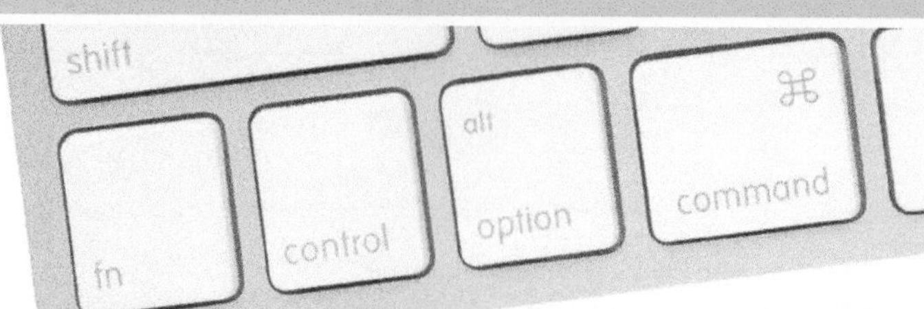

English Language Learner Resources

studysync

USERS ASSIGNMENTS

GRADE 8 › UNIT

Past and Present
Core ELA
Grade 8
30 Days

Unit Overview

Integrated Reading and Writing

Extended Writing Project

ELL Resources

Novel Study

End-of-Unit Assessment

Instructional Path

The Others

Mom's First Day

Skill: Classroom Vocabulary

Students will learn and recognize academic classroom vocabulary words and practice using them in a variety of contexts.

Assign

Skill: Generating Questions

Students will learn and practice the skill of generating questions when reading in order to demonstrate and improve comprehension.

Teacher Resources: Lesson Plan

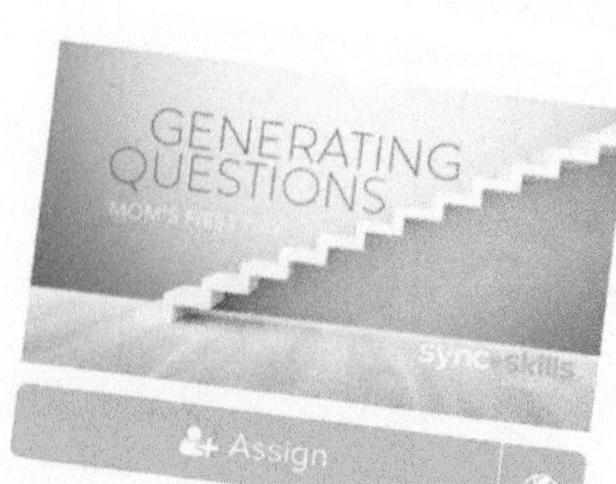

Assign

Lessons in the English Language Learner Resources section offer explicit ELL instruction. These lessons share a thematic and genre focus with all other lessons in the Core ELA unit.

The twenty ELL Resources are developed around two texts, "The Others" and "Mom's First Day," and an Extended Oral Project. Each text is written at four distinct levels. For ELLs, these texts serve as structural and thematic models of authentic texts in the Integrated Reading and Writing section of the unit. Thus, teachers may use the ELL texts in place of or as extensions for *The Outsiders* and "Abuela Invents the Zero."

ELL lessons modify the routines used with texts in the Integrated Reading and Writing section. Explicit vocabulary instruction is emphasized, and reading and writing Skills lessons focus strongly on language acquisition and reading comprehension.

After reading texts about identity and relationships, students will complete an Extended Oral Project that can be used in place of or as an extension to the Extended Writing Project. In this unit, students will plan and present the pros and cons of "fitting in" in the form of a debate.

Focus on English Language Proficiency Levels

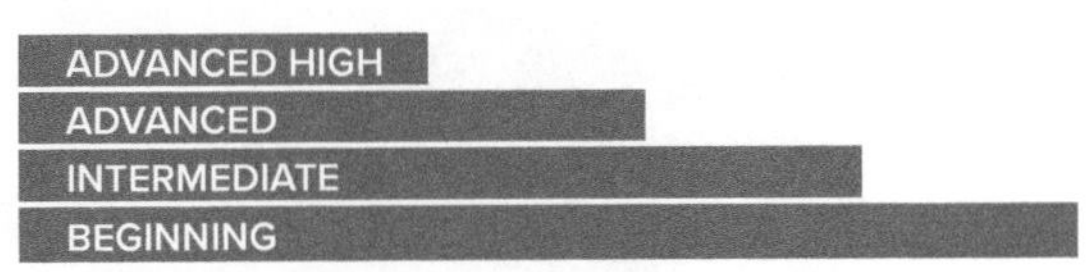

ELL Resources provide targeted support for four levels of proficiency: Beginning, Intermediate, Advanced, and Advanced High. Instruction and scaffolds, as well as the texts themselves, are differentiated based on these levels.

Additional differentiated scaffolds include visual glossaries, speaking and writing frames, and suggested grouping for peer and teacher support. Lessons also include suggested extension activities to challenge Advanced and Advanced High students as they progress through the year.

ELL Resources

ELL TEXTS

The Others

- Skill: Sight Vocabulary and High-Frequency Words
- Skill: Demonstrating Listening Comprehension
- First Read
- Skill: Analyzing Expressions
- Skill: Sharing Information
- Skill: Spelling Patterns and Rules
- Close Read

Mom's First Day

- Skill: Classroom Vocabulary
- Skill: Generating Questions
- First Read
- Skill: Language Structures
- Skill: Drawing Inferences and Conclusions
- Skill: Verb Tenses
- Close Read

EXTENDED ORAL PROJECT

- Introduction
- Skill: Acquiring Vocabulary
- Plan
- Skill: Connecting Words
- Practice
- Present

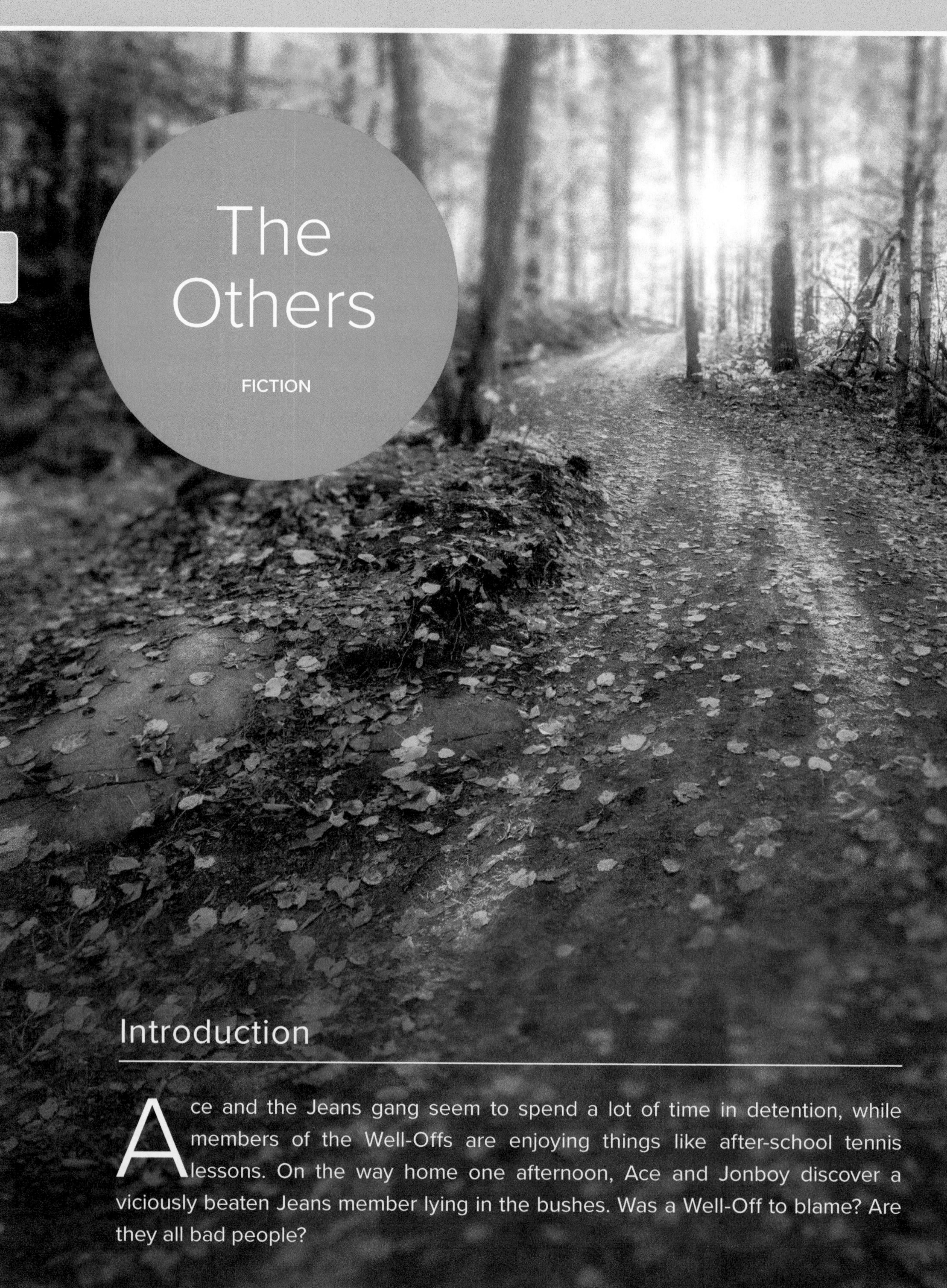

The Others

FICTION

Introduction

Ace and the Jeans gang seem to spend a lot of time in detention, while members of the Well-Offs are enjoying things like after-school tennis lessons. On the way home one afternoon, Ace and Jonboy discover a viciously beaten Jeans member lying in the bushes. Was a Well-Off to blame? Are they all bad people?

Ace and Jonboy, part of the Jeans clique composed of the poorer kids in the school, have just completed detention. The rich kids are called the Well-Offs, and they never end up in detention. Ace notices Madison and Brittany, two Well-Offs, walking with their tennis racquets. Then, Ace and Jonboy come upon their friend Brad lying in the bushes with his clothes torn and his face covered in blood. Instantly, Ace suspects that Brad was beaten up by Jason—a Well-Off whose father is an attorney with connections around town. When the girls see Brad, they are shocked. Ace confronts them about their friend Jason inflicting this kind of violence. However, the girls insist that they are not like Jason. They also point out that Bubba, a member of the Jeans clique, is also a vicious fighter. Madison tells Ace that money doesn't buy happiness and everyone has problems.

ELL Summaries in multiple languages are available digitally.

Audio and audio text highlighting are available with this text.

CONNECT TO ESSENTIAL QUESTION

What makes you, you?

In this short story, the Jeans and the Well-Offs are two gangs from different sides of the track. They attend the same school but don't trust each other. One day, Ace and Jonboy find another Jeans' member badly beaten and unconscious in the bushes. Are the Well-Offs to blame for this violent act?

Core ELA Connections

Texts	Theme	Genre
The Outsiders	When they find a member of the Jeans gang badly injured, Ace and Jonboy suspect the rival gang, the Well-Offs. This story builds on the theme of conflict between social groups.	Told from the first person, the readers witness the clash of social groups through the eyes of someone outside the conflict.

Differentiated Text Levels

ELL LEVEL	BEGINNING	INTERMEDIATE	ADVANCED	ADVANCED HIGH
WORD COUNT	259	357	443	543
LEXILE	270L	510L	590L	710L

Instructional Path

The print teacher's edition includes essential point-of-use instruction and planning tools. Complete lesson plans and program documents appear in your digital teacher account.

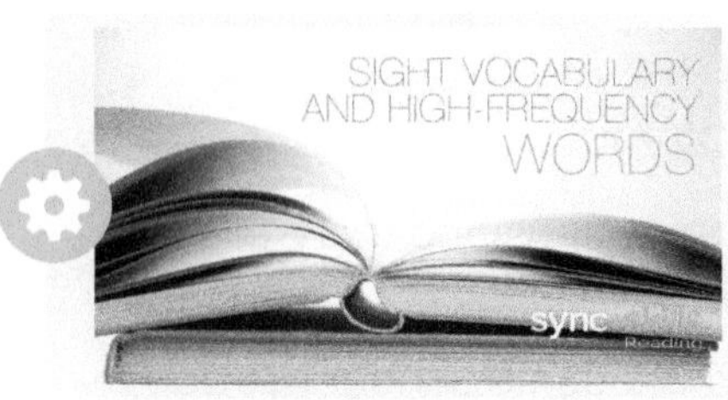

Skill: Sight Vocabulary and High-Frequency Words

DIGITAL ONLY

Objectives: Students will be able to learn and recognize sight vocabulary and high-frequency words in English.

Objectives: Students will be able to recognize sight vocabulary and high-frequency words when listening and reading, and produce sight vocabulary and high-frequency words when speaking and writing.

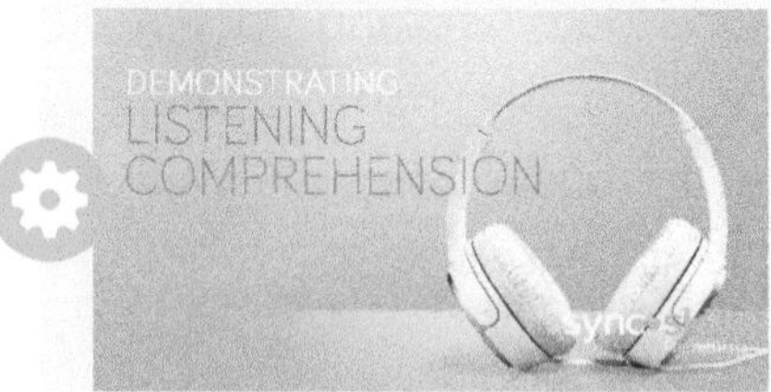

Skill: Demonstrating Listening Comprehension

DIGITAL ONLY

Objectives: Students will be able to learn and practice the skill of demonstrating listening comprehension.

Objectives: Students will be able to learn and practice the skill of demonstrating listening comprehension in discussions with peers and teacher.

First Read: The Others

Objectives: Students will be able to perform an initial reading of a text using the strategy of demonstrating listening comprehension.

Objectives: Students will be able to demonstrate comprehension of a text by demonstrating listening comprehension and responding to questions using textual evidence.

Skill: Analyzing Expressions

Objectives: Students will be able to analyze expressions when reading.

Objectives: Students will be able to analyze expressions when reading and justify their analysis when speaking.

Skill: Sharing Information

Objectives: Students will be able to share information when speaking.

Objectives: Students will be able to share information when writing.

Skill: Spelling Patterns and Rules

Objectives: Students will be able to recognize and apply spelling patterns and rules.

Objectives: Students will be able to recognize spelling patterns and rules when reading and apply spelling patterns and rules when writing.

Close Read: The Others

Objectives: Students will be able to perform a close reading of a text in order to share information with peers.

Objectives: Students will be able to demonstrate sharing information with peers by participating in a collaborative conversation and writing a short constructed response.

Progress Monitoring

Opportunities to Learn	Opportunities to Demonstrate Learning	Opportunities to Reteach
Sight Vocabulary and High-Frequency Words		
Skill: Sight Vocabulary and High-Frequency Words	Skill: Sight Vocabulary and High-Frequency Words • Your Turn First Read • Sight Vocabulary and High-Frequency Words	Spotlight Skill: Sight Vocabulary and High-Frequency Words
Demonstrating Listening Comprehension		
Skill: Demonstrating Listening Comprehension	Skill: Demonstrating Listening Comprehension • Your Turn First Read • Skills Focus	Spotlight Skill: Demonstrating Listening Comprehension
Analyzing Expressions		
Skill: Analyzing Expressions	Skill: Analyzing Expressions • Your Turn	Spotlight Skill: Analyzing Expressions
Sharing Information		
Skill: Sharing Information	Skill: Sharing Information • Your Turn Close Read • Complete Skills Focus • Write	Spotlight Skill: Sharing Information
Spelling Patterns and Rules		
Skill: Spelling Patterns and Rules	Skill: Spelling Patterns and Rules • Your Turn Close Read • Write	Spotlight Skill: Spelling Patterns and Rules

First Read

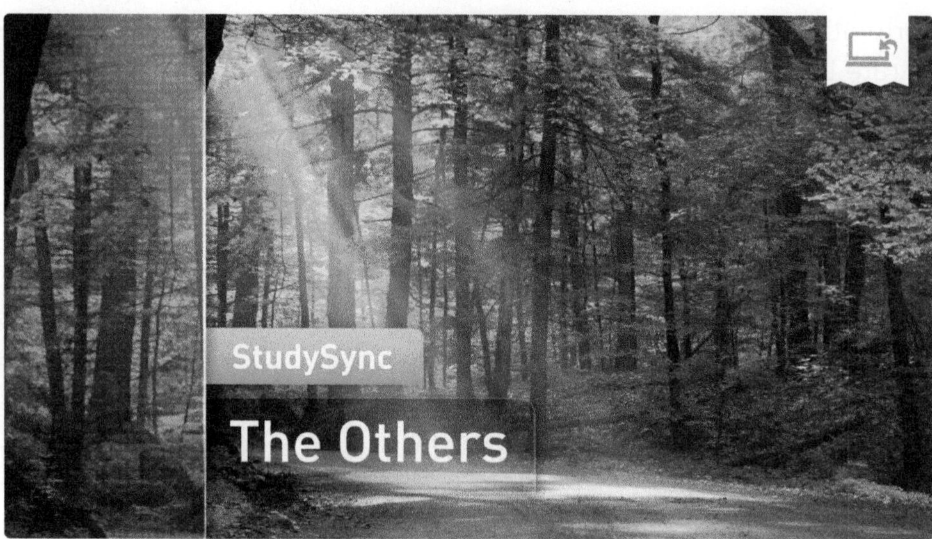

Introduce the Text

As a class, watch the video preview  and have students read the introduction in pairs to make connections to the video preview. Ask students various "wh" questions such as:

- What did you see in the video? How does it make you feel?
- What do you think the text will be about?
- Is there something in the video or introduction that surprised you?

ELL **Beginning & Intermediate**

SPEAKING FRAMES

- I see ____. I feel ____.
- I think the text will be about ____.
- I was surprised by ____.

Practice Prereading Skill

Remind students that Demonstrating Listening Comprehension:

helps you better understand the text. Listening to a story may help you notice details. Talking with another student can help you form new ideas. By listening closely and agreeing, disagreeing, and asking further questions about each other's ideas, you can develop a deeper understanding of the story than you would from just reading it alone.

To have students practice listening comprehension, have them listen to the audio of the summary and take notes. Then, pair students and allow them time to discuss what they recorded.

Activate Prior Knowledge and Experiences OPTIONAL

Have students make connections while practicing their oral language by discussing what they know about detention.

Generate a list (on the board or on paper) of any information or ideas your students have about detention.

Ask students to share where their background knowledge came from. For example, did their ideas come from a movie, friend, television show, book, or family member?

VOCABULARY

expensive
costly

assert
to state with confidence

inferior
lower in rank or position; closer to the bottom of the group

ferocious
very violent and fierce

brief
taking a very short time

READ

1 The school doors whooshed shut. I heard Jonboy's sigh of relief. We could finally go home. We had been in detention, again. The teachers seemed to like the fancy Well-Offs better. Those were the rich kids with no problems and no detentions, ever. Mr. Wilson ran detention. I think he hated the Jeans.

2 I noticed Madison and Brittany leaving school. They were holding their tennis racquets. They looked like **expensive** fly swatters. The girls had special lessons after school. We got detention. I usually ignored the Well-Off girls. They ignored us. We liked it that way.

3 We headed down the park path. Mom would be mad because of the detention. She wanted me to "better myself." I didn't feel **inferior**. Suddenly I heard Jonboy gasp. Brad was lying half in the bushes. His clothes were soaked in blood. We pulled him onto the grass. He looked badly beaten. His face was bleeding in a hundred places. He had a deep cut on his jaw.

AUDIO TEXT HIGHLIGHTING

Allow students to use the audio text highlight feature to follow along as they read. Alternately, you may wish to work directly with students or group them in twos or threes for partner reading or choral reading.

Preteach Vocabulary

Model the first word and example for the class.

1. The first word is *expensive,* and its meaning is "costly."
2. When I hear the word *expensive*, I think of fancy items.
3. For example, I'd like to get a sports car, but they're so *expensive*.
4. This is an example of something that is *expensive* because it costs a lot of money.

Continue this exercise with each word in the glossary, calling on individuals or groups of students to share out.

Beginning

PRETEACH VOCABULARY

Use the gestures to clarify meanings.

- **expensive** (Rub index and middle finger against thumb.)
- **inferior** (Look down on, as if in contempt, with hands on hips.)
- **brief** (Tap watch or wrist, or put thumb and index finger close together but not touching.)
- **assert** (Stand up straight, look confident, and make a statement with confidence.)
- **ferocious** (Imitate a wild animal.)

Sight Vocabulary and High-Frequency Words Focus

Remind students of the sight vocabulary and high-frequency words that they studied at the beginning of the unit. Point out that some of the words may be useful as they think about and discuss the text. For example:

- because (Mom would be mad **because** Ace received . . .)
- buy (Money does not **buy** . . .)
- their (They liked **their** new clothes and their . . .)
- pulled (They **pulled** Brad onto . . .)
- many (**Many** people have . . .)

4 I touched Brad's arm. He groaned. "I know who did this," I muttered. "It was Jason." He threatened Brad before. He called Brad a lowlife. He said he was "looking at" Tiffany. Tiffany was Jason's girl. Jason's dad was an attorney who had connections in town. Any trouble Jason got into was quickly fixed and forgotten. Jason got away with everything.

5 "What happened?" Madison whimpered. For a **brief** moment I thought Madison would burst into tears. Brittany stood frozen in horror.

6 "Who would do anything like this?"

7 "Jason did this," I **asserted**. "He's a Well-Off just like you."

8 "We are not all like Jason," Madison insisted. "Most of us are nice people. We just come from families who don't worry about money."

9 "Yeah, right," I growled.

10 "Are all you Jeans like Big Bubba?" she demanded. "I bet he has beaten up people who did not deserve it."

11 It was true. Big Bubba was a **ferocious** fighter. He could knock someone down with one blow of his massive fist.

12 Madison looked sad now. "We have problems, too. Money doesn't buy happiness." She looked at me. "Life is hard, Ace. It doesn't matter who you are."

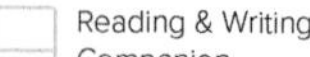

TEXT TALK

What is the story about?

1. Who are the story's characters?
2. Where does the story take place?
3. How does the story make you feel?

All Levels

SPEAKING FRAMES

Giving Information:

- This story is about ____.
- The story's characters are ____.
- This story takes place ____.
- This story makes me feel ____.

Asking for Information:

- Can you explain ____?
- What do you think about ____?
- Why do you think ____?

First Read

Read the story. After you read, answer the Think Questions below.

THINK QUESTIONS

1. What are the two groups in the story? What is the difference between them?

   The two groups are ________________________.

   The difference between them is ________________________.

2. Who do Ace and Jonboy find? What do they think happened?

   Ace and Jonboy find ________________________.

   Ace and Jonboy think ________________________.

3. Who is Big Bubba?

   Big Bubba is ________________________.

4. Use context to confirm the meaning of the word *brief* as it is used in "The Others." Write your definition of *brief* here.

   Brief means ________________________.

   A context clue is ________________________.

5. What is another way to say that something is *inferior*?

   Something is ________________________.

Think Questions

Circulate as students answer Think Questions independently. Answers will vary.

QUESTION 1: Comprehension

The Well-Offs and the Jeans. The Well-Offs are rich, and the Jeans are poor.

QUESTION 2: Comprehension

They find Brad, a Jean. They think Jason beat him up.

QUESTION 3: Comprehension

Big Bubba is a large and ferocious Jean.

QUESTION 4: Language

Brief is used to describe the moment Ace thinks that Madison will cry. It is a short moment, so *brief* must have something to do with time. *Brief* means "a small amount of time"

QUESTION 5: Language

It is not as good. It is worse.

Skill: Analyzing Expressions

Introduce the Skill

Watch the Concept Definition video and read the definition for Analyzing Expressions.

Skill: Analyzing Expressions

DEFINE

When you read, you may find English expressions that you do not know. An **expression** is a group of words that communicates an idea. Three types of expressions are idioms, sayings, and figurative language. They can be difficult to understand because the meanings of the words are different from their **literal**, or usual, meanings.

An **idiom** is an expression that is commonly known among a group of people. For example: "It's raining cats and dogs" means it is raining heavily. **Sayings** are short expressions that contain advice or wisdom. For instance: "Don't count your chickens before they hatch" means do not plan on something good happening before it happens. **Figurative** language is when you describe something by comparing it with something else, either directly (using the words *like* or *as*) or indirectly. For example, "I'm as hungry as a horse" means I'm very hungry. None of the expressions are about actual animals.

••• CHECKLIST FOR ANALYZING EXPRESSIONS

To determine the meaning of an expression, remember the following:

- ✓ If you find a confusing group of words, it may be an expression. The meaning of words in expressions may not be their literal meaning.
  - Ask yourself: Is this confusing because the words are new? Or because the words do not make sense together?
- ✓ Determining the overall meaning may require that you use one or more of the following:
  - context clues
  - a dictionary or other resource
  - teacher or peer support
- ✓ Highlight important information before and after the expression to look for clues.

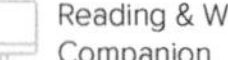

TURN AND TALK

1. Have you learned a phrase in English that you didn't understand at first?
2. How did you figure out its meaning?
3. What are some idioms or expressions in English that you know?

BEGINNING & INTERMEDIATE

SPEAKING FRAMES

- A phrase in English that I didn't understand at first is ____.
- I figured out its meaning using ____.
- An idiom or expression in English that I know is ____.

ADVANCED & ADVANCED HIGH

SPEAKING FRAMES

- A phrase in English that I didn't understand at first is ____.
- I figured out its meaning ____.
- Two idioms or expressions in English that I know are ____ and ____. The first one means ____. The second one means ____.

SKILL VOCABULARY

expression / la expresión ***noun*** a phrase used to express an idea COGNATE

literal / literal ***adjective*** describing the usual meaning of a word COGNATE

idiom / el modismo ***noun*** a common expression that cannot be taken literally

saying / el dicho ***noun*** an expression that contains advice or wisdom

YOUR TURN

Read paragraphs 10–12 from "The Others." Then, complete the multiple-choice questions below.

from **"The Others"**

"Are all you Jeans like Big Bubba?" she demanded. "I bet he has beaten up people who did not deserve it."

It was true. Big Bubba was a ferocious fighter. He could knock someone down with one blow of his massive fist.

Madison looked sad now. "We have problems, too. Money doesn't buy happiness." She looked at me. "Life is hard, Ace. It doesn't matter who you are."

1. **In paragraph 12, what is the meaning of the saying "Money doesn't buy happiness"?**
   - ○ A. Rich people are never happy.
   - ○ B. Happiness is too expensive to buy.
   - ○ C. Things you buy can make you sad.
   - ○ D. Having money doesn't make a person happy.

2. **A sentence that best supports the correct answer to question 1 is:**
   - ○ A. "Big Bubba was a ferocious fighter." (paragraph 11)
   - ○ B. "We have problems, too." (paragraph 12)
   - ○ C. "She looked at me." (paragraph 12)
   - ○ D. "Life is hard, Ace." (paragraph 12)

Your Turn

Ask students to complete the Your Turn activity.

QUESTION 1: D) The saying means that having money does not guarantee happiness.

QUESTION 2: B) Madison is saying that being rich does not mean being problem-free.

Discuss the Skill Model

1. What are the confusing words in the student's first annotation? Why does the student highlight these words?

   The confusing words in the annotation were *Well-Offs* and *Jeans*. They are capitalized; the word *jeans* is normally not capitalized.

2. How does the student figure out the meaning of *Well-Offs*?

   The student figures out the meaning by finding the context clues "fancy" and "rich kids."

3. How does the student figure out the meaning of *Jeans*?

   The student figures out the meaning by noticing that they are the opposite of *Well-Offs* and comparing the two.

4. What does the reader do last to check the conclusions about the meanings of the expressions?

   The reader talks about the story with the teacher or with peers.

ELL **Beginning & Intermediate**

Have students use the speaking frames and helpful terms to participate in the group discussion. If beginning students are hesitant to participate in a discussion, encourage them by prompting with *yes* or *no* questions.

Advanced & Advanced High

Have students use the speaking frames to participate in the group discussion.

SPEAKING FRAMES

- The confusing words are ____.
- The reader thinks ____ is usually not capitalized.
- The reader thinks *Well-Offs* means ____.
- The reader thinks *Jeans* means ____.
- The reader can ____.

HELPFUL TERMS FOR DISCUSSION

- saying
- people
- money
- rich
- literal
- jeans
- context
- detention

Skill: Sharing Information

Introduce the Skill

Watch the Concept Definition video ▶ and read the definition for Sharing Information.

TURN AND TALK

1. Do you ever talk to friends about a movie or TV show you saw? Why?
2. What are the advantages of discussing ideas in a group rather than thinking on your own?

BEGINNING & INTERMEDIATE

SPEAKING FRAMES

- I talk to friends about movies and TV shows because ____.
- Discussing in a group lets me ____.

ADVANCED & ADVANCED HIGH

SPEAKING FRAMES

- Talking about movies and TV shows lets me ____. For example, when my friends and I talked about ____, we realized that ____.
- Thinking on your own can let you ____, but discussing in a group lets you ____. This means that ____.

Skill:
Sharing Information

★ DEFINE

Sharing information involves asking for and giving information. The process of sharing information with other students can help all students learn more and better understand a text or a topic. You can share information when you participate in **brief** discussions or **extended** speaking assignments.

••• CHECKLIST FOR SHARING INFORMATION

When you have to speak for an extended period of time, as in a discussion, you ask for and share information. To ask for and share information, you may use the following sentence frames:

✓ To ask for information:

- What do you think about ____________________?
- Do you agree that ____________________?
- What is your understanding of ____________________?

✓ To give information:

- I think ____________________
- I agree because ____________________
- My understanding is ____________________

SKILL VOCABULARY

share / compartir *verb* to tell someone

brief / corto/a *adjective* short

extended / extendido/a *adjective* long COGNATE

YOUR TURN

Watch the "The Outsiders" StudySyncTV episode. After watching, sort the following statements from the episode into the chart below.:

	Statements
A	Even on the inside, you can still feel alone.
B	Both groups are outsiders.
C	Greasers are more emotional.
D	The two groups can connect through their differences.
E	Ponyboy is the first person Cherry has gotten through to.
F	Sharing the meanings of sympathy and empathy.

Information from "The Outsiders"	Shared Information

Your Turn Ask students to complete the Your Turn activity. ELPS: (3)(E)

Information from *The Outsiders*	Shared Information
Greasers are more emotional.	Sharing the meanings of *sympathy* and *empathy*.
Even on the inside, you can still feel alone.	The two groups can connect through their differences.
Ponyboy is the first person Cherry has gotten through to.	Both groups are outsiders.

Discuss the Skill Model

1. What is the difference between *empathy* and *sympathy*?

   Empathy means "understanding," and *sympathy* just means "feeling sorry for."

2. How does understanding the difference between *empathy* and *sympathy* support the group's answers?

   The idea that the groups can empathize rather than sympathize shows that they are similar.

3. What does Sam do after she learns the difference between *empathy* and *sympathy*?

   She shifts the conversation from comparing the groups to contrasting the groups.

4. What does Sam do to support her point?

   Sam reads an excerpt of the text to support her point.

5. What are some key words in the groups' discussion about the groups reconciling?

   Examples of key words are *peace offering*, *vulnerable*, and *trust*.

ELL

Beginning & Intermediate

Have students use the speaking frames and helpful terms to participate in the group discussion. If beginning students are hesitant to participate in a discussion, encourage them by prompting with *yes* or *no* questions.

Advanced & Advanced High

Have students use the speaking frames to participate in the group discussion.

SENTENCE FRAMES

- *Sympathy* is ____, and *empathy* is ____.
- Being able to empathize means the Greasers and Socs are ____.
- After learning the difference between *empathy* and *sympathy*, Sam ____.
- Sam supports her argument by ____.
- Key words in the conversation include ____, ____, and ____.

HELPFUL TERMS FOR DISCUSSION

- share
- sympathy
- compare
- disagree
- brief
- empathy
- contrast
- evidence

Close Read

Model Skills Focus

Remind students of the Reading Skill Sharing Information. Tell students that asking for and giving information about a text can help improve their understanding. Direct students to the Skills Focus and remind them to track as you read aloud. *Note similarities between the narrator and Madison.*

Model this activity for students:

- I am going to focus on the character of Madison.
- I am going to reread the story and look at her interactions with the narrator. Near the end, I notice the text says that Madison is sad. I underlined this sentence.
- When Madison says "Money doesn't buy happiness," I recognized that I had heard this before. This saying seems important. I want to better understand its meaning.
- I look at the context clues in the text. I see words like "problems" and "hard." I underlined these words. They help me to understand the meaning of the saying.
- I am going to add an annotation about it. I am going to highlight the sentence and rewrite it in my own words: "Having money does not mean you are going to be happy."
- Rewriting this expression shows that I understand it. Now I can see that it points to a similarity between the narrator and Madison. They both have problems, despite what the narrator thinks.

Complete Skills Focus

Divide students into three equal groups. Assign each group with one of the following focus areas:

- Write an annotation about the narrator's first mention of Madison.
- Write an annotation about the reactions of the narrator and Madison to Brad's injuries.
- Write an annotation about the narrator and Madison's conversation about Big Bubba.

Circulate and monitor groups as they work.

Close Read

WRITE

LITERARY ANALYSIS: The Well-Offs and the Jeans come from two different social classes. However, the two gangs have things in common. How are the Well-Offs and the Jeans similar? Pay attention to the *IE* and *EI* spelling rules as you write.

Use the checklist below to guide you as you write.

- ☐ Who are the Well-Offs and the Jeans?
- ☐ How are the social classes of the Well-Offs and the Jeans different?
- ☐ How are the Well-Offs and the Jeans similar?

Use the sentence frames to organize and write your literary analysis.

The Well-Offs and the Jeans are two ______________________.

The Well-Offs belong to a social class that is ______________________.

The Jeans belong to a social class that is ______________________.

Despite their differences, the Well-Offs and the Jeans are similar because ______________________
______________________.

One detail from the text to support this is ______________________.

Collaborative Conversation

Group students so they have a representative from each of the original three groups. Prompt groups to combine their annotations, making sure that each annotation is clear and makes sense.

- Did the annotations examine important parts of the text?
- Were the annotations focused on the prompt?
- Did sharing these annotations help me better understand the story?

Collaborative Conversation

BEGINNING, INTERMEDIATE Use the word bank to participate in the group discussion.

ADVANCED Use the speaking frames to participate in the group discussion.

BEGINNING, INTERMEDIATE	ADVANCED
Word Bank	**Speaking Frames**
• helped me understand • now I understand • examined • similarities • differences	• The annotations (did / did not) —— examine an important part of the text. • The annotations (did / did not) —— focus on the prompt. • The annotations (did / did not) —— help me better understand the story.

Write

Ask students to complete the writing assignment. Remind students to pay attention to spelling rules for *EI* and *IE* words and words with unstressed vowels.

BEGINNING Write a response using the paragraph and word bank.

INTERMEDIATE Write a response using the paragraph frames.

INTERMEDIATE / BEGINNING	BEGINNING
Paragraph Frames	**Word Bank**
The Well-Offs and the Jeans are two ____. The Well-Offs belong to a social class that is ____. The Jeans belong to a social class that is ____. Despite their differences, the Well-Offs and the Jeans are similar because ____. One detail from the text to support this is ____.	• struggle • problems • poor • gangs • rich

Mom's First Day

FICTION

Introduction

Sometimes life takes you by surprise and challenges you without warning. When this happens, you rely on your values to pull you through. In "Mom's First Day," Yvette is startled when her mother addresses her in a familiar way in front of her classmates. In a flash, this innocent, awkward encounter swells into a moment of truth.

On Monday morning, Yvette's father asks her to be kind to her mother, who will be Yvette's substitute teacher in science class this week. When her mother comes into the kitchen wearing one of her church outfits, Yvette is mortified. But remembering her father's words, she doesn't say anything. Her mother looks especially nervous, as she's only recently returned to teaching since giving birth to Yvette's brother, Pepe. In class, Yvette's mother does well, even making the kids laugh a couple times. Later, as Yvette is running out the classroom door, her mother calls her back. Yvette's mother gives her the lunch that Yvette forgot and quickly says, "Love you." Yvette is humiliated. When the kids around her laugh, she laughs with them. She notices the hurt look on her mother's face and feels guilty.

CONNECT TO ESSENTIAL QUESTION

What makes you, you?

Yvette's mom is going back to school after two years as a stay-at-home mom. She is going back to school as a substitute teacher—for Yvette's science class! Yvette is nervous, her mom is excited. Will Yvette survive the day?

Summaries in multiple languages are available digitally.

Audio and audio text highlighting are available with this text.

Core ELA Connections

Texts	Theme	Genre
Abuela Invents the Zero	Yvette is embarrassed when her mother starts a job in her new school. Her attitude and behavior reflect themes of respect, guilt, shame, and family.	This first-person narrative describes the complex emotions of a specific childhood moment.

Differentiated Text Levels

ELL LEVEL	BEGINNING	INTERMEDIATE	ADVANCED	ADVANCED HIGH
WORD COUNT	349	406	504	578
LEXILE	400L	590L	780L	760L

Instructional Path

The print teacher's edition includes essential point-of-use instruction and planning tools. Complete lesson plans and program documents appear in your digital teacher account.

Skill: Learning Classroom Vocabulary

DIGITAL ONLY

Objectives: Students will be able to learn and recognize academic classroom vocabulary words in English.

Objectives: Students will be able to recognize academic classroom vocabulary words when listening and reading, and produce academic classroom vocabulary words when speaking and writing.

Skill: Generating Questions

DIGITAL ONLY

Objectives: Students will be able to learn and practice the skill of generating questions when reading a new text.

Objectives: Students will be able to generate questions when reading in order to demonstrate and improve comprehension.

First Read: Mom's First Day

Objectives: Students will be able to perform an initial reading of a text using the strategy of generating questions.

Objectives: Students will be able to demonstrate comprehension of a text by responding to questions orally and in writing using textual evidence.

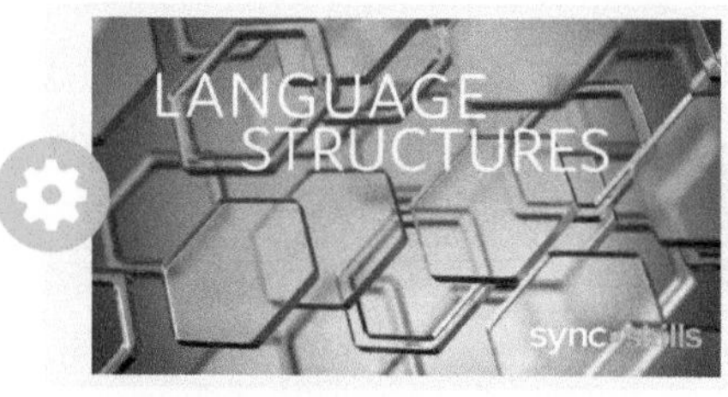

Skill: Language Structures

Objectives: Students will be able to analyze language structures.

Objectives: Students will be able to analyze language structures when reading.

Skill: Drawing Inferences and Conclusions

Objectives: Students will be able to draw inferences and conclusions.

Objectives: Students will be able to draw inferences and conclusions when reading.

Skill: Verb Tenses

DIGITAL ONLY

Objectives: Students will be able to use present, past, and future verb tenses.

Objectives: Students will be able to recognize present, past, and future verb tenses when reading and use present, past, and future verb tenses when writing.

Close Read: Mom's First Day

Objectives: Students will be able to perform a close reading of a text in order to draw inferences and conclusions.

Objectives: Students will be able to demonstrate drawing inferences and conclusions by participating in a collaborative conversation and writing a short constructed response.

Progress Monitoring

Opportunities to Learn	Opportunities to Demonstrate Learning	Opportunities to Reteach
Classroom Vocabulary		
Skill: Classroom Vocabulary	Skill: Classroom Vocabulary • Your Turn First Read • Classroom Vocabulary	Spotlight Skill: Classroom Vocabulary
Generating Questions		
Skill: Generating Questions	Skill: Generating Questions • Your Turn First Read • Skills Focus	Spotlight Skill: Generating Questions
Language Structures		
Skill: Language Structures	Skill: Language Structures • Your Turn	Spotlight Skill: Language Structures
Drawing Inferences and Conclusions		
Skill: Drawing Inferences and Conclusions	Skill: Drawing Inferences and Conclusions • Your Turn Close Read • Complete Skills Focus • Write	Spotlight Skill: Drawing Inferences and Conclusions
Verb Tenses		
Skill: Verb Tenses	Skill: Verb Tenses • Your Turn Close Read • Write	Spotlight Skill: Verb Tenses

First Read

Introduce the Text

As a class, watch the video preview and have students read the introduction in pairs to make connections to the video preview. Ask students various "wh" questions such as:

- What did you see in the video? How does it make you feel?
- What do you think the text will be about?
- Is there something in the video or introduction that surprised you?

Beginning & Intermediate

SPEAKING FRAMES

- I see ____. I feel ____.
- I think the text will be about ____.
- I was surprised by ____.

Practice Prereading Skill

Remind students that Generating Questions:

is the process of coming up with questions before, during, and after reading. Before reading, you can preview a text and then come up with questions. During reading, you can ask questions about unfamiliar terms or confusing parts. After reading, you can ask yourself questions that will help you determine the main idea or general message of the text. Generating questions helps you better understand a story or a text.

Have students work in small, homogeneous groups to generate questions about the summary.

As students are working in small groups, circulate to listen for sample questions such as:

- *What questions do you have when you read the title of the story?*
- *What questions do you have while you read the summary?*
- *What questions do you have after reading the summary?*

Activate Prior Knowledge and Experiences OPTIONAL

Have students make connections while practicing their oral language by discussing what they know about substitute teachers.

Generate a list (on the board or on paper) of any information or ideas your students have about substitute teachers.

Ask students to share where their background knowledge came from. For example, did their ideas come from a movie, friend, television show, book, or family member?

VOCABULARY

hover
to remain floating or suspended in the air

slump
to sink down or forward

outfits
a set of clothes worn together

humiliate
to make (someone) feel ashamed or foolish

dressy
formal or elegant in style

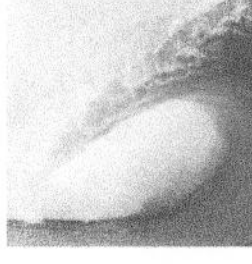

tidal wave
a very tall, strong wave that is sometimes dangerous

READ

1 "Be nice to Mom today," my dad tells me. He sets my sack lunch on the counter. It's not even 7:30 a.m. on Monday and already I'm wishing the week were over. How will I survive a week with my mother as my substitute teacher? "Make her feel welcome," Dad continues. "Remember what school felt like on *your* first day?"

2 Just then my mother enters the kitchen. She looks as nervous as the hummingbird that **hovers** outside the window. To my horror, she is dressed in one of her church **outfits:** a green silk dress with beige pumps. I am about to tell her she is *way* too **dressy** for school, when I remember my father's words.

3 None of this would be happening if Pepe hadn't been born. Mom used to be a teacher at a private school in town, but she quit during her pregnancy. Now she mostly stays home with Pepe. If I were her, I'd want to get out of the house, too. Don't get me wrong, Pepe is cute, but he cries a lot, and he's usually wet with something.

AUDIO TEXT HIGHLIGHTING

Allow students to use the audio text highlight feature to follow along as they read. Alternately, you may wish to work directly with students or group them in twos or threes for partner reading or choral reading.

Preteach Vocabulary

Model the first word and example for the class.

1. The first word is *hover,* and its meaning is "to remain floating or suspended in the air."
2. When I hear the word *hover*, I think of something in the air that is not moving forward.
3. For example, a helicopter can *hover* in one place above a ship.
4. This is an example of something that *hovers* because it is suspended in the air without moving forward.

Continue this exercise with each word in the glossary, calling on individuals or groups of students to share out.

Beginning

PRETEACH VOCABULARY

Use the gestures to clarify meanings.

- **hover** (Hold your hands just above a flat surface as if they were suspended there.)
- **outfits** (Touch or pinch different items of clothing you are wearing.)
- **dressy** (Strut like a model on a runway.)
- **slump** (Sit at your desk and slump forward.)
- **humiliate** (Look extremely embarrassed, sagging your shoulders.)
- **tidal wave** (Raise your arms and make a swooping motion with them.)

Classroom Language Focus

Remind students of the sight vocabulary and high-frequency words that they studied at the beginning of the unit. Point out that some of the words may be useful as they think about and discuss the text. For example:

- appropriate (The **appropriate** clothes for a teacher are . . .)
- conclude (This week at school will **conclude** with . . .)
- interpret (The mother **interprets** her daughter's actions to mean . . .)
- issue (The **issue** is that her mother . . .)
- section (The **section** of the story that I like is . . .)

NOTES

4 My best friend Katie and I have science class together. We get there early and sit in the back. As the class fills up, I **slump** low in my seat, keeping my head down. Suddenly, everybody gets quiet.

5 I look up. There's my mom, standing in front of the class. She smiles at me, and then introduces herself to the class.

6 To my surprise, Mom does a good job. She even makes the class laugh a few times. But I still can't wait for class to be over.

7 Finally the bell rings. Katie and I jump up. We are almost out the door when I hear her.

8 "Yvette," she says. She's holding my sack lunch. "You forgot your lunch."

9 "Thanks," I mumble. I take it from her without meeting her eyes.

10 "Love you," says Mom, just like she often does, only this time it's in front of my classmates. Everybody freezes. I'm so **humiliated**, all I can do is bury my face in Katie's shoulder. To my relief, the kids around me start to laugh and so I laugh, too. But then I see the sad expression on my mother's face. Her disappointment hits like a **tidal wave**. I don't know what to call this new feeling, but I know I'll be left thinking about it for a long time.

TEXT TALK

1. What is the story about?
2. Who are the story's characters?
3. Where does the story take place?
4. How does the story make you feel?

ELL **All Levels**

SPEAKING FRAMES

Giving Information:

- This story is about ____.
- The story's characters are ____.
- This story takes place in ____.
- This story makes me feel ____.

Asking for Information:

- Can you explain ____?
- What do you think about ____?
- Why do you think ____?

First Read

Read the story. After you read, answer the Think Questions below.

THINK QUESTIONS

1. Which three people speak in the story?

   The people that speak are ____________________.

2. Which class will Yvette's mother teach? Who are two students in this class?

   Yvette's mother will teach ____________________.

   Two students in the class are ____________________.

3. At the end of the story, what does Yvette's mother say to Yvette? How does Yvette feel at that moment?

   Yvette's mother says ____________________.

   Yvette feels ____________________.

4. Use context to confirm the meaning of the word *dressy* as it is used in "Mom's First Day." Write your definition of *dressy* here.

   Dressy means ____________________.

   A context clue is ____________________.

5. What is another way to say that someone is *humiliated*?

   Someone feels ____________________.

Think Questions

Circulate as students answer Think Questions independently. Answers will vary.

QUESTION 1: Comprehension

Yvette, Yvette's father, and Yvette's mother

QUESTION 2: Comprehension

She will teach science class. Katie and Yvette are in this class.

QUESTION 3: Comprehension

She says, "Love you." Yvette feels humiliated.

QUESTION 4: Language

Dressy describes what Yvette's mother is wearing. She is wearing a very nice dress. It is the same thing that she wears to church. *Dressy* must mean "formal or nice."

QUESTION 5: Language

The person feels extremely embarrassed.

Skill: Language Structures

Introduce the Skill

Watch the Concept Definition video and read the definition for Language Structures.

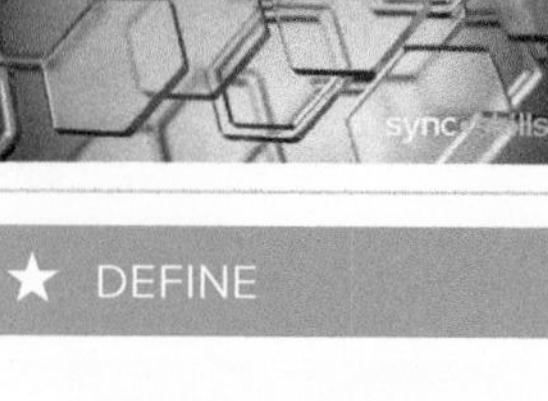

Skill: Language Structures

DEFINE

In every language, there are rules that tell how to **structure** sentences. These rules define the correct order of words. In the English language, for example, a **basic** structure for sentences is subject, verb, and object. Some sentences have more **complicated** structures.

You will encounter both basic and complicated **language structures** in the classroom materials you read. Being familiar with language structures will help you better understand the text.

CHECKLIST FOR LANGUAGE STRUCTURES

To improve your comprehension of language structures, do the following:

- ✓ Monitor your understanding.
  - Ask yourself: Why do I not understand this sentence? Is it because I do not understand some of the words? Or is it because I do not understand the way the words are ordered in the sentence?
- ✓ Break down the sentence into its parts.
  - In English, adjectives almost always come before the noun. Example: He had a **big dog.**
    - > A **noun** names a person, place, thing, or idea.
    - > An **adjective** modifies, or describes, a noun or a pronoun.
    - > If there is more than one adjective, they usually appear in the following order separated by a comma: quantity or number, quality or opinion, size, age, shape, color.
      Example: He had a **big, brown dog.**
    - > If there is more than one adjective from the same category, include the word *and.*
      Example: He had a **brown and white dog.**
  - Ask yourself: What are the nouns in this sentence? What adjectives describe them? In what order are the nouns and adjectives?
- ✓ Confirm your understanding with a peer or teacher.

TURN AND TALK

1. What kinds of sentences are difficult for you to understand?
2. How do you try to figure them out?
3. What makes some other kinds of sentences easy to understand?

ELL BEGINNING & INTERMEDIATE

SPEAKING FRAMES

- A sentence that is ____ is difficult for me to understand.
- A sentence that is ____ is easy for me to understand.

ELL ADVANCED & ADVANCED HIGH

SPEAKING FRAMES

- When I read a difficult sentence, I try to figure it out by ____.
- A sentence that is ____ is easy to understand because ____.

SKILL VOCABULARY

structure / la estructura ***noun*** the order of parts COGNATE

basic / básico/a ***adjective*** the most important parts without anything extra COGNATE

complicated / complicado/a ***adjective*** having many parts COGNATE

language structure / la estructura del lenguaje ***noun*** the order of words in a sentence COGNATE

YOUR TURN

Read each sentence in the first column. Then, complete the chart by writing the words and phrases into the "Adjective" and "Noun" columns. The first row has been done as an example.

Sentence	Adjective	Noun
You will complete a group project on conservation.	group	project
Bryan's role was to pick important passages from the text and explain their significance.		
His group asked a few times about his progress.		
Back in science class, Bryan tried to focus.		
Bryan, I gave you that role for a good reason.		

Your Turn

Ask students to complete the Your Turn activity.

Adjective	Noun
important	passages
few	times
science	class
good	reason

Discuss the Skill Model

1. Why does the reader highlight the sentence in yellow?

   She highlights the sentence because it contains unfamiliar words.

2. Why does the reader highlight the sentence in different colors?

   She uses different colors to identify the nouns and the adjectives.

3. How does this help the reader?

   She realizes that some unfamiliar words are probably adjectives because of their placement. She uses this to make a guess about the unfamiliar word.

4. What does the reader do to confirm her understanding?

   She asks her teacher if her understanding is right.

ELL

Beginning & Intermediate

Have students use the speaking frames and helpful terms to participate in the group discussion. If beginning students are hesitant to participate in a discussion, encourage them by prompting with *yes* or *no* questions.

Advanced & Advanced High

Have students use the speaking frames to participate in the group discussion.

SPEAKING FRAMES

- The reader highlights the sentence because she is ____.
- The reader highlights in different colors to identify ____.
- This helps the reader ____. She is able to ____.
- Finally, the reader asks her teacher to ____.

HELPFUL TERMS FOR DISCUSSION

- determine
- identify
- understanding
- analyze
- teacher
- noun
- confused
- confirm
- adjective

Skill: Drawing Inferences and Conclusions

Introduce the Skill

Watch the Concept Definition video ▶ and read the definition for Drawing Inferences and Conclusions.

TURN AND TALK

1. How can you sometimes tell how your best friend is feeling without even talking to him or her?
2. How can you use your own experiences to draw conclusions about your friend's feelings?
3. What are some things that people do that can help you conclude that they are sad/mad/happy?

BEGINNING & INTERMEDIATE

SPEAKING FRAMES

- I know how my friend is feeling by looking at ____.
- My own experiences help me understand when my friend feels ____.
- When people are sad/mad/happy, they might ____.

ADVANCED & ADVANCED HIGH

SPEAKING FRAMES

- When I see my friend ____, I know he/she feels ____.
- My own experiences with ____ help me understand when my friend feels ____.
- When people are sad/mad/happy, they might ____. For example, ____.

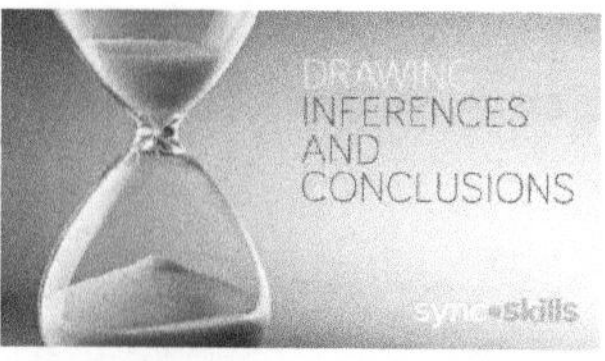

Skill: Drawing Inferences and Conclusions

★ DEFINE

Making **inferences** means connecting your experiences with what you read. Authors do not always tell readers directly everything that takes place in a story or text. You need to use clues to infer, or make a guess about, what is happening. To make an inference, first find facts, details, and examples in the text. Then think about what you already know. Combine the **textual evidence** with your **prior knowledge** to draw a **conclusion** about what the author is trying to communicate.

Making inferences and drawing conclusions can help you better understand what you are reading. It may also help you search for and find the author's message in the text.

••• CHECKLIST FOR DRAWING INFERENCES AND CONCLUSIONS

In order to make inferences and draw conclusions, do the following:

✓ Look for information that is missing from the text or that is not directly stated.
- Ask yourself: What is confusing? What is missing?

✓ Think about what you already know about the topic.
- Ask yourself: Have I had a similar experience in my life? Have I learned about this subject in another class?

✓ Combine clues from the text with prior knowledge to make an inference and draw a conclusion.
- Think: I can conclude ________________, because the text says ________________, and I know that ______________.

✓ Use textual evidence to support your inference and make sure that it is valid.

SKILL VOCABULARY

inference / la inferencia *noun* a conclusion or idea based on details from the text, as well as prior knowledge or experience COGNATE

text evidence / evidencia del texto *noun* details from the text that a reader can use to support his or her ideas COGNATE

background knowledge / conocimiento previo *noun* information a person has gained through reading and experience

conclusion / la conclusión *noun* a final opinion or decision COGNATE

YOUR TURN

Read the following excerpt from "Mom's First Day." Then, complete the multiple-choice questions below.

from **"Mom's First Day"**

None of this would be happening if Pepe hadn't been born. Mom used to be a teacher at a private school in town, but she quit during her pregnancy. Now she mostly stays home with Pepe. If I were her, I'd want to get out of the house, too. Don't get me wrong, Pepe is cute, but he cries a lot, and he's usually wet with something.

My best friend Katie and I have science class together. We get there early and sit in the back. As the class fills up, I slump low in my seat, keeping my head down. Suddenly, everybody gets quiet.

1. At the beginning of this excerpt, Yvette feels:
   - A. annoyed by her little brother.
   - B. proud to be a big sister.
   - C. jealous of her mother's past students.
   - D. worried that her mother will criticize her.

2. A detail that best supports this inference is:
   - A. "Mom used to be a teacher at a private school in town."
   - B. "She quit during her pregnancy."
   - C. "Don't get me wrong, Pepe is cute."
   - D. "He cries a lot, and he's usually wet with something."

3. Based on details at the end of the excerpt, Yvette:
   - A. does not like science class.
   - B. is mad at her friend Katie.
   - C. tries to avoid her mother.
   - D. does not get along with her classmates.

4. A detail that best supports this conclusion is:
   - A. "My best friend Katie and I have science class together."
   - B. "We get there early."
   - C. "I slump low in my seat."
   - D. "Everybody gets quiet."

Your Turn

Ask students to complete the Your Turn activity.

QUESTION 1: A) Yvette complains about her little brother, Pepe.

QUESTION 2: D) This shows that Yvette has negative feelings about her brother.

QUESTION 3: C) Yvette acts as if she is trying to hide from her mother.

QUESTION 4: C) This shows that Yvette is trying to avoid her mother..

Discuss the Skill Model

1. What does the reader wonder about?

   He wonders how Yvette feels about her mom being a substitute teacher.

2. What clues does the student highlight? What does he conclude in his annotation?

   "She is dressed in one of her church outfits," "she is way too dressy for school"; he concludes that Yvette is feeling embarrassed.

3. How does the reader use his own experience to make inferences and draw conclusions?

   He knows from personal experience that the mom's outfit is inappropriate for school.

4. What clues confirm his conclusion?

   Yvette's thoughts, like the word "horror" that describes her reaction

5. What can the reader do to check his conclusions about the text?

   He can share his ideas with a partner.

ELL **Beginning & Intermediate**

Have students use the sentence frames and helpful terms to participate in the group discussion. If beginning students are hesitant to participate in a discussion, encourage them by prompting with *yes* or *no* questions.

Advanced & Advanced High

Have students use the sentence frames to participate in the group discussion.

SENTENCE FRAMES

- The reader wonders how ____.
- The student highlights ____ in the text.
- The student concludes that ____.
- He thinks about ____.
- The reader confirms his conclusion by ____.
- The reader can also ____.

HELPFUL TERMS FOR DISCUSSION

- inference
- analyze
- actions
- personal
- clues
- confirm
- appearance
- partner
- evidence
- embarrassed
- experience
- background knowledge

Close Read

Model Skills Focus

Remind students of the Reading Skill Drawing Inferences and Conclusions. Tell students that one way to make inferences is to review text evidence and combine it with background knowledge. Direct students to the Skills Focus and remind them to track as you read aloud.

Build on the story by imagining what Yvette's mom is thinking at the end.

Model this activity for students:

- I am going to reread the last paragraph of the story to look for text evidence.
- I see the phrase "the sad expression on my mother's face."
- The mother must be surprised about how Yvette is behaving.
- I will try to use my background knowledge to think about how my parent would feel in this situation.
- I think my parent would also not be happy in this situation. I will make the inference that Yvette's mom is disappointed by Yvette's behavior.

Complete Skills Focus

Divide students into three equal groups. Assign each group with one of the following focus areas:

- Write two sentences about what Yvette's mom is thinking.
- Think of an experience from your own life that is similar to that of Yvette and her mom in the story.
- Write dialogue that Yvette's mom will say when she sees Yvette later in the day.

Circulate and monitor groups as they work.

Close Read

WRITE

NARRATIVE: How do you think Yvette's mom feels at the end of the story? Make an inference to decide. Then, write a few sentences from Mom's point of view. Pay attention to verb tenses as you write.

Use the checklist below to guide you as you write.

- ☐ Who is talking?
- ☐ What is she thinking and saying?
- ☐ What happens next?
- ☐ How does it end?

Use the sentence frames to organize and write your narrative.

Mom was surprised about what Yvette did at the end of class because ____.

Mom thought, "I feel ______________________________

that ______________________________."

At home that night, Mom said, "______________________________" to Yvette.

Mom hoped that next time Yvette would ______________________________.

Collaborative Conversation

Group students so they have a representative from each of the original three groups. Prompt groups to combine their additions, making sure that the story still makes sense once all the new pieces are included.

- Do the additions accurately address the jigsaw prompt?
- Did they make sense with the rest of the story?
- Did the additions enhance my understanding of the story?

Collaborative Conversation

SCAFFOLDS

 **BEGINNING, INTERMEDIATE** Use the word bank to participate in the group discussion.

ADVANCED Use the speaking frames to participate in the group discussion.

BEGINNING, INTERMEDIATE	ADVANCED
Word Bank	**Speaking Frames**
• made sense • showed • addressed • I understand • point of view • inferred	• The additions (did / did not) ____ accurately address the prompt. • The additions (did / did not) ____ make sense with the rest of the story. • The additions enhanced my understanding of the story because ____.

Write

Ask students to complete the writing assignment. Remind students to pay attention to verb tenses.

ELL **BEGINNING** Write a response using the paragraph frames and word bank.

INTERMEDIATE Write a response using the paragraph frames.

INTERMEDIATE
BEGINNING

Paragraph Frames	Word Bank
• Mom was surprised about what Yvette did at the end of class because ____. Mom thought, "I feel ____ that ____." • At home that night, Mom said, "____" to Yvette. Mom hoped that next time Yvette would ____.	• rude • embarrassed • expect • sad • school

In the Extended Oral Project, students plan, draft, practice, and deliver an oral presentation that ties into the theme of the unit and spans informative, argumentative, and narrative genres. Lessons provide explicit instruction to prepare students for the unique challenges of an oral presentation, and to help break down the genre characteristics of each prompt. At each step in the process, students focus in-depth on specific writing and speaking skills as they brainstorm, organize, and refine their presentation. Students also receive discussion prompts and frames to guide them in providing effective peer feedback as they practice and discuss in small groups before presenting to the class on the final day.

CONNECT TO ESSENTIAL QUESTION

What makes you, you?

In this unit, students practiced effective collaborative communication skills, as well as generating questions and drawing inferences and conclusions, while reading and analyzing two texts about identity. Now students will apply those skills to work together in writing and participating in a debate.

Developing Effective Presentations

Form	Language and Conventions	Oral Language Production
Students may struggle with the academic demands of developing the debate, such as claims and evidence.	Students should be encouraged to experiment with new sentence patterns and lengths to make their debate sound convincing and logical.	Students may make mistakes when they transfer grammatical forms from their native languages into English. Remind students to monitor their use of articles.

SCAFFOLDS

ELL ENGLISH LANGUAGE LEARNERS

Vocabulary, discussion, and peer and teacher support in the Extended Oral Project is differentiated for Beginning, Intermediate, Advanced, and Advanced High English Language Learners. See individual lesson plans for additional scaffolding and support.

Instructional Path

All Extended Oral Project lessons lesson plans appear in your digital teacher account.

Introduction

Objectives: Students will be able to identify the components of a debate in order to prepare for and participate in a debate in response to a prompt.

Objectives: Students will be able to record ideas for a debate in writing.

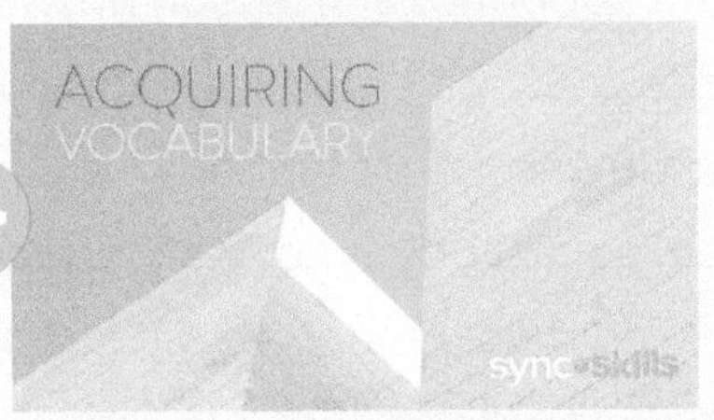

Skill: Acquiring Vocabulary

Objectives: Students will be able to use a graphic organizer to make comparisons between words and acquire new vocabulary in order to prepare for a debate.

Objectives: Students will be able to compare and contrast new words to use in a debate.

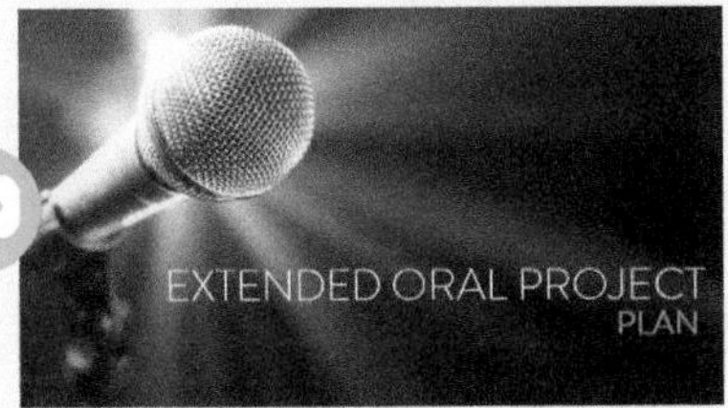

Plan

Objectives: Students will be able to plan and write a first draft of their presentation of debate points.

Objectives: Students will be able to organize their first draft using an outline.

Skill: Connecting Words

Objectives: Students will be able to apply knowledge of connecting words to revise their debate presentation.

Objectives: Students will be able to use connecting words orally and in writing.

Practice

Objectives: Students will be able to practice and revise their debate points based on peer feedback.

Objectives: Students will be able to practice a debate presentation orally and make revisions in writing.

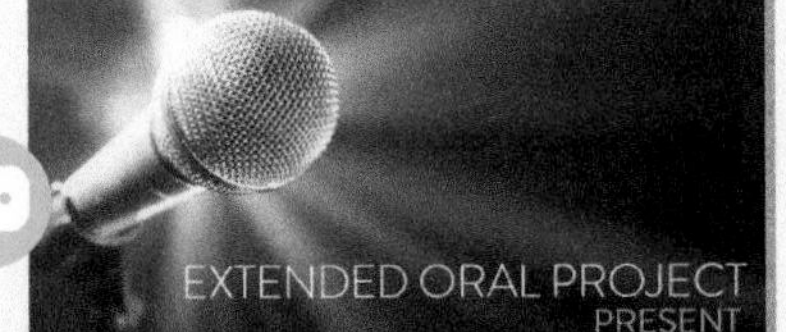

Present

Objectives: Students will be able to observe and participate in a debate in order to give and receive peer feedback.

Objectives: Students will be able to use connecting words in an oral presentation and give peer feedback orally and in writing.

Unit Overview

Integrated Reading and Writing

Extended Writing Project

English Language Learner Resources

Novel Study

End-of-Unit Assessment

Novel Study

Each Core ELAR Unit contains two texts designated for Novel Study. The Novel Study supports the close reading of the complete text through its associated Reading Guide and a series of comparative reading and writing lessons. Novel Studies are not a part of each grade-level's 180 days of instruction; however, teachers may choose to draw from them if they wish to incorporate materials from other disciplines or develop an alternative, novel-based approach to instruction.

Each novel comes with a **Reading Guide** that provides both teacher and student support. Each lesson provides key vocabulary words and close reading questions, as well as a key passage that will help teachers guide students through an exploration of the essential ideas, events, and character development in the novel. This passage will also serve as the point from which students will engage in their own StudySyncTV-style group discussion. Each novel study's **Comparative Reading and Writing** lessons contain resources to support comparative analyses. Students read passages of other texts drawn from across the disciplines and compare those passages to specific sections of the novel in written responses.

Suggested Novel Studies

Title	Genre	Summary	Themes and Topics
The Outsiders (1967)	Fiction	In 1960s Tulsa, Oklahoma, the Greasers and the Socs are at war. Ponyboy likes a Soc girl, but when Johnny stabs a Soc in self-defense, the two must go on the run.	• Adolescence • Friendship • Violence
Inside Out & Back Again (2011)	Fiction	Young Hà's father is missing in the war to the north. With the Viet Cong about to take their home city of Saigon, she flees—along with her mother and brothers—to a new life in America that is nearly as challenging as wartime.	• Refugees • Family Relationships • Immigrant Experience

OPTION 1

The Outsiders

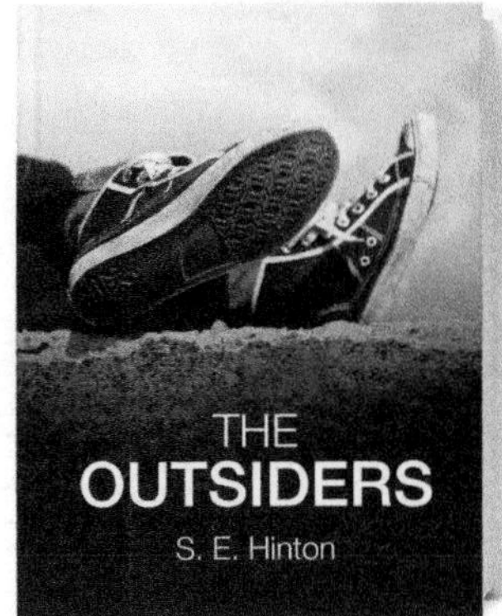

Fourteen-year-old Ponyboy is smart and thoughtful, but lives on the wrong side of the tracks. Like other "greasers," he slicks back his hair and gets into petty crimes, feuding with a gang of privileged kids called the "Socs" (SOH-shiz). Since their parents died, Ponyboy and his two brothers—handsome, foolish Sodapop and stern, serious Darry—have taken care of each other. When Ponyboy and Johnny, the most timid boys in the gang, are implicated in a murder, they flee the city and embark on a tragic and moving journey.

S. E. Hinton (b. 1948) grew up in Tulsa, Oklahoma. She wrote *The Outsiders* at the age of 16. The novel was published four years later and was adapted into a movie in 1983. Her other books include *That Was Then, This Is Now; Rumble Fish;* and *Tex*.

OPTION 2

Inside Out & Back Again

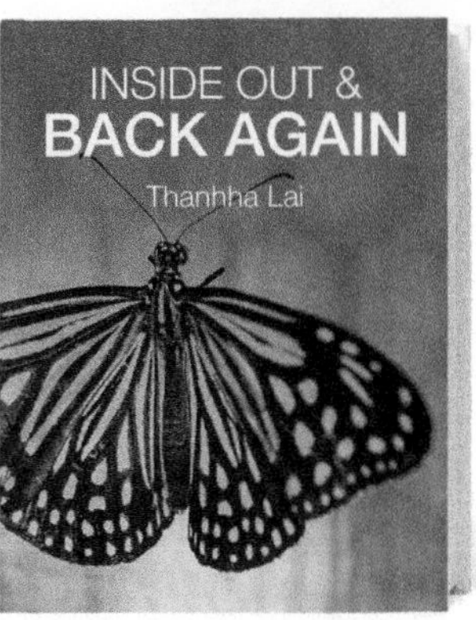

It's 1975 in Saigon—the Year of the Cat—and South Vietnam is on the brink of surrender. Ten-year-old Hà is wishing that her father would come home, but he's been missing from the family for nearly a decade. A fortune teller predicts their lives will "twist inside out" in the coming year. As Saigon falls to the North Vietnamese Army a couple of months later, Hà, her mother, and her three older brothers hatch a quick plan to escape.

Inside Out & Back Again is a National Book Award-winning novel in verse by Thanhha Lai (b. 1965) chronicling a turbulent year in young Hà's life, one that sweeps her and her family from the familiarity of Saigon to the loneliness of Alabama. Ten-year-old Hà's Year of the Cat closely resembles Lai's own story of fleeing the Vietnam War in 1975 and resettling in the American South.

Unit Overview

Integrated Reading and Writing

Extended Writing Project

English Language Learner Resources

Novel Study

End-of-Unit Assessment

Spotlight Skills Review

A review day before the end-of-unit assessment gives you an opportunity to review difficult concepts with students using Spotlight Skills lessons. Spotlight Skills are targeted lessons that provide you with resources to reteach or remediate without assigning additional readings. Every Core ELA Skill lesson has a corresponding Spotlight Skill lesson. Spotlight Skills can be assigned at any point in the year, but the end of each unit provides a natural moment to pause, review data collected throughout the unit, and reteach skills students have not yet mastered.

Progress Monitoring

The Progress Monitoring charts that appear before every text in this unit identify standards and associated Spotlight Skills. On review day, you may want to give preference to reteaching skills that are not revisited in later units. You can see where skills are covered again in the Opportunities to Reteach column.

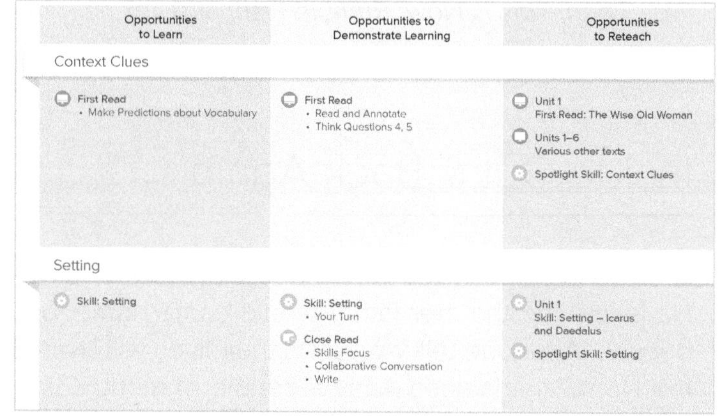

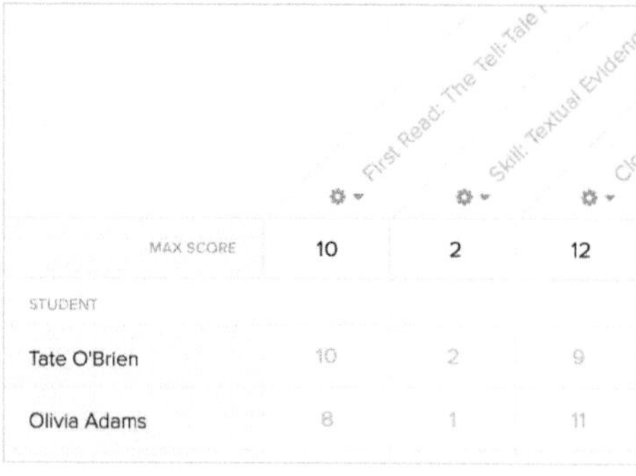

StudySync Gradebook

As students submit assignments on StudySync, their mastery of skills and standards is tracked via the gradebook. The gradebook can be sorted and viewed in a variety of ways. Sorting by assignment shows overall student performance, while sorting by standards or by Skill lessons displays student progress toward mastery goals.

Skills Library 

Spotlight Skills are located in the Skills section of the StudySync Library. You can assign Spotlight Skills to individual students or groups of students. Search tools allow you to search by skill type or name.

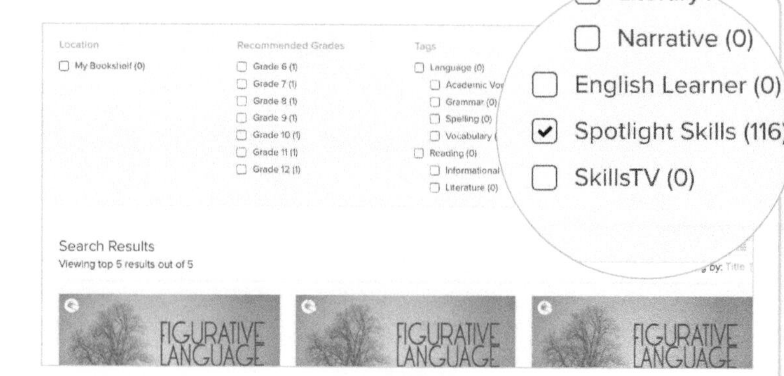

End-of-Unit Assessment

The end-of-unit assessment can be found in two places. The digital version of the assessment can be assigned from the Online Assessment tab inside your ConnectED account. The paper-based version of the assessment can be printed from the End-of-Unit Assessment tab inside this unit in your StudySync account.

Assessment Section	Content	Assessed Skills	
READING	The Emperor's Procession Genre: Fiction Word Count: 653 Lexile: 1080L	• Plot • Character • Textual Evidence	• Summarizing • Theme • Figures of Speech
	The Old Man Dreams Genre: Poem Word Count: 246 Lexile: N/A	• Figurative Language • Textual Evidence	• Theme • Poetic Elements and Structure
	What's in Your DNA? Genre: Nonfiction Word Count: 1,094 Lexile: 1100L	• Figures of Speech • Central or Main Idea	• Textual Evidence • Arguments and Claims
	The Path to Home Genre: Poem Word Count: 275 Lexile: N/A	• Figurative Language • Poetic Elements and Structure	• Theme
REVISING and EDITING	Student Passage #1	• Active and Passive Voice • Verb Moods	• Consistent Verb Voice and Mood
	Student Passage #2	• Organizing Argumentative Writing • Thesis	• Reasons and Relevant Evidence • Transitions • Conclusions
WRITING	Prompt: Literary Analysis	• Literary Analysis	

What's Next?

Assessment results can be viewed by item, standard, and skill to monitor mastery and make decisions for upcoming instruction.

RETEACH skills that students have not yet mastered, using Spotlight Skills or the Test Preparation and Practice book.

REVISE your teaching plan to provide more or less explicit instruction into a skill or text, using Beyond the Book activities for enrichment.

REGROUP students and levels of scaffolding based on standards progress.

No Risk, No Reward

Why do we take chances?

UNIT 3

No Risk, No Reward

ESSENTIAL QUESTION

Why do we take chances?

Why do we take chances? Every time a person takes a chance, he or she risks losing something for the possibility of a reward. Sometimes these chances pay off, and sometimes they don't. Yet, people still take risks every day. With a genre focus on informational texts, this Grade 8 unit prepares students to explore questions about why we take chances.

Nonfiction authors explore risk-taking from a variety of viewpoints. Walter Lord takes a historical approach to the topic, sharing an account of a real event with a surprising outcome that still affects people today. Anya Groner and Nina Gregory look at contemporary risk-takers who search for solutions in the face of environmental challenges, while essayist Thomas Ponce is a current risk-taker seeking environmental justice. President Ronald Reagan shares his perspective after a shocking national tragedy. Frederick Douglass explains risks he had to take in order to improve his own life as an enslaved person in the time before the Civil War; poets Langston Hughes and Frances Ellen Watkins Harper reveal how taking risks was historically necessary for African Americans. Classic American novelist Jack London depicts a risk-taking fictional character—a dog.

After reading about these ideas within and across genres, your students will write an informative essay, applying what they have learned from the unit's literature, speeches, and informational texts to an informative writing project.

Integrated Reading and Writing

Genre Focus: INFORMATIONAL TEXT

Extended Writing Project and Grammar

English Language Learner Resources

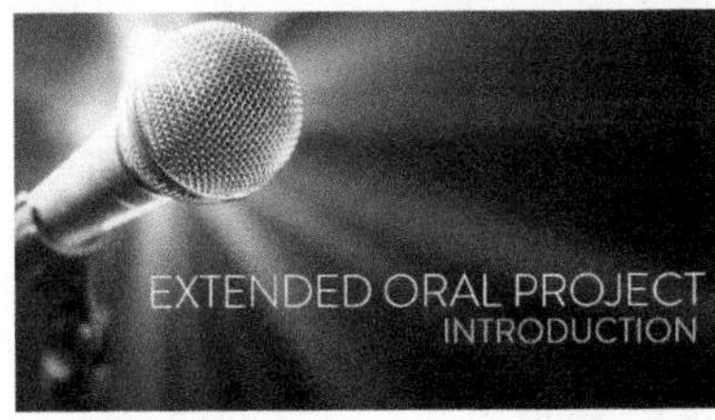

906 | Novel Study Choices

A Night to Remember
INFORMATIONAL TEXT
Walter Lord

Narrative of the Life of Frederick Douglass, An American Slave
INFORMATIONAL TEXT
Frederick Douglass

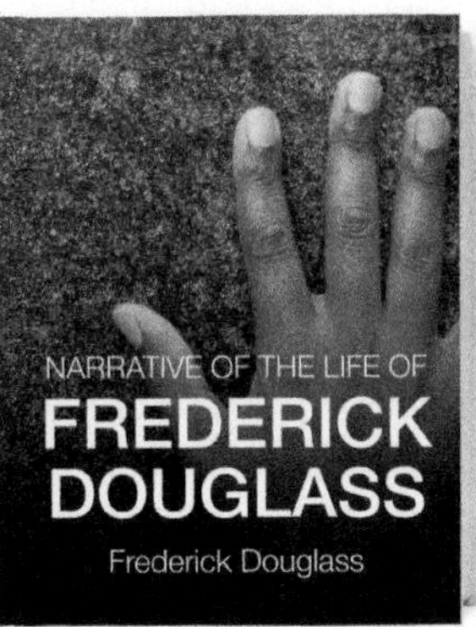

909 | End-of-Unit Assessment

THEMATIC PACING GUIDE

No Risk, No Reward

tv StudySyncTV or SkillsTV Episode

Pacing Guide

Days	Readings	Skill and Standard Instruction	Skill Practice and Spiraling
1–2	Essential Question **The Big Idea: Why do we take chances?** p. 630	• Recognizing Genre: Informational Text • Academic Vocabulary	• Write: Analyzing Genre
3–5	**The Vanishing Island** p. 634	• Evaluating Details • Greek and Latin Affixes and Roots • Media	• Textual Evidence • Informative Writing
6–9	PAIRED READINGS **A Night to Remember** tv p. 670 **Address to the Nation on the Explosion of the Space Shuttle *Challenger*** p. 680	• Summarizing • Informational Text Structure tv	• Textual Evidence • Comparative Writing • Collaborative Conversations
10–12	**A Kenyan Teen's Discovery: Let There Be Lights to Save Lions** p. 698	• Synthesizing • Media • Word Patterns and Relationships	• Textual Evidence • Summarizing • Informative Writing
13–17	PAIRED READINGS **Mother to Son** p. 716 **Learning to Read** p. 726 **Narrative of the Life of Frederick Douglass, An American Slave** tv p. 736	• Adjusting Fluency • Informational Text Elements • Figurative Language tv	• Textual Evidence • Central or Main Idea • Author's Purpose and Point of View • Comparative Writing • Collaborative Conversations

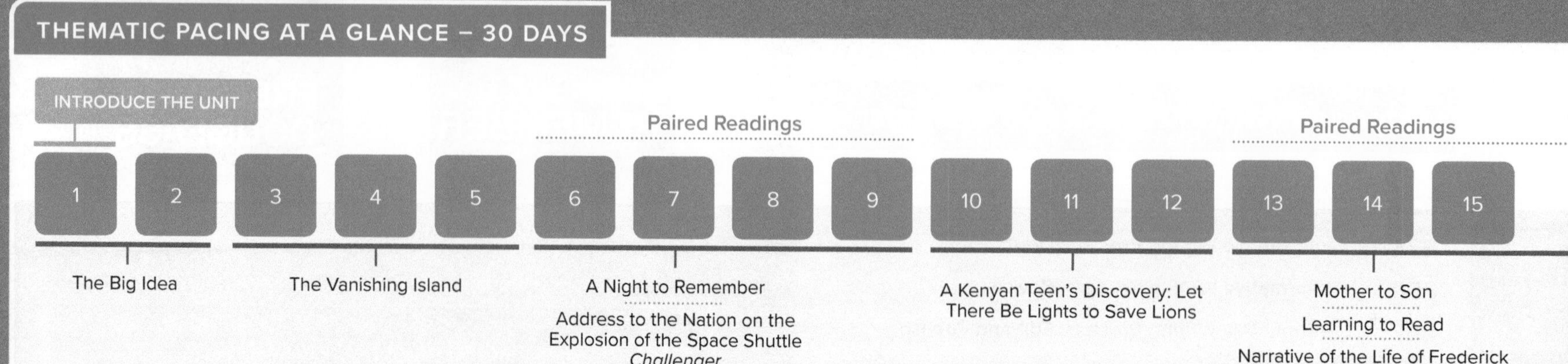

Days	Readings	Skill and Standard Instruction	Skill Practice and Spiraling
18–21	**The Day I Saved a Life** p. 758	• Context Clues • Technical Language • Write: Analyzing Genre	• Textual Evidence • Argumentative Writing
22–24	**The Call of the Wild** tv p. 778	• Language, Style, and Audience • Media	• Textual Evidence • Theme • Literary Analysis Writing • Collaborative Conversations
25–27	**Cocoon** p. 796	• Connotation and Denotation	• Textual Evidence • Literary Analysis Writing
28	**Self-Selected Reading and Response** p. 812	• Independent Reading	• Personal Response Writing

Review and Assessment See page 908.

Days	Review and Assessment	Skill Practice and Assessment
29	**Skills Review** p. 908	Students will have the opportunity to complete one or more Spotlight skill lessons in order to improve understanding and further practice skills from the unit that they found most challenging.
30	**End-of-Unit Assessment** p. 909	For more detail, please see the End-of-Unit Assessment information for Grade 8 Unit 3 on page 909.

Extended Writing Project and Grammar

Pacing Guide

In the second half of the unit, students continue exploring texts that address the unit's Essential Question and begin crafting a longer composition to share their own ideas about the Essential Question in the Extended Writing Project. The writing project will take your students through the writing process to produce an informative essay.

Extended Writing Project Prompt

What happens when we take risks?

Choose three informational texts from this unit, including research links in the Blasts, and explain how the authors inform readers about their risk-taking subjects. Identify the risks individuals take and the outcomes of those risks. Include a clear main idea or thesis statement, and cite evidence from each text to explain your conclusions.

Days	Extended Writing Project and Grammar	Skill and Standard Instruction	Connect to Mentor Texts
16	**Informative Writing Process: Plan** p. 822		
17-20	**Informative Writing Process: Draft** p. 838	• Thesis Statement • Organizing Informative Writing • Supporting Details	• Address to the Nation on the Explosion of the Space Shuttle *Challenger* • Narrative of the Life of Frederick Douglass, An American Slave • The Day I Saved a Life
21-25	**Informative Writing Process: Revise** p. 858	• Introductions • Transitions • Precise Language • Style • Conclusions	• The Vanishing Island • A Night to Remember • The Day I Saved a Life
26-28	**Informative Writing Process: Edit and Publish** p. 867	• Participles • Gerunds • Infinitives	Additional grammar lessons can be found in the StudySync Skills Library.

Research

The following lessons include opportunities for research:

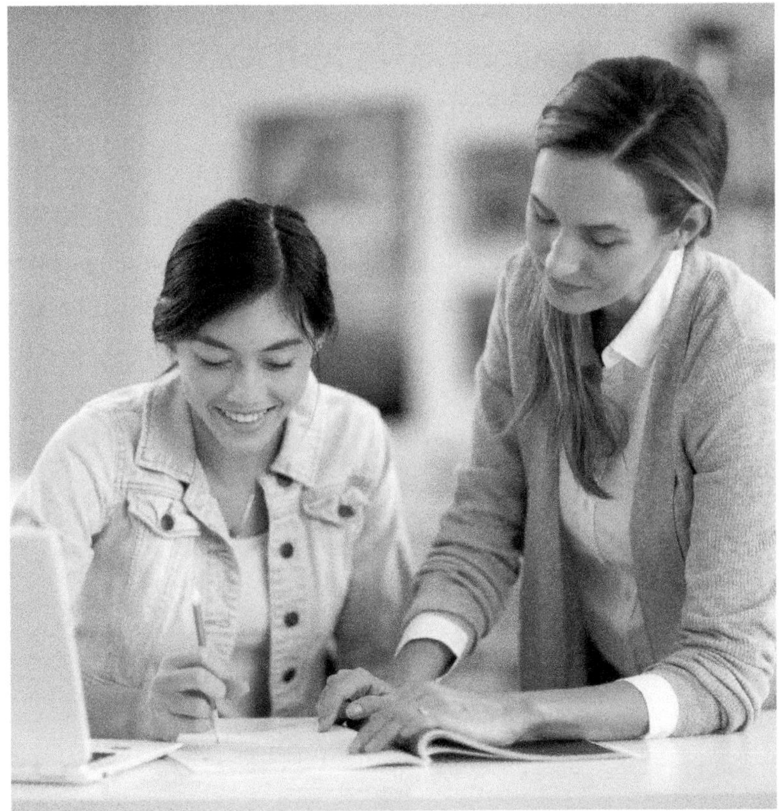

Blast **No Risk, No Reward** Research Links*

Close Read **The Vanishing Island** Beyond the Book

Blast **Risky Business** Research Links*

Close Read **Address to the Nation on the Explosion of the Space Shuttle *Challenger*** Beyond the Book

Close Read **A Kenyan Teen's Discovery: Let There Be Lights to Save Lions** Beyond the Book

Blast **Now, That's an Idea** Research Links*

Close Read **Narrative of the Life of Frederick Douglass, An American Slave** Beyond the Book

First Read **The Day I Saved a Life** Independent Research (Beyond)

First Read **The Day I Saved a Life** Beyond the Book

*See the teacher lesson plan online

Self-Selected Reading Prompt

After reading a self-selected text, students will respond to the following narrative prompt:

Have you ever heard the expression "walk a mile in someone else's shoes"? It means you can't really understand someone until you've spent some time imagining the world from his or her perspective.

Why do we take chances?

Assume the role of a character, individual, or narrator/speaker from your self-selected text. Imagine that a journalist has asked your chosen character to respond to the question "Why do we take chances?" Think about how your chosen character, individual, or narrator/speaker would respond, and write a personal response as this character, individual, or narrator/speaker.

Integrated Scaffolding

ELL and Approaching grade-level students receive scaffolds for every lesson, whether in the Thematic, Novel Study or ELL Resources sections of the unit. Specific scaffolds are intentionally designed to support the needs of English Language Learners and Approaching grade-level students in the ELA classroom. Other scaffolds exist as part of the many standard features in the StudySync digital platform and can be strategically utilized to support students' comprehension and engagement.

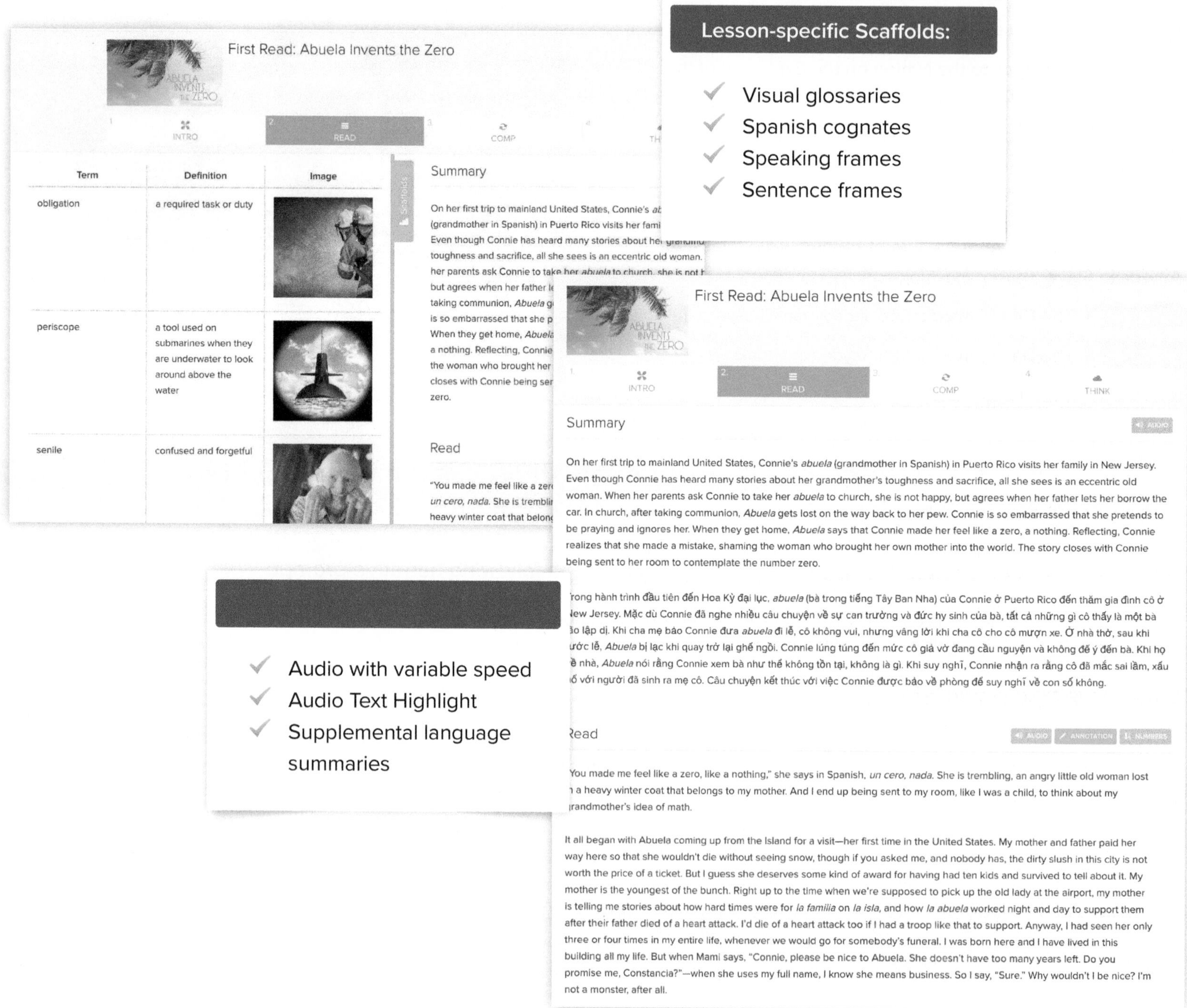

English Language Learner Resources

Both Thematic and Novel Study units include English Language Learner resources designed to match the thematic focus, text structures, and writing form of the unit. ELL resources include two leveled texts and an extended oral project.

ELL Texts	Differentiated Text Levels	Skill and Standard Instruction
	BEGINNING 540L | 377 words INTERMEDIATE 620L | 416 words ADVANCED 770L | 467 words ADVANCED HIGH 810L | 545 words Use this text in place of or as an extension to "Address to the Nation on the Explosion of the Space Shuttle *Challenger*."	• Sight Vocabulary and High-Frequency Words • Using Prereading Supports • Analyzing Expressions • Main Ideas and Details • Spelling Patterns and Rules
	BEGINNING 390L | 257 words INTERMEDIATE 700L | 416 words ADVANCED 830L | 456 words ADVANCED HIGH 900L | 567 words Use this text in place of or as an extension to *Narrative of the Life of Frederick Douglass, An American Slave.*	• Classroom Vocabulary • Making Connections • Language Structures • Comparing and Contrasting • Main and Helping Verbs
	In this Extended Oral Project, students will write and perform an informative presentation. This may be assigned in place of this unit's EWP.	• Acquiring Vocabulary • Sentence Types

Focus on English Language Proficiency Levels

ADVANCED HIGH
ADVANCED
INTERMEDIATE
BEGINNING

ELL Resources provide targeted support for four levels of proficiency: Beginning, Intermediate, Advanced, and Advanced High. Instruction and scaffolds, as well as the texts themselves, are differentiated based on these levels.

Additional differentiated scaffolds include visual glossaries, speaking and writing frames, and suggested grouping for peer and teacher support. Lessons also include suggested extension activities to challenge Advanced and Advanced High students as they progress through the year.

Assessment

DAYS 29-30

Assessment in StudySync is built upon a recursive cycle that includes assessment, instruction, and review. Screening, placement, and benchmark assessments help teachers establish baselines and determine scaffold needs. Throughout the course of instruction, teachers regularly assess student progress using formative and summative measures, and use the individualized data from those assessments to guide choices about instruction, review, remediation, and enrichment to bring all students to standards mastery and College and Career Readiness.

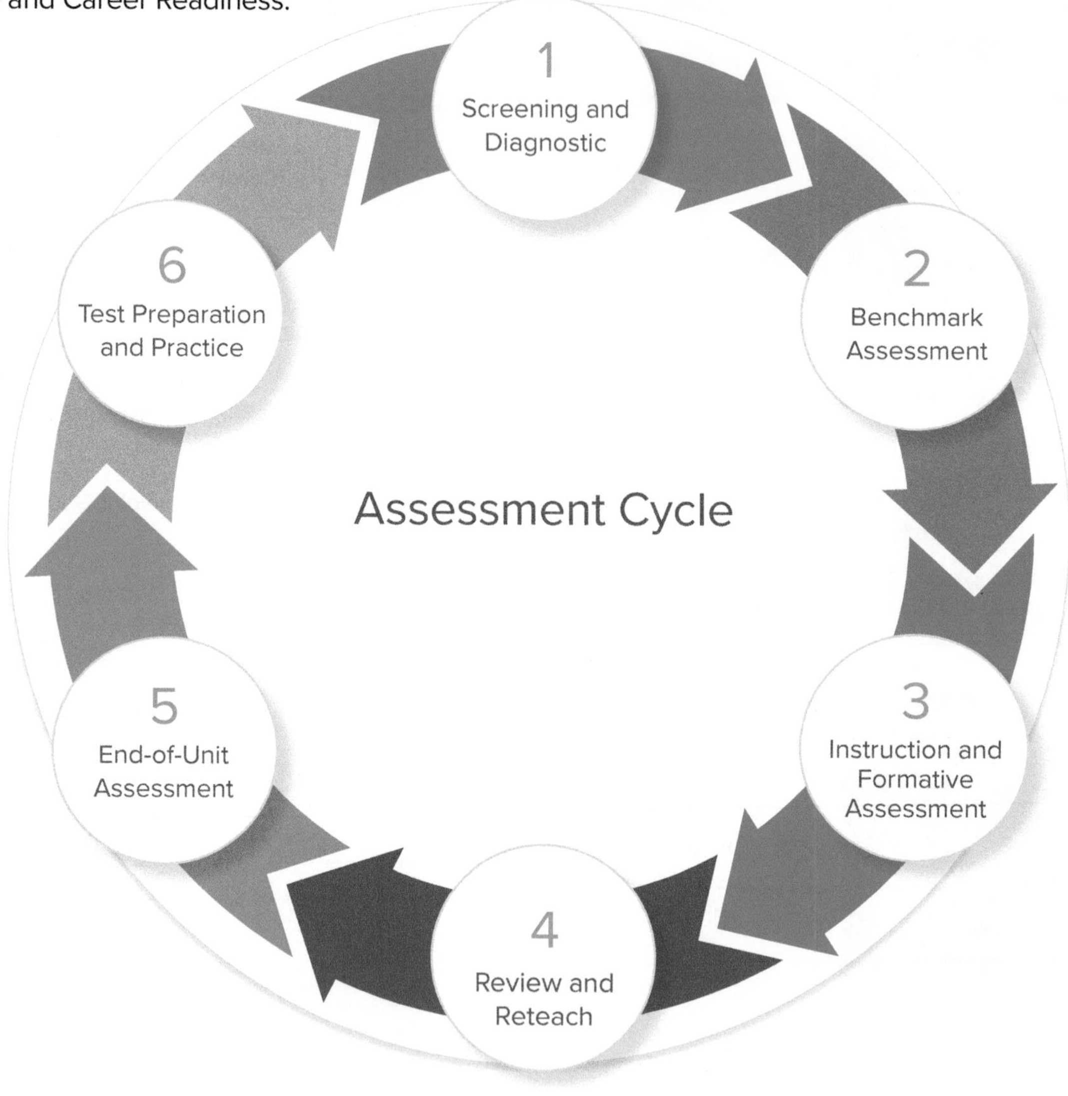

What's Next?

Assessment results can be viewed by item, standard, and skill to monitor mastery and make decisions for upcoming instruction.

- ✓ Reteach skills that students have not yet mastered, using Spotlight Skills or the Test Preparation and Practice book.
- ✓ Revise your teaching plan to provide more or less explicit instruction into a skill or text, using Beyond the Book activities for enrichment.
- ✓ Regroup students and levels of scaffolding based on standards progress.

Review

Spotlight Skills Review

A review day before the end-of-unit assessment gives you an opportunity to review difficult concepts with students using Spotlight Skills lessons. Spotlight Skills are targeted lessons that provide you resources to reteach or remediate without assigning additional readings. Every Core ELA Skill lesson has a corresponding Spotlight Skill lesson. Spotlight Skills can be assigned at any point in the year, but the end of each unit provides a natural moment to pause, review data collected throughout the unit, and reteach skills students have not yet mastered.

Progress Monitoring

The Progress Monitoring charts that appear before every text in this unit identify standards and associated Spotlight Skills. On review day, you may want to give preference to reteaching skills that are not revisited in later units. You can see where Skills are covered again in the Opportunities to Reteach column.

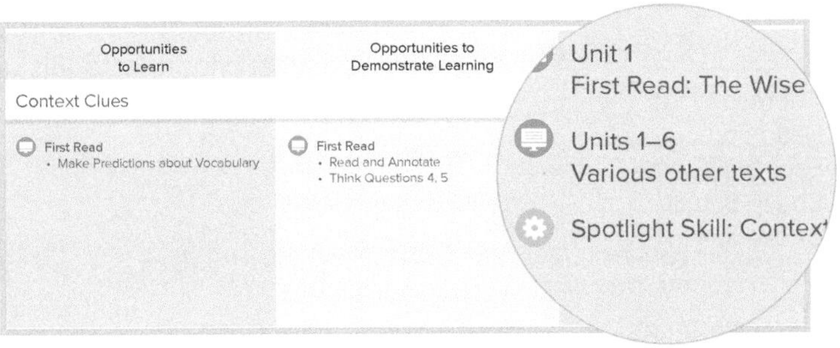

StudySync Gradebook

As students submit assignments on StudySync, their mastery of skills and standards is tracked via the gradebook. The gradebook can be sorted and viewed in a variety of ways. Sorting by assignment shows overall student performance, while sorting by standards or by Skill lessons displays student progress toward mastery goals.

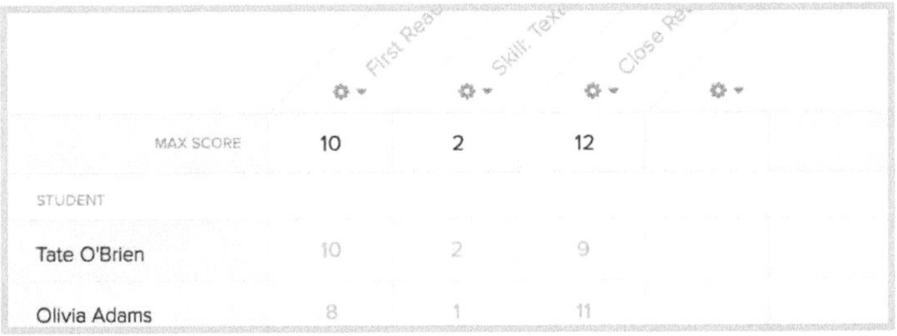

Skills Library

Spotlight Skills are located in the Skills section of the StudySync Library. You can assign Spotlight Skills to individual students or groups of students. Search tools allow you to search by Skill type or name.

End-of-Unit Assessment

Assessed Reading Skills

- ✓ Connotation and Denotation
- ✓ Context Clues
- ✓ Figurative Language
- ✓ Greek and Latin Affixes and Roots
- ✓ Informational Text Elements
- ✓ Informational Text Structure
- ✓ Language, Style, and Audience
- ✓ Point of View
- ✓ Summarizing
- ✓ Technical Language
- ✓ Textual Evidence
- ✓ Word Patterns and Relationships

Assessed Revising, Editing, and Writing Skills

- ✓ Conclusions
- ✓ Gerunds
- ✓ Infinitives
- ✓ Introductions
- ✓ Organizing Informative Writing
- ✓ Participles
- ✓ Precise Language
- ✓ Style
- ✓ Supporting Details
- ✓ Thesis Statement
- ✓ Transitions

Unit Preview

Introduce the Unit

As a class, watch the unit preview and discuss the questions below.

- What two words would you use to describe this video?
- What key words or images from the video do you think will be most important to this unit?

Instructional Path

Big Idea Blast

Objectives: After exploring background information and research links about a topic, students will respond to a question with a 140-character response.

DIGITAL ONLY

Skill: Recognize Genre

Objectives: After learning about the genre of informational text, students will be able to identify and describe characteristics of memoir, articles, speeches, biography, and essays.

DIGITAL ONLY

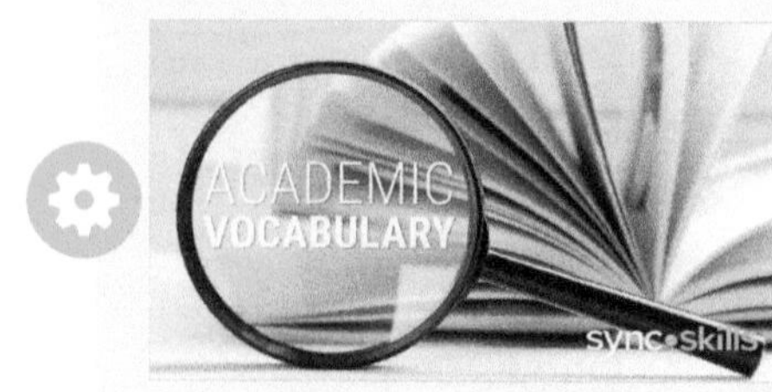

Skill: Academic Vocabulary

Objectives: After learning the meanings of ten academic vocabulary words, students will be able to recognize and use them in a variety of contexts.

DIGITAL ONLY

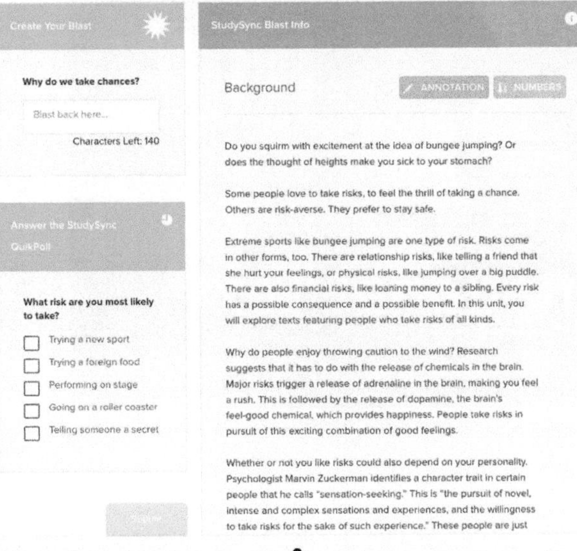

Blast: No Risk, No Reward

Why do we take chances?

Ask students:

- What do you think this Blast will be about? Make a prediction.

TEXT TALK

What are the possible results of taking a risk?

Risks have possible consequences and benefits.

Why do some people like taking risks more than others?

According to Marvin Zuckerman, some people have a "sensation-seeking" character trait.

Why do people sometimes take "senseless" risks?

They make emotional choices and base their choices on personal experience rather than logic.

Create Your Own Blast

SCAFFOLDS

Ask students to write a 140-character Blast after they complete the QuikPoll.

Use the scaffolds below to differentiate instruction for your ELL English Language Learners.

BEGINNING Write a response using the word bank to complete the sentence frame.

INTERMEDIATE Write a response using the sentence frame.

ADVANCED, ADVANCED HIGH Write a response using the sentence starter.

BEGINNING	INTERMEDIATE	ADVANCED, ADVANCED HIGH
Word Bank	**Sentence Frame**	**Sentence Starter**
fun a bad outcome reward improvement high low	A chance is worth taking when you think the likelihood of ____ is ____.	• A chance is worth taking when . . .

Skill: Recognize Genre

Introduce the Genre: Informational Text

Watch the Concept Definition video and read the following definition with your students.

Informational text presents readers information or ideas about real people, places, things, and events. In order to express information clearly, writers use a set of informational text elements, including a **thesis**, or main idea, and supporting **evidence** in the form of details, facts, examples, statistics, and expert opinions.

A typical informational text includes an introduction that builds to a thesis, body paragraphs that include key ideas and supporting evidence, and a conclusion that restates the most important ideas to remember.

Within body paragraphs, writers might use specific **text structures**, or organizational patterns. For instance, a writer may discuss ideas in order of importance, tell about events in chronological order, or present causes and then describe their effects.

Informational writing can take many forms, including essays, pamphlets, news and magazine articles, textbook articles, and nonfiction books.

TURN AND TALK

Use the questions to discuss informational texts.

- What features in an informational text convey information?
- What feature do you find the most useful and why?

SPEAKING FRAMES

- The text features that make up an informational text are ____, ____, ____, ____, and ____.

Your Turn

Ask students to complete the Your Turn activity.

Description	Text Feature
A chart shows the number of cases of the flu over the course of 12 months.	graphic feature
Ninety-eight percent of adults have drivers licenses.	statistics
The flu is a contagious viral infection of the respiratory passages and causes fever, severe aching, and catarrh, and often occurs in epidemics.	specialized vocabulary
The flu is a virus.	facts
The author interviewed several experts on the different techniques for treating the flu.	research

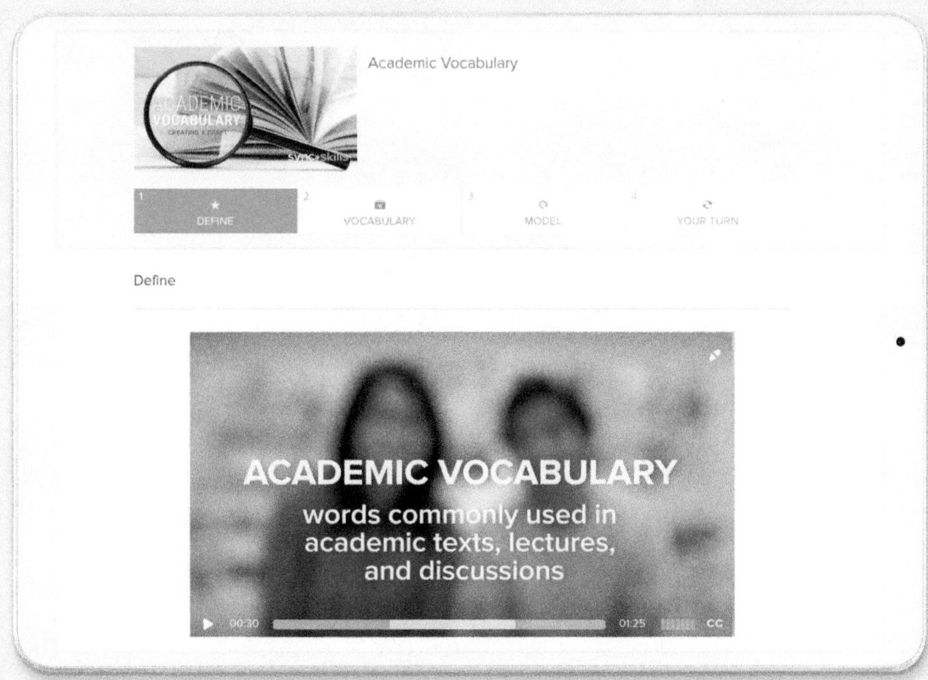

Skill: Academic Vocabulary

Introduce the Terms

asterisk / el asterisco *noun* a star-shaped character (*) used in printing COGNATE

asteroid / el asteroide *noun* a small space object made up of rock and metal that moves around the sun COGNATE

astronaut / el/la astronauta *noun* a person trained to travel in a spacecraft COGNATE

deduce / deducir *verb* to conclude by reasoning COGNATE

induce / inducir *verb* to bring about; to cause something to happen COGNATE

introduce / introducir *verb* to bring into notice, practice, or use, as in to introduce a new fashion COGNATE

apathetic / apático/a *adjective* showing little or no emotion

empathy / la empatía *noun* the feeling that you understand and share another person's experiences and emotions COGNATE

pathologist / el/la patólogo/a *noun* a doctor who specializes in medical diagnosis COGNATE

sympathy / la compasión *noun* sharing the feelings of others, especially feelings of sorrow or anguish

Your Turn

Ask students to complete the Your Turn activities.

Your Turn 1

Word	Root	How can the word part help you remember the meaning of the word?
introduce	duc (Latin) "lead"	If you introduce a topic, you are leading the discussion toward that topic.
deduce	duc (Latin) "lead"	When you deduce a solution, you follow where the evidence leads to draw a conclusion.
induce	duc (Latin) "lead"	When you try to induce someone to accept your opinion, you are trying to lead them toward your way of thinking.
apathetic	path (Greek) "feeling, disease"	If you are bored and don't care or have any feelings about a situation, you are apathetic.
asterisk	ast(er) (Greek) "star"	The star-shaped symbol you put next to an important item on a list is called an asterisk.

Your Turn 2

QUESTION 1: B **QUESTION 2:** D **QUESTION 3:** A **QUESTION 4:** C **QUESTION 5:** C

Your Turn 3

See digital teacher's edition for complete sample activity."

Practice Using Vocabulary

Divide the vocabulary words into two lists. Pair students and give each student one half of the list. Challenge students to have a casual conversation with each other that uses every word on their list. Students should aim to insert their vocabulary words in a way that sounds natural. You may wish to turn this activity into a game, allowing partners to award each other points if they effectively use each word on their list.

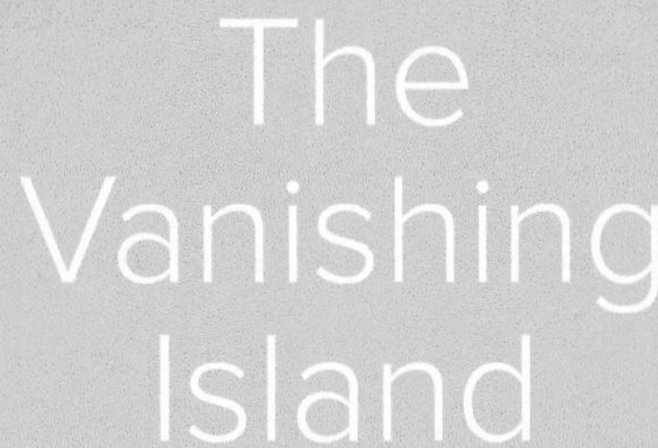

The Vanishing Island

INFORMATIONAL TEXT
Anya Groner
2017

Introduction

Author Anya Groner offers an intimate perspective of the Biloxi-Chitimacha-Choctaw Native American tribe and the trials they face as their ancestral homeland disappears before their eyes. As creeping water threatens the tribe and much of the Louisiana coast, the tribe must take on the challenge of seeking a new and safe place to live. In a race against the clock, the tribe seeks ways to preserve community and protect their culture from eroding along with the land.

The ancestral homeland of the Biloxi-Chitimacha-Choctaw Native American tribe, Isle de Jean Charles, is being threatened by rising sea levels. In the past, the small Louisiana island was eleven-by-five miles, but over time it has shrunk to only two miles long by a quarter mile wide. The tribe originally settled on the island in the early 1800s and was self-sufficient for years. However, the loss of land has meant that the tribe can no longer grow food to sustain themselves. In 2002, the tribe had an opportunity to relocate, but the residents voted against it. In 2009, after Hurricanes Katrina and Rita, the residents agreed to leave, but potential future neighbors did not want the tribe in their backyard. In 2016, the government gave the tribe a $48 million grant, which will allow the tribe to stay together and maintain their community when they find a new home.

ELL Proficiency-leveled summaries and summaries in multiple languages are available digitally.

Audio and audio text highlighting are available with this text.

CONNECT TO ESSENTIAL QUESTION

Why do we take chances?

Why would a group of people stay in a dangerous location? In this informational text, author Anya Groner describes the struggle faced by the Biloxi-Chitimacha-Choctaw Native American tribe as their homeland vanishes into the surrounding water.

Access Complex Text

LEXILE: 1000L **WORD COUNT:** 5,780

The following areas may be challenging for students, particularly ELL English Language Learners and A Approaching grade-level learners.

Prior Knowledge	Connection of Ideas	Specific Vocabulary
• Students may be unfamiliar with environmental and geological changes that cause massive land erosion. • References to historical events, such as the Indian Removal Act and the Trail of Tears, as well as references to French influence on Louisiana culture, may need explaining.	• This article interweaves information involving Louisiana geology, political and social history, the culture and lives of Native Americans, and historical events in a long and complex narrative, and the narration moves back and forth in time. Students may need support as the topics and time periods shift.	• Students may be unfamiliar with domain-specific vocabulary, such as *anhingas*, *arsenic*, and *palmetto(s)*, as well as French words, such as *bousillage*. • Using Greek and Latin roots, as well as a dictionary, can help students with words such as *biannual*.

SCAFFOLDS  ENGLISH LANGUAGE LEARNERS  APPROACHING GRADE LEVEL  BEYOND GRADE LEVEL

These icons identify differentiation strategies and scaffolded support for a variety of students. See the digital lesson plan for additional differentiation strategies and scaffolds.

Instructional Path

The print teacher's edition includes essential point-of-use instruction and planning tools. Complete lesson plans and program documents appear in your digital teacher account.

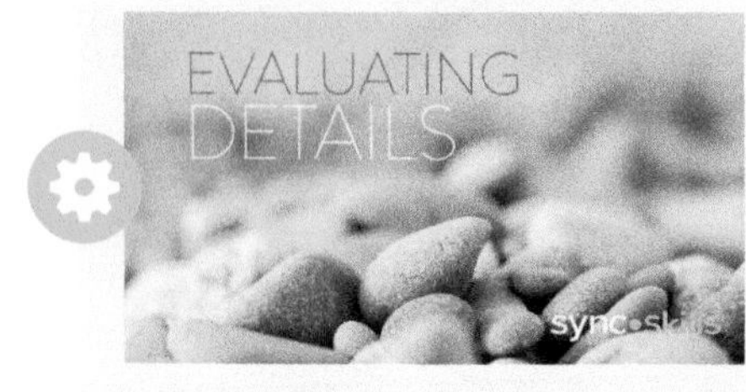

Skill: Evaluating Details

Objectives: After reading and discussing a model, students will be able to evaluate details in order to determine key ideas.

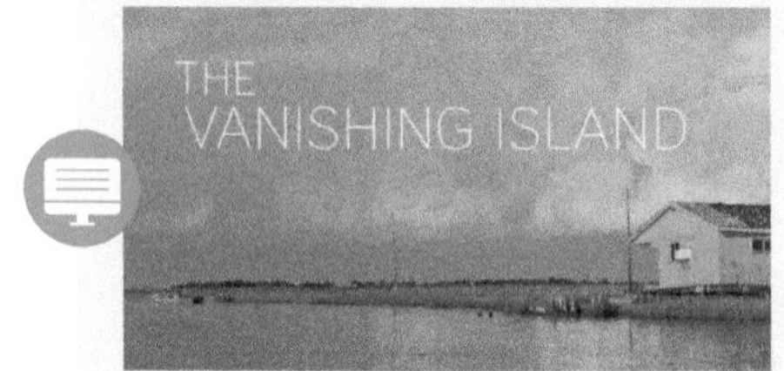

First Read: The Vanishing Island

Objectives: After an initial reading and discussion of an informational text, students will be able to identify and restate the text's key ideas and details.

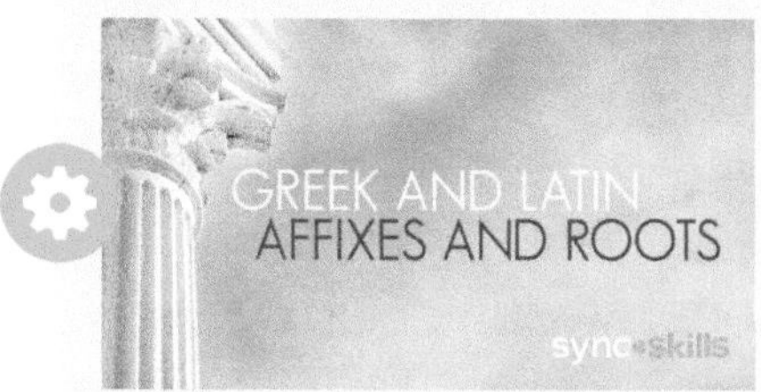

Skill: Greek and Latin Affixes and Roots

Objectives: After rereading and discussing a model of close reading, students will be able to determine the meaning and usage of grade-level academic English words derived from Greek and Latin roots.

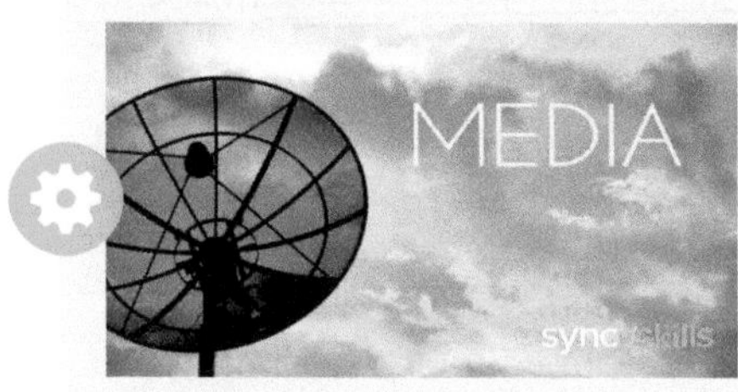

Skill: Media

Objectives: After rereading and discussing a model of close reading, students will be able to analyze and evaluate the author's use of media to achieve specific purposes.

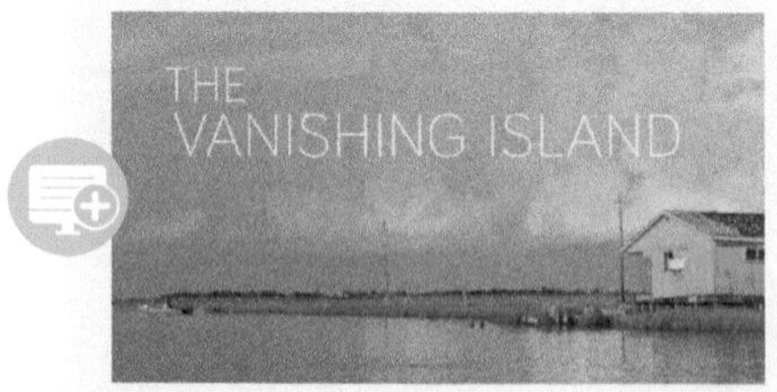

Close Read: The Vanishing Island

Objectives: After engaging in a close reading and discussion of the text, students will be able to explain why people fight hard for their cultural survival, citing different media in a short, written response.

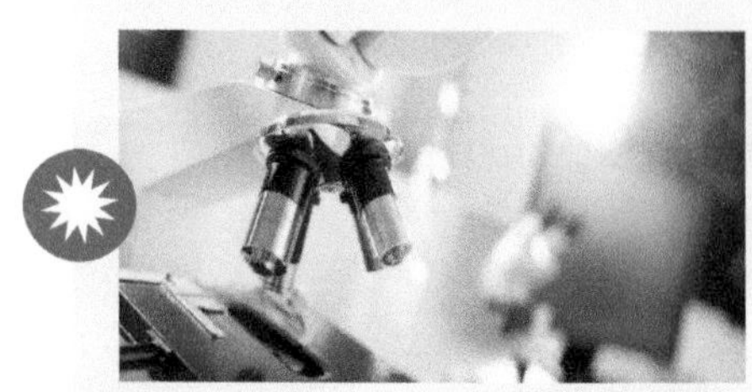

Blast: Risky Business

Objectives: After exploring background information and research links about a topic, students will respond to a question with a 140-character response.

Progress Monitoring

Opportunities to Learn	Opportunities to Demonstrate Learning	Opportunities to Reteach
Evaluating Details		
Skill: Evaluating Details	First Read • Read and Annotate	Spotlight Skill: Evaluating Details
Greek and Latin Affixes and Roots		
Skill: Greek and Latin Affixes and Roots	Skill: Greek and Latin Affixes and Roots • Your Turn Close Read • Skills Focus	Spotlight Skill: Greek and Latin Affixes and Roots
Media		
Skill: Media	Skill: Media • Your Turn Close Read • Skills Focus • Write	Unit 3 Skill: Media - A Kenyan Teen's Discovery: Let There Be Lights to Save Lions Unit 3 Skill: Media - The Call of the Wild Spotlight Skill: Media

First Read

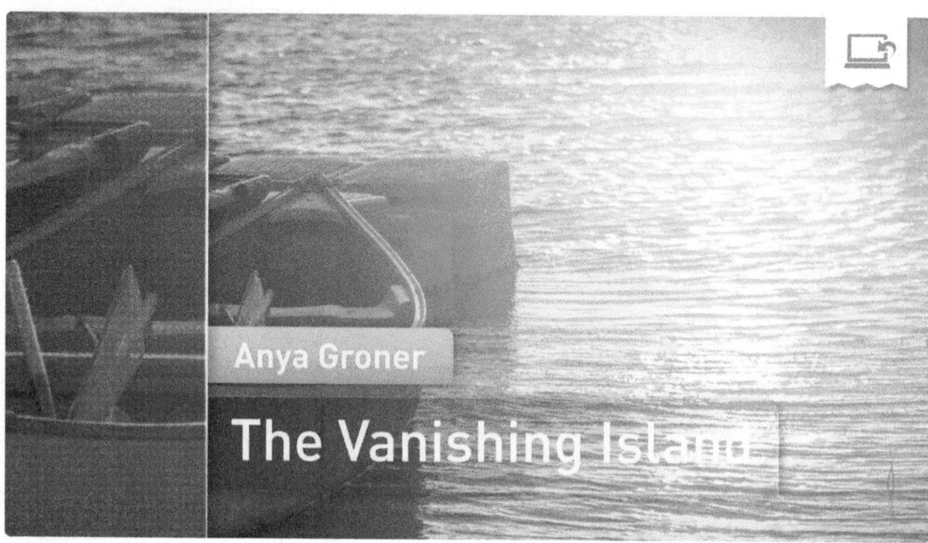

Introduce the Text

As a class, watch the video preview  and have students read the introduction in pairs to make connections to the video preview.

To activate prior knowledge and experiences, ask students:

- What key words or images from the video do you think will be most important to the text you are about to read?
- Why do you think it's important to learn about this topic?

ELL **SPEAKING FRAMES**

- The ____ in the video makes me think ____.
- The video shows ____. This makes me wonder ____.
- I think the text will ____. I think this because ____.
- I predict that there will be ____. I believe this because ____.

Entry Point

As students prepare to read "The Vanishing Island," share the following information with them to provide context.

✓ A coastal area can be protected from hurricane damage by barrier islands and wetlands. A barrier island lies just off the coast and takes the brunt of a storm as it approaches the coast from the ocean. During a hurricane, a wetland absorbs much of the water from the initial storm surge, as well as water from the pounding rains, reducing flooding in populated areas. When these natural protective features disappear through erosion or destruction, an area like Isle de Jean Charles is much more at the mercy of hurricanes.

✓ Louisiana was part of France's colonial empire in North America until the late 1700s. French culture remains strong in the area, influencing cuisine, place-names, religious practices, and other cultural characteristics.

✓ French-speaking Acadians (descendants from French settlers in North America) migrated from Canada to what is now Louisiana in the late 1700s and developed a distinct local culture, including a popular cuisine and the Cajun French dialect.

"We know we are going to lose it. We just don't know when."

NOTES

The Lay of the Land

1 At first glance, the Isle de Jean Charles, a skinny, two-mile long Louisiana island 75 miles south of New Orleans, looks like a tropical paradise. Beards of Spanish moss sway from the branches of oak trees. Orange and white wildflowers brighten both sides of the only street. Snow-white egrets, blue and green herons, and ebony anhingas stretch their necks, balancing on fallen trees. A flock of red-winged blackbirds takes flight, swooping before landing on the power lines. Even the houses have a bird-like quality. Teal, maroon, and gray, the buildings perch on stilts, fourteen feet off the ground. Wide porches and open front doors welcome visitors. A group has gathered for a fresh crawfish and crab boil. Everyone knows each other here: they grew up together, fishing and crabbing and catching game. Of the two dozen families that still live here, most are relatives and members of the Biloxi-Chitimacha-Choctaw Native American tribe. But the island is not what it used to be. In fact, the island is vanishing. By 2050, Isle de Jean Charles may be completely gone.

Skill: Media

The boldface text sitting on its own line shows that this is a heading. The heading gives clues about the information in this section. The word land indicates it will be about the geography of the island.

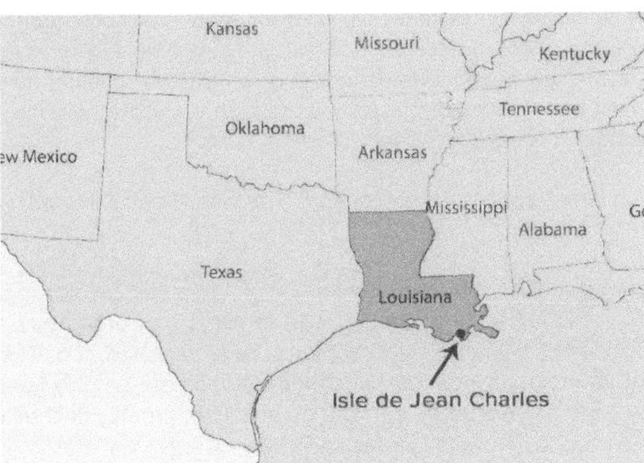

Analyze Vocabulary Using Context Clues

In paragraph 7, focus on the sentence that uses the word ***subsistence***. Point out these context clues:

1. First, I notice there is a phrase that follows the word *subsistence*.
2. The phrase seems to be the definition of the word.
3. I read the paragraph again. The meaning fits the context because the forests and fish nurseries are gone. That means people can no longer live off their natural surroundings.

Media

How did the reader use a feature of the print medium to better understand the text?

The reader used a boldface section heading and a key word to identify what information the author will give in that section.

TEXT TALK

How many people live on Isle de Jean Charles, and how are they related?

See paragraph 1: Two dozen people still live there. Most of them are relatives and members of the Biloxi-Chitimacha-Choctaw tribe.

NOTES

2 "Way back in the old days," lifetime resident Wenceslaus Billiot Sr. says in the film *Can't Stop the Waters,* "you had trees. There was no bay. All this water used to be marsh." Billiot Sr. is an 89-year-old boat builder and lifelong resident who has watched the landscape transform. "I built this house in the 1960s. I have another I built in '49. I built it all." Since 1955, the tribe has lost 98 percent of their land to encroaching waters. What was once an eleven-by-five mile island that contained forests and cattle farms is now just two miles long and a quarter of a mile wide. The land, composed of soft, silty dirt, has dissolved, much of it giving way to the waters of the Gulf of Mexico—and the population has shrunk along with the island.

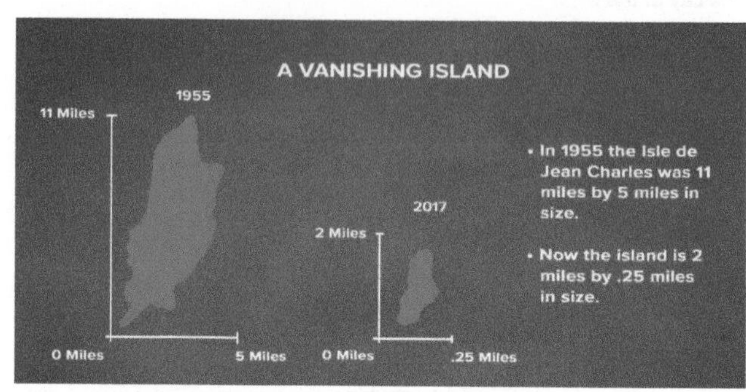

3 "Just in my lifetime, the amount of land loss is astonishing," says tribal secretary Chantel Comardelle. She spent her early years on the island, but her family left when she was four because life on the mainland is more stable than an uncertain future on Isle de Jean Charles. Nonetheless, like many tribal members who've moved away, the island remains her cultural home. She visits nearly every weekend, usually bringing her children with her. "Every time I go back, I see a little bit less."

4 "I grew up here," echoes Emray Naquin. "The land is going like you wouldn't believe."

5 When he was a child, the tribe's leader, Chief Albert Naquin, set traps in the woods with his father. Now, though, that forest is part of the bay, a place where fishermen search for crabs. Farms have vanished, too. There's no place for livestock. Even small vegetable gardens are hard to keep. Over time, the earth has absorbed salt and arsenic from the polluted waters that sweep across the land with increasing frequency.

TEXT TALK

Where has the lost land gone?

See paragraph 2: The land has disappeared under the waters of the Gulf of Mexico.

NOTES

6 “We were so self-sufficient as a tribe, that [in the past] we were unaware of the outside world,” explains Damian Naquin. He’s eighteen years old. He grew up in nearby Pointe-aux-Chenes. “When the Great Depression happened, the tribe didn’t know it.” He says that during the nation’s greatest economic collapse, tribe members suffered no shortage of food. “It didn’t affect us.”

7 Self-sufficiency used to be a point of pride for islanders who found freedom in working for themselves. **Subsistence**, the ability to live off one’s natural surroundings, is no longer possible because of land loss. The forests are gone, and without the marshes to sustain fish nurseries and provide habitats, the once abundant sea life has diminished.

8 “At one time, water was our life. Now it’s almost our enemy because it is driving us out,” says Comardelle. “It’s a double-edged sword. Our life and our death.”

9 Between August and October, the peak months of hurricane season, day-to-day erosion is worsened by storms. Since 1998, Terrebonne Parish, the region that encompasses the Isle de Jean Charles, has suffered a federally-declared disaster every two years. The big ones arrive with more strength and more frequency than in the past. The natural features that used to protect land—wetlands and barrier island—are gone. During hurricanes, waist-deep water rises over the only exit road, cutting off the island from rescue crews. Trees fall and wind rips walls and roofs from buildings. Before residents began elevating their homes atop stilts, biannual flood waters swept furniture and belongings into the bay. “Every time there’s a flood, we lose everything,” explains Damian. “We don’t have any valuables. We know, if we get something, the next storm that comes through, it’s going to ruin it. It’s going to carry it away.”

10 When storms subside, weary residents paddle through town checking up on one another and assessing the damage. After the waters recede, mold and mildew linger, which causes respiratory problems and makes residents ill. The cycle of devastation and rebuilding is exhausting. But it wasn’t always like this.

11 “Now [folks] evacuate for hurricanes. Back then they didn’t,” recalls Comardelles’s father, Deputy Chief Wenceslaus Billiot Jr. As a child in 1965, he spent Hurricane Betsy in his father’s boat, in the canal in front of their house. “We would get hit by storms but it wouldn’t be as bad because we had protection. When Camille hit we didn’t have any damage at all. Now, a hurricane like Betsy hits? Shooo.” His voice drops to a whisper and he shakes his head.

12 With such severe conditions, outsiders are often baffled to learn that many of the remaining residents of Isle de Jean Charles refuse to leave. The island, which some affectionately refer to as “the bathtub,” isn’t simply a place to

SELECTION VOCABULARY

subsistence / la subsistencia *noun* the tools and ability needed to survive COGNATE

Prepare for Advanced Courses

Use the activity below to differentiate instruction for your B Beyond grade-level learners.

Look at paragraph 6. Have students discuss what they already know about how Native Americans lived off the land and their treatment of the environment. Ask students to conduct informal research to answer the following questions: How do Native Americans rely on self-sufficiency? How have Native American survival practices changed over time?

live—it is the center of tribal life and a cultural homeland. Eight generations have grown up on Isle de Jean Charles, surviving off the bounty of the water and land around them: hunting, fishing, trapping, and gardening. As the land **erodes**, the Biloxi-Chitimacha-Choctaw tribal culture erodes with it. "Once our island goes, the core of our tribe is lost," says Comardelle. "We've lost our whole culture—that is what is on the line."

13 Many elder tribe members don't want another way of life. They grew up here. Though the island has changed, giving up on their homeland is simply too hard. For them, staying put is a way of maintaining traditional life. Others lack the financial resources to live elsewhere. They have come to terms with cleaning up flood damage every two to three years.

14 Island life has changed dramatically over the past few decades. "The old chief, a great-great-great-grandpa of mine, he owned the [island] store," remembers Comardelle. "The store was also the dance hall, it was the church, it was the wedding hall, it was everything." When the population began shrinking, the store shut down. Today the closest grocery store is fifteen miles away. Other community spaces have disappeared as well. There are no longer event grounds on the island. Grand Bois Park, a public event space on the mainland once used for pow wows, has been destroyed by flooding, too. The tribe hasn't held a pow wow—a traditional Native American festival—since before Hurricane Katrina hit Louisiana in 2005. "We have no place," says Comardelle. "I used to dance in pow wow dress. My kids have never experienced that."

15 What remains are the Isle de Jean Charles firehouse and the local marina. Above the tin roof, an orange flag flaps in the wind. It is the flag of Houma Nation, the name of another local Native American tribe. On weekends, visitors come to the island to eat fresh crawfish, shrimp, and crabs; the rest of the week the marina is quiet, as though already abandoned.

16 For more than fifteen years, Chief Naquin has been trying to relocate his people. "The longer we wait," Naquin says in the documentary *Can't Stop the Water*, "the more hurricane seasons we have to go through. We hate to let the island go, but we have to. It's like losing a family member. We know we are going to lose it. We just don't know when."

17 As chief, Naquin believes he must have a good heart in order to know right from wrong and determine what's good for his people. "We're washing away, one day at a time," he says. It is painful for him to admit, but Naquin believes the tribe's future lies elsewhere.

18 In January of 2016, Chief Naquin received good news. Through a Housing and Urban Development grant, his tribe received $48 million, about half the

Skills Focus

QUESTION 1: Greek and Latin Affixes and Roots

The word *education* has the Latin root *duc*. The root helps me understand the meaning of the word because education leads people to knowledge.

SELECTION VOCABULARY

erode / erosionar ***verb*** to become worn down or to deteriorate, usually caused by natural forces

- What is happening to the island?
- How do clues such as "once our island goes" show the meaning of *erode*?

NOTES

estimated cost of resettling the tribe. The money would help build a community center, medical facilities, and housing for tribe members. That includes the 600 or so people who left Isle de Jean Charles and scattered throughout Louisiana. The grant would also help fund an education program so visitors can learn about the island's history and the difficult process of relocation.

19 "I'm flying high as a kite," Naquin told the newspaper *Houma Today* after receiving the news. It's easy to understand why the grant would make him so happy. Though the island is vanishing, with this money the Biloxi-Chitimacha-Choctaw tribe just may have a future.

Eight Generations of History

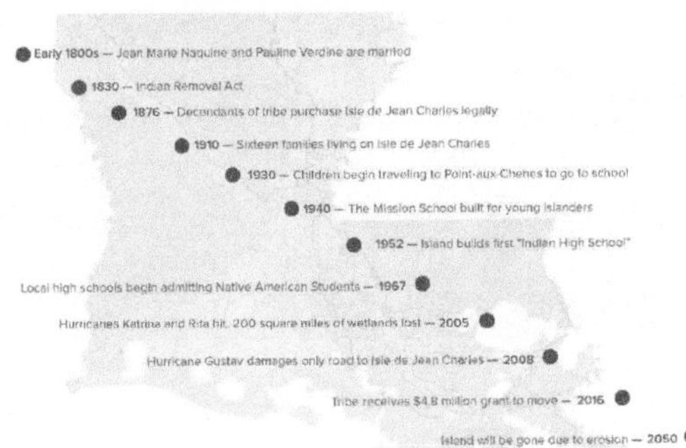

Early 1800s — Jean Marie Naquine and Pauline Verdine are married
1830 — Indian Removal Act
1876 — Decendants of tribe purchase Isle de Jean Charles legally
1910 — Sixteen families living on Isle de Jean Charles
1930 — Children begin traveling to Point-aux-Chenes to go to school
1940 — The Mission School built for young islanders
1952 — Island builds first "Indian High School"
Local high schools begin admitting Native American Students — 1967
Hurricanes Katrina and Rita hit. 200 square miles of wetlands lost — 2005
Hurricane Gustav damages only road to Isle de Jean Charles — 2008
Tribe receives $4.8 million grant to move — 2016
Island will be gone due to erosion — 2050

20 Jean Marie Naquin and Pauline Verdin married in the early 1800s. After their wedding, though, they needed to hide: Jean Marie was French and Pauline was Native American. At the time in Louisiana, interracial couples faced discrimination and even violence. Jean Marie's family disowned him because of the marriage. To escape persecution, Jean Marie and Pauline built their home on an "uninhabited" island. The landscape was rich with palmettos, alligators, crawfish, and sea birds.

21 Ironically, it was Jean Marie's disapproving father, Jean Charles, for whom the Isle de Jean Charles was likely named. He was the one who first showed his son the island, hidden in the coastal wetlands. Jean Charles had first come to the island while he was employed by the notorious privateer and outlaw, Jean Lafitte. At the time, Louisiana's wetlands were considered "uninhabitable" by the government. They weren't even mapped by Europeans. For a man like Jean Lafitte, a privateer who transported stolen goods and slaves to illegal markets, the maze of marshes provided a hiding place for his misdeeds.

Skills Focus

QUESTION 3: Media

The timeline is a good way to show me the events that happened over eight generations of history, but the disadvantage of a timeline is that it doesn't give any details about these events. When I go on to read the text, I see that it does explain the events with rich and interesting details.

TEXT TALK

What does Chief Naquin think about the tribe's future?

See paragraphs 16–19: He thinks the tribe can survive by resettling together in a new place.

Skills Focus

QUESTION 5: Connect to Essential Question

Jean Marie and Pauline took a risk when they built their home on an uninhabitable island. They took this chance because they were not safe on the mainland.

22 The coastal swamps provided safety for the newly married Jean Marie and Pauline. Not only was the island isolated, the land was also free. "Uninhabitable" land meant unwanted land, so Jean Marie and Pauline simply claimed it as their own. They built their home from mud, moss, and palmetto leaves, a kind of construction known as bousillage. Soon they started a family.

23 By the 1830s, Jean Marie and Pauline's children were having children of their own. Later, they married Native Americans from off the island and brought them to Isle de Jean Charles to live and start families as well. Once again, the remote location provided safety from a hostile society. In 1830, the United States Congress passed the Indian Removal Act, a federal law authorizing the forced removal of southern Native Americans from their ancestral land. The purpose of the law was to enable white settlers to move in. A few tribes, including the Mississippi Choctaws, signed treaties exchanging their homeland for payment and land rights west of the Mississippi. Other tribes resisted and the situation escalated. White men formed local and state militias, which forced southern and southeastern Native Americans to abandon their homes and march west to Oklahoma and Texas. The Native Americans were exposed to the elements. They lacked supplies. Thousands died and the march west became known as the Trail of Tears, in memory of the lives and culture lost.

24 Unlike so many other Native Americans, the growing Naquin family escaped the Trail of Tears because of their hidden island deep in the marshes. For the second time, the swamp saved their lives.

TEXT TALK

How did living in a hidden swamp help the people on Isle de Jean Charles survive in the past?

See paragraphs 23 and 24: The people on the island could stay on their ancestral land. Other Native Americans were forced off their land after the Indian Removal Act and lost their lives during the Trail of Tears.

NOTES

25 By 1876, Louisiana settlers were looking to expand their communities and build in new places. The state revoked the coastal marshes' official designation as "uninhabitable." It put the wetlands and their hidden islands up for sale. Four families, residents of Isle de Jean Charles and descendants of Jean Marie and Pauline, purchased the land they lived on, which gave them a legal claim to the island their families had been occupying for seven decades.

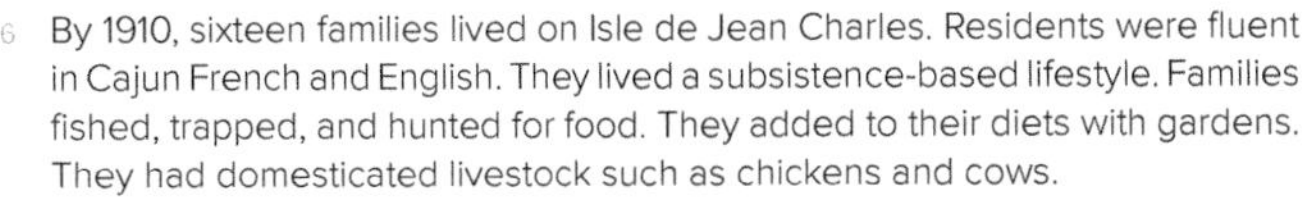

26 By 1910, sixteen families lived on Isle de Jean Charles. Residents were fluent in Cajun French and English. They lived a subsistence-based lifestyle. Families fished, trapped, and hunted for food. They added to their diets with gardens. They had domesticated livestock such as chickens and cows.

27 French, Native American, and African food cultures influenced their cuisine. For instance, Gumbo Fricassee, a popular dish, contains the following ingredients:

- Okra - a vegetable imported from West Africa during the slave trade
- Roux - a mixture of fat and flour often used as a base in French cooking
- Filé - a Choctaw spice made from ground sassafras leaves
- The Holy Trinity - a Catholic nickname for the celery, bell peppers, and onions, essential ingredients in any gumbo recipe
- Whatever seafood, chicken, or sausage is fresh and available

Skills Focus

QUESTION 2: Media

The photograph of gumbo fricassee shows the finished product of the recipe the author includes. This helps me understand the kind of food that is associated with the tribe's cultural heritage.

28 Religious practices on the island similarly combine French Catholic and Native American customs. To this day, many Biloxi-Chitimacha-Choctaw people attend both church and pow wows.

29 Masculinity was important in both games and government. On Christian or Native American holidays, men and boys often gathered to play pick, a game still played today. Damiann Naquin first played pick when he was six. Pick, he explains, is "a simple game. You have a circle in the mud. Everyone has a sharpened wooden stick, which you find from a tree and sharpen. . . . The point [is] to see who could keep their stick in the mud the longest [and] to knock another person's stick down."

30 The tribe's chief was always a man. As the tribal leader, he would **maintain** the grocery store, distribute mail, help **settle** disputes, represent the people of the island to outsiders, and gather residents for community service. Upon retirement, he chose his successor, a practice that continues to this day.

31 Despite the growing size of the community, for decades Isle de Jean Charles lacked a school. In the 1930s, children began traveling by small wooden boats called pirogues to the nearby town of Pointe-aux-Chenes, where a missionary school funded by donations and run by the Live Oak Baptist Church served both white and Native American children. At that time, though, Louisiana was committed to Jim Crow laws, which legalized racial segregation. The missionary school didn't last long. The superintendent visited, saw a racially mixed classroom, and shut the school down. The island children had nowhere to go.

 SELECTION VOCABULARY

maintain / mantener *verb* to keep or continue without changing COGNATE

- What goals are described in this paragraph?
- How do those goals show the meaning of *maintain*?

settle / resolver *verb* to resolve a problem or reach an agreement

- What is being "settled"?
- What other events are described in the sentence? Are they positive or negative?

NOTES

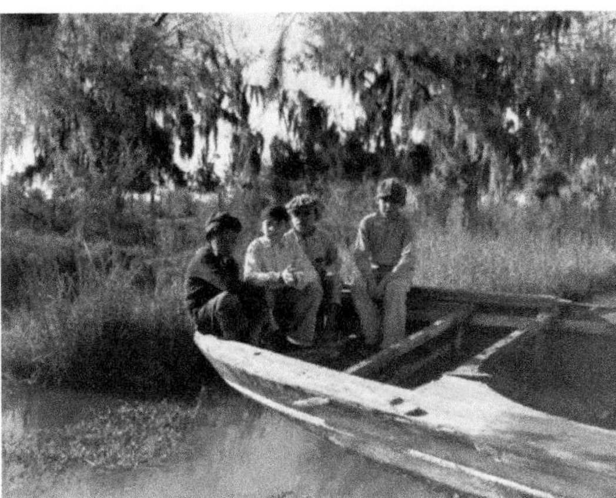

32 In 1940, Baptists tried again to provide education for the younger islanders by building the Mission School. It was a one room building on the Isle de Jean Charles. The mission school filled a gap, but it only ran to eighth grade. Eventually, some frustrated families moved off the island. In 1952, Louisiana built its first "Indian High School" in Houma, Louisiana. It was a segregated school for Native American teenagers 25 miles from Isle de Jean Charles. It was not until 1967 that local public schools admitted Native American students.

Prepare for Advanced Courses

Use the activity below to differentiate instruction for your **B** Beyond grade-level learners.

Direct students to reread paragraphs 31–33.

Ask students: How does the author's inclusion of the information about schools add complexity to the island problems?

Answers will vary; sample answer: The author shows that the island had to abide by state laws, which included racial segregation. Island life meant "traveling by small wooden boats," so a mix of geography, culture, and politics made attending school at times impossible. This made raising families there more stressful.

Media

How did the reader use a visual in the print medium to better understand the text?

The reader noticed a photograph that helped her visualize key details in the text about how flooding can trap people on the island.

Greek and Latin Affixes and Roots

How did knowledge of Greek roots and affixes help the reader define a word?

The reader combined the root *geo* and the affix *-logy* to confirm that *geological* had to do with the study of the earth.

NOTES

Skill: Media

The author talks about the road being low and easily flooded and then includes a photograph of it. The photo really helps me see how close to the water the road is. No one could get to school or work when it floods.

33 Even today, there are no schools on the island. The closest schools are on the mainland. In 2008, Hurricane Gustav damaged the only road connecting the mainland to the island, turning it from a two-lane road into a one-lane road. After that, school buses stopped coming to Isle de Jean Charles. All but one family with school-age children have moved away. Though the road has been repaired, it still sits only inches above open water. High winds can cause flooding over the pavement. "If you live on the island and the road is flooded then you can't go to school or go to work," explains Sheila Billiot.

Stomping Out the Boot

34 If you open a United States atlas or search the Internet for "Louisiana map," you'll discover a state shaped roughly like a boot. Louisiana is bordered by the Mississippi River to the east, Arkansas to the north, and Texas to the west. The foot of the boot stretches south and east into the Gulf of Mexico.

Skill: Greek and Latin Affixes and Roots

I see the word geological, and I think it has to do with a study of Earth. I know that it combines the Greek root geo, meaning "earth," and the Greek root logy, meaning "the study of."

35 A state's shape sounds unchangeable, but some Louisianans believe their map needs to be redrawn. "The boot is at best an inaccurate approximation," writes Brett Anderson, staff writer for the New Orleans newspaper *The Times-Picayune*. Anderson isn't disputing Louisiana's borders with surrounding states; his contention lies with the southernmost border, where the state's marshy edges are rapidly slipping into the gulf.

36 Because marshlands are largely impassable except by boat, it's difficult to understand the magnitude of Louisiana's land loss unless viewing it from a plane. The United States Geological Service (USGS) reports that between 1932 and 2000, roughly 1,900 square miles of Louisiana's land vanished into the Gulf of Mexico. That's an area about the size of Delaware. Today, an

TEXT TALK

Why is it difficult for residents to travel off the island?

See paragraph 33: There is only one road that connects the island to the mainland. If that road is flooded, people cannot go to school or work.

Why do Louisiana residents want their state to be redrawn on maps?

See paragraphs 35 and 36: Land is disappearing into the Gulf of Mexico.

NOTES

estimated football field of land is lost every 45 minutes. That rate of land loss is higher than almost anywhere else on the planet. If no measures are put in place to prevent more erosion, another 1,750 square miles—a landmass larger than Rhode Island—will give way by 2064. "Our coast is going away faster than pretty much any other coast in the world," explains Pat Forbes. He's the Executive Director of the Louisiana State Office of Community and Development. Currently, Louisiana's greatest land loss occurs during storms. In 2005, the year Hurricanes Katrina and Rita hit, Louisiana lost more than 200 square miles of coastal wetlands in a single summer.

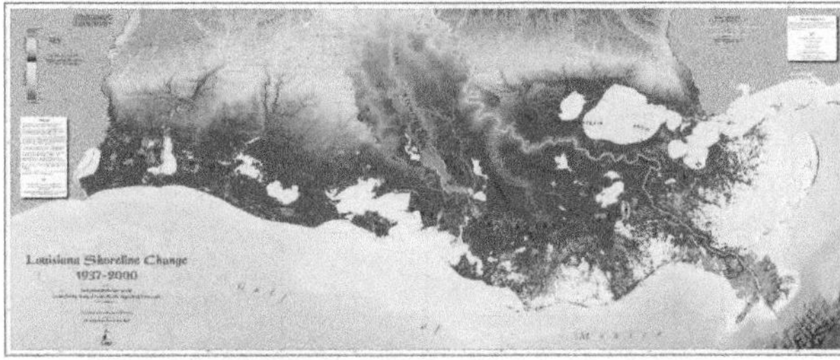

37 In addition to hurricane damage and global sea level rise, other factors also contribute to land loss. The engineering of the Mississippi River, the land's natural propensity to sink and erode, and the dredging of canals throughout the wetlands have also contributed to the loss of land in Louisiana.

38 From its source in Minnesota, the Mississippi River winds its way through nine more states before spilling into the Gulf of Mexico: Wisconsin, Iowa, Illinois, Missouri, Kentucky, Tennessee, Arkansas, Mississippi, and Louisiana. The river, nicknamed the Big Muddy, picks up dirt and carries it downstream. Eventually, this dirt is deposited along the Louisiana Gulf Coast, a process that has replenished and maintained coastline marshes and islands that would otherwise erode into the sea. "Essentially," explains Forbes, "most of Southern Louisiana has been built up by sediment carried down the Mississippi over thousands of years." Without this sediment to constantly build back the land, Louisiana's coastline would naturally diminish.

39 In 1927, unusually heavy rains overwhelmed the Mississippi River, flooding an area the size of Ireland and causing the current to run backwards. Levees broke. Floodwaters swept away farms and towns. In some places the swollen river stretched more than 60 miles wide. More than 700,000 people lost their homes. The damage cost about $1 billion at the time to fix.

Prepare for Advanced Courses

Use the activity below to differentiate instruction for your B Beyond grade-level learners.

Note the word *dredge* in paragraph 37. Explain to students the idiomatic use of *dredge*. Ask students to consider how the idiomatic usage plays into the text. Have students look up meanings of the word *dredge* and explore how those various meanings are connected.

NOTES

40 To prevent such a disaster from happening again, the US government constructed the world's largest river containment system around the Big Muddy. The Army Corps of Engineers built dirt barriers called levees on either side of the river to prevent the floodwaters from spilling over the banks. They also dug man-made canals, called floodways. That way, when the river swelled, the water could be released along predictable routes. Rather than carving a new riverbed every spring, as the Mississippi had done annually since the last Ice Age, the massive waterway was given a fixed path which ended in the Gulf of Mexico.

41 The levees and floodways prevented the Mississippi from overflowing its banks, but they also stopped the river from carrying out many of the natural processes that surrounding states relied on. The levee system cut the Louisiana coast off from the sediment that nourished and created the land. The dirt that gave the Big Muddy its nickname no longer reached Louisiana's marshes.

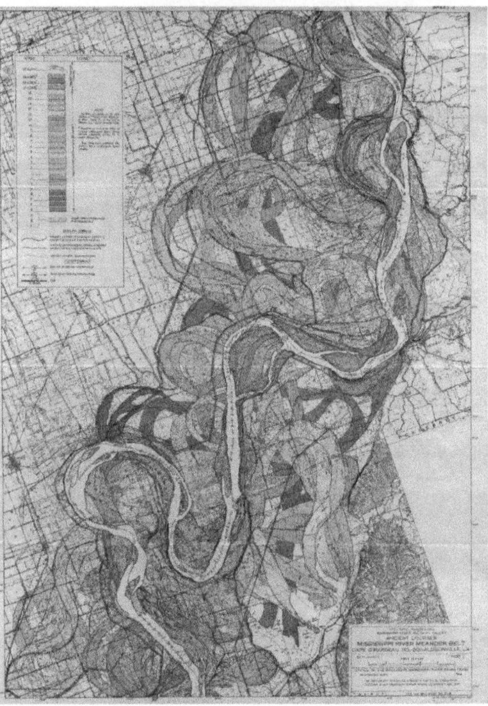

NOTES

42 The problems caused by river engineering are worsened by subsidence, or the natural propensity for wetlands to sink and erode. Louisiana contains 40% of the nation's wetlands. These marshes make up more than a third of the state. They provide habitats for shrimp, fish, crawfish, and crabs. These animals are crucial to Louisiana's fisheries. Built from soft mud, these wetlands are constantly sinking and eroding, a natural process called subsidence. When the river dumps sediment into the marshes, the wetlands rebuild and the lost land replenishes. Without river sediment to continually build them back up, Louisiana's wetlands shrink, then vanish, a process that's been charted repeatedly along the coast.

43 In addition to subsidence, a system of canals crisscrosses the state's wetlands, further damaging the fragile ecosystem. In the swamp, these waterways function as roads, providing boats easy access to oil, gas, and fisheries; over time, however, they've created pathways for saltwater from the Gulf of Mexico to leach into the freshwater wetlands. Salt is poisonous to wetland plants such as Cypress and Tupelo Gum trees. As the flora dies off, the wetlands give way to open water.

44 The disappearance of the wetlands has had another unintended consequence. Marshes and swamps are like sponges; they can expand and soak up water, protecting the mainland and inland islands from storm surges and flooding—but without wetlands to provide natural barriers, hurricane damage can be even more **catastrophic.**

45 For Louisianans, restoring the coast is a race against time. The goal is not only to protect the land, but also to care for the humans, plants, and animals that live there. The US economy is deeply linked to Louisiana's wellbeing. The state's commercial fishing industry produces a quarter of US seafood, and nearly half of the nation's grain supply passes through the port of New Orleans. Since 2007, the state has built 250 miles of levees and constructed 45 miles of barrier islands and berms. But this massive effort has not been able to keep up with the rate of land loss.

Stay or Go?

46 The first opportunity for the Biloxi-Chitimacha-Choctaw tribe to relocate came in 2002. The Army Corps of Engineers redrew the path of the Morganza-to-the-Gulf Levee. This 98-mile earthen wall was designed to protect people and property from hurricanes and storm surges. Originally, Isle de Jean Charles was included in this plan. The levee would keep water off the island and the land would regenerate. However, in 2002, the Army Corps of Engineers decided to bypass Isle de Jean Charles. For islanders, the news was devastating.

SELECTION VOCABULARY

catastrophic / catastrófico/a *adjective* causing ruin; disastrous COGNATE

- What effects are being described in these paragraphs?
- Are the effects positive or negative?

TEXT TALK

Why is hurricane damage worse since the disappearance of wetlands in the area?

See paragraph 44: Marshes and swamps soak up extra water, so hurricane-related flooding is worse without them.

Greek and Latin Affixes and Roots

How did the reader determine the meaning of the word *relocate*?

The reader looked up the word in a dictionary. He learned the prefix *re-* means "again," the root *loc* means "place," and the verb suffix *-ate* means "to make."

Greek and Latin Affixes and Roots

How does the reader determine the meaning of the word *relocation*?

The reader used his knowledge of the root and affixes of *relocate* and the noun suffix *-tion* to make a guess before looking up the word in a dictionary.

Skill: Greek and Latin Affixes and Roots

I'm not sure what the word relocate means. I can tell it is a verb because the word to comes before it. I think it may have a Greek or Latin root, but I need to look it up to be sure.

Skill: Greek and Latin Affixes and Roots

Relocation looks like relocate, so the words probably have a similar meaning. I know the suffix -ion forms nouns. Based on these clues, I think the word relocation might mean "the act of moving to a new place."

47 The Army Corps of Engineers offered to relocate the community. But it would only happen if the residents voted unanimously in favor of resettling. "The plan was dead in the water," Comardelle recalls. "At the time, we'd had a lot of land loss, but we hadn't had major structural issues [with buildings and infrastructure]." The majority of residents were in favor of the relocation. However, some residents, particularly tribal elders, were reluctant to leave. "It's home for them, you know," Dominick explains. "They were born, raised, grew up, lived their whole entire lives there. Even though their home is being stripped away, they still don't want to leave because of the sentimental value." Others worried the relocation was part of a dishonest effort to take over their island. In the end, the tribe couldn't get unanimous support. The relocation was voted down by the people.

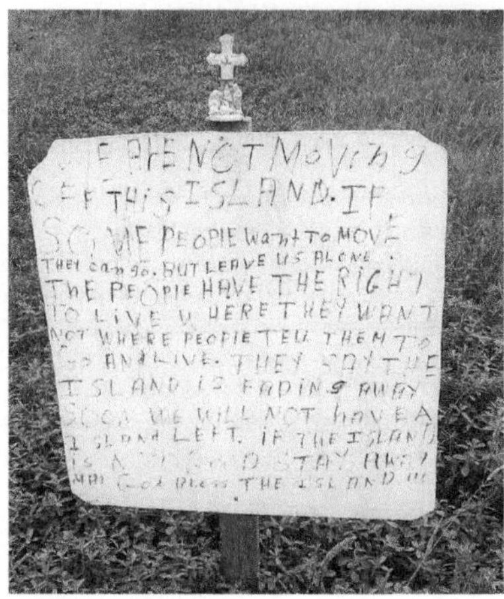

48 Several years after the vote, storm damage caused tribe members to reconsider their stance. In 2005, Hurricanes Katrina and Rita flooded the island, badly damaging the land. Three years later, when Hurricane Gustav hit Isle de Jean Charles directly, houses lost roofs and walls, gas lines broke, and the utility company refused to replace the lines. Many residents left, and those who stayed behind reconsidered their options.

49 In 2009, the tribal council restarted the relocation process. This time, plans progressed much further. Most residents were ready to leave. The tribal

TEXT TALK

How did the tribe's feelings about relocating change over time?

See paragraphs 47 and 48: People reconsidered the option of relocating after hurricanes badly damaged the land.

NOTES

council found land to purchase. This time the relocation was halted by their future neighbors. "We were going forward and some issues came up with the [adjacent] neighborhood," remembers Comardelle. "That community rose up and said they didn't want [us] in their backyard." With no place to move, tribe members wondered if their culture was fated to vanish along with the island.

50 Good news came in early 2016. That's when the Biloxi-Chitimacha-Choctaw tribe learned they would receive the $48 million relocation grant from the federal office of Housing and Urban Development. Beginning with the marriage of Jean Marie Naquin and Pauline Verdin, eight generations of tribal members made their home on the Isle de Jean Charles. The relocation grant meant the tribe could have a future, but it would have to be elsewhere. Though he was thrilled to receive the grant, in an article in *National Geographic* Chief Naquin compared "losing the island" with "losing a family member."

51 Federal grants have supported resettlement projects for storm victims for decades. They've enabled, for example, families who lost houses in Hurricane Katrina and Hurricane Sandy to live elsewhere. The Isle de Jean Charles relocation, however, is an entirely new endeavor. "Resettling a community is entirely different from relocating individuals," explains Pat Forbes. "In the past, when an area's been declared unsafe to live, the state or federal government has offered buyouts to affected landowners. In other words, they pay residents to leave. The problem with buyouts is that communities don't stay together."

52 In contrast, the primary goal of the Isle de Jean Charles relocation is to preserve the community and culture of the Biloxi-Chitimacha-Choctaw tribe. Rather than splitting up tribe members, the grant aims to bring people together. The grant proposal explains, "The tribe has physically and culturally been torn apart with the scattering of members. . . . A new settlement offers an opportunity for the tribe to rebuild their homes and secure their culture on safe ground." With this funding, island residents and tribal members who left their homeland due to land loss and flooding can also rejoin their community in a new location.

53 "The people of the Isle de Jean Charles Band of Biloxi-Chitimacha-Choctaw tribe are situated on the front line of Louisiana's coastal land loss disaster and their ancestral home is sinking into the marsh," explains Forbes. "This $48 million grant will allow the state to help them resettle their entire community to a safer place with minimum of disruption to livelihoods and lifestyles.

Skills Focus

QUESTION 4: Textual Evidence

Most groups have to split up when they relocate. However, the federal grant money will help the tribe rebuild their community in a new location.

TEXT TALK

How will the relocation grant help the community?

See paragraphs 50–52: The grant will help the community move together to a new location.

Together we'll be creating a model for resettlement of endangered coastal communities throughout the United States."

54 To accomplish this lofty goal, tribal members have been dreaming big. "We could have our own community center," says secretary Comardelle. "We could have room to grow. We could have our own crops, our own industry if we wanted. We want to be our own place again."

55 Community members are working hard to make the relocation happen. "It's about family," says Dominick Naquin. "No matter how many times we've been shot down, we came back stronger and kept fighting." Perhaps everything that the Isle de Jean Charles' residents and their ancestors have overcome has set them up for this moment. With ancestors who escaped the Trail of Tears and families who've survived numerous hurricanes, they're well equipped to triumph despite unfavorable odds.

A Vision of Community

56 "I want you to feel like you have just walked onto the original island, with the way the trees look, the way the vegetation looks," says Chantel Comardelle. She's leaning back in a brown armchair in her two-bedroom house in Houma, Louisiana, 45 minutes from the Isle de Jean Charles. To her right sits her daughter's three-story plastic dollhouse; to her left, giant containers filled with quilts and photo albums. Heirlooms inherited when her mother-in-law passed away. One room over, one of her young sons is crying. Comardelle's mother, Sheila Billiot, is talking to him softly, comforting him. The emphasis on family, a value nearly every member of her tribe seems to cherish, is abundant in this house.

57 Comardelle's eyes are closed as she talks. Physically, she's here, in her living room. Spiritually, she's in the future, imagining what her tribe's relocation will look like. What will it mean for her family and for the future of her people? Her voice is confident as if she's describing a place that already exists.

58 "When you pull up, when you approach the community, the center grounds are also pow wow grounds." In the front of the facility, she imagines a museum. It's a wooden building with a front porch. When visitors enter, they feel like they're walking into someone's house. "I want guests to walk through the history of the island with the original settlers. The ceiling, I want it to be the road to show how it progressed. With no road, just water and canoes, and then you have the road, and then you start to see the road on the floor. I want to have a big map on the wall and show the island. I want it to be digitized to show you how the island's progressed in digital pictures as far as land loss, how it's shrunk."

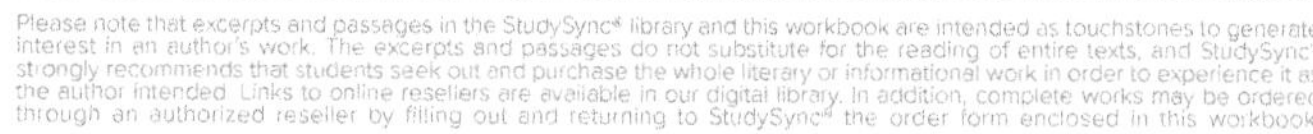

NOTES

59 Comardelle's belief in the museum is so great that she's begun taking online graduate courses in museum studies, using her class assignments to start planning exhibits and features. "Even the sounds will be like you're on the island," she says. "I want French music playing in some sections. I want people talking in other sections. I want animal sounds in other sections. I want you to be fully immersed." Comardelle's vision is so detailed and her belief so firm that it's hard to imagine the future panning out any other way.

60 Besides the museum, Comardelle imagines the new site hosting other public facilities. There will be a store, a clinic, and a restaurant. "We hope to have a kitchen. The food's traditional Cajun food. Gumbo. Gumbo fricassee. We're going to have a healthcare facility. We want to have a 24-hour nurse, and we'll also service the outside, so it'll be like a both-ways kind of thing. We also want to have a childcare facility. An elderly senior center. Our kitchen will cook and serve food for the outside, but daily they'll make a plate lunch for our residents who are elderly."

61 Comardelle's idealism is intentional. In 2010, the tribe began working with a non-profit called the Lowlander Center, a community-run organization aimed at helping lowland residents build a future while adapting to an ever-changing coastline. After Hurricane Gustav, volunteers at the Lowlander Center heard about the tribe's resettlement plan. They encouraged the council of elders to come up with their best-case scenario. "All the bells and whistles," recalls Comardelle. "Everything you want. Everything you desire."

62 Beyond the pow wow grounds, the museum, and the restaurant, Comardelle envisions a less public part of the community where residents live. Designed to accommodate up to 400 members, the houses will be arranged, as they were on the the island, so that extended families share backyards. Aunts and uncles and grandparents will be able watch each other's children. They'll call across to each other from porch to porch. "I want to build that family unit back," says Comardelle.

63 Comardelle isn't the only one to prioritize shared responsibility and familial interactions. At eighteen, Damian and Dominick Naquin are the youngest members of the resettlement committee. They see blood relationships as the glue that holds their community together.

64 "As a future, I would love to see us stay as a family," explains Damian. "Some elders don't want to give up what they remember, what they hold onto, but their grandchildren, they would love to see another future for them. They want to save the family values and the culture so that the younger generation can experience what they experienced."

TEXT TALK

What is being planned for the tribe's new community?

See paragraphs 56–62: The plans include a museum, pow wow grounds, a store, a clinic, a childcare facility, a senior center, and a restaurant.

Prepare for Advanced Courses

Use the activity below to differentiate instruction for your B Beyond grade-level learners.

Look at the accomplishments and desires of Comardelle in paragraphs 60–65.

Initiatives like Comardelle's museum and public facilities are often driven by a variety of social and cultural values. Ask students: What is the driving force of Comardelle's museum and future plans? What controversies might emerge from Comardelle's idealism?

65 "If we're successful with the relocation," adds Dominick, "then the elders will know the younger generation will experience what they experienced."

66 As for their own future, the twin brothers hope to return to their tribe equipped with skills to help their community thrive. Both are currently freshmen at Louisiana State University in Baton Rouge. "I'm trying to become a pediatrician, a child doctor," says Damian. "If I achieve that goal, I know I'm able to bring a very valuable resource back. I see my role in the future of the tribe, to support wherever the tribe goes."

67 Dominick, who's majoring in computer science, echoes his brother's wish to contribute to the well-being of his people. His ideal day in the new community includes multigenerational activities. "I'll wake up. I'll do my job, whatever that may be," he says. "Hopefully, when the time comes, I would have the privilege to sit down with a whole bunch of children and be able to sit down in a circle drum and teach them how to drum and sing. To pass down our culture, that would bring me great joy."

68 Damian and Dominick's plans are exactly what the tribe needs for the resettlement to work. Maintaining a cultural identity is the primary goal of the resettlement, but the only way that can happen is through interaction across age groups. Already, the culture is being lost. Comardelle's grandmother was a medicinal herbalist, who used teas and plants to cure others. Those skills weren't passed down and the tradition was lost.

69 Until the relocation is complete, Comardelle does her best to transfer culture by taking her children to Isle de Jean Charles, explaining, "If you can keep the younger generation connected with the oldest generation, you can keep that transition. I notice it with my kids, when we go visit my grandma. They're learning French in school and they're tickled to go over there and talk French with my grandma."

70 Perhaps, years from now, Comardelle's children will recall these trips to Isle de Jean Charles, an island homeland that no longer exists. Sitting on a back porch, they'll tell their children about how they caught crabs in the bayou. How they listened to their grandparents speak in Cajun French about weddings in general stores and waiting out hurricanes in their daddy's boats. Around them the egrets will take flight as Spanish moss sways in the breeze. Relatives might wave from nearby porches. After all, history isn't just what happened a long time ago. The creation of a new homeland, the tribe's relocation, and the council's efforts to maintain culture are all history in action. If the relocation works, Comardelle, the Naquins, and the other members of

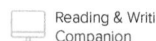

the Biloxi-Chitimacha-Choctaw tribe will achieve something amazing. Their people and their culture will have a safe home in coastal Louisiana for centuries to come.

NOTES

Anya Groner's essays and stories can be read in journals including *The New York Times, Ecotone, The Oxford American*, and *The Atlantic*. A resident of New Orleans, Groner teaches creative writing at the New Orleans Center for Creative Arts and through the New Orleans Writers Workshop.

TEXT TALK

How is preserving the Biloxi-Chitimacha-Choctaw Native American tribe's land like preserving their culture?

Answers will vary.

B Ask each Beyond grade-level student to write one additional discussion question. Then have one or two students facilitate a discussion, using their questions to guide the conversation.

Think Questions

Circulate as students answer Think Questions independently. Scaffolds for these questions are shown on the opposite page.

QUESTION 1: Textual Evidence

Jean Marie Naquin and Pauline Verdin were the first people to move to Isle de Jean Charles. They were an interracial married couple who moved to the uninhabited island "to escape persecution." Later, their children married Native Americans from areas near the island and "brought them to Isle de Jean Charles to live and start families."

QUESTION 2: Textual Evidence

The tribe used to subsist on food they got for themselves on the island. They used to be able to trap animals, farm, and keep livestock. But "since 1955, the tribe lost 98% of their land to encroaching waters," so land loss prevents them from being able to support themselves.

QUESTION 3: Textual Evidence

Containment of the Mississippi River stopped natural processes that used to maintain the coastline: "The levee system cut the Louisiana coast off from the sediment that nourished and created the land." This has had long-term effects: "Without river sediment to continually build them back up, Louisiana's wetlands shrink, then vanish, a process that's been charted repeatedly along the coast."

QUESTION 4: Context Clues

I think *erodes* must mean "to disappear slowly over a long period of time." The word is used to tell what happens to the land, and the text is mostly about how the land is vanishing over time.

QUESTION 5: Word Meaning

Definition e most closely matches the meaning of the word *settle* in paragraph 30. In the text, the chief helps people end disputes, or arguments.

First Read

Read "The Vanishing Island." After you read, complete the Think Questions below.

THINK QUESTIONS

1. Why did people move to the Isle de Jean Charles? Provide two specific examples from the text to support your response.

2. Why is the Biloxi-Chitimacha-Choctaw tribe no longer able to subsist? Provide specific evidence from the text to support your response.

3. How does containment of the Mississippi River affect the Louisiana coastline? Provide specific evidence from the text to support your response.

4. Find the word **erodes** in paragraph 12 of "The Vanishing Island." Use context clues in the surrounding sentences, as well as the sentence in which the word appears, to determine the word's meaning. Write your definition here and identify clues that helped you figure out its meaning.

5. Read the following dictionary entry:

   settle
   set•tle \sedl\ *verb*

   a. to decide something
   b. to put things in order
   c. to move to a place to live
   d. to pay money that is owed
   e. to end an argument
   f. to get into a more comfortable position

   Which definition most closely matches the meaning of **settle** as it is used in paragraph 30? Write the correct definition of *settle* here and explain how you figured out the correct meaning.

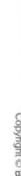

SCAFFOLDS

Think Questions

Use the scaffolds below to differentiate instruction for your ELL English Language Learners and A Approaching grade-level learners.

ELL **BEGINNING** Write a response using the word bank and sentence frames.

INTERMEDIATE Write a response using the sentence frames.

ADVANCED, ADVANCED HIGH Write a response using the Text-Dependent Question Guide.

A APPROACHING Write a response using the Text-Dependent Question Guide.

BEGINNING	INTERMEDIATE	APPROACHING / ADVANCED, ADVANCED HIGH
Word Bank	**Sentence Frames**	**Text-Dependent Question Guide**
fish smaller accepted land loss disappear farm shrink married sediment Native Americans	The first people to move to the island were a ____ couple. They moved to the uninhabited island because interracial couples were not ____ at the time. Later, their children married ____ from nearby areas and brought them to the island to live.	1. • Why did they move to the island? • How did their children contribute to the island's population?
	The tribe used to ____ and ____ to live. Over time, ____ has made this impossible.	2. • How did people on the island subsist, or live off the land, in the past? • What changed on the island?
	The ____ from the Mississippi River used to naturally build up Louisiana's wetlands. Now that the river has been contained, these areas ____ and eventually vanish.	3. • What happened naturally before the containment of the Mississippi River? • What happened after the containment was complete? • How did the Louisiana coastline change?
	The island is getting ____. This gives me a clue that *erodes* means "to ____ over time."	4. • Read: "As the land **erodes**, the Biloxi-Chitimacha-Choctaw tribal culture **erodes** with it." • What is eroding? • What does that tell me about the meaning of the word *erodes*?
	Settle as used in the text matches definition ____.	5. • "As the tribal leader, he would maintain the grocery store, distribute mail, help **settle** disputes, represent the people of the island to outsiders, and gather residents for community service." • Does *settle* mean "make a decision" (a), "put things in order" (b), "move" (c), "pay back money" (d), "end an argument" (e), or "get more comfortable" (f)?

Reading Comprehension OPTIONAL

Have students complete the digital reading comprehension questions ✓ when they finish reading.

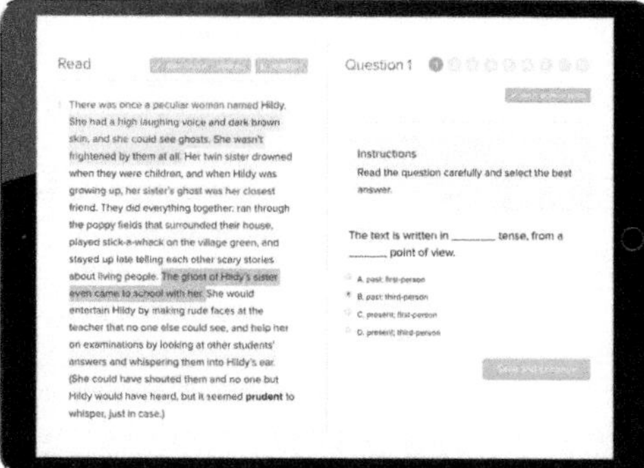

ANSWER KEY

QUESTION 1: D
QUESTION 2: B
QUESTION 3: C
QUESTION 4: D
QUESTION 5: A
QUESTION 6: B
QUESTION 7: A
QUESTION 8: C
QUESTION 9: *See first chart.*
QUESTION 10: *See second chart.*

Synonym	Word
continue	maintain
disastrous	catastrophic
upkeep	subsistence
crumble	erode
occupy	settle

Quote	Person
"I want to build that family unit back."	Chantel Comardelle
"To pass down our culture, that would bring me great joy."	Dominik Naquin
"We hate to let the island go, but we have to. It's like losing a family member."	Chief Albert Naquin
"I built this house in the 1960s. I have another I built in '49. I built it all."	Wenceslaus Billiot Sr.

Connect and Extend OPTIONAL

CONNECT TO EXTENDED WRITING PROJECT

Students can use "The Vanishing Island" as a resource when writing their informational essays. Have students analyze Anya Groner's use of details to help them in their own writing.

BEYOND THE BOOK

Research Project: Rising Waters

Isle de Jean Charles is one community being impacted by rising sea levels, but there are many more communities in danger. Break students into small groups and ask them to:

- Identify another coastal community or island being impacted by rising sea levels.
- Research the impact of rising sea levels on the geographic location, people's lifestyle and customs, access to services (e.g., hospitals and schools), food sources, and work.
- Explore how the community they selected is dealing with their changing environment.
- Create a multimedia presentation to present their research to the class.
- Present their findings in a formal group presentation.

To reflect, ask students:

- What similarities did you notice about the different locations and the impact of rising sea levels?
- How are communities dealing with these changes? What creative solutions are people developing?
- Many locations in the United States (e.g., New Orleans, San Francisco, Miami, Manhattan) are extremely vulnerable to rising sea levels. How can highly populated cities deal with this threat?

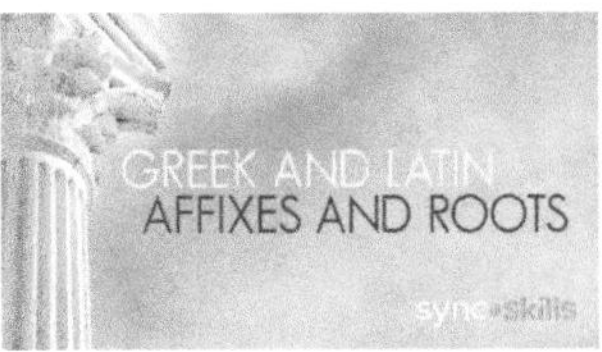

Skill: Greek and Latin Affixes and Roots

Use the Checklist to analyze Greek and Latin Affixes and Roots in "The Vanishing Island." Refer to the sample student annotations about Greek and Latin Affixes and Roots in the text.

••• CHECKLIST FOR GREEK AND LATIN AFFIXES AND ROOTS

In order to identify Greek and Latin affixes and roots, note the following:

- ✓ the root
- ✓ the prefix and/or suffix

To use common, grade-appropriate Greek or Latin affixes and roots as clues to the meaning of a word, use the following questions as a guide:

- ✓ Can I identify the root of this word? Should I look in a dictionary or other resource?
- ✓ What is the meaning of the root?
- ✓ Can I identify the prefix and/or suffix of this word? Should I look in a dictionary or other resource?
- ✓ What is the meaning of the prefix and/or suffix?
- ✓ Does this affix change the word's part of speech?
- ✓ How do the word parts work together to define the word's meaning and part of speech?

SKILL VOCABULARY

root / la raíz ***noun*** the most basic part of a word that gives a word its meaning

affix / el afijo ***noun*** a word part added to a root that can change the word's part of speech or meaning

prefix / el prefijo ***noun*** an affix added to the beginning of a word COGNATE

suffix / el sufijo ***noun*** an affix attached to the end of a word; may change the spelling of the base word depending on the suffix COGNATE

Skill: Greek and Latin Affixes and Roots

Introduce the Skill

Watch the Concept Definition video ▶ and read the following definition with your students.

A **root** is the basic part of a word that gives the word its meaning. An **affix** is a word part that is added to a root. Affixes can change the word's meaning or its part of speech. **Prefixes** are affixes added to the beginning of a word, and **suffixes** are added to the end of a word.

For example, the word *acid* is the root in the word *acidic*. The suffix *-ic* changes the word *acid* from a noun to an adjective.

Many words in English come from ancient Greek and Latin. Knowing the meanings of Greek and Latin affixes and roots can often help readers figure out the meanings of unfamiliar words.

TURN AND TALK

1. What are some of your favorite words? Why do you like these words?
2. What word parts can be added to the beginnings or ends of those words to create new words? For example, the word *script*, meaning "something written," can be changed to *transcript, manuscript,* or *description.*

SPEAKING FRAMES

- One of my favorite words is ____. I like this word because ____.
- A word part that is added to the beginning of the word is ____. This changes the ____.
- A word part that is added to the end of the word is ____. This changes the ____.

Your Turn

Ask students to complete the Your Turn activity.

QUESTION 1

A. Incorrect. The context does not support this meaning.

B. Incorrect. The word *marina* is not used as a verb.

C. Incorrect. Neither the context nor the root supports this meaning.

D. Correct. Both the context and the root support this meaning.

QUESTION 2

A. Incorrect. The context does not support this meaning.

B. Correct. Both the context and the root support this meaning.

C. Incorrect. Neither the context nor the root supports this meaning.

D. Incorrect. Neither the context nor the root supports this meaning.

QUESTION 3

A. Correct. The context and the root support this meaning.

B. Incorrect. The context and the root do not support this meaning.

C. Incorrect. The context does not support this meaning.

D. Incorrect. The context does not support this meaning.

QUESTION 4

A. Incorrect. The context and the root do not support this meaning.

B. Incorrect. The context and the root do not support this meaning.

C. Correct. The context and root support this meaning.

D. Incorrect. While the root *port* means "carry," the context does not support this meaning.

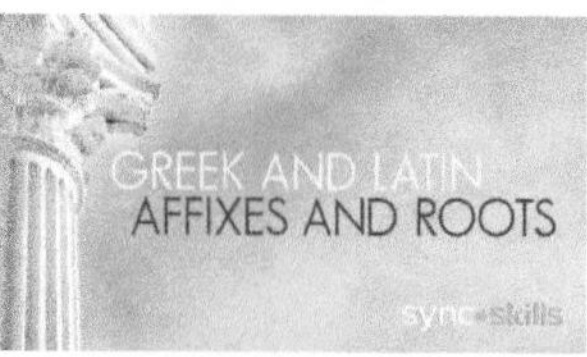

Skill: Greek and Latin Affixes and Roots

Reread paragraphs 15 and 21 of "The Vanishing Island." Then, using the Checklist on the previous page, answer the multiple-choice questions below.

YOUR TURN

marina mar•in•a \mə 'rē-nə\
Origin: from the Latin root *mar* meaning "sea"

local loc•al \lō-kəl\
Origin: from the Latin root *loc* meaning "place"

quiet qui•et \kwī-ət\
Origin: from the Latin root *qui* meaning "rest"

transport trans•port \tran(t)s-pôrt\
Origin: from the Latin root *trans* meaning "across" and *port* meaning "carry"

misdeed mis•deed \mis-dēd\
Origin: from the Greek root *mis* meaning "bad"

1. Based on its context and root, what is the most likely meaning of *marina*?
   - A. an island
   - B. to go swimming
   - C. a group of sailors
   - D. a dock in the water
2. Based on its context and root, what is the most likely meaning of *local*?
   - A. below
   - B. nearby
   - C. healthy
   - D. well-known
3. Based on its context and root, what is the most likely meaning of *quiet*?
   - A. calm
   - B. noisy
   - C. alive
   - D. asleep
4. Based on the Greek or Latin root and context, which of the words listed above best completes the following sentence?
   The men were on trial for several ________, including carrying money out of the country.
   - A. locals
   - B. marinas
   - C. misdeeds
   - D. transports

Skill: Media

Use the Checklist to analyze Media in "The Vanishing Island." Refer to the sample student annotations about Media in the text.

••• CHECKLIST FOR MEDIA

In order to identify the advantages and disadvantages of using different media, note the following:

- ✓ the features of each medium, such as print or digital text, video, and multimedia
- ✓ how different media present a particular topic, idea, or historical event—such as World War II or the first moon landing—and can include diaries, eyewitness accounts, films, books, news and feature articles, photographs, and so on
- ✓ which details are stressed in each type of media presentation
- ✓ how readers and historians compare and contrast accounts in different media as they analyze and interpret events
- ✓ the reliability of each medium
- ✓ when presentations contradict each other

To evaluate the advantages and disadvantages of using different media to present a particular topic or idea, ask the following questions:

- ✓ What are the advantages and disadvantages of using different media to present a particular topic or idea?
- ✓ Which account of the event or topic is better supported by objective facts?
- ✓ Is an eyewitness account of an event more valuable than a film or book about the same subject? Why or why not?

SKILL VOCABULARY

media / los medios *noun* the plural form of the word medium; a means of sending a communication to an intended audience

medium / el medio *noun* a form of communication, such as television, the Internet, and radio COGNATE

Skill: Media

Introduce the Skill

Watch the Concept Definition video and read the following definition with your students.

Media is the plural form of the word *medium.* A **medium** is a means of sending a communication to an intended audience. Throughout most of human history, people communicated through three main media: speech, writing, and visual arts such as drawing, painting, and sculpture. But in the 19th century, media options suddenly exploded. The invention of photography, and then the telegraph and the telephone, changed the world. Within a century radio, motion pictures, and television followed.

Stories and ideas change as they are translated from one medium to another. A dialogue between two characters in a novel, for example, becomes very different when it is delivered by actors in a film—with close-ups, sound effects such as music, and other elements unique to the medium of film itself.

Today, new media are being invented at a much faster pace than ever before, and each of these forms of online communication has its own "language" and creates its own experience.

TURN AND TALK

1. What types of media have you used?
2. Do you like it when something you read combines text with other media like visuals? Why or why not?

ELL **SPEAKING FRAMES**

- I have used ____.
- I (do / do not) like text with other media.
- Other media like visuals (are / are not) helpful because ____.

Your Turn

Ask students to complete the Your Turn activity.

QUESTION 1

A. Correct. The text feature of the print medium is the boldface heading "Eight Generations of History."

B. Incorrect. The boldface heading "Eight Generations of History" does not support this inference.

C. Incorrect. The boldface heading "Eight Generations of History" does not support this inference.

D. Incorrect. The boldface heading "Eight Generations of History" does not support this inference.

QUESTION 2

A. Incorrect. The photograph does not give information about Jean Lafitte.

B. Incorrect. The photograph does not show how the island has changed.

C. Correct. The photograph provides information about how people once lived on the island, such as their houses and clothes and how many children they might have.

D. Incorrect. The photograph does not give information about why the land was once declared uninhabitable.

QUESTION 3

A. Incorrect. This is not an accurate explanation of the difference between the two types of media.

B. Correct. Both the print text and the visual photograph help the reader understand the author's key ideas.

C. Incorrect. This is not a main advantage of including both types of media.

D. Incorrect. This is not a main advantage of including both types of media.

Skill: Media

Reread paragraphs 20–22 of "The Vanishing Island." Then, using the Checklist on the previous page, answer the multiple-choice questions below.

YOUR TURN

1. Based on a text feature of the print medium in this excerpt, the reader can identify that the section is about—

   - A. the tribe's experiences on the island.
   - B. Native American traditions.
   - C. possible places for relocation.
   - D. environmental factors that affect the island.

2. The photograph in this excerpt provides information about—

   - A. Jean Lafitte.
   - B. how the island has changed.
   - C. how people on the island lived.
   - D. why the land was "uninhabitable."

3. The main advantage to including both types of media is that—

   - A. the photograph gives readers information that printed text cannot possibly give.
   - B. the two types of media work together to provide a clear idea and explanation for the reader's benefit.
   - C. it shows that the author did extensive research on the subject and is a reliable source of information.
   - D. the photograph helps break up the printed words on the page and makes it appear more readable.

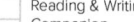

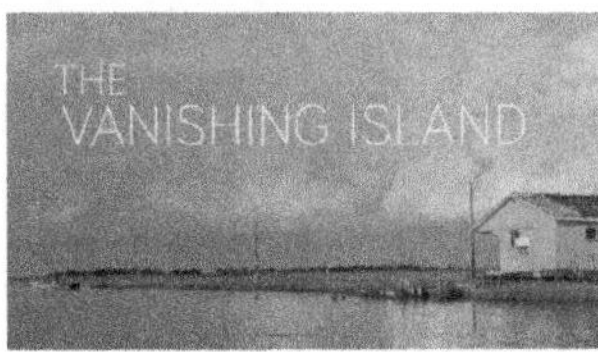

Close Read

Reread "The Vanishing Island." As you reread, complete the Skills Focus questions below. Then use your answers and annotations from the questions to help you complete the Write activity.

SKILLS FOCUS

1. The Latin root *duc* means "to lead." Identify a word with this root, and explain how the meaning of the root helps you understand the meaning of the word in context.
2. Identify a detail in the text that is clarified by a visual media item. Explain how the visual item deepens your understanding of the author's ideas.
3. For visual media items, what are some possible advantages and disadvantages of including them with the text? Be specific in your response and cite at least two examples for each situation.
4. Identify specific textual evidence that shows how relocation is a good way for the tribe to preserve their unique heritage. Explain your response.
5. Identify an example from some type of medium in "The Vanishing Island" of a risk members of the tribe took and explain why they took that chance.

WRITE

INFORMATIONAL: Based on the information in the article, what makes people care so deeply about this "vanishing island" that nothing can induce them to leave? Why do people still continue to inhabit it and work so hard for its cultural survival? Use evidence from the text, including different media, to support your understanding of the reading.

Close Read

Skills Focus

QUESTION 1: Greek and Latin Affixes and Roots

See paragraph 18.

QUESTION 2: Media

See paragraph 27.

QUESTION 3: Media

See paragraph 20.

QUESTION 4: Textual Evidence

See paragraphs 51 and 52.

QUESTION 5: Connect to Essential Question

See paragraph 22.

CHECK FOR SUCCESS

If students struggle to respond to Skills Focus question 1, ask them the following questions:

1. What word do you see with *duc* in paragraph 18?
2. How is "to lead" part of the word's meaning?

Writer's Notebook

Give students time to reflect on how "The Vanishing Island" connects to the unit's essential question: "Why do we take chances?" by freewriting in their Writer's Notebooks.

Beginning & Intermediate

Read aloud the unit's essential question: "Why do we take chances?" Encourage students to draw their reflections or allow students to write in their native language. Circulate the room, prompting students for their thoughts as they respond orally or through pantomime.

Advanced & Advanced High

Allow students to share their reflections orally in pairs or small groups before freewriting.

Collaborative Conversation

SCAFFOLDS

Break students into collaborative conversation groups to discuss the Close Read prompt. Ask students to use the StudySyncTV episode as a model for their discussion. Remind them to reference their Skills Focus annotations in their discussion.

Based on the information in the article, what makes people care so deeply about this "vanishing island" that nothing can induce them to leave? Why do people still continue to inhabit it and work so hard for its cultural survival? Use evidence from the text, including different media, to support your understanding of the reading.

Use the scaffolds below to differentiate instruction for your ELL English Language Learners and A Approaching grade-level learners.

ELL **BEGINNING, INTERMEDIATE** Use the discussion guide and speaking frames to facilitate the discussion with support from the teacher.

ADVANCED, ADVANCED HIGH Use the discussion guide and speaking frames to facilitate the discussion in mixed-level groups.

A **APPROACHING** Use the discussion guide to facilitate the discussion in mixed-level groups.

APPROACHING
ADVANCED, ADVANCED HIGH
BEGINNING, INTERMEDIATE

Discussion Guide	Speaking Frames
1. Which key details explain an important idea?	• ____ is a key detail. • It helps develop the author's ideas because ____.
2. What printed text explains an important idea?	• ____ is important text. • It helps develop the author's ideas because ____.
3. Which visual media explain an important idea?	• ____ is an important visual. • It helps develop the author's ideas because ____.
4. How do the key details and different media work together to tell why people stay on the island?	• The key details and different media work together to explain ____.

Review Prompt and Rubric

Before students begin writing, review the writing prompt and rubric with the class.

INFORMATIONAL: Based on the information in the article, what makes people care so deeply about this "vanishing island" that nothing can induce them to leave? Why do people still continue to inhabit it and work so hard for its cultural survival? Use evidence from the text, including different media, to support your understanding of the reading.

ELL A **PROMPT GUIDE**

- Which key details explain an important idea?
- What printed text explains an important idea?
- Which visual media explain an important idea?
- How do the key details and different media work together to tell why people stay on the island?

Score	Media	Language and Conventions
4	The writer clearly analyzes and explains how different media support their ideas. The writer provides exemplary analysis, using relevant evidence from the text.	The writer demonstrates a consistent command of grammar, punctuation, and usage conventions. Although minor errors may be evident, they do not detract from the fluency or the clarity of the writing.
3	The writer analyzes and explains how different media support their ideas. The writer provides sufficient analysis, using relevant evidence from the text most of the time.	The writer demonstrates an adequate command of grammar, punctuation, and usage conventions. Although some errors may be evident, they create few (if any) disruptions in the fluency or clarity of the writing.
2	The writer begins to analyze or explain how different media support their ideas, but the analysis is incomplete. The writer uses relevant evidence from the text only some of the time.	The writer demonstrates a partial command of grammar, punctuation, and usage conventions. Some distracting errors may be evident, at times creating minor disruptions in the fluency or clarity of the writing.
1	The writer attempts to analyze or explain how different media support their ideas, but the analysis is not successful. The writer uses little or no relevant evidence from the text.	The writer demonstrates little or no command of grammar, punctuation, and usage conventions. Serious and persistent errors create disruptions in the fluency of the writing and sometimes interfere with meaning.
0	The writer does not provide a relevant response to the prompt or does not provide a response at all.	Serious and persistent errors overwhelm the writing and interfere with the meaning of the response as a whole, making the writer's meaning impossible to understand.

Write

SCAFFOLDS

Ask students to complete the writing assignment using textual evidence to support their answers.

Use the scaffolds below to differentiate instruction for your ELL English Language Learners and A Approaching grade-level learners.

ELL **BEGINNING** With the help of the word bank, write a response using paragraph frame 1.

INTERMEDIATE With the help of the word bank, write a response using paragraph frames 1 and 2.

ADVANCED, ADVANCED HIGH Write a response of differentiated length using the sentence starters.

A **APPROACHING** Write a response of differentiated length using the sentence starters.

BEGINNING / INTERMEDIATE	BEGINNING / INTERMEDIATE	INTERMEDIATE	ADVANCED, ADVANCED HIGH / APPROACHING
Word Bank	**Paragraph Frame 1**	**Paragraph Frame 2**	**Sentence Starters**
Indian Removal Act photographs culture heading history	The residents of Isle de Jean Charles care about the island because of its ____. Printed text, such as the ____ "Eight Generations of History," provides information about the island's people. Visual media, such as ____, show the generations that lived there before them. Key details, such as information about the ____, show that the island has kept them safe. Tribe members worry that their ____ will disappear along with the island.	Many tribe members feel like the island is ____. Even though only two dozen people remain on the island, they want to stay because ____. A key detail in the text that supports this is Text that supports this is ____. A visual that develops this is ____.	• People care about the island because . . . • People stayed on the island even after . . . because . . . • A key detail in the text that explains this is . . . • Text that supports this idea is . . . • A visual that supports this idea is . . .

Peer Review

Rate

Respond to the following with a point rating that reflects your opinion.

	1	2	3	4
Ideas				
Evidence				
Language and Conventions				

Submit

Students should submit substantive feedback to two peers using the review instructions below.

- How well does this response answer the prompt?
- How well does the writer support his or her ideas with details and examples from the text?
- Does the writer identify media that also support his or her ideas?
- What did the writer do well in this response? What does the writer need to work on?

SENTENCE FRAMES

- You were able to (completely / partly / almost) answer the prompt because ____.
- You could answer the prompt more completely by ____.
- You supported the idea of ____ with the detail of ____.
- You identified at least one example of printed text that ____.
- You identified at least one visual media item that ____.
- One idea that needs more support is ____.
- My favorite part of your response is ____ because ____.

A Night to Remember

INFORMATIONAL TEXT
Walter Lord
1955

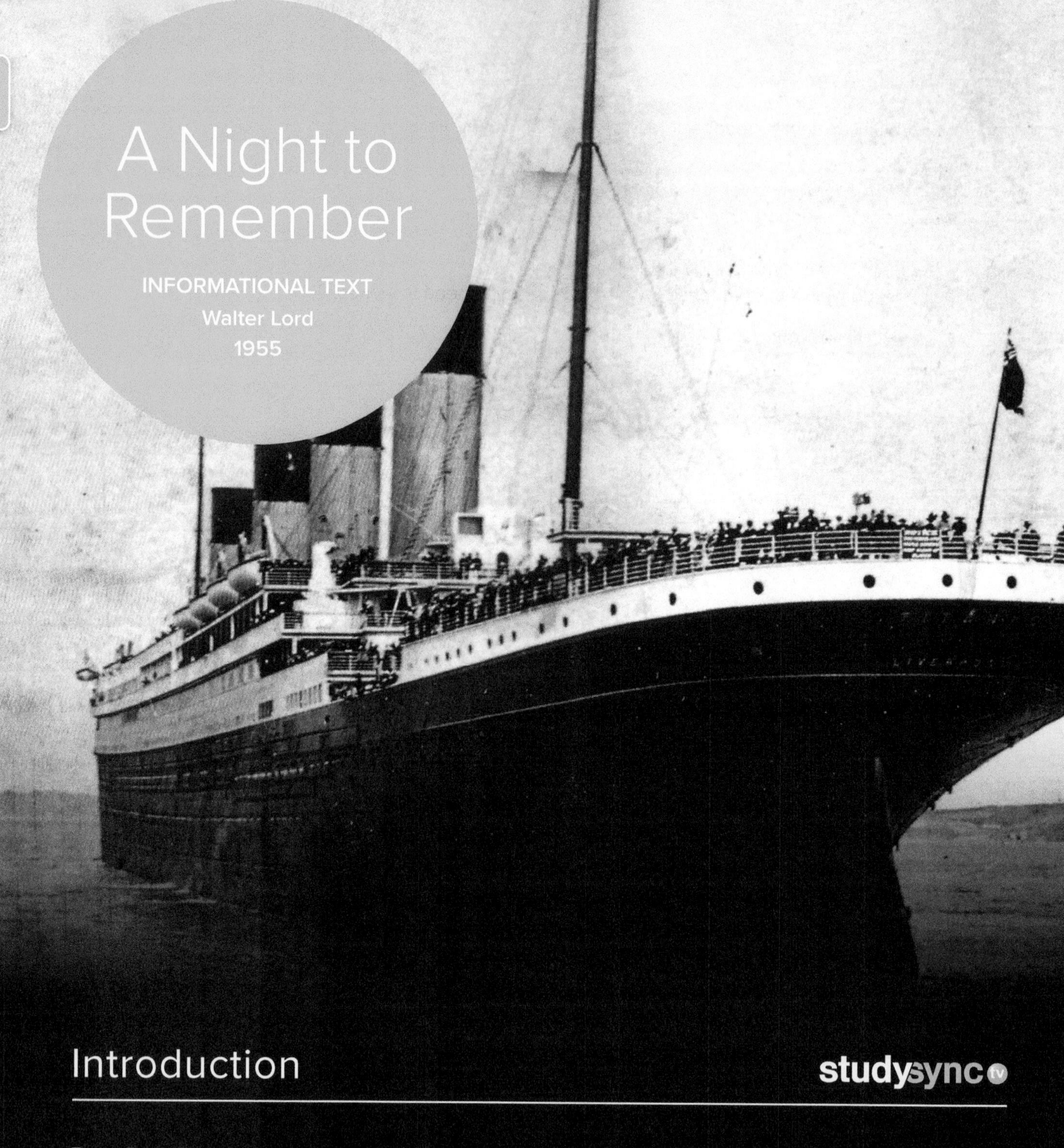

Introduction

studysync tv

Walter Lord interviewed scores of *Titanic* survivors to create a powerful account of the ship's sinking in the calm, frigid North Atlantic on April 14, 1912. In this passage, we hear a variety of reactions at the beginning of the disaster, from the first sighting of an iceberg by the ship's lookout to the mysterious jolt heard and felt by crew members and passengers alike, each observer interpreting the impact differently.

In this excerpt, *Titanic* survivors recount their varied impressions when the ship collided with the iceberg. The quartermaster remembered seeing ice crystals flashing in the lights outside; when the ship passed the iceberg, he initially thought it was a large sailboat. Below deck, the stewards heard the impact as a grinding sound, which they thought was a broken propeller blade. Consequently, they were looking forward to spending a few days in port while the ship would be repaired. The night baker was upset because the impact knocked over a tray of rolls he was preparing for the morning. Some passengers said it sounded like a wave striking the hull. Others stated that it was like rolling over "a thousand marbles," while some claimed that it reminded them of the San Francisco earthquake in 1906. However, none of them suspected what an awful night they had in store.

 Proficiency-leveled summaries and summaries in multiple languages are available digitally.

 Audio and audio text highlighting are available with this text.

COMPARING WITHIN AND ACROSS GENRES

 Read together, this excerpt from *A Night to Remember* and President Ronald Reagan's "Address to the Nation on the Explosion of the Space Shuttle *Challenger*" will allow students to analyze what happens when a big risk has a negative outcome.

Access Complex Text

LEXILE: 1050L **WORD COUNT:** 1,147

The following areas may be challenging for students, particularly ELL English Language Learners and A Approaching grade-level learners.

Prior Knowledge	Organization	Specific Vocabulary
• Students may not know the significance of the *Titanic*. There were over 2,000 passengers—who were organized by class, or type of ticket—and crew members. There were too few lifeboats, and a passenger's gender and class of ticket affected who survived.	• The text retells one event from the points of view of several passengers and crew members. Students may need help tracking the shifts in point of view as they read the text.	• Nautical terms, such as *knots, bow, starboard,* and *stern*, may present a challenge to some readers. Remind students to use a dictionary to define unfamiliar words.

SCAFFOLDS ELL **ENGLISH LANGUAGE LEARNERS**  **APPROACHING GRADE LEVEL**  **BEYOND GRADE LEVEL**

These icons identify differentiation strategies and scaffolded support for a variety of students. See the digital lesson plan for additional differentiation strategies and scaffolds.

Instructional Path

The print teacher's edition includes essential point-of-use instruction and planning tools. Complete lesson plans and program documents appear in your digital teacher account.

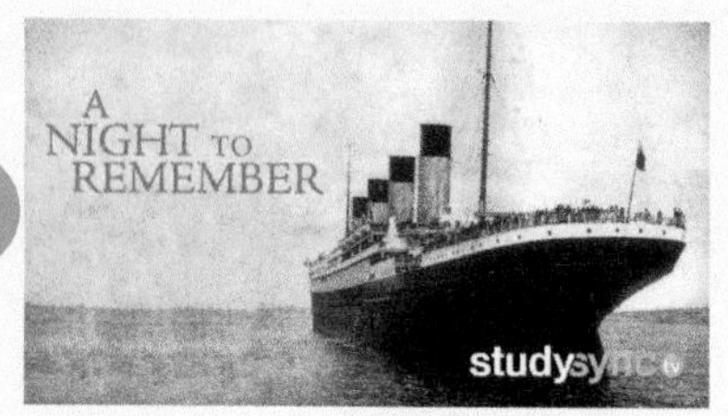

Independent Read: A Night to Remember

Objectives: After reading the text, students will write a short response that demonstrates their understanding of the text through a personal connection.

Independent Read

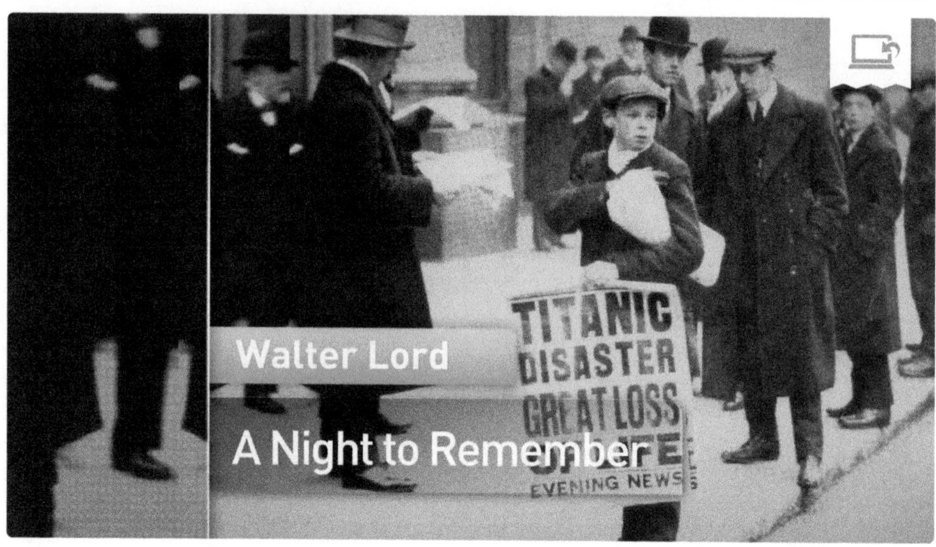

Walter Lord
A Night to Remember
TITANIC
DISASTER
GREAT LOSS
EVENING NEWS

Introduce the Text

As a class, watch the video preview and have students read the introduction in pairs to make connections to the video preview.

- What two words would you use to describe this video?
- What is one prediction you can make about the text you're going to read?

ELL **SPEAKING FRAMES**

- Two words I would use to describe it are ____.
- I think the text will ____. I think this because ____.
- I predict that there will be ____. I believe this because ____.

Entry Point

As students prepare to read *A Night to Remember*, share the following information with them to provide context.

- ✓ In the early 1900s, passenger ships gave travelers a way to cross the Atlantic. One of these ships was an enormous luxury liner called the *Titanic*. Due to its design, many people thought that this ship could not sink.
- ✓ On its maiden voyage, however, the *Titanic* hit an iceberg. There were about 2,200 people on the ship, and over 1,500 people died. The majority of deaths occurred among the crew and the third-class passengers.
- ✓ The author of this text is Walter Lord (1917–2002). In the mid-20th century, he took a new approach to recording history in this book: He gathered and shared stories from people who survived the tragedy. This is now called a documentary style of writing.

"It was almost 11:40 P.M. on Sunday, the 14th of April, 1912."

NOTES

from Chapter: "Another Belfast Trip"

1 High in the crow's-nest[1] of the New White Star Liner *Titanic*, Lookout Frederick Fleet peered into a dazzling night. It was calm, clear and bitterly cold. There was no moon, but the cloudless sky blazed with stars. The Atlantic was like polished plate glass; people later said they had never seen it so smooth.

2 This was the fifth night of the *Titanic's* maiden voyage to New York, and it was already clear that she was not only the largest but also the most **glamorous** ship in the world. Even the passengers' dogs were glamorous. John Jacob Astor had along his Airedale Kitty. Henry Sleeper Harper, of the publishing family, had his prize Pekingese Sun Yat-sen. Robert W. Daniel, the Philadelphia banker, was bringing back a champion French bulldog just purchased in Britain. Clarence Moore of Washington also had been dog-shopping, but the 50 pairs of English foxhounds he bought for the Loudoun Hunt weren't making the trip.

3 That was all another world to Frederick Fleet. He was one of six lookouts carried by the *Titanic*, and the lookouts didn't worry about passenger problems. They were the "eyes of the ship," and on this particular night Fleet had been warned to watch especially for icebergs.

4 So far, so good. On duty at 10 o'clock . . . a few words about the ice problem with Lookout Reginald Lee, who shared the same watch . . . a few more words about the cold . . . but mostly just silence, as the two men stared into the darkness.

5 Now the watch was almost over, and still there was nothing unusual. Just the night, the stars, the biting cold, the wind that whistled through the rigging as the *Titanic* raced across the calm, black sea at 22 1/2 knots[2]. It was almost 11:40 P.M. on Sunday, the 14th of April, 1912.

6 Suddenly Fleet saw something directly ahead, even darker than the darkness. At first it was small (about the size, he thought, of two tables put together), but every second it grew larger and closer. Quickly Fleet banged the crow's-nest

1. **crow's-nest** a platform on a ship's mast or in a high place used for lookout
2. **knots** nautical miles

SELECTION VOCABULARY

glamorous / glamoroso/a *adjective* extremely attractive; excitingly attractive COGNATE

Analyze Vocabulary Using Context Clues

As students read the text, ask them to make predictions about each bold vocabulary word based on the context clues in the sentence.

CHECK FOR SUCCESS

If students are unable to determine the meaning of one or more bolded vocabulary words, project the Checklist from the Grade 8 Context Clues lesson with the class. After revisiting, guide students as they make predictions about the bold word in paragraph 9 using the following routine:

- Is the word a noun, a verb, an adjective, or an adverb?
- What is described as "detached" in this paragraph?
- Is it a positive or negative description?

TURN AND TALK

Have students discuss their original vocabulary predictions with a neighbor. Come to a consensus as a class before confirming their definitions.

TEXT TALK

What was the weather and water like on the night the Titanic sank?

See paragraph 1: It was a cold, clear, and cloudless night. The water was calm and smooth.

bell three times, the warning of danger ahead. At the same time he lifted the phone and rang the bridge.

7 "What did you see?" asked a calm voice at the other end.

8 "Iceberg right ahead," replied Fleet.

9 "Thank you," acknowledged the voice with curiously **detached** courtesy. Nothing more was said.

10 For the next 37 seconds, Fleet and Lee stood quietly side by side, watching the ice **draw** nearer. Now they were almost on top of it, and still the ship didn't turn. The berg towered wet and glistening far above the forecastle deck, and both men braced themselves for a crash. Then, miraculously, the bow began to swing to port. At the last second the stem shot into the clear, and the ice glided swiftly by along the starboard side. It looked to Fleet like a very close shave.

11 At this moment Quartermaster George Thomas Rowe was standing watch on the after bridge. For him too, it had been an uneventful night—just the sea, the stars, the biting cold. As he paced the deck, he noticed what he and his mates called "Whiskers 'round the Light"—tiny splinters of ice in the air, fine as dust, that gave off **myriads** of bright colors whenever caught in the glow of the deck lights.

12 Then suddenly he felt a curious motion break the steady rhythm of the engines. It was a little like coming alongside a dock wall rather heavily. He glanced forward—and stared again. A windjammer,[3] sails set, seemed to be passing along the starboard side. Then he realized it was an iceberg, towering perhaps 100 feet above the water. The next instant it was gone, drifting astern into the dark.

13 Meanwhile, down below in the First Class dining saloon on D Deck, four other members of the *Titanic's* crew were sitting around one of the tables. The last diner had long since departed, and now the big white Jacobean[4] room was empty except for this single group. They were dining-saloon stewards, indulging in the time-honored pastime of all stewards off duty—they were gossiping about their passengers.

14 Then, as they sat there talking, a faint grinding jar seemed to come from somewhere deep inside the ship. It was not much, but enough to break the conversation and rattle the silver that was set for breakfast next morning.

15 Steward James Johnson felt he knew just what it was. He recognized the kind of shudder a ship gives when she drops a propeller blade, and he knew this sort of mishap meant a trip back to the Harland & Wolff Shipyard at Belfast—with plenty of free time to enjoy the hospitality of the port.

3. **windjammer** a type of large sailing ship for passengers or cargo
4. **Jacobean** design or literature from Britain during the reign of King James IV (1567–1625)

TEXT TALK

What did Fleet do when he spotted an iceberg?

See paragraphs 6–9: He rings a warning bell and calls the bridge to report the iceberg ahead of the ship.

On which side of the ship did the iceberg hit the *Titanic*?

See paragraph 10: The iceberg hit the starboard side of the ship.

What did Steward James Johnson think happened to the *Titanic*?

See paragraph 15: Johnson thought the ship had dropped a propeller blade.

SELECTION VOCABULARY

detached / indiferente ***adjective*** unemotional; unconcerned

- What is described as "detached" in this paragraph?
- Is it a positive or negative description?

draw / avanzar ***verb*** to move to one side COGNATE

- What is happening to the ship in this paragraph? Where might it draw?
- What does the amount of time that Fleet and Lee wait suggest about the ship's movement?

myriads / la miríada ***noun*** large numbers; multitudes COGNATE

- What is there myriads of in this paragraph?
- What do the myriads help describe?

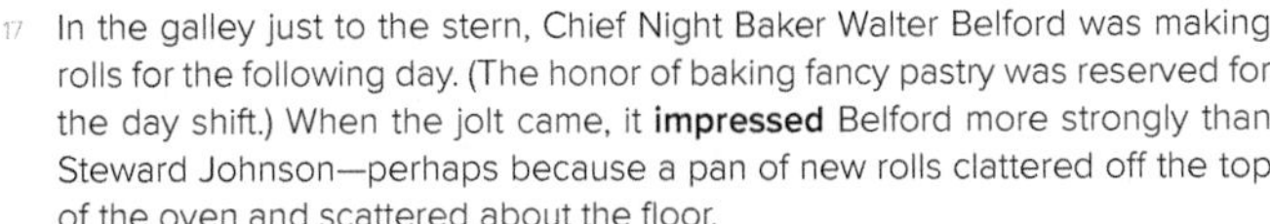

NOTES

16 Somebody near him agreed and sang out cheerfully, "Another Belfast trip!"

17 In the galley just to the stern, Chief Night Baker Walter Belford was making rolls for the following day. (The honor of baking fancy pastry was reserved for the day shift.) When the jolt came, it **impressed** Belford more strongly than Steward Johnson—perhaps because a pan of new rolls clattered off the top of the oven and scattered about the floor.

18 The passengers in their cabins felt the jar too, and tried to connect it with something familiar. Marguerite Frolicher, a young Swiss girl accompanying her father on a business trip, woke up with a start. Half-asleep, she could think only of the little white lake ferries at Zurich making a sloppy landing. Softly she said to herself, "Isn't it funny . . . we're landing!"

19 Major Arthur Godfrey Peuchen, starting to undress for the night, thought it was like a heavy wave striking the ship. Mrs. J. Stuart White was sitting on the edge of her bed, just reaching to turn out the light, when the ship seemed to roll over "a thousand marbles." To Lady Cosmo Duff Gordon, waking up from the jolt, it seemed "as though somebody had drawn a giant finger along the side of the ship." Mrs. John Jacob Astor thought it was some mishap in the kitchen.

20 It seemed stronger to some than to others. Mrs. Albert Caldwell pictured a large dog that had a baby kitten in its mouth and was shaking it. Mrs. Walter B. Stephenson recalled the first **ominous** jolt when she was in the San Francisco earthquake—then decided this wasn't that bad. Mrs. E. D. Appleton felt hardly any shock at all, but she noticed an unpleasant ripping sound . . . like someone tearing a long, long strip of calico.[5]

21 The jar meant more to J. Bruce Ismay, Managing Director of the White Star Line, who in a festive mood was going along for the ride on the *Titanic's* first trip. Ismay woke up with a start in his deluxe suite on B Deck—he felt sure the ship had struck something, but he didn't know what.

Excerpted from *A Night to Remember* by Walter Lord, published by Bantam Books.

5. **calico** a type of rough fabric of woven cotton

WRITE

PERSONAL RESPONSE: How do the reactions of the *Titanic* passengers affect your feelings, such as sympathy, about the collision? How does reading these personal reactions help you better understand what happened? Be sure to use evidence to support your response.

TEXT TALK

Where was Marguerite Frolicher when the *Titanic* hit the iceberg? What did she think was happening?

See paragraph 18: She was in her cabin. She thought the boat was landing.

What did J. Bruce Ismay believe caused the jar?

See paragraph 21: He thought the ship had struck something.

The ship was described as "glamorous," but it had a devastating end. Do you think the expectations of the ship made the tragedy that much more shocking for the passengers? Why or why not?

Answers will vary.

B Ask each Beyond grade-level student to write one additional discussion question. Then have one or two students facilitate a discussion, using their questions to guide the conversation.

SELECTION VOCABULARY

impressed / impresionar *verb* to create a strong effect; to have a forceful impact COGNATE

- Who does the jolt impress?
- What smaller words can you see in *impress*?

ominous / ominoso/a *adjective* threatening; suggesting that something bad will happen COGNATE

- What word does *ominous* describe?
- What previous event is the character describing?

Reading Comprehension OPTIONAL

Have students complete the digital reading comprehension questions ✓ when they finish reading.

ANSWER KEY

QUESTION 1: D
QUESTION 2: B
QUESTION 3: C
QUESTION 4: C
QUESTION 5: D
QUESTION 6: B
QUESTION 7: A
QUESTION 8: C
QUESTION 9: D
QUESTION 10: *See chart.*

First	Second	Third	Fourth
Lookouts Fleet and Lee prepare themselves mentally for a possible crash into the iceberg.	Quartermaster George Thomas Rowe paces the deck.	In the galley, Night Baker Belford notices the jolt more than Steward Johnson in the dining area.	Passengers Peuchen, White, Gordon, and Astor use metaphors to describe the iceberg's impact upon the ship.

Connect and Extend OPTIONAL

CONNECT TO EXTENDED WRITING PROJECT

Students can use *A Night to Remember* as a resource when writing their informational essays. Have students use Walter Lord's style of reporting the events as an inspiration for their own writing.

BEYOND THE BOOK

Art: A Google Doodle Tribute to the *Titanic*

Students will design a Google Doodle to be displayed on April 14 to remember the *Titanic*. Students should include details from *A Night to Remember* in their Google Doodle. They can create pieces of artwork with moveable parts to demonstrate how it should be animated or use an online design tool to create their Google Doodle.

StudySyncTV

Project the StudySyncTV episode and pause at the following times to prompt discussion:

0:12 What do you think it would feel like to be in the middle of the ocean at night with the stars providing the only light you can see?

0:24 What would you do if you were a passenger and you felt the impact?

0:36 What do you predict the passengers and crew did when the *Titanic* began to sink?

Collaborative Conversation

SCAFFOLDS

Post the writing prompt to generate a discussion in small groups. Ask students to first break down the prompt before they discuss relevant ideas and textual evidence. Ask students to use the StudySyncTV episode as a model for their discussion.

How do the reactions of the *Titanic* passengers affect your feelings, such as sympathy, about the collision? How does reading these personal reactions help you better understand what happened? Be sure to use evidence to support your response.

Use the scaffolds below to differentiate instruction for your ELL English Language Learners and A Approaching grade-level learners.

ELL **BEGINNING, INTERMEDIATE** Use the discussion guide and speaking frames to facilitate the discussion with support from the teacher.

ADVANCED, ADVANCED HIGH Use the discussion guide and speaking frames to facilitate the discussion in mixed-level groups.

A **APPROACHING** Use the discussion guide to facilitate the discussion in mixed-level groups.

APPROACHING

ADVANCED, ADVANCED HIGH

BEGINNING, INTERMEDIATE

Discussion Guide	Speaking Frames
1. How do you feel when you read the reactions of the *Titanic* passengers?	• I feel ___ and ___.
2. Which person did you feel sympathy for?	• I felt sympathy for ___ because ___.
3. What do you know about the disaster from reading the personal reactions?	• From reading the reactions I know ___.

Review Prompt and Rubric

Before students begin writing, review the writing prompt and rubric with the class.

PERSONAL RESPONSE: How do the reactions of the *Titanic* passengers affect your feelings, such as sympathy, about the collision? How does reading these personal reactions help you better understand what happened? Be sure to use evidence to support your response.

PROMPT GUIDE

- What feelings do you have when you read the reactions of the *Titanic* passengers?
- What do you learn from reading the reactions?
- What evidence from the text can you include to help explain your feelings and what you learned?

Score	Personal Response	Language and Conventions
4	The writer clearly explains his or her personal feelings about the text, using relevant evidence from the text as needed.	The writer demonstrates a consistent command of grammar, punctuation, and usage conventions. Although minor errors may be evident, they do not detract from the fluency or the clarity of the writing.
3	The writer sufficiently explains his or her personal feelings about the text, using relevant evidence from the text most of the time.	The writer demonstrates an adequate command of grammar, punctuation, and usage conventions. Although some errors may be evident, they create few (if any) disruptions in the fluency or clarity of the writing.
2	The writer begins to explain his or her personal feelings about the text, but the explanation is incomplete. The writer uses relevant evidence from the text only some of the time.	The writer demonstrates a partial command of grammar, punctuation, and usage conventions. Some distracting errors may be evident, at times creating minor disruptions in the fluency or clarity of the writing.
1	The writer attempts to explain his or her personal feelings about the text, but the explanation is not successful. The writer uses little or no relevant evidence from the text.	The writer demonstrates little or no command of grammar, punctuation, and usage conventions. Serious and persistent errors create disruptions in the fluency of the writing and sometimes interfere with meaning.
0	The writer does not provide a relevant response to the prompt or does not provide a response at all.	Serious and persistent errors overwhelm the writing and interfere with the meaning of the response as a whole, making the writer's meaning impossible to understand.

Write

SCAFFOLDS

Ask students to complete the writing assignment using textual evidence to support their answers.

Use the scaffolds below to differentiate instruction for your ELL English Language Learners and A Approaching grade-level learners.

ELL **BEGINNING** With the help of the word bank, write a response using paragraph frame 1.

INTERMEDIATE With the help of the word bank, write a response using paragraph frames 1 and 2.

ADVANCED, ADVANCED HIGH Write a response of differentiated length using the sentence starters.

A **APPROACHING** Write a response of differentiated length using the sentence starters.

BEGINNING | INTERMEDIATE | ADVANCED, ADVANCED HIGH | APPROACHING

Word Bank	Paragraph Frame 1	Paragraph Frame 2	Sentence Starters
lookout danger collision iceberg imagine	Reading the reactions of the *Titanic* passengers makes me feel like I actually got to talk to the real people. I can more easily ____ what it was like for them to experience the disaster, so I better understand what happened. I feel sympathy for them because I know what actually happened to them. For example, Frederick Fleet was a ____ on the *Titanic* who first saw the ____. The ship turned at the last minute, and Fleet thought the *Titanic* had avoided a ____. I feel sympathy for Fleet because he did not understand the ____ that he was in.	Another passenger who was on the *Titanic* during the crash was ____. He reacted by ____. Reading that helps me ____. He thought ____. Reading about his experience, I feel ____ because he ____.	• Reading the reactions of the *Titanic* passengers makes me feel . . . • I can more easily imagine what it was like for them to . . . • I feel sympathy for them because . . . • For example . . .

Peer Review

Rate

Respond to the following with a point rating that reflects your opinion.

	1 2 3 4
Ideas	■■■□
Evidence	■■■■
Language and Conventions	■■□□

Submit

Students should submit substantive feedback to two peers using the review instructions below.

- How well does this response answer the prompt?
- Which of the author's comments inspired you to think differently about the text?
- What did the writer do well in this response? What does the writer need to work on?

ELL A **SENTENCE FRAMES**

- You were able to (completely / partly / almost) answer the prompt because ____.
- You could answer the prompt more completely by ____.
- You supported the idea of ____ with the detail of ____.
- One idea that needs more support is ____.
- I thought differently about the text after reading ____.
- My favorite part of your response is ____.

Address to the Nation on the Explosion of the Space Shuttle *Challenger*

INFORMATIONAL TEXT
Ronald Reagan
1986

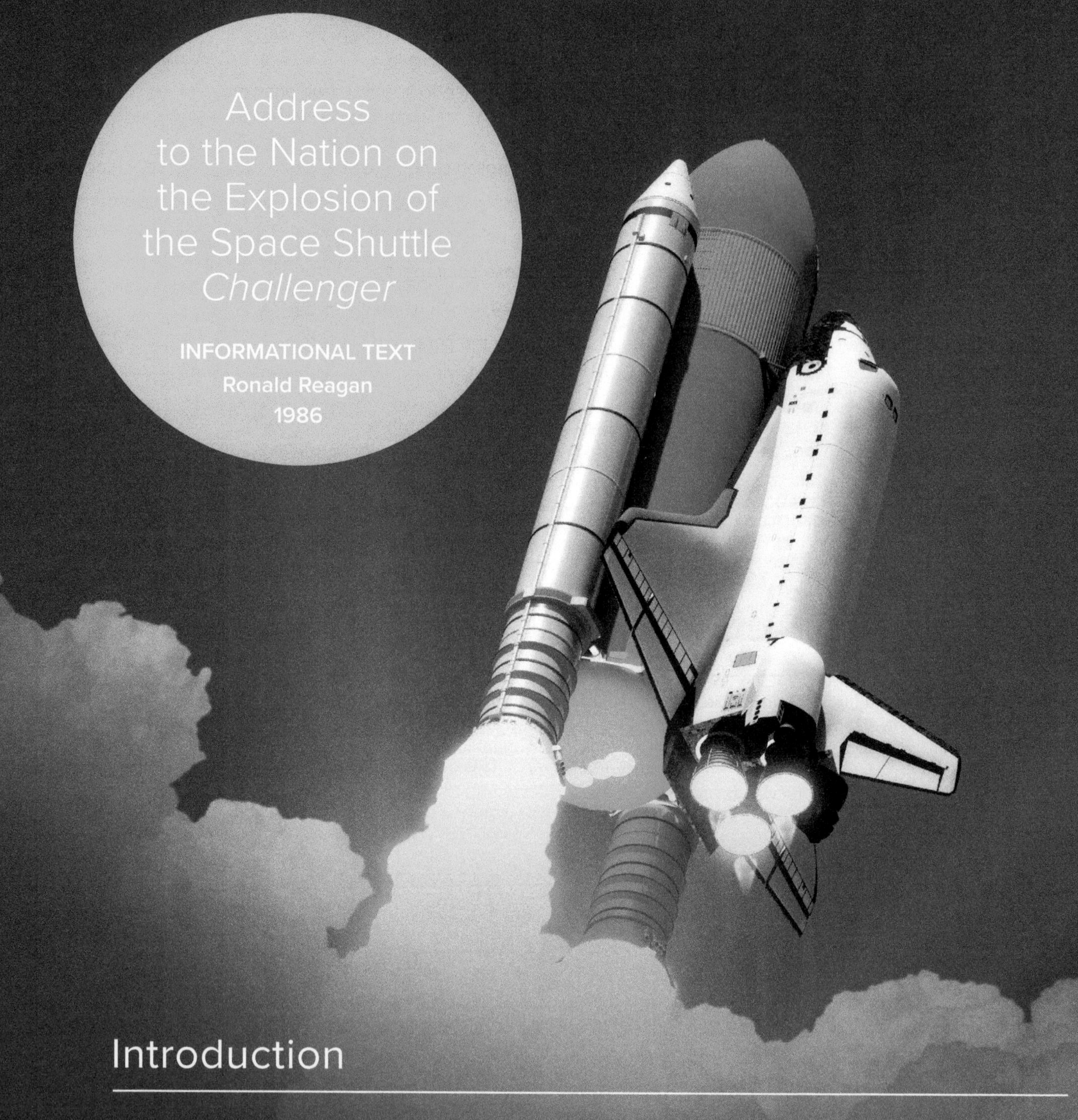

Introduction

On January 28, 1986, millions of Americans watched on live TV as the Space Shuttle *Challenger* violently exploded just 73 seconds after takeoff, killing all seven people on board. It was the tenth mission for *Challenger*, but the first scheduled to carry an ordinary citizen into space, a teacher from New Hampshire named Christa McAuliffe. That evening, President Ronald Reagan (1911–2004) addressed the nation, including the many school children who witnessed the disaster, and lauded the bravery of the fallen crew.

On January 28, 1986, U.S. President Reagan preempted his State of the Union speech to address the nation. Earlier that morning, the space shuttle *Challenger* exploded during its nationally televised launch, killing everyone on board. Reagan began by praising the crew members, who knew the risks yet courageously went ahead with the mission. He also tried to console their family members with the reminder that the nation was thinking of them. As the launch was televised in schools across the country, Reagan also spoke to the American children, explaining that the *Challenger* crew were pioneers and discovery is undertaken by the brave, not the fainthearted. Praising all the men and women who work at NASA, Reagan concluded his speech by affirming that the space program would proceed with future missions, and the journey of discovery would continue.

 Proficiency-leveled summaries and summaries in multiple languages are available digitally.

 Audio and audio text highlighting are available with this text.

COMPARING WITHIN AND ACROSS GENRES

 What happens when a big risk has a negative outcome? In the wake of the *Challenger* explosion, President Ronald Reagan speaks to a shocked and grieving nation about the crew who gave their lives for science and why space exploration is worth the risk.

Access Complex Text

LEXILE: 780L **WORD COUNT:** 651

The following areas may be challenging for students, particularly ELL English Language Learners and A Approaching grade-level learners.

Genre	Purpose	Prior Knowledge
• The text is a speech, a public statement meant to be heard and seen. A speech reflects the speaker's point of view. • In the speech, President Reagan uses the pronoun *we* to indicate not only himself and the First Lady, but also all Americans.	• The speech contains a eulogy, or memorial speech, of the astronauts who died, as well as reassurances to the nation's children. • One role of the president is to speak to the nation in times of crisis or tragedy.	• Students may not be familiar with NASA and the U.S. space program, from the first flights to the space shuttle missions. • Reagan ends his speech with a quote from John Gillespie Magee, Jr., a pilot who was killed during a flight in 1941.

SCAFFOLDS  ENGLISH LANGUAGE LEARNERS  APPROACHING GRADE LEVEL  BEYOND GRADE LEVEL

These icons identify differentiation strategies and scaffolded support for a variety of students. See the digital lesson plan for additional differentiation strategies and scaffolds.

Instructional Path

The print teacher's edition includes essential point-of-use instruction and planning tools. Complete lesson plans and program documents appear in your digital teacher account.

First Read: Address to the Nation on the Explosion of the Space Shuttle *Challenger*

Objectives: After an initial reading and discussion of the Presidential address, students will be able to identify and restate the text's key ideas and details.

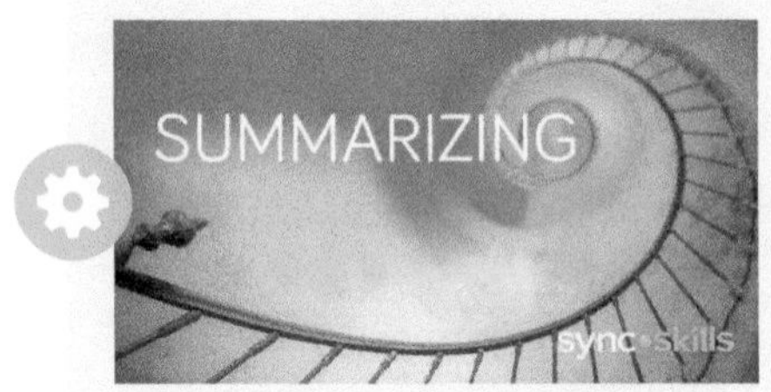

Skill: Summarizing

Objectives: After rereading and discussing a model of close reading, students will be able to determine how to write an objective summary of a text.

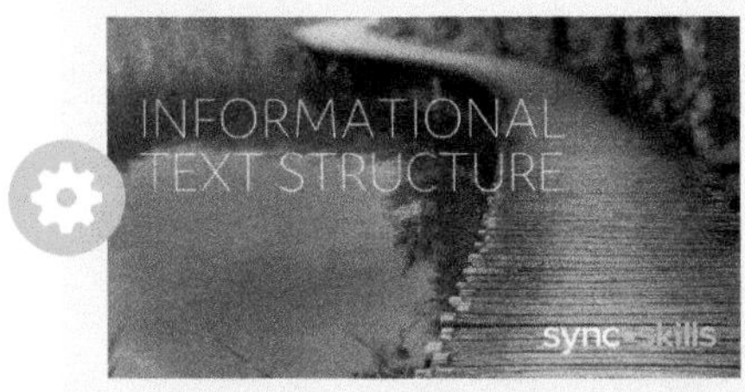

Skill: Informational Text Structure

Objectives: After rereading and discussing a model of close reading, students will be able to analyze how multiple organizational patterns within a text help develop the thesis.

Close Read: Address to the Nation on the Explosion of the Space Shuttle *Challenger*

Objectives: After engaging in a close reading and discussion of the text, students will be able to analyze how different structures of the text help to effectively communicate information.

Progress Monitoring

Opportunities to Learn	Opportunities to Demonstrate Learning	Opportunities to Reteach
Summarizing		
Skill: Summarizing	Skill: Summarizing • Your Turn Close Read • Skills Focus • Write	Spotlight Skill: Summarizing
Informational Text Structure		
Skill: Informational Text Structure	Skill: Informational Text Structure • Your Turn Close Read • Skills Focus • Write	Unit 6 Skill: Informational Text Structure - Blood, Toil, Tears and Sweat Unit 6 Skill: Informational Text Structure - Nobel Prize Acceptance Speech Spotlight Skill: Informational Text Structure

First Read

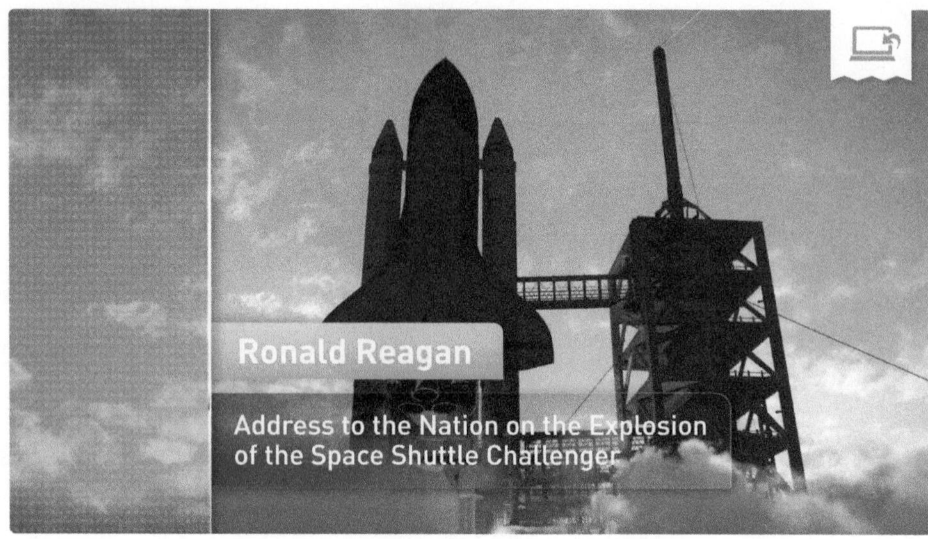

Introduce the Text

As a class, watch the video preview and have students read the introduction in pairs to make connections to the video preview.

To activate prior knowledge and experiences, ask students:

- What part of the video stood out to you the most?
- What kind of speech are you about to read? How can you tell?

SPEAKING FRAMES

- The ____ in the video makes me think ____.
- The video shows ____. This makes me wonder ____.
- I think the text will ____. I think this because ____.
- I predict that there will be ____. I believe this because ____.

Entry Point

As students prepare to read "Address to the Nation on the Explosion of the Space Shuttle *Challenger*," share the following information with them to provide context.

✓ NASA launched the space shuttle *Challenger* on the morning of January 28, 1986, but it exploded 73 seconds after liftoff. The *Challenger* was carrying six crew members and one passenger, and they all lost their lives.

✓ The passenger was a teacher named Christa McAuliffe, and NASA had selected her to be the first teacher in space. As a result, many students were watching the launch.

✓ Ronald Reagan delivered a speech about the *Challenger* disaster later that evening. It was written by speechwriter Peggy Noonan, and it was meant for an audience of all ages. The speech was widely acclaimed, and it became one of Reagan's most historic speeches.

"We're still pioneers. They, the members of the *Challenger* crew, were pioneers."

January 28, 1986

NOTES

1 Ladies and gentlemen, I'd planned to speak to you tonight to report on the state of the Union,[1] but the events of earlier today have led me to change those plans. Today is a day for mourning and remembering. Nancy and I are pained to the core by the tragedy of the shuttle *Challenger*. We know we share this pain with all of the people of our country. This is truly a national loss.

2 Nineteen years ago, almost to the day, we lost three astronauts in a terrible accident on the ground. But we've never lost an astronaut in flight; we've never had a tragedy like this. And perhaps we've forgotten the courage it took for the crew of the shuttle. But they, the *Challenger* Seven, were aware of the dangers, but overcame them and did their jobs brilliantly. We mourn seven heroes: Michael Smith, Dick Scobee, Judith Resnik, Ronald McNair, Ellison Onizuka, Gregory Jarvis, and Christa McAuliffe. We mourn their loss as a nation together.

Five astronauts and two payload specialists make up the STS 51-L crew, scheduled to fly aboard the Space Shuttle *Challenger* in January of 1986. Crew members are (left to right, front row) astronauts Michael J. Smith, Francis R. (Dick) Scobee, and Ronald E. McNair; and (left to right, back row) Ellison S. Onizuka, Sharon Christa McAuliffe, Gregory Jarvis, and Judith A. Resnik.

Skill: Summarizing

Reagan calls members of the Challenger crew pioneers. Although we have become used to the idea of space, we must remember we are all still pioneers. The Challenger crew wished to serve and met the challenge with joy. We feel their loss.

3 For the families of the seven, we cannot bear, as you do, the full impact of this tragedy. But we feel the loss, and we're thinking about you so very much. Your loved ones were daring and brave, and they had that special **grace,** that special spirit that says, "Give me a challenge, and I'll meet it with joy." They had a hunger to explore the universe and discover its truths. They wished to serve, and they did. They served all of us. We've grown used to wonders in

1. **state of the Union** Reagan had previously planned to deliver the State of the Union, an annual speech given by U.S. presidents before Congress on general topics

Analyze Vocabulary Using Context Clues

In paragraph 3, focus on the sentence that uses the word *grace*. Point out these context clues:

1. First, I notice who the sentence is about—"your loved ones"—which means the astronauts who died.
2. I see that *grace* was something "your loved ones" had, and that it was "that special spirit."
3. I think *grace* means a special quality of someone's personality, such as the ability to welcome challenges.

Summarizing

What does the reader notice Reagan talking about in the third paragraph?

Reagan talks about the seven members of the *Challenger* crew and the grace, bravery, and special spirit they possessed.

SELECTION VOCABULARY

grace / la gentileza *noun* polite and pleasant behavior

horizon / el horizonte *noun* the limit of possibility or knowledge COGNATE

- Whose horizons are described in this paragraph?
- What does "the process of exploration and discovery" help us see?

TEXT TALK

What event led to this speech?

See the Introduction and paragraph 1: The space shuttle *Challenger* exploded, killing seven astronauts.

Who were the astronauts killed in the *Challenger* disaster?

See paragraph 2: The astronauts were Michael Smith, Dick Scobee, Judith Resnik, Ronald McNair, Ellison Onizuka, Gregory Jarvis, and Christa McAuliffe.

How did the president explain the disaster to the schoolchildren of America?

See paragraph 4: He explains that risk and danger are part of the process of exploration and discovery, which is why the astronauts were brave.

Informational Text Structure

How does the reader use signal words to identify a secondary structure?

The reader recognizes that the word *like* suggests a comparison, and a compare-and-contrast text structure is used in the last two paragraphs. This reinforces a key concept about the nature and perils of exploration.

NOTES

this century. It's hard to dazzle us. But for 25 years the United States space program has been doing just that. We've grown used to the idea of space, and perhaps we forget that we've only just begun. We're still pioneers. They, the members of the *Challenger* crew, were pioneers.

4 And I want to say something to the schoolchildren of America who were watching the live coverage of the shuttle's takeoff. I know it is hard to understand, but sometimes painful things like this happen. It's all part of the process of exploration and discovery. It's all part of taking a chance and expanding man's **horizons**. The future doesn't belong to the fainthearted; it belongs to the brave. The *Challenger* crew was pulling us into the future, and we'll continue to follow them.

5 I've always had great faith in and respect for our space program, and what happened today does nothing to diminish it. We don't hide our space program. We don't keep secrets and cover things up. We do it all up front and in public. That's the way freedom is, and we wouldn't change it for a minute. We'll continue our quest in space. There will be more shuttle flights and more shuttle crews and, yes, more volunteers, more civilians, more teachers in space. Nothing ends here; our hopes and our journeys continue. I want to add that I wish I could talk to every man and woman who works for NASA or who worked on this mission and tell them: "Your dedication and **professionalism** have moved and impressed us for decades. And we know of your **anguish.** We share it."

Skill: Informational Text Structure

In the second-to-last paragraph, Reagan mentions Sir Francis Drake. He was an ocean explorer who died at sea 390 years ago. Here Reagan uses a compare-and-contrast text structure to compare the Challenger crew to another explorer.

6 There's a **coincidence** today. On this day 390 years ago, the great explorer Sir Francis Drake died aboard ship off the coast of Panama. In his lifetime the great frontiers were the oceans, and an historian later said, "He lived by the sea, died on it, and was buried in it." Well, today we can say of the *Challenger* crew: Their dedication was, like Drake's, complete.

7 The crew of the space shuttle *Challenger* honored us by the manner in which they lived their lives. We will never forget them, nor the last time we saw them, this morning, as they prepared for their journey and waved goodbye and "slipped the surly bonds of earth" to "touch the face of God."

TEXT TALK

What does President Reagan promise will happen with the space program?

See paragraph 5: He promises that the program will continue and expand.

What coincidence does President Reagan talk about?

See paragraph 6: The explorer Sir Francis Drake died on his ship on the same day 390 years before; he was dedicated to exploration.

What did the *Challenger* explosion teach the nation? What lessons were learned from the tragedy?

Answers will vary.

SELECTION VOCABULARY

professionalism / el profesionalismo ***noun*** skill and competence COGNATE

- What smaller word do you see in *professionalism*?
- Who is described as having professionalism in this paragraph?

anguish / la angustia ***noun*** severe suffering or distress COGNATE

- How did the people at NASA feel after the explosion?
- Is the word positive or negative?

coincidence / la coincidencia ***noun*** two things that happen by chance at the same time or place COGNATE

- What two events happened on January 28?
- Did the two events happen by chance or by human planning?

Reading Comprehension OPTIONAL

Have students complete the digital reading comprehension questions when they finish reading.

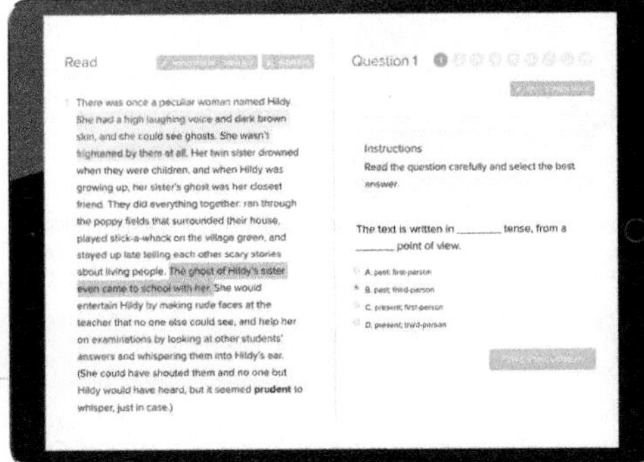

ANSWER KEY

QUESTION 1: A
QUESTION 2: A
QUESTION 3: D
QUESTION 4: C
QUESTION 5: A
QUESTION 6: C
QUESTION 7: C
QUESTION 8: B
QUESTION 9: *See first chart.*
QUESTION 10: *See second chart.*

Excerpt	Significance
". . . as they prepared for their journey and waved goodbye and 'slipped the surly bonds of earth' . . ."	Quoting a poem as an elegy to the astronauts
"We don't hide our space program. We don't keep secrets and cover things up."	Calling out the USSR and their way of governing
"Their dedication was, like Drake's, complete."	Comparing the astronauts to the European explorers from centuries ago
". . . but the events of earlier today have led me to change those plans."	Canceling a major national address

Synonym	Word
dignity	grace
suffering	anguish
chance happening	coincidence
competence	professionalism

Connect and Extend

CONNECT TO EXTENDED WRITING PROJECT

Students can use "Address to the Nation on the Explosion of the Space Shuttle *Challenger*" as a resource when writing their informational essays. Students may consider ways to structure their own writing.

BEYOND THE BOOK

Writing: Obituaries for *Challenger* Astronauts

Break students into seven groups and give each group the name of one of the people who died in the 1986 *Challenger* explosion: Michael Smith, Dick Scobee, Judith Resnik, Ronald McNair, Ellison Onizuka, Gregory Jarvis, or Christa McAuliffe.

Ask students to:

- Research the person's life to learn about his/her family, work, and accomplishments.
- Read examples of obituaries in the local paper or online.
  - > How long is the average obituary?
  - > What types of details and information do obituaries contain about people who have died?
- Write an obituary announcing the astronaut's death and celebrating his/her life and accomplishments.

Allow each group to read their obituary for the class.

Then discuss the following:

- What did these individuals have in common?
- After learning more about them, how does this change the way you think about the 1986 *Challenger* explosion?

Think Questions

Circulate as students answer Think Questions independently. Scaffolds for these questions are shown on the opposite page.

QUESTION 1: Textual Evidence

The *Challenger* explosion was significant because seven astronauts died and they were the first astronauts to die after takeoff. President Reagan said, "We've never lost an astronaut in flight; we've never had a tragedy like this." Also, the *Challenger* tragedy was significant because a teacher, Christa McAuliffe, was one of the astronauts who died.

QUESTION 2: Textual Evidence

President Reagan calls the astronauts "the *Challenger* Seven." He describes the astronauts as brave and willing to take risks. The President said they "were aware of the dangers, but overcame them and did their jobs brilliantly."

QUESTION 3: Textual Evidence

President Reagan is proud of the space program because it is a symbol of freedom, and he wants the United States to continue to explore space. He promises, "There will be more shuttle flights and more shuttle crews and, yes, more volunteers, more civilians, more teachers in space."

QUESTION 4: Context Clues

The horizon is the farthest distance you can see, the boundary between the earth and the sky. Reagan uses *horizons* to mean the boundaries of human knowledge. "Expanding man's *horizons*" means expanding our knowledge through "the process of exploration and discovery."

QUESTION 5: Greek and Latin Affixes and Roots

An *incident* is something that happens. So *coincidence* must mean things that happen together, such as at the same time or place. Also, coincidences happen just by chance. For example, in this case, two tragedies happened to take place on the same date: the death of Sir Francis Drake and the deaths of seven astronauts.

First Read

Read "Address to the Nation on the Explosion of the Space Shuttle *Challenger*." After you read, complete the Think Questions below.

THINK QUESTIONS

1. Refer to one or more details from the text to support your understanding of the significance of the *Challenger* tragedy. What words and phrases in the first two paragraphs indicate this significance?

2. How does President Reagan describe the astronauts? Use details from the text to write two or three sentences that summarize his description.

3. Write two or three sentences explaining how President Reagan feels about the space program. What details does he offer to support his ideas? Cite evidence from the text to support your answer.

4. Use context to determine the meaning of the word **horizons** as it is used in this speech. Write your definition of *horizons* here and tell how you found it.

5. Remembering that the Latin prefix *co-* means "together," use the context clues provided in the passage to determine the meaning of **coincidence**. Write your definition of *coincidence* here and tell how you got it.

Think Questions

SCAFFOLDS

Use the scaffolds below to differentiate instruction for your ELL English Language Learners and A Approaching grade-level learners.

ELL **BEGINNING** Write a response using the word bank and sentence frames.

INTERMEDIATE Write a response using the sentence frames.

ADVANCED, ADVANCED HIGH Write a response using the Text-Dependent Question Guide.

A **APPROACHING** Write a response using the Text-Dependent Question Guide.

BEGINNING	INTERMEDIATE	APPROACHING / ADVANCED, ADVANCED HIGH
Word Bank	**Sentence Frames**	**Text-Dependent Question Guide**
NASA *Challenger* discovery loss time space program shuttle heroes ideas pioneers	The president talked about "the tragedy of the _____. *Challenger*." The president said, "We mourn seven _____." The president called the tragedy a national _____.	1. • What did the president mean by "the events of earlier today"? • How many astronauts died in the *Challenger* tragedy? • Who is mourning the deaths of the astronauts?
	The president referred to the astronauts as the _____ Seven. The president said that the members of the crew were _____.	2. • What group name does the president give to the astronauts? • What word does the president use to describe "the members of the *Challenger* crew"?
	President Reagan had "great faith in and respect for our space _____." The president said, "We'll continue our quest in _____." The president said, "I wish I could talk to every man and woman who works for _____."	3. • What does President Reagan have "great faith in and respect for"? • How will we "continue our quest"? • Who does the president wish he could talk to?
	Horizons are the limits of our _____. The president said, "It's all part of the process of exploration and _____."	4. • Read: "It's all part of taking a chance and expanding man's **horizons**." • When you expand your view, or horizons, what happens to your mind? • What process is "expanding man's horizons" a part of?
	Coincidence means "two events that happen by chance at the same _____."	5. • Read: "There's a **coincidence** today. On this day 390 years ago, the great explorer Sir Francis Drake died aboard ship off the coast of Panama." • What event happened 390 years earlier on the same day as the *Challenger* disaster? • Were the two events planned so they would happen on the same day?

Skill: Summarizing

Introduce the Skill

Watch the Concept Definition video and read the following definition with your students.

When you **summarize** a text, you briefly state the main points and most important details in your own words. Summarizing can help you organize, explain, and remember concepts in an informational text or the events that take place in a story.

To summarize, you must decide what is most important as you read. Ask the basic questions: *who, what, when, where, why,* and *how.* Using your own words, write your answers to these questions from an **objective** point of view, without inserting your own feelings and opinions.

Summarizing is sometimes confused with paraphrasing. When you **paraphrase**, you do not condense a text to its most important details. Instead, you restate the entire text in your own words. A summary is much shorter than the original text, while a paraphrase may be the same length as the original text.

Skill: Summarizing

Use the Checklist to analyze Summarizing in "Address to the Nation on the Explosion of the Space Shuttle *Challenger*." Refer to the sample student annotations about Summarizing in the text.

••• CHECKLIST FOR SUMMARIZING

In order to determine how to write an objective summary of a text, note the following:

- ✓ in a nonfiction text, examine the details, making notations in a notebook or graphic organizer
  - ask basic questions such as *who, what, when, where, why,* and *how*
  - identify what each of the details describe or have in common
  - determine what central or main idea ties all the information together
- ✓ use the main idea as the topic sentence of the summary
- ✓ stay objective and do not add your own personal thoughts, judgments, or opinions to the summary

To provide an objective summary of a text, consider the following questions:

- ✓ What are the answers to basic *who, what, where, when, why,* and *how* questions in works of nonfiction?
- ✓ Have I determined what each of the details have in common and what central or main idea ties them together?
- ✓ In what order should I put the main ideas and most important details in a work of nonfiction to make my summary clear and logical?
- ✓ Is my summary objective, or have I added my own thoughts, judgments, and personal opinions?

TURN AND TALK

1. Think about your favorite book or movie. Can you describe who did what, where, when, why, and how without including your thoughts and feelings about it?
2. Why is it important to leave out our thoughts and feelings when we summarize?

ELL SPEAKING FRAMES

- The [book / movie] took place in ____.
- In [book or movie title], the main character was ____ and in the [book / movie] they ____.
- The reason the main character did what they did was to ____.
- It is important to leave out our thoughts and feelings when we summarize because ____.

V SKILL VOCABULARY

summarize / resumir ***verb*** to restate briefly the most important points in a text

objective / objetivo/a ***adjective*** undistorted by emotion or personal bias COGNATE

paraphrase / parafrasear ***verb*** to restate the author's words in your own words COGNATE

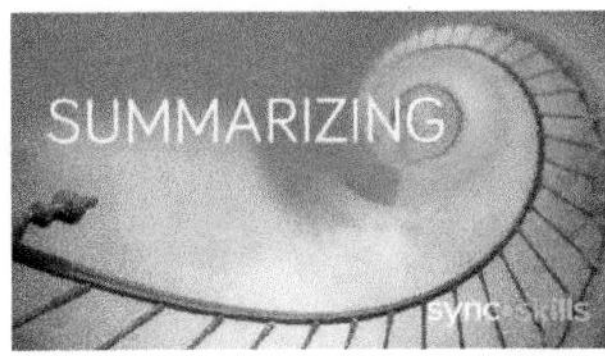

Skill: Summarizing

Reread paragraph 5 of "Address to the Nation on the Explosion of the Space Shuttle *Challenger*." Then, using the Checklist on the previous page, answer the multiple-choice questions below.

YOUR TURN

1. This question has two parts. First, answer Part A. Then, answer Part B.

Part A: What is the main idea of paragraph 5?

- ○ A. It is important to keep the space program hidden from the public.
- ○ B. NASA will continue with their space exploration program.
- ○ C. President Reagan wants to talk to everyone at NASA who worked on this mission.
- ○ D. More teachers will be in space one day.

Part B: Which two details from the paragraph support your answer to Part A?

- ○ A. "We don't hide our space program" and "we know of your anguish."
- ○ B. "We don't hide our space program" and "we don't keep secrets and cover things up."
- ○ C. "There will be more shuttle flights and more shuttle crews and, yes, more volunteers, more civilians, more teachers in space" and "nothing ends here; our hopes and our journeys continue."
- ○ D. "We do it all up front and in public" and "we know of your anguish."

2. In paragraph 5, what is the important link between Reagan's statements about the space program and the people who work at NASA that supports the main idea and should be included in a summary?

- ○ A. President Reagan says that we don't hide our space program, and we don't keep secrets and cover things up.
- ○ B. Reagan states that there will be more shuttle flights and more shuttle crews, more volunteers, more civilians, and more teachers in space.
- ○ C. Reagan says that "our journeys continue," and this is supported by his statements that he has great faith in the space program, and that the professionalism and dedication of the people who work at NASA have impressed us for decades.
- ○ D. President Reagan says that he has to talk to every man and woman who works for NASA or this mission about hiding the space program so tragedies like *Challenger* do not happen again.

Your Turn

Ask students to complete the Your Turn activity.

QUESTION 1

Part A

A. Incorrect. Reagan says that the United States doesn't hide its space program and we don't keep secrets or cover things up.

B. Correct. The entire paragraph is about the importance of continuing the space program.

C. Incorrect. This is only one detail from the paragraph that supports the main idea.

D. Incorrect. This is only one detail from the paragraph that supports the main idea.

Part B

A. Incorrect. These phrases do not support the idea of continuing the space program.

B. Incorrect. These phrases do not support the idea of continuing the space program.

C. Correct. These statements support the idea that the NASA space program will continue.

D. Incorrect. These phrases do not support the idea of continuing the space program.

QUESTION 2

A. Incorrect. This is not a link between his two statements related to the continuation of the space program.

B. Incorrect. This is an important detail, but it does not specifically refer to the link between his opening statement and his opinion of the employees at NASA.

C. Correct. These details support the fact that he feels the space program should continue despite the *Challenger* tragedy, and they should be included in a summary.

D. Incorrect. Reagan does say that he wants to talk to everyone at NASA, but he does not want to "hide" the space program.

Skill: Informational Text Structure

Introduce the Skill

Watch the Concept Definition video and read the following definition with your students.

Text structure refers to the organizational pattern authors of nonfiction use to present information. Some of the most common informational text structures include **sequential**, **problem and solution**, **cause and effect**, and **comparison and contrast**. In a sequential text structure, authors present information about events or steps in a process, in the order in which they take or have taken place. Writers who specialize in history or science topics often use a cause and effect text structure to explain how or why something happened. Many authors use a compare and contrast text structure to present information about things that are different but have something in common, such as two points of view on a subject. Or a writer may present a problem or a series of problems, and offers solutions on how to solve them.

Authors may also use text structure to organize information about multiple topics, or use more than one organizational pattern within the same text.

Address to the Nation on the Explosion of the Space Shuttle *Challenger*

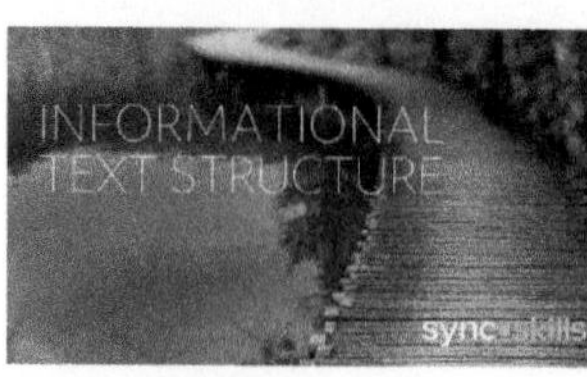

Skill: Informational Text Structure

Use the Checklist to analyze Informational Text Structure in "Address to the Nation on the Explosion of the Space Shuttle *Challenger*." Refer to the sample student annotations about Informational Text Structure in the text.

CHECKLIST FOR INFORMATIONAL TEXT STRUCTURE

In order to determine the structure of a specific paragraph in a text, note the following:

- ✓ details and signal words that reveal the text structure in a paragraph of the text
- ✓ a key concept in the paragraph that is revealed by the text structure the author has chosen to organize the text
- ✓ particular sentences in the paragraph and the role they play in defining and refining a key concept

To analyze in detail the structure of a specific paragraph in a text, including the role of particular sentences in developing and refining a key concept, consider the following questions:

- ✓ What is the structure of the paragraph?
- ✓ Which sentences in the paragraph reveal the text structure the author is using?
- ✓ What role do these sentences play in developing and refining a key concept?

TURN AND TALK

1. What is one informational text you've read recently?
2. What kind of text structures did the author use?

ELL SPEAKING FRAMES

- One informational text I read recently is ____.
- The author used a ____ structure.
- This text structure helped the author develop the key concept that ____.

SKILL VOCABULARY

text structure / la estructura del texto ***noun*** the order or pattern a writer uses to organize ideas or events COGNATE

sequential text structure / la estructura secuencial del texto ***noun*** a text structure in which events or steps are presented in the order in which they have taken place COGNATE

problem and solution text structure / el problema y la solución ***noun*** a text structure that identifies a problem and offers a solution COGNATE

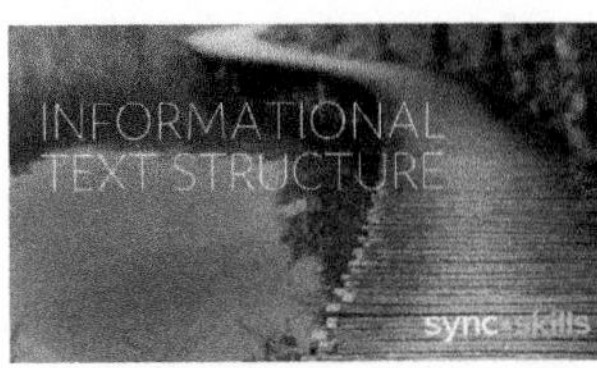

Skill: Informational Text Structure

Reread paragraph 3 of "Address to the Nation on the Explosion of the Space Shuttle *Challenger*." Then, using the Checklist on the previous page, answer the multiple-choice questions below.

YOUR TURN

1. The primary text structure in paragraph 3 is—
   - A. description.
   - B. cause and effect.
   - C. problem and solution.
   - D. compare and contrast.

2. The author develops this text structure by—
   - A. using the word *but* to identify differences.
   - B. discussing change over time to describe a solution to a problem.
   - C. starting many of the clauses with similar phrases to describe or define the qualities of two groups.
   - D. describing two groups' feelings after the *Challenger* disaster to develop its effect.

3. This text structure helps develop the author's thesis by—
   - A. developing the key concept that the disaster was a great loss because the astronauts had families.
   - B. developing the key concept that the disaster was a great loss because it was the end result of decades of research.
   - C. developing the key concept that the disaster was a great loss because many Americans were saddened by the disaster.
   - D. developing the key concept that the disaster was a great loss because Americans lost a group of special people who were willing to take on an important challenge for their country.

SkillsTV

Project the SkillsTV episode and pause at the following times to prompt discussion:

0:34 How do the students use the title to help them understand the text?

1:38 How do the students use textual evidence to recognize a change in text structure?

2:06 How do the students use textual evidence to understand the purpose of a change in text structure?

Your Turn

Ask students to complete the Your Turn activity.

QUESTION 1

A. Correct. Reagan describes or defines the qualities of the *Challenger* astronauts and the nation they served.

B. Incorrect. Although Reagan mentions the effect of the *Challenger* disaster, cause and effect is not the primary organizational pattern in the paragraph.

C. Incorrect. Reagan does not identify a problem or solution in this paragraph.

D. Incorrect. Compare and contrast is not the primary organizational pattern in the paragraph.

QUESTION 2

A. Incorrect. Reagan's use of the word does not develop the primary organizational pattern.

B. Incorrect. The idea or key concept of change does not develop the primary organizational pattern.

C. Correct. Reagan starts many of the clauses with *they* and a verb that describe the astronauts' qualities or actions. Then he uses *we* to discuss Americans in a similar manner.

D. Incorrect. Reagan's description of feelings is not the primary organizational pattern in the paragraph.

QUESTION 3

A. Incorrect. Reagan's description of the astronauts and other Americans emphasizes that their deaths are a loss to the families and to the nation.

B. Incorrect. Reagan does not discuss the research involved in creating and launching the *Challenger* shuttle.

C. Incorrect. Reagan's structure emphasizes the astronauts' contributions rather than Americans' feelings after the disaster.

D. Correct. Emphasizing the astronauts' qualities and contributions to an important program helps develop the significance of the loss for the nation.

Close Read

Skills Focus

QUESTION 1: Informational Text Structure

See paragraph 6: President Reagan notes that Sir Francis Drake died on the same day as the astronauts on *Challenger*. By comparing the astronauts to Sir Francis Drake, he is suggesting that the astronauts are great explorers, and it makes losing them seem more significant and tragic.

QUESTION 2: Summarizing

See paragraph 5: Reagan believes that the space program is something to be proud of and a representation of freedom in the United States. Even after the *Challenger* tragedy, Reagan makes a point to say that we as a country will continue to explore space, which emphasizes his support of the space program.

QUESTION 3: Connect to Essential Question

See paragraph 2: Space exploration is dangerous and can cost an astronaut his or her life, but astronauts take the risk because they are courageous and committed to their jobs.

Close Read

Reread "Address to the Nation on the Explosion of the Space Shuttle *Challenger*." As you reread, complete the Skills Focus questions below. Then use your answers and annotations from the questions to help you complete the Write activity.

SKILLS FOCUS

1. Identify examples of compare-and-contrast structure in the text. Explain how these comparisons help develop the thesis, or central message, in Reagan's speech.
2. Identify Reagan's stance on the space program. Write one or two sentences summarizing his message.
3. Identify details in the text that show the risks of the space program. Explain why astronauts are willing to take chances and explore space.

WRITE

COMPARATIVE: In "Address to the Nation on the Explosion of the Space Shuttle *Challenger*," President Reagan addresses the public about a national tragedy. In *A Night to Remember*, the tragedy is recounted through interviews with various people who experienced the *Titanic's* crash. How do the different structures of the texts help to effectively communicate information regarding the tragedies? Are there advantages or disadvantages to the structure of either text? Which one do you prefer? Cite specific examples from the text to explain which structure better helps to effectively communicate information and make the author's point.

Writer's Notebook

Connect to Essential Question: Give students time to reflect on how "Address to the Nation on the Explosion of the Space Shuttle *Challenger*" connects to the unit's essential question "Why do we take chances?" by freewriting in their Writer's Notebooks.

Beginning & Intermediate

Read aloud the unit's essential question: "Why do we take chances?" Encourage students to draw their connections or allow students to write in their native language. Circulate the room, prompting students for their thoughts as they respond orally or through pantomime.

Advanced & Advanced High

Allow students to share their reflections orally in pairs or small groups before freewriting.

Collaborative Conversation

SCAFFOLDS

Break students into collaborative conversation groups to discuss the Close Read prompt. Ask students to use the StudySyncTV episode as a model for their discussion. Remind them to reference their Skills Focus annotations in their discussion.

In "Address to the Nation on the Explosion of the Space Shuttle *Challenger*," President Reagan addresses the public about a national tragedy. In *A Night to Remember*, the tragedy is recounted through interviews with various people who experienced the *Titanic's* crash. How do the different structures of the texts help to effectively communicate information regarding the tragedies? Are there advantages or disadvantages to the structure of either text? Which one do you prefer? Cite specific examples from the texts to explain which structure better helps to effectively communicate information and make the author's point.

Use the scaffolds below to differentiate instruction for your ELL English Language Learners and A Approaching grade-level learners.

ELL **BEGINNING, INTERMEDIATE** Use the discussion guide and speaking frames to facilitate the discussion with support from the teacher.

ADVANCED, ADVANCED HIGH Use the discussion guide and speaking frames to facilitate the discussion in mixed-level groups.

A **APPROACHING** Use the discussion guide to facilitate the discussion in mixed-level groups.

APPROACHING

ADVANCED, ADVANCED HIGH

BEGINNING, INTERMEDIATE

Discussion Guide	Speaking Frames
1. What is one type of text structure that Reagan uses in the speech?	• In paragraph ____ (number), Reagan uses ____ text structure.
2. How does this text structure help communicate information?	• Reagan uses this text structure to communicate ____.
3. What is one type of text structure that Lord uses in the excerpt?	• In paragraph ____ (number), Lord uses a ____ text structure.
4. How does this text structure help communicate information?	• Lord uses this text structure to communicate ____.

Review Prompt and Rubric

Before students begin writing, review the writing prompt and rubric with the class.

Comparative: In "Address to the Nation on the Explosion of the Space Shuttle *Challenger*," President Reagan addresses the public about a national tragedy. In *A Night to Remember*, the tragedy is recounted through interviews with various people who experienced the *Titanic's* crash. How do the different structures of the texts help to effectively communicate information regarding the tragedies? Are there advantages or disadvantages to the structure of either text? Which one do you prefer? Cite specific examples from the texts to explain which structure better helps to effectively communicate information and make the author's point.

PROMPT GUIDE

- What types of text structures do Reagan and Lord use?
- How does the use of these text structures help to communicate information?
- What are the advantages and disadvantages of using these text structures?

Score	Informational Text Structure	Language and Conventions
4	The writer clearly analyzes and explains the author's use of informational text structure. The writer provides exemplary analysis, using relevant evidence from the text.	The writer demonstrates a consistent command of grammar, punctuation, and usage conventions. Although minor errors may be evident, they do not detract from the fluency or the clarity of the writing.
3	The writer analyzes and explains the author's use of informational text structure. The writer provides sufficient analysis, using relevant evidence from the text most of the time.	The writer demonstrates an adequate command of grammar, punctuation, and usage conventions. Although some errors may be evident, they create few (if any) disruptions in the fluency or clarity of the writing.
2	The writer begins to analyze or explain the author's use of informational text structure, but the analysis is incomplete. The writer uses relevant evidence from the text only some of the time.	The writer demonstrates a partial command of grammar, punctuation, and usage conventions. Some distracting errors may be evident, at times creating minor disruptions in the fluency or clarity of the writing.
1	The writer attempts to analyze or explain the author's use of informational text structure, but the analysis is not successful. The writer uses little or no relevant evidence from the text.	The writer demonstrates little or no command of grammar, punctuation, and usage conventions. Serious and persistent errors create disruptions in the fluency of the writing and sometimes interfere with meaning.
0	The writer does not provide a relevant response to the prompt or does not provide a response at all.	Serious and persistent errors overwhelm the writing and interfere with the meaning of the response as a whole, making the writer's meaning impossible to understand.

Write

SCAFFOLDS

Ask students to complete the writing assignment using textual evidence to support their answers.

Use the scaffolds below to differentiate instruction for your ELL English Language Learners and A Approaching grade-level learners.

ELL **BEGINNING** With the help of the word bank, write a response using paragraph frame 1.

INTERMEDIATE With the help of the word bank, write a response using paragraph frames 1 and 2.

ADVANCED, ADVANCED HIGH Write a response of differentiated length using the sentence starters.

A **APPROACHING** Write a response of differentiated length using the sentence starters.

BEGINNING / INTERMEDIATE | ADVANCED, ADVANCED HIGH / APPROACHING

Word Bank	Paragraph Frame 1	Paragraph Frame 2	Sentence Starters
sequential order explanation depends compare and contrast	____ was one text structure used in "Address to the Nation on the Explosion of the Space Shuttle *Challenger*." This structure effectively communicated why the *Challenger* explosion was tragic by comparing it to another hardship in exploration. The ____ text structure used in *A Night to Remember* effectively communicated what it was like to be on the *Titanic* the night it sank. Compare-and-contrast text structure has the advantage of explaining the explosion by connecting it to other tragedies, but a disadvantage is that the information it communicates ____ on comparing it to another event. Sequential text structure has the advantage of providing a detailed ____ of the events, but it forces the writer to tell the story of what happened in ____.	I think ____ text structure is ____ because ____.	• The compare and contrast text structure used in . . . • The sequential text structure used in . . . • Compare and contrast text structure has the advantage of . . . • Sequential text structure has the advantage of . . . • I prefer the . . . structure of . . .

Peer Review

Students should submit substantive feedback to two peers using the instructions below.

- How well does this response answer the prompt?
- How well does the writer support his or her ideas with details from the text?
- What did the writer do well in this response? What does the writer need to work on?

Rate

Respond to the following with a point rating that reflects your opinion.

	1	2	3	4
Ideas				
Evidence				
Language and Conventions				

Submit

SENTENCE FRAMES

- You were able to (completely / partly / almost) answer the prompt.
- You supported the idea of ____ with the detail of ____.
- One idea that needs more support is ____.
- My favorite part of your response is ____.

A Kenyan Teen's Discovery:

Let There Be Lights to Save Lions

INFORMATIONAL TEXT
Nina Gregory
2013

Introduction

Having roamed the lands of present-day Kenya and Tanzania for thousands of years, the Maasai tribe had long coexisted with the region's lion population. But now, the lion population is in sharp decline—and their next-door neighbors are a big reason why. Richard Turere is one of those neighbors, a thirteen-year-old inventor who lives among the Maasai near Nairobi National Park, which hosts many of the endangered lions of Kenya. Living in such close proximity, some lions have begun to prey on the livestock owned by locals like Richard's family. A struggle has emerged between the locals and the encroaching lions, resulting in deaths of a highly threatened and endangered species (there are fewer than 2,000 lions remaining in Kenya). In this article and its accompanying video, explore how young Richard devised an inventive way to save both livestock and lions from harm.

In 2013, Richard Turere, a 13-year-old inventor from Kenya, was invited to give a TED Talk to explain how he created a way to prevent lions from attacking livestock. Richard lives near the Nairobi National Park, a sanctuary for endangered lions in close proximity to surrounding farms. Richard explains that cows are kept in sheds in the evenings, which makes them easy prey. In an effort to protect livestock, many local farmers resorted to killing lions, and as a result, only an estimated 2,000 lions remain in the region. One night, Richard realized that lions are scared of flashlights. This led him to create a system he named Lion Lights, which uses flashing lights to mimic human activity. Richard's system has worked so well that many of his neighbors asked him to build one for them. Currently, Lion Lights are employed throughout Kenya.

ELL Proficiency-leveled summaries and summaries in multiple languages are available digitally.

Audio and audio text highlighting are available with this text.

CONNECT TO ESSENTIAL QUESTION

Why do we take chances?

What happens when protecting one group of animals puts another group of animals at risk? This informational text and video show how Richard Turere drew inspiration from this problem.

Access Complex Text

LEXILE: 950L WORD COUNT: 502

The following areas may be challenging for students, particularly ELL English Language Learners and A Approaching grade-level learners.

Connection of Ideas	Purpose	Organization
• Readers synthesize information from the video and article to better understand the importance of Richard's invention.	• The text is from a news source, and it gives information about a real person and real events. • The author's purpose is to explain how Richard got his idea and invented his Lion Lights.	• The text shows a cause and effect. The cause is the conflict between humans and lions. The effect is Richard's invention. • Clues such as "from ages 6 to 9" and "one night" show chronological order.

SCAFFOLDS ELL ENGLISH LANGUAGE LEARNERS  APPROACHING GRADE LEVEL  BEYOND GRADE LEVEL

These icons identify differentiation strategies and scaffolded support for a variety of students. See the digital lesson plan for additional differentiation strategies and scaffolds.

Instructional Path

The print teacher's edition includes essential point-of-use instruction and planning tools. Complete lesson plans and program documents appear in your digital teacher account.

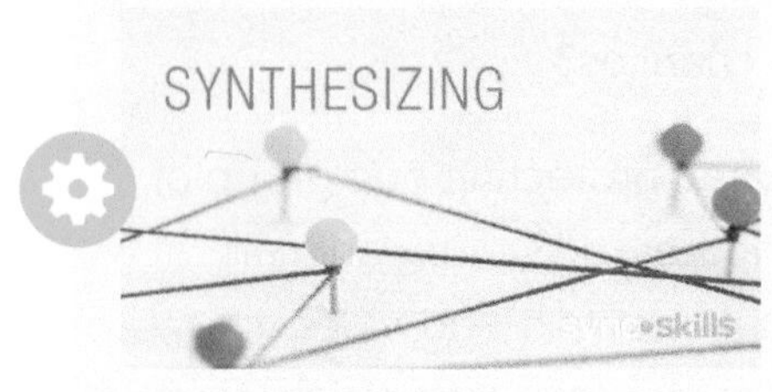

Skill: Synthesizing

Objectives: After reading and discussing a model, students will be able synthesize information from multiple texts to create new understanding in order to improve reading comprehension.

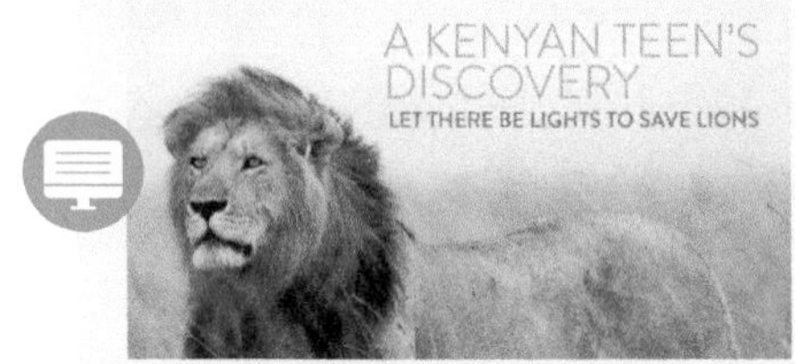

First Read: A Kenyan Teen's Discovery: Let There Be Lights to Save Lions

Objectives: After an initial reading and discussion of the informational text and viewing of the video, students will be able to identify and restate the text's key ideas and details.

Skill: Media

Objectives: After rereading and discussing a model of close reading, students will be able to analyze and evaluate characteristics, purpose, advantages, and disadvantages of different types of media.

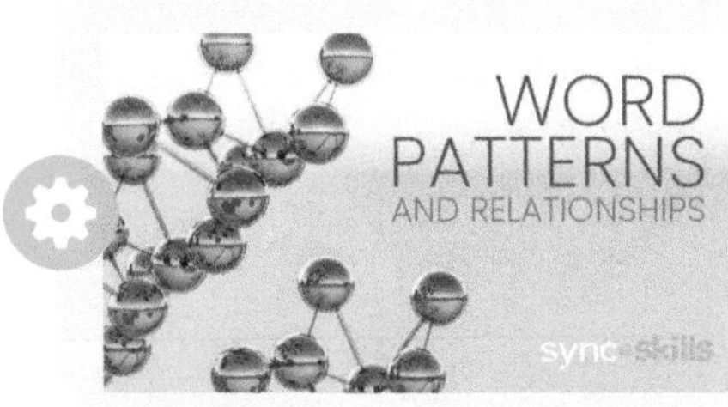

Skill: Word Patterns and Relationships

Objectives: After rereading and discussing a model of close reading, students will be able to analyze word patterns and relationships to better understand vocabulary in a text.

Close Read: A Kenyan Teen's Discovery: Let There Be Lights to Save Lions

Objectives: After engaging in a close reading and discussion of the text, students will be able to analyze the use and advantages and disadvantages of different mediums to convey information in a short written response.

Blast: Now, That's an Idea

Objectives: After exploring background information and research links about a topic, students will respond to a question with a 140-character response.

Progress Monitoring

Opportunities to Learn	Opportunities to Demonstrate Learning	Opportunities to Reteach
Synthesizing		
Skill: Synthesizing	First Read • Read and Annotate	Spotlight Skill: Synthesizing
Media		
Skill: Media	Skill: Media • Your Turn Close Read • Skills Focus • Write	Unit 3 Skill: Media - The Call of the Wild Unit 4 Skill: Media - Across Five Aprils Spotlight Skill: Media
Word Patterns and Relationships		
Skill: Word Patterns and Relationships	Skill: Word Patterns and Relationships • Your Turn	Unit 4 Skill: Word Patterns and Relationships - Blind Spotlight Skill: Word Patterns and Relationships

First Read

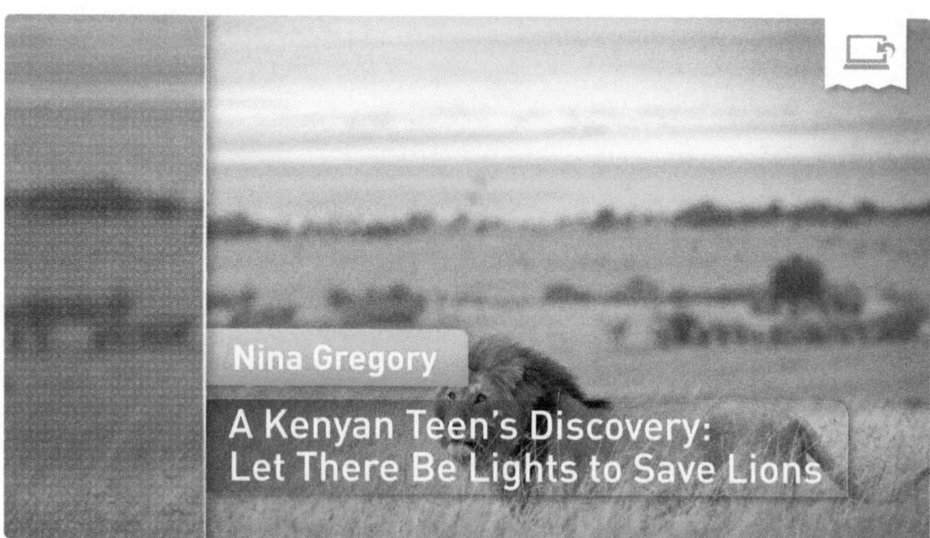

Introduce the Text

As a class, watch the video preview and have students read the introduction in pairs to make connections to the video preview.

To activate prior knowledge and experiences, ask students:

- What image was your favorite from the video? Why?
- How do the images, words, and music in the video connect to the information in the introduction?

SPEAKING FRAMES

- The ____ in the video makes me think ____.
- The video shows ____. This makes me wonder ____.
- I think the text will ____. I think this because ____.
- I predict that there will be ____. I believe this because ____.

Entry Point

As students prepare to read "A Kenyan Teen's Discovery: Let There Be Lights to Save Lions," share the following information with them to provide context.

✓ The Maasai live in the Great Rift Valley of East Africa, which is also the location of the Serengeti, the Maasai Mara, and other extensive areas of savanna (grassland) that have been set aside to preserve African wildlife, including lions, elephants, cheetahs, zebras, and hippos.

✓ The Maasai lead a semi-nomadic life, herding their cattle in this semi-arid land according to the seasonal rains. Since formal education of children was established, adults have taken over the main responsibility of herding the cattle, with boys resuming the job only when school is out, such as weekends.

✓ TED Talks are free online lectures given on a wide range of topics by experts in their fields. Lists of TED Talks that are especially interesting and beneficial to middle-school students are also available online.

"A light went on inside him and an idea was born."

NOTES

1 One of the talks from the TED stage in Long Beach, Calif., this week came from Richard Turere, an inventor. He is a Maasai from Kenya. And he's 13.

2 "From ages 6 to 9, I started looking after my father's cows," Richard says. "I'd take them out in the morning and bring them back in the evening. We put them in a small cow shed at night," and that's when the trouble would start. Lions would jump in the shed and kill the cows, which are enclosed and an easy target.

3 Lions are the top tourist attraction to Kenya, especially in the Nairobi National Park, which is near where Richard lives. Lions are also considered **critically** endangered in Kenya.

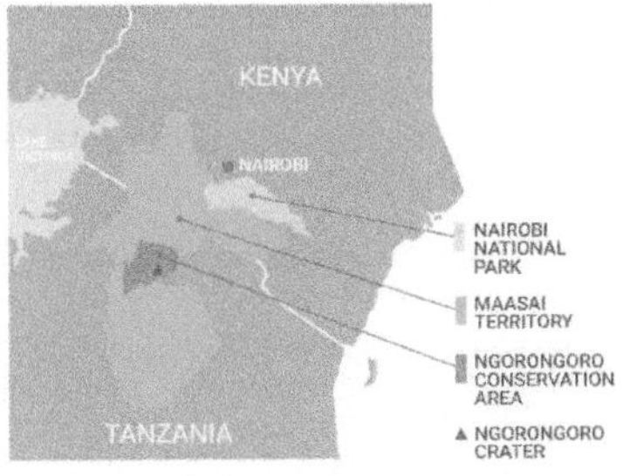

Map showing Maasai Territory, Nairobi National Park area, Ngorongoro Conservation Area, and Ngorongoro Crater.*
*Approximate sizes of areas and locations.

Skill: Media

According to the video I saw, killing lions can also be cultural. However, this seems to be the bigger problem. The article and the video showing the lions and livestock offer a variety of ways to understand why Richard's invention is so important.

4 The Kenya Wildlife Service estimates there are just 2,000 lions left in the country. One of the main causes of their demise, "is that people kill them in **retaliation** for lions attacking their livestock," says Paula Kahumbu, executive director of Wildlife Direct, a wildlife **conservation** organization in Africa.

Analyze Vocabulary Using Context Clues

In paragraph 3, focus on the sentence that uses the word *critically*. Point out these context clues:

1. First, I notice the word *critical* inside the word *critically*. It means "near a turning point or crisis."
2. When I read the sentence again, I think that the danger to lions is close to a crisis.
3. This meaning fits because the text is about stopping the killing of endangered lions.

Media

How does the student relate the video to the article?

The student says that seeing the livestock in the video increased his understanding of the need for Richard's invention discussed in the article.

TEXT TALK

How did Richard learn lions were killing cows?

See paragraph 2: Richard was caring for cows and knew lions killed cows by jumping in the shed at night.

What put lions in Kenya in danger?

See paragraph 4: People were killing them because lions attacked their livestock.

SELECTION VOCABULARY

critically / críticamente ***adverb*** in a serious manner

retaliation / la represalia ***noun*** action taken in return for being hurt

- What is happening to the lions?
- Why are people taking action?

conservation / la preservación ***noun*** protection of the natural environment

- What does Paula Kahumbu do as part of Wildlife Direct?
- How does that give you a clue to the meaning of *conservation*?

Word Patterns and Relationships

What was the relationship that the reader used in the second annotation, and why?

The reader used an synonym/antonym relationship to eventually determine the meaning of the word *crisis*.

Skills Focus

QUESTION 2: Summarizing

Richard Turere saw that lions are scared of people's moving flashlights. He used spare parts and a solar panel to create an invention that protects cows from lions with moving lights.

5 She has been studying the **conflict** between humans and lions, and her work led her to Richard. In one week, she **monitored** over 50 cases where lions attacked livestock. "It's a very, very serious problem," she says.

6 Her work studying the problem led her to Richard.

7 One night he was walking around with a flashlight and discovered the lions were scared of a moving light. A light went on inside him and an idea was born.

8 Three weeks and much tinkering later, Richard had invented a system of lights that flash around the cow shed, **mimicking** a human walking around with a flashlight. His system is made from broken flashlight parts and an indicator box from a motorcycle.

9 "The only thing I bought was a solar panel," which charges a battery that supplies power to the lights at night, Richard says. He calls the system Lion Lights.

10 "There have been a lot of efforts to try to protect the lions," Kahumbu says. "It's a crisis and everyone is looking for a solution. One idea was land leases, another was lion-proof fences. And basically no one even knew that Richard had already come up with something that worked."

11 His simple solution was so successful, his neighbors heard about it and wanted Lion Lights, too. He installed the lights for them and for six other homes in his community. From there, the lights spread and are now being used all around Kenya. Someone in India is trying them out for tigers. In Zambia and Tanzania they're being used, as well.

12 To get to the TED stage, Richard traveled on an airplane for the first time in his life. He says he has a lot to tell his friends about when he goes back home, and among the scholars and prize winners, scientists and poets, what impressed him the most on his trip was something he saw at the nearby Aquarium of the Pacific: "It was my first time seeing a shark. I've never seen a shark."

NOTES

Skill: Word Patterns and Relationships

Kahumbu says protecting lions is a crisis and everyone is looking for a solution. An antonym for solution is problem. But this seems like more than just a problem as there have been so many efforts to solve it. So, a crisis must mean an emergency.

TEXT TALK

What did Paula Kahumbu study?

See paragraph 5: She studied the conflict between lions and humans.

How did Richard discover lions are afraid of moving lights?

See paragraph 7: One night Richard walked around with a flashlight and made the discovery.

What did Richard invent?

See paragraphs 7–9: He invented Lion Lights. They act like a person walking around with a flashlight.

SELECTION VOCABULARY

conflict / el conflicto *noun* a state of opposition between persons, ideas, or interests; a disagreement COGNATE

ELL
- Who is in "conflict"?
- Why is the conflict a problem?

monitor / monitorear *verb* to check, track, and observe COGNATE

- What was "monitored" in a week?
- How does that give you a clue to the meaning of *monitor*?

mimic / imitar *verb* to copy or imitate

- What did Richard discover about the lions?
- How do the words around *mimicking* help you understand its meaning?

Reading Comprehension OPTIONAL

Have students complete the digital reading comprehension questions when they finish reading.

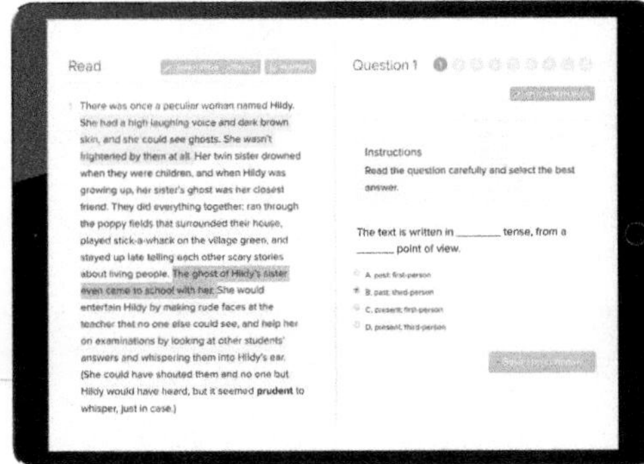

ANSWER KEY

QUESTION 1: D
QUESTION 2: A
QUESTION 3: C
QUESTION 4: A
QUESTION 5: D
QUESTION 6: C
QUESTION 7: B
QUESTION 8: B
QUESTION 9: *See first chart.*
QUESTION 10: *See second chart.*

First	Second	Third	Fourth
A conflict begins between locals who own livestock and the lions that attack the livestock, resulting in more lion deaths.	Richard notices that the lions are afraid of his flashlight when he is out walking at night.	Using his idea and the materials around him, Richard invents Lion Lights to keep the lions away from livestock.	Richard's invention becomes so popular that his neighbors and people in other countries use them as well.

Synonym	Word
protection	conservation
revenge	retaliation
seriously	critically
struggle	conflict
observed	monitored
copying	mimicking

Connect and Extend OPTIONAL

CONNECT TO EXTENDED WRITING PROJECT

Students can use "A Kenyan Teen's Discovery: Let There Be Lights to Save Lions" as a mentor text for their Extended Writing Project. They may use the text as a resource for their informational essays.

BEYOND THE BOOK

Infographic: Man vs. Nature

Conflicts between people and nature are increasing as humans infringe on land that has belonged to other animals. Students will select another example of this conflict between human beings and animals to research. They will transform this research into a dynamic infographic designed to raise awareness about this man-versus-nature conflict.

Ask students to:

- Clearly identify the conflict between humans and animals they want to research.
- Research this conflict to find out more about it.
  - > Where is this conflict taking place?
  - > What is causing the conflict?
  - > In what way are humans and/or animals threatened?
  - > What damage has already been done?
  - > What are possible solutions to this conflict?
- Design an infographic that identifies the conflict and location, provides visual data to show the impact of the conflict, and communicates a clear call to action. Infographics can be done on paper or online.

Once students have posted their infographics in class or online, allow students to do a gallery walk to see what their peers have created.

To reflect, ask students:

- Which infographics were most effective at communicating information?

Think Questions

Circulate as students answer Think Questions independently. Scaffolds for these questions are shown on the opposite page.

QUESTION 1: Textual Evidence

Richard's invention works well because it imitates "a human walking around with a flashlight." Richard discovered that lions are afraid of a moving light. His Lion Lights frighten the lions away from livestock without hurting them.

QUESTION 2: Textual Evidence

Richard did not buy a lot of expensive things to create Lion Lights because he used old parts from flashlights and a motorcycle. The only thing he bought was a solar panel to power the lights at night when the lions attack the livestock.

QUESTION 3: Textual Evidence

Paula Kahumbu, the executive director of Wildlife Direct, says, "There have been a lot of efforts to try to protect the lions." She mentions the idea of land leases and the idea of fences that would keep the lions out. Richard's solution was successful because it was simple and not expensive to make.

QUESTION 4: Context Clues; Greek and Latin Affixes and Roots

I think *conservation* must mean "saving or guarding resources." The word is used to describe an organization that is concerned about lions being killed. The organization wants to save or protect animals that are in danger of becoming extinct.

QUESTION 5: Context Clues

I think *retaliation* must mean "hurting someone because they have hurt you." The context clues in the sentence support this meaning. People are killing lions because lions are killing their livestock. The people need their livestock because it is their livelihood. They take out their revenge on the lions.

First Read

Read "A Kenyan Teen's Discovery: Let There Be Lights to Save Lions." After you read, complete the Think Questions below.

THINK QUESTIONS

1. Why does Richard's invention work so well? How does it keep the lions away from the livestock without harming them? Use specific evidence from the text to support your answer.
2. What items did Richard use to create his invention? Did he have to buy a lot of expensive equipment? Why or why not?
3. Before Richard's idea became known, what were some of the other ideas people had to keep the lions from attacking livestock? Cite specific examples from the text.
4. The root *serv* comes from the Latin word *servare*, meaning "to save or guard." With this in mind, write a definition of **conservation** in your own words, indicating any words or phrases that helped you understand.
5. Use context clues to find the meaning of the word **retaliation** as it is used in paragraph 4. Write your own definition of *retaliation*, identifying any context clues that helped you unlock the meaning of the word.

SCAFFOLDS

Think Questions

Use the scaffolds below to differentiate instruction for your ELL English Language Learners and A Approaching grade-level learners.

ELL **BEGINNING** Write a response using the word bank and sentence frames.

INTERMEDIATE Write a response using the sentence frames.

ADVANCED, ADVANCED HIGH Write a response using the Text-Dependent Question Guide.

A APPROACHING Write a response using the Text-Dependent Question Guide.

BEGINNING	INTERMEDIATE	APPROACHING / ADVANCED, ADVANCED HIGH
Word Bank	**Sentence Frames**	**Text-Dependent Question Guide**
fences hurting human motorcycle wildlife lions saving scare solar panel revenge parts simple	Richard's invention works well because the flashing lights act like a ____ walking around with a flashlight. The lights ____ the lions away. The invention saves the cows without hurting the ____.	1. • What is Richard's invention? • How does the invention work? • Why doesn't the invention harm lions?
	Richard uses old flashlight ____ and an indicator box from a ____. His invention was not expensive because he only bought a ____.	2. • What things does Richard use for his Lion Lights? • What does Richard buy? • Was the invention expensive to make?
	Before Richard's invention, people tried land leases and ____. Richard's invention was better because it was ____ and didn't cost much to make.	3. • Why was it important to keep the lions from attacking livestock? • What other ideas did people try? • Why was Richard's invention better than the other ideas?
	Conservation describes a ____ organization. This gives me a clue that *conservation* means "____ wildlife."	4. • Read: "One of the main causes of their demise 'is that people kill them in retaliation for lions attacking their livestock,' says Paula Kahumbu, executive director of Wildlife Direct, a wildlife **conservation** organization in Africa." • What does *servare* mean? • What does *conservation* describe in this sentence? • What does that tell me about the meaning of the word *conservation*?
	Retaliation means "taking ____." The people are ____ the lions because the lions are attacking their livestock.	1. • Read: ". . . people kill them in **retaliation** for lions attacking their livestock . . ." • What are the lions doing? • Is *retaliation* a reward or revenge?

Skill: Media

Introduce the Skill

Watch the Concept Definition video and read the following definition with your students.

Media is the plural form of the word *medium*. A **medium** is a means of sending a communication to an intended audience. Throughout most of human history, people communicated through three main media: speech, writing, and visual arts such as drawing, painting, and sculpture. But in the 19th century, media options suddenly exploded. The invention of photography, and then the telegraph and the telephone, changed the world. Within a century radio, motion pictures, and television followed.

Stories and ideas change as they are translated from one medium to another. A dialogue between two characters in a novel, for example, becomes very different when it is delivered by actors in a film—with close-ups, sound effects such as music, and other elements unique to the medium of film itself.

Today, new media are being invented at a much faster pace than ever before, and each of these forms of online communication has its own "language" and creates its own experience.

Skill: Media

Use the Checklist to analyze Media in "A Kenyan Teen's Discovery: Let There Be Lights to Save Lions." Refer to the sample student annotations about Media in the text.

••• CHECKLIST FOR MEDIA

In order to identify the purpose of information and the advantages and disadvantages of presenting it in different forms of media, note the following:

- ✓ the features of each medium, such as print or digital text, video, and multimedia
- ✓ how the medium contributes to the information in the text
- ✓ how the same information can be treated, or presented, in more than one medium, including visually, quantitatively, or orally
- ✓ how different media present a particular topic, idea, or historical event and can include diaries, eyewitness accounts, films, books, news and feature articles, or photographs
- ✓ which details are emphasized or absent in each medium and the reasons behind these choices
- ✓ how readers and historians compare and contrast accounts in different media as they analyze and interpret events
- ✓ the reliability of each medium, including specific words and images that can help you identify the motive or motives behind a video, oral, quantitative, or written work

To evaluate the advantages and disadvantages of using different media to present a particular topic or idea and analyze the purpose of presenting information in diverse formats, ask the following questions:

- ✓ What are the advantages and disadvantages of using different media to present a particular topic or idea?
- ✓ What was the purpose behind the creation of this video, speech, book, or article?
- ✓ What were the motives behind its presentation? How do you know?

TURN AND TALK

1 What types of media have you used?

2 Do you like it when something you read combines text with other media, such as visuals? Why or why not?

SPEAKING FRAMES

- I have used ____.
- I (do / do not) like text with other media.
- Other media, such as visuals, (are / are not) helpful because ____.

SKILL VOCABULARY

medium / el medio *noun* a form of communication, such as television, the Internet, and radio COGNATE

media / los medios *noun* the plural form of the word *medium*; a means of sending a communication to an intended audience

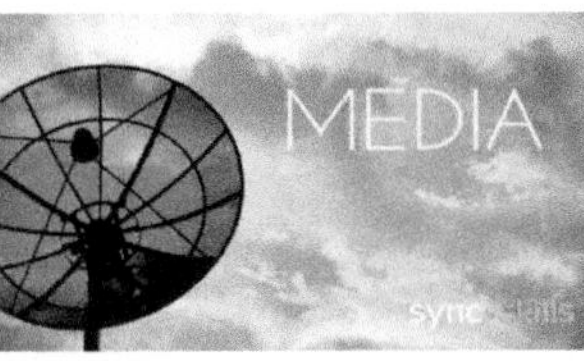

Skill: Media

Watch the video clips from "Inside Africa" on the StudySync site as indicated for each question. Then, using the Checklist on the previous page, answer the multiple-choice questions below.

YOUR TURN

1. Watch from the beginning of the video to 00:24. Both types of media—video and audio—of the Maasai man and his herd are intended to—
   - O A. provide background information about Maasai life.
   - O B. emphasize threats to cattle in the region.
   - O C. show that the cattle suffer during seasonal changes.
   - O D. show the distance the cattle travel.

2. Watch the video from 03:47 to 04:13. The interaction of visual and audio in the video clip in the explanation of the lion-killing ritual is intended to—
   - O A. suggest that lion hunting is dangerous.
   - O B. show that it is difficult to kill a lion.
   - O C. emphasize the symbolic importance of the ritual.
   - O D. explain why the ritual has been outlawed in the region.

3. The main advantage of using both digital text and the video clip is to make sure that the reader—
   - O A. knows where the region is located and what the land looks like.
   - O B. is provided with background knowledge about Kenyan culture.
   - O C. understands the key ideas of the lion problem and its solution.
   - O D. grasps how Richard Turere's invention works.

Your Turn

Ask students to complete the Your Turn activity.

QUESTION 1

A. Correct. The purpose of the video clip is to give background information about Maasai practices.

B. Incorrect. The video clip does not focus on threats to cattle in the region.

C. Incorrect. The video clip does not suggest that the cattle suffer during seasonal changes.

D. Incorrect. This video clip does not show any distance measurements.

QUESTION 2

A. Incorrect. The clip is not intended to suggest that lion killing is dangerous.

B. Incorrect. The clip is not intended to show how difficult it is to kill a lion.

C. Correct. The camera's focus on the lions and the spear tip, combined with the audio explanation of the ritual, emphasizes its symbolic importance.

D. Incorrect. The clip is not intended to explain why the ritual has been outlawed in the region.

QUESTION 3

A. Incorrect. The location and appearance of the region are not the main advantages of using both types of media.

B. Incorrect. Both kinds of media were not used to provide background about Kenyan culture.

C. Correct. The digital text article and the video, taken together, enable a reader to better understand the lion problem and Richard Turere's solution.

D. Incorrect. Both kinds of media were not used to show how the invention works.

Skill: Words Patterns and Relationships

Introduce the Skill

Watch the Concept Definition video and read the following definition with your students.

Understanding how words relate to other words is an important part of creating meaning in both reading and writing, and it can also help build vocabulary. **Cause/effect** is a relationship where one thing is the result of the other. For example, if someone is described as a catalyst for change, the reader can infer that *catalyst* means someone who causes change to happen. **Part/whole** is a relationship in which a part of something is compared to the whole. For example, the knowledge that a gearshift is a mechanism that is part of a whole automobile can help a reader define *gearshift* as well as *mechanism*. **Item/category** is a relationship in which a word can be seen to belong to larger category. For example, categorizing poodles, beagles, and schnauzers as canines shows that *canine* is another word for *dog*. Recognizing **word patterns** is another way to help you determine a word's meaning and part of speech, as when *analyze* becomes *analysis*.

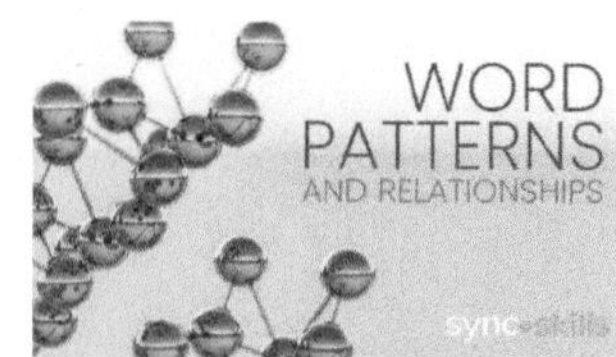

Skill: Word Patterns and Relationships

Use the Checklist to analyze Word Patterns and Relationships in "A Kenyan Teen's Discovery: Let There Be Lights to Save Lions." Refer to the sample student annotations about Word Patterns and Relationships in the text.

••• CHECKLIST FOR WORD PATTERNS AND RELATIONSHIPS

In order to determine the relationship between specific words to better understand each one, note the following:

- ✓ any unfamiliar words in the text
- ✓ surrounding words and phrases to better understand word meanings or any possible relationships between words
- ✓ examples of part/whole, item/category, or other relationships between words, such as cause/effect, analogies, or synonym/antonym relationships
- ✓ ways that the specific words relate to each other

To analyze the relationship between specific words to better understand each one, consider the following questions:

- ✓ Are these words related to each other in some way? How?
- ✓ What kind of relationship do these words have?
- ✓ How can I use the relationship between two or more specific words to better understand each of the words?
- ✓ Can any of these words be defined by identifying a synonym/antonym or cause/effect relationship?

TURN AND TALK

1 What are two words that come to mind when you think about word relationships?

2 What are ways in which the two words are related?

ELL SPEAKING FRAMES

- Two words that I think of when I think about word relationships are ____ and ____.
- The two words are related ____.
- The two words have a ____ relationship.

SKILL VOCABULARY

cause / la causa ***noun*** something that brings about an action or effect COGNATE

effect / el efecto ***noun*** a result; that which has been brought about COGNATE

part / la parte ***noun*** a piece or fragment of something COGNATE

whole / el todo ***noun*** a complete unit or entity

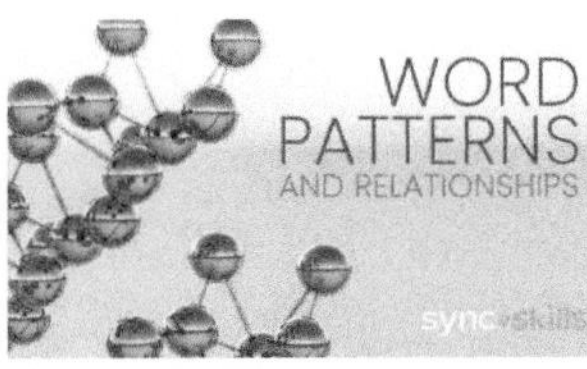

Skill: Word Patterns and Relationships

Reread paragraphs 5–9 of "A Kenyan Teen's Discovery: Let There Be Lights to Save Lions." Then, using the Checklist on the previous page, answer the multiple-choice questions below.

YOUR TURN

1. The word *light* appears twice in the paragraph 7. How is the meaning of the word in the first sentence different from the way the word is used in the second sentence of the paragraph?

   ○ A. In the first sentence the world *light* means "something that is moving," and in the second sentence it refers to the beginnings of an idea.
   ○ B. In the first sentence the word *light* means "illumination that makes things visible," and in the second sentence it refers to Richard shining the flashlight on himself.
   ○ C. In the first sentence the word *light* means "illumination that makes things visible," and in the second sentence it refers to the beginnings of an idea.
   ○ D. In the first sentence the word *light* means "something that comes out of a flashlight," and in the second sentence it refers to the beginnings of an idea.

2. How does the relationship between the two meanings of the word *light* help you to better understand how the author uses the word to create and highlight meaning in the text?

   ○ A. The first meaning of the word *light* helps Richard to make a discovery about the lions and their behavior because he is using a flashlight. The meaning of the word in the second sentence refers to the idea that Richard had to solve a problem.
   ○ B. The meanings of the word *light* and the way they are used are related because in the first sentence, *light* means actual illumination that Richard uses to see the lions in the darkness. In the second sentence it means the light Richard uses to see something within himself.
   ○ C. The meanings are related because one refers to the flashlight Richard uses while walking around at night, and the other indicates that Richard has a light within him, or an idea, to help him "see" a solution to his problem.
   ○ D. The meaning of the word *light* and the way the word is used in the first and second sentences are related. In the first sentence it means the actual illumination that makes things visible. In the second sentence it is used in a symbolic way to refer to a sudden idea. While not an actual light, it indicates that Richard has a light within him, or an idea, to help him "see" a solution.

SKILL VOCABULARY

item / el elemento ***noun*** one part or component of a group or collection

category / la categoría ***noun*** a collection of things that share a common quality COGNATE

word pattern / el patrón de las palabras ***noun*** the changes in a word depending on usage, as with the verb *analyze* and the noun *analysis*

Your Turn

Ask students to complete the Your Turn activity.

QUESTION 1

A. Incorrect. Although Richard is moving the source of the light around by using a flashlight, the definition of *light* in the first sentence is not "something that moves or is moving."

B. Incorrect. The word *light* in the second sentence does not mean that a light is shining on Richard. This is a description of how Richard is using the flashlight and not a definition for the word.

C. Correct. The definition of *light* in the first sentence means illumination, as from the sun or a light bulb, that makes things visible. The second definition means a symbolic light.

D. Incorrect. The fact that light, or illumination, comes out of a flashlight is not a definition for the word *light* because it can come from many different sources.

QUESTION 2

A. Incorrect. This does not explain how the meanings of the two words are related.

B. Incorrect. Richard does not use an actual light to see the solution to the problem.

C. Incorrect. A flashlight creates light, but it is not related to the meaning of the word *light* as it is used in the first sentence.

D. Correct. The two uses of the word are related because *light* means illumination that makes things visible, yet it can also be used in a symbolic way to mean an idea or realization that points the way out of the "darkness" of a troubling problem.

Close Read

Skills Focus

QUESTION 1: Media

See paragraph 3: The article says that Richard Turere lives near Nairobi National Park. The map shows me exactly where this national park is, so including it is an advantage to the reader.

QUESTION 2: Summarizing

See paragraphs 7–9.

QUESTION 3: Media

See paragraph 10: The text explains that people have tried lots of different methods to protect lions. The video shows footage from the Ngorongoro Conservation Area, which helps protect lions. The video helps me understand how giving lions their own land helps protect them.

QUESTION 4: Connect to Essential Question

See paragraph 11: Richard's invention helps people in many places. This shows that creating something new is worth taking a chance because you never know who will benefit from your efforts.

Close Read

Reread "A Kenyan Teen's Discovery: Let There Be Lights to Save Lions" and rewatch the video "Inside Africa" on the StudySync site. As you reread, complete the Skills Focus questions below. Then use your answers and annotations from the questions to help you complete the Write activity.

SKILLS FOCUS

1. Identify a detail from the article that is clarified by the map. Explain the advantage of including the map to convey information.
2. Identify evidence that shows how Richard Turere's invention works. Write a two-sentence summary of his process.
3. Identify a detail from the article that is developed by the video. Explain the advantage of including the video to understand this information.
4. How and why did Richard Turere take a chance with the creation of his invention? What was risky about this venture? How did his invention impact his community once it was introduced?

WRITE

INFORMATIONAL: How do the video and the text work together to introduce and explain the impact of Richard Turere's invention? What are the advantages and disadvantages of using these different media in the article? Cite evidence from both the text and the video in your response.

Writer's Notebook

Connect to Essential Question: Give students time to reflect on how "A Kenyan Teen's Discovery: Let There Be Lights to Save Lions" and the video clip from "Inside Africa" connect to the unit's essential question "Why do we take chances?" by freewriting in their Writer's Notebooks.

Beginning & Intermediate

Read aloud the unit's essential question: "Why do we take chances?" Encourage students to draw their connections or allow students to write in their native language. Circulate the room, prompting students for their thoughts as they respond orally or through pantomime.

Advanced & Advanced High

Allow students to share their reflections orally in pairs or small groups before freewriting.

Collaborative Conversation

Break students into collaborative conversation groups to discuss the Close Read prompt. Ask students to use the StudySyncTV episode as a model for their discussion. Remind them to reference their Skills Focus annotations in their discussion.

How do the video and the text work together to introduce and explain the impact of Richard Turere's invention? What are the advantages and disadvantages of using these different media in the article? Cite evidence from both the text and the video in your response.

Use the scaffolds below to differentiate instruction for your ELL English Language Learners and A Approaching grade-level learners.

ELL **BEGINNING, INTERMEDIATE** Use the discussion guide and speaking frames to facilitate the discussion with support from the teacher.

ADVANCED, ADVANCED HIGH Use the discussion guide and speaking frames to facilitate the discussion in mixed-level groups.

A **APPROACHING** Use the discussion guide to facilitate the discussion in mixed-level groups.

APPROACHING
ADVANCED, ADVANCED HIGH
BEGINNING, INTERMEDIATE

Discussion Guide	Speaking Frames
1. How does the text provide information about the impact of Richard Turere's invention?	• The text gives information about ____. • This helps me understand ____.
2. How does the video provide information about the impact of Richard Turere's invention?	• The video gives information about ____. • This helps me understand ____.
3. What are the advantages and disadvantages of using these different media in the text?	• One advantage of using these different media is ____. • A disadvantage of using these different media is ____.

Review Prompt and Rubric

Before students begin writing, review the writing prompt and rubric with the class.

INFORMATIONAL: How do the video and the text work together to introduce and explain the impact of Richard Turere's invention? What are the advantages and disadvantages of using these different media in the article? Cite evidence from both the text and the video in your response.

PROMPT GUIDE

- How does the text introduce and explain the impact of Richard Turere's invention?
- What information does the video provide that shows the impact of Richard Turere's invention?
- How do the text and video work together to convey information?
- What are the advantages and disadvantages of using these different media in the text?

Score	Media	Language and Conventions
4	The writer clearly analyzes and explains information from different media and the advantages and disadvantages of using them. The writer provides exemplary analysis, using relevant evidence from the text and video.	The writer demonstrates a consistent command of grammar, punctuation, and usage conventions. Although minor errors may be evident, they do not detract from the fluency or the clarity of the writing.
3	The writer analyzes and explains information from different media and the advantages and disadvantages of using them. The writer provides sufficient analysis, using relevant evidence from the text and video most of the time.	The writer demonstrates an adequate command of grammar, punctuation, and usage conventions. Although some errors may be evident, they create few (if any) disruptions in the fluency or clarity of the writing.
2	The writer begins to analyze or explain information from different media and the advantages and disadvantages of using them, but the analysis is incomplete. The writer uses relevant evidence from the text and video only some of the time.	The writer demonstrates a partial command of grammar, punctuation, and usage conventions. Some distracting errors may be evident, at times creating minor disruptions in the fluency or clarity of the writing.
1	The writer attempts to analyze or explain information from different media and the advantages and disadvantages of using them, but the analysis is not successful. The writer uses little or no relevant evidence from the text and video.	The writer demonstrates little or no command of grammar, punctuation, and usage conventions. Serious and persistent errors create disruptions in the fluency of the writing and sometimes interfere with meaning.
0	The writer does not provide a relevant response to the prompt or does not provide a response at all.	Serious and persistent errors overwhelm the writing and interfere with the meaning of the response as a whole, making the writer's meaning impossible to understand.

Write

SCAFFOLDS

Ask students to complete the writing assignment using textual evidence to support their answers.

Use the scaffolds below to differentiate instruction for your ELL English Language Learners and A Approaching grade-level learners.

ELL **BEGINNING** With the help of the word bank, write a response using paragraph frame 1.

INTERMEDIATE With the help of the word bank, write a response using paragraph frames 1 and 2.

ADVANCED, ADVANCED HIGH Write a response of differentiated length using the sentence starters.

A **APPROACHING** Write a response of differentiated length using the sentence starters.

Word Bank	Paragraph Frame 1	Paragraph Frame 2	Sentence Starters
BEGINNING / INTERMEDIATE	BEGINNING / INTERMEDIATE	INTERMEDIATE	ADVANCED, ADVANCED HIGH / APPROACHING
cows Maasai lions both saves	The text introduces Richard Turere's invention to protect his family's ____. The video shows a conservation area to protect ____. It explains that both cattle and lions are vital to ____ culture. Together the media show that saving ____ animals is important which is an advantage of using both media. Just one medium would be a disadvantage because the message would not be as strong. The impact of Richard's invention is that it ____ these animals' lives.	An important text detail is ____. An important visual element is ____. An important audio element is ____. Together, these details work together to emphasize that ____.	• The text gives information about . . . • An example of this is . . . This shows the impact of the invention by . . . • The video builds on this idea by . . . • One advantage of using both media is . . . • A disadvantage of using both media is . . . • This helps me understand the impact of the invention because . . .

Peer Review

Rate

Respond to the following with a point rating that reflects your opinion.

	1 2 3 4
Ideas	
Evidence	
Language and Conventions	

Submit

Students should submit substantive feedback to two peers using the instructions below.

- How well does this response answer the prompt?
- How well does the writer support his or her ideas?
- How well does the writer explain the advantages and disadvantages of using the different media?

ELL **SENTENCE FRAMES**

- You were able to (completely / partly / almost) ____ answer the prompt.
- You supported the idea of ____ with the detail of ____.
- One idea that needs more support is ____.
- You explained the advantages and disadvantages ____.

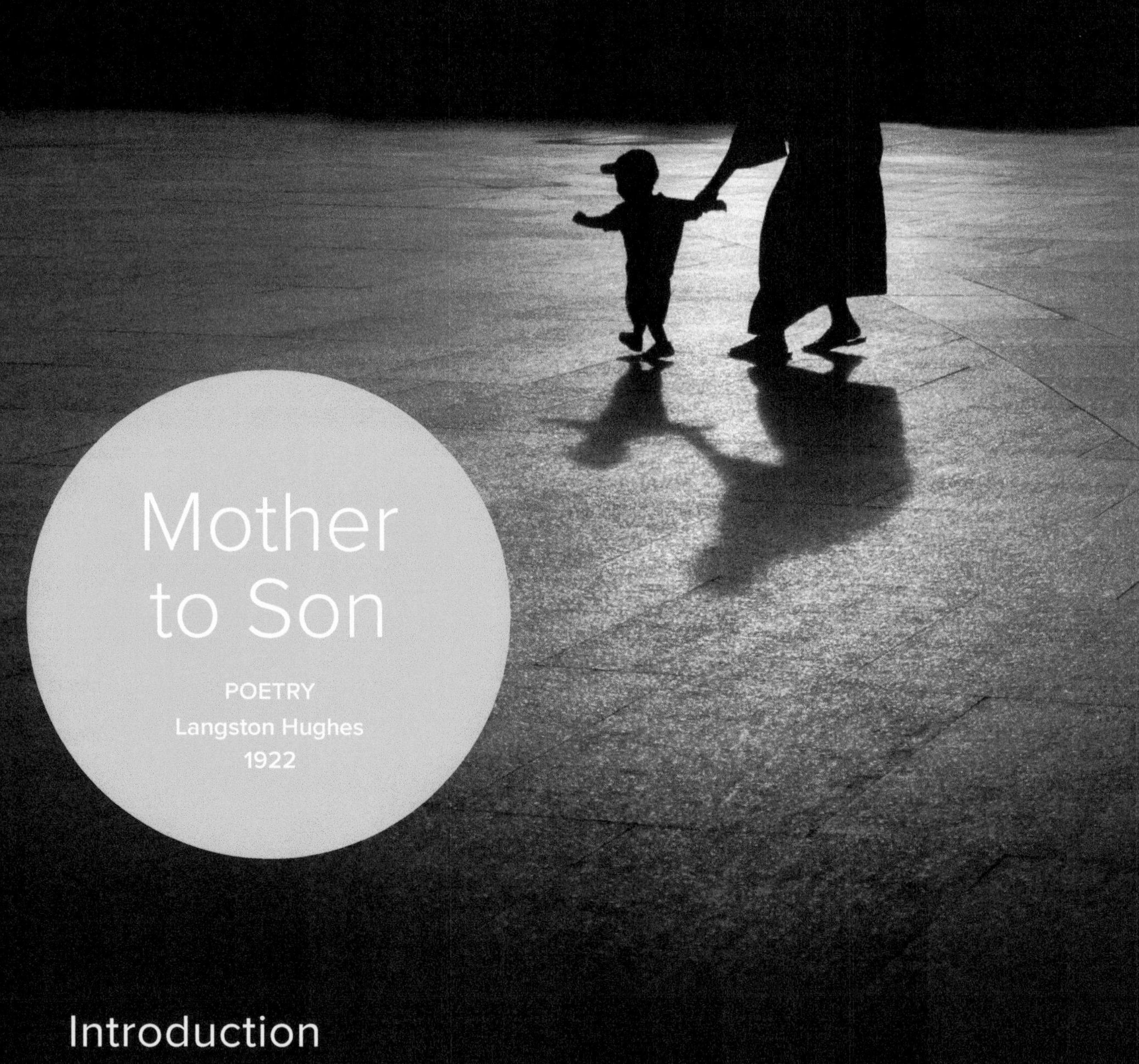

Mother to Son

POETRY

Langston Hughes

1922

Introduction

African American poet Langston Hughes (1902–1967) is one of the best-known poets of the Harlem Renaissance, a cultural and intellectual movement that began in the 1920s and resulted in the production of African American literature, art, and music that challenged racism and promoted progressive politics, such as racial and social integration. In Hughes's poem "Mother to Son," the speaker is a mother who draws on her own experiences to teach her son about perseverance.

In this poem, the speaker is a mother giving advice to her son. Using an extended metaphor of ascending a staircase, the mother explains how her life has not been easy. She begins by saying that her journey has "been no crystal stair," describing her staircase as filled with splinters and torn-up floorboards. Her metaphoric climb continues as she turns blind corners and moves through darkened sections. Despite the difficulties, she reminds her son to not turn back or sit down, which she asserts would be even more difficult. She concludes by saying that she is still climbing, even though life is hard.

 Proficiency-leveled summaries and summaries in multiple languages are available digitally.

 Audio and audio text highlighting are available with this text.

COMPARING WITHIN AND ACROSS GENRES

 Read with the poem "Learning to Read" and *Narrative of the Life of Frederick Douglass, An American Slave*, Langston Hughes's classic poem "Mother to Son" invites students to compare and contrast the risks taken by African Americans.

Access Complex Text

LEXILE: N/A **WORD COUNT:** 99

The following areas may be challenging for students, particularly ELL English Language Learners and A Approaching grade-level learners.

Prior Knowledge	Sentence Structure	Connection of Ideas
• Students should know that Hughes was an African American poet associated with the Harlem Renaissance, an arts movement during the 1920s that sought to express African Americans' experiences.	• Sentences written in dialect may challenge readers. Several lines do not follow the rules of standard grammar (e.g., "ain't been no") and may include contractions and other words spelled as they would be pronounced by the speaker, such as *I'se* and *kinder*. • Students may need guidance following the author's free verse style, including his use of punctuation (e.g., colon, dashes) to connect and emphasize ideas in the lines of the poem.	• Understanding the poem's extended metaphor, which compares life to a staircase, is key to determining the theme.

SCAFFOLDS  **ENGLISH LANGUAGE LEARNERS**  **APPROACHING GRADE LEVEL**  **BEYOND GRADE LEVEL**

These icons identify differentiation strategies and scaffolded support for a variety of students. See the digital lesson plan for additional differentiation strategies and scaffolds.

Instructional Path

The print teacher's edition includes essential point-of-use instruction and planning tools. Complete lesson plans and program documents appear in your digital teacher account.

Independent Read: Mother to Son

Objectives: After reading the text, students will demonstrate their understanding of metaphor by writing a short, personal response.

Skill: Adjusting Fluency

Objectives: Adjust fluency when reading grade-level text, based on the reading purpose.

Independent Read

Introduce the Text

As a class, watch the video preview and have students read the introduction in pairs to make connections to the video preview.

- How do the images, words, and music in this video make you feel?
- How do the images, words, and music in the video connect to the information in the introduction?
- How do you think this poem will make you feel?

Entry Point

As students prepare to read "Mother to Son," share the following information with them to provide context.

✓ Langston Hughes (1902–1967) was a poet, novelist, playwright, and columnist. He was among the first poets to use jazz rhythms and urban African American dialect in his poems. His literary works reflect his passionate efforts for racial equality and social justice.

Analyze Vocabulary Using Context Clues

As students read the text, ask them to make predictions about each bold vocabulary word based on the context clues in the sentence.

“Well, son, I’ll tell you:
Life for me ain’t been no crystal stair.”

Well, son, I’ll tell you:
Life for me ain’t been no **crystal** stair.
It’s had tacks in it,
And **splinters,**
And boards torn up,
And places with no carpet on the floor—
Bare.
But all the time
I’se been a-climbin’ on,
And reachin’ **landin’s,**
And turnin’ corners,
And sometimes goin’ in the dark
Where there ain’t been no light.
So, boy, don’t you turn back.
Don’t you set down on the steps
’Cause you finds it’s kinder hard.
Don’t you fall now—
For I’se still goin’, honey,
I’se still climbin’,
And life for me ain’t been no crystal stair.

TEXT TALK

To what does the speaker compare life?

See line 2: She compares life to a staircase, which for her is not like crystal.

What images does the speaker use to describe stairs?

See lines 3–7: She describes the stairs as worn out and full of splinters.

How does the speaker describe the way she moves on the stairs?

See lines 9–12: She describes herself as climbing, reaching landings, turning corners, and going on in the dark.

What does the speaker tell her son to do?

See lines 14–17: She tells him not to stop climbing, not to sit down, and not to fall.

SELECTION VOCABULARY

crystal / el cristal ***adjective*** having qualities like crystal, or glassware that is very clear and that suggests elegance COGNATE

- What object does the speaker describe as “crystal”?
- What comparison does the speaker make between her life and this object? How does she describe her life?

splinter / la astilla ***noun*** a small, thin, sharp bit of wood that has broken off from a larger board

- What shape is the staircase in?
- What else does the stair have?

WRITE

PERSONAL RESPONSE: The mother of the poem's title shows sympathy for her son, but she does not let him dwell on defeat. What did you think about the mother's advice in "Mother to Son"? What kind of advice have you received from an adult in your life? What kind of a metaphor could you use to share the advice with a friend?

V SELECTION VOCABULARY

landin's (landing) / el descanso ***noun*** a wide, flat place between sections of stairs in a staircase

- How does the speaker get to "landin's"?
- What does she do after she reaches these landings?

Reading Comprehension OPTIONAL

Have students complete the digital reading comprehension questions ✓ when they finish reading.

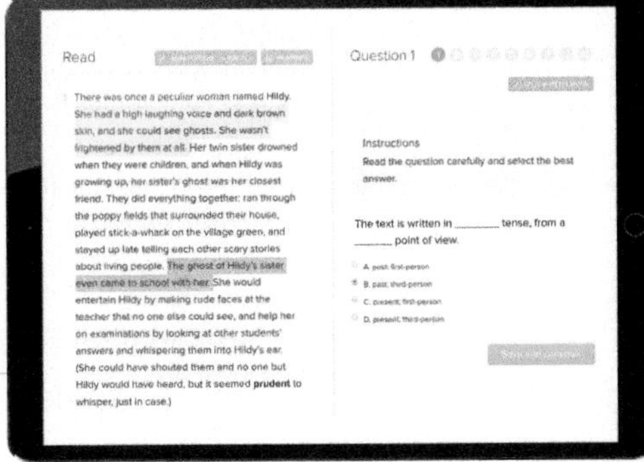

ANSWER KEY

QUESTION 1: B
QUESTION 2: C
QUESTION 3: A
QUESTION 4: D
QUESTION 5: *See chart.*

Mother Says of Herself	Mother Says to Son
"Life for me ain't been no crystal stair." "And sometimes goin' in the dark"	"Don't you set down on the steps" "Don't you fall now—"

Connect and Extend OPTIONAL

CONNECT TO EXTENDED WRITING PROJECT

Students can find inspiration from the poem "Mother to Son" when writing their informational essays. Have students relate Langston Hughes's metaphor to the challenges real people may face.

BEYOND THE BOOK

Art: Visual Metaphor for Life

Langston Hughes's poem "Mother to Son" compares life to a staircase to teach about perseverance. Students will create their own visual metaphors about life to teach an important life lesson.

Ask students to:

- Imagine you are going to give a younger sibling, family member, or friend advice about life.
  - > What is the most important lesson you have learned?
  - > What piece of advice would you want to give someone you care about?
- As Hughes does in his poem, select an object that can be used to represent life's ups and downs.
- Create a visual metaphor using the artistic medium of your choice (e.g., papier-mâché, clay, paint) to reveal this life lesson.
- Write a 20-line poem that articulates this life lesson and weaves in details from your visual metaphor.

Host a gallery walk for parents and student to show off the students' artwork and poems.

To reflect, ask students:

- How did you decide what metaphor to use?
- Did creating the visual metaphor make the poem easier to write?

Collaborative Conversation

SCAFFOLDS

Post the writing prompt to generate a discussion in small groups. Ask students to first break down the prompt before they discuss relevant ideas and textual evidence.

The mother of the poem's title shows sympathy for her son, but she does not let him dwell on defeat. What did you think about the mother's advice in "Mother to Son"? What kind of advice have you received from an adult in your life? What kind of a metaphor could you use to share the advice with a friend?

Use the scaffolds below to differentiate instruction for your ELL English Language Learners and A Approaching grade-level learners.

ELL **BEGINNING, INTERMEDIATE** Use the discussion guide and speaking frames to facilitate the discussion with support from the teacher.

ADVANCED, ADVANCED HIGH Use the discussion guide and speaking frames to facilitate the discussion in mixed-level groups.

A **APPROACHING** Use the discussion guide to facilitate the discussion in mixed-level groups.

APPROACHING
ADVANCED, ADVANCED HIGH
BEGINNING, INTERMEDIATE

Discussion Guide	Speaking Frames
1. What did you think about the mother's advice in "Mother to Son"?	• I think the mother's advice (is / is not) good because ____.
2. What kind of advice have you received from an adult in your life?	• I have received advice from ____. (He / she) told me ____.
3. What kind of a metaphor could you use to share the advice with a friend?	• I can use the metaphor of ____ to share this advice with a friend.

Review Prompt and Rubric

Before students begin writing, review the writing prompt and rubric with the class.

PERSONAL RESPONSE: The mother of the poem's title shows sympathy for her son, but she does not let him dwell on defeat. What did you think about the mother's advice in "Mother to Son"? What kind of advice have you received from an adult in your life? What kind of a metaphor could you use to share the advice with a friend?

ELL A **PROMPT GUIDE**

- What did you think about the mother's advice in "Mother to Son"?
- What kind of advice have you received from an adult in your life?
- What kind of a metaphor could you use to share the advice with a friend?

Score	Personal Response	Language and Conventions
4	The writer clearly explains his or her personal connection to the text, using relevant evidence from the text as needed.	The writer demonstrates a consistent command of grammar, punctuation, and usage conventions. Although minor errors may be evident, they do not detract from the fluency or the clarity of the writing.
3	The writer sufficiently explains his or her personal connection to the text, using relevant evidence from the text most of the time.	The writer demonstrates an adequate command of grammar, punctuation, and usage conventions. Although some errors may be evident, they create few (if any) disruptions in the fluency or clarity of the writing.
2	The writer begins to explain his or her personal connection to the text, but the explanation is incomplete. The writer uses relevant evidence from the text only some of the time.	The writer demonstrates a partial command of grammar, punctuation, and usage conventions. Some distracting errors may be evident, at times creating minor disruptions in the fluency or clarity of the writing.
1	The writer attempts to explain his or her personal connection to the text, but the explanation is not successful. The writer uses little or no relevant evidence from the text.	The writer demonstrates little or no command of grammar, punctuation, and usage conventions. Serious and persistent errors create disruptions in the fluency of the writing and sometimes interfere with meaning.
0	The writer does not provide a relevant response to the prompt or does not provide a response at all.	Serious and persistent errors overwhelm the writing and interfere with the meaning of the response as a whole, making the writer's meaning impossible to understand.

Write

SCAFFOLDS

Ask students to complete the writing assignment using textual evidence to support their answers.

Use the scaffolds below to differentiate instruction for your ELL English Language Learners and A Approaching grade-level learners.

ELL **BEGINNING** With the help of the word bank, write a response using paragraph frame 1.

INTERMEDIATE With the help of the word bank, write a response using paragraph frames 1 and 2.

ADVANCED, ADVANCED HIGH Write a response of differentiated length using the sentence starters.

A **APPROACHING** Write a response of differentiated length using the sentence starters.

BEGINNING / INTERMEDIATE	BEGINNING / INTERMEDIATE	INTERMEDIATE	ADVANCED, ADVANCED HIGH / APPROACHING
Word Bank	**Paragraph Frame 1**	**Paragraph Frame 2**	**Sentence Starters**
flying a kite grandmother persevere wise follow my dreams	In "Mother to Son," the mother tells her son to ____. I think that this advice is ____. I have received advice from my ____. (He / she) told me to ____. I would use the metaphor of ____ to share this advice with a friend.	When you persevere, you stick to a goal even though ____. In my metaphor, sticking to a goal is represented by ____. The challenges come when ____. If you stick to your goal, ____.	• The mother tells her son to . . . • I think that this advice is . . . because . . . • I have received advice from . . . • (He / she) told me to . . . • To share this advice with a friend, I would use the metaphor of . . . • In this metaphor, . . . would represent . . .

Peer Review

Students should submit substantive feedback to two peers using the review instructions below.

- How well does this response answer the prompt?
- Which of the author's comments inspired you to think differently about the text?
- What did the writer do well in this response? What does the writer need to work on?

Rate

Respond to the following with a point rating that reflects your opinion.

	1	2	3	4
Ideas	■	■	■	□
Evidence	■	■	■	■
Language and Conventions	■	■	□	□

SENTENCE FRAMES

A

- You were able to (completely / partly / almost) answer the prompt.
- You could answer the prompt more completely by ____.
- I thought differently about the text after reading ____.
- My favorite part of your response is ____.

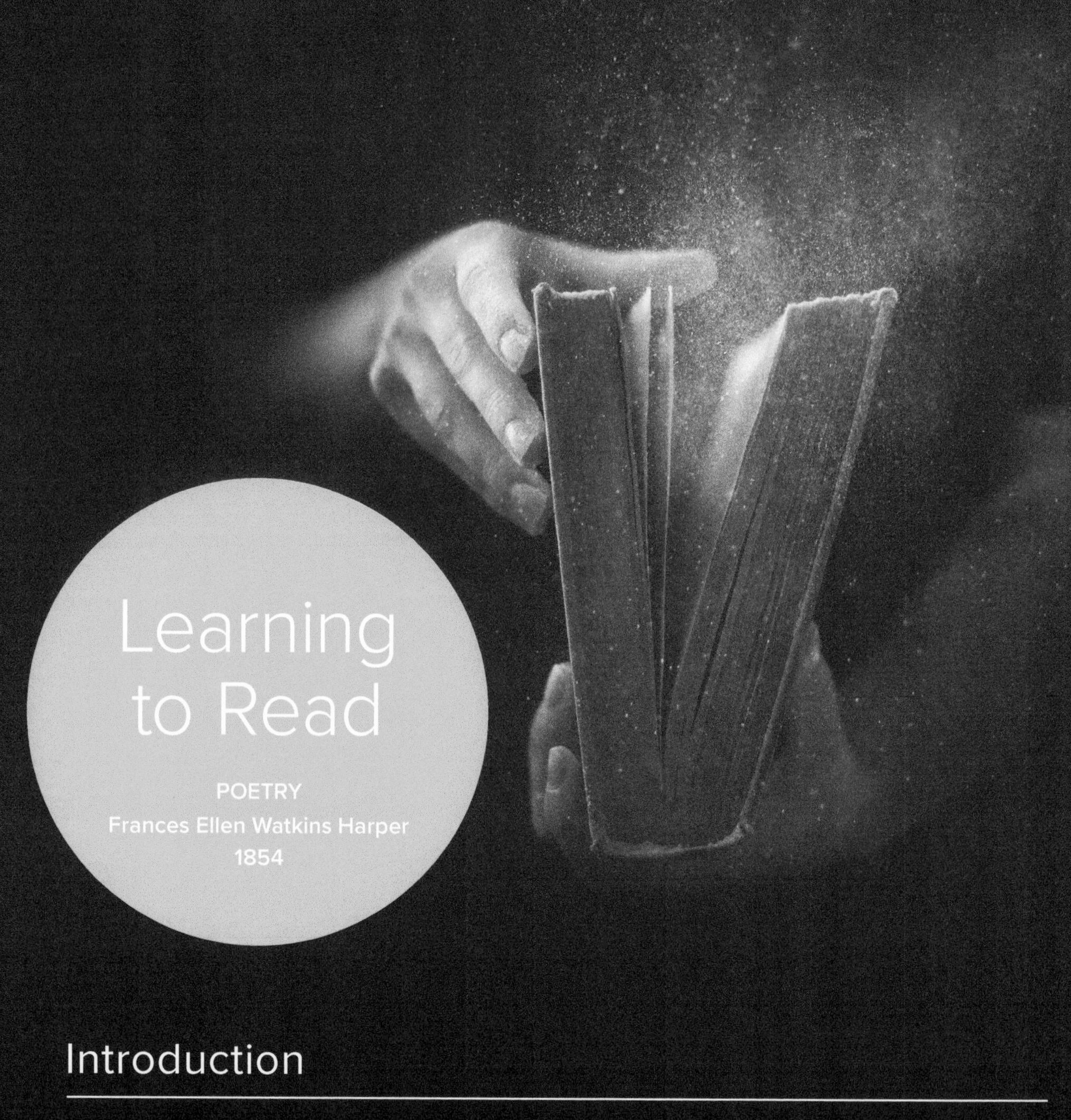

Learning to Read

POETRY
Frances Ellen Watkins Harper
1854

Introduction

Born a free woman in Baltimore, Frances Ellen Watkins Harper (1825–1911) is known by some as the mother of African American journalism. Harper experienced commercial success as a poet and novelist, and she is credited with establishing the tradition of African American protest poetry. Harper also helped enslaved people escape along the Underground Railroad and was a well-known public speaker and civil rights activist. In the poem "Learning to Read," she animates her real-life experiences talking to newly-freed enslaved people. "Learning to Read" is told from the perspective of a woman who fights to earn her education late in life.

Sixty-year-old Chloe opens this poem by recounting how teachers in the North set up schools in the South, but the Southern masters did not want enslaved people to read because they understood that knowledge would give them power. Nonetheless, the enslaved people were able to learn covertly. The speaker's uncle, Caldwell, hid pages of a book under his hat, and an enslaved person named Ben learned to read by eavesdropping on the master's children while they were taking lessons. When Chloe had an opportunity to learn how to read, people told her that she was too old. Chloe felt like she had no time to waste and wanted to learn how to read the Bible. By the end of the poem, she has learned how to read, and she describes feeling like a queen in her little cabin.

 Proficiency-leveled summaries and summaries in multiple languages are available digitally.

 Audio and audio text highlighting are available with this text.

COMPARING WITHIN AND ACROSS GENRES

 In her poem "Learning to Read," poet Frances Ellen Watkins Harper uses biblical allusions and details of life after the Civil War to recount the joys and complications of education. Along with "Mother to Son" and *Narrative of the Life of Frederick Douglass, An American Slave,* students will continue to explore the African American experience through this text.

Access Complex Text

LEXILE: N/A **WORD COUNT:** 258

The following areas may be challenging for students, particularly ELL English Language Learners and A Approaching grade-level learners.

Prior Knowledge	Specific Vocabulary	Connection of Ideas
• The poem is set in the South during the Civil War. Students may be unfamiliar with the history of slavery in America. It is especially important for students to understand that enslaved people were forbidden from reading by slaveholders.	• Terms related to the Civil War era—such as *Rebs* and *Yankees*—may challenge readers. Remind students to use context clues or a reference work to learn the meaning of unfamiliar terms. • Some dialect or expressions of the time may need explanation.	• Some readers may not immediately connect the poem's allusions to the Bible. Direct students who have trouble explaining the connections among *Bible*, *hymns*, and *Testament* to a relevant reference source.

SCAFFOLDS  **ENGLISH LANGUAGE LEARNERS**  **APPROACHING GRADE LEVEL**  **BEYOND GRADE LEVEL**

These icons identify differentiation strategies and scaffolded support for a variety of students. See the digital lesson plan for additional differentiation strategies and scaffolds.

Instructional Path

The print teacher's edition includes essential point-of-use instruction and planning tools. Complete lesson plans and program documents appear in your digital teacher account.

Independent Read: Learning to Read

Objectives: Students will closely read the text in order to participate in a collaborative conversation in response to a prompt and write a reflection on participation in the discussion.

Independent Read

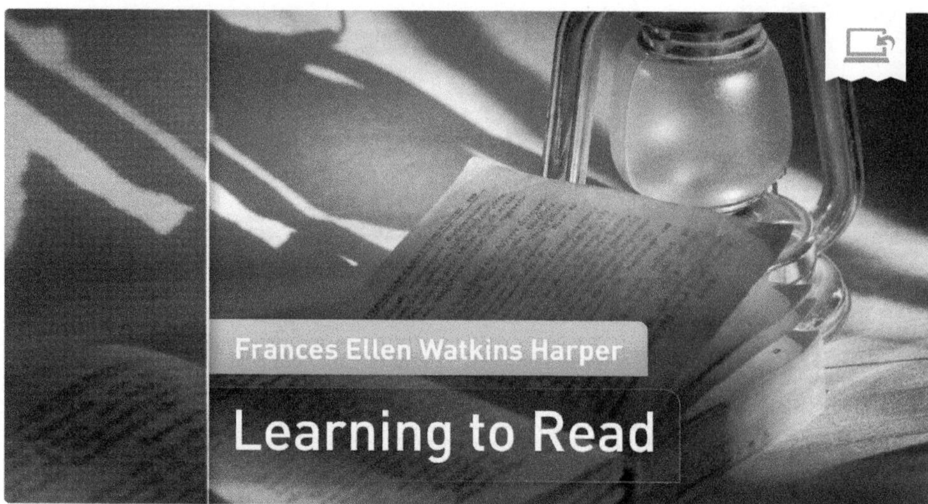

Introduce the Text

As a class, watch the video preview and have students read the introduction in pairs to make connections to the video preview.

- What is one prediction you can make about the poem you're going to read?
- How do you think this poem will make you feel?

ELL SENTENCE FRAMES

- I think the text will ____. I think this because ____.
- I predict that there will be ____. I believe this because ____.

Entry Point

As students prepare to read "Learning to Read," share the following information with them to provide context.

✓ Frances Ellen Watkins Harper (1825–1911) was an avid reader, a pioneering writer, and an active abolitionist. She was born free in Baltimore and worked to end slavery by helping enslaved people escape on the Underground Railroad. She also taught at a school, delivered speeches, and wrote articles in anti-slavery newspapers. Harper became known as the "mother of African American journalism."

✓ Before the end of the Civil War, it had been illegal to educate enslaved people in many southern states. After the war, local groups of African Americans and several aid organizations set out to establish schools for learners of all ages in the southern states. However, many white Southerners still resisted efforts to educate people who had been enslaved.

"Knowledge didn't agree with slavery—
'Twould make us all too wise."

NOTES

Very soon the **Yankee** teachers
  Came down and set up school;
But, oh! how the **Rebs** did hate it,—
  It was agin' their rule.

Our masters always tried to hide
  Book learning from our eyes;
Knowledge didn't agree with slavery—
  'Twould make us all too wise.

But some of us would try to steal
  A little from the book.
And put the words together,
  And learn by **hook or crook**.

I remember Uncle Caldwell,
  Who took pot liquor fat
And greased the pages of his book,
  And hid it in his hat.

And had his master ever seen
  The **leaves** upon his head,
He'd have thought them greasy papers,
  But nothing to be read.

And there was Mr. Turner's Ben,
  Who heard the children spell,
And picked the words right up by heart,
  And learned to read 'em well.

Well, the Northern folks kept sending
  The Yankee teachers down;
And they stood right up and helped us,
  Though Rebs did **sneer** and frown.

SELECTION VOCABULARY

yankee / yanqui *noun* someone who supported the North during the Civil War COGNATE

reb / el/la confederado/a *noun* someone who supported the Confederacy during the Civil War

 ELL

- Who are the Rebs in this stanza?
- Does the speaker describe the Rebs positively or negatively?

Analyze Vocabulary Using Context Clues

As students read the text, ask them to make predictions about each bold vocabulary word based on the context clues in the sentence.

CHECK FOR SUCCESS

If students are unable to determine the meaning of one or more bolded vocabulary words, project the Checklist from the Grade 8 Context Clues lesson with the class. After revisiting, guide students as they make predictions about the bold word in line 1 using the following routine:

- Is the word a noun, a verb, an adjective, or an adverb?
- Who are the *Yankees* in this stanza?
- Where are the *Yankees* coming from? Where are they going?

TEXT TALK

Who is this narrator and in what time period does the narrator live?

See lines 1–4: The speaker begins by talking about "Yankee teachers" and "Rebs," so it is the time of the Civil War. The narrator must live in the South.

What inference can you make about the speaker's background in the second stanza?

See lines 5 and 7: The speaker was an enslaved person, since she refers to "masters" and "slavery."

How does Uncle Caldwell hide the pages he reads?

See lines 16–18: He hides them in his hat.

Why is it that formerly enslaved people are learning to read at this time, according to the speaker?

See lines 25–27: The Northerners who won the war are coming down to the South to teach them.

Prepare for Advanced Courses

Use the activity below to differentiate instruction for your B Beyond grade-level learners.

Direct students to reread lines 29–44.

Ask students: What kind of voice does the poet create in the speaker, and how does she do it?

Answers will vary; sample answer: The rhythm of the poem is regular and very strong, and this gives the speaker's voice strength. The speaker describes a journey from her decision to learn to read to getting "a pair of glasses." She then goes "straight to work" and "never stopped" until she could read the Bible. The rhythm and details show her steady determination to succeed.

NOTES

And I longed to read my Bible,
For precious words it said;
But when I begun to learn it,
Folks just shook their heads,

And said there is no use trying,
Oh! Chloe, you're too late;
But as I was rising sixty,
I had no time to wait.

So I got a pair of glasses,
And straight to work I went,
And never stopped till I could read
The hymns and Testament.[1]

Then I got a little cabin
A place to call my own—
And I felt independent
As the queen upon her throne.

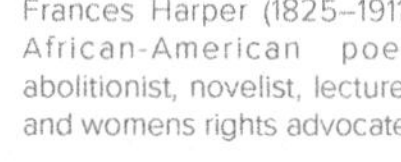

Frances Harper (1825–1911), African-American poet, abolitionist, novelist, lecturer, and womens rights advocate

1. **Testament** the Christian bible is split into two Testaments, Old and New

WRITE

DISCUSSION: It's often said that "knowledge is power." The speaker of the poem presents the reason enslaved people were not allowed to learn to read: "Knowledge didn't agree with slavery— / 'Twould make us all too wise." Discuss these ideas and your response to the poem.

TEXT TALK

Why do people think it's too late for the speaker to learn to read?

See lines 32–36: She is sixty, so people tell her it is too late for her to learn.

Why did so many Southerners oppose formerly enslaved people learning how to read? What does that tell you about discrimination in the South around the time of the Civil War?

Answers will vary.

SELECTION VOCABULARY

by hook or crook / como sea ***phrase*** by any possible way

- What is done "by hook or crook" in this stanza?
- Is it easy or difficult to do?

leaf / la hoja ***noun*** page in a book

- Where are the "leaves" in this stanza?
- How does the master feel about the leaves?

sneer / burlarse ***verb*** to smile meanly

ELL

- Who is "sneering" in this stanza?
- What makes them sneer?

Reading Comprehension OPTIONAL

Have students complete the digital reading comprehension questions ✓ when they finish reading.

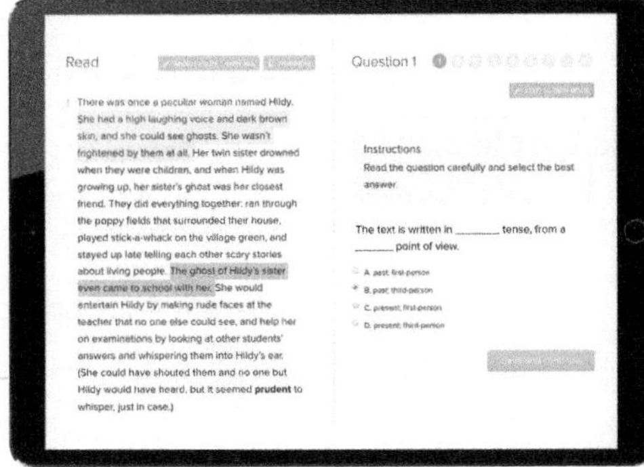

ANSWER KEY

QUESTION 1: C
QUESTION 2: D
QUESTION 3: C
QUESTION 4: D

QUESTION 5:
See chart.

First	Second	Third	Fourth
Uncle Caldwell greases the book pages with fat.	Ben learns to read after listening to children spell words.	The speaker gets a pair of glasses and learns to read the Bible.	The speaker gets a cabin of her own.

Connect and Extend OPTIONAL

CONNECT TO EXTENDED WRITING PROJECT

Students can find inspiration from the poem "Learning to Read" when writing their informational essays. Have students reflect on Frances Ellen Watkins Harper's details about risk-taking and reward.

BEYOND THE BOOK

Analysis: Rap as Modern Day Protest Poetry

Frances Ellen Watkins Harper is credited with establishing the tradition of African American protest poetry. This poetry was designed to shine a light on the struggles and inequalities that African Americans face in society. Similarly, modern day rap continues to emphasize the inequalities among races and in socioeconomic status in America.

Ask students to:

- Select a rap song that they believe is a modern example of protest poetry. [Note: Teachers can provide a list of songs to ensure the language is appropriate.]
- Analyze the lyrics of the song to identify the specific racial and socioeconomic inequalities identified in this song. Think about the following questions:
  - > What specific inequalities does the artist identify in this song?
  - > What is causing these inequalities?
  - > How can these inequalities be corrected?
  - > Why do you think this song qualifies as "protest poetry"?

Once students have selected their song and written an analytical paragraph, put them into small groups to discuss the songs they selected and why they believe they are examples of modern day protest poetry. They should use the questions above to guide their conversation.

Collaborative Conversation

Post the writing prompt to generate a discussion in small groups. Ask students to first break down the prompt before they discuss relevant ideas and textual evidence.

It's often said that "knowledge is power." The speaker of the poem presents the reason enslaved people were not allowed to learn to read: "Knowledge didn't agree with slavery— / 'Twould make us all too wise." Discuss these ideas and your response to the poem

Use the scaffolds below to differentiate instruction for your ELL English Language Learners and A Approaching grade-level learners.

ELL **BEGINNING, INTERMEDIATE** Use the discussion guide and speaking frames to facilitate the discussion with support from the teacher.

ADVANCED, ADVANCED HIGH Use the discussion guide and speaking frames to facilitate the discussion in mixed-level groups.

A **APPROACHING** Use the discussion guide to facilitate the discussion in mixed-level groups.

APPROACHING
ADVANCED, ADVANCED HIGH
BEGINNING, INTERMEDIATE

Discussion Guide	Speaking Frames
1. Do you think knowledge is power? Why or why not?	• I think knowledge (is / is not) power because ____.
2. Why would being able to read make someone more knowledgeable?	• I think being able to read makes someone more knowledgeable because ____.
3. Why do you think enslaved people were not allowed to read?	• I think enslaved people were not allowed to read because ____.
4. What do you think would be able to happen if enslaved people were allowed to become more knowledgeable?	• If enslaved people were allowed to become more knowledgeable ____.

Review Prompt and Rubric

Before students begin writing, review the writing prompt and rubric with the class.

REFLECTION: As you write, make sure to

- evaluate how well everyone followed the rules when making decisions affecting the group
- evaluate your own participation in the discussion
- reflect on how well you posed questions that connected the ideas of several speakers and responded to others' questions and comments with relevant evidence, observations, and ideas

PROMPT GUIDE

- What does "knowledge is power" mean?
- Where do you see the idea of knowledge in the poem? Where do you see the idea of power in the poem?
- What did the poem make you feel about knowledge and power?

Score	Reflection	Language and Conventions
4	The writer clearly reflects on how well he or she posed questions that connected the ideas of several speakers and responded to others' questions and comments, and also clearly reflects on his or her own participation. The writer consistently refers to specific examples from the discussion.	The writer demonstrates a consistent command of grammar, punctuation, and usage conventions. Although minor errors may be evident, they do not detract from the fluency or the clarity of the writing.
3	The writer reflects on how well he or she posed questions that connected the ideas of several speakers and responded to others' questions and comments, and also reflects on his or her own participation. The writer refers to specific examples from the discussion most of the time.	The writer demonstrates an adequate command of grammar, punctuation, and usage conventions. Although some errors may be evident, they create few (if any) disruptions in the fluency or clarity of the writing.
2	The writer begins to reflect on how well he or she posed questions that connected the ideas of several speakers and responded to others' questions and comments, and also begins to reflect on his or her own participation. The writer refers to specific examples from the discussion some of the time.	The writer demonstrates a partial command of grammar, punctuation, and usage conventions. Some distracting errors may be evident, at times creating minor disruptions in the fluency or clarity of the writing.
1	The writer attempts to reflect on how well he or she posed questions that connected the ideas of several speakers and responded to others' questions and comments, and also attempts to reflect on as well as his or her own participation. The writer refers to few, if any examples from the discussion.	The writer demonstrates little or no command of grammar, punctuation, and usage conventions. Serious and persistent errors create disruptions in the fluency of the writing and sometimes interfere with meaning.
0	The writer does not provide a relevant response to the prompt or does not provide a response at all.	Serious and persistent errors overwhelm the writing and interfere with the meaning of the response as a whole, making the writer's meaning impossible to understand.

Write

SCAFFOLDS

Ask students to complete the writing assignment using textual evidence to support their answers.

Use the scaffolds below to differentiate instruction for your ELL English Language Learners and A Approaching grade–level learners.

ELL **BEGINNING** With the help of the word bank, write a response using paragraph frame 1.

INTERMEDIATE With the help of the word bank, write a response using paragraph frames 1 and 2.

ADVANCED, ADVANCED HIGH Write a response of differentiated length using the sentence starters.

A **APPROACHING** Write a response of differentiated length using the sentence starters.

BEGINNING
INTERMEDIATE

ADVANCED, ADVANCED HIGH
APPROACHING

Word Bank	Paragraph Frame 1	Paragraph Frame 2	Sentence Starters
knowledge average slavery good gain freedom reading power	My discussion group talked about ____. I think my group did a(n) ____ job connecting to each other's ideas. I think this because ____. I added to the discussion by ____.	One person said that reading helps people ____ knowledge, and another person said people with knowledge have ____. I asked "what would happen if ____ people had more power?" This led to our group to talking about enslaved people fighting for their ____ with their new power.	• My discussion group talked about . . . • I think my group did a(n) . . . job . . . • I added to the discussion by . . . • One person said . . . • Another person said . . . • This led to our group to talking about . . .

Peer Review

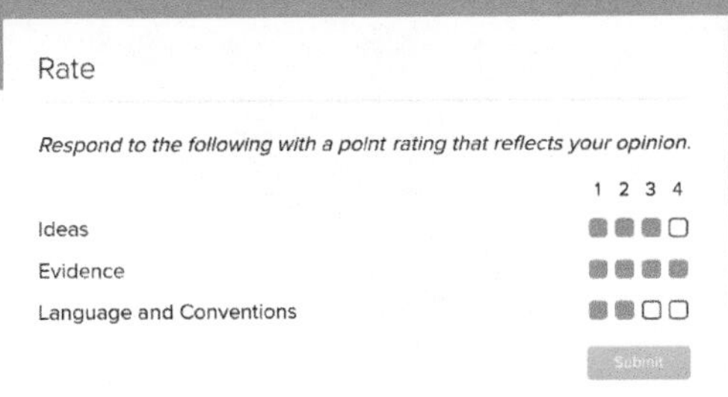

Students should submit substantive feedback to two peers using the review instructions below.

- How well does the writer refer to specific examples from the discussion?
- What does the writer do well in this reflection? What does the writer need to work on?

SENTENCE FRAMES

A

- The writer does a ____ job referring to specific examples from the discussion.
- The writer does ____ well in this reflection.
- The writer need to work on ____.

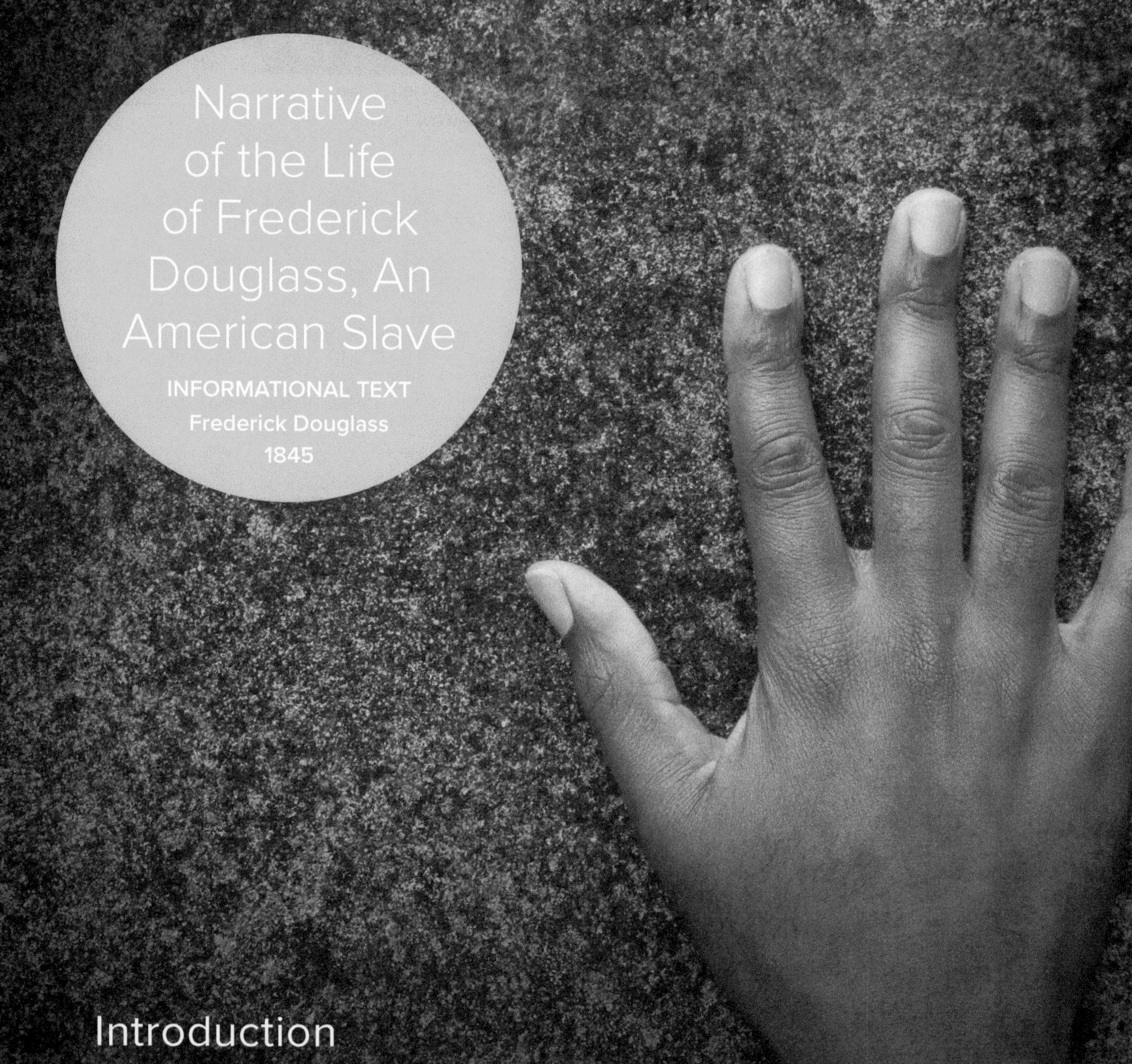

Narrative of the Life of Frederick Douglass, An American Slave

INFORMATIONAL TEXT

Frederick Douglass

1845

Introduction

Published in 1845, *Narrative of the Life of Frederick Douglass, An American Slave* describes Douglass's journey from slavery to freedom. This great American orator provides a factual account of his struggle to educate and free himself and others from the oppression of his times. The memoir's vivid descriptions of life as an enslaved person played a key role in fueling the abolitionist movement in the North prior to the Civil War. In the following excerpt from the middle of the text, Douglass overcomes the odds against him, procuring the assistance of others in teaching himself to read despite laws prohibiting slaves from learning such skills.

In this excerpt from Frederick Douglass's autobiography, he recounts how he struggled to learn to read and write while he was enslaved. While living with Master Hugh, the master's mistress started to teach Douglass how to read, but then she took on the views of her husband—it was dangerous for slaves to have access to knowledge—and she stopped. Douglass found willing teachers in the white children he would encounter around the neighborhood. When he was sent on errands, Douglass would trade bread in return for reading lessons. At 12 years old, Douglass found a life-changing book that depicted a conversation between an enslaved man and his master, in which the enslaved man convinced the master to set him free. Douglass explained that this book gave voice to feelings that he did not know how to express.

 Proficiency-leveled summaries and summaries in multiple languages are available digitally.

 Audio and audio text highlighting are available with this text.

COMPARING WITHIN AND ACROSS GENRES

 In the powerful memoir *Narrative of the Life of Frederick Douglass, An American Slave*, Douglass recounts how he came to learn to read and write, the risks involved, and the powerful impact this learning had on his life.

Access Complex Text

LEXILE: 1010L **WORD COUNT:** 945

The following areas may be challenging for students, particularly ELL English Language Learners and A Approaching grade-level learners.

Prior Knowledge	Sentence Structure	Genre
• Frederick Douglass was born into slavery around 1820. He escaped and became a notable writer and abolitionist. • Douglass alludes to the speeches of Richard Brinsley Sheridan, who argued for the freedom of the Irish from British rule.	• The language in the selection is complex. Douglass uses long sentences with many clauses. Students may benefit from breaking these long sentences into smaller parts.	• *Narrative of the Life of Frederick Douglass, An American Slave* is a memoir that tells of the author's experiences. Remind students that the selection is part of a longer work. • Douglass uses first-person point of view to tell his story.

SCAFFOLDS ELL **ENGLISH LANGUAGE LEARNERS**  **APPROACHING GRADE LEVEL**  **BEYOND GRADE LEVEL**

These icons identify differentiation strategies and scaffolded support for a variety of students. See the digital lesson plan for additional differentiation strategies and scaffolds.

Instructional Path

The print teacher's edition includes essential point-of-use instruction and planning tools. Complete lesson plans and program documents appear in your digital teacher account.

First Read: Narrative of the Life of Frederick Douglass

Objectives: After an initial reading and discussion of the excerpt, students will be able to identify and restate the text's key ideas and details.

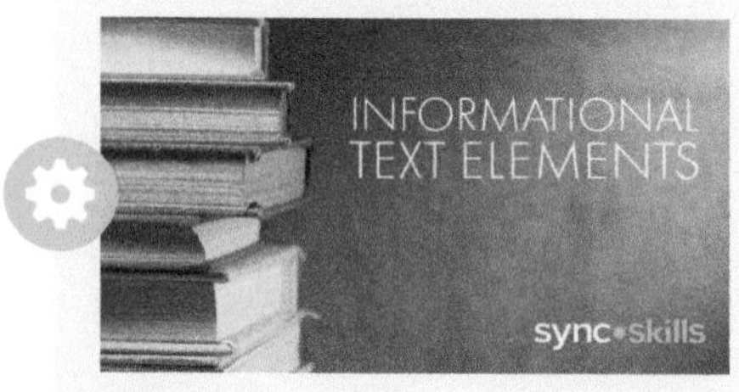

Skill: Informational Text Elements

Objectives: After rereading and discussing a model of close reading, students will be able to analyze how an author makes connections between individuals, events, and ideas through various informational text elements.

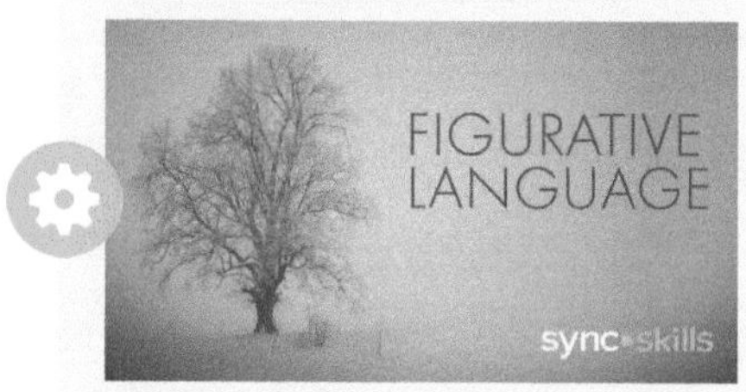

Skill: Figurative Language

Objectives: After rereading and discussing a model of close reading, students will be able to determine the meaning of figures of speech in a text.

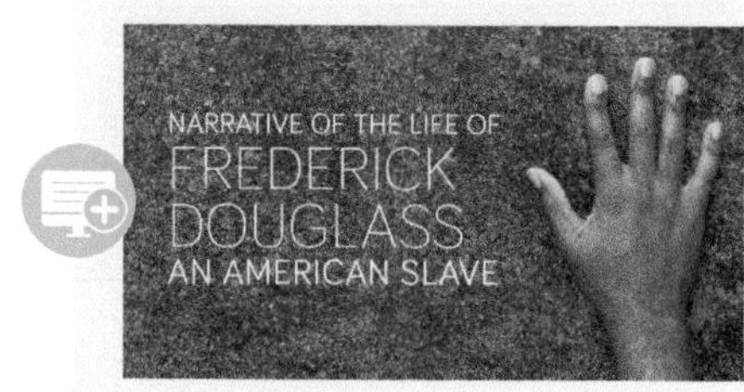

Close Read: Narrative of the Life of Frederick Douglass

Objectives: After engaging in a close reading and discussion of the text, students will be able to analyze informational text elements and figurative language in a short, written response.

Progress Monitoring

Opportunities to Learn	Opportunities to Demonstrate Learning	Opportunities to Reteach
Informational Text Elements		
Skill: Informational Text Elements	Skill: Informational Text Elements • Your Turn Close Read • Skills Focus • Write	Unit 5 Skill: Informational Text Elements - Parallel Journeys Unit 5 Skill: Informational Text Elements - Long Walk to Freedom Spotlight Skill: Informational Text Elements
Figurative Language		
Skill: Figurative Language	Skill: Figurative Language • Your Turn Close Read • Complete Vocabulary Chart • Skills Focus • Write	Spotlight Skill: Figurative Language

First Read

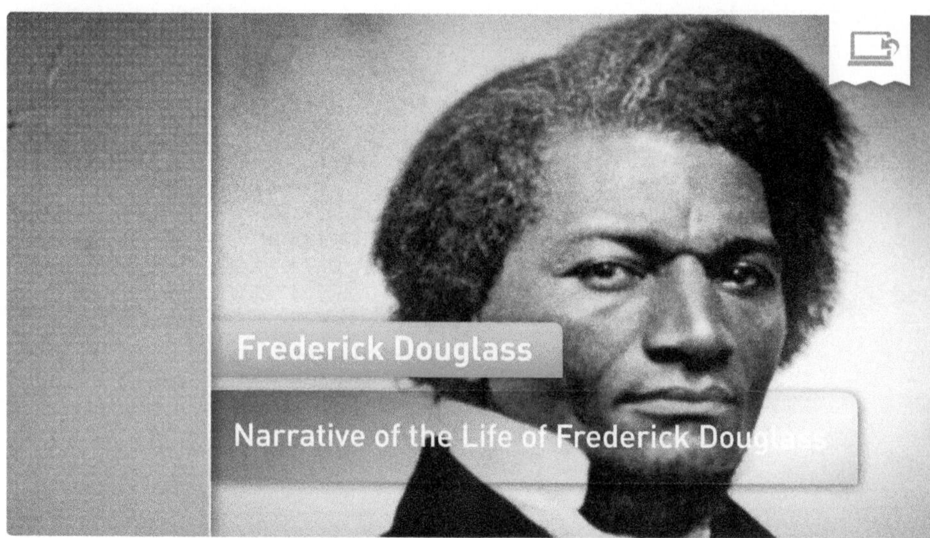

Introduce the Text

As a class, watch the video preview  **and have students read the introduction in pairs to make connections to the video preview.**

To activate prior knowledge and experiences, ask students:

- How does the information in this video connect to what you already know?
- Why do you think it's important to learn about this person?

ELL SPEAKING FRAMES

- The ____ in the video makes me think ____.
- The video shows ____. This makes me wonder ____.
- I think the text will ____. I think this because ____.
- I predict that there will be ____. I believe this because ____.

Entry Point

As students prepare to read *Narrative of the Life of Frederick Douglass*, share the following information with them to provide context.

✓ Frederick Douglass (1818–1895) was an abolitionist and U.S. diplomat. He was originally named "Frederick Augustus Washington Bailey," and he was born into slavery in Tuckahoe, Maryland. He secretly managed to learn to read and write, even though it was illegal for him to be educated at the time. He then escaped from slavery, changed his last name, and became a leading abolitionist. Douglass was famous for his exceptional writing and speaking skills.

✓ Douglass first published *Narrative of the Life of Frederick Douglass, An American Slave* in 1845. It was one of Douglass's responses to anyone who doubted that such an eloquent speaker could have been enslaved. The book was widely read in the United States and Europe.

"The silver trump of freedom had roused my soul to eternal wakefulness."

NOTES

from Chapter VII

1 I lived in Master Hugh's family about seven years. During this time, I succeeded in learning to read and write. In accomplishing this, I was compelled to resort to various stratagems.[1] I had no regular teacher. My mistress, who had kindly commenced to instruct me, had, in compliance with the advice and direction of her husband, not only ceased to instruct, but had set her face against my being instructed by any one else. It is due, however, to my mistress to say of her, that she did not adopt this course of treatment immediately. She at first lacked the depravity indispensable to shutting me up in mental darkness. It was at least necessary for her to have some training in the exercise of irresponsible power, to make her equal to the task of treating me as though I were a brute.

2 My mistress was, as I have said, a kind and tender-hearted woman; and in the simplicity of her soul she commenced, when I first went to live with her, to treat me as she supposed one human being ought to treat another. In entering upon the duties of a slaveholder, she did not seem to perceive that I sustained to her the relation of a mere chattel, and that for her to treat me as a human being was not only wrong, but dangerously so. Slavery proved as injurious to her as it did to me. When I went there, she was a pious, warm, and tender-hearted woman. There was no sorrow or suffering for which she had not a tear. She had bread for the hungry, clothes for the naked, and comfort for every mourner that came within her reach. Slavery soon proved its ability to divest her of these heavenly qualities. Under its influence, the tender heart became stone, and the lamblike disposition gave way to one of tiger-like fierceness. The first step in her downward course was in her ceasing to instruct me. She now commenced to practise her husband's precepts. She finally became even more violent in her opposition than her husband himself. She was not satisfied with simply doing as well as he had commanded; she seemed anxious to do better. Nothing seemed to make her more angry than to see me with a newspaper. She seemed to think that here lay the danger. I have had her rush at me with a face made all up of fury, and snatch from me a newspaper, in a manner that fully revealed her apprehension. She was an

Skill: Figurative Language

A lamb and a tiger remind me of the lamb and the lion in the Bible. The allusion continues as Douglass describes how his mistress changes from having kind and generous qualities to having a hardened heart and the fierceness of a tiger.

1. **stratagems** plans or strategies

Analyze Vocabulary Using Context Clues

In paragraph 4, focus on the sentence that uses the word *bestow*. Point out these context clues:

1. First, I notice that the word *bestow* follows the helping verb phrase "used to." That tells me that *bestow* is a verb.
2. When I read the sentence again, I notice the verb *give*. I think this is a synonym. I read the sentence again using the word *give* in place of *bestow*.
3. It fits within the context of the sentence, in which Douglass describes how he and the children gave each other help.

Figurative Language

What does the reader notice about the way that the mistress is described?

The reader notices that she is described as turning from a lamb to a tiger, which the reminds the reader of an allusion to lions and lambs in the Bible.

TEXT TALK

How did Douglass's mistress treat him?

See paragraphs 1 and 2: At first, she treated him well and began to teach him to read, but later, she was unkind and prevented him from learning.

Informational Text Elements

How does the reader identify the connections between the individuals in paragraph 2 and paragraph 4?

The reader explains that Douglass's mistress and the white boys are all key figures in his quest for knowledge.

Skills Focus

QUESTION 2: Central or Main Idea

Douglass points out how unfair it is that he has to be enslaved for life when the other boys would be "free" when they grew up. This textual evidence develops Douglass's thesis that slavery was an extremely unfair system.

TEXT TALK

How did Douglass continue learning to read on his own?

See paragraph 4: Douglass continued learning to read by trading bread to poor white boys in exchange for lessons.

apt woman; and a little experience soon demonstrated, to her satisfaction, that education and slavery were incompatible with each other.

3 From this time I was most narrowly watched. If I was in a separate room any considerable length of time, I was sure to be suspected of having a book, and was at once called to give an account of myself. All this, however, was too late. The first step had been taken. Mistress, in teaching me the alphabet, had given me the *inch,* and no precaution could prevent me from taking the ell.[2]

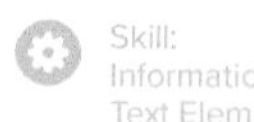

Skill: Informational Text Elements

Earlier in the text, Douglass's mistress refused to teach him anymore, so he had to find another way to learn to read. The mistress became cruel, but these white boys are helpful. The white boys and the mistress are connected because they are key to Douglass's ability to read.

4 The plan which I adopted, and the one by which I was most successful, was that of making friends of all the little white boys whom I met in the street. As many of these as I could, I converted into teachers. With their kindly aid, obtained at different times and in different places, I finally succeeded in learning to read. When I was sent of errands, I always took my book with me, and by going one part of my errand quickly, I found time to get a lesson before my return. I used also to carry bread with me, enough of which was always in the house, and to which I was always welcome; for I was much better off in this regard than many of the poor white children in our neighborhood. This bread I used to **bestow** upon the hungry little urchins, who, in return, would give me that more valuable bread of knowledge. I am strongly tempted to give the names of two or three of those little boys, as a testimonial of the gratitude and affection I bear them; but **prudence** forbids;—not that it would injure me, but it might embarrass them; for it is almost an unpardonable offence to teach slaves to read in this Christian country. It is enough to say of the dear little fellows, that they lived on Philpot Street, very near Durgin and Bailey's ship-yard. I used to talk this matter of slavery over with them. I would sometimes say to them, I wished I could be as free as they would be when they got to be men. "You will be free as soon as you are twenty-one, but I am a slave for life! Have not I as good a right to be free as you have?" These words used to trouble them; they would express for me the liveliest sympathy, and **console** me with the hope that something would occur by which I might be free.

5 I was now about twelve years old, and the thought of being a slave for life began to **bear** heavily upon my heart. Just about this time, I got hold of a book entitled "The Columbian Orator." Every opportunity I got, I used to read this book. Among much of other interesting matter, I found in it a dialogue between a master and his slave. The slave was represented as having run away from his master three times. The dialogue represented the conversation which took place between them, when the slave was retaken the third time. In this dialogue, the whole argument in behalf of slavery was brought forward by the master, all of which was disposed of by the slave. The slave was made to say some very smart as well as impressive things in reply to his

2. ***ell*** (archaic) a six hand-width measurement used in textile-making

SELECTION VOCABULARY

bestow / otorgar *verb* to give

prudence / la prudencia *noun* good judgment that helps a person avoid problems COGNATE

- What does "prudence" forbid Douglass from doing?
- Would the consequences of that action be positive or negative?

console / consolar *verb* to comfort COGNATE

- How does the word *sympathy* give a clue about *console*?
- How does the word *hope* give a clue about *console*?

bear / pesar *verb* to be oppressive, to weigh down

- How does Douglass feel in this part of the text?
- What nearby word describes *bear*? Is it positive or negative?

Narrative of the Life of Frederick Douglass, An American Slave

NOTES

master—things which had the desired though unexpected effect; for the conversation resulted in the voluntary emancipation of the slave on the part of the master.

6 In the same book, I met with one of Sheridan's mighty speeches on and in behalf of Catholic emancipation. These were choice documents to me. I read them over and over again with unabated interest. They gave tongue to interesting thoughts of my own soul, which had frequently flashed through my mind, and died away for want of utterance. The moral which I gained from the dialogue was the power of truth over the conscience of even a slaveholder. What I got from Sheridan was a bold denunciation of slavery, and a powerful vindication of human rights.

7 The reading of these documents enabled me to utter my thoughts, and to meet the arguments brought forward to sustain slavery; but while they relieved me of one difficulty, they brought on another even more painful than the one of which I was relieved. The more I read, the more I was led to abhor and detest my enslavers. I could regard them in no other light than a band of successful robbers, who had left their homes, and gone to Africa, and stolen us from our homes, and in a strange land reduced us to slavery. I loathed them as being the meanest as well as the most wicked of men. As I read and contemplated the subject, behold! that very discontentment which Master Hugh had predicted would follow my learning to read had already come, to torment and sting my soul to unutterable **anguish.** As I writhed under it, I would at times feel that learning to read had been a curse rather than a blessing. It had given me a view of my wretched condition, without the remedy. It opened my eyes to the horrible pit, but to no ladder upon which to get out. In moments of agony, I envied my fellow-slaves for their stupidity. I have often wished myself a beast. I preferred the condition of the meanest reptile to my own. Any thing, no matter what, to get rid of thinking! It was this everlasting thinking of my condition that tormented me. There was no getting rid of it. It was pressed upon me by every object within sight or hearing, animate or inanimate. The silver trump of freedom had roused my soul to eternal wakefulness. Freedom now appeared, to disappear no more forever. It was heard in every sound, and seen in every thing. It was ever present to torment me with a sense of my wretched condition. I saw nothing without seeing it, I heard nothing without hearing it, and felt nothing without feeling it. It looked from every star, it smiled in every calm, breathed in every wind, and moved in every storm.

8 I often found myself regretting my own existence, and wishing myself dead; and but for the hope of being free, I have no doubt but that I should have killed myself, or done something for which I should have been killed. While in this state of mind, I was eager to hear any one speak of slavery. I was a ready listener. Every little while, I could hear something about the abolitionists. It

Skills Focus

QUESTION 4: Figurative Language

Douglass uses this metaphor to express his feelings about being enslaved and not knowing how to free himself. This comparison shows that he feels trapped and that he wants to gain his freedom. This helps me understand why he is so committed to learning. He sees it as a tool to gain his freedom.

Skills Focus

QUESTION 3: Informational Text Elements

A problem that Douglass has is that knowing about freedom while being enslaved makes him feel depressed. He talks about his depression just before introducing the abolitionists, which signifies that they are important to the "hope of being free."

V SELECTION VOCABULARY

anguish / la angustia *noun* severe suffering or distress COGNATE

- How do the words *sting* and *torment* give clues about *anguish*?
- What other nearby words describe *anguish*? Are they positive or negative?

TEXT TALK

What did Douglass learn about that gave him hope?

See paragraph 8: Douglass felt hopeful after learning about abolition and abolitionists.

What did the Irishmen tell Douglass to do?

See paragraph 8: The Irishmen told Douglass that he should escape to the North.

Prepare for Advanced Courses

Use the activity below to differentiate instruction for your B Beyond grade-level learners.

Look at the word *abolition* in paragraph 8.

"...it was spoken of as the fruit of abolition. *Hearing the word in this connection very often, I set about learning what it meant. The dictionary afforded me little or no help. I found it was "the act of abolishing;" but then I did not know what was to be abolished."*

Ask students to examine the word abolition. An abolitionist is someone who wanted to end slavery. The Latin root *abolere* means "destroy." Have students discuss the meaning and transformation of the word. Ask students: How does Douglass feel about the use of the word *abolition*? Do you think he would feel differently had he known the meaning?

was some time before I found what the word meant. It was always used in such connections as to make it an interesting word to me. If a slave ran away and succeeded in getting clear, or if a slave killed his master, set fire to a barn, or did any thing very wrong in the mind of a slaveholder, it was spoken of as the fruit of *abolition*. Hearing the word in this connection very often, I set about learning what it meant. The dictionary afforded me little or no help. I found it was "the act of abolishing;" but then I did not know what was to be abolished. Here I was perplexed. I did not dare to ask any one about its meaning, for I was satisfied that it was something they wanted me to know very little about. After a patient waiting, I got one of our city papers, containing an account of the number of petitions from the north, praying for the abolition of slavery in the District of Columbia, and of the slave trade between the States. From this time I understood the words *abolition* and *abolitionist*, and always drew near when that word was spoken, expecting to hear something of importance to myself and fellow-slaves. The light broke in upon me by degrees. I went one day down on the wharf of Mr. Waters; and seeing two Irishmen unloading a scow of stone, I went, unasked, and helped them. When we had finished, one of them came to me and asked me if I were a slave. I told him I was. He asked, "Are ye a slave for life?" I told him that I was. The good Irishman seemed to be deeply affected by the statement. He said to the other that it was a pity so fine a little fellow as myself should be a slave for life. He said it was a shame to hold me. They both advised me to run away to the north; that I should find friends there, and that I should be free. I pretended not to be interested in what they said, and treated them as if I did not understand them; for I feared they might be treacherous. White men have been known to encourage slaves to escape, and then, to get the reward, catch them and return them to their masters. I was afraid that these seemingly good men might use me so; but I nevertheless remembered their advice, and from that time I resolved to run away. I looked forward to a time at which it would be safe for me to escape. I was too young to think of doing so immediately; besides, I wished to learn how to write, as I might have occasion to write my own pass. I consoled myself with the hope that I should one day find a good chance. Meanwhile, I would learn to write.

American orator, editor, author, abolitionist, and former enslaved person Frederick Douglass (1818–1895) edits a journal at his desk, late 1870s.

9 The idea as to how I might learn to write was suggested to me by being in Durgin and Bailey's ship-yard, and frequently seeing the ship carpenters, after hewing, and getting a piece of timber ready for use, write on the timber the name of that part of the ship for which it was intended. When a piece of timber was intended for the larboard side, it would be marked thus—"L."

TEXT TALK

How did Douglass learn to write his first letters?

See paragraph 9: Douglass copied letters he saw on timber that was labeled to show what part of a ship it would form.

B Ask each Beyond grade-level student to write one additional discussion question. Then have one or two students facilitate a discussion, using their questions to guide the conversation.

When a piece was for the starboard side, it would be marked thus—"S." A piece for the larboard side forward, would be marked thus—"L. F." When a piece was for starboard side forward, it would be marked thus—"S. F." For larboard aft, it would be marked thus—"L. A." For starboard aft, it would be marked thus—"S. A." I soon learned the names of these letters, and for what they were intended when placed upon a piece of timber in the ship-yard. I immediately commenced copying them, and in a short time was able to make the four letters named. After that, when I met with any boy who I knew could write, I would tell him I could write as well as he. The next word would be, "I don't believe you. Let me see you try it." I would then make the letters which I had been so fortunate as to learn, and ask him to beat that. In this way I got a good many lessons in writing, which it is quite possible I should never have gotten in any other way. During this time, my copy-book was the board fence, brick wall, and pavement; my pen and ink was a lump of chalk. With these, I learned mainly how to write. I then commenced and continued copying the Italics in Webster's Spelling Book, until I could make them all without looking on the book. By this time, my little Master Thomas had gone to school, and learned how to write, and had written over a number of copy-books. These had been brought home, and shown to some of our near neighbors, and then laid aside. My mistress used to go to class meeting at the Wilk Street meetinghouse every Monday afternoon, and leave me to take care of the house. When left thus, I used to spend the time in writing in the spaces left in Master Thomas's copy-book, copying what he had written. I continued to do this until I could write a hand very similar to that of Master Thomas. Thus, after a long, tedious effort for years, I finally succeeded in learning how to write.

TEXT TALK

How does Douglass's journey to learning how to read and write reflect the abolition movement and purpose?

Answers will vary.

Think Questions

Circulate as students answer Think Questions independently. Scaffolds for these questions are shown on the opposite page.

QUESTION 1: Textual Evidence

Douglass believed that learning to read would be a valuable skill. He calls reading "that more valuable bread of knowledge." Reading helped Douglass convey his own ideas and argue against slavery.

QUESTION 2: Textual Evidence

Douglass was briefly instructed by his mistress, who was the wife of a slave owner. Later, when she stopped helping him, he traded bread with little white boys in exchange for knowledge. In *The Columbian Orator*, Douglass read a dialogue between a master and an enslaved person and a speech by Sheridan in favor of Catholic emancipation. These related to Douglass's own life because he was enslaved and wanted freedom. He found both texts to be inspirational because they reflected thoughts he'd already had about his condition. He says, "They gave tongue to interesting thoughts of my own soul, which had frequently flashed through my mind, and died away for want of utterance."

QUESTION 3: Textual Evidence

As he read more about slavery, Douglass thought more about his terrible condition and felt tortured by not having a way to change it. He says, "It had given me a view of my wretched condition, without the remedy. It opened my eyes to the horrible pit, but to no ladder upon which to get out."

QUESTION 4: Context Clues

I think *console* must mean "to comfort." The word is used to describe the ideas that would make Douglass feel hopeful that he might gain his freedom someday.

QUESTION 5: Word Meaning

Definition d most closely matches the meaning of the word *bear* in paragraph 5. Douglass describes a heavy feeling on his heart, so *bear* must mean "to weigh on or burden."

Narrative of the Life of Frederick Douglass, An American Slave

First Read

Read *Narrative of the Life of Frederick Douglass, An American Slave*. After you read, complete the Think Questions below.

THINK QUESTIONS

1. Identify evidence from the excerpt that reveals why learning to read was so important to Frederick Douglass when he was a boy.
2. How did Douglass learn to read? Describe how he was affected by the texts he read.
3. Over time, Douglass begins to think that "learning to read had been a curse rather than a blessing." Why does he come to feel this way? Explain, citing evidence from the excerpt.
4. Based on context clues, what is the meaning of the word **console** as it is used in paragraph 4? Write your best definition of *console* here, explaining how you figured it out.
5. Read the following dictionary entry:

   bear
   bear \ber\ *verb*

   a. to carry
   b. to bring forth or produce
   c. to endure
   d. to weigh on or burden

   Which definition most closely matches the meaning of **bear** as it is used in paragraph 5? Write the correct definition of *bear* here and explain how you figured out the correct meaning.

 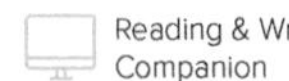

Think Questions

Use the scaffolds below to differentiate instruction for your ELL English Language Learners and A Approaching grade-level learners.

ELL **BEGINNING** Write a response using the word bank and sentence frames.

INTERMEDIATE Write a response using the sentence frames.

ADVANCED, ADVANCED HIGH Write a response using the Text-Dependent Question Guide.

A **APPROACHING** Write a response using the Text-Dependent Question Guide.

BEGINNING	INTERMEDIATE	APPROACHING / ADVANCED, ADVANCED HIGH
Word Bank	**Sentence Frames**	**Text-Dependent Question Guide**
terrible freedom valuable comfort slavery escape hopeful upset thoughts trades	Douglass thought that learning how to read would be a ____ skill. Reading helped Douglass express his own ideas and make an argument against ____.	1. • What descriptive words and phrases does Douglass use to describe reading? • How did reading help Douglass?
	Douglass ____ bread with white boys. The dialogue and the speech in *The Columbian Orator* are both about the value of ____. Reading these texts made Douglass feel inspired because they reflected his own ____ about his condition as an enslaved person.	2. • Who does Douglass trade bread with? What does he get in return? • What ideas are in the dialogue and speech Douglass reads? • How do those ideas relate to Douglass?
	As he learned more, Douglass thought more about how ____ his condition was. It made him feel ____ because he doubted that he would ever be able to ____.	3. • How does reading expand Douglass's perspective on slavery? • How do Douglass's feelings change as his perspective changes? • Why does he feel this way?
	The words made Douglass feel ____. This gives me a clue that *console* means "to ____."	4. • Read: "'You will be free as soon as you are twenty-one, but I am a slave for life! Have not I as good a right to be free as you have?' These words used to trouble them; they would express for me the liveliest sympathy, and **console** me with the hope that something would occur by which I might be free." • What feelings are being described in this paragraph? • What does that tell me about the meaning of the word *console*?
	Bear as used in the text matches definition ____.	5. • Read: "I was now about twelve years old, and the thought of being a slave for life began to **bear** heavily upon my heart." • Does *bear* refer to carrying something? (#1) • Does *bear* refer to producing something? (#2) • Does *bear* refer to enduring? (#3) • Does *bear* refer to weighing on something? (#4)

Reading Comprehension OPTIONAL

Have students complete the digital reading comprehension questions when they finish reading.

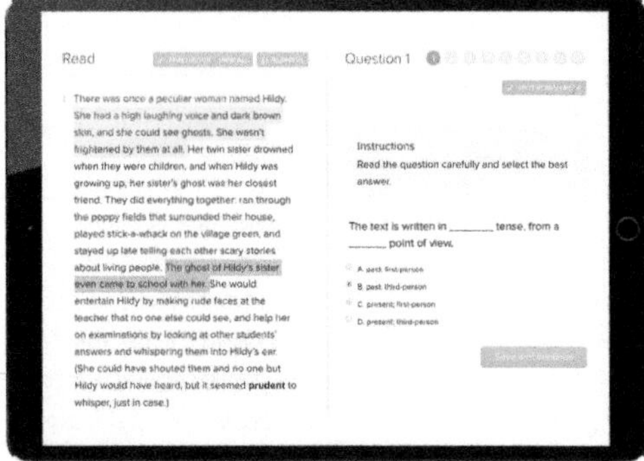

ANSWER KEY

QUESTION 1: B
QUESTION 2: C
QUESTION 3: D
QUESTION 4: A
QUESTION 5: C
QUESTION 6: A
QUESTION 7: B
QUESTION 8: C
QUESTION 9: *See first chart.*
QUESTION 10: *See second chart.*

Effect Reading Had on Him	Not an Effect from Reading
Obsessed with the idea of freedom	Developed a deeper affection for his owner
Felt tortured by the idea of being stuck as an enslaved person	Got whipped for taking bread in exchange for his lessons
Took a book with him whenever he went out on an errand	Refused to share his feelings on slavery with the white children who lived near him

Definition	Word
to give or confer something formally	bestow
to weigh or impact	bear
intense suffering or pain	anguish
to comfort at a difficult time	console
good judgment	prudence

Connect and Extend OPTIONAL

CONNECT TO EXTENDED WRITING PROJECT

Students can use *Narrative of the Life of Frederick Douglass, An American Slave* as a resource when writing their informational essays. Have students analyze the impact of Douglass's personal risk.

BEYOND THE BOOK

Writing: Changing the Face of American Currency

Imagine that the United States Treasury is planning to change the face on the $20 bill. Students will need to write an argumentative paragraph making a strong case for putting Frederick Douglass on the American bill.

Ask students to:

- Research Frederick Douglass's life and achievements to gather relevant information to use in their argumentative paragraph.
- Write a clear claim stating why they believe Frederick Douglass should appear on the $20 bill, and support that claim with credible evidence collected during their research and thoughtful analysis.
- Include citations for all of the resources they included in their paragraph.

Pair up students so they can provide one another with peer edits on their paragraphs.

To reflect, ask students:

- How would changing the faces that appear on our currency impact our national identity?
- What do the images on our currency reveal about our country and its history?

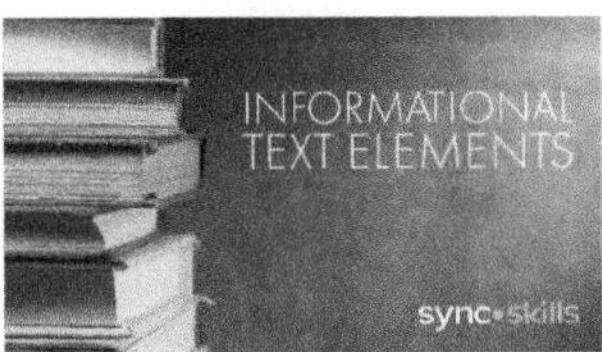

Skill: Informational Text Elements

Use the Checklist to analyze Informational Text Elements in *Narrative of the Life of Frederick Douglass, An American Slave*. Refer to the sample student annotations about Informational Text Elements in the text.

••• CHECKLIST FOR INFORMATIONAL TEXT ELEMENTS

In order to determine how a text makes connections among and distinctions between individuals, ideas, or events, note the following:

- ✓ key details in the text that describe or explain important ideas, events, or individuals
- ✓ connections as well as distinctions between different individuals, ideas, and events, such as:
    - particular characteristics
    - shared experiences
    - similar or different ideas
    - important conversations
- ✓ analogies the author uses to determine the similarities between two pieces of information (e.g., a heart and a pump)
- ✓ comparisons the author makes between individuals, ideas, or events

To analyze how a text makes connections among and distinctions between individuals, ideas, or events, consider the following questions:

- ✓ What kinds of connections and distinctions does the author make in the text?
- ✓ Does the author include any analogies or comparisons? What do they add to the text?
- ✓ What other features, if any, help readers to analyze the events, ideas, or individuals in the text?

Skill: Informational Text Elements

Introduce the Skill

Watch the Concept Definition video ▶ and read the following definition with your students.

An **informational text** presents readers with information or ideas about real people, places, things, and events. To present information clearly, writers use a common set of **informational text elements**, or features, that link key individuals, events, and ideas. Some examples of informational text include biographies, diaries, interviews, articles, letters, editorials, essays, and speeches. Many of these texts will include **supporting evidence**, or any relevant fact that an author includes to support his or her ideas, as well as **pertinent examples**. These examples have a logical connection to a subject, such as discussing the Gettysburg Address in an article on Civil War battles. To identify informational text elements, readers should look for key details in the text, as well as any photographs, charts, or maps the author includes, and analyze the connections and relationships among them. Analyzing the elements of an informational text helps the reader understand how they work together to support a central idea.

V SKILL VOCABULARY

informational text / el texto informativo *noun* nonfiction writing that presents information about real people, places, things, and events COGNATE

informational text elements / los elementos del texto informativo *noun* characteristics of informational texts COGNATE

supporting evidence / la evidencia de apoyo *noun* textual evidence, descriptions, examples, reasons, expert opinions, facts, and statistics that further explain key aspects of the controlling idea

TURN AND TALK

1. What is the last nonfiction text you read?
2. How did the author make connections between the events or individuals?

SPEAKING FRAMES

- The last nonfiction text I read was ____. It was about ____.
- The author made connections between the events and the individuals by ____.

Your Turn

Ask students to complete the Your Turn activity.

QUESTION 1

A. Incorrect. While Douglass did enjoy reading and often read this book, this is not the strongest answer.

B. Incorrect. While Douglass wanted to be free, nothing in this paragraph indicates that reading helped him feel free.

C. Correct. Douglass's position weighed "heavily upon [his] heart," and this text presented the story of an enslaved person whose master emancipated him.

D. Incorrect. The enslaved person in the text is made free.

QUESTION 2

A. Incorrect. This detail introduces the part of the book that affected Douglass.

B. Incorrect. This detail shows that Douglass enjoyed the book, but not why it was important.

C. Incorrect. This detail does show why the book was important, but it is not the strongest answer.

D. Correct. This detail explicitly states why the book was so important to Douglass.

QUESTION 3

A. Incorrect. This answer is true but does not address the realization Douglass presents in paragraph 6.

B. Correct. Douglass makes the connection between the way the enslaved person in the story uses dialogue to get his master to set him free and the ways that Douglass could gain his own freedom.

C. Incorrect. This answer is not supported by the details in the text.

D. Incorrect. This answer is true but does not address the realization Douglass presents in paragraph 5.

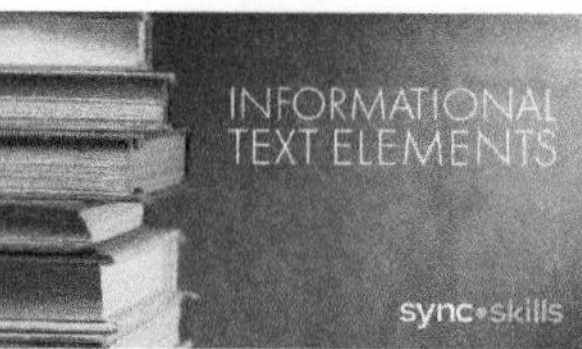

Skill: Informational Text Elements

Reread paragraphs 5 and 6 of *Narrative of the Life of Frederick Douglass, An American Slave*. Then, using the Checklist on the previous page, answer the multiple-choice questions below.

YOUR TURN

1. According to the information in paragraph 5, why was discovering the *The Columbian Orator* important to Douglass?

   - A. Douglass enjoyed reading and could read this book often.
   - B. Douglass wanted to be free, and reading helped him feel free.
   - C. Douglass felt that he would always be an enslaved person, but this text gave him hope.
   - D. Douglass felt that he would always be an enslaved person, and this text presented a similar fate for another enslaved person.

2. Which detail from paragraph 6 best supports the idea that discovering *The Columbian Orator* was a key event in Douglass's life?

   - A. "In the same book, I met with one of Sheridan's mighty speeches on and in behalf of Catholic emancipation."
   - B. "These were choice documents to me. I read them over and over again with unabated interest."
   - C. "They gave tongue to interesting thoughts of my own soul, which had frequently flashed through my mind, and died away for want of utterance."
   - D. "What I got from Sheridan was a bold denunciation of slavery, and a powerful vindication of human rights."

3. What connection does Douglass make between the ideas in the *The Columbian Orator* and his own situation?

   - A. Douglass realizes that he is just like the enslaved person in the book.
   - B. Douglass realizes that like the enslaved person in the book, he could use the power of the truth to gain his own freedom.
   - C. Douglass realizes that he is like the enslaved person in the book, but he will never be free.
   - D. Douglass realizes that human rights are important.

Skill: Figurative Language

Use the Checklist to analyze Figurative Language in *Narrative of the Life of Frederick Douglass, An American Slave*. Refer to the sample student annotations about Figurative Language in the text.

••• CHECKLIST FOR FIGURATIVE LANGUAGE

To determine the meanings of figures of speech in a text, note the following:

- ✓ words that mean one thing literally and suggest something else
- ✓ similes, such as "strong as an ox"
- ✓ metaphors, such as "her eyes were stars"
- ✓ allusions, or indirect references to people, texts, events, or ideas, such as
  - saying of a setting, "the place was a Garden of Eden" (biblical allusion)
  - saying of a character whose snooping caused problems, "he opened a Pandora's box" (allusion to mythology)
  - calling someone who likes romance "a real Romeo" (allusion to Shakespeare)
- ✓ verbal irony, or people saying one thing and meaning another, such as
  - referring to a stormy day as "beautiful weather"
  - a character saying how happy he is to be somewhere when he is not
- ✓ analogies, or comparisons of two unlike things based on a specific similarity and used for clarification, such as
  - remarking, "Life is like a ball game; anybody can have a losing day."
  - in Shakespeare's Sonnet 18, "Shall I compare thee to a summer's day? / Thou art more lovely and more temperate."
- ✓ other language in the text used in a nonliteral way

Skill: Figurative Language

Introduce the Skill

Watch the Concept Definition video and read the following definition with your students.

Figurative language is language used for descriptive effect, often to illustrate or imply ideas indirectly. Types of figurative language include simile, metaphor, and personification. A **simile** uses the words *like* or *as* to compare two seemingly unlike things. A **metaphor** directly compares two seemingly unlike things without using *like* or *as*. **Personification** is a **figure of speech** in which an animal, object, force of nature, or an idea is given human qualities.

When reading prose, and especially poetry, readers use **context**—including when and where a text was written, for example—to analyze the impact of word choice and to help determine or interpret the meaning of figurative words and phrases.

TURN AND TALK

1. What are some examples of figurative language that you use or hear often?
2. Why do people and writers use figurative language?

ELL SPEAKING FRAMES

- One example of figurative language that I often hear is ____.
- When people use that figure of speech, what they mean is ____.
- Writers use figurative language because ____.

SKILL VOCABULARY

figurative language / el lenguaje figurativo ***noun*** expressions used for descriptive or rhetorical effect that are not literally true but express some truth beyond the literal level COGNATE

simile / el símil ***noun*** a figure of speech that uses the words *like* or *as* to compare two seemingly unlike things COGNATE

metaphor / la metáfora ***noun*** a figure of speech that compares two seemingly unlike things but implies a comparison instead of stating it directly with the words *like* or *as* COGNATE

In order to interpret the meaning of a figure of speech in context, ask the following questions:

- ✓ Does any of the descriptive language in the text compare two seemingly unlike things?
- ✓ Do any descriptions include *like* or *as,* indicating a simile?
- ✓ Is there a direct comparison that suggests a metaphor?
- ✓ What literary, biblical, or mythological allusions do you recognize?
- ✓ Can you detect humor or sarcasm in the tone of the word or phrase, or a character saying one thing and clearly meaning the opposite?
- ✓ How does the use of this figure of speech change your understanding of the thing or person being described?

In order to analyze the impact of figurative language on the meaning of a text, use the following questions as a guide:

- ✓ Where does figurative language appear in the text? What does it mean?
- ✓ Why does the author use figurative language rather than literal language?

SKILL VOCABULARY

personification / la personificación ***noun*** a figure of speech in which an animal, object, force of nature, or idea is given human form or qualities COGNATE

figure of speech / la figura literaria ***noun*** a word or phrase not meant to be taken literally, but rather used for effect

context / el contexto ***noun*** the set of facts or circumstances that surround a situation or event COGNATE

Skill: Figurative Language

Reread paragraph 4 of *Narrative of the Life of Frederick Douglass, An American Slave*. Then, using the Checklist on the previous page, answer the multiple-choice questions below.

YOUR TURN

1. In paragraph 4, how does Douglass show his feelings for America?
   - A. He literally calls it a "Christian country," which means he likes it and thinks enslaved people shouldn't be taught to read.
   - B. He seems to sarcastically refer to it as a "Christian country," which shows that he doesn't think he should be taught to read.
   - C. He literally calls it a "Christian country," which shows that he doesn't like it very much.
   - D. He seems to sarcastically refer to it as a "Christian country," which shows that he doesn't like it because slavery exists and teaching enslaved people to read is not allowed.

2. This question has two parts. First, answer Part A. Then, answer Part B.

   Part A: What kind of figurative language is Douglass using when he writes, "This bread I used to **bestow** upon the hungry little urchins, who, in return, would give me that more valuable bread of knowledge"?
   - A. simile
   - B. metaphor
   - C. personification
   - D. verbal Irony

   Part B: What does the figurative language identified in Part A tell us about how Douglass feels about knowledge?
   - A. Douglass knows that the boys should value knowledge as much as he does, but they prefer bread.
   - B. Douglass knows that he needs to share knowledge, just like he shared bread with the boys from his neighborhood.
   - C. Douglass sees knowledge as a form of nourishment. Bread can nourish people who are hungry, and knowledge can nourish people who want to learn.
   - D. Douglass sees knowledge as something that can go stale if you do not use it, so he shares bread and knowledge with the boys in his neighborhood.

SkillsTV

Project the SkillsTV episode and pause at the following times to prompt discussion:

1:15 One student reads aloud some text from the selection. What do the students take away from the content of this passage?

2:14 When the second passage is read aloud, what is revealed about Douglass's skills as a writer?

3:43 What do the metaphors Douglass uses say about who he has become through reading?

Your Turn

Ask students to complete the Your Turn activity.

QUESTION 1

A. Incorrect. His tone is sarcastic in this phrase, and we know this because Douglass believes enslaved people should be able to read.

B. Incorrect. His tone is sarcastic in this phrase, and we know this because Douglass believes enslaved people should be able to read.

C. Incorrect. His tone is sarcastic in this phrase, and we know this because Douglass believes enslaved people should be able to read.

D. Correct. Douglass believes enslaved people should be able to read, and so by calling America a "Christian country," he uses a sarcastic phrase.

QUESTION 2

Part A

A. Incorrect. Douglass compares bread to knowledge, but he does not use *like* or *as*.

B. Correct. Douglass compares bread and knowledge without using *like* or *as*.

C. Incorrect. Douglass does not give human qualities to an object in this description.

D. Incorrect. Douglass uses a metaphor to compare bread and knowledge without using *like* or *as*.

Part B

A. Incorrect. The boys have access to an education, but they are hungry.

B. Incorrect. Douglass gives bread to the boys so they will teach him how to read and write in return. As a result, he is sharing bread, but not sharing knowledge yet.

C. Correct. Douglass sees knowledge as something that is as necessary for him as food is necessary for people who are hungry.

D. Incorrect. There is no textual evidence that relates to knowledge becoming stale in this passage.

Close Read

Skills Focus

QUESTION 1: Author's Purpose and Point of View

See paragraph 1: Douglass chooses words that convey a strong opinion about not being allowed to read. He calls it "mental darkness" and compares it to being treated like an animal. His point of view, or opinion, helps reveal that his purpose in writing is to critique his enslavement.

QUESTION 2: Central or Main Idea

See paragraph 4.

QUESTION 3: Informational Text Elements

See paragraph 8.

QUESTION 4: Figurative Language

See paragraph 7.

QUESTION 5: Connect to Essential Question

See paragraph 7: Douglass uses personification to explain how often he thought about gaining his freedom. This use of figurative language helps show how tortured he feels by the desire for freedom and why he would feel driven to find a way to attain it. This also helps me understand why he is so committed to learning. He is desperate to gain his freedom.

Close Read

Reread *Narrative of the Life of Frederick Douglass, An American Slave*. As you reread, complete the Skills Focus questions below. Then use your answers and annotations from the questions to help you complete the Write activity.

SKILLS FOCUS

1. Autobiographical texts such as *Narrative of the Life of Frederick Douglass, An American Slave* utilize key details from the author's perspective. Identify a strong opinion that Douglass shares, and explain how it helps to reveal his purpose.
2. Identify details that reveal Douglass's central or main idea in this excerpt from *Narrative of the Life of Frederick Douglass, An American Slave*. Explain how the textual evidence supports that central or main idea.
3. Reread the final two paragraphs in the excerpt. Identify the informational elements within these two paragraphs. Use and cite at least two specific examples in your response.
4. Identify specific instances of figurative language Douglass uses to describe slavery and freedom, and explain what the language helps you understand about Douglass's message.
5. In "Mother to Son," "Learning to Read," and *Narrative of the Life of Frederick Douglass, An American Slave,* the authors use figurative language to develop ideas about hardship and perseverance. In "Mother to Son," Hughes uses an extended metaphor to describe the hardship the speaker experiences as she pursues a better life. In "Learning to Read," Watkins uses a simile to describe the positive outcome of the speaker's persistence in learning to read. Identify figurative language Douglass uses to describe slavery and freedom, and explain what the language helps you understand about why he took chances to learn how to read and write.

WRITE

COMPARATIVE: The speakers of the poems "Mother to Son" and "Learning to Read," and Frederick Douglass in his autobiography, describe the risks involved to make successes of their lives. While Douglass's autobiography uses informational text elements to convey his experience, all three texts send a message about the importance of education. Think about the use of language, descriptions, and events, and explain how they contribute to this message.

Writer's Notebook

Connect to Essential Question: Give students time to reflect on how *Narrative of the Life of Frederick Douglass, An American Slave* connects to the unit's essential question "Why do we take chances?" by freewriting in their Writer's Notebooks.

Beginning & Intermediate

Read aloud the unit's essential question: "Why do we take chances?" Encourage students to draw their connections or allow students to write in their native language. Circulate the room, prompting students for their thoughts as they respond orally or through pantomime.

Advanced & Advanced High

Allow students to share their connections orally in pairs or small groups before freewriting.

StudySyncTV

Project the StudySyncTV episode and pause at the following times to prompt discussion:

0:50 How do the students use textual evidence to determine that the children are taking a risk by teaching Douglass how to read?

2:08 Pattelynn says that "sometimes the road to good things can be painful." How does the group use textual evidence and make inferences to develop her idea?

4:17 How do the students use details from the text to draw connections to their own experiences? What evidence do they use to support their ideas?

Collaborative Conversation

SCAFFOLDS

Break students into collaborative conversation groups to discuss the Close Read prompt. Ask students to use the StudySyncTV episode as a model for their discussion. Remind them to reference their Skills Focus annotations in their discussion.

The speakers of the poems "Mother to Son" and "Learning to Read," and Frederick Douglass in his autobiography, describe the risks involved to make successes of their lives. While Douglass's autobiography uses informational text elements to convey his experience, all three texts send a message about the importance of education. Think about the use of language, descriptions, and events, and explain how they contribute to this message.

Use the scaffolds below to differentiate instruction for your ELL English Language Learners and A Approaching grade-level learners.

ELL **BEGINNING, INTERMEDIATE** Use the discussion guide and speaking frames to facilitate the discussion with support from the teacher.

ADVANCED, ADVANCED HIGH Use the discussion guide and speaking frames to facilitate the discussion in mixed-level groups.

A **APPROACHING** Use the discussion guide to facilitate the discussion in mixed-level groups.

APPROACHING
ADVANCED, ADVANCED HIGH
BEGINNING, INTERMEDIATE

Discussion Guide	Speaking Frames
1. How does "Mother to Son" use language and descriptions? How does it contribute to the text's message about the importance of education?	• The text describes ____. • It reveals the message of ____ because ____.
2. How does "Learning to Read" use language and descriptions? How does it contribute to the text's message about the importance of education?	• The text describes ____. • It reveals the message of ____________ because ____.
3. What informational text elements are used in *Narrative of the Life of Frederick Douglass, An American Slave*? How do they contribute to the text's message about the importance of education?	• The informational text elements used are ____. • It reveals the message of ____ because ____.

Review Prompt and Rubric

Before students begin writing, review the writing prompt and rubric with the class.

COMPARATIVE: The speakers of the poems "Mother to Son" and "Learning to Read," and Frederick Douglass in his autobiography, describe the risks involved to make successes of their lives. While Douglass's autobiography uses informational text elements to convey his experience, all three texts send a message about the importance of education. Think about the use of language, descriptions, and events, and explain how they contribute to this message.

PROMPT GUIDE

- What language and descriptions does each author use?
- What informational text elements are used by Douglass?
- How do these elements contribute to the message of the text?
- How are the texts' messages revealed through the language?

An additional rubric item for Language and Conventions appears in your digital teacher and student accounts.

Score	Informational Text Elements	Figurative Language
4	The writer clearly analyzes and explains how the texts make connections among and distinctions between individuals, ideas, or events. The writer provides exemplary analysis, using relevant evidence from the text.	The writer clearly determines the meanings of words and phrases as they are used in the texts, including figurative and connotative meanings. The writer provides an exemplary analysis of the impact of specific word choices on meaning and tone, using relevant evidence from the text.
3	The writer analyzes and explains how the texts make connections among and distinctions between individuals, ideas, or events. The writer provides sufficient analysis, using relevant evidence from the text most of the time.	The writer determines the meanings of words and phrases as they are used in the texts, including figurative and connotative meanings. The writer sufficiently analyzes the impact of specific word choices on meaning and tone and the writer mostly uses relevant evidence from the text.
2	The writer begins to analyze or explain how the texts make connections among and distinctions between individuals, ideas, or events, but the analysis is incomplete. The writer uses relevant evidence from the text only some of the time.	The writer begins to determine the meanings of words and phrases as they are used in the texts, including figurative and connotative meanings. The writer provides an incomplete analysis of the impact of specific word choices on meaning and tone and occasionally uses relevant evidence from the text.
1	The writer attempts to analyze or explain, but the analysis is not successful. The writer uses little or no relevant evidence from the text.	The writer attempts to determine the meanings of words and phrases as they are used in the texts, including figurative and connotative meanings. The writer's analysis of the impact of specific word choices on meaning and tone is not successful and uses little or no relevant evidence from the text.
0	The writer does not provide a relevant response to the prompt or does not provide a response at all.	The writer does not provide a relevant response to the prompt or does not provide a response at all.

Write

SCAFFOLDS

Ask students to complete the writing assignment using textual evidence to support their answers.

Use the scaffolds below to differentiate instruction for your ELL English Language Learners and A Approaching grade-level learners.

ELL **BEGINNING** With the help of the word bank, write a response using paragraph frame 1.

INTERMEDIATE With the help of the word bank, write a response using paragraph frames 1 and 2.

ADVANCED, ADVANCED HIGH Write a response of differentiated length using the sentence starters.

A **APPROACHING** Write a response of differentiated length using the sentence starters.

BEGINNING / INTERMEDIATE	BEGINNING / INTERMEDIATE	INTERMEDIATE	ADVANCED, ADVANCED HIGH / APPROACHING
Word Bank	**Paragraph Frame 1**	**Paragraph Frame 2**	**Sentence Starters**
desire communicate images importance metaphor	All three texts use descriptive language to ____ the importance of education. "Mother to Son" creates _____ of two sets of stairs: the crystal stairs and the splintered torn up stairs. These descriptions reveal the possible benefits of education through a ____. In "Learning to Read," Harper describes learning to read by "hook or crook." This language reveals the ____ of education. The informational text elements in *Narrative of the Life of Frederick Douglass, An American Slave* help the author reveal his strong ____ to be able to read. He describes in detail the lengths he went to in order to learn.	All of these texts use descriptive language and metaphor to express ____. The importance of a good education is also revealed through the ____ in each text. Reading each text provides the reader with ____ that reveal the importance of education. Though each text presents its message in a different manner, they all convey ____.	• All three texts use descriptive language to . . . • "Mother to Son" creates . . . of . . . • These descriptions reveal . . . • In "Learning to Read," Harper describes . . . • This language reveals . . . • The . . . in *Narrative of the Life of Frederick Douglass, An American Slave* helps the author reveal . . . • He describes in detail . . .

Peer Review

Students should submit substantive feedback to two peers using the review instructions below.

- How well does this response answer the prompt?
- How well does the writer support his or her ideas with details from the text?
- What did the writer do well in this response? What does the writer need to work on?

Rate

Respond to the following with a point rating that reflects your opinion.

	1	2	3	4
Ideas	■	■	■	□
Evidence	■	■	■	■
Language and Conventions	■	■	□	□

Submit

ELL A **SENTENCE FRAMES**

- You were able to (completely / partly / almost) answer the prompt.
- You supported the idea of ____ with the detail of ____.
- One idea that needs more support is ____.
- My favorite part of your response is ____.

The Day I Saved a Life

INFORMATIONAL TEXT
Thomas Ponce
2018

Introduction

Thomas Ponce (b. 2000) is a Florida native, animal rights activist, and citizen lobbyist. He has been a vegetarian since age four, and at age five began writing about animal rights. He is the creator of the group Lobby for Animals, and he has received awards from major organizations such as PETA and the Farm Animal Rights Movement. In "The Day I Saved a Life," Ponce describes a key day in his life, which would lead directly to a greater awareness about the plight of sharks and his decision to actively work to improve their conditions.

For his 11th birthday, Thomas Ponce's family took him to Venice Beach. For Thomas, this trip wasn't about swimming. Thomas knew that Venice is also known as "Shark Tooth Beach," and he was excited to comb the sands in search of ancient shark teeth. With his sifter in hand, he began searching and quickly found teeth from bull sharks and great whites, but then he hit the jackpot: a black four-inch tooth which belonged to a Megalodon. Later, he and his family went to the pier to watch the sun set on a perfect day. Nearby, Thomas saw a fisherman pull a baby shark out of the water and proclaim that he was going to eat well tonight. Thomas ran over and talked to the man about how important sharks are for the ocean's ecosystem, and how their slow reproductive rate makes every shark important. Thomas succeeded in convincing the fisherman to release the shark, and ever since then, he's been working to advocate for shark's rights.

ELL Proficiency-leveled summaries and summaries in multiple languages are available digitally.

 Audio and audio text highlighting are available with this text.

CONNECT TO ESSENTIAL QUESTION

Why do we take chances?

Standing up for what you believe sometimes involves risk. In this personal narrative, a young man stands up for animal rights when a fisherman intends to kill a shark.

Access Complex Text

LEXILE: 970L **WORD COUNT:** 1,084

The following areas may be challenging for students, particularly ELL English Language Learners and A Approaching grade-level learners.

Prior Knowledge	Specific Vocabulary
• The text refers to biological concepts such as the ocean ecosystem and the shark's role in it as a predator. • Explain that sharks are generally at the top of a food chain, although killer whales have been known to prey on them. Because sharks are major predators, they keep the populations of the species they prey on in check.	• Higher-level vocabulary, such as *inhumane* (without humanity, compassion, or kindness), and technical language, such as *vivisection* (operating on a live animal for scientific research), may need defining. • Students will have focused skill lessons on using context clues and determining the meaning of technical language after the First Read.

SCAFFOLDS  **ENGLISH LANGUAGE LEARNERS**  **APPROACHING GRADE LEVEL**  **BEYOND GRADE LEVEL**

These icons identify differentiation strategies and scaffolded support for a variety of students. See the digital lesson plan for additional differentiation strategies and scaffolds.

Instructional Path

The print teacher's edition includes essential point-of-use instruction and planning tools. Complete lesson plans and program documents appear in your digital teacher account.

First Read: The Day I Saved a Life

Objectives: After an initial reading and discussion of the informational text, students will be able to identify and restate the text's key ideas and details.

Skill: Context Clues

Objectives: After rereading and discussing a model of close reading, students will be able to use context clues, such as definition, comparison, contrast, and examples, to clarify the meanings of words.

Skill: Technical Language

Objectives: After rereading and discussing a model of close reading, students will be able to identify and determine the meaning of technical language in a text.

Close Read: The Day I Saved a Life

Objectives: After engaging in a close reading and discussion of the text, students will be able to tell of an experience with a subject and use technical language from the subject in a short, written response.

Progress Monitoring

Opportunities to Learn	Opportunities to Demonstrate Learning	Opportunities to Reteach
Context Clues		
Skill: Context Clues	Skill: Context Clues • Your Turn Close Read • Complete Vocabulary Chart • Skills Focus • Write	Spotlight Skill: Context Clues
Technical Language		
Skill: Technical Language	Skill: Technical Language • Your Turn Close Read • Complete Vocabulary Chart • Skills Focus • Write	Unit 4 Skill: Technical Language - Cover Letter to LucasArts Unit 6 Skill: Technical Language - Everybody Out (from 'What If?') Spotlight Skill: Technical Language

First Read

Introduce the Text

As a class, watch the video preview  and have students read the introduction in pairs to make connections to the video preview.

To activate prior knowledge and experiences, ask students:

- What key words or images from the video do you think will be most important to the text you are about to read?

ELL SPEAKING FRAMES

- The ____ in the video makes me think ____.
- The video shows ____. This makes me wonder ____.
- I think the text will ____. I think this because ____.
- I predict that there will be ____. I believe this because ____.

Entry Point

As students prepare to read "The Day I Saved a Life," share the following information with them to provide context.

- ✓ There are more than 500 species of sharks, ranging in size from hand length to 39 feet long. Half of all shark species are less than one yard long. A person is more likely to be killed by lightning than by a shark. It is estimated fishing practices kill 100 million sharks each year.
- ✓ A green flash is an optical phenomenon that sometimes occurs at sunset or sunrise, especially over ocean waters. As the upper edge of the sun touches the horizon, a green spot of light flashes, caused by refraction in Earth's atmosphere.
- ✓ *Vivisection*, while literally meaning "live cutting," is sometimes applied to all experimentation on live animals. Some people believe such experimentation is necessary to advance medical knowledge; others oppose it entirely as cruel. Those in the middle advocate restricting animal experimentation to essential medical research, using alternative methods when possible, and eliminating unnecessarily cruel practices.

"I swear the shark looked at me with gratitude. He was alive because I spoke up for him and he knew it."

Skill: Technical Language

Fossilized is technical language. The context tells me fossilized teeth are really old. The dictionary definition of fossilized supports this: "to change into a fossil," which is "the remains or trace of an ancient life form." Now I know both fossil and fossilized.

Skill: Context Clues

I'm not sure what a scooper is, but it's a noun because my comes before it. He uses it to dig into the sand. I see scoop in scooper, and later he uses scoop to mean the same thing. It must be a tool used to scoop up sand.

1 We've all seen Hollywood's depiction of sharks, the media's over-dramatization of shark attacks and felt that pit in our stomach at the sight of a shark. Movies like *Jaws*, *Day of the Shark*, *Shark Night*, *Deep Blue Sea*, etc., give us the impression of a mindless killing machine out to kill all human beings. Well, I've seen another side of the shark and I've seen it up close and personal.

2 It all started on December 16, 2011, my birthday. My family took me to Venice Beach, which is also known as Shark Tooth Beach. This was the trip I had been waiting for. I had seen this location on the Discovery Channel over a year ago and had wanted to go ever since. Having the opportunity to find fossilized shark teeth that have been in the waters for over millions of years was something I was **ecstatic** about! When we arrived at our destination, I was amazed at all the sights, sounds and smells. The water was crystal clear and blue and the sand was so warm between my toes. The occasional breeze whisked my mind away to a beautiful tropical paradise. It was a perfect day to go sifting for shark teeth. I walked into the water up to my knees, sifter in hand, and began sifting. I dug my scooper into the sand, beneath the water, and pulled up many small teeth. I found great white teeth, bull shark teeth, tiger shark teeth and a few I was unsure about, it was amazing. Then it happened. I hit the jackpot! I discovered in my scoop the largest tooth I had ever seen. It was four inches long and black in color. Its edges were serrated and you could still see the gum line. The great white teeth I found paled in comparison to this massive tooth. It was a Megalodon tooth! My dream had come true, I had found one! This was the best birthday present I could have ever gotten, or so I thought.

3 As we were leaving the beach, a friendly local told us about a pier close by that was a perfect place to watch the sunset. I was determined to see the green flash that everyone talks about when the sun sets. We headed back to our hotel to change and then went straight to the pier. The view from the pier was miraculous. The skies were clear and the weather was perfect for being outside, not too hot and there was a cool breeze coming off the water. As we watched the sunset, the sky turned orange and pink as the sun went down. It was absolutely breathtaking! In the water we saw dolphins swimming and a man painting sea turtles at the edge of the pier. It was a night right out of a novel.

SELECTION VOCABULARY

ecstatic / eufórico/a ***adjective*** feeling overwhelming joy or excitement

- What is the author talking about when he uses the word *ecstatic*?

keystone / la especie clave ***adjective*** a group of organisms essential to an ecosystem

Analyze Vocabulary Using Context Clues

In paragraph 4, focus on the sentence that uses the word *keystone*. Point out these context clues:

1. I know that predators prey on, or eat, other animals, and *keystone* is an adjective describing *predator*. I think *keystone* means something like "important," maybe even "essential"—something the environment depends on
2. When I read the sentence again, using *essential* in place of *keystone*, the sentence makes sense: "I told him how sharks are *essential* predators."

Technical Language

What technical term did the reader notice, and how did she first determine its meaning?

The reader noticed *fossilized* and first used context to determine its meaning.

Context Clues

How does the reader determine the part of speech of the word *scooper*?

The reader notices that the word *my* comes before *scooper*, which suggests the scooper is a thing. A word that is a thing must be a noun.

TEXT TALK

What is the author doing at the beginning of the day he writes about?

See paragraph 2: It's his birthday, and he goes to the beach with his family to look for shark teeth.

Skills Focus

QUESTION 5: Connect to Essential Question

Ponce steps in and tries everything he can do to persuade the fisherman not to kill the shark. That was taking a chance because who knows how the fisherman would react, and he still might go ahead and kill the shark anyway. I'd like to think I would have done the same thing, but I'm not sure. Ponce begins to fight for sharks' rights after this experience.

Skills Focus

QUESTION 1: Technical Language

Finning must refer to cutting off the fins of sharks. I don't know why people just want the fins, but it's cruel. It helps prove Ponce's point that sharks need protecting.

Skills Focus

QUESTION 3: Context Clues

If killing sharks in huge numbers brings them close to extinction, then extinction must mean the removal of all sharks from the planet. There would be no more sharks left. That's obviously a negative because, at the very least, it would upset the balance of life in the ocean.

Skills Focus

QUESTION 4: Technical Language

I know vegetarians don't eat meat, but he says now he's a vegan. Maybe that's taking it one step further and not eating anything from an animal. I'll check this in a dictionary. Using this term supports his argument for protecting animals.

NOTES

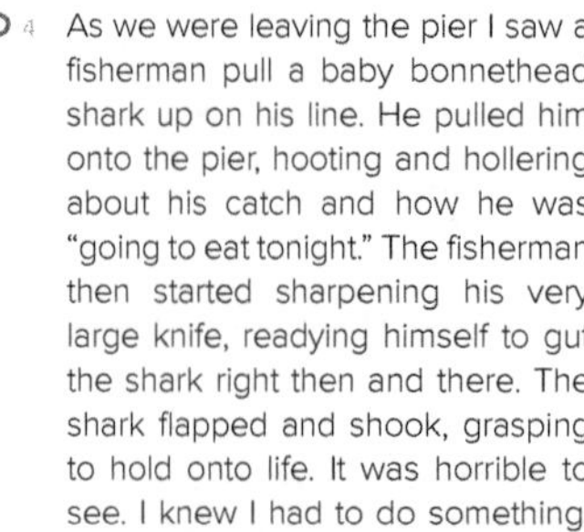

4 As we were leaving the pier I saw a fisherman pull a baby bonnethead shark up on his line. He pulled him onto the pier, hooting and hollering about his catch and how he was "going to eat tonight." The fisherman then started sharpening his very large knife, readying himself to gut the shark right then and there. The shark flapped and shook, grasping to hold onto life. It was horrible to see. I knew I had to do something, so I approached the fisherman and asked him to set the shark free. I explained how it was a living creature, a baby with a family and that it deserved to live. I explained to him the important role sharks play in our ecosystem. I pleaded with him to free him and not eat him. I even offered to buy him dinner. I told him how sharks are **keystone** species and how they keep the ocean ecosystem in balance; I explained about their slow reproductive rate and how we needed every shark in the ocean to keep it healthy. I explained how the effects of removing sharks would be felt throughout the ecosystem like a domino effect. I was not letting up, I knew I had to keep fighting for that shark. After what seemed like an eternity, the fisherman finally **conceded** and told me that I could set him free. I couldn't believe it, I did it! I immediately walked over, picked up the shark and placed him back into the water and told him to live free. I swear the shark looked at me with gratitude. He was alive because I spoke up for him and he knew it. I saw the understanding in his eyes and knew there was much more to sharks than what I had been led to believe.

One of a pair of new Bonnethead sharks at Chessington World of Adventures, Surrey, England

5 That day changed me forever and now I fight for sharks' rights. I have always been an active animal and environmental advocate and a vegetarian and now vegan. I had run many fundraisers for farm animals and for spaying and neutering your pets. I had leafletted about animals in captivity and in **vivisection** labs; I had signed petitions against animal cruelty and protested at various sites where cruelty had been taking place, but until that day I hadn't really concentrated my efforts on sharks. I started doing some research and I watched a documentary called *Sharkwater* and it gave me insight into the plight of the shark. It showed me the horrors they faced due to finning. They were being killed in huge quantities for their fins and were becoming extremely close to extinction. The sharks are stripped of their fins then discarded, while still alive, back into the ocean. It was a horrible discovery and one that moved me to act and speak up for the sharks. From that moment on, I have dedicated myself to making as many people aware of what's going on with sharks as I can. My hope is that through educating people on the cruel and inhumane acts being done to sharks and by explaining the importance of sharks to the ocean ecosystem, as well as our own environment,

TEXT TALK

What happens in the evening at the pier?

See paragraph 4: A fisherman catches a shark and is going to kill it, but the author persuades him not to.

What does the author do now as a result of that incident?

See paragraph 5: He is an advocate for sharks' rights.

SELECTION VOCABULARY

conceded / admitir *verb* to surrender or give up

 ELL • What does the fisherman do after he concedes?

vivisection / la vivisección *noun* dissecting a living body for scientific research COGNATE

 ELL • What has the writer leafletted and signed petitions about?

that I can make a difference in helping to preserve this beautiful species. I hope to one day soon be speaking at Congress on behalf of sharks and **lobbying** to bring change to the finning laws in our country.

6 December 16, 2011 the ocean gave me two gifts, a Megalodon tooth and an appreciation and love of sharks. In return, I gave it back one of its own and a voice that could be heard and would never be silenced.

By Thomas Ponce, President and Founder of Lobby For Animals. Used by permission of Thomas Ponce.

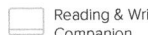

SELECTION VOCABULARY

lobby / cabildear *verb* to try to influence a politician on behalf of a cause

- Why will the speaker be lobbying?

TEXT TALK

What did Thomas Ponce see in sharks that other people overlooked? What does this teach you about being misunderstood?

Answers will vary.

Think Questions

Circulate as students answer Think Questions independently. Scaffolds for these questions are shown on the opposite page.

QUESTION 1: Textual Evidence

The author gets ecstatic just at the thought of finding fossilized shark teeth. More important, he saves the life of a shark. He persuades a fisherman not to kill the shark by explaining how important sharks are to the ocean ecosystem. He also speaks up for sharks by educating people about them and intending to lobby Congress to pass laws protecting them from finning.

QUESTION 2: Textual Evidence

The description of the evening at the pier creates a peaceful and beautiful scene with words and phrases like "miraculous," "skies were clear," "the sky turned pink and orange," and "breathtaking." The images of dolphins swimming and a man painting add to the quiet nature of the scene. This peace is broken and in sharp contrast to what follows: a fisherman catching a shark, "hollering" about eating it, and getting ready to kill it with a knife.

QUESTION 3: Textual Evidence

On December 16, 2011, the author became an advocate for shark's rights. He had always worked to protect animals; from that day on, he concentrated his efforts on doing research about sharks and then educating people on the need to protect sharks—particularly from the finning industry.

QUESTION 4: Context Clues

The author says that going to Shark Tooth Beach "was the trip I had been waiting for." He calls it an "opportunity" and ends the sentence with an exclamation point, so *ecstatic* must mean "very happy."

QUESTION 5: Context Clues

The fisherman was going to kill the shark, but after the author keep trying to persuade him not to, he "conceded" and let the shark go free. So *conceded* probably means something like "agreed." An online dictionary says *concede* means "admit to be true" but also includes "agree," so my meaning was close.

First Read

Read "The Day I Saved a Life." After you read, complete the Think Questions below.

THINK QUESTIONS

1. How does the author show his love of sharks? Provide specific examples from the text.
2. What effect does the author's sensory description of the beautiful evening at the pier have on the story? What is its function in the text? Use specific evidence from the text to support your answer.
3. What changed specifically for the author on this particular day? How was his life different afterward? Provide specific examples from the text.
4. Based on the context, what do you think the word **ecstatic** means? Write your definition here, and indicate which context clues informed your thinking.
5. Use context clues to determine the meaning of the word **concede** as it used in the text. Write your definition of *concede* here, and state which clues from the text helped you determine the answer. Confirm your definition using a print or online dictionary.

SCAFFOLDS

Think Questions

Use the scaffolds below to differentiate instruction for your ELL English Language Learners and A Approaching grade-level learners.

ELL **BEGINNING** Write a response using the word bank and sentence frames.

INTERMEDIATE Write a response using the sentence frames.

ADVANCED, ADVANCED HIGH Write a response using the Text-Dependent Question Guide.

A **APPROACHING** Write a response using the Text-Dependent Question Guide.

BEGINNING	INTERMEDIATE	APPROACHING / ADVANCED, ADVANCED HIGH
Word Bank	**Sentence Frames**	**Text-Dependent Question Guide**
life contrast rights happy admit ecstatic important peaceful lobby waiting protecting ends	The author gets ____ about finding shark teeth. He saves the ____ of a shark. He talks to people about ____ sharks.	1. • What event does the title refer to? • How does the author react to going to Shark Tooth Beach? • What does the author do now concerning sharks?
	The description of the evening creates a ____ scene. The quiet ____ when the fisherman catches a shark. This event is a ____ to the peace.	2. • What are some words and phrases that describe the evening on the pier? • What feeling do these images create? • What happens as the author is leaving the pier? • What effect does this event have?
	On December 16, 2011, the author began to work for sharks' ____. He wants to ____ for laws to stop finning.	3. • What did the author do before December 16, 2011? • What has he done since then? • What specifically changed?
	The author says that he had been ____ for the trip. He really wants to find shark teeth. This is a clue that *ecstatic* means "very ____."	4. • Read: "This was the trip I had been waiting for," "had wanted to go ever since," and "opportunity." • How does the author feel about going to the beach? • What does *ecstatic* likely mean?
	The author told the fisherman that sharks were ____. The fisherman conceded and set the shark free. This is a clue that *concede* means "____ to be true," or "agree."	5. • Read: "I explained how the effects of removing sharks would be felt throughout the ecosystem like a domino effect. I was not letting up, I knew I had to keep fighting for that shark. After what seemed like an eternity, the fisherman finally **conceded** and told me that I could set him free." • What was the fisherman going to do with the shark? • What did he do after he conceded? • What does *conceded* likely mean?

Reading Comprehension OPTIONAL

Have students complete the digital reading comprehension questions ✓ when they finish reading.

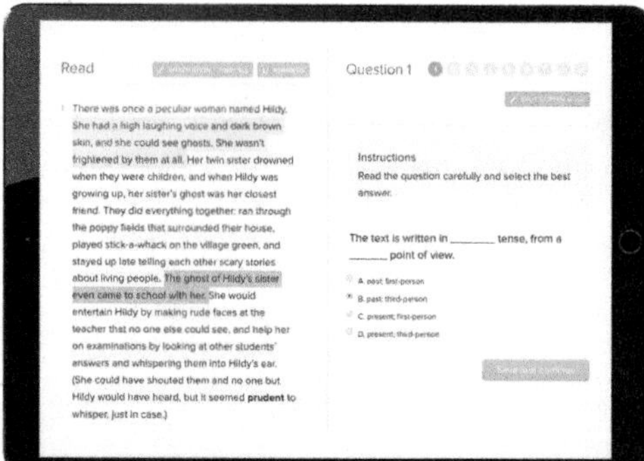

ANSWER KEY

QUESTION 1: C
QUESTION 2: A
QUESTION 3: D
QUESTION 4: A
QUESTION 5: C
QUESTION 6: A
QUESTION 7: C
QUESTION 8: D
QUESTION 9:
See first chart.
QUESTION 10:
See second chart.

Definition	Word
feeling overwhelming happiness or excitement	ecstatic
something on which associated things depend	keystone
to surrender, yield	concede
the practice of performing operations of live animals for scientific research	vivisection
to seek to influence a politician about an issue	lobby

First	Second	Third	Fourth	Fifth
The narrator enjoys the sights, sounds, and smells of Shark Tooth Beach.	The narrator finds a Megalodon tooth.	A fisherman pulls a baby Bonnethead shark up on his line.	As it is set free, the shark looks back gratefully at the narrator.	The narrator learns more about the plight of sharks from a documentary.

Connect and Extend OPTIONAL

CONNECT TO EXTENDED WRITING PROJECT

Students can find inspiration from "The Day I Saved a Life" when writing their informational essays. Have them reflect on Thomas Ponce's decision to take action about sharks.

BEYOND THE BOOK

Research: Going Vegan

In his essay, Thomas Ponce says that he is vegan. Have your students conduct research about what it means to be vegan. Veganism can be a broad subject, so consider having students choose one of the following as a basis for their research:

- Following a vegan, or plant-based, diet that abstains from all animal products (meat, fish, dairy, honey, etc.) because of animal rights.
- Being vegan because you're an environmental advocate.
- Eating a vegan diet for health reasons.
- Promoting veganism in different aspects of life (vegan cosmetics, accessories, clothes, etc.) as a stand against animal cruelty.

Have students present their research. In addition, you may also choose to have your students give their opinions about adopting a vegan lifestyle. Their opinions may accompany their research in order to have a classroom discussion or debate.

To reflect, ask students:

- Why do people choose to be vegan?
- What effects can veganism have on the world?
- Do you think veganism will continue to gain in popularity? Why or why not?

Skill: Context Clues

Use the Checklist to analyze Context Clues in "The Day I Saved a Life." Refer to the sample student annotations about Context Clues in the text.

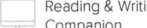

••• CHECKLIST FOR CONTEXT CLUES

In order to use context as a clue to infer the meaning of a word or phrase, note the following:

- ✓ clues about the word's part of speech
- ✓ clues about the word's meaning in the surrounding text
- ✓ signal words that cue a type of context clue, such as:
  - *for example* or *for instance* to signal an example clue
  - *like, similarly,* or *just as* to signal a comparison clue
  - *but, however,* or *unlike* to signal a contrast clue

To determine the meaning of a word or phrase as it is used in a text, consider the following questions:

- ✓ What is the overall sentence, paragraph, or text about?
- ✓ How does the word function in the sentence?
- ✓ What clues can help me determine the word's part of speech?
- ✓ What text clues can help me figure out the word's definition?
- ✓ Are there any examples that show what the word means?
- ✓ What do I think the word means?

To verify the preliminary determination of the meaning of the word or phrase based on context, consider the following questions:

- ✓ Does the definition I inferred make sense within the context of the sentence?
- ✓ Which of the dictionary's definitions makes sense within the context of the sentence?

SKILL VOCABULARY

context clue / la clave del contexto ***noun*** a hint in the surrounding text that can help a reader infer the meaning of an unfamiliar word, phrase, or description

infer / inferir ***verb*** to determine something by using reasoning and evidence from the text COGNATE

definition context clue / la clave del contexto de definición ***noun*** text that provides a definition of a word

Skill: Context Clues

Introduce the Skill

Watch the Concept Definition video ▶ and read the following definition with your students.

When readers come across words they don't know, they often use context to determine the meanings of the unfamiliar words. **Context clues** are hints in the surrounding text that a reader can use to **infer** the meaning of an unfamiliar word. Some common types of context clues include the following:

- **Definition:** an explanation of the word's meaning before or after the word appears, usually set off by a comma
- **Example:** one or more examples in a text that may demonstrate the meaning of a word
- **Comparison**: determining a word's meaning based on how it is like something else in the text
- **Contrast**: determining a word's meaning based on how it is unlike something else in the text

In addition, the genre of a text and what it is about also provide context clues for a word's meaning. Readers can verify their preliminary definitions of words or phrases by using a print or digital resource.

TURN AND TALK

1. What are context clues?
2. What are four different types of context clues?

SPEAKING FRAMES

- Context clues are ____.
- A reader uses context clues to ____.
- One type of context clue is ____.
- It provides a clue to the meaning of a word through ____.

Your Turn

Ask students to complete the Your Turn activity.

QUESTION 1

A. Incorrect. This is not the meaning of the phrase "domino effect."

B. Correct. With a "domino effect," one thing causes another to happen, which in turn causes another, and so on, like lined-up dominoes falling one after the other once you push over the first one.

C. Incorrect. This is not the meaning of the phrase "domino effect."

D. Incorrect. This is not the meaning of the phrase "domino effect."

QUESTION 2

A. Incorrect. This quote does not contain context suggesting the meaning of "domino effect."

B. Incorrect. This quote does not contain context suggesting the meaning of "domino effect."

C. Correct. This quote is a context clue that removing sharks affects other parts of the ecosystem.

D. Incorrect. This quote does not contain context suggesting the meaning of "domino effect."

QUESTION 3

A. Incorrect. The context after *conceded* does not suggest that the fisherman refused.

B. Incorrect. The context after *conceded* does not suggest that the fisherman argued.

C. Correct. The context clue "the fisherman finally . . . told me that I could set him free" helps you infer that *conceded* means the fisherman gave up on wanting to kill the shark and let the author free it.

D. Incorrect. The context after *conceded* does not suggest that the fisherman refused.

The Day I Saved a Life

Skill: Context Clues

Reread paragraph 4 of "The Day I Saved a Life." Then, using the Checklist on the previous page, answer the multiple-choice questions below.

YOUR TURN

1. What is the meaning of "domino effect"? Use context clues to figure out what the phrase means.

   ○ A. Killing is a serious thing and not to be taken lightly, like a game.
   ○ B. If one thing happens, it will cause another, and so on.
   ○ C. One good turn deserves another.
   ○ D. The world is a complex place, intricately structured.

2. Which quote from the text best supports the reasoning you used in question 1?

   ○ A. "The shark flapped and shook, grasping to hold onto life. It was horrible to see."
   ○ B. "I was not letting up, I knew I had to keep fighting for that shark."
   ○ C. "I explained to him the important role sharks play in our ecosystem. . . . I explained how the effects of removing sharks would be felt throughout the ecosystem."
   ○ D. "I swear the shark looked at me with gratitude. He was alive because I spoke up for him and he knew it."

3. What is the meaning of *conceded* as it used in the paragraph? Use context clues to figure out what the word means.

   ○ A. refused
   ○ B. argued
   ○ C. gave up
   ○ D. insisted

SKILL VOCABULARY

example context clue / la clave del contexto de ejemplo ***noun*** text that provides a clue to the meaning of a word through one or more examples

comparison context clue / la clave del contexto de comparación ***noun*** text that provides a clue to the meaning of a word through a comparison

contrast context clue / la clave del contexto de contraste ***noun*** text that provides a clue to the meaning of a word through a contrast

Skill: Technical Language

Use the Checklist to analyze Technical Language in "The Day I Saved a Life." Refer to the sample student annotations about Technical Language in the text.

••• CHECKLIST FOR TECHNICAL LANGUAGE

In order to determine the meaning of words and phrases as they are used in a text, note the following:

- ✓ the subject of the book or article
- ✓ any unfamiliar words that you think might be technical terms
- ✓ words that have multiple meanings that change when used with a specific subject
- ✓ the possible contextual meaning of a word, or the definition from a dictionary

To determine the meaning of words and phrases as they are used in a text, including technical meanings, consider the following questions:

- ✓ What is the subject of the informational text?
- ✓ How does the use of technical language help establish the author as an authority on the subject?
- ✓ Are there any technical words that have an impact on the meaning and tone, or quality, of the book or article?
- ✓ Does the writer use analogies, or a comparison between two things for the purpose of explanation or clarification? What impact do they have on your understanding of the subject?
- ✓ Does the writer use any allusions to another topic or subject as a way to explain something? What impact do they have on the author's treatment of the main subject?

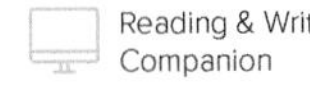

SKILL VOCABULARY

technical language / el lenguaje técnico ***noun*** words that are used in certain fields of knowledge, such as astronomy or computer science COGNATE

subject / la materia ***noun*** an area of knowledge to study

precise / preciso/a ***adjective*** clearly defined and accurate COGNATE

authority / la autoridad ***noun*** the power or right to give orders or make decisions; the power to be in charge COGNATE

Skill: Technical Language

Introduce the Skill

Watch the Concept Definition video and read the following definition with your students.

Technical language refers to words that are used in certain fields of knowledge. The **subject** is the field of knowledge the author writes about, such as astronomy or computer science, and it is an important part of determining the meaning of technical language. For example, if you know that archaeologists study human history based on things found in ancient ruins, and you read that an archaeologist has discovered an important artifact, you can guess that in this context the word *artifact* refers to an object made by a human being, usually an item of cultural or historical interest. Writers include technical language to educate readers, to make their explanation more **precise** and accurate, or to establish their **authority** on a subject. When a writer is being precise, they must be detailed but straightforward in their explanations of complex ideas and concepts. Being an authority, or expert, on a subject gives the writer credibility with readers.

TURN AND TALK

1. What is a particular subject you are interested in?
2. What are some terms that only people who know about that subject area will likely be familiar with?

SPEAKING FRAMES

- I am interested in the subject of ____.
- A word in that subject area is ____.
- Another word from that subject is ____.

Your Turn

Ask students to complete the Your Turn activity.

QUESTION 1

A. Incorrect. This is not the meaning of the technical term *ecosystem*.

B. Correct. An ecosystem consists of all the living organisms in a particular environment and their interactions with one another.

C. Incorrect. This is not the meaning of the technical term *ecosystem*.

D. Incorrect. This is not the meaning of the technical term *ecosystem*.

QUESTION 2

A. Incorrect. A keystone species is not an animal that eats both plants and animals.

B. Incorrect. A keystone species is not an animal that can survive in only one place.

C. Incorrect. A keystone species is not an animal that preys constantly and never stops hunting.

D. Correct. If a keystone species is removed from its environment, the environment changes drastically.

QUESTION 3

A. Incorrect. The fact that the shark tried to hold on to its life does not relate to its being a keystone species.

B. Incorrect. The fact that the shark is alive does not relate to its being a keystone species.

C. Incorrect. The fact that the shark has a slow reproductive rate does not relate to its being a keystone species.

D. Correct. This information helps explain what a keystone species is.

Skill: Technical Language

Reread paragraph 4 of "The Day I Saved a Life." Then, using the Checklist on the previous page, answer the multiple-choice questions below.

YOUR TURN

1. What is the meaning of the technical term *ecosystem*?

    - A. the world's oceans and the flow of water between them
    - B. the network of animals and plants that interact in an environment
    - C. a species of animal that lives in one place
    - D. planet Earth and all the living things on it

2. What is the meaning of the technical term *keystone species*?

    - A. an animal that eats both plants and animals
    - B. an animal that can survive in only one place
    - C. an animal that preys constantly and never stops hunting
    - D. an animal that plays a crucial role in its environment

3. Which quote from the text best supports the reasoning you used in question 2?

    - A. "The shark flapped and shook, grasping to hold onto life."
    - B. "I explained how it was a living creature, a baby with a family"
    - C. "I explained about their slow reproductive rate"
    - D. "I explained how the effects of removing sharks would be felt throughout the ecosystem"

Close Read

Reread "The Day I Saved a Life." As you reread, complete the Skills Focus questions below. Then use your answers and annotations from the questions to help you complete the Write activity.

SKILLS FOCUS

1. Explain the meaning of *finning* in paragraph 5, and discuss how and why this technical term helps make Ponce's argument more meaningful and gives it more of an impact.
2. Use context clues to determine the meaning of *jackpot*. How does this help to describe Ponce's discoveries? Does it make everything else he describes seem more important or less so? Use specific evidence from the text to support your answer.
3. Use context clues to determine the meaning of *extinction*. Is this word positive or negative? Is it contrasted with any other word in the text? How does it compare to the rest of the text that surrounds it? Use specific evidence from the text to support your response.
4. What is the meaning of the technical term *vegan*? Does it help Ponce's argument to use this term? Why or why not? Cite specific evidence from the text to support your answer.
5. What was risky about Thomas Ponce's actions? Would you have made the same decision that he did? Why or why not? What does Ponce seem to have learned from his experience?

WRITE

NARRATIVE: Using Ponce's essay as a point of reference, write a persuasive narrative essay where you defend a subject about which you are passionate. Be sure to include technical language where applicable, as this can lend authority to your opinions and ideas.

Close Read

Skills Focus

QUESTION 1: Technical Language

See paragraph 5.

QUESTION 2: Context Clues

See paragraph 2: Hitting the jackpot is obviously a good thing because he equates it with finding a huge tooth, which is important to him. It must be like the biggest prize.

QUESTION 3: Context Clues

See paragraph 5.

QUESTION 4: Technical Language

See paragraph 5.

QUESTION 5: Connect to Essential Question

See paragraph 4.

CHECK FOR SUCCESS

If students struggle to respond to Skills Focus question 1, ask them the following questions:

1. Which sentence in paragraph 5 helps explain what finning is?
2. How do you feel when you read about finning?

Writer's Notebook

Connect to Essential Question: Give students time to reflect on how "The Day I Saved a Life" connects to the unit's essential question "Why do we take chances?" by freewriting in their Writer's Notebooks.

Beginning & Intermediate

Read aloud the unit's essential question: "Why do we take chances?" Encourage students to draw their connections or allow students to write in their native language. Circulate the room, prompting students for their thoughts as they respond orally or through pantomime.

Advanced & Advanced High

Allow students to share their connections orally in pairs or small groups before freewriting.

Collaborative Conversation

Break students into collaborative conversation groups to discuss the Close Read prompt. Ask students to use the StudySyncTV episode as a model for their discussion. Remind them to reference their Skills Focus annotations in their discussion.

Using Ponce's essay as a point of reference, write a persuasive narrative essay where you defend a subject about which you are passionate. Be sure to include technical language where applicable, as this can lend authority to your opinions and ideas.

Use the scaffolds below to differentiate instruction for your ELL English Language Learners and A Approaching grade-level learners.

ELL **BEGINNING, INTERMEDIATE** Use the discussion guide and speaking frames to facilitate the discussion with support from the teacher.

ADVANCED, ADVANCED HIGH Use the discussion guide and speaking frames to facilitate the discussion in mixed-level groups.

A **APPROACHING** Use the discussion guide to facilitate the discussion in mixed-level groups.

APPROACHING
ADVANCED, ADVANCED HIGH
BEGINNING, INTERMEDIATE

Discussion Guide	Speaking Frames
1. What subject area does Ponce talk about?	• The subject area is ____.
2. What happened to Ponce that led him to learn about this subject?	• Ponce met a fisherman who ____. • Ponce tried to persuade the fisherman to ____.
3. What role does technical language have in Ponce's essay?	• Technical language in the essay includes ____. • This language helps Ponce ____.

Review Prompt and Rubric

Before students begin writing, review the writing prompt and rubric with the class.

NARRATIVE: Using Ponce's essay as a point of reference, write a persuasive narrative essay where you defend a subject about which you are passionate. Be sure to include technical language where applicable, as this can lend authority to your opinions and ideas.

ELL PROMPT GUIDE

A
- What subject area does Ponce talk about?
- What happened to Ponce that led him to learn about this subject?
- What role does technical language have in Ponce's essay?
- Like Ponce's essay, what can you write your essay about?
- What technical language can you use?

Score	Technical Language	Language and Conventions
4	The writer effectively defends a subject about which he or she is passionate. The writer skillfully includes technical language that lends authority to his or her words.	The writer demonstrates a consistent command of grammar, punctuation, and usage conventions. Although minor errors may be evident, they do not detract from the fluency or the clarity of the writing.
3	The writer defends a subject about which he or she is passionate. The writer includes some technical language that lends authority to his or her words.	The writer demonstrates an adequate command of grammar, punctuation, and usage conventions. Although some errors may be evident, they create few (if any) disruptions in the fluency or clarity of the writing.
2	The writer attempts to defend a subject about which he or she is passionate but is not entirely successful. The writer includes one or two examples of technical language.	The writer demonstrates a partial command of grammar, punctuation, and usage conventions. Some distracting errors may be evident, at times creating minor disruptions in the fluency or clarity of the writing.
1	The writer does not successfully defend a subject about which he or she is passionate. The writer includes no technical language.	The writer demonstrates little or no command of grammar, punctuation, and usage conventions. Serious and persistent errors create disruptions in the fluency of the writing and sometimes interfere with meaning.
0	The writer does not provide a relevant response to the prompt or does not provide a response at all.	Serious and persistent errors overwhelm the writing and interfere with the meaning of the response as a whole, making the writer's meaning impossible to understand.

Write

SCAFFOLDS

Ask students to complete the writing assignment using textual evidence to support their answers.

Use the scaffolds below to differentiate instruction for your ELL English Language Learners and A Approaching grade-level learners.

ELL **BEGINNING** With the help of the word bank, write a response using paragraph frame 1.

INTERMEDIATE With the help of the word bank, write a response using paragraph frames 1 and 2.

ADVANCED, ADVANCED HIGH Write a response of differentiated length using the sentence starters.

A **APPROACHING** Write a response of differentiated length using the sentence starters.

BEGINNING / INTERMEDIATE	BEGINNING / INTERMEDIATE	INTERMEDIATE	ADVANCED, ADVANCED HIGH / APPROACHING
Word Bank	**Paragraph Frame 1**	**Paragraph Frame 2**	**Sentence Starters**
plastic effect reused ecosystems ecstatic	One time I went to the store with my mother. We ____ our own bags. Many people did not. They got ____ bags. I saw plastic bags blowing around the parking lot. Some were stuck in trees. Plastic bags have a negative ____. I learned they can harm ____. Now I work hard to ban plastic bags. I will be ____ when plastic bags are banned.	I am passionate about this subject because ____. Now I understand that ____. I hope ____.	• One time I . . . • What happened next was . . . • I learned that . . . • Now I am passionate about . . .

Peer Review

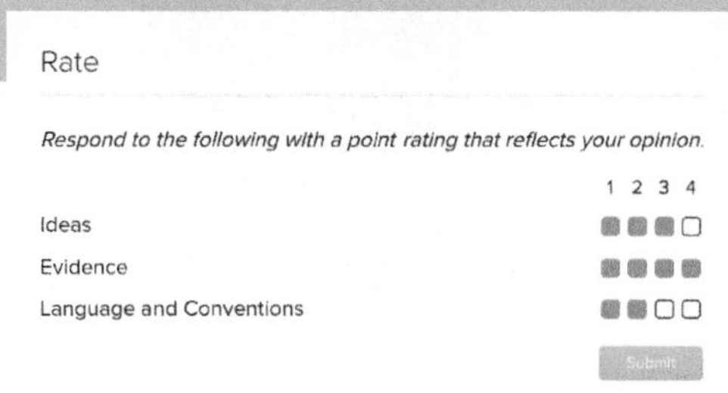

Students should submit substantive feedback to two peers using the review instructions below.

- How well does this response answer the prompt?
- How well does the writer defend a subject with a personal narrative?
- Does the essay use technical language that lends authority to the writer?
- What did the writer do well in this response? What does the writer need to work on?

SENTENCE FRAMES

A

- You were able to (completely / partly / almost) answer the prompt because ____.
- You could answer the prompt better by ____.
- You could make the essay sound more persuasive by ____.
- You might also include the technical term ____.
- My favorite part of your essay is ____.

The Call of the Wild

FICTION
Jack London
1903

Introduction

studysync tv

Author Jack London (1876–1916) was a writer and adventurer, beginning his life in the San Francisco Bay area, and then traveling the world—seal hunting in the Far East, mucking for gold in the Yukon Territory, sailing the South Pacific, and more. While participating in the Klondike Gold Rush, he reportedly encountered a mythical wolf that served as the inspiration for *The Call of the Wild*, his most popular novel. The book details the adventures of Buck, a large and powerful St. Bernard mix, as he experiences both love and abuse from a succession of owners. In this excerpt, Buck, by now a sled dog, stirs up rebellion among the team when he stands up to the aggressive alpha dog, Spitz.

In this excerpt, Buck, a sled dog, stirs up rebellion among the team after he stands up to the aggressive alpha dog, Spitz. Traveling across the Yukon, the team is making great progress, but their driver Francois has trouble keeping the dogs in line. Due to Buck's rebelliousness, the rest of the team has begun to challenge Spitz, stealing his fish and starting fights. Francois knows that Buck is the instigator, but Buck is too clever to be caught causing trouble. When he is in the harness, he runs tirelessly. One night after supper, the dogs catch sight of a rabbit and proceed to chase it. Even though the rabbit continues to stay one step ahead, Buck is ecstatic living in the moment. Driven only by his instincts, Buck is aglow with happiness.

ELL Proficiency-leveled summaries and summaries in multiple languages are available digitally.

Audio and audio text highlighting are available with this text.

CONNECT TO ESSENTIAL QUESTION

Why do we take chances?

In Jack London's classic novel *The Call of the Wild*, the sled dog Buck stirs up a rebellion when he risks standing up to the aggressive alpha dog, Spitz.

Access Complex Text

LEXILE: 1160L WORD COUNT: 759

The following areas may be challenging for students, particularly ELL English Language Learners and A Approaching grade-level learners.

Prior Knowledge	Sentence Structure	Organization
• Students unfamiliar with Alaska and snowy climates may struggle to visualize the setting. • Students who have never seen a dogsled may not understand the significance of the dogs not getting along with one another.	• The combination of compound sentences and complex sentences in some paragraphs will challenge students. • Visualizing the actions may help students understand what is being described in compound sentences and complex sentences.	• Students may find it confusing that the viewpoints of the dogs are included in places. • The description of various incidents among the dogs may cause students to struggle with tracking the chronology of events.

SCAFFOLDS ELL ENGLISH LANGUAGE LEARNERS  APPROACHING GRADE LEVEL  BEYOND GRADE LEVEL

These icons identify differentiation strategies and scaffolded support for a variety of students. See the digital lesson plan for additional differentiation strategies and scaffolds.

Instructional Path

The print teacher's edition includes essential point-of-use instruction and planning tools. Complete lesson plans and program documents appear in your digital teacher account.

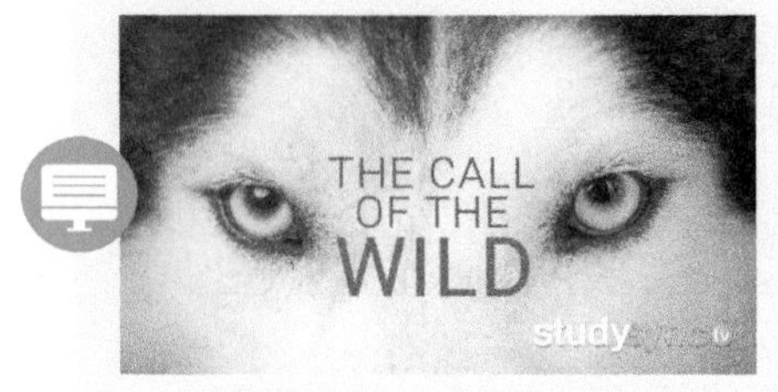

First Read: The Call of the Wild

Objectives: After an initial reading and discussion of the excerpt, students will be able to identify and describe character traits and setting details, as well as articulate the conflict that is integral to the story's plot.

Skill: Language, Style, and Audience

Objectives: After rereading and discussing a model of close reading, students will be able to analyze the impact of specific word choice on meaning and tone in the text.

Skill: Media

Objectives: After rereading and discussing a model of close reading, students will be able to analyze the extent to which a filmed production of a story stays faithful to or departs from the text, and will be able to evaluate the choices made by the director or actors.

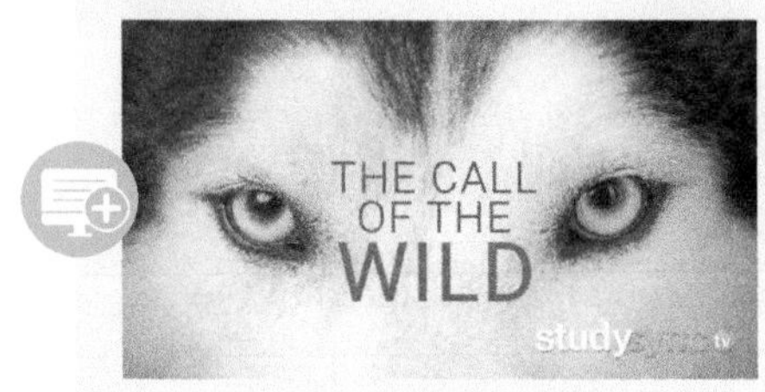

Close Read: The Call of the Wild

Objectives: After engaging in a close reading and discussion of the text, students will be able to write a short response analyzing how word choice affects meaning and tone and how the text aligns with a video version of the same story.

Progress Monitoring

Opportunities to Learn	Opportunities to Demonstrate Learning	Opportunities to Reteach
Language, Style, and Audience		
Skill: Language, Style, and Audience	Skill: Language, Style, and Audience • Your Turn Close Read • Complete Vocabulary Chart • Skills Focus • Write	Unit 4 Skill: Language, Style, and Audience - Speech to the Ohio Women's Conference: Ain't I a Woman? Unit 5 Skill: Language, Style, and Audience - Refugee Spotlight Skill: Language, Style, and Audience
Media		
Skill: Media	Skill: Media • Your Turn Close Read • Skills Focus • Write	Unit 4 Skill: Media - Across Five Aprils Spotlight Skill: Media

First Read

Introduce the Text

As a class, watch the video preview  and have students read the introduction in pairs to make connections to the video preview.

To activate prior knowledge and experiences, ask students:

- What part of the video stood out to you the most?
- What questions do you have after reading the introduction?
- How does this information connect to something you already know?

ELL **SPEAKING FRAMES**

- The ___ in the video makes me think ___.
- The video shows ___. This makes me wonder ___.
- I think the text will ___. I think this because ___.
- I predict that there will be ___. I believe this because ___.

Entry Point

As students prepare to read *The Call of the Wild,* share the following information with them to provide context.

- ✓ Jack London (1876–1916) was a writer who often wrote about adventures in the wilderness. He was born in San Francisco, California, and he moved frequently as a child. He became an avid reader by going to public libraries.
- ✓ London left school at 14 to earn money and go on adventures. He then returned to California to complete his education when he was 19. After completing high school and briefly attending college, London continued to travel. He took part in the Klondike Gold Rush in Alaska and Canada.
- ✓ London did not strike gold, but he dedicated himself to writing once he returned home in 1898. By 1899, magazines began to publish London's short stories about adventures. London's first novel, *The Call of the Wild,* was then published in 1903. It quickly became popular and brought him international fame.

"He was ranging at the head of the pack, running the wild thing down"

NOTES

from Chapter III, The Dominant Primordial Beast

Dog sled in Alaska, circa 1890s

1 They made Sixty Mile, which is a fifty-mile run, on the first day; and the second day saw them booming up the Yukon well on their way to Pelly. But such splendid running was achieved not without great trouble and vexation on the part of Francois. The insidious revolt led by Buck had destroyed the **solidarity** of the team. It no longer was as one dog leaping in the traces. The encouragement Buck gave the rebels led them into all kinds of petty misdemeanors. No more was Spitz a leader greatly to be feared. The old awe departed, and they grew equal to challenging his authority. Pike robbed him of half a fish one night, and gulped it down under the protection of Buck. Another night Dub and Joe fought Spitz and made him forego the punishment they deserved. And even Billee, the good-natured, was less good-natured, and whined not half so **placatingly** as in former days. Buck never came near Spitz without snarling and bristling menacingly. In fact, his conduct approached that of a bully, and he was given to swaggering up and down before Spitz's very nose.

 Skill: Media

In both types of media, Buck's attitude about work changed. In the video, Buck wants to please his master, and so he happily changes his mind. The text is different. Buck seems to enjoy working but also enjoys causing trouble.

2 The breaking down of discipline likewise affected the dogs in their relations with one another. They quarrelled and bickered more than ever among themselves, till at times the camp was a howling bedlam. Dave and Sol-leks alone were unaltered, though they were made irritable by the unending squabbling. Francois swore strange barbarous oaths, and stamped the snow in futile rage, and tore his hair. His lash was always singing among the dogs, but it was of small avail. Directly his back was turned they were at it again. He backed up Spitz with his whip, while Buck backed up the remainder of the team. Francois knew he was behind all the trouble, and Buck knew he knew; but Buck was too clever ever again to be caught red-handed. He worked faithfully in the harness, for the toil had become a delight to him; yet it was a

V SELECTION VOCABULARY

solidarity / la solidaridad *noun* a feeling of being united COGNATE

placatingly / pacíficamente *adverb* to act in a way that causes others to feel less angry

 ELL

- How does a dog with a good nature behave toward other dogs?
- How does this behavior change if other dogs misbehave?

Analyze Vocabulary Using Context Clues

In paragraph 1, focus on the sentence that uses the word *solidarity*. Point out these context clues:

1. I know that solidarity is something the team had, and Buck's revolt destroyed it. I think solidarity is like team work or unity, because it makes sense that a revolt would destroy those things.
2. When I read the sentence again, using *unity* in place of *solidarity*, the sentence makes sense: "The insidious revolt led by Buck had destroyed the *unity* of the team."

Media

What similarity and difference does the reader notice between paragraph 2 of the text and the video?

The reader notices that in both media, Buck has changed. However, the degree to which he has changed varies between the written text and the video.

TEXT TALK

What is the main problem that Francois faces?

See paragraph 1: The dogs pulling his sled do not get along.

Which dog is making the strongest challenge to Spitz's leadership?

See paragraph 1: Buck is strongly challenging Spitz's leadership.

What type of discipline does Francois use unsuccessfully on the dogs? What can you infer about this?

See paragraph 2: He tries to use a whip on the dogs. Force is not what makes the dogs work.

Language, Style, and Audience

What analogy and word choices did the reader notice in the paragraph 3, and how did they affect her understanding of the text?

The reader highlighted the repeated use of "leap by leap" and the analogy referring to "flashed." She said the word choices draw her in and make the story more real and more active.

Skills Focus

QUESTION 2: Language, Style, and Audience

The analogy here compares Buck to both an artist and a soldier. London phrased the comparison this way to help the reader understand what he means by the "ecstasy, this forgetfulness of living." The analogy compares Buck's ecstasy to the passion and intense concentration of an artist caught up in her art, or a soldier in war.

TEXT TALK

Buck is compared to two types of people during the chase. What are they?

See paragraph 5: Buck is compared to an artist and a soldier.

greater delight slyly to **precipitate** a fight amongst his mates and tangle the traces.

3 At the mouth of the Tahkeena, one night after supper, Dub turned up a snowshoe rabbit, blundered it, and missed. In a second the whole team was in full cry. A hundred yards away was a camp of the Northwest Police, with fifty dogs, huskies all, who joined the chase. The rabbit sped down the river, turned off into a small creek, up the frozen bed of which it held steadily. It ran lightly on the surface of the snow, while the dogs ploughed through by main strength. Buck led the pack, sixty strong, around bend after bend, but he could not gain. He lay down low to the race, whining eagerly, his splendid body flashing forward, leap by leap, in the wan white moonlight. And leap by leap, like some pale frost wraith, the snowshoe rabbit flashed on ahead.

Skill: Language, Style, and Audience

The author compares the speed of Buck and the rabbit using "leap by leap" and the word "flashed." Buck's chase of the rabbit comes alive through this analogy. It is written in an active way and draws me into the story.

4 All that stirring of old instincts which at stated periods drives men out from the sounding cities to forest and plain to kill things by chemically **propelled** leaden pellets, the blood lust, the joy to kill—all this was Buck's, only it was infinitely more intimate. He was ranging at the head of the pack, running the wild thing down, the living meat, to kill with his own teeth and wash his muzzle to the eyes in warm blood.

5 There is an ecstasy that marks the summit of life, and beyond which life cannot rise. And such is the **paradox** of living, this ecstasy comes when one is most alive, and it comes as a complete forgetfulness that one is alive. This ecstasy, this forgetfulness of living, comes to the artist, caught up and out of himself in a sheet of flame; it comes to the soldier, war-mad on a stricken field and refusing quarter; and it came to Buck, leading the pack, sounding the old wolf-cry, straining after the food that was alive and that fled swiftly before him through the moonlight. He was sounding the deeps of his nature, and of the parts of his nature that were deeper than he, going back into the womb of Time. He was mastered by the sheer surging of life, the tidal wave of being, the perfect joy of each separate muscle, joint, and sinew in that it was everything that was not death, that it was aglow and rampant, expressing itself in movement, flying exultantly under the stars and over the face of dead matter that did not move.

London, Jack. *The Call of the Wild*. 1903. Scholastic Paperbacks, 2001.

SELECTION VOCABULARY

precipitate / precipitar ***verb*** to cause something to happen quickly and unexpectedly, usually something bad or undesirable COGNATE

- What does Buck want to do?

propel / propulsar ***verb*** to cause something to move forward with force COGNATE

- How do the "leaden pellets" travel?

paradox / la paradoja ***noun*** a statement that is seemingly contradictory or impossible and yet often reveals a larger truth COGNATE

ELL

- What two feelings can one have about being alive, as described by London?
- What is unusual about having these feelings at the same time?

Reading Comprehension OPTIONAL

Have students complete the digital reading comprehension questions ✔ when they finish reading.

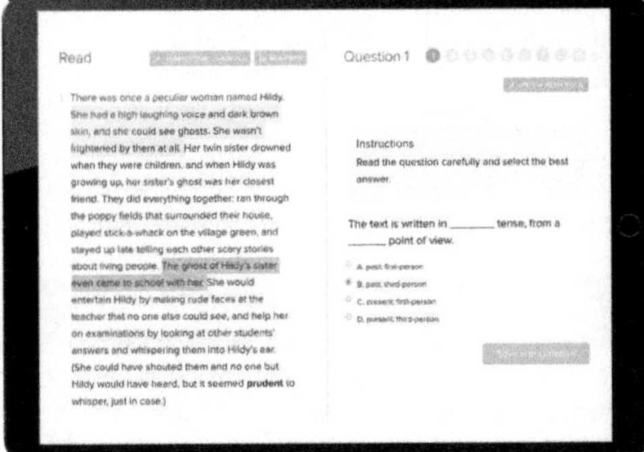

ANSWER KEY

QUESTION 1: A
QUESTION 2: A
QUESTION 3: D
QUESTION 4: D
QUESTION 5: B
QUESTION 6: A
QUESTION 7: C
QUESTION 8: C
QUESTION 9: *See first chart.*
QUESTION 10: *See second chart.*

Synonym	Word
unity	solidarity
pushed forward	propelled
please	placate
come before	precipitate
a seemingly absurd or contradictory statement	paradox

Character	Description
Buck	"He was ranging at the head of the pack, running the wild thing down"
Francois	"swore strange barbarous oaths, and stamped the snow in futile rage, and tore his hair"
Pike	"robbed him of half a fish one night, and gulped it down under the protection of Buck"
Billee	"the good-natured, was less good-natured, and whined not half so placatingly as in former days"

Connect and Extend OPTIONAL

CONNECT TO EXTENDED WRITING PROJECT

Students can find inspiration from *The Call of the Wild* when writing their informational essays. Have them reflect on Jack London's characterization of Buck as he takes chances.

BEYOND THE BOOK

Writing: Mimicking a Master

Students will mimic the writing of Jack London to write a descriptive paragraph about events in their own lives.

Ask students to:

- Reread paragraph 3 of the excerpt from *The Call of the Wild.*
- Change the characters, setting, and events to something from their own lives.
- As closely as possible, mimic London's writing style to write about their own experience.
- Read the finished piece aloud to a partner.

To reflect, ask students:

- How did this writing style affect your story? Why do you think that was?

Think Questions

Circulate as students answer Think Questions independently. Scaffolds for these questions are shown on the opposite page.

QUESTION 1: Textual Evidence

Buck "destroyed the solidarity of the team" by encouraging the rebels. The rebels stopped following the leadership of Spitz, they stole fish, and they fought and bullied Spitz. By challenging the leader, Buck also challenged the rules that had reinforced the solidarity of the team.

QUESTION 2: Textual Evidence

In paragraph 2, Buck's cleverness and ability to stir up trouble without getting caught shows that he took pleasure in causing trouble for Francois.

QUESTION 3: Textual Evidence

Buck led all the dogs to chase the snowshoe rabbit that Dub turned up, including the fifty dogs from a nearby camp. This shows that Buck is a leader of dogs, but he is not disciplined.

QUESTION 4: Context Clues

The word *paradox* is used to describe forgetting that one is alive while feeling the ecstasy that comes when one is most alive. I think *paradox* means "two things that seem contradictory but are both true."

QUESTION 5: Greek and Latin Affixes and Roots

I think *placatingly* means "calmly." I determined this meaning because the root placare means "to calm down," and *calmly* fits in the sentence if I use it to replace *placatingly*: "And even Billee, the good-natured, was less good-natured, and whined not half so *calmly* as in former days."

First Read

Read *The Call of the Wild*. After you read, complete the Think Questions below.

THINK QUESTIONS

1. Refer to several details in paragraph 1 to explain how Buck "destroyed the solidarity of the team." Cite evidence that is directly stated in the text, and make inferences to support your explanation.
2. What evidence is there in paragraph 2 that Buck took pleasure in causing trouble for Francois?
3. How did Buck react when Dub turned up a snowshoe rabbit? What inferences can you make about Buck from his behavior? Support your answer with specific evidence from the text.
4. Use context to determine the meaning of the word **paradox** as it is used in paragraph 5. Write your definition of *paradox* and tell how you determined the meaning of the word. Then check your definition in a print or digital dictionary to confirm the word's meaning.
5. By understanding that the Latin word *placare* means "to calm down" or "appease," use the context clues provided in paragraph 1 to determine the meaning of **placatingly**. Write your definition of *placatingly* and tell how you determined the meaning of the word.

Think Questions

Use the scaffolds below to differentiate instruction for your ELL English Language Learners and A Approaching grade-level learners.

ELL **BEGINNING** Write a response using the word bank and sentence frames.

INTERMEDIATE Write a response using the sentence frames.

ADVANCED, ADVANCED HIGH Write a response using the Text-Dependent Question Guide.

A **APPROACHING** Write a response using the Text-Dependent Question Guide.

BEGINNING	INTERMEDIATE	APPROACHING / ADVANCED, ADVANCED HIGH
Word Bank	**Sentence Frames**	**Text-Dependent Question Guide**
contradictory calmly led leadership reinforced disciplined rules trouble forgetting encouraging sentence cleverness	Buck "destroyed the solidarity of the team" by _____ the rebels. The rebels stopped following the _____ of Spitz, they stole fish, and they fought and bullied Spitz. By challenging the leader Buck, also challenged the _____ that had _____ the solidarity of the team.	1. • How does the team behave at the beginning of the paragraph? • What does it mean for a team to have solidarity? • What does Buck do? • What is the team like without solidarity?
	In paragraph 2, Buck's _____ and ability to stir up _____ without getting caught shows that he took pleasure in causing trouble for Francois.	2. • What things does Buck do that cause trouble? • What would it look like to take pleasure in causing trouble? • What is it about Buck that makes it seem like he enjoys causing trouble?
	Buck _____ all the dogs to chase the snowshoe rabbit that Dub turned up, including the fifty dogs from a nearby camp. This shows that Buck is a leader of dogs, but he is not _____.	3. • What happened when Dub turned up the snowshoe rabbit? • Who was chasing the rabbit? • Who was leading the chase?
	The word *paradox* is used to describe _____ that one is alive while feeling the ecstasy that comes when one is most alive. I think *paradox* means two things that seem _____ but are both true.	4. • Read: "There is an ecstasy that marks the summit of life, and beyond which life cannot rise. And such is the **paradox** of living, this ecstasy comes when one is most alive, and it comes as a complete forgetfulness that one is alive." • What two things is the word *paradox* describing? • How do those two things relate to each other?
	I think *placatingly* means _____. I determined this meaning because the root *placare* means "to calm down," and "calmly" fits in the _____if I use it to replace *placatingly*: "And even Billee, the good-natured, was less good-natured, and whined not half so *calmly* as in former days."	5. • Read: "And even Billee, the good-natured, was less good-natured, and whined not half so **placatingly** as in former days." • Is *placatingly* a noun, a verb, an adjective, or an adverb? • How does a dog with a good nature behave toward other dogs? • How does this behavior change if other dogs misbehave?

Skill: Language, Style, and Audience

Introduce the Skill

Watch the Concept Definition video ▶ and read the following definition with your students.

Authors use language to convey meaning or to affect the way their audience thinks and perceives. An **audience** is the intended reader or listener. Readers can analyze an author's style to better understand the tone and meaning of a text.

Style refers to the way an author uses language (words, sentences, paragraphs) to achieve a purpose. One element of style is word choice. **Word choice** is a technique in which writers choose specific words for precise meaning or to convey a certain tone. **Meaning** is a reader's interpretation of the text's deeper messages, themes, or ideas. **Tone** expresses a writer's **attitude** (or thoughts and feelings) toward his or her subject. Tone can be described, for example, as formal, casual, conversational, ironic, sad, bitter, humorous, or serious.

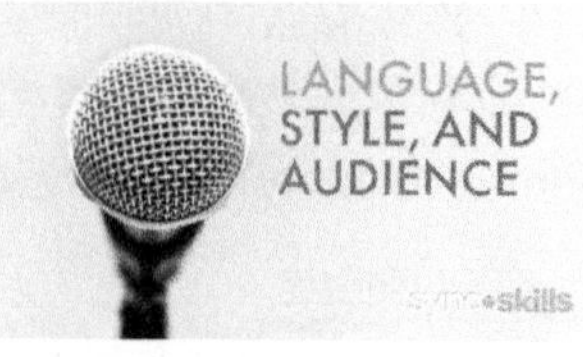

Skill: Language, Style, and Audience

Use the Checklist to analyze Language, Style, and Audience in *The Call of the Wild*. Refer to the sample student annotations about Language, Style, and Audience in the text.

••• CHECKLIST FOR LANGUAGE, STYLE, AND AUDIENCE

In order to determine an author's style, do the following:

- ✓ identify and define any unfamiliar words or phrases
- ✓ use context, including the meaning of surrounding words and phrases
- ✓ note possible reactions to the author's word choice
- ✓ examine your reaction to the author's word choice
- ✓ identify any analogies, or comparisons in which one part of the comparison helps explain the other

To analyze the impact of specific word choice on meaning and tone, ask the following questions:

- ✓ How did your understanding of the language change during your analysis?
- ✓ How does the writer's word choice impact or create meaning in the text?
- ✓ How does the writer's word choice impact or create a specific tone in the text?
- ✓ How could various audiences interpret this language? What different possible emotional responses can you list?
- ✓ What analogies do I see here? Where might an analogy have clarified meaning or created a specific tone?

TURN AND TALK

1. Think of your favorite story by a particular author. Would it be the same story if it were written by someone else?
2. Why is word choice so important? How do the choices that an author makes affect the reader?

ELL SPEAKING FRAMES

- My favorite story is by ____. If the story were written by another author it would ____.
- Word choice is important because ____.
- The word choices an author makes affect the reader by ____.

SKILL VOCABULARY

style / el estilo *noun* a way of expressing something that is characteristic of the person or time period COGNATE

word choice / la elección de palabras *noun* specific words chosen for precise meaning or to generate an emotional response

tone / el tono *noun* the writer's or speaker's attitude toward his or her subject matter COGNATE

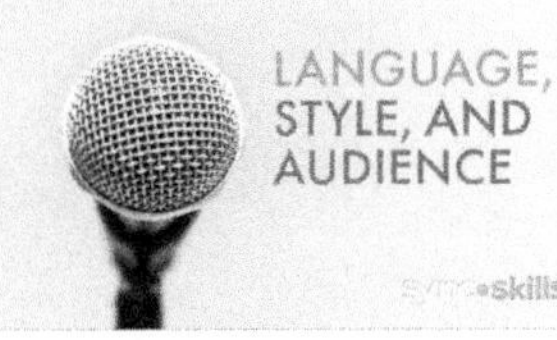

Skill: Language, Style, and Audience

Reread paragraph 5 of *The Call of the Wild*. Then, using the Checklist on the previous page, answer the multiple-choice questions below.

YOUR TURN

1. By using the phrase "There is an ecstasy that marks the summit of life, and beyond which life cannot rise," what is Jack London trying to say about Buck?

   - A. That Buck is not fast enough to catch and kill the rabbit.
   - B. That Buck is about to kill the rabbit.
   - C. That Buck could not possibly feel more alive than he is right now.
   - D. That Buck is about to die.

2. Why does Jack London mention life and death throughout his analogies about Buck and the rabbit?

   - A. He wants to suggest that Buck will die once he kills the rabbit.
   - B. He is trying to say that Buck is dying.
   - C. He wants to draw a comparison between life and death and the act of Buck chasing the rabbit.
   - D. He is trying to make everyone who reads the story feel bad for the rabbit.

3. What is the meaning behind the author's phrase "it comes to the soldier, war-mad and refusing quarter"?

   - A. That a soldier driven crazy by battle will still fight on and refuse the safety of shelter.
   - B. That a soldier driven crazy by battle will not be paid.
   - C. That a soldier driven crazy by battle will refuse to get paid.
   - D. That soldiers always refuse safety in order to get paid.

 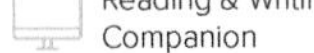

SKILL VOCABULARY

attitude / la actitud *noun* a state involving beliefs and feelings that causes a person to think or act in a certain way COGNATE

audience / la audiencia *noun* the people who read a written text, listen to an oral response or presentation, or watch a performance COGNATE

meaning / el significado *noun* what is meant by a word; the general message of a text or idea

Your Turn

Ask students to complete the Your Turn activity.

QUESTION 1

A. Incorrect. The author is talking about Buck's experience of his life, not his speed.

B. Incorrect. The author is talking about Buck's experience of his life, not if he will be able to kill the rabbit.

C. Correct. The author is talking about Buck's experience of his life and how Buck is feeling very good in the chase.

D. Incorrect. There is nothing to indicate the author is saying this.

QUESTION 2

A. Incorrect. The text does not suggest that this might happen.

B. Incorrect. Although Buck may be hungry, the excerpt does not focus on whether Buck is dying.

C. Correct. He wants the reader to understand how alive Buck feels in this moment and that the rabbit may die.

D. Incorrect. There is no textual evidence to support this idea.

QUESTION 3

A. Correct. *Quarter* means "a place where soldiers take shelter," and when soldiers are feeling that ecstasy, they will keep fighting instead of seeking the safety of shelter.

B. Incorrect. *Quarter* does not refer to money here.

C. Incorrect. *Quarter* does not refer to money here.

D. Incorrect. *Quarter* does not refer to money here.

Skill: Media

Introduce the Skill

Watch the Concept Definition video ▶ and read the following definition with your students.

Media is the plural form of the word *medium*. A **medium** is a means of sending a communication to an intended audience. Throughout most of human history, people communicated through three main media: speech, writing, and visual arts such as drawing, painting, and sculpture. But in the 19th century, media options suddenly exploded. The invention of photography, and then the telegraph and the telephone, changed the world. Within a century radio, motion pictures, and television followed.

Stories and ideas change as they are translated from one medium to another. A dialogue between two characters in a novel, for example, becomes very different when it is delivered by actors in a film—with close-ups, sound effects such as music, and other elements unique to the medium of film itself.

Today, new media are being invented at a much faster pace than ever before, and each of these forms of online communication has its own "language" and creates its own experience.

Skill: Media

Use the Checklist to analyze Media in *The Call of the Wild*. Refer to the sample student annotations about Media in the text.

••• CHECKLIST FOR MEDIA

In order to determine the extent to which a filmed or live production of a story or drama stays faithful to or departs from the text or script, do the following:

- ✓ note key elements from the text and how they changed or were removed in the film
- ✓ think about the advantages and disadvantages of using different media to present a particular topic, idea, or event
- ✓ consider the choices made by the director of a film, and how they may emphasize or minimize an event or even a line of dialogue from a written work
- ✓ weigh and understand the strengths and weaknesses of different media

To analyze the extent to which a filmed or live production of a story or drama stays faithful to or departs from the text or script, and to evaluate the choices made by the director or actors, ask the following questions:

- ✓ How does the filmed production of a story stay faithful to or depart from the text?
- ✓ What are the strengths of different media, such as novels or motion pictures, when telling a story? What are their weaknesses?
- ✓ How might the choices a director makes when making a film based on a novel completely change the point of view?

TURN AND TALK

1. Are there any books that you've read that have been turned into a television show or movie?
2. Do you like the book version better or the film? Why? What are the differences?

SPEAKING FRAMES

- [Book title] was turned into a [movie / television show] called ____.
- The reason I like the [book / movie / television show] better is ____.
- The differences between the versions are ____.

SKILL VOCABULARY

medium / el medio ***noun*** a form of communication, such as television, the Internet, and radio COGNATE

media / los medios ***noun*** the plural form of the word *medium*; a means of sending a communication to an intended audience

Skill: Media

Reread paragraph 4 of *The Call of the Wild,* and rewatch the video clip of *The Call of the Wild* from 03:57 to 05:20, available on the StudySync site. Then, using the Checklist on the previous page, answer the multiple-choice questions below.

YOUR TURN

1. What is Buck's reason for pursuing food in the text?
   - A. Francois didn't give him any food, and he was hungry.
   - B. He pulled 1,000 pounds, and that made him really hungry.
   - C. He was going to eat the snowshoe rabbit, but Dub stole it from him.
   - D. His instincts—in particular, the joy to kill—are what give him the desire to pursue food.

2. In the video, why does Buck finally eat so hungrily?
   - A. He seems to trust and understand that John Thornton is there to help him and wants him to be happy.
   - B. He pulled 1,000 pounds, and that made him really hungry.
   - C. He has to sneak food from John Thornton, so he eats it as quickly as he can.
   - D. His instincts as a dog make him eat quickly.

3. What is the difference in the portrayal of these scenes in the text and in the video clip?
   - A. In the text, the food is rabbit, but in the video, the food is moose.
   - B. Buck has different reasons for seeking food. Also, he relies on Francois in the text, but he relies only on himself in the video.
   - C. Buck has different reasons for seeking food. Also, he relies on Thornton in the video, but he relies only on himself in the text.
   - D. Buck moves slowly in the text and quickly in the video.

Your Turn

Ask students to complete the Your Turn activity.

QUESTION 1

A. Incorrect. The text doesn't mention if Francois fed him well or not.

B. Incorrect. This happens in the video, not the text.

C. Incorrect. Dub "turned up a snowshoe rabbit," and Buck pursued it for food.

D. Correct. The text talks about "the blood lust, the joy to kill."

QUESTION 2

A. Correct. Thornton doesn't push Buck, he lets Buck decide to trust him.

B. Incorrect. Buck eats in the video before pulling the 1,000 pounds.

C. Incorrect. Thornton brings him the food.

D. Incorrect. The movie doesn't talk about Buck's instincts or say anything about all dogs eating quickly.

QUESTION 3

A. Incorrect. We don't know what animal the meat in the video comes from.

B. Incorrect. Buck does have different reasons for seeking food. However, he does not rely on Francois in the text, and he does not rely on Thornton in the video.

C. Correct. Buck has different motivations, and in the video he is learning to trust Thornton.

D. Incorrect. Buck moves quickly when chasing the rabbit in the text, and he moves slowly—but eats hungrily—in the video.

Close Read

Skills Focus

QUESTION 1: Theme

See paragraph 2: The author explains how much Francois wants control and tries to get it with his lash. Whenever he turns away, though, he no longer has control. I think the author is trying to say that real control comes from more than yelling and lashing out.

QUESTION 2: Language, Style, and Audience

See paragraph 5.

QUESTION 3: Media

See paragraph 2: When I read that Francois yelled and lashed at the dogs, I could tell he was angry, but when I saw it in the video it seemed really mean. The interactions between Francois and the dogs seem much harsher and abusive when I can see and hear them than they do when I am reading them.

QUESTION 4: Connect to Essential Question

See paragraph 2: After reading the excerpt and watching the video, I think Buck is taking the biggest chance. In the video, Buck takes a chance on trusting Thornton, even after he has experienced how mean a human can be through his interactions with Francois, which is shown in both the text and the video.

Close Read

Reread *The Call of the Wild* and rewatch the video clip of *The Call of the Wild* available on the StudySync site. As you reread, complete the Skills Focus questions below. Then use your answers and annotations from the questions to help you complete the Write activity.

SKILLS FOCUS

1. Reread paragraph 2. What message is the author trying to convey about control? Include important details from the text that support your answer.
2. Reread paragraph 5 and identify an analogy. Explain what the analogy means and why you think it was important for Jack London to phrase his text that way.
3. Identify a part in the excerpt where humans interact with Buck and the dogs. Explain their interaction(s), and contrast this scene with what you saw in the video. How is this scene treated differently between the two types of media?
4. Based on your observations of the video and having read the text, who was taking a bigger chance: Buck, Thornton, the pack, or Francois? Make specific references from both the video and the text to support your response.

WRITE

LITERARY ANALYSIS: In the final paragraph, Jack London writes, "such is the paradox of living, this ecstasy comes when one is most alive, and it comes as a complete forgetfulness that one is alive." Based on his language, what sort of response was he likely looking for from his audience? Is there a difference in the impact of the text and the impact of the video? Which medium is more powerful and effective? Use textual evidence as well as references from the video to support your response.

Writer's Notebook

Connect to Essential Question: Give students time to reflect on how *The Call of the Wild* connects to the unit's essential question "Why do we take chances?" by freewriting in their Writer's Notebooks.

Beginning & Intermediate

Read aloud the unit's essential question: "Why do we take chances?" Encourage students to draw their connections or allow students to write in their native language. Circulate the room, prompting students for their thoughts as they respond orally or through pantomime.

Advanced & Advanced High

Allow students to share their connections orally in pairs or small groups before freewriting.

StudySyncTV

Project the StudySyncTV episode and pause at the following times to prompt discussion:

1:43 What difficulty does Jasmine have with the prompt?

4:03 What opposing interpretations do Ben and Jasmine have of the description of Buck?

7:38 What human activity does the end of the excerpt remind Ben and Alicia of? Do you think this is a valid comparison?

Collaborative Conversation

SCAFFOLDS

Break students into collaborative conversation groups to discuss the Close Read prompt. Ask students to use the StudySyncTV episode as a model for their discussion. Remind them to reference their Skills Focus annotations in their discussion.

In the final paragraph, Jack London writes, "such is the paradox of living, this ecstasy comes when one is most alive, and it comes as a complete forgetfulness that one is alive." Based on his language, what sort of response was he likely looking for from his audience? Is there a difference in the impact of the text and the impact of the video? Which medium is more powerful and effective? Use textual evidence as well as references from the video to support your response.

Use the scaffolds below to differentiate instruction for your ELL English Language Learners and A Approaching grade-level learners.

ELL **BEGINNING, INTERMEDIATE** Use the discussion guide and speaking frames to facilitate the discussion with support from the teacher.

ADVANCED, ADVANCED HIGH Use the discussion guide and speaking frames to facilitate the discussion in mixed-level groups.

A **APPROACHING** Use the discussion guide to facilitate the discussion in mixed-level groups.

APPROACHING

ADVANCED, ADVANCED HIGH

BEGINNING, INTERMEDIATE

Discussion Guide	Speaking Frames
1. Where does the author use language designed to get a response from the audience?	• The phrase ____ in paragraph ____ seems designed to get a response from the audience. • The response the audience is likely to have is ____.
2. What happened in the video that seems designed to get a response from the audience?	• The scene in the video that seems designed to get a response from the audience is ____.

Review Prompt and Rubric

Before students begin writing, review the writing prompt and rubric with the class.

LITERARY ANALYSIS: In the final paragraph, Jack London writes, "such is the paradox of living, this ecstasy comes when one is most alive, and it comes as a complete forgetfulness that one is alive." Based on his language, what sort of response was he likely looking for from his audience? Is there a difference in the impact of the text and the impact of the video? Which medium is more powerful and effective? Use textual evidence as well as references from the video to support your response.

 PROMPT GUIDE

- What is the difference between the impact of the text and the video?
- Which is more powerful?
- Which medium is more effective at getting a reaction from the audience? Why?

An additional rubric item for Language and Conventions appears in your digital teacher and student accounts.

Score	Media	Language, Style, and Audience
4	The writer clearly analyzes and explains information from different media and the advantages and disadvantages of using them. The writer provides exemplary analysis, using relevant evidence from the text and video.	The writer clearly analyzes and explains the author's word choice and tone. The writer provides exemplary analysis, using relevant evidence from the text.
3	The writer analyzes and explains information from different media and the advantages and disadvantages of using them. The writer provides sufficient analysis, using relevant evidence from the text and video most of the time.	The writer analyzes and explains the author's word choice and tone. The writer provides sufficient analysis, using relevant evidence from the text most of the time.
2	The writer begins to analyze or explain information from different media and the advantages and disadvantages of using them, but the analysis is incomplete. The writer uses relevant evidence from the text and video only some of the time.	The writer begins to analyze or explain the author's word choice and tone, but the analysis is incomplete. The writer uses relevant evidence from the text only some of the time.
1	The writer attempts to analyze or explain information from different media and the advantages and disadvantages of using them, but the analysis is not successful. The writer uses little or no relevant evidence from the text and video.	The writer attempts to analyze or explain the author's word choice and tone, but the analysis is not successful. The writer uses little or no relevant evidence from the text.
0	The writer does not provide a relevant response to the prompt or does not provide a response at all.	The writer does not provide a relevant response to the prompt or does not provide a response at all.

Write

SCAFFOLDS

Ask students to complete the writing assignment using textual evidence to support their answers.

Use the scaffolds below to differentiate instruction for your ELL English Language Learners and A Approaching grade-level learners.

ELL **BEGINNING** With the help of the word bank, write a response using paragraph frame 1.

INTERMEDIATE With the help of the word bank, write a response using paragraph frames 1 and 2.

ADVANCED, ADVANCED HIGH Write a response of differentiated length using the sentence starters.

A **APPROACHING** Write a response of differentiated length using the sentence starters.

BEGINNING / INTERMEDIATE — ADVANCED, ADVANCED HIGH / APPROACHING

Word Bank	Paragraph Frame 1	Paragraph Frame 2	Sentence Starters
best friend powerful understand relate ecstasy	Jack London wants his audience to ____ to Buck, or understand him. London compares the ____ Buck feels to what human artists and soldiers feel, which shows London wants humans to relate to Buck. In the video, Thornton calls Buck his ____, which a person can ____. The text is a more ____ tool for the response London wants, because when I am reading about Buck, he seems like a person, but it's harder to relate when I see the video of Buck and the dogs.	When I am reading, my mind ____, so my imagination can start with whatever the author has written and ____. For this reason the ____ is a more powerful and effective tool for communicating ____. When I watch a video instead, I am watching how the director and actors have ____. Also, because there are already images, my ____ has much less to do.	• London is looking for his . . . • London compares the . . . • In the video . . . • The . . . is a more . . .

Peer Review

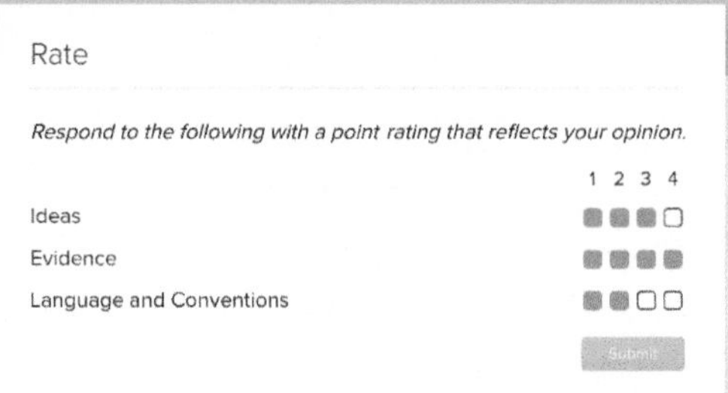

Students should submit substantive feedback to two peers using the instructions below.

- How well does this response answer the prompt?
- How well does the writer analyze the differences between the text and the video?
- What did the writer do well in this response? What does the writer need to work on?

SENTENCE FRAMES

- You were able to (completely / partly / almost) answer the prompt.
- You could answer the prompt better by ____.
- The reference to the video that was really helpful was ____.
- I think you could work on ____.

Cocoon

POETRY
Mahvash Sabet
2013

Introduction

Mahvash Sabet (b. 1953), a leader in the Bahá'í community in Tehran, Iran, was arrested and imprisoned at Evin Prison in March of 2008 because of her faith. The Iranian government does not recognize the Bahá'í Faith as an official religion, even though it is the largest religious minority in the country. Before her arrest, Sabet worked as a teacher, collaborating with the National Literacy Committee and serving as director of the Bahá'í Institute for Higher Education for 15 years. While in prison, Sabet began writing poems, which were smuggled out by relatives and were eventually translated into English by Bahiyyih Nakhjavani. *Prison Poems*, a collection of about 70 of Sabet's poems, was published in 2013. After nearly ten years of imprisonment, Sabet was released in September of 2017. "Cocoon" depicts a speaker wrestling with contradictory feelings.

The speaker mourns for the cocoon, the chrysalis that had been smashed and destroyed before her eyes. She feels tossed to and fro, caught between compulsions, longing for both freedom and the security of her old cocoon. Initially, when her soul had broken out of the cocoon, she felt thrilled at the feeling of freedom. However, a part of her was afraid, feeling threatened by the fire that awaited her. So she wonders about contrary desires. She loves to fly and applauds bravely dying, but she also weeps for the security of how it used to be.

ELL Proficiency-leveled summaries and summaries in multiple languages are available digitally.

Audio and audio text highlighting are available with this text.

CONNECT TO ESSENTIAL QUESTION

Why do we take chances?

Poet Mahvash Sabet was a leader in the Bahá'í community in Tehran, Iran, where she was arrested for practicing her faith. She wrote poems such as "Cocoon" during her imprisonment, which were a risk in themselves to write.

Access Complex Text

LEXILE: N/A WORD COUNT: 132

The following areas may be challenging for students, particularly ELL English Language Learners and A Approaching grade-level learners.

Prior Knowledge

- Some students may be unfamiliar with the Bahá'í faith, a religion that teaches the essential worth of all religions and the unity and equality of all people.
- Established in 1863, it initially grew in Iran and parts of the Middle East, where it has faced ongoing persecution since its inception.

Specific Vocabulary

- Difficult vocabulary, such as *cowering* (to crouch, or kneel-down with the upper body brought forward, usually in fear), *pining* (suffering because of a broken heart), and *demise* (a person or thing's death), may need to be explained.
- Remind students to use context clues while reading and to use a dictionary to define any unfamiliar words.

SCAFFOLDS ELL ENGLISH LANGUAGE LEARNERS A APPROACHING GRADE LEVEL 
B BEYOND GRADE LEVEL

These icons identify differentiation strategies and scaffolded support for a variety of students. See the digital lesson plan for additional differentiation strategies and scaffolds.

Instructional Path

The print teacher's edition includes essential point-of-use instruction and planning tools. Complete lesson plans and program documents appear in your digital teacher account.

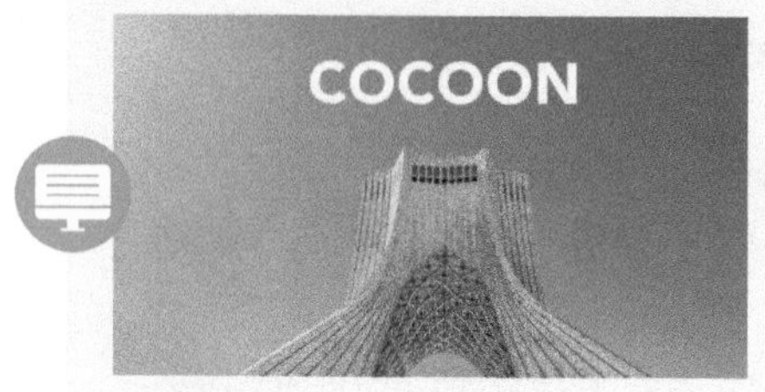

First Read: Cocoon

Objectives: After an initial reading and discussion of the poem, students will be able to make inferences to analyze and understand the ideas presented in the poem.

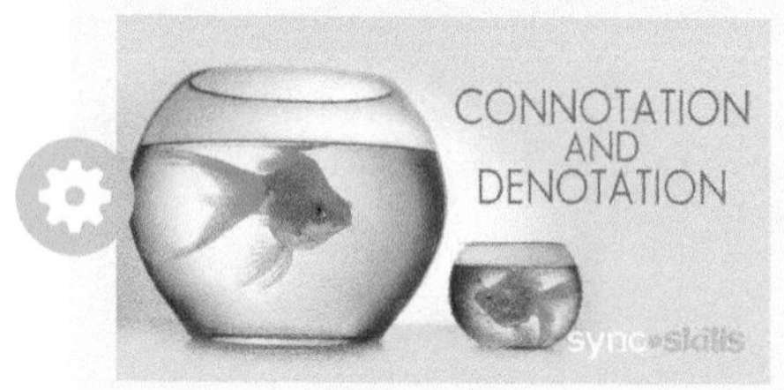

Skill: Connotation and Denotation

Objectives: After rereading and discussing a model of close reading, students will be able to determine the meanings of words and phrases as they are used in a text, including connotative and denotative meanings.

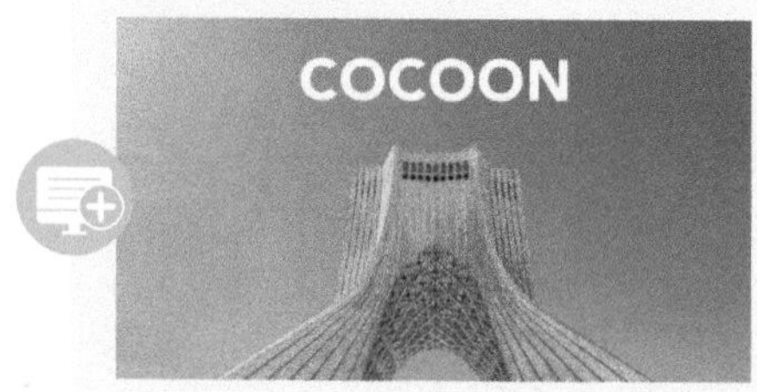

Close Read: Cocoon

Objectives: After engaging in a close reading and discussion of the text, students will be able to analyze the author's use of connotations and denotations and explain the author's purpose for writing in a short, written response.

Progress Monitoring

Opportunities to Learn	Opportunities to Demonstrate Learning	Opportunities to Reteach
Connotation and Denotation		
Skill: Connotation and Denotation	Skill: Connotation and Denotation • Your Turn Close Read • Complete Vocabulary Chart • Skills Focus • Write	Unit 4 Skill: Connotation and Denotation - Gettysburg Address Unit 4 Skill: Connotation and Denotation - Blind Spotlight Skill: Connotation and Denotation

First Read

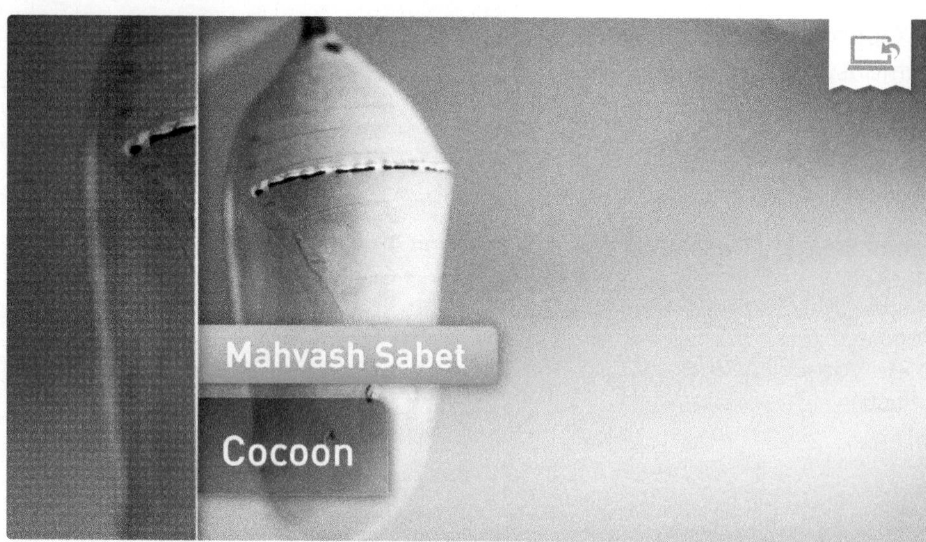

Introduce the Text

As a class, watch the video preview  and have students read the introduction in pairs to make connections to the video preview.

To activate prior knowledge and experiences, ask students:

- What key words or images from the video do you think will be most important to the poem you are about to read?
- What behaviors would you consider to be bizarre, and why?

ELL **SPEAKING FRAMES**

- The ____ in the video makes me think ____.
- The video shows ____. This makes me wonder ____.
- I think the text will ____. I think this because ____.
- I predict that there will be ____. I believe this because ____.

Entry Point

As students prepare to read "Cocoon," share the following information with them to provide context.

- ✓ In 1979, Iran—once called Persia, and now officially the Islamic Republic of Iran—underwent a revolution that overthrew its ruler, the shah, and installed a government run by conservative Islamic clergymen according to Islamic law. Restrictions on free speech, women's activity and dress, and many social practices were instituted. Bahá'í was banned and its followers persecuted because its founder claimed to be a prophet, but Muslims believe Mohammad was the last prophet. Anyone who publicly criticizes the government may be put in jail.
- ✓ Women's rights are restricted in Iranian society under the Islamic government. For example, a married woman cannot leave the country without her husband's permission, and women cannot watch men play sports in stadiums.
- ✓ According to Sabet, writing poetry was her "means of survival" in prison. Prison poems form a subgroup of poetry. Some prisons in the United States have poetry writing programs for inmates.

"I'm tossed to and fro, from here to there . . ."

There's a part of me that keeps mourning
for the soft cocoon where I lay,
a part of me that keeps pining
for the delicate **chrysalis** smashed and destroyed
before my eyes that day.

I'm tossed to and fro, from here to there,
caught between **compulsions**;
I'm thrown left and right and back and forth,
longing for the freedom of flight and yet
craving those soft consolations.

When my soul broke free, a part of me
thrilled at the lift of its arc,
but another shrank back in cowering fear
from the threatening fires, from the lowering smoke
that awaited me in here.

All this makes me wonder greatly
about **contrary** desires.
There's something in me approves of flying,
applauds the thought of bravely dying,
yet I weep for the cocoon's demise.

From *Prison Poems*, 2013. Used by permission of George Ronald Publishing Ltd.

NOTES

Skill: Connotation and Denotation

The denotative meaning of cocoon is a case that insect larva spin as protection when turning into an adult. The connotative meaning here seems to be a bed, a safe place that the speaker remembers before she was arrested and imprisoned.

SELECTION VOCABULARY

chrysalis / la crisálida ***noun*** pupa of a moth or butterfly enclosed in a cocoon COGNATE

compulsion / la compulsión ***noun*** an urge to do or say something COGNATE

Analyze Vocabulary Using Context Clues

In lines 1–5, focus on that part of the poem that uses the word *chrysalis*. Point out these context clues:

1. I know that *delicate* is an adjective and that it describes the word *chrysalis*. That means *chrysalis* must be a noun. In a previous line, the speaker says she is in mourning for a "soft cocoon." *Cocoon* is also a noun, because the adjective *soft* describes it.
2. The speaker says she is in mourning for the cocoon and she is pining for the chrysalis that was destroyed that day. I'm thinking that a *chrysalis* might be a synonym of *cocoon*, or maybe part of a cocoon.
3. When I look up the word in a dictionary, I see my second guess was right. A chrysalis is the hard, outer case that protects the cocoon inside of it.

CHECK FOR SUCCESS

If students are unable to make predictions, revisit the Checklist section of the Grade 8 Context Clues lesson with the class. After revisiting, guide students as they make predictions about the next bold word, appearing in line 7 of the poem, using the following routine:

- Is the word a noun, a verb, an adjective, or an adverb?
- Why would someone be "thrown back and forth" when trying to make up their mind?
- How can longing for something, such as freedom or safety, become a "compulsion"?

Connotation and Denotation

What does the author notice about the denotation of the word *cocoon* and the way the speaker uses it?

The reader notes that the denotative meaning of *cocoon* is an envelope an insect forms to change into a butterfly or moth. The way it is used in the poem gives it a positive connotation: a safe, warm place.

TEXT TALK

Why is the speaker in mourning?

See lines 1–5: She is in mourning for the "soft cocoon" where she lay, and the "chrysalis" where she felt safe.

Why does the speaker feel as if she's being tossed to and fro, and thrown left and right?

See lines 6–10: She longs for freedom, but at the same time she also longs for the safety of the "cocoon" she describes in the first part of the poem.

Skills Focus

QUESTION 1: Connotation and Denotation

See lines 1–5: Both *smashed* and *destroyed* have negative connotations. They both suggest that something has been ruined or broken. But *destroyed* has a more negative connotation than *smashed*. If something is *smashed*, like a vase, it might still be repaired. If something is destroyed, however, it no longer exists. It cannot be saved or rebuilt. For this reason, *destroyed* has a more negative connotation.

QUESTION 2: Connotation and Denotation

See lines 1–10: The word *cocoon*, which is also the title of the poem, has a very strong, positive emotional connotation. The author could have chosen a word such as *bed* or even *sofa*, but *cocoon* suggests something that surrounds you and keeps you safe. *Craving* also has a strong emotional connotation. The author could have said that she wanted soft consolations. But if you crave something, you have a very strong desire for it.

QUESTION 3: Connotation and Denotation

See lines 11–15: *Broke* is the past tense of *break*. The denotation of the word *break* is to shatter something into parts with suddenness or violence. It can have a negative connotation, if someone threatens another person with violence, but here it has a positive connotation. The poet uses broke here to mean that she has freed herself from bonds that hold her back or "imprison" her. This connotation makes sense because in the twelfth line she says that she is "thrilled" when her soul breaks free.

SELECTION VOCABULARY

crave / antojarse ***verb*** to have a great desire for

- What is the author longing for?
- How might *craving* be similar to *longing*?

thrill / entusiasmar ***verb*** to feel sudden intense sensation or emotion

- When your feelings are "lifted," are you happy or sad?
- How would you feel if you were suddenly free of something?

contrary / contrario/a ***adjective*** very opposed in nature, character, or purpose COGNATE

- What two desires does the speaker have?
- How are these two desires different?

Reading Comprehension OPTIONAL

Have students complete the digital reading comprehension questions when they finish reading.

ANSWER KEY

QUESTION 1: C
QUESTION 2: B
QUESTION 3: A
QUESTION 4: D
QUESTION 5: *See chart.*

First	Second	Third	Fourth
The speaker feels sorrow and longing for the security and comfort that was ripped away from her on "that day."	The speaker is experiencing an internal conflict between wanting to face the world as her true self and craving comfort and compassion.	When the speaker existed as her true self, a part of her was joyful, but a part of her was afraid of the personal costs of that freedom.	The speaker thinks it is important to be her true self even if it means she will die, but she is sad that in order to do so she must sacrifice security and comfort.

Connect and Extend OPTIONAL

CONNECT TO EXTENDED WRITING PROJECT

Students can find inspiration from "Cocoon" when writing their informational essays. Have them reflect on the denotations and connotations of words when describing the risks that some people take, why they take them, and the outcomes.

BEYOND THE BOOK

Photography: Risk Takers

Taking a risk can mean many things to many different people. For Mahvash Sabet, it meant confronting her fears about freedom. To explore the concept of "taking a risk," have students do the following:

Find a photograph in a magazine or online that they feel shows someone taking a risk. It might be an Olympic champion, or someone who pushes themselves to achieve some goal.

- The photo may be of someone famous, someone not many people know about, or someone only they know.
- The portrait may be in color or black and white.

Choose one type of brief caption to write that tells the story of the person in the photo.

- A narrative describing the person and circumstances
- Why they think this person is taking a risk.

Display the portraits and stories. To reflect, ask students:

- What do the portraits and captions make you think about?
- How might you look at the concept of taking a risk in a new way?

Think Questions

Circulate as students answer Think Questions independently. Scaffolds for these questions are shown on the opposite page.

QUESTION 1: Textual Evidence

The very first line of the poem—"There's a part of me that keeps mourning"—suggests that the author is clearly upset over something. The word *mourning* means "the expression or feeling of extreme sadness." The speaker says she mourns the "soft cocoon where I lay." A cocoon is a case spun by some insects as protection when they change into a butterfly or a moth. The speaker must be mourning a sense of security, perhaps her home.

QUESTION 2: Textual Evidence

While a part of the speaker seems to long for "the freedom of flight," she is torn between wanting that freedom and yet craving those "soft consolations." I think the "soft consolations" is another reference to the cocoon that she mentions in the first part of the poem. She seems torn between wanting freedom and, at the same time, the "consolation" of her "cocoon."

QUESTION 3: Textual Evidence

The speaker says that part of her was thrilled when her "soul broke free," but another part of her "shrank back in cowering fear." The idea of being free frightens the speaker. She imagines that "threatening fires" and "lowering smoke" wait for her now that she is free.

QUESTION 4: Context Clues

In the lines 9 and 10, the speaker says that she is "longing for the freedom of flight," but at the same time she is "craving those soft consolations." The "soft consolations" must refer to the "soft cocoon" she mentions in the first part of the poem. I know *longing* means having a great desire for something, so *craving* must have a meaning very similar to *longing* because the speaker wants both freedom and consolation.

QUESTION 5: Greek and Latin Roots and Affixes

The word *desires* is a noun used in the same line where the word *contrary* appears, so *contrary* must be an adjective that describes *desires*. I know the writer keeps saying that a part of her wants one thing and another part of her wants something else, so her desires are pitted against one another. The word *contrary* must mean "to oppose or contradict."

First Read

Read "Cocoon." After you read, complete the Think Questions below.

THINK QUESTIONS

1. In lines 1–5, what is the speaker mourning? Cite evidence from the text to support your answer.
2. What do lines 6–10 tell you about the speaker's state of mind? Support your answer with evidence from the text.
3. The speaker says in lines 11–15 that a part of her felt thrilled "when my soul broke free." What other emotion does she describe? Cite evidence from the text to support your answer.
4. What is the meaning of the word **craving** as it is used in the text? Write your best definition here, along with a brief explanation of how you arrived at its meaning, and then consult a dictionary to check your answer.
5. The Latin word *contra* means "against." With this information in mind and using context clues from the text, write your best definition of the word **contrary** here.

SCAFFOLDS

Think Questions

Use the scaffolds below to differentiate instruction for your ELL English Language Learners and A Approaching grade-level learners.

ELL **BEGINNING** Write a response using the word bank and sentence frames.

INTERMEDIATE Write a response using the sentence frames.

ADVANCED, ADVANCED HIGH Write a response using the Text-Dependent Question Guide.

A **APPROACHING** Write a response using the Text-Dependent Question Guide.

BEGINNING	INTERMEDIATE	APPROACHING / ADVANCED, ADVANCED HIGH
Word Bank	**Sentence Frames**	**Text-Dependent Question Guide**
safe consolations shrank mournful demise applauds against cocoon thrilled fear safety freedom flying	The speaker is sad and ____. She is mournful for the soft ____ where she lay. The speaker misses a feeling of ____.	1. • Where did the speaker lay and why did she like it? • What happened to the chrysalis? • Why is the speaker sad? • How do I know this?
	The speaker wants to feel the ____ of flight. At the same time, she also wants the ____ of home. She wants to feel ____.	2. • How does the speaker feel about freedom? • In what ways are the "soft consolations" like the "soft cocoon" in lines 1–5? • What is the speaker caught between and why can't she make up her mind?
	The speaker felt ____ when her "soul broke free." But a part of her also ____ back in ____.	3. • What two feelings does the speaker describe in lines 11–15? • What does part of the author feel when her "soul breaks free"? • What is the author afraid of?
	There is something in the speaker that approves of ____. She also ____ the thought of bravely dying. But she still weeps for the cocoon's ____.	4. • Read: "I'm thrown left and right and back and forth / longing for the freedom of flight and yet / **craving** those soft consolations." • What does *longing* mean? • What was smashed and destroyed before the speaker's eyes? • What else does the author want besides freedom?
	The Latin word *contra* means "____."	5. • Read: "All this makes me wonder greatly / about **contrary** desires." • What does the author approve of? • What does the author weep for? • How are these desires different?

Skill: Connotation and Dentotation

Introduce the Skill

Watch the Concept Definition video and read the following definition with your students.

The **denotation** of a word is its dictionary definition. The **connotation** of a word is the idea or feeling that a word suggests, or that our culture or our emotions give the word. A word's connotation can be positive, negative, or neutral. For example, the words *cheap* and *affordable* both denote "inexpensive." However, *cheap* connotes something that is of low quality.

To determine the connotation of a word, readers must use **context**, such as the genre or subject of a text. They also use **context clues**, or the surrounding words that help a reader determine a word's meaning. To verify the denotation of a word and check for possible connotations, readers can consult reference materials such as dictionaries, glossaries, and thesauruses. To **analyze** an author's word choices, readers consider the emotional impact of language in the text for its potential effect on readers.

Skill: Connotation and Denotation

Use the Checklist to analyze Connotation and Denotation in "Cocoon." Refer to the sample student annotations about Connotation and Denotation in the text.

••• CHECKLIST FOR CONNOTATION AND DENOTATION

In order to identify the denotative meanings of words, use the following steps:

- ✓ first, note unfamiliar words and phrases, keywords used to describe important characters, events, and ideas, or words that inspire or cause an emotional reaction
- ✓ next, determine and note the denotative meaning of a word by checking a reference source, such as a dictionary, glossary, or thesaurus

To better understand the meanings of words and phrases as they are used in a text, including connotative meanings, use the following questions:

- ✓ How do synonyms or context help you identify the connotative meaning of the word?
- ✓ How could you say this word or phrase differently? Would it change or maintain the meaning of the sentence/line/paragraph?
- ✓ How can you note differences between words with similar denotations and their connotations?

To determine the meaning of words and phrases as they are used in a text, including connotative meanings, use the following questions:

- ✓ What is the meaning of the word or phrase? What is its denotation, and what connotations does the word or phrase have?
- ✓ If I substitute a synonym based on denotation, is the meaning the same? How does it change the meaning of the text?

TURN AND TALK

1. Can you think of a time when knowing the dictionary definition of a word might not be enough to understand how it is used in a text?
2. What words can you think of that carry different connotations depending on the context, or the way in which they are used?

ELL SPEAKING FRAMES

- I needed to know more than the dictionary definition for the word ____. The reason is ____.
- The word ____ means different things in different situations. Sometimes it means ____, and other times it means ____.

SKILL VOCABULARY

denotation / la denotación ***noun*** the literal or dictionary meaning of a word, in contrast to the feelings or ideas that the word suggests COGNATE

connotation / la connotación ***noun*** an idea or feeling that a word suggests in addition to its literal or primary meaning COGNATE

context / el contexto ***noun*** the set of facts or circumstances that surround a situation or event COGNATE

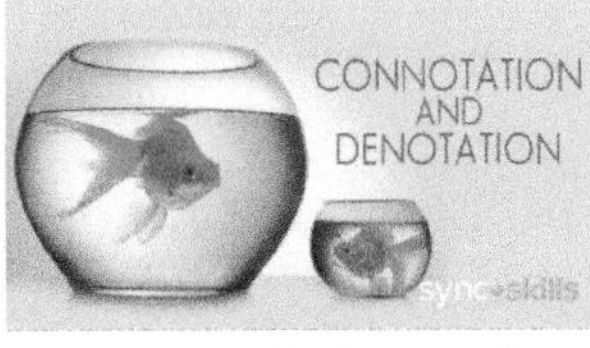

Skill: Connotation and Denotation

Reread lines 11–20 of "Cocoon." Then, using the Checklist on the previous page, answer the multiple-choice questions below.

YOUR TURN

1. In lines 11 and 12, the speaker writes, "When my soul broke free, a part of me / thrilled at the lift of its arc." What word could you use in place of *thrilled* that would have the same connotation and maintain, or keep, the meaning of the line?

   - A. When my soul broke free, a part of me / was happy at the lift of its arc
   - B. When my soul broke free, a part of me / was surprised at the lift of its arc.
   - C. When my soul broke free, a part of me / was exhilarated at the lift of its arc.
   - D. When my soul broke free, a part of me / was pleased at the lift of its arc.

2. *Shrank* is the past tense of *shrink*, which means "to become smaller because of cold, heat, or moisture." Does the way the speaker uses the word *shrank* in line 13 have a negative or a positive connotation?

   - A. Since only part of the author shrank back in cowering fear, the use of the word has a neutral connotation, neither positive nor negative.
   - B. The speaker shrinks because of heat from a threatening fire, so *shrank* has a negative connotation.
   - C. The speaker is thrilled because her soul has broken free, so the use of *shrank* in the third line has a positive connotation.
   - D. The speaker shrinks because of fear, not because of heat, cold, or moisture, so she uses its negative connotation.

SKILL VOCABULARY

context clue / la clave del contexto ***noun*** a hint in the surrounding text that can help a reader infer the meaning of an unfamiliar word, phrase, or description

analyze / analizar ***verb*** to consider in detail and discover essential features or meaning COGNATE

Your Turn

Ask students to complete the Your Turn activity.

QUESTION 1

A. Incorrect. The denotation of *happy* is contentment, which does not have the same connotation as *thrilled*, which means "a sudden feeling of excitement and pleasure."

B. Incorrect. To be *surprised* means "to come upon or encounter something suddenly and unexpectedly."

C. Correct. *Exhilarated* means "to be energized and excited" and has the same connotation as *thrilled*, so substituting this word would keep the meaning of the line.

D. Incorrect. To be *pleased* means "to be glad or satisfied," which would not have the same connotation as *thrilled*.

QUESTION 2

A. Incorrect. The fact that the author was divided about whether she felt thrilled or shrank back in fear because she was so frightened does not affect the negative connotation of *shrank*, because it only describes her reaction to the fear the speaker felt.

B. Incorrect. Although exposure to heat can cause some objects to shrink in size, in this case the fire is threatening the speaker's security and even her life, so it is not causing her to literally shrink from the heat of the fire.

C. Incorrect. The speaker says she is thrilled in the second line, yet the word *but* that opens the third line indicates that she is going to explain how her feelings have changed.

D. Correct. The speaker uses the word *shrank* to imply that she has become so frightened, she has figuratively grown small to increase the distance between herself and the source of her fear. This gives the word a negative connotation.

Close Read

Skills Focus

QUESTION 1: Connotation and Denotation

See lines 1–5.

QUESTION 2: Connotation and Denotation

See lines 1–10.

QUESTION 3: Connotation and Denotation

See lines 11–15.

QUESTION 4: Connect to Essential Question

See lines 11–20: For the speaker, the idea of freedom is frightening because she won't feel protected. She says she "weeps for the cocoon's demise," a place where she had felt safe. Though freedom is "thrilling," it brings with it the possibility of danger. To enjoy freedom, the speaker had to overcome her fear and take a chance even though there is the possibility of "bravely dying."

CHECK FOR SUCCESS

If students struggle to respond to Skills Focus question 1, ask them the following questions:

1. What is the denotation for *smashed?* What is the denotation for *destroyed?* Which word has more connotations?
2. Which word do you think has a stronger connotation? Why?

Close Read

Reread "Cocoon." As you reread, complete the Skills Focus questions below. Then use your answers and annotations from the questions to help you complete the Write activity.

SKILLS FOCUS

1. The words *smashed* and *destroyed* in the first stanza (lines 1–5) have similar denotations. Which word has a stronger connotation, and why?
2. Reread lines 1–10. Identify words the author uses that have specific emotional connotations. Explain why you think the author chose these specific words.
3. Reread lines 11 and 12 in the third stanza. Does the word *broke* have a positive or a negative connotation the way it is used here? How could it be used so that it has a different connotation?
4. Why does the speaker consider the idea of freedom as taking a chance?

WRITE

LITERARY ANALYSIS: In this poem, Mahvash Sabet describes the conflicting emotions she feels when she is arrested in her home and watches as it is destroyed. She then reflects on why she should feel torn between desiring freedom and wanting the security she once had. Some of the words she chooses to describe her feelings have powerful connotations that help her describe her experience. Write an analysis of at least 250 words in which you explain Sabet's purpose for telling this story about her personal experience. Use textual evidence to support your response, including the author's use of connotation and denotation.

Writer's Notebook

Connect to Essential Question: Give students time to reflect on how "Cocoon" connects to the unit's essential question "Why do we take chances?" by freewriting in their Writer's Notebooks.

Beginning & Intermediate

Read aloud the unit's essential question: "Why do we take chances?" Encourage students to draw their connections or allow students to write in their native language. Circulate the room, prompting students for their thoughts as they respond orally or through pantomime.

Advanced & Advanced High

Allow students to share their connections orally in pairs or small groups before freewriting.

Collaborative Conversation

Break students into collaborative conversation groups to discuss the Close Read prompt. Ask students to use the StudySyncTV episode as a model for their discussion. Remind them to reference their Skills Focus annotations in their discussion.

In this poem, Mahvash Sabet describes the conflicting emotions she feels when she is arrested in her home and watches as it is destroyed. She then reflects on why she should feel torn between desiring freedom and wanting the security she once had. Some of the words she chooses to describe her feelings have powerful connotations that help her to describe her experience. Write an analysis of at least 250 words in which you explain Sabet's purpose for telling this story about her personal experience. Use textual evidence to support your response, including the author's use of connotation and denotation.

Use the scaffolds below to differentiate instruction for your ELL English Language Learners and A Approaching grade-level learners.

ELL **BEGINNING, INTERMEDIATE** Use the discussion guide and speaking frames to facilitate the discussion with support from the teacher.

ADVANCED, ADVANCED HIGH Use the discussion guide and speaking frames to facilitate the discussion in mixed-level groups.

A **APPROACHING** Use the discussion guide to facilitate the discussion in mixed-level groups.

APPROACHING
ADVANCED, ADVANCED HIGH
BEGINNING, INTERMEDIATE

Discussion Guide	Speaking Frames
1. What is the author's purpose for telling her story?	• A part of the author keeps ____ for the soft ____ where she once felt safe. • Another part of the author wants ____, but she also ____ it. • The author wants people to know how hard it is to have ____ desires.
2. How did the author use connotations and denotations to describe this experience?	• ____ is one word the author uses that has a more powerful connotation than *wanting*. • When the speaker says she is "cowering in fear," it is a stronger connotation than just saying she is ____.

Review Prompt and Rubric

Before students begin writing, review the writing prompt and rubric with the class.

LITERARY ANALYSIS: In this poem, Mahvash Sabet describes the conflicting emotions she feels when she is arrested in her home and watches as it is destroyed. She then reflects on why she should feel torn between desiring freedom and wanting the security she once had. Some of the words she chooses to describe her feelings have powerful connotations that help her to describe her experience. Write an analysis of at least 250 words in which you explain Sabet's purpose for telling this story about her personal experience. Use textual evidence to support your response, including the author's use of connotation and denotation.

ELL PROMPT GUIDE

- What conflicting emotions does the speaker feel?
- What powerful words does the speaker use to explain how she feels?
- How does the speaker feel at the end of the poem?

Score	Connotation and Denotation	Language and Conventions
4	The writer clearly and effectively identifies the connotations and denotations of words from the poem. The writer provides exemplary analysis of connotations and denotations, using relevant evidence from the text all of the time.	The writer demonstrates a consistent command of grammar, punctuation, and usage conventions. Although minor errors may be evident, they do not detract from the fluency or the clarity of the writing.
3	The writer identifies the connotations and denotations of words from the poem. The writer provides sufficient analysis of connotations and denotations, using relevant evidence from the text most of the time.	The writer demonstrates an adequate command of grammar, punctuation, and usage conventions. Although some errors may be evident, they create few (if any) disruptions in the fluency or clarity of the writing.
2	The writer begins to analyze or explain the connotations and denotations of words from the poem. The writer provides an incomplete analysis, using relevant evidence from the text only some of the time.	The writer demonstrates a partial command of grammar, punctuation, and usage conventions. Some distracting errors may be evident, at times creating minor disruptions in the fluency or clarity of the writing.
1	The writer attempts to analyze or explain the connotations and denotations of words from the poem. The writer provides an unsuccessful analysis, using little or no relevant evidence from the text.	The writer demonstrates little or no command of grammar, punctuation, and usage conventions. Serious and persistent errors create disruptions in the fluency of the writing and sometimes interfere with meaning.
0	The writer does not provide a relevant response to the prompt or does not provide a response at all.	Serious and persistent errors overwhelm the writing and interfere with the meaning of the response as a whole, making the writer's meaning impossible to understand.

Write

SCAFFOLDS

Ask students to complete the writing assignment using textual evidence to support their answers.

Use the scaffolds below to differentiate instruction for your ELL English Language Learners and A Approaching grade-level learners.

ELL **BEGINNING** With the help of the word bank, write a response using paragraph frame 1.

INTERMEDIATE With the help of the word bank, write a response using paragraph frames 1 and 2.

ADVANCED, ADVANCED HIGH Write a response of differentiated length using the sentence starters.

A **APPROACHING** Write a response of differentiated length using the sentence starters.

BEGINNING / INTERMEDIATE | ADVANCED, ADVANCED HIGH / APPROACHING

Word Bank	Paragraph Frame 1	Paragraph Frame 2	Sentence Starters
freedom inform safe experiences protected	The author's purpose is to ____ the reader about her ____. She was arrested in Iran because she was a member of the Bahá'í faith. She describes an experience when she saw a place she felt ____ "smashed and destroyed." These are words with negative connotations. Now the author is confused. She likes the idea of ____. But a part of her sees it as a threatening fire where she is cowering in fear. "The Cowering" and "threatening" also have negative connotations. She also misses the "cocoon" where she was ____. The author wonders how she can have two different emotions at the same time.	The author uses words with strong ____. Instead of just being afraid, she is "____ in fear." She is not caught between two choices or decisions. She is caught between "____." Each of these word choices helps the reader to know how strong her ____ are.	• In the opening, stanza the author . . . • When the speaker's soul "breaks free," she is afraid of . . . • The speaker questions . . . • The speaker's purpose for writing seems to be . . .

Peer Review

Students should submit substantive feedback to two peers using the instructions below.

- How well does this response answer the prompt?
- Does the writer support the analysis with textual evidence?
- What did the writer do well in his or her literary analysis? What does the writer need to work on?

Rate

Respond to the following with a point rating that reflects your opinion.

	1	2	3	4
Ideas				
Evidence				
Language and Conventions				

Submit

ELL A **SENTENCE FRAMES**

- You were able to (completely / partly / almost) answer the prompt.
- You could answer the prompt better by ____.
- Your use of textual evidence to support the author's purpose was ____.
- I thought the best part of your analysis was ____.

Unit Overview

Integrated Reading and Writing

THE BIG IDEA

The Vanishing Island

A Night to Remember

Address to the Nation on the Explosion of the Space Shuttle *Challenger*

A Kenyan Teen's Discovery: Let There Be Lights to Save Lions

Mother to Son

Learning to Read

Narrative of the Life of Frederick Douglass, An American Slave

The Day I Saved a Life

The Call of the Wild

Cocoon

Self-Selected Reading

Extended Writing Project

English Language Learner Resources

Novel Study

End-of-Unit Assessment

Blast: A Single Line

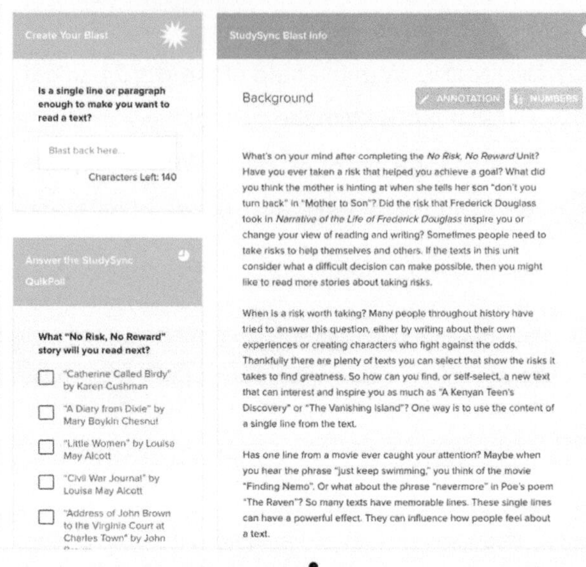

TEXT TALK

What are you thinking after finishing the *No Risk, No Reward* unit? What is your opinion of this genre based on the unit's selections? Answers may vary.

What is one strategy you can use for self-selecting a new text? How does it work? I can use the content of a single line from the text.

What should you do once you choose a text that interests you? Start reading the text to confirm my interest. If I like it, I should keep reading.

Create Your Own Blast

SCAFFOLDS

Ask students to write a 140-character Blast after they complete the QuikPoll.

Use the scaffolds below to differentiate instruction for your ELL English Language Learners.

ELL **BEGINNING** Write a response using the word bank to complete the sentence frame.

INTERMEDIATE Write a response using the sentence frame.

ADVANCED, ADVANCED HIGH Write a response using the sentence starter.

BEGINNING	BEGINNING / INTERMEDIATE	ADVANCED, ADVANCED HIGH
Word Bank	**Sentence Frame**	**Sentence Starter**
line decide phrases events curious	I can read a ___ from a text in order to ___ what to read. ___ and ___ can help me become ___ about a story.	• I can read a text's . . . • I can select a text by reading . . .

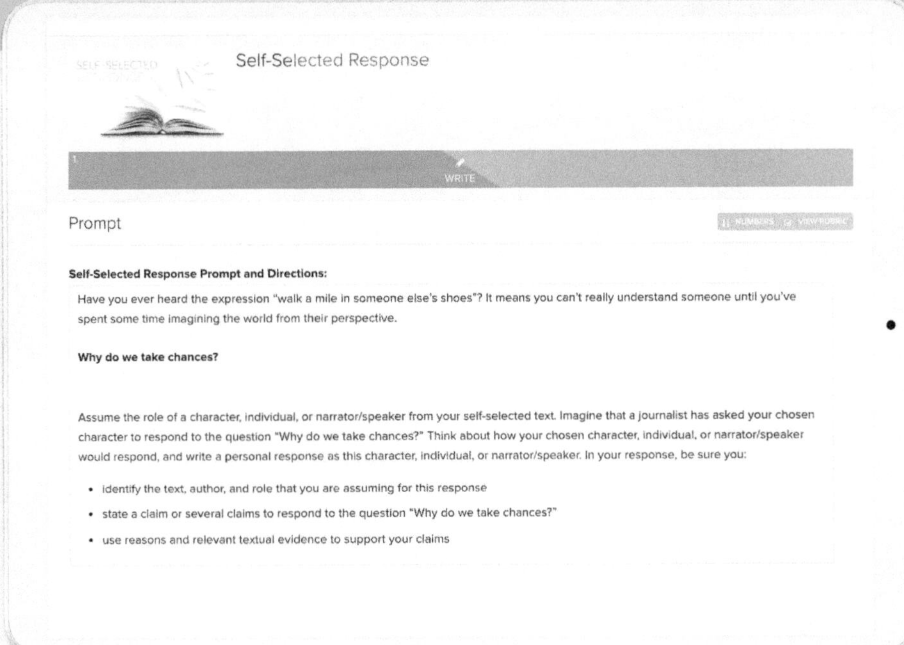
Self-Selected Response

WRITE

Prompt

Self-Selected Response Prompt and Directions:

Have you ever heard the expression "walk a mile in someone else's shoes"? It means you can't really understand someone until you've spent some time imagining the world from their perspective.

Why do we take chances?

Assume the role of a character, individual, or narrator/speaker from your self-selected text. Imagine that a journalist has asked your chosen character to respond to the question "Why do we take chances?" Think about how your chosen character, individual, or narrator/speaker would respond, and write a personal response as this character, individual, or narrator/speaker. In your response, be sure you:

- identify the text, author, and role that you are assuming for this response
- state a claim or several claims to respond to the question "Why do we take chances?"
- use reasons and relevant textual evidence to support your claims

Self-Selected Response

Introduce the Prompt

Read aloud the prompt. Ask students to discuss:

- What is the prompt asking you to do?
- Why might it be helpful to think about the world from another person's point of view?

Write

SCAFFOLDS

Ask students to complete the writing assignment using text evidence to support their answers.

Use the scaffolds below to differentiate instruction for your ELL English Language Learners and A Approaching grade level readers.

ELL **BEGINNING** With the help of the word bank, write a response using paragraph frame 1.

INTERMEDIATE With the help of the word bank, write a response using paragraph frames 1 and 2.

ADVANCED, ADVANCED HIGH Write a response of differentiated length using the sentence starters.

A **APPROACHING** Write a response of differentiated length using the sentence starters.

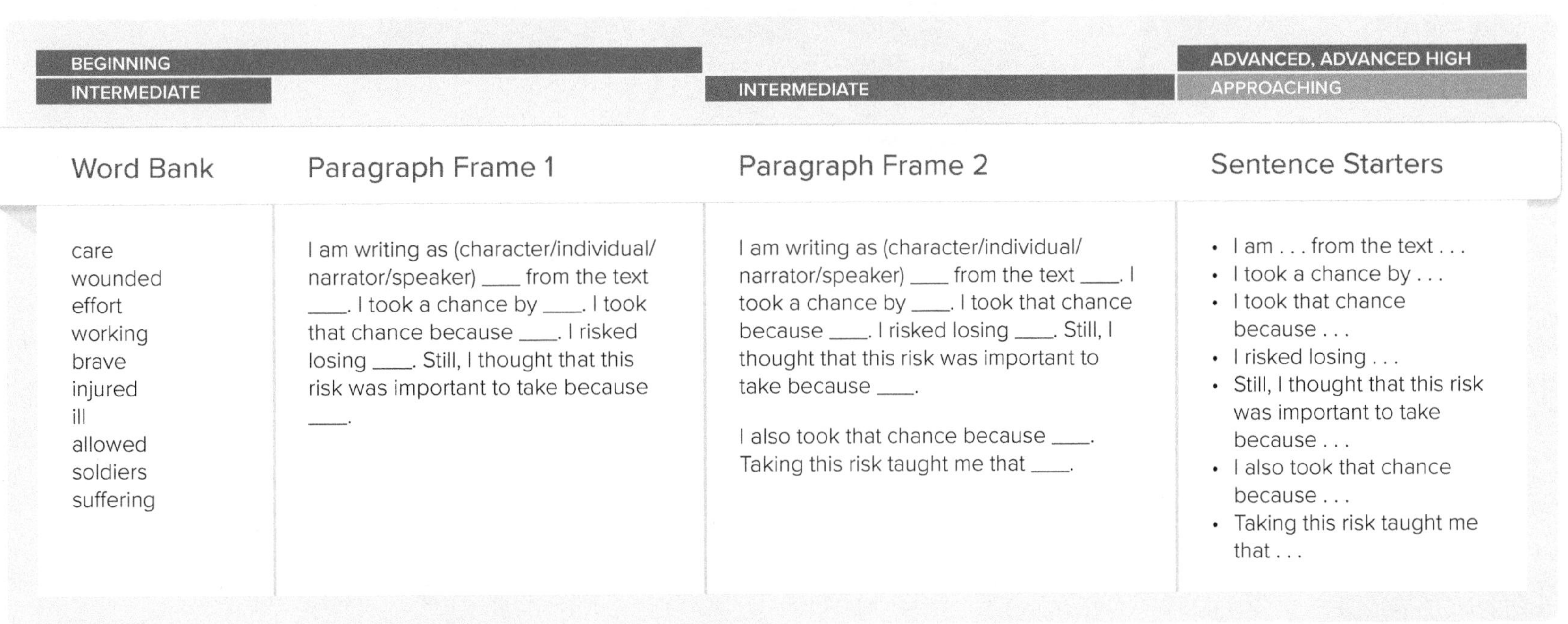

BEGINNING / INTERMEDIATE	BEGINNING	INTERMEDIATE	ADVANCED, ADVANCED HIGH / APPROACHING
Word Bank	**Paragraph Frame 1**	**Paragraph Frame 2**	**Sentence Starters**
care wounded effort working brave injured ill allowed soldiers suffering	I am writing as (character/individual/narrator/speaker) ____ from the text ____. I took a chance by ____. I took that chance because ____. I risked losing ____. Still, I thought that this risk was important to take because ____.	I am writing as (character/individual/narrator/speaker) ____ from the text ____. I took a chance by ____. I took that chance because ____. I risked losing ____. Still, I thought that this risk was important to take because ____. I also took that chance because ____. Taking this risk taught me that ____.	• I am . . . from the text . . . • I took a chance by . . . • I took that chance because . . . • I risked losing . . . • Still, I thought that this risk was important to take because . . . • I also took that chance because . . . • Taking this risk taught me that . . .

Extended Writing Project

The Extended Writing Project (EWP) in Grade 8, Unit 3 focuses on informative writing. The students probe the unit's essential question—Why do we take chances?—as they write an informative text about what happens when people take risks. The multiple informative texts in the unit, as well as fiction and poetry, serve as resources for students in crafting their writing. Specific skill lessons teach developing ideas, thesis statements, organization, and conventions, while other skill lessons focus on supporting details, introductions, and conclusions to help students craft a strong informative text. Directed revision leads students through the process of revising for clarity, development, organization, word choice, and sentence variety. Throughout the EWP, students have the opportunity to practice using created student writing, authentic texts, and their own work.

CONNECT TO ESSENTIAL QUESTION

Why do we take chances?

After finishing the texts in this unit, students have read about many characters and subjects who took risks to achieve rewards. Students will explore how authors inform readers about risk-taking subjects and characters through an informative essay that requires a controlling idea or thesis.

 Audio and audio text highlighting are available in select lessons in the Extended Writing Project.

Extended Writing Project Prompt

What happens when we take risks?

Choose three informative texts from this unit, including research links in the Blasts, and explain how the authors inform readers about their risk-taking subjects. Identify the risks individuals take and the outcomes of those risks. Include a clear main idea or thesis statement, and cite evidence from each text to explain your conclusions.

 APPROACHING GRADE LEVEL

 BEYOND GRADE LEVEL

These icons identify differentiation strategies and scaffolded support for a variety of students. See the digital lesson plan for additional differentiation strategies and scaffolds.

Instructional Path

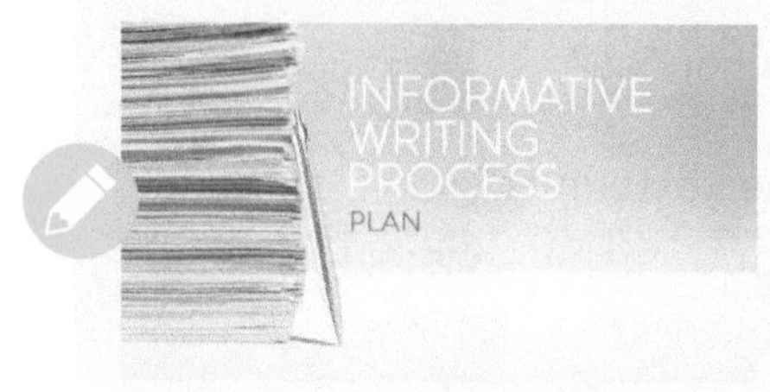

Informative Writing Process: Plan

Objectives: After learning about genre characteristics and craft, students will analyze a sample Student Model and plan a meaningful informative essay in response to a prompt.

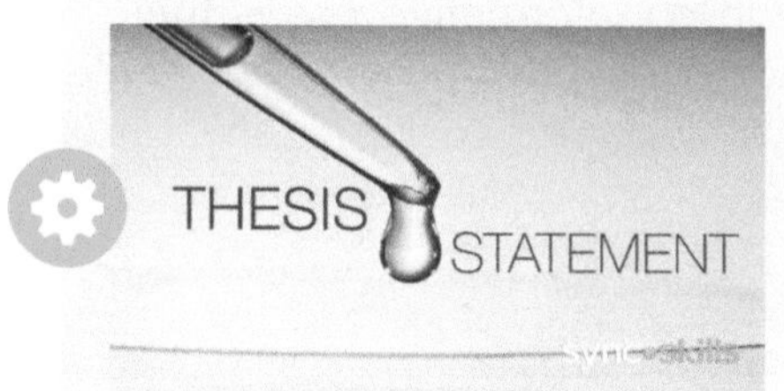

Skill: Thesis Statement

Objectives: After reading and discussing a model of student writing, students will develop and clearly introduce a main idea about a topic.

Skill: Organizing Informative Writing

Objectives: After reading and discussing a model of student writing, students will develop their drafts by organizing ideas, concepts, and information effectively.

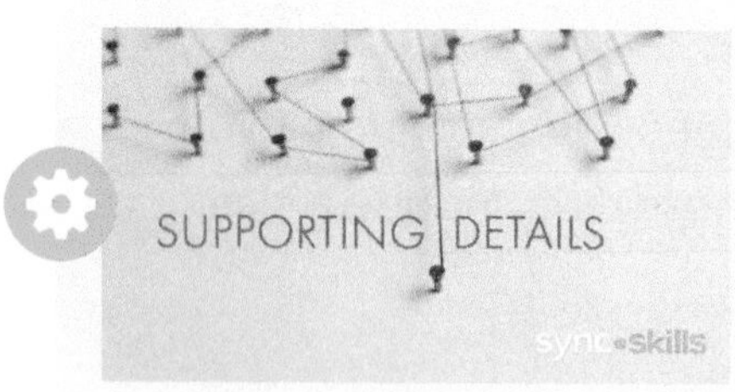

Skill: Supporting Details

Objectives: After reading and discussing a model of student writing, students will develop their drafts by using supporting details.

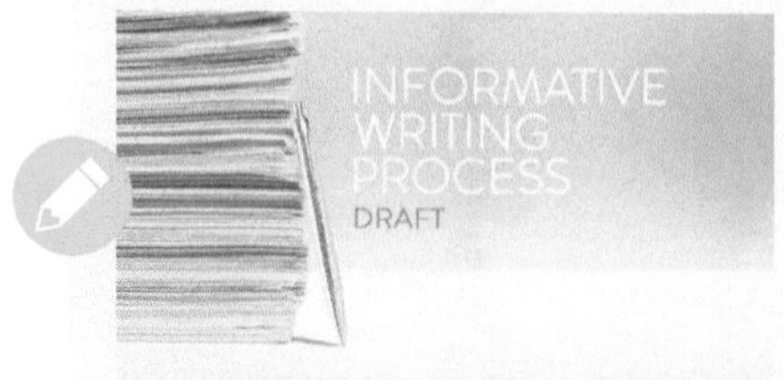

Informative Writing Process: Draft

Objectives: After reading a Student Model draft and reviewing a writing checklist, students will draft a meaningful informative essay in response to a prompt.

The print teacher's edition includes essential point-of-use instruction and planning tools. Complete lesson plans and program documents appear in your digital teacher account.

Skill: Introductions

Objectives: After reading and discussing a model of student writing, students will develop their drafts by improving their introductions.

Skill: Transitions

Objectives: After reading and discussing a model of student writing, students will develop their drafts by using appropriate and varied transitions to create cohesion and clarify the relationships among ideas and concepts.

Skill: Precise Language

Objectives: After reading and discussing a model of student writing, students will develop their drafts by using precise language and domain-specific vocabulary to inform about or explain the topic.

Skill: Style

Objectives: After reading and discussing a model of student writing, students will develop their drafts by establishing and maintaining a formal style.

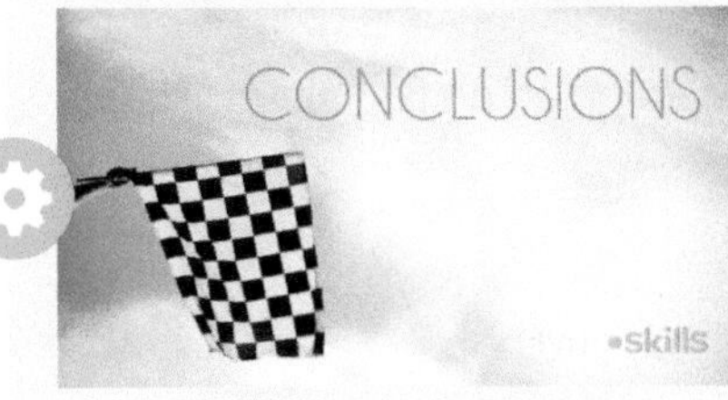

Skill: Conclusions

Objectives: After reading and discussing a model of student writing, students will develop their drafts by improving their conclusions.

Instructional Path

The print teacher's edition includes essential point-of-use instruction and planning tools. Complete lesson plans and program documents appear in your digital teacher account.

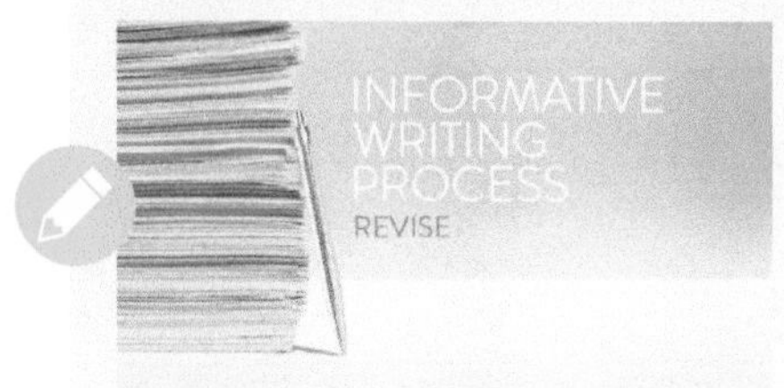

Informative Writing Process: Revise

Objectives: Students will use a revision guide to revise the draft of their informative essay for clarity, development, organization, style, diction, and sentence effectiveness.

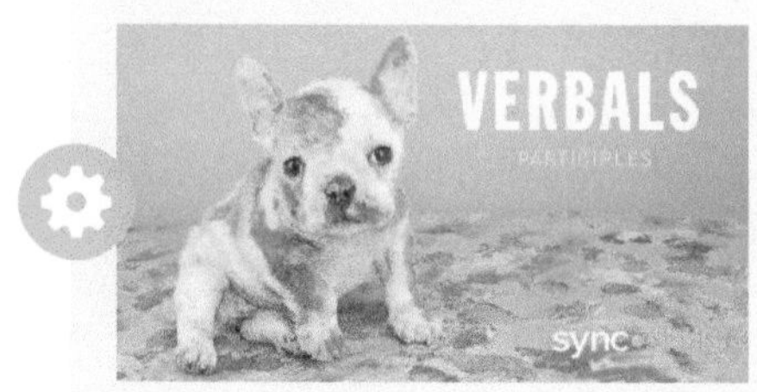

Grammar: Participles

Objectives: After learning about participles and seeing how they are used in text examples, students will practice using participles correctly.

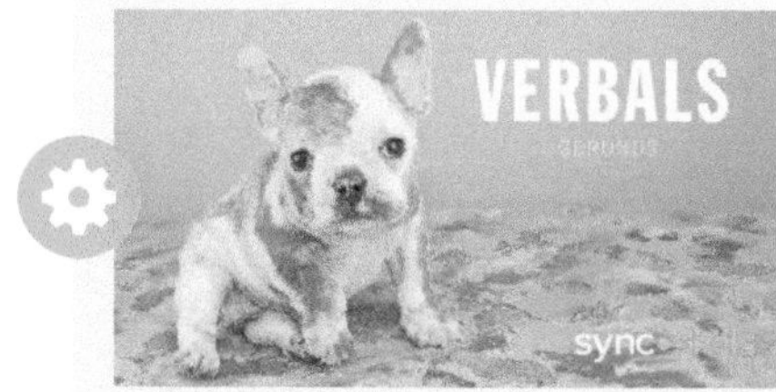

Grammar: Gerunds

Objectives: After learning about gerunds and seeing how they are used in text examples, students will practice using gerunds correctly.

Grammar: Infinitives

Objectives: After learning about infinitives and seeing how they are used in text examples, students will practice using infinitives correctly.

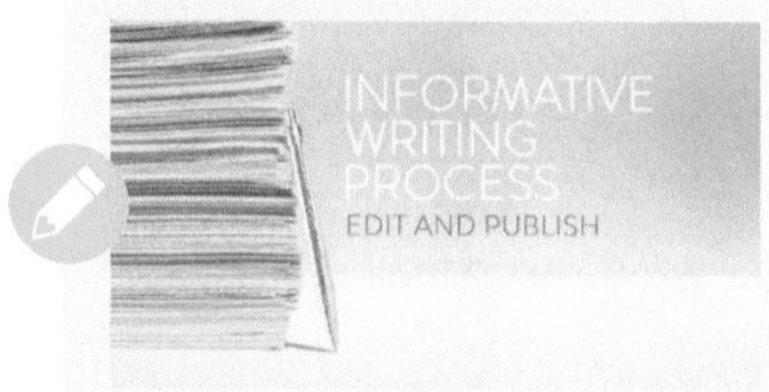

Informative Writing Process: Edit and Publish

Objectives: After seeing an example of editing in the Student Model and reviewing an editing checklist, students will edit and publish the final draft of their informative essay.

Progress Monitoring

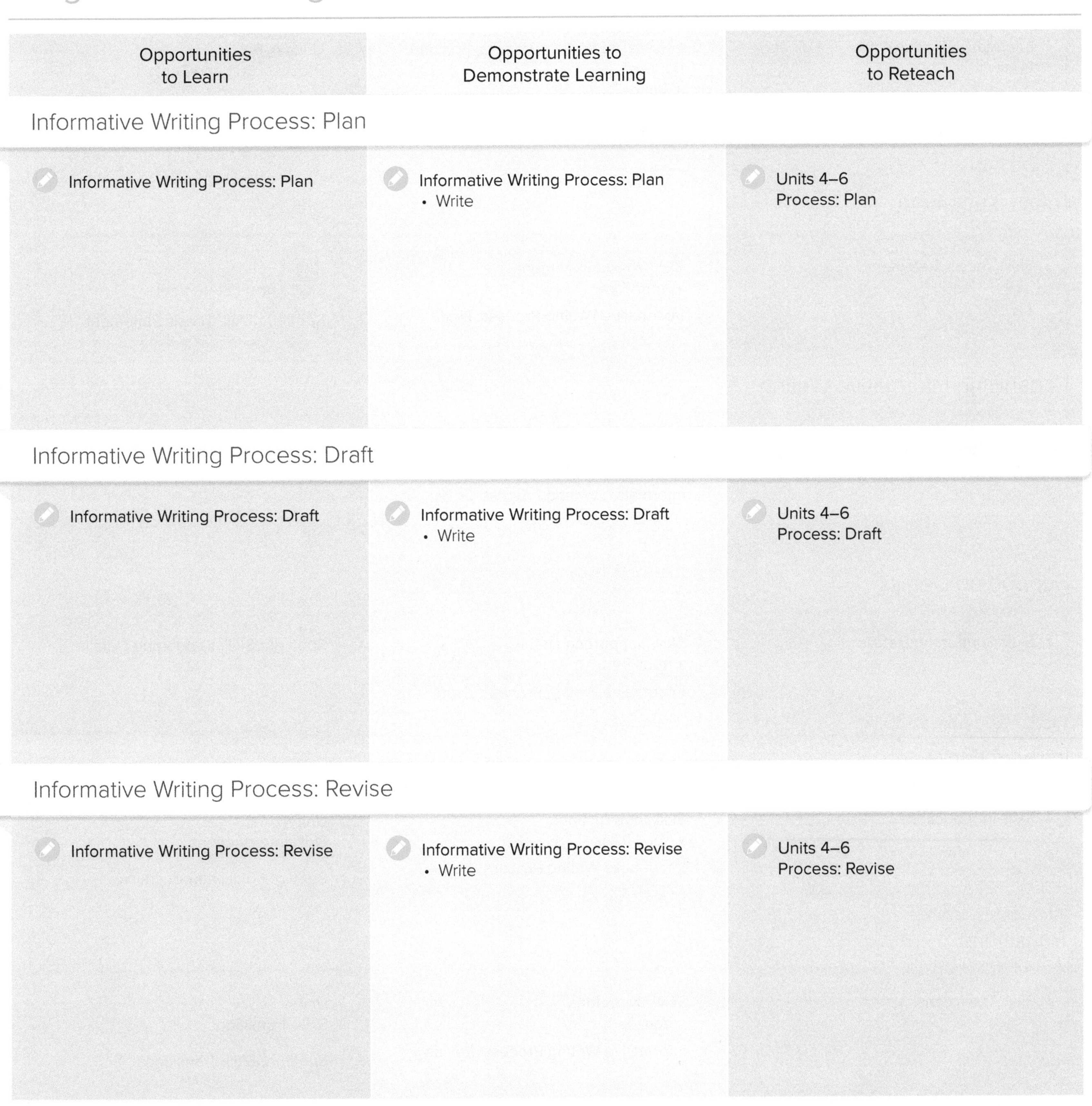

Opportunities to Learn	Opportunities to Demonstrate Learning	Opportunities to Reteach
Informative Writing Process: Plan		
Informative Writing Process: Plan	Informative Writing Process: Plan • Write	Units 4–6 Process: Plan
Informative Writing Process: Draft		
Informative Writing Process: Draft	Informative Writing Process: Draft • Write	Units 4–6 Process: Draft
Informative Writing Process: Revise		
Informative Writing Process: Revise	Informative Writing Process: Revise • Write	Units 4–6 Process: Revise

Informative Writing Process: Edit and Publish

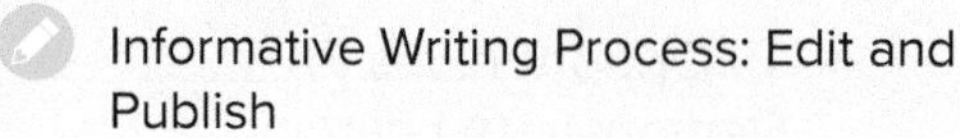

Informative Writing Process: Edit and Publish	Informative Writing Process: Edit and Publish • Write	Units 4, 6 Process: Edit and Publish Unit 5 Process: Edit and Present

Thesis Statement

Skill: Thesis Statement	Skill: Thesis Statement • Your Turn Informative Writing Process: Draft	Unit 4 Skill: Thesis Statement Spotlight Skill: Thesis Statement

Organizing Informative Writing

Skill: Organizing Informative Writing	Skill: Organizing Informative Writing • Your Turn Informative Writing Process: Draft	Spotlight Skill: Organizing Informative Writing

Supporting Details

Skill: Supporting Details	Skill: Supporting Details • Your Turn Informative Writing Process: Draft	Spotlight Skill: Supporting Details

Introductions

Skill: Introductions	Skill: Introductions • Your Turn Informative Writing Process: Revise	Unit 4 Skill: Introductions Spotlight Skill: Introductions

Transitions

Skill: Transitions	Skill: Transitions • Your Turn Informative Writing Process: Revise	Unit 4 Skill: Transitions Spotlight Skill: Transitions

Precise Language

Skill: Precise Language	Skill: Precise Language • Your Turn Informative Writing Process: Revise	Spotlight Skill: Precise Language

Style

Skill: Style	Skill: Style • Your Turn Informative Writing Process: Revise	Unit 4 Skill: Style Spotlight Skill: Style

Conclusions

Skill: Conclusions	Skill: Conclusions • Your Turn Informative Writing Process: Revise	Unit 4 Skill: Conclusions Spotlight Skill: Conclusions

Participles

Grammar: Participle	Grammar: Participle • Your Turn Informative Writing Process: Edit and Publish	Grammar: Commas—With Introductory Phrases

Gerunds

Grammar: Gerunds	Grammar: Gerunds • Your Turn Informative Writing Process: Edit and Publish	Grammar: Verbs—Progressive Tense

Infinitives

Grammar: Infinitives	Grammar: Infinitives • Your Turn Informative Writing Process: Edit and Publish	Grammar: Verbs—Regular Verbs

Informative Writing Process: Plan

Introduce the Extended Writing Project

- What is the prompt asking you to do?
- Which characteristics of informative writing will you need to learn more about in order to respond to the prompt?
- What are the five characteristics of informative writing?
- What elements of craft do informative writers use?

DIFFERENTIATED QUESTIONS

- What does **risk-taking subjects** mean?
- What kinds of risks do people take in the texts you read?
- What can the outcomes or results of the risks teach us?

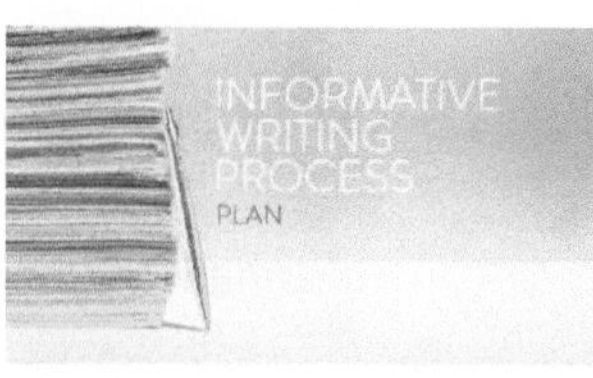

Informative Writing Process: Plan

PLAN | DRAFT | REVISE | EDIT AND PUBLISH

In a variety of genres, the authors of the texts in this unit explore the value of taking risks to achieve rewards. Whether one is learning to read, overcoming a terrible tragedy, or simply getting on with life, any decision can involve a risk. While there is always a chance that something will go wrong, often great, unforeseen opportunities come from risk-taking.

WRITING PROMPT

What happens when we take risks?

Choose three informational texts from this unit, including research links in the Blasts, and explain how the authors inform readers about their risk-taking subjects. Identify the risks individuals take and the outcomes of those risks. Include a clear main idea or thesis statement, and cite evidence from each text to explain your conclusions. Regardless of which sources you choose, be sure your essay includes the following:

- an introduction
- a main idea or thesis statement
- a clear text structure
- supporting details
- a conclusion

Introduction to Informative Writing

Informative writing informs readers about real people, places, things, and events. It includes ideas, concepts, and information that needs to be organized in a logical way such as definition, classification, compare/contrast, and cause/effect. Good informative writing also includes a clear thesis statement or main idea of the essay, and the writer develops that main idea with supporting details, such as descriptions, examples, reasons, quotations, and relevant facts. The characteristics of informative writing include:

- an introduction with a thesis statement or main idea
- supporting details that develop the thesis statement or main idea
- a clear and logical text structure
- a formal style
- a conclusion that wraps up your ideas

As you continue with this Extended Writing Project, you'll receive more instruction and practice at crafting each of the characteristics of informative writing to create your own informative essay.

Review the Rubric

Have students examine the "Informative Writing Rubric—Grade 8" grading rubric. Inform students that this is the same rubric that will be used to evaluate their completed Informative Extended Writing Project.

Read and Annotate

As students read, have them use the Annotation Tool to identify and label the genre characteristics and craft of informative writing, including:

- an introduction with a thesis statement or main idea
- supporting details that develop the thesis statement or main idea
- a clear and logical text structure
- a formal style
- a conclusion that wraps up your ideas

When students finish reading, ask them to share their annotations in small groups.

ANNOTATION GUIDE

Find the following quotes in the Student Model. Then, use the Annotation Tool to label each quote as an example of introduction, main idea or thesis statement, clear text structure, supporting detail, or conclusion.

- People take risks every day.
- Even though these risks and the outcomes of these risks differ, they all teach essential lessons.
- Douglass recalls the rage: "I have had her rush at me with a face made all up of fury, and snatch from me a newspaper, in a manner that fully revealed her apprehension."
- In his speech "Address to the Nation on the Explosion of the Space Shuttle *Challenger*," President Ronald Reagan reminds Americans that the crew was willing to do a dangerous job.
- As a result, many members of the tribe will risk giving up their land and homes to relocate the community.
- They set examples that readers can follow when they need to decide if they want to take a risk for an important goal.

READ AND ANNOTATE

Pair students with on-grade-level peers to complete the annotation activity.

Before you get started on your own informative essay, read this essay that one student, Aiko, wrote in response to the writing prompt. As you read the Model, highlight and annotate the features of informative writing that Aiko included in her essay.

STUDENT MODEL

NOTES

Risks Teach Valuable Lessons

1 People take risks every day. Many risks are small, such as trying a new type of food. Other risks are bigger, such as moving across the country. Whether big or small, all risks have something in common. People can never be certain of how a risk will turn out. Every time a person takes a risk, there is a chance that they will lose something valuable. Frederick Douglass, the crew of the *Challenger*, and members of the Biloxi-Chitimacha-Choctaw Native American tribe are examples of people who have risked devastating losses to pursue worthy goals. Even though these risks and the outcomes of these risks differ, they all teach essential lessons.

2 In his autobiography *Narrative of the Life of Frederick Douglass, an American Slave*, Douglass describes dangerous risks that he took on the road to freedom. Born into slavery, Douglass was legally denied an education. When he was young, however, the mistress of one house started to teach him how to read until her husband told her to stop. She then became angry and violent when Douglass tried to learn on his own. Douglas recalls the rage: "I have had her rush at me with a face made all up of fury, and snatch from me a newspaper, in a manner that fully revealed her apprehension." Douglass knew that there could be serious personal and legal consequences if he were caught, but he decided that knowledge was worth the risk. Douglass saw knowledge as part of his long-term plan to escape slavery. He explains, "I looked forward to a time at which it would be safe for me to escape. I was too young to think of doing so immediately; besides, I wished to learn how to write, as I might have occasion to write my own pass." Douglass's efforts gave him a way to pursue freedom. After several years, he learned how to read and write. The risks Douglass took in pursuit of his goal also teach readers valuable lessons. His success teaches the values of perseverance and faith in one's own abilities.

TEXT TALK

Structure and Organization

What is the purpose of Aiko's essay?

See paragraph 1: Aiko states that she will compare informative texts about risks that historical figures have taken. She will use those texts to show what we can learn from them.

Organization and Focus

Where does Aiko identify her thesis or main idea?

See paragraph 1: The thesis or main idea is stated in the last sentence of the introduction: "Even though these risks and the outcomes of these risks differ, they all teach essential lessons."

NOTES

3 However, failure teaches lessons, too. In 1986, the crew of the space shuttle *Challenger* set out to make new discoveries in space, but they lost their lives in a space shuttle disaster. In his speech "Address to the Nation on the Explosion of the Space Shuttle *Challenger*," President Ronald Reagan reminds Americans that the crew was willing to do a dangerous job. They wanted to travel into space because they believed that the mission would be worth the risk. He says, "They had a hunger to explore the universe and discover its truths." The *Challenger* crew was well prepared and planning to study important questions about the universe. Unfortunately, they never had a chance to achieve that goal because the space shuttle exploded after takeoff. Despite this tragic end, Americans can still learn a valuable lesson from the *Challenger* crew. Reagan explains that "the future doesn't belong to the fainthearted; it belongs to the brave. The *Challenger* crew was pulling us into the future, and we'll continue to follow them." The crew was willing to risk their lives in search of knowledge about the universe. Their efforts teach the values of selflessness and bravery.

4 The risks that one needs to take to pursue a goal can also change over time. This is evident in "Vanishing Island," an informational article by Anya Groner. In the early 1800s, many members of the Biloxi-Chitimacha-Choctaw Native American tribe established a community on a small island off the coast of Louisiana, and it became a "cultural homeland." The island is called Isle de Jean Charles. Since the mid-twentieth century, however, the land on the island has been rapidly eroding, or wearing away. Storms, river engineering, and pollution are causing this to happen, and the landform may not even exist by 2050. As a result, many members of the tribe will risk giving up their land and homes to relocate the community. Chief Naquin, the current chief of the Biloxi-Chitimacha-Choctaw Native American tribe, compared the loss of this island to "the loss of a family member." Leaving that land will be painful, but members are dedicated to preserving their history, community, and culture on the new site. For example, tribal secretary Chantel Comardelle envisions a museum that guides visitors through the history of the island. Many members of the community also value family. To encourage interactions among family members on the new site, they want to build groups of houses with shared backyards. These plans address important issues, but many residents on Isle de Jean Charles will

TEXT TALK

Organization and Coherence

Where does Aiko use a transition to connect ideas from one paragraph to another?

Answers will vary. Sample answer: Aiko uses the word "risks" at the end of paragraph 1 and in the first sentence of paragraph 2 to connect her main idea to a text.

Development of Ideas and Details

How does Aiko use specific details to contribute to the development of her essay?

Answers will vary. Sample answer: In paragraph 2, Aiko quotes passages from *Narrative of the Life of Frederick Douglass, an American Slave* to support her ideas.

Development of Ideas

In what ways does Aiko connect the texts to the world and life in general?

Answers will vary. Sample answer: In paragraph 3, Aiko states, "However, failure teaches lessons, too." In this way, she engages readers by showing them that this informative text is still relevant.

Word Choice

Where do you find Aiko's word choice especially strong or expressive?

Answers will vary. Sample answer: In paragraph 3, Aiko uses the word "selflessness" to describe a quality of the *Challenger* crew and their sacrifice.

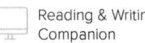

NOTES

still need to endure a difficult move. Their sacrifices teach readers the values of determination and resilience, the ability to recover from a loss.

5 *Narrative of the Life of Frederick Douglass, an American Slave,* "Address to the Nation on the Explosion of the Space Shuttle *Challenger*," and "Vanishing Island" inform readers about historic risks that people have taken to pursue their goals. They show that each person faced hardships as a result of their decisions, and the *Challenger* crew tragically lost their lives. However, their stories continue to teach lessons about honorable qualities. They set examples that readers can follow when they need to decide if they want to take a risk for an important goal.

TEXT TALK

Sentence Fluency

Choose one sentence that you think is really effective. Why do you think it's so strong?

Answers will vary. Sample answer: I think that this sentence from paragraph 4 is strong: "Storms, river engineering, and pollution are causing this to happen, and the landform may not even exist by 2050." The facts in this sentence surprised me because I did not realize that there are a number of reasons why water can take over land, and I was stunned to read that this island could completely vanish in a few decades.

Conventions

Did Aiko use verbals in a logical and correct way? Find one verbal that Aiko used correctly and identify what kind of verbal it is.

Answers will vary. Sample answer: In paragraph 4, Aiko writes, "Leaving that land will be painful." In this clause, "leaving" is a gerund because it ends in "-ing," and it acts like a noun. It is the subject of this independent clause.

 WRITE

Writers often take notes about their ideas before they sit down to write. Think about what you've learned so far about informative writing to help you begin prewriting.

- What are your ideas about what happens when people take risks? Is risk-taking positive or negative behavior? Why?
- Which three informational texts in the unit best reflect your ideas? Why?
- What risks do the people in those texts take?
- What do the outcomes of their risks tell you about risk-taking?
- How do the authors of those texts express their ideas about risk-taking?
- What textual evidence might you use to support your ideas?

Response Instructions

Use the questions in the bulleted list to write a one-paragraph summary. Your summary should describe the ideas that you want to share and how the texts support them.

Don't worry about including all of the details now; focus only on the most essential and important elements. You will refer back to this short summary as you continue through the steps of the writing process.

Write

Circulate as students use the questions in the bulleted list to plan their writing. See the instructions for scaffolding and differentiation that follow.

CHECK FOR SUCCESS

If students struggle to come up with answers for the questions in the lesson, work with students to provide an answer to one question and then help them build from there.

For example, start by asking students, "Do you think risk-taking is good or bad?" or "What happens as a result of the risks taken in the unit?" Once students have answered one question, help them to work through a second question until they've begun to build some momentum. It may be helpful to start with a different question than the one that's listed first in the lesson.

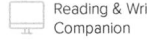

Review Prompt and Rubric

Before students begin writing, review the writing prompt and rubric with the class.

Response Instructions

Use the questions in the bulleted list to write a one-paragraph summary. Your summary should describe the ideas that you want to share and how the texts support them.

Don't worry about including all of the details now; focus only on the most essential and important elements. You will refer back to this short summary as you continue through the steps of the writing process.

Score	Plan	Language and Conventions
4	The writer responds to the questions, and the writing is clear and focused.	The writer demonstrates a consistent command of grammar, punctuation, and usage conventions. Although minor errors may be evident, they do not detract from the fluency or clarity of the writing.
3	The writer responds to the questions, but the writing is not always clear or focused.	The writer demonstrates an adequate command of grammar, punctuation, and usage conventions. Although some errors may be evident, they create few (if any) disruptions in the fluency or clarity of the writing.
2	The writer responds to the questions, but the writing is somewhat unclear and unfocused.	The writer demonstrates a partial command of grammar, punctuation, and usage conventions. Some distracting errors may be evident, at times creating minor disruptions in the fluency or clarity of the writing.
1	The writer responds to the questions, but the writing is very unclear and unfocused.	The writer demonstrates little or no command of grammar, punctuation, and usage conventions. Serious and persistent errors create disruptions in the fluency of the writing and sometimes interfere with meaning.
0	The writer fails to respond to the questions.	Serious and persistent errors overwhelm the writing and interfere with the meaning of the response as a whole, making the writer's meaning impossible to understand.

Write

SCAFFOLDS

Use the scaffolds below to differentiate instruction for your ELL English Language Learners and A Approaching grade-level learners.

ELL **BEGINNING, INTERMEDIATE** With the help of the word bank, write a response using the paragraph frame.

ADVANCED, ADVANCED HIGH Write a response using the sentence starters.

A **APPROACHING** Write a response using the sentence starters.

BEGINNING / INTERMEDIATE		ADVANCED, ADVANCED HIGH / APPROACHING
Word Bank	**Paragraph Frame**	**Sentence Starters**
resilience Anya Groner Frederick Douglass Ronald Reagan perseverance lessons selflessness	The main idea or thesis is that risks teach valuable ____. In his autobiography, ____ takes a risk when he teaches himself how to read. His risk teaches readers about ____. In his speech about the *Challenger* explosion, ____ explains that the crew was willing to risk their lives for science. The story of the *Challenger* crew teaches about ____. In the article "Vanishing Island," the author ____ describes how many residents on Isle de Jean Charles are about to risk losing their home and historic land to preserve their history and continue to develop as a culture. Their risk teaches readers the importance of ____.	• My essay will be about . . . • When people take risks . . . • In the text . . . by . . . • One person who takes a risk is . . . • The outcome of the risk is . . . • This shows readers that . . .

Peer Review

Students should submit substantive feedback to two peers using the review instructions below.

- How well does this response answer the prompt?
- What part of the informative essay are you most interested in reading?
- Are there any ideas that could be improved on? How so?

Rate

Respond to the following with a point rating that reflects your opinion.

	1	2	3	4
Ideas				
Evidence				
Language and Conventions				

ELL A **SENTENCE FRAMES**

- The response does a good job of addressing ____ from the prompt.
- The response would improve by addressing ____ from the prompt.
- I am most interested in reading about ____.
- I think you could improve ____ by (adding / clarifying / describing) ____.

Skill: Thesis Statement

Introduce the Skill

Watch the Concept Definition video and read the following definition with your students.

In an essay, a **thesis statement** expresses the writer's main idea about a topic. The thesis statement usually appears in the **introduction**, or opening paragraph of your essay, and is often the last sentence of the introduction. The **body paragraphs** of the essay should offer a thorough explanation of the thesis statement as well as supporting details, reasons, and relevant evidence. The thesis is often restated in the **conclusion** of an essay.

Skill: Thesis Statement

CHECKLIST FOR THESIS STATEMENT

Before you begin writing your thesis statement, ask yourself the following questions:

- What is the prompt asking me to write about?
- What is the topic of my essay? How can I state it clearly for the reader?
- What claim do I want to make about the topic of this essay? Is my statement clear to my reader?
- Does my thesis statement introduce the body of my essay?
- Where should I place my thesis statement?

Here are some methods to introduce and develop your claim and topic clearly:

- Think about the topic and central idea of your essay.
  - > The central idea of an argument is stated as a claim, or what will be proven or shown to be true.
  - > Identify as many claims as you intend to prove.
- Write a clear statement about the central idea or claim. Your thesis statement should:
  - > let the reader anticipate the body of your essay
  - > respond completely to the writing prompt
- Consider the best placement for your thesis statement.
  - > If your response is short, you may want to get right to the point. Your thesis statement may be presented in the first sentence of the essay.
  - > If your response is longer (as in a formal essay), you can build up your thesis statement. In this case, you can place your thesis statement at the end of your introductory paragraph.

TURN AND TALK

Turn to your partner and discuss online articles you have read that have interesting thesis statements or main ideas. Discuss how using a version of the thesis statement as the headline draws your attention.

SPEAKING FRAMES

- An article I read with an interesting thesis statement is ____.
- The headline caught my attention by ____.

SKILL VOCABULARY

thesis statement / la presentación de la tesis ***noun*** a statement that shares the main idea of an argumentative or informational essay

introduction / la introducción ***noun*** the opening paragraph or section of an essay COGNATE

body paragraph / el párrafo del cuerpo ***noun*** a paragraph that appears between the introduction and the conclusion of an essay

conclusion / la conclusión ***noun*** the closing paragraph or section of an essay; a closing argument in an argumentative text COGNATE

YOUR TURN

Read the phrases below. Then, complete the chart by sorting them into those that are thesis statements and those that are supporting details.

	Phrases
A	I lived in Master Hugh's family about seven years. During this time, I succeeded in learning to read and write. —From *Narrative of the Life of Frederick Douglass*
B	I immediately walked over, picked up the shark and placed him back into the water and told him to live free. I swear the shark looked at me with gratitude. He was alive because I spoke up for him and he knew it. —From "The Day I Saved a Life"
C	Today is a day for mourning and remembering. —From "Address to the Nation on the Explosion of the Space Shuttle *Challenger*"
D	If I was in a separate room any considerable length of time, I was sure to be suspected of having a book, and was at once called to give an account of myself. —From *Narrative of the Life of Frederick Douglass*
E	And perhaps we've forgotten the courage it took for the crew of the shuttle. But they, the *Challenger* Seven, were aware of the dangers, but overcame them and did their jobs brilliantly. —From "Address to the Nation on the Explosion of the Space Shuttle *Challenger*"
F	Movies like Jaws, Day of The Shark, Shark Night, Deep Blue Sea etc., give us the impression of a mindless killing machine out to kill all human beings. Well, I've seen another side of the shark and I've seen it up close and personal. —From "The Day I Saved a Life"

Your Turn

Ask students to complete the Your Turn activity.

Thesis Statement	Supporting Details
A	D
C	E
F	B

Writer's Notebook

Ask students to pretend that they are writing an article for a class newsletter that tells about local places to visit. Have them write a thesis statement about a local place to visit.

TURN AND TALK

Allow students to share their ideas orally in pairs or small groups before writing.

Write

Ask students to complete the writing assignment.

ELL REWRITE CHECKLIST

A Main Idea

- ☐ What selections will you write about?
- ☐ What is the main idea of each selection?
- ☐ How are the main ideas related?

Responding to the Prompt

- ☐ How do the main ideas of each selection relate to the prompt?
- ☐ What makes the risks in each selection different?
- ☐ What makes the risks in each selection similar?
- ☐ How can you clearly state your ideas?

Placement

- ☐ Is there information that you need to share before stating your thesis?
- ☐ Where will your thesis statement appear in your essay?
- ☐ Why will it work best in that location?

Thesis Statement	Supporting Details

WRITE

Use the questions in the checklist to revise the beginning of your informative essay.

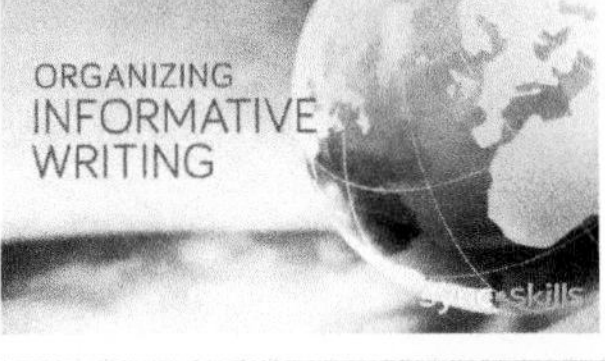

Skill: Organizing Informative Writing

CHECKLIST FOR ORGANIZING INFORMATIVE WRITING

As you consider how to organize your writing for your informative essay, use the following questions as a guide:

- What is my topic? How can I summarize the main idea?
- How can I organize the information from the text into broad categories?
- What is the logical order of my ideas, concepts, and information? Do I see a pattern that is similar to a specific text structure?
- Which organizing structure should I use to present my information?
- How might using graphics, headings, or some form of multimedia help to present my information?

Here are some broader categories that can help you organize ideas, concepts, and information and aid comprehension:

- topic or main idea
- definitions, including restatements and examples
- classifications, including subcategories of a topic
- comparisons of ideas or concepts
- cause-and-effect relationships

SKILL VOCABULARY

informative writing / la escritura informativa ***noun*** nonfiction writing that presents information about real people, places, things, and events

organizational structure / la estructura organizativa ***noun*** the order or pattern that a writer uses to organize information, such as cause-and-effect or compare-and-contrast COGNATE

heading / el título ***noun*** the title given to a particular section of text

Skill: Organizing Informative Writing

Introduce the Skill

Watch the Concept Definition video and read the following definition with your students.

The purpose of **informative writing** is to inform readers about real people, places, things, and events, so authors need to organize their ideas, concepts, and information in a logical way. Experienced authors carefully choose an **organizational structure**, such as definition, classification, compare/contrast, and cause/effect, that best suits their material. Writers often use an outline to decide which organizational structure will help them express their ideas. For example, texts about historical topics might need a cause/effect structure to explain why something happened. **Headings** that divide a series of paragraphs can make organization obvious. They tell readers how information is arranged and presented. A reader can scan a document and find specific information. Some writers also use **graphics**, such as charts and tables, or **multimedia**, such as video, sound, and hypertext links, to make complex information easier to understand. The organizational structure should always be appropriate for the writing purpose.

TURN AND TALK

Turn to your partner and discuss a time you followed directions to complete a task, such as cooking with a recipe or assembling something with an instruction manual.

SPEAKING FRAMES

- I followed directions to ____.
- The structure of the directions was / was not clear because ____

Your Turn

Ask students to complete the Your Turn activity.

"What Is Ornithology?"	definition
"On Puffins and Penguins: An Exclusive Look at Their Similarities and Differences"	compare/contrast
"Why Can't Ostriches Fly?"	cause and effect
"A Guide to Flightless Birds"	classification

Your Turn

Ask students to complete the Your Turn activity. Answers will vary.

Introduction:	Richard Turere, Frederick Douglass, and the *Challenger* crew show that taking risks brings out the best in people.
Body Paragraph 1:	Richard Turere took a risk when he used a flashlight to scare away lions. This risk gave him an idea for a set of lights that scare away lions. These lights protect people, the livestock that lions hunt, and the lions themselves.
Body Paragraph 2:	Like Richard Turere, Frederick Douglass helped a lot of people because he secretly learned how to read and write even though he could have been punished. His success changed his own life, and it continues to inspire others.
Body Paragraph 3:	The *Challenger* crew also inspired many people even though their story ended in tragedy. In his speech about the disaster, President Reagan says that people will follow their example because they took a risk for important reasons.
Conclusion:	Taking risks can help people develop bravery and strength. It can also inspire others to do the same.

YOUR TURN

Read the informational text titles below. Then, complete the chart by writing the organizational structure that would best convey the ideas of each text.

Organizational Structure Options			
compare/contrast	definition	classification	cause and effect

Informational Text Title	Organizational Structure
"What Is Ornithology?"	
"On Puffins and Penguins: An Exclusive Look at Their Similarities and Differences"	
"Why Can't Ostriches Fly?"	
"A Guide to Flightless Birds"	

YOUR TURN

Complete the chart below by writing a short summary of what you will focus on in each paragraph of your essay.

Outline	Summary
Introduction:	
Body Paragraph 1:	
Body Paragraph 2:	
Body Paragraph 3:	
Conclusion:	

SKILL VOCABULARY

graphics / las gráficas ***noun*** charts or tables that can make complex information easier to understand COGNATE

multimedia / multimedia ***adjective*** using several communications media at the same time COGNATE

Skill:
Supporting Details

••• CHECKLIST FOR SUPPORTING DETAILS

As you look for supporting details to develop your topic, claim, or thesis statement, ask yourself the following questions:

- What is my main idea about this topic?
- What does a reader need to know about the topic in order to understand the main idea?
- What details will support my thesis statement?
- Is this information necessary to the reader's understanding of the topic?
- Does this information help to develop and refine my key concept or idea?
- Does this information relate closely to my thesis statement or claim?
- Where can I find better evidence that will provide stronger support for my point?

Here are some suggestions for how you can develop your topic:

- Review your thesis statement or claim.
- Consider your main idea.
- Note what the reader will need to know in order to understand the topic.
- Be sure to consult credible sources.
- Use different types of supporting details, such as:
  > well-chosen facts that are specific to your topic and enhance your discussion to establish credibility with your reader and build information
  > definitions to explain difficult concepts, terms, or ideas in your topic, claim, or thesis statement
  > concrete details that will add descriptive and detailed material to your topic
  > quotations to directly connect your thesis statement or claim to the text
  > examples and other information to deepen your claim, topic, or thesis statement

Skill: Supporting Details

Introduce the Skill

Watch the Concept Definition video and read the following definition with your students.

In informative and argumentative writing, writers develop their thesis statements or claims with information called **supporting details**. These details can include any kind of textual evidence, such as descriptions, examples, reasons, quotations that reveal expert opinions, facts, and statistics. Supporting details help explain key ideas and are closely related to the topic.

Supporting details that develop a thesis statement or claim must be relevant, necessary, or concrete. **Relevant** supporting details are appropriate and logically related to the topic. **Necessary** details are essential and required for developing a writer's thesis statement or proving a writer's claim. A **concrete detail** is very specific. It helps readers visualize and understand the topic or the idea in the writer's mind.

Though information is plentiful, the writer must be careful to **evaluate**, or judge, the quality of information to determine what is most important and most closely related to the thesis statement or claim.

TURN AND TALK

Turn to your partner and share a "fun fact" about the natural world. It could relate to an animal species, the human body, space, or another topic. Discuss how that fun fact would make a strong supporting detail in a paper on that topic.

SPEAKING FRAMES

- A "fun fact" I know is ____.
- This fact relates to the topic of ____.
- This fact would make a good supporting detail because ____.

Your Turn

Ask students to complete the Your Turn activitiy.

QUESTION 1

A. Incorrect. This quotation does not support the idea that teaching was also risky.

B. Incorrect. This quotation does not support the idea that teaching was also risky.

C. Correct. This quotation supports the idea that teaching was also risky.

D. Incorrect. This quotation does not support the idea that teaching was also risky.

QUESTION 2

A. Incorrect. This quotation does not support Aiko's idea that failure is part of success.

B. Correct. This quotation best supports Aiko's idea that failure is part of success, "part of the process."

C. Incorrect. This quotation does not support Aiko's idea that failure is part of success.

D. Incorrect. This quotation states that more work is to be done, but it does not support Aiko's idea that failure is part of success.

YOUR TURN

Choose the best answer to each question.

1. Aiko wants to improve the supporting details of a previous draft of her informative essay. How can she rewrite the underlined sentence to provide more support?

> In his autobiography *Narrative of the Life of Frederick Douglass, an American Slave*, Douglass describes many risks he took. However, Douglass is not the only person who took risks. <u>Some kids helped him</u>. This shows that it was also risky to agree to teach an enslaved person at the time.

- ○ A. Douglass knew some white children, and he says, "As many of these as I could, I converted into teachers."
- ○ B. Douglass gave bread to some boys, "who, in return, would give me that more valuable bread of knowledge."
- ○ C. Even though it was "almost an unpardonable offence to teach slaves to read in this Christian country," some local boys agreed to teach him.
- ○ D. Douglass recalls chatting with some white boys about slavery: "These words used to trouble them; they would express for me the liveliest sympathy."

2. Aiko would like to add a supporting detail to a previous draft of her paragraph on "Address to the Nation on the Explosion of the Space Shuttle *Challenger*." Which quotation could best follow and provide support for her last sentence?

> Failure can have a great impact on people, too. For example, when the crew of the *Challenger* died on their mission, the American people were deeply affected by the loss. The tragedy was a reminder that failure is part of success.

- ○ A. "Nineteen years ago, almost to the day, we lost three astronauts in a terrible accident on the ground. But we've never lost an astronaut in flight; we've never had a tragedy like this. And perhaps we've forgotten the courage it took for the crew of the shuttle."
- ○ B. "I know it is hard to understand, but sometimes painful things like this happen. It's all part of the process of exploration and discovery. It's all part of taking a chance and expanding man's horizons."
- ○ C. "I've always had great faith in and respect for our space program, and what happened today does nothing to diminish it. We don't hide our space program."
- ○ D. "We'll continue our quest in space. There will be more shuttle flights and more shuttle crews and, yes, more volunteers, more civilians, more teachers in space. Nothing ends here; our hopes and our journeys continue."

SKILL VOCABULARY

supporting detail / el detalle de apoyo ***noun*** a piece of text evidence, a description, an example, a reason, an expert opinion, a fact, or a statistic that further explains a key idea and closely relates to the thesis or claim

relevant / relevante ***adjective*** appropriate and logically related to the topic COGNATE

necessary / necesario/a ***adjective*** essential and required COGNATE

concrete detail / el detalle concreto ***noun*** a specific detail that helps readers visualize or understand the topic or the idea in the writer's mind COGNATE

evaluate / evaluar ***verb*** to judge or decide; to estimate the quality of COGNATE

YOUR TURN

Complete the chart below by identifying evidence from each text you've chosen. Identifying evidence will help you develop your own thesis statement.

Text	Evidence
Selection #1:	
Selection #2:	
Selection #3:	

Your Turn

Ask students to complete the Your Turn activity. Answers will vary.

Selection #1:	Taking a risk to walk outside near wild animals at night led Richard Turere to come up with an invention that helped a lot of people.
Selection #2:	Because asking for help was too risky, Frederick Douglass came up with a way to trick other boys into helping him when he challenged them to write as well as he could.
Selection #3:	The *Challenger* crew reminded hard-to-impress Americans that space is still a new frontier for exploration and discovery.

Writer's Notebook

Ask students to think of a topic they know a lot about, such as their favorite class, TV show, or sport. Ask them to pretend they are writing a study guide on that topic. Have students write a list of supporting details that are important to understanding the topic.

TURN AND TALK

Allow students to share their topics and list of supporting details orally in pairs or small groups.

Informative Writing Process: Draft

Write

Ask students to complete the writing assignment.

CHECK FOR SUCCESS

If students struggle to begin drafting their informative essay, ask them the following questions:

- What is your thesis statement or the main idea of your informative essay?
- What is your main idea about each selection that you chose?
- How do those ideas support your thesis statement or the main idea of your essay?
- What supporting details help explain key ideas and are closely related to your topic?

DRAFT CHECKLIST

- ☐ Does your introduction clearly include your thesis statement or main idea of the essay?
- ☐ Do the main ideas in your body paragraphs help develop your thesis statement?
- ☐ Does your conclusion wrap up your ideas?

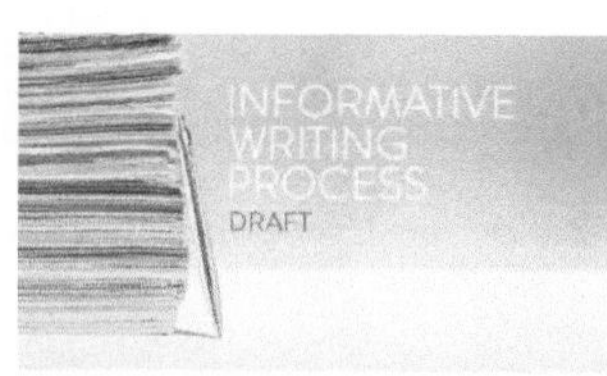

Informative Writing Process: Draft

PLAN | DRAFT | REVISE | EDIT AND PUBLISH

You have already made progress toward writing your informative essay. Now it is time to draft your informative essay.

WRITE

Use your plan and other responses in your Binder to draft your informative essay. You may also have new ideas as you begin drafting. Feel free to explore those new ideas as you have them. You can also ask yourself these questions:

- Does my thesis statement or main idea of the essay clearly respond to the prompt?
- Does the organization of my essay make sense?
- Have I developed my thesis statement by using supporting details that help explain key ideas and are closely related to my topic?
- Have I made my ideas clear to readers?

Before you submit your draft, read it over carefully. You want to be sure that you've responded to all aspects of the prompt.

Peer Review

Students should submit substantive feedback to two peers using the review instructions below.

- Has the writer stated a thesis that clearly responds to the prompt?
- What suggestions can you make to help the writer improve the organization of this informative essay?
- Are there any ideas that could be improved on? How so?
- Does the writer use relevant supporting details to develop the thesis statement? Are there any supporting details that could be added or improved?

SENTENCE FRAMES

- You clearly stated your thesis that ____.
- Your thesis does / does not respond to the entire prompt because ____.
- Each supporting detail does / does not help develop your thesis because ____.
- I would suggest improving your ____ by ____.

Here is Aiko's informative essay draft. As you read, identify Aiko's main ideas. As she continues to revise and edit her essay, she will find and improve weak spots in her writing, as well as correct any language or punctuation mistakes.

NOTES

STUDENT MODEL: FIRST DRAFT

Risks Teach Valuable Lessons

~~Everybody takes risks even through they can never be certain of how a risk will turn out. Some risks are small. Some are big. Every time a person takes a risk, risking losing something. Frederick Douglass, the crew of the Challenger, and members of the Biloxi-Chitimacha-Choctaw Native American tribe all risked losses in to pursue their goals. The risks that they took were very different, but they all show that risk-taking can help people learn lessons.~~

People take risks every day. Many risks are small, such as trying a new type of food. Other risks are bigger, such as moving across the country. Whether big or small, all risks have something in common. People can never be certain of how a risk will turn out. Every time a person takes a risk, there is a chance that they will lose something valuable. Frederick Douglass, the crew of the *Challenger*, and members of the Biloxi-Chitimacha-Choctaw Native American tribe are examples of people who have risked devastating losses to pursue worthy goals. Even though these risks and the outcomes of these risks differ, they all teach essential lessons.

Skill: Introductions

Aiko adds more information about the people she will write about to clarify why she chose to analyze their stories in her essay. After reviewing these changes, Aiko sees that she still needs to engage readers at the beginning of her paragraph, so she adds a new sentence as a hook. After making those changes, Aiko then revises her thesis statement so that it flows from her new ideas.

In his autobiography *Narrative of the Life of Frederick Douglass, An American Slave*, Douglass describes many dangerous risks taking. Born into slavery, Douglass was legaly denied an education. When he was young, the mistress of one house started to teach him how to read until her husband telling her to stop. She then got angry and violent when Douglass tried to learn on his own. Douglass says, "I have had her rush at me with a face made all up of fury, and snatch from me a newspaper, in a manner that fully revealed her apprehension." Still, Douglass, wanting to learn, he explains, "All this, however, was too late. The first step had been taken. Mistress, in teaching me the alphabet, had given me the *inch*, and no precaution could prevent me from taking the *ell*." Douglass's efforts made a difference. After several years, he learned how to read and writing.

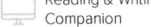

B **GRAPHIC ORGANIZER**

Before students write their draft, have them think about the Student Model (and process) and the prompt. Challenge students to create an original graphic organizer to help plan their thoughts before beginning their draft. Students can share/compare their graphic organizers with their peers.

Analyze Student Model

Have students discuss the questions in the lesson as well as the Student Model draft. Ask:

- What thesis statement or main idea does Aiko present in the introduction?
- What main idea does Aiko share in her first body paragraph?
- How does the main idea in the body paragraph support her thesis statement or the main idea of the essay?

Encourage students to share ideas for their own informative essays based on the questions in the lesson.

ELL **SPEAKING FRAMES**

- The writer's thesis statement or main idea of the essay is ____.
- The main idea in the writer's first body paragraph is ____.
- The writer uses the main idea of the first body paragraph to develop her thesis statement by ____.

Introductions

Discuss the Model

1. Why does Aiko replace the first sentence in her introduction? Answers will vary. Sample answer: Her original sentence was not engaging, so Aiko decides to add a stronger hook. She writes a short sentence that shows how the topic of risk-taking is an important part of everyone's life.
2. Why does Aiko decide to revise her thesis statement? Aiko has revised some information in her introduction, so she needs to make sure that her thesis statement flows from her updated set of ideas.

ELL **SPEAKING FRAMES**

- Aiko replaces the first sentence in her introduction because ____.
- Aiko revises her thesis statement because ____.

Transitions

Discuss the Model

1. What is Aiko searching for as she rereads her draft? any unclear relationships among ideas and concepts
2. What is an example of a transition that Aiko adds to create cohesion? What relationship does it show among ideas in her draft? Answers will vary. Sample answer: Aiko uses the word "however" to show the difference in outcomes for Douglass and the *Challenger* crew.

ELL **SPEAKING FRAMES**

- As Aiko rereads her draft, she searches for ____.
- Aiko uses the transition ____ to show the relationship between ____ and ____.

Style

Discuss the Model

1. How does Aiko revise the language in her draft to make it more formal? She uses a third-person instead of a second-person pronoun. She replaces a conversational phrase with a more formal one.
2. How does domain-specific vocabulary improve Aiko's essay? Answers will vary. Sample answer: Domain-specific vocabulary shows readers that Aiko is knowledgeable about her topic, and it makes the information that she shares more accurate.

Style

Connect to Mentor Text

Project the following example of style and discuss with your students:

Then it happened. I hit the jackpot! I discovered in my scoop the largest tooth I had ever seen. It was four inches long and black in color. Its edges were serrated and you could still see the gum line. The great white teeth I found paled in comparison to this massive tooth. It was a Megalodon tooth! ("The Day I Saved a Life")

Ask students:

- Which style of writing does the example show?
- Which style will be appropriate for your informative essay?

NOTES

~~The risks Douglass took in pursuit of his goal also teach readers valuable lessons. His success teaches the values of perseverance and faith in one's own abilities.~~

~~In 1986, The crew of the space shuttle *Challenger* set out to making new discoveries in space. They lost they're lives in a space shuttle disaster. In his speech, "Address to the Nation on the Explosion of the Space Shuttle *Challenger*," President Ronald Reagan reminds Americans that the crew was willed to do a dangerous job. Believing that their mission would be worth the risk.~~

The risks Douglass took in pursuit of his goal also teach readers valuable lessons. His success teaches the values of perseverance and faith in one's own abilities.

However, failure teaches lessons, too. In 1986, the crew of the space shuttle *Challenger* set out to make new discoveries in space, but they lost their lives in a space shuttle disaster. In his speech "Address to the Nation on the Explosion of the Space Shuttle *Challenger*," President Ronald Reagan reminds Americans that the crew was willing to do a dangerous job. They wanted to travel into space because they believed that the mission would be worth the risk.

And well prepared, there were important questions about the universe that the *Challenger* crew was planning to study. Unfortunately, they never had a chance to acheive that goal because the Space Shuttle exploded after takeoff despite this tragic end, Americans are still to learn a valuable lessen from the *Challenger* crew. Reagan's explaining "The future doesn't belong to the fainthearted; it belongs to the brave. The *Challenger* crew was pulling us into the future, and we'll continue to follow them." The crew was willing to risk their lives to find out new information about the universe. The crew also teaches the values of putting others before yourself and bravery.

~~The risks that you need to take to go after a goal aren't always the same over time. This is evident in "Vanishing Island," an informational article by Anya Groner. In the early 1800s, many members of the Biloxi-Chitimacha-Choctaw Native American tribe established a community on a small island off the coast of Louisiana called Isle de Jean Charles, and it became a "cultural homeland." Since the~~

Skill: Transitions

Aiko sees that the ideas in this paragraph do not logically follow from the ideas in the first body paragraph about Frederick Douglass's risk. She searches for a way to use a transition word and a clear topic sentence to show the relationship between the two paragraphs. She uses the linking word "However" to show readers that the outcome of the Challenger crew's risk contrasts with the successful outcome of Frederick Douglass's risk.

ELL **SPEAKING FRAMES**

- Aiko revises the language in her draft to make it more formal by ____.
- Domain-specific vocabulary improves Aiko's essay because ____.

NOTES

~~mid-twentieth century, however, the land on the Island been disappearing into the water that's around the Island at a fast rate. It may not even exist by 2050. As a result, many members of the tribe will risk to give up their land and homes to relocate the community.~~

The risks that one needs to take to pursue a goal can also change over time. This is evident in "Vanishing Island," an informational article by Anya Groner. In the early 1800s, many members of the Biloxi-Chitimacha-Choctaw Native American tribe established a community on a small island off the coast of Louisiana, and it became a "cultural homeland." The island is called Isle de Jean Charles. Since the mid-twentieth century, however, the land on the island has been rapidly eroding, or wearing away. Storms, river engineering, and pollution are causing this to happen, and the landform may not even exist by 2050.

Skill: Style

Aiko starts by looking for sentences that sound conversational, and she finds three issues in her first sentence: It includes a second-person pronoun, the conversational phrase "go after a goal," and a contraction. Since this sentence needs several changes, she decides to rewrite it by using third-person pronouns, replacing the conversational phrase, and avoiding contractions.

~~Chief Naquin, the current chief of the Biloxi-Chitimacha-Choctaw Native American tribe, compared the loss of this island to "the loss of a family member." But the members' not giving up and dedicated to preserving their history, community, and culture on the new site. The tribal secretary Chantel Comardelle wants a museum that guides visitor's through the history of the island. Many members of the community also value family. And building houses that give extended families shared backyards. These plans address important issues, but many residents on Isle de Jean Charles will still need to go through a major move, and that teaches readers a lot.~~

Chief Naquin, the current chief of the Biloxi-Chitimacha-Choctaw Native American tribe, compared the loss of this island to "the loss of a family member." Leaving that land will be painful, but members are dedicated to preserving their history, community, and culture on the new site. For example, tribal secretary Chantel Comardelle envisions a museum that guides visitors through the history of the island. Many members of the community also value family. To encourage interactions among family members on the new site, they want to build groups of houses with shared backyards. These plans address important issues, but many residents on Isle de Jean Charles will still need to endure a difficult move. Their sacrifices teach readers the values of determination and resilience, the ability to recover from a loss.

Skill: Precise Language

Aiko searches for other language that needs to be more specific and vivid. For example, she replaces "wants" with "envisions" and elaborates on the purpose of the museum that the tribal secretary describes.

Precise Language

Discuss the Model

1. In this section of her draft, why doesn't Aiko successfully convey information to readers? Vague, general, and overused language makes the information in this section unclear.
2. What is one example of precise language that Aiko adds to the draft? Answers will vary. Sample answer: Aiko replaces "wants a museum" with "envisions a museum."
3. How does that change improve her essay? Answers will vary. Sample answer: This change makes the sentence more accurate. It shows that Chantel Comardelle is imagining and designing a museum that has not been built yet.

SPEAKING FRAMES

- In this section of her draft, Aiko doesn't successfully convey information because ____.
- One example of precise language that Aiko adds to the draft is ____.
- That change improves her essay because ____.

Precise Language

Connect to Mentor Text

Project the following excerpt from "A Night to Remember" as an example of precise language and discuss with your students:

For the next 37 seconds, Fleet and Lee stood quietly side by side, watching the ice draw nearer. Now they were almost on top of it, and still the ship didn't turn. The berg towered wet and glistening far above the forecastle deck, and both men braced themselves for a crash. Then, miraculously, the bow began to swing to port. At the last second the stem shot into the clear, and the ice glided swiftly by along the starboard side. It looked to Fleet like a very close shave.

Ask students:

- What information is the author trying to convey?
- What is one example of precise language that the author uses?
- What domain-specific vocabulary does the author use?

Conclusions

Discuss the Model

1. Why does Aiko delete the first sentence in her conclusion? Aiko sees that the first sentence in her conclusion is not clearly related to her thesis statement or the information that she presents in her essay.
2. Why does Aiko update the thesis statement or main idea in her conclusion? Aiko has already revised the thesis statement or main idea in her introduction, so she needs to revise the main idea in her conclusion as well. She wants to make sure that both statements convey the same ideas.
3. Aiko wanted to motivate readers with her last line. How well did she do? Can you suggest any ways to improve the last line? Answers will vary.

Conclusions

Connect to Mentor Text

Project the following example of a conclusion from "Vanishing Island" and discuss with your students:

Perhaps, years from now, Comardelle's children will recall these trips to Isle de Jean Charles, an island homeland that no longer exists. Sitting on a back porch, they'll tell their children about how they caught crabs in the bayou. How they listened to their grandparents speak in Cajun French about weddings in general stores and waiting out hurricanes in their daddy's boats. Around them the egrets will take flight as Spanish moss sways in the breeze. Relatives might wave from nearby porches. After all, history isn't just what happened a long time ago. The creation of a new homeland, the tribe's relocation, and the council's efforts to maintain culture are all history in action. If the relocation works, Comardelle, the Naquins, and the other members of the Biloxi-Chitimacha-Choctaw tribe will achieve something amazing. Their people and their culture will have a safe home in coastal Louisiana for centuries to come.

Ask students:

- What do you notice about this conclusion?
- Did the author restate the thesis or main idea of this essay?
- What important ideas from the article did the author include in this conclusion?
- What impression might the author have wanted to make on you as a reader? How do you know?

NOTES

~~People need to consider when risks are worth taking and when they are not worth taken. *Narrative of the Life of Frederick Douglass, An American Slave*, "Address to the Nation on the Explosion of the Space Shuttle *Challenger*," and "Vanishing Island" are stories about people who took major risks. The risks that they took were very different, but they all show that risk-taking can help people learn lessons.~~

Narrative of the Life of Frederick Douglass, an American Slave, "Address to the Nation on the Explosion of the Space Shuttle *Challenger*," and "Vanishing Island" inform readers about historic risks that people have taken to pursue their goals. They show that each person faced hardships as a result of their decisions, and the *Challenger* crew tragically lost their lives. However, their stories continue to teach lessons about honorable qualities. They set examples that readers can follow when they need to decide if they want to take a risk for an important goal.

Skill: Conclusions

Aiko's revision brings her essay to a close by clearly reviewing her thesis statement and supporting details. To leave her readers with a lasting impression, she also tried to motivate them by adding the final line. It reminds readers that they can use the information in this essay when they need to decide whether or not to take a risk.

SPEAKING FRAMES

- Aiko deletes the first sentence in her conclusion because ____.
- Aiko updates the thesis statement in her conclusion because ____.
- Aiko's last line (did / did not) motivate me because ____.
- Aiko could improve the last line by ____.

Skill: Introductions

CHECKLIST FOR INTRODUCTIONS

Before you write your introduction, ask yourself the following questions:

- What is my claim?
- How can I introduce my topic clearly?
- How will you "hook" your reader's interest? You might:
    - > start with an attention-grabbing statement
    - > begin with an intriguing question
    - > use descriptive words to set a scene

Below are two strategies to help you introduce your claim and topic clearly in an introduction:

- Peer Discussion
    - > Talk about your topic with a partner, explaining what you already know and your ideas about your topic.
    - > Write notes about the ideas you have discussed and any new questions you may have.
    - > Review your notes and think about what will be your claim or main idea.
    - > Briefly state your claim or thesis statement.
    - > Write ways you can give readers a "preview" of what they will read in the rest of your essay.
    - > Write a possible "hook."
- Freewriting
    - > Freewrite for ten minutes about your topic. Don't worry about grammar, punctuation, or having fully formed ideas. The point of freewriting is to discover ideas.
    - > Review your notes and think about what will be your claim or main idea.
    - > Briefly state your claim or thesis.
    - > Write ways you can give readers a "preview" of what they will read in the rest of your essay.
    - > Write a possible "hook."

SKILL VOCABULARY

introduction / la introducción *noun* the opening paragraph or section of an essay COGNATE

topic / el tema *noun* the subject of a literary work, usually expressed as a single word or phrase in the form of a noun

thesis statement / la presentación de la tesis *noun* a statement that shares the main idea of an argumentative or informational essay

claim / la afirmación *noun* the writer's or speaker's position on a debatable issue or problem

Skill: Introductions

Introduce the Skill

Watch the Concept Definition video and read the following definition with your students.

The **introduction** is the opening paragraph or section of an essay or other nonfiction text. To begin an argumentative essay, writers identify the **topic**, or what the essay will be about. The most important part of the introduction in an argumentative essay is the **thesis statement**. This statement contains the writer's **claim**, or main argument, and it states something that the writer believes to be true.

In an informative/explanatory text, the introduction should provide readers with necessary information in order to introduce a topic. It should state the thesis, which in an informative/explanatory essay is a short statement that summarizes the main point of the essay and previews the ideas that will follow in the text. In an informative/explanatory essay, many writers also include one or two sentences that are called a "hook." They are intended to engage readers' interest and grab their attention so they keep reading.

TURN AND TALK

Turn to your partner and discuss the last time you had to introduce someone new to a friend or family member. Tell how you chose which details to include in your introduction.

ELL SPEAKING FRAMES

- I introduced ____ to ____.
- A detail I chose to include was ____ because ____.

Your Turn

Ask students to complete the Your Turn activity.

QUESTION 1

A. Correct. Asking an intriguing question is a good way to grab readers' attention.

B. Incorrect. This sentence states the writer's opinion. It does not introduce her main ideas.

C. Incorrect. This sentence does not reflect the main ideas of the essay.

D. Incorrect. This sentence introduces a supporting detail, not the main idea of the essay.

QUESTION 2

A. Incorrect. The word "teachers" could cause confusion. Although each person's story teaches a valuable lesson, the people whom the writer mentions are not all teachers.

B. Incorrect. This sentence does not add information that shows readers why these people are noteworthy.

C. Incorrect. The thesis statement that follows this sentence already makes this point, so it does not add new information.

D. Correct. Their stories teach readers why difficult risks are sometimes important to take.

YOUR TURN

Choose the best answer to each question.

1. The following introduction is from a previous draft of Aiko's essay. Aiko would like to replace the underlined sentence with a sentence that better grabs readers' attention and introduces her main idea. Which of these would be the BEST replacement for the underlined sentence?

> Lots of different people take risks. Even if a risk leads to failure, there is always a lesson to learn. There are lessons for the people who have taken the risks, but there are also lessons for people who learn about them. Frederick Douglass, the *Challenger* crew, and the Biloxi-Chitimacha-Choctaw Native American tribe are examples of risk-takers. Their risks and the outcomes of their risks differ, but their stories all teach valuable lessons.

- A. Have you ever taken a risk that didn't work out?
- B. I don't like taking risks.
- C. Sometimes people should not take risks.
- D. Members of the Biloxi-Chitimacha-Choctaw Native American tribe are taking a risk.

2. The following introduction is from a previous draft of Aiko's essay. Aiko would like to replace the underlined sentence with a sentence that explains why she has chosen Frederick Douglass, the *Challenger* crew, and the Biloxi-Chitimacha-Choctaw Native American tribe as examples of risk-takers. Which of these would be the BEST replacement for the underlined sentence?

> Lots of different people take risks. Even if a risk leads to failure, there is always a lesson to learn. There are lessons for the people who have taken the risks, but there are also lessons for people who learn about them. Frederick Douglass, the *Challenger* crew, and the Biloxi-Chitimacha-Choctaw Native American tribe are examples of risk-takers. Their risks and the outcomes of their risks differ, but their stories all teach valuable lessons.

- A. Frederick Douglass, the *Challenger* crew, and the Biloxi-Chitimacha-Choctaw Native American tribe are risk-takers and teachers.
- B. Frederick Douglass, the *Challenger* crew, and the Biloxi-Chitimacha-Choctaw Native American tribe are risk-takers who are noteworthy.
- C. Frederick Douglass, the *Challenger* crew, and the Biloxi-Chitimacha-Choctaw Native American tribe are examples of people who took risks with different outcomes.
- D. Frederick Douglass, the *Challenger* crew, and the Biloxi-Chitimacha-Choctaw Native American tribe are examples of people who took difficult risks for important causes.

Writer's Notebook

Ask students to imagine that they are writing an informative article about a game for the school newspaper. That could include a board game, a video game, a sports game, or a game played in class. Have them write the introduction of the article. Remind them to use the questions in the checklist as a guide.

TURN AND TALK

Allow students to share their ideas orally in pairs or small groups before writing.

WRITE

Use the steps in the checklist to revise the introduction of your informative essay.

Write

Ask students to complete the writing assignment.

ELL **REWRITE CHECKLIST**

A **Hook**

- ☐ What attention-grabbing statement could you include?
- ☐ How might an intriguing question grab your readers' attention?
- ☐ How could descriptive details establish a scene that introduces your ideas?

Development

- ☐ Have you provided readers with the information necessary to introduce your claim?
- ☐ Does the introduction show readers how you will organize your ideas?

Thesis Statement

- ☐ Does your thesis statement answer all parts of the prompt?
- ☐ Does your thesis statement summarize the main point of the essay?
- ☐ Does your thesis statement preview the ideas that will follow in the text?

Skill: Transitions

Introduce the Skill

Watch the Concept Definition video ▶ and read the following definition with your students.

Transitions are connecting words, phrases, and clauses that writers use to **clarify** the relationships among ideas and details in a text. Transitions have different functions depending on whether the text is argumentative, informative, or narrative.

In an argumentative essay, writers state claims and provide reasons and evidence for their claims. To clarify a relationship between a claim and a reason or supporting evidence, transitions such as *although* and *on the other hand* help make connections clear.

For informative essays, transitions such as *however, in addition,* and *for example* may help create **cohesion** among ideas and concepts.

In narrative writing, authors use a variety of words, phrases, and clauses to signal shifts in time, setting, and action. Transitions such as *until now, meanwhile,* and *once it was over* may make narrative events more **coherent**.

Transitions also help to connect ideas both within and across paragraphs and between major sections of text.

Skill: Transitions

••• CHECKLIST FOR TRANSITIONS

Before you revise your current draft to include transitions, think about:

- the key ideas you discuss in your body paragraphs
- how your paragraphs connect together to support your claim(s)
- the relationships among your ideas and concepts
- the logical progression of your ideas

Next, reread your current draft and note areas in your essay where:

- the relationships among your ideas and concepts are unclear, identifying places where you could add linking words or other transitional devices to make your essay more cohesive. Look for:
  - > sudden jumps in your ideas
  - > breaks between paragraphs where the ideas in the next paragraph are not logically following from the previous one

Revise your draft to use words, phrases, and clauses to create cohesion and clarify the relationships among your ideas and concepts, using the following questions as a guide:

- Are there unifying relationships between the ideas I present in my essay?
- Have I clarified, or made clear, these relationships?
- What linking words (such as conjunctions), phrases, or clauses could I add to my essay to clarify the relationships among the ideas and concepts I present?

TURN AND TALK

Turn to your partner and inform your partner about one routine you follow to complete homework or a project at home. Use a variety of transitions to describe your routine.

SPEAKING FRAMES

- One routine I follow to complete (my homework / a project) is ____.
- When I follow this routine, I ____.
- If we needed to show the class how our routines are related, we could use this transition: ____.
- For example, we could say ____.

SKILL VOCABULARY

transition / la transición ***noun*** a connecting word or phrase that a writer may use to clarify the relationship between ideas in a text; set off with a comma COGNATE

clarify / aclarar ***verb*** to make clear and more comprehensible

cohesion / la cohesión ***noun*** the quality of parts working together as a whole COGNATE

coherent / coherente ***adjective*** marked by being orderly and logical; easy to understand COGNATE

YOUR TURN

Choose the best answer to each question.

1. Below is an excerpt from a previous draft of Aiko's informative essay. Aiko notices that her introduction and first body paragraphs are not clearly connected to one another, so she wants to revise the underlined sentence. Which of the following sentences clearly shows how the main idea of the first body paragraph relates to the topic of the essay?

> Frederick Douglass, the crew of the *Challenger*, and members of the Biloxi-Chitimacha-Choctaw Native American tribe all risked losses in pursuit of their goals. Even though their risks and the outcomes of their risks differ, they all required courage.
>
> <u>Douglass describes a major risk that he took in his autobiography.</u> Born into slavery, Douglass was legally denied an education. At first, his mistress started teaching him how to read, but after she changed her mind about teaching him, she became angry and violent when he tried to learn on his own.

- ○ A. In Frederick Douglass's autobiography, Douglass described how he learned to read and write while risking severe punishment.
- ○ B. In Frederick Douglass's autobiography, Douglass described his effort to learn how to read and write, and the outcome of this risk was positive.
- ○ C. As an example, Frederick Douglass described major risks that he took while learning how to read and write.
- ○ D. As an example, Frederick Douglass wrote about acts of courage in his autobiography.

2. Below is a body paragraph from a previous draft of Aiko's informative essay. Aiko would like to add a transition word or phrase to help readers move from sentence 2 to sentence 3. Which transition will work best?

> (1) Risks can also have tragic outcomes. (2) For example, the space shuttle *Challenger* exploded after takeoff in 1986. (3) After the disaster occurred, President Reagan reflected on this tragedy in his speech "Address to the Nation on the Explosion of the Space Shuttle *Challenger*." (4) He mourned the loss of the crew and emphasized that their risks took great courage. (5) He said, "And perhaps we've forgotten the courage it took for the crew of the shuttle. (6) But they, the *Challenger* Seven, were aware of the dangers, but overcame them and did their jobs brilliantly."

- ○ A. Similarly,
- ○ B. For example,
- ○ C. In addition to that detail,
- ○ D. As a result,

Your Turn

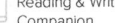

Ask students to complete the Your Turn activity.

QUESTION 1

A. Correct. This sentence indicates which text this paragraph will focus on, and it clearly describes an example of a risk that requires courage.

B. Incorrect. This sentence indicates which text this paragraph will focus on, but the main idea does not clearly relate to the thesis statement.

C. Incorrect. This sentence relates to the thesis statement, but it does not clearly indicate which text this paragraph will focus on.

D. Incorrect. This sentence mentions courage, but it does not clearly relate to the thesis statement about risks that require courage.

QUESTION 2

A. Incorrect. "Similarly" is a word used to show how one idea relates to another idea that is like it.

B. Correct. "For example" introduces a supporting detail that helps develop the topic sentence.

C. Incorrect. "In addition to that detail" adds evidence to information that has already been presented.

D. Incorrect. "As a result" is a phrase that shows the relationship between a cause and its effect.

Writer's Notebook

In one paragraph, write about a risk that you once took and the outcome. Write one thesis statement about what you learned from that risk in a sentence and use supporting details to develop that claim. Then, look for ways to use a variety of transitions to show how your ideas and/or concepts are connected.

TURN AND TALK

Allow students to share their paragraphs orally in pairs or small groups before writing.

Write

Ask students to complete the writing assignment.

ELL REWRITE CHECKLIST

A **Logical Progression of Your Argument**

- ☐ Is there a clear relationship among all paragraphs in this essay, including this one?
- ☐ Is there a clear connection between this paragraph and the paragraph before it?
- ☐ Is there a clear flow of information from one idea to another within the paragraph?
- ☐ Do you use a variety of transition words, phrases, or clauses to make those connections clear?

Relationships Among the Topic and Supporting Details

- ☐ What is your thesis statement about the topic of your essay?
- ☐ How does the topic sentence relate to that thesis statement?
- ☐ Do you clearly show readers the relationship between the topic sentence and each supporting detail?
- ☐ Is there a clear relationship among the supporting details?
- ☐ Do you use a variety of transition words, phrases, or clauses to show those connections?

WRITE

Use the questions in the checklist to revise one of your body paragraphs. Look for a variety of ways to use words, phrases, and clauses to create cohesion and clarify the relationships among ideas in this section. Those ideas may include your claim, counterclaims, reasons, and evidence.

Skill: Precise Language

••• CHECKLIST FOR PRECISE LANGUAGE

As you consider precise language and domain-specific vocabulary related to a subject or topic, use the following questions as a guide:

- What information am I trying to convey or explain to my audience?
- Are there any key concepts that need to be explained or understood?
- What domain-specific vocabulary is relevant to my topic and explanation?
- Where can I use more precise vocabulary in my explanation?

Here are some suggestions that will help guide you in using precise language and domain-specific vocabulary to inform about or explain a topic:

- Determine the topic or area of study you will be writing about.
- Identify key concepts that need explanation in order to inform readers.
- Research any domain-specific vocabulary that you may need to define.
- Substitute precise, descriptive, and domain-specific language for vague, general, or overused words and phrases.
- Reread your writing to refine and revise if needed.

SKILL VOCABULARY

precise language / el lenguaje preciso *noun* exact language that includes specific nouns and action verbs COGNATE

domain-specific vocabulary / el vocabulario específico de un campo *noun* words and phrases that are limited to specific domains, or fields of study, such as law or medicine

Skill: Precise Language

Introduce the Skill

Watch the Concept Definition video ▶ and read the following definition with your students.

Precise language refers to clear and direct words or phrases that have very specific meanings. **Domain-specific vocabulary** are words and phrases that are used to explain concepts that are related to a particular subject or topic. A scientist writing about astronomy might use terms such as "airglow," for example, which is a glow in the night sky caused by radiation from the upper atmosphere.

When writers have to explain a complicated subject or topic, using precise language allows readers to develop a deeper understanding of the text and make connections between facts and other information. For example, the word *observe* is a synonym for the words *notice* or *see*, but it has a more precise meaning. To observe something means "to notice something and recognize it as significant." This difference, when used to describe a scientific experiment, can help readers develop their own ideas about the subject matter.

TURN AND TALK

Turn to your partner and practice using precise language and domain-specific vocabulary to describe a song that you heard, a photo that you viewed, or an object that you observed this past week.

SPEAKING FRAMES

- One memorable (song / object / photo) I (heard / observed / viewed) this past week is ____.
- I chose that (song / object / photo) because ____.
- One observation I want to convey is ____.
- I can convey that observation by saying, ____.

Your Turn

Ask students to complete the Your Turn activity.

QUESTION 1

A. Incorrect. This sentence includes domain-specific vocabulary, but some of the language is vague and unclear.

B. Incorrect. No domain-specific vocabulary is evident, and some of the language in this sentence is unclear.

C. Incorrect. No domain-specific vocabulary is evident, and some of the language in this sentence is unclear.

D. Correct. This sentence includes domain-specific vocabulary and precise language.

QUESTION 2

A. Incorrect. The language in this sentence is still vague and unclear.

B. Correct. This sentence includes more precise language.

C. Incorrect. The language in this sentence is still vague and unclear.

D. Incorrect. The language in this sentence is still vague and unclear.

YOUR TURN

Choose the best answer to each question.

1. Aiko wants to improve the underlined sentence from a previous draft that included a paragraph about "The Day I Saved a Life." How can she use domain-specific vocabulary and more precise language in the underlined sentence?

> In "The Day I Saved a Life," Thomas Ponce took a risk by dedicating himself to protecting a shark. Due to their roles in horror movies like *Jaws*, sharks are often seen as evil predators who do not need to be saved. However, Ponce pointed out that sharks are necessary in the ocean, and they are often hurt by human beings. He used that knowledge to speak on behalf of a shark that a fisherman had caught, and Ponce saved the shark's life as a result. That risk took courage because Ponce decided to do something difficult that needed to be done quickly.

- ○ A. However, Ponce informs readers that sharks are needed in oceans, and human beings often cause harm to them.
- ○ B. However, Ponce adds that they are very important in the ocean, and they are often unnecessarily removed from it or hurt by human beings.
- ○ C. However, Ponce says that sharks are absolutely necessary in the ocean, and they are often the victims.
- ○ D. However, Ponce explains that sharks are vital parts of their ecosystems, and they are often victims of cruelty by human beings.

2. Aiko wants to improve the underlined sentence from one of her previous drafts by revising and refining the language. How can she use more precise language in the underlined sentence?

> In "The Day I Saved a Life," Thomas Ponce took a risk by dedicating himself to protecting a shark. Due to their roles in horror movies like *Jaws*, sharks are often seen as evil predators who do not need to be saved. However, Ponce pointed out that sharks are necessary in the ocean, and they are often hurt by human beings. He used that knowledge to speak on behalf of a shark that a fisherman had caught, and Ponce saved the shark's life as a result. That risk took courage because Ponce decided to do something difficult that needed to be done quickly.

- ○ A. That risk took courage because Ponce took action, and he could have done nothing instead.
- ○ B. That risk took courage because the situation was urgent, and Ponce's goal was difficult to achieve.
- ○ C. That risk took courage because Ponce could have failed to do something difficult.
- ○ D. That risk took courage because it involved a shark and someone else achieving his goal of catching that shark.

Writer's Notebook

Ask students to use precise language to describe one risk that a person has taken for a cause that is important to him or her. Students should look for opportunities to add domain-specific vocabulary to their descriptions as well.

TURN AND TALK

Allow students to share the information they want to convey orally in pairs or small groups before freewriting.

YOUR TURN

Identify at least five sentences from your draft that need more precise language and write them in the first column. Then, complete the chart by writing a revised sentence in the second column.

Draft Sentence	Revised Sentence

Your Turn

Ask students to complete the Your Turn activity. Answers will vary.

Draft Sentence	Revised Sentence
Richard Turere, Thomas Ponce, and Tom Sawyer are examples of young people who learn new things while taking risks.	Richard Turere, Thomas Ponce, and Tom Sawyer are examples of young people who make discoveries while taking risks.
The articles about Richard Turere and Thomas Ponce are true, while the passage about Tom Sawyer is not.	The articles about Richard Turere and Thomas Ponce are informative articles, while the passage about Tom Sawyer is from a work of fiction.
"Lion lights" aren't that expensive to make, and they're a solution that works.	"Lion lights" are an inexpensive and effective solution.
To get the fisherman to let the baby bonnethead shark go, Thomas Ponce shared several facts that he knew about sharks.	To persuade the fisherman to release the baby bonnethead shark, Thomas Ponce shared several facts about the need to save sharks.
Tom did not want to spend the day doing work for Aunt Polly, so he tried to think of ways to get out of it.	Tom dreaded spending the day doing work for his Aunt Polly, so he brainstormed ways to avoid it.

Skill: Style

Introduce the Skill

Watch the Concept Definition video and read the following definition with your students.

Style is the way a writer uses language to express ideas and convey information. It is revealed through the writer's choice of words and sentence construction. Style also involves being aware of the rules for writing standard English.

Choosing an appropriate style depends on the audience and the purpose for writing. Different subjects require different styles of writing. For both argumentative and informative writing, writers must use a formal style. With a **formal style**, a writer chooses **academic** language—the type of vocabulary used in school texts, for example—rather than informal or conversational language. The writer might also use special vocabulary unique to a particular topic, sometimes called **domain-specific** language.

Finally, to help maintain a formal style, writers must be sure to follow conventional rules for grammar, spelling, capitalization, and punctuation.

Skill: Style

••• CHECKLIST FOR STYLE

First, reread the draft of your informative essay and identify the following:

- places where you use slang, contractions, abbreviations, and a conversational tone
- areas where you could use subject-specific or academic language in order to help persuade or inform your readers
- moments where you use first person (*I*) or second person (*you*)
- areas where sentence structure lacks variety
- incorrect uses of the conventions of standard English for grammar, spelling, capitalization, and punctuation

Establish and maintain a formal style in your essay, using the following questions as a guide:

- Have I avoided slang in favor of academic language?
- Did I consistently use a third-person point of view, using third-person pronouns (*he*, *she*, *they*)?
- Have I varied my sentence structure and the length of my sentences? Apply these specific questions where appropriate:
  - > Where should I make some sentences longer by using conjunctions to connect independent clauses, dependent clauses, and phrases?
  - > Where should I make some sentences shorter by separating any independent clauses?
- Did I follow the conventions of standard English, including:
  - > grammar?
  - > spelling?
  - > capitalization?
  - > punctuation?

TURN AND TALK

Turn to your partner and brainstorm situations in which a speaker or writer should use formal language and situations in which a speaker or writer should use informal language. For each example, explain which style would work best and why it would work best.

SPEAKING FRAMES

- A (speaker / writer) should use an informal style when ____.
- This style would work well because ____.
- A (speaker / writer) should use a formal style when ____.
- This style would work well because ____.

SKILL VOCABULARY

style / el estilo *noun* a way of expressing something that is characteristic of the person or time period COGNATE

formal style / el estilo formal *noun* a writing style or way of writing for academic essays

academic / académico/a *adjective* having to do with school COGNATE

domain-specific / específico/a del campo *adjective* having to do with a particular topic

YOUR TURN

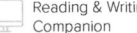

Choose the best answer to each question.

1. Below is a section from a previous draft of Aiko's informative essay. She sees that she needs to revise the language in the underlined sentence to make sure that it is written in a formal style. Which of the following sentences is a successful revision that is written in a formal style?

> A resettlement committee is working on a design for the new site, and their plan should help the community achieve their goals. To preserve the community's history on Isle de Jean Charles, the site may include a museum. <u>It'd guide us through information about the island and what it was like to live on it.</u> Many members of the community also value family, and they'd like to build houses that give extended families a shared backyard.

- A. It would guide you through information about the island and what it was like to live on it.
- B. It guides you through information about the island and what it was like to live on it.
- C. It would guide visitors through information about the island and the community's experiences on it.
- D. It guides visitors through information about the island and the communitys experiences on it.

2. Below is a section from a previous draft of Aiko's informative essay. Aiko wants to vary the length of her sentences, so she decides to rewrite the underlined sentence as two separate independent clauses. Which of the following sentences successfully divide the underlined sentence into separate independent clauses that are written in a formal style?

> A resettlement committee is working on a design for the new site, and their plan should help the community achieve their goals. To preserve the community's history on Isle de Jean Charles, the site may include a museum. It'd guide us through information about the island and what it was like to live on it. <u>Many members of the community also value family, and they'd like to build houses that give extended families a shared backyard.</u>

- A. Many members of the community also value family and would like to build houses for them. They'll give extended families a shared backyard.
- B. Many members of the community also value family and would like to build houses for them. Giving extended families backyards to share.
- C. Many members of the community also value family. And they would like to build houses that give extended families a shared backyard.
- D. Many members of the community also value family. For this reason, they would like to build houses that give extended families a shared backyard.

Your Turn

Ask students to complete the Your Turn activity.

QUESTION 1

A. Incorrect. This sentence uses the second-person point of view, and "what it was like" is written in a conversational tone.

B. Incorrect. This sentence is not accurate since the museum had not been built when the article was written. In addition, the sentence also uses the second-person point of view, and "what it was like" is written in a conversational tone.

C. Correct. This sentence uses the third-person point of view and a formal tone. It also avoids using contractions.

D. Incorrect. This sentence is not accurate since the museum had not been built when the article was written. In addition, "community's" needs an apostrophe before the "s."

QUESTION 2

A. Incorrect. The noun that "They" represents is not clear, and "They'll" is a contraction.

B. Incorrect. The second sentence is a sentence fragment, not an independent clause.

C. Incorrect. In formal writing, a sentence should not start with a conjunction like "and."

D. Correct. The sentence has been divided into two independent clauses, and the contraction "they'd" has been spelled out as "they would." This change makes the sentence more formal.

Writer's Notebook

Can you switch your writing style? Rewrite one paragraph from your draft for different audiences. Use an informal style to write the first version for students in your class. Then, use a formal style to write the second version for an audience that is made of leaders in the community.

TURN AND TALK

Allow students to share both versions of a sentence orally in pairs or small groups before writing.

Write

Ask students to complete the writing assignment.

ELL REWRITE CHECKLIST

A Language

- ☐ Can you find examples of slang in this paragraph?
- ☐ How can you replace those words or phrases with more formal language?
- ☐ Do you see opportunities to add academic language to this paragraph?

Sentence Structure

- ☐ Do all of your sentences follow the same pattern, or do they have different structures?
- ☐ Where can you make some sentences longer and clearer?
- ☐ Where can you make some hard-to-follow sentences shorter?

Conventions

- ☐ Did you follow the conventions of standard English, including:
  - ☐ grammar?
  - ☐ spelling?
  - ☐ capitalization?
  - ☐ punctuation?

WRITE

Use the steps in the checklist to add to or revise the language of one paragraph from your draft by establishing and maintaining a formal style.

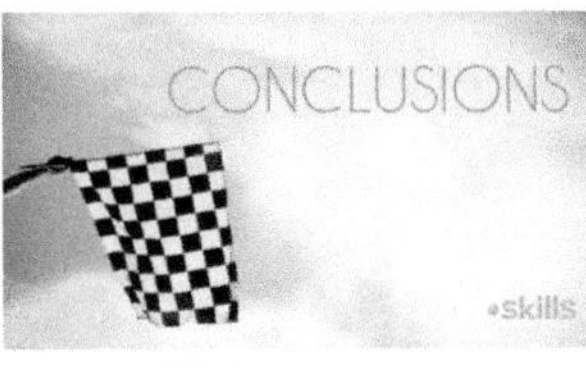

Skill: Conclusions

••• CHECKLIST FOR CONCLUSIONS

Before you write your conclusion, ask yourself the following questions:

- How can I restate the thesis or main idea in my concluding section or statement? What impression can I make on my reader?
- How can I write my conclusion so that it supports and follows logically from my argument?
- How can I conclude with a memorable comment?

Below are two strategies to help you provide a concluding statement or section that follows from and supports the argument presented:

- Peer Discussion
  - > After you have written your introduction and body paragraphs, talk with a partner and tell him or her what you want readers to remember, writing notes about your discussion.
  - > Review your notes and think about what you wish to express in your conclusion.
  - > Do not simply restate your claim or thesis statement. Rephrase your main idea to show the depth of your knowledge and the importance of your idea.
  - > Write your conclusion.
- Freewriting
  - > Freewrite for ten minutes about what you might include in your conclusion. Don't worry about grammar, punctuation, or having fully formed ideas. The point of freewriting is to discover ideas.
  - > Review your notes and think about what you wish to express in your conclusion.
  - > Do not simply restate your claim or thesis statement. Rephrase your main idea to show the depth of your knowledge and the importance of your idea.
  - > Write your conclusion.

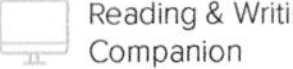

SKILL VOCABULARY

conclusion / la conclusión ***noun*** the closing paragraph or section of an essay; a closing argument in an argumentative text COGNATE

thesis statement / la presentación de la tesis ***noun*** a statement that shares the main idea of an argumentative or informational essay

claim / la afirmación ***noun*** the writer's or speaker's position on a debatable issue or problem

narrative / la narración ***noun*** a story, real or imagined, consisting of connected events

Skill: Conclusions

Introduce the Skill

Watch the Concept Definition video ▶ and read the following definition with your students.

A **conclusion** is the closing paragraph or section of an essay, argument, or narrative. It is where the writer brings an essay to a close by restating the main idea or **thesis statement** or the **claim** in an argument. It also summarizes the evidence and research that support the claim or thesis. The conclusion should follow logically from the information, explanations, or claim that has been presented. A conclusion is a good way to suggest to your readers that you have accomplished what you set out to do. In addition, try to leave readers with an interesting final impression. This might be accomplished by closing with a quote, an anecdote, or a call to action.

In a **narrative**, a conclusion should follow logically from the events of the plot and what the characters have experienced. It might include characters reflecting on events, why they matter, and how they feel about them.

TURN AND TALK

Turn to your partner and brainstorm ways to end an article that informs readers about after-school activities for students in your community.

SPEAKING FRAMES

- If I were writing a conclusion for an article about after-school activities, I would start by ____.
- I would then ____ because ____.
- I would also want my readers to remember ____.
- So, I might end the paragraph with a(n) ____.

Your Turn

Ask students to complete the Your Turn activity.

QUESTION 1

A. Correct. This sentence rephrases the thesis statement and includes each part of it.

B. Incorrect. This sentence does not follow from the sentence before it, and the writer is discussing three risks, not every risk.

C. Incorrect. This sentence rephrases a part of the thesis statement, but it leaves out some important information.

D. Incorrect. This sentence restates the topic sentence of this paragraph instead of the thesis statement.

QUESTION 2

A. Incorrect. This sentence comments on one text, rather than on all three.

B. Incorrect. This sentence asks a question, rather than bringing Aiko's ideas to a close.

C. Incorrect. This sentence states a personal connection, rather than bringing Aiko's ideas to a close.

D. Correct. This sentence brings Aiko's ideas to a close and conveys the information that she wants readers to remember.

YOUR TURN

Choose the best answer to each question.

1. The following conclusion is from a previous draft of Aiko's essay. Aiko sees that she copied the thesis statement from the introduction and pasted it at the end of her conclusion. As a result, she would like to rephrase the underlined sentence so that it engages readers. Which of the following sentences would be the BEST replacement for the underlined sentence?

> Frederick Douglass, the *Challenger* crew, and members of the Biloxi-Chitimacha-Choctaw Native American tribe all took risks to pursue important goals. Frederick Douglass found ways to learn how to read and write even though it was illegal for him to get an education at the time. The *Challenger* crew wanted to explore space, but they lost their lives just after their shuttle took off. Members of the Biloxi-Chitimacha-Choctaw Native American tribe wanted to reestablish their homes and culture on new land, and the outcome of their work was not known when "Vanishing Island" was published. <u>Even though these risks and their outcomes differ, they all teach essential lessons.</u>

- A. These risks and their outcomes widely vary, but they all teach valuable lessons.
- B. It is also evident that every risk teaches readers a valuable lesson.
- C. Readers can learn valuable lessons from each risk.
- D. These are the risks that each person took to pursue an important goal.

2. The following conclusion is from a previous draft of Aiko's essay. Aiko would like to add a sentence to bring her essay to a more effective close. Which sentence could she add after the last sentence to help achieve this goal?

> Frederick Douglass, the *Challenger* crew, and members of the Biloxi-Chitimacha-Choctaw Native American tribe all took risks to pursue important goals. Frederick Douglass found ways to learn how to read and write even though it was illegal for him to get an education at the time. The *Challenger* crew wanted to explore space, but they lost their lives just after their shuttle took off. Members of the Biloxi-Chitimacha-Choctaw Native American tribe wanted to reestablish their homes and culture on new land, and the outcome of their work was not known when "Vanishing Island" was published. Even though these risks and their outcomes differ, they all teach essential lessons.

- A. The lesson from the Biloxi-Chitimacha-Choctaw Native American tribe is the most recent example.
- B. What is an example of a lesson that you learned from each selection?
- C. I think that the lessons I learned from each story apply to my life and my classmates' lives as well.
- D. Each story shows readers personal qualities that everyone can work to develop.

WRITE

Use the steps in the checklist to revise the conclusion of your informative essay.

Write

Ask students to complete the writing assignment.

ELL **REWRITE CHECKLIST**

A **Restated Thesis Statement or Main Idea**

- ☐ Have you clearly restated the thesis or main idea of this informative essay?
- ☐ Is the main idea in your introduction the same as the main idea that you restated in your conclusion?
- ☐ Does the thesis statement in your conclusion show a deeper understanding of the main idea?

Coherence

- ☐ Does your conclusion bring your essay to a close in a logical way?
- ☐ Does your conclusion review important information from your essay?

Impression

- ☐ Does the information in your conclusion show readers that your main idea is important?
- ☐ Have you concluded this paragraph with a memorable comment?

Writer's Notebook

Ask students to imagine that they are writing an informative article about a game for the school newspaper. That could include a board game, a video game, a sports game, or a game played in class. Have them write the conclusion of the article. Remind them to use the questions in the checklist as a guide.

TURN AND TALK

Allow students to share their ideas orally in pairs or small groups before writing.

Informative Writing Process: Revise

Review Revision Guide

Break the class into five groups, and assign each group a category of the revision guide. Ask:

- What is the purpose of this section of the guide?
- How did it improve Aiko's writing?
- How will it help to improve your writing?

Allow groups to share their ideas with the class.

SPEAKING FRAMES

- I think ___ (clarity / development / organization / word choice / sentence variety) improved Aiko's writing by ___.
- I think ___ (clarity / development / organization / word choice / sentence variety) will improve my writing because ___.

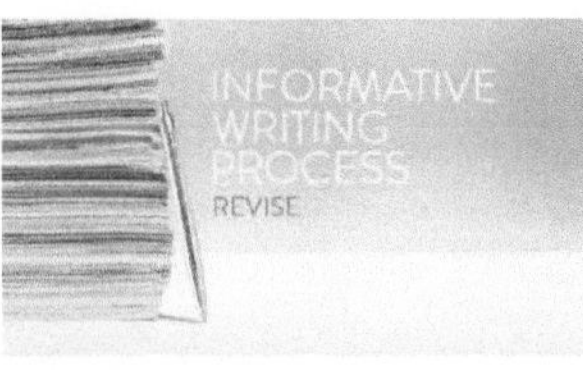

Informative Writing Process: Revise

PLAN | DRAFT | REVISE | EDIT AND PUBLISH

You have written a draft of your informative essay. You have also received input from your peers about how to improve it. Now you are going to revise your draft.

REVISION GUIDE

Examine your draft to find areas for revision. Keep in mind your purpose and audience as you revise for clarity, development, organization, and style. Use the guide below to help you review:

Review	Revise	Example
	Clarity	
Identify the information you want to convey and any concepts that need to be explained. Annotate places where you can add domain-specific vocabulary to clarify information or explain a concept.	Clarify information or explain a concept by using domain-specific vocabulary. Remember to think about whether or not you need to define a term for your audience.	Since the mid-twentieth century, however, the land on the island has been rapidly eroding, or wearing away;. ~~It~~ Storms, river engineering, and pollution are causing this to happen, and the landform may not even exist by 2050.

Review	Revise	Example
Development		
Identify your main idea about the topic. Annotate places where you need to add, replace, or remove supporting details. Each detail should clearly help develop the main idea.	Make sure to include textual evidence from the selections that you have read, and use quotation marks when you are quoting a source directly.	In his speech "Address to the Nation on the Explosion of the Space Shuttle *Challenger*," President Ronald Reagan reminds Americans that the crew was willing to do a dangerous job. They wanted to travel into space because they believed that the mission would be worth the risk. He says, "They had a hunger to explore the universe and discover its truths."
Organization		
Review your body paragraphs. Identify and annotate any sentences that don't flow in a clear and logical way.	Rewrite the sentences so that the information flows from one idea to another. Make sure that you have clearly expressed the relationships between ideas.	Leaving that land will be painful~~. On the new site~~, but members are dedicated to preserving their history, community, and culture on the new site. ~~The~~ For example, tribal secretary Chantel Comardelle envisions a museum that guides visitors through the history of the island.
Style: Word Choice		
Identify weak or repetitive words or phrases that do not clearly express your ideas to the reader.	Replace weak and repetitive words and phrases with more descriptive ones that better convey your ideas.	The crew was willing to risk their lives ~~to find out new information~~ in search of knowledge about the universe. ~~The crew also~~ Their efforts teach the values of ~~putting others before yourself~~ selflessness and bravery.

Revise

Students should start this activity with a copy of their drafts either printed on paper or open in a word-processing program, such as Google Docs. Allow students time to revise their drafts using the instructions in the revision guide. Once students have finished revising their narrative, have them submit their work.

CHECK FOR SUCCESS

Circulate around the room to spend time with individual students. Ask:

- What category are you working on?
- Why are you revising this specific section?
- How are you revising it?
- How does this change support your purpose?
- Does this change make your writing appropriate for your audience?

If students struggle while revising their drafts, choose an exemplary revision to share with the class while the student talks through the process. You could also invite a student to share a dilemma in the revision process and allow the class to offer feedback or suggestions.

ORGANIZATION

Revise your draft, focusing on organization. One way to clarify the organization of ideas in your text is by using transitions.

ORGANIZATION

Tell students to revise their drafts using the revision guide, focusing on organization and development.

Write

Ask students to complete their writing assignment.

ELL REWRITE CHECKLIST

- ☐ Find ideas that are not clearly connected.
- ☐ Identify the relationship between those ideas.
- ☐ Clarify the relationship by using a transition word, phrase, or clause.

Review	Revise	Example
Style: Sentence Variety		
Read your informational essay aloud. Annotate places where you have too many long or short sentences in a row.	Revise short sentences by linking them together. Shorten longer sentences for clarity of emphasis.	Many members of the community also value family;. To encourage interactions among family members on the new site, ~~so~~ they want to build groups of houses with shared backyards.

WRITE

Use the guide above, as well as your peer reviews, to help you evaluate your informative essay to determine areas that should be revised.

Grammar: Participles

A present participle is formed by adding *-ing* to a verb. As part of a verb phrase, the present participle is used with forms of the helping verb *to be*.

A past participle is usually formed by adding *-ed* to a verb. The past participle of some verbs has other endings, as in *broken*. When a participle acts as the main verb in a verb phrase, it is used with forms of the helping verb *to have*.

A present or past participle can also act as an adjective to describe, or modify, a noun or a pronoun. When a participle acts as an adjective, it is called a verbal.

Participle as a Verb	Participle as an Adjective
They looked the same as the other people from Africa who had been **coming** over, who had dark skin. The People Could Fly: American Black Folktales	A poor, bare, miserable room it was, with **broken** windows, no fire, ragged bedclothes, a sick mother, **wailing** baby, and a group of pale, hungry children **cuddled** under one old quilt, **trying** to keep warm. Little Women

Both present and past participles can function as either verbs or adjectives.

Text	Function	Explanation
But Coach had **spoken**, and his word was law on the court. Middle School Madness	verb	**Spoken** is a past participle. It works with the helping verb *had* to tell what *Coach* had done.
The magical time of childhood stood still, and the pulse of the **living** earth pressed its mystery into my **living** blood. A Celebration of Grandfathers	adjective	**Living** is a present participle. It modifies the nouns *earth* and *blood*.

Grammar: Participles

Introduce the Skill

Review the image and definition for participles as a class.

- participle (verb phrase) - a form of a verb used with a helping verb
- present participle - formed by adding *-ing* to a verb; can act as an adjective
- past participle - usually formed by adding *-ed* to a verb; can act as an adjective

Discuss the Model

1. How is a present participle formed? To form a present participle, add *-ing* to a verb. For example, "try" becomes "trying."
2. How is a past participle formed? To form a past participle, you can usually add *-ed* to a verb. For example, "cuddle" becomes "cuddled." However, there are past participles with other endings as well. For example, "speak" becomes "spoken."
3. How can a participle be used as a verb? Both past and present participles follow helping verbs. Present participles follow a version of "to be," as in "I am climbing"; past participles follow a version of "to have," as in "I have climbed."
4. How can a participle be used as an adjective? You may be able to use a present participle or a past participle to describe a noun, as in "the wailing baby" and "the broken window."

Your Turn

Ask students to complete the Your Turn activity.

QUESTION 1

A. Incorrect.

B. Incorrect.

C. Correct. *Rising* is used as an adjective to modify *sun*.

D. Incorrect.

QUESTION 2

A. Incorrect.

B. Correct. *Chirping* is used as an adjective to modify *crickets*.

C. Incorrect.

D. Incorrect.

QUESTION 3

A. Incorrect.

B. Incorrect.

C. Incorrect.

D. Correct. *Pleasing* is used as an adjective to modify *star*.

QUESTION 4

A. Incorrect.

B. Incorrect.

C. Correct. *Challenging* is used as an adjective to modify *time*.

D. Incorrect.

YOUR TURN

1. Choose the revision that uses a participle as an adjective.

   The sun rises slowly, and its light spreads along the horizon.

   - A. The sun rises slowly, and its light is spreading along the horizon.
   - B. The sun has been rising slowly, and its light spreads along the horizon.
   - C. The rising sun spreads light slowly along the horizon.
   - D. No change needs to be made to this sentence.

2. Choose the revision that uses a participle as an adjective.

   Ruby struggled to sleep through the sound of the crickets that chirped all night.

   - A. Ruby struggled to sleep through the sound of the crickets that were chirping all night.
   - B. All night, Ruby struggled to sleep through the sound of the chirping crickets.
   - C. Ruby was struggling to sleep through the sound of the crickets that chirped all night.
   - D. No change needs to be made to this sentence.

3. Choose the revision that uses a participle as an adjective.

   The pleasing film star has smiled and posed for pictures with fans all day.

   - A. The film star is pleasing her fans by smiling and posing for pictures.
   - B. The film star has smiled and posed for pictures to please her fans.
   - C. Smiling and posing for pictures are good ways for a film star to please fans.
   - D. No change needs to be made to this sentence.

4. Choose the revision that uses a participle as an adjective.

   The Civil War challenged Americans and reshaped their ideas about freedom.

   - A. The Civil War was challenging to Americans and reshaped their ideas about freedom.
   - B. The Civil War is challenging to Americans and has been reshaping their ideas about freedom.
   - C. The Civil War was a challenging time for Americans and reshaped their ideas about freedom.
   - D. No change needs to be made to this sentence.

Grammar: Gerunds

A gerund is a noun that is formed from the present participle of a verb.

A present participle is formed by adding *-ing* to the base form of a verb. When used as verbs, present participles always follow a form of the verb *to be* (for example, *We are going to the car*). Without a helping verb, present participles can be used as adjectives.

A gerund is determined by its use in a sentence. A gerund can be the subject of a sentence, the direct object of a verb, or the object of a preposition.

Remember that gerunds are used as nouns and present participles are used as adjectives.

Text	Explanation
High in the crow's-nest of the New White Star Liner Titanic, Lookout Frederick Fleet peered into a **dazzling** night. A Night to Remember	*Dazzling* is the present participle of the verb *to dazzle*. Here it is used as an adjective modifying the noun *night*.
"Yes," I replied, answering for her, "I paid her for everything, and the **eating** was the worst I ever tried." Ten Days in a Mad-House	The gerund *eating* is used as the subject of the last clause. Note that *answering* is part of the participial phrase *answering for her*, used as an adjective modifying *I*.
He never stopped **growling**. Cujo	The gerund *growling* is used as the direct object of the verb *stopped*.
The ringing became more distinct: it continued and became more distinct; I talked more freely to get rid of the **feeling**: but it continued and gained definitiveness--until, at length, I found that the noise was *not* within my ears. The Tell-Tale Heart	The gerund *feeling* is the object of the preposition *of*.

Grammar: Gerunds

Introduce the Skill

Review the image and definition for gerunds as a class.

- present participle - formed by adding *-ing* to a verb; can act as an adjective
- gerund - a verb form that ends in *-ing* and is used as a noun

Discuss the Model

1. How is a gerund formed? A gerund is formed from the present participle of a verb, so *-ing* is added to a verb.
2. What is the difference between a present participle and a gerund? A present participle is an adjective, while a gerund is a noun. As a result, a gerund may be the subject of a sentence, direct object of a verb, or object of a preposition.

Your Turn

Ask students to complete the Your Turn activity.

QUESTION 1

A. Incorrect.

B. Correct. *Viewing* is the gerund form of the verb to *view*.

C. Incorrect.

D. Incorrect.

QUESTION 2

A. Correct. *Coping* is the gerund of the verb to *cope*.

B. Incorrect.

C. Incorrect.

D. Incorrect.

QUESTION 3

A. Incorrect.

B. Incorrect.

C. Correct. *Delivering* is the gerund form of the verb to *deliver*.

D. Incorrect.

QUESTION 4

A. Correct. *Reading* is the gerund form of the verb *to read*.

B. Incorrect.

C. Incorrect.

D. Incorrect.

YOUR TURN

1. Replace the words in bold with a gerund.

> A study by six leading medical organizations concludes that "**to view** entertainment violence can lead to an increase in aggressive attitudes, values, and behavior, particularly in children."

- A. viewer
- B. viewing
- C. viewed
- D. None of the above

2. Replace the word in bold with a gerund.

> The young man's **cope** with impossible situations such as those in the Japanese internment camps took an amazing amount of strength along with a positive attitude.

- A. coping
- B. coped
- C. is coping
- D. None of the above

3. Replace the word in bold with a gerund.

> I think Reanna is training to be a spy—no one could be more discreet in **deliver** secret messages!

- A. delivers
- B. delivered
- C. delivering
- D. None of the above

4. Replace the words in bold with a gerund.

> Mia prefers **to read** about real-life unsolved mysteries, while most of her friends choose to read mind-bending science fiction or engaging crime novels.

- A. reading
- B. to read
- C. has read
- D. None of the above

Grammar: Infinitives

The function of a verb is to name an action or state of being, or to describe "having." An infinitive is a verb form that may function as a noun, an adjective, or an adverb. An infinitive is formed from the word *to* followed by the base form of a verb. The word *to* is not a preposition when it is used immediately before a verb.

An infinitive used as a noun can be the subject of a sentence or the direct object of a verb.

Infinitives Are Not Prepositions	Example
When the word *to* appears before a noun or a pronoun, it is a preposition. When *to* appears before the base form of a verb, the two words form an infinitive.	Then, miraculously, the bow began **to swing** to port. A Night to Remember
Infinitives Used as Nouns	**Example**
The infinitive can be the subject of a sentence.	**To resist** takes courage.
The infinitive can be the direct object of a verb.	I smiled,—for what had I **to fear**? The Tell-Tale Heart
Infinitives Used as Adjectives or Adverbs	**Example**
The infinitive can be used as an adjective to modify a noun or a pronoun.	That's the worst of living so far out," bawled Mr. White, with sudden and unlooked-for violence; "of all the beastly, slushy, out-of-the-way places **to live** in, this is the worst. . . ." The Monkey's Paw
The infinitive can be used as an adverb to modify a verb, an adjective, or another adverb.	But I guess she deserves some kind of award for having had ten kids and survived **to tell** about it. Abuela Invents the Zero

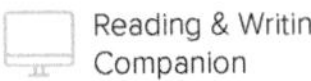

Grammar: Infinitives

Introduce the Skill

Review the image and definition for infinitives as a class.

- prepositional phrase - group of words that begins with a preposition and ends with a noun or pronoun called the object of the preposition
- verb - a word that names an action or state of being or having
- infinitive - a verb that is usually preceded by the word *to*; functions as a noun, adjective, or adverb

Discuss the Model

1. How are infinitives formed? Infinitives are formed by adding the word *to* in front of a base form of a verb. One example of an infinitive is *to go*. The word *to* has been added before the base form of the verb *go*.
2. What is the difference between an infinitive and a prepositional phrase? An infinitive and a prepositional phrase are different because they end with words that function in different ways. A prepositional phrase may start with the word *to*, but it always ends with a noun. In contrast, an infinitive always starts with the word *to* and ends with a verb.
3. When an infinitive is used as a noun, how can it function in a sentence? When used as a noun, an infinitive can act as a subject or direct object.
4. What other functions can an infinitive have in a sentence? An infinitive can also act as an adjective or adverb in a sentence.

Your Turn

Ask students to complete the Your Turn activity.

QUESTION 1

A. Incorrect.

B. Correct. The word *to* is followed by the base form of a verb, so this is an infinitive.

C. Incorrect.

D. Incorrect.

QUESTION 2

A. Correct. The word *to* is followed by the base form of a verb, so this is an infinitive.

B. Incorrect.

C. Incorrect.

D. Incorrect.

QUESTION 3

A. Incorrect.

B. Correct. The word *to* is followed by the base form of a verb, so this is an infinitive.

C. Incorrect.

D. Incorrect.

QUESTION 4

A. Incorrect.

B. Correct. The word *to* is followed by the base form of a verb, so this is an infinitive.

C. Incorrect.

D. Incorrect.

YOUR TURN

1. Identify the infinitive in this sentence.

   We went to the park to find the bench that she usually went to when she needed time to herself.

   - A. to the park
   - B. to find
   - C. to herself
   - D. There is no infinitive in this sentence.

2. Identify the infinitive in this sentence.

   To develop her ear for music, she went to as many free concerts as possible, while also adhering to her daily practice schedule.

   - A. To develop
   - B. to as many
   - C. to her daily practice schedule
   - D. There is no infinitive in this sentence.

3. Identify the infinitive in this sentence.

   From eight to ten candidates have registered to participate in the debates that have been assigned to Ellen for scheduling.

   - A. to ten
   - B. to participate
   - C. to Ellen
   - D. There is no infinitive in this sentence.

4. Identify the infinitive in this sentence.

   Why would I bow to her demand for another cake to serve when she did not invite me to the party?

   - A. to her demand
   - B. to serve
   - C. to the party
   - D. There is no infinitive in this sentence.

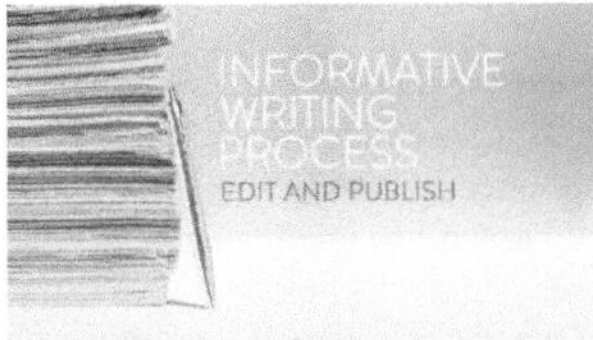

Informative Writing Process: Edit and Publish

PLAN | DRAFT | REVISE | EDIT AND PUBLISH

You have revised your informative essay based on your peer feedback and your own examination.

Now, it is time to edit your informative essay. When you revised, you focused on the content of your informative essay. You probably looked at your essay's introduction, supporting ideas, and conclusion. When you edit, you focus on the mechanics of your essay, paying close attention to things like grammar and punctuation.

Use the checklist below to guide you as you edit:

- ☐ Have I used participles correctly?
- ☐ Have I used gerunds correctly?
- ☐ Have I used infinitives correctly?
- ☐ Do I have any sentence fragments or run-on sentences?
- ☐ Have I spelled everything correctly?

Notice some edits Aiko has made:

- Rewrote a sentence with a participle that did not clearly describe a noun, adjective, or adverb.
- Corrected a spelling mistake.
- Fixed a run-on sentence by dividing it into two separate sentences.
- Replaced an infinitive that did not make sense with a verb.
- Fixed a sentence fragment by replacing a gerund with a verb.

Informative Writing Process: Edit and Publish

Practice with Student Model (optional)

Provide groups with a different section of Aiko's draft. Each group should practice editing Aiko's model using the checklist in the lesson. Has she:

- ☐ used participles correctly?
- ☐ used gerunds correctly?
- ☐ used infinitives correctly?
- ☐ corrected any sentence fragments or run-on sentences?
- ☐ spelled everything correctly?

After the groups have finished, call on volunteers from each group to make edits until all the mistakes have been found and edited, pausing to discuss points of disagreement.

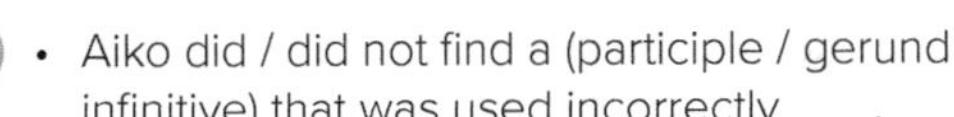

ELL **SPEAKING FRAMES**

A

- Aiko did / did not find a (participle / gerund / infinitive) that was used incorrectly ____.
- Aiko did / did not successfully revise the sentence with that error by ____.
- ____ is an example of a run-on sentence that Aiko has / has not corrected.
- ____ is an example of a sentence fragment that Aiko has / has not corrected.
- ____ is spelled incorrectly. The correct spelling is ____.

Write

After students finish editing, suggest, if there's time, that they set their essays aside for a few minutes, and that they then proofread them one more time. Once students have completed their writing, have them submit their work.

CHECK FOR SUCCESS

If students struggle to edit successfully, help them determine where edits are needed and what changes need to be made.

Direct students to the grammar lessons in this unit if they are uncertain about the rules for specific concepts.

ELL READ ALOUD

Encourage students to read their stories aloud to themselves or to a partner in order to catch any remaining mistakes.

READ ALOUD

Encourage students to read their stories aloud to themselves or to an on-grade-level peer in order to catch any remaining mistakes.

PLAY CRITIC

Have students review their writing for any potential weaknesses or places in which they might have gone in different directions. Invite them to operate as their own critics—how might the ending of their creative piece be resolved differently? How might someone with an opposing point of view challenge a point made in their essay? What other piece of evidence might have been included in their research paper? Have students critically analyze an aspect of their own work from an outsider's perspective.

~~And~~ The *Challenger* crew was well prepared~~, there were important questions about the universe that the *Challenger* crew was~~ and planning to study important questions about the universe. Unfortunately, they never had a chance to ~~acheive~~ achieve that goal because the space shuttle exploded after takeoff ~~despite~~. Despite this tragic end, Americans can ~~are~~ still ~~to~~ learn a valuable ~~lessen~~ lesson from the *Challenger* crew. Reagan~~'s explaining~~ explains that "the future doesn't belong to the fainthearted; it belongs to the brave. The *Challenger* crew was pulling us into the future, and we'll continue to follow them." The crew was willing to risk their lives in search of knowledge about the universe. Their efforts teach the values of selflessness and bravery.

WRITE

Use the questions on the previous page, as well as your peer reviews, to help you evaluate your informative essay to determine areas that need editing. Then edit your essay to correct those errors.

Once you have made all your corrections, you are ready to publish your work. You can distribute your writing to family and friends, hang it on a bulletin board, or post it on your blog. If you publish online, share the link with your family, friends, and classmates.

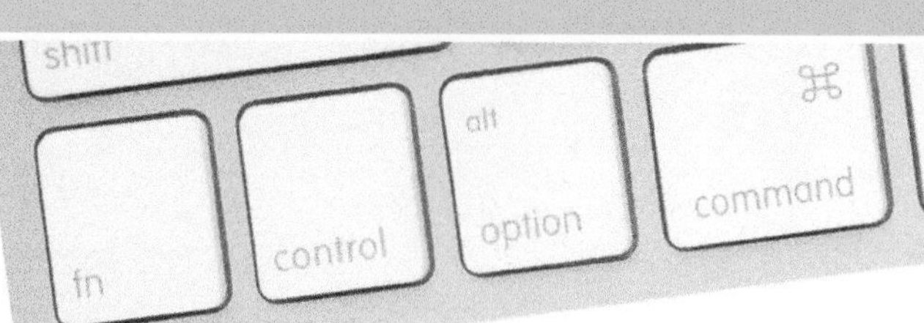

English Language Learner Resources

studysync

USERS ASSIGNMENTS

GRADE 8 › UNIT

No Risk, No Reward

Core ELA

Grade 8

30 Days

Unit Overview

Integrated Reading and Writing

Extended Writing Project

ELL Resources

Novel Study

End-of-Unit Assessment

Instructional Path

Add to book

The History of the Space Shuttle

Narrative of the Life of Ada Lee, an American Farm Girl

Skill: Classroom Vocabulary

Students will learn and recognize classroom vocabulary words and practice using them in a variety of contexts.

Assign

Skill: Making Connections

Students will learn and practice the skill of making connections when reading in order to demonstrate and improve comprehension.

Teacher Resources: Lesson Plan

Assign

Lessons in the English Language Learner Resources section offer explicit ELL instruction. These lessons share a thematic and genre focus with all other lessons in the Core ELA unit.

The twenty ELL Resources are developed around two texts, "The History of the Space Shuttle" and "Narrative of the Life of Ada Lee, an American Farm Girl," and an Extended Oral Project. Each text is written at four distinct levels. For ELLs, these texts serve as structural and thematic models of authentic texts in the Integrated Reading and Writing section of the unit. Thus, teachers may use the ELL texts in place of or as extensions for "Address to the Nation on the Explosion of the Space Shuttle *Challenger*" and *Narrative of the Life of Frederick Douglass, an American Slave*.

ELL lessons modify the routines used with texts in the Integrated Reading and Writing section. Explicit vocabulary instruction is emphasized, and reading and writing Skills lessons focus strongly on language acquisition and reading comprehension.

After reading texts about risks people have taken and why they chose to take them, students will complete an Extended Oral Project that can be used in place of or as an extension to the Extended Writing Project. In this unit, students will plan and present advice for risk-takers in the form of an informational presentation.

Focus on English Language Proficiency Levels

ADVANCED HIGH
ADVANCED
INTERMEDIATE
BEGINNING

ELL Resources provide targeted support for four levels of proficiency: Beginning, Intermediate, Advanced, and Advanced High. Instruction and scaffolds, as well as the texts themselves, are differentiated based on these levels.

Additional differentiated scaffolds include visual glossaries, speaking and writing frames, and suggested grouping for peer and teacher support. Lessons also include suggested extension activities to challenge Advanced and Advanced High students as they progress through the year.

ELL Resources

ELL TEXTS

The History of the Space Shuttle

- Skill: Sight Vocabulary and High-Frequency Words
- Skill: Using Prereading Supports
- First Read
- Skill: Analyzing Expressions
- Skill: Main Ideas and Details
- Skill: Spelling Patterns and Rules
- Close Read

The Narrative of Ada Lee

- Skill: Classroom Vocabulary
- Skill: Making Connections
- First Read
- Skill: Language Structures
- Skill: Comparing and Contrasting
- Skill: Main and Helping Verbs
- Close Read

EXTENDED ORAL PROJECT

- Introduction
- Skill: Acquiring Vocabulary
- Plan
- Skill: Sentence Types
- Practice
- Present

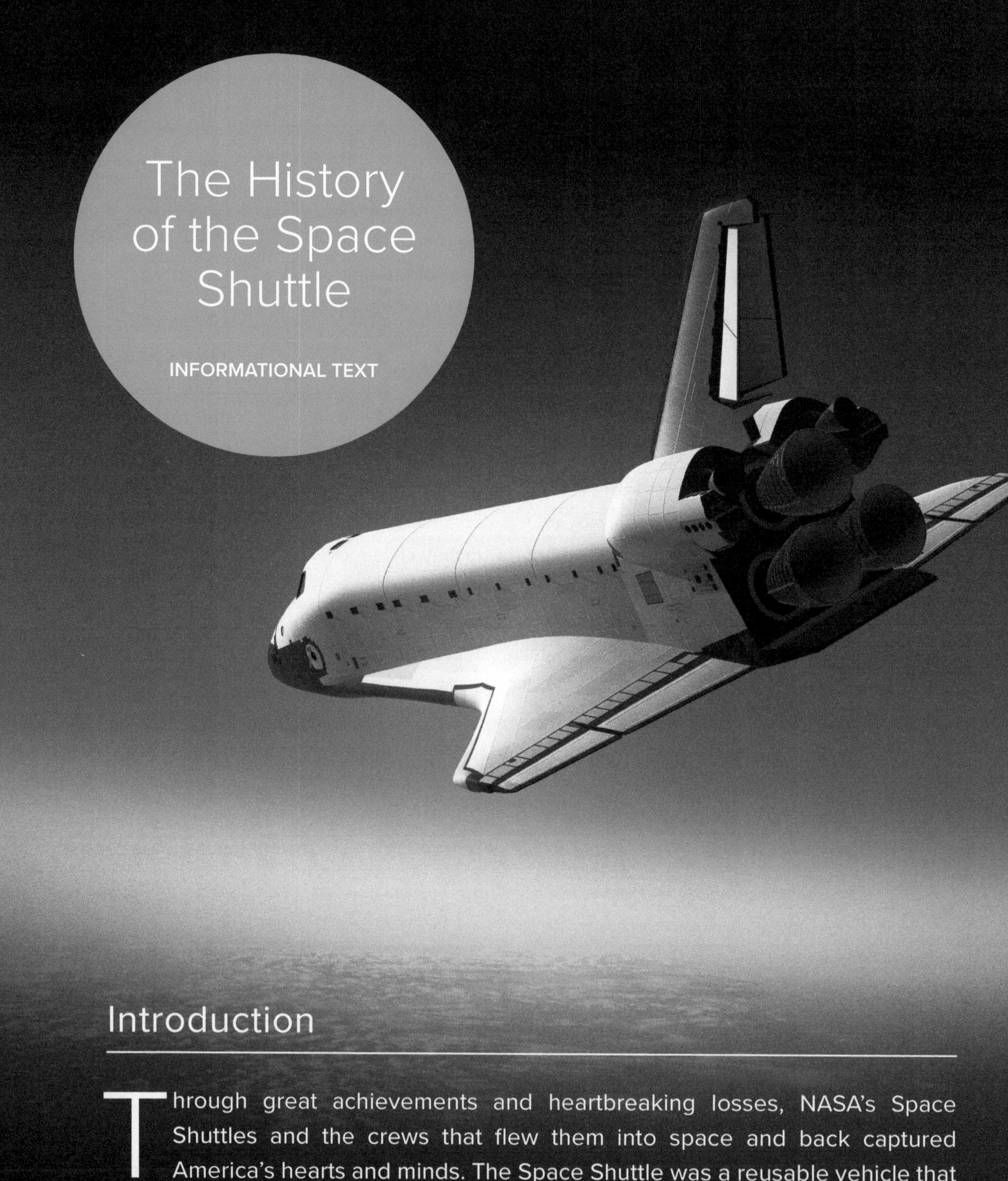

The History of the Space Shuttle

INFORMATIONAL TEXT

Introduction

Through great achievements and heartbreaking losses, NASA's Space Shuttles and the crews that flew them into space and back captured America's hearts and minds. The Space Shuttle was a reusable vehicle that allowed NASA to carry out 135 missions as well as send more than 350 people and 3 million pounds of cargo into space. Although the program ended in 2011, its triumphs and tragedies remain an important part of American history.

NASA's Space Shuttle program lasted for more than thirty years. There were 135 space missions, and 350 people went into space. The program started in 1958. The goal was to compete with the Soviet space program. Americans were very interested in space exploration. There were many successes. The most famous achievement was the 1969 moon landing. Later, NASA scientists created a reusable space vehicle. By the early 1980s, NASA built the *Columbia, Challenger,* and *Discovery* space crafts. However, in 1986, NASA experienced a very big failure. The *Challenger* exploded. Despite this loss, the Space Shuttle program continued. The astronauts worked on the Hubble Space Telescope and the International Space Station. Unfortunately, there was another disaster in 2003. The space shuttle *Columbia* broke into pieces as it returned to Earth. This was one reason that the Space Shuttle program ended in 2004.

ELL Summaries in multiple languages are available digitally.

Audio and audio text highlighting are available with this text.

CONNECT TO ESSENTIAL QUESTION

Why do we take chances?

This informational text explores the triumphs and tragedies of NASA's Space Shuttle program. Many brave astronauts flew over 100 space shuttle missions, but not everyone survived to return home to Earth. Knowing the dangers, why would astronauts continue to risk their lives on the space shuttle?

Core ELA Connections

Texts	Theme	Genre
"Address to the Nation on the Explosion of the Space Shuttle Challenger"	NASA's space shuttle was a reusable vehicle that completed 135 missions in space. This text builds on ideas of space travel, achievements, and losses.	An informational text, "The History of the Space Shuttle" provides a thorough background of the NASA vehicle.

Differentiated Text Levels

ELL LEVEL	BEGINNING	INTERMEDIATE	ADVANCED	ADVANCED HIGH
WORD COUNT	377	416	467	545
LEXILE	540L	620L	770L	810L

Instructional Path

The print teacher's edition includes essential point-of-use instruction and planning tools. Complete lesson plans and program documents appear in your digital teacher account.

Skill: Sight Vocabulary and High-Frequency Words

Objectives: Students will be able to learn and recognize sight vocabulary and high-frequency words in English.

Objectives: Students will be able to recognize sight vocabulary and high-frequency words when listening and reading, and produce sight vocabulary and high-frequency words when speaking and writing.

Skill: Using Prereading Supports

Objectives: Students will be able to learn and practice the skill of using prereading supports when reading a new text.

Objectives: Students will be able to read a new or unfamiliar text using prereading supports such as graphic organizers, illustrations, and topic vocabulary.

DIGITAL ONLY

First Read: The History of the Space Shuttle

Objectives: Students will be able to perform an initial reading of a text using the strategy of using prereading supports.

Objectives: Students will be able to demonstrate comprehension of a text by responding to questions orally and in writing using textual evidence.

Skill: Analyzing Expressions

Objectives: Students will be able to analyze expressions.

Objectives: Students will be able to analyze expressions when reading.

Skill: Main Ideas and Details

Objectives: Students will be able to distinguish between main ideas and details.

Objectives: Students will be able to distinguish between main ideas and details when reading and justify their decision when speaking.

Skill: Spelling Patterns and Rules

Objectives: Students will be able to recognize and apply spelling patterns and rules.

Objectives: Students will be able to recognize spelling patterns and rules when reading and apply spelling patterns and rules when writing

Close Read: The History of the Space Shuttle

Objectives: Students will be able to perform a close reading of a text in order to analyze main ideas and details.

Objectives: Students will be able to demonstrate analysis of main ideas and details by participating in a collaborative conversation and writing a short constructed response.

Progress Monitoring

Opportunities to Learn	Opportunities to Demonstrate Learning	Opportunities to Reteach
Sight Vocabulary and High-Frequency Words		
Skill: Sight Vocabulary and High-Frequency Words	Skill: Sight Vocabulary and High-Frequency Words • Your Turn First Read • Sight Vocabulary and High-Frequency Words Focus	Spotlight Skill: Sight Vocabulary and High-Frequency Words
Using Prereading Supports		
Skill: Using Prereading Supports	Skill: Using Prereading Supports • Your Turn First Read • Practice Prereading Skill	Spotlight Skill: Using Prereading Supports
Analyzing Expressions		
Skill: Analyzing Expressions	Skill: Analyzing Expressions • Your Turn	Spotlight Skill: Analyzing Expressions
Main Ideas and Details		
Skill: Main Ideas and Details	Skill: Main Ideas and Details • Your Turn Close Read • Skills Focus • Write	Spotlight Skill: Main Ideas and Details
Spelling Patterns and Rules		
Skill: Spelling Patterns and Rules	Skill: Spelling Patterns and Rules • Your Turn Close Read • Write	Spotlight Skill: Spelling Patterns and Rules

First Read

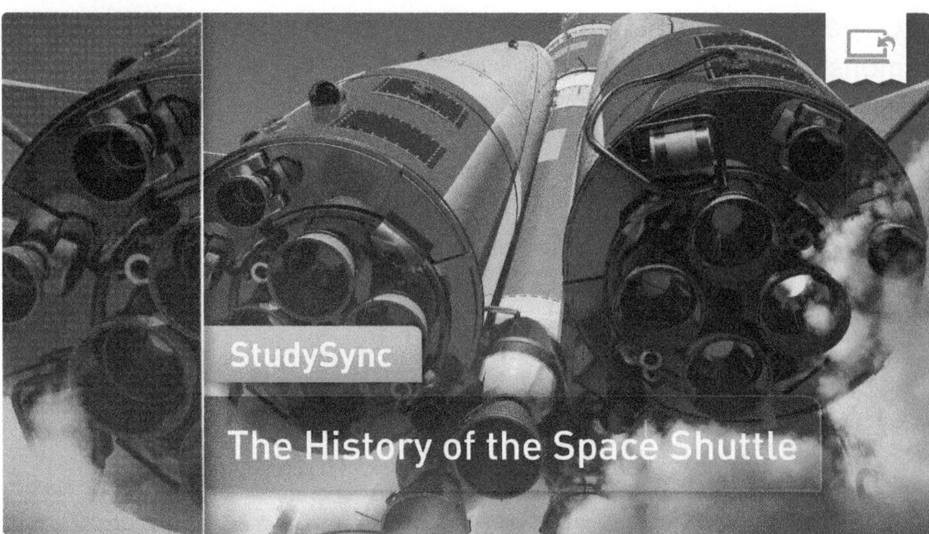

Introduce the Text

As a class, watch the video preview and have students read the introduction in pairs to make connections to the video preview. Ask students various "wh" questions such as:

- What did you see in the video? How does it make you feel?
- What do you think the text will be about?
- Is there something in the video or introduction that surprised you?

Beginning & Intermediate

SPEAKING FRAMES

- I see ____. I feel ____.
- I think the text will be about ____.
- I was surprised by ____.

Practice Prereading Skill

Remind students that Using Prereading Supports:

helps you prepare to read a text. An example of this is learning topic vocabulary to prepare to read a text. When you scan a text and discover words that are important to the topic, you can look them up in a dictionary or ask your teacher or peers for support.

Have students work in small, mixed-level groups to skim the passage looking for topic vocabulary related to space exploration. Prompt students to use a dictionary, context clues, and each other to define unknown words.

As students are working in small groups, circulate to listen for sample questions such as:

- *What does this word mean?*
- *What meaning does the dictionary give?*

Activate Prior Knowledge and Experiences OPTIONAL

Have students make connections while practicing their oral language by discussing what they know about space exploration.

Generate a list (on the board or on paper) of any information or ideas your students have about space exploration.

Ask students to share where their background knowledge came from. For example, did their ideas come from a movie, friend, television show, book, or family member?

VOCABULARY

satellite
an object that follows a consistent course around a larger object

fleet
a group of vehicles that are owned and operated by the same company

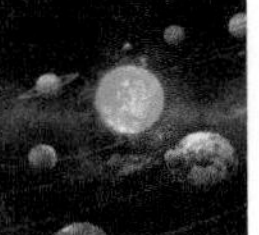

orbit
to revolve around a large object in a curved path

disintegrate
to fall apart or separate into pieces

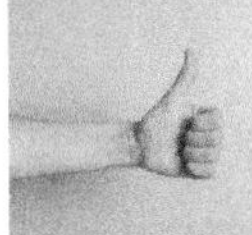

clear
to approve or give official permission

READ

1 The Space Shuttle program ran for three decades and 135 missions. It launched more than 350 people and 3 million pounds of cargo into space. Some of these missions ended in joyful celebrations. Others led to tragedy. Overall, the Space Shuttle program was an impressive achievement.

2 The National Aeronautics and Space Administration (NASA) was founded in 1958. Americans wanted to enter the Space Race. The Soviet Union launched the world's first made-man **satellite** in 1957. Interest in space exploration grew. In 1962, President John F. Kennedy said that NASA would put a man on the Moon. On July 20, 1969, Neil Armstrong achieved that goal.

3 With the success of the Moon landing behind them, NASA's scientists needed a new goal. A task force wanted to design a reusable space vehicle. They also wanted to build a space station and launch missions to Mars. President Richard Nixon told them to focus on the vehicle. The Space Shuttle program was born.

AUDIO TEXT HIGHLIGHTING

Allow students to use the audio text highlight feature to follow along as they read. Alternately, you may wish to work directly with students or group them in twos or threes for partner reading or choral reading.

Preteach Vocabulary

Model the first word and example for the class.

1. The first word is *satellite,* and its meaning is "an object that follows a consistent course around a larger object."
2. When I hear the word *satellite*, I think of devices in space that send information to Earth. These devices gather information by moving around the Earth in a set path.
3. For example: The weather is predicted using *satellites* in space.
4. This is an example of something that is a *satellite* because it works by traveling around the planet and sending information to Earth.

Continue this exercise with each word in the glossary, calling on individuals or groups of students to share out.

Beginning

PRETEACH VOCABULARY

Use the gestures to clarify meanings.

- **satellite** (Use a balled-up piece of paper and a smaller object, such as an eraser, to show how satellites orbit Earth.)
- **orbit** (Walk around your desk two or three times.)
- **clear** (Nod your head and give a thumbs up.)
- **fleet** (Use several objects of the same type, such as books, to model a fleet.)
- **disintegrate** (Put your hands together and then wiggle your fingers in a downward motion as your hands separate, to model something coming apart as it falls.)

Sight Vocabulary and High-Frequency Words Focus

Remind students of the sight vocabulary and high-frequency words that they studied at the beginning of the unit. Point out that some of the words may be useful as they think about and discuss the text. For example:

- goes (The crew **goes** into space to . . .)
- first (The **first** Space Shuttle . . .)
- about (I learned **about** . . .)
- show (The reactions to the tragic accidents **show** that people . . .)
- keep (I don't know if NASA should **keep** . . .)

4 Each shuttle has three main parts. The orbiter is the astronauts' home in space. There are two solid rocket boosters (SRBs). The SRBs create the force needed to launch. They break off. The last piece of the puzzle is the external fuel tank (ET). The ET provides fuel for launch. It also separates. The orbiter carries fuel for the mission and reentry.

5 The first shuttle, *Enterprise*, was never **cleared** for space. In April 1981, *Columbia* **orbited** the Earth 37 times before its arrival home. *Challenger* was built in 1983. *Discovery* followed in 1984. *Atlantis* joined the **fleet** a year later. With many successes under their belt, NASA had a failure. The shuttles were not reliable. On January 28, 1986, *Challenger* exploded 73 seconds after liftoff. The crew was killed. The likelihood of the disaster seemed low. America wept. NASA didn't launch another mission for two years.

6 The Space Shuttle program continued. *Challenger's* replacement, *Endeavour*, was built in 1992. The shuttles' crews worked to put satellites into orbit. They launched and repaired the Hubble Space Telescope. They worked on the International Space Station.

7 Another tragedy struck on February 1, 2003. *Columbia* **disintegrated** coming back to Earth. The crew was killed. The loss shook the nation. The program carried on.

8 The end of the historic Space Shuttle program was announced in 2004. NASA's budget grew smaller. Its priorities changed. The orbiters and SRBs were reusable, but they were expensive to maintain. The final mission ended on July 21, 2011. *Atlantis* landed safely. It joined the other shuttles in retirement.

TEXT TALK

1. What is the text about?
2. What is the author mainly discussing?
3. What are some examples that the author gives?
4. Does the text change the way you think about the topic?

All Levels

SPEAKING FRAMES

Giving Information:

- This text is about ____.
- The main idea is ____.
- Some examples the author gives about ____ include ____.
- This text makes me think ____.

Asking for Information:

- Can you explain ____?
- What do you think about ____?
- Why do you think ____?

First Read

Read the text. After you read, answer the Think Questions below.

THINK QUESTIONS

1. When and why was NASA founded?

   NASA was founded in ______________________________.

   It was founded because ______________________________.

2. What are the parts of a Space Shuttle?

   The parts of the Space Shuttle are ______________________________

   ______________________________.

3. What type of work did crews use Space Shuttles to do?

   Crews used the Space Shuttle to ______________________________

   ______________________________.

4. Use context to confirm the meaning of the word *fleet* as it is used in "The History of the Space Shuttle." Write your definition of *fleet* here.

   Fleet means ______________________________.

   A context clue is ______________________________.

5. What is another way to say that someone has *cleared* a plan?

   Someone has ______________________________.

Think Questions

Circulate as students answer Think Questions independently. Answers will vary.

QUESTION 1: Comprehension

NASA was founded in 1958. NASA was founded because there was a lot of interest in space.

QUESTION 2: Comprehension

The Space Shuttle has three parts: the orbiter, the solid rocket boosters, and the external fuel tank.

QUESTION 3: Comprehension

Answers will vary, but may include the following examples:

- "The Space Shuttles' crews put satellites into orbit."
- "They launched and repaired the Hubble Space Telescope."
- "They worked on the International Space Station."

Student responses should provide an example from the text and an explanation that describes how crews used the Space Shuttle to do tasks in space.

QUESTION 4: Language

The author uses the word *fleet* to explain when each of NASA's Space Shuttles was built. Together, the Space Shuttles make a fleet. A definition for *fleet* is "a group of vehicles."

QUESTION 5: Language

Someone has approved a plan.

Skill: Analyzing Expressions

Introduce the Skill

Watch the Concept Definition video and read the definition for Analyzing Expressions.

Skill: Analyzing Expressions

 DEFINE

When you read, you may find English expressions that you do not know. An **expression** is a group of words that communicates an idea. Three types of expressions are idioms, sayings, and figurative language. They can be difficult to understand because the meanings of the words are different from their **literal**, or usual, meanings.

An idiom is an expression that is commonly known among a group of people. For example: "It's raining cats and dogs" means it is raining heavily. **Sayings** are short expressions that contain advice or wisdom. For instance: "Don't count your chickens before they hatch" means do not plan on something good happening before it happens. **Figurative** language is when you describe something by comparing it with something else, either directly (using the words *like* or *as*) or indirectly. For example, "I'm as hungry as a horse" means I'm very hungry. None of the expressions are about actual animals.

••• CHECKLIST FOR ANALYZING EXPRESSIONS

To determine the meaning of an expression, remember the following:

- ✓ If you find a confusing group of words, it may be an expression. The meaning of words in expressions may not be their literal meaning.
  - Ask yourself: Is this confusing because the words are new? Or because the words do not make sense together?
- ✓ Determining the overall meaning may require that you use one or more of the following:
  - context clues
  - a dictionary or other resource
  - teacher or peer support
- ✓ Highlight important information before and after the expression to look for clues.

TURN AND TALK

1. What does it mean to analyze expressions?
2. Why might it be difficult to understand expressions?
3. What can you do if you are struggling to analyze expressions?

 **Beginning & Intermediate**

SPEAKING FRAMES

- To analyze expressions means to understand ____.
- You may not be able to ____.
- You could look at ____.
- You could think about ____.

 **Advanced & Advanced High**

SPEAKING FRAMES

- To analyze expressions means to ____.
- You may not be able to ____ because ____.
- You could look at ____, such as ____.
- You could think about ____. For example, ____.

 SKILL VOCABULARY

expression / la expresión *noun* a phrase used to express an idea COGNATE

literal / literal *adjective* describing the usual meaning of a word COGNATE

idiom / el modismo *noun* a common expression that cannot be taken literally

saying / el dicho *noun* an expression that contains advice or wisdom

The History of the Space Shuttle

YOUR TURN

Read paragraphs 4–7 from the text. Then, complete the multiple-choice questions below.

from "The History of the Space Shuttle"

Each shuttle has three main parts. The orbiter is the astronauts' home in space. There are two solid rocket boosters (SRBs). The SRBs create the force needed to launch. They break off. The last piece of the puzzle is the external fuel tank (ET). The ET provides fuel for launch. It also separates. The orbiter carries fuel for the mission and reentry.

The first shuttle, *Enterprise*, was never cleared for space. In April 1981, *Columbia* orbited the Earth 37 times before its arrival home. *Challenger* was built in 1983. *Discovery* followed in 1984. *Atlantis* joined the fleet a year later. With many successes under their belt, NASA had a failure. The shuttles were not reliable. On January 28, 1986, *Challenger* exploded 73 seconds after liftoff. The crew was killed. The likelihood of the disaster seemed low. America wept. NASA didn't launch another mission for two years.

The Space Shuttle program continued. *Challenger's* replacement, *Endeavour*, was built in 1992. The shuttles' crews worked to put satellites into orbit. They launched and repaired the Hubble Space Telescope. They worked on the International Space Station.

Another tragedy struck on February 1, 2003. *Columbia* disintegrated coming back to Earth. The crew was killed. The loss shook the nation. The program carried on.

1. In paragraph 4, the sentence "The last piece of the puzzle is the external fuel tank (ET)" means that the ET:
   - ○ A. was hard to put together.
   - ○ B. had a lot of parts.
   - ○ C. was part of the shuttle.
   - ○ D. was hard to understand.

2. In paragraph 5, the phrase "With many successes under their belt" means that NASA:
   - ○ A. got new uniforms.
   - ○ B. had many achievements.
   - ○ C. made a mistake.
   - ○ D. discovered an asteroid belt.

Discuss the Skill Model

1. What is the student trying to understand?

   The student is trying to understand the sentence "With the success of the Moon landing behind them, NASA's scientists needed a new goal."

2. Why is the student struggling?

   The student does not understand the meaning of the words in the sentence.

3. What strategies does the student use?

   The student asks for help.

Beginning & Intermediate

Have students use the speaking frames and helpful terms to participate in the group discussion. If beginning students are hesitant to participate in a discussion, encourage them by prompting with *yes* or *no* questions.

Advanced & Advanced High

Have students use the speaking frames to participate in the group discussion.

SPEAKING FRAMES

- The student is trying to ____.
- The student is struggling because ____.
- The student ____ in order to ____.
- The teacher's response helps him understand ____.

HELPFUL TERMS FOR DISCUSSION

- literal
- expression
- asks
- figurative
- describes
- help

Your Turn

Ask students to complete the Your Turn activity.

QUESTION 1: C) This meaning is supported by the passage. The ET was part of the shuttle.

QUESTION 2: B) This meaning is supported by the passage. NASA had many achievements.

QUESTION 3: A) This meaning is supported by the passage. Americans felt very sad after the accident.

QUESTION 4: B) This meaning is supported by the passage. Americans had a strong reaction to the accident.

3. In paragraph 5, the sentence “America wept” means that Americans felt:

   - A. sad.
   - B. mad.
   - C. joyful.
   - D. surprised.

4. In paragraph 7, the sentence “The loss shook the nation” means that Americans:

   - A. had an earthquake.
   - B. had a strong reaction.
   - C. did not support NASA.
   - D. felt strong winds.

Skill: Main Ideas and Details

Introduce the Skill

Watch the Concept Definition video and read the definition for Main Ideas and Details.

TURN AND TALK

1. How do you distinguish between the main idea and supporting details?
2. How do supporting details relate to the main idea?
3. What can you do if you are struggling to identify a main idea?

Beginning & Intermediate

SPEAKING FRAMES

- A main idea is ____.
- Supporting details ____ a main idea.
- You could look at ____.
- You could also scan ____.

Advanced & Advanced High

SPEAKING FRAMES

- A main idea is ____.
- Supporting details ____ a main idea because ____.
- You could look at ____, such as ____.
- You could also try using strategies like ____ or ____.

SKILL VOCABULARY

main idea / la idea principal *noun* the most important idea of a paragraph, a section, or an entire text

supporting details / los detalles que desarrollan la idea central *noun* details that describe or explain the main idea

distinguish / distinguir *verb* to determine the difference between two things COGNATE

Skill: Main Ideas and Details

★ DEFINE

The **main ideas** are the most important ideas of a paragraph, a section, or an entire text. The **supporting details** are details that describe or explain the main idea.

To **distinguish** between the main ideas and the supporting details, you will need to decide what information is the most important and supports or explains the main ideas.

••• CHECKLIST FOR MAIN IDEAS AND DETAILS

In order to distinguish between main ideas and supporting details, do the following:

- ✓ Preview the text. Look at headings, topic sentences, and boldface vocabulary.
  - Ask yourself: What seem to be the main ideas in this text?
- ✓ Read the text.
  - Ask yourself: What are the most important ideas? What details support or explain the most important ideas?
- ✓ Take notes or use a graphic organizer to distinguish between main ideas and supporting details.

Discuss the Skill Model

1. What is the student looking for?

   The student is looking for main ideas and supporting details.

2. What strategy does the student use to identify a main idea?

   The student reads the topic sentence of the paragraph.

3. What strategy does the student use to identify supporting details?

   The student looks for details that develop the main idea.

ELL **Beginning & Intermediate**

Have students use the speaking frames and helpful terms to participate in the group discussion. If beginning students are hesitant to participate in a discussion, encourage them by prompting with *yes* or *no* questions.

Advanced & Advanced High

Have students use the speaking frames to participate in the group discussion.

SENTENCE FRAMES

- The student is looking for ____.
- First, the student reads ____ because ____.
- Then, the student looks for ____ in order to ____.
- The student also thinks about ____ to help him ____.

HELPFUL TERMS FOR DISCUSSION

- identify
- supporting
- highlight
- topic
- details
- consider

YOUR TURN

Read paragraphs 7–8 from the text. Then, complete the multiple-choice questions below.

from "The History of the Space Shuttle"

Another tragedy struck on February 1, 2003. *Columbia* disintegrated coming back to Earth. The crew was killed. The loss shook the nation. The program carried on.

The end of the historic Space Shuttle program was announced in 2004. NASA's budget grew smaller. Its priorities changed. The orbiters and SRBs were reusable, but they were expensive to maintain. The final mission ended on July 21, 2011. Atlantis landed safely. It joined the other shuttles in retirement.

1. The main idea of paragraph 7 is that NASA:
   - O A. kept going.
   - O B. had an accident.
   - O C. was shocked.
   - O D. did not know what to do.

2. A supporting detail that best develops this main idea is:
   - O A. "Another tragedy struck on February 1, 2003."
   - O B. "*Columbia* disintegrated coming back to Earth."
   - O C. "The loss shook the nation."
   - O D. "The program carried on."

3. The main idea of paragraph 8 is that the Space Shuttle program:
   - O A. was expensive.
   - O B. reused some parts.
   - O C. had many shuttles.
   - O D. came to an end.

4. A supporting detail that best develops this main idea is:
   - O A. "NASA's budget grew smaller. Its priorities changed."
   - O B. "The orbiters and SRBs were reusable, but they were expensive to maintain."
   - O C. "The final mission ended on July 21, 2011."
   - O D. "Atlantis landed safely."

Your Turn

Ask students to complete the Your Turn activity.

QUESTION 1: B) This is the main idea of the paragraph.

QUESTION 2: B) This detail supports the main idea that NASA had an accident.

QUESTION 3: D) This is the main idea of the paragraph.

QUESTION 4: C) This detail supports the main idea that the Space Shuttle program came to an end.

Close Read

✎ WRITE

ARGUMENTATIVE: Should NASA restart the Space Shuttle program? Why or why not? Write a short paragraph in which you state your opinion on this topic. Support your claim with details from the text. Pay attention to correctly spelling words with suffixes as you write.

Use the checklist below to guide you as you write.

- ☐ Do you think NASA should restart the Space Shuttle program?
- ☐ Why do you feel that way?
- ☐ What details in the text support your opinion?

Use the sentence frames to organize and write your argument.

NASA (should / should not) restart the Space Shuttle program.

Restarting the Space Shuttle program would be ______________________________.

I think this because ______________________________.

Overall, the Space Shuttle program was ______________________________,

but it was also ______________________________.

Details that support this opinion are ____________________ and ______________________________.

Close Read

Model Skills Focus

Remind students of the Reading Skill Main Ideas and Details. Tell students that one way you can identify main ideas and details is to determine what information is most important and how the text supports it. Direct students to the Skills Focus and remind them to track as you read aloud.

Find the main ideas and details of the text.

Model Main Ideas and Details for students:

- I am going to focus on the first paragraph.
- I reread the paragraph and look at my annotations. I notice that I highlighted the last sentence.
- *Overall* seems like an important key word. I think the words that follow tell the author's main idea: *the Space Shuttle program was an impressive achievement*.
- With this idea in mind, I look at the paragraph again and look for supporting details. The author gives facts about the Space Shuttle program. The paragraph says there were 135 missions in 30 years. That seems like a lot! It also says that 350 people went into space. That also seems like a big number. These details support the main idea that the program was "an impressive achievement."

Complete Skills Focus

Use a Jigsaw strategy to have students complete the Skills Focus. Divide students into three groups. Assign each group the beginning, middle, or end of the text (paragraphs 1–3, 4 and 5, and 6–8). Prompt groups to:

- Find the main ideas and details of each paragraph in their section.
- Decide on the main idea of the section as a whole.

Circulate and monitor groups as they work.

Collaborative Conversation

Rearrange students so they have at least one representative from each of the original groups. Prompt partners to combine the main ideas and details they found to better understand the whole text.

- How did you determine the main ideas?
- How did you determine supporting details?
- How did distinguishing main ideas from details help you better understand the text?

Collaborative Conversation

BEGINNING, INTERMEDIATE Use the word bank to participate in the group discussion.

ADVANCED Use the speaking frames to participate in the group discussion.

BEGINNING, INTERMEDIATE	ADVANCED
Word Bank	**Speaking Frames**
• helped me identify • now I understand • key word • phrase • main idea • supporting detail	• Key words and phrases helped me because ____. • Looking for supporting details helped me because ____. • Identifying main ideas helped me better understand the text because ____.

SCAFFOLDS

Write

Ask students to complete the writing assignment. Remind students to pay attention to spelling patterns in words.

ELL **BEGINNING** Write a response using the paragraph frames and word bank.

INTERMEDIATE Write a response using the paragraph frames.

INTERMEDIATE

BEGINNING

Paragraph Frames

- NASA should / should not restart the Space Shuttle program.
- Restarting the Space Shuttle program would be ____. I think this because ____.
- Overall, the Space Shuttle program was ____, but it was also ____. Details that support this opinion are ____ and ____.

Word Bank

- wrong
- good
- helpful
- expensive
- successful

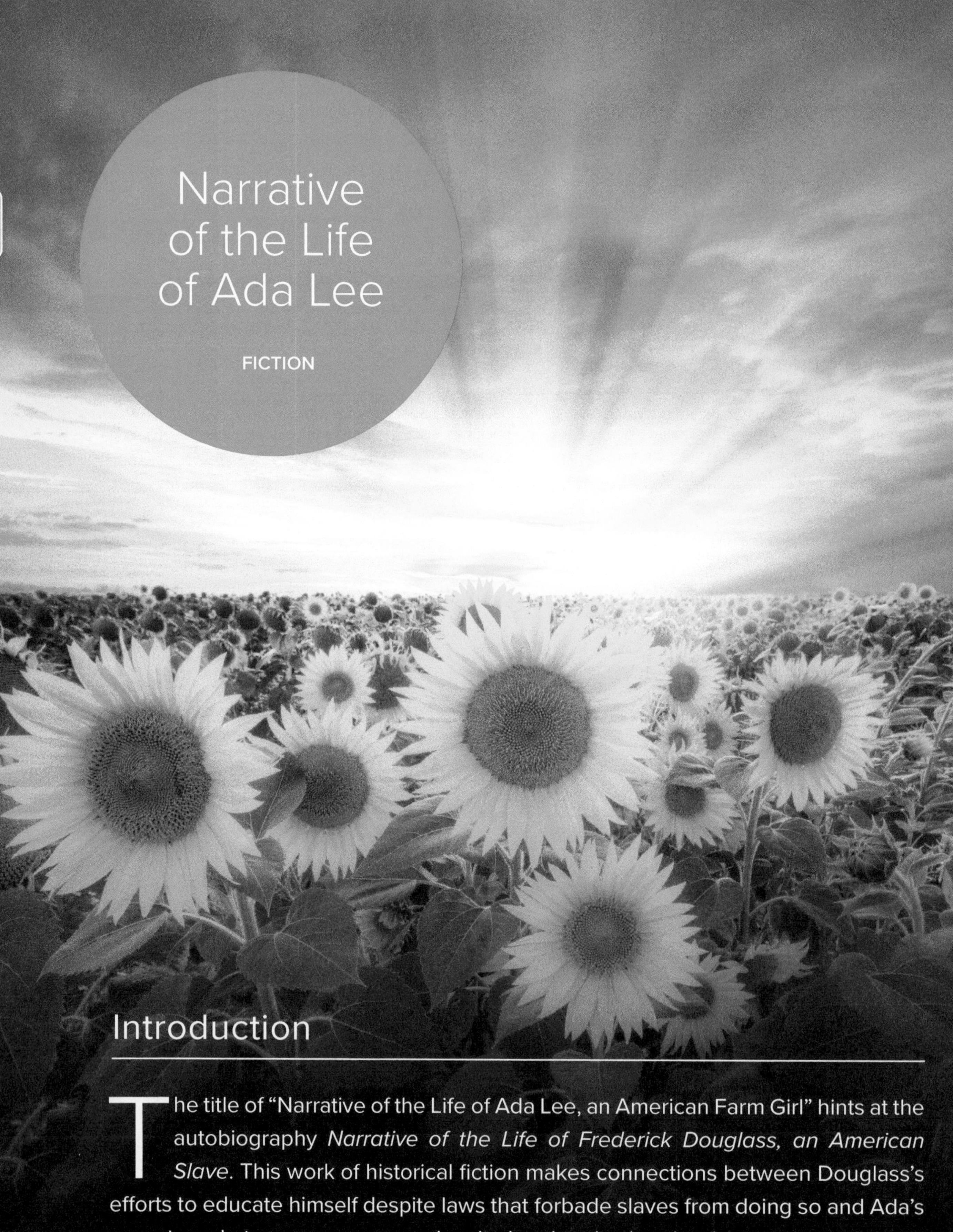

Narrative of the Life of Ada Lee

FICTION

Introduction

The title of "Narrative of the Life of Ada Lee, an American Farm Girl" hints at the autobiography *Narrative of the Life of Frederick Douglass, an American Slave*. This work of historical fiction makes connections between Douglass's efforts to educate himself despite laws that forbade slaves from doing so and Ada's own struggle to pursue a career despite legal and cultural unfairness to women

Ada Lee is sitting in her barn. She is whispering a secret to the family's dairy cow. She will soon leave for college. Women are not allowed to attend most colleges. But Ada found one on the East Coast that accepted her. She is worried that the work will be hard. Ada taught herself to read. So she thinks that she can do the work. When she gets to the college, the work is very difficult. Ada has a tall pile of books. The books are filled with legal terminology. Ada meets another student named John Wilson. John offers to tutor Ada. In exchange, Ada will give him some home-cooked meals. John and Ada spend a lot of time studying together. They earn their law degrees. They decide to get married. Ada wants to start a law practice with John. However, the state does not allow women to practice law. As a result, Ada tries to change the law. She believes that women can do anything they put their minds to.

ELL Summaries in multiple languages are available digitally.

Audio and audio text highlighting are available with this text.

CONNECT TO ESSENTIAL QUESTION

Why do we take chances?

In this short story, young women do not receive much education or have careers. Ada Lee knows she can be more than what society says she can be. Despite challenges and risks to come, Ada Lee leaves behind her life on the farm to pursue her dream of becoming a lawyer. Will her decision pay off?

Core ELA Connections

Texts	Theme	Genre
Narrative of the Life of Frederick Douglass, an American Slave	Ada Lee struggles to pursue a career in spite of legal and cultural unfairness to women. This text builds on the ideas of education, adversity, and ambition.	"Narrative of the Life of Ada Lee" is a work of historical fiction.

Differentiated Text Levels

ELL LEVEL	BEGINNING	INTERMEDIATE	ADVANCED	ADVANCED HIGH
WORD COUNT	257	416	456	567
LEXILE	390L	700L	830L	900L

Instructional Path

The print teacher's edition includes essential point-of-use instruction and planning tools. Complete lesson plans and program documents appear in your digital teacher account.

Skill: Classroom Vocabulary

Objectives: Students will be able to learn and recognize routine classroom vocabulary in English.

Objectives: Students will be able to recognize routine classroom vocabulary when listening and reading, and produce classroom vocabulary when speaking and writing.

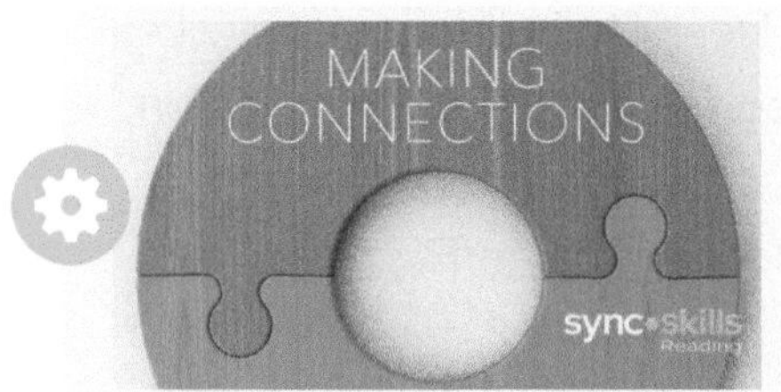

Skill: Making Connections

Objectives: Students will be able to learn and practice the skill of making connections when reading a text.

Objectives: Students will be able to make connections when reading.

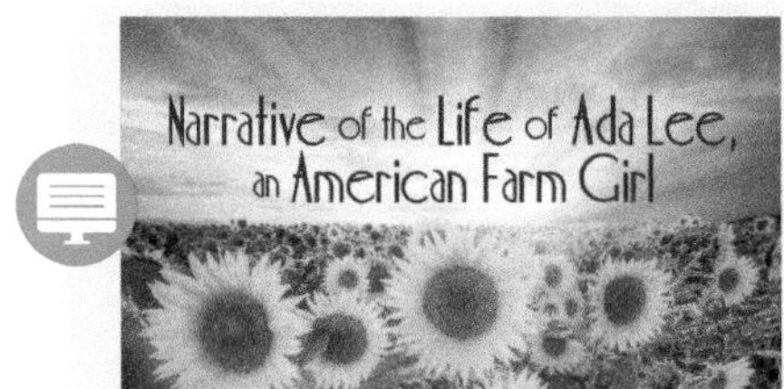

First Read: Narrative of the Life of Ada Lee, an American Farm Girl

Objectives: Students will be able to perform an initial reading of a text using the strategy of using prereading supports.

Objectives: Students will be able to demonstrate comprehension of a text by responding to questions orally and in writing using textual evidence.

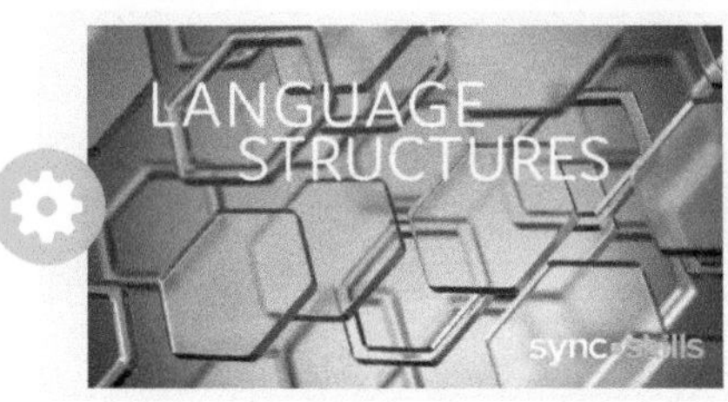

Skill: Language Structures

Objectives: Students will be able to grasp language structures.

Objectives: Students will be able to grasp language structures when reading.

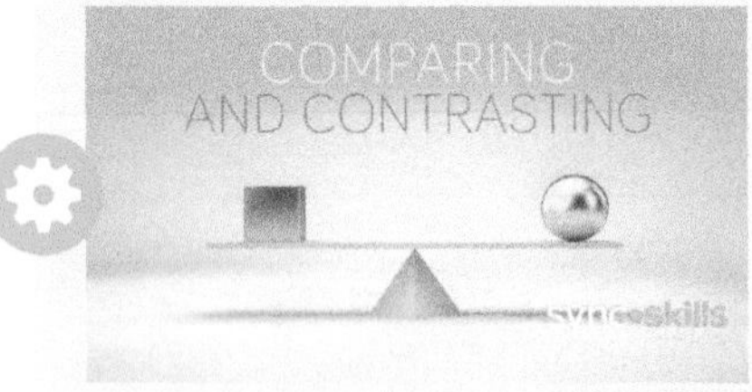

Skill: Comparing and Contrasting

Objectives: Students will be able to compare and contrast.

Objectives: Students will be able to compare and contrast when reading.

Skill: Main and Helping Verbs

Objectives: Students will be able to identify main and helping verbs.

Objectives: Students will be able to identify main and helping verbs when reading.

Close Read: Narrative of the Life of Ada Lee, an American Farm Girl

Objectives: Students will be able to perform a close reading of a text in order to compare and contrast.

Objectives: Students will be able to demonstrate comparing and contrasting by participating in a collaborative conversation and writing a short constructed response.

Progress Monitoring

Opportunities to Learn	Opportunities to Demonstrate Learning	Opportunities to Reteach
Classroom Vocabulary		
Skill: Classroom Vocabulary	Skill: Classroom Vocabulary • Your Turn First Read • Classroom Vocabulary Focus	Spotlight Skill: Classroom Vocabulary
Making Connections		
Skill: Making Connections	Skill: Making Connections • Your Turn First Read • Practice Prereading Skill	Spotlight Skill: Making Connections
Language Structures		
Skill: Language Structures	Skill: Language Structures • Your Turn	Spotlight Skill: Language Structures
Comparing and Contrasting		
Skill: Comparing and Contrasting	Skill: Comparing and Contrasting • Your Turn Close Read • Skills Focus • Write	Spotlight Skill: Comparing and Contrasting
Main and Helping Verbs		
Skill: Main and Helping Verbs	Skill: Main and Helping Verbs • Your Turn Close Read • Write	Spotlight Skill: Main and Helping Verbs

First Read

StudySync
Narrative of the Life of Ada Lee, An American Farm Girl

Introduce the Text

As a class, watch the video preview and have students read the introduction in pairs to make connections to the video preview. Ask students various "wh" questions such as:

- What did you see in the video? How does it make you feel?
- What do you think the text will be about?
- Is there something in the video or introduction that surprised you?

Beginning & Intermediate

SPEAKING FRAMES

- I see ____. I feel ____.
- I think the text will be about ____.
- I was surprised by ____.

Practice Prereading Skill

Remind students that Making Connections:

helps you better understand a text by connecting what you read to your own experiences, to other texts you have read, or to the world around you.

Have students work in small, homogeneous groups to make connections.

As students are working in small groups, circulate to listen for sample connections such as:

- *What happened to Ada reminds me of the time . . .*
- *This is really similar to the book . . .*

Activate Prior Knowledge and Experiences OPTIONAL

Have students make connections while practicing their oral language by discussing what they know about careers.

Generate a list (on the board or on paper) of any information or ideas your students have about careers.

Ask students to share where their background knowledge came from. For example, did their ideas come from a movie, friend, television show, book, or family member?

VOCABULARY

secret
known by only a few people

earnest
sincere and serious

enroll
to register for or enter

grieving
to feel deep sadness

incomprehensible
unable to be understood

READ

1 I sat down on the stool and dug my heels into the barn's dirt floor. "You know I love you, Bessie," I whispered dreamily to our dairy cow, "but I'm not going to be with you for much longer. I am going to college." A **secret** grin spread slowly across my face. It was the first time I had said my plan out loud. "I know what you're thinking, Bessie," I continued, patting her gently. Women could not go to college, but I had heard about a college on the east coast that would accept female students. The school was far away. The workload might be very hard, given my limited education. But I was determined to **enroll**. After all, I had taught myself to read. Learning from a teacher couldn't be harder than that. "It's going to be hard, but I will go to school and become a lawyer."

2 College was different than I had expected it to be. I missed my life on the farm, and the pile of books that rested on my desk practically reached the ceiling. They were filled with **incomprehensible** legal terminology that I hadn't much use for back home. I knew I needed to get some help if I were to

AUDIO TEXT HIGHLIGHTING

Allow students to use the audio text highlight feature to follow along as they read. Alternately, you may wish to work directly with students or group them in twos or threes for partner reading or choral reading.

Preteach Vocabulary

Model the first word and example for the class.

1. The first word is *secret,* and its meaning is "known by only a few people."
2. When I hear the word *secret*, I think of wishes or embarrassing stories I don't want anyone else to know.
3. For example, I have a *secret* crush on my brother's best friend.
4. This is an example of something that is *secret* because not many people know.

Continue this exercise with each word in the glossary, calling on individuals or groups of students to share out.

Beginning

PRETEACH VOCABULARY

Use the gestures to clarify meanings.

- **secret** ("Zip" your lips and then hold an index finger in front of your lips to signal "shhhh.")
- **enroll** (Pantomime filling out a form at a desk.)
- **incomprehensible** (Shrug, raise your eyebrows, shake your head, and hold your hands out with your palms up.)
- **earnest** (Hold your hands to your heart and smile with your mouth closed.)
- **grieving** (Sit with your head in your hands looking downward so your face can't be seen.)

Classroom Language Focus

Remind students of the sight vocabulary and high-frequency words that they studied at the beginning of the unit. Point out that some of the words may be useful as they think about and discuss the text. For example:

- grow up (Ada **grew up** on a farm.)
- show up (When Ada **shows up** at college . . .)
- keep up (Ada struggles to **keep up** with her reading.)
- give up (Ada did not **give up** when . . .)
- grow up (When Ada **grows up**, she wants to . . .)

succeed. John Wilson was a young man in the law program who came from a long line of lawyers. One day, I flashed John a smile and told him I'd exchange home-cooked meals for some tutoring. He gladly accepted.

3 John and I worked together from then on. By the time we had earned our law degrees, we had grown quite close. We were married after graduation. It was my **earnest** wish that we would open a law office and continue working side by side. The state legislature had other plans. The state would not grant me a license to practice law because I was a woman.

4 My husband was not bothered by this turn of events. He had loved studying with me, but he was happy to provide for his family while I ran our home. I was devastated. I didn't have to go to college to be a homemaker. I spent my days **grieving** for the career I'd never have. I wished that I had never heard of the college, because then I'd be a happy wife. But then I wished something else. I wished that women could do anything we wanted to. I set out to find a way to change the law so we could.

TEXT TALK

1. What is the story about?
2. Who are the story's characters?
3. Where does the story take place?
4. How does the story make you feel?

All Levels

SPEAKING FRAMES

Giving Information:

- This story is about ____.
- The story's characters are ____.
- This story takes place in ____.
- This story makes me feel ____.

Asking for Information:

- Can you explain ____?
- What do you think about ____?
- Why do you think ____?

Narrative of the Life of Ada Lee, an American Farm Girl

First Read

Read the story. After you read, answer the Think Questions below.

THINK QUESTIONS

1. Where does Ada live in the beginning of the story? How do you know?

   Ada lives ______________________________.

2. Write two or three sentences describing what happens when Ada goes to college.

   When Ada goes to college ______________________________

   ______________________________.

3. What problem(s) does Ada face at the end of the story? Cite text evidence in your response.

   The problems Ada faces ______________________________

   ______________________________.

4. Use context clues to confirm the meaning of the word *earnest* as it is used in "Narrative of the Life of Ada Lee, an American Farm Girl." Write your definition of *earnest* here.

   Earnest means ______________________________.

   A context clue is ______________________________.

5. What is another way to say that a text is *incomprehensible*?

   A text is ______________________________.

Think Questions

Circulate as students answer Think Questions independently. Answers will vary.

QUESTION 1: Comprehension

Ada lives on a farm. She sits in a barn and talks to a cow.

QUESTION 2: Comprehension

Ada works hard. She meets a man named John. They get married.

QUESTION 3: Comprehension

Answers will vary, but may include the following examples:

- "The state would not grant me a license to practice law because I was a woman."
- "I spent my days grieving for the career I'd never have."

Student responses should provide an example from the text and an explanation that describes how the state did not allow Ada to become a lawyer.

QUESTION 4: Language

The author uses the word *earnest* when Ada tells about her deepest wish. This is a clue that *earnest* means "sincere."

QUESTION 5: Language

A text is impossible to understand.

Skill: Language Structures

Introduce the Skill

Watch the Concept Definition video ▶ and read the definition for Language Structures.

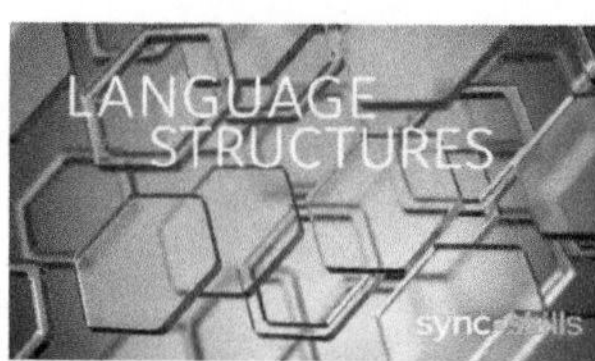

Skill: Language Structures

 DEFINE

In every language, there are rules that tell how to **structure** sentences. These rules define the correct order of words. In the English language, for example, a **basic** structure for sentences is subject, verb, and object. Some sentences have more **complicated** structures.

You will encounter both basic and complicated **language structures** in the classroom materials you read. Being familiar with language structures will help you better understand the text.

••• CHECKLIST FOR LANGUAGE STRUCTURES

To improve your comprehension of language structures, do the following:

✓ Monitor your understanding.

- Ask yourself: Why do I not understand this sentence? Is it because I do not understand some of the words? Or is it because I do not understand the way the words are ordered in the sentence?

✓ Pay attention to **perfect tenses** as you read. There are three perfect tenses in the English language: the present perfect, past perfect, and future perfect. The word *perfect* means "completed." These tenses describe actions that are completed or finished.

- **Present perfect tense** expresses an action that occurred at some indefinite time in the past.
  > Combine *have* or *has* with the past participle of the main verb.
  Example: I **have played** basketball for three years.
- **Past perfect tense** describes an action that happened before another action or event in the past.
  > Combine *had* with the past participle of the main verb.
  Example: I **had learned** how to dribble a ball before I could walk!

TURN AND TALK

1. What does it mean to grasp language structures?
2. Why might it be difficult to understand language?
3. What can you do if you are struggling to grasp language structures?

 **Beginning & Intermediate**

SPEAKING FRAMES
- To grasp language structures means to understand ____.
- Language can be difficult because you may not understand ____.
- You could look at ____.
- You could think about ____.

 **Advanced & Advanced High**

SPEAKING FRAMES
- To grasp language structures means to ____.
- Language can be difficult because ____.
- You could look at ____, such as ____.
- You could think about ____. For example, ____.

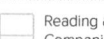

 SKILL VOCABULARY

structure / la estructura *noun* the order of parts COGNATE

basic / básico *adjective* the most important parts without anything extra COGNATE

complicated / complicado *adjective* having many parts COGNATE

language structure / la estructura de lenguaje *noun* the order of words in a sentence COGNATE

Narrative of the Life of Ada Lee, an American Farm Girl

- **Future perfect tense** expresses one future action that will begin and end before another future event begins.
  - > Use *will have* or *shall have* with the past participle of a verb.
    Example: Before the end of the year, I **will have played** more than 100 games!

✓ Break down the sentence into its parts.

- Ask yourself: What actions are expressed in this sentence? Are they completed or are they ongoing? What words give me clues about when an action is taking place?

✓ Confirm your understanding with a peer or teacher.

Discuss the Skill Model

1. What is the student trying to understand?

   The student is trying to understand the sentence "By the time we had earned our law degrees, we had grown quite close."

2. Why is the student struggling?

   The student is confused by the number of verbs in the sentence.

3. What strategies does the student use?

   Answers will vary, but should include: The student asks for help. The student thinks about verb tense. The student looks for clues.

Beginning & Intermediate

Have students use the speaking frames and helpful terms to participate in the group discussion. If beginning students are hesitant to participate in a discussion, encourage them by prompting with *yes* or *no* questions.

Advanced & Advanced High

Have students use the speaking frames to participate in the group discussion.

SPEAKING FRAMES

- The student is trying to ____.
- The student is confused because ____.
- First, the student ____ in order to ____.
- The student also ____ to help her ____.

HELPFUL TERMS FOR DISCUSSION

- tense
- past
- asks
- subject
- perfect
- help

YOUR TURN

Read the following excerpt from the text. Look at the bold-faced examples of past perfect tense. Remember that past perfect tense describes events that started and ended in the past. Then, sort the events into the order in which they happened. Place the correct letter in the chart below.

from "**Narrative of the Life of Ada Lee, an American Farm Girl**"

I sat down on the stool and dug my heels into the barn's dirt floor. "You know I love you, Bessie," I whispered dreamily to our dairy cow, "but I'm not going to be with you for much longer. I am going to college." A secret grin spread slowly across my face. It was the first time **I had said** my plan out loud. "I know what you're thinking, Bessie," I continued, patting her gently. Women could not go to college, but **I had heard** about a college on the east coast that would accept female students. The school was far away. The workload might be very hard, given my limited education. But I was determined to enroll. After all, **I had taught** myself to read. Learning from a teacher couldn't be harder than that. "It's going to be hard, but I will go to school and become a lawyer."

	Events
A	Ada teaches herself how to read.
B	Ada talks to Bessie about her plan to go to college.
C	Ada hears about a college that accepts female students.

First	Next	Last

Your Turn

Ask students to complete the Your Turn activity.

First	Next	Last
Ada teaches herself how to read.	Ada hears about a college that accepts female students.	Ada talks to Bessie about her plan to go to college.

Narrative of the Life of Ada Lee, an American Farm Girl

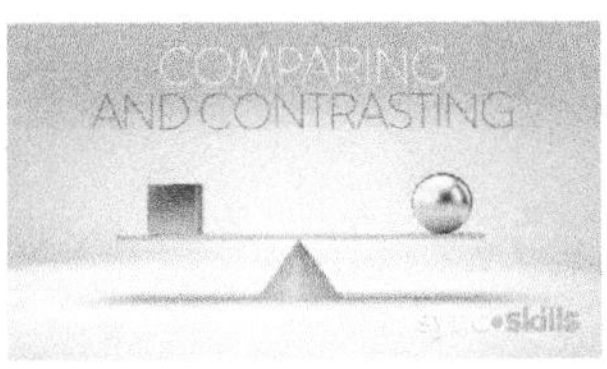

Skill: Comparing and Contrasting

★ DEFINE

To **compare** is to show how two or more pieces of information or literary elements in a text are similar. To **contrast** is to show how two or more pieces of information or literary elements in a text are different. By comparing and contrasting, you can better understand the **meaning** and the **purpose** of the text you are reading.

••• CHECKLIST FOR COMPARING AND CONTRASTING

In order to compare and contrast, do the following:

✓ Look for information or elements that you can compare and contrast.
- Ask yourself: How are these two things similar? How are they different?

✓ Look for signal words that indicate a compare-and-contrast relationship.
- Ask yourself: Are there any words that indicate the writer is trying to compare and contrast two or more things?

✓ Use a graphic organizer, such as a Venn diagram, to compare and contrast information.

SKILL VOCABULARY

compare / comparar *verb* to explain how two or more things are similar COGNATE

contrast / contrastar *verb* to explain how two or more things are different COGNATE

meaning / el significado *noun* the general message of a text

purpose / el propósito *noun* the reason the writer wrote a text

Skill: Comparing and Contrasting

Introduce the Skill

Watch the Concept Definition video ▶ and read the definition for Comparing and Contrasting.

TURN AND TALK

1. What does it mean to compare and contrast?
2. What type of information can be compared and contrasted in a text?
3. What can you do if you are struggling to determine what to compare and contrast in a text?

Beginning & Intermediate

SPEAKING FRAMES
- To compare and contrast means to show how ____.
- You can compare and contrast information that is ____ or ____.
- You could look for ____.
- You could also use a ____

Advanced & Advanced High

SPEAKING FRAMES
- To compare and contrast means ____.
- You can compare and contrast ____, such as ____.
- You could look for ____. For example, ____.
- You could also use a ____, like a ____.

Discuss the Skill Model

1. What does the student notice when he starts reading the text?

   He notices that there is a difference between what Ada expected college to be like and her actual experience.

2. What does the student do first?

   The student makes a note that shows what Ada's life was like before college.

3. What does the student do second?

   The student makes a note that shows what Ada's life was like during college.

4. What does the student do with this information?

   Answers will vary, but should include: The student makes a chart to compare and contrast the experiences. He shares his conclusion with a peer.

ELL **Beginning & Intermediate**

Have students use the speaking frames and helpful terms to participate in the group discussion. If beginning students are hesitant to participate in a discussion, encourage them by prompting with *yes* or *no* questions.

Advanced & Advanced High

Have students use the speaking frames to participate in the group discussion.

SPEAKING FRAMES

- The student notices that there is a difference between what Ada ____ and her ____.
- He makes a note that shows ____. For example, ____.
- He makes a note that shows ____. For example, ____.
- He decides to ____. He also ____.

HELPFUL TERMS FOR DISCUSSION

- text
- during
- before
- expected
- chart
- conclusion

YOUR TURN

Read the following excerpt from the text. Then, complete the Compare-and-Contrast chart by writing the letter of the correct example in the chart below.

from "Narrative of the Life of Ada Lee, an American Farm Girl"

John and I worked together from then on. By the time we had earned our law degrees, we had grown quite close. We were married after graduation. It was my earnest wish that we would open a law office and continue working side by side. The state legislature had other plans. The state would not grant me a license to practice law because I was a woman.

My husband was not bothered by this turn of events. He had loved studying with me, but he was happy to provide for his family while I ran our home. I was devastated. I didn't have to go to college to be a homemaker. I spent my days grieving for the career I'd never have. I wished that I had never heard of the college, because then I'd be a happy wife. But then I wished something else. I wished that women could do anything we wanted to. I set out to find a way to change the law so we could.

	Examples
A	loved studying together in college
B	wasn't allowed to get a license
C	was allowed to get a license
D	wasn't bothered by the laws against women working
E	wanted to continue working together
F	was unhappy about not being able to have a career

Ada's Experience	Both	John's Experience

Your Turn

Ask students to complete the Your Turn activity.

Ada's Experience	Both	John's Experience
wasn't allowed to get a license	wanted to continue working together	was allowed to get a license
was unhappy about not being able to have a career	loved studying together in college	wasn't bothered by the laws against women working

Close Read

WRITE

PERSONAL RESPONSE: Think of a goal that you are trying to achieve. Are there any challenges? Is there anything stopping you? Write a short paragraph comparing and contrasting your experience to Ada Lee's story. Pay attention to main and helping verbs as you write.

Use the checklist below to guide you as you write.

- ☐ What is a goal you have?
- ☐ What problems do you have to face?
- ☐ How does your experience compare to Ada Lee's experiences?
- ☐ How does your experience contrast with Ada Lee's experiences?

Use the sentence frames to organize and write your personal response.

A goal I have is ______________________________.

This goal is important to me because ______________________________.

A problem I have is ______________________________.

To solve the problem, I ______________________________.

My experience is like Ada Lee's because ______________________________.

Unlike Ada Lee, ______________________________.

Close Read

Model Skills Focus

Remind students of the Reading Skill Comparing and Contrasting. Tell students they can compare and contrast information within the text, across different texts, or even with their personal experiences. Direct students to the Skills Focus and remind them to track as you read aloud.

Compare and contrast Ada Lee's experience with a similar personal experience

Model Comparing and Contrasting for students:

- I am going to focus on Ada Lee's plan to go to college.
- When I was younger, I made a plan to go to a soccer camp during the summer.
- Just like Ada Lee, I was excited about my plan and I told my closest friends.
- However, my experience was easier. There were no rules or laws saying that I wasn't allowed to go. I didn't have to travel far to find a camp that I liked.

Complete Skills Focus

Use a Jigsaw strategy to have students complete the Skills Focus. Divide students into pairs. Have each pair focus on a single point of comparison, for example:

- Ada Lee teaches herself a skill
- Ada Lee struggles with a challenge
- Ada Lee asks for help
- Ada Lee achieves a goal
- Ada Lee decides to make a change

Circulate and monitor groups as they work.

Collaborative Conversation

Rearrange partners so that they are talking with someone who worked on a different point of comparison. Prompt partners to take turns sharing their personal comparisons with the events in text.

- How did your experience compare with Ada Lee's experience?
- How did your experience contrast with Ada Lee's experience?
- How did comparing and contrasting help your understanding of the story?

Collaborative Conversation

SCAFFOLDS

BEGINNING, INTERMEDIATE Use the word bank to participate in the group discussion.

ADVANCED Use the speaking frames to participate in the group discussion.

BEGINNING, INTERMEDIATE		ADVANCED
Word Bank		**Speaking Frames**
• experience • like • same • unlike	• different • connect • understand • realize	• I focused on ____. • It is similar because ____. • It is different because ____. • This helps me understand the text because ____

Write

SCAFFOLDS

Ask students to complete the writing assignment. Remind students to pay attention to verb tenses as they write.

ELL **BEGINNING** Write a response using the paragraph frames and word bank.

INTERMEDIATE Write a response using the paragraph frames.

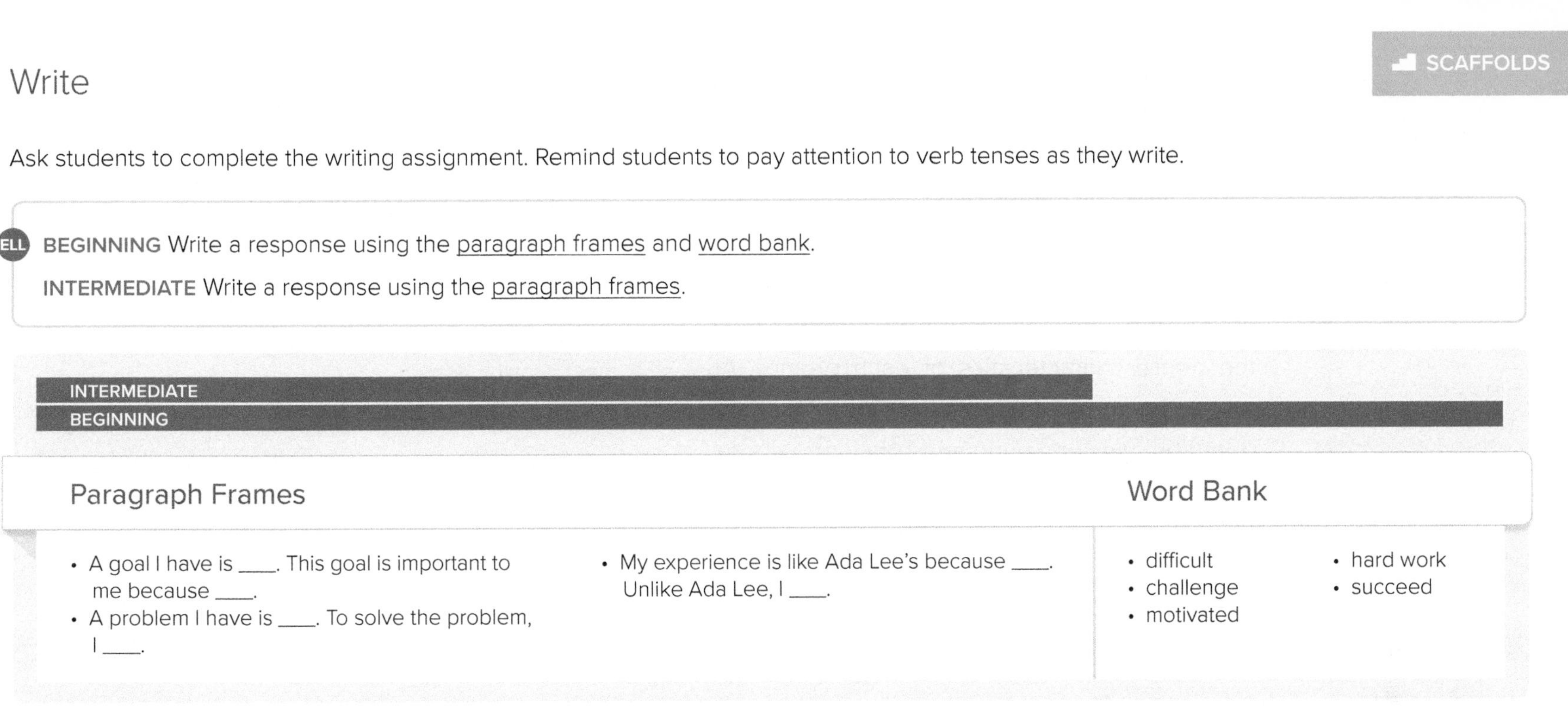

INTERMEDIATE

BEGINNING

Paragraph Frames

- A goal I have is ____. This goal is important to me because ____.
- A problem I have is ____. To solve the problem, I ____.
- My experience is like Ada Lee's because ____. Unlike Ada Lee, I ____.

Word Bank

- difficult
- challenge
- motivated
- hard work
- succeed

In the Extended Oral Project, students plan, draft, practice, and deliver an oral presentation that ties into the theme of the unit and spans informative, argumentative, and narrative genres. Lessons provide explicit instruction to prepare students for the unique challenges of an oral presentation, and to help break down the genre characteristics of each prompt. At each step in the process, students focus in-depth on specific writing and speaking skills as they brainstorm, organize, and refine their presentation. Students also receive discussion prompts and frames to guide them in providing effective peer feedback as they practice and discuss in small groups before presenting to the class on the final day.

CONNECT TO ESSENTIAL QUESTION

Why do we take chances?

In this unit, students practiced effective collaborative communication skills, as well as making connections and comparing and contrasting, while reading and analyzing two texts about risks. Now students will apply those skills to work together in writing and delivering an informational presentation.

Developing Effective Presentations

The presentation revolves around the conflicts that arise when people can read each other's thoughts.

Form	Language and Conventions	Oral Language Production
Students may struggle with the demands of developing the presentation, such as breaking out advice into steps.	Students should be encouraged to experiment with new sentence patterns and types to make their presentation sound natural and logical.	Students may make mistakes when they transfer grammatical forms from their native languages into English. Remind students to monitor their use of pronouns.

SCAFFOLDS

ELL ENGLISH LANGUAGE LEARNERS

Vocabulary, discussion, and peer and teacher support in the Extended Oral Project is differentiated for Beginning, Intermediate, Advanced, and Advanced High English Language Learners. See individual lesson plans for additional scaffolding and support.

Instructional Path

All Extended Oral Project lessons lesson plans appear in your digital teacher account.

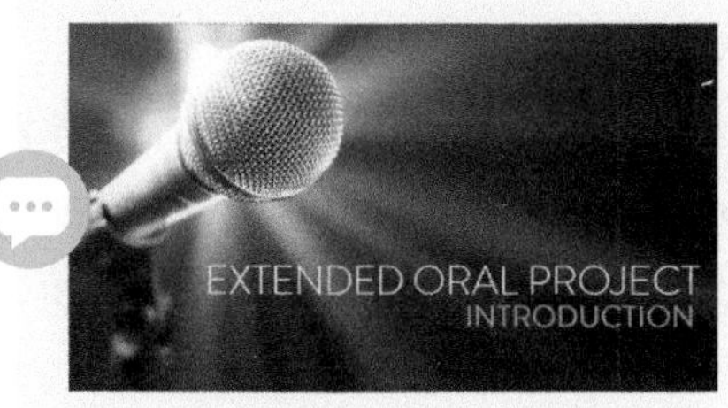

Introduction

Objectives: Students will be able to identify the components of an informational presentation in order to brainstorm and plan their own presentation.

Objectives: Students will be able to record ideas for an informational presentation in writing.

DIGITAL ONLY

Skill: Acquiring Vocabulary

Objectives: Students will be able to use a graphic organizer to make connections between words and acquire new vocabulary for their informational presentation.

Objectives: Students will be able to brainstorm new words to use in writing their informational presentation.

DIGITAL ONLY

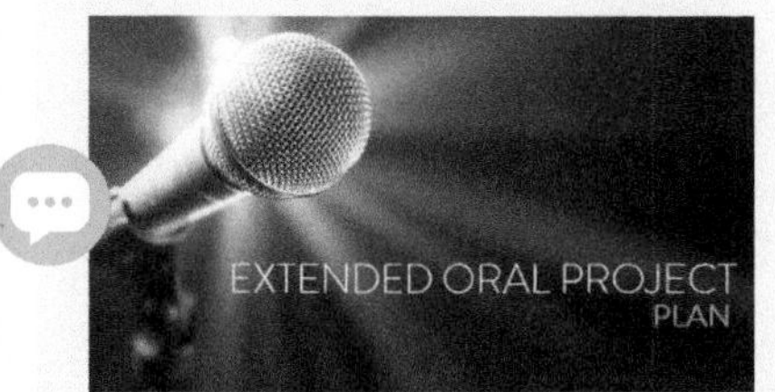

Plan

Objectives: Students will be able to plan and write a first draft of their informational presentation.

Objectives: Students will be able to organize their first draft using an outline.

DIGITAL ONLY

Skill: Sentence Types

Objectives: Students will be able to apply knowledge of sentence types to revise the sentences in their informational presentations.

Objectives: Students will be able to vary sentence types orally and in writing.

DIGITAL ONLY

Practice

Objectives: Students will be able to practice and revise their informational presentation based on peer feedback.

Objectives: Students will be able to practice an informational presentation orally and make revisions in writing.

DIGITAL ONLY

Present

Objectives: Students will be able to observe and deliver an informational presentation in order to give and receive peer feedback.

Objectives: Students will be able to use varied sentence types in an informational presentation and give peer feedback orally and in writing.

DIGITAL ONLY

Novel Study

Each Core ELAR Unit contains two texts designated for Novel Study. The Novel Study supports the close reading of the complete text through its associated Reading Guide and a series of comparative reading and writing lessons. Novel Studies are not a part of each grade-level's 180 days of instruction; however, teachers may choose to draw from them if they wish to incorporate materials from other disciplines or develop an alternative, novel-based approach to instruction.

Each novel comes with a **Reading Guide** that provides both teacher and student support. Each lesson provides key vocabulary words and close reading questions, as well as a key passage that will help teachers guide students through an exploration of the essential ideas, events, and character development in the novel. This passage will also serve as the point from which students will engage in their own StudySyncTV-style group discussion. Each novel study's **Comparative Reading and Writing** lessons contain resources to support comparative analyses. Students read passages of other texts drawn from across the disciplines and compare those passages to specific sections of the novel in written responses.

Suggested Novel Studies

Title	Genre	Summary	Themes and Topics
A Night to Remember (1955)	History	The biggest ocean liner ever built, the RMS *Titanic* was dubbed "unsinkable" because of its fifteen interior bulkheads. No one suspected an iceberg could rip them open.	• Disaster • Ocean • Eyewitness Account
Narrative of the Life of Frederick Douglass (1845)	Autobiography	The first widely published narrative by a formerly enslaved person was a sensation, helping to turn public sentiment against slavery in 19th-century America.	• Autobiography • Slavery • Freedom

OPTION 1

A Night to Remember

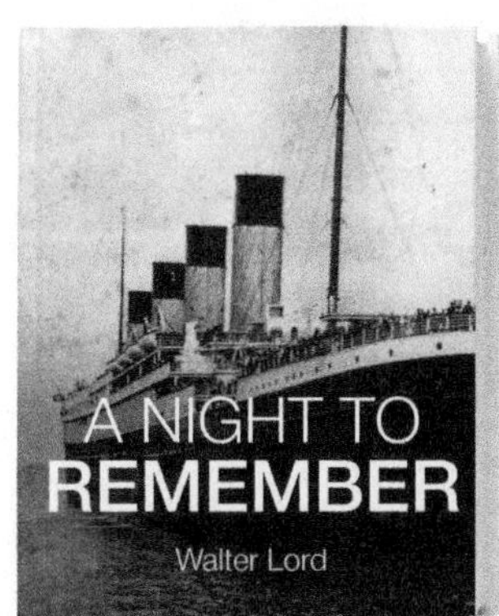

Published 43 years after the legendary 1912 sinking of the *Titanic*, Walter Lord's *A Night to Remember* is the definitive account of the disaster. Chilling details from interviews with more than 60 survivors as well as from several other sources recount the collision with an iceberg, the filling of the lifeboats, and the rescue by the ship *Carpathia*. Through the experiences of passengers and crew, readers relive the last moments of the "village" aboard the world's largest ocean liner.

Walter Lord (1917–2002) wrote 11 books, but *A Night to Remember* is by far his most famous. On account of his expertise, he often lectured at meetings of the Titanic Historical Society, and when director James Cameron began filming the 1997 movie about the disaster, Lord was called in as a consultant.

OPTION 2

Narrative of the Life of Frederick Douglass

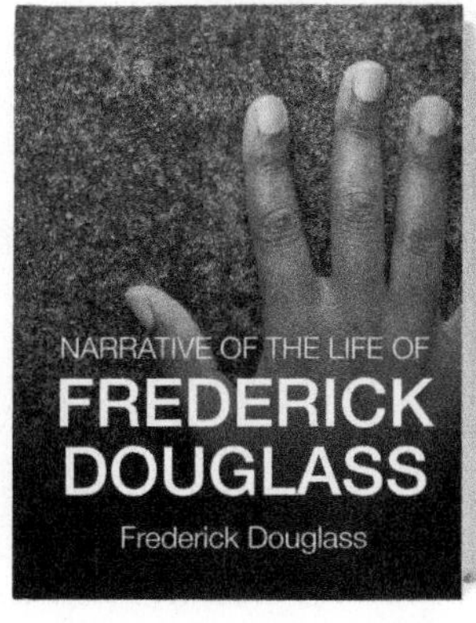

This autobiography by America's most famous formerly enslaved abolitionist chronicles his journey from the plantation—where he witnessed firsthand the brutality and injustices of slavery—through his years in Baltimore, where he learned to read. Marked by a series of epiphanies that continue even after Douglass's emancipation, the narrative is a meditation on the meaning of liberty and the shared responsibility of members of a society.

Frederick Douglass (1818–1895) was an activist, orator, and statesman who escaped slavery in Maryland to become one of the national leaders of the antislavery movement. In 1845, *Narrative of the Life of Frederick Douglass* was published; its vivid testimony leads readers along the road that led Douglass from chains to emancipation.

Spotlight Skills Review

A review day before the end-of-unit assessment gives you an opportunity to review difficult concepts with students using Spotlight Skills lessons. Spotlight Skills are targeted lessons that provide you with resources to reteach or remediate without assigning additional readings. Every Core ELA Skill lesson has a corresponding Spotlight Skill lesson. Spotlight Skills can be assigned at any point in the year, but the end of each unit provides a natural moment to pause, review data collected throughout the unit, and reteach skills students have not yet mastered.

Progress Monitoring

The Progress Monitoring charts that appear before every text in this unit identify standards and associated Spotlight Skills. On review day, you may want to give preference to reteaching skills that are not revisited in later units. You can see where skills are covered again in the Opportunities to Reteach column.

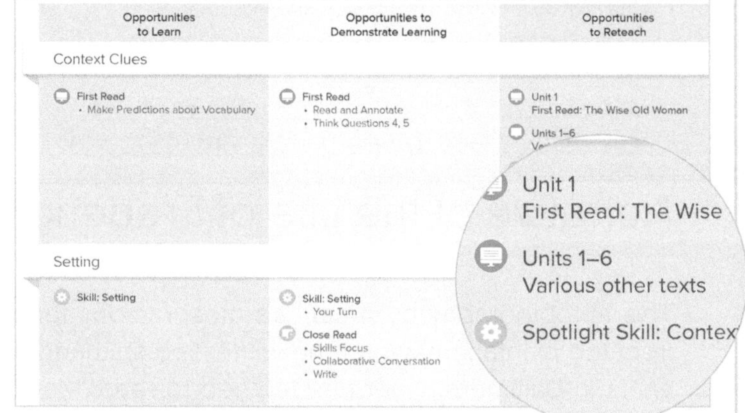

StudySync Gradebook

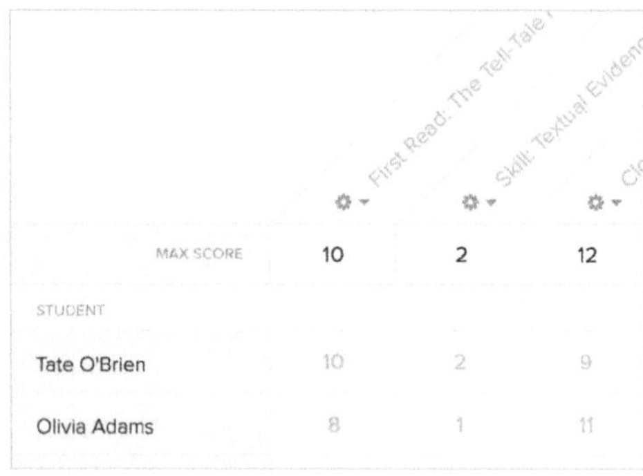

As students submit assignments on StudySync, their mastery of skills and standards is tracked via the gradebook. The gradebook can be sorted and viewed in a variety of ways. Sorting by assignment shows overall student performance, while sorting by standards or by Skill lessons displays student progress toward mastery goals.

Skills Library 

Spotlight Skills are located in the Skills section of the StudySync Library. You can assign Spotlight Skills to individual students or groups of students. Search tools allow you to search by skill type or name.

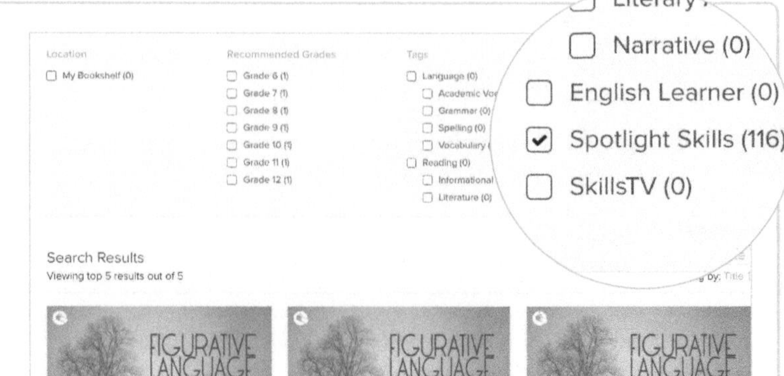

End-of-Unit Assessment

The end-of-unit assessment can be found in two places. The digital version of the assessment can be assigned from the Online Assessment tab inside your ConnectED account. The paper-based version of the assessment can be printed from the End-of-Unit Assessment tab inside this unit in your StudySync account.

Assessment Section	Content	Assessed Skills	
READING	The Scientific Revolution Genre: Nonfiction Word Count: 829 Lexile: 1060L	• Greek and Latin Affixes and Roots • Informational Text Structure	• Textual Evidence • Informational Text Elements • Summarizing • Figurative Language
	The *Friendship 7* Genre: Nonfiction Word Count: 463 Lexile: 1100L	• Informational Text Elements • Technical Language • Textual Evidence	• Summarizing • Informational Text Structure • Word Patterns and Relationships
	The Building of the Transcontinental Railroad Genre: Nonfiction Word Count: 495 Lexile: 1100L	• Informational Text Elements • Context Clues • Textual Evidence	• Summarizing • Informational Text Structure
	No Risk, No Reward Genre: Nonfiction Word Count: 872 Lexile: 1080L	• Greek and Latin Affixes and Roots • Informational Text Structure	• Context Clues • Informational Text Elements • Summarizing
REVISING and EDITING	Student Passage #1	• Infinitives • Gerunds	• Participles
	Student Passage #2	• Organizing Informational Writing • Introductions	• Supporting Details • Conclusions • Thesis
WRITING	Prompt: Informative Writing	• Informative Writing	

What's Next?

Assessment results can be viewed by item, standard, and skill to monitor mastery and make decisions for upcoming instruction.

RETEACH skills that students have not yet mastered, using Spotlight Skills or the Test Preparation and Practice book.

REVISE your teaching plan to provide more or less explicit instruction into a skill or text, using Beyond the Book activities for enrichment.

REGROUP students and levels of scaffolding based on standards progress.

Teacher's Edition Credits

Cover, iStock.com/
p. iii, iStock/FatCamera
p. vii, iStock.com/den-belitsky
p. vii, iStock.com/DNY59
p. vii, ©iStock.com/Arsty
p. vii, bortn76/iStock.com
p. vii, iStock.com/DenisTangneyJr
p. vii, Nellie Bly - Public Domain
p. viii, Nellie Bly - Public Domain
p. viii, Paul Laurence Dunbar - Anthony Barboza/Contributor/Archive Photos
p. viii, Rudolph Fisher - Science History Images/Alamy Stock Photo
p. viii, Neil Gaiman - Jeremy Sutton-Hibbert/Contributor/Getty Images Entertainment
p. viii, Alfred Hitchcock - CBS Photo Archive/Contributor/CBS
p. ix, W.W. Jacobs - Bettmann/Contributor/Bettmann/Getty Images
p. ix, Shirley Jackson - Bloomberg/Contributor/Bloomberg/Getty Images
p. ix, Walter Dean Myers - New York Daily News Archive/Contributor/New York Daily News/Getty Images
p. ix, Edgar Allen Poe - Universal History Archive/Contributor/Universal Images Group/Getty Images
p. xi, iStock.com/swissmediavision
p. xii, Swin Cash - Taylor Hill/Contributor/FilmMagic/Getty Images
p. xii, Sandra Cisneros - Ulf Andersen/Contributor/Getty Images Entertainment
p. xii, Judith Ortiz Cofer - University of Georgia Marketing & Communications. All rights reserved.
p. xii, Emily Dickinson - Culture Club/Contributor/Hulton Archive/Getty Images
p. xiii, Robert Frost - Bachrach/Contributor/Archive Photos/Getty Images
p. xiii, S.E. Hinton - Ron Galella/Contributor/Ron Galella Collection/Getty Images
p. xiii, Yusef Komunyakaa - Neilson Barnard/Stringer/Getty Images Entertainment
p. xiii, Michelle Obama - Gilbert Carrasquillo/Contributor/FilmMagic/Getty Images
p. xiii, Natasha Trethewey - The Washington Post/Contributor/The Washington Post/Getty Images
p. xv, istock.com/Figure8Photos
p. xvi, Frederick Douglass - Archive Photos/Library of Congress/Stringer/Getty Images
p. xvi, Anya Groner - courtesey of Anya Groner
p. xvi, Frances Ellen Watkins Harper - Library of Congress/Contributor/Corbis Historical/Getty Images
p. xvi, Langston Hughes - Underwood Archives/Contributor/Archive Photos/Getty Images
p. xvii, Jack London - Chronicle/Alamy Stock Photo
p. xvii, Thomas Ponce - Courtesey of Thomas Ponce
p. xvii, Ronald Reagan - IanDagnall Computing/Alamy Stock Photo
p. 1, iStock.com/den-belitsky
p. 2, iStock.com/DNY59
p. 2, ©iStock.com/Arsty
p. 2, bortn76/iStock.com
p. 2, iStock.com/DenisTangneyJr
p. 10, iStock.com/Ivan Bajic
p. 12, iStock.com/Brainsil
p. 14, ©iStock.com/anskuw
p. 16, yacobchuk/iStock
p. 16, iStock.com/simarik
p. 16, iStock.com/donatas1205
p. 16, iStock.com/malerapaso
p. 16, ©iStock.com/anskuw
p. 16, iStock.com/Delpixart
p. 17, iStock.com/urbancow
p. 17, iStock.com/antoni_halim
p. 17, ©iStock.com/anskuw
p. 17, iStock.com/JayKJay21
p. 17, iStock.com/sara_winter
p. 17, iStock.com/medlar
p. 22, iStock.com/yacobchuk
p. 22, iStock.com/borchee
p. 23, iStock.com/borchee
p. 23, iStock.com/simarik
p. 24, iStock.com/borchee
p. 24, iStock.com/donatas1205
p. 25, iStock.com/borchee
p. 25, iStock.com/malerapaso
p. 26, NiseriN/iStock.com
p. 31, ©iStock.com/cougarsan
p. 41, iStock.com/borchee
p. 41, iStock.com/JayKJay21
p. 44, iStock.com/borchee
p. 44, iStock.com/sara_winter
p. 45, iStock.com/borchee
p. 45, iStock.com/medlar
p. 48, iStock.com/den-belitsky
p. 48, iStock.com/simonbradfield
p. 48, iStock.com/hkeita
p. 48, iStock.com/5second
p. 49, iStock.com/borchee
p. 49, iStock.com/simonbradfield
p. 50, iStock.com/NiseriN
p. 50, iStock.com/borchee
p. 51, iStock.com/borchee
p. 51, iStock.com/5second
p. 52, iStock.com/bortn76
p. 54, iStock.com/bortn76
p. 54, iStock.com/deimagine
p. 54, iStock.com/alejandrophotography
p. 56, iStock.com/HaizhanZheng
p. 64, ©iStock.com/cougarsan
p. 72, iStock.com/jeancliclac
p. 74, iStock.com/from2015
p. 74, iStock.com/jeancliclac
p. 74, iStock.com/Brostock
p. 76, iStock.com/Claudiad
p. 79, ©iStock.com/cougarsan
p. 90, iStock.com/LisaValder
p. 92, iStock.com/LisaValder
p. 92, iStock.com/BeachcottagePhotography
p. 95, ©iStock.com/cougarsan
p. 100, iStock.com/DenisTangneyJr
p. 102, iStock.com/DenisTangneyJr
p. 102, iStock.com/Brostock
p. 102, iStock.com/Martin Barraud
p. 104, iStock.com/Mathier
p. 112, ©iStock.com/cougarsan
p. 122, iStock.com/SoulOfAutumn/
p. 124, iStock.com/SoulOfAutumn/
p. 124, iStock.com/natasaadzic
p. 124, iStock.com/Dominique_Lavoie
p. 124, iStock.com/ooyoo
p. 126, iStock.com/IakovKalinin
p. 138, ©iStock.com/cougarsan
p. 148, iStock.com/Snowshill
p. 150, iStock.com/Snowshill
p. 150, iStock.com/shayes17
p. 174, ©iStock.com/cougarsan
p. 178, ©iStock.com/GuidoVrola
p. 180, ©iStock.com/GuidoVrola
p. 180, iStock.com/B&M Noskowski
p. 187, ©iStock.com/cougarsan
p. 192, iStock.com/vesilvio
p. 194, iStock.com/vesilvio
p. 194, iStock.com/Gemini-Create
p. 194, iStock.com/ValentinaPhotos
p. 194, iStock.com/essentialimage
p. 196, iStock.com/johnnorth
p. 210, ©iStock.com/cougarsan
p. 220, ©iStock.com/BlackJack3D
p. 222, ©iStock.com/BlackJack3D
p. 222, iStock.com/ThomasVogel
p. 222, iStock.com/urbancow
p. 224, iStock.com/HaizhanZheng
p. 229, ©iStock.com/cougarsan
p. 240, iStock.com/borchee
p. 240, iStock.com/shironosov
p. 241, iStock.com/borchee
p. 241, iStock.com/EasternLightcraft
p. 242, iStock.com/hanibaram, iStock.com/seb_ra, iStock.com/Martin Barraud
p. 242, iStock.com/Martin Barraud
p. 244, iStock.com/oonal
p. 244, iStock.com/truelight
p. 244, iStock.com/Jinnawat
p. 244, iStock/Jasmina007
p. 245, iStock.com/Jeff_Hu
p. 245, iStock.com/stevedangers
p. 245, iStock.com/Martin Barraud
p. 245, iStock.com/efks
p. 245, ©iStock.com/Thomas Shanahan
p. 245, iStock.com/wwing
p. 245, iStock.com/efks
p. 294, iStock.com/den-belitsky
p. 294, iStock.com/eskymaks
p. 294, iStock.com/ThomasVogel
p. 294, iStock.com/borchee
p. 296, iStock.com/DNY59
p. 298, iStock.com/blackred
p. 298, iStock.com/greenphotoKK
p. 298, iStock.com/DNY59
p. 298, iStock.com/Ales_Utovko
p. 298, iStock.com/BlackJack3D
p. 298, iStock.com/eugenesergeev
p. 300, iStock.com/Denisfilm
p. 310, ©iStock.com/Arsty
p. 312, iStock.com/eskymaks
p. 312, iStock.com/ThomasVogel
p. 312, ©iStock.com/Arsty
p. 312, iStock.com/BlackJack3D
p. 312, iStock.com/eugenesergeev
p. 312, iStock.com/RomoloTavani
p. 314, iStock.com/Ababsolutum
p. 325, iStock.com/nikkytok
p. 325, iStock.com/juhide
p. 325, iStock.com/Ivan Bajic
p. 327, iStock.com/SonerCdem
p. 327, iStock.com/DenisTangneyJr

Student Edition Credits

PHOTO/IMAGE CREDITS:

Cover, iStock.com/anskuw
p. 1, iStock.com/PEDRE
p. 5, iStock.com/Delpixart
p. 6, iStock.com/Delpixart
p. 7, iStock.com/anskuw
p. 8, iStock.com/urbancow
p. 9, iStock.com/urbancow
p. 10, iStock.com/antoni_halim
p. 11, iStock.com/antoni_halim
p. 12, iStock.com/anskuw
p. 13, iStock.com/bortn76
p. 19, iStock.com/bortn77
p. 20, iStock.com/deimagine
p. 21, iStock.com/deimagine
p. 22, iStock.com/bortn76
p. 23, iStock.com/jeancliclac
p. 26, iStock.com/jeancliclac
p. 27, iStock.com/Brostock
p. 28, iStock.com/Brostock
p. 30, iStock.com/jeancliclac
p. 31, iStock.com/LisaValder
p. 34, iStock.com/DenisTangneyJr
p. 36, The New York Historical Society/ Archive Photos/Getty Images
p. 40, iStock.com/DenisTangneyJr
p. 41, iStock.com/Brostock
p. 42, iStock.com/Brostock
p. 43, iStock.com/Martin Barraud
p. 44, iStock.com/Martin Barraud
p. 45, iStock.com/DenisTangneyJr
p. 46, iStock.com/SoulOfAutumn
p. 56, iStock.com/SoulOfAutumn
p. 57, iStock.com/Dominique_Lavoie
p. 58, iStock.com/Dominique_Lavoie
p. 60, iStock.com/ooyoo
p. 61, iStock.com/ooyoo
p. 62, iStock.com/SoulOfAutumn
p. 63, iStock.com/Snowshill
p. 64–85, Text copyright © 2008 by Neil Gaiman. Illustrations copyright © 2014 by P. Craig Russell. Used by permission of HarperCollins Publishers
p. 87, iStock.com/GuidoVrola
p. 94, iStock.com/vesilvio
p. 96, Transcendental Graphics/Archive Photos/ GettyImages
p. 106, iStock.com/vesilvio
p. 107, iStock.com/Gemini-Create
p. 108, iStock.com/Gemini-Create
p. 109, iStock.com/ValentinaPhotos
p. 110, iStock.com/ValentinaPhotos
p. 111, iStock.com/vesilvio
p. 112, iStock.com/BlackJack3D
p. 117, iStock.com/BlackJack3D
p. 118, iStock.com/ThomasVogel
p. 119, iStock.com/ThomasVogel
p. 120, iStock.com/urbancow
p. 121, iStock.com/urbancow
p. 122, iStock.com/BlackJack3D
p. 123, iStock.com/Martin Barraud
p. 124, iStock.com/Martin Barraud
p. 130, iStock.com/oonal
p. 133, iStock.com/Martin Barraud
p. 140, iStock.com/truelight
p. 142, iStock.com/Jinnawat
p. 145, iStock.com/Jasmina007
p. 148, iStock.com/Jeff_Hu
p. 151, iStock.com/stevedangers
p. 154, iStock.com/Martin Barraud
p. 157, iStock.com/Martin Barraud
p. 159, iStock.com/DNY59
p. 160, iStock.com/EHStock
p. 160, iStock.com/Pamela Moore
p. 160, iStock.com/YinYang
p. 160, iStock.com/RapidEye
p. 160, iStock.com/sdominick
p. 162, iStock.com/DNY59
p. 163, iStock.com/Ales_Utovko
p. 165, iStock.com/BlackJack3D
p. 167, iStock.com/DNY59
p. 168, iStock.com/Arsty
p. 169, iStock.com/AleksandarGeorgiev
p. 169, iStock.com
p. 169, iStock.com
p. 169, iStock.com
p. 169, iStock.com
p. 171, iStock.com/Arsty
p. 172, iStock.com/BlackJack3D
p. 174, iStock.com/eugenesergeev
p. 176, iStock.com/Arsty

Teacher's Edition Credits

p. 331, iStock.com/swissmediavision
p. 332, iStock.com/SHSPhotography
p. 332, ©iStock.com/fstop123
p. 332, iStock.com/Jasmina007
p. 332, ©iStock.com/Jangnhut
p. 340, iStock.com/Ivan Bajic
p. 342, iStock.com/friendwithlove
p. 342, iStock.com/praetorianphoto
p. 342, iStock.com/hkeita
p. 342, iStock.com/5second
p. 343, iStock.com/borchee
p. 343, iStock.com/praetorianphoto
p. 344, iStock.com/NiseriN
p. 344, iStock.com/borchee
p. 345, iStock.com/borchee
p. 345, iStock.com/5second
p. 346, ©iStock.com/coffeekai
p. 348, ©iStock.com/coffeekai
p. 348, iStock.com/Andrey_A
p. 350, fotorince/iStock.com
p. 353, ©iStock.com/cougarsan
p. 362, ©iStock.com/fstop123
p. 364, iStock.com/mycola
p. 364, ©iStock.com/fstop123
p. 364, iStock.com/DNY59
p. 366, iStock.com/stockce/
p. 376, ©iStock.com/cougarsan
p. 384, ©iStock.com/35007
p. 386, ©iStock.com/35007
p. 386, iStock.com/kadirkaplan
p. 389, ©iStock.com/cougarsan
p. 394, ©iStock.com/oneinchpunch
p. 396, iStock.com/LoveTheWind
p. 396, iStock.com/ThomasVogel
p. 396, iStock.com/peshkov
p. 398, iStock.com/Delbars
p. 401, ©iStock.com/cougarsan
p. 410, iStock.com/Jasmina007
p. 412, iStock.com/Jasmina007
p. 412, iStock.com/deimagine
p. 412, iStock.com/urbancow
p. 414, iStock.com/BrianBrownImages
p. 420, ©iStock.com/cougarsan
p. 430, ©iStock.com/Kameleon007
p. 432, ©iStock.com/Kameleon007
p. 432, iStock.com/Andrey_A
p. 432, iStock.com/ooyoo
p. 432, iStock.com/77studio
p. 434, iStock.com/chat9780
p. 437, ©iStock.com/cougarsan
p. 448, iStock.com/Maksymowicz
p. 450, iStock.com/Maksymowicz
p. 450, iStock.com/Gemini-Create
p. 450, iStock.com/Dominique_Lavoie
p. 452, iStock.com/jrothe
p. 457, ©iStock.com/cougarsan
p. 468, ©iStock.com/Jangnhut
p. 470, ©iStock.com/Jangnhut
p. 470, iStock.com/KariHoglund
p. 477, ©iStock.com/cougarsan
p. 482, ©iStock.com/dszc
p. 484, ©iStock.com/dszc
p. 484, iStock.com/sdbower
p. 487, ©iStock.com/cougarsan
p. 492, iStock.com/xelf
p. 494, iStock.com/xelf
p. 494, iStock.com/Andrey_A
p. 494, iStock.com/fotogaby
p. 496, iStock.com/oksix
p. 499, ©iStock.com/cougarsan
p. 510, iStock.com/anskuw/
p. 512, iStock.com/anskuw/
p. 512, iStock.com/Smithore
p. 512, iStock.com/fotogaby
p. 514, iStock.com/gdagys/
p. 520, ©iStock.com/cougarsan
p. 530, iStock.com/borchee
p. 530, iStock.com/shironosov
p. 531, iStock.com/borchee
p. 531, iStock.com/EasternLightcraft
p. 532, iStock.com/hanibaram, iStock.com/seb_ra, iStock.com/Martin Barraud
p. 534, iStock.com/Martin Barraud
p. 534, iStock.com/oonal
p. 534, iStock.com/gopixa
p. 534, iStock.com/Domin_domin
p. 535, iStock.com/bo1982
p. 535, iStock.com/Jeff_Hu
p. 535, iStock/Fodor90
p. 535, iStock.com/stevedangers
p. 535, iStock.com/Martin Barraud
p. 536, iStock.com/peeterv
p. 536, iStock.com/Martin Barraud
p. 536, iStock.com/borchee
p. 582, iStock.com/borchee
p. 582, iStock.com/swissmediavision
p. 582, iStock.com/eskymaks
p. 582, iStock.com/from2015
p. 584, SHSPhotography/iStock.com
p. 586, iStock.com/blackred
p. 586, iStock.com/artisteer
p. 586, SHSPhotography/iStock.com
p. 586, iStock.com/Ales_Utovko
p. 586, iStock.com/Zoran Kolundzija
p. 586, iStock.com/eugenesergeev
p. 588, iStock.com/AdirondackZack
p. 598, ©iStock.com/fstop123
p. 600, iStock.com/eskymaks
p. 600, iStock.com/from2015
p. 600, ©iStock.com/fstop123
p. 600, iStock.com/BlackJack3D
p. 600, iStock.com/serggn
p. 600, iStock.com/BlackJack3D
p. 602, iStock.com/manley099
p. 613, iStock.com/nikkytok
p. 613, iStock.com/juhide
p. 613, iStock.com/Aslan Alphan
p. 615, iStock.com/Jasmina007
p. 615, ©iStock.com/Jangnhut

Student Edition Credits

PHOTO/IMAGE CREDITS:

Cover, iStock.com/coffeekai
p. 2, iStock.com/coffeekai
p. 3, iStock.com/
p. 4, iStock.com/
p. 5, iStock.com/coffeekai
p. 6, iStock.com/
p. 9, Public Domain Image
p. 14, iStock.com/
p. 15, iStock.com/DNY59
p. 16, iStock.com/DNY60
p. 17, iStock.com/
p. 18, iStock.com/35007
p. 21 -iStock.com/oneinchpunch
p. 23, iStock.com/Andrii Yalanskyi
p. 24, iStock.com/oneinchpunch
p. 25, iStock.com/ThomasVogel
p. 26, iStock.com/ThomasVogel
p. 27, iStock.com/oneinchpunch
p. 28, iStock.com/Jasmina007
p. 32, iStock.com/Jasmina008
p. 33, iStock.com/deimagine
p. 34, iStock.com/deimagine
p. 35, @istock.com/urbancow
p. 36, @istock.com/urbancow
p. 38, ©iStock.com/Kameleon008
p. 41, ©iStock.com/Kameleon008
p. 42, ©iStock.com/Andrey_A
p. 43, ©iStock.com/Andrey_A
p. 44, ©iStock.com/ooyoo
p. 45, ©iStock.com/ooyoo
p. 46, ©iStock.com/Kameleon008
p. 47, ©iStock.com/Maksymowicz
p. 52, ©iStock.com/Maksymowicz
p. 53, iStock.com/Gemini-Create
p. 54, iStock.com/Gemini-Create
p. 55, iStock.com/Dominique_Lavoie
p. 56, iStock.com/Dominique_Lavoie
p. 57, ©iStock.com/Maksymowicz
p. 58, iStock.com/Jangnhut
p. 65, iStock.com/dszc
p. 68, iStock.com/xelf
p. 69, iStock.com/Alex
p. 70, iStock.com/xelf
p. 71, ©iStock.com/Andrey_A
p. 72, ©iStock.com/Andrey_A
p. 73, iStock.com/fotogaby
p. 74, iStock.com/fotogaby
p. 80, iStock.com/anskuw
p. 81, iStock.com/fotogaby
p. 82, iStock.com/fotogaby
p. 83, iStock.com/
p. 84, iStock.com/
p. 86, iStock.com/anskuw
p. 87, iStock.com/hanibaram, iStock.com/seb_ra, iStock.com/Martin Barraud
p. 88, iStock.com/Martin Barraud
p. 94, iStock.com/fstop123
p. 97, iStock.com/gopixa
p. 102, iStock.com/Martin Barraud
p. 107, iStock.com/bo1982
p. 109, iStock.com/Jeff_Hu
p. 112, iStock/Fodor90
p. 115, iStock.com/stevedangers
p. 118, iStock.com/Martin Barraud
p. 120, iStock.com/Martin Barraud
p. 123, iStock/tetmc/
p. 123, iStock/Marilyn Nieves
p. 123, iStock/ariwasabi
p. 123, iStock/Chrisds
p. 123, iStock/m-1975
p. 125, iStock.com/SHSPhotography
p. 126, iStock.com/Ales_Utovko
p. 128, iStock.com/Zoran Kolundzija
p. 130, iStock.com/SHSPhotography
p. 131, iStock.com/fstop123
p. 132, iStock/alphaspirit
p. 132, iStock/abadonian
p. 132, iStock/Dean Mitchell
p. 132, iStock/sdominick
p. 132, iStock/Reniw-Imagery
p. 132, iStock/blindtoy99
p. 134, iStock.com/fstop123
p. 135, iStock.com/BlackJack3D
p. 137, iStock.com/serggn
p. 139, iStock.com/fstop123

Teacher's Edition Credits

p. 618, istock.com/Figure8Photos
p. 621, iStock.com/3DSculptor
p. 621, Jag_cz/iStock.com
p. 621, istock.com/jaminwell
p. 621, Public Domain
p. 628, iStock.com/Ivan Bajic
p. 630, istock.com/Toltek
p. 630, istock.com/Bondariev
p. 630, iStock.com/hkeita
p. 630, iStock.com/5second
p. 631, iStock.com/borchee
p. 631, istock.com/Bondariev
p. 632, iStock.com/borchee
p. 632, istock.com/Sergey Tinyakov
p. 633, iStock.com/borchee
p. 633, iStock.com/5second
p. 634, Julie Dermansky/Contributor/Corbis News/Getty Images
p. 636, istock.com/feyyazalacam
p. 636, Julie Dermansky/Contributor/Corbis News/Getty Images
p. 636, iStock.com/GreenPimp
p. 636, iStock.com/Hohenhaus
p. 636, istock.com/nicolas_
p. 638, istock.com/DWalker44
p. 660, ©iStock.com/cougarsan
p. 670, Public Domain
p. 672, Public Domain
p. 672, Public Domain
p. 676, ©iStock.com/cougarsan
p. 680, 3DSculptor/iStock.com
p. 682, 3DSculptor/iStock.com
p. 682, iStock.com/igmarx
p. 682, iStock.com/Caval
p. 684, 3DSculptor/iStock.com
p. 687, ©iStock.com/cougarsan
p. 698, WLDavies/iStock.com
p. 700, iStock.com/coscaron
p. 700, WLDavies/iStock.com
p. 700, iStock.com/Hohenhaus
p. 700, iStock.com/Murat Göçmen
p. 700, GLENN CHAPMAN/Staff/AFP/Getty Images
p. 702, WLDavies/iStock.com
p. 705, ©iStock.com/cougarsan
p. 716, szefei/iStock.com
p. 718, szefei/iStock.com
p. 718, iStock.com/KM6064
p. 718, gettyimages.com/yucanchen
p. 721, ©iStock.com/cougarsan
p. 726, istock.com/kevron2001
p. 728, istock.com/kevron2001
p. 728, Ladida/iStock.com
p. 731, ©iStock.com/cougarsan
p. 736, istock.com/jaminwell
p. 738, istock.com/jaminwell
p. 738, iStock.com/eskaylim
p. 738, iStock.com/fotogaby
p. 740, Bettmann/Contributor/Bettmann/Getty Images
p. 748, ©iStock.com/cougarsan
p. 758, istock.com/iLexx
p. 760, istock.com/iLexx
p. 760, iStock.com/donatas1205
p. 760, iStock.com/Orla
p. 762, istock.com/WilliamBunce
p. 768, ©iStock.com/cougarsan
p. 778, KrivoTIFF/iStock.com
p. 780, KrivoTIFF/iStock.com
p. 780, iStock.com/antoni_halim
p. 780, iStock.com/Hohenhaus
p. 782, KrivoTIFF/iStock.com
p. 785, ©iStock.com/cougarsan
p. 796, Hendra Su/Contributor/EyeEm/Getty Images
p. 798, istock.com/guenterguni
p. 798, iStock.com/Orla
p. 800, skhoward/istock.com
p. 803, ©iStock.com/cougarsan
p. 812, iStock/shironosov
p. 812, iStock.com/borchee
p. 813, iStock.com/EasternLightcraft
p. 813, iStock.com/borchee
p. 814, iStock.com/hanibaram, iStock.com/seb_ra, iStock.com/Martin Barraud
p. 814, iStock.com/Martin Barraud
p. 816, iStock.com/gopixa
p. 816, iStock.com/oonal
p. 816, iStock.com/Tevarak
p. 817, iStock.com/bo1982
p. 817, iStock.com/Jeff_Hu
p. 817, iStock/Fodor90
p. 817, iStock.com/peepo
p. 817, iStock.com/stevedangers
p. 818, iStock.com/Martin Barraud
p. 818, ©iStock.com/JStaley401
p. 818, ©iStock.com/JStaley401
p. 870, iStock.com/borchee
p. 870, istock.com/Figure8Photos
p. 870, iStock.com/eskymaks
p. 870, iStock.com/NUMAX3D
p. 872, iStock.com/3DSculptor
p. 874, iStock.com/blackred
p. 874, iStock.com/mukem
p. 874, iStock.com/3DSculptor
p. 874, iStock.com/Ales_Utovko
p. 874, iStock.com/14951893
p. 874, iStock.com/eugenesergeev
p. 876, 1971yes/iStock.com
p. 888, Jag_cz/iStock.com
p. 890, iStock.com/eskymaks
p. 890, iStock.com/NUMAX3D
p. 890, Jag_cz/iStock.com
p. 890, iStock.com/BlackJack3D
p. 890, iStock.com/RazvanDP
p. 890, iStock.com/m63085
p. 892, kellyvandellen/iStock.com
p. 905, iStock.com/nikkytok
p. 905, iStock.com/juhide
p. 905, iStock.com/DNY59
p. 907, Public Domain
p. 907, istock.com/jaminwell

Student Edition Credits

PHOTO/IMAGE CREDITS:

Cover, Julie Dermansky / Contributor / GettyImages
p. 1, Isle de Jean Charles Biloxi-Chitimacha-Choctaw Tribe
p. 2–14, Isle de Jean Charles Biloxi-Chitimacha-Choctaw Tribe
p. 20, Julie Dermansky / Contributor / GettyImages
p. 21, iStock.com/GreenPimp
p. 22, iStock.com/GreenPimp
p. 23, ©iStock.com/Hohenhaus
p. 24, ©iStock.com/Hohenhaus
p. 25, Julie Dermansky / Contributor / GettyImages
p. 26, Public Domain
p. 30, iStock.com/3DSculptor
p. 31, Bettmann/Bettmann/Getty Images
p. 33, iStock.com/3DSculptor
p. 34, iStock.com/
p. 35, iStock.com/
p. 36, iStock.com/Caval
p. 37, iStock.com/Caval
p. 38, iStock.com/3DSculptor
p. 39, iStock.com/MaggyMeyer
p. 40, ©2013 National Public Radio, Inc. NPR news report titled "A Kenyan Teen's Discovery: Let There Be Lights To Save Lions" by Nina Gregory as originally published on npr.org on March 1, 2013, and is used with the permission of NPR. Any unauthorized duplication is strictly prohibited.
p. 42, ©iStock.com/MaggyMeyer
p. 43, ©iStock.com/Hohenhaus
p. 44, ©iStock.com/Hohenhaus
p. 45, ©iStock.com/Murat Göçmen
p. 46, ©iStock.com/Murat Göçmen
p. 47, ©iStock.com/MaggyMeyer
p. 48, ©iStock.com/szefei
p. 51, ©iStock.com/kevron2001
p. 53, Library of Congress/Corbis Historical/Getty Images
p. 54, ©iStock.com/jaminwell
p. 58, Hulton Archive/Hulton Archive/Getty Images
p. 60, ©iStock.com/jaminwell
p. 61, ©iStock.com/eskaylim
p. 62, ©iStock.com/eskaylim
p. 63, ©iStock.com/fotogaby
p. 65, ©iStock.com/fotogaby
p. 66, ©iStock.com/jaminwell
p. 67, ©iStock.com/iLexx
p. 69, Steve Parsons - PA Images/PA Images/Getty Images
p. 71, ©iStock.com/iLexx
p. 72, ©iStock.com/donatas1205
p. 73, ©iStock.com/donatas1205
p. 74, ©iStock.com/Orla
p. 75, ©iStock.com/Orla
p. 76, ©iStock.com/iLexx
p. 77, ©iStock.com/KrivoTIFF
p. 80, ©iStock.com/KrivoTIFF
p. 81, ©iStock.com/antoni_halim
p. 82, ©iStock.com/antoni_halim
p. 83, ©iStock.com/Hohenhaus
p. 84, ©iStock.com/Hohenhaus
p. 85, ©iStock.com/KrivoTIFF
p. 86, Hendra Su / EyeEm/ Getty
p. 88, Hendra Su / EyeEm/ Getty
p. 89, ©iStock.com/Orla
p. 90, ©iStock.com/Orla
p. 91, Hendra Su / EyeEm/ Getty
p. 92, iStock.com/hanibaram, iStock.com/seb_ra, iStock.com/Martin Barraud
p. 93, ©iStock.com/Martin Barraud
p. 99, ©iStock.com/gopixa
p. 102, ©iStock.com/ThomasVogel
p. 104, ©iStock.com/Tevarak
p. 107, ©iStock.com/Martin Barraud
p. 112, ©iStock.com/bo1982
p. 115, ©iStock/Jeff_Hu
p. 118, ©iStock.com/peepo
p. 121, ©iStock/Fodor90
p. 124, ©iStock.com/stevedangers
p. 127, ©iStock.com/Martin Barraud
p. 130, ©iStock.com/Martin Barraud
p. 132, ©iStock.com/3DSculptor
p. 133, ©iStock.com/lolostock
p. 133, ©iStock.com/
p. 133, ©iStock.com/PeskyMonkey
p. 133, ©iStock.com/adventtr
p. 133, ©iStock.com/3DSculptor
p. 135, ©iStock.com/3DSculptor
p. 136, ©iStock.com/Ales_Utovko
p. 139, ©iStock.com/14951893
p. 141, ©iStock.com/3DSculptor
p. 142, ©iStock.com/Jag_cz
p. 143, Susan Chiang/iStock
p. 143, Pamela Moore/iStock
p. 143, Wavebreak/iStock
p. 143, Christopher Futcher/iStock
p. 143, iStock.com/
p. 145, ©iStock.com/Jag_cz
p. 146, ©iStock.com/BlackJack3D
p. 149, ©iStock.com/RazvanDP
p. 151, ©iStock.com/Jag_cz

Text Fulfillment Through StudySync

If you are interested in specific titles, please fill out the form below and we will check availability through our partners.

ORDER DETAILS

Date:

TITLE	AUTHOR	Paperback/ Hardcover	Specific Edition *If Applicable*	Quantity

SHIPPING INFORMATION

Contact:

Title:

School/District:

Address Line 1:

Address Line 2:

Zip or Postal Code:

Phone:

Mobile:

Email:

BILLING INFORMATION

☐ *SAME AS SHIPPING*

Contact:

Title:

School/District:

Address Line 1:

Address Line 2:

Zip or Postal Code:

Phone:

Mobile:

Email:

PAYMENT INFORMATION

☐ CREDIT CARD

Name on Card:

Card Number: Expiration Date: Security Code:

☐ PO

Purchase Order Number:

StudySync Text Fulfillment, BookheadEd Learning, LLC
610 Daniel Young Drive | Sonoma, CA 95476